Thomas Bros. Maps®
SINCE 1915

CALIFORNIA ROAD ATLAS & DRIVER'S GUIDE

W0010504

TABLE OF CONTENTS

	Page	
Key Map & General Charts	B - E	GENERAL
Cities & Communities Index	F - K	CITIES
Major Metro Highway Maps	L - V	METRO
State Highway Maps	1 - 112	HIGHWAYS
Detail Street Maps	113-217	DETAIL
Driving Tours	218-242	TOURS
Indexes	243-308	INDEXES

Indexes
- List of Abbreviations 243
- Street Index 244 - 274
- Highway Index 275 - 279
- Points of Interest 280 - 308

Irvine • 17331 Cowan, Irvine, CA 92614 • (714) 863-1984
Los Angeles • 521 W. 6th St., Los Angeles, CA 90014 • (213) 627-4018
San Francisco • 550 Jackson St., San Francisco, CA 94133 • (415) 981-7520

Thomas Bros. Maps®
SINCE 1915
1-800-899-6277

GENERAL

CALIFORNIA STATE KEY MAP TO HIGHWAY PAGES

Three Easy Ways to find your destination:

1. Refer to this Key Map to find your page;
2. Refer to the Fold Out Map inside the back cover; or,
3. Use the Cities and Communities Index on pages F through K.

To find a specific Street, Highway or Point of Interest, use the handy index in the back of the book.

See the Fold Out Map inside the Back Cover of this guide for a larger scale Key Map of Statewide Arterial Pages.

SPECIAL FEATURE MAPS

MAP	PAGE
LOS ANGELES/ORANGE COUNTY FREEWAY SYSTEM MAPS	97-98
BAY AREA FREEWAY SYSTEM MAPS	45-46

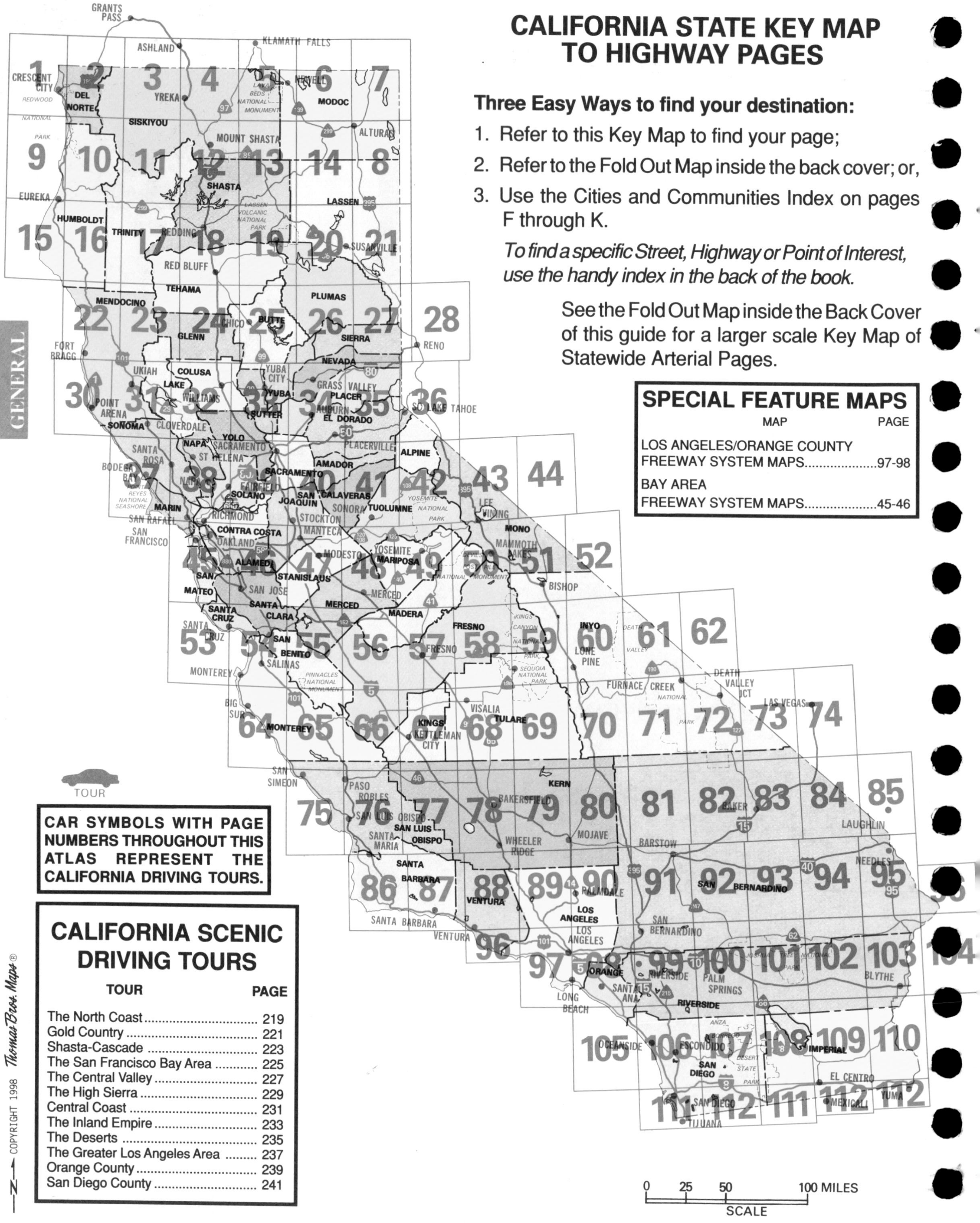

TOUR

CAR SYMBOLS WITH PAGE NUMBERS THROUGHOUT THIS ATLAS REPRESENT THE CALIFORNIA DRIVING TOURS.

CALIFORNIA SCENIC DRIVING TOURS

TOUR	PAGE
The North Coast	219
Gold Country	221
Shasta-Cascade	223
The San Francisco Bay Area	225
The Central Valley	227
The High Sierra	229
Central Coast	231
The Inland Empire	233
The Deserts	235
The Greater Los Angeles Area	237
Orange County	239
San Diego County	241

Legend of Map Symbols

- Interstate Highway (BUS =Business)
- U.S. Highway (BYP =Bypass)
- State Highway
- State Highway
- Ariz, Oregon, Nevada State Hwy
- County Route
- State Scenic Route
- Carpool Lane
- Historic Highway 66
- Tour Route
- Airport (Major)
- Airport (Minor)
- Amusement Park
- Beach
- Boat Launch
- Building
- Campground
- University or College
- Fire Station *(FS)*
- Forest, State or National Park
- Gate, Lock, Barricade
- Golf Course
- Harbor
- Historic Feature
- Hospital
- Hotel
- Library
- Lighthouse
- Mission
- Mountain Peak
- Miscellaneous Feature
- Recreation Feature (Water)
- Rest Area
- Rest Area (Seasonal)
- Public Elementary School
- Public JR HS or High School
- Private Elementary School
- Private JR HS or High School
- Point of Interest
- Shopping Center
- Ski Area
- Station (Train or Bus)
- Theatre
- Truck Scales
- Winery

- Freeway
- Toll Road
- Highway
- Primary Road
- Secondary Road
- Minor Road
- Restricted Road
- Alley, Trail, Walkway
- Unpaved Road
- Gold Country Route
- Ramp
- Tunnel
- High Occupancy Lane
- Stacked Roadways
- Freeway Proposed
- Toll Road Proposed
- Highway Proposed
- Primary Road Proposed
- Freeway Construction
- Toll Road Construction
- One-Way Road
- Two-Way Road
- Stairs
- Railroad
- Rapid Transit
- Rapid Transit (Underground)
- City Boundary
- County Boundary
- State Boundary
- International Boundary
- Military Boundary
- Park Boundary
- Ferry
- River, Creek
- Shoreline
- *CC* Chamber of Commerce
- *CH* *CHP* City Hall, Calif. Highway Patrol
- *CON CTR* Convention Center
- *CTH* Court House
- *DMV* Department of Motor Vehicles
- *MUS* *PO* Museum, Post Office
- *PS* *VIS BUR* Police Station, Visitors Bureau
- *T2N* Township or Range Line
- Section Corner and Number
- *RANCHO TRABUCO* *RANCHO BERNARDO* Rancho Line

- County Seat
- City · Community
- City
- City
- City
- City
- County Area
- County Area
- County Area
- County Area
- County Area
- County Area
- Beach
- Beach
- Cemetery
- Cemetery
- Golf Course
- Golf Course
- Major Parking Area
- Military
- Lake or Ocean
- Lake (Intermittent)
- Lake (Dry)
- Large Dam
- Park (City, County or State)
- Park (City or County)
- Park (National Park or Forest)
- Point of Interest
- Structure Footprint
- Regional Shopping Center
- Regional Shopping Center
- Major Department Stores
- BD Bloomingdale's
- BN The Bon Marche
- D Diamonds
- FN Frederick & Nelson
- G GT Goldwaters, Gottschalks
- H IM Harris, I Magnin
- L MA Lamonts, Macy's
- ME MF Mervyn's, Meier & Frank
- MW N Montgomery Ward, Nordstrom
- NM P Neiman-Marcus, J. C. Penney
- RM S Robinsons-May, Sears
- SF Saks Fifth Avenue
- W Weinstocks

Scale of Detail Maps One Inch = 2200 feet (Unless otherwise noted)

0 1/4 1/2 3/4 1 Mile

0 .25 .5 .75 1 Kilometer

Scale of Arterial Maps One Inch = 5 Miles (Unless otherwise noted)

0 1 2 3 4 5 Miles

0 1 2 3 4 5 Kilometers

D

DISTANCE MAP

DISTANCE BETWEEN POINTS GIVEN IN MILES. MILEAGE DETERMINED BY MOST DIRECT DRIVING ROUTE.

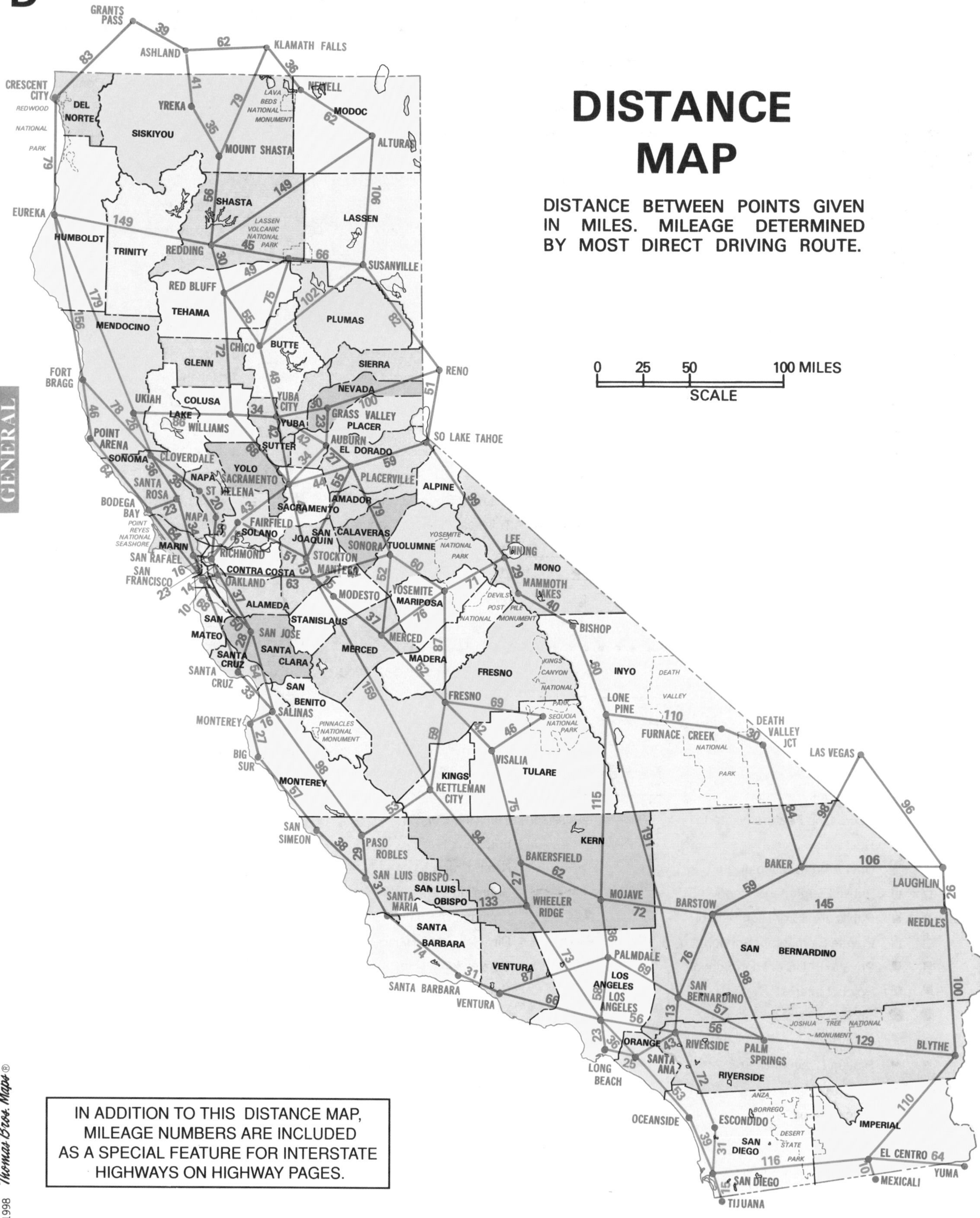

IN ADDITION TO THIS DISTANCE MAP, MILEAGE NUMBERS ARE INCLUDED AS A SPECIAL FEATURE FOR INTERSTATE HIGHWAYS ON HIGHWAY PAGES.

MILEAGE CHART

MILEAGE DETERMINED BY MOST DIRECT DRIVING ROUTE

	BAKERSFIELD	CHICO	EUREKA	FRESNO	LAS VEGAS	LONG BEACH	LOS ANGELES	MERCED	MODESTO	OAKLAND	PALM SPRINGS	REDDING	RIVERSIDE	SACRAMENTO	SALINAS	SAN DIEGO	SAN FRANCISCO	SAN JOSE	SAN LUIS OBISPO	SANTA ANA	SANTA BARBARA	SANTA ROSA	SOUTH LAKE TAHOE	STOCKTON	VENTURA
ALTURAS	577	207	292	470	624	705	650	415	374	379	720	142	645	297	471	741	360	392	577	683	737	367	241	342	692
ANAHEIM	138	505	718	245	274	24	30	302	341	443	100	577	42	415	346	86	449	403	235	4	128	485	490	370	102
AUBURN	306	90	321	199	601	441	420	143	106	115	518	175	473	34	207	539	121	151	339	452	444	131	86	70	421
BAKERSFIELD		362	555	109	284	132	113	163	200	285	209	433	177	272	206	232	283	241	114	143	146	340	360	227	115
BARSTOW	129	491	684	236	155	123	131	292	330	414	123	559	78	401	335	180	412	385	264	116	205	469	395	356	174
BENICIA	292	144	287	177	578	429	396	123	84	37	510	187	466	58	106	513	43	49	236	456	341	61	164	74	374
BISHOP	222	360	553	235	284	308	277	223	252	314	308	396	264	265	347	360	335	321	357	301	327	382	176	240	296
BLYTHE	339	705	918	446	208	228	230	501	521	622	129	775	171	616	530	222	619	575	433	202	314	676	686	568	287
BODEGA BAY	404	189	266	249	632	491	451	194	156	74	568	246	527	141	165	594	64	109	294	516	400	23	256	152	431
BURBANK	104	465	659	210	294	31	9	266	304	383	111	536	67	376	304	127	377	334	200	45	93	421	446	330	64
CHICO	362		218	254	620	498	475	198	160	172	575	73	543	89	264	638	180	212	389	509	490	166	170	134	477
CLAREMONT	135	497	691	308	246	47	26	298	336	415	79	568	23	408	336	107	409	366	226	23	118	453	469	360	88
DAVIS	287	83	282	180	582	422	399	134	87	66	499	155	454	15	158	520	74	102	320	433	425	83	127	60	402
DEATH VALLEY	238	530	703	395	182	229	288	393	422	484	241	566	262	435	475	407	505	491	352	324	366	552	346	410	336
EL CENTRO	322	706	872	427	303	219	213	482	520	615	110	775	154	618	536	110	601	561	413	201	308	660	596	554	279
EUREKA	555	218		446	797	683	669	390	353	288	788	149	743	287	381	776	269	323	508	722	614	219	388	332	643
FAIRFIELD	278	132	276	171	561	412	391	118	79	45	489	173	457	43	132	554	55	78	260	423	362	57	150	51	389
FORT BRAGG	460	199	156	353	730	597	551	292	255	180	674	288	629	217	280	669	176	216	401	608	507	119	319	233	534
FRESNO	109	254	446		416	239	220	56	93	178	316	325	272	165	134	339	185	151	140	250	245	233	251	120	222
GRASS VALLEY	329	78	320	222	624	464	443	166	129	138	541	163	496	57	230	562	144	174	362	475	467	154	115	93	444
LAGUNA BEACH	162	528	741	269	288	34	55	324	363	465	115	598	62	437	368	75	471	425	257	19	150	507	511	391	123
LA JOLLA	219	625	763	326	319	90	103	382	419	507	122	667	79	492	428	13	517	449	309	79	203	536	529	450	172
LASSEN NATIONAL PK	437	102	202	329	695	573	550	273	235	247	650	45	618	164	339	713	255	287	459	584	562	241	199	209	552
LAS VEGAS	284	620	797	408		314	302	446	484	567	276	640	231	567	488	332	568	524	414	269	354	610	466	510	323
LONE PINE	159	420	593	285	224	232	209	283	312	374	277	456	204	325	365	307	395	381	273	245	285	442	236	300	254
LONG BEACH	132	498	683	239	314		24	294	333	417	118	568	60	407	338	103	427	383	218	25	120	477	479	361	93
LOS ANGELES	113	475	669	220	302	24		276	314	393	103	546	56	386	314	119	387	344	204	35	96	431	456	340	66
MAMMOTH LAKES	262	320	513	195	324	348	317	283	212	274	348	356	305	225	307	400	295	281	397	341	367	342	130	200	336
MANTECA	215	147	345	108	499	348	329	54	15	63	425	219	380	44	99	447	73	65	248	382	354	123	144	13	330
MARTINEZ	288	146	290	172	571	424	391	118	79	28	507	191	460	61	101	509	38	47	233	453	338	64	168	70	369
MERCED	163	198	390	56	446	294	276		37	123	368	269	326	109	105	395	130	115	195	305	300	172	194	64	278
MODESTO	200	160	353	93	484	333	314	37		84	410	232	365	72	104	432	92	77	233	344	339	135	156	27	315
MOJAVE	62	424	617	169	229	117	94	225	262	347	162	495	118	334	268	213	345	303	190	130	116	402	351	289	123
MONTEREY	216	278	399	149	504	356	334	115	138	111	433	350	388	190	18	442	122	75	145	367	250	170	272	141	273
NAPA	331	150	255	224	613	463	439	169	130	46	540	191	495	61	145	566	56	88	270	492	363	36	168	69	390
NEEDLES	281	638	821	383	108	269	279	439	476	560	190	729	224	548	481	311	561	517	416	262	352	603	552	508	316
NEVADA CITY	334	83	325	227	629	469	448	171	134	143	546	168	501	62	235	567	149	179	367	480	472	159	110	98	449
NEWPORT BEACH	155	519	735	262	279	21	43	317	366	458	108	592	55	430	361	81	465	418	230	12	141	498	502	382	114
OAKLAND	285	172	288	178	567	417	393	123	84		494	218	449	81	99	520	10	42	224	446	317	60	195	73	344
ONTARIO	141	493	696	247	222	44	37	303	341	420	77	573	21	413	341	125	414	371	232	33	123	458	483	367	103
OXNARD	122	485	650	229	316	85	59	271	322	351	165	555	117	395	252	178	379	329	142	97	38	421	478	349	7
PALMDALE	98	460	653	205	244	81	58	261	298	383	126	531	82	370	304	182	381	339	221	94	116	438	387	325	87
PALM SPRINGS	209	575	788	316	276	118	103	368	410	494		658	56	484	415	135	504	460	306	96	199	554	435	438	172
PALO ALTO	261	213	302	171	544	403	364	135	97	43	480	251	433	120	74	482	33	20	205	426	311	89	223	92	342
PASADENA	109	475	688	216	259	31	7	271	310	394	104	554	52	384	315	134	404	360	210	42	95	454	463	338	68
PLACERVILLE	282	133	331	175	525	416	395	122	83	125	493	205	461	44	177	548	131	127	309	427	429	141	59	55	397
REDDING	433	73	149	325	640	568	546	269	232	218	658		600	161	334	680	218	246	431	579	537	223	249	206	548
RENO	432	172	342	297	444	510	504	241	209	216	510	196	465	132	308	561	223	249	434	503	507	229	61	177	496
RICHMOND	299	163	276	192	581	431	407	137	98	14	508	204	462	74	113	534	24	56	238	460	331	50	181	82	358
RIVERSIDE	177	543	743	272	231	60	56	326	365	449	56	600		439	367	92	463	413	259	43	147	509	379	406	125
SACRAMENTO	272	89	287	165	567	407	386	109	72	81	484	161	439		173	505	87	117	305	418	410	97	107	45	387
SALINAS	206	264	381	134	488	338	314	105	104	99	415	334	367	173		441	101	57	125	349	218	160	251	122	245
SAN BERNARDINO	167	534	714	269	228	63	59	325	362	439	57	595	13	436	360	104	444	401	260	48	154	486	436	389	123
SAN DIEGO	232	638	776	339	332	103	119	395	432	520	135	680	92	505	441		530	462	322	84	216	549	542	493	185
SAN FRANCISCO	283	180	269	185	568	427	387	130	92	10	504	218	463	87	101	530		45	230	452	336	56	192	88	367
SAN JOSE	241	212	323	151	524	383	344	115	77	42	460	246	413	117	57	462	45		185	406	291	96	197	72	322
SAN JUAN CAPISTRANO	163	529	742	270	289	40	55	325	364	466	116	599	63	438	369	66	472	426	258	20	151	508	512	395	124
SAN LUIS OBISPO	114	384	508	140	414	218	204	195	233	224	306	431	259	305	125	322	230	185		238	106	281	382	254	137
SAN MATEO	313	199	288	181	554	413	374	125	86	29	490	237	443	106	84	492	19	30	215	436	321	75	209	78	352
SAN PEDRO	134	496	690	242	285	9	22	298	336	415	126	568	68	408	336	118	409	366	213	37	108	454	478	362	75
SAN RAFAEL	306	167	260	199	588	438	414	144	105	21	515	243	470	83	121	559	18	64	246	470	339	39	181	94	366
SANTA ANA	143	509	722	250	269	25	35	305	344	446	96	579	43	418	349	84	452	406	238		131	488	492	372	104
SANTA BARBARA	146	490	614	245	354	120	96	300	339	317	199	537	147	410	218	216	336	291	106	131		387	490	374	31
SANTA CRUZ	239	230	354	150	524	379	344	116	109	75	456	275	411	146	33	462	74	29	162	390	268	129	229	101	300
SANTA MARIA	145	415	539	171	428	194	170	226	264	255	273	462	221	336	156	290	261	216	31	205	74	312	413	285	103
SANTA ROSA	340	166	219	233	610	477	431	172	135	60	554	223	509	97	160	549	56	96	281	488	387		199	113	414
SAUSALITO	298	183	276	200	583	442	402	145	107	25	519	259	478	99	116	545	15	60	245	467	351	55	207	103	382
SEQUOIA NATIONAL PK	129	343	556	84	408	258	234	139	178	335	235	385	303	252	209	361	272	228	178	269	276	329	335	206	262
SONOMA	331	163	239	224	613	468	439	170	130	46	540	204	495	75	146	584	43	89	271	495	364	20	181	82	391
SONORA	215	189	387	108	498	380	366	52	42	105	420	261	391	86	157	447	115	107	247	357	352	165	139	55	330
SOUTH LAKE TAHOE	360	170	388	251	466	479	456	194	156	195	435	249	379	107	251	542	192	197	382	492	490	199		131	471
STOCKTON	227	134	332	120	510	361	340	64	27	73	438	206	406	45	122	493	88	72	254	372	374	113	131		342
SUSANVILLE	465	105	257	356	599	600	577	299	262	275	677	110	645	191	369	714	252	280	465	613	571	257	133	240	582
UKIAH	402	147	179	295	672	539	493	234	197	135	616	184	571	159	222	611	118	158	343	550	449	62	253	175	476
VALLEJO	310	147	265	203	592	442	418	131	92	25	519	186	474	57	124	545	35	67	249	471	342	46	266	65	370
VENTURA	115	477	643	222	323	93	66	278	315	344	172	548	125	387	245	185	367	322	137	104	31	414	471	342	
YOSEMITE NATIONAL PK	199	263	476	92	435	331	307	83	122	174	408	333	364	172	188	434	184	178	236	342	329	234	133	129	330
YREKA	531	171	205	427	698	657	638	372	335	307	747	98	689	263	423	756	317	346	534	668	630	325	315	297	645
YUBA CITY	313	48	290	206	608	448	427	150	113	122	525	133	480	41	214	546	128	158	346	459	451	201	145	86	428
YUMA	379	742	922	491	299	278	271	545	584	674	169	816	221	655	595	173	655	614	473	260	368	702	646	603	337

CITIES AND COMMUNITIES

A

COMMUNITY NAME	CO.	ZIP CODE	POP.	PG.	GD.
ACADEMY	FRCO	93612		57	E2
ACAMPO	SJCO	95220		40	A4
ACTON	LACO	93510		89	E4
ADAMS	LAK	95496		31	E4
ADELAIDA	SLO	93446		75	E1
* ADELANTO	SBD	92301	13,350	91	A3
ADIN	MOD	96006		14	D3
AERIAL ACRES	KER	93523		80	D5
AETNA SPRINGS	NAPA	94567		32	B5
AFTON	GLE	95920		25	A5
AGATE BAY	PLA	95711		35	E1
AGOURA	LACO	91301		97	A1
* AGOURA HILLS	LACO	91301	21,150	97	A1
AGUA CALIENTE	SDCO	92086		107	C2
AGUA CALIENTE	SON	95476		38	B3
AGUA CALIENTE HOT SPGS	SDCO	92036		107	E4
AGUA DULCE	LACO	91350		89	D4
AGUANGA	RCO	92302		107	A1
AGUEREBERRY POINT	INY	92328		71	D1
AHWAHNEE	MAD	93601		49	C4
AINSWORTH CORNER	SIS			5	C2
* ALAMEDA	ALA	94501	78,300	L	D5
-- ALAMEDA COUNTY	ALA		1,356,100		
ALAMO	CC	94507		M	A4
ALAMORIO	IMP	92227		109	B4
ALAMO SQUARE	SFCO	94115		142	B3
* ALBANY	ALA	94706	17,100	L	D4
ALBERHILL	RCO	92303		99	A4
ALBION	MEN	95410		30	B1
ALDER CREEK	SAC	95670		40	B1
ALDERCROFT HEIGHTS	SC	95030		46	A5
ALDERPOINT	HUM	95411		16	D5
ALDER SPRINGS	FRCO	93602		58	A1
ALDER SPRINGS	GLE	95939		23	E3
ALGODONES	BAJA			112	C5
* ALHAMBRA	LACO	91801	88,500	R	C3
ALISO VIEJO	ORCO	92656		98	D5
ALLEGHANY	SIE	95910		26	D4
ALLENDALE	SOL	95688		39	A2
ALLENSWORTH	TUL	93219		68	A4
ALMANOR	PLU	95911		20	B4
ALPAUGH	TUL	93201		67	E4
ALPINE	SDCO	92001		107	B5
-- ALPINE COUNTY	ALP		1,180		
ALPINE HEIGHTS	SDCO	92001		107	B5
ALPINE HIGHLANDS	SDCO	92001		107	B5
ALPINE HILLS	SDCO	92001		107	B5
ALPINE HILLS	SMCO	94025		N	D3
ALPINE MEADOWS	PLA	95730		35	D2
ALPINE PEAKS	PLA	95730		35	D2
ALTA	PLA	95701		34	E1
ALTADENA	LACO	91001		R	C2
ALTA LOMA	SBD	91701		U	D2
ALTAMONT	ALA	94550		M	D5
ALTAMONT	KLAM			5	C1
ALTA SIERRA	KER	93285		69	C5
ALTAVILLE	CAL	95221		41	B4
ALTA VISTA	INY	93514		51	C3
ALTON	HUM	95540		15	D2
* ALTURAS	MOD	96101	3,160	8	A1
ALUM ROCK	SCL	95127		P	C3
ALVISO	SCL	95002		P	B2
* AMADOR CITY	AMA	95601	210	40	D2
-- AMADOR COUNTY	AMA		34,000		
AMARGOSA VALLEY	NYE			62	E4
AMBLER	TUL	93277		68	B1
AMBOY	SBD	92304		93	E3
* AMERICAN CANYON	NAPA	94590	8,900	L	D1
AMERICAN HOUSE	PLU	95981		26	C3
* ANAHEIM	ORCO	92801	293,200	T	D2
ANAHEIM HILLS	ORCO	92807		U	C5
* ANDERSON	SHA	96007	8,650	18	C3
ANDERSON SPRINGS	LAK	95461		31	E4
ANDRADE	IMP	92283		112	C5
ANGEL ISLAND	MAR	94920		45	B1
* ANGELS CAMP	CAL	95222	2,840	41	B4
ANGELUS OAKS	SBD	92305		99	E1
ANGWIN	NAPA	94508		38	C1
ANNAPOLIS	SON	95412		30	E5
ANTELOPE	SAC	95621		34	A5
ANTELOPE ACRES	LACO	93534		89	D2
* ANTIOCH	CC	94509	74,800	M	C3
ANZA	RCO	92306		100	C5
APPLEGATE	PLA	95703		34	D3
* APPLE VALLEY	SBD	92307	52,800	91	C4
APTOS	SCR	95003		54	B2
ARABIA	RCO	92274		101	B5
ARBUCKLE	COL	95912		32	E5
* ARCADIA	LACO	91006	52,100	R	C3
* ARCATA	HUM	95521	16,300	9	E5
ARDEN	CLK			74	D3
ARDEN	SAC	95864		40	A1
ARGUS	SBD	93562		71	B5
ARLINGTON	RCO	92503		99	A3
ARMONA	KIN	93202		67	D1
ARNOLD	CAL	95223		41	C3
ARNOLD HEIGHTS	RCO	92508		99	B3
AROMAS	MON	95004		54	C2
ARROWBEAR LAKE	SBD	92308		99	D1
ARROWHEAD SPRINGS	SBD	92404		99	C1
* ARROYO GRANDE	SLO	93420	15,150	76	B4
* ARTESIA	LACO	90701	16,400	T	A1
ARTOIS	GLE	95913		24	D4
* ARVIN	KER	93203	10,700	78	E4
ASHFORD JUNCTION	INY	92328		72	C4
* ASHLAND	JKSN		16,200	3	E1
ASPENDELL	INY	93514		51	B5
ASTI	SON	95425		31	C5
* ATASCADERO	SLO	93422	24,750	76	A2
* ATHERTON	SMCO	94025	7,300	N	D2
ATOLIA	SBD	93558		80	E3
* ATWATER	MCO	95301	20,900	48	B4
ATWOOD	ORCO	92601		T	E1
* AUBURN	PLA	95603	11,450	34	C3
* AVALON	LACO	90704	3,400	97	E5
* AVENAL	KIN	93204	12,350	66	E3
AVERY	CAL	95224		41	C3
AVILA BEACH	SLO	93424		76	A4
AVON	CC	94553		L	E3
* AZUSA	LACO	91702	43,950	U	A1

B

COMMUNITY NAME	CO.	ZIP CODE	POP.	PG.	GD.
BABBITT	MIN			44	B1
BACHELOR VALLEY	LAK	95493		31	D2
BADGER	TUL	93603		58	D4
BADWATER	INY	92328		72	A2
BAKER	SBD	92309		83	B3
* BAKERSFIELD	KER	93301	212,700	78	D3
BALBOA	ORCO	92661		T	C4
BALBOA ISLAND	ORCO	92662		T	C4
BALCH CAMP	FRCO	93657		58	C2
* BALDWIN PARK	LACO	91706	73,500	R	D3
BALLARAT	INY	93562		71	C3
BALLARD	SB	93463		86	E3
BALLENA	SDCO	92065		107	B4
BALLICO	MCO	95303		48	A3
BANGOR	BUT	95914		25	E5
BANKHEAD SPRINGS	SDCO	92034		111	A4
BANNER	SDCO	92036		107	D4
* BANNING	RCO	92220	23,850	100	A3
BARD	IMP	92222		112	D5
BARDSDALE	VEN	93015		88	D4
BARRETT JUNCTION	SDCO	92017		112	B2
BARRIO LOGAN	SDCO	92113		216	A5
BARSTOW	FRCO	93702		57	B3
* BARSTOW	SBD	92311	22,300	91	E1
BARTLE	SIS	96057		13	B2
BARTLETT	INY	93545		60	B5
BARTLETT SPRINGS	LAK	95443		32	A2
BARTON	AMA	92309		41	B2
BARTON FLATS	SBD			100	A1
BASSETT	LACO	91746		R	D4
BASSETTS	SIE	96125		27	A4
BASS LAKE	MAD	93604		49	E4
BAXTER	PLA	95704		34	E1
BAY FARM ISLAND	ALA			L	D5
BAY POINT	CC	94565		M	B3
BAYSHORE	SMCO	94005		L	C5
BAYSIDE	HUM	95524		9	E5
BAYWOOD PARK	SLO	93402		75	E3
BEAR HARBOR	MEN	95489		22	B2
BEAR VALLEY	ALP	95223		41	E2
BEAR VALLEY	MPA	95338		48	E3
BEAR VALLEY	SDCO	92082		106	E3
BEAR VALLEY SPRINGS	KER	93561		79	B4
BEATTY	NYE			62	B2
BEATTY JUNCTION	INYO	92328		61	E4
* BEAUMONT	RCO	92223	10,450	99	E3
BECKWOURTH	PLU	96129		27	C2
BEE ROCK	SLO	93426		65	D5
BEL AIRE	MAR	94920		L	B4
BEL AIR ESTATES	LACO	90077		Q	B4
BELDEN	PLU	95915		26	A1
* BELL	LACO	90201	36,400	R	B5
BELLA VISTA	KER	93283		79	E1
BELLA VISTA	SHA	96008		18	D4
* BELLFLOWER	LACO	90706	65,300	S	E1
* BELL GARDENS	LACO	90201	43,750	R	B5
BELLOTA	SJCO	95236		40	C4
BELL SPRINGS	MEN	95440		22	D1
BELL STATION	SC	95020		55	A2
BEL MARIN KEYS	MAR	94949		L	B2
* BELMONT	SMCO	94002	24,950	N	C2
* BELVEDERE	MAR	94920	2,250	L	B4
BELVEDERE GARDENS	MAR	94920		L	B4
BENBOW	HUM	95440		22	C1
BEND	TEH	96008		18	D4
* BENICIA	SOL	94510	27,200	L	E2
BEN LOMOND	SCR	95005		N	E5
BENTON	MNO	93512		51	C1
BERENDA	MAD	93637		56	E1
* BERKELEY	ALA	94710	104,700	L	D4
BERKELEY CAMP	SON	95421		37	C1
BERMUDA DUNES	RCO	92201		101	A4
BERRY CREEK	BUT	95916		25	E3
BERRYESSA HIGHLANDS	NAPA	94558		38	D1
BERRYESSA PINES	NAPA	94567		38	C1
BERTELEDA	DN	95531		2	A4
BERTSCH TERRACE	DN	95531		1	E4
BETHANY	SJCO	95376		M	E5
BETHEL ISLAND	CC	94511		M	D3
BETTERAVIA	SB	93455		86	B1
* BEVERLY HILLS	LACO	90210	33,300	Q	C3
BIEBER	LAS	96009		14	B3
BIG BAR	AMA	95704		41	A2
BIG BEAR CITY	SBD	92314		92	A5
* BIG BEAR LAKE	SBD	92315	5,950	92	A5
BIG BEND	SHA	96011		13	A4
BIG BEND	SON	95476		38	B3
BIG CREEK	FRCO	93605		50	B5
* BIGGS	BUT	95917	1,640	25	B5
BIG MEADOW	CAL	95223		41	E2
BIG OAK FLAT	TUO	95305		48	D1
BIG PINE	INY	93513		51	E5
BIG RIVER	SBD	92242		104	A1
BIG SPRINGS	SIS			4	C5
BIG SUR	MON	93920		64	B2
BINGHAMTON	SOL	95625		39	B2
BIOLA	FRCO	93606		57	B3
BIRCH HILL	SDCO	92060		107	A2
BIRCHVILLE	NEV			34	C1
BIRDS LANDING	SOL	94512		39	B4
* BISHOP	INY	93514	3,520	51	D4
BITTERWATER	SBT	93930		65	C1
BLACKHAWK	CC	94526		M	B4
BLACK POINT	MAR	94945		L	B2
BLACKWELLS CORNER	KER	93249		77	C1
BLAIRSDEN	PLU	96103		27	A2
BLOCKSBURG	HUM	95414		16	D4
BLOOMFIELD	SON	94952		37	D3
BLOOMINGTON	SBD	92316		99	A2
BLOSSOM	TEH	96080		18	B5
BLOSSOM VALLEY	SDCO	92021		107	A5
BLUE DIAMOND	CLK			74	B3
BLUE JAY	SBD	92317		91	C5
* BLUE LAKE	HUM	95525	1,240	10	A5
BLUE LAKES	LAK	95493		31	C2
* BLYTHE	RCO	92225	18,350	103	D5
BOCA	NEV	95737		27	E5
BODEGA	SON	94922		37	C3
BODEGA BAY	SON	94923		37	C3
BODFISH	KER	93205		79	C1
BODIE	MNO	93517		43	D3
BOLINAS	MAR	94924		37	E5
BOLSA KNOLLS	MON	93906		54	C3
BOMBAY BEACH	IMP	92257		108	E2
* BONANZA	KLAM		340	5	E1
BONDS CORNER	IMP	92250		112	C4
BONITA	SDCO	92002		V	D4
BONNEFOY	AMA	95642		41	A2
BONSALL	SDCO	92003		106	C2
BOONVILLE	MEN	95415		30	E3
BOOTJACK	MPA	95338		49	B3
BORON	KER	93516		80	E5
BORREGO SPRINGS	SDCO	92004		107	E2
BOSTONIA	SDCO	92021		V	E2
BOULDER CREEK	SCR	95006		N	E5
BOULDER OAKS	SDCO	92062		112	D1
BOULEVARD	SDCO	92005		111	A4
BOUQUET CANYON	LA	91355		89	C4
BOUSE	LPAZ	92363		104	D3
BOWLES	FRCO	93725		57	C4
BOWMAN	PLA	95603		34	C3
BOYES HOT SPRINGS	SON	95416		38	B3
BOYLE HEIGHTS	LACO	90033		R	A4
* BRADBURY	LACO	91010	890	R	E3
BRADLEY	MON	93426		65	E4
BRANSCOMB	MEN	95417		22	D3
* BRAWLEY	IMP	92227	21,550	109	A4
* BREA	ORCO	92621	34,800	T	D1
BRENDA	LPAZ			104	D4
* BRENTWOOD	CC	94513	13,200	M	D3
BRENTWOOD	LACO	90049		Q	B4
BRICEBURG	MPA	95345		49	B2
BRICELAND	HUM	95440		16	B5
BRIDGE HAVEN	SON	95450		37	C2
BRIDGE HOUSE	SAC	95683		40	C2
BRIDGEPORT	MPA	95306		49	A4
BRIDGEPORT	MNO	93517		43	B3
BRIDGEPORT	NEV	95975		34	B1
BRIDGEVIEW	JOS			2	D1
BRIDGEVILLE	HUM	95526		16	C3
* BRISBANE	SMCO	94005	3,120	L	C5
BRITE VALLEY	KER	93561		79	C4
BROOKDALE	SCR	95007		N	E5
* BROOKINGS	CUR		4,450	1	D2
BROOKS	YOL	95606		32	D5
BROWNS VALLEY	YUB	95918		33	E1
BROWNSVILLE	YUB	95919		26	A4
BRUCEVILLE	SAC	95758		39	E3
BRUSH CREEK	BUT	95916		25	E3
BRYN MAWR	SBD	92318		99	C2
BUCKEYE	ED	95634		34	E3
BUCKEYE	SHA	96003		18	B2
BUCKHORN	AMA	95666		41	B2
BUCKHORN SPRINGS	JKSN			4	B2
BUCKMAN SPRINGS	SDCO	92062		112	D1
BUCK MEADOWS	MPA	95321		49	A1
BUCKS BAR	ED	95684		35	A5
BUCKS LAKE	PLU	95971		26	B2
* BUELLTON	SB	93427	3,510	86	D3
BUENA	SDCO	92083		106	C3
* BUENA PARK	ORCO	90620	72,700	T	B1
BUENA VISTA	AMA	95640		40	D3
BUHACH	MCO	95340		48	B4
* BULLHEAD CITY	MOH		26,940	85	D4
BUMMERVILLE	CAL	95257		41	B2
BUNTINGVILLE	LAS	96114		21	B4
* BURBANK	LACO	91501	101,400	Q	E2
BURDELL	MAR	94945		L	A2
* BURLINGAME	SMCO	94010	28,100	N	C1
BURNEY	SHA	96013		13	C5
BURNT RANCH	TRI	95527		10	D5
BURREL	FRCO	93607		57	B5
BURSON	CAL	95225		40	D4
BUTTE CITY	GLE	95920		25	A5
-- BUTTE COUNTY	BUT		197,000		
BUTTE MEADOWS	BUT	95921		25	D1
BUTTONWILLOW	KER	93206		78	A3
BYRON	CC	94514		M	D4

C

COMMUNITY NAME	CO.	ZIP CODE	POP.	PG.	GD.
CABAZON	RCO	92230		100	B3
CABBAGE PATCH	CAL	95223		41	E2
CADENASSO	YOL	95607		32	E5
CADIZ	SBD	92319		94	B4
CADWELL	SON	95472		37	E2
CAIRNS CORNER	TUL	93247		68	C2
CAJON JUNCTION	SBD	92358		91	A5
* CALABASAS	LACO	91302	18,800	97	B1
-- CALAVERAS COUNTY	CAL		36,950		
CALAVERITAS	CAL	95249		41	A3
* CALEXICO	IMP	92231	24,700	112	B4
CALICO GHOST TOWN	SBD	92398		82	A5
CALIENTE	KER	93518		79	B3
* CALIFORNIA CITY	KER	93505	8,825	80	B4
CALIFORNIA HOT SPRINGS	TUL	93207		69	B4
CALIFORNIA VALLEY	SLO	93453		77	B3
* CALIMESA	RCO	92320	7,300	99	D2
* CALIPATRIA	IMP	92233	7,275	109	B3
* CALISTOGA	NAPA	94515	4,710	38	A1
CALLAHAN	SIS	96014		11	D2
CALNEVA	LAS	96113		21	E5
CALPELLA	MEN	95418		31	B1
CALPINE	SIE	96124		27	B3
CALWA	FRCO	93725		57	C3
* CAMARILLO	VEN	93010	58,200	96	C1
CAMBRIA	SLO	93428		75	C2
CAMDEN	FRCO	93656		57	C5
CAMERON CORNERS	SDCO	92006		112	D2
CAMERON PARK	ED	95682		34	C5
CAMINO	ED	95709		35	A4
* CAMPBELL	SCL	95008	38,250	P	B4
CAMP CONIFER	TUL	93271		59	A5
CAMP CONNELL	CAL	95223		41	D3
CAMP KLAMATH	DN	95548		2	A5
CAMP MEEKER	SON	95419		37	D2
CAMPO	SDCO	92006		112	D2
CAMPO SECO	CAL	95226		40	E3
CAMP SIERRA	FRCO	93634		50	B5
CAMPTONVILLE	YUB	95922		26	B5
CANBY	MOD	96015		14	D1
CANE BRAKE	KER	93255		70	B5
CANOGA PARK	LACO	91303		Q	A2
CANTIL	KER	93519		80	C3
CANTUA CREEK	FRCO	93608		56	D5
CANYON	CC			L	E4
CANYON CITY	SDCO	92006		112	D2
CANYON COUNTRY	LACO	91351		89	C4
CANYON CREST HEIGHTS	RCO	92507		99	B2
CANYON DAM	PLU	95923		20	C5
* CANYON LAKE	RCO	92380	11,300	99	C4
CAPAY	YOL	95607		32	E5
CAPETOWN	HUM	95536		15	C3
CAPISTRANO BEACH	ORCO	92624		105	D1
* CAPITOLA	SCR	95010	10,800	54	A2
CARBONDALE	AMA	95640		40	C2
CARDIFF-BY-THE-SEA	SDCO	92007		106	B4
CARL INN	TUO	95321		49	C1
CARLOTTA	HUM	95528		16	A2
* CARLSBAD	SDCO	92008	68,200	106	B3
* CARMEL-BY-THE-SEA	MON	93921	4,460	54	A5
CARMEL HIGHLANDS	MON	93923		54	A5
CARMEL VALLEY VILLAGE	MON	93924		54	C5
CARMET	SON	94923		37	C2
CARMICHAEL	SAC	95608		34	A5
CARNELIAN BAY	PLA	95711		36	A1
CARPENTERVILLE	CUR			1	C1
* CARPINTERIA	SB	93013	14,500	87	E4
CARQUINEZ HEIGHTS	SOL	94590		38	C4
* CARSON	LACO	90745	88,100	S	C2
* CARSON CITY	CRSN		40,443	36	C2
-- CARSON CITY COUNTY	CRSN		40,443		
CARSON HILL	CAL	95222		41	B4
CARTAGO	INY	93549		70	B1
CARUTHERS	FRCO	93609		57	C5
CASA BLANCA	RCO	92504		99	B3
CASA DE ORO	SDCO	92077		V	E3
CASA DIABLO HOT SPGS	MNO	93546		50	E2
CASITAS SPRINGS	VEN	93001		88	A4
CASMALIA	SB	93429		86	B1
CASPAR	MEN	95420		22	B5
CASSEL	SHA	96016		13	D5
CASTAIC	LACO	91310		89	B4
CASTELLA	SHA	96017		12	C3
CASTELLAMMARE	LACO	90290		Q	A4
CASTLE CRAG	SHA	96013		12	C3
CASTLE PARK	SDCO	92011		V	D5
CASTRO VALLEY	ALA	94546		L	E5
CASTROVILLE	MON	95012		54	B3
* CATHEDRAL CITY	RCO	92234	35,400	100	D4
CATHEYS VALLEY	MPA	95306		49	A3
CAVE JUNCTION	JOS			2	D1
CAYTON	SHA	96013		13	C4
CAYUCOS	SLO	93430		75	D2
CAZADERO	SON	95421		37	C1
CECILVILLE	SIS	96018		11	B3
CEDAR BROOK	FRCO	93641		58	D3
CEDAR CREST	FRCO	93605		50	C5
CEDAR FLAT	PLA	95711		35	E1
CEDAR GLEN	SBD	92321		91	D5
CEDAR GROVE	ED	95709		35	A4
CEDAR GROVE	FRCO	93641		59	B3
CEDARPINES PARK	SBD	92322		91	B5
CEDAR RIDGE	NEV	95924		34	C2
CEDAR VALLEY	MAD	93644		49	D4
CEDARVILLE	MOD	96104		7	D5
CENTERVILLE	ALA	94536		P	A2
CENTERVILLE	DGL			36	C3
CENTERVILLE	FRCO	93654		57	E3
CENTERVILLE	SHA	96001		18	B2
CENTRAL VALLEY	SHA	96019		18	C1
CENTRE CITY	SDCO	92101		215	D3
CENTURY CITY	LACO	90067		Q	D4
* CERES	STA	95307	31,100	47	D3
* CERRITOS	LACO	90701	55,300	T	B1
CHALFANT	MNO	93514		51	D3
CHALK HILL VALLEY	SON	95448		37	E1
CHALLENGE	YUB	95925		26	B4
CHAMBERS LODGE	PLA	95718		35	E2
CHATSWORTH	LACO	91311		Q	A1
CHAWANAKEE	FRCO	93602		50	A5
CHEMEKETA PARK	SCL	95030		P	A4
CHEROKEE	BUT	95965		25	D3
CHEROKEE	NEV	95602		26	C5
CHERRY VALLEY	RCO	92223		99	E2
CHESTER	PLU	96020		20	A4
CHICAGO PARK	NEV	95712		34	C2
* CHICO	BUT	95926	47,200	25	B3
CHILCOOT	PLU	96105		27	D2
CHINATOWN	SFCO	94108		142	D2
CHINESE CAMP	TUO	95309		41	B5
* CHINO	SBD	91710	63,400	U	D3
* CHINO HILLS	SBD	91709	49,750	98	D2
CHINQUAPIN	MPA	95389		49	D2
CHIQUITA LAKE	ED	95634		35	A3
CHIRIACO SUMMIT	RCO			101	E4

*** INDICATES INCORPORATED CITY**

CITIES

COMMUNITY NAME	CO.	ZIP CODE	POP.	PG.	GD.
CHLORIDE CITY	INY	92328		62	A4
CHOCTAW VALLEY	KER	93306		78	E2
CHOLAME	SLO	93431		66	D5
* CHOWCHILLA	MAD	93610	6,600	48	D5
CHROME	GLE	95963		24	A3
CHUALAR	MON	93925		54	D4
* CHULA VISTA	SDCO	92010	153,200	V	D4
CIBOLA	LPAZ			110	D2
CIENEGA SPRINGS	LPAZ			104	C1
CIMA	SBD	92323		84	B4
CIRCLE OAKS	NAPA	94599		38	D2
CISCO	PLA	95728		35	B1
CITRUS HEIGHTS	SAC	95610		34	A5
CITY HEIGHTS	SDCO	92105		V	C3
* CITY OF COMMERCE	LACO	90040	12,700	R	B4
* CITY OF INDUSTRY	LACO	91744	690	R	E4
CLAIREMONT MESA	SDCO	92117		V	B2
* CLAREMONT	LACO	91711	34,050	U	C2
CLARENDON HEIGHTS	SFCO	94114		141	E5
CLARK	STOR			28	E4
-- CLARK COUNTY	CLK		741,459		
CLARKSBURG	YOL	95612		39	D2
CLARKSVILLE	ED	95682		34	C5
CLAY	SAC	95638		40	B3
* CLAYTON	CC	94517	9,400	M	B3
CLEAR CREEK	SIS	96039		2	E4
* CLEARLAKE	LAK	95422	12,050	32	A3
CLEARLAKE KEYS	LAK	95423		32	A3
CLEARLAKE OAKS	LAK	95423		32	A3
CLEMENTS	SJCO	95227		40	C3
CLEONE	MEN	95437		22	C4
CLIFF HOUSE	TUO	95321		49	B1
CLINTON	AMA	95232		41	A2
CLIO	PLU	96106		27	A3
CLIPPER GAP	PLA	95703		34	C3
CLIPPER MILLS	BUT	95930		26	A4
CLOVERDALE	SHA	96007		18	B3
* CLOVERDALE	SON	95425	5,475	31	C4
* CLOVIS	FRCO	93612	65,000	57	D3
CLYDE	CC	94520		M	A3
* COACHELLA	RCO	92236	21,050	101	B4
* COALINGA	FRCO	93210	9,925	66	D3
COALINGA MINERAL SPGS	FRCO	93210		66	B2
COARSEGOLD	MAD	93614		49	C4
COBB	LAK	95426		31	E4
CODORA	GLE	95970		25	A5
COFFEE CREEK	TRI	96091		11	E3
COHASSET	BUT	95926		25	C1
COLD SPRINGS	TUO	95370		42	A3
COLES STATION	ED	95684		35	B5
COLEVILLE	MNO	96107		42	D1
* COLFAX	PLA	95713	1,450	34	D2
COLLEGE CITY	COL	95931		33	A3
COLLEGEVILLE	SJCO	95206		40	B5
COLLIERVILLE	SJCO	95220		40	B3
COLLINSVILLE	SOL	94585		39	B4
* COLMA	SMCO	94014	1,230	L	B5
COLOMA	ED	95613		34	D4
COLONIA	VEN	93030		176	C3
* COLTON	SBD	92324	44,500	99	B2
COLUMBIA	TUO	95310		41	C4
* COLUSA	COL	95932	5,275	32	E2
-- COLUSA COUNTY	COL		17,950		
COMPTCHE	MEN	95427		30	C1
* COMPTON	LACO	90220	93,300	S	C1
* CONCORD	CC	94520	111,800	M	A3
CONFIDENCE	TUO	95370		41	D4
CONSTANTIA	LAS	96019		27	E1
-- CONTRA COSTA COUNTY	CC		870,700		
COOKS STATION	AMA	95666		41	C1
COOL	ED	95614		34	C4
COOLIDGE SPRING	IMP	92274		108	C1
COPCO	SIS	96044		4	C2
COPPEROPOLIS	CAL	95228		41	A5
* CORCORAN	KIN	93212	14,600	67	E3
CORDELIA	SOL	93063		L	E1
* CORNING	TEH	96021	6,150	24	D2
* CORONA	RCO	91720	99,500	U	E4
CORONA DEL MAR	ORCO	92625		T	C5
* CORONADO	SDCO	92118	28,500	V	B4
CORONA HEIGHTS	SFCO	94114		142	A5
CORONITA	RCO	91720		98	E3
* CORTE MADERA	MAR	94925	8,600	L	A3
COSO JUNCTION	INY	93542		70	C3
* COSTA MESA	ORCO	92626	102,100	T	C4
COSUMNES	SAC	95683		40	B2
* COTATI	SON	94931	6,500	37	E3
COTO DE CAZA	ORCO	92679		98	E4
COTTAGE SPRINGS	CAL	95223		41	D2
COTTON CENTER	TUL	93257		68	C3
COTTONWOOD	SHA	96022		18	C3
COULTERVILLE	MPA	95311		48	D2
COURTLAND	SAC	95615		39	D3
COVELO	MEN	95428		23	A3
* COVINA	LACO	91722	45,950	U	A2
COVINGTON MILL	TRI	96052		11	E5
COWAN HEIGHTS	ORCO	92705		98	C4
COW HOLLOW	SFCO	94123		142	A4
COYOTE	SCL	95013		P	D4
COYOTE WELLS	IMP	92259		111	C3
COZZENS CORNERS	SON	95441		31	D5
CRAFTON	SBD	92374		99	D2
CRANMORE	SUT	95645		33	B3
CRANNELL	HUM	95530		9	E4
* CRESCENT CITY	DN	95531	8,800	1	D4
CRESCENT MILLS	PLU	95934		20	C5
CRESSEY	MCO	95312		48	A4
CREST	SDCO	92021		112	A1
CRESTLINE	SBD	92325		91	C5
CRESTMORE	SBD	92316		99	B2
CRESTON	SLO	93432		76	B2
CRESTVIEW	MNO	93514		50	D1
CROCKETT	CC	94525		L	D2
CROMBERG	PLU	96103		27	A2
CROWN POINT	SDCO	92109		V	A3
CROWS LANDING	STA	95313		47	C4

COMMUNITY NAME	CO.	ZIP CODE	POP.	PG.	GD.
* CRYSTAL BAY	WSH		1,200	36	A1
* CUDAHY	LACO	90201	24,400	R	B5
CUESTA BY THE SEA	SLO	93402		75	D3
* CULVER CITY	LACO	90230	40,500	Q	D4
CUMMINGS	MEN	95477		22	D2
CUMMINGS VALLEY	KER	93561		79	B4
CUNNINGHAM	SON	95472		37	E2
* CUPERTINO	SCL	95014	43,650	P	A3
-- CURRY COUNTY	CUR		21,300		
CURRY VILLAGE	MPA	95389		49	D2
CUTLER	TUL	93615		58	B5
CUTTEN	HUM	95534		15	E1
CUYAMA	SB	93214		87	D1
CUYAMACA	SDCO	92335		107	C4
* CYPRESS	ORCO	90630	46,400	T	B2

D

COMMUNITY NAME	CO.	ZIP CODE	POP.	PG.	GD.
DAGGETT	SBD	92327		92	A1
DAIRY	KLAM			5	D1
DAIRYVILLE	TEH	96080		18	D5
DALES	TEH	96080		18	E4
* DALY CITY	SMCO	94014	99,500	L	B5
DANA	SHA	96036		13	D3
* DANA POINT	ORCO	92629	36,000	105	D1
* DANVILLE	CC	94526	37,050	M	A4
DARDANELLE	TUO	95314		42	B2
DARLINGTONIA	DN	95543		2	B3
DARRAH	MPA	95338		49	C3
DARWIN	INY	93522		70	E2
DATE CITY	IMP	92250		112	C3
DAULTON	MAD	93653		57	B1
DAVENPORT	SCR			53	D2
* DAVIS	YOL	95616	52,600	39	C1
DAVIS CREEK	MOD	96108		7	C4
DAVIS DAM	MOH			85	D4
DAY	MOD	96056		13	E3
DAYTON	BUT	95926		25	B3
DAYTON	LYON			36	D1
DEATH VALLEY JCT	INY			72	D1
DEER PARK	NAPA	94576		38	B1
DEHESA	SDCO	92021		112	A1
* DELANO	KER	93215	31,450	68	B3
DEL CERRO	SDCO	92120		V	D3
DEL DIOS	SDCO	92025		106	D3
DELEVAN	COL	95988		24	D5
DELFT COLONY	TUL	93619		58	A5
DELHI	MCO	95315		47	E4
DEL LOMA	TRI	96010		17	A1
* DEL MAR	SDCO	92014	5,125	V	A1
-- DEL NORTE COUNTY	DN		28,650		
DEL PASO HEIGHTS	SAC	95838		33	E5
DEL REY	FRCO	93616		57	E4
* DEL REY OAKS	MON	93940	1,670	54	B4
DEL RIO WOODS	SON	95448		37	E1
DEL ROSA	SBD	92404		99	C1
DELTA	SHA	96051		12	B4
DE LUZ	SDCO	92055		106	B1
DEMOCRAT HOT SPRINGS	KER	93301		79	B2
DENAIR	STA	95316		47	E3
DENNY	TRI	95538		10	E5
DENVERTON	SOL	94585		39	A3
DERBY ACRES	KER	93268		77	E3
DE SABLA	BUT	95978		25	C2
DESCANSO	SDCO	92016		107	C5
DESCANSO JUNCTION	SDCO	92016		107	C5
DESERT BEACH	RCO	92254		101	D5
DESERT CENTER	RCO	92239		102	C4
DESERT HAVEN	RCO	92240		100	D3
* DESERT HOT SPRINGS	RCO	92240	14,850	100	D2
DESERT LAKE	KER	93516		80	D5
DESERT SHORES	IMP	92274		108	C1
DEVILS DEN	KER	93204		67	B5
DEVORE	SBD	92405		99	B1
DIABLO	CC	94528		M	B4
* DIAMOND BAR	LACO	91765	56,000	U	B3
DIAMOND SPRINGS	ED	95619		34	E5
DI GIORGIO	KER	93217		79	A3
DILLON BEACH	MAR	94929		37	D3
DINKEY CREEK	FRCO	93617		58	C1
* DINUBA	TUL	93618	14,650	58	A5
DISCOVERY BAY	CC	94514		39	D5
DIXIELAND	IMP	92251		108	D5
* DIXON	SOL	95620	13,100	39	B2
DOBBINS	YUB	95935		26	B5
DOG TOWN	CAL	95249		41	B4
DOGTOWN	MPA	95311		48	E2
DOGTOWN	SJCO	95220		40	C3
DORRINGTON	CAL	95223		41	D3
* DORRIS	SIS	96023	890	5	A2
* DOS PALOS	MCO	93620	4,360	56	B2
DOS PALOS Y	MCO	93620		56	A1
DOS RIOS	MEN	95429		23	A3
DOUGHERTY	ALA	94566		46	B2
DOUGLAS CITY	TRI	96024		17	D2
-- DOUGLAS COUNTY	DGL		27,637		
DOVE CANYON	ORCO	92679		98	E4
* DOWNEY	LACO	90241	97,600	R	B5
DOWNIEVILLE	SIE	95936		26	D4
DOYLE	LAS	96019		27	E1
DOYLES CORNER	SHA	96040		13	D5
DOZIER	SOL	94535		39	B3
DRAKES BEACH	MAR	94956		37	D5
DRYTOWN	AMA	95699		40	E2
* DUARTE	LACO	91010	21,900	R	D3
* DUBLIN	ALA	94566	26,250	M	B5
DUBOCE TRIANGLE	SFCO	94114		142	B4
DUCOR	TUL	93218		68	D4
DULZURA	SDCO	92017		112	B2
DUNCANS MILLS	SON	95430		37	C2
DUNLAP	FRCO	93621		58	C3
DUNLAP	MEN	95490		30	D1
DUNMOVIN	INY	93542		70	C3
DUNNEVILLE	SBT			54	E2
DUNNIGAN	YOL	95937		33	A4

COMMUNITY NAME	CO.	ZIP CODE	POP.	PG.	GD.
* DUNSMUIR	SIS	96025	2,020	12	D3
DURHAM	BUT	95938		25	B3
DUSTIN ACRES	KER	93268		78	A4
DUTCH FLAT	PLA	95714		34	D1
DYER	ESM			52	B2

E

COMMUNITY NAME	CO.	ZIP CODE	POP.	PG.	GD.
EAGLE LAKE RESORT	LAS	96130		20	D2
EAGLE MOUNTAIN	RCO	92241		102	B3
EAGLE ROCK	LACO	90041		R	A3
EAGLES NEST	SDCO	92086		107	C2
EAGLEVILLE	MOD	96110		8	D2
EARLIMART	TUL	93219		68	B4
EARP	SBD	92242		104	B1
EAST BAKERSFIELD	KER	93307		78	D3
EAST GUERNEWOOD	SON	95446		37	C1
EAST HIGHLANDS	SBD	92346		99	C1
EAST IRVINE	ORCO	92650		T	E4
EAST LAKE	ORCO	92686		T	E1
EASTLAKE	SDCO	91913		V	D4
EAST NICOLAUS	SUT	95622		33	D3
EASTON	FRCO	93706		57	C4
EAST OROSI	TUL	93647		58	B5
* EAST PALO ALTO	SMCO	94303	24,800	N	E2
EAST QUINCY	PLU	95971		26	D1
EAST SAN DIEGO	SDCO	92105		V	C3
EAST SAN JOSE	SC	95127		46	B4
EASTSIDE ACRES	MAD	93622		56	C3
EASTSIDE RANCH	MAD	93622		56	C3
ECHO DELL	SDCO	92016		107	C5
ECHO LAKE	ED	95721		35	E4
EDEN GARDENS	SDCO	92075		106	B4
EDEN HOT SPRINGS	RCO	92353		99	D3
EDGEWOOD	SIS	96094		12	C1
EDISON	KER	93220		78	E3
EDNA	SLO	93401		76	B4
EDWARDS AIR FORCE BASE	KER	93523		90	C1
EEL ROCK	HUM	95554		16	C4
EHRENBERG	LPAZ			103	E5
EL BONITA	SON	95446		37	C1
* EL CAJON	SDCO	92020	93,400	V	E3
EL CARISO	RCO	92530		99	A4
* EL CENTRO	IMP	92243	37,800	109	A5
* EL CERRITO	CC	94530	23,250	L	C3
ELDERS CORNERS	PLA	95603		34	C3
ELDERWOOD	TUL	93286		58	C5
EL DORADO	ED	95623		34	D5
-- EL DORADO COUNTY	ED		144,900		
EL DORADO HILLS	ED	95630		34	C5
ELDRIDGE	SON	95431		38	B3
ELECTRA	AMA	95642		41	A2
EL GRANADA	SMCO	94018		N	B2
ELIZABETH LAKE	LACO	93550		89	D3
ELK	MEN	95432		30	C2
ELK CREEK	GLE	95939		24	A4
ELK GROVE	SAC	95624		39	E2
ELK VALLEY	DN	95543		2	C2
ELLWOOD	SB	93117		87	B4
EL MACERO	YOL	95618		39	C1
ELMIRA	SOL	95625		39	B2
EL MODENA	ORCO	92669		T	E2
* EL MONTE	LACO	91731	113,300	R	D3
ELMORE	IMP	92227		108	D3
ELM VIEW	FRCO	93725		57	C4
EL NIDO	MCO	95317		56	C1
* EL PASO DE ROBLES	SLO	93446	21,450	76	A1
EL PORTAL	MPA	95318		49	C2
EL PORVENIR	FRE	93608		56	C5
EL RIO	VEN	93030		176	D1
* EL SEGUNDO	LACO	90245	16,050	Q	C5
EL SERENO	LACO	90031		R	A3
EL SOBRANTE	CC	94803		L	D3
EL TORO	ORCO	92630		98	D4
EL TORO MARINE BASE	ORCO	92709		98	D4
EL VERANO	SON	95433		L	B1
ELVERTA	SAC	95626		33	E5
EMERALD BAY	ED	95733		35	E3
EMERALD BAY	ORCO	92651		T	D5
* EMERYVILLE	ALA	94608	6,450	L	C4
EMIGRANT GAP	PLA	95715		35	A1
EMMATON	SAC			M	D2
EMPIRE	STA	95319		47	D2
ENCANTO	SDCO	92114		V	D4
* ENCINITAS	SDCO	92024	57,100	106	B4
ENCINO	LACO	91316		Q	B3
ENGINEER SPRINGS	SDCO	92017		112	B2
ENTERPRISE	SHA	96001		18	C2
* ESCALON	SJCO	95320	5,275	47	C1
* ESCONDIDO	SDCO	92025	118,300	106	D3
-- ESMERALDA COUNTY	ESM		1,344		
ESPARTO	YOL	95627		33	A5
ESSEX	SBD	92332		94	D2
ESTRELLA	SLO	93451		76	B1
ETHEDA SPRINGS	FRCO	93633		58	D4
* ETNA	SIS	96027	780	11	D1
ETTERSBURG	HUM	95440		16	A5
EUCALYPTUS HILLS	SDCO	92040		V	E2
* EUREKA	HUM	95501	27,500	15	E1
EUREKA VLY/DOLORES HTS	SFCO	94114		45	B2
EVELYN	INY	92384		72	E2
EVERGREEN	SC	95121		46	C4
* EXETER	TUL	93221	8,275	68	C1

F

COMMUNITY NAME	CO.	ZIP CODE	POP.	PG.	GD.
* FAIRFAX	MAR	94930	7,025	L	A3
* FAIRFIELD	SOL	94533	86,900	M	A1
FAIRHAVEN	HUM	95564		15	D1
FAIRMEAD	MAD	93610		56	D1
FAIRMONT	LACO	93534		89	C2
FAIR OAKS	SAC	95628		34	A5
FAIR PLAY	ED	95684		41	A1
FAIRVIEW	TUL	93238		69	C4
FALES HOT SPRINGS	MNO	93517		43	A2
FALLBROOK	SDCO	92028		106	C2
FALLEN LEAF	ED	95716		35	E4
FALLON	MAR	94952		37	D3
FALL RIVER MILLS	SHA	96028		13	E4
FAMOSO	KER	93250		78	C1
* FARMERSVILLE	TUL	93223	7,125	68	C1
FARMINGTON	SJCO	95230		40	C5
FAWNSKIN	SBD	92333		91	E5
FEATHER FALLS	BUT	95940		26	A4
FELICITY	IMP			112	C5
FELIX	CAL	95228		41	A4
FELLOWS	KER	93224		77	E4
FELTON	SCR	95018		N	E5
FERN	SHA	96096		19	A1
FERNBROOK	SDCO	92065		107	A4
* FERNDALE	HUM	95536	1,240	15	D2
FETTERS HOT SPRINGS	SON	95416		38	B3
FIDDLETOWN	AMA	95629		40	E1
FIELDBROOK	HUM	95521		10	A4
FIELDS LANDING	HUM	95537		15	E1
* FILLMORE	VEN	93015	12,800	88	D4
FINANCIAL DISTRICT	SFCO	94104		142	E2
FINE GOLD	MAD	93643		49	D5
FINLEY	LAK	95435		31	D3
* FIREBAUGH	FRCO	93622	5,825	56	C3
FISH CAMP	MPA	93623		49	D3
FISH ROCK	MEN	95445		30	D4
FISH SPRINGS	INY	93513		59	E1
FIVE CORNERS	LAKE			7	B1
FIVE CORNERS	SJCO	95336		47	C1
FIVE POINTS	FRCO	93624		57	A5
FIVE POINTS	LACO	91732		R	D4
FLEETRIDGE	SDCO	92106		V	A3
FLETCHER HILLS	SDCO	92020		V	D2
FLINN SPRINGS	SDCO	92021		107	A5
FLORIN	SAC	95828		39	E2
FLOURNOY	TEH	96029		24	B2
FLOWING WELLS	RCO	92254		101	C5
* FOLSOM	SAC	95630	41,450	34	B5
* FONTANA	SBD	92335	103,300	99	B1
FOOTHILL FARMS	SAC	95841		34	A5
FOOTHILL RANCH	ORCO	92610		98	D4
FORBESTOWN	BUT	95963		26	A4
FORD CITY	KER	93268		78	A4
FOREST	SIE	95910		26	D4
FORESTA	MPA	95389		49	C2
FORESTHILL	PLA	95631		34	D3
FOREST FALLS	SBD	92339		100	A2
FOREST GLEN	TRI	96030		17	A3
FOREST HOME	AMA	95640		40	C2
FOREST KNOLLS	MAR	94933		38	A5
FOREST KNOLLS	SFCO	94116		141	D5
FOREST LAKE	LAK	95461		32	A4
FOREST RANCH	BUT	95942		25	C2
FOREST SPRINGS	NEV	95945		34	C2
FORESTVILLE	SON	95436		37	D2
FORKS OF SALMON	SIS	96031		11	A2
FORREST PARK	LACO	91350		89	C4
FORT BIDWELL	MOD	96112		7	D3
* FORT BRAGG	MEN	95437	6,200	22	C5
FORT DICK	DN	95538		1	D3
FORT IRWIN	SBD	92310		82	B3
* FORT JONES	SIS	96032	610	3	D5
FORT ROSS	SON	95450		37	B1
FORT SEWARD	HUM	95438		16	D5
* FORTUNA	HUM	95540	9,825	15	E2
FOSTER	SDCO	92040		V	E1
* FOSTER CITY	SMCO	94404	29,300	N	D1
FOSTER PARK	VEN	93001		88	A5
FOUNTAIN SPRINGS	TUL	93257		68	E4
* FOUNTAIN VALLEY	ORCO	92708	54,300	T	C3
FOUR CORNERS	SHA	96016		13	C4
FOUTS SPRINGS	COL	95979		24	A5
* FOWLER	FRCO	93625	3,740	57	D4
FRANKLIN	SAC	95758		39	E2
FRAZIER PARK	KER	93225		88	D1
FREDALBA	SBD	92382		99	D1
FREDERICKSBURG	ALP	96120		36	B4
FREDS PLACE	ED	95720		35	D4
FREEDOM	SCR	95019		54	B2
FREEMAN	KER	93527		80	C1
FREEPORT	SAC	95832		39	E2
FREESTONE	SON	95472		37	D2
* FREMONT	ALA	94536	78,300	P	A2
FREMONT VALLEY	KER	93519		80	B4
FRENCH CAMP	SJCO	95231		40	B5
FRENCH CORRAL	NEV	95975		34	B1
FRENCH GULCH	SHA	96033		18	A1
FRENCH POND	ED	95725		35	B4
FRESHWATER	HUM	95504		16	A1
* FRESNO	FRCO	93706	400,400	57	C3
-- FRESNO COUNTY	FRCO		760,900		
FRIANT	FRCO	93626		57	D2
FROGTOWN	CAL	95222		41	B4
FRUITRIDGE	SAC	95820		39	E1
FRUITVALE	KER	93308		78	C3
FRUTO	GLE	95988		24	B4
FULLER ACRES	KER	93307		78	E3
* FULLERTON	ORCO	92631	122,100	T	C1
FULTON	SON	95439		37	E1
FURNACE CREEK RANCH	INY	92328		62	A5

G

COMMUNITY NAME	CO.	ZIP CODE	POP.	PG.	GD.
GALLINAS	MAR	94903		L	B3
* GALT	SAC	95632	15,400	40	A3
GANNS	CAL	95223		41	D2
GARBERVILLE	HUM	95440		16	C5
* GARDENA	LACO	90247	56,800	S	C1
GARDEN FARMS	SLO	93422		76	B2
* GARDEN GROVE	ORCO	92640	151,400	T	C2
GARDEN PARK	ED	95633		34	D4
GARDEN VALLEY	ED	95633		34	D4
GARDNERVILLE	DGL			36	C3

CITIES AND COMMUNITIES

COMMUNITY NAME	CO.	ZIP CODE	POP.	PG.	GD.
GAREY	SB	93454		86	C1
GARLOCK	KER	93519		80	D2
GARNET	RCO	92258		100	C3
GASQUET	DN	95543		2	A3
GAVIOTA	SB	93117		86	D4
GAZELLE	SIS	96034		4	B5
GENESEE	PLU	95983		26	E1
GENOA	DGL			36	B3
GEORGETOWN	ED	95634		34	E3
GERBER	TEH	96035		24	E1
GEYSERVILLE	SON	95441		31	D5
GIANT FOREST	TUL	93271		59	A4
GIBSONVILLE	SIE	95981		26	D3
GILMAN HOT SPRINGS	RCO	92340		99	E3
* GILROY	SCL	95020	34,000	54	D2
GLAMIS	IMP	92248		109	E4
GLANNVALE	SAC	95758		39	E3
GLEN AVON	RCO	92509		99	A2
GLENBROOK	DGL			36	A2
GLENBURN	SHA	96036		13	D4
GLENCOE	CAL	95232		41	B2
* GLENDALE	LACO	91201	193,500	Q	E3
* GLENDORA	LACO	91740	51,200	U	A1
GLEN ELLEN	SON	95442		38	B2
GLENHAVEN	LAK	95443		31	E3
GLENN	GLE	95943		25	A4
-- GLENN COUNTY	GLE		26,600		
GLENNVILLE	KER	93226		69	A5
GLEN OAKS	SDCO	92001		107	A5
GLEN VALLEY	RCO	92370		99	B3
GLENVIEW	LAK	95451		31	E4
GLENVIEW	LACO	90290		Q	A3
GLENVIEW	SDCO	92021		107	A5
GOFFS	SBD	92332		94	E1
GOLDEN GATE HEIGHTS	SFCO	94112		141	D5
GOLDEN HILL	SDCO	92102		216	A3
GOLDEN HILLS	KER	93561		79	C4
GOLDEN SHORES	MOH	92363		95	E1
GOLDEN VALLEY	WSH			28	B3
GOLD HILL	ED	95651		34	D4
GOLD HILL	STOR			36	D1
GOLD RIVER	SAC	95670		40	B1
GOLD RUN	PLA	95717		34	D2
GOLD SPRINGS	TUO	95370		41	C4
GOLETA	SB	93111		87	B4
* GONZALES	MON	93926	6,050	54	E5
GONZALEZ ORTEGA	BAJA			112	C4
GOOD HOPE	RCO	92370		99	B4
GOODSPRINGS	CLK			74	B4
GOODYEARS BAR	SIE	95944		26	D4
GORDONS WELL	IMP			112	A5
GORMAN	LACO	93534		88	E2
GOSHEN	TUL	93227		68	A1
GOTTVILLE	SIS	96050		3	E3
GOVERNMENT FLAT	TEH	95939		23	D2
GRAEAGLE	PLU	96103		27	A3
GRANADA HILLS	LACO	91344		Q	A1
* GRAND TERRACE	SBD	92324	13,200	99	B2
GRANGEVILLE	KIN	93230		67	D1
GRANITEVILLE	NEV	95959		26	E5
GRANT HILL	SDCO	92102		216	B4
GRANTVILLE	SDCO	92120		V	C3
GRAPEVINE	KER	93301		88	D1
* GRASS VALLEY	NEV	95945	9,350	34	C1
GRATON	SON	95444		37	D2
GRAVESBORO	FRCO	93657		58	A3
GRAYSON	STA	95363		47	B3
GRAYS WELL	IMP			112	B5
GREELEY HILL	MPA	95311		48	E1
GREEN ACRES	RCO	92343		99	D4
GREENACRES	KER	93308		78	C3
GREENBRAE	MAR	94904		L	B3
GREENFIELD	KER	93309		78	D3
* GREENFIELD	MON	93927	9,325	65	B1
GREENHAVEN	SAC	95831		39	D1
GREEN POINT	MAR	94945		L	B2
GREEN VALLEY	LACO	91350		89	C3
GREEN VALLEY ESTATES	SOL	94585		38	D3
GREEN VALLEY FALLS	SDCO	92016		107	C5
GREEN VALLEY LAKE	SBD	92341		91	D5
GREENVIEW	SIS	96037		3	D5
GREENVILLE	PLU	95947		20	C5
GREENWOOD	ED	95635		34	D3
GRENADA	SIS	96038		4	B4
* GRIDLEY	BUT	95948	4,780	25	C5
GRIMES	COL	95950		33	B2
GRIZZLY FLAT	ED	95636		35	B5
GROSSMONT	SDCO	92041		V	D3
GROVELAND	TUO	95321		48	E1
* GROVER BEACH	SLO	93433	12,100	76	A4
GROVERS HOT SPRINGS	ALP	96120		36	B5
* GUADALUPE	SB	93434	6,250	76	B5
GUALALA	MEN	95445		30	D4
GUASTI	SBD	91743		U	E2
GUATAY	SDCO	92031		107	C5
GUERNEVILLE	SON	95446		37	C2
GUERNEWOOD PARK	SON	95446		37	C2
GUINDA	YOL	95637		32	D4
* GUSTINE	MCO	95322	4,140	47	C5
H					
HACIENDA	SON	95436		37	D1
HACIENDA HEIGHTS	LACO	91745		R	E5
HAIGHT-ASHBURY	SFCO	94117		142	A4
* HALF MOON BAY	SMCO	94019	10,600	N	C2
HALLELUJAH JUNCTION	LAS	96135		27	E2
HALLWOOD	YUB	95901		33	D2
HAMBURG	SIS	96045		3	C4
HAMILTON BRANCH	PLU	96137		20	C4
HAMILTON CITY	GLE	95951		24	E3
HAMMOND	TUL	93271		58	E5
HAMMONTON	YUB	95901		33	E2
HAM'S STATION	AMA	95666		41	C1
* HANFORD	KIN	93230	38,450	67	D1
HAPPY CAMP	SIS	96039		3	A4
HARBIN SPRINGS	LAK	95461		32	A4
HARBISON CANYON	SDCO	92021		107	A5
HARBOR	CUR			1	D2

COMMUNITY NAME	CO.	ZIP CODE	POP.	PG.	GD.
HARBOR CITY	LACO	90710		S	C2
HARDWICK	KIN	93230		67	D1
HARMONY	SLO	93435		75	C2
HARMONY GROVE	SDCO	92025		106	D3
HARRIS	HUM	95447		16	D5
HARRISBURG	INY	92328		71	C1
HARRISON PARK	SDCO	92036		107	C4
HART PARK	KER	93306		78	E2
HASKELL CREEK	SIE	96124		27	B3
HAT CREEK	SHA	96040		13	D5
HATFIELD	SIS	96134		5	D2
HAVILAH	KER	93518		79	C2
* HAWAIIAN GARDENS	LACO	90716	14,500	T	A2
HAWKINSVILLE	SIS	96097		4	A4
* HAWTHORNE	LACO	90250	76,700	Q	D5
HAWTHORNE	MIN			44	B1
HAYES VALLEY	SFCO	94102		142	B4
HAYFORK	TRI	96041		17	B2
* HAYWARD	ALA	94544	122,200	L	E5
HAZEL CREEK	SHA	96017		12	C4
* HEALDSBURG	SON	95448	9,575	37	D1
HEBER	IMP	92249		112	A3
HELENA	TRI	96042		17	B1
HELENDALE	SBD	92342		91	B2
HELLS GATE	INY	92328		61	E3
HELM	FRCO	93627		57	A5
* HEMET	RCO	92343	52,600	99	E4
* HENDERSON	CLK		120,196	74	E3
HENDERSON VILLAGE	SJCO	95240		40	A4
HENLEY	KLAM			5	C1
HENLEY	SIS	96044		4	A3
HENLEYVILLE	TEH	96021		24	C1
HERALD	SAC	95632		40	B3
* HERCULES	CC	94547	18,800	L	C3
HERMIT VALLEY	ALP	95314		42	B1
* HERMOSA BEACH	LACO	90254	18,700	S	A1
HERNANDEZ	SBT	95043		65	E1
HERNDON	FRCO	93721		57	B3
* HESPERIA	SBD	92345	59,400	91	B4
HESSEL	SON	95472		37	E3
HICKMAN	STA	95323		47	E2
HIDDEN GLEN	SDCO	92001		112	B1
* HIDDEN HILLS	LACO	91302	1,860	97	A5
HIDDEN MEADOWS	SDCO	92026		106	D3
HIDDEN VALLEY	PLA	95650		34	B4
HIDDEN VALLEY LAKE	LAK	95461		32	B4
HIGGINS CORNER	NEV	95603		34	C3
* HIGHLAND	SBD	92346	40,500	99	C1
HIGHLAND PARK	LACO	90042		R	A3
HIGHLANDS HARBOR	LAK	95457		32	A3
HIGHTS CORNER	KER	93308		78	C2
HIGHWAY CITY	FRCO	93705		57	C3
HILLCREST	SHA	96065		13	B5
HILL HAVEN	MAR	94920		L	B4
* HILLSBOROUGH	SMCO	94010	11,200	N	C1
HILMAR	MCO	95324		47	E4
HILT	SIS	96043		4	A2
HINKLEY	SBD	92347		91	C1
HOAGLIN	TRI	95495		16	E5
HOBART MILLS	NEV	95734		27	D5
HOBERGS	LAK	95496		31	E4
HODSON	CAL	95228		41	A5
HOLLAND	JOS			2	D1
* HOLLISTER	SBT	95023	24,700	54	E3
HOLLOW TREE	MEN	95455		22	B2
HOLLYWOOD	LACO	90028		Q	D3
HOLLYWOOD BEACH	VEN	93035		96	A1
HOLLYWOOD-BY-THE-SEA	VEN	93035		96	A1
HOLMES	HUM	95569		16	B3
HOLT	SJCO	95234		39	E5
* HOLTVILLE	IMP	92250	5,500	109	B5
HOLY CITY	SCL	95026		P	B5
HOME GARDENS	RCO	91720		99	A3
HOMELAND	RCO	92348		99	D4
HONCUT	BUT	95965		33	D1
HONEYDEW	HUM	95545		15	E4
HOOD	SAC	95639		39	D2
HOOPA	HUM	95546		10	C4
HOPETON	MCO	95369		48	B3
HOPE VLY FOREST CAMP	ALP	96120		36	B5
HOPLAND	MEN	95449		31	B3
HORNBROOK	SIS	96044		4	B3
HORNITOS	MPA	95325		48	E3
HORSE CREEK	SIS	96045		3	C3
HOT SPRINGS	KLAM			6	A1
HOUGH SPRINGS	LAK	95443		32	A2
HOWLAND FLAT	SIE	95981		26	D3
HUASNA	SLO	93402		76	D4
HUGHSON	STA	95326	3,530	47	E2
HULBURD GROVE	SDCO	92016		107	C5
HULLVILLE	LAK	95469		23	C5
-- HUMBOLDT COUNTY	HUM		125,500		
HUME	FRCO	93628		58	E3
HUMPHREYS STATION	FRCO	93612		58	A2
* HUNTINGTON BEACH	ORCO	92646	187,200	T	B4
HUNTINGTON LAKE	FRCO	93629		50	B5
* HUNTINGTON PARK	LACO	90255	60,200	R	A5
HURLETON	BUT	95962		25	E4
* HURON	FRCO	93234	5,525	67	A2
HYAMPOM	TRI	96046		16	E2
HYDESVILLE	HUM	95547		15	E2
I					
IDYLLWILD	RCO	92349		100	B4
IDYLWILD	SCL	95030		P	B4
IGNACIO	MAR	94947		L	B2
IGO	SHA	96047		18	B3
ILLINOIS VALLEY	JOS			2	C2
* IMPERIAL	IMP	92251	6,950	109	A5
* IMPERIAL BEACH	SDCO	92032	27,850	V	B5
-- IMPERIAL COUNTY	IMP		140,100		
IMPERIAL GABLES	IMP	92266		110	A3
INCLINE	MPA	95318		49	C2
INCLINE VILLAGE	WSH			36	A1
INDEPENDENCE	CAL	95245		41	B2
INDEPENDENCE	INY	93526		60	A3
INDIAN FALLS	PLU	95952		26	C1
INDIAN SPRINGS	SDCO	92035		112	A1

COMMUNITY NAME	CO.	ZIP CODE	POP.	PG.	GD.
* INDIAN WELLS	RCO	92260	3,080	100	E4
* INDIO	RCO	92201	42,100	101	A4
INDIO HILLS	RCO			101	B3
* INGLEWOOD	LACO	90301	116,000	Q	D5
INGOT	SHA	96008		18	E1
INSKIP	BUT	95921		25	D1
INVERNESS	MAR	94937		37	D4
INVERNESS PARK	MAR	94937		37	D4
INWOOD	SHA	96088		19	A2
-- INYO COUNTY	INY		18,500		
INYOKERN	KER	93527		80	D1
* IONE	AMA	95640	7,200	40	D2
IOWA HILL	PLA	95713		34	D2
* IRVINE	ORCO	92715	127,200	T	E4
IRVING'S CREST	SDCO	92065		107	A4
IRVINGTON	ALA	94538		P	A2
IRWIN	MCO	95380		47	E4
* IRWINDALE	LACO	91706	1,090	R	E3
ISLA VISTA	SB	93117		87	B4
* ISLETON	SAC	95641	830	M	D2
IVANHOE	TUL	93235		68	B1
IVANPAH	SBD	92364		84	C3
J					
* JACKSON	AMA	95642	3,880	40	E2
-- JACKSON COUNTY	JKSN		164,400		
JACKSON GATE	AMA	95642		40	E2
JACUMBA	SDCO	92034		111	B4
JAMACHA	SDCO	92035		106	E4
JAMESBURG	MON	93924		64	D1
JAMESTOWN	TUO	95327		41	C5
JAMUL	SDCO	92035		112	A1
JANESVILLE	LAS	96114		21	A4
JARBO GAP	BUT	95916		25	D3
JEAN	CLK			74	C5
JENNER	SON	95450		37	B2
JENNY LIND	CAL	95252		40	D4
JESMOND DENE	SDCO	92026		106	D3
JIMTOWN	SON	95959		31	E5
JOHANNESBURG	KER	93528		80	D3
JOHNSONDALE	TUL	93236		69	C4
JOHNSON PARK	SHA	96013		13	C5
JOHNSONS	HUM	95546		10	B2
JOHNSTONVILLE	LAS	96130		21	A3
JOHNSTOWN	SDCO	92021		107	A5
JOHNSVILLE	PLU	95921		26	E3
JOLON	MON	93928		65	B4
JONESVILLE	BUT	95921		19	E5
JORDAN HTS/LAUREL HTS	SFCO	94118		141	E3
-- JOSEPHINE COUNTY	JOS		71,100		
JOSHUA TREE	SBD	92252		100	E1
JULIAN	SDCO	92036		107	C3
JUNCTION CITY	TRI	96048		17	C1
JUNE LAKE	MNO	93529		50	D1
JUNE LAKE JUNCTION	MNO	93529		50	D1
JUNIPER FLATS	RCO	92367		99	D3
JUNIPER LAKE RESORT	LAS	96020		20	A3
K					
KAGEL CANYON	LACO	91342		Q	D1
KANE SPRING	IMP	92227		108	D3
KARNAK	SUT	95676		33	C4
KAWEAH	TUL	93237		58	E5
KEARNEY PARK	FRCO	93706		57	B3
KEARNY MESA	SDCO	92111		V	B2
KEARSARGE	INY	93526		60	A3
KEDDIE	PLU	95952		26	C1
KEELER	INY	93530		60	C5
KEENE	KER	93531		79	B4
KELLOGG	SON	94515		31	E5
KELSEY	ED	95643		34	D4
KELSEYVILLE	LAK	95451		31	D3
KELSO	SBD	92351		83	E5
KENO	KLAM			5	A1
KENSINGTON	CC	94708		L	D3
KENSINGTON	SDCO	92116		V	C3
KENTFIELD	MAR	94904		L	A3
KENTWOOD IN THE PINES	SDCO	92036		107	C4
KENWOOD	SON	95452		38	B2
KEOUGH HOT SPRINGS	INY	93514		51	D4
KERBY	JOS			2	D1
KERCKHOFF POWERHOUSE	FRCO	93602		57	E1
* KERMAN	FRCO	93630	6,725	57	A3
KERN CITY	KER	93309		78	C3
-- KERN COUNTY	KER		624,700		
KERNVALE	KER	93240		79	C1
KERNVILLE	KER	93238		69	C5
KESWICK	SHA	96001		18	B2
KETTLEMAN CITY	KIN	93239		67	B3
KEYES	STA	95328		47	D3
KILKARE	ALA	94586		P	B1
* KING CITY	MON	93930	9,900	65	C2
KING COLE	KLAM			4	D1
KINGS BEACH	PLA	95719		36	A1
* KINGSBURG	FRCO	93631	8,450	57	D5
KINGSBURY	DGL			36	B3
-- KINGS COUNTY	KIN		118,900		
KINGS MOUNTAIN	SMCO	94062		N	C3
KINGSVILLE	ED	95623		34	D5
KINGVALE	NEV	95728		35	C1
KINSLEY	MPA	95311		49	B2
KIRKVILLE	SUT	95645		33	B3
KIRKWOOD	ALP	95646		36	A5
KIRKWOOD	TEH	96021		24	D2
KIT CARSON	AMA	95644		35	E5
KLAMATH	DN	95548		2	A5
-- KLAMATH COUNTY	KLAM		61,600		
* KLAMATH FALLS	KLAM		18,680	5	B1
KLAMATH GLEN	DN	95548		2	A5
KLAMATH RIVER	SIS	96050		3	D3
KLAU	SLO	93465		75	D1
KNEELAND	HUM	95549		16	B1
KNIGHTSEN	CC	94548		M	D3
KNIGHTS FERRY	STA	95367		48	A1
KNIGHTS LANDING	YOL	95645		33	C4
KNOB	SHA	96076		17	C3

COMMUNITY NAME	CO.	ZIP CODE	POP.	PG.	GD.
KNOWLES	MAD	93653		49	B5
KNOWLES CORNER	SON	95472		37	D2
KNOXVILLE	NAPA	95637		32	C4
KONO TAYEE	LAK	95458		31	E3
KORBEL	HUM	95550		10	B5
KRAMER	SBD	93516		80	E5
KYBURZ	ED	95720		35	D4
L					
LA BARR MEADOWS	NEV	95945		34	C2
* LA CANADA FLINTRIDGE	LACO	91011	20,000	R	B2
LA CONCHITA	VEN	93001		87	E5
LA COSTA	SDCO	92008		106	C3
LA CRESCENTA	LACO	91214		R	A2
LADERA	SMCO	94025		N	D3
* LAFAYETTE	CC	94549	23,550	L	E4
LA GRANGE	STA	95329		48	C2
* LAGUNA BEACH	ORCO	92651	23,800	T	E5
LAGUNA CREEK	SAC	95758		39	E2
* LAGUNA HILLS	ORCO	92653	25,000	98	D5
* LAGUNA NIGUEL	ORCO	92677	55,600	98	D5
LAGUNA WEST	SAC	95758		39	E2
LAGUNITAS	MAR	94938		38	A5
* LA HABRA	ORCO	90631	54,100	R	E5
* LA HABRA HEIGHTS	LACO	90631	6,550	R	D5
LA HONDA	SMCO	94020		45	D4
LA HONDA PARK	CAL	94020		41	B4
LAIRDS CORNER	TUL	93257		68	B3
LA JOLLA	SDCO	92037		105	G3
LA JOLLA AMAGO	SDCO	92060		107	A2
LA JOLLA SHORES	SDCO	92037		211	A1
LAKE	SFCO	94118		141	D3
LAKE ALPINE	ALP	95235		42	A1
LAKE ARROWHEAD	SBD	92352		91	C5
LAKE BERRYESSA ESTATES	NAPA	94567		32	C5
LAKE CITY	MOD	96115		7	D5
LAKE CITY	NEV	95959		26	D5
-- LAKE COUNTY (CA)	LAE		55,300		
-- LAKE COUNTY (OR)	LAKE		7,550		
* LAKE ELSINORE	RCO	92330	25,600	99	B4
* LAKE FOREST	ORCO	92630	57,600	98	D4
LAKE FOREST	PLA	95730		35	E2
* LAKE HAVASU CITY	MOH		36,285	96	B4
LAKEHEAD	SHA	96051		12	C5
LAKE HENSHAW	SDCO	92070		107	B3
LAKE HILLS EST	ED	95630		34	C5
LAKE HUGHES	LACO	93532		89	C3
LAKE ISABELLA	KER	93240		79	C1
LAKELAND VILLAGE	RCO	92330		99	B5
LAKE OF THE WOODS	KER	93225		88	C2
* LAKEPORT	LAK	95453	4,580	31	D3
LAKE RIVERSIDE	RCO	92302		100	B5
LAKESHORE	FRCO	93634		50	C5
LAKESHORE	SHA	96051		12	B5
LAKESIDE	SDCO	92040		V	E2
* LAKEVIEW	LAKE		2,645	7	C1
LAKEVIEW	RCO	92353		99	D3
LAKEVIEW	SDCO	92040		107	A5
LAKEVIEW TERRACE	LACO	91340		Q	D1
LAKEVILLE	SON	95954		L	B1
* LAKEWOOD	LACO	90712	77,100	S	E2
LA LOMA	STA	95354		47	D2
* LA MESA	SDCO	92041	56,600	V	D3
* LA MIRADA	LACO	90638	45,800	T	B1
LA MOINE	SHA	96017		12	C4
LAMONT	KER	93241		78	E3
LANARE	FRCO	93656		57	B5
* LANCASTER	LACO	93534	121,000	90	A3
LANDERS	SBD	92284		92	E5
LANGELL VALLEY	KLAM			6	B2
* LA PALMA	ORCO	90623	15,500	T	B2
-- LA PAZ COUNTY	LPAZ		16,550		
LA PLAYA	SDCO	92106		V	A3
LA PORTE	PLU	95981		26	C3
LA PRESA	SDCO	92077		V	E4
* LA PUENTE	LACO	91744	40,400	R	E4
* LA QUINTA	RCO	92253	18,050	100	E4
* LARKSPUR	MAR	94939	11,600	L	A3
LAS CRUCES	SB	93117		86	D4
LA SIERRA	RCO	92505		99	A3
LAS LOMAS	MON	95076		54	C3
LAS LOMAS	SON	95412		31	B5
-- LASSEN COUNTY	LAS		31,050		
* LAS VEGAS	CLK	89114	383,369	74	D2
* LATHROP	SJCO	95330	8,850	47	B1
LATON	FRCO	93242		57	D5
LATROBE	ED	95682		40	C1
LAUGHLIN	CLK			85	D4
LAUREL HEIGHTS	SFCO	94118		141	E3
* LA VERNE	LACO	91750	32,300	U	B2
* LAWNDALE	LACO	90260	29,450	S	B1
LAYTONVILLE	MEN	95454		22	D3
LEBEC	KER	93243		88	D1
LE GRAND	MCO	95333		48	D5
LEESVILLE	COL	95987		32	B2
LEE VINING	MNO	93541		43	C5
LEGGETT	MEN	95455		22	C2
LEISURE TOWN	SOL	95688		39	A2
LEISURE WORLD	ORCO	90740		98	A4
LEISURE WORLD	ORCO	92653		98	D5
LELITER	KER	93527		70	D5
LEMONCOVE	TUL	93244		68	D1
* LEMON GROVE	SDCO	92045	24,700	V	D3
LEMON HEIGHTS	ORCO	92705		T	E3
LEMON VALLEY	WSH	96109		28	B3
* LEMOORE	KIN	93245	16,350	67	C1
LENWOOD	SBD	92311		91	D1
LEONA VALLEY	LACO	93551		89	D3
LEUCADIA	SDCO	92024		106	B3
LEWISTON	TRI	96052		17	D1
LIBERTY FARMS	SOL	95647		39	C3
LIDO ISLE	ORCO	92660		T	C4
LIKELY	MOD	96116		8	B3
LINCOLN	JKSN			4	C2
* LINCOLN	PLA	95648	7,950	34	A3
LINCOLN ACRES	SDCO	92050		V	D4
LINCOLN VILLAGE	SJCO	95207		40	A5
LINDA	YUB	95961		33	D2

* INDICATES INCORPORATED CITY

CITIES

COMMUNITY NAME	CO.	ZIP CODE	POP.	PG.	GD.
LINDA MAR	SMCO	94044		N	B1
LINDA VISTA	SDCO	92111		V	B3
LINDCOVE	TUL	93221		68	C1
LINDEN	SJCO	95236		40	C5
* LINDSAY	TUL	93247	8,825	68	D2
LINGARD	MCO	95340		48	C5
LITCHFIELD	LAS	96117		21	C3
LITTLE LAKE	INY	93542		70	C4
LITTLE RIVER	MEN	95456		30	B1
LITTLEROCK	LACO	93543		90	B3
LITTLE SHASTA	SIS	96064		4	C4
LITTLE VALLEY	LAS	96053		14	B5
* LIVE OAK	SUT	95953	5,275	33	C1
LIVE OAK PARK	SDCO	92028		106	C2
LIVE OAK SPRINGS	SDCO	92005		112	E1
* LIVERMORE	ALA	94550	65,400	M	C5
* LIVINGSTON	MCO	95334	10,450	48	A4
LOCH LOMOND	LAK	95426		31	E4
LOCKE	SAC	95690		39	D3
LOCKEFORD	SJCO	95237		40	B4
LOCKWOOD	MON	93932		65	C4
LOCKWOOD VALLEY	VEN	93225		88	C2
LODGE POLE	TUL	93271		59	B4
* LODI	SJCO	95240	54,500	40	A4
LODOGA	COL	95979		32	B4
LOGAN HEIGHTS	SDCO	92113		V	B4
LOG CABIN	YUB	95922		26	C5
LOG SPRING	TEH	96074		14	E4
LOLETA	HUM	95551		15	E2
* LOMA LINDA	SBD	92354	21,200	99	C2
LOMA MAR	SMCO	94021		N	C4
LOMA PARK	KER	93306		78	E3
LOMA RICA	YUB	95901		33	E1
* LOMITA	LACO	90717	20,100	S	C2
LOMO	BUT	95942		25	C1
* LOMPOC	SB	93436	41,000	86	B3
LONDON	TUL	93631		58	A5
LONE MOUNTAIN	SFCO	94118		141	E3
LONE PINE	INY	93545		60	B4
LONG BARN	TUO	95335		41	E4
* LONG BEACH	LACO	90801	437,800	S	D3
LONGVALE	MEN	95490		22	E4
LONGVIEW	LACO	93553		90	C4
LOOKOUT	MOD	96054		14	B3
* LOOMIS	PLA	95650	6,025	34	B4
LOOMIS CORNERS	SHA	96003		18	C2
LORAINE	KER	93518		79	D3
LORELLA	KLAM			6	A1
* LOS ALAMITOS	ORCO	90720	12,300	T	A2
LOS ALAMOS	SB	93440		86	C2
* LOS ALTOS	SCL	94022	27,300	N	E3
* LOS ALTOS HILLS	SCL	94022	7,800	N	E3
* LOS ANGELES	LACO	90001	3,638,100	R	A4
-- LOS ANGELES COUNTY	LACO		9,369,800		
* LOS BANOS	MCO	93635	20,100	55	E1
* LOS GATOS	SCL	95030	28,950	P	A4
LOS MOLINOS	TEH	96055		24	E1
LOS OLIVOS	SB	93441		86	E3
LOS OSOS	SLO	93402		75	E3
LOS RANCHITOS	MAR	94903		L	A3
LOS SERRANOS	SBD	91709		U	C3
LOST HILLS	KER	93249		77	D1
LOS TRANCOS WOODS	SMCO	94025		N	D3
LOTUS	ED	95651		34	D4
LOVELOCK	BUT	95978		25	D2
LOWER LAKE	LAK	95457		32	A4
* LOYALTON	SIE	96118	890	27	C3
LUCERNE	LAK	95458		31	D2
LUCERNE VALLEY	SBD	92356		91	E4
LUCIA	MON	93920		64	D3
LUDLOW	SBD	92357		93	B2
LUNDY	MNO	93541		43	B4
LUNING	MIN			44	E1
* LYNWOOD	LACO	90262	65,900	S	D1
LYNWOOD HILLS	SDCO	92010		V	D4
-- LYON COUNTY	LYON		20,001		
LYONSVILLE	TEH	96075		19	C4
LYTLE CREEK	SBD	92358		91	A5
LYTTON	SON	95448		31	D5
M					
MACDOEL	SIS	96058		4	E3
MADELINE	LAS	96119		8	B4
* MADERA	MAD	93637	34,650	57	A2
-- MADERA COUNTY	MAD		108,900		
MADISON	YOL	95653		33	A5
MAD RIVER	TRI	95552		16	E3
MADRONE	SCL	95037		P	D5
MAGALIA	BUT	95954		25	C2
MAGUNDEN	KER	93306		78	E3
MALAGA	FRCO	93725		57	D4
* MALIBU	LACO	90265	12,200	97	B2
MALIBU BEACH	LACO	90265		97	B2
* MALIN	KLAM		730	5	E2
* MAMMOTH LAKES	MNO	93546	5,275	50	D2
MANCHESTER	MEN	95459		30	C3
* MANHATTAN BEACH	LACO	90266	33,900	S	A1
MANKAS CORNER	SOL	94533		L	E1
* MANTECA	SJCO	95336	44,950	47	B1
MANTON	TEH	96059		19	A3
MANZANITA	SDCO	92005		111	A4
MAPLE CREEK	HUM	95550		16	B1
MARCH AFB	RCO	92508		99	C3
* MARICOPA	KER	93252	1,240	78	A5
* MARINA	MON	93933	17,750	54	B4
MARINA	SFCO	94123		142	B1
MARINA DEL REY	LACO	90291		Q	B5
MARIN CITY	MAR	94965		L	B4
-- MARIN COUNTY	MAR		239,500		
MARINWOOD	MAR	94903		L	A3
MARIPOSA	MPA	95338		49	B3
-- MARIPOSA COUNTY	MPA		16,050		
MARIPOSA PINES	MPA	95338		49	B2
MARKLEEVILLE	ALP	96120		36	C5
MARK WEST	SON	95492		37	E2

COMMUNITY NAME	CO.	ZIP CODE	POP.	PG.	GD.
MARK WEST SPRINGS	SON	95492		37	E1
MARSHALL	MAR	94950		37	D4
MARSHALL STATION	FRCO	93651		57	E2
MARTELL	AMA	95654		40	E2
* MARTINEZ	CC	94553	35,150	L	E3
MARTINS FERRY	HUM	95556		10	C3
MAR VISTA	LACO	90066		Q	C4
* MARYSVILLE	YUB	95901	62,200	33	D2
MASONIC	MNO	93517		43	C2
MATHER	TUO	95339		42	B5
MAXWELL	COL	95955		32	D1
MAYFAIR	KER	93307		78	E3
* MAYWOOD	LACO	90270	29,150	R	A4
MCARTHUR	SHA	96056		13	E4
MCCANN	HUM	95569		16	B4
MCCAULEY	MPA	93518		49	C2
MCCLOUD	SIS	96057		12	D2
* MCFARLAND	KER	93250	7,950	78	B1
MCKAYS POINT	TUL	93286		68	D1
MCKEE BRIDGE	JKSN			3	C1
MCKINLEYVILLE	HUM	95521		9	E4
MCKITTRICK	KER	93251		77	D3
MCMULLIN	FRCO	93706		57	B4
MEADOW LAKES	FRCO	93602		58	A1
MEADOW VALLEY	PLU	95956		26	B2
MEADOW VISTA	PLA	95722		34	C3
MECCA	RCO	92254		101	C5
MEEKS BAY	ED	95723		35	E2
MEINERS OAKS	VEN	93023		88	A4
MELOLAND	IMP	92243		112	B3
MENDOCINO	MEN	95460		30	B1
MENDOCINO COAST	MEN	95459		30	C3
-- MENDOCINO COUNTY	MEN		84,500		
* MENDOTA	FRCO	93640	7,400	56	D3
* MENLO PARK	SMCO	94025	30,200	N	D2
MENTONE	SBD	92359		99	D2
* MERCED	MCO	95340	61,000	48	C4
-- MERCED COUNTY	MCO	95369	198,800	48	D3
MERCED FALLS	MCO	95369		48	D3
MERCY HOT SPRINGS	FRCO	95043		55	E4
MERIDIAN	SUT	95957		33	B2
* MERRILL	KLAM		837	5	D2
MESA GRANDE	SDCO	92070		107	B3
MESQUITE SPRING	INY	92328		61	B2
METTLER	KER	93301		78	E5
MEXICALI	BAJA			112	B4
MEYERS	ED	95731		36	A4
MICHIGAN BAR	SAC	95683		40	C1
MICHIGAN BLUFF	PLA	95631		35	A2
MIDDLE RIVER	SJCO	95234		39	D5
MIDDLETOWN	LAK	95461		32	A5
MIDDLETOWN	SDCO	92103		215	D2
MIDLAND	KLAM			5	B1
MIDLAND	RCO	92255		103	B3
MIDPINES	MPA	95345		49	B3
MIDWAY	ALA	94550		M	E5
MIDWAY	SHA	96088		19	A2
MIDWAY CITY	ORCO	92655		T	C3
MIDWAY WELL	IMP			112	E3
MILFORD	LAS	96121		21	C5
* MILLBRAE	SMCO	94030	21,250	N	C1
MILL CREEK	TEH	96061		19	D4
MILLERS CORNER	MAD	93614		57	C1
MILLS ORCHARDS	COL	95955		32	C1
* MILL VALLEY	MAR	94941	13,750	L	A3
MILLVILLE	SHA	96062		18	D2
MILO	TUL	93265		68	E2
* MILPITAS	SCL	95035	59,700	P	B3
MILTON	CAL	95230		40	E4
MINA	MIN			44	E2
* MINDEN	DGL		1,441	36	C3
MINERAL	TEH	96063		19	C4
-- MINERAL COUNTY	MIN		6,475		
MINERAL KING	TUL	93271		59	B5
MINKLER	FRCO	93657		58	A3
MINNESOTA	SHA	96001		18	B2
MINTER VILLAGE	KER	93301		78	C2
MIRABEL PARK	SON	95436		37	D2
MIRACLE HOT SPRINGS	KER	93288		79	C1
MIRA LOMA	RCO	91752		98	E2
MIRAMAR	SDCO	92145		V	B1
MIRAMAR	SMCO	94019		N	B2
MIRAMONTE	FRCO	93641		58	C3
MIRA MONTE	VEN	93023		88	A4
MIRANDA	HUM	95553		16	C4
MIRA VISTA	LAK	95461		31	E4
MISSION BAY PARK	SDCO	92109		212	C4
MISSION BEACH	SDCO	92109		V	A3
MISSION DELORES	SFCO	94110		142	C5
MISSION HILLS	SDCO	92103		V	B3
MISSION SAN JOSE	ALA	94538		P	B2
MISSION VALLEY	SDCO	92108		214	A3
* MISSION VIEJO	ORCO	92690	89,900	98	D5
MISSION VILLAGE	SDCO	92123		V	C2
MITCHELL MILL	CAL	95255		41	B2
MI-WUK VILLAGE	TUO	95346		41	E4
MOCCASIN	TUO	95347		48	D1
* MODESTO	MDO	95350	178,700	47	D2
MODJESKA	ORCO	92669		98	E4
-- MODOC COUNTY	MOD	95350	10,150	6	C3
-- MOHAVE COUNTY	MOH		124,500		
MOJAVE	KER	93501		80	A5
MOKELUMNE HILL	CAL	95245		41	A3
MONARCH BEACH	ORCO	92677		98	D5
MONMOUTH	FRCO	93725		57	C4
MONO CAMP	MPA	95338		49	B3
MONO CITY	MNO	93541		43	C4
MONO HOT SPRINGS	FRCO	93642		50	D4
MONO LAKE	MNO	93541		43	C5
MONOLITH	KER	93548		79	D4
MONO VISTA	TUO	95370		41	D4
* MONROVIA	LACO	91016	38,900	R	D3
MONSON	TUL	93618		58	B5
* MONTAGUE	SIS	96064	1,370	4	B4
MONTALVO	VEN	93003		88	B5
MONTARA	SMCO	94037		N	B2

COMMUNITY NAME	CO.	ZIP CODE	POP.	PG.	GD.
MONTCLAIR	ALA			L	D4
* MONTCLAIR	SBD	91763	29,950	U	C2
* MONTEBELLO	LACO	90640	62,100	R	C4
MONTECITO	SB	93108		87	D4
MONTE MARIA	MAR	94947		L	A2
MONTE NIDO	LACO	91302		97	B2
* MONTEREY	MON	93940	32,200	54	B4
-- MONTEREY COUNTY	MON		364,500		
MONTEREY HILLS	LACO	90032		R	B3
* MONTEREY PARK	LACO	91754	64,000	R	B4
MONTE RIO	SON	95462		37	C2
* MONTE SERENO	SCL	95030	3,280	P	A4
MONTEZUMA	SOL	94512		39	B4
MONTGOMERY CREEK	SHA	96065		13	A5
MONTROSE	LACO	91020		Q	E2
MOONRIDGE	SBD	92315		92	A5
MOONSTONE	HUM	95570		9	E4
* MOORPARK	VEN	93021	27,750	88	D5
MOORPARK HOME ACRES	VEN	93021		88	D5
* MORAGA	CC	94556	16,300	L	E4
MORENA VILLAGE	SDCO	92006		112	D1
MORENO	SDCO	92040		107	A5
* MORENO VALLEY	RCO	92388	133,400	99	D3
MORETTIS	SDCO	92070		107	B3
* MORGAN HILL	SCL	95037	27,950	P	D5
MORMON BAR	MPA	95338		49	B3
MORONGO VALLEY	SBD	92256		100	C2
* MORRO BAY	SLO	93442	9,675	75	E3
MOSS BEACH	SMCO	94038		N	B2
MOSS LANDING	MON	95039		54	B3
MOUNTAIN CENTER	RCO	92361		100	B4
MOUNTAIN GATE	SHA	96003		18	C1
MOUNTAIN HOME VILLAGE	SBD	92359		99	E1
MOUNTAIN HOUSE	ALA	94550		46	D2
MOUNTAIN MESA	KER	93240		79	D1
MOUNTAIN RANCH	CAL	95246		41	B3
MOUNTAIN REST	FRCO	93667		58	B1
MOUNTAIN SPRINGS	CLK			74	A3
* MOUNTAIN VIEW	SCL	94040	71,300	N	E3
MOUNTAIN VIEW	SDCO	92102		216	D4
MOUNT AUKUM	ED	95656		40	E1
MOUNT BALDY VILLAGE	SBD	91759		90	E5
MOUNT BULLION	MPA	95338		49	A3
MOUNT CHARLESTON	CLK			74	A2
MOUNT HEBRON	SIS	96066		5	A4
MOUNT HELIX	SDCO	92041		V	D3
MOUNT HERMON	SCR	95041		P	A5
MOUNT HOPE	SDCO	92102		216	D3
MOUNT LAGUNA	SDCO	92048		107	E5
* MOUNT SHASTA	SIS	96067	3,520	12	C2
MOUNT SIGNAL	IMP	92231		112	A4
MOUNT VIEW	JKSN			4	C1
MOUNT WILSON	LACO	91023		R	C2
MUGGINSVILLE	SIS	96032		3	C5
MUIR BEACH	MAR	94965		L	A4
MULFORD GARDENS	ALA			L	D5
MURPHYS	CAL	95247		41	C4
MURPHYS RANCH	CAL	95247		41	C4
* MURRIETA	RCO	92362	34,550	99	C5
MURRIETA HOT SPRINGS	RCO	92362		99	C5
MUSCOY	SBD	92405		99	B1
MYERS FLAT	HUM	95554		16	B4
N					
NAIRN	MCO	95340		48	B4
NANCEVILLE	TUL	93257		68	D3
* NAPA	NAPA	94558	66,900	L	D1
-- NAPA COUNTY	NAP		119,000		
NAPLES	LACO	90803		S	E3
NAPLES	SB	93117		87	A4
NASHVILLE	ED	95675		40	E1
* NATIONAL CITY	SDCO	92050	54,700	V	C4
NATOMA	SAC	95630		34	B5
NAVARRO	MEN	95463		30	D2
NAVELENCIA	FRCO	93654		58	A4
* NEEDLES	SBD	92363	5,750	95	D2
NEENACH	LACO	93534		89	B2
NELSON	BUT	95958		25	B4
NESTOR	SDCO	92154		V	C5
* NEVADA CITY	NEV	95959	2,830	34	C1
-- NEVADA COUNTY	NEV		87,000		
NEW ALMADEN	SCL	95042		P	C4
* NEWARK	ALA	94560	40,000	P	A2
NEW AUBERRY	FRCO	93602		57	E1
NEWBERRY SPRINGS	SBD	92365		92	B2
NEWBURY PARK	VEN	91320		96	D1
NEWCASTLE	PLA	95658		34	C4
NEW CUYAMA	SB	93254		87	C1
NEWELL	MOD	96134		5	E3
NEWHALL	LACO	91321		89	C5
NEWHOPE LANDING	SJCO			39	D3
NEW IDAHO	LAKE			7	B1
NEW IDRIA	SBT	95027		66	A1
* NEWMAN	STA	95360	5,750	47	C4
NEW PINE CREEK	MOD	97635		7	C2
* NEWPORT BEACH	ORCO	92660	69,100	T	C4
NEWPORT CENTER	ORCO	92660		T	D4
NEWTOWN	ED	95709		35	A5
NEWVILLE	GLE	95963		24	B3
NEW WASHOE CITY	WSH	95611		36	C1
NICASIO	MAR	94946		37	E4
NICE	LAK	95464		31	D2
NICHOLLS WARM SPRINGS	RCO	92225		103	C5
NICHOLS	CC	94565		39	A4
NICOLAUS	SUT	95659		33	D3
NILAND	IMP	92257		109	B2
NIMBUS	SAC	94536		40	B1
NIPINNAWASSEE	MAD	93601		49	C4
NIPOMO	SLO	93444		76	C5
NIPTON	SBD	92364		84	C2
NIXON	WSH	96109		28	E2
NOB HILL	SFCO	94108		142	D2
NOE VALLEY	SFCO	94114		142	A5
* NORCO	RCO	91760	24,500	U	E4

COMMUNITY NAME	CO.	ZIP CODE	POP.	PG.	GD.
NORD	BUT	95926		25	A3
NORDEN	NEV	95724		35	C1
NORMAN	GLE	95988		24	D5
NORTH BEACH	SFCO	94133		142	D1
NORTH BLOOMFIELD	NEV	95959		26	D5
NORTH COLUMBIA	NEV	95959		26	C5
NORTH EDWARDS	KER	93523		80	D5
NORTH FORK	MAD	93643		49	E5
NORTH HIGHLANDS	SAC	95660		34	A5
NORTH HILLS	LA	91335		Q	B2
NORTH HOLLYWOOD	LACO	91601		Q	C2
NORTH JAMUL	SDCO	92035		112	A1
* NORTH LAS VEGAS	CLK		80,991	74	D2
NORTH LONG BEACH	LACO	90805		S	D2
NORTH PARK	SDCO	92104		216	B1
NORTH RICHMOND	CC	94807		L	C3
NORTHRIDGE	LACO	91324		Q	B2
NORTH SAN JUAN	NEV	95960		26	B5
NORTH SHORE	RCO	92254		101	D5
NORTHSTAR	PLA	95732		35	E1
NORTH WATERFRONT	SFCO	94113		142	D1
NORTHWOOD	ORCO	92714		T	E3
NORTHWOOD	SON	95462		37	C2
* NORWALK	LACO	90650	99,800	T	A1
* NOVATO	MAR	94949	46,500	L	A2
NOYO	MEN	95437		22	C5
NUBIEBER	LAS	96068		14	B3
NUEVO	RCO	92367		99	D3
-- NYE COUNTY	NYE		17,781		
NYLAND ACRES	VEN	93030		88	C5
O					
* OAKDALE	STA	95361	14,300	47	D1
OAK GLEN	SBD	92399		99	E2
OAK GROVE	SDCO	92302		107	B1
OAKGROVE	TUL	93271		59	A5
OAKHURST	MAD	93644		49	D4
* OAKLAND	ALA	94601	383,900	L	C4
OAKLEY	CC	94561		M	D3
OAK PARK	SDCO	92105		V	C3
OAK RUN	SHA	96069		18	E1
OAK VIEW	VEN	93022		88	A4
OAKVILLE	NAPA	94562		38	B2
OASIS	RCO	92274		108	B1
OATMAN	MOH			85	E5
OBRIEN	JOS			2	C2
O'BRIEN	SHA	96070		12	C5
OCCIDENTAL	SON	95465		37	C2
OCEAN BEACH	SDCO	92107		V	A3
OCEANO	SLO	93445		76	B5
* OCEANSIDE	SDCO	92054	147,200	106	B3
OCEAN VIEW	SON	95450		37	C2
OCOTILLO	IMP	92259		111	C3
OCOTILLO WELLS	SDCO	92004		108	B3
OGILBY	IMP	92222		110	B5
OILDALE	KER	93308		78	D2
* OJAI	VEN	93023	8,075	88	B4
OLANCHA	INY	93549		70	B1
OLD BORREGO	SDCO	92004		107	E3
OLD RIVER	KER	93307		78	C3
OLD STATION	SHA	96071		19	D1
OLD TOWN	LAS	96137		20	C4
OLEMA	MAR	94950		37	E4
OLENE	KLAM			5	C1
OLINDA	ORCO	92621		T	D1
OLINDA	SHA	96007		18	C3
OLINGHOUSE	WSH			28	E3
OLIVE	ORCO	92665		T	D2
OLIVEHURST	YUB	95961		33	D2
OLIVENHAIN	SDCO	92024		106	C4
OLIVE VIEW	LACO	91342		Q	C1
OLYMPIC VALLEY	PLA	95730		35	D1
OMO RANCH	ED	95661		41	B1
ONEALS	MAD	93645		57	D1
ONO	SHA	96072		18	A3
* ONTARIO	SBD	91761	142,400	U	D2
ONYX	KER	93255		69	E5
OPHIR	PLA	95603		34	C4
* ORANGE	ORCO	92666	119,700	T	D2
-- ORANGE COUNTY	ORCO		2,624,300		
* ORANGE COVE	FRCO	93646		58	B4
ORANGE PARK ACRES	ORCO	92669		U	C5
ORANGEVALE	SAC	95662		34	B5
ORCHARD SHORES	LAK	95423		32	A3
ORCUTT	SB	93455		86	C1
ORDBEND	GLE	95943		25	A3
OREGON HOUSE	YUB	95962		26	A5
ORICK	HUM	95555		10	A2
* ORINDA	CC	94563	16,850	L	D4
ORINDA VILLAGE	CC	94563		L	D4
* ORLAND	GLE	95963	5,625	24	D3
ORLEANS	HUM	95556		10	D2
ORO FINO	SIS	96032		3	D5
ORO GRANDE	SBD	92368		91	B3
ORO LOMA	FRCO	93622		56	A2
OROSI	TUL	93647		58	B4
* OROVILLE	BUT	95965	12,400	25	C4
ORR SPRINGS	MEN	95482		31	A1
OTAY	SDCO	92011		V	C5
OUTINGDALE	ED	95684		34	E5
* OXNARD	VEN	93030	153,300	96	B1
P					
PACHECO	CC	94553		L	E3
* PACIFICA	SMCO	94044	39,150	N	B1
PACIFIC BEACH	SDCO	92109		V	A2
* PACIFIC GROVE	MON	93950	17,150	54	A4
PACIFIC HEIGHTS	SFCO	94115		142	B2
PACIFIC HOUSE	ED	95725		35	B4
PACIFIC PALISADES	LACO	90272		Q	B4
PACOIMA	LACO	91331		Q	C1
PAHRUMP	NYE			73	C2
PAICINES	SBT	95043		55	B3

* INDICATES INCORPORATED CITY

CITIES

CITIES AND COMMUNITIES

COMMUNITY NAME	CO.	ZIP CODE	POP.	PG.	GD.
PAINTED HILLS	RCO	92282		100	C2
PAINTERSVILLE	SAC	95615		39	D3
PAJARO	MON	95076		54	C2
PALA	SDCO	92059		106	D2
PALA MESA VILLAGE	SDCO	92028		106	D2
PALERMO	BUT	95968		25	D5
PALISADES HIGHLANDS	LACO	90272		Q	B4
PALM CITY	SDCO	92154		V	C5
* PALMDALE	LACO	93550	112,000	90	A3
* PALM DESERT	RCO	92260	33,450	100	D4
PALMS	LACO	90034		Q	C4
* PALM SPRINGS	RCO	92262	41,700	100	D3
* PALO ALTO	SCL	94301	58,500	N	E2
PALO CEDRO	SHA	96073		18	D2
PALOMA	CAL	95252		40	E3
PALOMAR MOUNTAIN	SDCO	92060		107	A2
* PALOS VERDES ESTATES	LACO	90274	13,950	S	A2
PALO VERDE	IMP	92266		110	C1
PALO VERDE	SDCO	92001		107	B5
PANAMA	KER	93309		78	D3
PANAMINT SPRINGS	INY	93545		71	A1
PANOCHE	SBT	95043		55	D4
PANORAMA CITY	LACO	91402		Q	C2
* PARADISE	BUT	95969	25,950	25	C3
PARADISE CAY	MAR	94920		38	B5
PARADISE VALLEY	SCL	95037		P	D5
PARAISO SPRINGS	MON	93960		64	E1
* PARAMOUNT	LACO	90723	53,900	S	E1
* PARKER	LPAZ		2,950	104	B1
PARKFIELD	MON	93451		66	C4
PARK VILLAGE	INY	92328		62	A5
* PARLIER	FRCO	93648	9,450	57	E4
PARNASSUS/ASHBURY HTS	SFCO	94117		142	A4
* PASADENA	LACO	91101	137,100	R	B3
PASKENTA	TEH	96074		24	B2
PASO PICACHO	SDCO	92036		107	C4
* PASO ROBLES	SLO	93446	21,450	76	A1
PATRICK CREEK	DN	95543		2	B3
* PATTERSON	STA	95363	9,600	47	B3
PATTON VILLAGE	LAS	96113		21	D5
PAUMA VALLEY	SDCO	92061		106	E2
PAYNES CREEK	TEH	96075		19	B4
PAYNESVILLE	ALP	96120		36	B4
PEANUT	TRI	96041		17	B3
PEARBLOSSOM	LACO	93553		90	C4
PEARDALE	NEV	95945		34	C1
PEARLAND	LACO	93550		90	B3
PEARSONVILLE	INY	93542		70	C5
PEBBLE BEACH	MON	93953		54	A4
PECWAN	HUM	95546		10	B2
PEDLEY	RCO	92509		99	A2
PELICAN CITY	KLAM			5	B1
PENNGROVE	SON	94951		38	A3
PENNINGTON	SUT	95953		33	C1
PENTZ	BUT	95965		25	D3
PEPPERWOOD	HUM	95565		16	A3
PERKINS	SAC	95826		39	E1
* PERRIS	RCO	92370	30,500	99	C4
PESCADERO	SMCO	94060		N	C4
* PETALUMA	SON	94952	47,700	L	A1
PETER PAM	TUO	95335		41	E4
PETERS	SJCO	95236		40	C5
PETROLIA	HUM	95558		15	D4
PHELAN	SBD	92371		90	E4
PHILLIPS	ED	95735		35	E4
PHILLIPSVILLE	HUM	95558		16	B5
PHILO	MEN	95466		30	E3
PICACHO	IMP	92222		110	D4
* PICO RIVERA	LACO	90660	61,100	R	C4
* PIEDMONT	ALA	94611	11,150	L	D4
PIERCY	MEN	95467		22	C1
PIERPONT BAY	VEN	93003		175	D4
PIKE	SIE	95922		26	C5
PILOT HILL	ED	95664		34	C4
PINE COVE	RCO	92349		100	B4
PINECREST	TUO	95364		42	A3
PINEDALE	FRCO	93650		57	C3
PINE FLAT	TUL	93207		69	B4
PINE GROVE	AMA	95665		41	A2
PINE GROVE	LAK	95426		31	E4
PINE GROVE	MEN	95460		30	B1
PINE GROVE	SHA	96003		18	C2
PINE HILLS	SDCO	92036		107	C4
PINEHURST	FRCO	93641		58	D3
PINEHURST	JKSN			4	C1
PINELAND	PLA	95718		35	E2
PINE MEADOW	RCO	92361		100	C5
PINE MOUNTAIN CLUB	KER	93225		88	B1
PINE RIDGE	FRCO	93602		58	B1
PINE VALLEY	SDCO	92062		107	D5
PINO GRANDE	ED	95634		35	A4
* PINOLE	CC	94564	18,100	L	C3
PINOLE ESTATES	CC	94564		L	D3
PINON PINES	KER	93225		88	C1
PINYON PINES	RCO	92361		100	D5
PIONEER STATION	AMA	95666		41	B2
PIONEERTOWN	SBD	92268		100	D1
PIRU	VEN	93040		88	E4
* PISMO BEACH	SLO	93449	8,175	76	B4
* PITTSBURG	CC	94565	50,400	M	B3
PITTVILLE	SHA	96056		13	E4
PIXLEY	TUL	93256		68	B4
* PLACENTIA	ORCO	92670	45,000	T	D1
-- PLACER COUNTY	PLA		206,000		
* PLACERVILLE	ED	95667	8,825	34	E5
PLAINSBURG	MCO	95333		48	D5
PLAINVIEW	TUL	93267		68	C2
PLANADA	MCO	95365		48	D4
PLASSE	AMA	95666		35	E5
PLASTER CITY	IMP	92269		108	D5
PLATINA	SHA	96076		17	D3
PLAYA DEL REY	LACO	90291		97	C2
PLEASANT GROVE	SUT	95668		33	D4
* PLEASANT HILL	CC	94523	31,450	L	E3
* PLEASANTON	ALA	94566	57,800	P	B1
PLEASANT VALLEY	ED	95709		35	A5

COMMUNITY NAME	CO.	ZIP CODE	POP.	PG.	GD.
-- PLUMAS COUNTY	PLU		20,450		
* PLYMOUTH	AMA	95669	830	40	D2
* POINT ARENA	MEN	95468	420	30	C4
POINT LOMA	SDCO	92106		V	A3
POINT PLEASANT	SAC	95758		39	D3
POINT REYES STATION	MAR	94956		37	D4
POLLARD FLAT	SHA	96017		12	C4
POLLOCK PINES	ED	95726		35	A4
POMINS	ED	95733		35	E2
POMO	MEN	95469		31	C1
* POMONA	LACO	91766	139,800	U	C2
POND	KER	93280		68	B5
PONDEROSA	TUL	93208		69	C3
PONDEROSA BASIN	MPA	95338		49	C3
PONDEROSA SKY RANCH	TEH			19	B4
PONDOSA	SIS	96077		13	C3
POPE VALLEY	NAPA	94567		32	C5
POPLAR	TUL	93257		68	C3
POPPET FLATS	RCO			100	A3
PORT COSTA	CC	94569		L	D3
PORTER RANCH	LACO	91311		Q	A1
* PORTERVILLE	TUL	93257	34,550	68	D3
* PORT HUENEME	VEN	93041	22,250	96	B1
* PORTOLA	PLU	96122	2,140	27	B2
PORTOLA HILLS	ORCO	92679		98	D4
* PORTOLA VALLEY	SMCO	94025	4,410	N	D3
POSEY	TUL	93260		69	B5
POSTON	LPAZ			104	A2
POSTON 2	LPAZ			104	A3
POTRERO	SDCO	92063		112	C2
POTTER VALLEY	MEN	95469		31	B1
* POWAY	SDCO	92064	45,450	V	D1
POZO	SLO	93453		76	D3
PRATHER	FRCO	93651		57	E1
PRATTVILLE	PLU	95923		20	B4
PRESIDIO HEIGHTS	SFCO	94118		141	D2
PRESIDIO OF SAN FRAN	SFCO	94129		141	D2
PRESTON	SON	95425		31	C4
PRIEST	TUO	95305		48	D1
PRIMM	CLK			84	C1
PRINCETON	COL	95970		25	A5
PRINCETON BY THE SEA	SMCO	94018		N	B2
PROBERTA	TEH	96078		24	D1
PROGRESO	BAJA			112	A4
PROJECT CITY	SHA	96079		18	C1
PRUNEDALE	MON	93901		54	C3
PUERTA LA CRUZ	SDCO	92086		107	C2
PULGA	BUT	95965		25	D2
PUMPKIN CENTER	KER	93309		78	D3

Q

COMMUNITY NAME	CO.	ZIP CODE	POP.	PG.	GD.
QUAIL VALLEY	RCO	92380		99	C4
QUAKING ASPEN	TUL	93208		69	C3
QUARTZ HILL	LACO	93536		89	E3
QUARTZSITE	LPAZ		2,005	104	B4
QUINCY	PLU	95971		26	C1
QUINCY JUNCTION	PLU	95971		26	D1

R

COMMUNITY NAME	CO.	ZIP CODE	POP.	PG.	GD.
RACKERBY	YUB	95972		25	E5
RAFAEL VILLAGE	MAR	94949		L	A2
RAILROAD FLAT	CAL	95248		41	B2
RAINBOW	SDCO	92028		106	D1
RAISIN CITY	FRCO	93652		57	B4
RAMONA	SDCO	92065		107	A4
RAMSEY	LPAZ			104	D4
RANCHITA	SDCO	92066		107	D3
RANCHO BERNARDO	SDCO	92128		106	D4
RANCHO CALIFORNIA	RCO	92390		106	D1
RANCHO CORDOVA	SAC	95670		40	B1
* RANCHO CUCAMONGA	SBD	91730	115,900	U	D2
* RANCHO MIRAGE	RCO	92270	10,550	100	D4
RANCHO MURIETA	SAC	95683		40	C1
* RANCHO PALOS VERDES	LACO	90274	42,650	S	B3
RANCHO PENASQUITOS	SDCO	92129		106	D4
RANCHO SAN DIEGO	SDCO	92078		V	E3
RANCHO SANTA FE	SDCO	92067		106	C4
RCHO SANTA MARGARITA	ORCO	92688		989	E4
RANCHO TEHAMA	TEH	96021		24	C1
RANDOLF	SIE	96126		27	C4
RANDSBURG	KER	93554		80	D3
RAVENDALE	LAS	96123		8	C5
RAYMOND	MAD	93653		49	B5
RED APPLE	CAL	95224		41	C3
REDBANK	TEH	96080		18	B5
* RED BLUFF	TEH	96080	13,050	18	C5
REDCREST	HUM	95569		16	A3
* REDDING	SHA	96001	76,700	18	C2
RED HILL	ORCO	92705		T	E3
* REDLANDS	SBD	92373	65,600	99	C2
RED MOUNTAIN	SBD	93558		80	E3
* REDONDO BEACH	LACO	90277	63,900	S	A2
REDWAY	HUM	95560		16	B5
* REDWOOD CITY	SMCO	94061	71,800	N	D2
REDWOOD ESTATES	SCL	95044		P	B4
REDWOOD SHORES	SMCO	94065		N	D2
REDWOOD VALLEY	MEN	95470		31	B1
* REEDLEY	FRCO	93654	19,100	58	A4
* RENO	WSH		158,249	28	B4
RENO-STEAD	WSH			28	B3
REPRESA	SAC	95671		34	B5
REQUA	DN	95561		1	E5
RESCUE	ED	95672		34	D5
RESEDA	LACO	91335		Q	B2
REWARD	INY	93526		60	B3
RHEEM VALLEY	CC	94556		L	E4
* RIALTO	SBD	92376	80,300	99	B1
RICARDO	KER	93519		80	B3
RICE	SBD	92280		103	B2
RICHARDSON SPRINGS	BUT	95978		25	B2
RICH BAR	PLU	95915		26	B1
RICHFIELD	TEH	96083		24	D1
RICHGROVE	TUL	93261		68	C5
* RICHMOND	CC	94801	90,900	L	C3
RICHMOND	SFCO	94121		141	B4
RICHVALE	BUT	95974		25	C4
* RIDGECREST	KER	93555	29,000	80	D1
RIMFOREST	SBD	92378		99	C1
RIMROCK	SBD	92268		100	D1
RINCON	SDCO	92082		106	E2
RIO BRAVO	KER	93306		78	E2
* RIO DELL	HUM	95562	2,890	15	E3
RIO DELL	SON	95486		37	D2
RIO LINDA	SAC	95673		33	E5
RIO NIDO	SON	95471		37	D1
RIO OSO	SUT	95674		33	D3
* RIO VISTA	SOL	94571	3,660	M	D2
RIPLEY	RCO	92272		103	D5
* RIPON	SJCO	95366	9,100	47	C2
* RIVERBANK	STA	95367	13,350	47	D2
RIVERDALE	FRCO	93656		57	B5
RIVER KERN	KER	93238		69	D5
RIVER PINES	AMA	95675		40	E1
* RIVERSIDE	RCO	92501	243,400	99	B2
-- RIVERSIDE COUNTY	RCO		1,381,900		
RIVERTON	ED	95806		35	B4
RIVIERA	MOH			85	D4
RIVIERA HEIGHTS	LAK	95443		31	D3
RIVIERA WEST	LAK	95422		31	E3
ROADS END	TUL	93236		69	C4
ROBBINS	SUT	95676		33	C4
ROBINSONS CORNER	BUT	95948		25	C5
ROBLA	SAC	95673		33	E5
ROCKAWAY BEACH	SMCO	94044		N	B1
ROCK HAVEN	SDCO	92065		106	E4
* ROCKLIN	PLA	95677	26,900	34	B4
ROCKPORT	MEN	95488		22	B3
ROCKVILLE	SOL	94585		38	E3
RODEO	CC	94572		L	D3
ROGERS LANDING	MOH			85	D4
* ROHNERT PARK	SON	94928	38,350	38	A2
ROHNERVILLE	HUM	95540		15	E2
ROLANDO	SDCO	92115		V	C3
ROLINDA	FRCO	93705		57	B3
* ROLLING HILLS	LACO	90274	1,980	S	B3
* ROLLING HILLS ESTATES	LACO	90274	8,200	S	B2
ROMOLAND	RCO	92380		99	D4
ROSAMOND	KER	93560		90	A1
ROSEDALE	KER	93308		78	C3
* ROSEMEAD	LACO	91770	54,500	R	C3
ROSEMONT	SAC	95826		40	A1
ROSEMONT	SDCO	92065		106	E4
* ROSEVILLE	PLA	95678	59,700	34	A4
ROSEVILLE	SDCO	92106		V	A3
ROSEWOOD	TEH	96022		18	B4
* ROSS	MAR	94957	2,240	L	A3
ROSSMOOR	ORCO	90720		T	A2
ROUGH AND READY	NEV	95975		34	B1
ROUND MOUNTAIN	SHA	96084		13	A5
ROVANA	INY	93514		51	B3
ROWLAND HEIGHTS	LACO	91745		U	A3
RUBIDOUX	RCO	92509		99	A2
RUCH	JKSN			3	C1
RUCKER	SCL	95020		P	D5
RUMSEY	YOL	95679		32	D4
RUNNING SPRINGS	SBD	92382		99	D1
RUSSIAN HILL	SFCO	94133		142	C2
RUTH	TRI	95526		17	A4
RUTHERFORD	NAPA	94573		38	B2
RYDE	SAC	95680		M	E1

S

COMMUNITY NAME	CO.	ZIP CODE	POP.	PG.	GD.
SABRE CITY	PLA	95660		34	A5
* SACRAMENTO	SAC	95801	384,800	39	E1
-- SACRAMENTO COUNTY	SAC		1,123,400		
* SAINT HELENA	NAPA	94574	5,575	38	B1
SALIDA	STA	95368		47	C2
* SALINAS	MON	93901	122,500	54	C4
SALMON CREEK	SON	94923		37	C2
SALT CREEK LODGE	SHA	96051		12	C5
SALTDALE	KER	93519		80	C3
SALTON	RCO	92257		108	D1
SALTON CITY	IMP	92274		108	C2
SALTON SEA BEACH	IMP	92274		108	C1
SALVADOR	NAPA	94558		38	C3
SALYER	TRI	95563		10	D5
SAMOA	HUM	95560		9	D5
SAN ANDREAS	CAL	95249		41	A3
* SAN ANSELMO	MAR	94960	12,150	L	A3
SAN ANTONIO HEIGHTS	SBD	91786		U	D1
SAN ARDO	MON	93450		65	D3
SAN BENITO	SBT	95023		55	C5
-- SAN BENITO COUNTY	SBT		43,350		
* SAN BERNARDINO	SBD	92402	181,700	99	C1
-- SAN BERNARDINO COUNTY	SBD		1,589,500		
SANBORN	KER	93501		80	A5
* SAN BRUNO	SMCO	94066	40,450	N	C1
SAN CARLOS	SDCO	92119		V	D2
* SAN CARLOS	SMCO	94070	27,800	N	D2
* SAN CLEMENTE	ORCO	92672	46,600	105	D1
SANDBERG	LACO	93532		89	A2
* SAND CITY	MON	93955	190	54	B4
* SAN DIEGO	SDCO	92101	1,183,100	V	B3
SAN DIEGO COUNTRY EST	SDCO	92065		107	A4
-- SAN DIEGO COUNTY	SDCO		2,690,300		
* SAN DIMAS	LACO	91773	35,100	U	B2
SANDY	CLK			74	A5
SAN FELIPE	SDCO	92086		107	C3
* SAN FERNANDO	LACO	91341	23,600	Q	C1
* SAN FRANCISCO	SFCO	94101	755,300	L	B4
-- SAN FRANCISCO COUNTY	SFCO		755,300		
* SAN GABRIEL	LACO	91776	39,600	R	C3
* SANGER	FRCO	93657	18,300	57	E3
SAN GERONIMO	MAR	94963		38	A5
SAN GORGONIO	RCO	92282		100	B3
SAN GREGORIO	SMCO	94074		N	C3
* SAN JACINTO	RCO	92383	23,900	99	E3
* SAN JOAQUIN	FRCO	93660	2,920	56	E4
* SAN JOSE	SCL	95103	849,400	P	B3
* SAN JUAN BAUTISTA	SBT	95045	1,620	54	D3
* SAN JUAN CAPISTRANO	ORCO	92675	28,950	98	D5
SAN JUAN HOT SPRINGS	ORCO	92675		98	E5
* SAN LEANDRO	ALA	94577	71,500	L	D5
SAN LORENZO	ALA	94580		L	E5
SAN LUCAS	MON	93954		65	D3
* SAN LUIS OBISPO	SLO	93401	41,950	76	B3
-- SAN LUIS OBISPO COUNTY	SLO		232,400		
SAN LUIS REY	SDCO	92068		106	B2
SAN LUIS REY HEIGHTS	SDCO	92028		106	C2
* SAN MARCOS	SDCO	92069	48,100	106	D3
SAN MARIN	MAR	94945		L	A2
* SAN MARINO	LACO	91108	13,400	R	C3
SAN MARTIN	SCL	95046		P	D5
* SAN MATEO	SMCO	94401	91,200	N	C1
-- SAN MATEO COUNTY	SMCO		691,500		
SAN MIGUEL	SLO	93451		66	A5
SAN ONOFRE	SDCO	92672		105	E1
* SAN PABLO	CC	94806	25,950	L	C3
SAN PASQUAL	SDCO	92025		106	E3
SAN PEDRO	LACO	90731		S	C3
SAN PEDRO TERRACE	SM	94044		45	B3
SAN QUENTIN	MAR	94964		L	B3
* SAN RAFAEL	MAR	94901	52,400	L	B3
* SAN RAMON	CC	94583	40,650	M	B4
SAN SIMEON	SLO	93452		75	B1
* SANTA ANA	ORCO	92701	305,800	T	D3
* SANTA BARBARA	SB	93101	89,400	87	C4
-- SANTA BARBARA COUNTY	SB		394,600		
* SANTA CLARA	SCL	95050	98,000	P	B3
-- SANTA CLARA COUNTY	SCL		1,612,300		
* SANTA CLARITA	LACO	91321	129,900	89	C4
* SANTA CRUZ	SCR	95060	52,700	53	E2
-- SANTA CRUZ COUNTY	SCR		243,000		
* SANTA FE SPRINGS	LACO	90670	15,700	R	C5
SANTA MARGARITA	SLO	93453		76	B3
* SANTA MARIA	SB	93454	68,900	86	B1
* SANTA MONICA	LACO	90402	90,300	Q	B4
SANTA NELLA	MCO	95322		55	C1
* SANTA PAULA	VEN	93060	26,700	88	C5
SANTA RITA	ALA	94566		M	C5
SANTA RITA PARK	MER	93660		56	B1
* SANTA ROSA	SON	95402	125,700	37	E2
SANTA SUSANA	VEN	93063		89	A5
SANTA VENETIA	MAR	94903		L	B3
SANTA YNEZ	SB	93460		86	E3
SANTA YSABEL	SDCO	92070		107	C3
* SANTEE	SDCO	92071	54,400	V	D2
SAN YSIDRO	SDCO	92073		V	D5
* SARATOGA	SCL	95070	29,600	P	A4
SATICOY	VEN	93004		88	C5
SATTLEY	SIE	96124		27	C3
SAUGUS	LACO	91350		89	B4
* SAUSALITO	MAR	94965	7,650	L	B4
SAWYERS BAR	SIS	96027		11	B2
SCALES	SIE	95981		26	C4
SCHELLVILLE	SON	95476		L	B1
SCISSORS CROSSING	SDCO	92036		107	D3
SCOTIA	HUM	95565		16	A3
SCOTT BAR	SIS	96085		3	C4
SCOTT DAM	LAK	95469		23	C5
SCOTTS CORNER	ALA	94586		P	B1
* SCOTTS VALLEY	SCR	95060	9,825	P	A5
SCOTTYS CASTLE	INY	92328		61	B1
SCRIPPS MIRAMAR RANCH	SDCO	92131		V	C1
SEACLIFF	SFCO	94121		141	C2
SEACLIFF	VEN	93001		87	E5
* SEAL BEACH	ORCO	90740	26,350	T	A3
SEA RANCH	SON	95497		30	E5
SEARCHLIGHT	CLK			85	A2
SEARCHLIGHT JUNCTION	SBD	92332		95	B1
SEARS POINT	SON	95476		L	B2
* SEASIDE	MON	93955	28,300	54	B4
* SEBASTOPOL	SON	95472	7,525	37	E2
SEDCO HILLS	RCO	92330		99	C4
SEELEY	IMP	92273		108	E5
SEIAD VALLEY	SIS	96086		3	B3
* SELMA	FRCO	93662	17,300	57	E4
SENECA	PLU	95923		20	C5
SERENE LAKES	PLA	95728		35	C1
SERENO DEL MAR	SON	94923		37	C2
SERRA MESA	SDCO	92123		V	C3
SEVEN PINES	INY	93526		59	E3
SHADY DELL	SDCO	92065		V	E1
SHADY GLEN	PLA	95713		34	D2
* SHAFTER	KER	93263	11,000	78	B2
SHANDON	SLO	93461		76	D1
SHASTA	SHA	96087		18	B2
-- SHASTA COUNTY	SHA		161,600		
* SHASTA LAKE	SHA	96079	9,200	18	C1
SHAVER LAKE	FRCO	93664		58	B1
SHAVER LAKE POINT	FRCO	93664		50	B5
SHEEP RANCH	CAL	95250		41	B3
SHEFFIELD VILLAGE	ALA			L	E5
SHELDON	SAC	95624		40	A2
SHELL BEACH	SLO	93449		76	B4
SHELTER VALLEY RANCHOS	SDCO	92036		107	D4
SHERIDAN	SON	95462		37	C2
SHERIDAN DUNCAN MILLS	SON	95462		37	C2
SHERMAN HEIGHTS	SDCO	92102		216	A4
SHERMAN OAKS	LACO	91403		Q	C3
SHINGLE MILL	SON	95480		31	A5
SHINGLE SPRINGS	ED	95682		34	D5
SHINGLETOWN	SHA	96088		19	A3
SHIVELY	HUM	95565		16	B3
SHOSHONE	INY	92384		73	A4
SHUMWAY	LAS			21	B1
SIERRA BROOKS	SIE	96135		27	D3
SIERRA CITY	SIE	96125		27	A4
-- SIERRA COUNTY	SIE		3,390		
* SIERRA MADRE	LACO	91024	11,150	R	D2
SIERRA VILLAGE	TUO			41	E4
SIERRAVILLE	SIE	96126		27	C4
* SIGNAL HILL	LACO	90806	8,775	S	D2

*** INDICATES INCORPORATED CITY**

COMMUNITY NAME	CO.	ZIP CODE	POP.	PG.	GD.
SILVERADO	ORCO	92676		98	E4
SILVERADO CANYON	ORCO	92676		98	E4
SILVER CITY	LYON			36	C1
SILVER CITY	TUL	93271		59	B5
SILVER FORK	ED	95728		35	C4
SILVER LAKE	LACO	90039		Q	E3
SILVER PEAK	ESM			52	D1
SILVER STRAND	VEN	93030		96	B1
* SIMI VALLEY	VEN	93065	103,200	89	A5
SIMMLER	SLO	93453		77	B3
-- SISKIYOU COUNTY	SIS		44,600		
SISQUOC	SB	93454		86	C1
SITES	COL	95979		32	C1
SKAGGS SPRINGS	SON	95448		31	C5
SKIDOO	INY	92328		61	D5
SKYFOREST	SBD	92385		99	C1
SKY LONDA	SMCO	94062		N	D3
SKY VALLEY	RCO	92240		100	E3
SLEEPY HOLLOW	MAR	94960		L	A3
SLEEPY HOLLOW	SBD			U	C4
SLEEPY VALLEY	LACO	91350		89	D4
SLIDE INN	TUO	95335		41	E4
SLOAN	CLK			74	D4
SLOAT	PLU	96127		26	E2
SLOUGHHOUSE	SAC	95683		40	B1
SMARTVILLE	YUB	95977		34	A2
SMITHFLAT	ED	95727		34	E5
SMITH RIVER	DN	95567		1	E3
SMITH STATION	TUO	95321		49	A1
SNELLING	MCO	95369		48	C3
SOBOBA HOT SPRINGS	RCO	92383		99	E3
SODA BAY	LAK	95443		31	D3
SODA SPRINGS	NEV	95728		27	C5
SODA SPRINGS	SON	95412		31	A5
* SOLANA BEACH	SDCO	92075	13,600	106	B4
-- SOLANO COUNTY	SOL		373,100		
* SOLEDAD	MON	93960	15,700	55	A5
* SOLVANG	SB	93463	5,100	86	E3
SOMERSET	ED	95684		35	A5
SOMES BAR	SIS	95568		10	E2
SOMIS	VEN	93066		88	D5
* SONOMA	SON	95476	8,750	L	B1
-- SONOMA COUNTY	SON		421,500		
* SONORA	TUO	95370	4,280	41	C5
SONORA JUNCTION	MNO	93517		42	E2
SOQUEL	SCR	95073		54	A2
SORRENTO VALLEY	SDCO	92121		V	B1
SOULSBYVILLE	TUO	95372		41	D5
SOUSA CORNERS	SON	95444		37	D2
SOUTH BELRIDGE	KER	93251		77	D2
SOUTHCREST	SDCO	92113		216	D5
SOUTH DOS PALOS	MCO	93665		56	A2
* SOUTH EL MONTE	LACO	91733	21,750	R	C4
SOUTH FORK	MAD			49	E5
SOUTH FORK	MPA	95318		49	B2
* SOUTH GATE	LACO	90280	91,100	R	A5
SOUTH LAGUNA	ORCO	92677		T	E5
SOUTH LAKE	KER	93283		79	D1
* SOUTH LAKE TAHOE	ED	95705	23,100	36	A3
SOUTH OF MARKET	SFCO	94103		143	C4
SOUTH OROVILLE	BUT	95965		25	D4
SOUTH PARK	SON	95404		38	A2
* SOUTH PASADENA	LACO	91030	24,850	R	B3
* SOUTH SAN FRANCISCO	SMCO	94080	57,000	N	C1
SOUTH SAN GABRIEL	LACO	91770		R	B4
SOUTH SHORE	ALA			L	D5
SOUTH TAFT	KER	93268		78	A4
SPANISH CREEK	PLU	95971		26	D1
SPANISH FLAT WOODLNDS	NAPA	94558		38	D1
SPANISH RANCH	PLU	95956		26	C1
* SPARKS	WSH		62,118	28	C4
SPAULDING	LAS	96130		20	D1
SPENCEVILLE	NEV	95945		34	B2
SPRECKELS	MON	93962		54	D4
SPRING GARDEN	PLU	95971		26	E2
SPRING TOWN	ALA	94550		M	C5
SPRING VALLEY	SDCO	92077		V	D3
SPRINGVILLE	TUL	93265		68	E2
SQUAW VALLEY	FRCO	93646		58	B3
SQUIRREL MTN VALLEY	KER	93240		79	D1
STAFFORD	HUM	95565		16	A3
STAGECOACH	LYON			28	E5
STANDISH	LAS	96128		21	B3
STANFIELD HILL	YUB	95918		34	A1
STANFORD	SCL	94305		N	D2
STANISLAUS	TUO	95247		41	C4
-- STANISLAUS COUNTY	STA		415,300		
* STANTON	ORCO	90680	31,900	T	B2
STATELINE	DGL			36	B3
STENT	TUO	95347		41	C5
STEVINSON	MCO	95374		47	E4
STEWART	CRSN			36	C2
STEWART-LENNOX	KLAM			5	B1
STEWARTS POINT	SON	95480		30	E5
STINSON BEACH	MAR	94970		L	A4
STIRLING CITY	BUT	95978		25	D2
STOCKTON	SDCO	92102		216	C3
* STOCKTON	SJCO	95201	233,600	40	B5
STONYFORD	COL	95979		24	B5
-- STOREY COUNTY	STOR		2,526		
STOVEPIPE WELLS	INY	92328		61	D4
STRATFORD	KIN	93266		67	C2
STRATHMORE	TUL	93267		68	D2
STRAWBERRY	ED	95735		35	D4
STRAWBERRY	TUO	95375		42	A3
STRAWBERRY VALLEY	YUB	95981		26	B4
STRONGHOLD	MOD	96431		5	E3
STUDIO CITY	LACO	91604		Q	C3
SUGAR LOAF	SBD	92386		92	A5
SUGARLOAF VILLAGE	TUL	93260		69	B4
SUGAR PINE	MAD	95389		49	D3
SUGARPINE	TUO	95346		41	D4
* SUISUN CITY	SOL	94585	25,500	M	A1
SULTANA	TUL	93666		58	B5
SUMMERHOME PARK	SON	95436		37	D2
SUMMERLAND	SB	93067		87	D4

COMMUNITY NAME	CO.	ZIP CODE	POP.	PG.	GD.
SUMMIT	VEN	93023		88	C4
SUMMIT CITY	SHA	96089		18	B1
SUN CITY	RCO	92381		99	C4
SUNLAND	LACO	91040		Q	D1
SUNNYBROOK	AMA	95640		40	D2
SUNNYSIDE	SDCO	92002		V	D4
SUNNYSLOPE	RCO	93656		99	A2
* SUNNYVALE	SCL	94086	126,100	P	A3
SUNNY VISTA	SDCO	92010		V	D4
SUNOL	ALA	94586		P	B1
SUNSET	SFCO	94122		141	B5
SUNSET BEACH	ORCO	90742		T	A3
SUNSET ESTATES	PLA	95678		33	E4
SUN VALLEY	LACO	91352		Q	D2
SUN VALLEY	WSH			28	B4
SURFSIDE	ORCO	90743		T	A3
* SUSANVILLE	LAS	96130	14,700	20	E3
SUTCLIFFE	WSH			28	C1
SUTTER	SUT	95982		33	C2
-- SUTTER COUNTY	SUT		74,100		
* SUTTER CREEK	AMA	95685	2,060	40	E2
SWANSBORO COUNTRY	ED	95727		35	A4
SWANSEA	INY	93545		60	C5
SWEETBRIER	SHA	96017		12	C3
SWEETLAND	NEV	95959		26	B5
SYCAMORE	COL	95957		33	A2
SYLMAR	LACO	91342		Q	B1
SYLMAR SQUARE	LACO	91342		Q	C1
SYLVIA PARK	LACO	90290		Q	A3

T

COMMUNITY NAME	CO.	ZIP CODE	POP.	PG.	GD.
* TAFT	KER	93268	6,600	78	A4
TAFT HEIGHTS	KER	93268		77	E4
TAHOE CITY	PLA	95730		35	E2
TAHOE PINES	PLA	95718		35	D2
TAHOE VILLAGE	DGL	25		36	B3
TAHOE VISTA	PLA	95732		36	A1
TAHOMA	PLA	95733		35	E2
TAKILMA	JOS			2	D2
* TALENT	JKSN		3,650	3	E1
TALMAGE	MEN	95481		31	B2
TAMALPAIS VALLEY	MAR	94941		L	A4
TAMARACK	CAL	95223		41	E2
TANCRED	YOL	95606		32	D5
TARZANA	LACO	91356		Q	A3
TASSAJARA	CC	94526		46	B1
TASSAJARA HOT SPGS	MON	93924		64	D2
TAYLORSVILLE	PLU	95983		20	D5
TECATE	BAJA			112	C2
TECATE	SDCO	92080		112	C2
TECOPA	INY	92389		73	A4
TECOPA HOT SPRINGS	INY	92389		73	A4
* TEHACHAPI	KER	93561	6,550	79	D4
TEHACHAPI EAST	KER	93561		79	D4
* TEHAMA	TEH	96090	430	24	D1
-- TEHAMA COUNTY	TEH		54,400		
TELEGRAPH CITY	CAL	95228		40	E5
TELEGRAPH HILL	SFCO	94133		142	D1
* TEMECULA	RCO	92390	41,850	106	C1
* TEMPLE CITY	LACO	91780	33,050	R	C3
TEMPLETON	SLO	93465		76	A2
TENNANT	SIS	96012		5	B5
TERMINAL ISLAND	LACO			S	C3
TERMINOUS	SJCO	95240		39	E4
TERMO	LAS	96132		8	B5
TERRA BELLA	TUL	93270		68	D3
TERRA LINDA	MAR	94903		L	A3
THE HIGHLANDS	SMCO	94402		N	C2
THE NARROWS	SDCO	92004		108	A3
THERMAL	RCO	92274		101	B5
THERMALANDS	PLA	95648		34	B3
THE WILLOWS	SDCO	92001		107	B5
THORNE	MIN			44	B1
THORNTON	SJCO	95686		39	E3
* THOUSAND OAKS	VEN	91360	112,000	96	E1
THOUSAND PALMS	RCO	92276		100	E3
THREE ARCH BAY	ORCO	92677		98	D5
THREE RIVERS	TUL	93271		58	D5
* TIBURON	MAR	94920	8,400	L	B4
TIERRA BUENA	SUT	95991		33	C2
TIERRA DEL SOL	SDCO	92005		112	E2
TIERRASANTA	SDCO	92124		V	C2
TIJUANA	BAJA			111	D2
TIMBER LODGE	MPA	95345		49	B3
TIPTON	TUL	93272		68	B3
TISDALE	SUT	95957		33	B3
TOBIN	PLU	95965		26	A1
TOLLHOUSE	FRCO	93667		58	A2
TOMALES	MAR	94971		37	D3
TOMS PLACE	MNO	93546		51	B3
TOPANGA	LACO	90290		Q	A3
TOPANGA PARK	LACO	90290		97	B1
TOPAZ	MNO	96133		36	D5
TOPOCK	MOH			95	E2
* TORRANCE	LACO	90505	139,800	S	B2
TOWER HOUSE	SHA	96095		18	A2
TOYON	SHA	96019		18	C1
TRABUCO CANYON	ORCO	92679		98	E4
* TRACY	SJCO	95376	44,900	46	E2
TRAIL PARK	ED	95651		34	E4
TRANQUILLITY	FRCO	93668		56	D4
TRAVER	TUL	93673		57	E5
TRAVIS AIR FORCE BASE	SOL	94535		39	A3
TRES PINOS	SBT	95075		55	A3
* TRINIDAD	HUM	95570	360	9	E4
TRINITY CENTER	TRI	96091		11	E4
-- TRINITY COUNTY	TRI		13,400		
TRONA	SBD	93562		71	B5
TROPICO	KER	93560		89	E1
TROWBRIDGE	SUT	95687		33	D3
TROY	PLA	95728		35	B1
* TRUCKEE	NEV	95734	2,400	35	D1
TUDOR	SUT	95991		33	C3
TUJUNGA	LACO	91042		Q	E1
* TULARE	TUL	93274	39,750	68	A2
-- TULARE COUNTY	TUL		351,500		
* TULELAKE	SIS	96134	920	5	D2
TUOLUMNE	TUO	95379		41	D5
-- TUOLUMNE COUNTY	TUO		52,700		
TUOLUMNE MEADOWS	TUO	95379		43	A5
TUPMAN	KER	93276		78	B3
* TURLOCK	STA	95380	49,200	47	E3
TURTLE ROCK	ORCO	92715		98	C4
* TUSTIN	ORCO	92680	63,600	T	E3
TUTTLE	MCO	95340		48	D4
TUTTLETOWN	TUO			41	C5
TWAIN	PLU	95984		26	B1
TWAIN HARTE	TUO	95383		41	D4
TWAIN HARTE VALLEY	TUO	95383		41	D4
* TWENTYNINE PALMS	SBD	92277	14,800	101	B1
TWIN BRIDGES	ED	95735		35	E4
TWIN CITIES	SAC	95632		40	A3
TWIN OAKS	SDCO	92083		106	C3
TWIN PEAKS	SBD	92391		91	C5
TWIN PEAKS	SFCO	94116		142	A5
TWIN PINES	RCO			100	B3
TYNDALL LANDING	YOL	95698		33	B4

U

COMMUNITY NAME	CO.	ZIP CODE	POP.	PG.	GD.
* UKIAH	MEN	95482	14,700	31	B2
ULTRA	TUL	93256		68	D3
* UNION CITY	ALA	94587	58,300	P	A1
UNIVERSAL CITY	LACO	91608		Q	D3
UNIVERSITY CITY	SDCO	92122		V	A2
UNIVERSITY HEIGHTS	SDCO	92116		214	A4
* UPLAND	SBD	91786	66,200	U	D2
UPPER LAKE	LAK	95485		31	D2
UPTOWN	SDCO	92103		213	B5

V

COMMUNITY NAME	CO.	ZIP CODE	POP.	PG.	GD.
VACATION BEACH	SON	95446		37	C2
* VACAVILLE	SOL	95688	84,200	39	A2
VALENCIA	LACO	91355		89	B4
VALERIE	RCO	92274		101	A5
VALINDA	LACO	91744		R	E4
VALLECITO	CAL	95251		41	C4
VALLECITO	SDCO	92036		107	E4
* VALLEJO	SOL	94590	112,300	L	D2
VALLEJO HEIGHTS	SOL	94590		38	D4
VALLE VISTA	RCO	92343		99	E4
VALLEY ACRES	KER	93268		78	A4
VALLEY CENTER	SDCO	92082		106	E2
VALLEY FORD	SON	94972		37	D3
VALLEY HOME	STA	95384		47	D1
VALLEY OF ENCHANTMENT	SBD	92322		91	B5
VALLEY SPRINGS	CAL	95252		40	D3
VALLEY WELLS	INY	92366		71	C4
VAL VERDE	LACO	91350		89	A4
VANDENBERG VILLAGE	STB	93436		86	B2
VAN NUYS	LACO	91408		Q	C2
VENICE	LACO	90291		Q	B5
VENTUCOPA	SB	93252		87	E1
VEN-TU PARK	VEN	91320		96	D1
* VENTURA	VEN	93001	100,300	88	B5
-- VENTURA COUNTY	VEN		716,100		
VERDEMONT	SBD	92407		99	B1
VERDI	WSH			28	A4
VERDI SIERRA PINES	SIE	95737		27	E4
VERDUGO CITY	LACO	91046		Q	E2
VERNALIS	SJCO			47	A2
* VERNON	LACO	90058	80	R	A4
VERONA	SUT	95659		33	D4
VICHY SPRINGS	MEN	95482		31	B2
VICHY SPRINGS	NAPA	94558		38	D3
VICTOR	SJCO	95253		40	B4
VICTORIA	SDCO	92001		107	B5
* VICTORVILLE	SBD	92392	60,000	91	C3
VIDAL	SBD	92280		103	E1
VIDAL JUNCTION	SBD	92280		103	D1
VILLA GRANDE	SON	95486		37	C2
* VILLA PARK	ORCO	92667	6,375	T	E2
VINA	TEH	96092		24	E2
VINEBURG	SON	95487		L	C1
VINTON	PLU	96135		27	D2
VIOLA	SHA	96088		19	C2
VIRGILIA	PLU	95984		26	B1
* VIRGINIA CITY	STOR		950	36	D1
* VISALIA	TUL	93277	91,300	68	B1
* VISTA	SDCO	92083	80,000	106	C3
VISTA VERDE	SMCO	94025		N	D3
VOLCANO	AMA	95689		41	A2
VOLCANOVILLE	ED	95634		34	E3
VOLLMERS	SHA	96051		12	B4
VOLTA	MER	93635		55	D1
VORDEN	SAC	95690		M	E1

W

COMMUNITY NAME	CO.	ZIP CODE	POP.	PG.	GD.
WAHTOKE PARK	FRCO	93654		58	A4
WALKER	MNO	96107		42	E1
WALLACE	CAL	95254		40	D3
* WALNUT	LACO	91789	31,600	U	A3
* WALNUT CREEK	CC	94595	62,000	M	A4
WALNUT GROVE	SAC	95690		M	E1
WALSH LANDING	SON	95450		37	A1
WARM SPRINGS	ALA	94538		P	B2
WARNER SPRINGS	SDCO	92086		107	C2
* WASCO	KER	93280	18,200	78	B1
WASHINGTON	NEV	95986		26	E5
WASHOE	SON	94931		37	E3
WASHOE CITY	WSH			28	B5
-- WASHOE COUNTY	WSH		254,667		
* WATERFORD	STA	95386	6,375	48	A2
WATERLOO	SJCO	95201		40	B4
* WATSONVILLE	SCR	95076	34,250	54	C2
WATTS	LACO	90002		Q	E5
WAWONA	MPA	95389		49	D3
WEAVERVILLE	TRI	96093		17	D1
* WEED	SIS	96094	3,080	12	C1
WEED PATCH	KER	93307		78	E4
WEIMAR	PLA	95736		34	D3
WEITCHPEC	HUM	95546		10	C3
WELDON	KER	93283		79	D1
WELLSONA	SLO	93446		76	A1
WENDEL	LAS	96136		21	D3
WENTWORTH SPRINGS	ED	95725		35	C3
WEOTT	HUM	95571		16	B4
WEST BRANCH	BUT	95941		25	C1
WEST BUTTE	SUT	95953		33	B2
* WEST COVINA	LACO	91790	101,900	U	A2
WESTERN ADDITION	SFCO	94115		143	A4
WEST HAVEN	FRCO	93234		67	B2
* WEST HOLLYWOOD	LACO	90069	37,200	Q	D3
* WESTLAKE VILLAGE	LACO	91361	7,825	96	E1
WESTLEY	STA	95387		47	B3
WEST LOS ANGELES	LACO	90025		Q	C4
* WESTMINSTER	ORCO	92683	82,500	T	B3
* WESTMORELAND	IMP	92281	1,690	109	A4
WEST OF TWIN PEAKS	SFCO	94122		141	D5
WEST POINT	CAL	95255		41	B2
WESTPORT	MEN	95488		22	C4
* WEST SACRAMENTO	YOL	95691	30,250	39	D1
WEST SIDE	LAKE			7	B1
WESTVILLE	PLA	95631		35	A2
WESTWOOD	LAS	96137		20	C4
WESTWOOD	LACO	90024		97	C2
* WHEATLAND	YUB	95692	1,960	33	E3
WHEATON SPRINGS	SBD	92364		84	B2
WHEATVILLE	FRCO	93656		57	A5
WHEELER RIDGE	KER	93284		78	D5
WHEELER SPRINGS	VEN	93023		88	A4
WHISKEYTOWN	SHA	96095		18	A2
WHISPERING PINES	LAK	95461		32	A4
WHITE HALL	ED	95725		35	C4
WHITE HORSE	MOD	96054		13	E2
WHITE PINES	CAL	95223		41	C3
WHITE RIVER	TUL	93257		68	E4
WHITETHORN	HUM	95489		22	B1
WHITEWATER	RCO	92282		100	C3
WHITLEY GARDENS	SLO	93451		76	C1
WHITLOW	HUM	95554		16	C4
WHITMORE	SHA	96096		19	A2
* WHITTIER	LACO	90605	82,500	R	D5
WILBUR SPRINGS	COL	95987		32	C3
WILDOMAR	RCO	92395		99	C5
WILDROSE	INY	93562		71	C2
* WILLIAMS	COL	95987	3,020	32	D2
WILLIAMS	JOS			3	A1
* WILLITS	MEN	95490	5,100	23	A5
WILLOW CREEK	HUM	95573		10	D5
WILLOW RANCH	MOD	96138		7	C3
* WILLOWS	GLE	95988	6,350	24	D4
WILLOW SPRINGS	KER	93550		89	D1
WILMINGTON	LACO	90744		S	C2
WILSEYVILLE	CAL	95257		41	B2
WILSONIA	TUL	93633		58	E3
WILTON	SAC	95693		40	B2
WINCHESTER	RCO	92396		99	D4
WINCHUCK	CUR			1	D2
* WINDSOR	SON	95492	18,750	37	E1
WINTER GARDENS	SDCO	92040		V	E2
WINTERHAVEN	IMP	92283		112	C5
* WINTERS	YOL	95694	5,175	39	A1
WINTERWARM	SDCO	92028		106	C2
WINTON	MER	95388		48	A4
WISHON	MAD	93669		49	E4
WITCH CREEK	SDCO	92065		107	B3
WOFFORD HEIGHTS	KER	93285		69	C5
WOLF	NEV	95945		34	B2
WONDER VALLEY	FRCO	93657		58	B3
WOODACRE	MAR	94973		L	A3
WOODBRIDGE	ORCO	92714		T	E4
WOODCREST	RCO	92504		99	B3
WOODFORD	KER	96120		79	B4
WOODFORDS	ALP	96120		36	B4
* WOODLAKE	TUL	93286	6,175	58	D5
* WOODLAND	YOL	95695	43,250	33	B5
WOODLAND HILLS	LACO	91364		Q	A3
* WOODSIDE	SMCO	94062	5,375	N	D2
WOODSIDE VILLAGE	LACO	91792		U	A3
WOODVILLE	TUL	93257		68	C3
WOODY	KER	93287		69	A5
WOOLSEY	SON	95436		37	D2
WORDEN	KLAM			5	B2
WRIGHTS LAKE	ED	95720		35	D4
WRIGHTWOOD	SBD	92397		90	E5
WYANDOTTE	BUT	95965		25	D5
WYNOLA	SDCO	92036		107	C3

Y

COMMUNITY NAME	CO.	ZIP CODE	POP.	PG.	GD.
YANKEE HILL	BUT	95969		25	D3
YANKEE JIMS	PLA	95631		34	D3
YERMO	SBD	92398		92	A1
YETTEM	TUL	93670		58	B5
YOLO	YOL	95697		33	B5
-- YOLO COUNTY	YOL		152,100		
* YORBA LINDA	ORCO	92686	57,600	T	D1
YORKVILLE	MEN	95494		31	B4
YOSEMITE FORKS	MAD	93644		49	D4
YOSEMITE VILLAGE	MPA	95389		49	D1
YOUNGSTOWN	SJCO	95220		40	B4
* YOUNTVILLE	NAPA	94599	3,460	38	C2
* YREKA	SIS	96097	7,175	4	A4
* YUBA CITY	SUT	95991	33,900	33	C2
-- YUBA COUNTY	YUB		62,200		
* YUCAIPA	SBD	92399	37,450	99	D2
* YUCCA VALLEY	SBD	92284	18,650	100	E1
* YUMA	YUMA		60,475	112	D5
-- YUMA COUNTY	YUMA		121,875		

Z

COMMUNITY NAME	CO.	ZIP CODE	POP.	PG.	GD.
ZAMORA	YOL	95698		33	B4
ZENIA	TRI	95495		16	E4
ZEPHYR COVE	DGL			36	A3

*** INDICATES INCORPORATED CITY**

CITIES

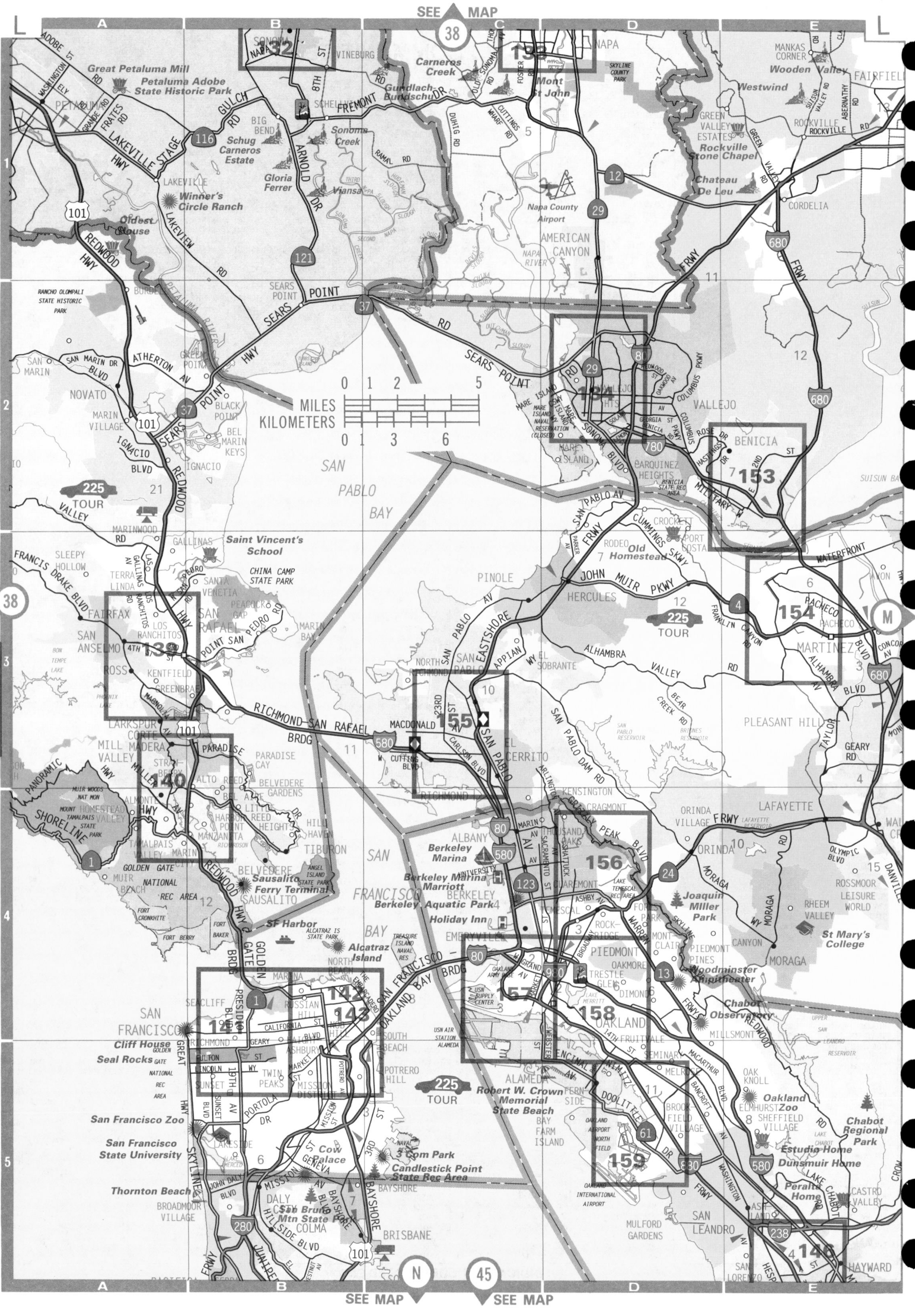

SEE MAP 38
SEE MAP 38
SEE MAP 45
SEE MAP
M
N
METRO
MILES
KILOMETERS
0 1 2 5
0 1 3 6
SAN PABLO BAY
SAN FRANCISCO BAY
Great Petaluma Mill
Petaluma Adobe State Historic Park
PETALUMA
LAKEVILLE
Winner's Circle Ranch
Oldest House
Schug Carneros Estate
Gloria Ferrer
Viansa
Sonoma Creek
Carneros Creek
Gundlach Bundschu
VINEBURG
BIG BEND
SCHELLVILLE
FREMONT
Mont St John
NAPA
SKYLINE COUNTY PARK
Napa County Airport
AMERICAN CANYON
NAPA RIVER
MANKAS CORNER
Wooden Valley
Westwind
FAIRFIELD
GREEN VALLEY ESTATES
Rockville Stone Chapel
ROCKVILLE
Chateau De Leu
CORDELIA
SEARS POINT
RANCHO OLOMPALI STATE HISTORIC PARK
BURDELL
SAN MARIN
NOVATO
MARIN VILLAGE
BLACK POINT
BEL MARIN KEYS
IGNACIO
225 TOUR
MARINWOOD
GALLINAS
Saint Vincent's School
CHINA CAMP STATE PARK
SLEEPY HOLLOW
TERRA LINDA
SANTA VENETIA
FAIRFAX
SAN ANSELMO
SAN RAFAEL
LOS RANCHITOS
ROSS
KENTFIELD
GREENBRAE
LARKSPUR
CORTE MADERA
MILL VALLEY
PARADISE CAY
BELVEDERE GARDENS
ALTO
STRAWBERRY
HOMESTEAD VALLEY
ALMONTE
MUIR WOODS NAT MON
MOUNT TAMALPAIS STATE PARK
TAMALPAIS VALLEY
MARIN CITY
MANZANITA
HARBOR POINT
LITTLE REED HEIGHTS
HILL HAVEN
TIBURON
BELVEDERE
ANGEL ISLAND STATE PARK
Sausalito Ferry Terminal
SAUSALITO
GOLDEN GATE NATIONAL REC AREA
MUIR BEACH
FORT CRONKHITE
FORT BAKER
FORT BERRY
SF Harbor
ALCATRAZ IS STATE PARK
Alcatraz Island
TREASURE ISLAND NAVAL RES
VALLEJO
VALLEJO HTS
MARE ISLAND
MARE ISLAND NAVAL RESERVATION (CLOSED)
CARQUINEZ HEIGHTS
BENICIA STATE REC AREA
BENICIA
SUISUN BAY
CROCKETT
PORT COSTA
RODEO
Old Homestead
PINOLE
HERCULES
225 TOUR
MARTINEZ
PACHECO
ALHAMBRA VALLEY
NORTH RICHMOND
SAN PABLO
EL SOBRANTE
RICHMOND
EL CERRITO
SAN PABLO RESERVOIR
BRIONES RESERVOIR
PLEASANT HILL
KENSINGTON
CRAGMONT
ORINDA VILLAGE
LAFAYETTE
LAFAYETTE RESERVOIR
ALBANY
Berkeley Marina
Berkeley Marina Marriott
BERKELEY
UNIVERSITY
Berkeley Aquatic Park
Holiday Inn
EMERYVILLE
THOUSAND OAKS
CLAREMONT
LAKE TEMESCAL REC AREA
TEMESCAL
ROCKRIDGE
ORINDA
Joaquin Miller Park
MONTCLAIR
PIEDMONT PINES
MORAGA
RHEEM VALLEY
ROSSMOOR LEISURE WORLD
St Mary's College
CANYON
PIEDMONT
OAKMORE
TRESTLE GLEN
Woodminster Amphitheater
DIMOND
OAKLAND
LAKE MERRITT
USN SUPPLY CENTER
OAKLAND ARMY BASE
Chabot Observatory
MILLSMONT
UPPER SAN LEANDRO RESERVOIR
FRUITVALE
SEMINARY
MELROSE
USN AIR STATION ALAMEDA
ALAMEDA
FERNSIDE
Robert W. Crown Memorial State Beach
BAY FARM ISLAND
OAK KNOLL
ELMHURST
Oakland Zoo
SHEFFIELD VILLAGE
BROOKFIELD VILLAGE
OAKLAND AIRPORT NORTH FIELD
OAKLAND INTERNATIONAL AIRPORT
Chabot Regional Park
Estudillo Home
Dunsmuir Home
Peralta Home
CASTRO VALLEY
SAN LEANDRO
MULFORD GARDENS
ASHLAND
SAN LORENZO
HAYWARD
SAN FRANCISCO
SEACLIFF
PRESIDIO
MARINA
NORTH BEACH
RUSSIAN HILL
NOB HILL
Cliff House
Seal Rocks
GOLDEN GATE NATIONAL REC AREA
RICHMOND
ASHBURY
TWIN PEAKS
SUNSET
MISSION DISTRICT
SOUTH BEACH
POTRERO HILL
225 TOUR
San Francisco Zoo
San Francisco State University
LAKESIDE
Cow Palace
3 Com Park
Candlestick Point State Rec Area
BAYSHORE
Thornton Beach
BROADMOOR VILLAGE
DALY CITY
San Bruno Mtn State Park
COLMA
BRISBANE
RICHMOND-SAN RAFAEL BRDG
SAN FRANCISCO-OAKLAND BAY BRDG
GOLDEN GATE BRDG
EASTSHORE FRWY
JOHN MUIR PKWY
SIR FRANCIS DRAKE BLVD
SEARS POINT RD
LAKEVILLE HWY
REDWOOD HWY
SHORELINE HWY
SKYLINE BLVD
132 153 154 155 156 157 158 159 139 140 141 142 143 146

SEE MAP 39

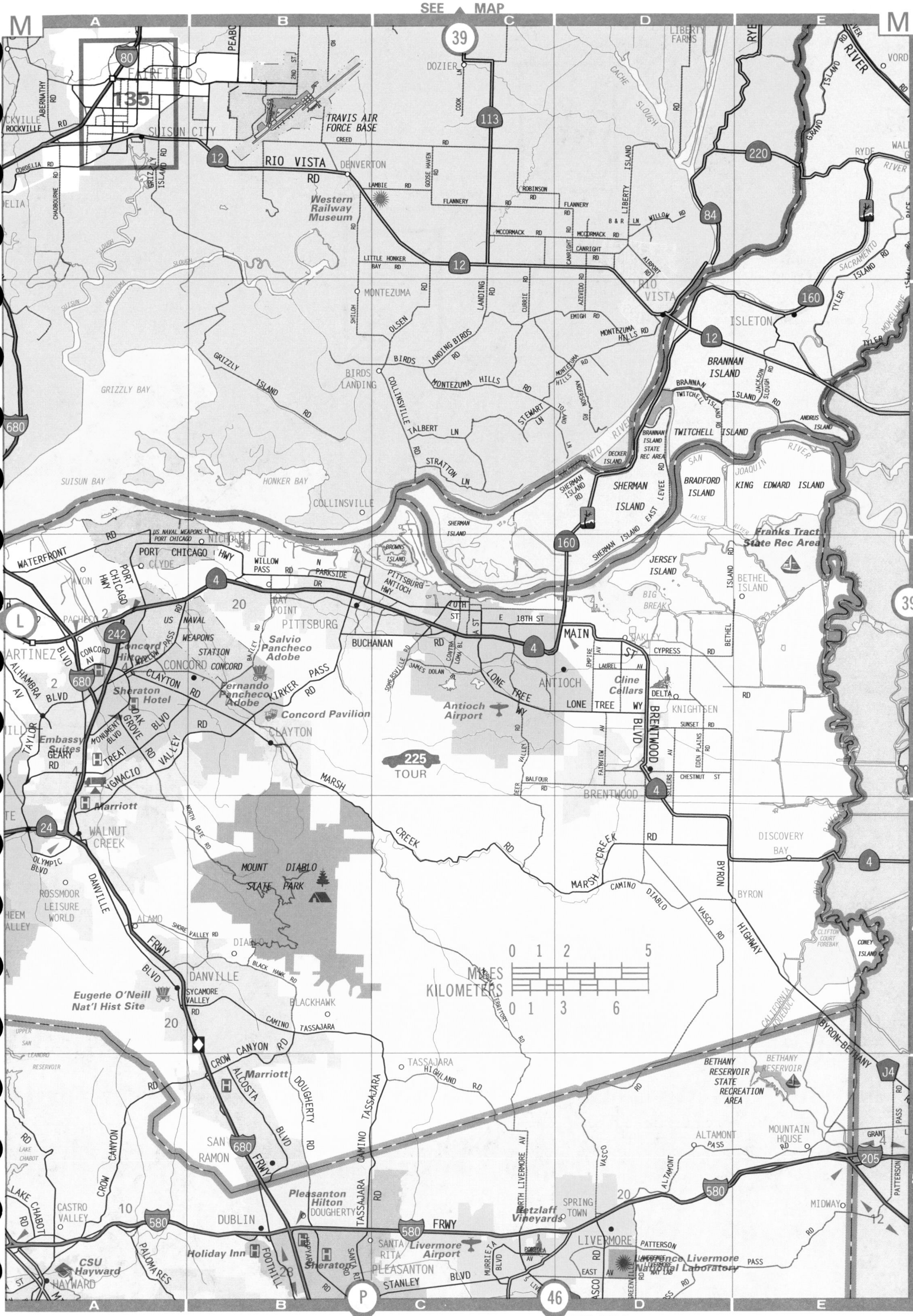

SEE MAP P
SEE MAP 46
SEE MAP L
SEE MAP 39

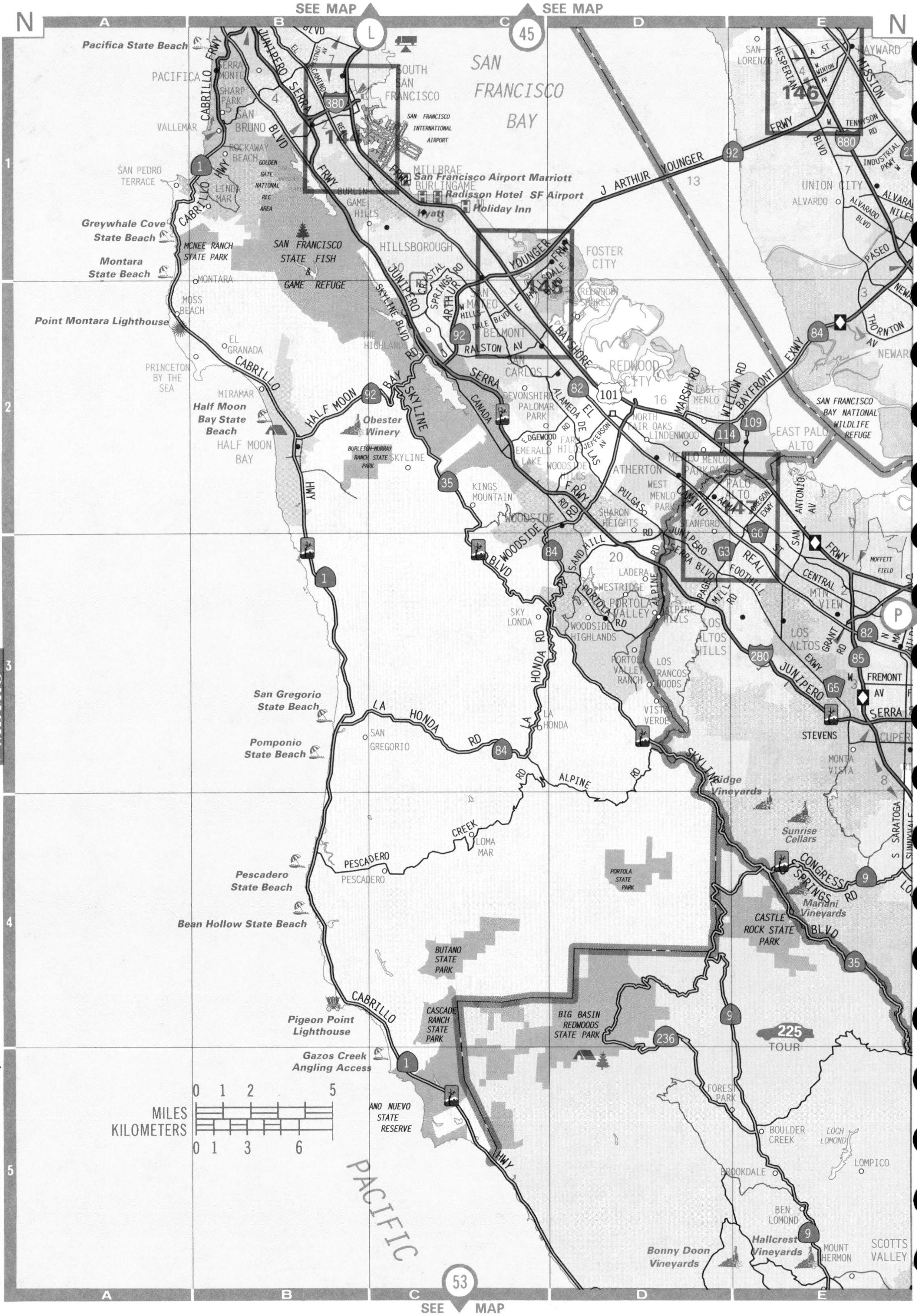
SEE MAP
L
SEE MAP
45
N
A
B
C
D
E
Pacifica State Beach
PACIFICA
SERRA MONTE
SHARP PARK
SAN BRUNO
VALLEMAR
ROCKAWAY BEACH
GOLDEN GATE NATIONAL REC AREA
SAN PEDRO TERRACE
LINDA MAR
CABRILLO FRWY
CABRILLO HWY
JUNIPERO SERRA BLVD
FRWY
EL CAMINO REAL
380
SOUTH SAN FRANCISCO
SAN FRANCISCO INTERNATIONAL AIRPORT
144
SAN FRANCISCO BAY
MILLBRAE
BURLINGAME
BURLINGAME HILLS
San Francisco Airport Marriott
Radisson Hotel SF Airport
Holiday Inn
Hyatt
Greywhale Cove State Beach
MCNEE RANCH STATE PARK
Montara State Beach
MONTARA
SAN FRANCISCO STATE FISH & GAME REFUGE
HILLSBOROUGH
MOSS BEACH
Point Montara Lighthouse
EL GRANADA
PRINCETON BY THE SEA
CABRILLO
MIRAMAR
Half Moon Bay State Beach
HALF MOON BAY
HALF MOON BAY
92
SKYLINE BLVD
SKYLINE
Obester Winery
BURLEIGH-MURRAY RANCH STATE PARK
SKYLINE
THE HIGHLANDS
CRYSTAL SPRINGS RD
ARTHUR
SAN MATEO
BELMONT
RALSTON AV
SAN CARLOS
YOUNGER
J ARTHUR YOUNGER
HILLSDALE
145
FOSTER CITY
REDWOOD SHORES
BAYSHORE
REDWOOD CITY
82
101
EL CAMINO
DEVONSHIRE
PALOMAR PARK
EDGEWOOD
EMERALD LAKE
FARM HILLS
WOODSIDE HILLS
ALAMEDA DE LAS PULGAS
JEFFERSON AV
NORTH FAIR OAKS
LINDENWOOD
ATHERTON
WEST MENLO PARK
MENLO PARK
EAST MENLO
MARSH RD
WILLOW RD
BAYFRONT EXWY
114
109
EAST PALO ALTO
SAN FRANCISCO BAY NATIONAL WILDLIFE REFUGE
PALO ALTO
OREGON EXWY
STANFORD
SHARON HEIGHTS
KINGS MOUNTAIN
35
WOODSIDE
WOODSIDE RD
84
SAND HILL RD
LADERA
WESTRIDGE
PORTOLA VALLEY
PORTOLA RD
ALPINE RD
ALPINE HILLS
WOODSIDE HIGHLANDS
PORTOLA VALLEY RANCH
LOS TRANCOS WOODS
LOS ALTOS HILLS
VISTA VERDE
SKY LONDA
JUNIPERO SERRA BLVD
G3
G6
FOOTHILL
PAGE MILL RD
CENTRAL
MTN VIEW
MOFFETT FIELD
LOS ALTOS
GRANT RD
85
280
JUNIPERO SERRA
G5
FREMONT AV
STEVENS
MONTA VISTA
SAN ANTONIO AV
SAN FRANCISCO
CAMINO REAL
P
SAN LORENZO
HESPERIAN
A ST
W WINTON AV
146
HAYWARD
MISSION
TENNYSON RD
FRWY
BLVD
880
92
13
INDUSTRIAL PKWY W
UNION CITY
ALVARADO
ALVARADO NILES
PASEO
NEWARK
THORNTON AV
84
16
20
San Gregorio State Beach
LA HONDA RD
LA HONDA
SAN GREGORIO
Pomponio State Beach
ALPINE RD
Ridge Vineyards
SKYLINE
CREEK
LOMA MAR
PESCADERO
Pescadero State Beach
Bean Hollow State Beach
PORTOLA STATE PARK
Sunrise Cellars
CONGRESS SPRINGS RD
Mariani Vineyards
9
SARATOGA
CASTLE ROCK STATE PARK
35
BUTANO STATE PARK
CABRILLO
Pigeon Point Lighthouse
CASCADE RANCH STATE PARK
BIG BASIN REDWOODS STATE PARK
236
225 TOUR
Gazos Creek Angling Access
1
ANO NUEVO STATE RESERVE
HWY
0 1 2 5
MILES
KILOMETERS
0 1 3 6
FOREST PARK
BOULDER CREEK
LOCH LOMOND
LOMPICO
BROOKDALE
BEN LOMOND
PACIFIC
Bonny Doon Vineyards
Hallcrest Vineyards
MOUNT HERMON
SCOTTS VALLEY
53
SEE MAP
METRO

P
SEE MAP
M
46
SEE MAP
P
A
B
C
D
E
HAYWARD
MISSION
TENNYSON
880
238
INDUSTRIAL PKWY W
225 TOUR
UNION CITY
BLVD
ALVARADO NILES RD
NILES
MISSION
FREMONT
PASEO PADRE
84
NEWARK
THORNTON AV
CENTERVILLE
IRVINGTON
MOWRY
STEVENSON
Hilton
238
MISSION SAN JOSE
Mission San Jose
680
Weibel Champagne Vineyards
WARM SPRINGS
262
SAN FRANCISCO BAY NATIONAL WILDLIFE REFUGE
NIMITZ
SINCLAIR
WARM SPRINGS BLVD
STANLEY BLVD
PLEASANTON
Shadow Cliffs Regional Recreation Area
KILKARE RD
SUNOL
CANYON RD
E VALLECITOS
SCOTTS CORNER
Leland Stanford Winery
LIVERMORE
Livermore Memorial Monument
J2
Concannon Vineyard
Wente Bros
Wente Bros Sparkling Wine Cellars
LAKE DEL VALLE RECREATION AREA
Livermore Valley Cellars
SAN ANTONIO RESERVOIR
LAKE DEL VALLE
DEL VALLE RD
MINES RD
TESLA RD
CROSS RD
Carnegie State Vehicular Area
0 1 2 5
MILES
KILOMETERS
0 1 3 6
CALAVERAS RESERVOIR
JACKLIN RD
E CALAVERAS BLVD
MILPITAS
ALVISO
Holiday Inn
Crown Sterling Suites
Westin
Marriott
Great America
Embassy Suites
Hilton
237
SOUTHBAY FRWY
LANDESS AV
BERRYESSA
880
148
101
MONTAGUE EXWY
OLD OAKLAND
N KING
ALUM ROCK AV
MOUNT HAMILTON RD
130
EAST SAN JOSE
ALUM ROCK
Lick Observatory
MT HAMILTON RD
SAN ANTONIO VALLEY RD
85
82
G6
G4
SUNNYVALE
FREMONT AV
EL CAMINO REAL
149
150
151
152
SANTA CLARA
SERRA FRWY
CUPERTINO
STEVENS CREEK BLVD
SAN CARLOS ST
SAN JOSE
TULLY
KING RD
CAPITOL EXWY
Mirassou Vineyards
Rancho Rinconada
MONTA VISTA
LAWRENCE EXWY
SARATOGA AV
SAN TOMAS
HAMILTON AV
CAMPBELL
BASCOM AV
MERIDIAN
CURTNER AV
87
MONTEREY
HILLSDALE AV
CAMDEN AV
BAYSHORE FRWY
101
EVERGREEN
SAN FELIPE RD
SILVER CREEK VALLEY
SOUTH VALLEY FRWY
SARATOGA
9
Hakone Gardens
LOS GATOS
MONTE SERENO
BLOSSOM HILL RD
G10
ALMADEN
G8
SANTA TERESA BLVD
MONTEREY RD
COYOTE
35
17
Byington Winery
Lexington Reservoir
David Bruce Winery
Almaden Golf & Country Club
MCKEAN RD
IDYLWILD
CHEMEKETA PARK
ALDERCROFT HEIGHTS
REDWOOD ESTATES
HOLY CITY
SUMMIT RD
Henry Coe State Park
Pedrizzetti Winery
ANDERSON RESERVOIR
Emilio Gugielmo
E DUNNE AV
Flying Lady Museum
MADRONE
CHESBRO RESERVOIR
COYOTE RESERVOIR
LOCH LOMOND
LOMPICO
Roudon-Smith Tasting
Roaring Camp & Big Trees Narrow Gauge
MOUNT HERMON
SCOTTS VALLEY
Felton Covered Bridge
The Forest of Nisene Marks State Park
UVAS
Sycamore Creek Vineyards
WATSONVILLE RD
SAN MARTIN
San Martin Winery
Kirigen Cellars
54
SEE MAP
46 SEE MAP
N SEE MAP
METRO
COPYRIGHT 1998 Thomas Bros. Maps ®
1
2
3
4
5

SEE MAP 89
SEE MAP 97
SEE MAP S
METRO
Angeles National Forest
OLIVE VIEW
SYLMAR
210
FOOTHILL
PACOIMA RESERVOIR
KAGEL CYN
LAKE VIEW TERRACE
LITTLE TUJUNGA RD
BIG TUJUNGA CANYON
SAN FERNANDO
San Fernando Mission
PORTER RANCH
RONALD REAGAN FRWY
118
MISSION HILLS
GRANADA HILLS
CHATSWORTH
NORTHRIDGE
NORTH HILLS
CSU Northridge
NORDHOFF
405
PANORAMA CITY
ARLETA
PACOIMA
5
HANSEN LAKE
SUNLAND
TUJUNGA
SHADOW HILLS
LA TUNA CANYON
LA CRESCENTA
210
VERDUGO CITY
VAN NUYS AIRPORT
ROSCOE BLVD
170
SUN VALLEY
Burbank-Glendale-Pasadena Airport
BURBANK
Holiday Inn
San Rafael Adobe
CANOGA PARK
WINNETKA
RESEDA
VICTORY
VAN NUYS
NORTH HOLLYWOOD
WARNER CENTER
177
178
179
TARZANA
WOODLAND HILLS
VENTURA
101
MAGNOLIA
VALLEY VILLAGE
134
ENCINO
ENCINO RESERVOIR
Los Encinos State Historic Park
SHERMAN OAKS
STUDIO CITY
TOLUCA LAKE
UNIVERSAL CITY
GLENDALE
ATWATER VILLAGE
27
MULHOLLAND
237 TOUR
STONE CANYON RESERVOIR
BEVERLY GLEN
Harold Lloyd Estates
TROUSDALE ESTATES
Greystone Mansion
MOUNT OLYMPUS
HOLLYWOOD HILLS
181
182
LOS FELIZ
SILVER LAKE
HOLLYWOOD
GLENVIEW
OLD CANYON
SYLVIA PARK
STATE OWNED LANDS
TOPANGA STATE PARK
TOPANGA
PALISADES HIGHLANDS
BEL AIR ESTATES
2
WEST HOLLYWOOD
HANCOCK PARK
ECHO PARK
HOLLYWOOD FRWY
Getty Center
BRENTWOOD
WESTWOOD
BEVERLY HILLS
FERNWOOD
Will Rogers State Historic Park
PACIFIC PALISADES
BIG ROCK
180
183
184
185
CENTURY CITY
PARK LA BREA
WESTLAKE
KOREATOWN
WEST LOS ANGELES
RANCHO PARK
CHEVIOT HILLS
MID-CITY
COUNTRY CLUB PARK
J Paul Getty Museum
Riviera Country Club
PACIFIC COAST HWY
1
CASTELLAMMARE
Las Tunas Beach
Topanga State Beach
Will Rogers State Beach
SAWTELLE
10
PALMS
JEFFERSON PARK
110
Miramar Sheraton Hotel
Santa Monica State Beach
Santa Monica Pier
SANTA MONICA
Loews Santa Monica Beach Hotel
Holiday Inn Bayview
OCEAN PARK
MAR VISTA
CULVER CITY
CRENSHAW
BALDWIN HILLS
LEIMERT PARK
VERNON
LA Co Museums Exposition Pk
LA Coliseum
FOX HILLS
VIEW PARK
WINDSOR HILLS
187
188
90
VENICE
LADERA HEIGHTS
HYDE PARK
FLORENCE
MARINA DEL REY
WESTCHESTER
INGLEWOOD
MORNINGSIDE PARK
42
The Forum
Hollywood Park
PLAYA DEL REY
LOS ANGELES INTERNATIONAL AIRPORT
CENTURY
LENNOX
WATTS
189
EL SEGUNDO
105
ATHENS
HAWTHORNE
EL PORTO
MILES 0 1 2 5
KILOMETERS 0 1 2 5

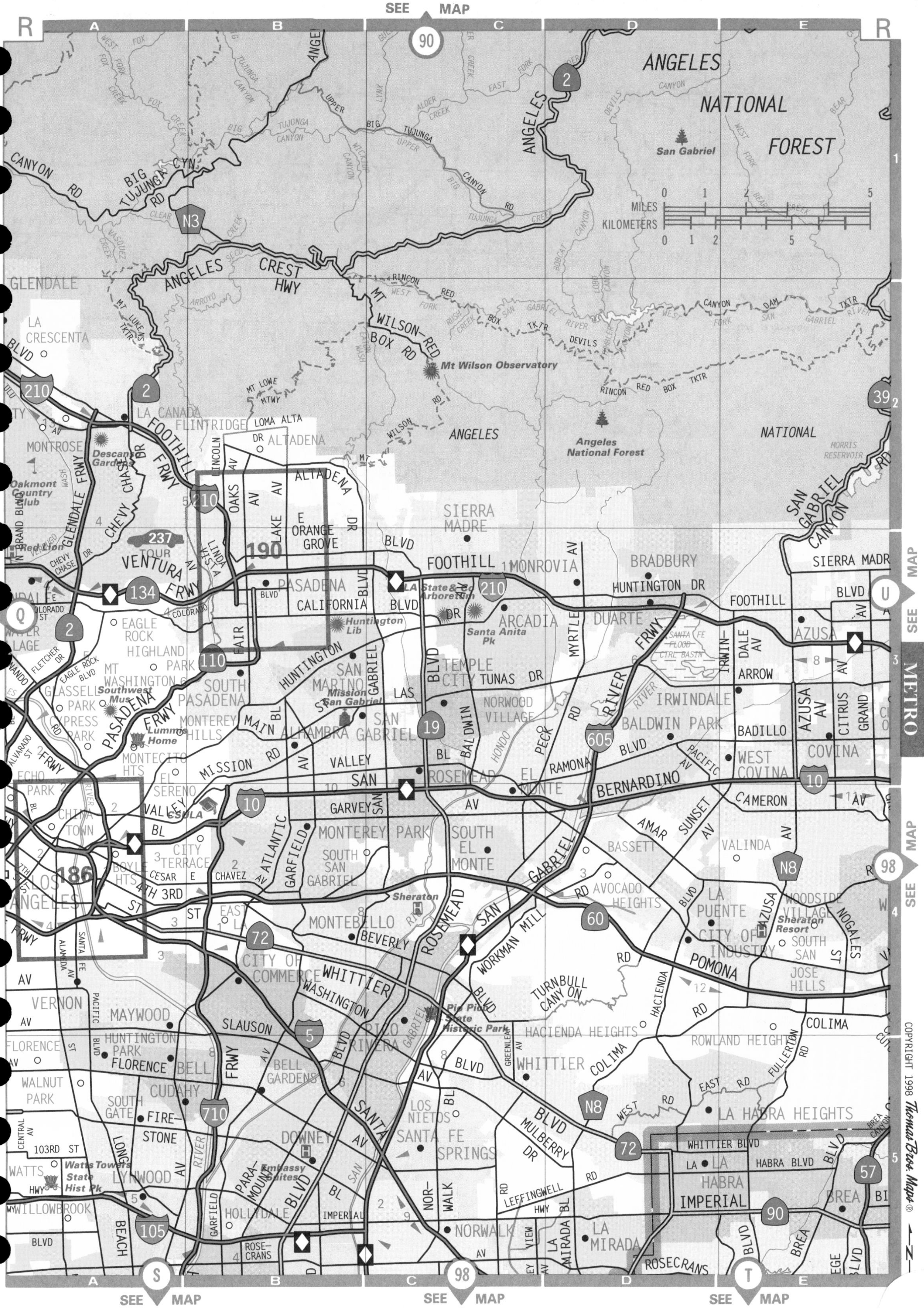
SEE MAP 90
R
A
B
C
D
E
ANGELES NATIONAL FOREST
San Gabriel
MILES
KILOMETERS
0 1 2 5
BIG TUJUNGA CYN RD
CANYON RD
ANGELES CREST HWY
UPPER BIG TUJUNGA CANYON RD
MT WILSON-RED BOX RD
Mt Wilson Observatory
RINCON RED BOX TKTR
WEST FORK SAN GABRIEL RIVER
ANGELES
Angeles National Forest
NATIONAL
MORRIS RESERVOIR
SAN GABRIEL CANYON RD
GLENDALE
LA CRESCENTA
MONTROSE
LA CANADA FLINTRIDGE
ALTADENA
Descanso Gardens
Oakmont Country Club
GLENDALE FRWY
FOOTHILL FRWY
CHEVY CHASE DR
VENTURA FRWY
TOUR 237
PASADENA
LAKE AV
E ORANGE GROVE
CALIFORNIA BLVD
FOOTHILL BLVD
SIERRA MADRE
MONROVIA
BRADBURY
HUNTINGTON DR
ARCADIA
DUARTE
LA State & Co Arboretum
Huntington Lib
Santa Anita Pk
EAGLE ROCK
HIGHLAND PARK
MT WASHINGTON
SOUTH PASADENA
Southwest Mus
GLASSELL PARK
CYPRESS PARK
Lummis Home
MONTEREY HILLS
SAN MARINO
Mission San Gabriel
SAN GABRIEL
ALHAMBRA
TEMPLE CITY
TUNAS DR
NORWOOD VILLAGE
IRWINDALE
BALDWIN PARK
AZUSA
COVINA
WEST COVINA
FOOTHILL BLVD
SIERRA MADRE
ARROW
BADILLO
CITRUS
GRAND
METRO
SEE MAP U
SEE MAP Q
ECHO PARK
CHINA TOWN
EL SERENO
CSULA
VALLEY BL
MISSION RD
VALLEY
SAN BERNARDINO
ROSEMEAD
EL MONTE
RAMONA
CAMERON
LOS ANGELES
BOYLE HTS
CITY TERRACE
CESAR E CHAVEZ
MONTEREY PARK
SOUTH EL MONTE
SOUTH SAN GABRIEL
GARVEY AV
ATLANTIC
GARFIELD
BASSETT
VALINDA
AMAR
SUNSET AV
AVOCADO HEIGHTS
LA PUENTE
CITY OF INDUSTRY
WOODSIDE VILLAGE
Sheraton Resort
SOUTH SAN JOSE HILLS
POMONA
NOGALES
SEE MAP 98
EAST LA
MONTEBELLO
BEVERLY
Sheraton
CITY OF COMMERCE
WHITTIER
WASHINGTON
ROSEMEAD
SAN GABRIEL
WORKMAN MILL
TURNBULL CANYON
HACIENDA
HACIENDA HEIGHTS
ROWLAND HEIGHTS
COLIMA
VERNON
MAYWOOD
SLAUSON
Pio Pico State Historic Park
PICO RIVERA
HUNTINGTON PARK
FLORENCE
BELL
BELL GARDENS
WALNUT PARK
CUDAHY
SOUTH GATE
FIRESTONE
WHITTIER
FULLERTON RD
LA HABRA HEIGHTS
LOS NIETOS
SANTA FE SPRINGS
DOWNEY
Embassy Suites
PARAMOUNT
MULBERRY DR
WHITTIER BLVD
LA HABRA
HABRA BLVD
IMPERIAL
BREA
WATTS
Watts Towers State Hist Pk
LYNWOOD
WILLOWBROOK
103RD ST
LONG BEACH
HOLLYDALE
LEFFINGWELL RD
NORWALK
LA MIRADA
ROSECRANS
SEE MAP S
SEE MAP 98
SEE MAP T
COPYRIGHT 1998 Thomas Bros Maps ®

SEE MAP Q
SEE MAP 97
SEE MAP R
S
A
B
C
D
E
1
2
3
4
5
LOS ANGELES INTERNATIONAL AIRPORT
VISTA DEL MAR
CENTURY
LENNOX
IMPERIAL
ANDERSON
WATTS
103RD ST
STONE
LYNWOOD
DOWNEY
EL SEGUNDO
WILLOWBROOK
HOLLYDALE
HAWTHORNE
ROSECRANS
ATHENS
EL SEGUNDO BLVD
EL PORTO
Manhattan Beach
MANHATTAN BEACH
LAWNDALE
EL CAMINO VILLAGE
GARDENA
ROSEWOOD
COMPTON
PARAMOUNT
BELLFLOWER
ALONDRA
MONETA
ARTESIA
Hermosa Beach
HERMOSA BEACH
EL NIDO
190TH ST
Holiday Inn Crowne Plaza
REDONDO BEACH
Redondo Beach
NORTH LONG BEACH
MAYFAIR
SOUTH
LAKEWOOD
RANCHO DOMINGUEZ
CSU Dominquez Hills
DEL AMO BLVD
HARBOR GATEWAY
TORRANCE
CARSON
Marriott
Holiday Inn
DOMINGUEZ
BIXBY KNOLLS
LONG BEACH MUNICIPAL AIRPORT
LOS COYOTES DIAG
Airport Marriott
HOLLYWOOD RIVIERA
HARBOR CITY
LOMITA
WALTERIA
WILMINGTON
WILLOW ST
WRIGLEY
SIGNAL HILL
LOS ALTOS
ATHERTON ST
Banning Pk
PALOS VERDES ESTATES
ROLLING HILLS ESTATES
South Coast Botanic Gardens
ROLLING HILLS
ANAHEIM ST
LONG BEACH
ROSE PARK
7TH
BELMONT
BELMONT SHORE
2ND ST
CSU Long Beach
RANCHO PALOS VERDES
MIRALESTE
TOUR
Wayfarer's Chapel
PORTUGUESE BEND
SAN PEDRO
TERMINAL ISLAND
LOS ANGELES HARBOR
Long Beach Marina & Marine Stadium
NAPLES
SEAL BEACH
LONG BEACH HARBOR
ISLAND GRISSOM
ISLAND WHITE
ISLAND FREEMAN
ISLAND CHAFFEE
Royal Palms Beach
Cabrillo Beach
Cabrillo Marine Mus
Point Fermin Historic Lighthouse
PACIFIC OCEAN
191
192
1
5
91
105
107
110
213
237
405
19
103
710
MILES
KILOMETERS
0
1
2
5

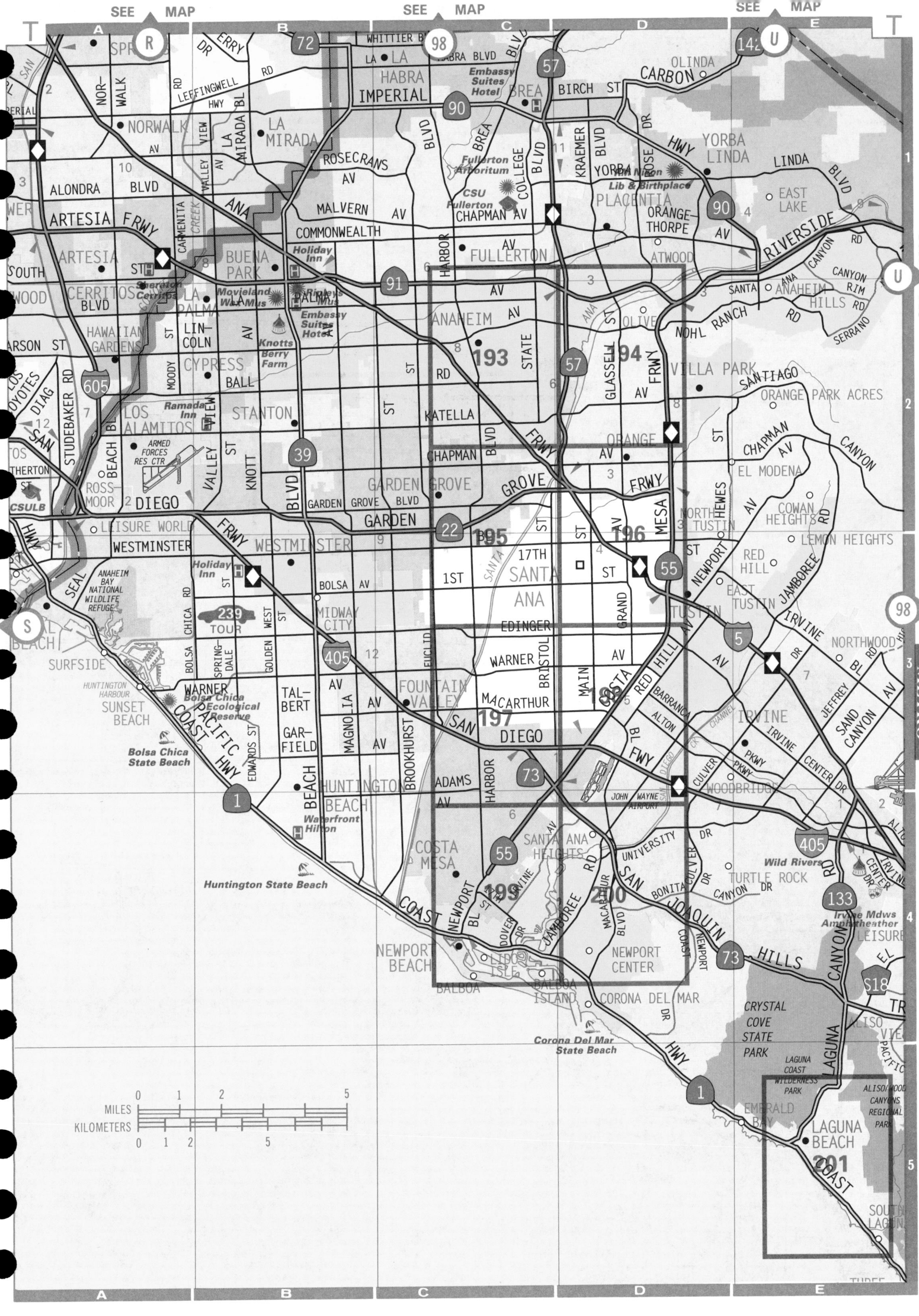
SEE MAP R
SEE MAP 98
SEE MAP U
SEE MAP S
A
B
C
D
E
T
1
2
3
4
5
METRO
WHITTIER BL
LA HABRA
HABRA BLVD
IMPERIAL
Embassy Suites Hotel
BREA
BIRCH ST
CARBON
OLINDA
NORWALK
LEFFINGWELL RD
LA MIRADA
ROSECRANS AV
ALONDRA BLVD
ARTESIA FRWY
MALVERN AV
COMMONWEALTH
CHAPMAN AV
Fullerton Arboritum
CSU Fullerton
COLLEGE BLVD
KRAEMER BLVD
YORBA LINDA
Nixon Lib & Birthplace
PLACENTIA
ORANGE-THORPE AV
EAST LAKE
LINDA BLVD
RIVERSIDE
ARTESIA
CERRITOS
Sheraton Cerritos
BUENA PARK
Holiday Inn
Movieland Wax Mus
Ripleys Mus
Embassy Suites Hotel
Knotts Berry Farm
FULLERTON
ATWOOD
ANAHEIM HILLS
CANYON RIM RD
SANTA ANA
NOHL RANCH RD
SERRANO
OLIVE
LA PALMA
HAWAIIAN GARDENS
LINCOLN
CARSON ST
CYPRESS
BALL
MOODY
ANAHEIM
193
194
STATE
GLASSELL
VILLA PARK
SANTIAGO
ORANGE PARK ACRES
STUDEBAKER RD
LOS ALAMITOS
Ramada Inn
STANTON
KATELLA
ORANGE
ARMED FORCES RES CTR
ROSSMOOR
CSULB
LEISURE WORLD
CHAPMAN
GARDEN GROVE
GARDEN GROVE BLVD
EL MODENA
COWAN HEIGHTS
LEMON HEIGHTS
NORTH TUSTIN
HEWES
WESTMINSTER
Holiday Inn
BOLSA AV
195
196
17TH
1ST
SANTA ANA
GRAND
RED HILL
EAST TUSTIN
TUSTIN
JAMBOREE
IRVINE
NORTHWOOD
ANAHEIM BAY NATIONAL WILDLIFE REFUGE
SEAL BEACH
SURFSIDE
HUNTINGTON HARBOUR
SUNSET BEACH
239 TOUR
MIDWAY CITY
EDINGER
WARNER
MACARTHUR
FOUNTAIN VALLEY
197
198
BRISTOL
MAIN
BARRANCA
ALTON
IRVINE
JEFFREY
SAND CANYON
Bolsa Chica Ecological Reserve
Bolsa Chica State Beach
PACIFIC COAST HWY
TALBERT
GARFIELD
MAGNOLIA
BROOKHURST
EUCLID
EDWARDS ST
HUNTINGTON BEACH
ADAMS AV
HARBOR
SAN DIEGO FWY
JOHN WAYNE AIRPORT
WOODBRIDGE
CULVER
Waterfront Hilton
Huntington State Beach
COSTA MESA
SANTA ANA HEIGHTS
UNIVERSITY DR
TURTLE ROCK
Wild Rivers
199
200
NEWPORT BL
DOVER DR
JAMBOREE
MACARTHUR BLVD
SAN JOAQUIN HILLS
BONITA CANYON DR
Irvine Mdws Amphitheather
LEISURE
NEWPORT BEACH
LIDO ISLE
BALBOA
BALBOA ISLAND
NEWPORT CENTER
CORONA DEL MAR
Corona Del Mar State Beach
CRYSTAL COVE STATE PARK
LAGUNA CANYON
LAGUNA COAST WILDERNESS PARK
ALISO/WOOD CANYONS REGIONAL PARK
EMERALD BAY
LAGUNA BEACH
201
COAST
SOUTH LAGUNA
MILES
KILOMETERS
0 1 2 5
0 1 2 5

SEE 98 MAP

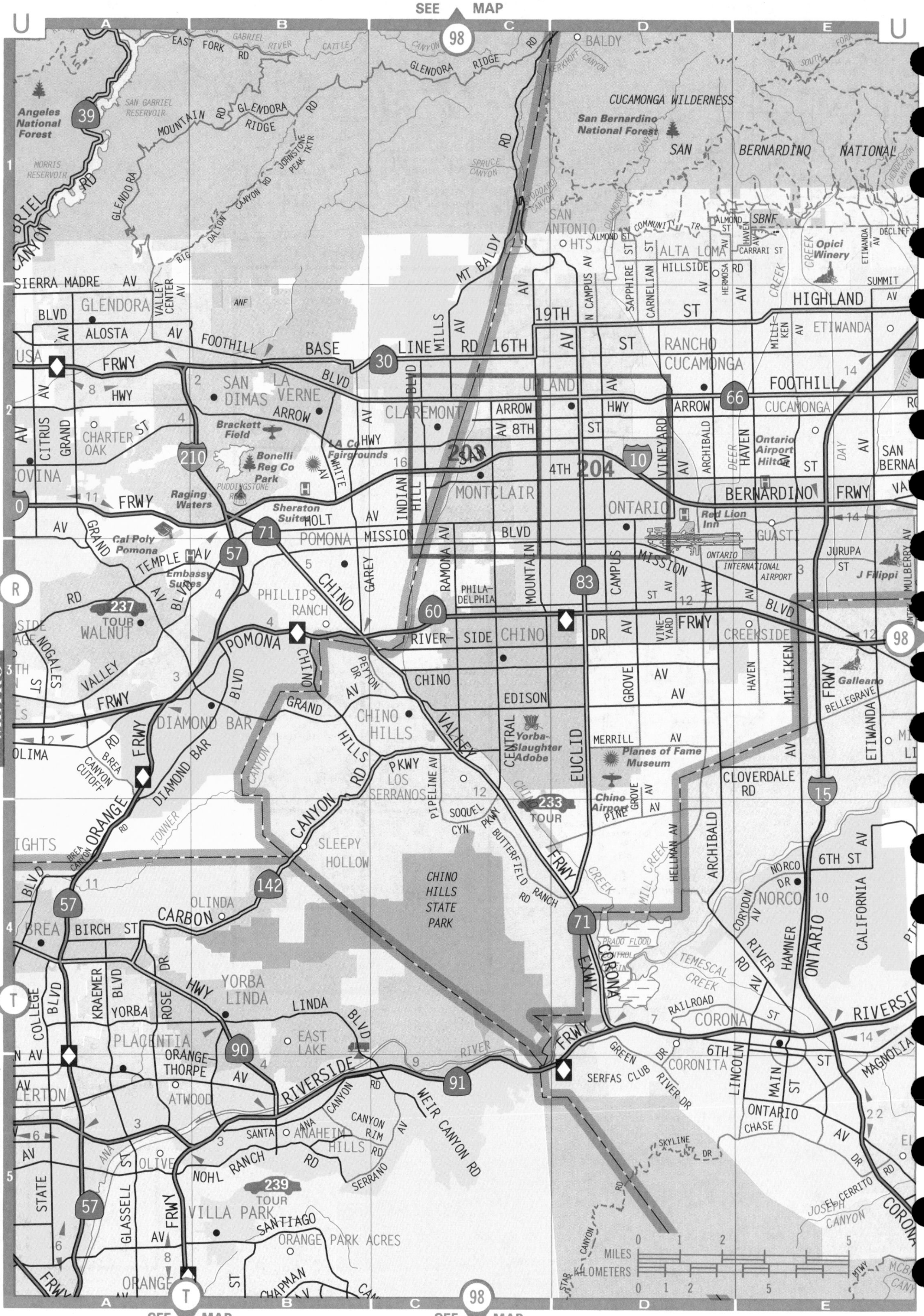

SEE R MAP

SEE T MAP

SEE 98 MAP

SEE T MAP

SEE 98 MAP

SEE MAP 106
SEE MAP 107
SEE MAP 112
SEE MAP 111
METRO
DEL MAR
TORREY PINES
CARMEL VALLEY
TED WILLIAMS FRWY
LOS PENASQUITOS CANYON PRESERVE
TORREY PINES STATE RESERVE
San Diego La Jolla Underwater Park
Torrey Pines State Beach
Torrey Pines Golf Course
Sheraton
UC San Diego
Hyatt Regency
La Jolla Marriott
Embassy Suites
SORRENTO VALLEY
SORRENTO MESA
MIRA MESA
MIRAMAR
POWAY
FERNBROOK
SAN VICENTE RESERVOIR
SYCAMORE CANYON COUNTY OPEN SPACE PRESERVE
FOSTER
EUCALYPTUS HILLS
SCRIPPS MIRAMAR RANCH
MIRAMAR RESERVOIR
MIRAMAR NAVAL AIR STATION
SANTEE
SANTEE RECREATION LAKES
Carlton Oaks Lodge & Country Club
EAST ELLIOTT
MISSION TRAILS REGIONAL PARK
LA JOLLA
UNIVERSITY
CLAIREMONT
KEARNY MESA
TIERRASANTA
TOUR
SAN CARLOS
FLETCHER HILLS
WINTER GARDENS
GILLESPIE FIELD
BOSTONIA
EL CAJON
GROSSMONT
MOUNT HELIX
PACIFIC BEACH
MISSION BAY
MISSION BEACH
MISSION BAY PARK
LINDA VISTA
SERRA MESA
BAY PARK
MISSION VALLEY
KENSINGTON
SD State Univ
TALMADGE
ROLANDO
Pacific SW Railway Museum (La Mesa Depot)
LA MESA
Open Air Theater
MISSION HILLS
OCEAN BEACH
MIDDLETOWN
SAN DIEGO ZOO
BALBOA PARK
NORTH PARK
SAN DIEGO
OAK PARK
LEMON GROVE
SPRING VALLEY
RANCHO SAN DIEGO
LA PRESA
SAN DIEGO INTERNATIONAL AIRPORT LINDBERGH FIELD
Holiday Inn
SWEETWATER RESERVOIR
Cabrillo National Monument
PT LOMA
NORTH ISLAND NAVAL AIR STATION
Hotel Del Coronado
CORONADO
NATIONAL CITY
PARADISE HILLS
Old Point Loma Lighthouse
Point Loma
Chula Vista Nature Interpretive Center
SAN DIEGO BAY
CHULA VISTA
BONITA
EASTLAKE
EASTLAKE GREENS
Otay Reservoir
Silver Strand State Beach
CORONADO CAYS
Loews Coronado Bay Resort
OTAY
OTAY MESA
IMPERIAL BEACH
NESTOR
SAN YSIDRO
TIJUANA RIVER NATIONAL ESTUARINE SANCTUARY
Border Field State Park
AEROPUERTO DE TIJUANA
OCEAN
MILES
KILOMETERS
0 1 2 5
0 1 2 5
COPYRIGHT 1998 Thomas Bros. Maps ®

1
A
B
C
D
E
1
2
3
4
5
CARPENTERVILLE
OREGON
THOMAS CK
101
BOWMAN CK
N FORK
CHETCO RIVER
S FORK
CHETCO RIVER
CHETCO RD
BOULDER CK
COON CK
HORSE CK
Siskiyou National Forest
CURRY CO.
NORTH BANK CHETCO RD
SOUTH BANK CHETCO RD
WINCHUCK RIVER
E FORK
FOURTH OF JULY CK
BROOKINGS
HARBOR
Harris Beach State Park
BENHAM LN
OCEANVIEW DR
ELK MTN 1688'
WINCHUCK
CURRY CO
DEL NORTE CO
OREGON
Pelican State Beach
D5
S FORK
Smith River National Recreation Area
HUNTER ROCK
PRINCE ISLAND
OCEAN VIEW DR
WESTBROOK LN
SMITH RIVER
1ST ST
ROWDY CK
SNAVELY RD
D4
PALA RD
LOWER LAKE RD
SMITH RD
BAILEY RD
HAIGHT RD
REDWOOD HWY
TELL BLVD
MOSELEY RD
LAKE EARL STATE PARK
KELLOGG RD
FORT DICK
DEL NORTE CO.
LOW DIVIDE
MILL CK
HARDSCRABBLE CK
DISTLERATH DR
MOREHEAD RD
CLOUTIER ST
MIDDLETON DR
OCEAN DR
LOWER LAKE RD
D3
KINGS VLY RD
S BANK RD
197
SIGNAL PK 2055'
SHUTT ST
STUKEL ST
LAKE TALAWA
Lake Earl State Park
PELICAN BAY
LAKE EARL
EARL WONDER STUMP RD
WALKER RD
RIVER RD
MYRTLE CK
199
OLD HWY
SOUTH FORK
OLD MILL RD
CROSS
D3
J. Smith Redwoods State Park
BERTELEDA
PT ST GEORGE
LAKE RAILROAD AV
PARKWAY DR
VALLEY
D2
John McNamara Field
D1
WASHINGTON BL
PEBBLE BEACH DR
PACIFIC
CRESCENT CITY
HOWLAND HILL RD
Redwood Natl Park
HILLS RD
Undersea World
ELK
BERTSCH TERRACE
Del Norte County Historical Society Museum
WHALER ISLAND
HUMBOLDT RD
HAMILTON RD
Battery Point Lighthouse
ENDERTS BEACH RD
CHILDS HILL 2330'
Del Norte Coast Redwoods State Park
MILL CK
101
REDWOODS ST PK
CREEK
219
TOUR
SISTER ROCKS
20
WILSON CREEK
WILSON
CREEK
FOOTSTEPS ROCK
FALSE KLAMATH COVE
FALSE KLAMATH ROCK
Trees of Mystery
HUNTER CREEK RD
REDWOOD HWY
MYNOT CK
REQUA
CAMP KLAMATH
KLAMATH
FLINT ROCK HEAD
WHITE ROCK
KLAMATH BCH RD
169
MCBETH AIRPORT
2

SEE 9 MAP

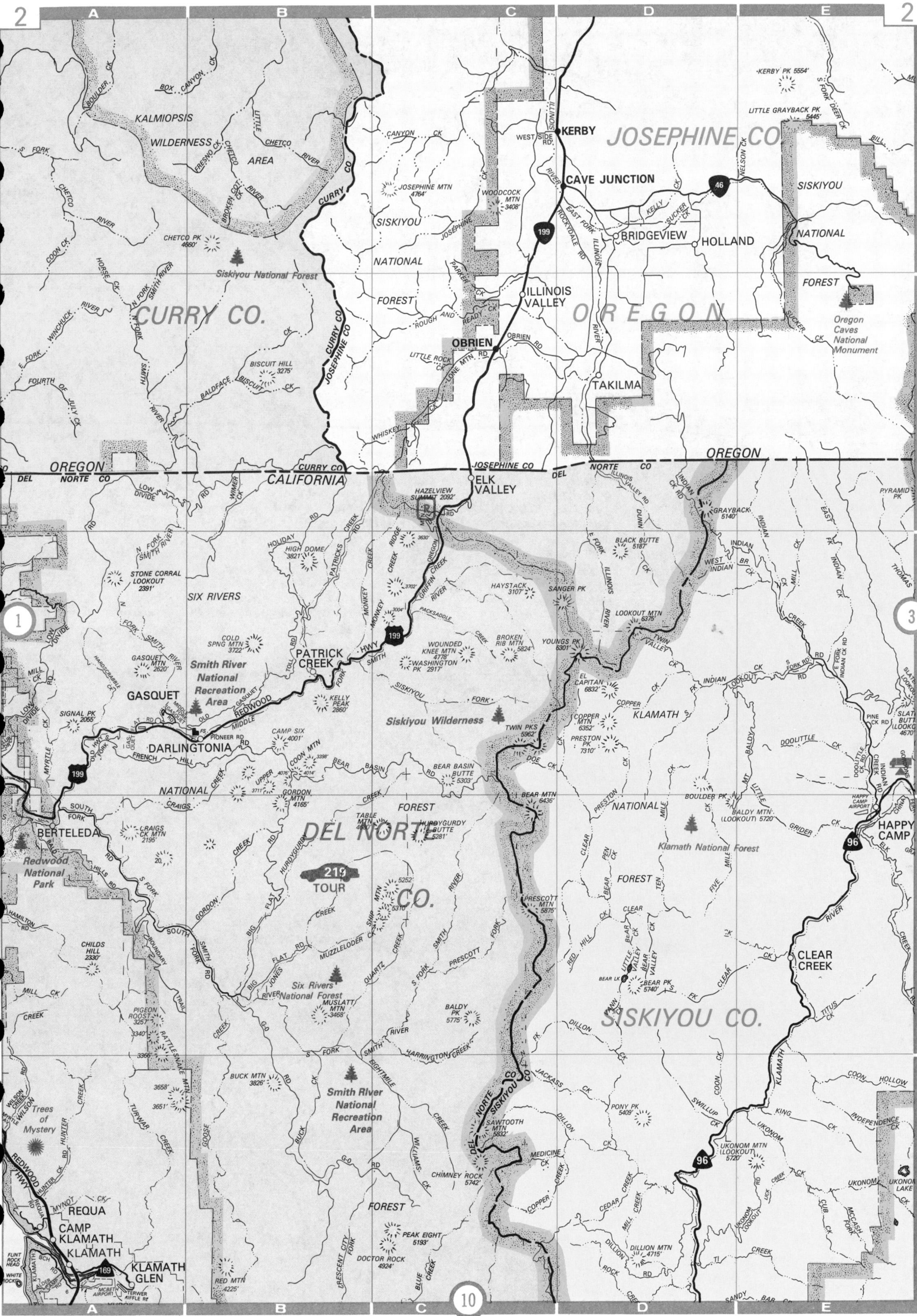

SEE MAP 1
SEE MAP 3
SEE MAP 10

HIGHWAYS

3

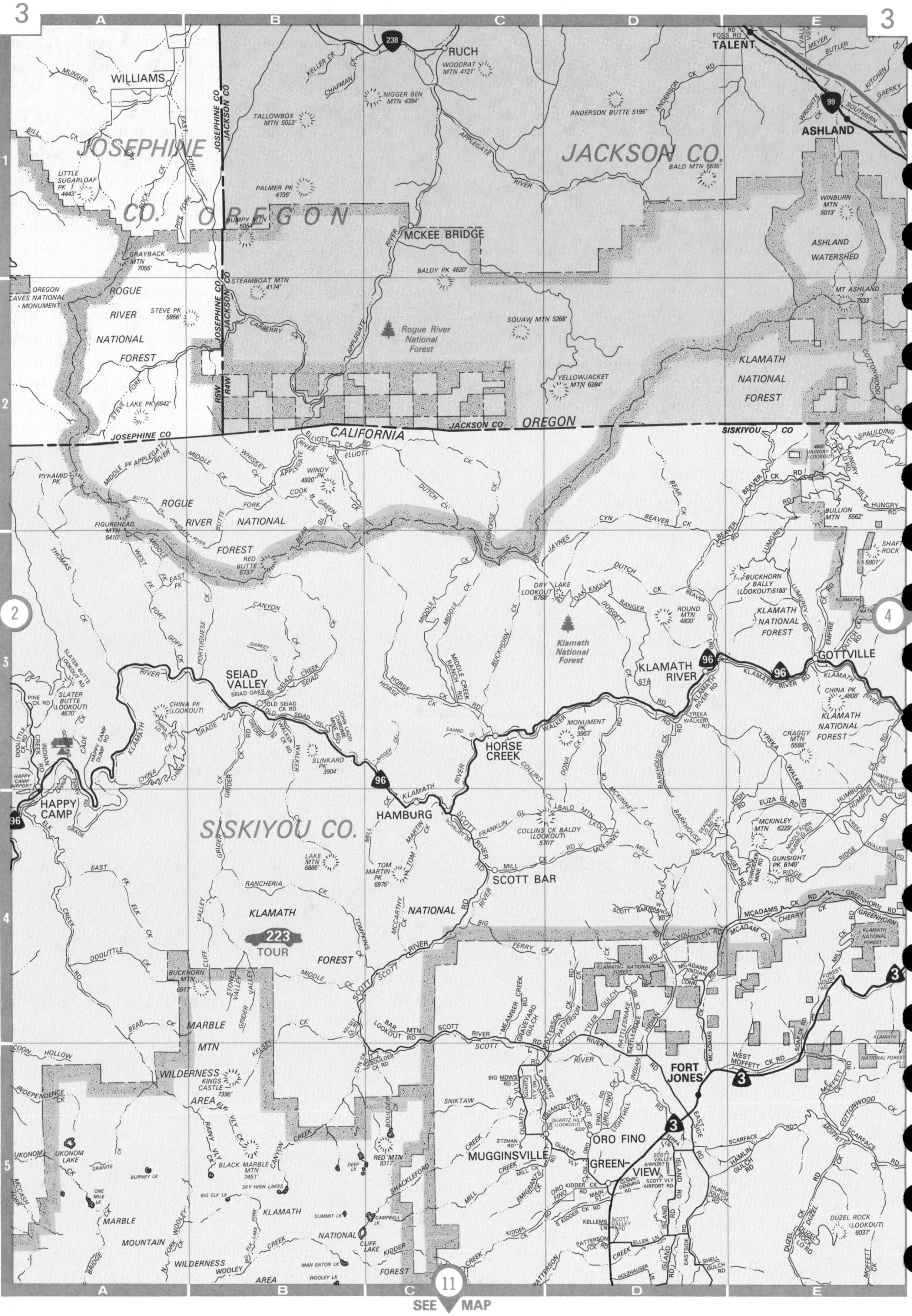
A
B
C
D
E
1
2
3
4
5
JOSEPHINE CO.
OREGON
JACKSON CO.
JOSEPHINE CO
JACKSON CO
WILLIAMS
RUCH
TALENT
ASHLAND
MCKEE BRIDGE
WOODRAT MTN 4121'
TALLOWBOX MTN 5023'
ANDERSON BUTTE 5195'
BALD MTN 5635'
LITTLE SUGARLOAF PK 4443'
PALMER PK 4736'
HUMPY MTN 5054'
GRAYBACK MTN 7055'
OREGON CAVES NATIONAL MONUMENT
STEAMBOAT MTN 4174'
BALDY PK 4620'
WINBURN MTN 5013'
ASHLAND WATERSHED
MT ASHLAND 7533'
ROGUE RIVER NATIONAL FOREST
Rogue River National Forest
STEVE PK 5866'
SQUAW MTN 5268'
YELLOWJACKET MTN 6284'
STEVE LAKE PK 6642'
KLAMATH NATIONAL FOREST
CALIFORNIA
SISKIYOU CO
R5W
R4W
APPLEGATE RIVER
PYRAMID PK
WINDY PK 4920'
FIGUREHEAD MTN 6410'
RED BUTTE 6737'
BULLION MTN 5562'
SHAFT ROCK 5801'
DRY LAKE LOOKOUT 6768'
BUCKHORN BALLY (LOOKOUT) 5183'
ROUND MTN 4800'
Klamath National Forest
SLATER BUTTE LOOKOUT 4670'
SEIAD VALLEY
KLAMATH RIVER
GOTTVILLE
CHINA PK (LOOKOUT)
CHINA PK 4808'
MONUMENT PK 3963'
CRAGGY MTN 5588'
SLINKARD PK 3904'
HORSE CREEK
HAPPY CAMP
HAMBURG
SISKIYOU CO.
COLLINS CK BALDY (LOOKOUT) 5707'
MCKINLEY MTN 6229'
GUNSIGHT PK 6140'
LAKE MTN 6886'
TOM MARTIN PK 6975'
SCOTT BAR
KLAMATH NATIONAL FOREST
223 TOUR
BUCKHORN MTN 6917'
MARBLE MTN WILDERNESS AREA
KINGS CASTLE 7396'
FORT JONES
RED MTN 8317'
BLACK MARBLE MTN 7451'
UKONOM LAKE
ORO FINO
MUGGINSVILLE
GREENVIEW
QUARTZ HILL (LOOKOUT) 4229'
DUZEL ROCK (LOOKOUT) 6037'
MARBLE MOUNTAIN WILDERNESS
SCOTT RIVER
SCOTT VALLEY AIRPORT
96
3
99
238
SEE MAP 2
SEE MAP 4
SEE MAP 11

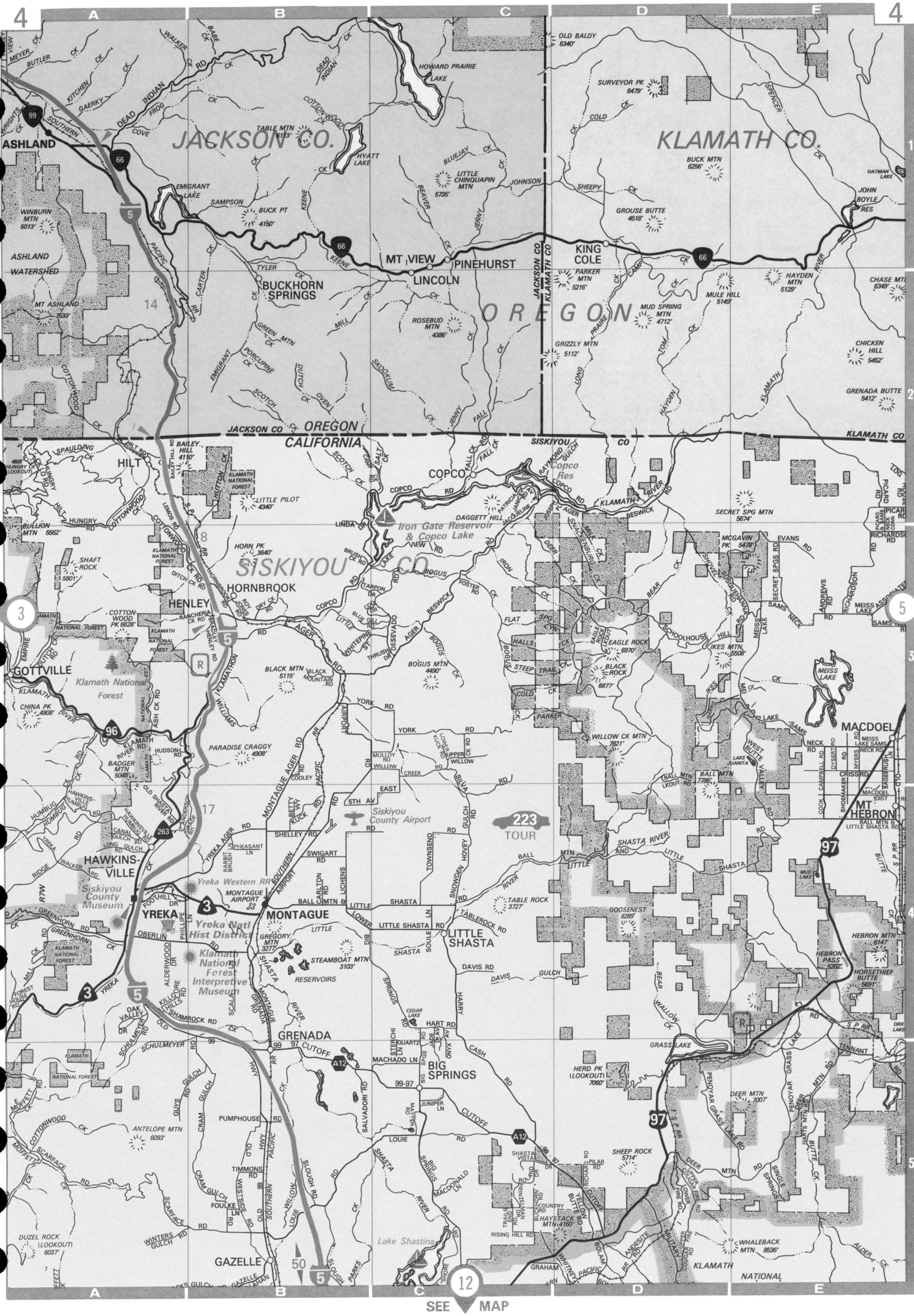
JACKSON CO.
KLAMATH CO.
OREGON
CALIFORNIA
SISKIYOU CO.
ASHLAND
EMIGRANT LAKE
HOWARD PRAIRIE LAKE
HYATT LAKE
TABLE MTN 6113'
BUCK PT 4150'
LITTLE CHINQUAPIN MTN 5735'
MT VIEW
PINEHURST
LINCOLN
BUCKHORN SPRINGS
KING COLE
OLD BALDY 6340'
SURVEYOR PK 6479'
BUCK MTN 6256'
GROUSE BUTTE 4518'
PARKER MTN 5216'
MUD SPRING MTN 4712'
MULE HILL 5149'
HAYDEN MTN 5129'
GRIZZLY MTN 5112'
CHICKEN HILL 5452'
GRENADA BUTTE 5412'
ROSEBUD MTN 4386'
JOHN BOYLE RES
OATMAN LAKE
WINBURN MTN 5013'
ASHLAND WATERSHED
MT ASHLAND 7533'
HILT
BAILEY HILL 4110'
KLAMATH NATIONAL FOREST
LITTLE PILOT 4340'
COPCO
Copco Res
Iron Gate Reservoir & Copco Lake
HORN PK 3640'
HORNBROOK
HENLEY
SHAFT ROCK 5801'
BULLION MTN 5562'
COTTONWOOD PK 6628'
SECRET SPG MTN 5674'
MCGAVIN PK 5478'
EAGLE ROCK 6970'
BLACK ROCK 6877'
IKES MTN 5508'
MEISS LAKE
MACDOEL
GOTTVILLE
Klamath National Forest
CHINA PK 4808'
BLACK MTN 5115'
BOGUS MTN 4490'
PARADISE CRAGGY 4908'
WILLOW CK MTN 7821'
BALL MTN 7786'
MT HEBRON
BADGER MTN 5048'
HAWKINSVILLE
Siskiyou County Museum
Yreka Western RR
YREKA
Yreka Natl Hist District
Klamath National Forest Interpretive Museum
MONTAGUE
Siskiyou County Airport
223 TOUR
TABLE ROCK 3727'
GOOSENEST 8289'
LITTLE SHASTA
GREGORY MTN 3277'
STEAMBOAT MTN 3103'
RESERVOIRS
HEBRON MTN 6147'
HEBRON PASS 5202'
HORSETHIEF BUTTE 5691'
GRENADA
BIG SPRINGS
HERD PK (LOOKOUT) 7060'
GRASS LAKE
TENNANT
DEER MTN 7007'
ANTELOPE MTN 6093'
SHEEP ROCK 5714'
SHASTA VISTA
HAYSTACK MTN 4160'
DUZEL ROCK (LOOKOUT) 6037'
GAZELLE
Lake Shastina
WHALEBACK MTN 8536'
KLAMATH NATIONAL
SEE MAP 3
SEE MAP 5
SEE MAP 12
HIGHWAYS

4

SEE MAP 4
SEE MAP 6
SEE MAP 13

HIGHWAYS

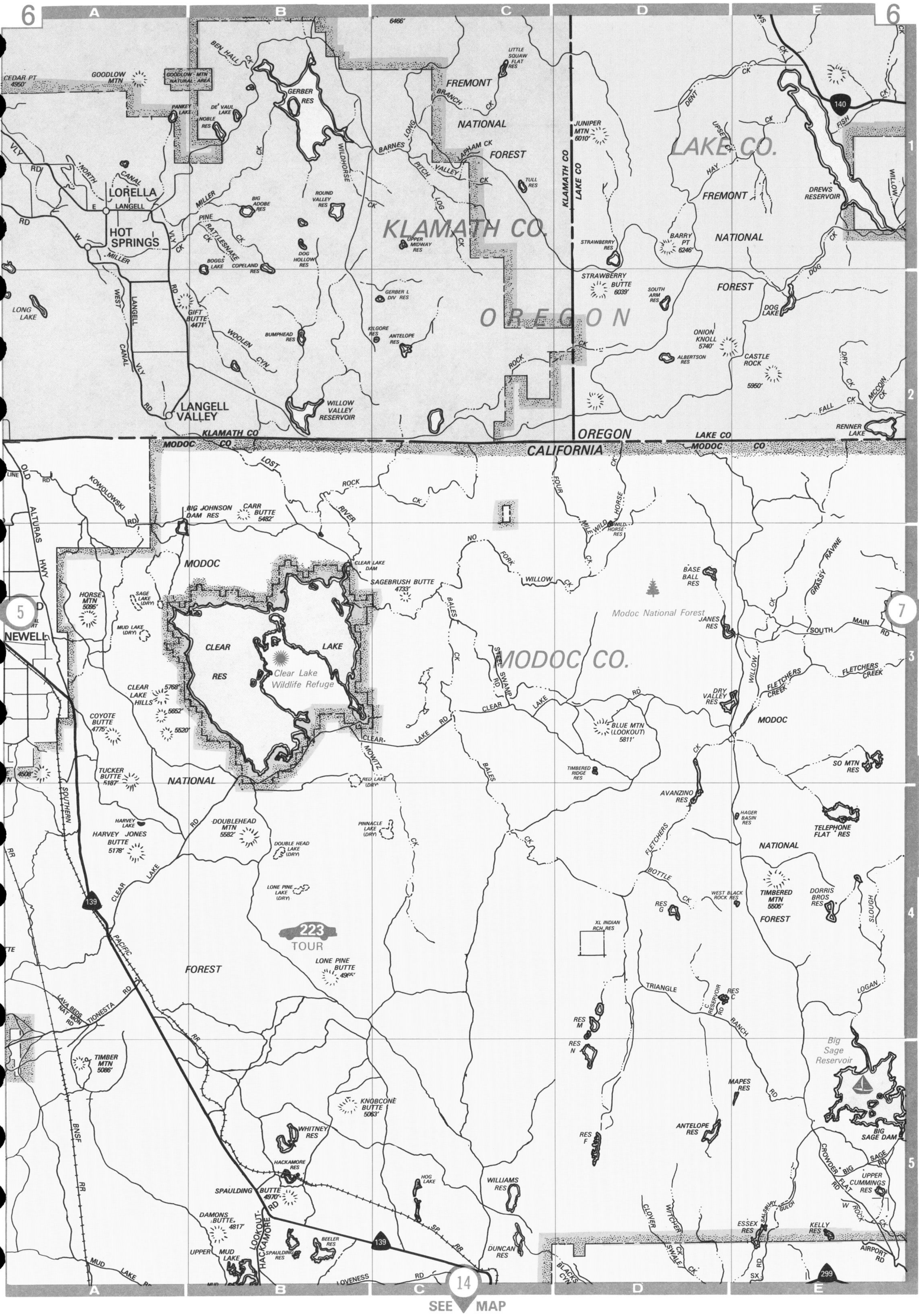
A
B
C
D
E
6466'
CEDAR PT 4950'
GOODLOW MTN
GOODLOW MTN NATURAL AREA
BEN HALL CK
LITTLE SQUAW FLAT RES
FREMONT
NATIONAL
FOREST
GERBER RES
PANKEY LAKE
DE' VAUL LAKE
NOBLE RES
BRANCH
JUNIPER MTN 6010'
DENT
UPSET
LAKE CO.
140
FISH
BARNES
LONG
PITCH
VALLEY
LAPHAM CK
WILDHORSE
VLY
RD
NORTH
CANAL
LORELLA
LANGELL
HOT SPRINGS
MILLER
PINE
RATTLESNAKE
BIG ADOBE RES
ROUND VALLEY RES
KLAMATH CO.
KLAMATH CO
LAKE CO
TULL RES
HAY
FREMONT
DREWS RESERVOIR
WILLOW
UPPER MIDWAY RES
DOG HOLLOW RES
BOGGS LAKE
COPELAND RES
STRAWBERRY RES
BARRY PT 6246'
NATIONAL
STRAWBERRY BUTTE 6039'
SOUTH ARM RES
FOREST
DOG LAKE
WEST
LANGELL
GIFT BUTTE 4471'
LONG LAKE
GERBER L DIV RES
OREGON
WOOLEN CYN
BUMPHEAD RES
KILGORE RES
ANTELOPE RES
ONION KNOLL 5740'
ALBERTSON RES
CASTLE ROCK
5950'
DRY
MCCOIN
FALL
CANAL
ROCK
LANGELL VALLEY
WILLOW VALLEY RESERVOIR
KLAMATH CO
MODOC CO
OREGON
CALIFORNIA
LAKE CO
MODOC CO
RENNER LAKE
LINE
OLD
RD
KOWOLOWSKI
LOST
ROCK
RIVER
FOUR
MILE
WILD HORSE
WILD HORSE RES
ALTURAS HWY
BIG JOHNSON DAM RES
CARR BUTTE 5482'
MODOC
NO FORK
WILLOW
BASE BALL RES
GRASSY
RAVINE
CLEAR LAKE DAM
SAGEBRUSH BUTTE 4733'
HORSE MTN 5095'
SAGE LAKE (DRY)
MUD LAKE (DRY)
Modoc National Forest
JANES RES
SOUTH
MAIN
5
NEWELL
7
SEE MAP
CLEAR
LAKE
RES
Clear Lake Wildlife Refuge
BALES
STEELE SWAMP
MODOC CO.
WILLOW
FLETCHERS CREEK
CLEAR LAKE HILLS
5768'
5652'
5520'
COYOTE BUTTE 4775'
CLEAR
LAKE
RD
DRY VALLEY RES
BLUE MTN (LOOKOUT) 5811'
MODOC
4608'
TUCKER BUTTE 5187'
NATIONAL
MOWITZ
RED LAKE (DRY)
TIMBERED RIDGE RES
SO MTN RES
AVANZINO RES
HIGHWAYS
SOUTHERN
HARVEY LAKE
HARVEY JONES BUTTE 5178'
DOUBLEHEAD MTN 5582'
PINNACLE LAKE (DRY)
DOUBLE HEAD LAKE (DRY)
FLETCHERS
HAGER BASIN RES
TELEPHONE FLAT RES
NATIONAL
BOTTLE
CK
LONE PINE LAKE (DRY)
RES G
WEST BLACK ROCK RES
TIMBERED MTN 5505'
DORRIS BROS RES
SLOUGH
FOREST
139
RR
CLEAR
223
TOUR
XL INDIAN RCH RES
PACIFIC
FOREST
LONE PINE BUTTE 4965'
TRIANGLE
RESERVOIR
RES C
RANCH
LOGAN
LAVA BEDS NAT MON RD
TIONESTA
RES M
RES N
Big Sage Reservoir
TIMBER MTN 5086'
KNOBCONE BUTTE 5063'
MAPES RES
WHITNEY RES
BNSF
RES F
ANTELOPE RES
BIG SAGE DAM
HACKAMORE RES
HOG LAKE
WILLIAMS RES
CROWDER FLAT RD
BIG SAGE
UPPER CUMMINGS RES
SPAULDING
BUTTE 4970'
SP
DAMONS BUTTE 4817'
LOOKOUT-HACKAMORE RD
BEELER RES
SPAULDING RES
CLOVER
WITCHER
SWALE
ESSEX RES
SALSBURY
BULCH
W ROCK
KELLY RES
UPPER MUD LAKE
DUNCAN RES
AIRPORT RD
MUD
LAKE
LOVENESS
RD
BLACKS CYN
SX
299
14
SEE MAP
1
2
3
4
5

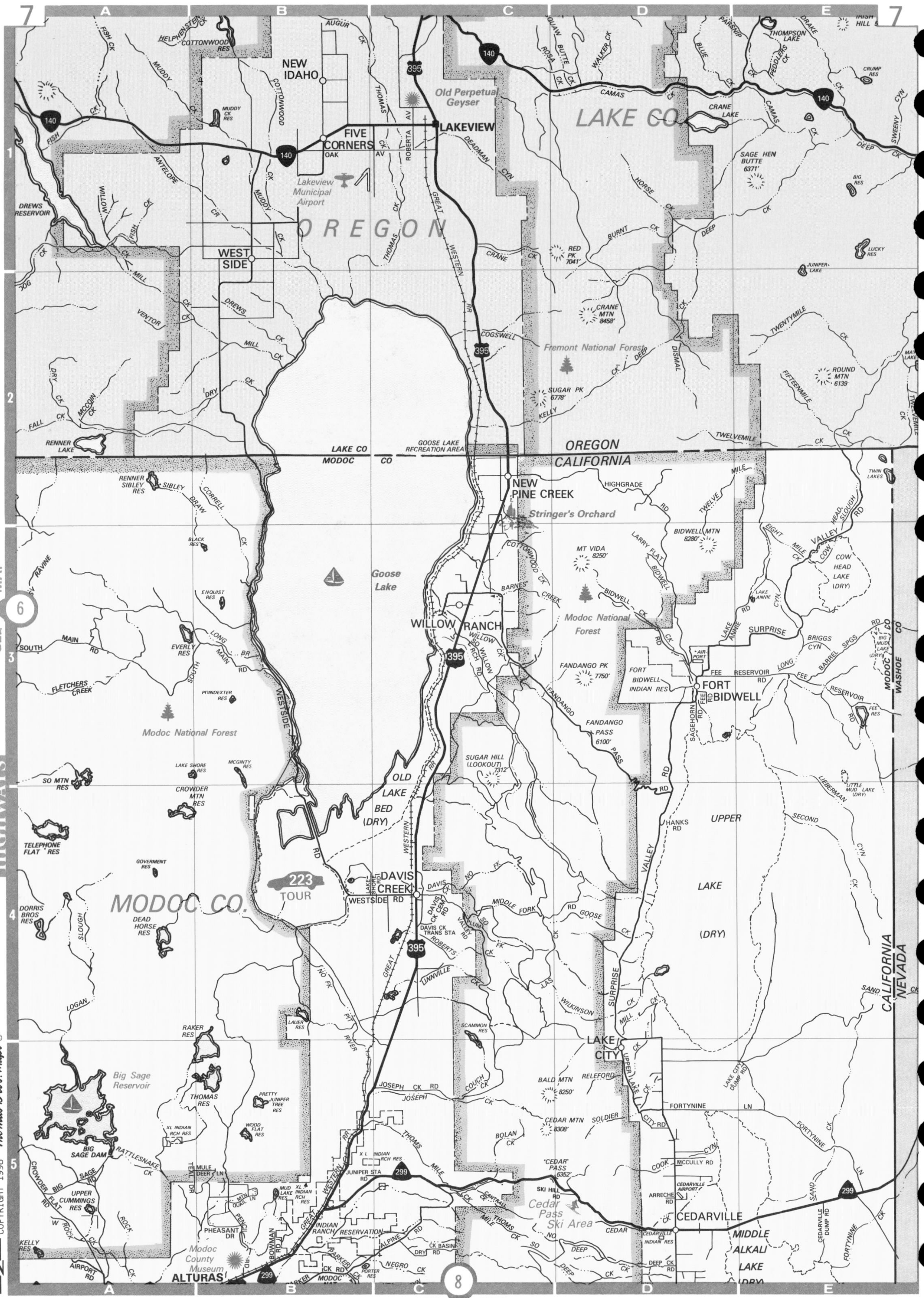

SEE MAP 6

HIGHWAYS

SEE 8 MAP

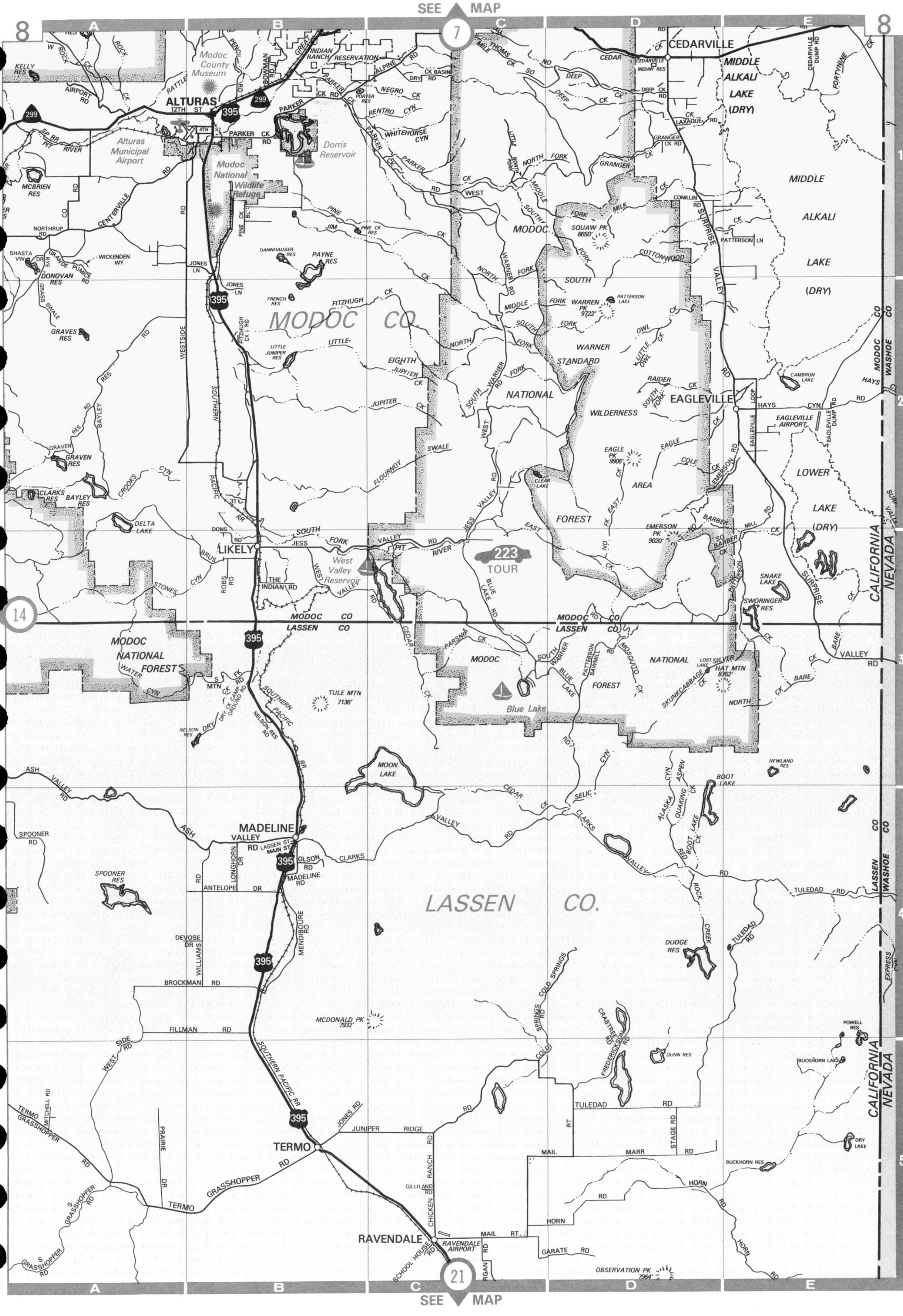
SEE MAP 7
SEE MAP 21
SEE MAP 14
A
B
C
D
E
1
2
3
4
5
ALTURAS
12TH ST
4TH ST
PARKER CK RD
Modoc County Museum
Alturas Municipal Airport
Modoc National Wildlife Refuge
Dorris Reservoir
INDIAN RANCH RESERVATION
299
395
KELLY RES
AIRPORT RD
SP RR
PIT RIVER
MCBRIEN RES
CENTERVILLE RD
NORTHRUP RD
SHASTA VW
GRANDE PUMICE
WICKENDEN WY
DONOVAN RES
GRASS SWALE
GRAVES RES
JONES LN
WESTSIDE RD
SOUTHERN PACIFIC RR
FITZHUGH CK RD
DANNHAUSER RES
PAYNE RES
FRENCH RES
LITTLE JUNIPER RES
MODOC CO.
FITZHUGH CK
LITTLE CK
EIGHTH CK
JUPITER CK
FLOURNOY
SWALE
BAYLEY RES RD
GRAVEN RES
CROOKS CYN
CLARKS RES
BAYLEY RES
DELTA LAKE
DONS RD
LIKELY
SOUTH FORK
JESS
West Valley Reservoir
THE INDIAN RD
ROBS RD
BRUS RD
STONES CYN
PIT RIVER RD
223 TOUR
BLUE LAKE RD
JESS VALLEY RD
CEDARVILLE
CEDARVILLE INDIAN RES
DEEP CK
LAXAQUE RD
GRANGER CK RD
MIDDLE ALKALI LAKE (DRY)
CEDARVILLE DUMP RD
FORTYNINE
CONKLIN RD
PATTERSON LN
SURPRISE VALLEY RD
MODOC
SQUAW PK 8650'
COTTONWOOD
SOUTH WARNER
WARREN PK 9722'
PATTERSON LAKE
NORTH WARNER RD
MIDDLE FORK
SOUTH FORK
NORTH FORK
STANDARD
OWL CK
LITTLE OWL CK
RAIDER CK
NATIONAL
WILDERNESS
EAGLEVILLE
HAYS CYN RD
EAGLEVILLE AIRPORT
EAGLEVILLE DUMP RD
EAGLE PK 9906'
EAGLE CK
COLE CK
EMERSON RD
AREA
CLEAR LAKE
FOREST
EMERSON PK 9020'
BARBER CK
LOWER LAKE (DRY)
SNAKE LAKE
SWORINGER RES
CAMBRON LAKE
MODOC CO
WASHOE CO
CALIFORNIA
NEVADA
MODOC CO
LASSEN CO
MODOC NATIONAL FORESTS
WATER CYN
S FK MTN
DRY CK CAMP GROUND RD
NELSON RES
TULE MTN 7136'
PARSNIP CK
CEDAR CK
SOUTH WARNER
BLUE LAKE
PATTERSON SAWMILL
MOSQUITO CK
NATIONAL
FOREST
Blue Lake
SKUNKCABBAGE CK
LOST LAKE
SILVER
HAT MTN 8762'
NORTH
BARE CK
VALLEY RD
MOON LAKE
NEWLAND RES
BOOT LAKE
ASPEN CYN
QUAKING ASPEN CK
ALASKA
ASH VALLEY RD
CEDAR CK
SELIC
CLARKS VALLEY RD
MADELINE
VALLEY RD
LASSEN ST
MAIN ST
OLSON RD
MADELINE RD
LONGHORN DR
ANTELOPE DR
SPOONER RD
SPOONER RES
LASSEN CO.
RED ROCK CREEK
TULEDAD RD
LASSEN CO
WASHOE CO
MENDIBOURE RD
DEVOSE DR
WILLIAMS
DODGE RES
TULEDAD
EXPRESS CYN
BROCKMAN RD
FILLMAN RD
COLD SPRINGS RD
CRABTREE RD
FREDERICKSON RD
MCDONALD PK 7932'
DUNN RES
POWELL RES
BUCKHORN LAKE
WEST SIDE RD
MITCHELL RD
TERMO GRASSHOPPER RD
PRAIRIE DR
JONES RD
JUNIPER RIDGE RD
TULEDAD RD
STAGE RD
TERMO
MAIL RT
MARR RD
DRY LAKE
BUCKHORN RES
GRASSHOPPER RD
TERMO
S GRASSHOPPER
GRASSHOPPER RD
GILLILAND
CHICKEN RANCH RD
HORN RD
RAVENDALE
RAVENDALE AIRPORT
SCHOOL HOUSE RD
MAIL RT.
GARATE RD
MORGAN
OBSERVATION PK 7964'
HORN RD

HIGHWAYS

SEE MAP 1

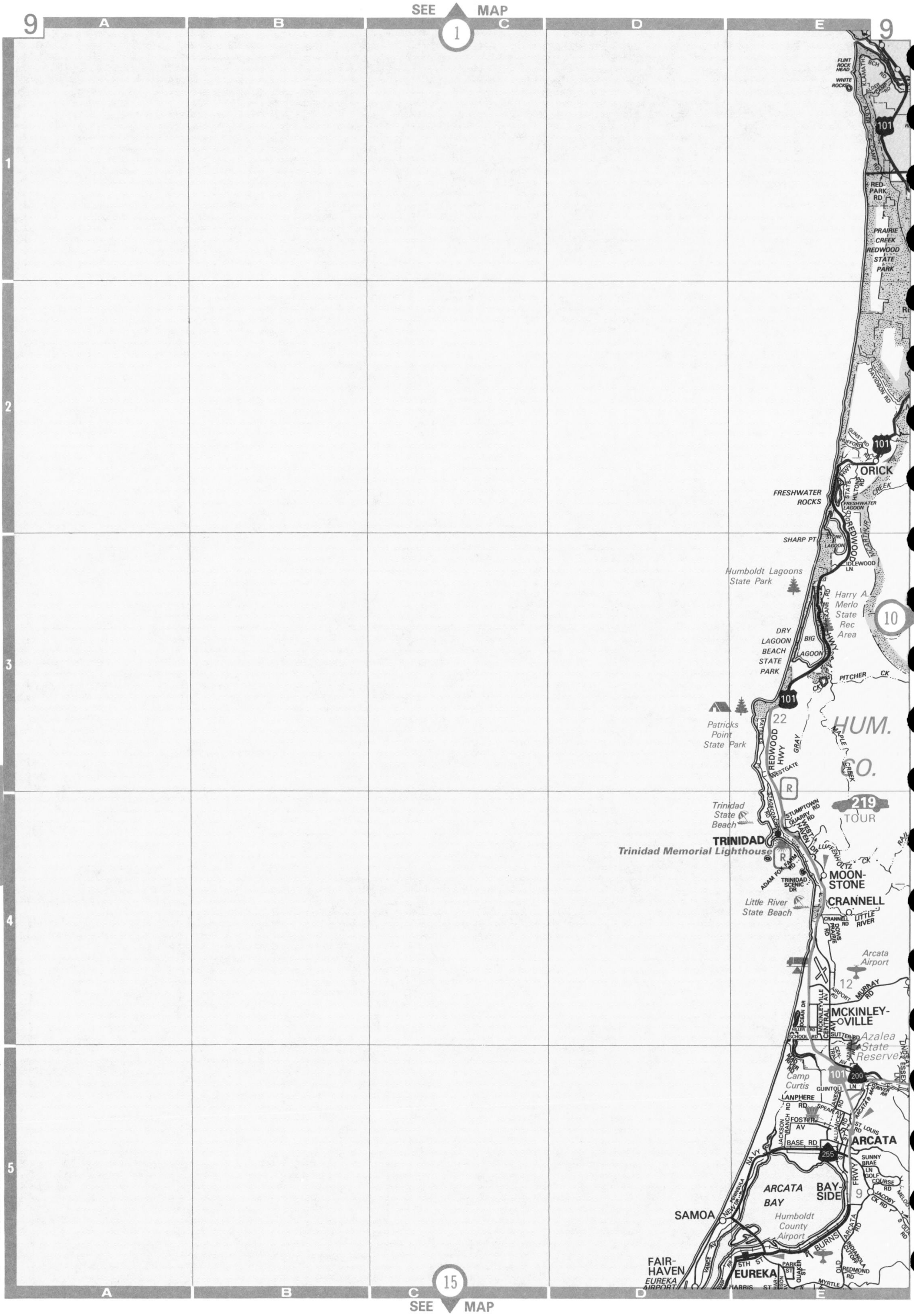

SEE MAP 10
SEE MAP 15

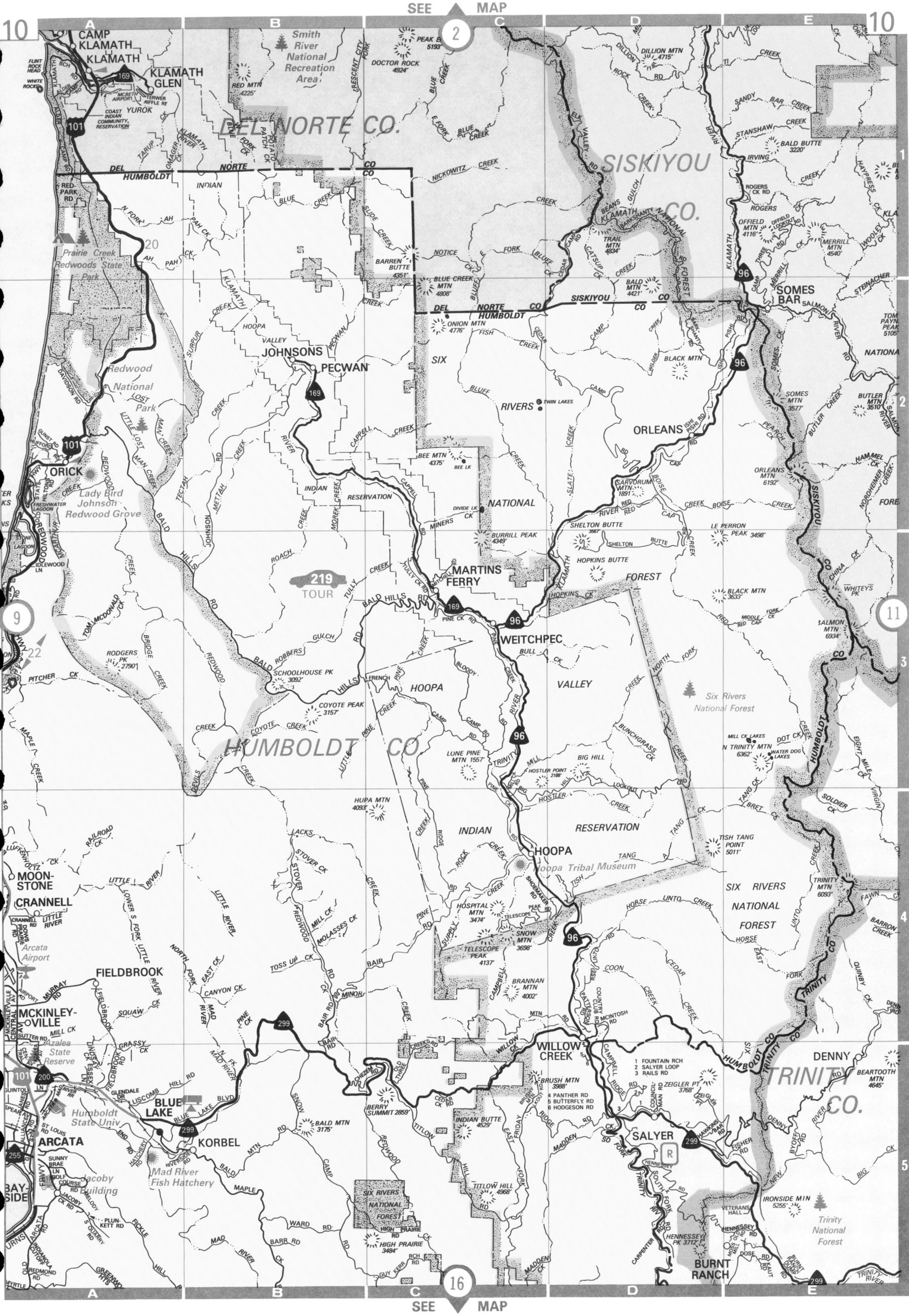

SEE MAP 2
SEE MAP 9
SEE MAP 11
SEE MAP 16
HIGHWAYS
CAMP KLAMATH
KLAMATH
KLAMATH GLEN
YUROK
COAST INDIAN COMMUNITY RESERVATION
Smith River National Recreation Area
DEL NORTE CO.
SISKIYOU CO.
HUMBOLDT CO.
TRINITY CO.
Prairie Creek Redwoods State Park
Redwood National Park
ORICK
Lady Bird Johnson Redwood Grove
JOHNSONS
PECWAN
HOOPA VALLEY INDIAN RESERVATION
219 TOUR
MARTINS FERRY
WEITCHPEC
HOOPA
Hoopa Tribal Museum
SIX RIVERS NATIONAL FOREST
Six Rivers National Forest
ORLEANS
SOMES BAR
MOONSTONE
CRANNELL
Arcata Airport
FIELDBROOK
MCKINLEYVILLE
Azalea State Reserve
Humboldt State Univ
ARCATA
BAYSIDE
BLUE LAKE
KORBEL
Mad River Fish Hatchery
Jacoby Building
WILLOW CREEK
SALYER
BURNT RANCH
DENNY
Trinity National Forest
1 FOUNTAIN RCH
2 SALYER LOOP
3 RAILS RD
4 PANTHER RD
5 BUTTERFLY RD
6 HODGESON RD
PEAK 8 5193'
DOCTOR ROCK 4924'
RED MTN 4225'
DILLION MTN 4715'
BALD BUTTE 3220'
OFFIELD MTN 4116'
MERRILL MTN 4540'
TRAIL MTN 4834'
BALD MTN 4421'
BARREN BUTTE 4351'
BLUE CREEK MTN 4808'
ONION MTN 4776'
BEE MTN 4375'
TOM PAYNE PEAK 5105'
SOMES MTN 3577'
BUTLER MTN 3610'
ORLEANS MTN 6192'
SARVORUM MTN 1891'
SHELTON BUTTE 3567'
LE PERRON PEAK 3498'
BURRILL PEAK 4349'
BLACK MTN 3633'
SALMON MTN 6934'
RODGERS PK 2790'
SCHOOLHOUSE PK 3092'
COYOTE PEAK 3157'
LONE PINE MTN 1557'
HOSTLER POINT 2188'
TRINITY MTN 6362'
HUPA MTN 4093'
TISH TANG POINT 5011'
TRINITY MTN 6093'
HOSPITAL MTN 3474'
SNOW MTN 3698'
TELESCOPE PEAK 4137'
BRANNAN MTN 4002'
BRUSH MTN 3988'
ZEIGLER PT 3768'
BEARTOOTH MTN 4645'
INDIAN BUTTE 4529'
BERRY SUMMIT 2859'
BALD MTN 3175'
TITLOW HILL 4968'
HENNESSEY PK 3712'
IRONSIDE MTN 5255'
HIGH PRAIRIE 3484'

SEE MAP 3

SEE MAP 10

SEE MAP 12

SEE MAP 17

HIGHWAYS

SEE MAP 4

SEE MAP 11

SEE MAP 13

SEE MAP 18

HIGHWAYS

SEE MAP 5

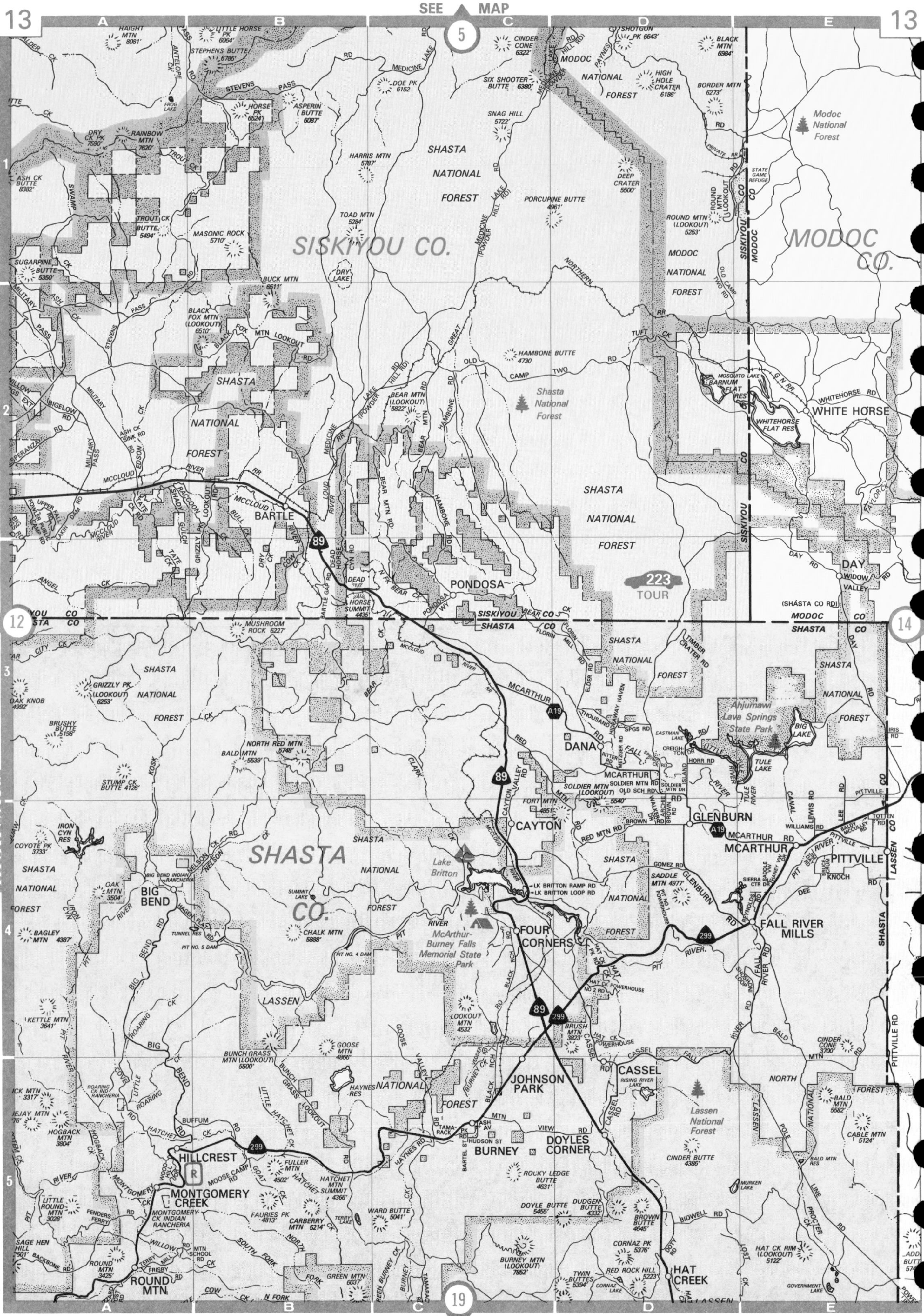

SEE MAP 12

SEE MAP 14

SEE MAP 19

HIGHWAYS

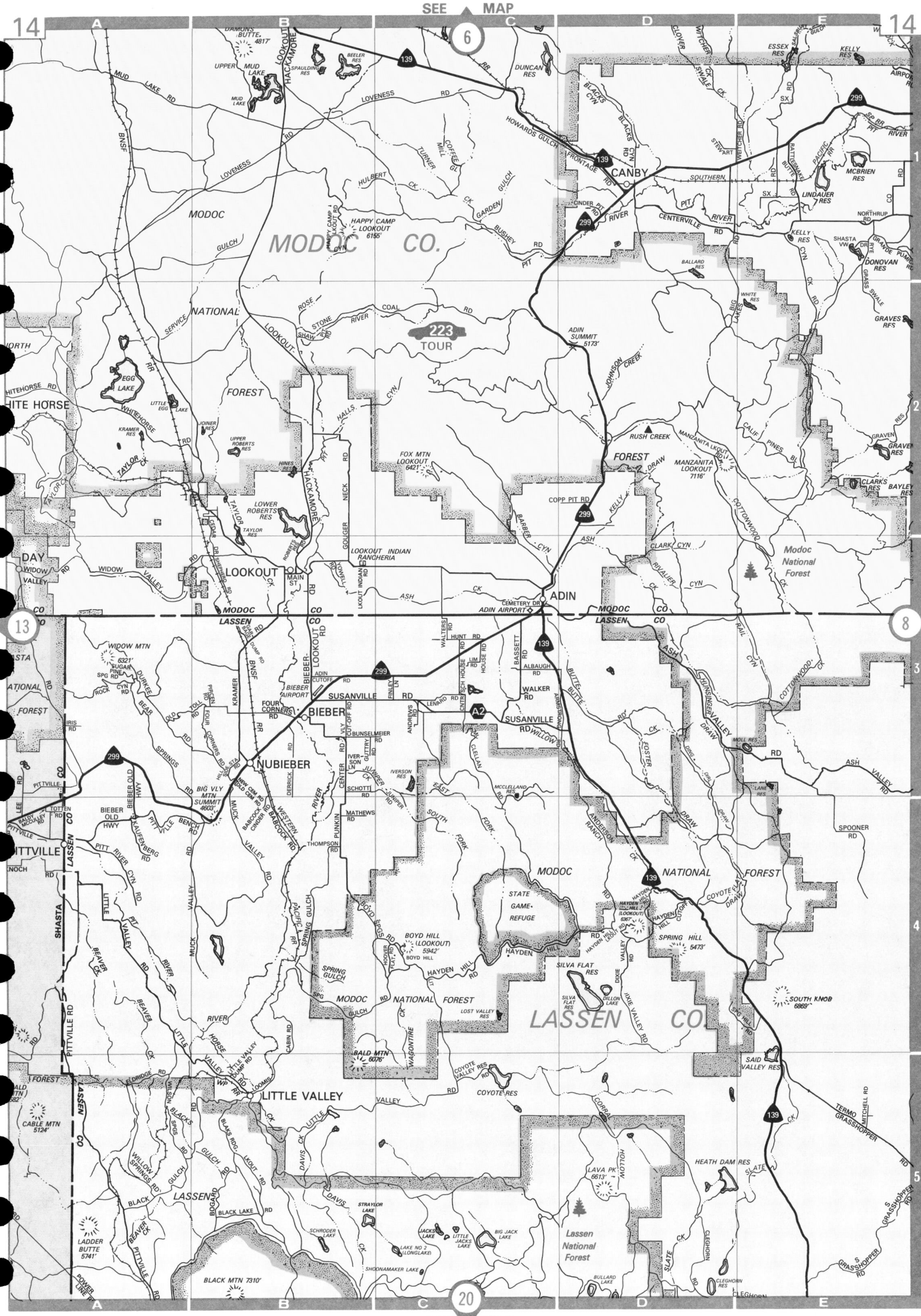
SEE MAP 6
SEE MAP 8
SEE MAP 13
SEE MAP 20
MODOC CO.
LASSEN CO.
MODOC CO
LASSEN CO
SHASTA CO
CANBY
ADIN
LOOKOUT
BIEBER
NUBIEBER
LITTLE VALLEY
PITTVILLE
DAY
WHITE HORSE
MODOC NATIONAL FOREST
Modoc National Forest
Lassen National Forest
STATE GAME REFUGE
223 TOUR
ADIN SUMMIT 5173'
HAPPY CAMP LOOKOUT 6155'
FOX MTN LOOKOUT 6421'
MANZANITA LOOKOUT 7116'
RUSH CREEK
DAMONS BUTTE 4817'
WIDOW MTN 6321'
BIG VLY MTN SUMMIT 4602'
BOYD HILL (LOOKOUT) 5942'
HAYDEN HILL (LOOKOUT) 6367'
SPRING HILL 5473'
SOUTH KNOB 6869'
BALD MTN 6076'
LAVA PK 6613'
CABLE MTN 5124'
LADDER BUTTE 5741'
BLACK MTN 7310'
EGG LAKE
MUD LAKE
LOWER ROBERTS RES
SILVA FLAT RES
DILLON LAKE
COYOTE RES
HEATH DAM RES
BIEBER AIRPORT
ADIN AIRPORT
LOOKOUT INDIAN RANCHERIA
A
B
C
D
E
1
2
3
4
5

SEE MAP 9

A
B
C
D
E
1
2
3
4
5
SAMOA
Humboldt Bay Maritime Museum
HUMBOLDT CO AIRPORT
FAIRHAVEN
EUREKA AIRPORT
EUREKA
5TH ST
HARRIS ST
CUTTEN
BURNS
MYRTLE AV
HUMBOLDT BAY
FIELDS LANDING
S JETTY RD
WESTGATE DR
RIDGEWOOD DR
WRIGLEY RD
N FORK ELK RIVER
ELK RIVER
PACIFIC
OCEAN
TABLE BLUFF RD
CANNIBAL RD
EEL RIVER
LOLETA
SALMON CK
OIL WELL RD
101
211
GOBLE LN
PALMER CK RD
FORTUNA
219 TOUR
ROHNERVILLE
FERNDALE
CENTERVILLE RD
GRIZZLY BLUFF RD
POOLE RD
FERNDALE DUMP DR
36
HYDESVILLE
ALTON
FALSE CAPE
MATTOLE RD
BEAR RIVER RDG RD
RIO DELL
SCOTIA
16
REDWOOD HWY
CAPETOWN
CAPE MENDOCINO
SUGAR LOAF ISLAND
HUMBOLDT CO
MT PIERCE 3188'
N FK MATTOLE RIVER
TAYLOR PK 3390'
OLD MATTOLE RD
PETROLIA
CHAMBERS RD
MOORE HILL 1245'
CONKLIN CK RD
LIGHTHOUSE RD
BIG HILL 3040'
CATHEYS PK 3070'
LITTLE CHAPARRAL MTN 2650'
COOSKIE MTN 2951'
HONEYDEW
KING RANGE NATIONAL CONSERVATION AREA
SQUAW CK
WILDER RIDGE
OAT HILL 2350'
NORTH SLIDE PK 3512'
HADLEY PK 3020'
King Range National Conservation Area
KINGS PK 4087'
SHUBRICK PK 2797'
SADDLE MTN 3290'
HORSE MTN 1929'
S KINGS PK RD

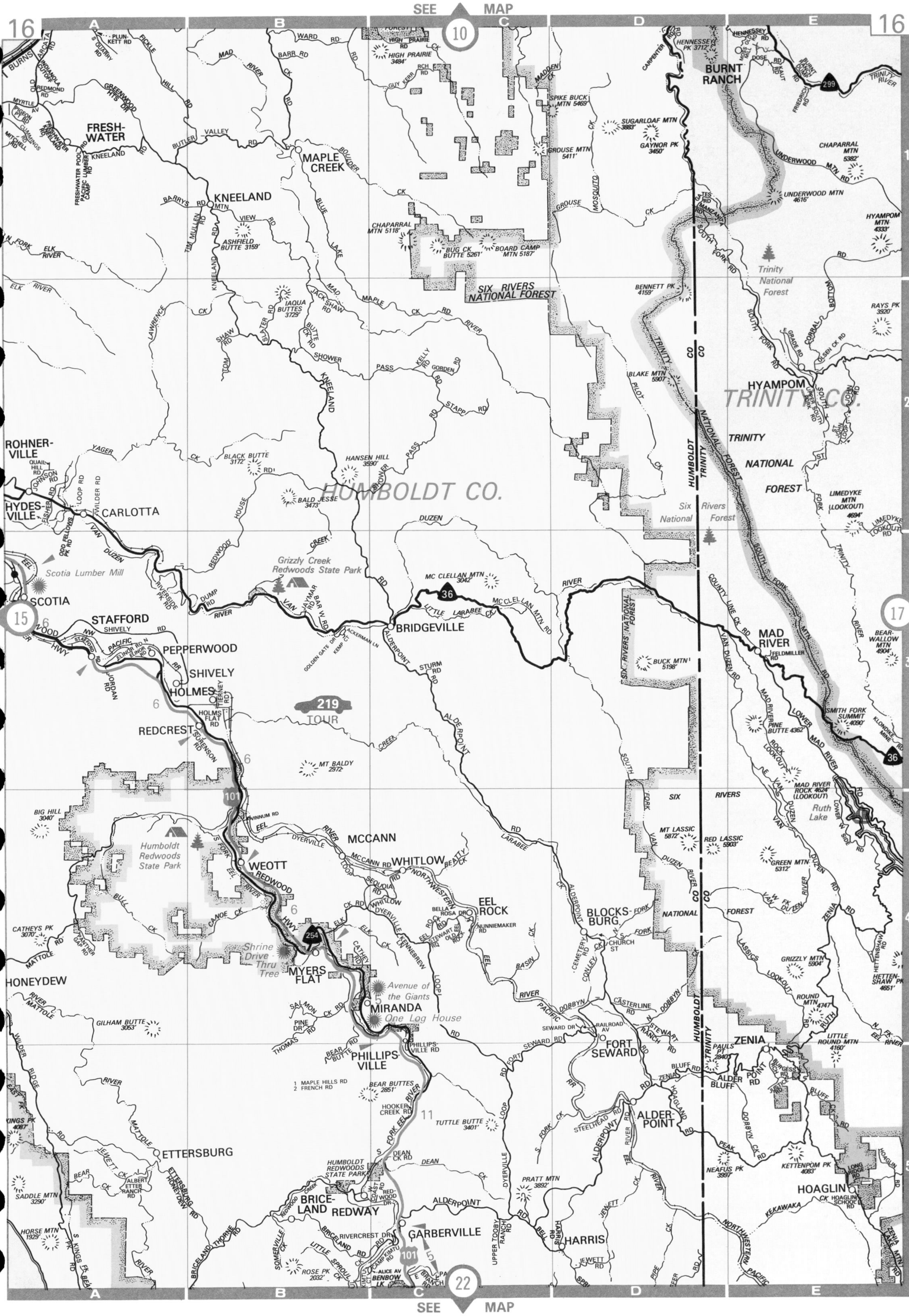
A
B
C
D
E
1
2
3
4
5
BURNS
ARCATA
PLUNKETT RD
FICKLE
HILL
WARD
BARR RD
HIGH PRAIRIE
HIGH PRAIRIE 3484'
HENNESSEY PK 3712'
BURNT RANCH
299
TRINITY RIVER
MAD RIVER
GREENWOOD HTS DR
RCH RD
GUY KERR RD
MADDEN CK
CARPENTER RD
FREDRICK RD
SPIKE BUCK MTN 5469'
SUGARLOAF MTN 3883'
GAYNOR PK 3450'
FRESHWATER
FRESHWATER POOL
BUTLER VALLEY RD
MAPLE CREEK
BOULDER
GROUSE MTN 5411'
CHAPARRAL MTN 5382'
UNDERWOOD MTN RD
KNEELAND RD
BARRYS RD
KNEELAND
MTN
TIM MULLEN RD
VIEW
BLUE
UNDERWOOD MTN 4616'
GROUSE
MOSQUITO
CK
ASHFIELD BUTTE 3159'
CHAPARRAL MTN 5118'
BUG CK BUTTE 5261'
BOARD CAMP MTN 5187'
HYAMPOM MTN 4333'
FORK ELK RIVER
ELK RIVER
LAKE
SIX RIVERS NATIONAL FOREST
BENNETT PK 4159'
Trinity National Forest
RD
IAQUA BUTTES 3729'
JACKSHAW RD
MAD
MAPLE CK RD
RIVER
LAWRENCE
SLATER RD
BUTTE CK RD
SHOWER PASS
KELLY RD
GORDEN RD
RAYS PK 3920'
TOM SHAW RD
KNEELAND
STAPP RD
BLAKE MTN 5907'
PILOT
CO CO
SOUTH FORK
GRADE RD
OLSEN CK RD
HYAMPOM
TRINITY CO.
HUMBOLDT TRINITY
NATIONAL FOREST
TRINITY NATIONAL FOREST
ROHNERVILLE
QUAIL HILL RD
JOHNSON RD
YAGER CK
BLACK BUTTE 3172'
HANSEN HILL 3590'
SHOWER PASS
HUMBOLDT CO.
Six Rivers National Forest
LIMEDYKE MTN (LOOKOUT) 4694'
LOOP RD
WILDER RD
HYDESVILLE
CARLOTTA
BALD JESSE 3473'
VAN DUZEN
HOUSE
REDWOOD
CREEK
DUZEN
ODD FELLOWS PK RD
EEL
Scotia Lumber Mill
Grizzly Creek Redwoods State Park
MC CLELLAN MTN 3042'
RIVER
COUNTY LINE CK RD
SCOTIA
RIVERSIDE PK RD
DUMP RD
RIVER
VAN
JAYMAR RD
BAR W RD
36
LITTLE LARABEE CK
MC CLELLAN MTN RD
15
STAFFORD
SHIVELY RD
BRIDGEVILLE
MAD RIVER
FELDMILLER
17
SEE MAP
BEARWALLOW MTN 4904'
WOOD
HWY
NW PACIFIC RR
ELINOR RD
PEPPERWOOD
ACKERMAN LN
GOLDEN GATE DR
KEMP CT
ALDERPOINT
STURM RD
SIX RIVERS NATIONAL FOREST
BUCK MTN 5198'
VAN DUZEN RD
JORDAN RD
SHIVELY
HOLMES
TIERNEY
HOLMS FLAT RD
219
TOUR
MAD RIVER
PINE BUTTE 4362'
SMITH FORK SUMMIT 4090'
KLONDIKE MINE
REDCREST
SORENSON
ALDERPOINT
CREEK
ROCK LOOKOUT
LOWER MAD RIVER
MT BALDY 2972'
SOUTH
MAD RIVER ROCK 4624' (LOOKOUT)
HIGHWAYS
101
BIG HILL 3040'
VINNUM RD
EEL
RIVER
FORK
SIX RIVERS
Ruth Lake
MCCANN
DYERVILLE
MCCANN RD
WHITLOW
BEATTY CK
LARABEE
MT LASSIC 5872'
RED LASSIC 5903'
GREEN MTN 5312'
Humboldt Redwoods State Park
WEOTT
REDWOOD
NORTHWESTERN
SEQUOIA
DUZEN RIVER
W FK DUZEN
BULL CK
CANOE CK
EEL RIVER
6
HWY
254
EEL ROCK
BELLA ROSA DR
NUNNIEMAKER RD
ALDERPOINT
BLOCKSBURG
FORK
NATIONAL
FOREST
CATHEYS PK 3070'
MATTOLE RD
GAPPER RD
Shrine Drive Thru Tree
ELK CK
CATHEY
KENNEBREW
STEWART RD
OLD ROCK
CEMETERY
CHURCH ST
LASSICS
HETTENSHAW
HONEYDEW
MYERS FLAT
Avenue of the Giants
LOOP
BASIN
CONLEY
GRIZZLY MTN 5904'
HETTENSHAW PK 4651'
RIVER MATTOLE
SALMON CK RD
MIRANDA
One Log House
RIVER
PACIFIC
DOBBYN
CASTERLINE RD
STEWART RANCH
DOBBYN
LOOKOUT
ROUND MTN 4747'
RUTH
GILHAM BUTTE 3053'
PINE DR
SEWARD DR
RAILROAD AV
HUMBOLDT TRINITY
ZENIA
LITTLE ROUND MTN 4160'
N FK EEL RIVER
THOMAS RD
BEAR BUTTE RD
PHILLIPSVILLE
PHILLIPSVILLE RD
FORT SEWARD
PAULS PT 2840'
ALDER BLUFF
POINT RD
WILDER
RIDGE
1 MAPLE HILLS RD
2 FRENCH RD
BEAR BUTTES 2851'
RIVER
BLUFF
ZENIA
HOAGLAND
MATTOLE
HOOKER CREEK RD
EEL RIVER
FORK EEL
11
TUTTLE BUTTE 3401'
LOOP
ALDERPOINT
KINGS PK 4087'
STEELHEAD RD
ALDERPOINT RD
ALDERPOINT
RIVER RD
DOBBYN CK RD
ETTERSBURG
DEAN CK RD
DEAN
CK
DYERVILLE
PEAK
KETTENPOM PK 4083'
HOAGLIN
BEAR
JEWETT CK
ALBERT ETTER RANCH RD
HUMBOLDT REDWOODS STATE PARK
REDWOOD DR
PRATT MTN 3892'
NEAFUS PK 3997'
SADDLE MTN 3290'
ETTERSBURG HONEYDEW
BRICELAND
REDWAY
ALDERPOINT
CK
JEWETT
HOAGLIN
HOAGLIN SCHOOL
LONG RIDGE RD
KEKAWAKA CK
HORSE MTN 1929'
S KINGS PK
THORNE
BRICELAND RD
RIVERCREST DR
GARBERVILLE
UPPER TOOBY RANCH RD
BELL
HARRIS RD
HARRIS
NORTHWESTERN
PACIFIC
ZENIA LAKE MTN RD
RIVER
BRICELAND THORNE RD
SOMERVILLE
LITTLE SPROUL CK
ROSE PK 2032'
CAMP KIMTU RD
ALICE AV
BENBOW LK
BRANCH
101
5
JEWETT RD
PIPE CK
RD
SPRING

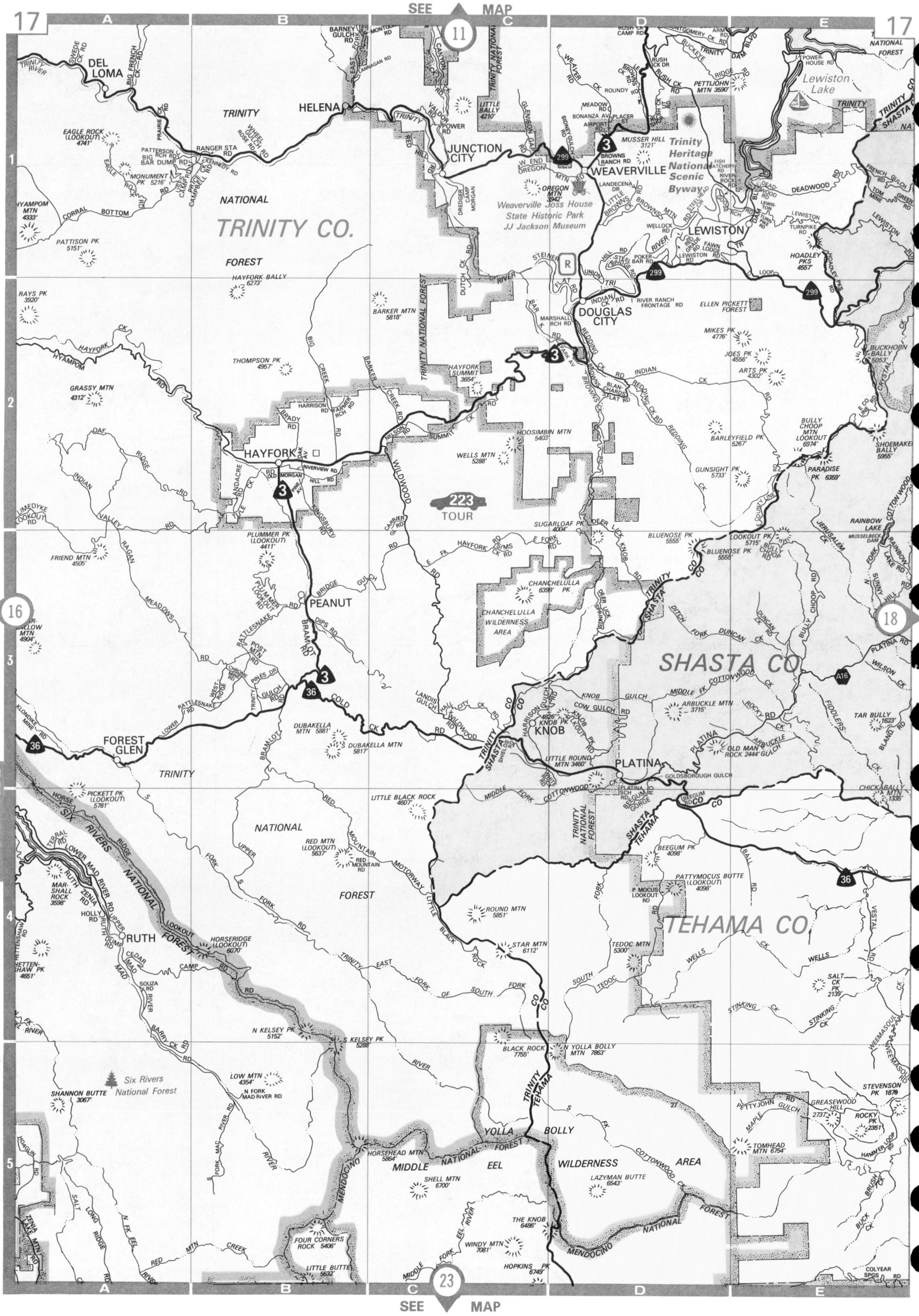
SEE MAP 11
SEE MAP 16
SEE MAP 18
SEE MAP 23
DEL LOMA
HELENA
JUNCTION CITY
WEAVERVILLE
Trinity Heritage National Scenic Byway
Weaverville Joss House State Historic Park
JJ Jackson Museum
Lewiston Lake
LEWISTON
DOUGLAS CITY
TRINITY CO.
TRINITY NATIONAL FOREST
HAYFORK
PEANUT
FOREST GLEN
SHASTA CO
KNOB
PLATINA
TEHAMA CO
RUTH
Six Rivers National Forest
CHANCHELULLA WILDERNESS AREA
YOLLA BOLLY MIDDLE EEL WILDERNESS AREA
MENDOCINO NATIONAL FOREST
SIX RIVERS NATIONAL FOREST
223 TOUR

HIGHWAYS

18

SEE MAP 12

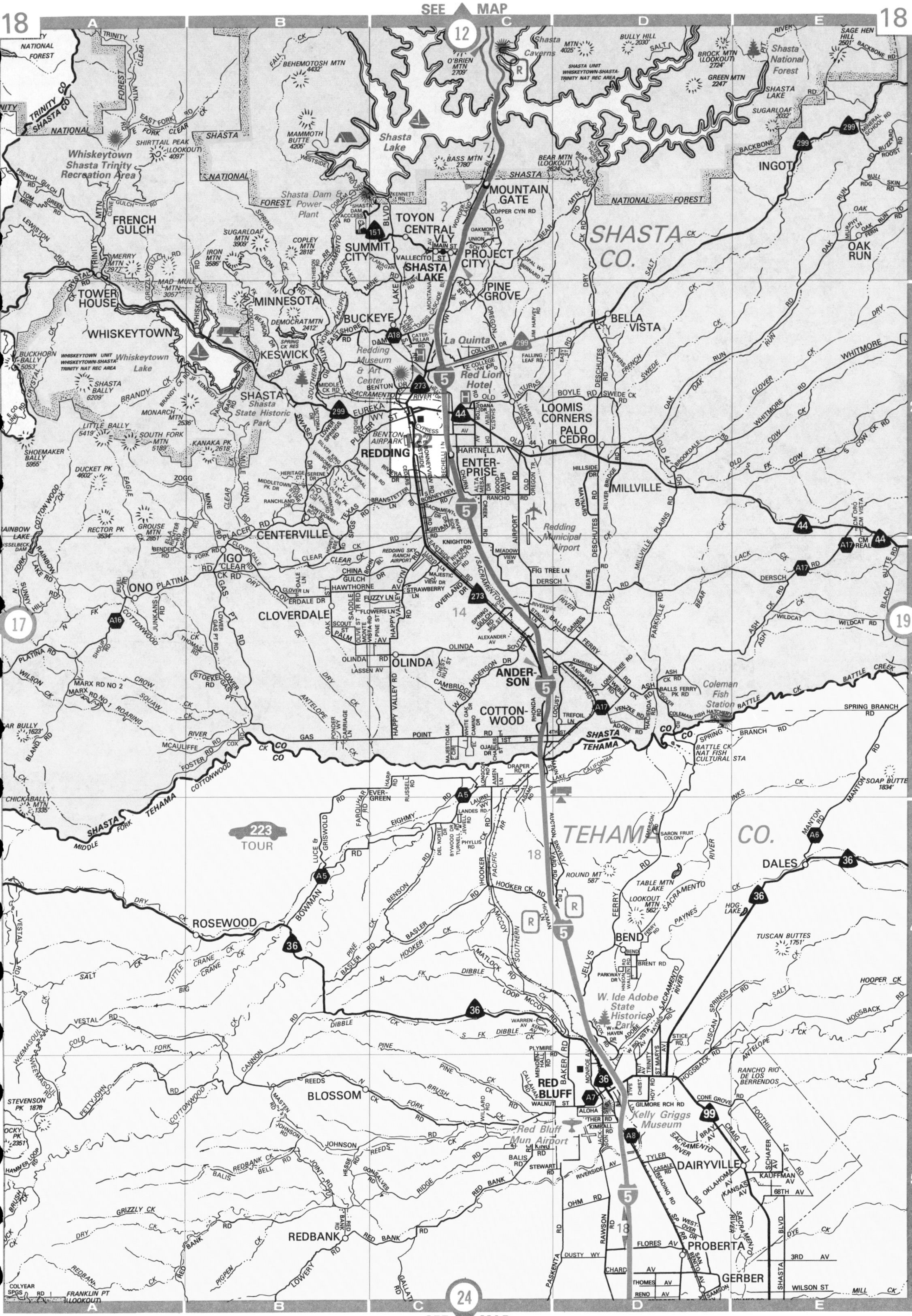

SEE MAP 17

SEE MAP 19

SEE MAP 24

HIGHWAYS

SEE MAP 13

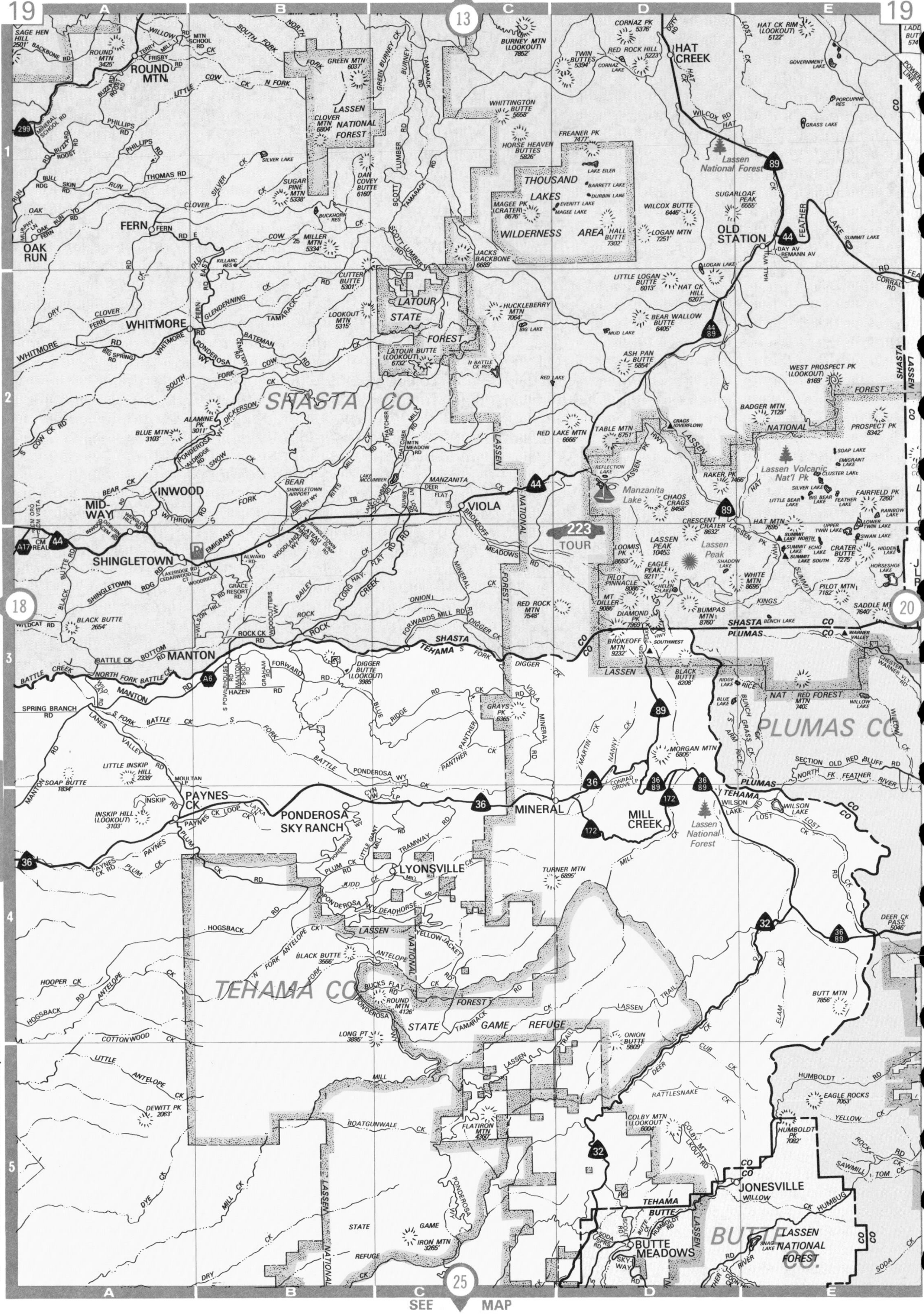

SEE MAP 18

20

SEE MAP 25

HIGHWAYS

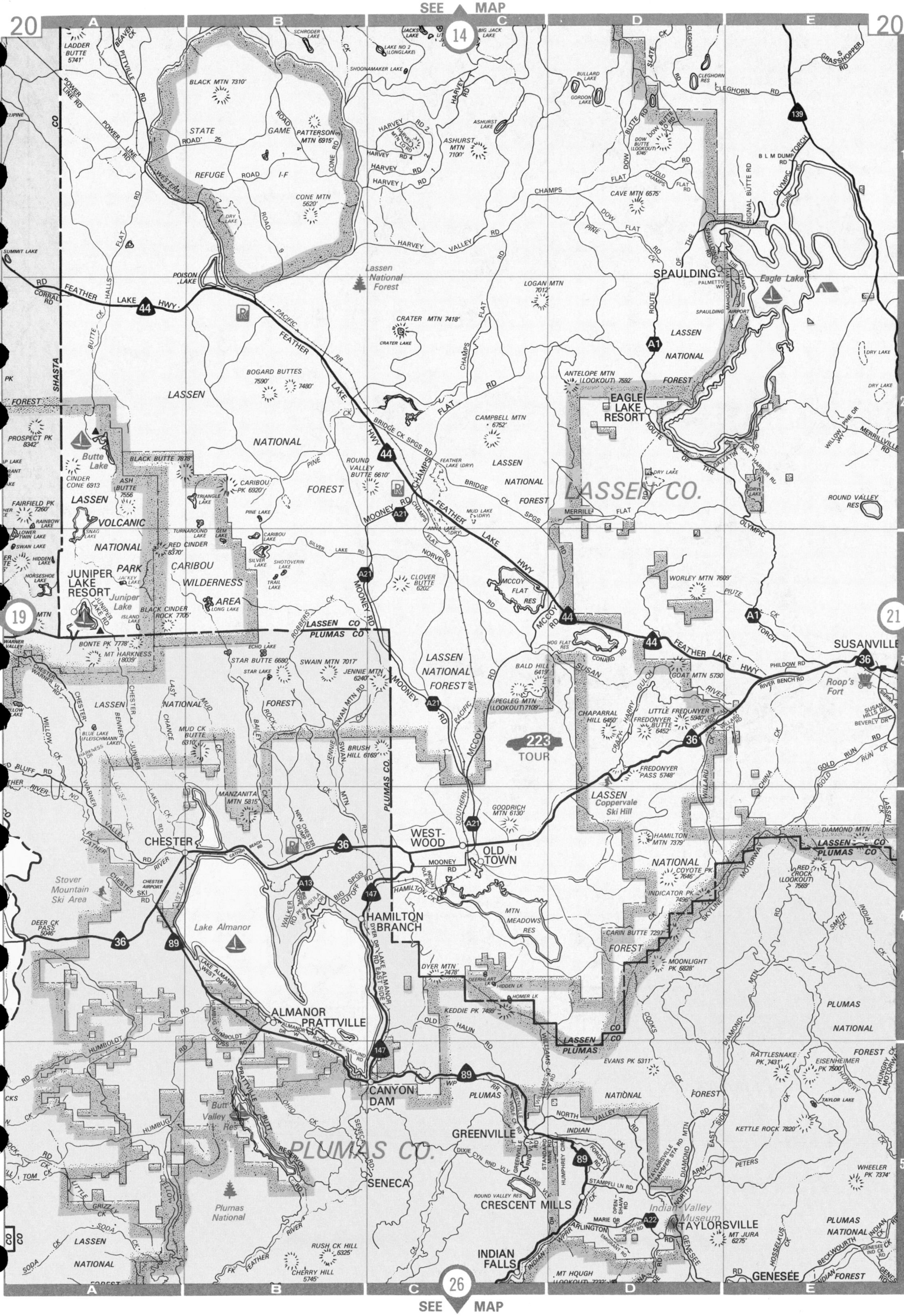
SEE MAP 14
SEE MAP 19
SEE MAP 21
SEE MAP 26
A
B
C
D
E
1
2
3
4
5
HIGHWAYS
LASSEN CO.
PLUMAS CO.
SHASTA CO
LASSEN NATIONAL FOREST
Lassen National Forest
LASSEN VOLCANIC NATIONAL PARK
CARIBOU WILDERNESS AREA
STATE GAME REFUGE 1-F
PLUMAS NATIONAL FOREST
Plumas National
SUSANVILLE
SPAULDING
EAGLE LAKE RESORT
Eagle Lake
JUNIPER LAKE RESORT
Juniper Lake
Butte Lake
CHESTER
WESTWOOD
OLD TOWN
HAMILTON BRANCH
ALMANOR
PRATTVILLE
CANYON DAM
GREENVILLE
SENECA
CRESCENT MILLS
INDIAN FALLS
TAYLORSVILLE
GENESEE
Indian Valley Museum
Lake Almanor
Butt Valley Res
Stover Mountain Ski Area
Coppervale Ski Hill
Roop's Fort
223 TOUR
FEATHER LAKE HWY
POISON LAKE
SUMMIT LAKE
BLACK MTN 7310'
PATTERSON MTN 6915'
CONE MTN 5620'
ASHURST MTN 7100'
CAVE MTN 6575'
LOGAN MTN 7012'
CRATER MTN 7418'
CRATER LAKE
BOGARD BUTTES 7590' 7480'
ANTELOPE MTN (LOOKOUT) 7592'
CAMPBELL MTN 6752'
ROUND VALLEY BUTTE 6610'
CARIBOU PK 6920'
PROSPECT PK 8342'
BLACK BUTTE 7878'
CINDER CONE 6913
FAIRFIELD PK 7260'
RED CINDER 8370'
BLACK CINDER ROCK 7705'
BONTE PK 7778'
MT HARKNESS 8039'
STAR BUTTE 6680
SWAIN MTN 7017'
JENNIE MTN 6240'
CLOVER BUTTE 6202'
BALD HILL 6419'
PEGLEG MTN (LOOKOUT) 7109'
WORLEY MTN 7609'
GOAT MTN 5730
CHAPARRAL HILL 6450'
LITTLE FREDONYER 5940'
FREDONYER BUTTE 6452'
FREDONYER PASS 5748'
MUD CK BUTTE 6310'
BRUSH HILL 6169'
MANZANITA MTN 5815'
GOODRICH MTN 6130'
HAMILTON MTN 7379'
COYOTE PK 7646'
INDICATOR PK 7496'
CARIN BUTTE 7297
MOONLIGHT PK 6826'
DYER MTN 7478'
KEDDIE PK 7499'
DIAMOND MTN
RED ROCK (LOOKOUT) 7569'
DEER CK PASS 5046
EVANS PK 5311'
RATTLESNAKE PK 7431'
EISENHEIMER PK 7500'
KETTLE ROCK 7820'
WHEELER PK 7374'
MT JURA 6275'
RUSH CK HILL 6325'
CHERRY HILL 5745'
MT HOUGH (LOOKOUT) 7232'
MCCOY FLAT RES
MTN MEADOWS RES
ROUND VALLEY RES
TAYLOR LAKE
DRY LAKE
HOMER LK
HIDDEN LK
DEERHEART LK
GRASSHOPPER RD
CLEGHORN RD
SIGNAL BUTTE RD
HARVEY VALLEY RD
CHAMPS FLAT RD
MOONEY RD
BRIDGE CK SPGS RD
PACIFIC RR
SOUTHERN PACIFIC RR
PIUTE CK
RIVER BENCH RD
PHILDOW RD
GOLD RUN RD
MERRILLVILLE RD
HAMILTON CK
LAKE ALMANOR WEST DR
LAKE ALMANOR EAST SIDE RD
ROCKY PT CP GROUND RD
HUMBOLDT RD
HUMBUG RD
PRATTVILLE BUTT RESERVOIR RD
DIXIE CYN RND VLY RD
NORTH VALLEY RD
STAMPFLI LN RD
ARLINGTON RD
BECKWOURTH GENESEE RD
36
44
89
139
147
A1
A13
A21
A22

SEE MAP 8

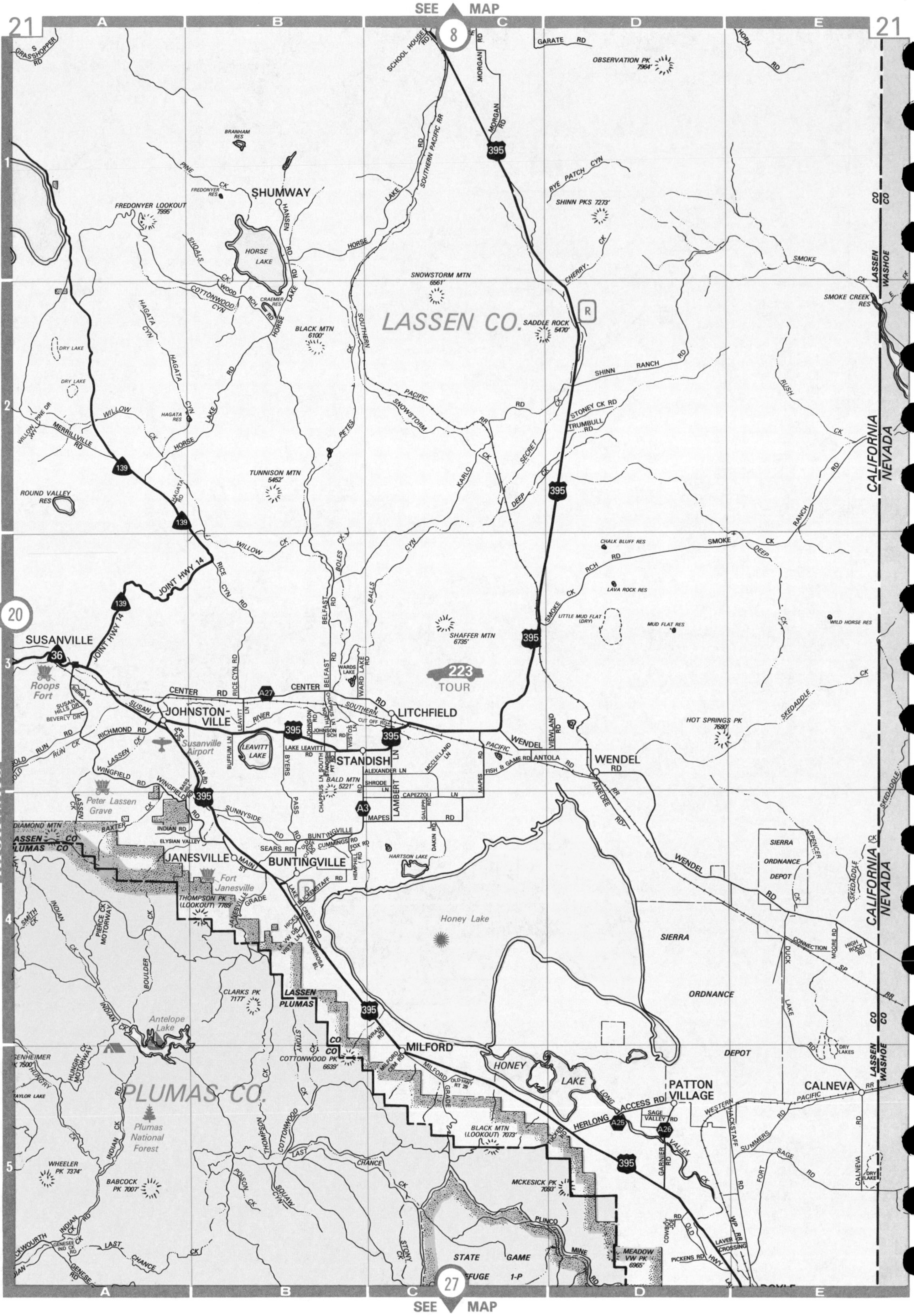

SEE MAP 20

SEE MAP 27

HIGHWAYS

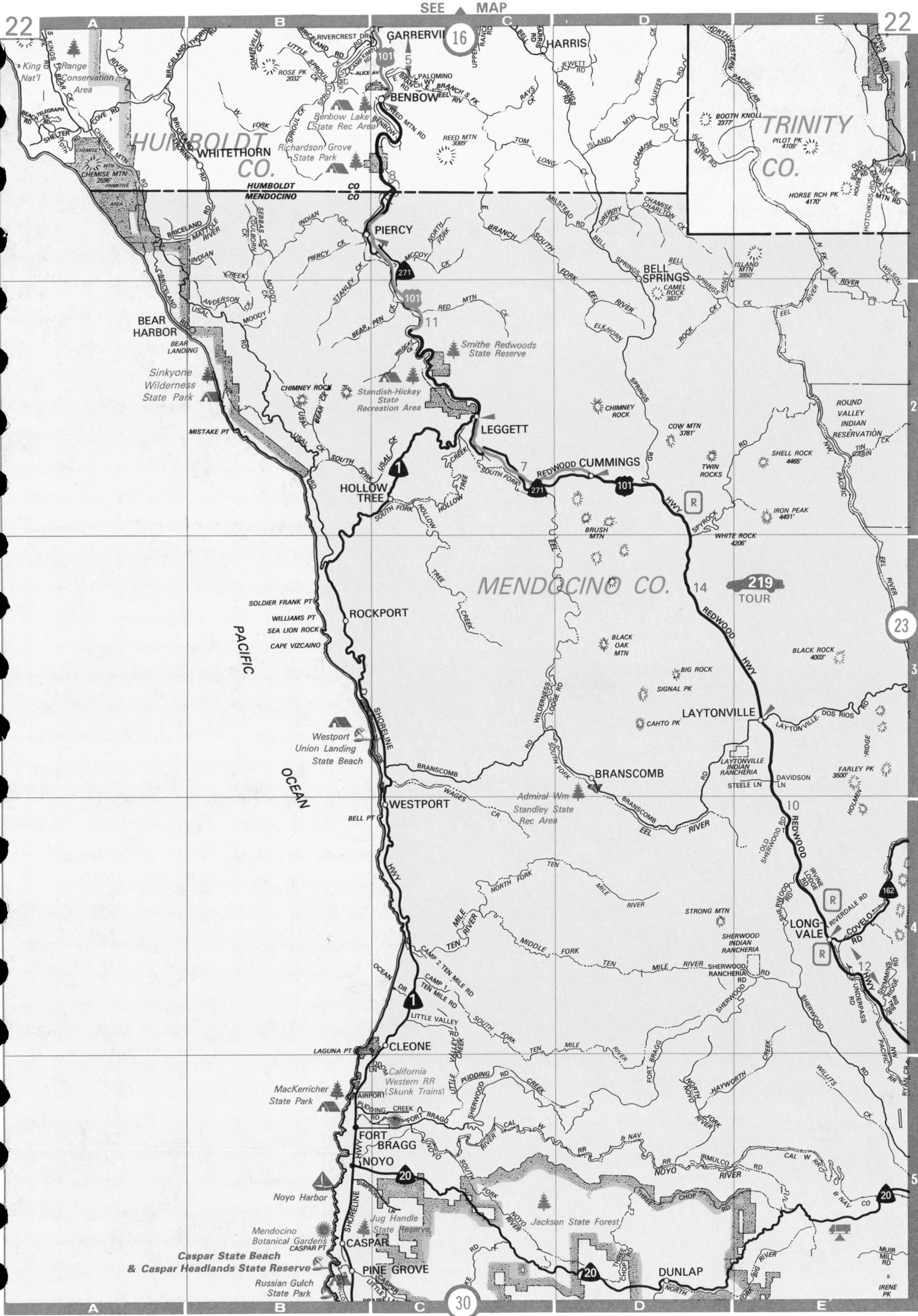

HIGHWAYS

SEE MAP 23

SEE MAP 17

SEE MAP 22
SEE MAP 24
SEE MAP 31

SEE MAP 18
SEE MAP 23
SEE MAP 25
SEE MAP 32
TEHAMA CO.
GLENN CO.
COLUSA CO.
BUTTE CO.
REDBANK
PROBERTA
GERBER
LOS MOLINOS
RANCHO TEHAMA
TEHAMA
RICHFIELD
HENLEYVILLE
VINA
CORNING
FLOURNOY
PASKENTA
KIRKWOOD
Woodson Bridge State Rec Area
MENDOCINO
NATIONAL
FOREST
NEWVILLE
Black Butte Lake
ORLAND
HAMILTON CITY
CHROME
GRINDSTONE RANCHERIA INDIAN RES
ELK CREEK
FRUTO
Mendocino National Forest
Stony Gorge Reservoir
ARTOIS
WILLOWS
BUTTE CITY
Sacramento National Wildlife Refuge
NORMAN
STONYFORD
FOUTS SPRINGS
EAST PARK RES
GRAPEVINE PASS
DELEVAN
HIGHWAYS
227 TOUR

SEE MAP 19

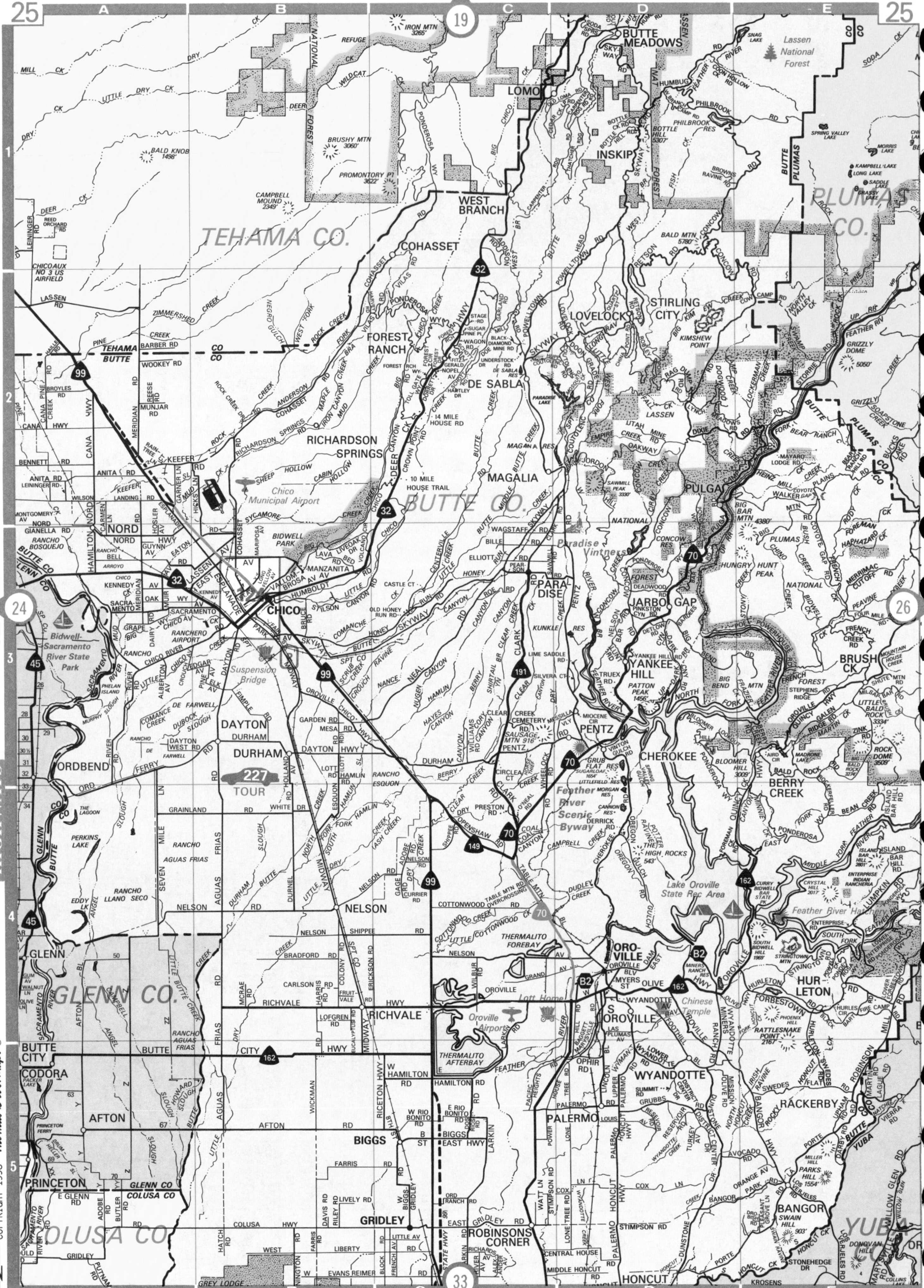

SEE MAP 24

SEE MAP 26

HIGHWAYS

SEE MAP 33

SEE MAP 20

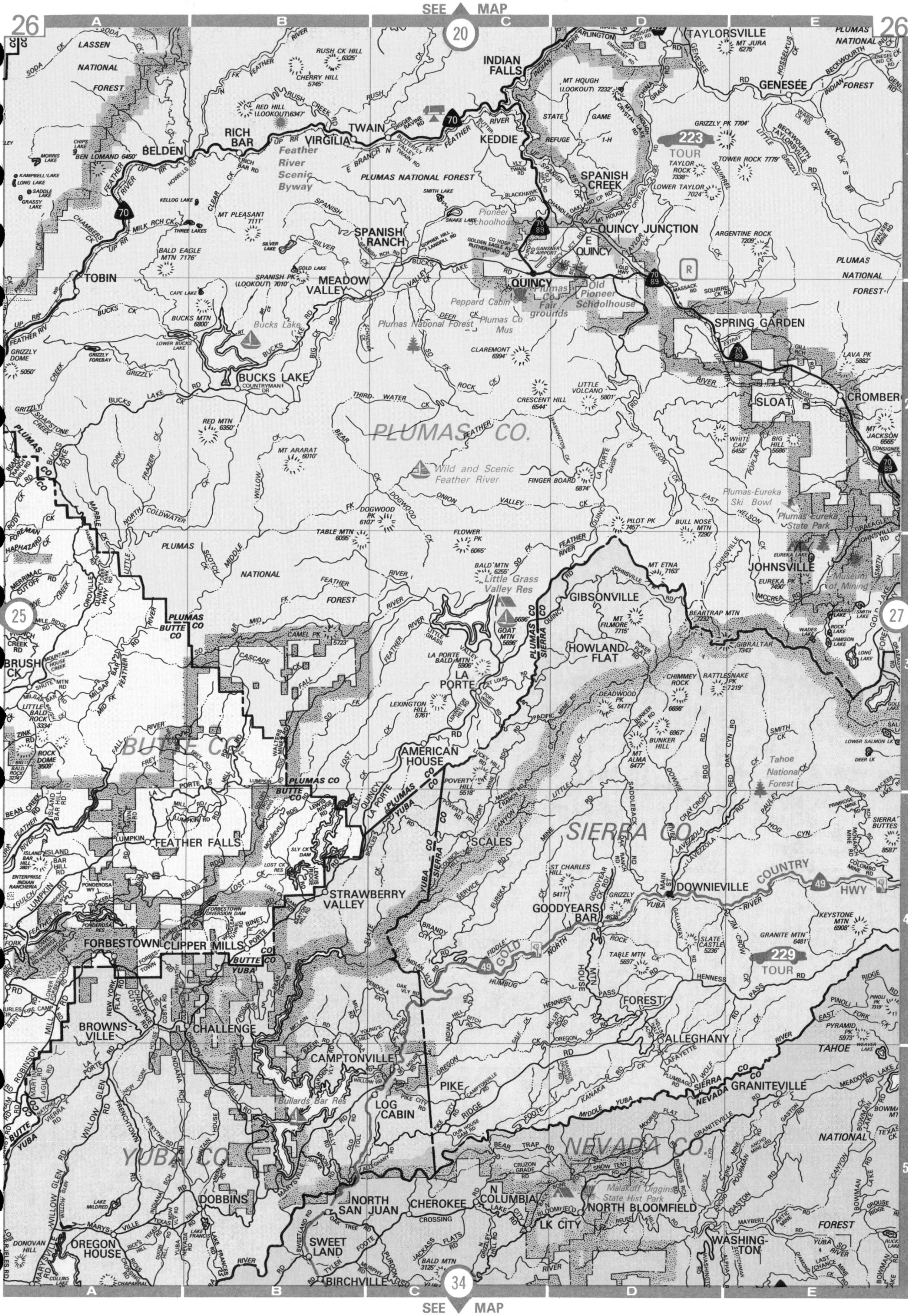

SEE MAP 34

SEE MAP 21
SEE MAP 26
SEE MAP 28
SEE MAP 35
PLUMAS CO.
LASSEN CO.
SIERRA CO.
NEVADA CO.
CALIFORNIA
NEVADA
Plumas National Forest
Tahoe National Forest
Toiyabe National Forest
STATE GAME REFUGE 1-P
STATE GAME REFUGE 1-V
DOYLE
CONSTANTIA
Frenchman Reservoir State Rec Area
Lake Davis
CROMBERG
BECKWOURTH
PORTOLA
Feather River Railroad Museum
Feather River Scenic Byway
VINTON
CHILCOOT
HALLELUJAH JUNCTION
BLAIRSDEN
Plumas Pines
Graeagle Meadows
Lakes Basin Recreation Area
CLIO
LOYALTON
Sierra Valley Museum
SIERRA BROOKS
CALPINE
HASKELL CREEK
BASSETTS
SATTLEY
SIERRAVILLE
RANDOLF
Kentucky Mine Historic Park
Sierra Buttes
GOLD COUNTRY
SIERRA CITY
GOLD COUNTRY HWY
Jackson Meadow Reservoir
Stampede Reservoir
VERDI
SIERRA PINES
Bowman Lake
HOBART MILLS
Prosser Creek Reservoir
Boca Res
BOCA
KINGVALE
SODA SPRINGS
Boreal Ridge
Tahoe Donner
TRUCKEE
Truckee Airport
223 TOUR
229 TOUR

HIGHWAYS

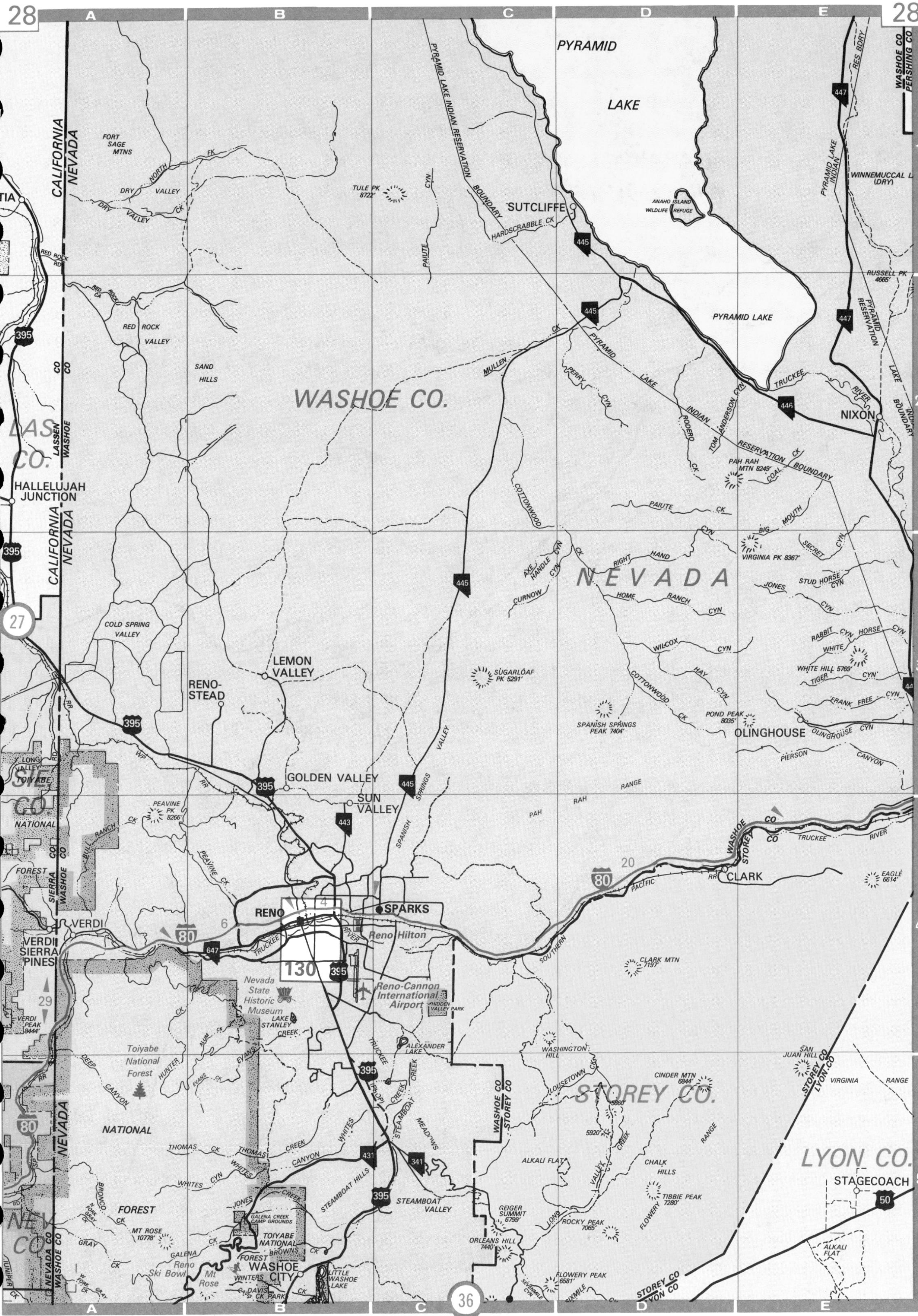

36
SEE MAP

HIGHWAYS

SEE MAP 38

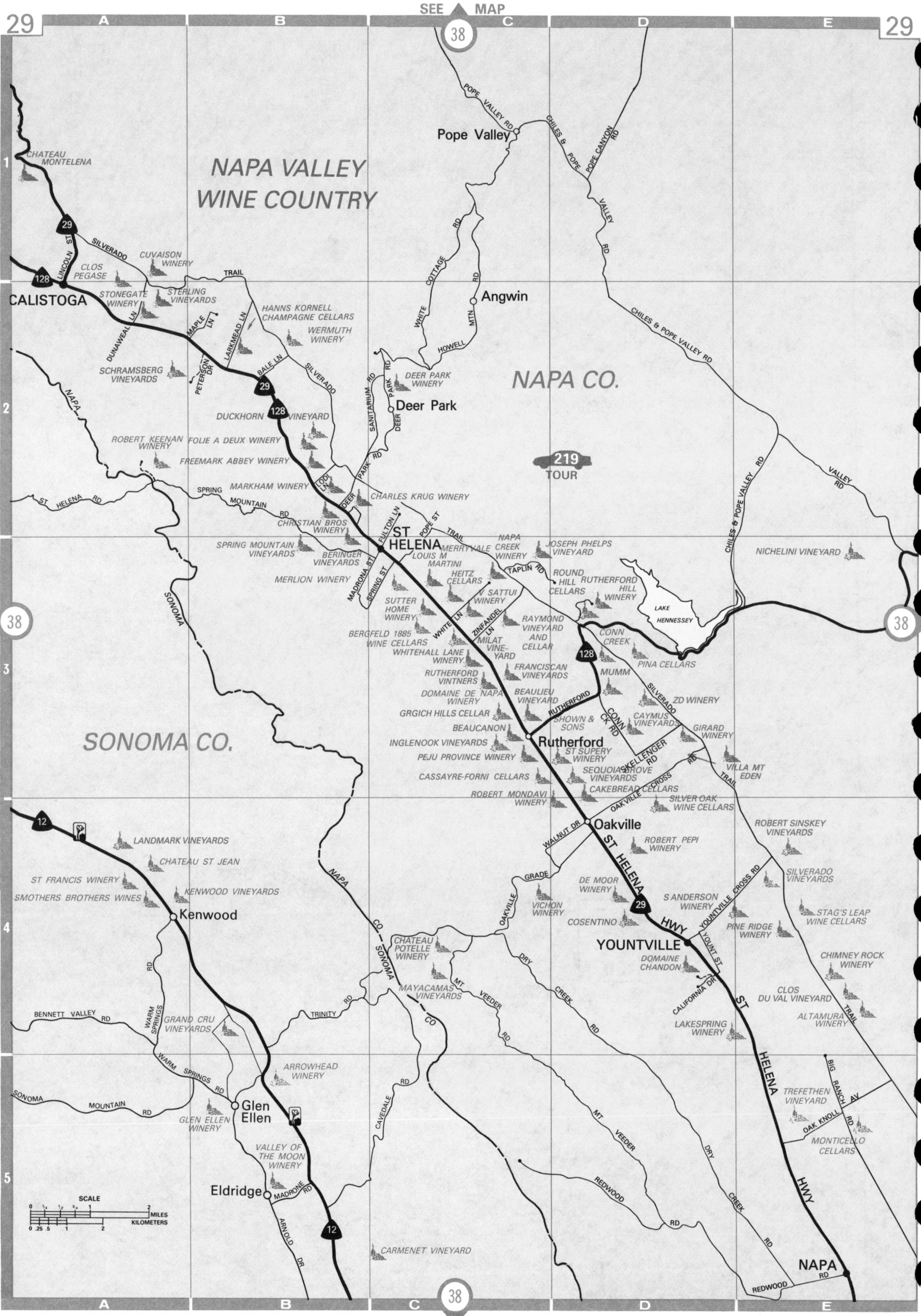

SEE MAP 38

HIGHWAYS

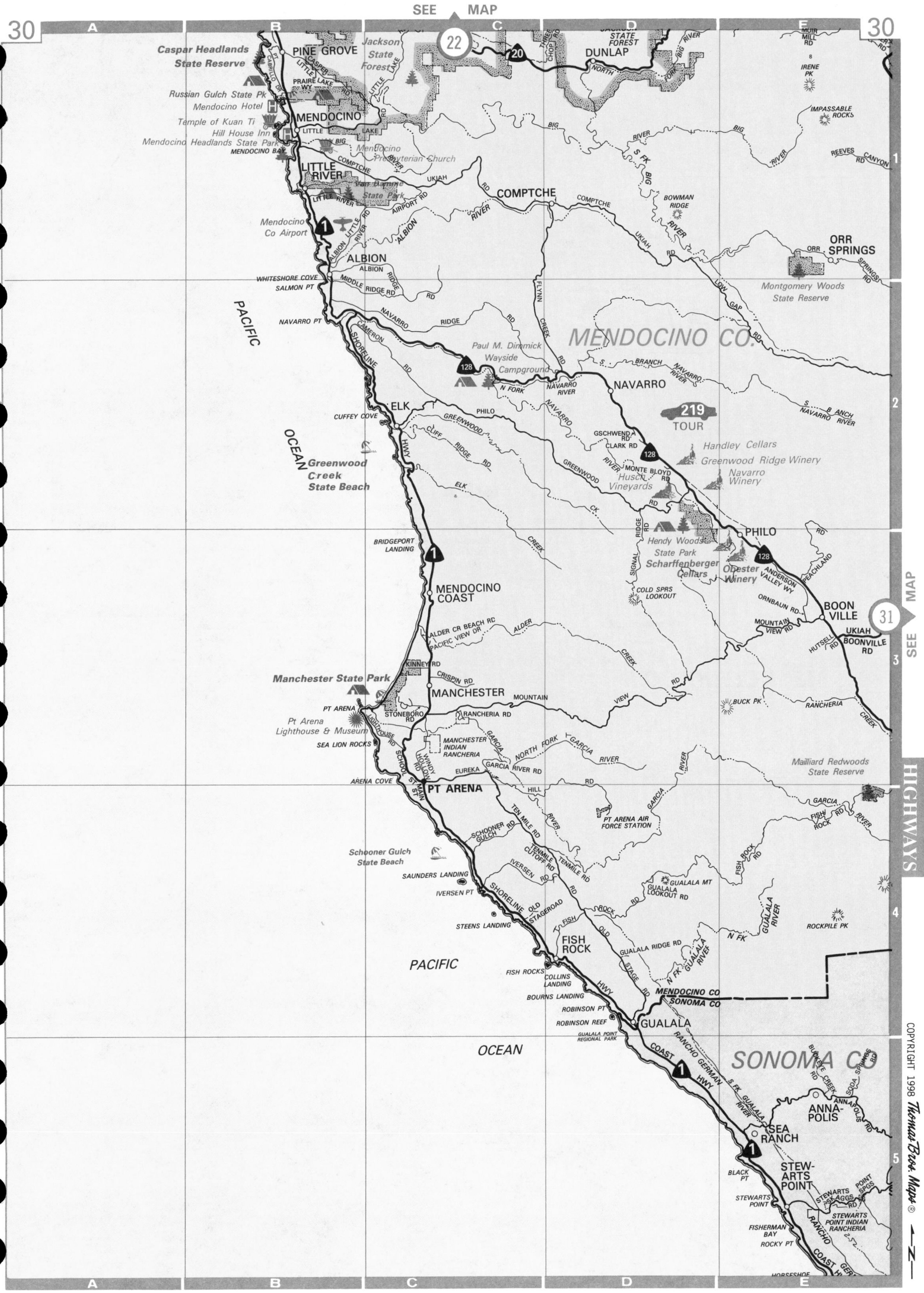
SEE MAP 22
SEE MAP 31
A
B
C
D
E
1
2
3
4
5
Caspar Headlands State Reserve
PINE GROVE
Jackson State Forest
JACKSON STATE FOREST
DUNLAP
Russian Gulch State Pk
Mendocino Hotel
Temple of Kuan Ti
Hill House Inn
Mendocino Headlands State Park
MENDOCINO BAY
MENDOCINO
Mendocino Presbyterian Church
LITTLE RIVER
Van Damme State Park
COMPTCHE
Mendocino Co Airport
ALBION
WHITESHORE COVE
SALMON PT
NAVARRO PT
PACIFIC
OCEAN
IRENE PK
IMPASSABLE ROCKS
BOWMAN RIDGE
ORR SPRINGS
Montgomery Woods State Reserve
MENDOCINO CO.
Paul M. Dimmick Wayside Campground
NAVARRO
219 TOUR
ELK
CUFFEY COVE
Greenwood Creek State Beach
Handley Cellars
Greenwood Ridge Winery
Navarro Winery
Husch Vineyards
PHILO
Hendy Woods State Park
Scharffenberger Cellars
Obester Winery
COLD SPRS LOOKOUT
BRIDGEPORT LANDING
MENDOCINO COAST
BOON VILLE
UKIAH BOONVILLE RD
Manchester State Park
MANCHESTER
PT ARENA
Pt Arena Lighthouse & Museum
SEA LION ROCKS
MANCHESTER INDIAN RANCHERIA
BUCK PK
Mailliard Redwoods State Reserve
ARENA COVE
PT ARENA
PT ARENA AIR FORCE STATION
Schooner Gulch State Beach
SAUNDERS LANDING
IVERSEN PT
GUALALA MT
GUALALA LOOKOUT RD
ROCKPILE PK
STEENS LANDING
FISH ROCK
PACIFIC
FISH ROCKS
COLLINS LANDING
BOURNS LANDING
ROBINSON PT
ROBINSON REEF
GUALALA POINT REGIONAL PARK
MENDOCINO CO
SONOMA CO
GUALALA
OCEAN
SONOMA CO
ANNAPOLIS
SEA RANCH
BLACK PT
STEW-ARTS POINT
STEWARTS POINT
STEWARTS POINT INDIAN RANCHERIA
FISHERMAN BAY
ROCKY PT
HORSESHOE
HIGHWAYS

SEE MAP 23
SEE MAP 30
SEE MAP 32
SEE MAP 37
A
B
C
D
E
1
2
3
4
5
POTTER VALLEY
POMO
REDWOOD VALLEY
RANCHO YOKAYO
ORR SPRINGS
CALPELLA
Lake Mendocino
Montgomery Woods State Reserve
Parducci Wine Cellars
Mendocino Vineyards
Frey Vineyards
Olson Vineyards
Wiebel Vinyards
VICHY SPRINGS
UKIAH
TALMAGE
BLUE LAKES
North Cow Mountain Recreation Area
South Cow Mountain OHV Rec Area
Hidden Cellars Winery
Whaler Vineyard
BACHELOR VALLEY
UPPER LAKE
NICE
LUCERNE
Clear Lake
LAKEPORT
Lakeport Historic Museum
Lake County Museum
George G Hoberg Vista Pt
Lake Co. Fairgrounds
Kendall-Jackson
Konocti Cellars
Clear Lake State Park
FINLEY
SODA BAY
RIVIERA HEIGHTS
RIVIERA WEST
KELSEYVILLE
Lampson Airport
KONO TAYEE
CLEARLAKE OAKS
GLEN HAVEN
LAKE CO.
COLUSA CO
MENDOCINO NATIONAL FOREST
Mendocino Nat'l Forest
BARTLETT SPGS
MENDOCINO CO.
RANCHO DE SANEL
Jepson Vineyards
Fetzer Vineyards
McDowell Valley Vineyards
HOPLAND
Milano Winery
YORKVILLE
Mailliard Redwoods State Reserve
PRESTON
CLOVERDALE
Bandiera Winery
Fritz Cellars
Lake Sonoma Winery
ASTI
Diamond Oaks Vineyards
Pastori
Geyser Peak Winery
Pedroncelli
COZZENS CORNERS
Chateau Souverain
Lake Sonoma Recreation Area
LAKE SONOMA
Ferrari-Carano Winery
Warm Springs Dam & Fish Hatchery
SKAGGS SPRINGS
LAS LOMAS
GEYSERVILLE
Nervo
Trentadue
JIMTOWN
Sausal Winery
Souverain
LYTTON
Lytton Springs
Robert Stemmler
Lambert Bridge
Dry Creek
River Oaks
Simi Winery
Soda Rock
Johnson's Alexander Valley
Alexander Valley
Field Stone
KELLOGG
HEALDSBURG
DEL RIO
Murphy-Goode
RANCHO CASLAMAYOMI
SONOMA CO.
ANNAPOLIS
SHINGLE MILL
SODA SPRINGS
GLEN VIEW
LOCH LOMOND
ADAMS
HOBERGS
COBB
Boggs Mtn State Forest
PINE GROVE
FOREST
WHISPERING PINES
ANDERSON SPRINGS
MENDOCINO CO
SONOMA CO
LAKE CO
101
20
29
175
253
128
281
123
219 TOUR

HIGHWAYS

SEE MAP 24

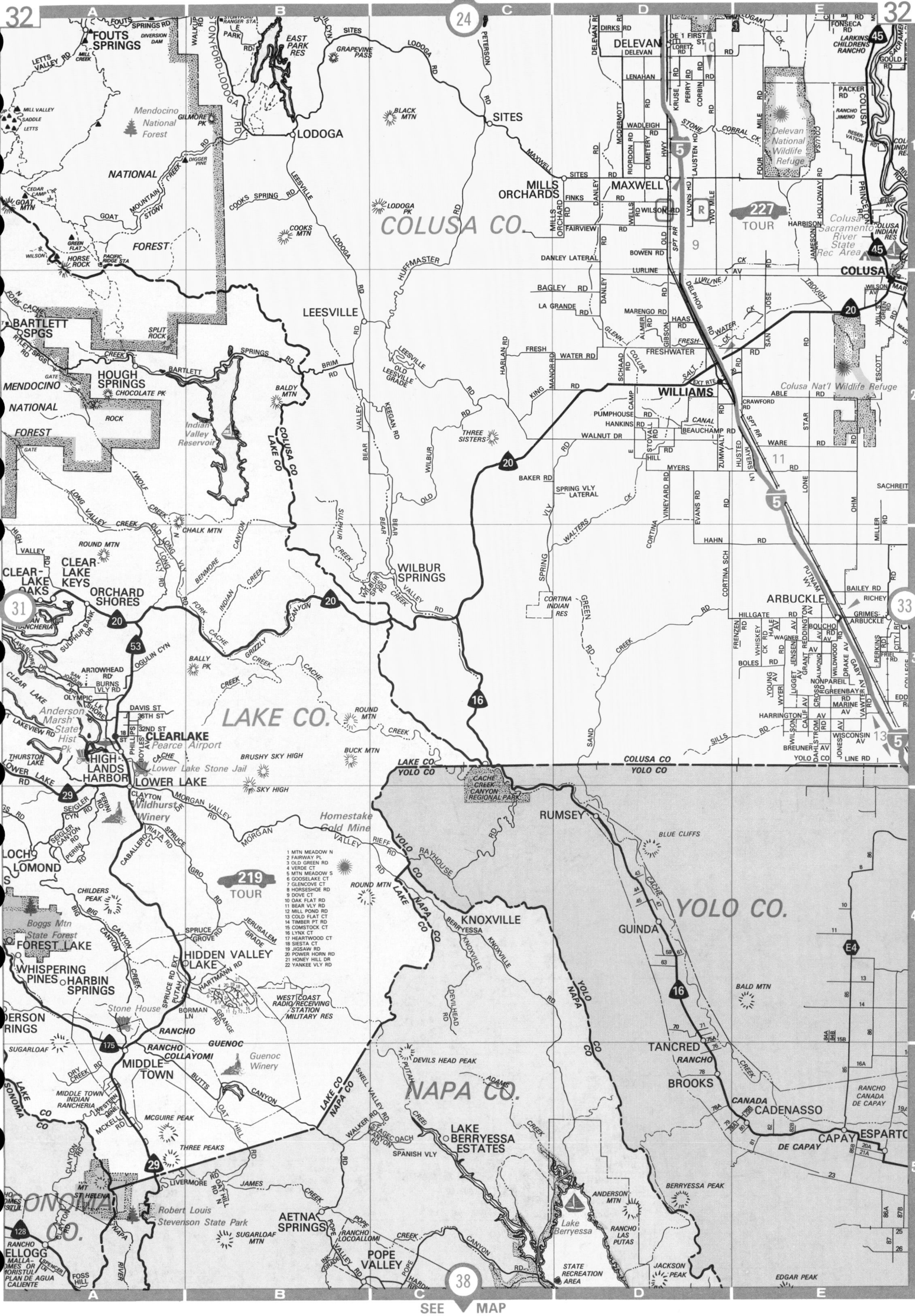

SEE MAP 31
SEE MAP 33
SEE MAP 38
HIGHWAYS

SEE MAP 25

SEE MAP 32
SEE MAP 34
SEE MAP 39

HIGHWAYS

SEE MAP 26

33

35 SEE MAP

HIGHWAYS

SEE MAP 40

SEE MAP 27

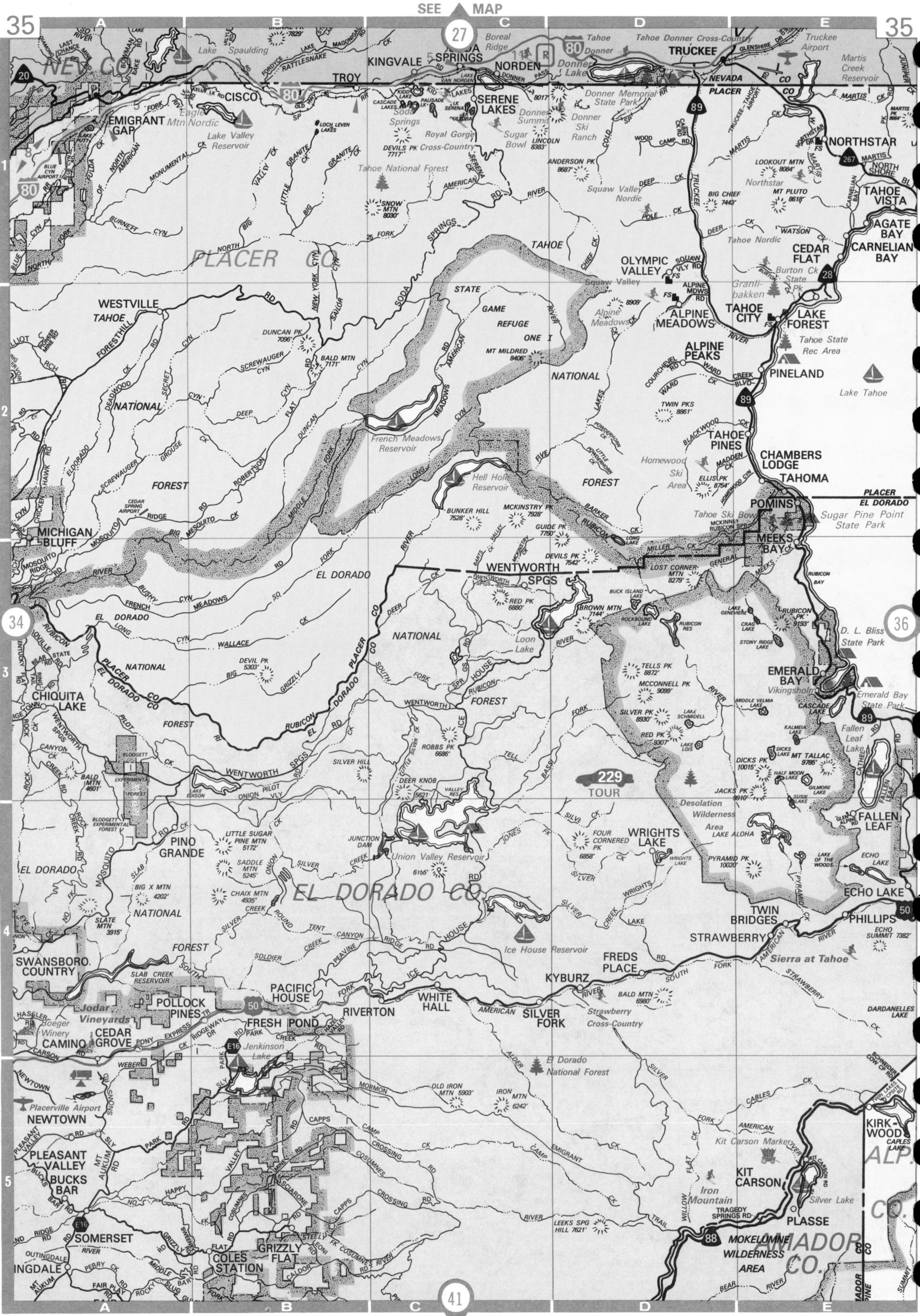

SEE MAP 41

HIGHWAYS

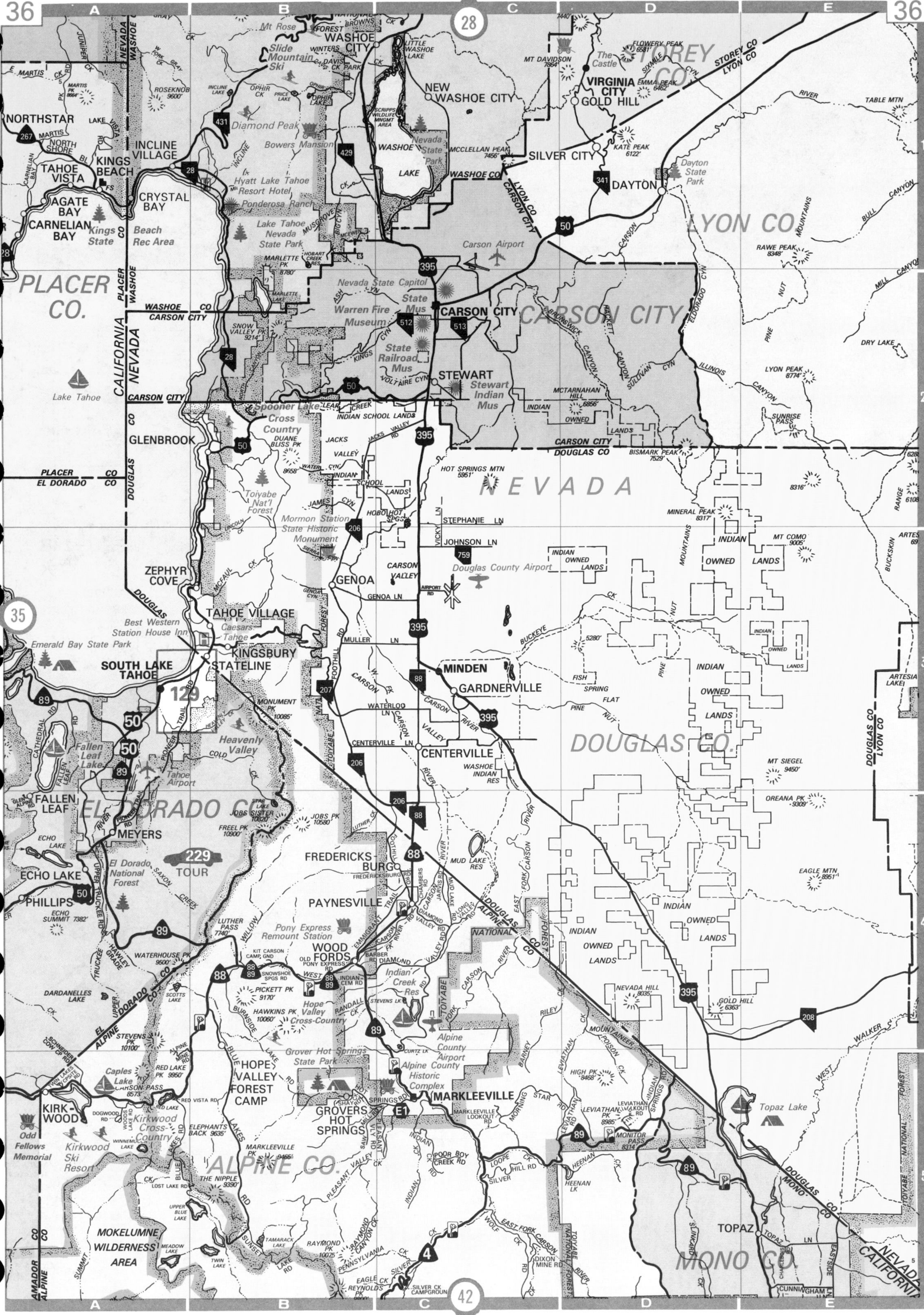
PLACER CO.
EL DORADO CO.
ALPINE CO.
MONO CO.
DOUGLAS CO.
LYON CO.
STOREY CO.
CARSON CITY
NEVADA
CALIFORNIA
NORTHSTAR
TAHOE VISTA
KINGS BEACH
INCLINE VILLAGE
CRYSTAL BAY
AGATE BAY
CARNELIAN BAY
Kings Beach State Rec Area
WASHOE CITY
NEW WASHOE CITY
VIRGINIA CITY
GOLD HILL
SILVER CITY
DAYTON
Dayton State Park
Slide Mountain Ski
Mt Rose
Diamond Peak
Bowers Mansion
Hyatt Lake Tahoe Resort Hotel
Ponderosa Ranch
Lake Tahoe Nevada State Park
WASHOE LAKE
Carson Airport
Nevada State Capitol
State Mus
Warren Fire Museum
State Railroad Mus
CARSON CITY
STEWART
Stewart Indian Mus
Lake Tahoe
GLENBROOK
Spooner Lake Cross Country
JACKS VALLEY
INDIAN OWNED LANDS
Toiyabe Nat'l Forest
Mormon Station State Historic Monument
GENOA
CARSON VALLEY
Douglas County Airport
ZEPHYR COVE
TAHOE VILLAGE
Best Western Station House Inn
Caesars Tahoe
KINGSBURY
STATELINE
SOUTH LAKE TAHOE
Emerald Bay State Park
MINDEN
GARDNERVILLE
CENTERVILLE
Heavenly Valley
Tahoe Airport
Fallen Leaf Lake
FALLEN LEAF
MEYERS
El Dorado National Forest
229 TOUR
ECHO LAKE
PHILLIPS
WASHOE INDIAN RES
MUD LAKE RES
FREDERICKSBURG
PAYNESVILLE
Pony Express Remount Station
WOODFORDS
Indian Creek Res
Hope Valley Cross-Country
Grover Hot Springs State Park
Alpine County Airport
Alpine County Historic Complex
MARKLEEVILLE
HOPE VALLEY FOREST CAMP
GROVERS HOT SPRINGS
Caples Lake
KIRKWOOD
Kirkwood Cross-Country
Kirkwood Ski Resort
Odd Fellows Memorial
MOKELUMNE WILDERNESS AREA
Topaz Lake
TOPAZ
MONITOR PASS
EAGLE MTN
MT SIEGEL
OREANA PK
LYON PEAK
MT COMO
MINERAL PEAK
HOT SPRINGS MTN
BISMARK PEAK
RAWE PEAK
NEVADA HILL
GOLD HILL
HIGH PK
LEVIATHAN PK
JOBS PK
JOBS SISTER
FREEL PK
MONUMENT PK
PICKETT PK
HAWKINS PK
STEVENS PK
RED LAKE PK
MARKLEEVILLE PK
THE NIPPLE
RAYMOND PK
ELEPHANTS BACK
WATERHOUSE PK
LUTHER PASS
CARSON PASS
ECHO SUMMIT
DARDANELLES LAKE
DRY LAKE
TABLE MTN
CARSON RIVER
EAST FORK CARSON RIVER
WEST FORK CARSON RIVER
DOUGLAS CO
ALPINE CO
AMADOR CO
ALPINE CO

HIGHWAYS

A
B
C
D
E
1
2
3
4
5
SONOMA CO.
MARIN CO.
PACIFIC OCEAN
219 TOUR
225 TOUR
HEALDSBURG
WINDSOR
SANTA ROSA
SEBASTOPOL
GUERNEVILLE
FORESTVILLE
GRATON
OCCIDENTAL
BODEGA BAY
BODEGA
VALLEY FORD
TOMALES
DILLON BEACH
MARSHALL
INVERNESS
PT REYES STATION
INVERNESS PARK
OLEMA
NICASIO
BOLINAS
DRAKES BEACH
DRAKES BAY
JENNER
FORT ROSS
WALSH LANDING
CAZADERO
MONTE RIO
CAMP MEEKER
FREESTONE
COTATI
ROHNERT PARK
WASHOE
TWO ROCK
FALLON
FULTON
CHALK HILL VALLEY
MARK WEST SPRINGS
KELLOGG
SOUTH PARK
Point Reyes National Seashore
Sonoma Coast State Beach
Salt Point State Park
Armstrong Redwoods State Reserve
Tomales Bay State Park

SEE MAP 32
SEE MAP 39
SEE MAP 45
SEE MAP 37
A
B
C
D
E
1
2
3
4
5
KELLOGG
Old Faithful Geyser of California
Mud Baths
CALISTOGA
Napa Valley Railroad Depot
WINE COUNTRY AREA
Bothe-Napa Valley State Park
Petrified Forest
DEER PARK
Silverado Museum
Bale Grist Mill St Historic Park
Hurd Candle Factory
ST HELENA
For Detail Page Locations SEE PAGE 29
AETNA SPRINGS
POPE VALLEY
ANGWIN
LAS POSADAS STATE FOREST
LAKE HENNESSEY
Lake Berryessa
BERRYESSA PINES
SPANISH FLAT WOODLANDS
BERRYESSA HIGHLANDS
YOLO CO.
NAPA CO.
SOLANO CO
SANTA ROSA
Annadel State Park
Sugarloaf Ridge St Pk
Chateau St Jean
RUTHERFORD
OAKVILLE
KENWOOD
Kenwood
Smothers Brothers Wines
St Francis Las Montanas Winery
Jack London St Hist Pk
Glen Ellen Winery
GLEN ELLEN
YOUNTVILLE
Napa Valley Lodge Best Western
CIRCLE OAKS
RANCHO CHIMILES
LAKE CURRY
Silverado Country Club Resort
SOUTH PARK
Matanzas Creek Winery
SONOMA CO.
ROHNERT PARK
Doubletree Hotel
Sonoma State University
PENNGROVE
Eagle Ridge Winery
ELDRIDGE
FETTERS HOT SPRINGS
AGUA CALIENTE
BOYES HOT SPRINGS
EL VERANO
SONOMA
Hacienda Cellars
SALVADOR
The Chateau
VICHY SPRINGS
219 TOUR
Gundlach Bundschu Winery
Carneros Creek Winery
VINEBURG
SCHELLVILLE
Mt St John Cellars
NAPA
SKYLINE COUNTY PARK
MANKAS CORNER
GREEN VALLEY ESTATES
ROCKVILLE
FAIRFIELD
SUISUN CITY
CORDELIA
PETALUMA
Petaluma Adobe State Historical Monument
BIG BEND
LAKEVILLE
Sonoma Creek Winery
Viansa Winery
US NAVAL RESERVATION
AMERICAN CANYON
MARINE WORLD
SOLANO CO.
VALLEJO HTS
VALLEJO
BURDELL
Rancho Olompali State Historic Park
SAN MARIN
NOVATO
SEARS POINT
GREEN POINT
BLACK POINT
IGNACIO
For Detail Page Locations SEE PAGE L
CARQUINEZ HTS
BENICIA
MONTEZUMA SLOUGH
GRIZZLY ISLAND
GRIZZLY BAY
SUISUN BAY
MARIN CO.
MARINWOOD
LUCAS VALLEY
NICASIO
NICASIO REDWOODS
FOREST
WOODACRE
SLEEPY HOLLOW
SAN PABLO BAY
GALLINAS
SANTA VENETIA
SAN RAFAEL
CROCKETT
PORT COSTA
AVON
RODEO
HERCULES
PINOLE
MARTINEZ
CLYDE
PACHECO
Concord Hilton
LAGUNITAS
SAN GERONIMO
FAIRFAX
SAN ANSELMO
ROSS
NORTH RICHMOND
EL SOBRANTE
225 TOUR
PLEASANT HILL
RICHMOND
SAN PABLO
CONTRA COSTA CO.
Audubon Canyon Ranch
LARKSPUR
SAN QUENTIN
CORTE MADERA
MILL VALLEY
PARADISE CAY
TIBURON
EL CERRITO
KENSINGTON
BRIONES REGIONAL PARK
LAFAYETTE
WALNUT CREEK
BOLINAS
STINSON
HIGHWAYS

SEE MAP 33

SEE MAP 38
40
SEE MAP 46

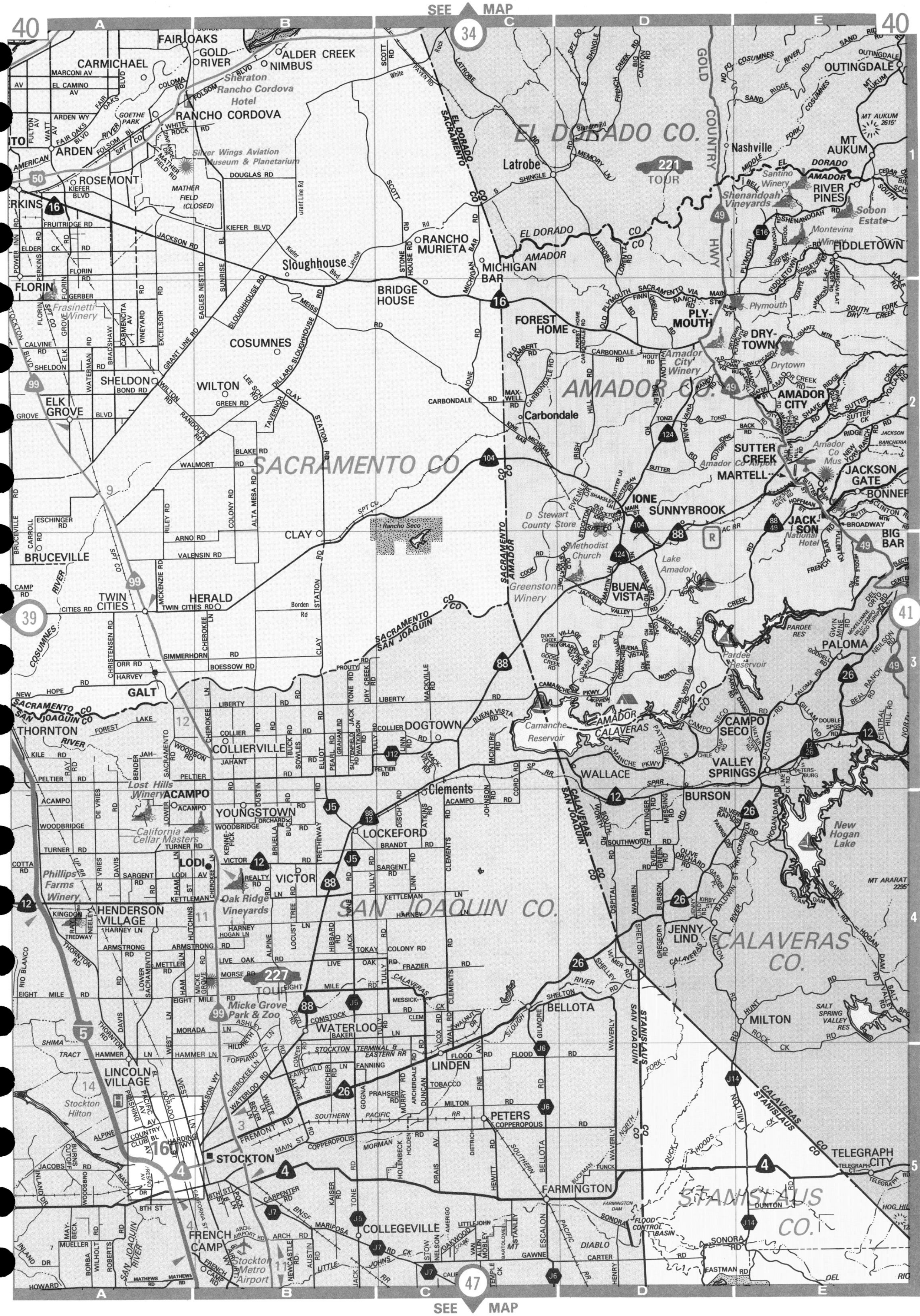

SEE MAP 34
SEE MAP 41
SEE MAP 39
SEE MAP 47
A
B
C
D
E
1
2
3
4
5
FAIR OAKS
GOLD RIVER
ALDER CREEK
NIMBUS
CARMICHAEL
Sheraton Rancho Cordova Hotel
RANCHO CORDOVA
ARDEN
Silver Wings Aviation Museum & Planetarium
ROSEMONT
MATHER FIELD (CLOSED)
FLORIN
Frasinetti Winery
SHELDON
ELK GROVE
WILTON
COSUMNES
Sloughhouse
RANCHO MURIETA
MICHIGAN BAR
BRIDGE HOUSE
EL DORADO CO.
Latrobe
221 TOUR
Nashville
MT AUKUM
OUTINGDALE
Santino Winery
Shenandoah Vineyards
RIVER PINES
Sobon Estate
Montevina Winery
FIDDLETOWN
PLYMOUTH
Plymouth
FOREST HOME
DRYTOWN
Drytown
Amador City Winery
AMADOR CO.
AMADOR CITY
Carbondale
SUTTER CREEK
Amador Co Airport
MARTELL
Amador Co Mus
JACKSON GATE
BONNEFF
SACRAMENTO CO.
IONE
SUNNYBROOK
D Stewart County Store
JACKSON
National Hotel
BIG BAR
Rancho Seco
CLAY
BRUCEVILLE
Methodist Church
Lake Amador
Greenstone Winery
BUENA VISTA
TWIN CITIES
HERALD
PARDEE RES
Pardee Reservoir
PALOMA
GALT
THORNTON
Camanche Reservoir
COLLIERVILLE
DOGTOWN
CAMPO SECO
VALLEY SPRINGS
WALLACE
Lost Hills Winery
ACAMPO
Clements
BURSON
YOUNGSTOWN
LOCKEFORD
New Hogan Lake
California Cellar Masters
LODI
VICTOR
Phillips Farms Winery
Oak Ridge Vineyards
HENDERSON VILLAGE
SAN JOAQUIN CO.
JENNY LIND
CALAVERAS CO.
227 TOUR
Micke Grove Park & Zoo
BELLOTA
MILTON
WATERLOO
LINDEN
LINCOLN VILLAGE
Stockton Hilton
PETERS
STOCKTON
TELEGRAPH CITY
FARMINGTON
STANISLAUS CO.
COLLEGEVILLE
FRENCH CAMP
Stockton Metro Airport
HIGHWAYS

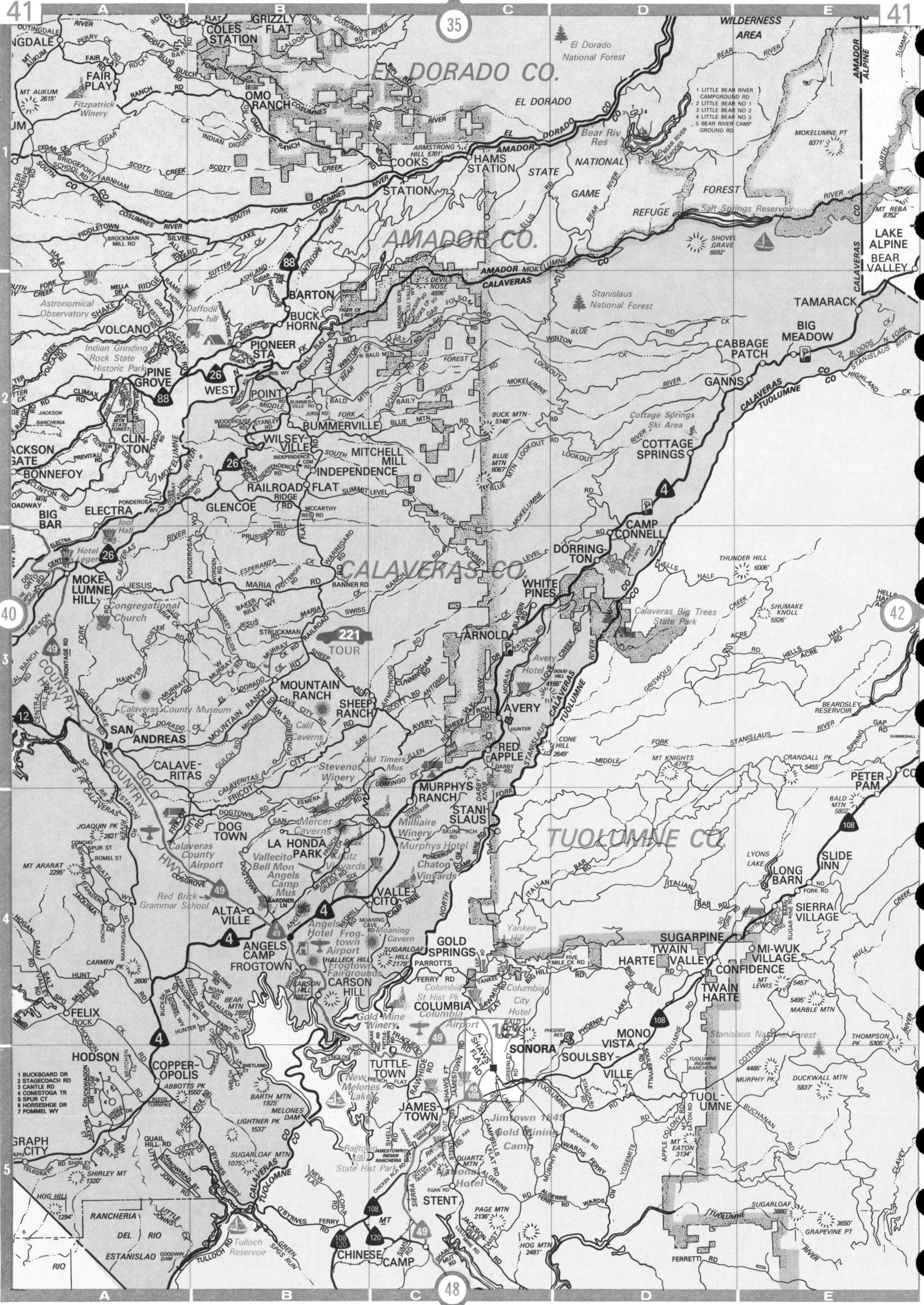

SEE MAP 40
SEE MAP 42
SEE MAP 48

HIGHWAYS

SEE MAP 36

41

SEE MAP 43

SEE MAP 49

HIGHWAYS

SEE MAP 42

44

50
SEE MAP

HIGHWAYS

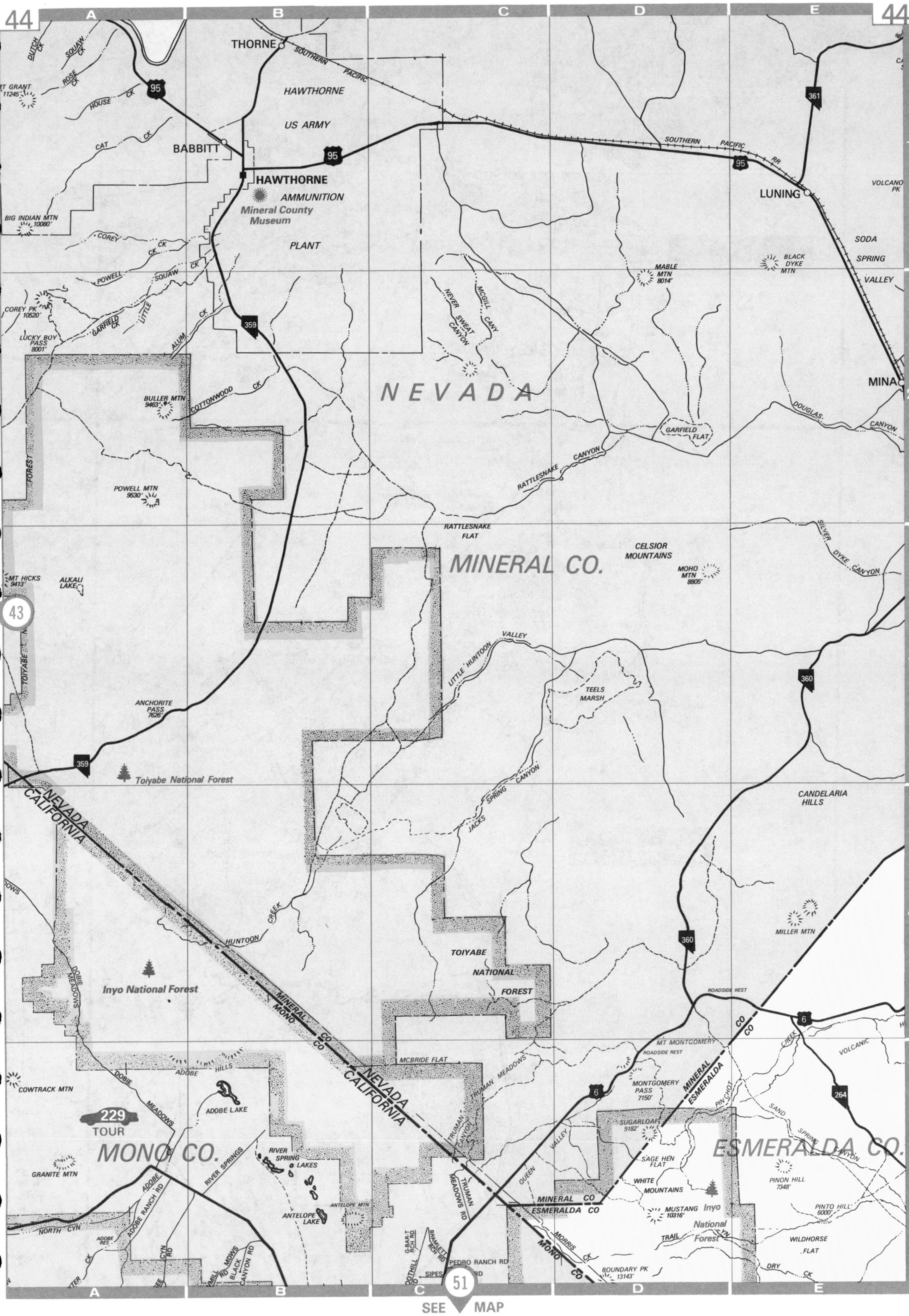

SEE 51 MAP

HIGHWAYS

A
B
C
D
E
1
2
3
4
5
STINSON BEACH
MUIR BEACH
MARIN CO.
SAUSALITO
MARIN CITY
TIBURON
BELVEDERE
ANGEL ISLAND
PARADISE CAY
GOLDEN GATE BRIDGE
SAN FRANCISCO
SF - OAKLAND BAY BRIDGE
ALBANY
BERKELEY
EMERYVILLE
ORINDA
ORINDA VILLAGE
LAFAYETTE
WALNUT CREEK
CONTRA COSTA CO.
Rheem Valley
MORAGA
Alamo
Canyon
Montclair
PIEDMONT
OAKLAND
CONTRA COSTA CO
ALAMEDA CO
UPPER SAN LEANDRO RES
ALAMEDA
South Shore
Bay Farm Island
OAKLAND INTERNATIONAL AIRPORT
SAN LEANDRO
Sheffield Village
Castro Valley
Mulford Gardens
ALAMEDA CO.
HAYWARD
San Lorenzo
SAN FRANCISCO CO.
SAN FRANCISCO CO
SAN MATEO CO
DALY CITY
COLMA
Bayshore
BRISBANE
PACIFICA
SOUTH SAN FRANCISCO
SAN BRUNO
225 TOUR
SAN FRANCISCO INTERNATIONAL AIRPORT
Rockaway Beach
MILLBRAE
SAN ANDREAS LAKE
San Pedro Terrace
Linda Mar
BURLINGAME
SAN MATEO
FOSTER CITY
SAN MATEO TOLL BRIDGE
UNION CITY
Alvarado
HILLSBOROUGH
Montara
Moss Beach
The Highlands
LOWER CRYSTAL SPRINGS RES
BELMONT
Redwood Shores
DUMBARTON BRIDGE
NEWARK
Princeton By The Sea
El Granada
SAN CARLOS
EAST PALO ALTO
MENLO PARK
Miramar
HALF MOON BAY
UPPER CRYSTAL SPRINGS RES
REDWOOD CITY
ATHERTON
PALO ALTO
Skyline
Kings Mtn
WOODSIDE
Stanford
MOUNTAIN VIEW
Ladera
LOS ALTOS
PORTOLA VALLEY
SAN MATEO CO.
Sky Londa
LOS ALTOS HILLS
SANTA CLARA CO.
CUPERTINO
Monte Vista
San Gregorio
La Honda
Loma Mar
Pescadero
SAN MATEO CO
SANTA CRUZ CO
SANTA CRUZ CO.
MONTE SERENO
LOS GATOS
Redwood
For Detail Page Locations SEE PAGE L
For Detail Page Locations SEE PAGE N
46
SEE MAP 53

HIGHWAYS

46

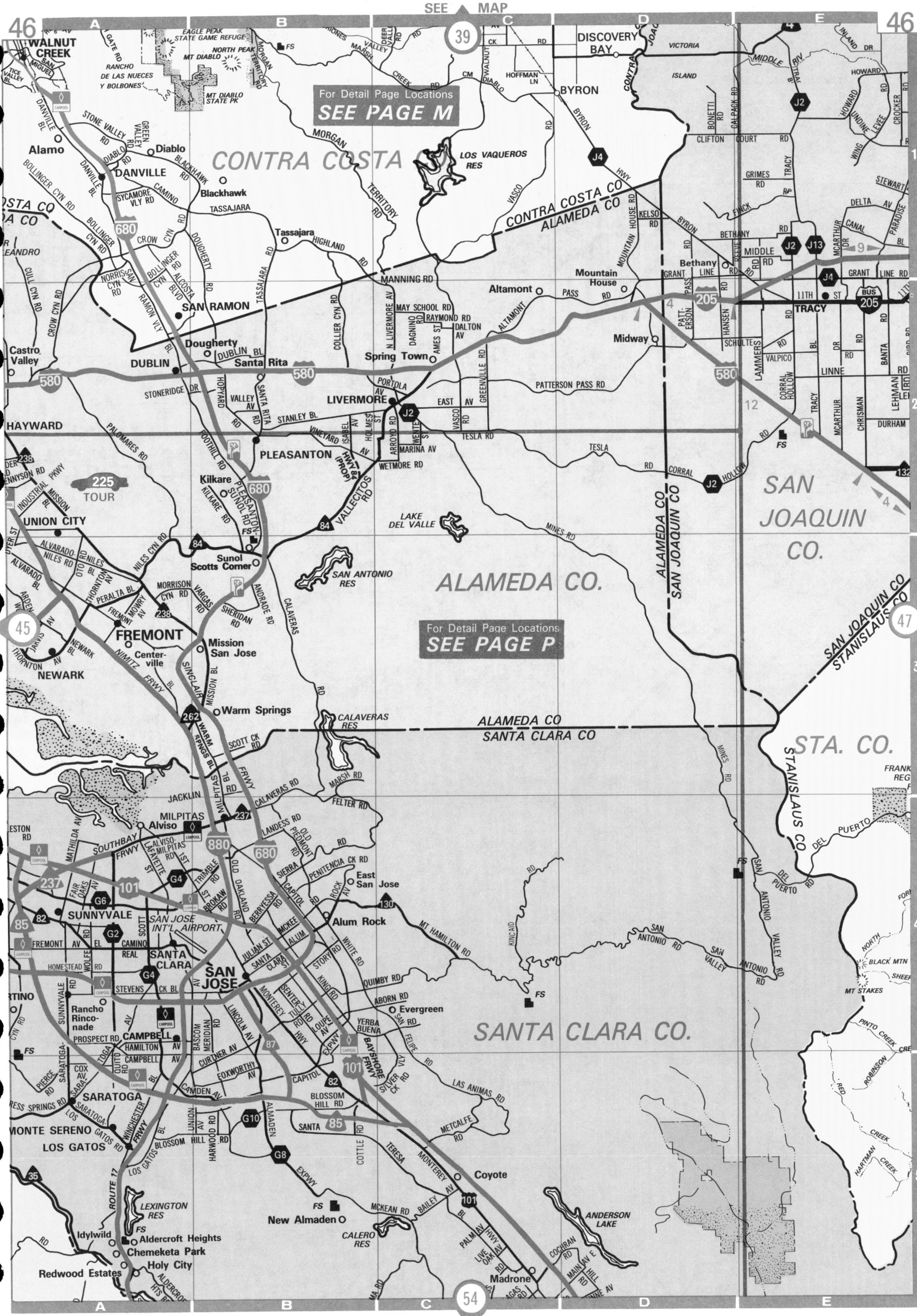
SEE MAP 39
For Detail Page Locations SEE PAGE M
For Detail Page Locations SEE PAGE P
SEE MAP 45
SEE MAP 47
SEE MAP 54
CONTRA COSTA CO.
ALAMEDA CO.
SAN JOAQUIN CO.
SANTA CLARA CO.
STA. CO.
CONTRA COSTA CO
ALAMEDA CO
SANTA CLARA CO
SAN JOAQUIN CO
STANISLAUS CO
WALNUT CREEK
EAGLE PEAK STATE GAME REFUGE
NORTH PEAK
MT DIABLO
MT DIABLO STATE PK
RANCHO DE LAS NUECES Y BOLBONES
DISCOVERY BAY
BYRON
VICTORIA ISLAND
LOS VAQUEROS RES
Alamo
Diablo
DANVILLE
Blackhawk
Tassajara
SAN RAMON
Dougherty
DUBLIN
Santa Rita
Castro Valley
HAYWARD
Spring Town
LIVERMORE
PLEASANTON
Altamont
Mountain House
Midway
TRACY
Bethany
Kilkare
225 TOUR
UNION CITY
Sunol
Scotts Corner
LAKE DEL VALLE
SAN ANTONIO RES
FREMONT
Mission San Jose
Centerville
NEWARK
Warm Springs
CALAVERAS RES
MILPITAS
Alviso
East San Jose
Alum Rock
SUNNYVALE
SAN JOSE INT'L AIRPORT
SANTA CLARA
SAN JOSE
Rancho Rinconade
Evergreen
CAMPBELL
SARATOGA
MONTE SERENO
LOS GATOS
Coyote
New Almaden
LEXINGTON RES
CALERO RES
ANDERSON LAKE
Idylwild
Aldercroft Heights
Chemeketa Park
Holy City
Redwood Estates
Madrone
MT STAKES
BLACK MTN
HIGHWAYS

SEE MAP 40

SEE MAP 46

SEE MAP 48

SEE MAP 55

HIGHWAYS

TUOLUMNE CO.
STANISLAUS CO.
MERCED CO.
MARIPOSA CO.
MADERA CO.
CAL. CO.
CHINESE CAMP
KNIGHTS FERRY
MOCCASIN
BIG OAK FLAT
PRIEST
GROVELAND
Groveland Hotel
SMITH STATION
GREELEY HILL
COULTERVILLE
DOGTOWN
Don Pedro Reservoir
MODESTO RES COUNTY PARK
WATERFORD
LA GRANGE
HICKMAN
Turlock Lake State Rec Area
Lake McClure
EXCHEQUER DAM
BEAR VALLEY
HIDALGO
SNELLING
MERCED FALLS
Lake McSwain
HORNITOS
HOPETON
Snelling Courthouse
Turlock Municipal Airport
BALLICO
McConnell State Rec Area
DELHI
CRESSEY
WINTON
LIVINGSTON
Castle Air Force Base
Castle Air Museum
NAIRN
ATWATER
BUHACH
Yosemite Lake & Park
Yosemite Wildlife Museum
MERCED
TUTTLE
PLANADA
LINGARD
PLAINSBURG
LE GRAND
MERCED NATIONAL WILDLIFE MANAGEMENT AREA
EL NIDO
CHOWCHILLA
221 TOUR
227 TOUR
Mariposa Reservoir
OWENS CREEK DAM
SEE MAP 47
SEE MAP 49
SEE MAP 56

SEE MAP 42

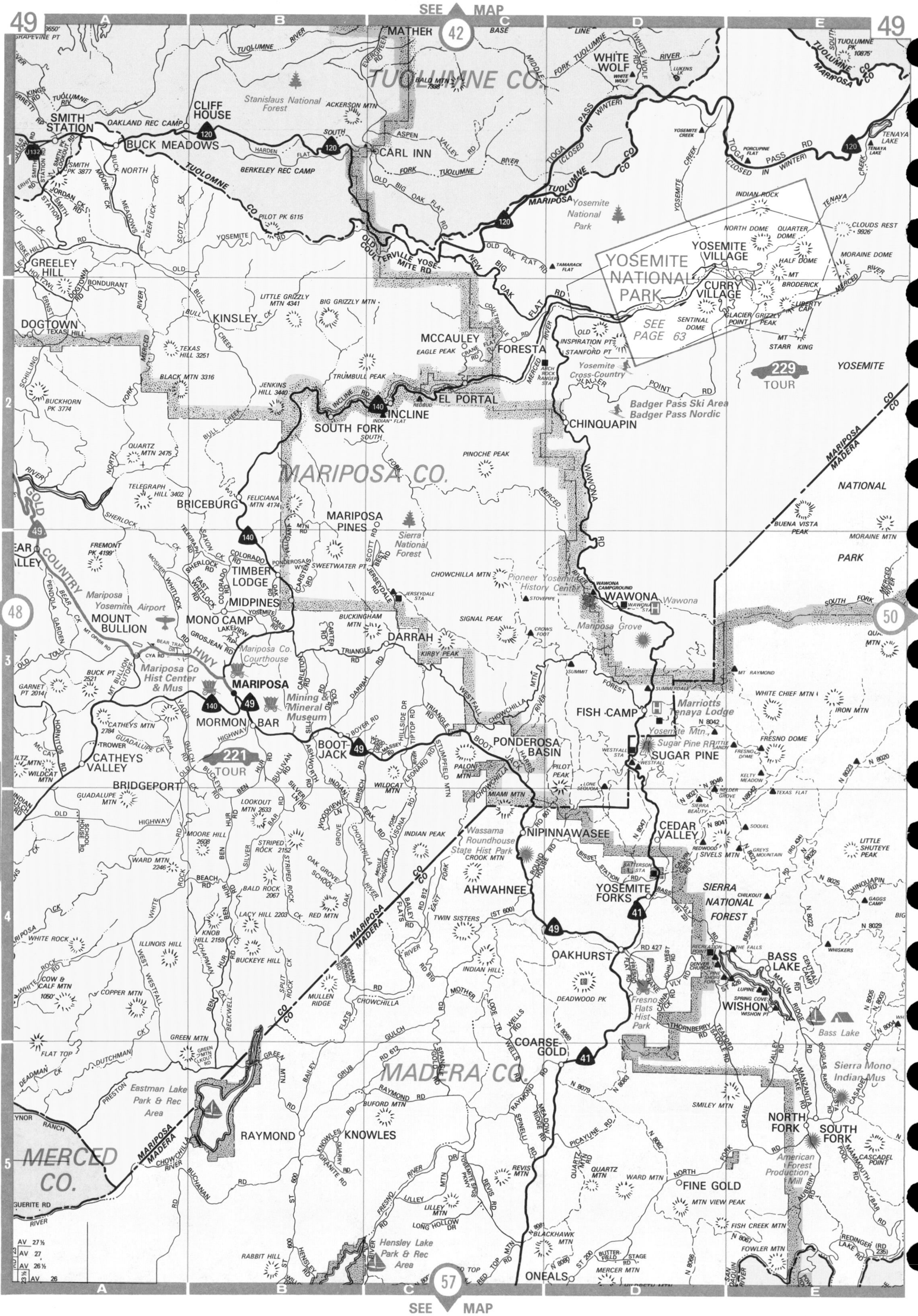

SEE MAP 57

HIGHWAYS

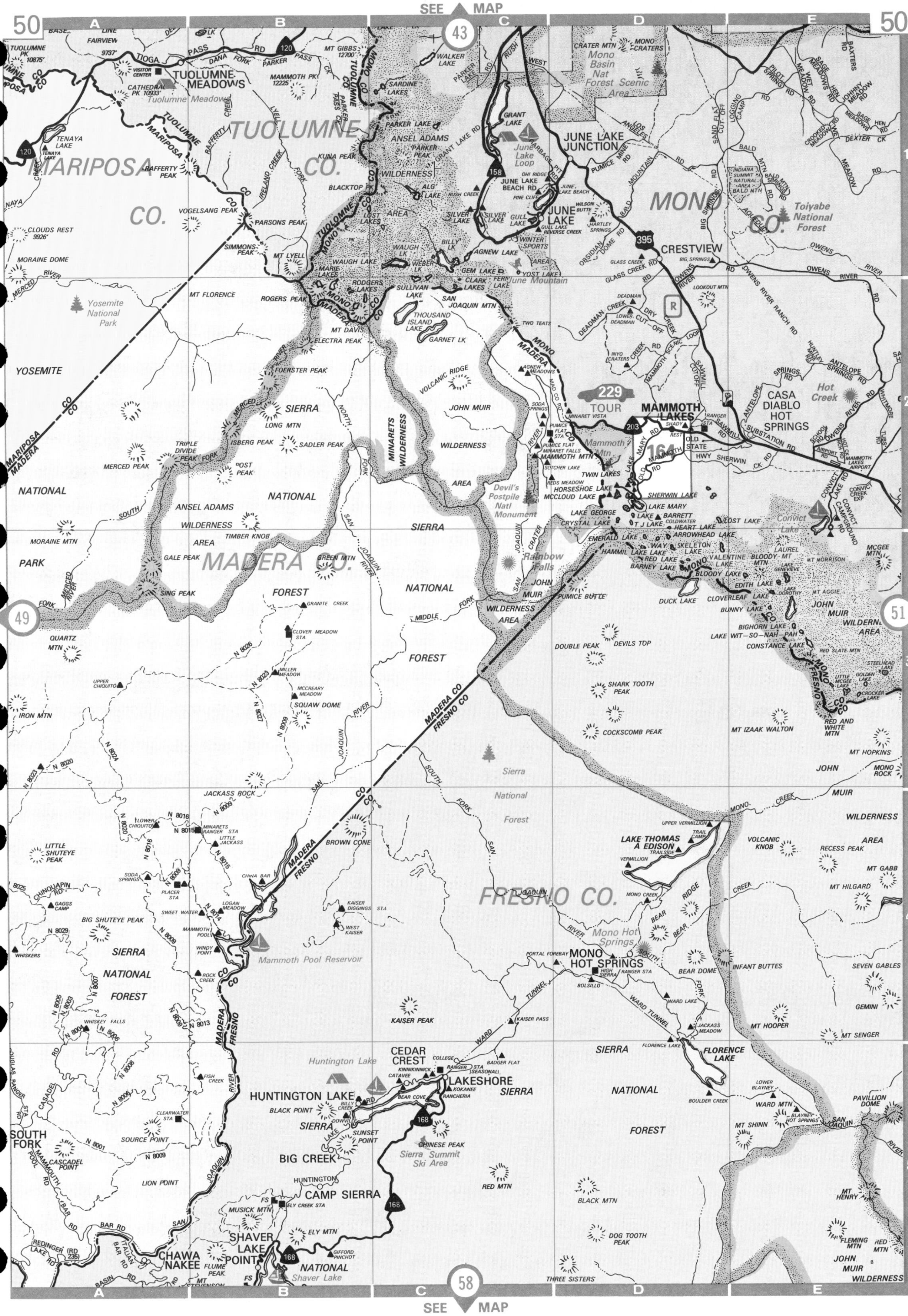
SEE MAP 43
SEE MAP 51
SEE MAP 58
49
A
B
C
D
E
1
2
3
4
5
TUOLUMNE PK 10875'
FAIRVIEW
TIOGA PASS RD
DANA FORK
PARKER PASS
MT GIBBS 12700'
MAMMOTH PK 12225'
VISITOR CENTER
TUOLUMNE MEADOWS
CATHEDRAL PK 10933'
Tuolumne Meadow
TUOLUMNE CO.
MONO CO
TUOLUMNE CO
WALKER LAKE
PARKER LAKE
SARDINE LAKES
CRATER MTN
MONO CRATERS
Mono Basin Nat Forest Scenic Area
GRANT LAKE
GRANT LAKE RD
JUNE LAKE JUNCTION
June Lake Loop
PUMICE MINE RD
LOS ANGELES AQUEDUCT
SAND FLAT
CUT OFF
LOGGING CAMP
PILOT SPRINGS RD
WET MEADOWS RD
SAGE HEN MEADOWS RD
BAXTERS RD
JOHNNY MEADOW RD
SAGE HEN
DEXTER CK
CROOKED MEADOW RD
BALD MTN RD
INDIANA SUMMIT RESEARCH NATURAL AREA
BALD MTN
MEADOW
TENAYA LAKE
MARIPOSA CO.
RAFFERTY PEAK
PARKER LAKE
ANSEL ADAMS
PARKER PEAK
KUNA PEAK
WILDERNESS
BLACKTOP PK
JUNE LAKE BEACH RD
OH! RIDGE
JUNE LAKE BEACH
PINE CLIFF
GULL LAKE
JUNE LAKE
SILVER LAKE
WILSON BUTTE
HARTLEY SPRINGS
GULL LAKE REVERSE CREEK
MONO CO.
Toiyabe National Forest
BIG SPRINGS RD
OWENS RIVER
OBSIDIAN DOME RD
BALD MOUNTAIN RD
CRESTVIEW
GLASS CREEK RD
BIG SPRINGS
VOGELSANG PEAK
PARSONS PEAK
CLOUDS REST 9926'
SIMMONS PEAK
MT LYELL
MORAINE DOME
MERCED RIVER
WAUGH LAKE
MARIE LAKES
RODGERS LAKES
AGNEW LAKE
GEM LAKE
CLARK LAKES
WINTER SPORTS AREA
YOST LAKE
June Mountain
Yosemite National Park
MT FLORENCE
ROGERS PEAK
SULLIVAN LAKE
SAN JOAQUIN MTN
THOUSAND ISLAND LAKE
GARNET LK
TWO TEATS
DEADMAN
DEADMAN CREEK
DRY CREEK
CUT-OFF
LOWER DEADMAN
LOOKOUT MTN
OWENS RIVER RANCH RD
MT DAVIS
ELECTRA PEAK
MONO MADERA CO
AGNEW MEADOWS
INYO CRATERS
MAMMOTH SCENIC LOOP
SAWMILL CUTOFF
HUNTLEY MINE
ANTELOPE SPRINGS RD
YOSEMITE
FOERSTER PEAK
VOLCANIC RIDGE
JOHN MUIR
WILDERNESS
MINARETS WILDERNESS
SODA SPRINGS
229 TOUR
MINARET VISTA
MAMMOTH LAKES
RANGER STA
SHADY REST
OLD STATE
SAWMILL
ANTELOPE
CASA DIABLO HOT SPRINGS
Hot Creek
SUBSTATION RD
SCHOOL RD
OWENS RIVER
WHITMORE
TUBBS
AIRPORT RD
MAMMOTH LAKES AIRPORT
HWY
SHERWIN CK RD
SIERRA
LONG MTN
SADLER PEAK
ISBERG PEAK
TRIPLE DIVIDE PEAK
MERCED PEAK
POST PEAK
NATIONAL
NATIONAL
AREA
Mammoth Mtn
PUMICE FLAT STA
MINARET FALLS
MAMMOTH MTN
SOTCHER LAKE
REDS MEADOW
Devil's Postpile Natl Monument
TWIN LAKES
HORSESHOE LAKE
MCCLOUD LAKE
SHERWIN LAKE
LAKE MARY
LAKE GEORGE
BARRETT
COLDWATER
T J LAKE
CRYSTAL LAKE
HEART LAKE
ARROWHEAD LAKE
LOST LAKE
Convict Lake
CONVICT LAKE RD
CONVICT CREEK CAMPGROUND
CONVICT CREEK EXP
ANSEL ADAMS WILDERNESS AREA
TIMBER KNOB
SOUTH
MORAINE MTN
PARK
GALE PEAK
MADERA CO.
GREEN MTN
SAN JOAQUIN RIVER
CRATER CREEK
Rainbow Falls
EMERALD LAKE
HAMMIL LAKE
WAY LAKE
SKELETON LAKE
VALENTINE LAKE
BLOODY MT
LAUREL MTN
MT MORRISON
MCGEE MTN
RED LAKE
BARNEY LAKE
BLOODY LAKE
EDITH LAKE
LAKE GENEVIEVE
LAKE DOROTHY
MT AGGIE
SING PEAK
FOREST
GRANITE CREEK
MERCED RIVER
FORK
NATIONAL
PUMICE BUTTE
DUCK LAKE
CLOVERLEAF LAKE
BUNNY LAKE
JOHN MUIR WILDERNESS AREA
CLOVER MEADOW STA
MIDDLE FORK
WILDERNESS AREA
QUARTZ MTN
BIGHORN LAKE
LAKE WIT-SO-NAH-PAH
CONSTANCE LAKE
DOUBLE PEAK
DEVILS TOP
RED SLATE MTN
N 8026
MILLER MEADOW
MCCREARY MEADOW
SQUAW DOME
UPPER CHIQUITO
FOREST
STEELHEAD LAKE
GOLDEN LAKE
LITTLE MCGEE LAKE
CROCKER LAKE
MADERA CO
FRESNO CO
SHARK TOOTH PEAK
IRON MTN
N 8023
N 8009
N 8024
N 8020
N 8022
RED AND WHITE MTN
COCKSCOMB PEAK
MT IZAAK WALTON
MT HOPKINS
Sierra National Forest
JOHN
MONO ROCK
SOUTH FORK
JACKASS ROCK
N 8016
LOWER CHIQUITO
N 8015
MINARETS RANGER STA
LITTLE JACKASS
BROWN CONE
SAN JOAQUIN
MONO CREEK
MUIR
WILDERNESS
AREA
UPPER VERMILLION
TRAIL CAMP
LAKE THOMAS A EDISON
VERMILLION
TRAILSIDE
VOLCANIC KNOB
RECESS PEAK
MT GABB
MT HILGARD
LITTLE SHUTEYE PEAK
SODA SPRINGS
PLACER STA
CHINQUAPIN
GAGGS CAMP
CHINA BAR
KAISER DIGGINGS STA
WEST KAISER
LOGAN MEADOW
SWEET WATER
FRESNO CO.
MONO CREEK
BEAR CREEK
BEAR RIDGE
BIG SHUTEYE PEAK
N 8029
MAMMOTH POOL
WINDY POINT
Mammoth Pool Reservoir
Mono Hot Springs
PORTAL FOREBAY
MONO HOT SPRINGS
HIGH SIERRA RANGER STA
BOLSILLO
INFANT BUTTES
BEAR DOME
SEVEN GABLES
WHISKERS
SIERRA
NATIONAL
FOREST
ROCK CREEK
WARD TUNNEL
WARD LAKE
GEMINI
WHISKEY FALLS
N 8013
KAISER PEAK
KAISER PASS
JACKASS MEADOW
MT HOOPER
MT SENGER
CEDAR CREST
COLLEGE
BADGER FLAT
FLORENCE LAKE
SIERRA
Huntington Lake
KINNIKINNICK
CATAVEE
RANGER STA (SEASONAL)
LAKESHORE
KOKANEE
RANCHERIA
FISH CREEK
HUNTINGTON LAKE
BEAR COVE
BILLY CREEK
BLACK POINT
DOWVILLE
SIERRA
NATIONAL
FOREST
LOWER BLAYNEY
WARD MTN
BLAYNEY HOT SPRINGS
PAVILLION DOME
CLEARWATER STA
SOUTH FORK
SOURCE POINT
N 8001
SUNSET POINT
CHINESE PEAK
Sierra Summit Ski Area
BIG CREEK
MT SHINN
SAN JOAQUIN RIVER
CASCADEL POINT
N 8009
LION POINT
HUNTINGTON
CAMP SIERRA
RED MTN
BLACK MTN
MT HENRY
MUSICK MTN
ELY CREEK STA
ELY MTN
DOG TOOTH PEAK
FLEMING MTN
RED MTN
BAR RD
REDINGER LAKE RD (RD 235)
CHAWANAKEE
SHAVER LAKE POINT
GIFFORD PINCHOT
NATIONAL
Shaver Lake
FLUME PEAK
MT STEVENSON
THREE SISTERS
JOHN MUIR WILDERNESS
HIGHWAYS

SEE MAP 44

SEE MAP 50

SEE MAP 52

SEE MAP 59

HIGHWAYS

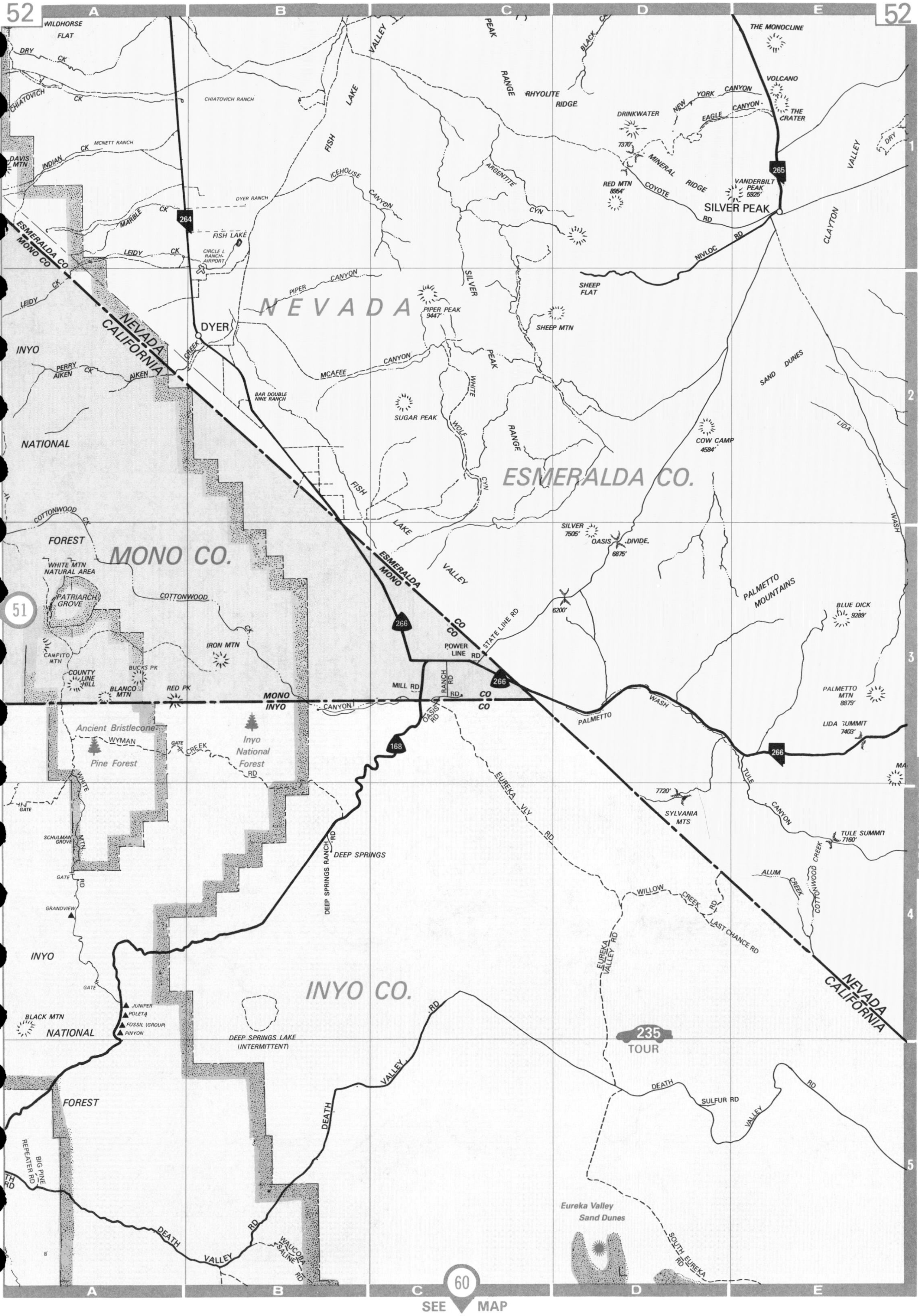

HIGHWAYS

SEE 60 MAP

SEE MAP 45
For Detail Page Locations
SEE PAGE N
SANTA CRUZ CO.
225 TOUR
Redwood Estates
Boulder Creek
Brookdale
Ben Lomond
Mt Hermon
Felton
Hallcrest Vineyards
Bonny Doon Vineyard
Davenport
SCOTTS
SANTA CRUZ
Wilder Ranch State Park
169
SEE MAP 167
17 MILE DRIVE
POINT JOE
MONTEREY PENINSULA COUNTRY CLUB
PRESIDIO OF MONTEREY
54
MONTEREY
231 TOUR
MONTEREY CO.
FOREST LAKE
BIRD ROCK
SEAL ROCK
FAN SHELL BEACH
CYPRESS POINT
Spyglass Hill Golf Club
Pebble Beach
Cypress Point Country Club
POPPY HILLS GOLF COURSE
PENINSULA COMMUNITY HOSP
SUNSET POINT
LONE CYPRESS TREE
MIDWAY POINT
The Lodge At Pebble Beach
PEBBLE BEACH
STILLWATER COVE
PESCADERO ROCKS
ARROWHEAD POINT
Pebble Beach Golf Links
PESCADERO POINT
PACIFIC
OCEAN
CARMEL BAY
CARMEL BY THE SEA
SEE MAP 168
HIGHWAYS

SEE MAP 46

SEE MAP 53

SEE MAP 55

HIGHWAYS

SEE MAP 64

SEE MAP 47

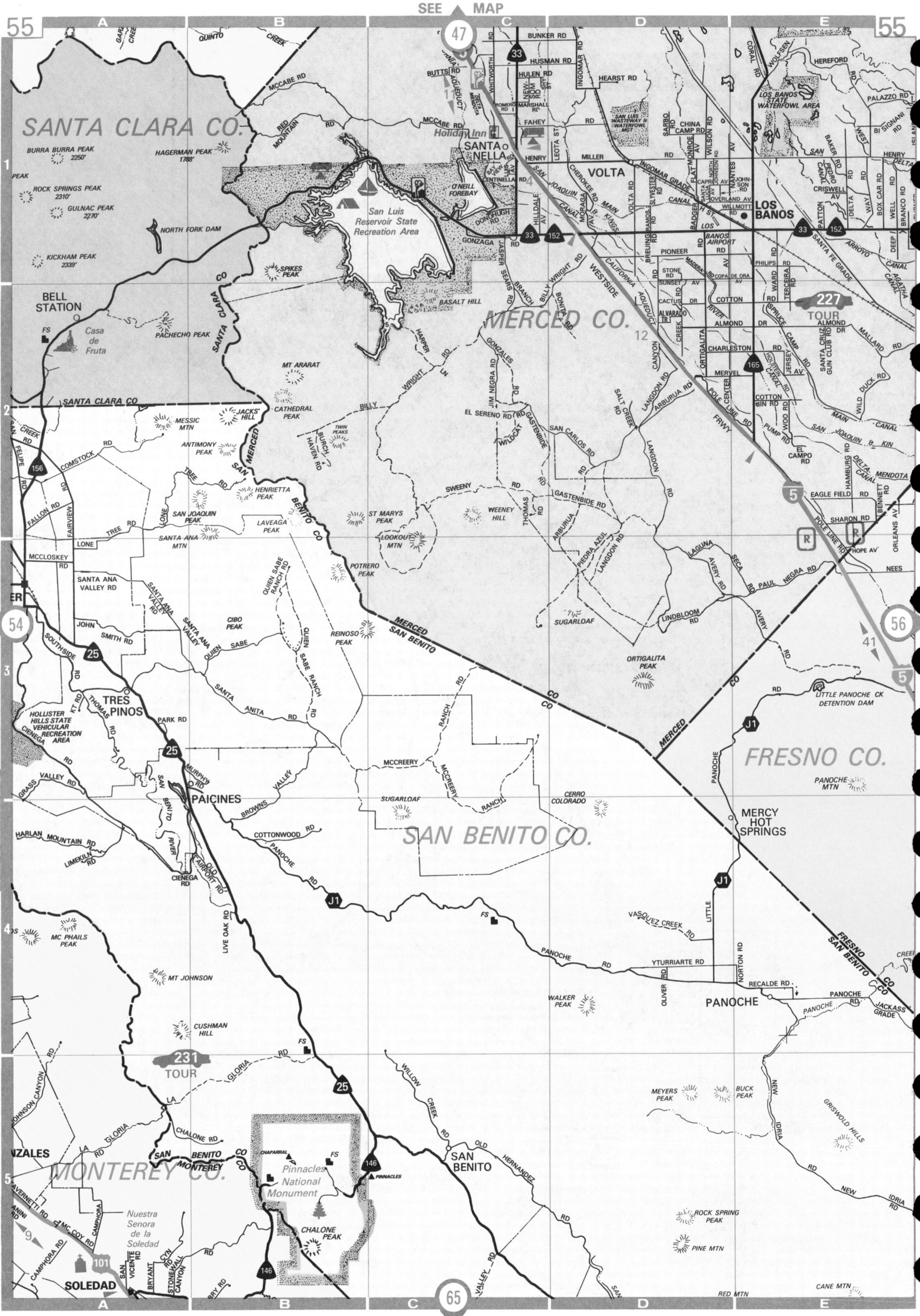

SEE MAP 54

SEE MAP 56

SEE MAP 65

HIGHWAYS

SEE MAP 48

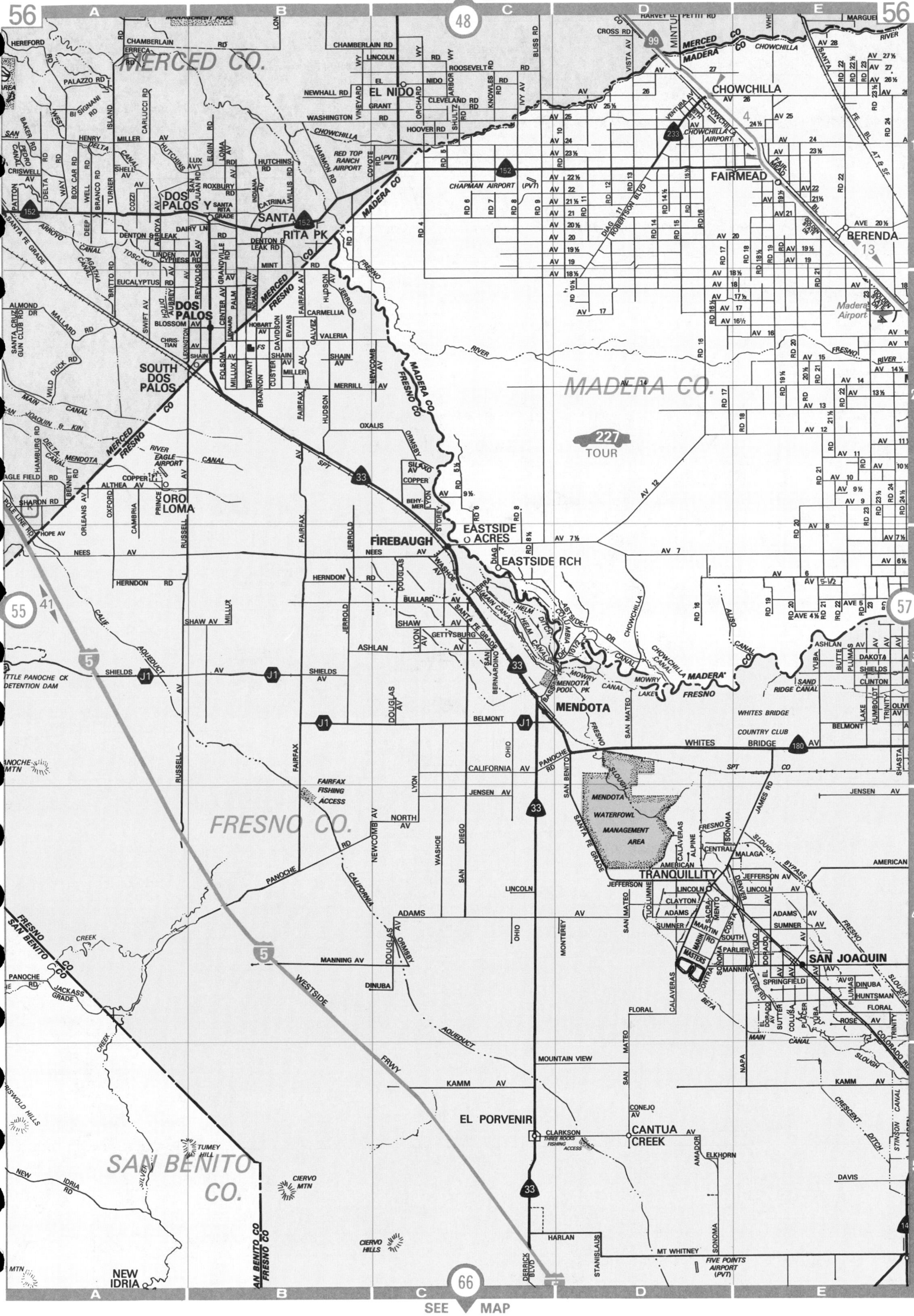

SEE MAP 66

SEE MAP 49

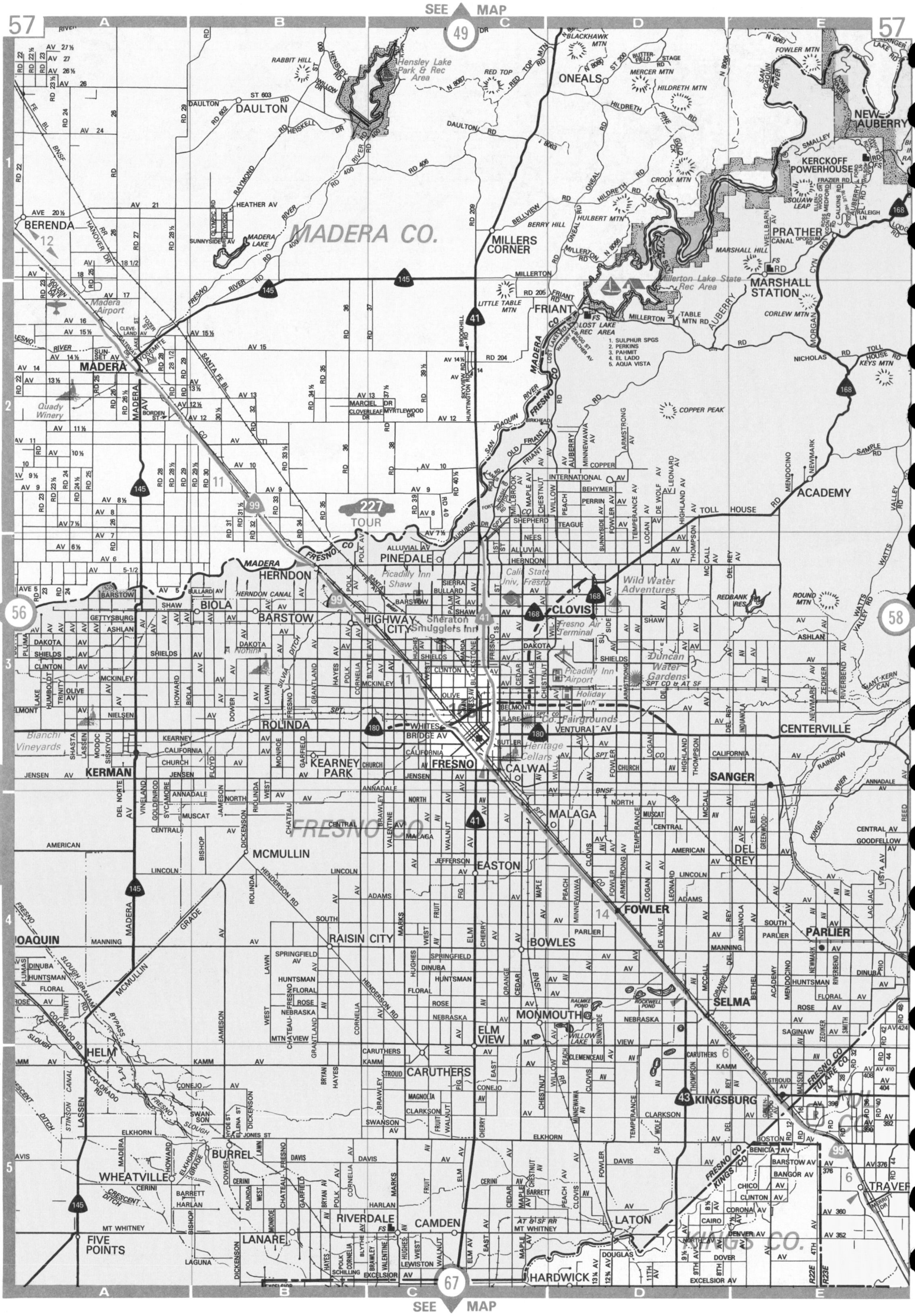

SEE MAP 67

HIGHWAYS

SEE MAP 50
SEE MAP 68
SEE MAP 57
SEE MAP 59
HIGHWAYS
FRESNO CO.
TULARE CO.
FRESNO CO
TULARE CO
Sierra National Forest
Sequoia National Forest
SIERRA NATIONAL FOREST
SEQUOIA NATIONAL FOREST
JOHN MUIR WILDERNESS AREA
KINGS CYN NATIONAL PARK
General Grant Grove
Montecito-Sequoia Cross-Country
229 TOUR
227 TOUR
Shaver Lake
Pine Flat Reservoir Rec Area
Lake Kaweah
SHAVER LAKE POINT
CHAWA NAKEE
NEW AUBERRY
SHAVER LAKE
ALDER SPRINGS
MDW LAKES
PINE RIDGE
MTN REST
TOLL HOUSE
HUMPHREYS STATION
DINKEY CREEK
BALCH CAMP
WONDER VALLEY
PRINCETON
WELDON
GRAVESBORO
SQUAW VALLEY
MINKLER
DUNLAP
MIRAMONTE
PINE HURST
CEDAR BROOK
WILSONIA
HUME
ETHEDA SPRINGS
NAVELENCIA
WAHTOKE PK
ORANGE COVE
REEDLEY
DINUBA
SULTANA
OROSI
EAST OROSI
DELFT COLONY
CUTLER
YETTEM
MONSON
LONDON
TRAVER
ELDERWOOD
WOODLAKE
NARANJO
LOMITAS
BADGER
KAWEAH
HAMMOND
THREE RIVERS
SEQUOIA AIRPORT
WOODLAKE AIRPORT
1 POND LN
2 LITTLEFIELD RD
3 GRANITE RD
1 CHECKERBLOOM LN
2 PITCHWOOD LN
3 RIDGE RD
4 MILKHOUSE LN
5 RED LEAF LN
6 HIGHCOUNTRY LN
1. QUARTZ LN
2. SANDPIPER LN
3. TOPAZ LN
4. WATERCRESS LN
NOTE: ALL NUMBERED STREETS ARE PRIVATE
1 BARBERRY
2 WAXBERRY
3 HAWTHORNE
4 CARDINAL
5 MIMOSA
6 MALLOW
7 SPEARMINT
8 BAY RD
9 SUMAC
10 BOXELDER
11 PRIMROSE
12 SWEETBRIAR
13 DEERBROOK
14 BAYWOOD
15 ARTESIA
16 FEATHER
17 ARGENBRIGHT
18 SQUAW VALLEY
19 CLEAR VIEW
20 MISTLETOE LN
21 COLUMBINE
23 PEBBLE
24 SCOUT
25 RIPPLE
26 SHADYBROOK
27 LOGAN BERRY
28 SHOREWOOD
29 WILLOWOOD
30 RUSTIC
32 PEPPERWOOD
33 KNOLLGLEN
34 LONG VIEW
35 PARTRIDGE
36 BADGER
37 IRIS
38 CLOVER
39 CORNFLOWER
40 COLUMBINE
41 TASSLE
42 BOBCAT
43 BUTTERFLY
44 CREEKSIDE
45 OAKLEAF
46 DIABLO
47 THUNDERHILL
48 PANORAMA
49 SASSAFRAS
50 WISTERIA
51 HIDDEN
52 BUTTERNUT
53 REDWING
54 DANDELION
55 HIGHOAKS
56 BLUEBELL
57 ROSEMARY
58 BEAR CLOVER
59 BRAMBLE
60 SUNDEW
61 CHUCKWAGON
62 BALDPATE
63 MOUND
64 DAFFODILL
65 LAVENDER
66 PINTAIL
67 GREENHILL
68 GERANIUM
69 MARIGOLD
70 SESAME
71 THISTLE
72 RED BUD
73 HUMMINGBIRD
74 MISTLETOE
75 COSTA LN
76 SIMON LN
77 PECK LN
78 LULLABY LN
79 BLOSSOM LN
80 WILDMINT LN
81 ROUNDTREE LN
82 TOTEM LN
83 WINESAP LN
84 ASTER LN
85 CROW LN
86 HONEYSUCKLE LN
87 BRYSON RD

59
SEE MAP 51

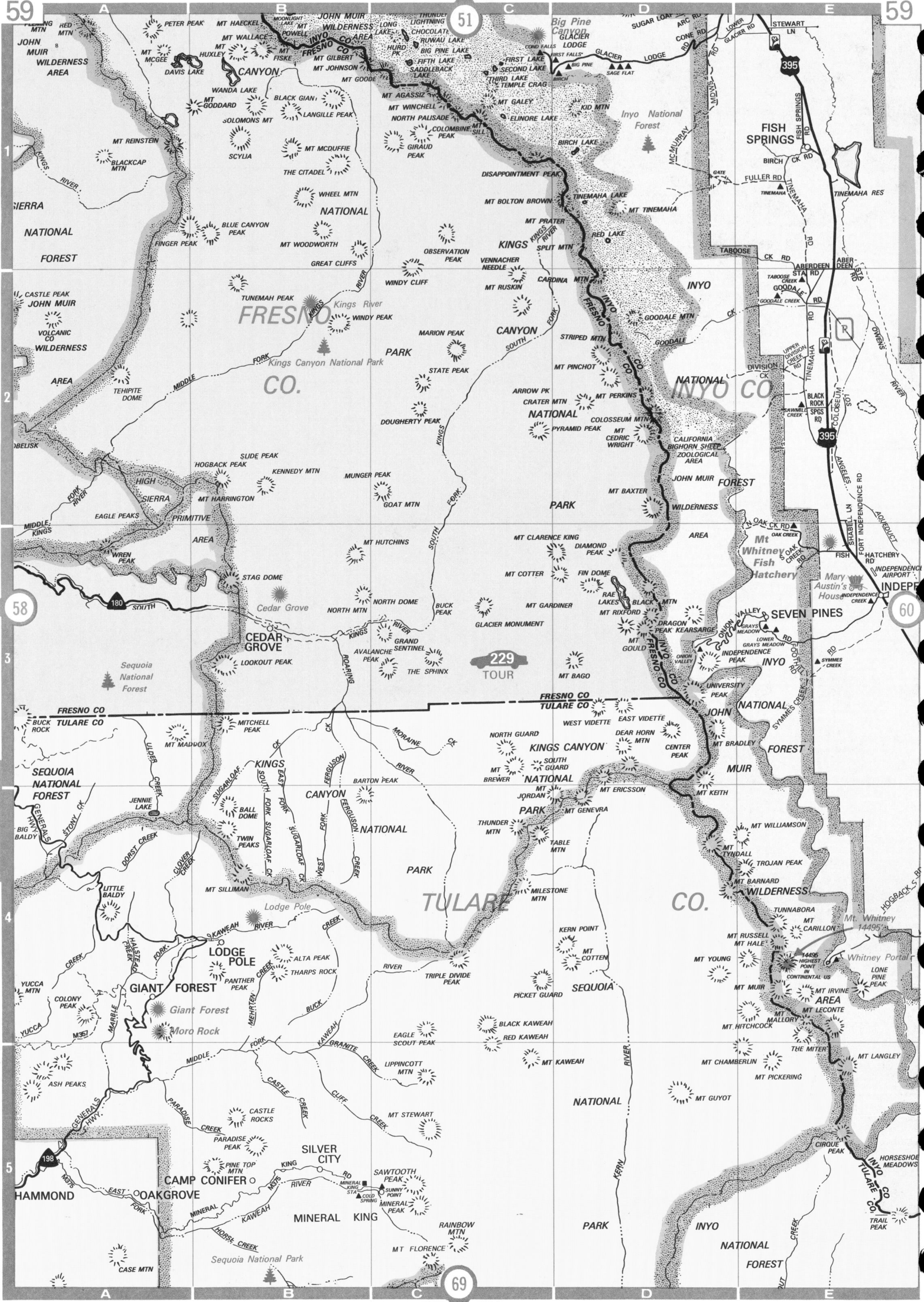

SEE MAP 58
60
HIGHWAYS

SEE MAP 69

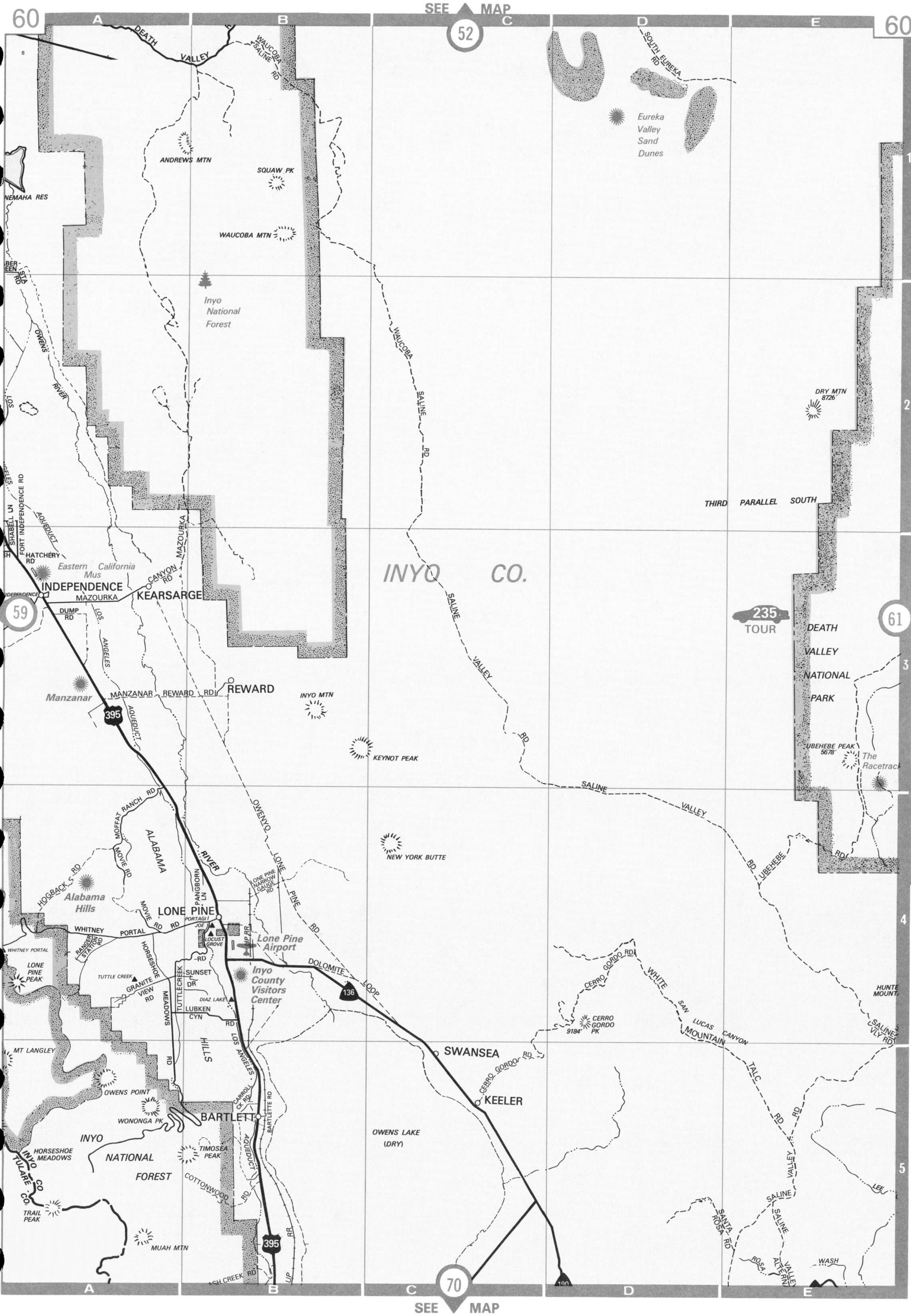
SEE MAP 52
SEE MAP 70
SEE MAP 61
59
A
B
C
D
E
1
2
3
4
5
DEATH VALLEY RD
WAUCOBA SALINE RD
SOUTH EUREKA RD
Eureka Valley Sand Dunes
ANDREWS MTN
SQUAW PK
NEMAHA RES
WAUCOBA MTN
Inyo National Forest
OWENS RIVER
LOS ANGELES AQUEDUCT
WAUCOBA SALINE RD
DRY MTN 8726'
THIRD PARALLEL SOUTH
FORT INDEPENDENCE RD
SHABELL LN
HATCHERY RD
Eastern California Mus
INDEPENDENCE
MAZOURKA CANYON RD
KEARSARGE
MAZOURKA
DUMP RD
INYO CO.
235 TOUR
DEATH VALLEY NATIONAL PARK
SALINE VALLEY RD
Manzanar
MANZANAR REWARD RD
REWARD
INYO MTN
395
KEYNOT PEAK
UBEHEBE PEAK 5678'
The Racetrack
MOFFAT RANCH RD
ALABAMA
OWENS RIVER
OWENYO LONE PINE RD
SALINE VALLEY RD
UBEHEBE RD
NEW YORK BUTTE
HOGBACK RD
MOVIE RD
Alabama Hills
PANGBORN LN
LONE PINE NARROW GAUGE RD
LONE PINE
WHITNEY PORTAL RD
PORTAGI JOE
LOCUST GROVE
Lone Pine Airport
WHITNEY PORTAL
RANGER STATION RD
HORSESHOE
LONE PINE PEAK
TUTTLE CREEK
SUNSET DR
GRANITE VIEW RD
TUTTLE CREEK
MEADOWS
Inyo County Visitors Center
DOLOMITE LOOP
136
DIAZ LAKE
LUBKEN CYN RD
CERRO GORDO RD
WHITE SAN LUCAS CANYON
MOUNTAIN
CERRO GORDO PK
9184'
HUNTER MOUNTAIN
SALINE VLY RD
MT LANGLEY
HILLS
SWANSEA
CERRO GORDO RD
TALC RD
OWENS POINT
KEELER
CARROLL CK RD
BARTLETT
BARTLETT RD
WONONGA PK
OWENS LAKE (DRY)
INYO NATIONAL FOREST
HORSESHOE MEADOWS
TIMOSEA PEAK
AQUEDUCT
INYO CO
TULARE CO.
COTTONWOOD RD
VALLEY RD
LEE
SALINE
SANTA ROSA RD
SALINE VALLEY ALTERNATE
TRAIL PEAK
MUAH MTN
395
ASH CREEK RD
UP RR
190
ROSA
WASH
HIGHWAYS

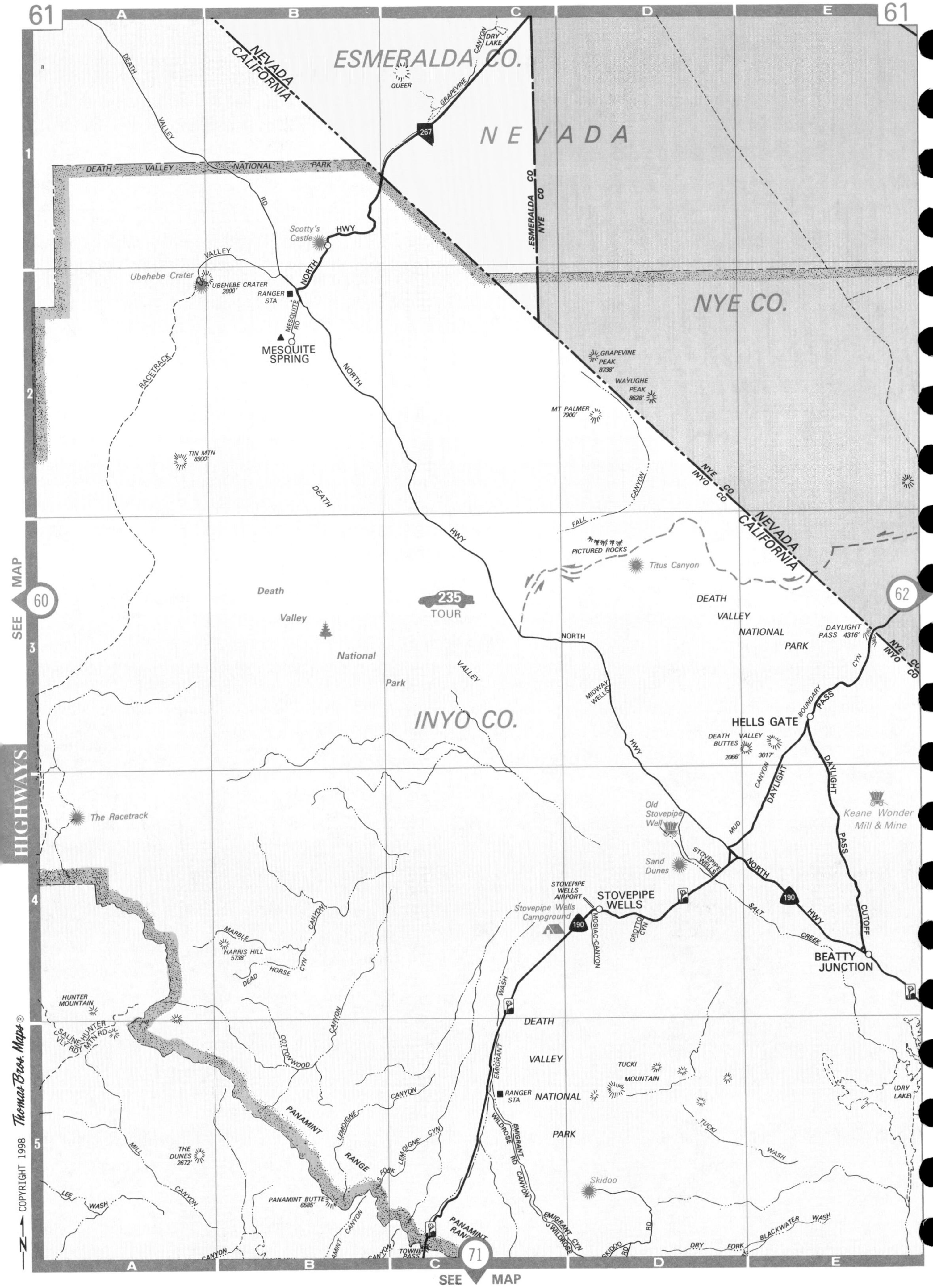
ESMERALDA CO.
NEVADA
CALIFORNIA
DRY LAKE
CANYON
QUEER
GRAPEVINE
267
N E V A D A
DEATH VALLEY RD
DEATH VALLEY NATIONAL PARK
ESMERALDA CO
NYE CO
Scotty's Castle
NORTH HWY
VALLEY
Ubehebe Crater
UBEHEBE CRATER 2800'
RANGER STA
MESQUITE RD
MESQUITE SPRING
NYE CO.
GRAPEVINE PEAK 8738'
WAYUGHE PEAK 8628'
MT PALMER 7900'
RACETRACK
TIN MTN 8900'
DEATH
NORTH
NYE CO
INYO CO
NEVADA
CALIFORNIA
FALL CANYON
PICTURED ROCKS
Titus Canyon
235 TOUR
Death Valley National Park
HWY
DEATH VALLEY NATIONAL PARK
DAYLIGHT PASS 4316'
CYN
NYE CO
INYO CO
NORTH
MIDWAY WELLS
VALLEY
INYO CO.
BOUNDARY
PASS
HELLS GATE
DEATH BUTTES 2066'
VALLEY 3017'
HWY
CANYON
DAYLIGHT
DAYLIGHT
The Racetrack
Old Stovepipe Well
MUD
Keane Wonder Mill & Mine
Sand Dunes
STOVEPIPE WELLS
NORTH
190
HWY
PASS
STOVEPIPE WELLS AIRPORT
STOVEPIPE WELLS
Stovepipe Wells Campground
190
MOSIAC CANYON
GROTTO CYN
SALT CREEK
CUTOFF
BEATTY JUNCTION
CANYON
MARBLE
HARRIS HILL 5738'
DEAD HORSE CYN
HUNTER MOUNTAIN
SALINE VLY RD
HUNTER MTN RD
WASH
DEATH VALLEY NATIONAL PARK
COTTONWOOD
CANYON
EMIGRANT
RANGER STA
TUCKI MOUNTAIN
(DRY LAKE)
PANAMINT RANGE
LEMOIGNE CANYON
LEMOIGNE CYN
CANYON
WILDROSE RD
EMIGRANT CANYON
TUCKI WASH
THE DUNES 2672'
MILL CANYON
S. FORK
Skidoo
LEE WASH
PANAMINT BUTTE 6585'
EMIGRANT CYN
WILDROSE
PANAMINT RANGE
SKIDOO RD
BLACKWATER WASH
DRY FORK
CANYON
TOWNE PASS
A B C D E
1 2 3 4 5
SEE MAP 60
SEE MAP 62
HIGHWAYS
Thomas Bros. Maps®
COPYRIGHT 1998
N

SEE 71 MAP

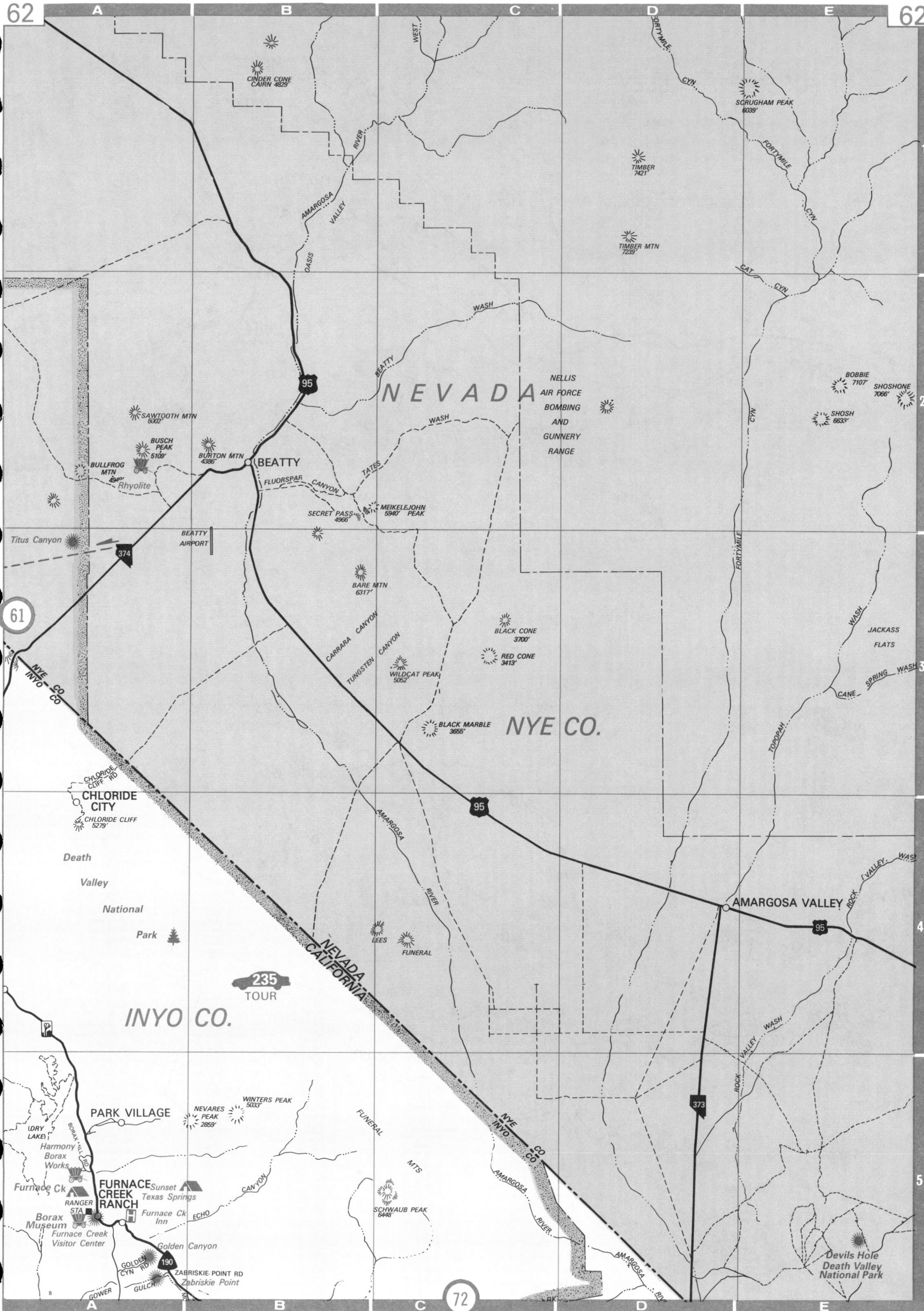

HIGHWAYS

SEE 72 MAP
61

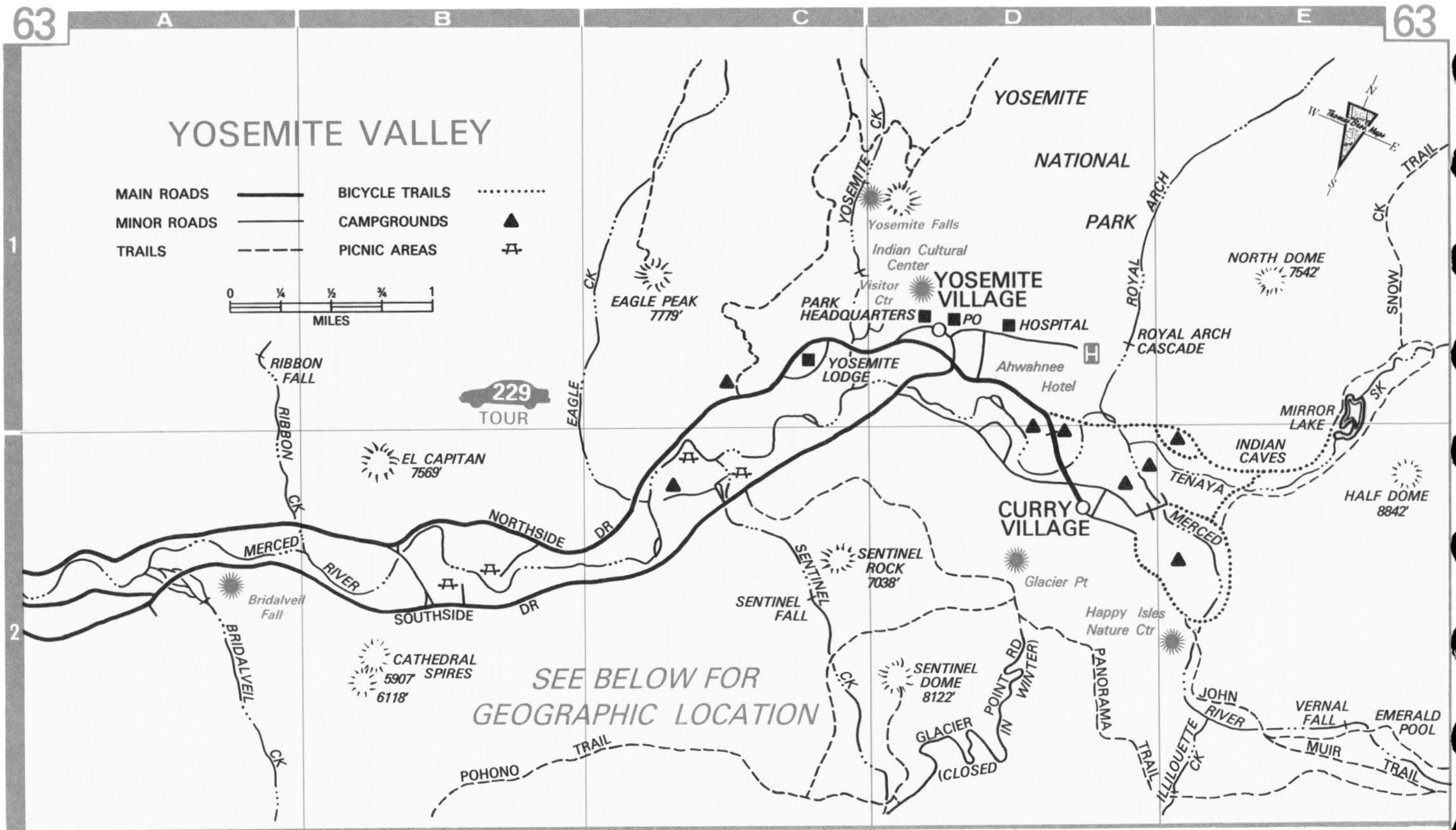

YOSEMITE NATIONAL PARK

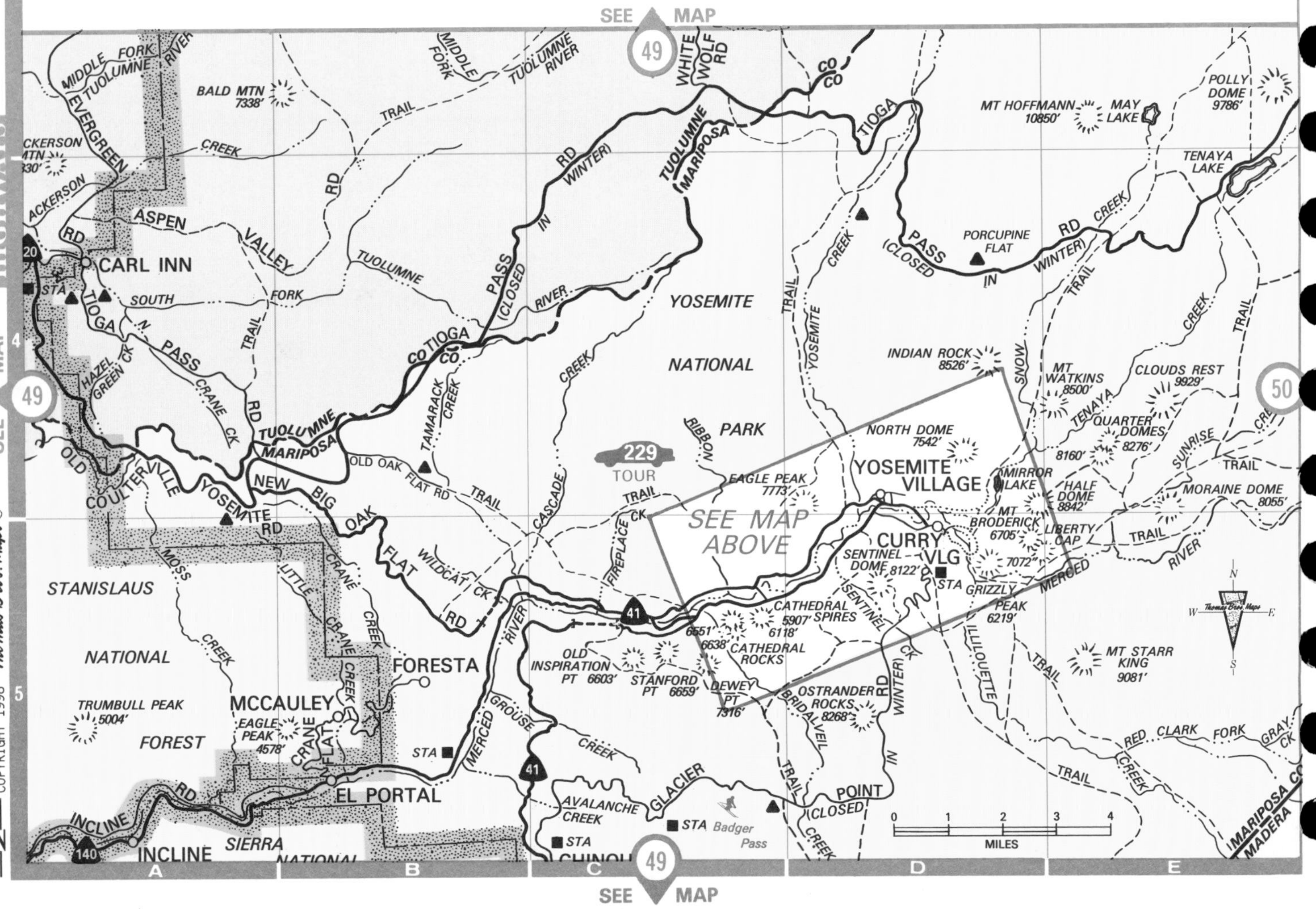

SEE MAP 54

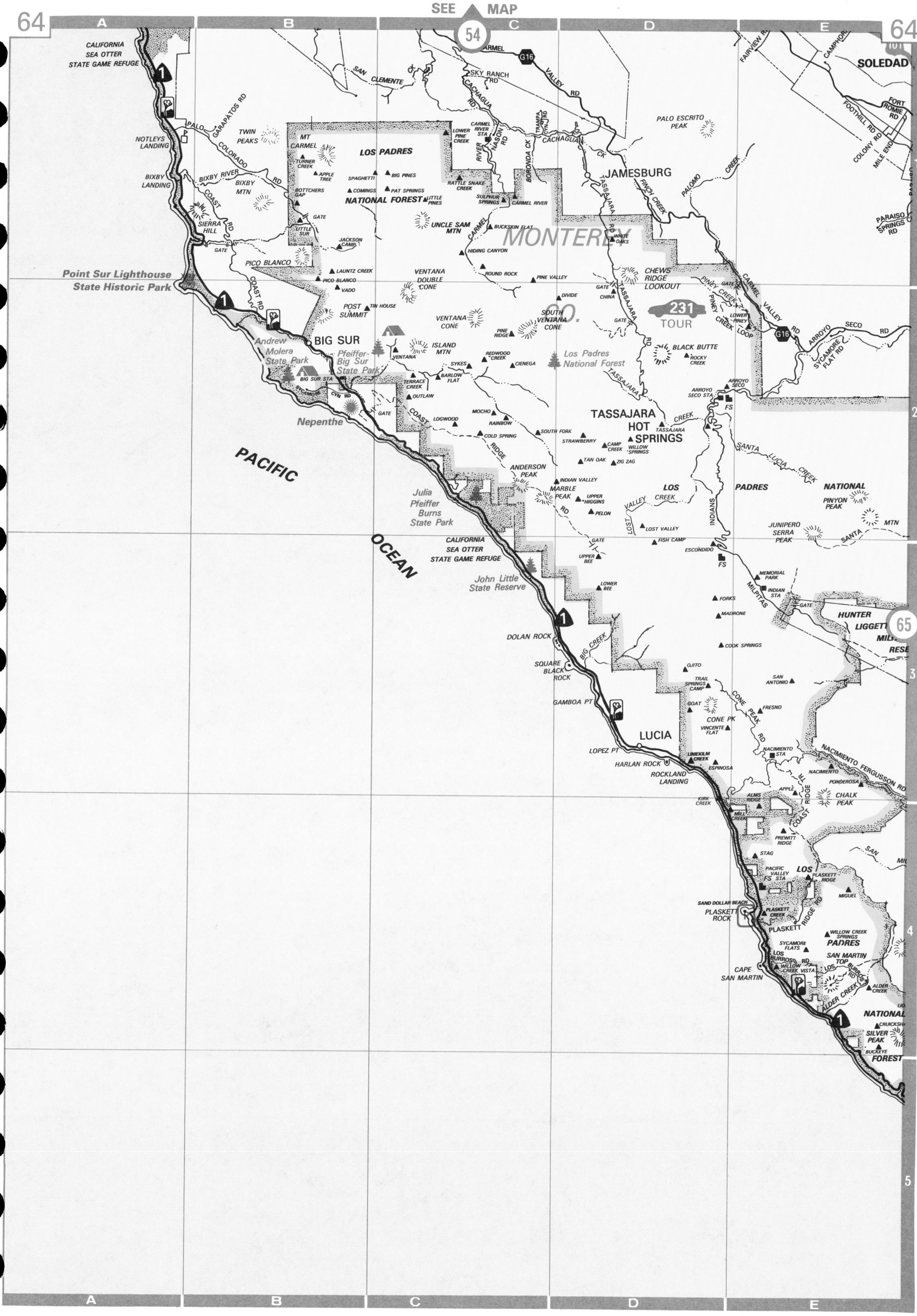

SEE MAP 65

HIGHWAYS

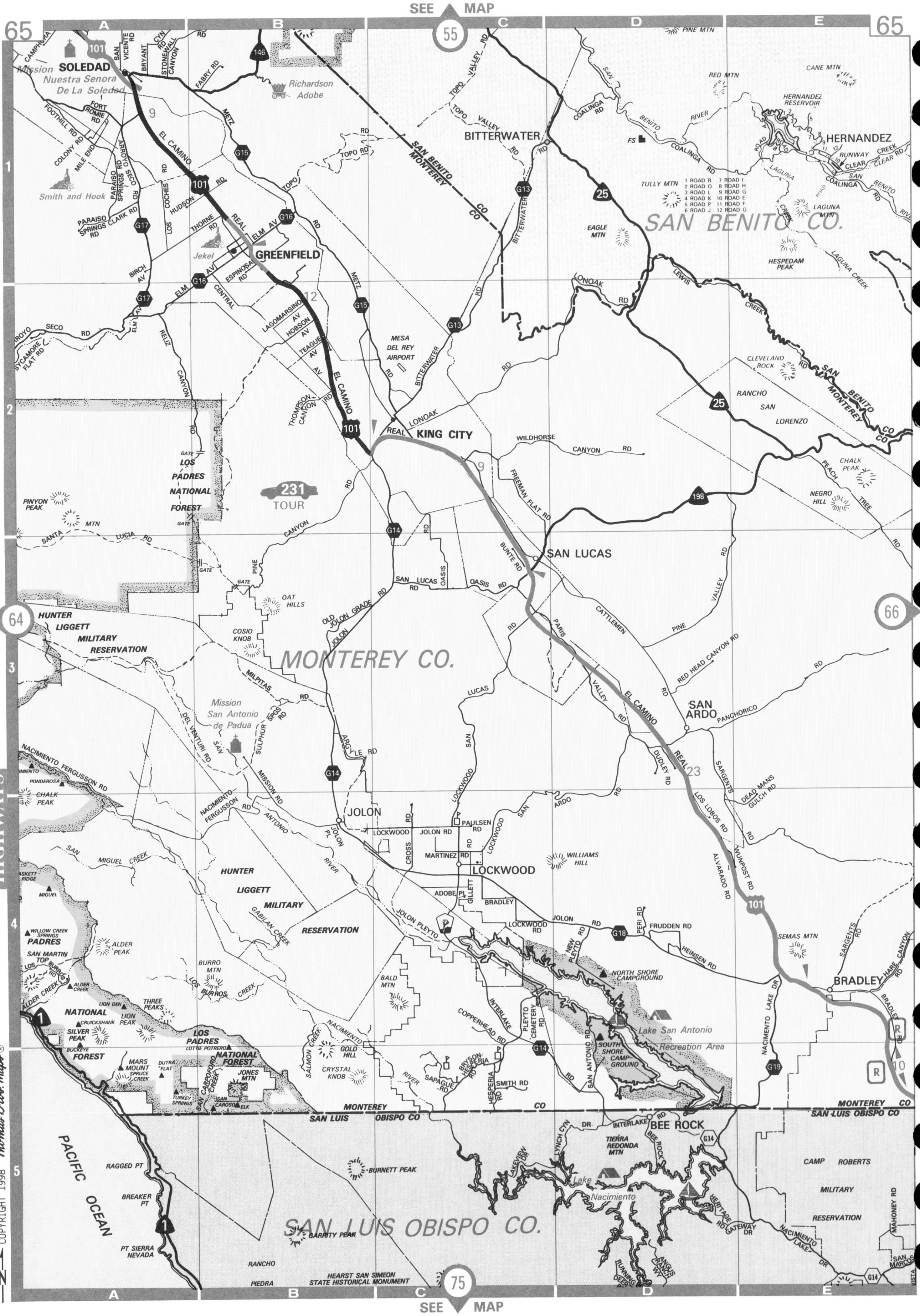
SEE MAP 55
SEE MAP 64
SEE MAP 66
SEE MAP 75
HIGHWAYS
SOLEDAD
Mission Nuestra Senora De La Soledad
Richardson Adobe
Smith and Hook
GREENFIELD
Jekel
BITTERWATER
SAN BENITO MONTEREY CO CO
HERNANDEZ
HERNANDEZ RESERVOIR
CANE MTN
RED MTN
TULLY MTN
1 ROAD R 7 ROAD I
2 ROAD Q 8 ROAD H
3 ROAD L 9 ROAD G
4 ROAD K 10 ROAD E
5 ROAD P 11 ROAD F
6 ROAD J 12 ROAD G
LAGUNA MTN
EAGLE MTN
HESPEDAM PEAK
SAN BENITO CO.
CLEVELAND ROCK
RANCHO SAN LORENZO
CHALK PEAK
NEGRO HILL
MESA DEL REY AIRPORT
KING CITY
231 TOUR
LOS PADRES NATIONAL FOREST
PINYON PEAK
SANTA LUCIA RD
SAN LUCAS
OAT HILLS
COSIO KNOB
HUNTER LIGGETT MILITARY RESERVATION
MONTEREY CO.
Mission San Antonio de Padua
SAN ARDO
JOLON
LOCKWOOD
WILLIAMS HILL
PONDEROSA
CHALK PEAK
ALDER PEAK
BURRO MTN
THREE PEAKS
LION PEAK
SILVER PEAK
BALD MTN
GOLD HILL
CRYSTAL KNOB
JONES MTN
NORTH SHORE CAMPGROUND
SOUTH SHORE CAMPGROUND
Lake San Antonio Recreation Area
SEMAS MTN
BRADLEY
MONTEREY CO
SAN LUIS OBISPO CO
BEE ROCK
TIERRA REDONDA MTN
Lake Nacimiento
CAMP ROBERTS MILITARY RESERVATION
PACIFIC OCEAN
RAGGED PT
BREAKER PT
PT SIERRA NEVADA
BURNETT PEAK
GARRITY PEAK
RANCHO PIEDRA
HEARST SAN SIMEON STATE HISTORICAL MONUMENT
SAN LUIS OBISPO CO.
SAN MARCOS

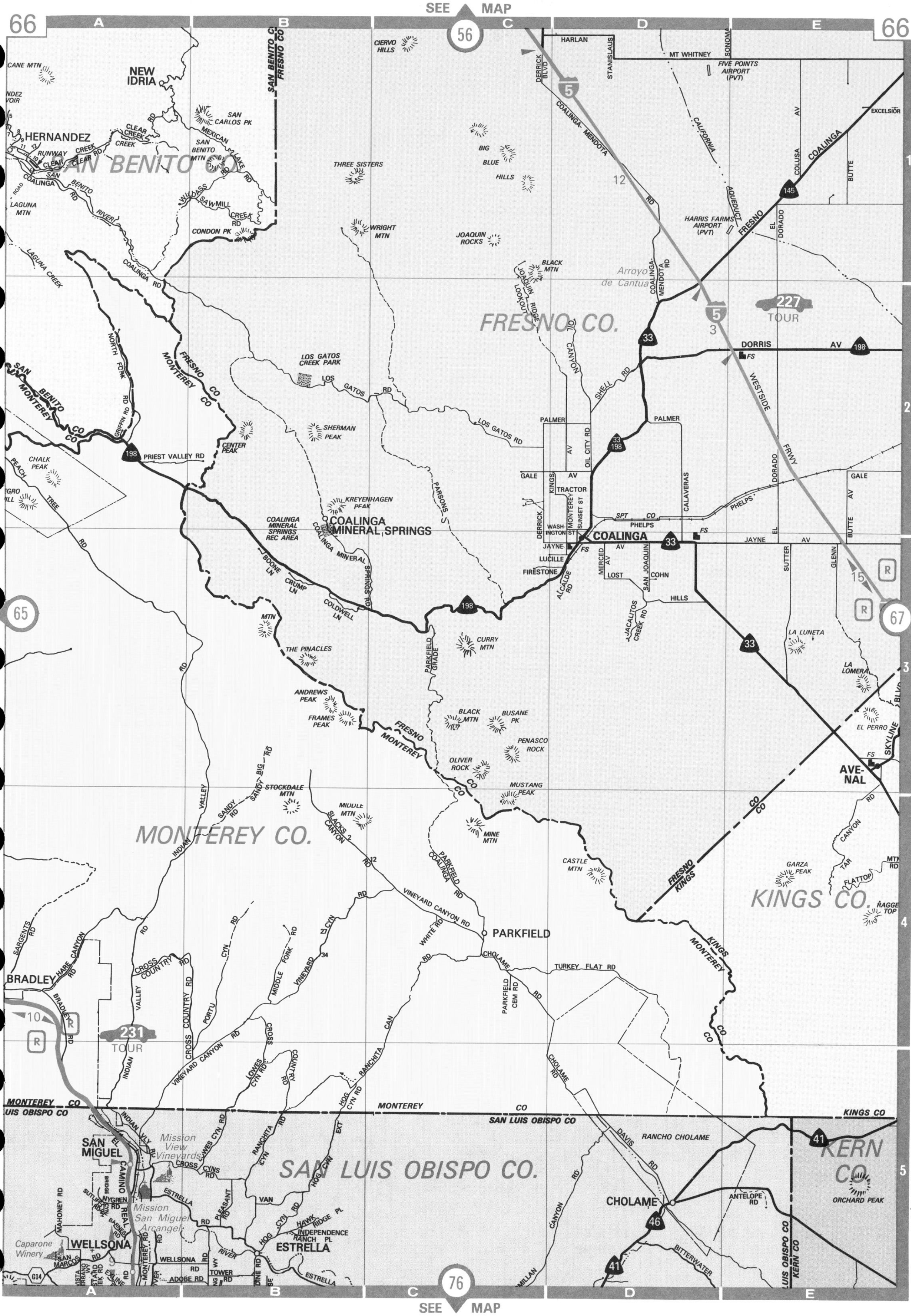

SEE MAP 56
SEE MAP 76
SEE MAP 65
SEE MAP 67
A
B
C
D
E
1
2
3
4
5
HIGHWAYS
NEW IDRIA
HERNANDEZ
CANE MTN
SAN CARLOS PK
SAN BENITO CO.
SAN BENITO CO
FRESNO CO
LAGUNA MTN
CONDON PK
CIERVO HILLS
HARLAN
MT WHITNEY
FIVE POINTS AIRPORT (PVT)
STANISLAUS
SONOMA
DERRICK BLVD
COALINGA- MENDOTA
CALIFORNIA
AQUEDUCT
EXCELSIOR
COALINGA
COLUSA
BUTTE
FRESNO
EL DORADO
HARRIS FARMS AIRPORT (PVT)
THREE SISTERS
BIG BLUE HILLS
WRIGHT MTN
JOAQUIN ROCKS
BLACK MTN
JOAQUIN RIDGE LOOKOUT
Arroyo de Cantua
FRESNO CO.
227 TOUR
DORRIS AV
WESTSIDE FRWY
LOS GATOS CREEK PARK
LOS GATOS RD
SHERMAN PEAK
CENTER PEAK
PRIEST VALLEY RD
CHALK PEAK
PEACH TREE RD
NORTH FORK
GRIFFIN RD
FRESNO MONTEREY CO
PALMER
OIL CITY RD
OIL CANYON
SHELL RD
PARSONS
GALE
KINGS AV
TRACTOR
MONTEREY
SUNSET ST
WASHINGTON ST
DERRICK
KREYENHAGEN PEAK
COALINGA MINERAL SPRINGS REC AREA
COALINGA MINERAL SPRINGS
COALINGA MINERAL SPRINGS RD
SPT CO
PHELPS
COALINGA
JAYNE AV
LUCILLE
FIRESTONE
ALCALDE RD
MERCED AV
LOST
SAN JOAQUIN
COHN
HILLS
CALAVERAS
SUTTER
GLENN
BOONE LN
CRUMP LN
COLDWELL LN
JACALITOS CREEK RD
LA LUNETA
LA LOMERA
EL PERRO
SKYLINE BLVD
AVENAL
CURRY MTN
PARKFIELD GRADE
THE PINACLES
ANDREWS PEAK
FRAMES PEAK
BLACK MTN
BUSANE PK
PENASCO ROCK
OLIVER ROCK
MUSTANG PEAK
STOCKDALE MTN
MIDDLE MTN
MINE MTN
SLACKS CANYON
SANDY
BIG
INDIAN VALLEY
MONTEREY CO.
CASTLE MTN
FRESNO KINGS CO CO
GARZA PEAK
TAR CANYON RD
FLATTOP
KINGS CO.
PARKFIELD COALINGA RD
VINEYARD CANYON RD
WHITE RD
PARKFIELD
CHOLAME RD
TURKEY FLAT RD
PARKFIELD CEM RD
KINGS MONTEREY CO
SARGENTS RD
BRADLEY
HARE CANYON RD
CROSS COUNTRY RD
MIDDLE FORK
VINEYARD
PORTU
231 TOUR
LOWES CYN RD
RANCHITA CAN
COUNTRY
MONTEREY CO
SAN LUIS OBISPO CO
KINGS CO
RANCHO CHOLAME
DAVIS RD
SAN MIGUEL
Mission View Vineyards
Mission San Miguel Arcangel
ESTRELLA
CROSS CYNS
VAN
HAWK RIDGE PL
INDEPENDENCE RANCH PL
SAN LUIS OBISPO CO.
CANYON
CHOLAME
ANTELOPE RD
BITTERWATER
KERN CO.
ORCHARD PEAK
LUIS OBISPO CO KERN CO
Caparone Winery
WELLSONA
WELLSONA RD
ADOBE RD
TOWER
MILLAN

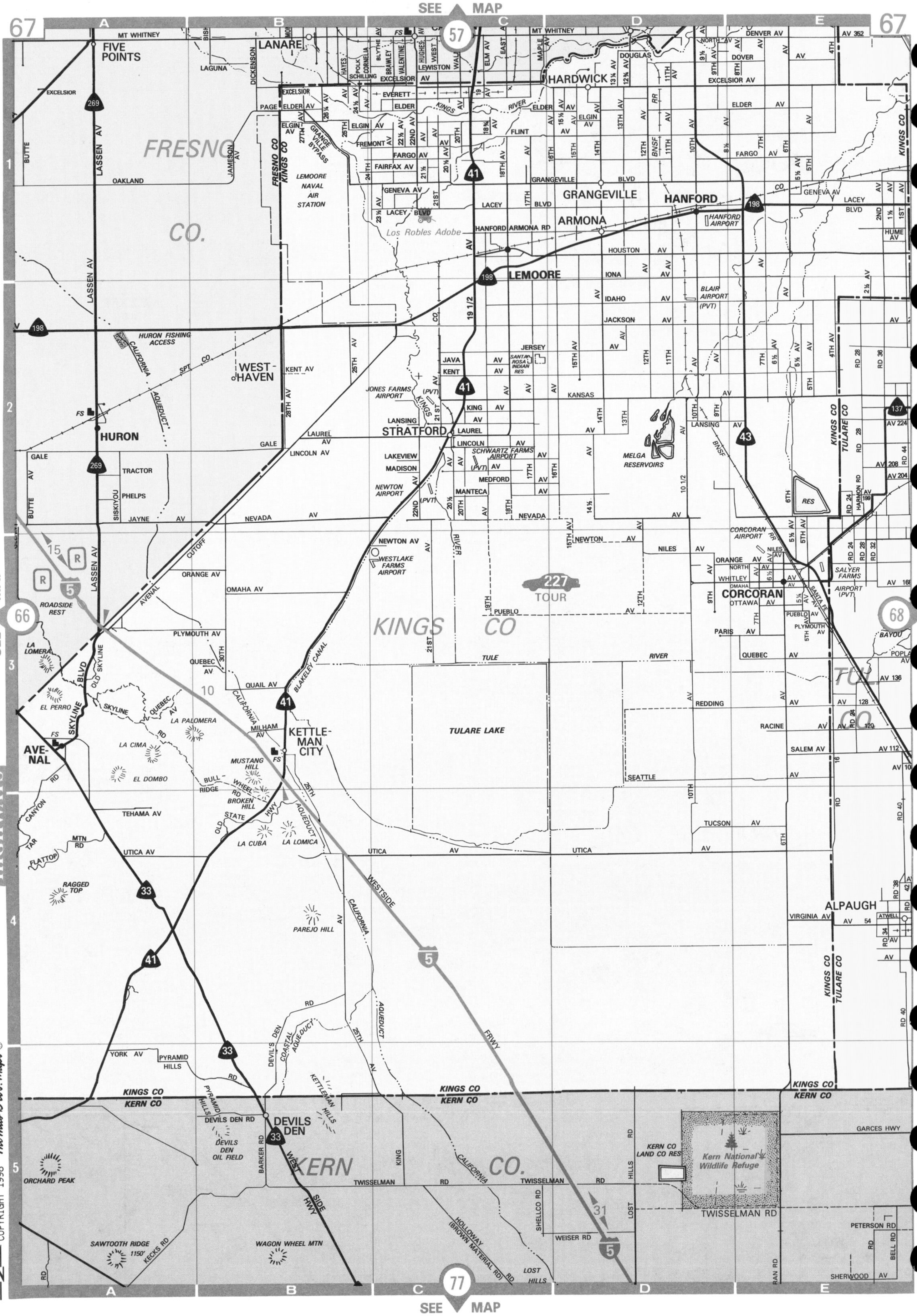
SEE MAP 57
SEE MAP 66
SEE MAP 68
SEE MAP 77
FIVE POINTS
LANARE
HARDWICK
GRANGEVILLE
HANFORD
ARMONA
LEMOORE
LEMOORE NAVAL AIR STATION
Los Robles Adobe
HANFORD AIRPORT
BLAIR AIRPORT (PVT)
FRESNO CO.
WEST-HAVEN
HURON
HURON FISHING ACCESS
CALIFORNIA AQUEDUCT
JONES FARMS AIRPORT
STRATFORD
SANTA ROSA INDIAN RES
SCHWARTZ FARMS AIRPORT
NEWTON AIRPORT
MELGA RESERVOIRS
CORCORAN AIRPORT
WESTLAKE FARMS AIRPORT
SALYER FARMS AIRPORT (PVT)
CORCORAN
227 TOUR
KINGS CO
ROADSIDE REST
LA LOMERA
EL PERRO
LA PALOMERA
LA CIMA
EL DOMBO
AVE-NAL
KETTLE-MAN CITY
MUSTANG HILL
BROKEN HILL
LA CUBA
LA LOMICA
TULARE LAKE
TUL CO
RAGGED TOP
PAREJO HILL
ALPAUGH
WESTSIDE FRWY
KINGS CO
KERN CO
KINGS CO TULARE CO
DEVILS DEN
DEVILS DEN OIL FIELD
KETTLEMAN HILLS
KERN CO LAND CO RES
Kern National Wildlife Refuge
ORCHARD PEAK
KERN CO.
SAWTOOTH RIDGE 1150'
WAGON WHEEL MTN
HOLLOWAY (BROWN MATERIAL RD)
LOST HILLS
TWISSELMAN RD
HIGHWAYS

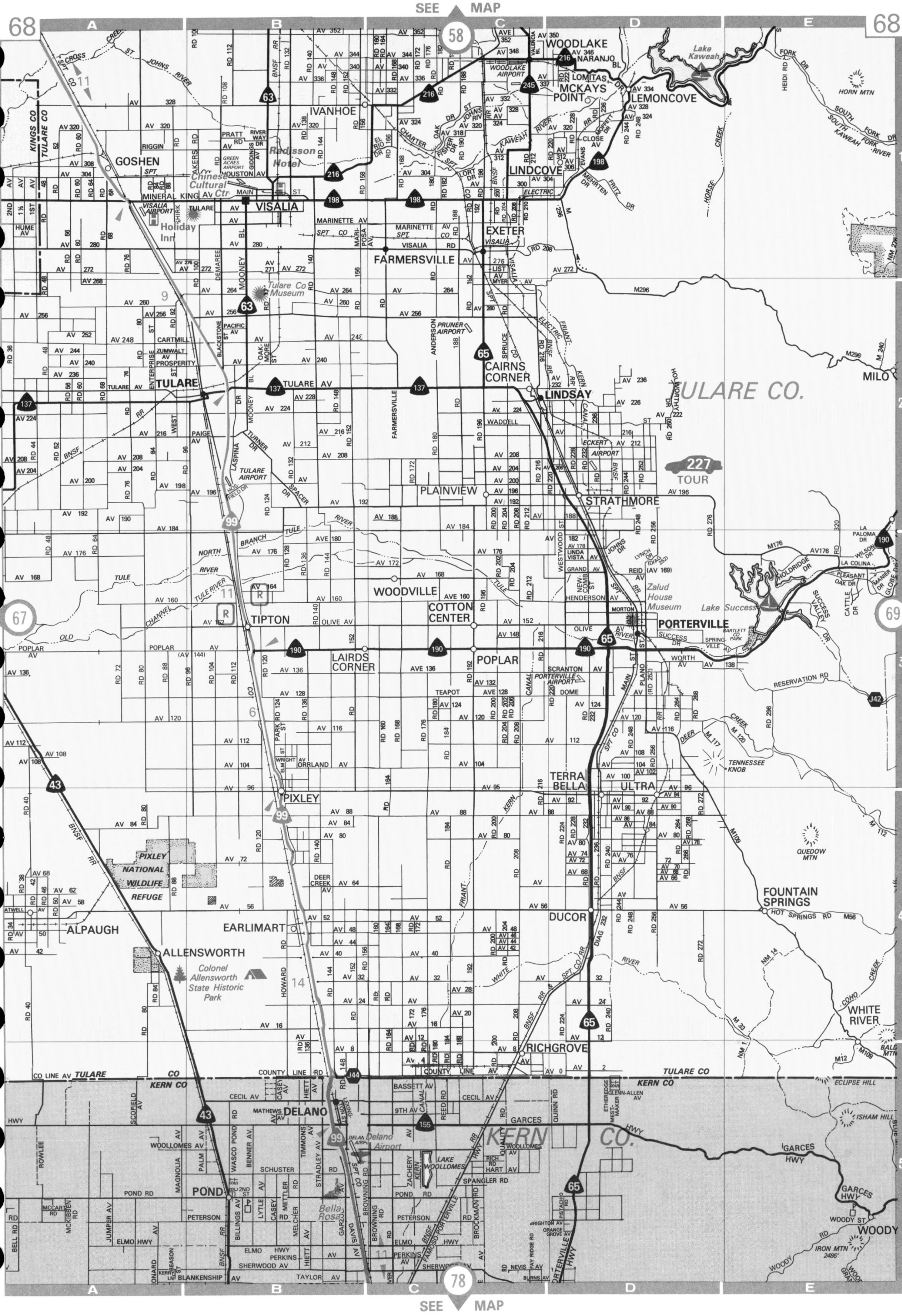
SEE MAP 58
SEE MAP 78
SEE MAP 67
SEE MAP 69
WOODLAKE
NARANJO
LOMITAS
MCKAYS POINT
LEMONCOVE
Lake Kaweah
HORN MTN
IVANHOE
Radisson Hotel
GOSHEN
Chinese Cultural Ctr
VISALIA
Holiday Inn
LINDCOVE
EXETER
FARMERSVILLE
Tulare Co Museum
PRUNER AIRPORT
CAIRNS CORNER
TULARE
LINDSAY
TULARE CO.
MILO
TULARE AIRPORT
PLAINVIEW
STRATHMORE
227 TOUR
WOODVILLE
COTTON CENTER
Zalud House Museum
PORTERVILLE
Lake Success
TIPTON
LAIRDS CORNER
POPLAR
PORTERVILLE AIRPORT
TERRA BELLA
ULTRA
TENNESSEE KNOB
PIXLEY
PIXLEY NATIONAL WILDLIFE REFUGE
QUEDOW MTN
FOUNTAIN SPRINGS
DUCOR
EARLIMART
ALPAUGH
ALLENSWORTH
Colonel Allensworth State Historic Park
WHITE RIVER
RICHGROVE
TULARE CO
KERN CO
DELANO
Delano Airport
LAKE WOOLLOMES
KERN CO.
POND
Bella Rosa
ECLIPSE HILL
ISHAM HILL
GARCES HWY
WOODY
IRON MTN 2486'

HIGHWAYS

SEE MAP 59

SEE MAP 68

70

SEE MAP 79

HIGHWAYS

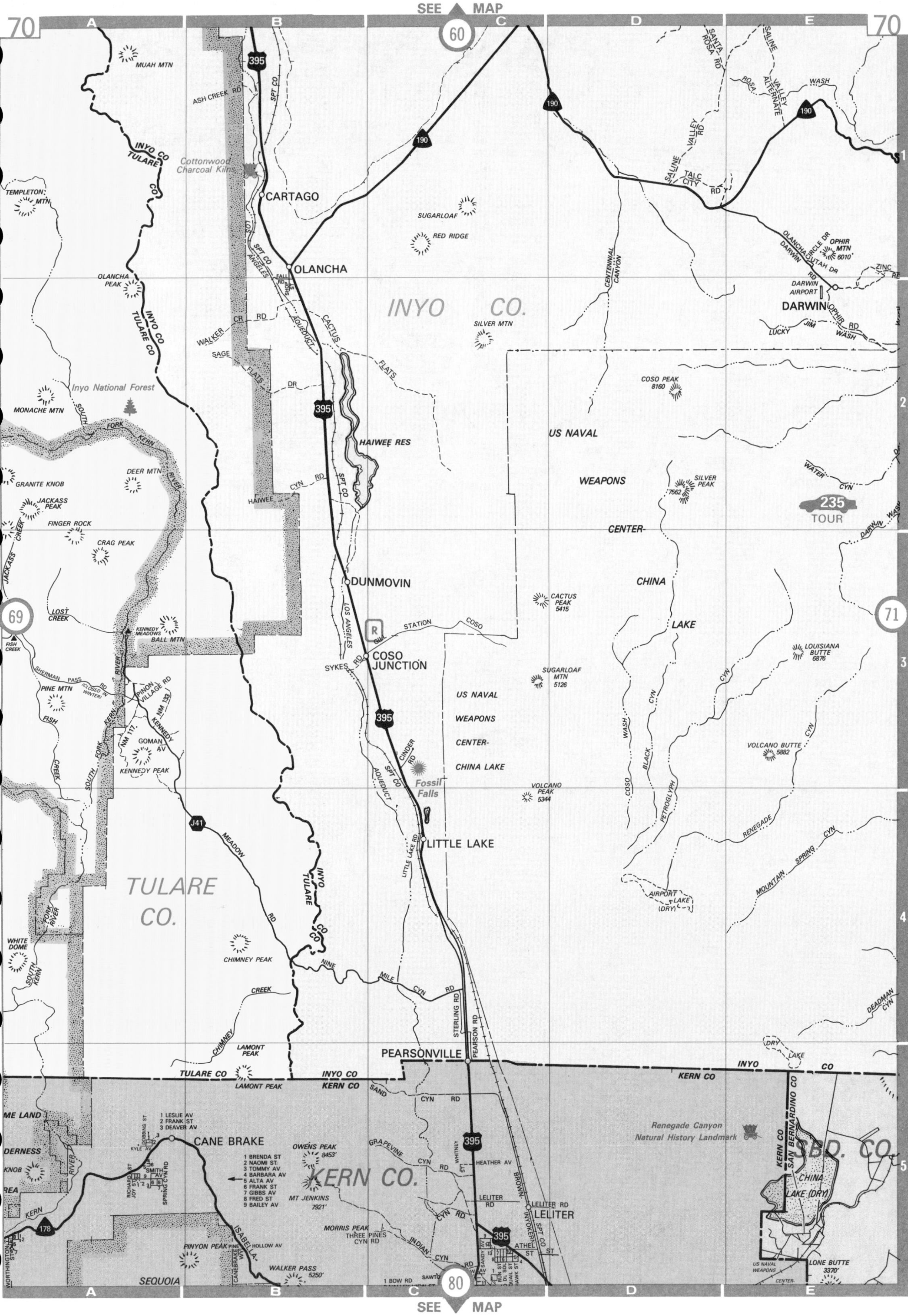
SEE MAP 60
SEE MAP 69
SEE MAP 71
SEE MAP 80
HIGHWAYS
A
B
C
D
E
1
2
3
4
5
INYO CO.
TULARE CO.
KERN CO.
SBD. CO.
US NAVAL WEAPONS CENTER-CHINA LAKE
CARTAGO
OLANCHA
DUNMOVIN
COSO JUNCTION
LITTLE LAKE
PEARSONVILLE
CANE BRAKE
LELITER
DARWIN
Cottonwood Charcoal Kilns
Inyo National Forest
HAIWEE RES
Fossil Falls
Renegade Canyon Natural History Landmark
CHINA LAKE (DRY)
AIRPORT LAKE (DRY)
DRY LAKE
MUAH MTN
TEMPLETON MTN
OLANCHA PEAK
MONACHE MTN
GRANITE KNOB
DEER MTN
JACKASS PEAK
FINGER ROCK
CRAG PEAK
BALL MTN
PINE MTN
KENNEDY PEAK
KENNEDY MEADOWS
FISH CREEK
CHIMNEY PEAK
LAMONT PEAK
WHITE DOME
OWENS PEAK 8453'
MT JENKINS 7921'
MORRIS PEAK
PINYON PEAK
WALKER PASS 5250'
SUGARLOAF
RED RIDGE
SILVER MTN
COSO PEAK 8160
SILVER PEAK 7562
CACTUS PEAK 5415
SUGARLOAF MTN 5126
VOLCANO PEAK 5344
LOUISIANA BUTTE 6876
VOLCANO BUTTE 5882
OPHIR MTN 6010'
LONE BUTTE 3370'
DARWIN AIRPORT
235 TOUR
395
190
178
J41
SHERMAN PASS RD (CLOSED IN WINTER)
NINE MILE CYN RD
STERLING RD
PEARSON RD
SAND CYN RD
GRAPEVINE CYN RD
HEATHER AV
LELITER RD
INDIAN CYN RD
THREE PINES CYN RD
BROWN RD
INYOKERN RD
1 LESLIE AV
2 FRANK ST
3 DEAVER AV
1 BRENDA ST
2 NAOMI ST
3 TOMMY AV
4 BARBARA AV
5 ALTA AV
6 FRANK ST
7 GIBBS AV
8 FRED ST
9 BAILEY AV
SALINE VALLEY RD
TALC CITY RD
OLANCHA DARWIN RD
WATER CYN
MOUNTAIN SPRING CYN
RENEGADE CYN
PETROGLYPH
COSO WASH
CENTENNIAL CANYON
DEADMAN CYN
SEQUOIA
1 BOW RD

SEE MAP 61

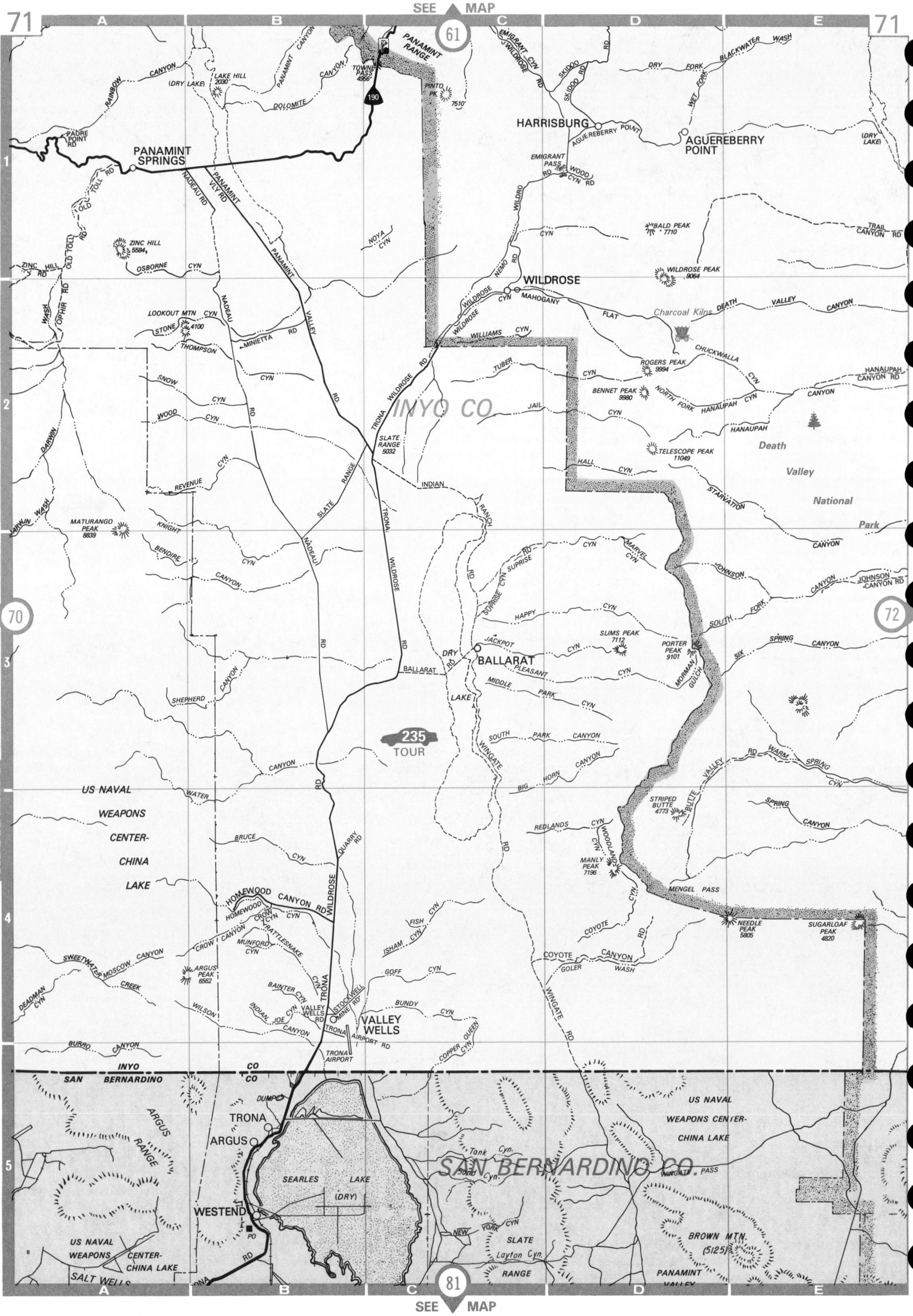

SEE MAP 70
72
SEE MAP 81

SEE MAP 62

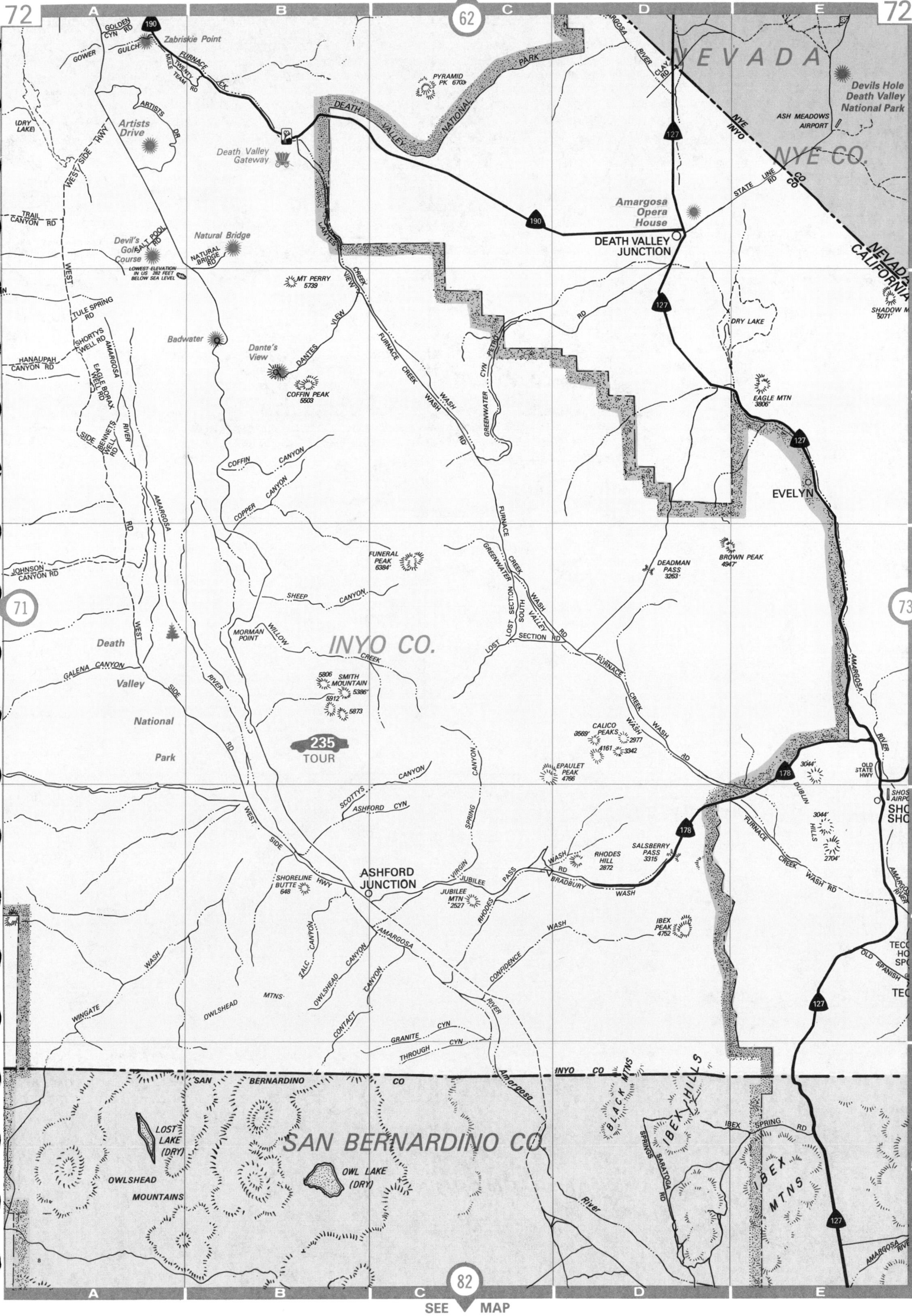

SEE MAP 71

SEE MAP 73

HIGHWAYS

SEE MAP 82

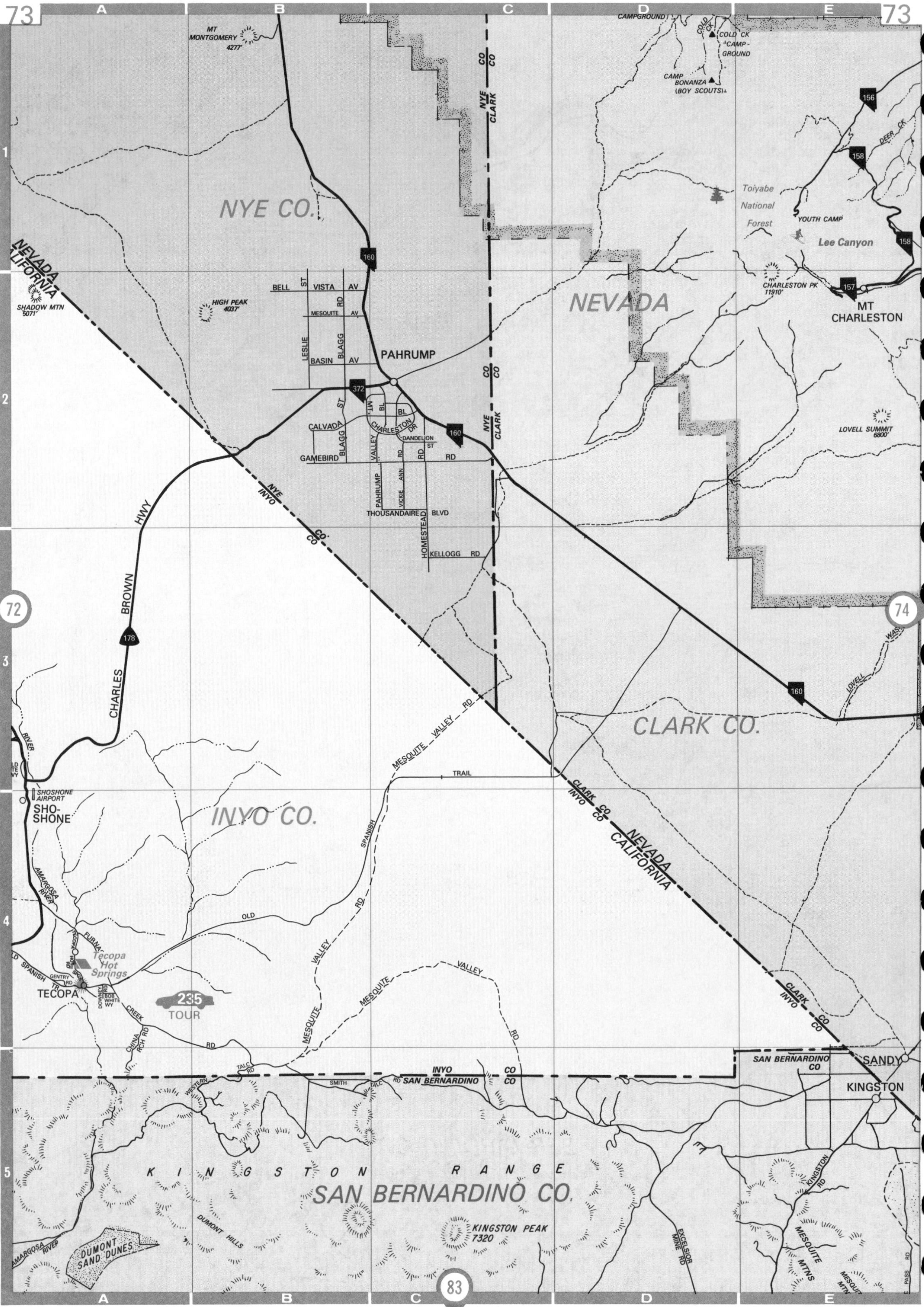

SEE 72 MAP
74
SEE 83 MAP

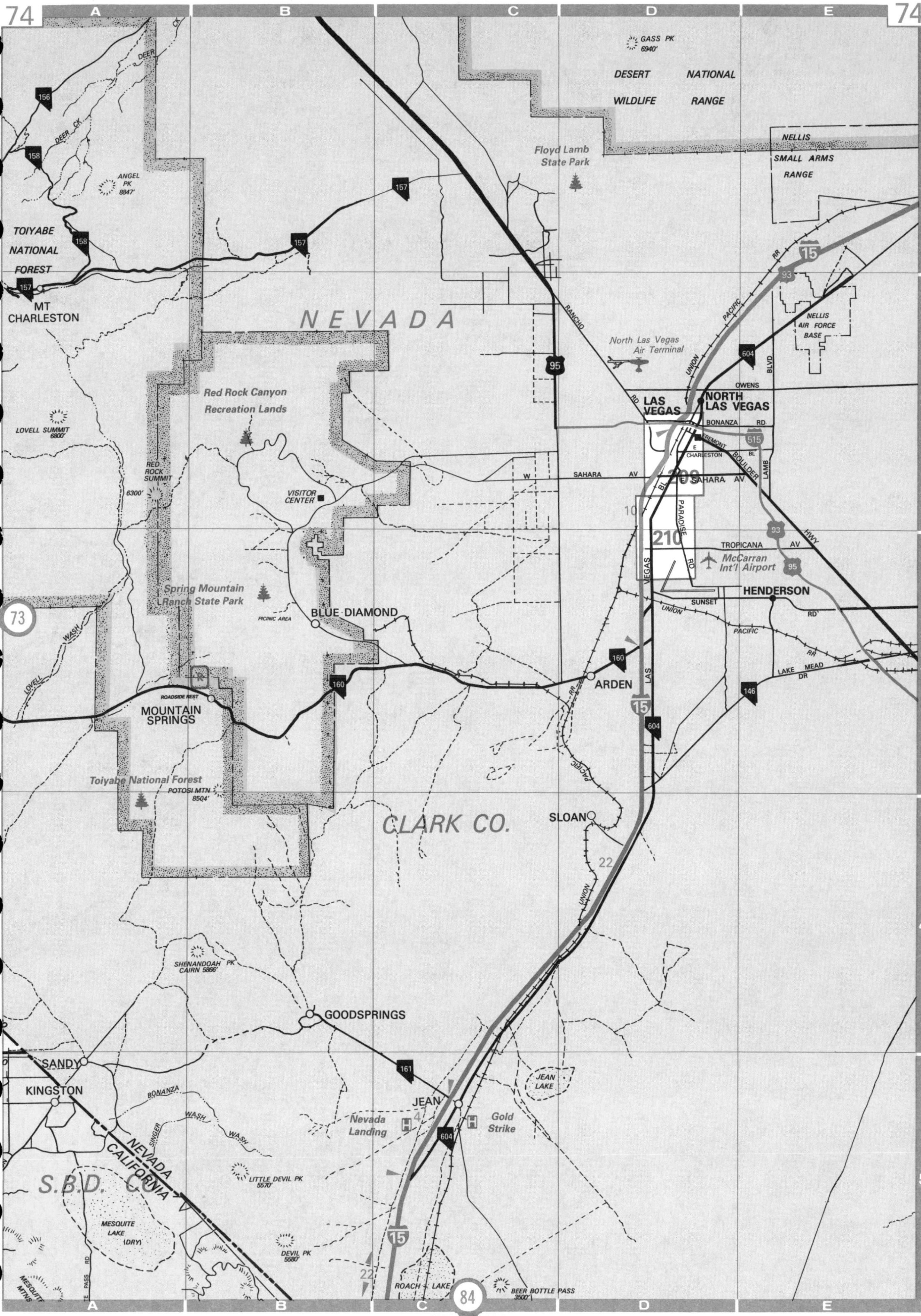
A
B
C
D
E
1
2
3
4
5
GASS PK 6940'
DESERT NATIONAL WILDLIFE RANGE
NELLIS SMALL ARMS RANGE
Floyd Lamb State Park
TOIYABE NATIONAL FOREST
MT CHARLESTON
ANGEL PK 8847'
DEER CK
156
158
157
NEVADA
RANCHO
95
North Las Vegas Air Terminal
UNION PACIFIC RR
15
93
604
NELLIS AIR FORCE BASE
OWENS
BLVD
LAS VEGAS
NORTH LAS VEGAS
BONANZA RD
515
FREMONT
CHARLESTON
BOULDER
LAMB
W SAHARA AV
209
SAHARA AV
10
BL
PARADISE RD
VEGAS
210
TROPICANA AV
McCarran Int'l Airport
HWY
HENDERSON
SUNSET
RD
Red Rock Canyon Recreation Lands
LOVELL SUMMIT 6800'
RED ROCK SUMMIT
6300'
VISITOR CENTER
Spring Mountain Ranch State Park
PICNIC AREA
BLUE DIAMOND
73
LOVELL WASH
ROADSIDE REST
MOUNTAIN SPRINGS
160
ARDEN
LAKE MEAD DR
146
Toiyabe National Forest
POTOSI MTN 8504'
CLARK CO.
SLOAN
PACIFIC
22
UNION
SHENANDOAH PK CAIRN 5866'
GOODSPRINGS
SANDY
KINGSTON
161
BONANZA
JEAN
JEAN LAKE
Nevada Landing
Gold Strike
4
SINGER WASH
NEVADA
CALIFORNIA
S.B.D. CO.
LITTLE DEVIL PK 5570'
MESQUITE LAKE (DRY)
DEVIL PK 5580'
MESQUITE MTNS
PASS RD
ROACH LAKE
BEER BOTTLE PASS 3500'

SEE 84 MAP

SEE MAP 65

HIGHWAYS

SEE MAP 66

SEE MAP 75
SEE MAP 77
SEE MAP 86

HIGHWAYS

SEE MAP 67

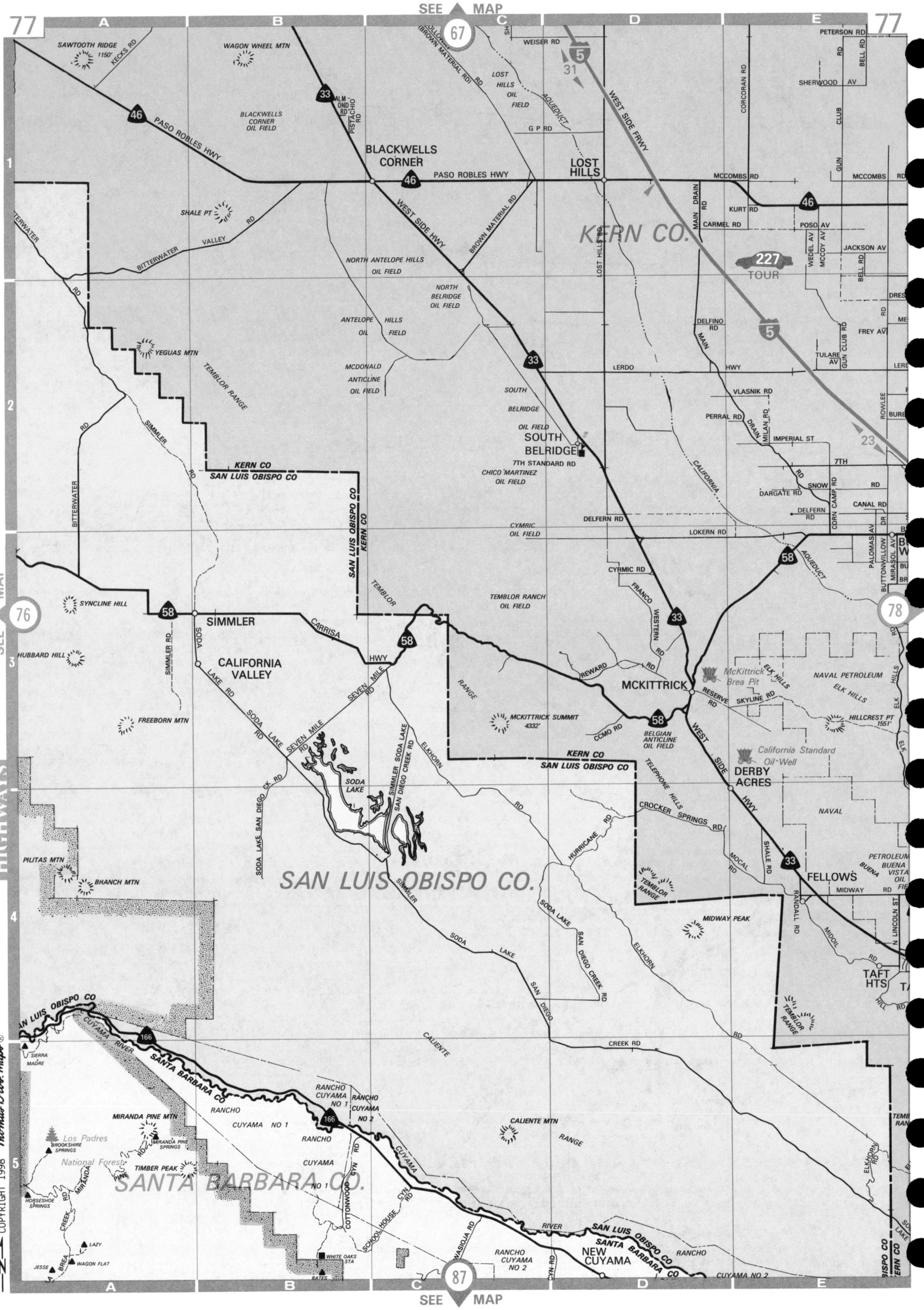

SEE MAP 76

SEE MAP 78

SEE MAP 87

SEE MAP 68

77
79 SEE MAP
SEE MAP 88

SEE MAP 69

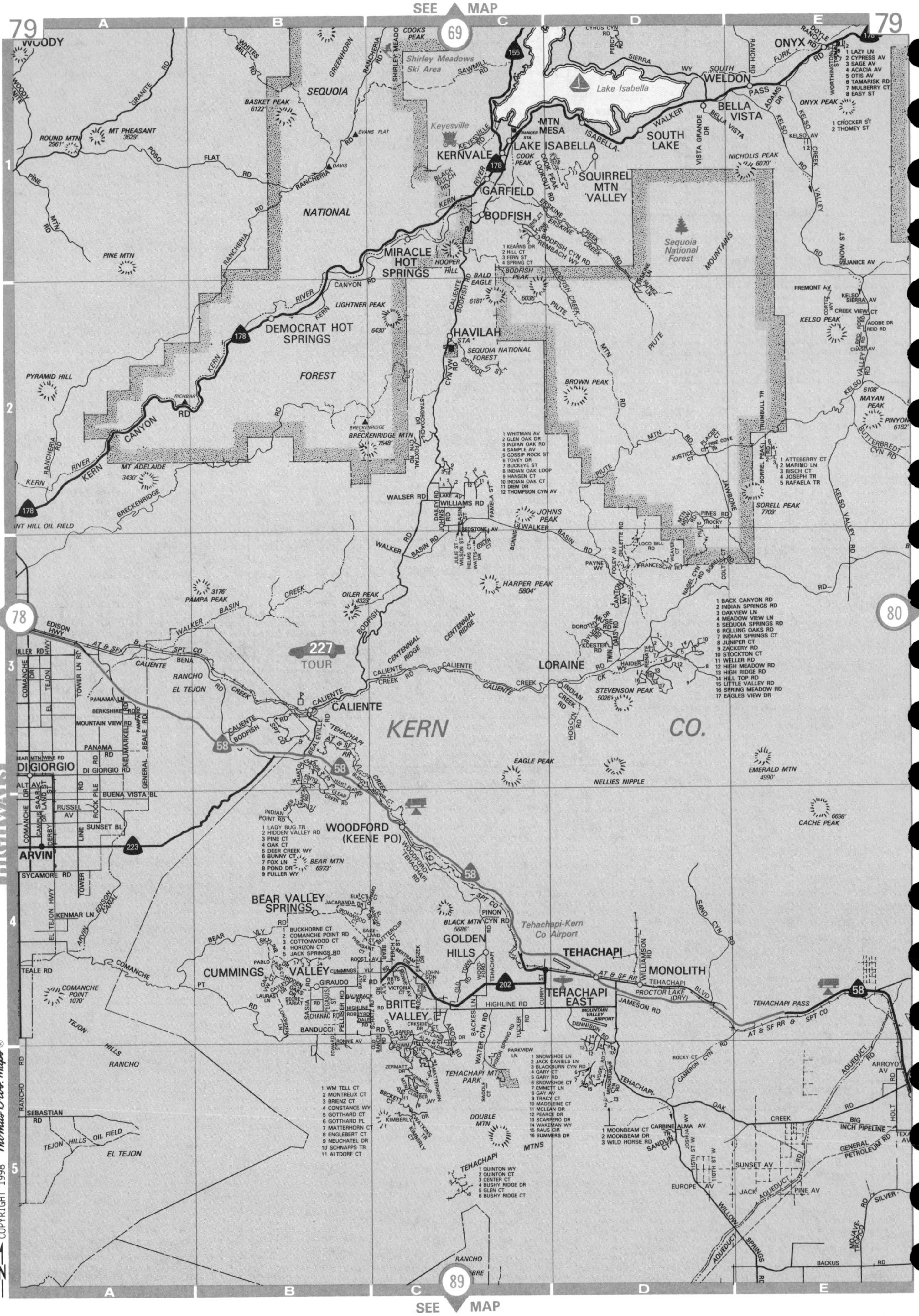

SEE MAP 78

SEE MAP 80

SEE MAP 89

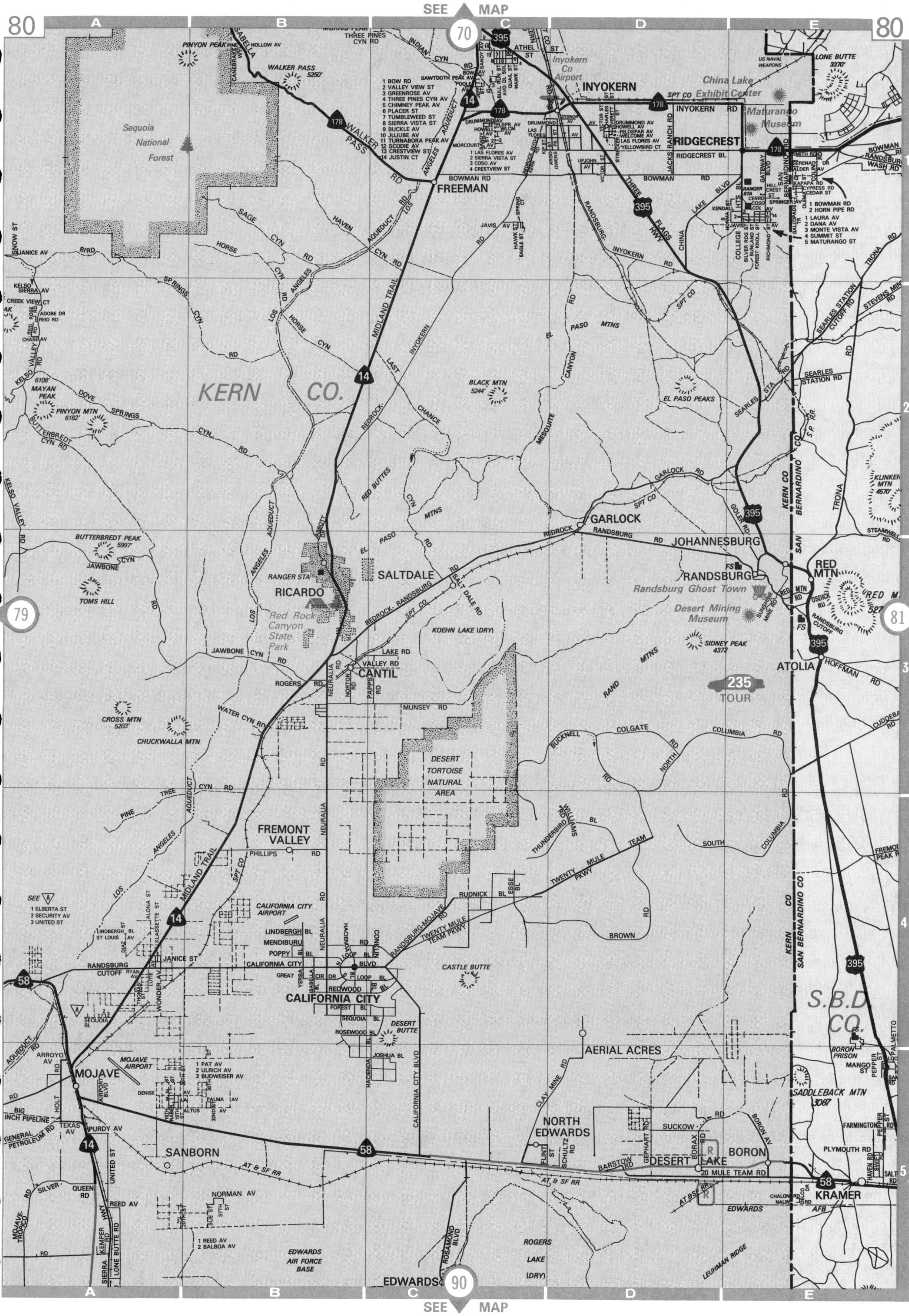
SEE MAP 70
SEE MAP 79
SEE MAP 81
SEE MAP 90
INYOKERN
Inyokern Co Airport
China Lake Exhibit Center
Maturango Museum
RIDGECREST
RIDGECREST BL
FREEMAN
Sequoia National Forest
WALKER PASS 5250'
PINYON PEAK
LONE BUTTE 3370'
US NAVAL WEAPONS
KERN CO.
BLACK MTN 5244'
EL PASO PEAKS
EL PASO MTNS
MAYAN PEAK
PINYON MTN 6182'
BUTTERBREDT PEAK 5997'
TOMS HILL
GARLOCK
JOHANNESBURG
RANDSBURG
Randsburg Ghost Town
Desert Mining Museum
RED MTN
ATOLIA
SIDNEY PEAK 4372
SALTDALE
RICARDO
RANGER STA
Red Rock Canyon State Park
KOEHN LAKE (DRY)
CANTIL
RAND MTNS
235 TOUR
CROSS MTN 5203'
CHUCKWALLA MTN
DESERT TORTOISE NATURAL AREA
FREMONT VALLEY
CALIFORNIA CITY AIRPORT
CALIFORNIA CITY
CASTLE BUTTE
DESERT BUTTE
MOJAVE
MOJAVE AIRPORT
SANBORN
AERIAL ACRES
NORTH EDWARDS
DESERT LAKE
BORON
KRAMER
EDWARDS
EDWARDS AIR FORCE BASE
ROGERS LAKE (DRY)
SADDLEBACK MTN 3087
KLINKER MTN 4570'
BORON PRISON
S.B.D. CO.
KERN CO
SAN BERNARDINO CO
MIDLAND TRAIL
TWENTY MULE TEAM PKWY
20 MULE TEAM RD
AT & SF RR
SPT CO
HIGHWAYS

SEE MAP 71
SEE MAP 80
SEE MAP 82
SEE MAP 91
HIGHWAYS
US NAVAL WEAPONS CENTER-CHINA LAKE
SALT WELLS VALLEY
TRONA RD
178
SALT WELLS CANYON
Trona Pinnacles
SLATE RANGE
Layton Cyn
BROWN MTN. (5125)
PANAMINT VALLEY
SPANGLER HILLS
PINNACLE RD
T27S
T.R.R.
Christmas Cyn
RANDSBURG RD
PILOT KNOB VALLEY
US NAVAL WEAPONS CENTER-CHINA LAKE
ROBBERS MTN. 4530
DOME MTN 4985
BLACK HILLS
PILOT KNOB 5428
EAGLE CRAGS
SAN BERNARDINO MERIDIAN
FORT IRWIN MILITARY RESERVATION
GRANIT
WELLS RD
CUDDEBACK LAKE
AF GUNNERY RANGE
CUDDEBACK LAKE (DRY)
CUDDEBACK
HOFFMAN
SAN BERNARDINO CO.
235 TOUR
GRASS VALLEY
SLOCUM MTN. 5124
SUPERIOR VALLEY
US NAVAL WEAPONS CENTER - CHINA LAKE
OLD COPPER CITY RD
SUPERIOR LAKE (DRY)
GOLDSTONE
COPPER CITY RD
INDIAN SPRINGS
BLACK CANYON RD
FREMONT PK 4584
FREMONT PEAK RD
GRAVEL HILLS
OPAL MTN. 3950
OPAL MOUNTAIN
BLACK MTN. 3939
CANYON RD
LOCKHART RD
PARADISE SPRINGS RD
COOLGARDIE RD
DOBSON
WILLIAMS WELL RD
STARBRIGHT MINE RD
LANE MTN. 4522
GEORGIA RD
LUCINDA RD
BLACK
Rainbow Basin National Natural Landmark
OWL CANYON
HARPER LAKE (DRY)
HOFFMAN RD
LOCKHART
HARPER
HALSTEAD
HOLSTEAD RD
FOSSIL BED RD
BURNT TREE RD
RAINBOW BASIN
COPPER CITY RD
IRWIN RD
PICKHANDLE
SANTA FE AV
BNSF RR
HINKLEY RD
MOUNTAIN VIEW RD
THOMPSON RD
1 PERA RD
2 DEARBORN RD
3 ALCUDIA RD
DUMP
BISHOP RD
LARK HAVEN RD
WEBSTER RD
FORT IRWIN RD
YERMO CUTOFF
SALINAS RD
ATLANTIC CT
PALMA RD
PACIFIC CT
LINDEN AV
MEDFORD AV
ASBURY CT
DELMONT AV
ALCUDIA RD
APACHE AV
MILFORD LN
SILVER PEAK RD
BROCKWAY LN
MANACOR RD
SALTON RD
PALMETTO ST
LOCUS AV
BALSAMO RD
A B C D E
1 2 3 4 5

SEE MAP 72
A
B
C
D
E
DEATH VALLEY NATIONAL PARK
OWL HOLE SPRING RD
SARATOGA (IRWIN
SPRINGS RD
RD)
SALT CK
AMARGOSA
SHEEP CREEK SPRING RD
FORT IRWIN
QUAIL MOUNTAINS
LEACH LAKE (DRY)
AVAWATZ MOUNTAINS
MILITARY RESERVATION
GRANITE MOUNTAINS
AVAWATZ
DRINKWATER LAKE (DRY)
MCLEAN LAKE (DRY)
MOUNTAINS
NELSON LAKE (DRY)
GRANITE
IRWIN RD
MOUNTAINS
FORT
FORT MILITARY RESERVATION IRWIN
GOLDSTONE LAKE (DRY)
AVAWATZ MOUNTAINS
SEE MAP 81
SEE MAP 83
FORT IRWIN MILITARY RESERVATION
SAN BERNARDINO CO.
FORT IRWIN RD
GRANITE
FORT IRWIN
(RD)
BICYCLE LAKE (DRY)
TIEFORT
235 TOUR
RED PASS LAKE (DRY)
MOUNTAINS
FORT IRWIN
LANGFORD WELL LAKE (DRY)
PARADISE RANGE
PARADISE SPRINGS
STARBRIGHT MINE RD
EAGLE POINT RD
FORT IRWIN MILITARY RES
M O
WEST CRONESE LAKE (DRY)
CRONESE
CRONESE MTNS
EAST LA
ARROWHEAD LAKE RD
ALVORD MTN 3456
19
MTN
FORT IRWIN RD
PARADISE SPRINGS RD
COYOTE LAKE RD
COYOTE LAKE (DRY)
ALVORD MTN RD
15
26
RASO
CAVE MOUNTAIN
BASIN RD
UNION
JACKHAMMER GAP
CALICO
PICKHANDLE PASS
R
CLYDE V KANE ROADSIDE REST
DUNN RD
AFTON CANYON
AFTON CANYON RECREATION AREA
RR
PACIFIC
River
RD
18
FIELD RD
15
YERMO RD
UNION
PARADISE
1 LA PEER RD
2 PICASSO RD
3 FLAX ST
CALICO MTNS.
Calico Mtns Archaeological Project
DORAN SCENIC DR
CALICO GHOST TOWN
PHILLIPS DR
CANYON RD
MULE
CEMETERY RD
FORT IRWIN RD
YERMO CUTOFF
CALICO MTNS ARCHAEOLOGICAL PROJECT
CARDIFF ST
DESERT VIEW
CHEROKEE RD
COYOTE LAKE RD
1
2
3
4
5
SEE MAP 92
HIGHWAYS

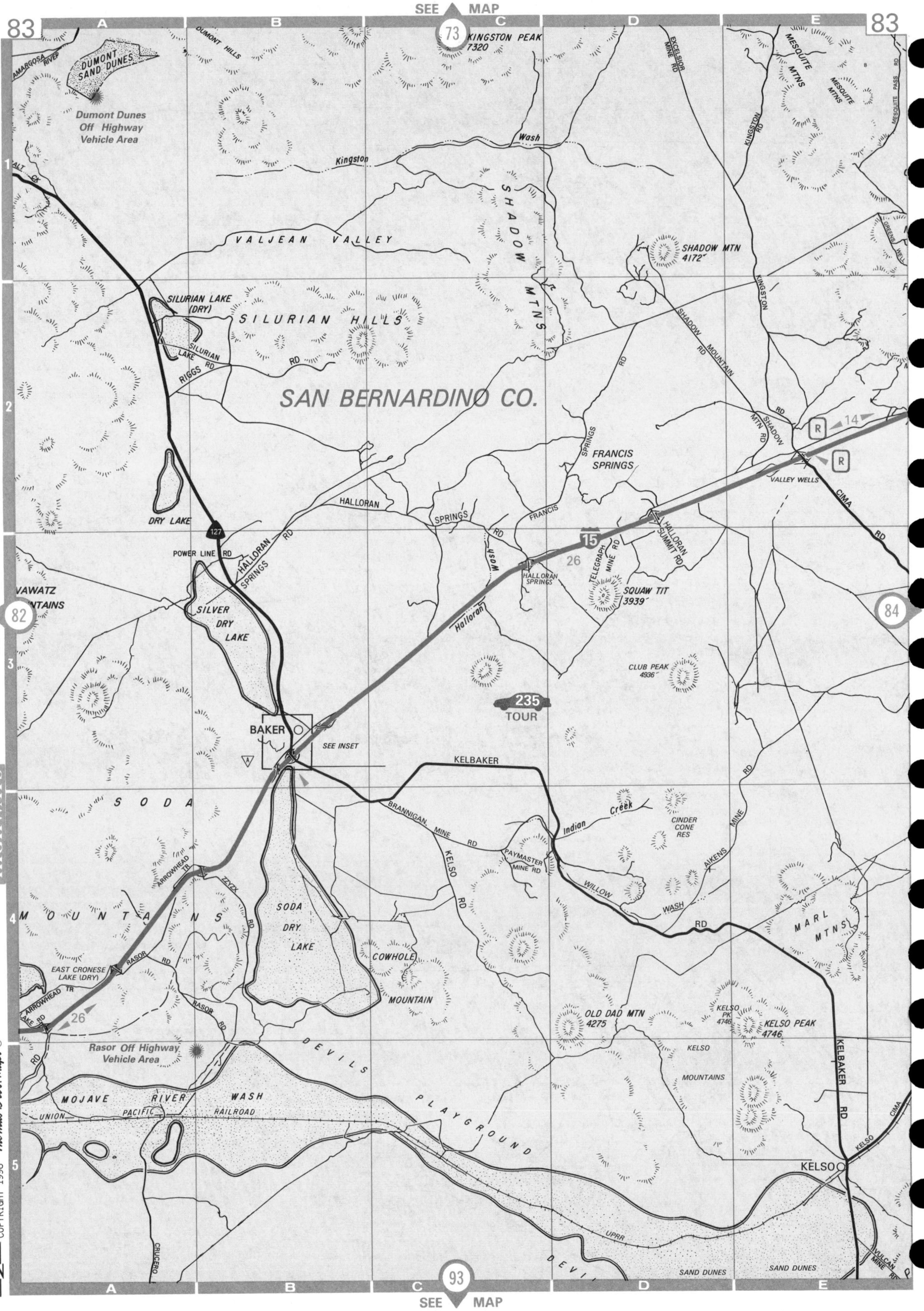
SEE MAP 73
KINGSTON PEAK 7320
DUMONT SAND DUNES
AMARGOSA RIVER
DUMONT HILLS
Dumont Dunes Off Highway Vehicle Area
EXCELSIOR MINE RD
MESQUITE MTNS
MESQUITE PASS RD
Kingston Wash
SHADOW MTNS
VALJEAN VALLEY
SHADOW MTN 4172
KINGSTON RD
SILURIAN LAKE (DRY)
SILURIAN HILLS
SILURIAN LAKE RD
RIGGS RD
SAN BERNARDINO CO.
SHADOW MOUNTAIN RD
SHADOW MTN RD
FRANCIS SPRINGS
VALLEY WELLS
CIMA RD
DRY LAKE
HALLORAN SPRINGS RD
FRANCIS SPRINGS RD
HALLORAN SUMMIT RD
TELEGRAPH MINE
HALLORAN SPRINGS
POWER LINE RD
Halloran Wash
SQUAW TIT 3939
SILVER DRY LAKE
AVAWATZ MOUNTAINS
SEE MAP 82
SEE MAP 84
CLUB PEAK 4936
235 TOUR
BAKER
SEE INSET
KELBAKER
SODA MOUNTAINS
BRANNIGAN MINE RD
Indian Creek
CINDER CONE RES
PAYMASTER MINE RD
KELSO RD
MINE RD
AIKENS
WILLOW WASH RD
ARROWHEAD TR
ZZYZX RD
SODA DRY LAKE
COWHOLE MOUNTAIN
MARL MTNS
EAST CRONESE LAKE (DRY)
RASOR RD
OLD DAD MTN 4275
KELSO PK 4746
KELSO PEAK 4746
Rasor Off Highway Vehicle Area
DEVILS PLAYGROUND
KELSO MOUNTAINS
KELBAKER RD
MOJAVE RIVER WASH
UNION PACIFIC RAILROAD
KELSO
UPRR
CRUCERO
SAND DUNES
VULCAN MINE RD
SEE MAP 93
HIGHWAYS

SEE MAP 74

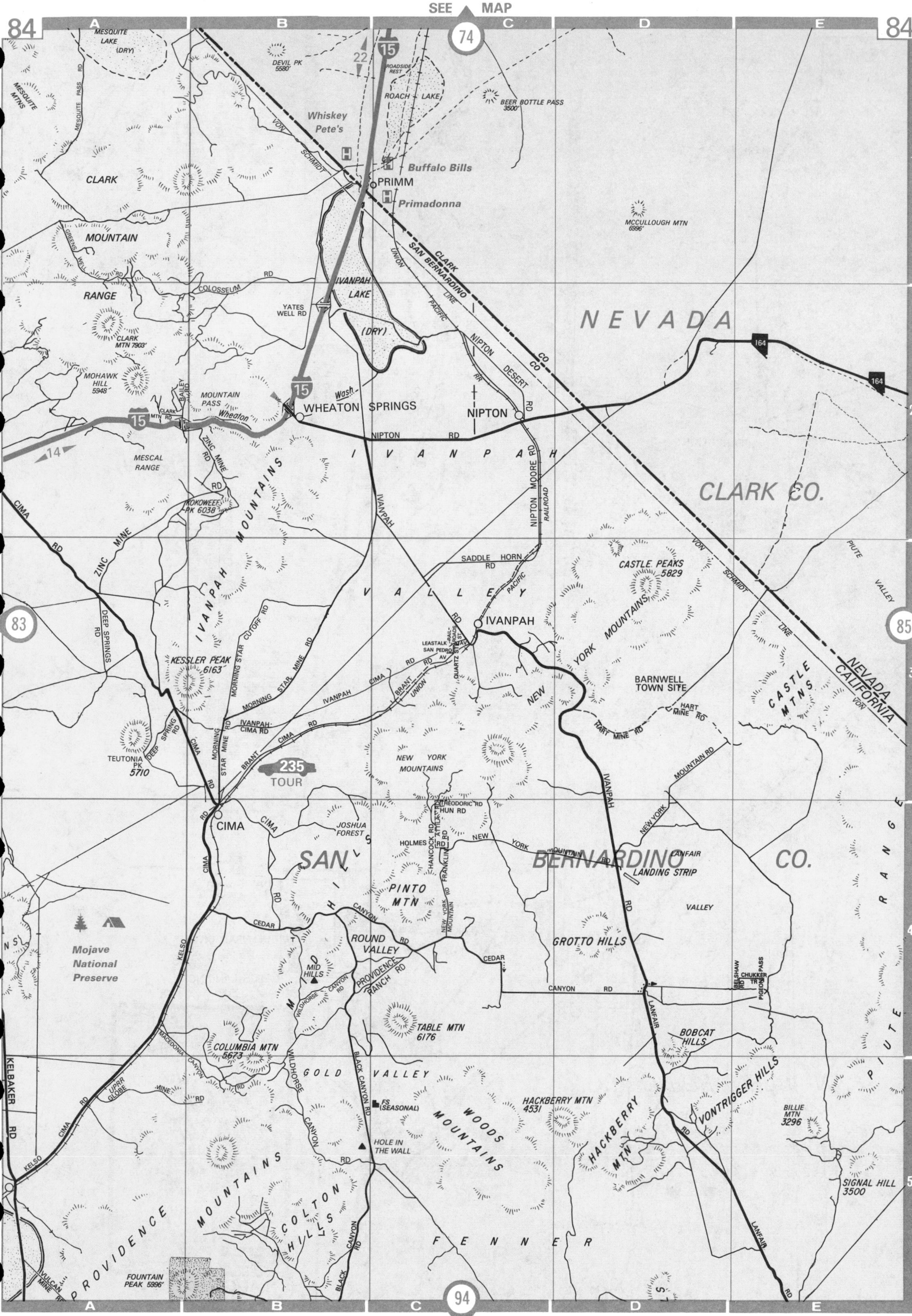

SEE MAP 83
SEE MAP 85
SEE MAP 94

HIGHWAYS

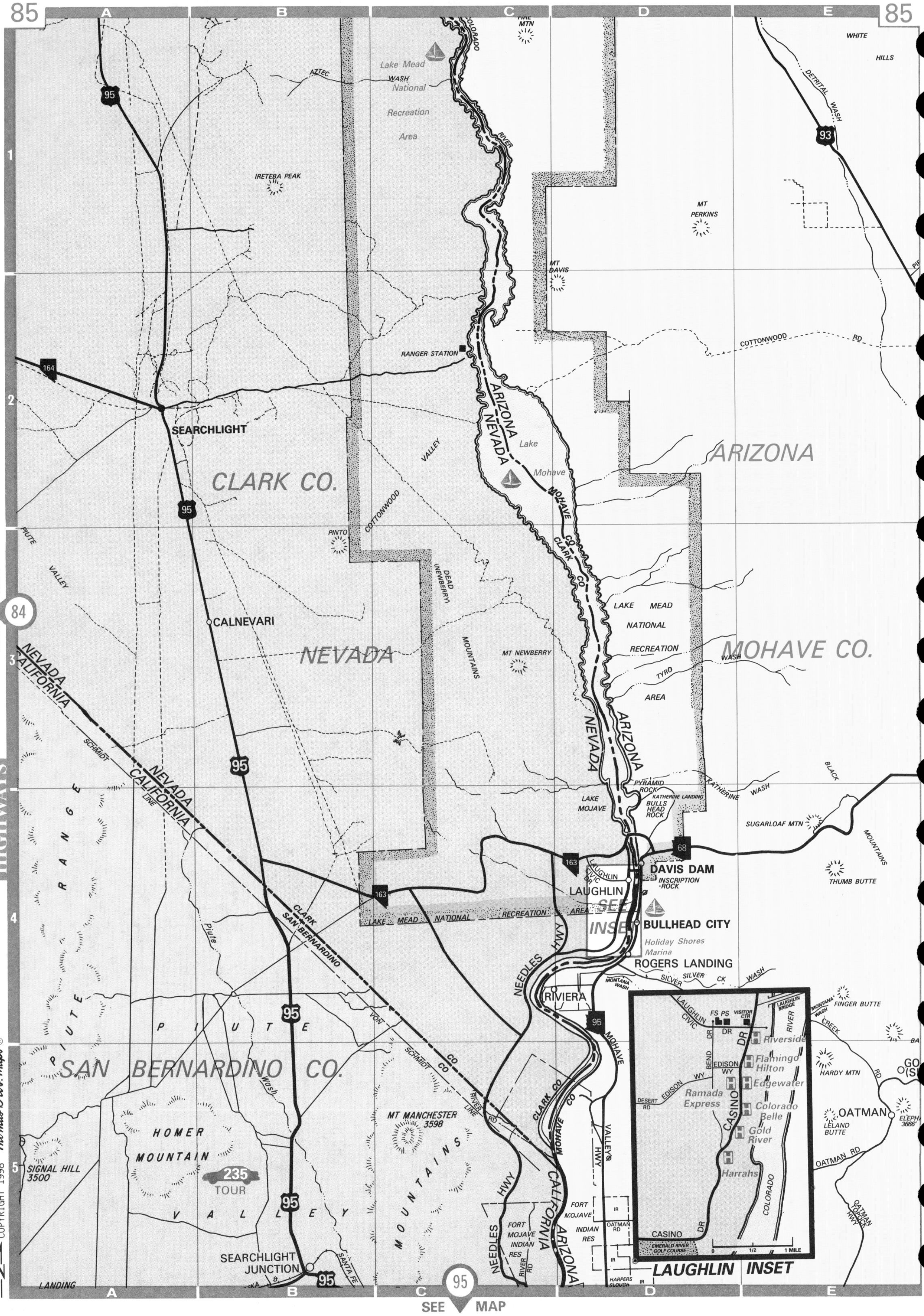
CLARK CO.
NEVADA
ARIZONA
MOHAVE CO.
SAN BERNARDINO CO.
SEARCHLIGHT
CALNEVARI
DAVIS DAM
LAUGHLIN
BULLHEAD CITY
RIVIERA
ROGERS LANDING
OATMAN
SEARCHLIGHT JUNCTION
Holiday Shores Marina
INSCRIPTION ROCK
Lake Mead National Recreation Area
Lake Mohave
LAKE MOJAVE
LAKE MEAD NATIONAL RECREATION AREA
RANGER STATION
IRETEBA PEAK
MT DAVIS
MT PERKINS
FIRE MTN
PINTO
MT NEWBERRY
DEAD (NEWBERRY) MOUNTAINS
COTTONWOOD VALLEY
COTTONWOOD RD
DETRITAL WASH
WHITE HILLS
TYRO WASH
KATHERINE WASH
KATHERINE LANDING
PYRAMID ROCK
BULLS HEAD ROCK
SUGARLOAF MTN
BLACK MOUNTAINS
THUMB BUTTE
FINGER BUTTE
HARDY MTN
LELAND BUTTE
SILVER CK WASH
MONTANA WASH
OATMAN RD
NEEDLES HWY
MOHAVE VALLEY HWY
FORT MOJAVE INDIAN RES
HARPERS SLOUGH
PIUTE VALLEY
PIUTE RANGE
SCHMIDT LINE
NEVADA CALIFORNIA
CLARK SAN BERNARDINO CO
ARIZONA CALIFORNIA
COLORADO RIVER
MT MANCHESTER 3598
NEWBERRY MOUNTAINS
HOMER MOUNTAIN
SIGNAL HILL 3500
PIUTE VALLEY
235 TOUR
AZTEC WASH
95
93
164
163
68
LAUGHLIN INSET
LAUGHLIN BRIDGE
VISITOR CTR
LAUGHLIN CIVIC DR
BEND DR
EDISON WY
DESERT RD
CASINO DR
Riverside
Flamingo Hilton
Edgewater
Ramada Express
Colorado Belle
Gold River
Harrahs
EMERALD RIVER GOLF COURSE
1 MILE
A B C D E
1 2 3 4 5
SEE 84 MAP
HIGHWAYS
Thomas Bros. Maps ®
COPYRIGHT 1998
SEE 95 MAP

SEE MAP 76

SEE MAP 87

HIGHWAYS

SEE MAP 77

SEE MAP 86
88

SEE MAP 78

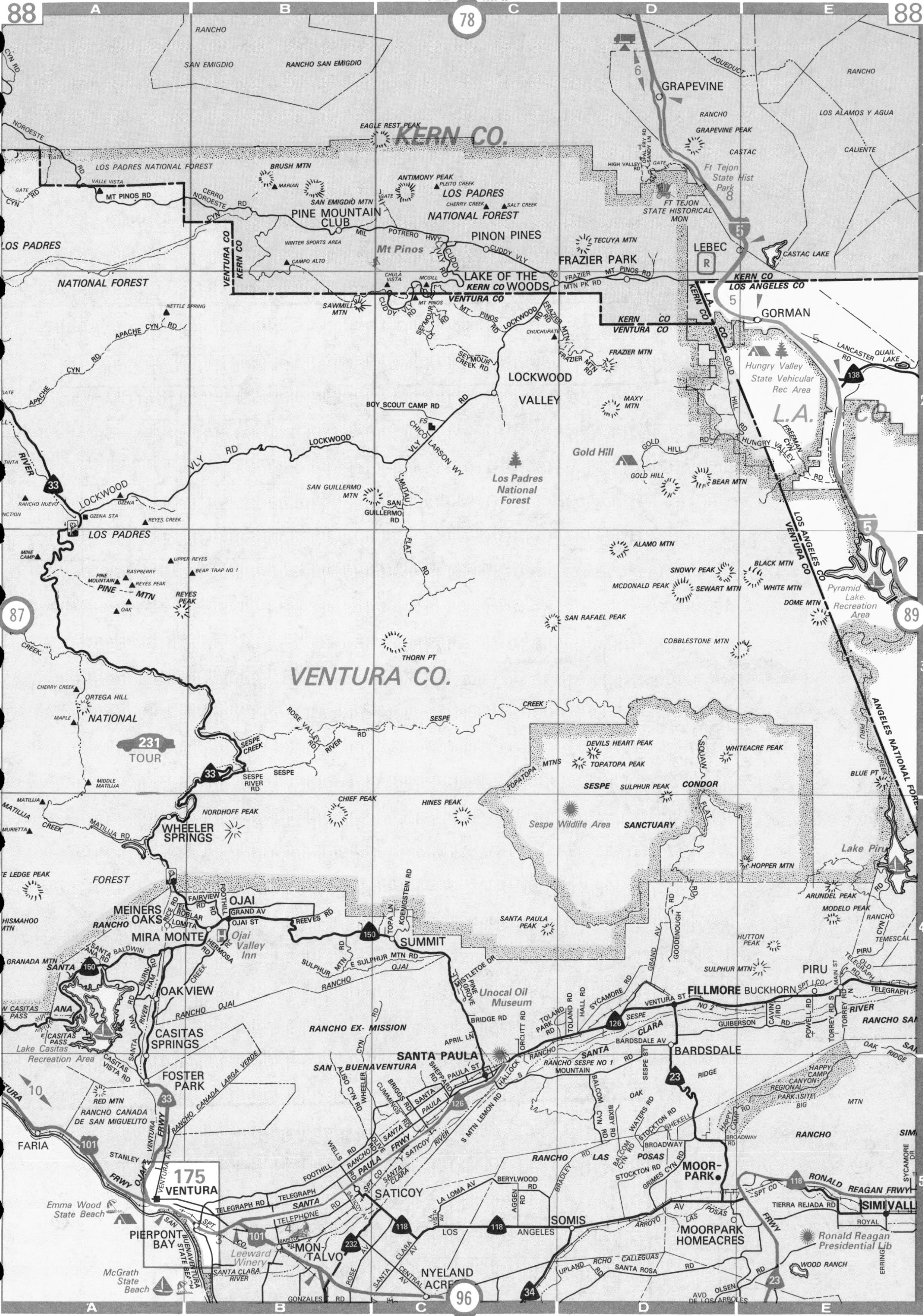

87

SEE MAP 89

SEE MAP 96

SEE MAP 79

SEE MAP 88
SEE MAP 90
SEE MAP 97

SEE MAP 80

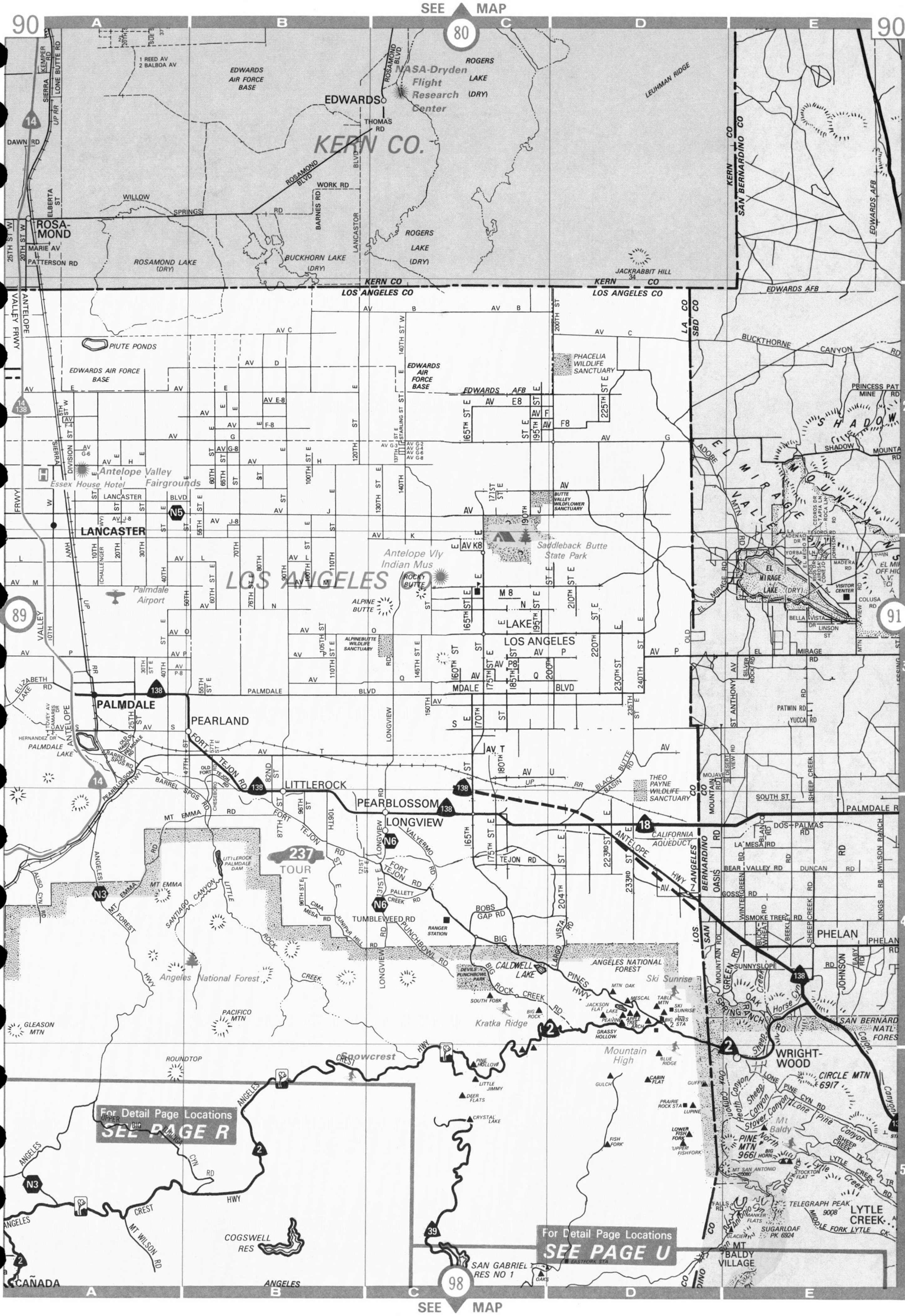

SEE MAP 89

SEE MAP 91

HIGHWAYS

SEE MAP 98

SEE MAP 90
92

KRAMER HILLS
HINKLEY
BARSTOW
LENWOOD
SILVER LAKES
HELENDALE
SAN BERNARDINO CO
Stoddard Valley Off Highway Vehicle Area
STODDARD VALLEY
STODDARD RIDGE
EL MIRAGE OFF HIGHWAY VEHICLE RECREATION AREA
ORO GRANDE
QUARTZITE MTN
ADELANTO
GEORGE AIR FORCE BASE
AIR BASE RD
VICTORVILLE
Roy Rogers Mus
CATHOLIC HILL 3646
BELL MTN 3897
FAIRVIEW MTN
DRY LAKE
APPLE VALLEY
LUCERNE DRY LAKE
RABBIT LAKE (DRY)
LUCERNE VALLEY
WEST ORD MTN
HESPERIA
JUNIPER FLATS
ROUND MTN 5283
WHITE MTN 7740
CRYSTAL CK REC AREA (PROP)
CAJON JCT
SUMMIT VALLEY
CLEGHORN MTN 5319
THE PINNACLE 5745
Silverwood Lake State Rec Area
PILOT ROCK 5260
SHAY MTN 6730
DEER MTN 5539
San Bernardino Nat'l Forest
LITTLE BEAR PK 7610
DELAMAR MTN 8367
BERTHA PK
FAWNSKIN
LYTLE CREEK
KEENBROOK
CEDARPINES PARK
SUGARPINE MTN 5478
VALLEY OF ENCHANTMENT
MONUMENT PK 5290
DEVORE
CRESTLINE
BLUE JAY
TWIN PEAKS
Lake Arrowhead
CEDAR GLEN
LAKE ARROWHEAD
RIMFOREST
SKY-FOREST
GREEN VALLEY LAKE
CRAFTS PK 8364
BUTLER PK 8537
BIG BEAR LAKE
Rim of the World Hwy
ARROWBEAR
HIGHWAYS

SEE MAP 82

SEE MAP 91

SEE MAP 93

SEE MAP 100

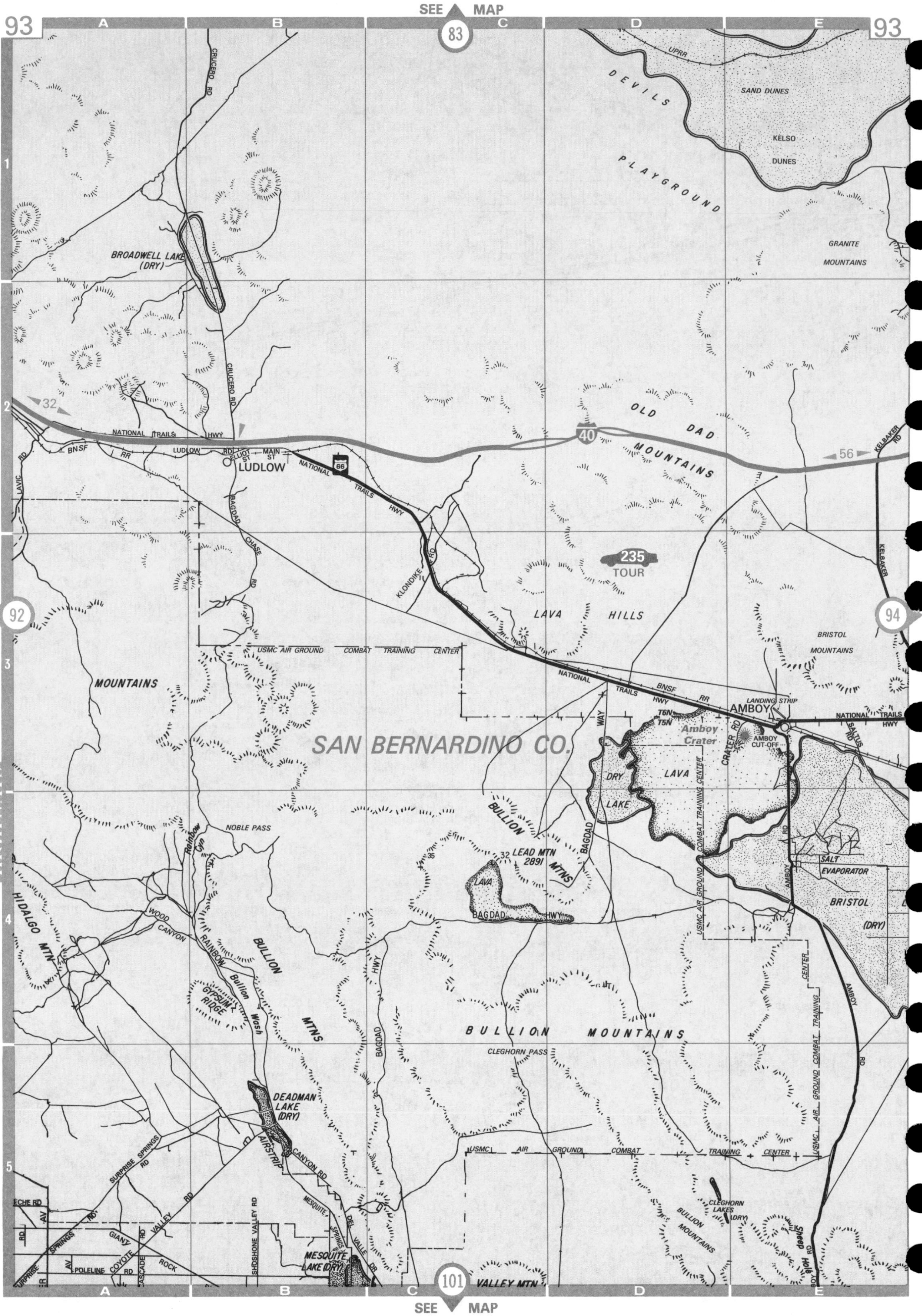

HIGHWAYS

Thomas Bros. Maps®

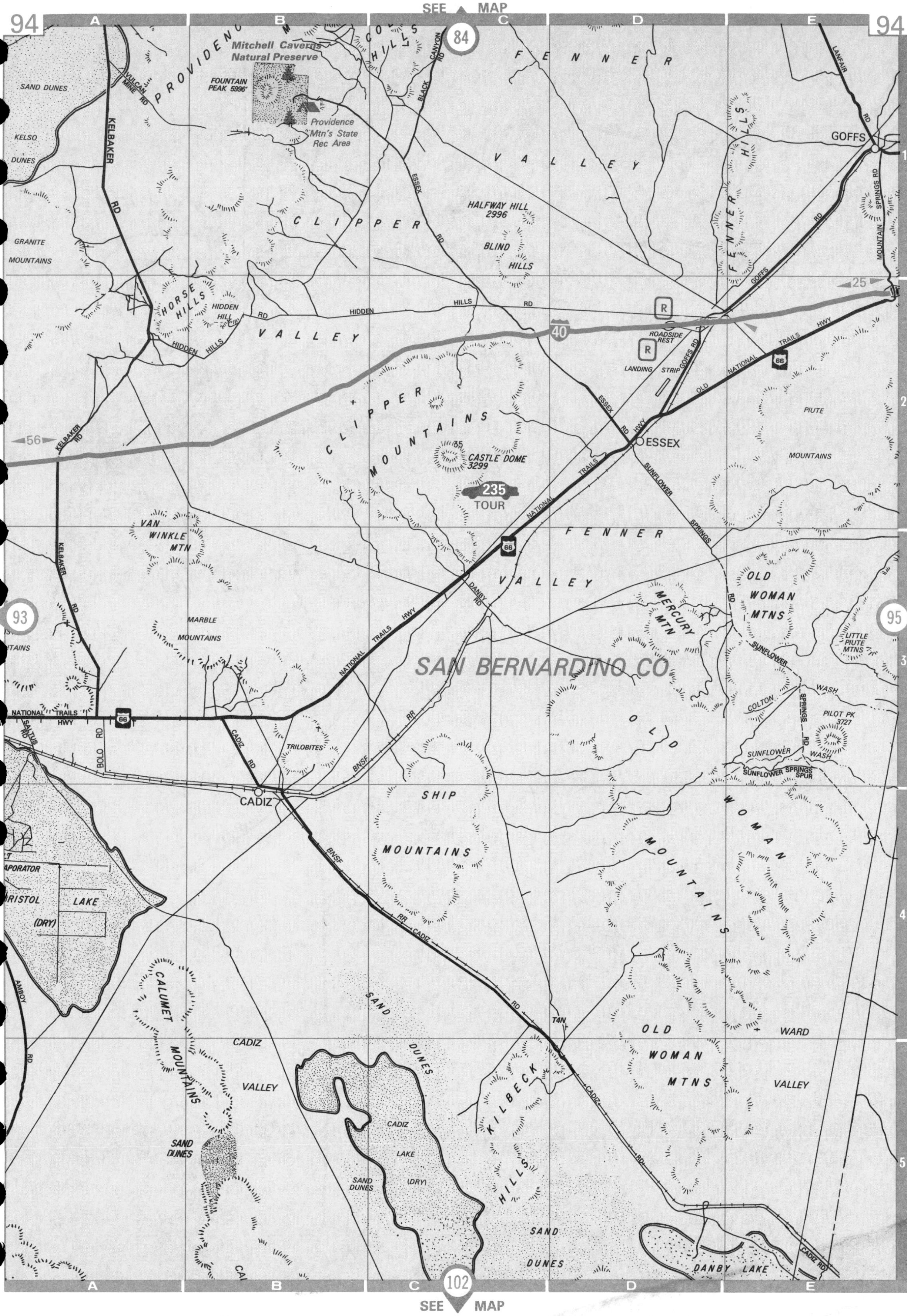
SEE MAP 84
Mitchell Caverns
Natural Preserve
FOUNTAIN PEAK 5996'
Providence
Mtn's State
Rec Area
PROVIDENCE
SAND DUNES
KELSO
DUNES
VULCAN MINE RD
KELBAKER RD
BLACK CANYON RD
F E N N E R
V A L L E Y
ESSEX RD
HALFWAY HILL
2996
BLIND
HILLS
C L I P P E R
GRANITE
MOUNTAINS
HORSE HILLS
HIDDEN HILL
HIDDEN HILLS RD
V A L L E Y
ROADSIDE REST
LANDING STRIP
GOFFS RD
GOFFS
LANFAIR RD
MOUNTAIN SPRINGS RD
FENNER HILLS
25
40
56
CLIPPER MOUNTAINS
CASTLE DOME
3299
235
TOUR
ESSEX
OLD NATIONAL TRAILS HWY
66
PIUTE
MOUNTAINS
SUNFLOWER SPRINGS RD
VAN WINKLE
MTN
FENNER
VALLEY
DANBY RD
MERCURY MTN
OLD WOMAN MTNS
LITTLE PIUTE MTNS
93
95
MARBLE
MOUNTAINS
SAN BERNARDINO CO.
SUNFLOWER
COLTON
WASH
PILOT PK
3727
SUNFLOWER WASH
SUNFLOWER SPRINGS SPUR
NATIONAL TRAILS HWY
SALTUS RD
BOLO RD
CADIZ RD
TRILOBITES
BNSF RR
CADIZ
SHIP
MOUNTAINS
OLD WOMAN MOUNTAINS
EVAPORATOR
BRISTOL
LAKE
(DRY)
AMBOY RD
CALUMET MOUNTAINS
CADIZ
VALLEY
SAND DUNES
T4N
OLD WOMAN MTNS
WARD
VALLEY
KILBECK HILLS
CADIZ
LAKE
(DRY)
SAND
DUNES
DANBY LAKE
CADIZ RD
102
SEE MAP

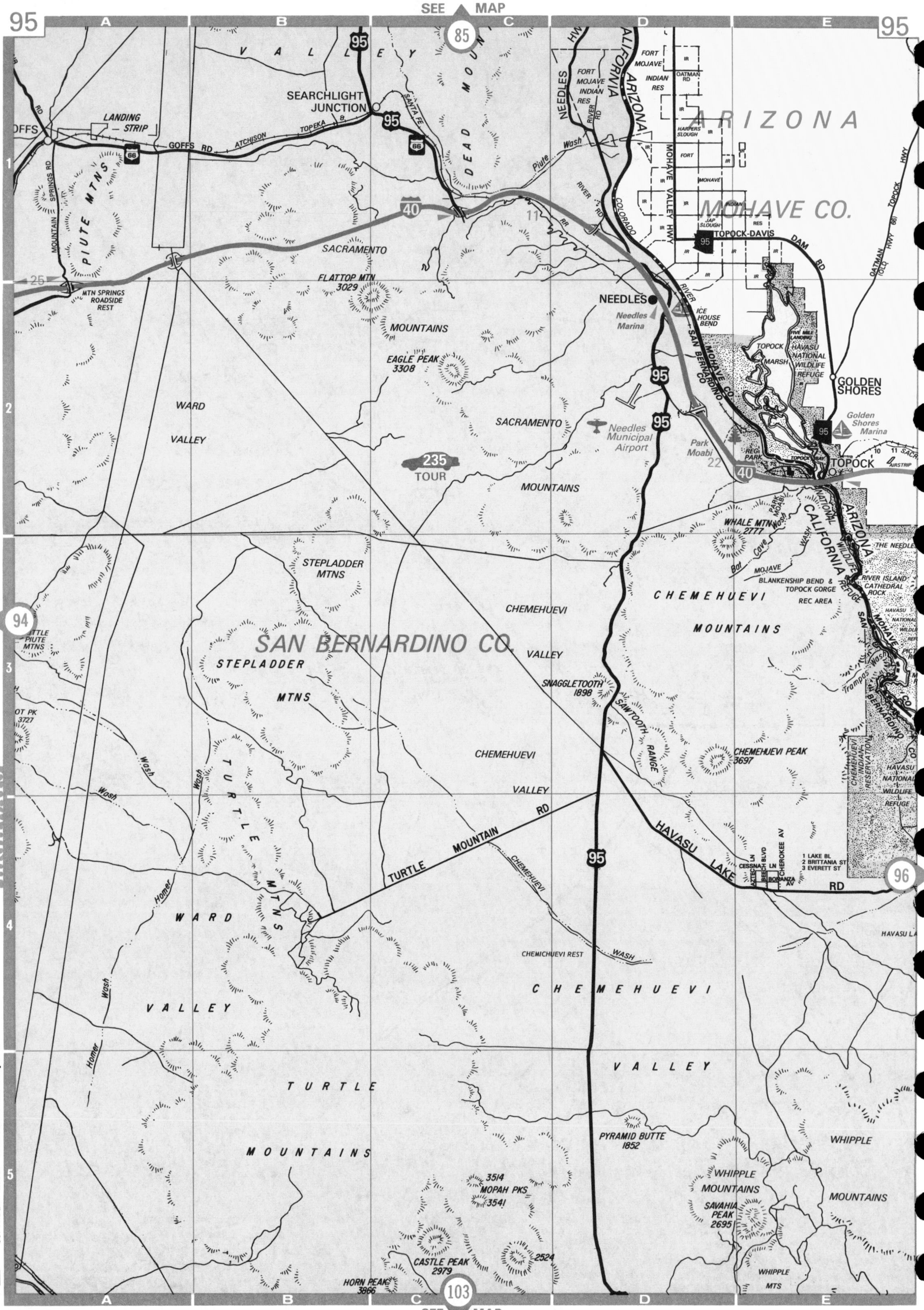
SEE MAP 85
A
B
C
D
E
VALLEY
95
SEARCHLIGHT JUNCTION
SANTA FE
LANDING STRIP
GOFFS
GOFFS RD
ATCHISON
TOPEKA
66
DEAD MOUNTAINS
MOUNTAIN SPRINGS RD
PIUTE MTNS
Piute Wash
40
11
SACRAMENTO
25
MTN SPRINGS ROADSIDE REST
FLATTOP MTN 3029
MOUNTAINS
EAGLE PEAK 3308
WARD VALLEY
SACRAMENTO
MOUNTAINS
235 TOUR
NEEDLES HWY
RIVER RD
CALIFORNIA
ARIZONA
FORT MOJAVE INDIAN RES
OATMAN RD
IR
HARPERS SLOUGH
FORT
MOHAVE
MOHAVE VALLEY HWY
JAP SLOUGH
RES
MOHAVE CO.
TOPOCK-DAVIS DAM RD
OATMAN (OLD) HWY 66
TOPOCK HWY
COLORADO RIVER
NEEDLES
Needles Marina
ICE HOUSE BEND
SAN BERNARDINO CO
MOHAVE CO
TOPOCK MARSH
FIVE MILE LANDING
HAVASU NATIONAL WILDLIFE REFUGE
GOLDEN SHORES
Golden Shores Marina
Needles Municipal Airport
Park Moabi
22
TOPOCK
AIRSTRIP
WHALE MTN 2777
Bat Cave Wash
MOJAVE
BLANKENSHIP BEND & TOPOCK GORGE REC AREA
THE NEEDLES
RIVER ISLAND
CATHEDRAL ROCK
STEPLADDER MTNS
CHEMEHUEVI
CHEMEHUEVI MOUNTAINS
SAN BERNARDINO CO.
LITTLE PIUTE MTNS
STEPLADDER MTNS
VALLEY
SNAGGLETOOTH 1898
SAWTOOTH RANGE
OT PK 3727
CHEMEHUEVI PEAK 3697
CHEMEHUEVI INDIAN RESERVATION
Trampas Wash
CHEMEHUEVI VALLEY
TURTLE MTNS
Wash
Homer Wash
TURTLE MOUNTAIN RD
HAVASU LAKE RD
CESSNA LN
CHEROKEE AV
BONANZA AV
1 LAKE BL
2 BRITTANIA ST
3 EVERETT ST
96
WARD
HAVASU LA
CHEMICHUEVI REST
CHEMEHUEVI WASH
CHEMEHUEVI
VALLEY
VALLEY
TURTLE
MOUNTAINS
PYRAMID BUTTE 1852
WHIPPLE
WHIPPLE MOUNTAINS
MOUNTAINS
SAVAHIA PEAK 2695
3514
MOPAH PKS 3541
2524
CASTLE PEAK 2979
HORN PEAK 3866
WHIPPLE MTS
SEE MAP 94
SEE MAP 103
HIGHWAYS

SEE MAP 88
SEE MAP 97
SEE MAP 104
95
PACIFIC OCEAN
PIERPONT BAY
San Buenaventura State Beach
McGrath State Beach
MONTALVO
NYELAND ACRES
CAMARILLO
OXNARD
HOLLYWOOD BEACH
HOLLYWOOD BY-THE-SEA
SILVER STRAND
PORT HUENEME
Channel Islands Harbor
Port Hueneme Harbor
Port Hueneme Beach
VENTURA CO.
MOORPARK HOMEACRES
NEWBURY PARK
VEN-TU PARK
LAKE SHERWOOD
THOUSAND OAKS
WESTLAKE VILLAGE
Seminole Hot Springs
Rancho Sierra Vista
SANTA MONICA MTNS
RANCHO EL CONEJO
Point Mugu State Park
LA JOLLA PEAK
LAGUNA PEAK
MUGU PEAK
MUGU NAVAL AIR MISSLE TEST CTR
LAGUNA PT
PT MUGU
POINT MUGU
PACIFIC COAST HWY
LOS ANGELES CO.
Santa Monica Mountains National Recreation Area
Leo Carrillo State Beach
Robert H. Meyer Mem. State Beach
Point Dume Beach
PT DUME
231 TOUR
Holiday Inn
Hyatt
MOHAVE CO
POWELL PEAK 2353'
RIVER ISLAND
CATHEDRAL ROCK
TUMARION PEAK 2093'
Havasu National Wildlife Refuge
PICTURE ROCK
MOHAVE ROCK
CASTLE ROCK
CHEMEHUEVI INDIAN RESERVATION
HAVASU NATIONAL WILDLIFE REFUGE
ARIZONA
CALIFORNIA
CROSSMAN PEAK
London Bridge
LAKE HAVASU CITY
Lake Havasu Marina
HAVASU LANDING
Lake Havasu City Airport
THOMPSON POINT
Lake Havasu State Park
CHEMEHUEVI INDIAN RES
ROADS END CAMP
SAN BERNARDINO CO.
BLACK MEADOWS CAMP
WHIPPLE MOUNTAINS
WHIPPLE MTNS RECREATION AREA (PROP)
235 TOUR
GENE WASH RES
COPPER BASIN RES
PARKER DAM
MONKEYS HEAD 1587'
CASTLE ROCK 1150'
BUCKSKIN MTN STATE PK
COLORADO RIVER INDIAN RES
LA PAZ COUNTY
LITTLE BLACK MTN
CASTANEDA HILLS
CASTANEDA PEAK
BLACK MOUNTAIN
MOHAVE SPGS MESA
BILL WILLIAMS RIVER
AUBREY 5078'
AIRSTRIP
HIGHWAYS

96

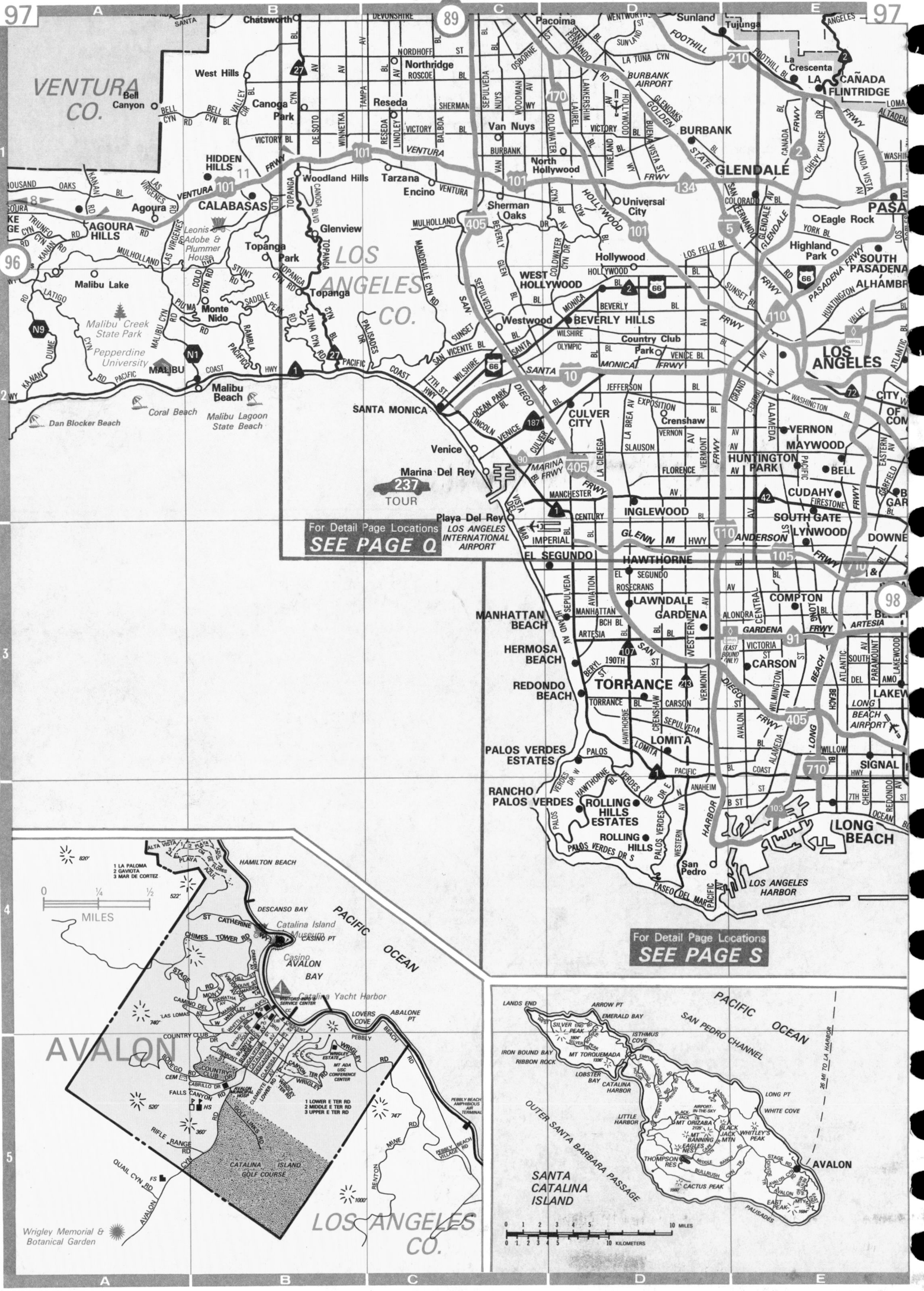
VENTURA CO.
LOS ANGELES CO.
SEE MAP 96
SEE MAP 98
A
B
C
D
E
1
2
3
4
5
Chatsworth
Pacoima
Sunland
Tujunga
La Crescenta
LA CAÑADA FLINTRIDGE
West Hills
Northridge
Reseda
Canoga Park
Bell Canyon
Van Nuys
BURBANK AIRPORT
BURBANK
GLENDALE
HIDDEN HILLS
Woodland Hills
Tarzana
Encino
North Hollywood
Universal City
CALABASAS
Agoura
AGOURA HILLS
Sherman Oaks
Leonis Adobe & Plummer House
Glenview
Topanga Park
Topanga
Malibu Lake
Monte Nido
Malibu Creek State Park
Pepperdine University
MALIBU
Malibu Beach
Coral Beach
Malibu Lagoon State Beach
Dan Blocker Beach
Hollywood
WEST HOLLYWOOD
Eagle Rock
Highland Park
SOUTH PASADENA
ALHAMBRA
Westwood
BEVERLY HILLS
Country Club Park
LOS ANGELES
SANTA MONICA
CULVER CITY
Crenshaw
VERNON
MAYWOOD
HUNTINGTON PARK
BELL
CUDAHY
Venice
Marina Del Rey
237 TOUR
SOUTH GATE
LYNWOOD
Playa Del Rey
LOS ANGELES INTERNATIONAL AIRPORT
INGLEWOOD
For Detail Page Locations
SEE PAGE Q
EL SEGUNDO
HAWTHORNE
LAWNDALE
COMPTON
MANHATTAN BEACH
GARDENA
HERMOSA BEACH
CARSON
REDONDO BEACH
TORRANCE
LONG BEACH AIRPORT
LOMITA
PALOS VERDES ESTATES
SIGNAL HILL
RANCHO PALOS VERDES
ROLLING HILLS ESTATES
ROLLING HILLS
LONG BEACH
San Pedro
LOS ANGELES HARBOR
For Detail Page Locations
SEE PAGE S
PACIFIC OCEAN
AVALON
HAMILTON BEACH
DESCANSO BAY
Catalina Island Museum
CASINO PT
AVALON BAY
Catalina Yacht Harbor
LOVERS COVE
ABALONE PT
1 LA PALOMA
2 GAVIOTA
3 MAR DE CORTEZ
1 LOWER E TER RD
2 MIDDLE E TER RD
3 UPPER E TER RD
MILES
CATALINA ISLAND GOLF COURSE
PEBBLY BEACH AMPHIBIOUS AIR TERMINAL
Wrigley Memorial & Botanical Garden
LANDS END
ARROW PT
EMERALD BAY
ISTHMUS COVE
SAN PEDRO CHANNEL
IRON BOUND BAY
RIBBON ROCK
MT TORQUEMADA
LOBSTER BAY
CATALINA HARBOR
LITTLE HARBOR
OUTER SANTA BARBARA PASSAGE
MT ORIZABA
BLACK JACK MTN
MT BANNING
EAGLES NEST
WHITLEY'S PEAK
LONG PT
WHITE COVE
THOMPSON RES
CACTUS PEAK
SANTA CATALINA ISLAND
26 MI TO LA HARBOR
10 MILES
10 KILOMETERS

HIGHWAYS

SEE MAP 90

SEE MAP 99
SEE MAP 97
SEE MAP 105

HIGHWAYS

SEE MAP 91
SEE MAP 98
SEE MAP 100
SEE MAP 106
KEENBROOK
DEVORE
MONUMENT PK 5290
PANORAMA PT 3775
ARROWHEAD PK 4237
SAN BERNARDINO NATIONAL FOREST
RIMFOREST
SKY-FOREST
LAKE ARROWHEAD
GREEN VALLEY LAKE
CRAFTS PK 8364
BUTLER PK 8537
Rim Of The World Hwy
BIG BEAR LAKE
ARROWBEAR LAKE
DEEP CREEK LAKE
RUNNING SPRINGS
FREDALBA
Snow Valley
VERDEMONT
ARROWHEAD SPRINGS
DEL ROSA
PATTON
MUSCOY
SAN BERNARDINO CO.
San Bernardino National Forest
ANGELUS OAKS
MOUNTAIN HOME VILLAGE
HIGHLAND
SAN BERNARDINO
EAST HIGHLANDS
FONTANA
RIALTO
COLTON
MENTONE
BLOOMINGTON
REDLANDS
CRAFTON
Yucaipa Adobe
YUCAIPA
OAK GLEN
LOMA LINDA
BRYN MAWR
GRAND TERRACE
SUNNYSLOPE
CRESTMORE
MIRA LOMA
GLEN AVON
RUBIDOUX
RIVERSIDE
CANYON CREST HEIGHTS
Riverside Botanical Gardens
Univ of Calif Riverside
CALIMESA
CHERRY VALLEY
PEDLEY
Riverside Muni Airport
MORENO VALLEY
NORTON YOUNGLOVE RESERVE
BEAUMONT
LA SIERRA
CASA BLANCA
ARLINGTON
MORENO
March Field Museum
ARNOLD HEIGHTS
MARCH AIR FORCE BASE
EDEN HOT SPRINGS
California Citrus State Historic Park
WOODCREST
HOME GARDENS
GLEN VALLEY
Lake Perris State Rec Area
RIVERSIDE CO.
LAKEVIEW
LAKE MATHEWS
MT RUDOLPH 2649
GILMAN HOT SPRINGS
JUNIPER FLATS
SOBOBA HOT SPRINGS
NUEVO
SAN JACINTO
ESTELLE MTN 2767
PERRIS
Orange Empire Railway Mus
GOOD HOPE
VALLE VISTA
HOMELAND
SANTIAGO PK 5696
TRABUCO PK 4578
ROMOLAND
GREEN ACRES
HEMET
ALBERHILL
WINCHESTER
Ramona Bowl & Museum
MENIFEE
SUN CITY
QUAIL VALLEY
LAKE ELSINORE
CANYON LAKE
CLEVELAND NATIONAL FOREST
ORANGE CO.
EL CARISO
Lake Elsinore State Rec
SEDCO HILLS
LAKELAND VILLAGE
SAN JUAN HOT SPRINGS
SITTON PK 3254
RANCHO LA CIENEGA
Cleveland National Forest
WILDOMAR
BLACK MTN 3040
BACHELOR MTN 2543
Lake Skinner
French Valley Vineyards
MURRIETA HOT SPRINGS
MURRIETA
Piconi Winery
Mt Palomar Winery
Callaway Vineyard
Hart Winery
Maurice Carrie
Cilurzo
Filsinger
Baily
Culbertson Winery
RANCHO CALIFORNIA
OAK MTN 2708
ROUNDTOP HILL 2583
HIGHWAYS

SEE 92 MAP

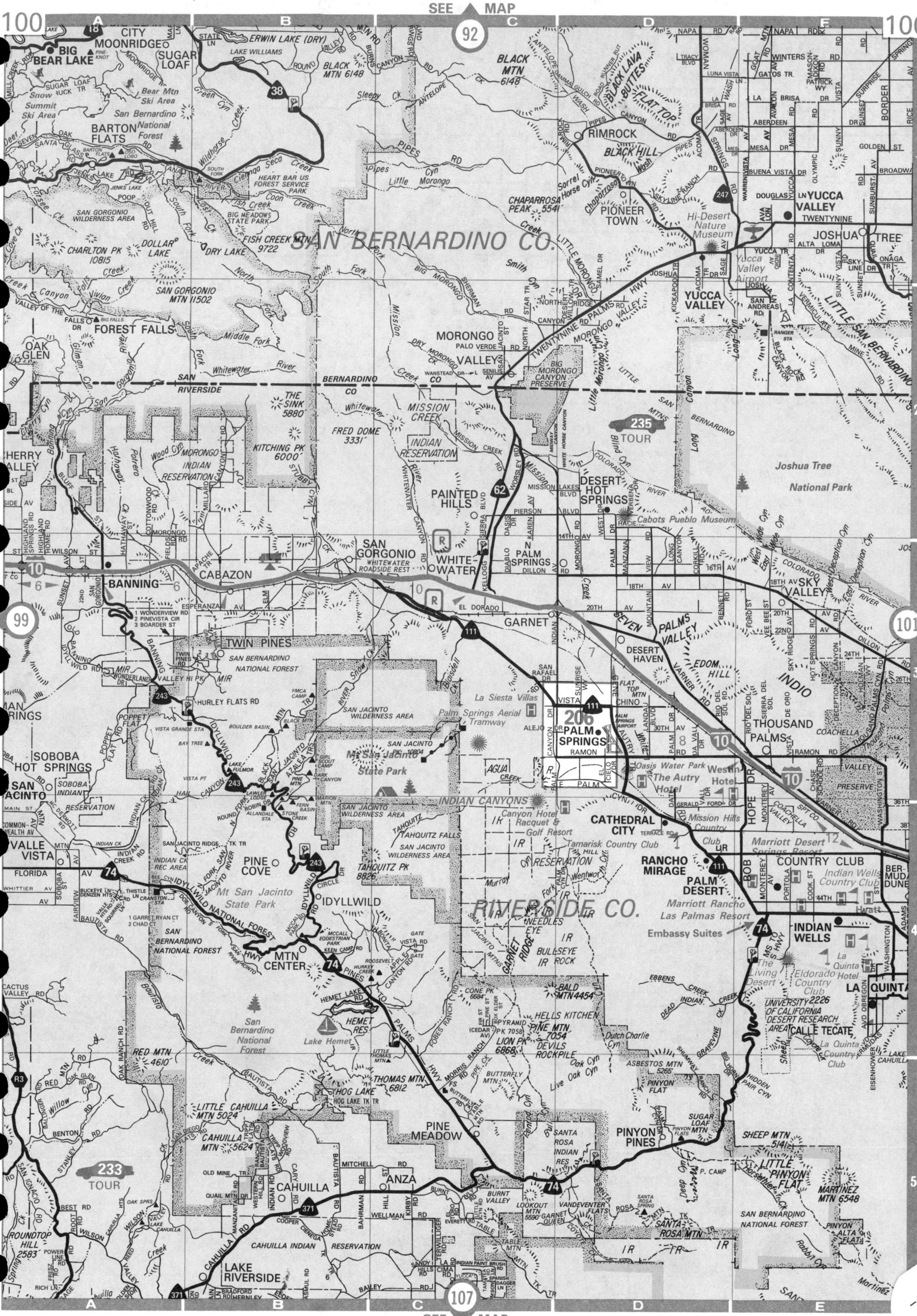

SEE 107 MAP

SEE MAP 93

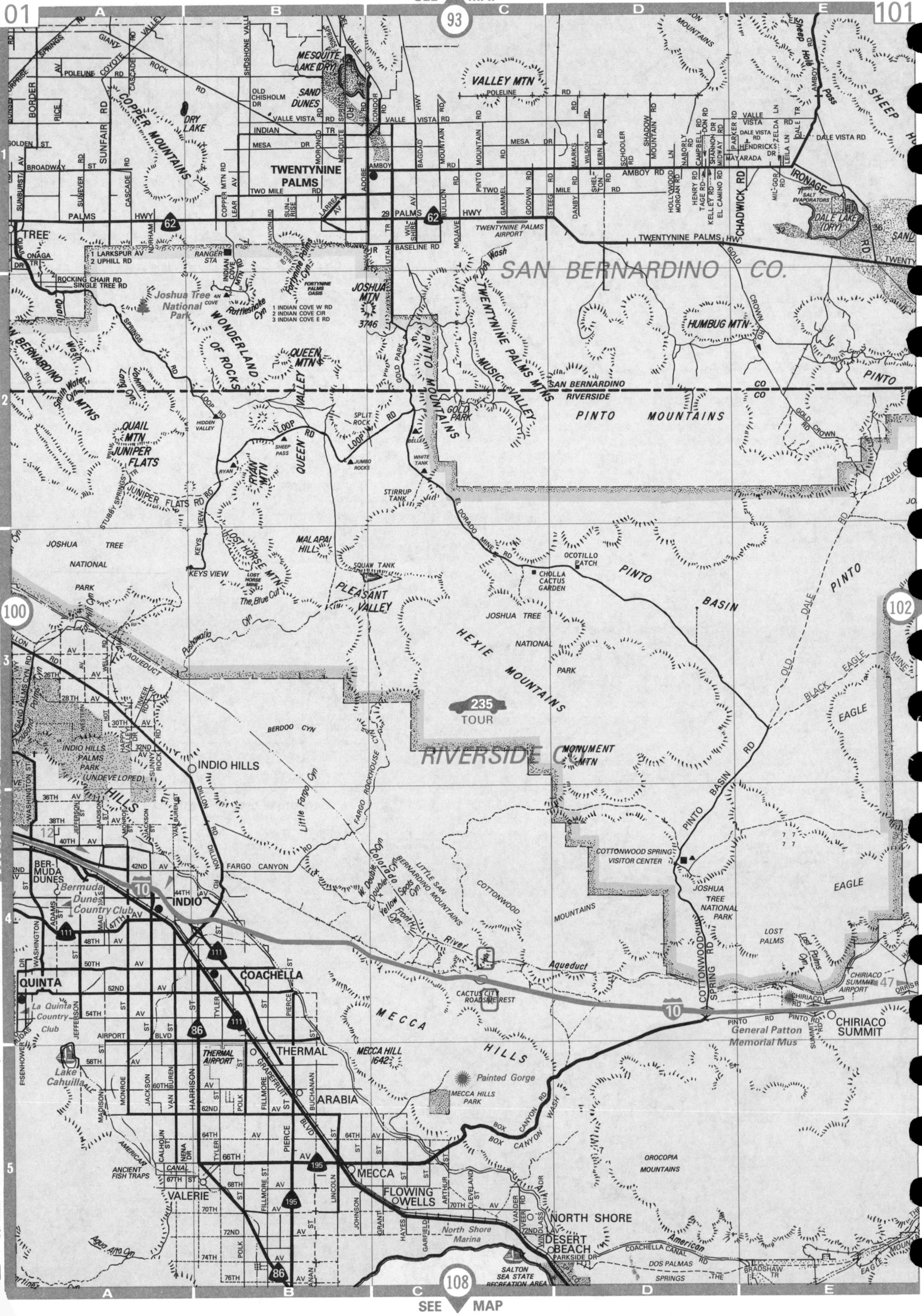

SEE MAP 100
SEE MAP 102
SEE MAP 108

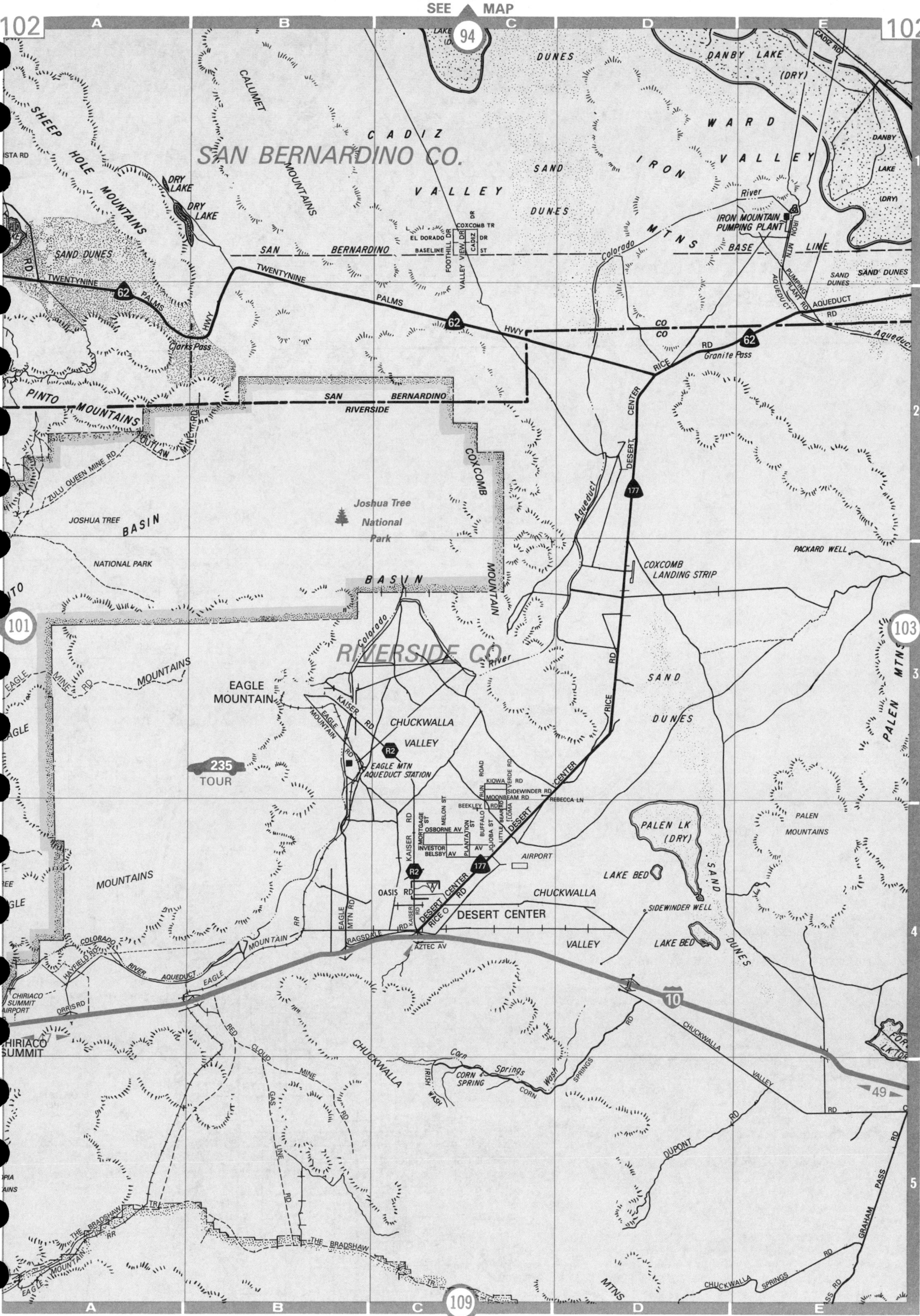
SEE MAP 94
SEE MAP 101
SEE MAP 103
SEE MAP 109
HIGHWAYS
SAN BERNARDINO CO.
RIVERSIDE CO.
SHEEP HOLE MOUNTAINS
CALUMET MOUNTAINS
CADIZ VALLEY
SAND DUNES
DUNES
DRY LAKE
DANBY LAKE (DRY)
WARD VALLEY
IRON MTNS
IRON MOUNTAIN PUMPING PLANT
SAN BERNARDINO BASE LINE
TWENTYNINE PALMS HWY
62
Clarks Pass
Granite Pass
RICE RD
PINTO MOUNTAINS
OUTLAW MINE RD
ZULU QUEEN MINE RD
JOSHUA TREE BASIN
NATIONAL PARK
Joshua Tree National Park
COXCOMB MOUNTAIN
DESERT CENTER RICE RD
177
Aqueduct
Colorado River
COXCOMB LANDING STRIP
PACKARD WELL
SAND DUNES
PALEN MTNS
PALEN MOUNTAINS
PALEN LK (DRY)
LAKE BED
SIDEWINDER WELL
EAGLE MOUNTAIN
EAGLE MOUNTAINS
EAGLE MINE RD
KAISER RD
CHUCKWALLA VALLEY
R2
EAGLE MTN AQUEDUCT STATION
235 TOUR
AIRPORT
DESERT CENTER
OASIS RD
RAGSDALE RD
AZTEC AV
10
CHIRIACO SUMMIT
CHIRIACO SUMMIT AIRPORT
HAYFIELD RD
ORR RD
COLORADO RIVER AQUEDUCT
RED CLOUD MINE RD
GAS LINE RD
CHUCKWALLA MOUNTAINS
Corn Springs Wash
CORN SPRING
IRISH WASH
DUPONT RD
CHUCKWALLA VALLEY RD
CHUCKWALLA SPRINGS RD
GRAHAM PASS RD
THE BRADSHAW TR

SEE MAP 95

SEE MAP 102
SEE MAP 104
SEE MAP 110
HIGHWAYS

SEE MAP 96

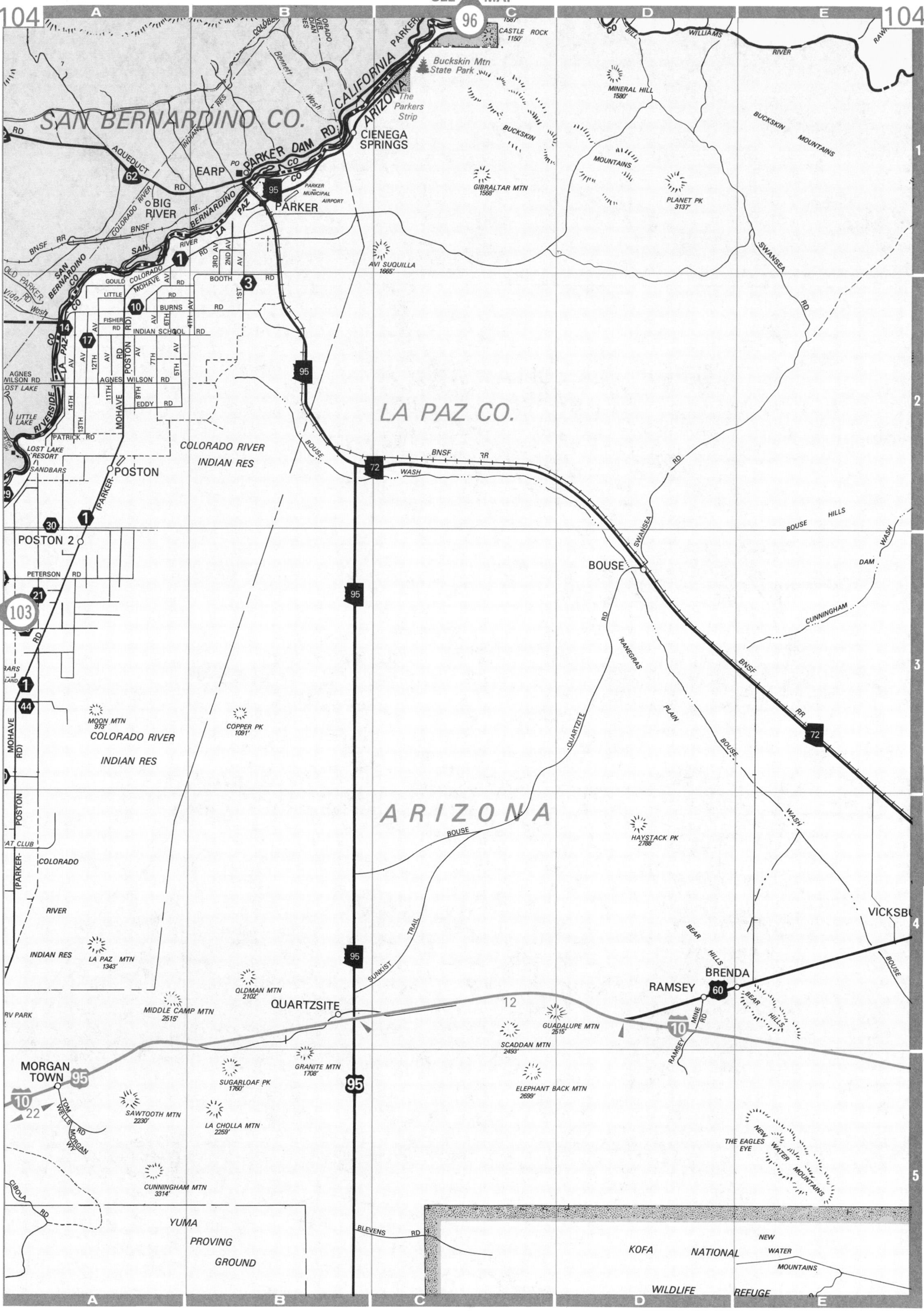
SAN BERNARDINO CO.
LA PAZ CO.
ARIZONA
CALIFORNIA
CASTLE ROCK 1150'
Buckskin Mtn State Park
The Parkers Strip
CIENEGA SPRINGS
EARP
PARKER
BIG RIVER
PARKER DAM RD
PARKER MUNICIPAL AIRPORT
AQUEDUCT
COLORADO RIVER
BNSF RR
MINERAL HILL 1580'
BUCKSKIN MOUNTAINS
GIBRALTAR MTN 1568'
PLANET PK 3137'
AVI SUQUILLA 1665'
WILLIAMS RIVER
SWANSEA RD
COLORADO RIVER INDIAN RES
POSTON
POSTON 2
PETERSON RD
LOST LAKE RESORT
LITTLE LAKE
RIVERSIDE
AGNES WILSON RD
INDIAN SCHOOL RD
BOUSE
BOUSE HILLS
BOUSE WASH
DAM
CUNNINGHAM
RANEGRAS PLAIN
QUARTZITE
MOON MTN 973'
COPPER PK 1091'
HAYSTACK PK 2788'
VICKSBU
LA PAZ MTN 1343'
OLDMAN MTN 2102'
MIDDLE CAMP MTN 2515'
QUARTZSITE
SUNKIST TRAIL
BRENDA
RAMSEY
BEAR HILLS
GUADALUPE MTN 2515'
SCADDAN MTN 2493'
ELEPHANT BACK MTN 2699'
MORGAN TOWN
TOM WELLS RD
MORGAN WY
SAWTOOTH MTN 2230'
SUGARLOAF PK 1760'
GRANITE MTN 1708'
LA CHOLLA MTN 2259'
CUNNINGHAM MTN 3314'
CIBOLA RD
THE EAGLES EYE
NEW WATER MOUNTAINS
YUMA PROVING GROUND
BLEVENS RD
KOFA NATIONAL WILDLIFE REFUGE
HIGHWAYS

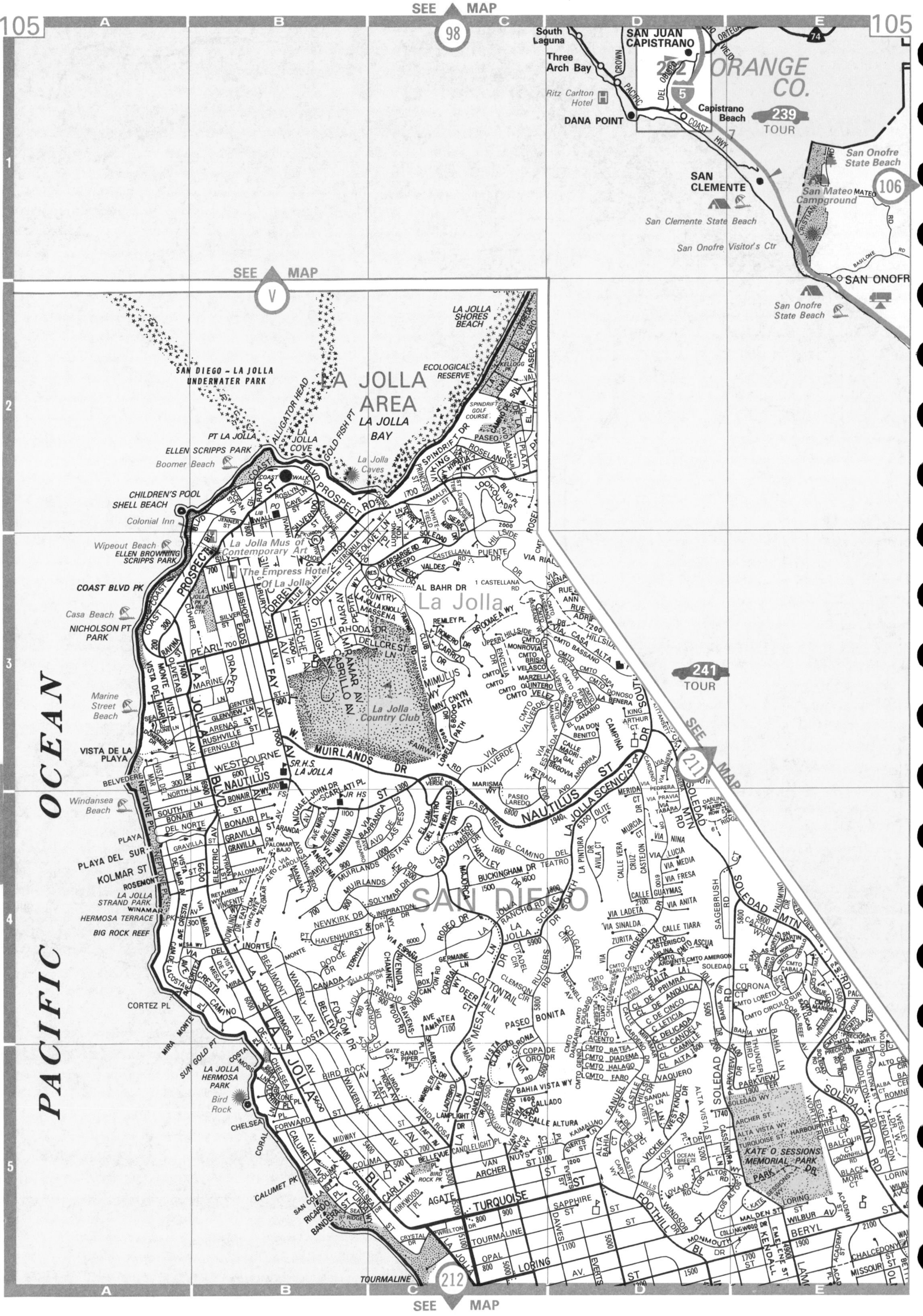

SEE MAP 98
SEE MAP V
SEE MAP 211
SEE MAP 212
106
South Laguna
Three Arch Bay
SAN JUAN CAPISTRANO
ORANGE CO.
Ritz Carlton Hotel
DANA POINT
Capistrano Beach
239 TOUR
SAN CLEMENTE
San Clemente State Beach
San Onofre State Beach
San Mateo Campground
San Onofre Visitor's Ctr
SAN ONOFRE
San Onofre State Beach
LA JOLLA AREA
LA JOLLA BAY
LA JOLLA SHORES BEACH
ECOLOGICAL RESERVE
SAN DIEGO - LA JOLLA UNDERWATER PARK
ALLIGATOR HEAD
LA JOLLA COVE
GOLD FISH PT
PT LA JOLLA
ELLEN SCRIPPS PARK
Boomer Beach
La Jolla Caves
CHILDREN'S POOL
SHELL BEACH
Colonial Inn
Wipeout Beach
ELLEN BROWNING SCRIPPS PARK
La Jolla Mus of Contemporary Art
The Empress Hotel Of La Jolla
COAST BLVD PK
Casa Beach
NICHOLSON PT PARK
La Jolla
La Jolla Country Club
241 TOUR
PACIFIC OCEAN
Marine Street Beach
VISTA DE LA PLAYA
BELVEDERE
Windansea Beach
PLAYA
PLAYA DEL SUR
KOLMAR ST
ROSEMONT
LA JOLLA STRAND PARK
WINAMAR
HERMOSA TERRACE
BIG ROCK REEF
SAN DIEGO
CORTEZ PL
MIRA MONTE
SUN GOLD PT
LA JOLLA HERMOSA PARK
Bird Rock
CHELSEA
CALUMET PK
KATE O SESSIONS MEMORIAL PARK
TOURMALINE
PROSPECT
TORREY PINES RD
MUIRLANDS DR
NAUTILUS ST
LA JOLLA SCENIC DR
SOLEDAD MTN RD
LA JOLLA BLVD
TURQUOISE
TOURMALINE
LORING

HIGHWAYS

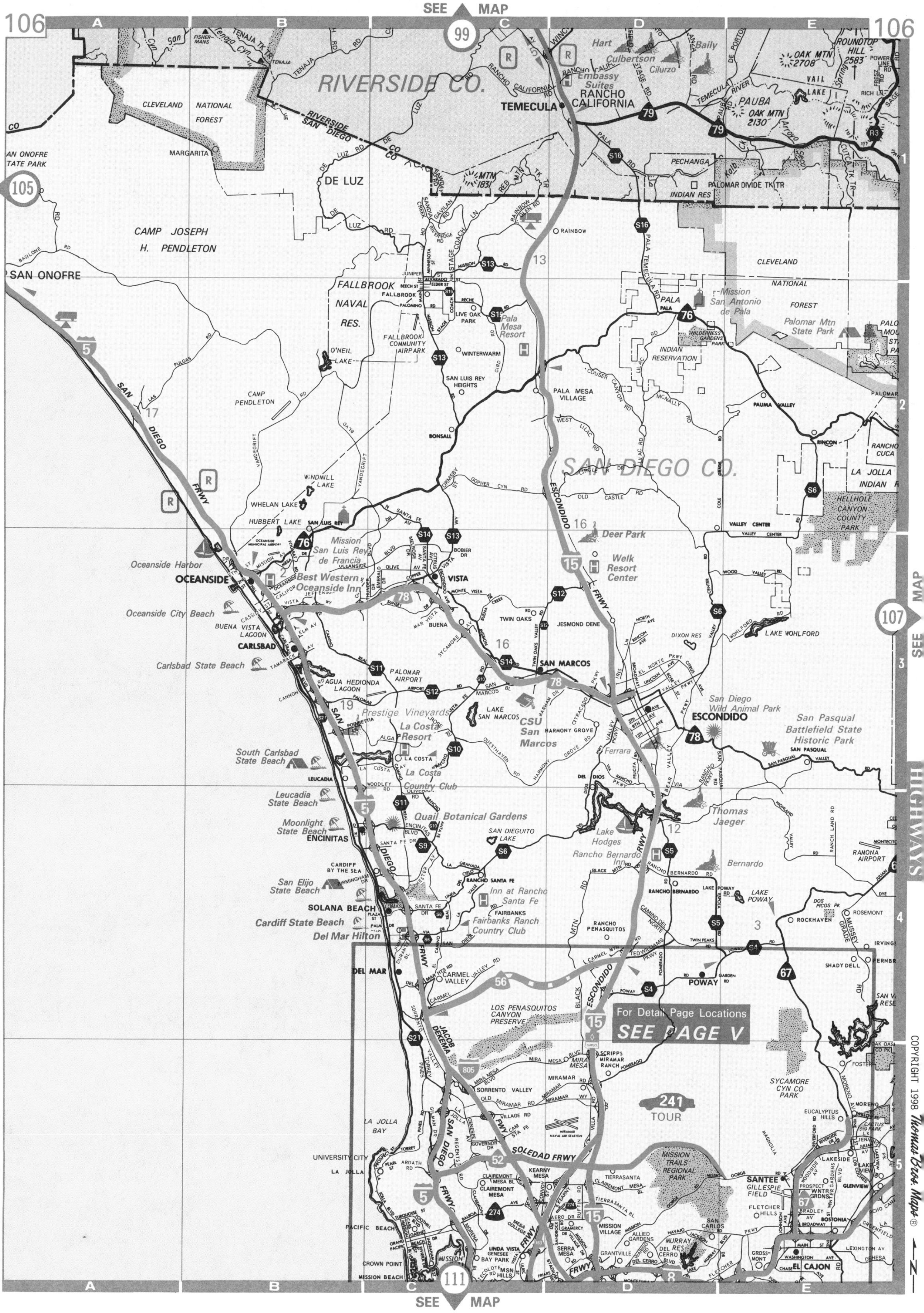
SEE MAP 99
SEE MAP 105
SEE MAP 107
SEE MAP 111
RIVERSIDE CO.
SAN DIEGO CO.
RIVERSIDE
SAN DIEGO
CO
TEMECULA
RANCHO CALIFORNIA
Embassy Suites
Hart
Culbertson
Baily
Cilurzo
OAK MTN 2708
ROUNDTOP HILL 2583
PAUBA
OAK MTN 2130
PECHANGA
INDIAN RES
PALOMAR DIVIDE TK TR
CLEVELAND NATIONAL FOREST
MARGARITA
SAN ONOFRE STATE PARK
DE LUZ
MTN 1831
RAINBOW
CAMP JOSEPH H. PENDLETON
SAN ONOFRE
FALLBROOK NAVAL RES.
FALLBROOK
LIVE OAK PARK
Pala Mesa Resort
FALLBROOK COMMUNITY AIRPARK
O'NEIL LAKE
WINTERWARM
SAN LUIS REY HEIGHTS
PALA
Mission San Antonio de Pala
INDIAN RESERVATION
WILDERNESS GARDENS PARK
Palomar Mtn State Park
CAMP PENDLETON
PALA MESA VILLAGE
PAUMA VALLEY
BONSALL
RINCON
RANCHO CUCA
LA JOLLA INDIAN R
SAN DIEGO FRWY
ESCONDIDO FRWY
WINDMILL LAKE
WHELAN LAKE
HUBBERT LAKE
SAN LUIS REY
Mission San Luis Rey de Francia
Deer Park
HELLHOLE CANYON COUNTY PARK
VALLEY CENTER
Oceanside Harbor
OCEANSIDE
Best Western Oceanside Inn
VISTA
Welk Resort Center
Oceanside City Beach
BUENA VISTA LAGOON
BUENA
TWIN OAKS
JESMOND DENE
DIXON RES
LAKE WOHLFORD
CARLSBAD
Carlsbad State Beach
SAN MARCOS
PALOMAR AIRPORT
AGUA HEDIONDA LAGOON
Prestige Vineyards
LAKE SAN MARCOS
CSU San Marcos
ESCONDIDO
San Diego Wild Animal Park
San Pasqual Battlefield State Historic Park
La Costa Resort
South Carlsbad State Beach
HARMONY GROVE
Ferrara
LA COSTA
La Costa Country Club
LEUCADIA
Leucadia State Beach
Quail Botanical Gardens
Moonlight State Beach
ENCINITAS
SAN DIEGUITO LAKE
Lake Hodges
Rancho Bernardo Inn
Thomas Jaeger
Bernardo
RAMONA AIRPORT
CARDIFF BY THE SEA
San Elijo State Beach
RANCHO SANTA FE
Inn at Rancho Santa Fe
FAIRBANKS
Fairbanks Ranch Country Club
RANCHO BERNARDO
LAKE POWAY
SOLANA BEACH
Cardiff State Beach
Del Mar Hilton
RANCHO PENASQUITOS
ROCKHAVEN
ROSEMONT
DEL MAR
CARMEL VALLEY
POWAY
SHADY DELL
LOS PENASQUITOS CANYON PRESERVE
For Detail Page Locations SEE PAGE V
SCRIPPS MIRAMAR RANCH
SORRENTO VALLEY
MIRAMAR
SYCAMORE CYN CO PARK
241 TOUR
LA JOLLA BAY
UNIVERSITY CITY
LA JOLLA
SOLEDAD FRWY
MIRAMAR NAVAL AIR STATION
KEARNY MESA
TIERRASANTA
MISSION TRAILS REGIONAL PARK
SANTEE
GILLESPIE FIELD
LAKESIDE
EUCALYPTUS HILLS
CLAIREMONT
FLETCHER HILLS
BOSTONIA
PACIFIC BEACH
SAN CARLOS
MISSION VILLAGE
ALLIED GARDENS
MURRAY DEL RES CERRO
GROSSMONT
EL CAJON
CROWN POINT
MISSION BEACH
LINDA VISTA
BAY PARK
SERRA MESA
GRANTVILLE
HIGHWAYS

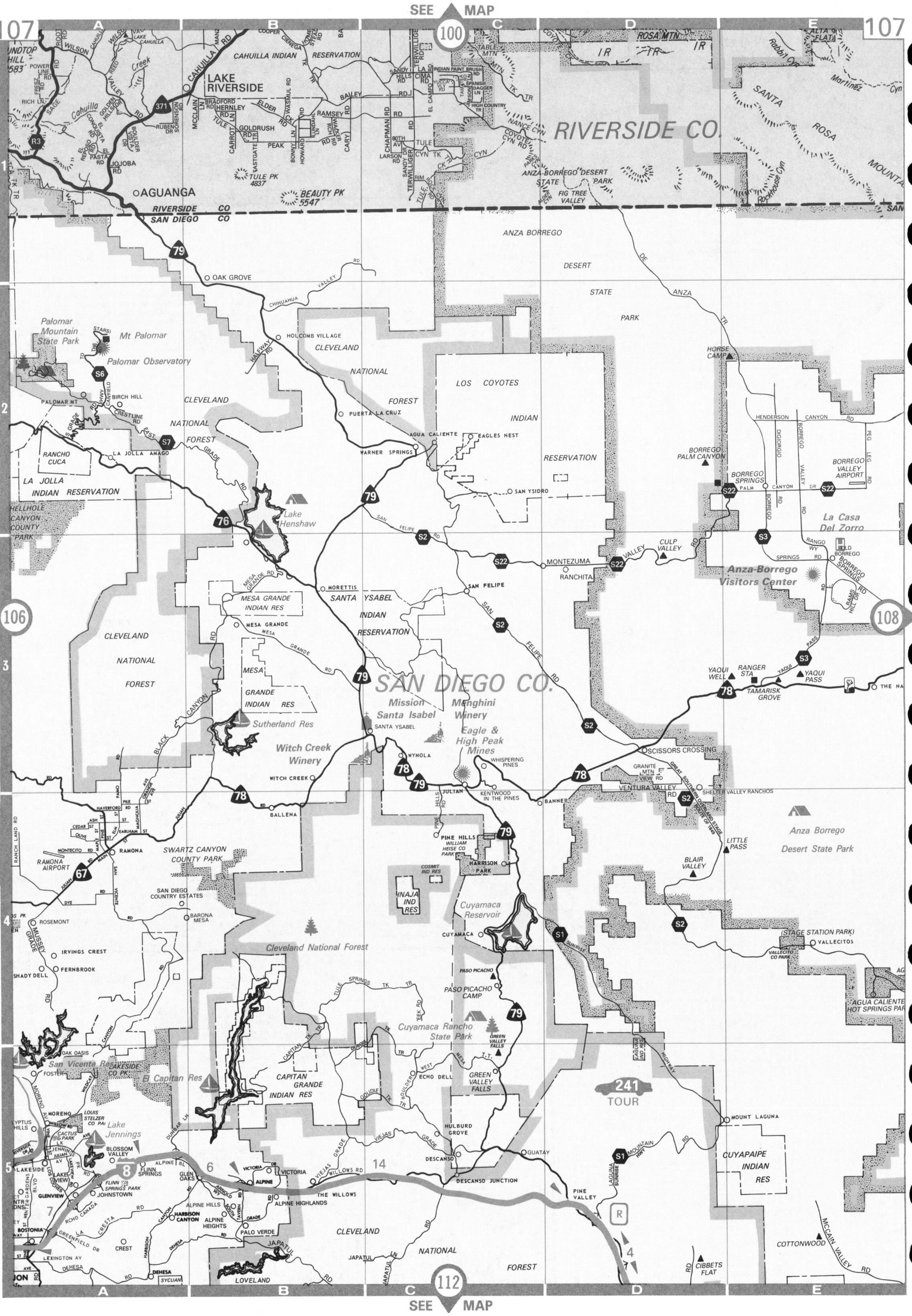
SEE MAP 100
SEE MAP 106
SEE MAP 108
SEE MAP 112
HIGHWAYS
RIVERSIDE CO.
RIVERSIDE CO
SAN DIEGO CO
SAN DIEGO CO.
LAKE RIVERSIDE
AGUANGA
CAHUILLA INDIAN RESERVATION
TULE PK 4837
BEAUTY PK 5547
ANZA-BORREGO DESERT STATE PARK
FIG TREE VALLEY
SANTA ROSA MOUNTA
ANZA BORREGO DESERT STATE PARK
OAK GROVE
HOLCOMB VILLAGE
CLEVELAND NATIONAL FOREST
LOS COYOTES INDIAN RESERVATION
Palomar Mountain State Park
Mt Palomar
Palomar Observatory
PALOMAR MT
BIRCH HILL
RANCHO CUCA
LA JOLLA INDIAN RESERVATION
HELLHOLE CANYON COUNTY PARK
PUERTA LA CRUZ
AGUA CALIENTE
EAGLES NEST
WARNER SPRINGS
SAN YSIDRO
Lake Henshaw
HORSE CAMP
BORREGO PALM CANYON
BORREGO SPRINGS
BORREGO VALLEY AIRPORT
La Casa Del Zorro
Anza-Borrego Visitors Center
CULP VALLEY
MONTEZUMA
RANCHITA
SAN FELIPE
MORETTIS
SANTA YSABEL INDIAN RESERVATION
MESA GRANDE INDIAN RES
MESA GRANDE
YAQUI WELL
RANGER STA
YAQUI PASS
TAMARISK GROVE
Sutherland Res
Mission Santa Isabel
Menghini Winery
Witch Creek Winery
Eagle & High Peak Mines
SANTA YSABEL
WYNOLA
WHISPERING PINES
SCISSORS CROSSING
GRANITE MTN VIEW
VENTURA VALLEY
SHELTER VALLEY RANCHOS
WITCH CREEK
JULIAN
KENTWOOD IN THE PINES
BANNER
BALLENA
RAMONA
RAMONA AIRPORT
SWARTZ CANYON COUNTY PARK
PINE HILLS
HARRISON PARK
LITTLE PASS
BLAIR VALLEY
Anza Borrego Desert State Park
SAN DIEGO COUNTRY ESTATES
BARONA MESA
INAJA IND RES
Cuyamaca Reservoir
CUYAMACA
STAGE STATION PARK
VALLECITOS
ROSEMONT
IRVINGS CREST
FERNBROOK
SHADY DELL
Cleveland National Forest
PASO PICACHO
PASO PICACHO CAMP
Cuyamaca Rancho State Park
GREEN VALLEY FALLS
AGUA CALIENTE HOT SPRINGS PAR
OAK OASIS
San Vicente Res
LAKESIDE CO PK
El Capitan Res
CAPITAN GRANDE INDIAN RES
ECHO DELL
LAGUNA IND RES
241 TOUR
MORENO
Lake Jennings
BLOSSOM VALLEY
LAKESIDE
FLINN SPRINGS
GLEN OAKS
VICTORIA
ALPINE
THE WILLOWS
HULBURD GROVE
DESCANSO
DESCANSO JUNCTION
GUATAY
MOUNT LAGUNA
CUYAPAIPE INDIAN RES
PINE VALLEY
ALPINE HIGHLANDS
ALPINE HILLS
HARBISON CANYON
ALPINE HEIGHTS
PALO VERDE
GLENVIEW
JOHNSTOWN
CREST
DEHESA
LOVELAND
CLEVELAND NATIONAL FOREST
COTTONWOOD
CIBBETS FLAT
Thomas Bros. Maps®
COPYRIGHT 1998

SEE MAP 101

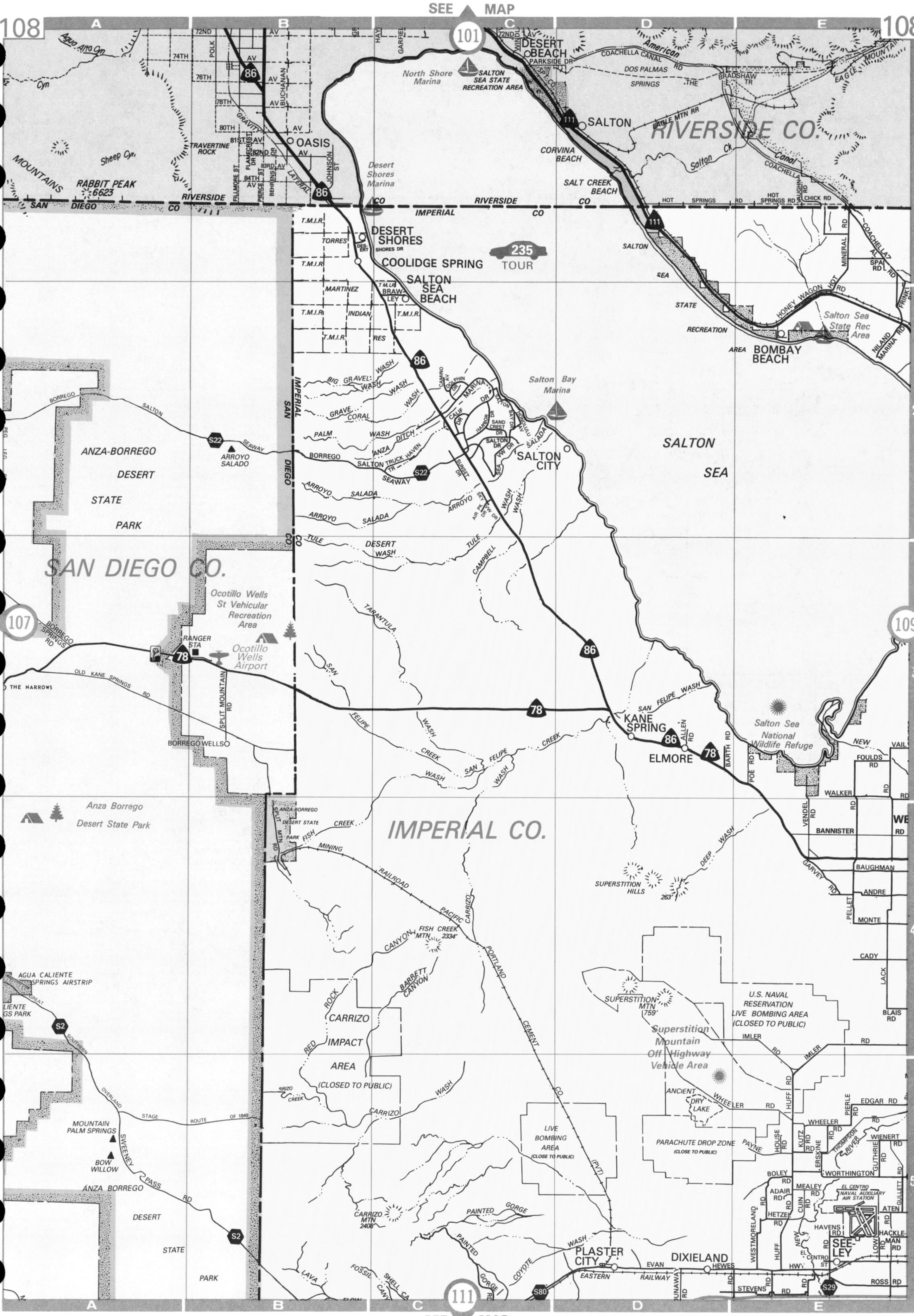

SEE MAP 107
SEE MAP 109
SEE MAP 111

SEE MAP 102

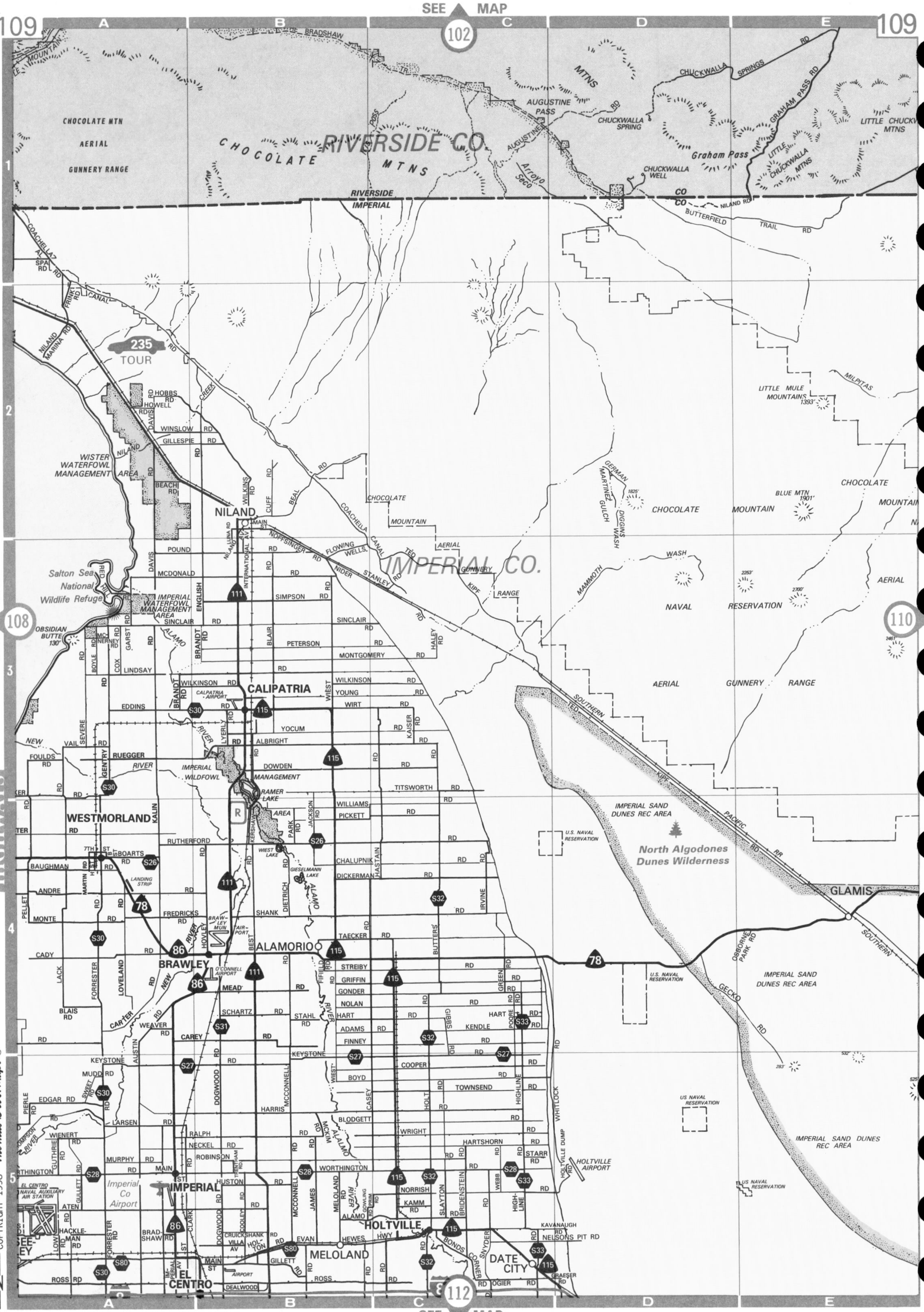

SEE MAP 108
110
SEE MAP 112
HIGHWAYS

SEE MAP 103

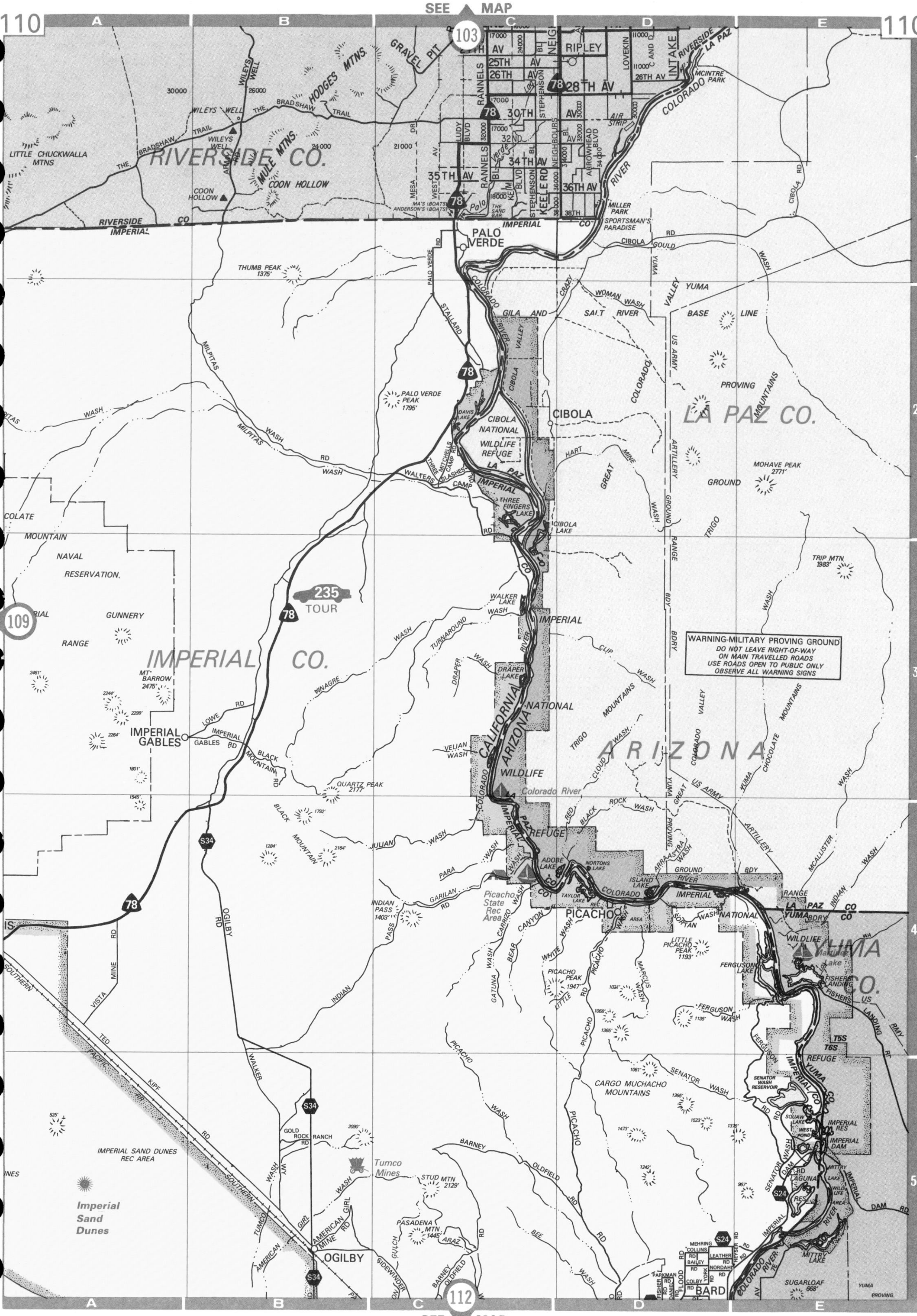

HIGHWAYS

SEE MAP 109

SEE MAP 112

111

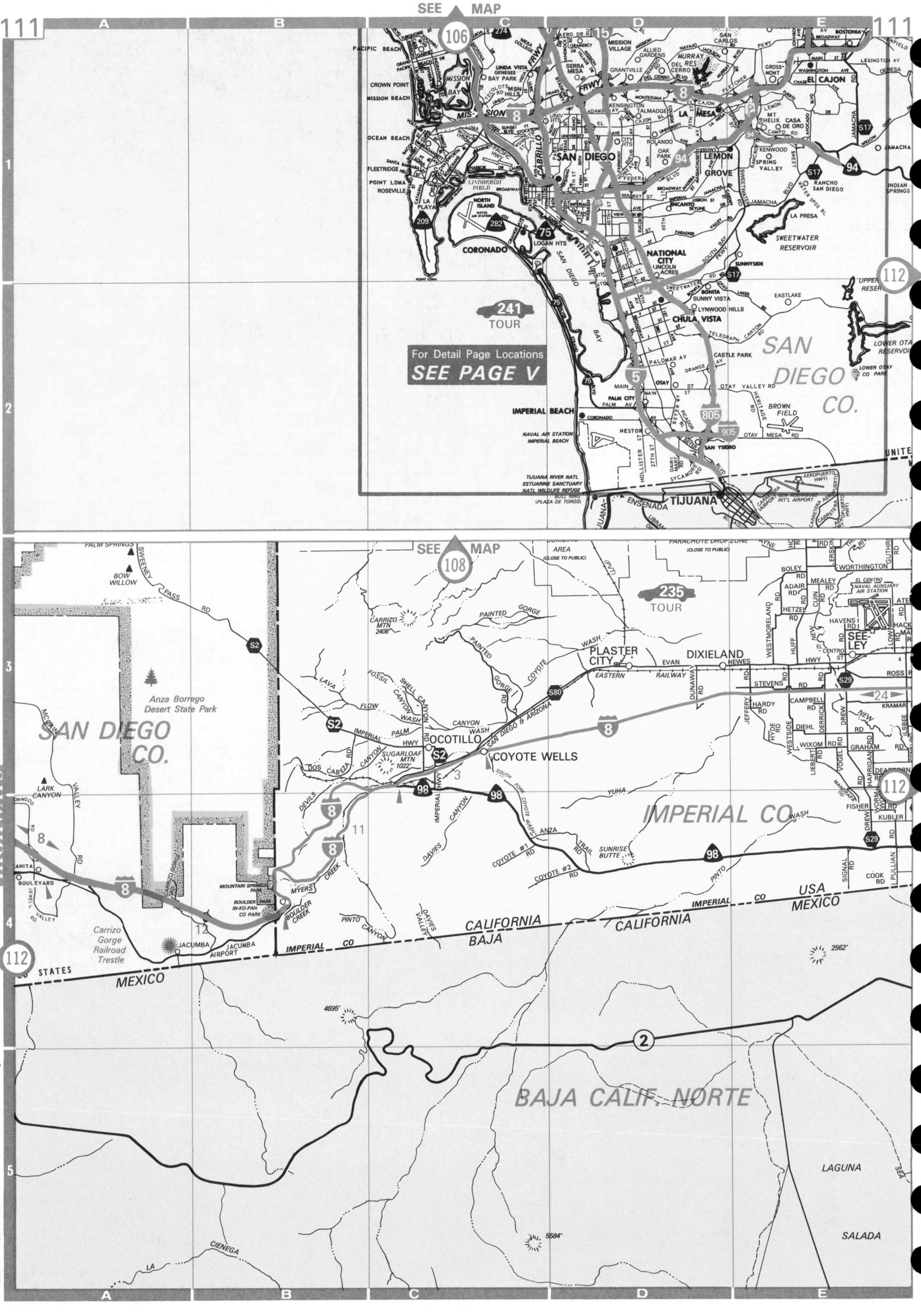
A
B
C
D
E
1
2
3
4
5
SEE MAP 106
SEE MAP 108
112
SEE MAP 112
PACIFIC BEACH
CROWN POINT
MISSION BEACH
MISSION BAY
OCEAN BEACH
FLEETRIDGE
POINT LOMA
ROSEVILLE
LA PLAYA
LINDBERGH FIELD
NORTH ISLAND
CORONADO
LOGAN HTS
LINDA VISTA
SERRA MESA
MISSION VILLAGE
ALLIED GARDENS
SAN CARLOS
MURRAY RES
DEL CERRO
GRANTVILLE
KENSINGTON
TALMADGE
LA MESA
EL CAJON
GROSSMONT
MT HELIX
CASA DE ORO
SAN DIEGO
LEMON GROVE
SPRING VALLEY
RANCHO SAN DIEGO
LA PRESA
SWEETWATER RESERVOIR
NATIONAL CITY
LINCOLN ACRES
BONITA
SUNNY VISTA
LYNWOOD HILLS
CHULA VISTA
EASTLAKE
UPPER OTAY RESERVOIR
LOWER OTAY RESERVOIR
LOWER OTAY CO PARK
INDIAN SPRINGS
JAMACHA
BOSTONIA
OTAY
PALM CITY
IMPERIAL BEACH
NAVAL AIR STATION IMPERIAL BEACH
NESTOR
SAN YSIDRO
BROWN FIELD
TIJUANA RIVER NATL ESTUARINE SANCTUARY NATL WILDLIFE REFUGE
BULL RING (PLAZA DE TOROS)
TIJUANA
ENSENADA
SAN DIEGO CO.
241 TOUR
For Detail Page Locations
SEE PAGE V
PALM SPRINGS
BOW WILLOW
SWEENEY PASS RD
Anza Borrego Desert State Park
SAN DIEGO CO.
LARK CANYON
BOULEVARD
JACUMBA
JACUMBA AIRPORT
Carrizo Gorge Railroad Trestle
MOUNTAIN SPRINGS PARK
BOULDER PARK
IN-KO-PAH CO PARK
BOULDER CREEK
MYERS CREEK
UNITED STATES
MEXICO
CARRIZO MTN 2408'
PAINTED GORGE
FOSSIL CANYON
SHELL CANYON
LAVA FLOW
IMPERIAL HWY
OCOTILLO
SUGARLOAF MTN 1022'
DOS CABEZA RD
DEVILS CANYON
COYOTE WELLS
SAN DIEGO & ARIZONA EASTERN RAILWAY
PLASTER CITY
DIXIELAND
HEWES
235 TOUR
IMPERIAL CO
YUHA WASH
SUNRISE BUTTE
COYOTE #1 RD
COYOTE #2 RD
PINTO CANYON
DAVIES VALLEY
SEELEY
EL CENTRO NAVAL AUXILIARY AIR STATION
CALIFORNIA
BAJA CALIFORNIA
USA
MEXICO
2562'
4695'
5584'
BAJA CALIF. NORTE
LAGUNA SALADA
CIENEGA
HIGHWAYS

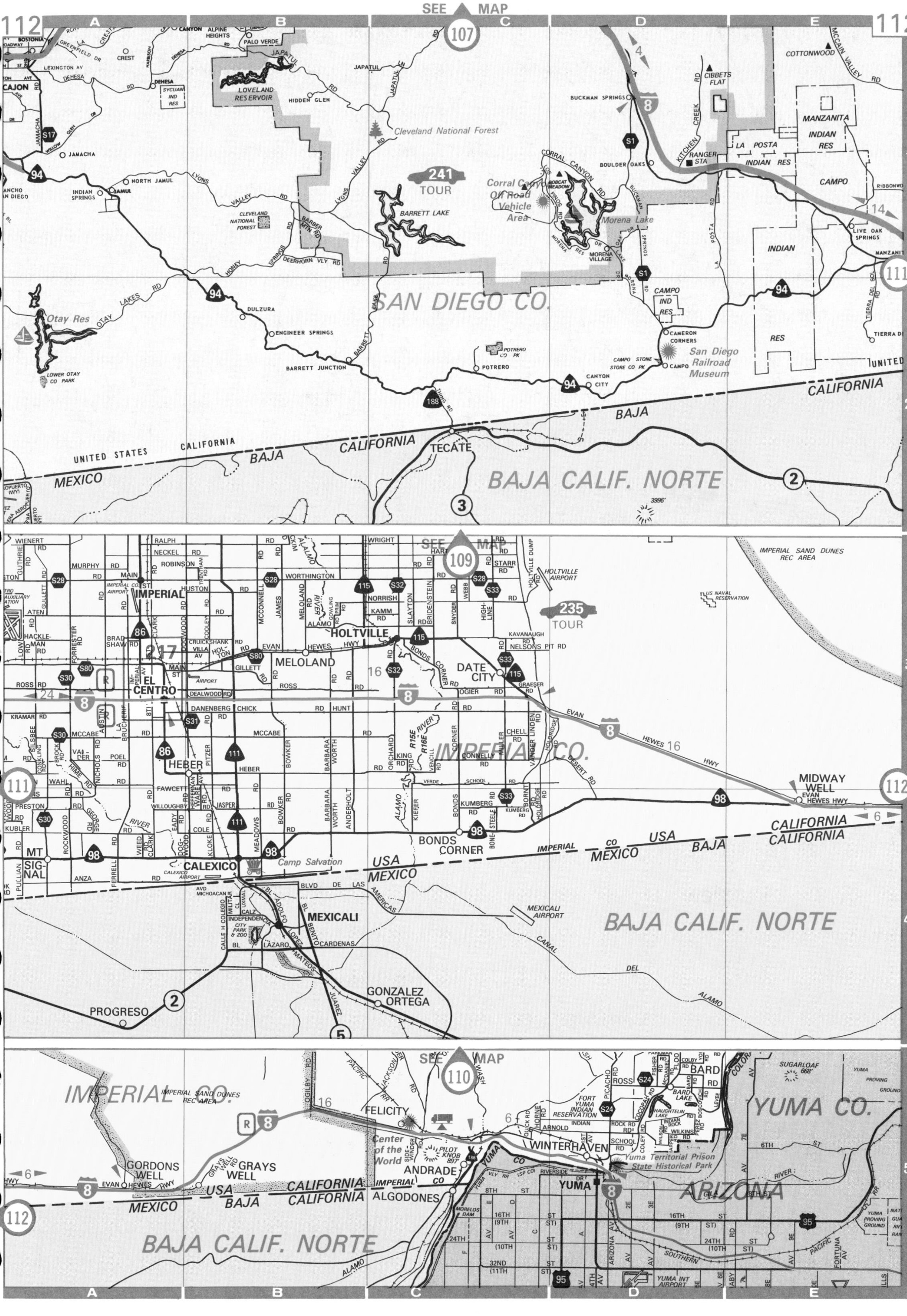
SEE MAP 107
SEE MAP 111
SEE MAP 109
SEE MAP 110
112
111
SAN DIEGO CO.
IMPERIAL CO.
YUMA CO.
ARIZONA
UNITED STATES
MEXICO
CALIFORNIA
BAJA
BAJA CALIF. NORTE
USA
Cleveland National Forest
LOVELAND RESERVOIR
BARRETT LAKE
Otay Res
LOWER OTAY CO PARK
Morena Lake
Corral Canyon Off Road Vehicle Area
241 TOUR
235 TOUR
San Diego Railroad Museum
CAMPO STONE STORE CO PK
POTRERO CO PK
SYCUAN IND RES
CAMPO IND RES
LA POSTA INDIAN RES
MANZANITA INDIAN RES
INDIAN RES
CAJON
JAMACHA
NORTH JAMUL
JAMUL
INDIAN SPRINGS
DEHESA
CREST
ALPINE HEIGHTS
PALO VERDE
HIDDEN GLEN
DULZURA
ENGINEER SPRINGS
BARRETT JUNCTION
POTRERO
CANYON CITY
CAMPO
CAMERON CORNERS
MORENA VILLAGE
BOULDER OAKS
BUCKMAN SPRINGS
CIBBETS FLAT
RANGER STA
COTTONWOOD
LIVE OAK SPRINGS
TIERRA DEL SOL
TECATE
3996'
IMPERIAL SAND DUNES REC AREA
US NAVAL RESERVATION
HOLTVILLE AIRPORT
IMPERIAL
EL CENTRO
HOLTVILLE
DATE CITY
HEBER
CALEXICO
MT SIGNAL
BONDS CORNER
MIDWAY WELL
Camp Salvation
MEXICALI
MEXICALI AIRPORT
CITY PARK & ZOO
GONZALEZ ORTEGA
PROGRESO
CANAL DEL ALAMO
GORDONS WELL
GRAYS WELL
FELICITY
Center of the World
PILOT KNOB 897'
ANDRADE
ALGODONES
WINTERHAVEN
FORT YUMA INDIAN RESERVATION
YUMA
Yuma Territorial Prison State Historical Park
YUMA INT AIRPORT
YUMA PROVING GROUND
SUGARLOAF 668'
BARD
MORELOS DAM
HIGHWAYS

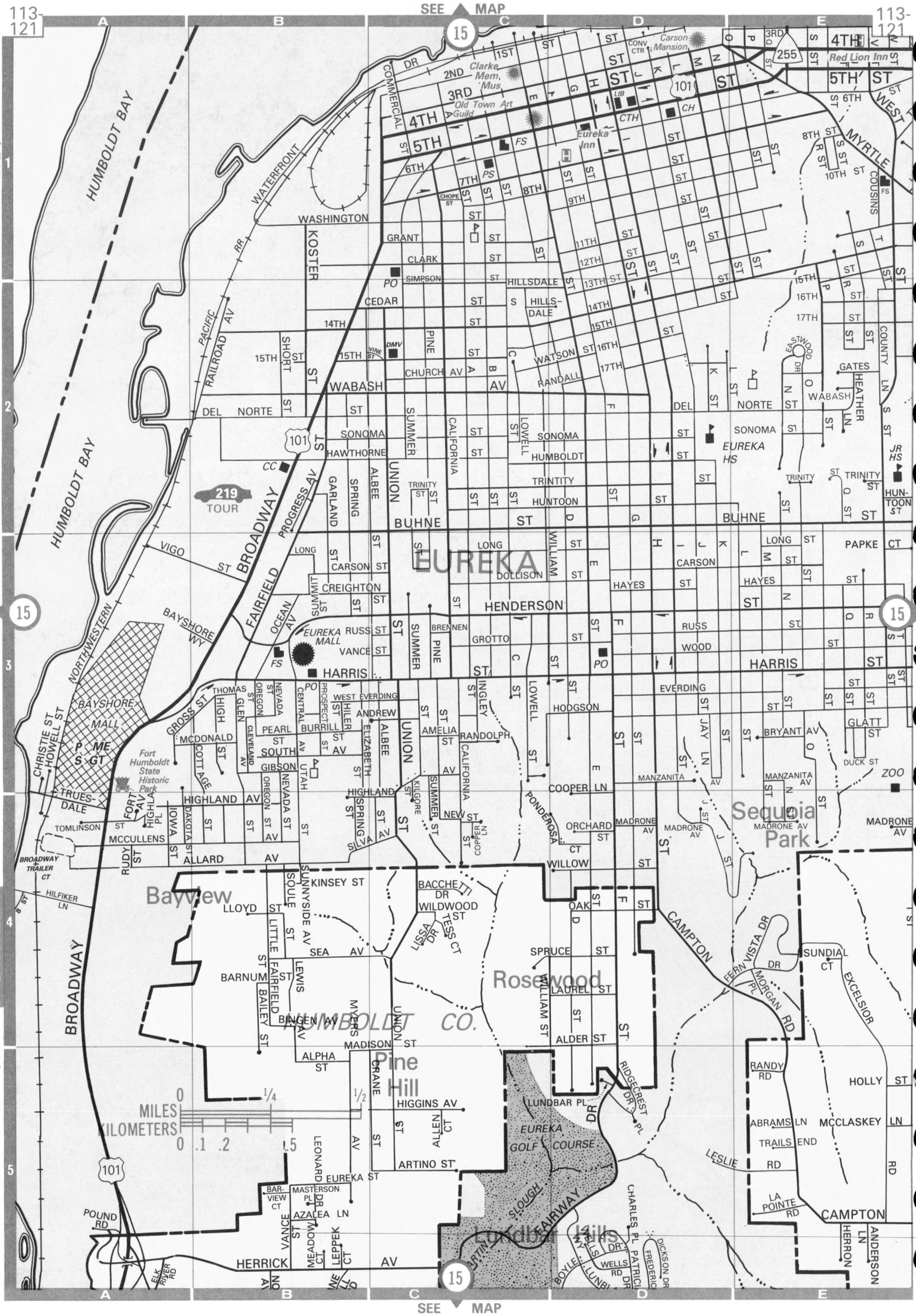
SEE MAP 15
EUREKA
HUMBOLDT BAY
WATERFRONT DR
COMMERCIAL ST
1ST ST
2ND ST
3RD ST
4TH ST
5TH ST
6TH ST
7TH ST
8TH ST
9TH ST
Clarke Mem Mus
Old Town Art Guild
Carson Mansion
CONV CTR
LIB
CTH
CH
FS
PS
Eureka Inn
Red Lion Inn
MYRTLE AV
WEST AV
COUSINS
WASHINGTON
GRANT
CLARK
SIMPSON
HILLSDALE
CEDAR
14TH
15TH
16TH
17TH
KOSTER ST
PO
DMV
VINE ST
CHURCH AV
PINE ST
WATSON ST
RANDALL
WABASH AV
DEL NORTE ST
SONOMA
HAWTHORNE
HUMBOLDT
TRINITY
HUNTOON
BUHNE ST
UNION ST
SUMMER ST
CALIFORNIA ST
ALBEE ST
SPRING ST
GARLAND ST
LOWELL ST
EUREKA HS
JR HS
EASTWOOD DR
GATES
HEATHER LN
COUNTY LN
PAPKE CT
PACIFIC RAILROAD AV
NORTHWESTERN PACIFIC RR
219 TOUR
CC
VIGO ST
BROADWAY
PROGRESS AV
FAIRFIELD
OCEAN AV
SUMMIT
LONG
CARSON ST
CREIGHTON
EUREKA
DOLLISON
WILLIAM ST
HENDERSON ST
HAYES ST
BAYSHORE WY
EUREKA MALL
RUSS ST
VANCE ST
BRENNEN
GROTTO
WOOD ST
HARRIS ST
FS
PO
BAYSHORE MALL
THOMAS ST
GROSS ST
HIGH ST
GLEN
OREGON ST
NEVADA ST
CENTRAL AV
PROSPECT
WEST EVERDING
EVERDING
HILER
ANDREW
PEARL
BURRILL
ELIZABETH
AMELIA
RANDOLPH
INGLEY
HODGSON
MCDONALD
COTTAGE
CLEVELAND AV
SOUTH AV
GIBSON
UTAH
Fort Humboldt State Historic Park
CHRISTIE ST
HOWELL ST
TRUESDALE
FORT AV
HIGHLAND AV
IOWA ST
DAKOTA ST
KILGORE
NEW ST
COPPER LN
SILVA AV
PONDEROSA
COOPER LN
ORCHARD ST
MADRONE AV
MANZANITA AV
JAY LN
BRYANT AV
GLATT
DUCK ST
ZOO
Sequoia Park
TOMLINSON
MCCULLENS
RUDY ST
ALLARD AV
BROADWAY TRAILER CT
HILFIKER LN
WILLOW
KINSEY ST
SOULE ST
SUNNYSIDE AV
BACCHETTI DR
WILDWOOD
TESS CT
LISSA DR
Bayview
LLOYD
LITTLE FAIRFIELD
SEA AV
BARNUM
LEWIS
BAILEY ST
BINGEN AV
HUMBOLDT CO.
MYERS
MADISON ST
ALPHA ST
Pine Hill
CRANE
HIGGINS AV
ALLEN CT
ARTINO ST
EUREKA ST
LEONARD
MASTERSON PL
BAR-VIEW CT
AZALEA LN
VANCE ST
MEADOW CT
LEPPEK CT
HERRICK AV
POUND RD
ELK RIVER RD
OAK ST
SPRUCE ST
Rosewood
LAUREL ST
ALDER ST
CAMPTON RD
FERN VISTA DR
MORGAN PL
SUNDIAL CT
EXCELSIOR
RIDGECREST DR
LUNDBAR PL
EUREKA GOLF COURSE
MARTIN SLOUGH
FAIRWAY DR
Lundbar Hills
CHARLES PL
PATRICIA
FREDERICK
DICKSON DR
WELLS RD
BOYLE
RANDY RD
ABRAMS LN
TRAILS END
LESLIE RD
LA POINTE RD
MCCLASKEY LN
HOLLY ST
HERRON LN
ANDERSON LN
MILES 0 1/4 1/2
KILOMETERS 0 .1 .2 .5
DETAIL

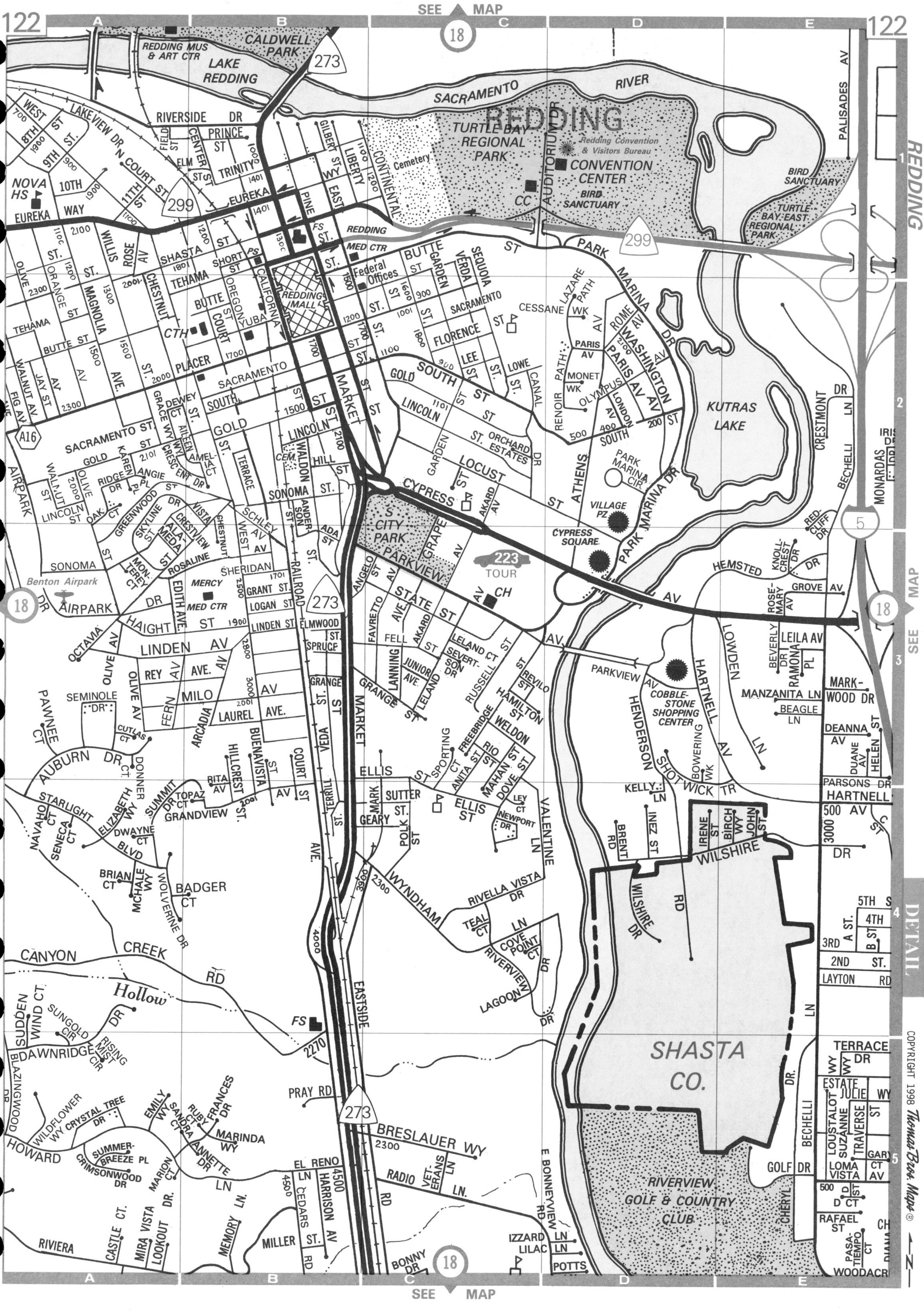
SEE MAP 18
A
B
C
D
E
1
2
3
4
5
REDDING
REDDING MUS & ART CTR
CALDWELL PARK
LAKE REDDING
273
SACRAMENTO RIVER
TURTLE BAY REGIONAL PARK
Redding Convention & Visitors Bureau
CONVENTION CENTER
CC
BIRD SANCTUARY
TURTLE BAY EAST REGIONAL PARK
PALISADES AV
AUDITORIUM DR
Cemetery
CONTINENTAL
RIVERSIDE DR
WEST ST
8TH ST
9TH ST
10TH
11TH ST
LAKEVIEW DR
N COURT ST
PRINCE ST
TRINITY
FIELD ST
CENTER ST
ELM ST
GILBERT ST
LIBERTY
EAST
PINE
EUREKA WAY
299
NOVA HS
WILLIS
ROSE AV
SHASTA ST
SHORT ST
TEHAMA ST
BUTTE ST
CHESTNUT
OREGON ST
COURT
YUBA
CALIFORNIA
REDDING MALL
CTH
PS
FS
MED CTR
Federal Offices
GARDEN
VERDA
SEQUOIA
SACRAMENTO
FLORENCE
LEE
LOWE
CANAL
CESSANE WK
LAZARE PATH
PARK MARINA DR
PARIS AV
ROME AV
WASHINGTON AV
MONET WK
OLYMPUS
LONDON
RENOIR PATH
SOUTH ST
KUTRAS LAKE
CRESTMONT DR
BECHELLI LN
MONARDAS
IRIS DR
OLIVE ST
ORANGE ST
MAGNOLIA AV
PLACER
SACRAMENTO
SOUTH
GOLD
LINCOLN
MARKET ST
WALNUT AV
JAY ST
FIG AV
A16
SACRAMENTO ST
DEWEY
GRACE WY
AILEEN
AMELIA CT
KAREN PL
ANGIE
CRESCENT DR
RIDGE DR
TERRACE
WALDON
CEM
HILL
LOCUST ST
ORCHARD ESTATES DR
ATHENS
PARK MARINA CIR
VILLAGE PZ
CYPRESS ST
CYPRESS SQUARE
AKARD AV
SONOMA ST
AIRPARK
WALNUT ST
LINCOLN ST
OAK CT
GREENWOOD
SKYLINE DR
VISTA
CRESTVIEW
ALAMEDA
ROSALINE
MONTEREY CT
CHESTNUT
WEST AV
SCHLEY
ANDERSON
ADA ST
S CITY PARK
PARKVIEW
GRAPE
223 TOUR
HEMSTED
KNOLLCREST DR
GROVE AV
RED CLIFF DR
5
18
Benton Airpark
SHERIDAN
MERCY MED CTR
EDITH AVE.
GRANT ST
LOGAN ST
LINDEN ST
RAILROAD
HAIGHT ST
OCTAVIA AV
LINDEN AV
ELMWOOD
SPRUCE
ANGELO
FAVRETTO
STATE ST
CH
FELL
LELAND CT
RUSSELL ST
PARKVIEW AV
COBBLESTONE SHOPPING CENTER
HARTNELL AV
LOWDEN LN
ROSEMARY
LEILA AV
BEVERLY DR
RAMONA PL
MARKWOOD DR
MANZANITA LN
BEAGLE LN
DEANNA AV
DUANE AV
HELEN ST
REY AV
AVE.
MILO AV
FERN
ARCADIA
LAUREL AVE.
GRANGE ST
LANNING AVE.
JUNIOR AVE.
SEVERTSON DR
REVILO ST
HAMILTON ST
WELDON
FREEBRIDGE
HENDERSON
SEMINOLE DR
PAWNEE CT
CUTLAS CT
AUBURN DR
DONNER CT
OLIVE AV
HILLCREST
BUENAVISTA
COURT ST
VEDA
ELLIS ST
SPORTING CT
ANITA ST
RIO ST
MAHAN ST
DOVE ST
SHOTWICK TR
BOWERING WK
KELLY LN
PARSONS DR
HARTNELL AV
STARLIGHT
SENECA CT
NAVAHO CT
ELIZABETH WY
SUMMIT DR
TOPAZ CT
RITA AV
GRANDVIEW
VERRILL
MARK
SUTTER
GEARY
POLK ST
LEY CT
NEWPORT DR
VALENTINE LN
BRENT RD
INEZ ST
IRENE ST
BIRCH WY
JOHN ST
WILSHIRE
DWAYNE CT
BLVD
BRIAN CT
MCHALE WY
WOLVERINE DR
BADGER CT
WYNDHAM
RIVELLA VISTA DR
TEAL CT
COVE POINT CT
RIVERVIEW DR
LAGOON DR
WILSHIRE DR
RD
5TH
4TH
A ST.
B ST
3RD
2ND ST.
LAYTON RD
DETAIL
CANYON CREEK RD
Hollow
EASTSIDE
SUDDEN WIND CT.
SUNGOLD CIR
RISING MIST CIR
DAWNRIDGE
BLAZINGWOOD DR
FS
2270
SHASTA CO.
TERRACE DR
ESTATE WY
JULIE WY
LOUSTALOT
SUZANNE
TRAVERSE ST
GARY CT
LOMA VISTA AV
PRAY RD
BRESLAUER WY
WILDFLOWER WY
CRYSTAL TREE DR
EMILY WY
SANDRA CT
RUBY CT
FRANCES DR
MARINDA WY
SUZANNE CT
ANNETTE DR
HOWARD
SUMMERBREEZE PL
CRIMSONWOOD DR
MARION CT
EL RENO LN
HARRISON AV
RADIO
VETERANS LN
E BONNEYVIEW RD
RIVERVIEW GOLF & COUNTRY CLUB
CHERYL
BECHELLI
GOLF DR
D CT
RAFAEL ST
PASATIEMPO CT
RIVIERA
CASTLE CT.
MIRA VISTA
LOOKOUT DR.
MEMORY LN.
MILLER
CEDARS ST.
IZZARD LN
LILAC LN
POTTS
BONNY DR
WOODACR

SEE MAP 31
UKIAH
DETAIL
A
B
C
D
E
1
2
3
4
5
UKIAH
MENDOCINO
CO.
RUSSIAN RIVER
101
222
219 TOUR
12TH DISTRICT FAIRGROUNDS
UKIAH HS
LOW GAP REGIONAL PARK
UKIAH MUNICIPAL GOLF COURSE
MENDOCINO COUNTY GOVERNMENTAL COMPLEX
TODD GROVE PK
ANTON STADIUM
MID
PEAR TREE CENTER
UKIAH VALLEY MEDICAL CENTER
DMV
PS
CO CTH
LIB
Grace Hudson Museum
OAK MANOR PARK
CC PS FS
UKIAH VALLEY MED CTR
Ukiah Airport
1 CABERNET PL
2 SAUVIGNON CT
3 RIESLING CT
LOVERS LN
TANYA LN
ALICANTE LN
GEORGE PL
CARRIGAN
MILLVIEW DR RD
ZINFANDEL
FEED LOT
CHARDONNAY
GAMAY PL
SAUTERNE PL
KUKI LN
MASONITE RD
FORD RD
REDEMEYER RD
MALAGA DR
BURGANDY ST
CONCORD
CHABLIS CT
SIRAH CT
SHERRY DR
TOKAY AV
EMPIRE DR
DONNER
HOMEWOOD DR
CRYSTAL BAY CT
INCLINE CT
TAHOE CT
CAPPS
SUMMIT CT
ZEPHYR COVE CT
DESPINA
BUSH ST
LOCKWOOD
IRVINGTON DR
BRICARELLI DR
GARRETT DR
CARLETON DR
BURLINGTON DR
ARLINGTON DR
PINE
VINEWOOD PK
MAGNOLIA ST
ELM
OAK ST
N STATE ST
MAZZONI RD
BRUNNER ST
BRIGGS ST
ORR ST
RIVER ST
VICHY SPGS RD
LOW GAP RD
GIBSON
BRUSH
GIBSON ST
EVANS ST
FORD
JOSEPH PL
MYRON ST
SIDNIE CT
HAMILTON
ORCHARD
FAIRWAY AV
MAPLE AV
DOMINICAN WY
FRANCIS
JACKSON AV
CK
RUDDOCK AV
CYPRUS AV
SCHOOL
CLARA
HOSPITAL DR
PERKINS ST (VICHY SPRINGS RD)
HAZEL
DORA AV
SNUFFIN
NORTON ST
MASON
LIVE OAK
GROVE AV
SCOTT ST
MORRIS ST
HENRY ST
MAIN ST
POMEROY
OAK MANOR CT
YOSEMITE DR
POMO
WASHO
RIO CT
EL RIO ST
WIYAT DR
MAYA WY
YAQUI DR
MOHAVE DR
PARK
WALNUT BLVD
TODD
WILLOW
SPRING
HORTENSE
STELLA DR
WARREN DR
PEACH CT
PLUM DR
KINGS CT
LESLIE
PARK CT
SMITH
STEPHENSON ST
GIORNO AV
STANDLEY
PERKINS
HOPE
BARNES
GIBSON CREEK
CLEVELAND LN
ORCHARD AV
HIGHLAND
CHURCH
THOMPSON
MCPEAK
CLAY ST
CLAY PL
HOLDEN
SEMINARY
DORA
JONES
MARSHALL ST
MYSZKA PL
MARY LN
EASTLICK
BETTY ST
CALVERT DR
OAK PARK AV
CAROLYN ST
BARBARA
MAE ST
PORZIO LN
WAUGH
CINDEE DR
MILL ST
GOBBI ST
COOPER LN
DEBORAH CT
MARLENE ST
MENDOCINO DR
HILLVIEW AV
HILLCREST AV
GARDENS AV
POMOLITA
LOUISE CT
COURT ST
FREITAS AV
CHERRY CT
APPLE AV
CHERRY ST
CUNNINGHAM
BETTY LN
LORRAINE ST
HENDERSON LN
MYRTLE LN
CALDWELL FRONTAGE RD
MENDOCINO PL
COCHRANE AV
ALICE AV
LUCE AV
SOUTH ST
THOMAS ST
RUPE ST
PERRY ST
TALMAGE FRONTAGE RD
TALMAGE RD
HASTINGS
BANKER BLVD
ALBRIGHT PL
OBSERVATORY
HELEN
NOKOMIS DR
NOKOMIS CT
NEHO CT
MARWEN DR
MULBERRY ST
LEWIS LN
REDWOOD AV
HASTINGS AV
COMMERCE DR
SAN JACINTA CT
FOOTHILL
WASHINGTON AV
YOKAYO DR
DOOLAN CT
CRESTA DR
WABASH AV
AIRPORT PARK BLVD
AIRPORT RD
FRONTAGE RD
DOOLAN CYN DR
BAYWOOD CT
LAUREL
ROSE AV
BERKLEY WY
BEACON WY
CYN VIEW
BEACON LN
TEDFORD AV
FAULL AV
THOMPSON AV
POULOS CT
LAWS AV
CANYON DR
ROSEMARY LN
ADAMS ST
MONROE ST
JEFFERSON LN
FIRCREST
DOOLAN CREEK
MILES 0 1/4 1/2
KILOMETERS 0 .1 .2 .5

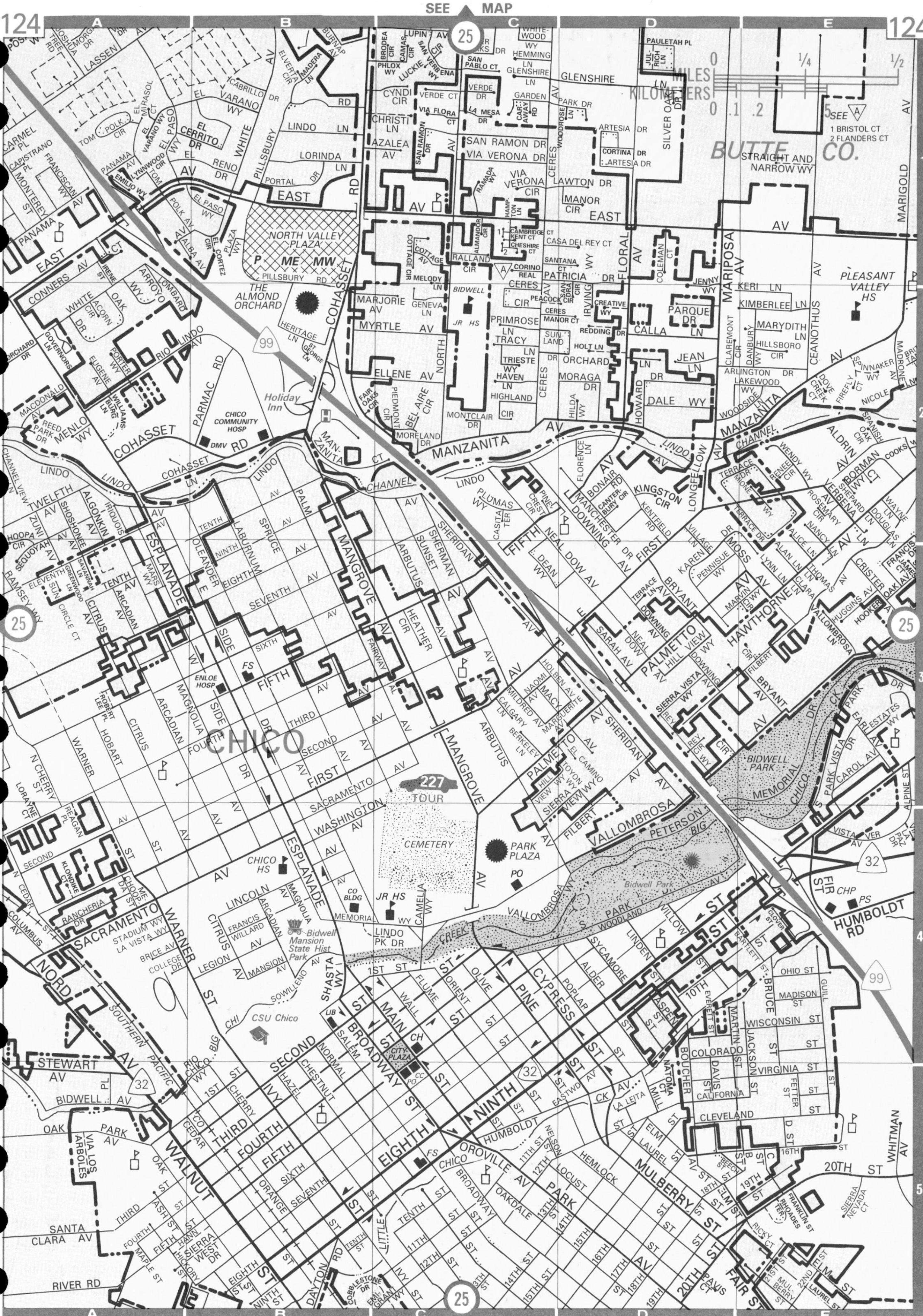
SEE MAP 25
CHICO
BUTTE CO.
MILES 0 1/4 1/2
KILOMETERS 0 .1 .2 .5
SEE A
1 BRISTOL CT
2 FLANDERS CT
EAST AV
COHASSET RD
MANGROVE AV
ESPLANADE
MANZANITA AV
VALLOMBROSA
NORTH VALLEY PLAZA
THE ALMOND ORCHARD
Holiday Inn
CHICO COMMUNITY HOSP
DMV
ENLOE HOSP
CHICO HS
BIDWELL JR HS
PLEASANT VALLEY HS
PARK PLAZA
CEMETERY
227 TOUR
Bidwell Mansion State Hist Park
CSU Chico
CITY PLAZA
BIDWELL PARK
Bidwell Park
HUMBOLDT RD
LINDO CHANNEL
BIG CHICO CREEK
FIRST ST
SECOND ST
FIFTH AV
EIGHTH ST
NINTH ST
WALNUT ST
BROADWAY
MAIN ST
OROVILLE AV
PARK AV
MULBERRY ST
20TH ST
RIVER RD
STEWART AV
BIDWELL AV
SACRAMENTO AV
NORD AV
SOUTHERN PACIFIC
CHP
PS
99
32
25
DETAIL
SEE MAP 25

SEE MAP 33

SEE MAP 33

SEE MAP 33

SEE MAP 33

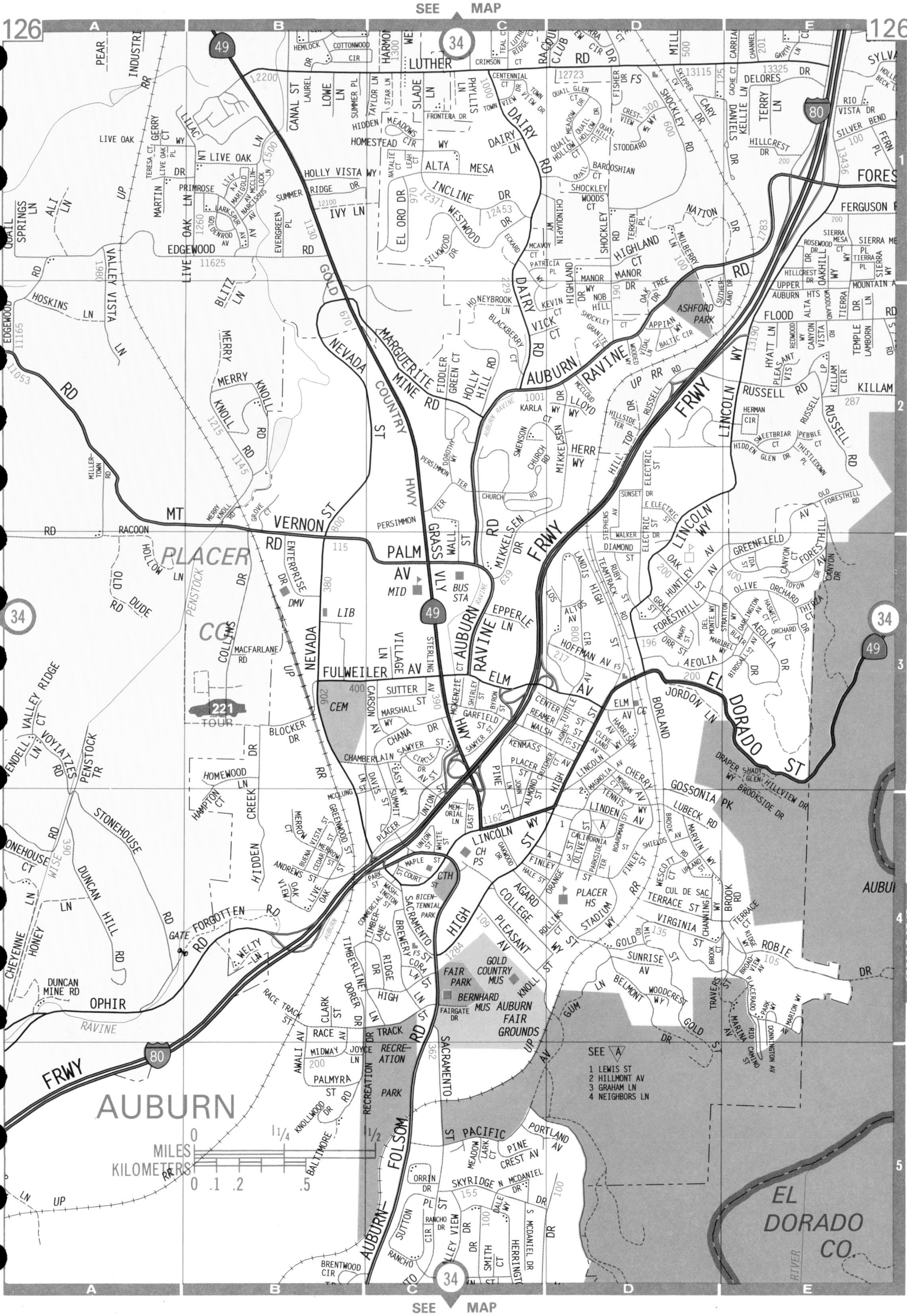
SEE MAP 34
AUBURN
PLACER CO
EL DORADO CO
AUBURN
DETAIL
MT VERNON RD
LUTHER RD
AUBURN RAVINE RD
NEVADA ST
GRASS VLY HWY
LINCOLN WY
EL DORADO ST
HIGH ST
FOLSOM RD
SACRAMENTO ST
AUBURN-FOLSOM RD
OPHIR RD
FRWY
DAIRY RD
MARGUERITE MINE RD
PALM AV
FULWEILER AV
ELM AV
AGARD
COLLEGE WY
PLEASANT AV
LINCOLN ST
CHERRY AV
ASHFORD PARK
BUS STA
MID
DMV
LIB
CEM
CTH
CH PS
PLACER HS
BICENTENNIAL PARK
FAIR PARK
GOLD COUNTRY MUS
BERNHARD MUS
AUBURN FAIR GROUNDS
RECREATION PARK
221 TOUR
SEE A
1 LEWIS ST
2 HILLMONT AV
3 GRAHAM LN
4 NEIGHBORS LN
MILES 0 1/4 1/2
KILOMETERS 0 .1 .2 .5
A B C D E

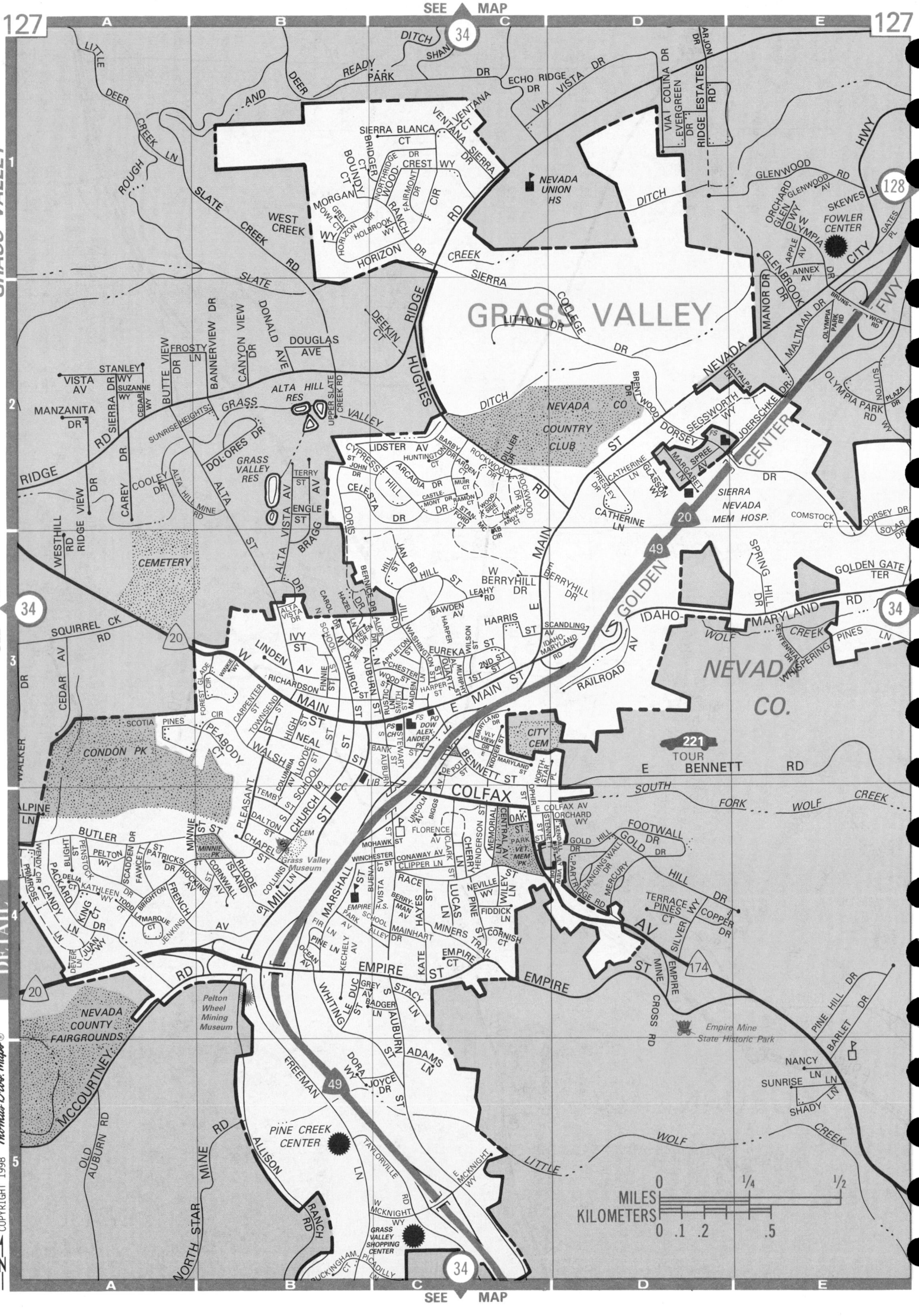
SEE MAP 34
GRASS VALLEY
NEVADA UNION HS
NEVADA COUNTRY CLUB
SIERRA NEVADA MEM HOSP.
FOWLER CENTER
CEMETERY
CONDON PK
CITY CEM
MINNIE PK
VET. MEM PK
Grass Valley Museum
Pelton Wheel Mining Museum
NEVADA COUNTY FAIRGROUNDS
Empire Mine State Historic Park
PINE CREEK CENTER
GRASS VALLEY SHOPPING CENTER
NEVADA CO.
ALTA HILL RES
GRASS VALLEY RES
221 TOUR
GOLDEN CENTER FWY
49
20
174
128
MAIN ST
COLFAX
EMPIRE ST
MILL ST
AUBURN ST
E BENNETT RD
IDAHO-MARYLAND RD
NEVADA CITY HWY
RIDGE RD
HUGHES RD
SIERRA COLLEGE DR
SLATE CREEK RD
MCCOURTNEY RD
OLD AUBURN RD
NORTH STAR MINE RD
ALLISON RANCH RD
SOUTH FORK WOLF CREEK
LITTLE WOLF CREEK
MILES 0 1/4 1/2
KILOMETERS 0 .1 .2 .5
A B C D E
1 2 3 4 5
DETAIL
Thomas Bros. Maps®

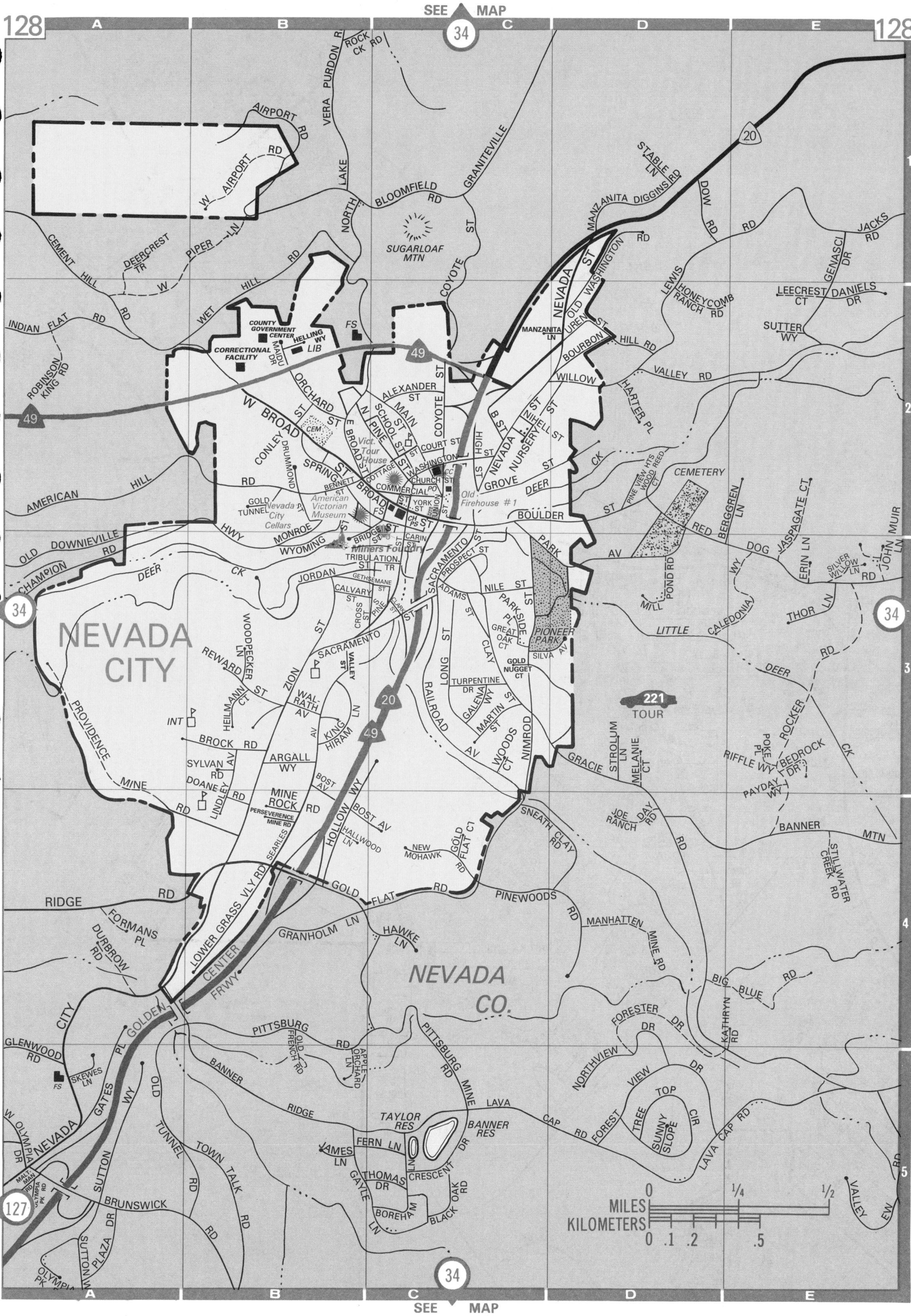

SEE MAP 34
NEVADA CITY
NEVADA CO.
DETAIL
SEE MAP 34
AIRPORT RD
W AIRPORT RD
VERA PURDON RD
ROCK CK RD
NORTH LAKE
BLOOMFIELD RD
GRANITEVILLE
SUGARLOAF MTN
COYOTE ST
CEMENT HILL RD
DEERCREST TR
W PIPER LN
WET HILL RD
INDIAN FLAT RD
ROBINSON KING RD
COUNTY GOVERNMENT CENTER
CORRECTIONAL FACILITY
HELLING WY
LIB
MAIDU DR
FS
W BROAD ST
ORCHARD ST
CEM
CONLEY
DRUMMOND
SPRING ST
E BROAD ST
N PINE ST
SCHOOL ST
MAIN ST
ALEXANDER ST
COURT ST
WASHINGTON ST
CHURCH ST
COMMERCIAL ST
BROAD ST
YORK ST
UNION ST
Vict. Tour House
American Victorian Museum
Nevada City Cellars
Old Firehouse #1
Miners Foundry
AMERICAN HILL RD
GOLD TUNNEL
MONROE
WYOMING
HWY
OLD DOWNIEVILLE RD
CHAMPION
DEER CK
TRIBULATION TR
JORDAN
GETHSEMANE
CALVARY ST
CROSS ST
PINE
CLARK
SACRAMENTO ST
PROSPECT ST
ADAMS
NILE ST
PARK SIDE PL
PARK AV
PIONEER PARK
SILVA AV
GREAT OAK CT
CLAY ST
GOLD NUGGET CT
LONG ST
TURPENTINE DR
GALENA WY
MARTIN ST
RAILROAD AV
WOODS CT
NIMROD ST
WOODPECKER LN
REWARD ST
ZION ST
VALLEY ST
WALRATH AV
KING HIRAM LN
HEILMANN CT
INT
BROCK RD
ARGALL WY
SYLVAN RD
DOANE RD
LINDLEY AV
MINE ROCK RD
PERSEVERENCE MINE RD
BOST AV
HOLLOW WY
HALLWOOD LN
NEW MOHAWK
GOLD FLAT CT
GOLD FLAT RD
SEARLES
LOWER GRASS VLY RD
PROVIDENCE MINE RD
RIDGE RD
FORMANS PL
DURBROW RD
NEVADA ST
OLD WASHINGTON RD
MANZANITA LN
BOURBON
UREN ST
HILL RD
MANZANITA DIGGINS RD
STABLE LN
DOW RD
WILLOW
B ST
HIGH ST
NEVADA ST
NURSERY ST
NIHELL ST
GROVE ST
DEER CK
BOULDER ST
HARTER PL
VALLEY RD
LEWIS RD
HONEYCOMB RANCH RD
LEECREST CT
DANIELS DR
GENASCI DR
JACKS RD
SUTTER WY
CEMETERY
PINE VIEW HTS
WOOD REED CT
BERGGREN LN
JASPAGATE CT
RED DOG AV
POND RD
MILL
ERIN LN
SILVER WILLOW LN
JOHN MUIR
THOR LN
LITTLE DEER CK
CALEDONIA
221 TOUR
STROLUM LN
MELANIE CT
GRACIE RD
ROCKER
POKE PL
BEDROCK DR
RIFFLE WY
PAYDAY WY
JOE RANCH RD
DAY RD
SNEATH CLAY RD
BANNER MTN
STILLWATER CREEK RD
PINEWOODS RD
MANHATTEN MINE RD
GRANHOLM LN
HAWKE LN
CENTER FRWY
GOLDEN CENTER FRWY
BIG BLUE RD
FORESTER DR
KATHRYN RD
NORTHVIEW DR
VIEW TOP CIR
TREE
SUNNY SLOPE
FOREST
LAVA CAP RD
VALLEY
EW
PITTSBURG RD
OLD FRENCH RD
APPLE ORCHARD LN
PITTSBURG MINE RD
BANNER RIDGE
TAYLOR RES
BANNER RES
CRESCENT DR
FERN LN
JAMES LN
THOMAS DR
GAYLE LN
BOREHAM
BLACK OAK RD
GLENWOOD RD
CITY
GATES PL
SKEWES LN
W OLYMPIA DR
NEVADA
OLD TUNNEL RD
TOWN TALK RD
WY
SUTTON WY
BRUNSWICK RD
PLAZA DR
OLYMPIA PK
MILES 0 1/4 1/2
KILOMETERS 0 .1 .2 .5
34
49
20
127

SEE MAP 36

SEE MAP 36
SEE MAP

Thomas Bros. Maps®

SEE 28 MAP

SEE 28 MAP

SEE MAP
37
SANTA ROSA
DETAIL
SANTA ROSA
SONOMA CO.
Roseland
South Park
A
B
C
D
E
1
2
3
4
5
KAISER PERMANENTE MED CTR
COUNTY ADM. CENTER
FISCAL DR
ADMINISTRATION
OAK CREST SANITARIUM
COMMUNITY HOSP
SANTA ROSA MEMORIAL PARK CEM
FRANKLIN PARK
CODDINGTON CENTER
SANTA ROSA JR COLLEGE
NATIONAL GUARD ARMORY
SANTA ROSA HS
219 TOUR
REDWOOD HWY
W STEELE LN
W COLLEGE AV
COLLEGE AV
MENDOCINO AV
MONTGOMERY
SONOMA AV
SEBASTOPOL RD
SEBASTOPOL FRWY
12
101
STONY POINT RD
PETALUMA HILL RD
FINLEY COMMUNITY PARK
NORTHWEST COMMUNITY PARK
SANTA ROSA MEMORIAL HOSPITAL
DOYLE PARK
SANTA ROSA PLAZA
Robt Ripley Mem Mus
Burbank Home & Gardens
Church Built From One Tree
GOLF COURSE
FAIR GROUNDS
MARTIN LUTHER KING JR PARK
WILSON SCHOOL PARK
JACOBS MEM PK
HEARN AV
BARHAM AV
KAWANA SPRINGS
SEE A
1 SPRUCE ST
2 E JASMINE CIR
3 LAUREL GROVE
4 FELDSPAR LN
1 FLAMINGO RD
2 ANGELUS ST
3 BILTMORE ST
4 COLUMBIA ST
1 GUADALAJARA CT
AQUISTAPACE

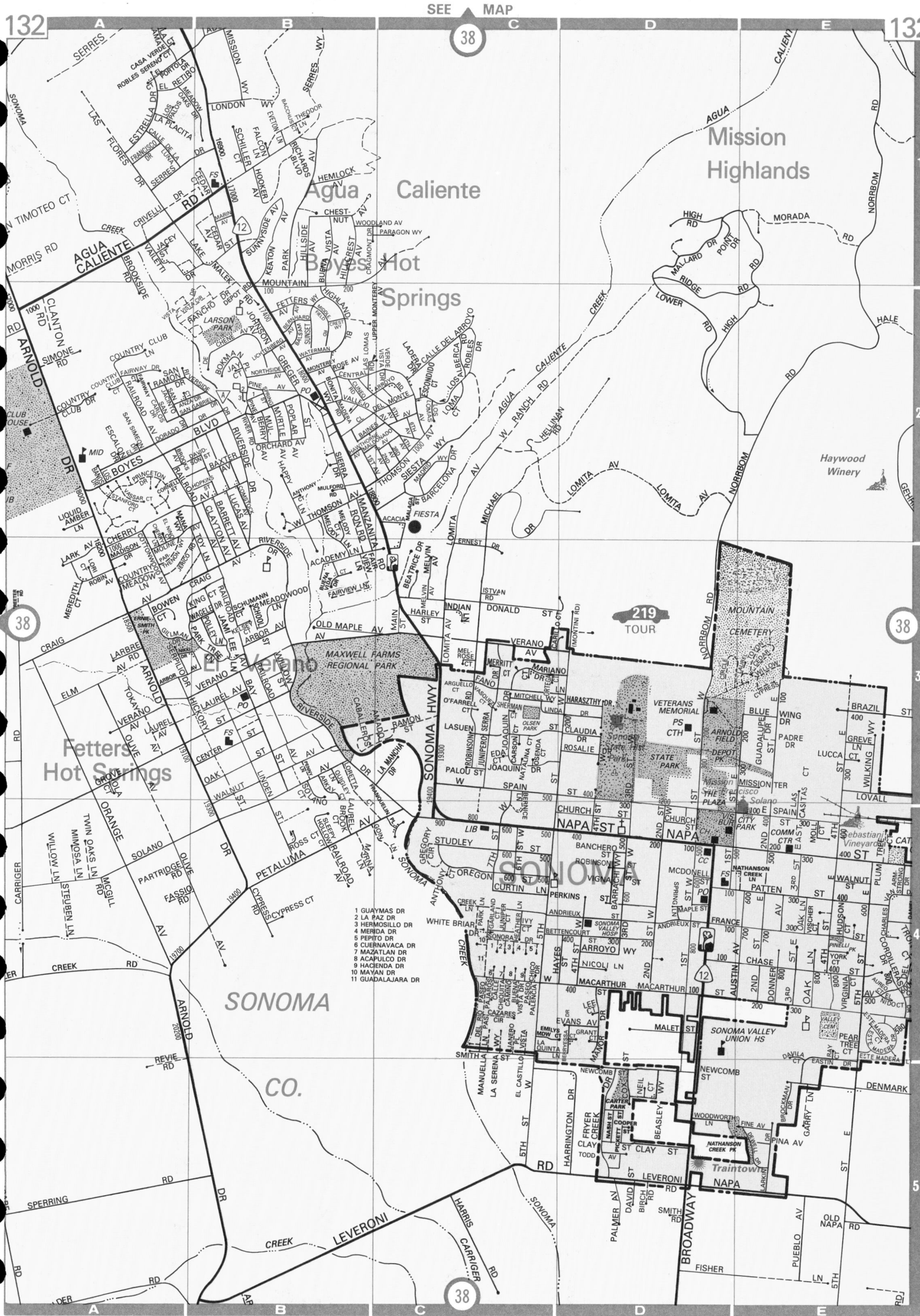

SEE MAP 38
Mission Highlands
Agua Caliente
Boyes Hot Springs
El Verano
Fetters Hot Springs
SONOMA
SONOMA CO.
MAXWELL FARMS REGIONAL PARK
MOUNTAIN CEMETERY
VETERANS MEMORIAL
Sonoma State Hist Park
ARNOLD FIELD
DEPOT PK
Mission San Francisco Solano
THE PLAZA
CITY PARK
SONOMA VALLEY UNION HS
SONOMA VALLEY HOSP
NATHANSON CREEK PK
CARTER PARK
Traintown
Haywood Winery
Sebastiani Vineyards
LARSON PARK
ERNIE SMITH PK
OLSEN PARK
CLUB HOUSE
219 TOUR
ARNOLD DR
SONOMA HWY
BROADWAY
NAPA ST
LEVERONI RD
AGUA CALIENTE RD
LOVALL VALLEY RD
NORRBOM RD
LOMITA AV
DENMARK
NAPA RD
1 GUAYMAS DR
2 LA PAZ DR
3 HERMOSILLO DR
4 MERIDA DR
5 PEPITO DR
6 CUERNAVACA DR
7 MAZATLAN DR
8 ACAPULCO DR
9 HACIENDA DR
10 MAYAN DR
11 GUADALAJARA DR
DETAIL

SEE MAP 38

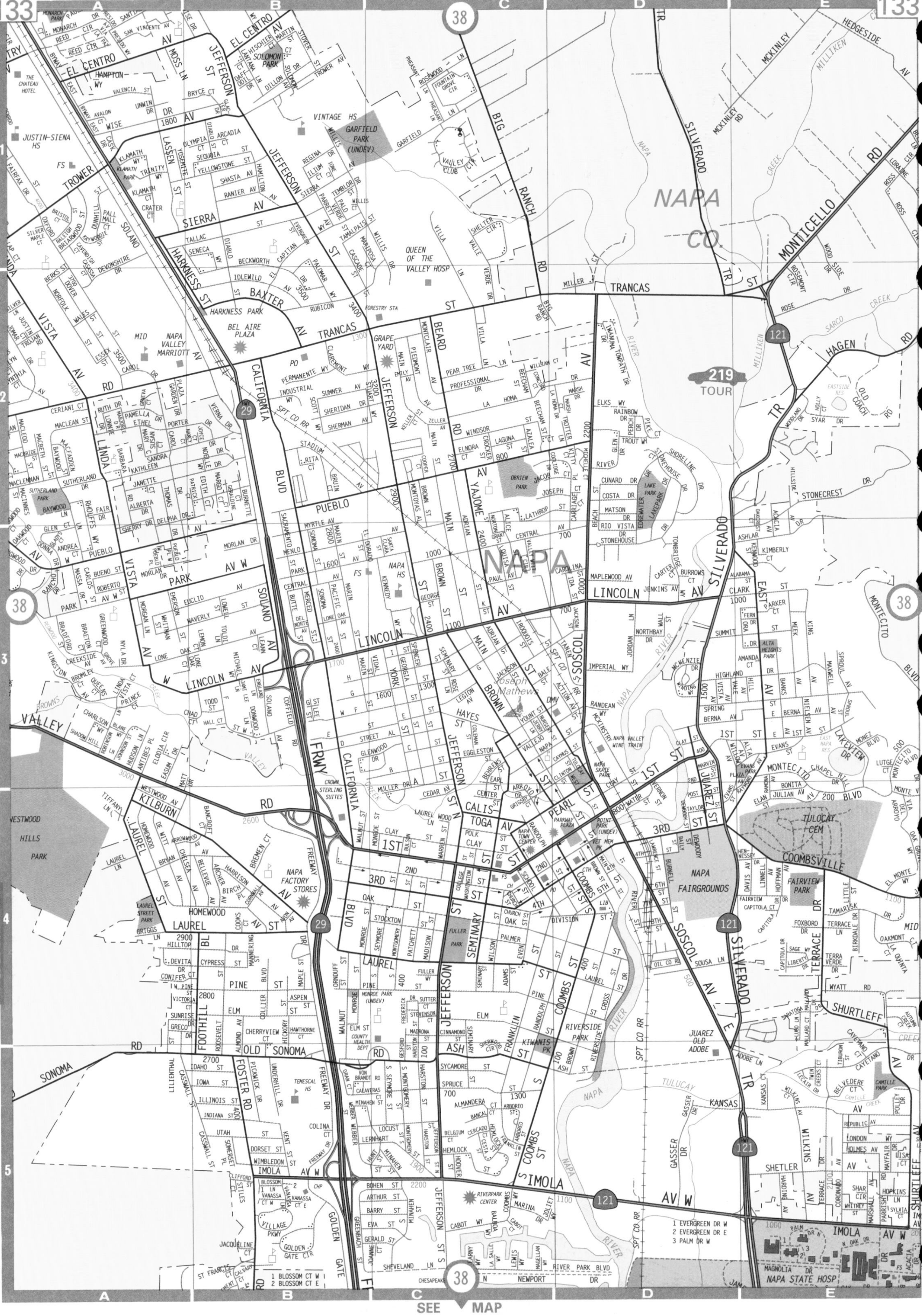

SEE MAP 38

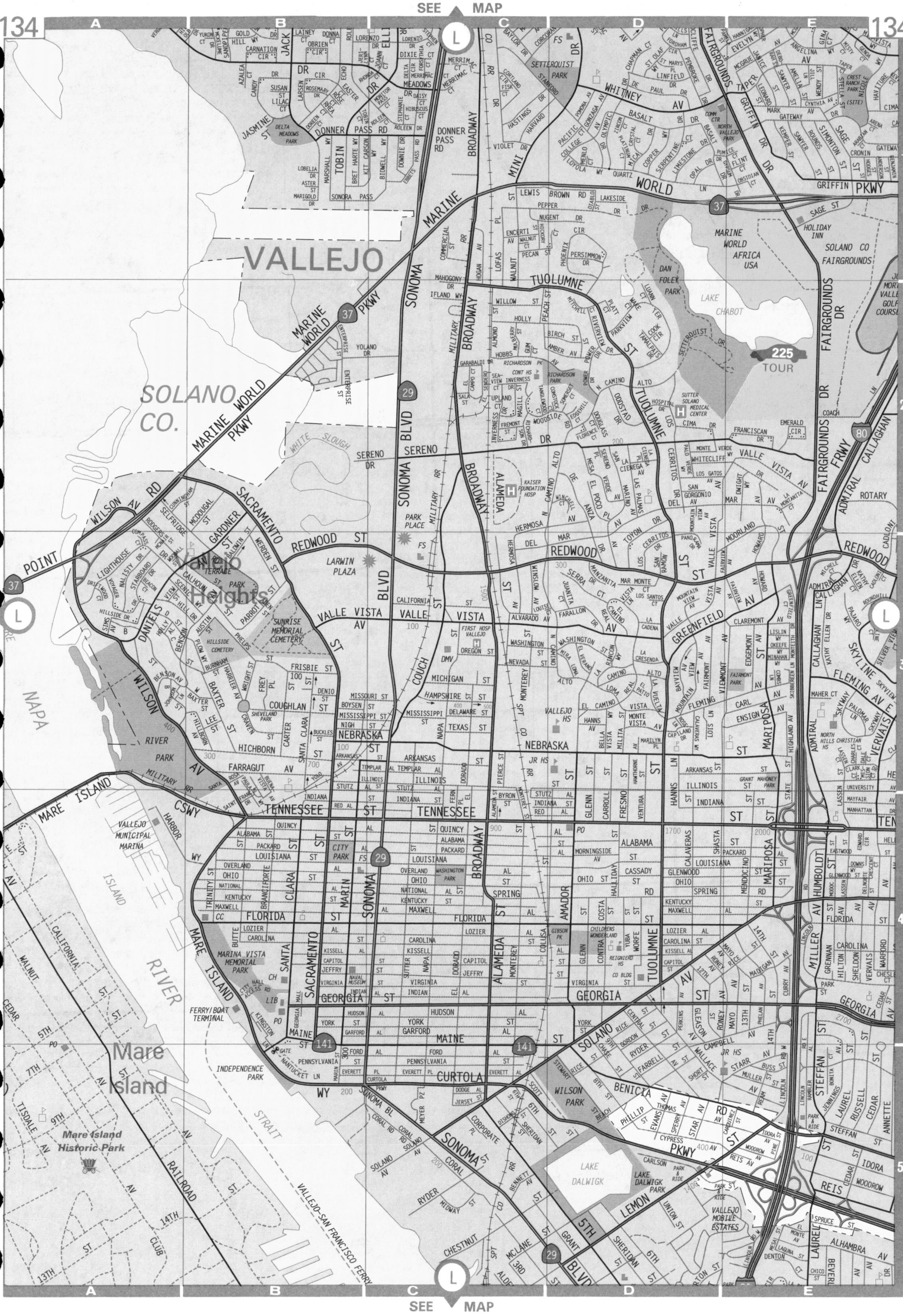
SEE MAP
L
VALLEJO
SOLANO CO.
Vallejo Heights
NAPA
RIVER
Mare Island
Mare Island Historic Park
MARE ISLAND STRAIT
MARINE WORLD AFRICA USA
SOLANO CO FAIRGROUNDS
HOLIDAY INN
LAKE CHABOT
DAN FOLEY PARK
LAKE DALWIGK
WILSON PARK
RIVER PARK
SUNRISE MEMORIAL CEMETERY
HILLSIDE CEMETERY
INDEPENDENCE PARK
VALLEJO MUNICIPAL MARINA
FERRY/BOAT TERMINAL
MARINA VISTA MEMORIAL PARK
CITY PARK
WASHINGTON PARK
LARWIN PLAZA
PARK PLACE
KAISER FOUNDATION HOSP
SUTTER SOLANO MEDICAL CENTER
FIRST HOSP VALLEJO
VALLEJO HS
SETTERQUIST PARK
NORTH VALLEJO PARK
NORTH HILLS CHRISTIAN
VALLEJO MOBILE ESTATES
WHITE SLOUGH
MARINE WORLD PKWY
SONOMA BLVD
BROADWAY
TENNESSEE ST
REDWOOD ST
GEORGIA ST
CURTOLA PKWY
FAIRGROUNDS DR
ADMIRAL CALLAGHAN
DETAIL
VALLEJO-SAN FRANCISCO FERRY
29
37
80
141
225 TOUR
A B C D E
1 2 3 4 5

SEE MAP

SEE MAP

SEE MAP 39

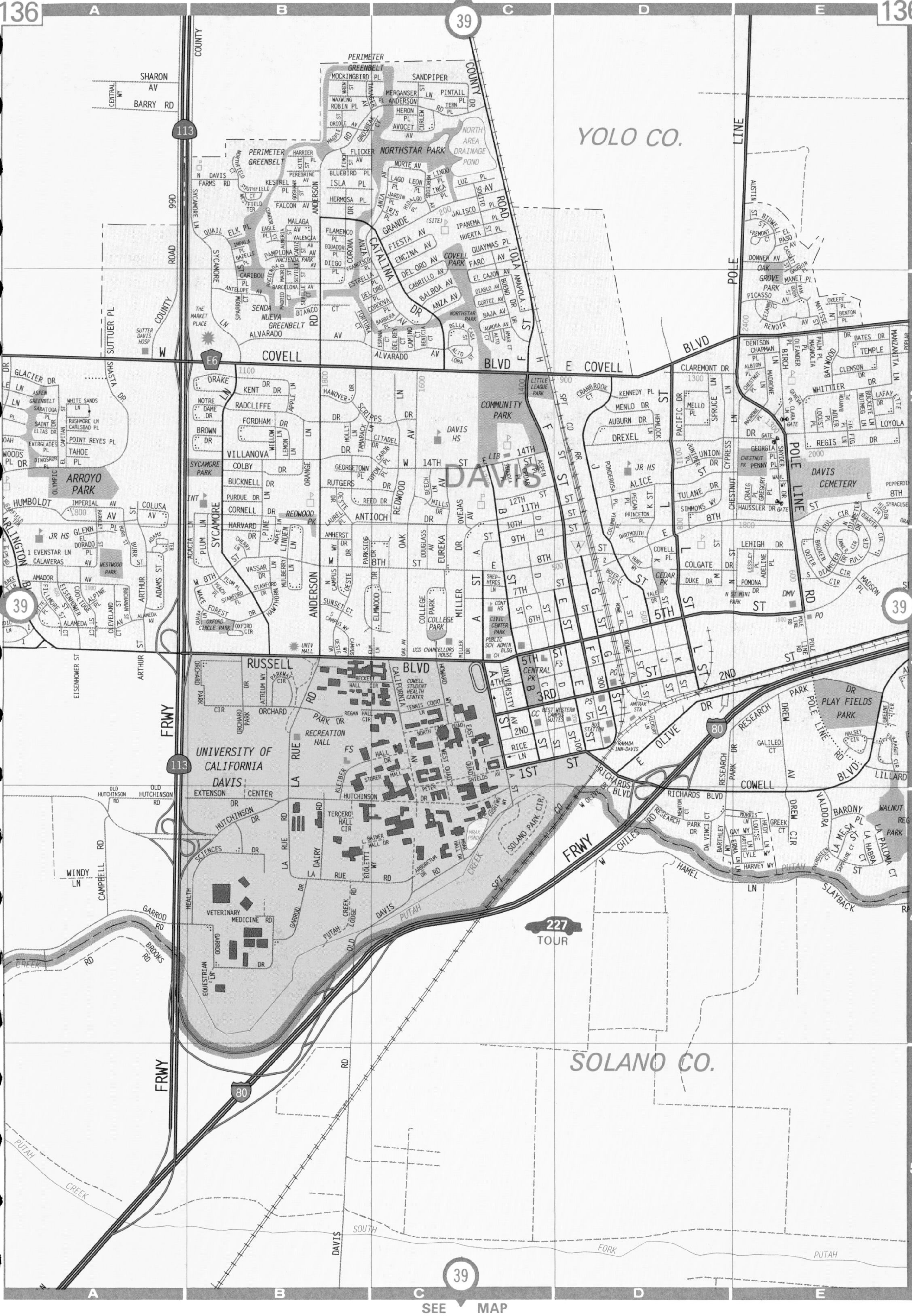

SEE MAP 39

SEE MAP 39

SEE MAP 39

SEE MAP 39

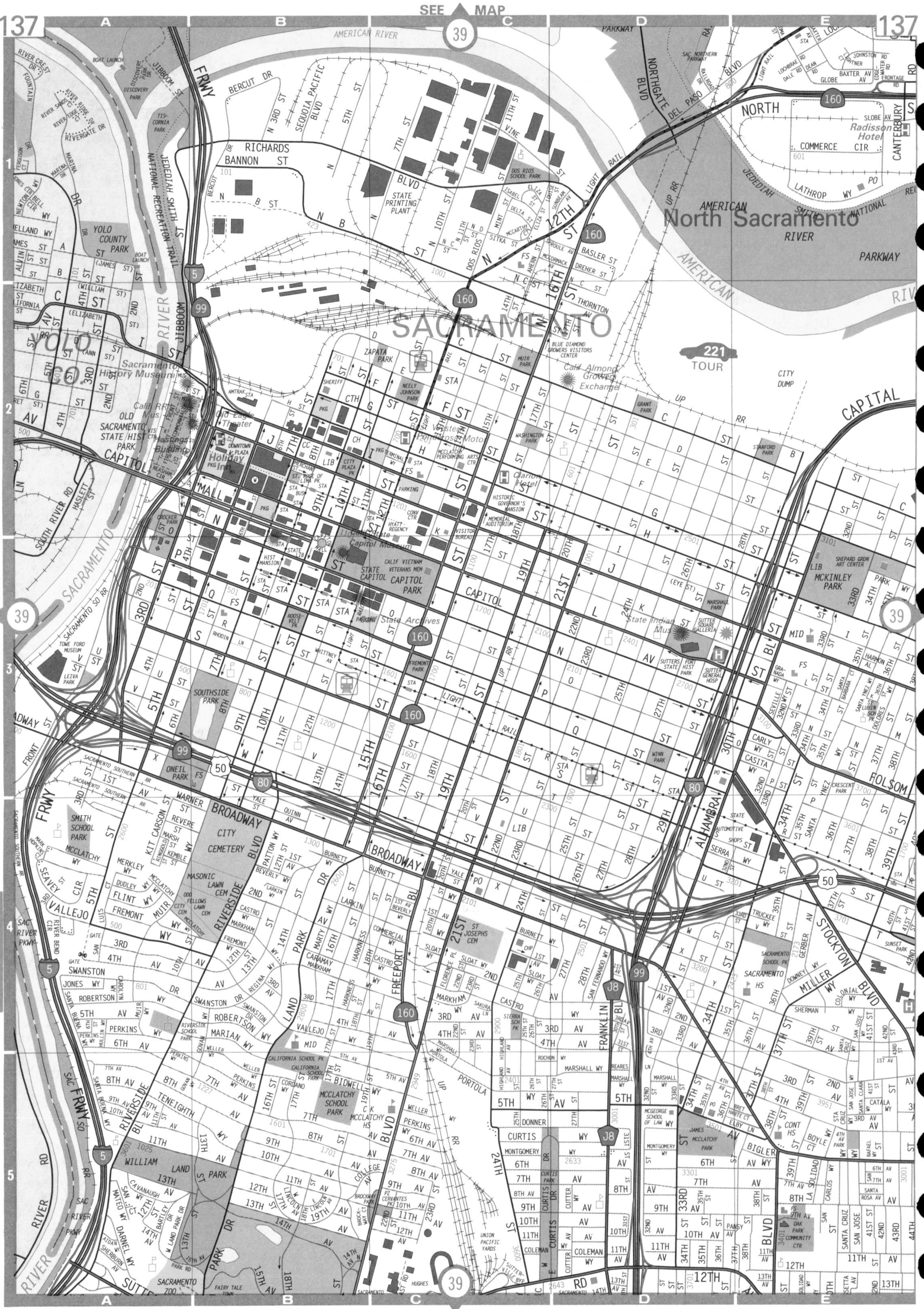

SEE MAP 39

SEE MAP 34

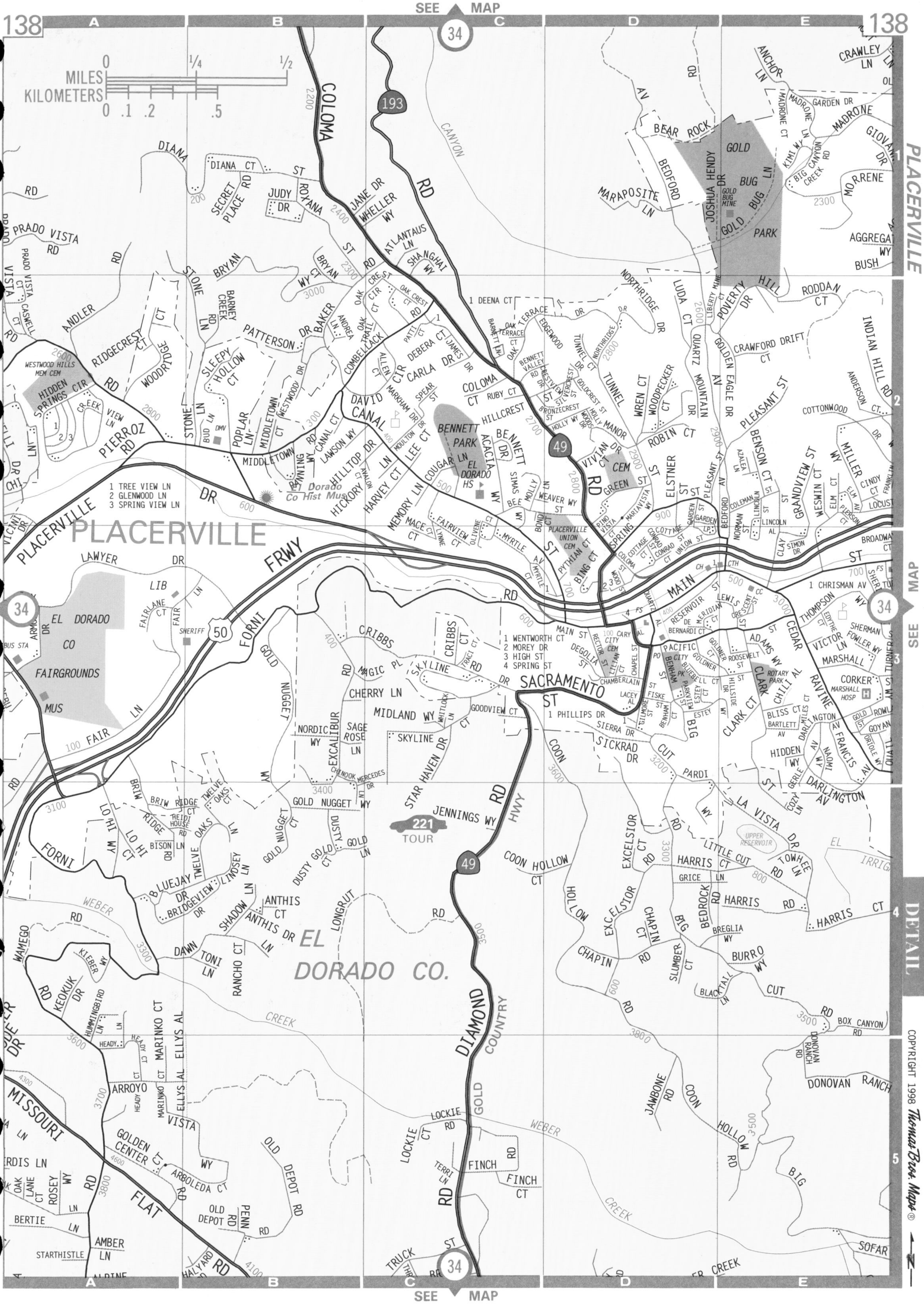

SEE MAP 34

SEE MAP L

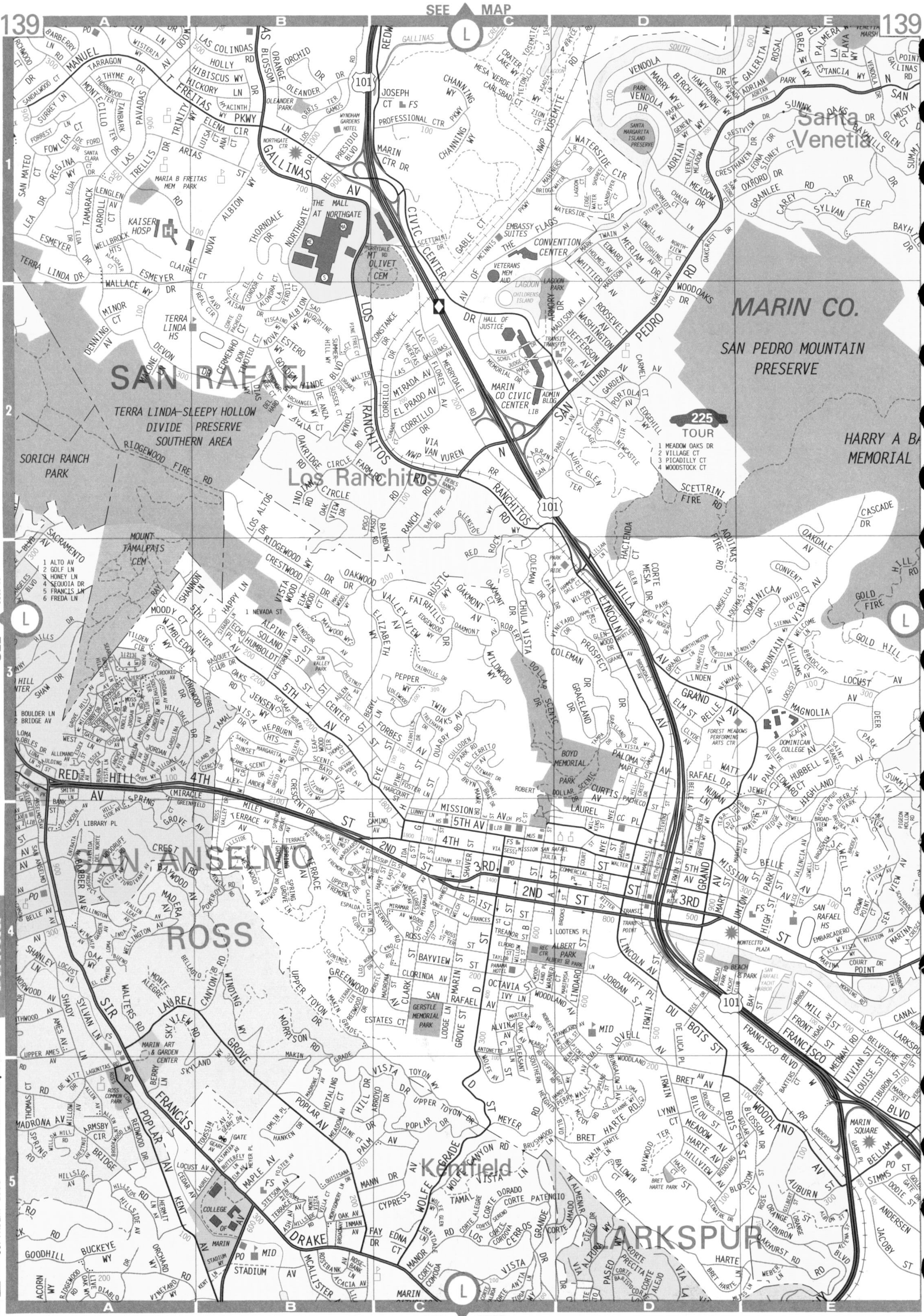

SEE MAP L

SEE MAP L

SEE MAP L

DETAIL

SEE MAP L

SEE MAP L

SEE MAP L

SEE MAP L

SEE MAP L

SEE MAP L

SEE MAP L
SAN FRANCISCO MARITIME NATIONAL HISTORICAL PARK
FISHERMANS WHARF
FISHERMANS MEMORIAL CHAPEL
PIER 39
MILES 1/4 1/2
KILOMETERS 0 .1 .2 .5
OAKLAND ALAMEDA FERRY
Golden Gate National Recreation Area
AQUATIC PARK
National Maritime Museum
FORT MASON CENTER
FORT MASON
GHIRARDELLI SQUARE
THE CANNERY
North Waterfront
Telegraph Hill
COIT TOWER
225 TOUR
SAN FRANCISCO
Russian Hill
North Beach
Chinatown
Nob Hill
Pacific Heights
LAFAYETTE PARK
Financial District
JAPAN CENTER
JEFFERSON SQUARE
HAYWARD PLGD
CIVIC CENTER
South of Market
MOSCONE CONV CTR
YERBA BUENA GARDENS
TRANSBAY TRANSIT TERMINAL
FERRY BUILDING
JUSTIN HERMAN PLAZA
GOLDEN GATEWAY CENTER
SEE A
1 ONE EMBARCADERO
2 TWO EMBARCADERO
3 THREE EMBARCADERO
4 FOUR EMBARCADERO
5 HYATT REGENCY
HALL OF JUSTICE
CALTRAIN YARD
Hayes Valley
THE EMBARCADERO
VAN NESS AV
MARKET
MISSION
FRWY
JOHN F FORAN
SEE MAP 142
DETAIL
SAN FRANCISCO

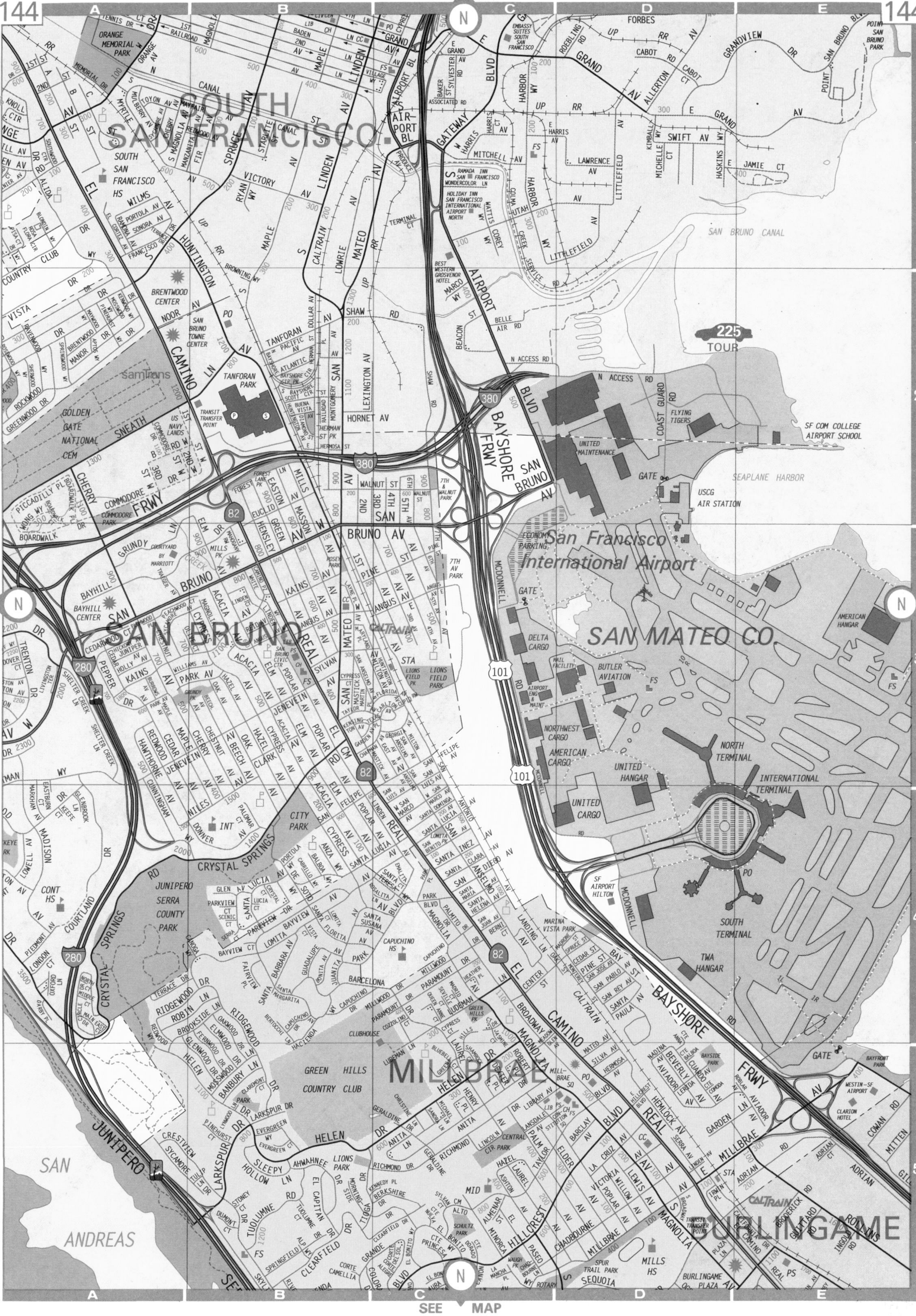

SAN BRUNO-SOUTH SAN FRANCISCO

SEE MAP

DETAIL

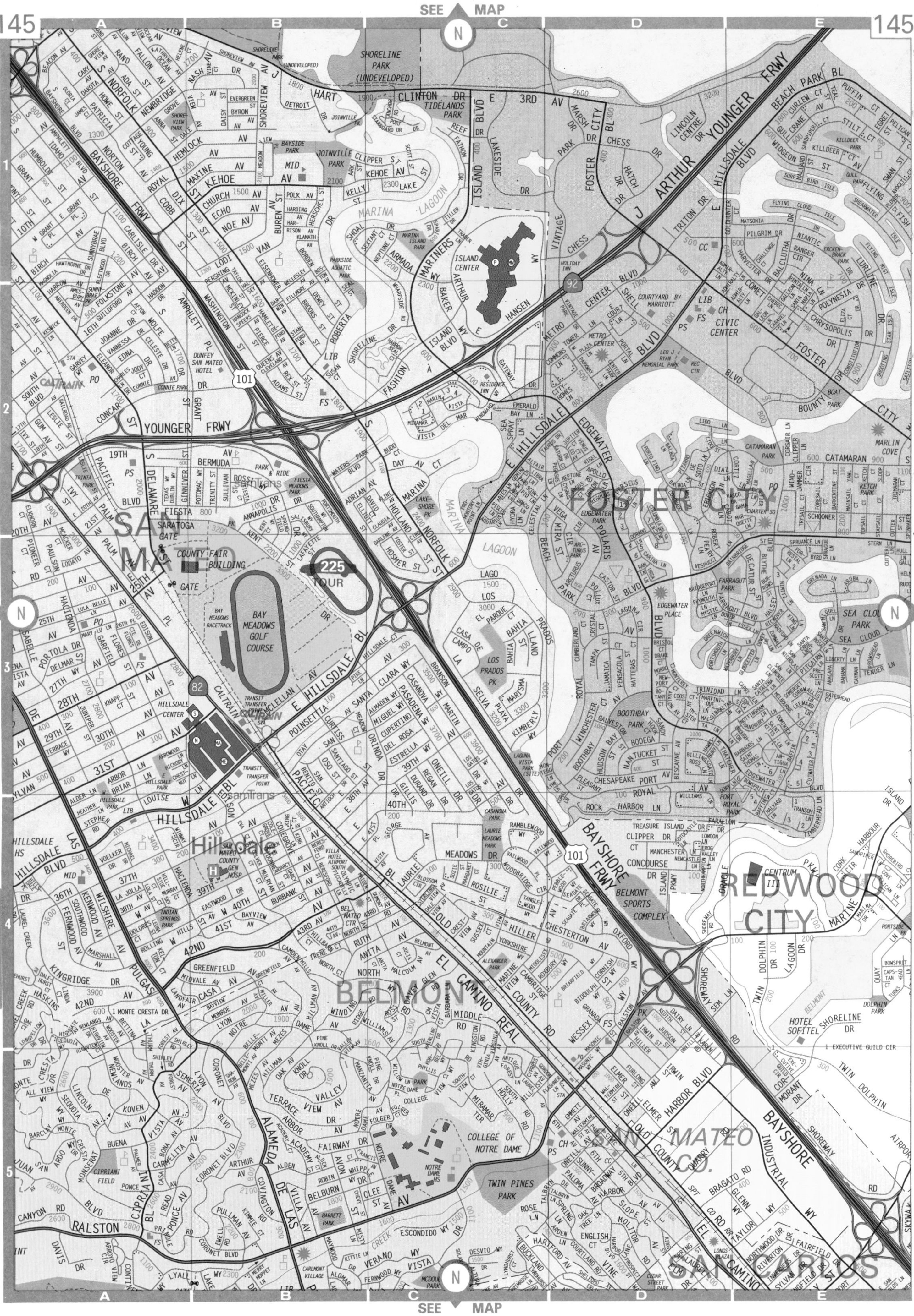

SAN MATEO
FOSTER CITY
BELMONT
REDWOOD CITY
SAN CARLOS
SAN MATEO CO.
BELMONT-FOSTER CITY
SHORELINE PARK (UNDEVELOPED)
MARINA LAGOON
BAY MEADOWS GOLF COURSE
COUNTY FAIR BUILDING
COLLEGE OF NOTRE DAME
TWIN PINES PARK
BELMONT SPORTS COMPLEX
HOTEL SOFITEL
J ARTHUR YOUNGER FRWY
BAYSHORE FRWY
EL CAMINO REAL
E HILLSDALE BL
HILLSDALE BLVD
ALAMEDA DE LAS PULGAS
RALSTON AV
FOSTER CITY BLVD

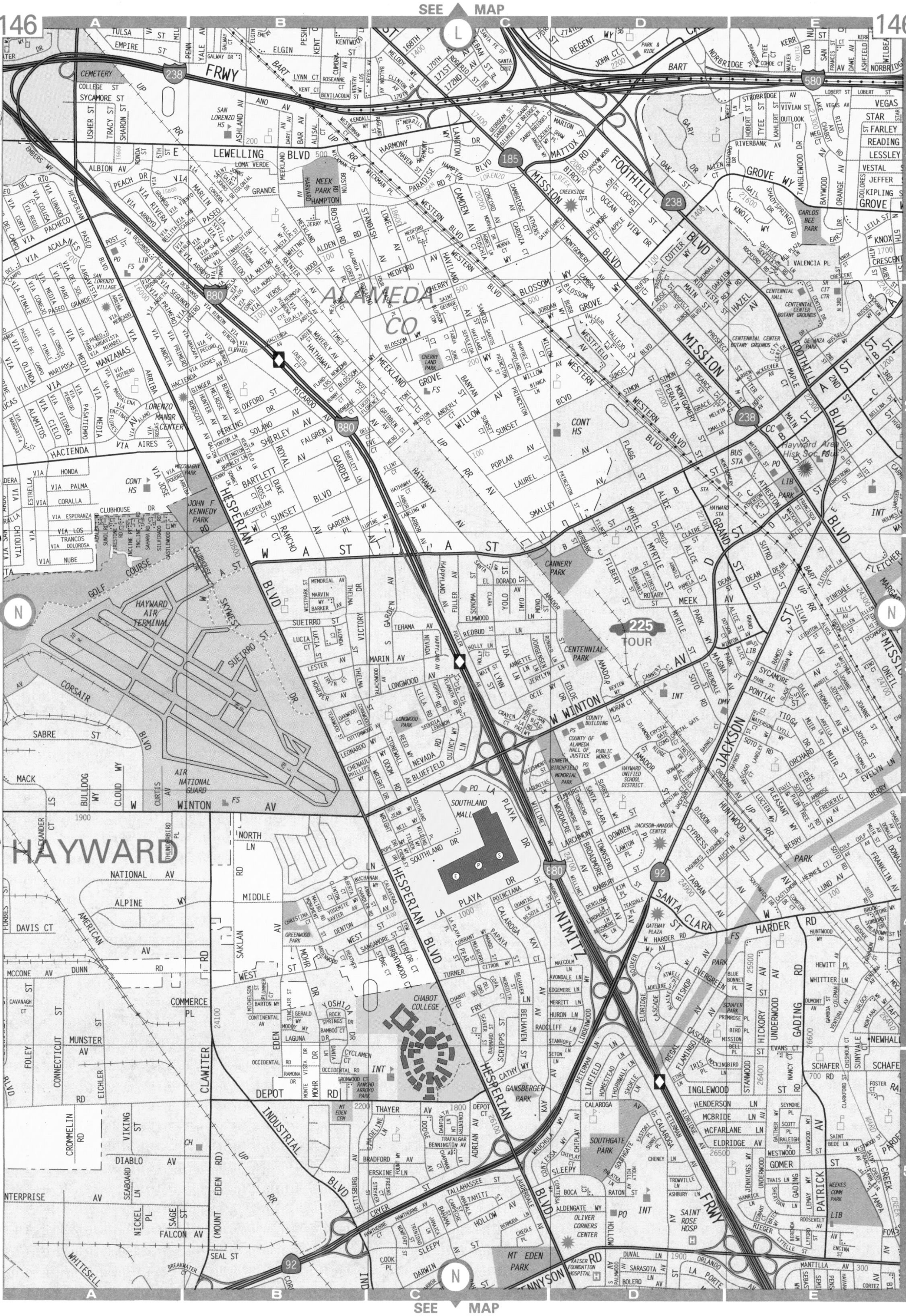
SEE MAP L
SEE MAP N
N
N
ALAMEDA CO
HAYWARD
HAYWARD
HAYWARD AIR TERMINAL
AIR NATIONAL GUARD
SOUTHLAND MALL
CHABOT COLLEGE
CENTENNIAL PARK
SOUTHGATE PARK
MT EDEN PARK
CANNERY PARK
JOHN F KENNEDY PARK
MEEK PARK HAMPTON
CARLOS BEE PARK
GANSBERGER PARK
COUNTY OF ALAMEDA HALL OF JUSTICE
HAYWARD UNIFIED SCHOOL DISTRICT
SAINT ROSE HOSP
KAISER FOUNDATION HOSPITAL
OLIVER CORNERS CENTER
GATEWAY PLAZA
JACKSON-AMADOR CENTER
Hayward Area Hist Soc Mus
225 TOUR
FRWY
MISSION BLVD
FOOTHILL BLVD
HESPERIAN BLVD
NIMITZ FRWY
JACKSON ST
W WINTON AV
W A ST
LEWELLING BLVD
HARDER RD
TENNYSON RD
SANTA CLARA ST
INDUSTRIAL BLVD
CLAWITER RD
238
580
880
185
92
DETAIL
SEE MAP

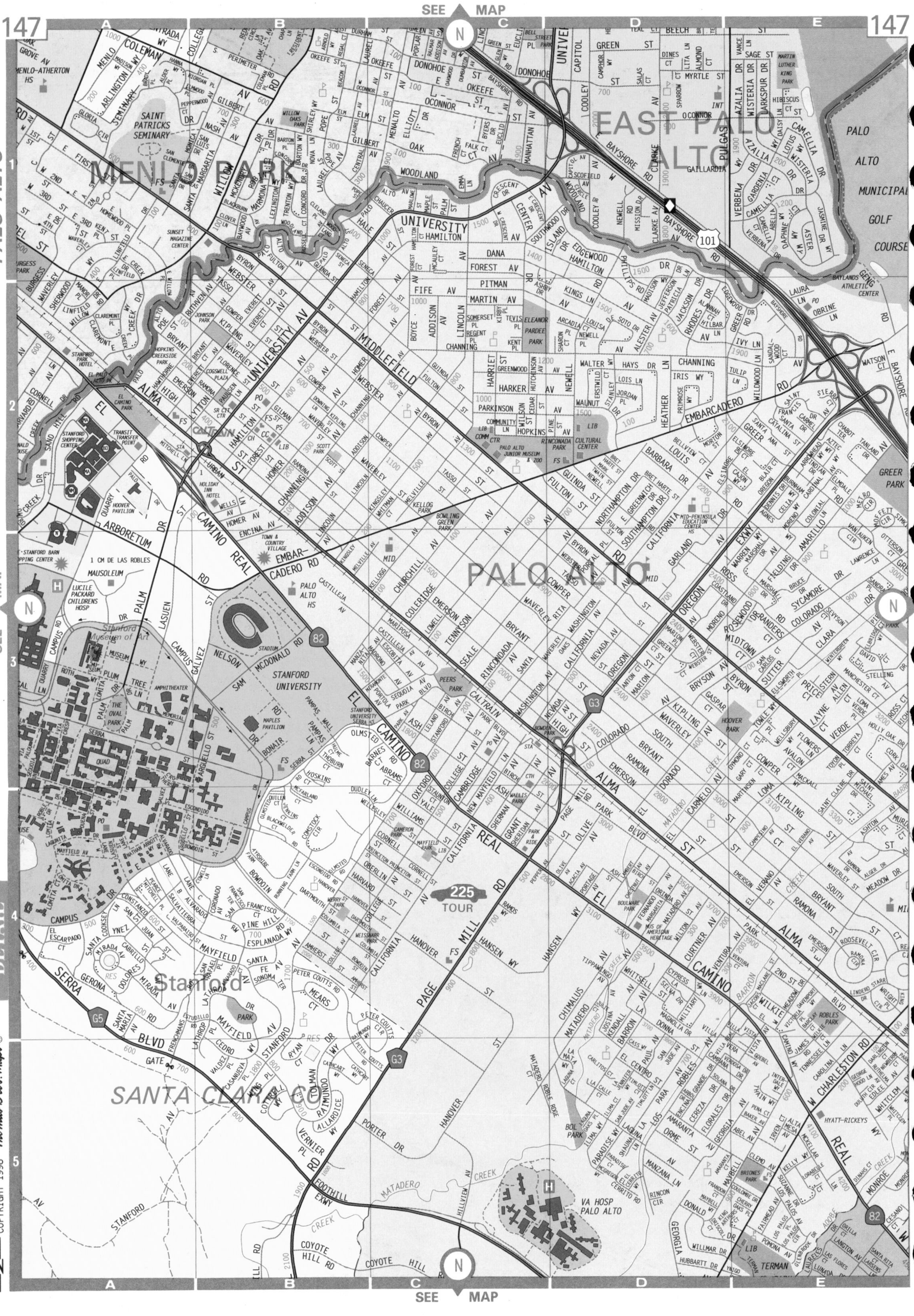
SEE MAP
MENLO PARK
EAST PALO ALTO
PALO ALTO
PALO ALTO
Stanford
SANTA CLARA CO
STANFORD UNIVERSITY
PALO ALTO MUNICIPAL GOLF COURSE
SAINT PATRICKS SEMINARY
MENLO-ATHERTON HS
STANFORD SHOPPING CENTER
LUCILE PACKARD CHILDRENS HOSP
PALO ALTO HS
VA HOSP PALO ALTO
UNIVERSITY AV
MIDDLEFIELD RD
EL CAMINO REAL
ALMA ST
EMBARCADERO RD
OREGON EXWY
PAGE MILL RD
FOOTHILL EXWY
JUNIPERO SERRA BLVD
W CHARLESTON RD
BAYSHORE FRWY
CALIFORNIA AV
225 TOUR
DETAIL

SEE MAP P

SEE MAP 149

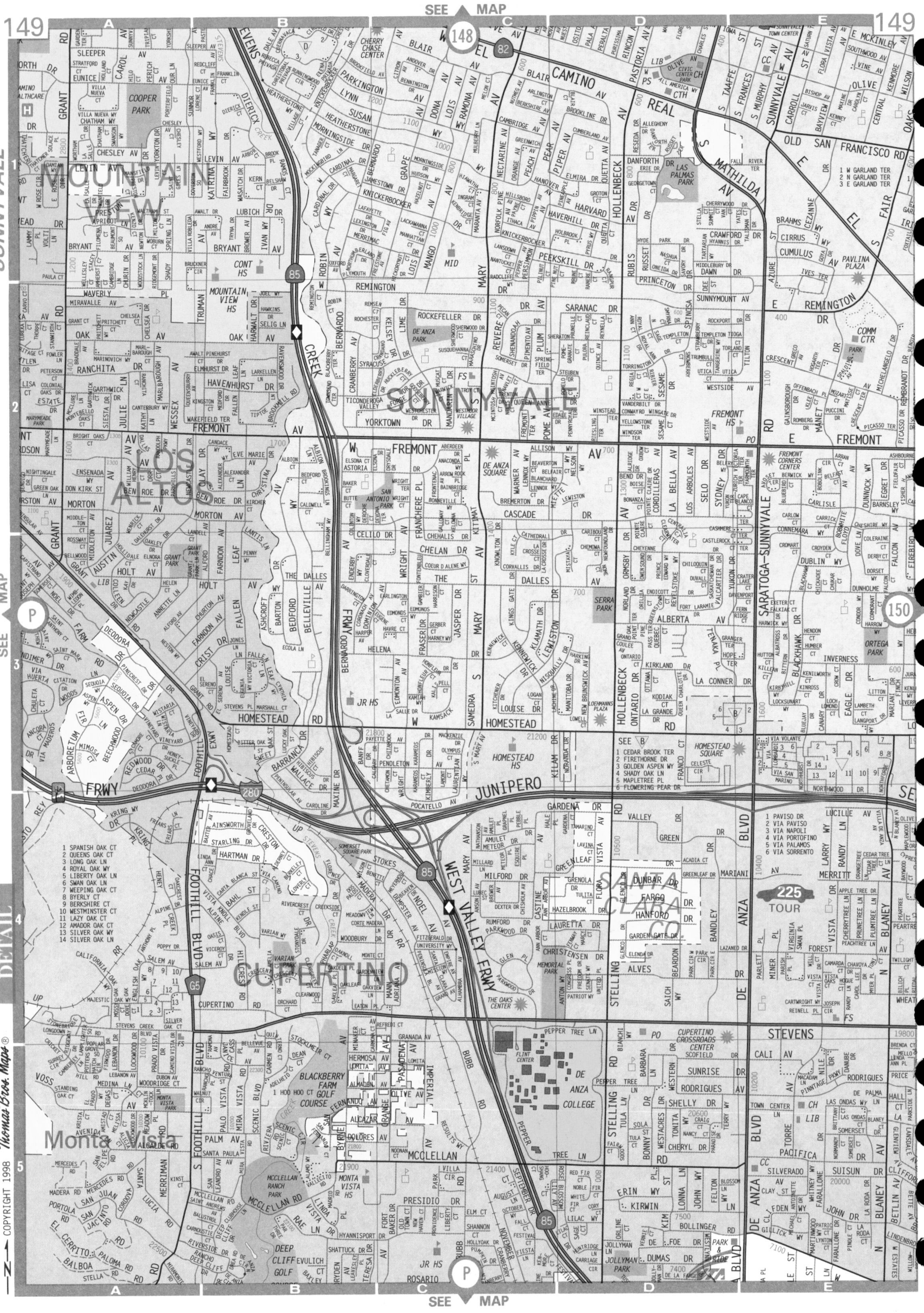
SEE 148 MAP
SEE 150 MAP
SEE P MAP
SUNNYVALE
MOUNTAIN VIEW
LOS ALTOS
CUPERTINO
Monta Vista
SANTA CLARA CO.
DETAIL
CAMINO REAL
FREMONT AV
W FREMONT AV
HOMESTEAD RD
JUNIPERO SERRA FRWY
STEVENS CREEK
S MATHILDA AV
OLD SAN FRANCISCO RD
REMINGTON DR
SARATOGA-SUNNYVALE RD
DE ANZA BLVD
FOOTHILL BLVD
WEST VALLEY FRWY
BERNARDO AV
HOLLENBECK AV
MARY AV
STELLING RD
MCCLELLAN RD
BOLLINGER RD
DE ANZA COLLEGE
BLACKBERRY FARM GOLF COURSE
DEEP CLIFF GOLF COURSE
MCCLELLAN RANCH PARK
COOPER PARK
LAS PALMAS PARK
DE ANZA PARK
SERRA PARK
ORTEGA PARK
JOLLYMAN PARK
MEMORIAL PARK
GRANT PARK
SAN ANTONIO PARK
MOUNTAIN VIEW HS
FREMONT HS
HOMESTEAD HS
CUPERTINO HS
MONTA VISTA HS
CONT HS
DE ANZA SQUARE
FREMONT CORNERS CENTER
HOMESTEAD SQUARE
CUPERTINO CROSSROADS CENTER
THE OAKS CENTER
PAVLINA PLAZA
LOEHMANNS PLAZA
VALLCO
1 W GARLAND TER
2 N GARLAND TER
3 E GARLAND TER
1 CEDAR BROOK TER
2 FIRETHORNE DR
3 GOLDEN ASPEN WY
4 SHADY OAK LN
5 MAPLETREE PL
6 FLOWERING PEAR DR
1 PAVISO DR
2 VIA PAVISO
3 VIA NAPOLI
4 VIA PORTOFINO
5 VIA PALAMOS
6 VIA SORRENTO
1 SPANISH OAK CT
2 QUEENS OAK CT
3 LONG OAK LN
4 ROYAL OAK WY
5 LIBERTY OAK LN
6 SWAN OAK LN
7 WEEPING OAK CT
8 BYERLY CT
9 BERKSHIRE CT
10 WESTMINSTER CT
11 LAZY OAK CT
12 AMADOR OAK CT
13 SILVER OAK WY
14 SILVER OAK LN
A B C D E
1 2 3 4 5
Thomas Bros. Maps ®
COPYRIGHT 1998

SEE MAP P
SEE MAP P
A B C D E
A B C D E
1 2 3 4 5
SANTA CLARA
DETAIL
SEE MAP 151
149
SUNNYVALE
SANTA CLARA
CUPERTINO
SAN JOSE
Rancho Rinconada
SANTA CLARA CO
EL CAMINO REAL
LAWRENCE EXWY
SAN TOMAS EXWY
WOLFE RD
STEVENS CREEK BLVD
HOMESTEAD RD
PRUNERIDGE AV
MONROE ST
BENTON ST
SARATOGA AV
KIELY BLVD
JUNIPERO SERRA FRWY
MOORPARK AV
BLACKFORD
CALTRAIN
STA CALTRAIN
SUNKEN GARDENS GOLF COURSE
CENTRAL PARK
VALLCO FASHION PARK
CUPERTINO HS
WILCOX HS
SANTA CLARA HS
KAISER FOUNDATION HOSPITAL
LAWRENCE STATION CTR
MARIPOSA GARDENS CENTER
CREEKSIDE PARK
SEE A
1 PERIWINKLE LN
2 VERBENA WY
3 RASPBERRY PL
4 VESCA WY
5 ALEXANDRIA LN
6 HOLLY BERRY CT
7 DAISYDELL CT
8 CHINABERRY CT
9 STRAWBERRY LN
10 BLUEBERRY TER
11 THIMBLEBERRY LN
12 CRYSTALBERRY TER
13 CARAWAY CT

SEE MAP P
SEE MAP 150
SEE MAP 152
SEE MAP P
SANTA CLARA
SAN JOSE
SANTA CLARA CO.
San Jose International Airport
TERMINAL A
TERMINAL C
SANTA CLARA UNIVERSITY
MISSION SANTA CLARA DE ASIS
SANTA CLARA CATHOLIC CEM
MISSION CITY MEMORIAL PARK CEM
VALLEY FAIR
SANTA CLARA VALLEY MEDICAL CENTER
SAN JOSE CITY COLLEGE
MUNICIPAL ROSE GARDEN
EGYPTIAN MUSEUM & PLANETARIUM
ROSICRUCIAN PARK
BELLARMINE COLLEGE PREP HS
LINCOLN HS
WINCHESTER MYSTERY HOUSE
CENTRAL EXWY
BAYSHORE FRWY
101
880
280
82
225 TOUR
NIMITZ FRWY
SINCLAIR FRWY
SAN TOMAS EXWY
LAFAYETTE ST
DE LA CRUZ BLVD
COLEMAN AV
AIRPORT BLVD
GUADALUPE PKWY
EL CAMINO REAL
HOMESTEAD RD
WINCHESTER BLVD
STEVENS CREEK BLVD
SAN CARLOS ST
HEDDING ST
THE ALAMEDA
BASCOM AV
MERIDIAN AV
MOORPARK AV
CALTRAIN
DETAIL

A
B
C
D
E
1
2
3
4
5
SAN JOSE
NIMITZ FRWY
BAYSHORE FRWY
OLD OAKLAND RD
BERRYESSA RD
MABURY RD
KING RD
SAN JOSE
HEDDING ST
TAYLOR ST
JULIAN ST
SANTA CLARA ST
SAN CARLOS ST
SAN SALVADOR ST
WILLIAM ST
REED ST
KEYES ST
ALMA AV
MONTEREY HWY
SINCLAIR FRWY
GUADALUPE FRWY
THE ALAMEDA
COLEMAN AV
VINE ST
MARKET ST
ALMADEN BLVD
SAN JOSE STATE UNIV
SAN JOSE CIVIC CENTER
WATSON PARK
BACKESTO PARK
ROOSEVELT PARK
WILLIAM STREET PARK
KELLEY PARK
HAPPY HOLLOW PARK
HAPPY HOLLOW ZOO
JAPANESE FRIENDSHIP TEA GARDEN
SPARTAN STADIUM
SAN JOSE MUNICIPAL BASEBALL STADIUM
SAN JOSE ARENA
GUADALUPE RIVER PARK
COLUMBUS PARK
MARTIN PARK
OVERFELT GARDENS
INDEPENDENCE HS
SAN JOSE ACADEMY HS
SAN JOSE CHRISTIAN COLLEGE
SAN JOSE MEDICAL CENTER
225 TOUR
101
880
280
87
82
151
COYOTE CREEK
CALTRAIN
SEE MAP P

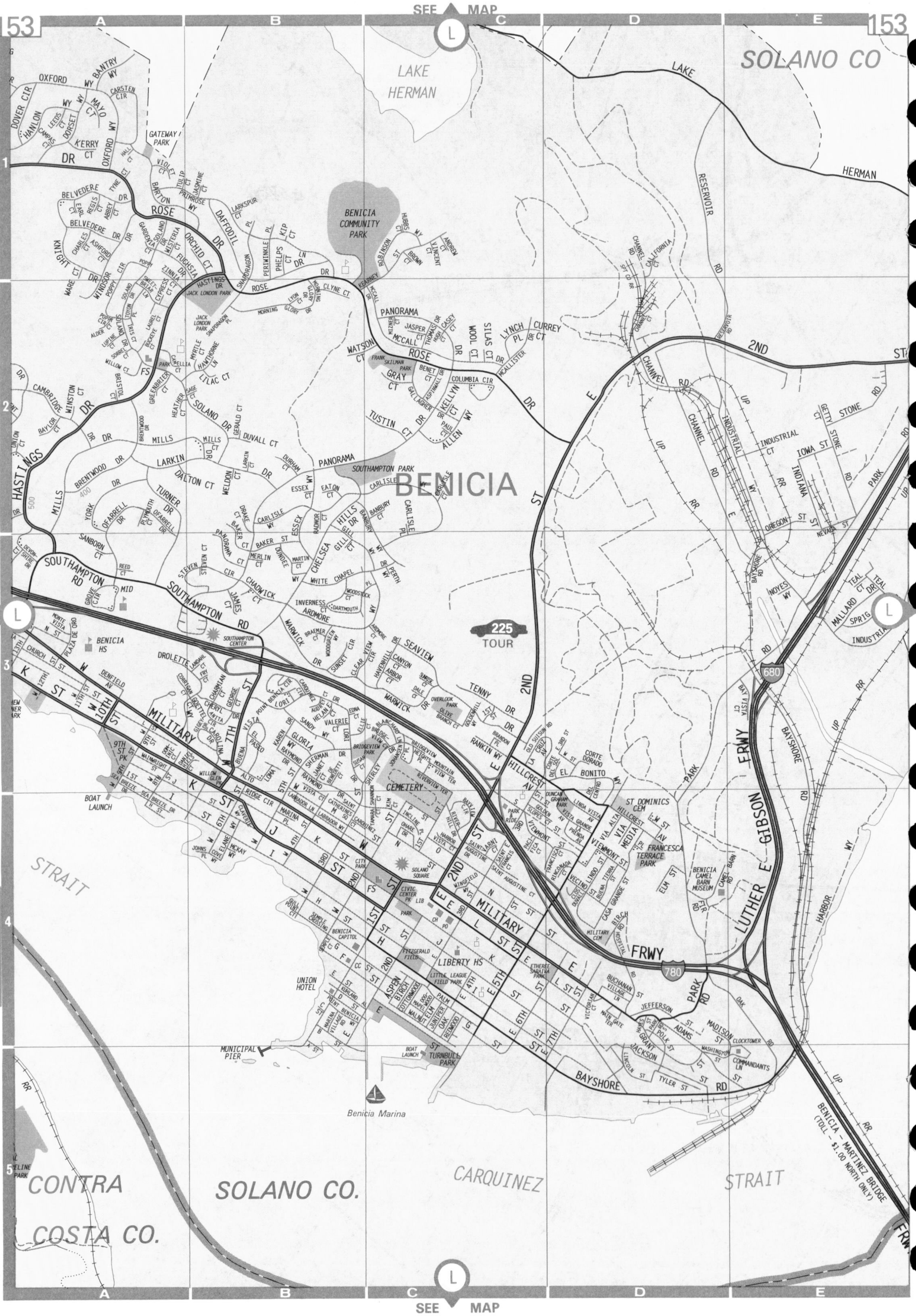

SEE MAP L
SOLANO CO
LAKE HERMAN
LAKE
HERMAN
BENICIA
BENICIA COMMUNITY PARK
GATEWAY PARK
JACK LONDON PARK
SOUTHAMPTON PARK
BENICIA HS
SOUTHAMPTON CENTER
225 TOUR
CEMETERY
BRIDGEVIEW PARK
OLIVE BRANCH CT
OVERLOOK PARK
ST DOMINICS CEM
FRANCESCA TERRACE PARK
BENICIA CAMEL BARN MUSEUM
CITY PARK
SOLANO SQUARE
CIVIC CENTER PK
FITZGERALD FIELD
LIBERTY HS
LITTLE LEAGUE FIELD PARK
BENICIA CAPITOL
UNION HOTEL
MUNICIPAL PIER
BOAT LAUNCH
TURNBULL PARK
Benicia Marina
MILITARY CEM
COMMANDANTS
CLOCKTOWER
BENICIA - MARTINEZ BRIDGE (TOLL - $1.00 NORTH ONLY)
I-680
I-780
FRWY
LUTHER E GIBSON FRWY
EAST 2ND ST
MILITARY
SOUTHAMPTON RD
HASTINGS DR
ROSE DR
PANORAMA DR
BAYSHORE RD
PARK RD
CHANNEL RD
INDUSTRIAL WY
STRAIT
CARQUINEZ STRAIT
SOLANO CO.
CONTRA COSTA CO.
DETAIL

SEE MAP L

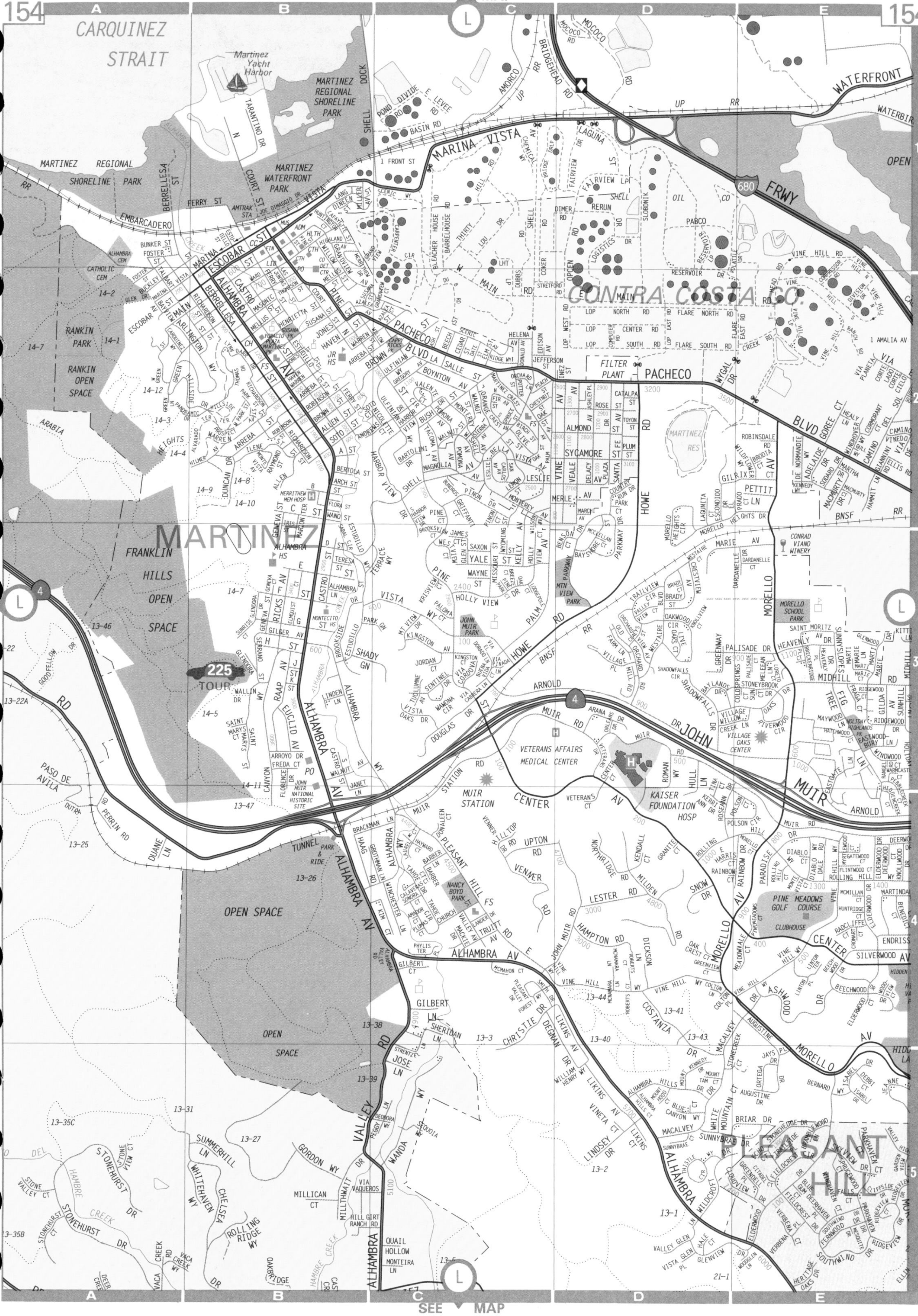

SEE MAP L

SEE MAP L

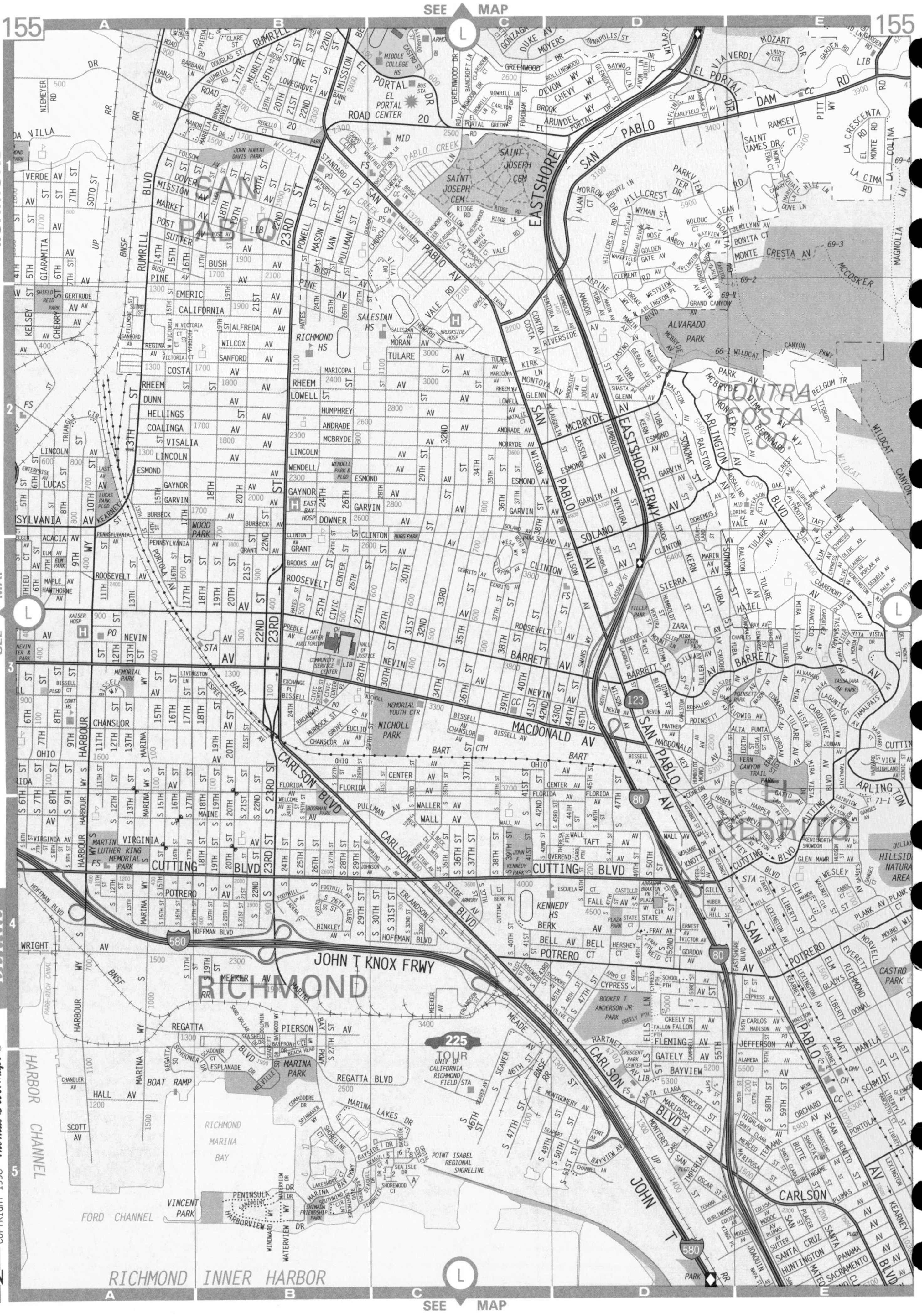
SEE MAP L
SEE MAP L
SEE MAP L
A
B
C
D
E
1
2
3
4
5
RICHMOND
DETAIL
SAN PABLO
RICHMOND
EL CERRITO
CONTRA COSTA CO
EL PORTAL CENTER
SAINT JOSEPH CEM
ALVARADO PARK
EASTSHORE FRWY
JOHN T KNOX FRWY
SAN PABLO AV
MACDONALD AV
CUTTING BLVD
CARLSON BLVD
BARRETT AV
NEVIN AV
POTRERO AV
REGATTA BLVD
MARINA BAY PKWY
RICHMOND HS
SALESIAN HS
MIDDLE COLLEGE HS
BROOKSIDE HOSP
KAISER HOSP
EAST BAY HOSP
NICHOLL PARK
MEMORIAL YOUTH CTR
KENNEDY HS
BOOKER T ANDERSON JR PARK
MARINA PARK
VINCENT PARK
POINT ISABEL REGIONAL SHORELINE
UNIV OF CALIFORNIA RICHMOND FIELD STA
225 TOUR
RICHMOND MARINA BAY
FORD CHANNEL
HARBOR CHANNEL
RICHMOND INNER HARBOR
FERN CANYON TRAIL PARK
HILLSIDE NATURAL AREA
CASTRO PARK
WILDCAT CANYON
80
580
123
N

SEE MAP L

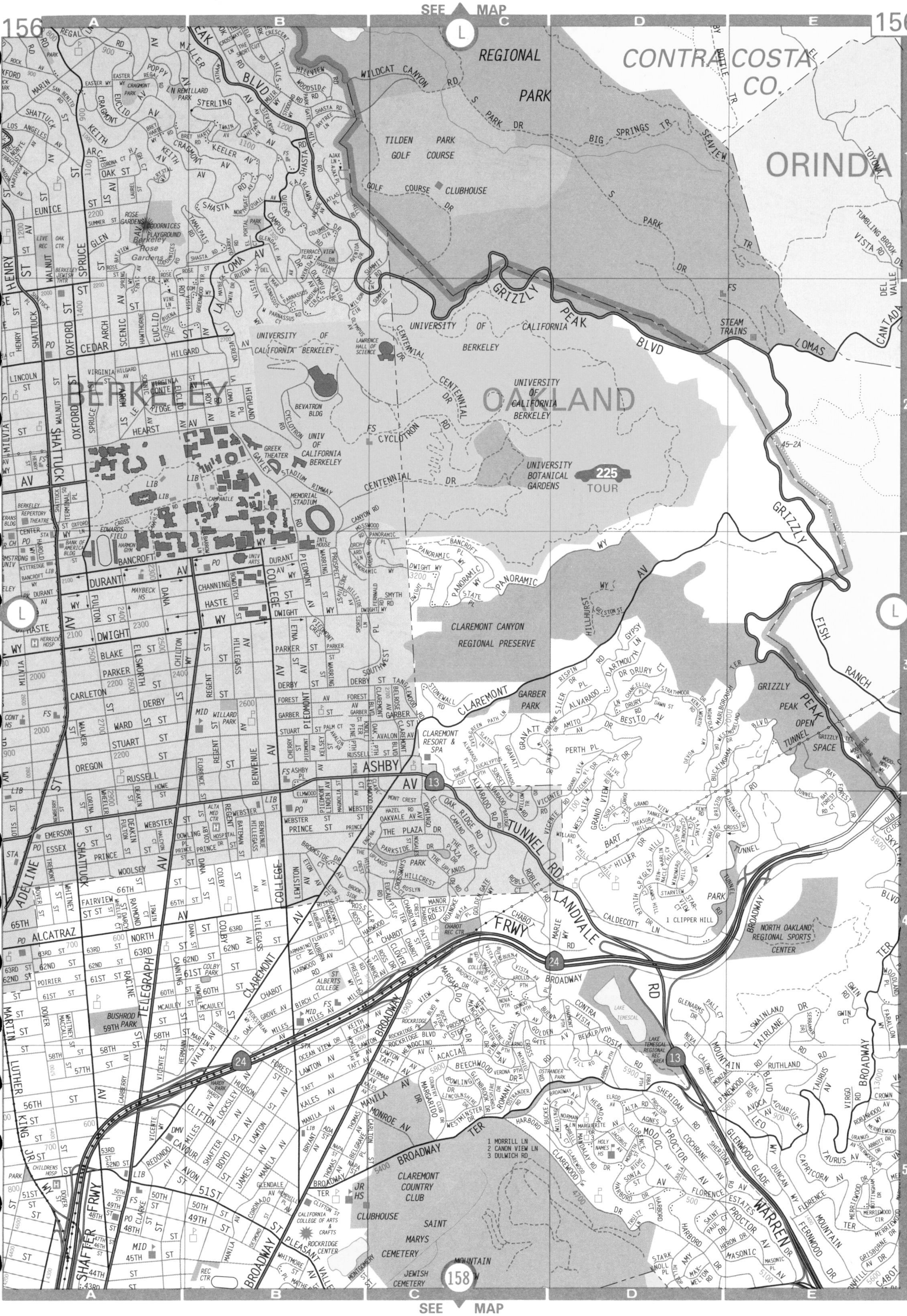

SEE MAP 158

SEE MAP L

SEE MAP L

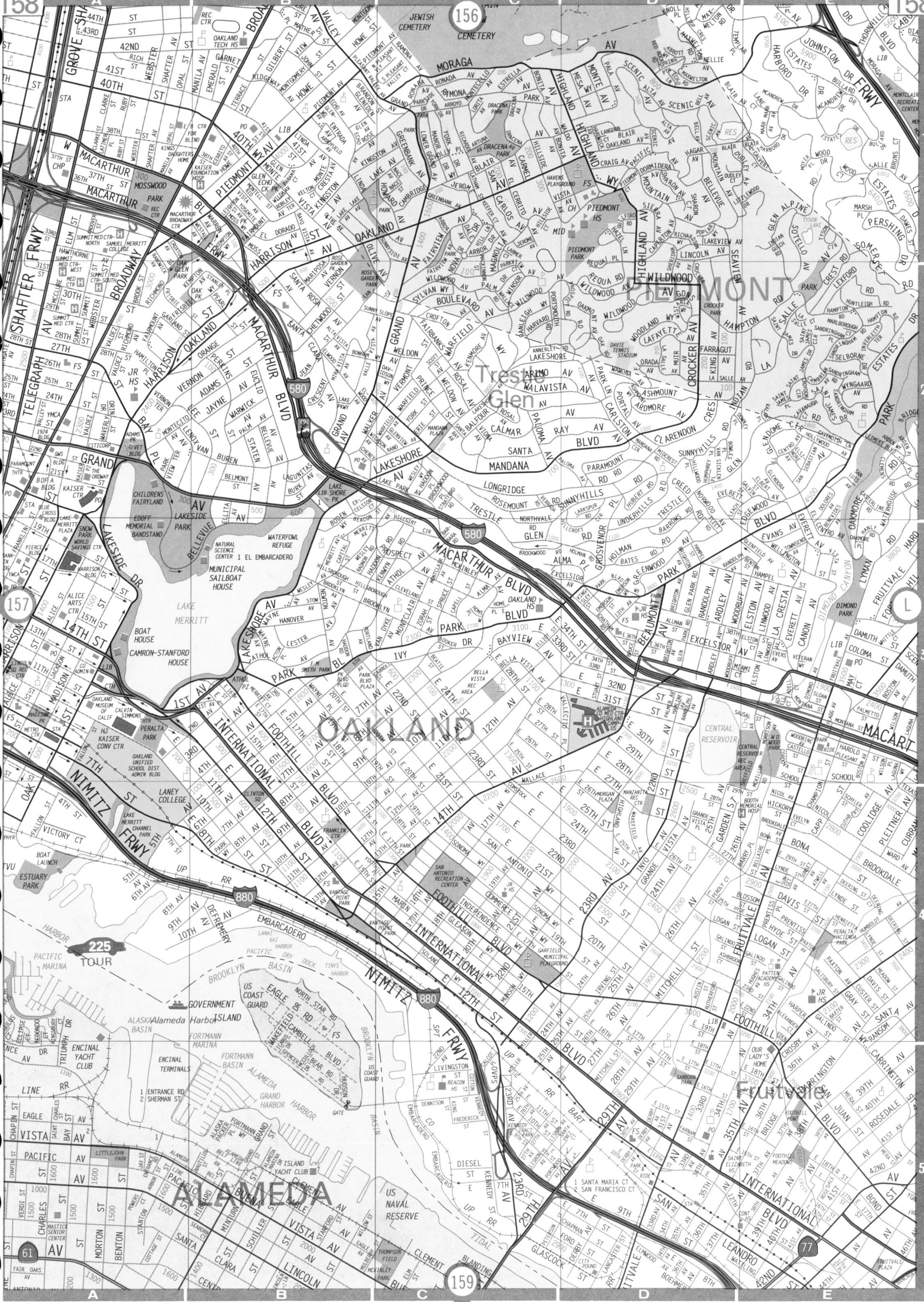

SEE MAP 157
SEE MAP L
SEE MAP 159

ALAMEDA-OAKLAND-PIEDMONT

DETAIL

SEE 158 MAP

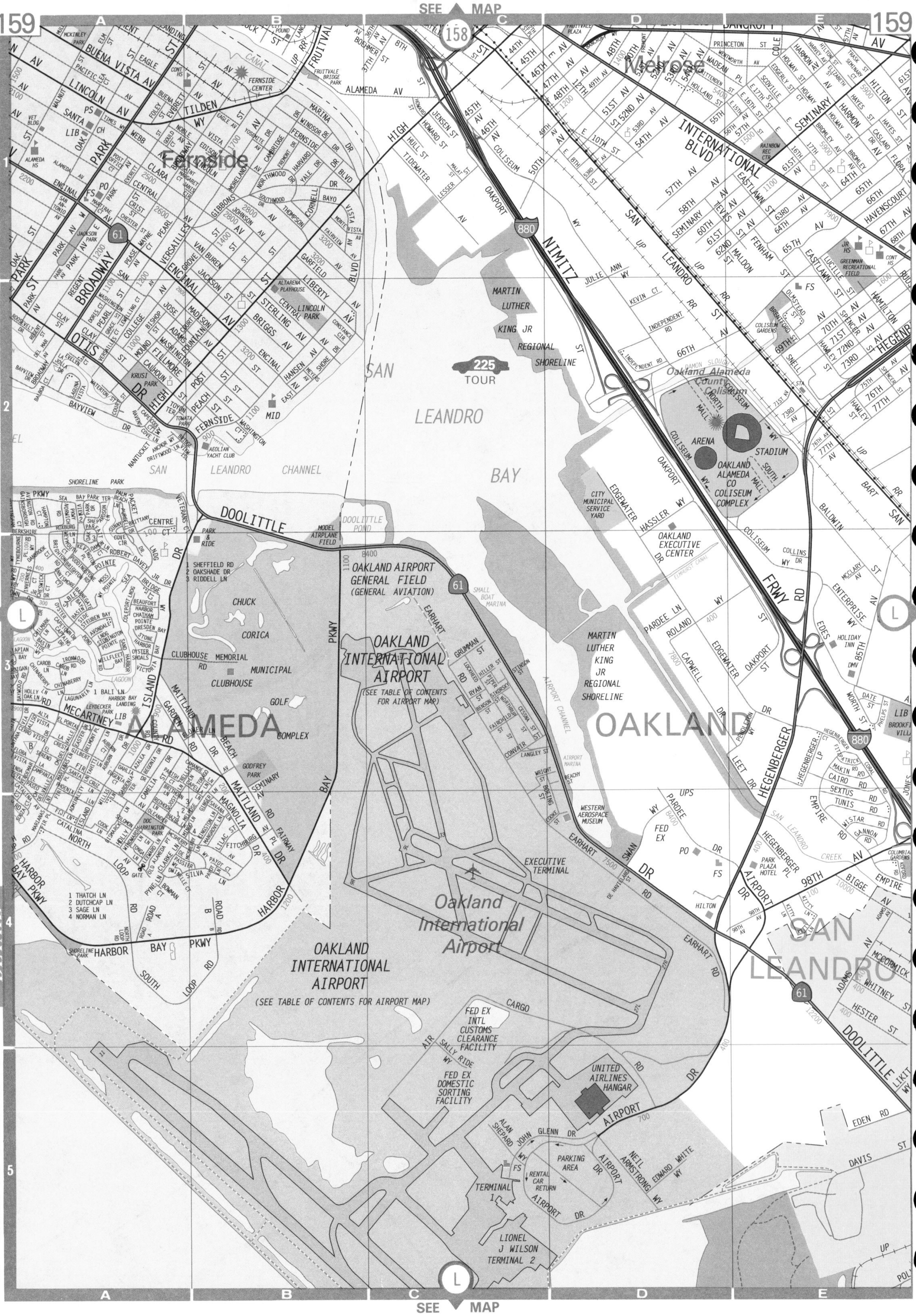

SEE L MAP

SEE L MAP

DETAIL

SEE MAP 40
A
B
C
D
E
1
2
3
4
5
STOCKTON
SAN JOAQUIN CO
SAN JOAQUIN DELTA COLLEGE
SHERWOOD MALL
WEBERSTOWN MALL
Plaza Inn
COLLEGE SQUARE
STAGG HS
University of the Pacific
HEBERT FIELD
OAK PARK
CEMETERY
VILLAGE AT WEBER RANCH
CALAVERAS RIVER
MARCH LN
PERSHING AV
PACIFIC AV
EL DORADO ST
WEST LN
AIRPORT WY
HARDING WY
CHARTER WAY
STOCKTON DEEP WATER CHANNEL
Port of Stockton
MORMAN SLOUGH
McLEOD LAKE
Haggin Museum
VICTORY PK
Childrens Museum of Stockton
BOGGS TRACT PK
227 TOUR
DETAIL

SEE 47 MAP

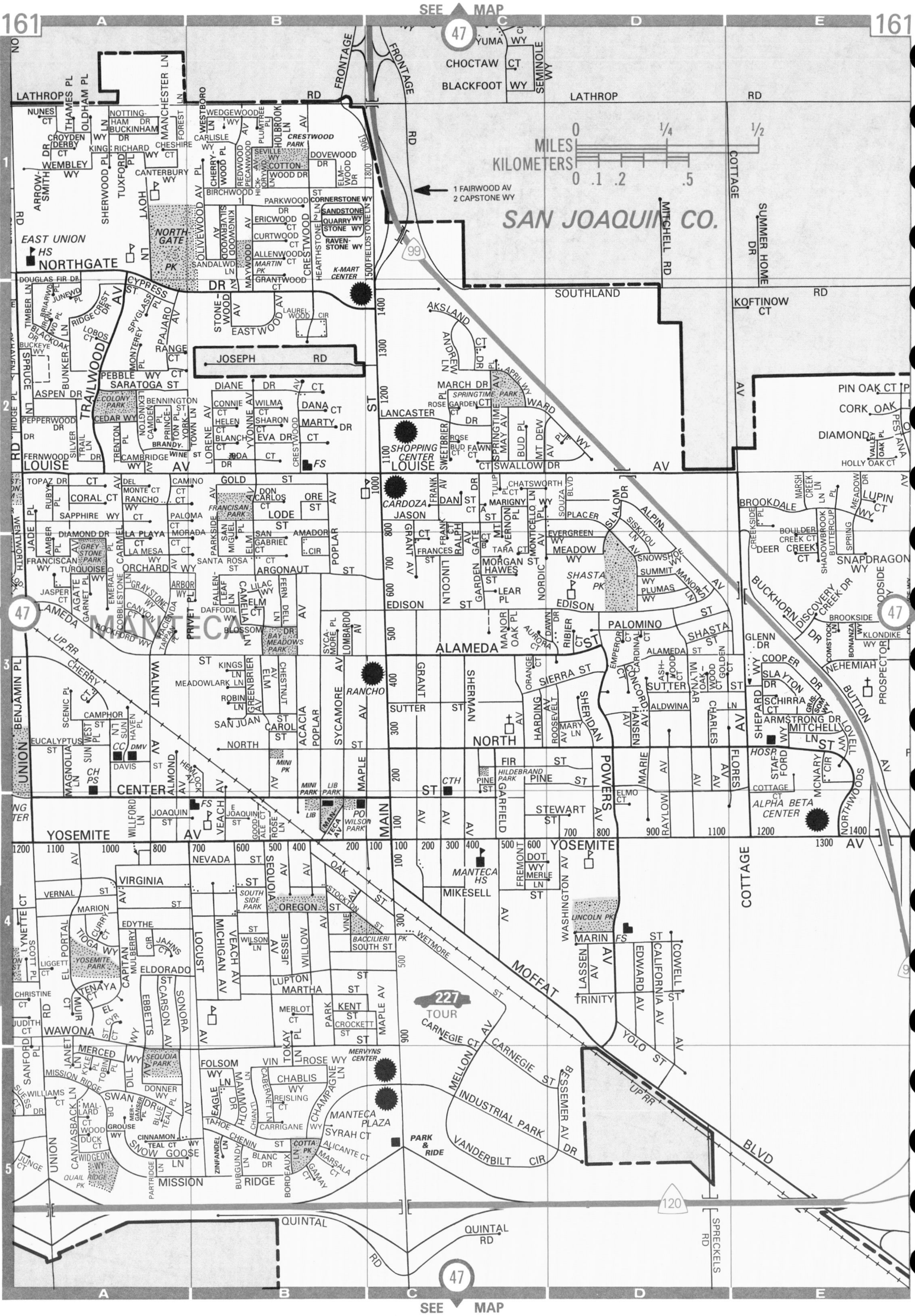

SEE 47 MAP

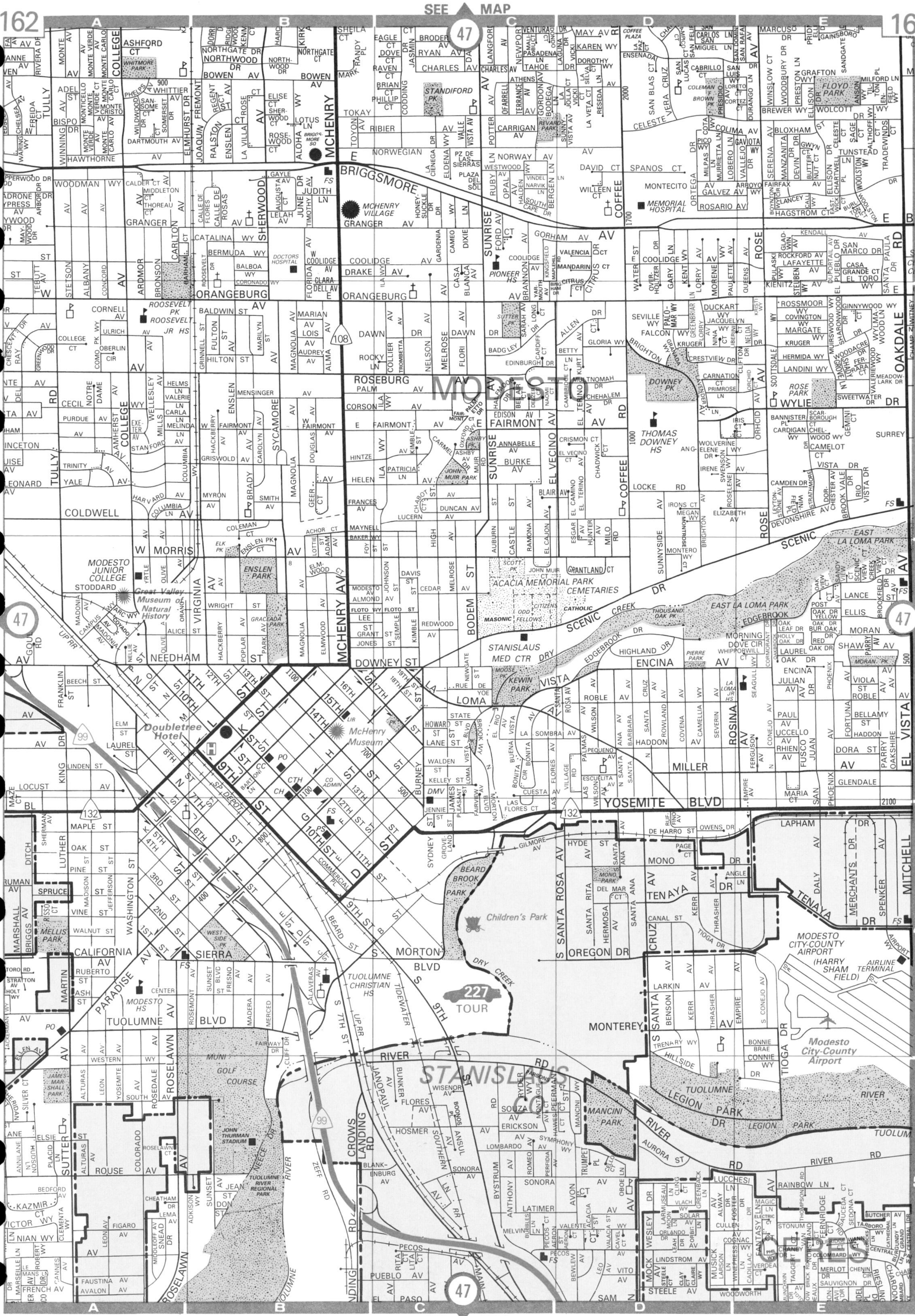
MODESTO
STANISLAUS CO
CERES
MODESTO JUNIOR COLLEGE
Great Valley Museum of Natural History
Doubletree Hotel
McHenry Museum
THOMAS DOWNEY HS
MODESTO HS
TUOLUMNE CHRISTIAN HS
ACACIA MEMORIAL PARK CEMETARIES
STANISLAUS MED CTR
MEMORIAL HOSPITAL
DOCTORS HOSPITAL
MODESTO CITY-COUNTY AIRPORT (HARRY SHAM FIELD)
AIRLINE TERMINAL
Modesto City-County Airport
Children's Park
MUNI GOLF COURSE
JOHN THURMAN STADIUM
TUOLUMNE RIVER REGIONAL PARK
LEGION PARK
MANCINI PARK
BEARD BROOK PARK
EAST LA LOMA PARK
ENSLEN PARK
GRACEADA PARK
JOHN MUIR PARK
FLOYD PARK
DOWNEY PK
ROSE PARK
McHENRY VILLAGE
BRIGGSMORE
YOSEMITE BLVD
TUOLUMNE BLVD
SCENIC DR
TUOLUMNE RIVER
DRY CREEK
227 TOUR
MODESTO DETAIL
SEE 47 MAP

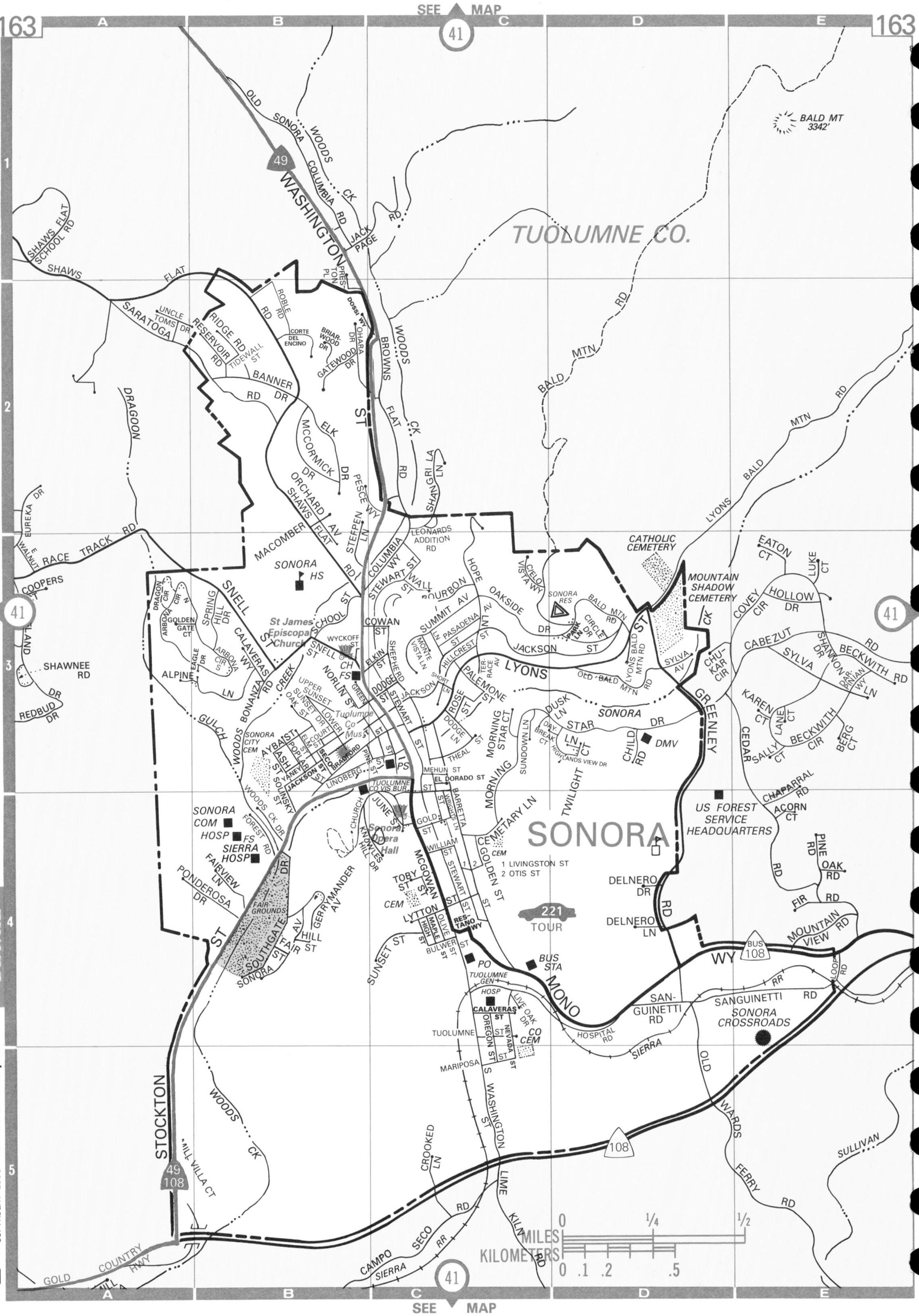
SEE MAP 41
A
B
C
D
E
1
2
3
4
5
SONORA
DETAIL
SEE MAP 41
TUOLUMNE CO.
BALD MT 3342'
OLD SONORA WOODS CK
COLUMBIA RD
JACK PAGE RD
WASHINGTON ST
49
SHAWS FLAT SCHOOL RD
SHAWS FLAT RD
SARATOGA RD
UNCLE TOMS DR
RESERVOIR RD
RIDGE RD
TIDEWALL ST
BANNER RD
BANNER DR
ROBLE RD
PRESTON PL
CORTE DEL ENCINO
BRIARWOOD DR
DOSSI WY
OHARA DR
GATEWOOD DR
BROWNS FLAT RD
WOODS CK
SHANGRI LA LN
BALD MTN RD
DRAGOON
ELK DR
MCCORMICK DR
ORCHARD AV
SHAWS FLAT RD
PESCE WY
STEFFEN LN
MACOMBER RD
EUREKA DR
E WALNUT
RACE TRACK RD
COOPERS CT
LEONARDS ADDITION RD
SONORA HS
COLUMBIA WY
STEWART ST
WALL ST
HOPE LN
CIELO VISTA WY
SONORA RES
BALD MTN RD
CIRCLE DR
PARK LN
OAKSIDE DR
BOURBON
SUMMIT AV
PASADENA AV
MONTE VISTA LN
HILLCREST
TERRACE AV
JACKSON ST
LYONS
OLD BALD MTN RD
LYONS BALD MTN RD
SYLVA AV
GREENLEY RD
CATHOLIC CEMETERY
MOUNTAIN SHADOW CEMETERY
LYONS BALD MTN RD
EATON CT
LUKE CT
COVEY CIR
HOLLOW DR
CHUKAR CIR
CABEZUT
SYLVA
SHANNON DR
BECKWITH RD
DARBINIAN WY
KAREN CT
LANE CT
BECKWITH CIR
BERG CT
CEDAR
SALLY CT
CHAPARRAL RD
ACORN CT
SNELL ST
DRAGON CIR
ARBONA CIR
GOLDEN GATE CT
SPRING HILL DR
CALAVERAS WY
ARBONA CIR
EAGLE DR
ALPINE LN
SHAWNEE RD
REDBUD DR
CREEK
SCHOOL ST
St James Episcopal Church
WYCKOFF ST
COWAN ST
CH
FS
NORLIN ST
GREEN
ELKIN ST
DODGE ST
SHEPHERD
STEWART ST
JACKSON
SHORT LN
PALEMONE ST
ROSE ST
DODGE ST
THEAL ST
MORNING STAR CT
SUNDOWN LN
DUSK LN
DAYBREAK CT
STAR DR
SONORA DR
HIGHLANDS VIEW DR
CHILD RD
DMV
GULCH
WOODS
BONANZA
SONORA CITY CEM
UPPER SUNSET
SUNSET DR
LOWER
OAK ST
COURT
Tuolumne Co Mus
AYBAST
ASH ST
POPLAR
ELM
SECO
BRADFORD
PINE ST
YANEY
SOLINSKY ST
JACKSON ST
LINOBERG
PS
MEHUN ST
EL DORADO ST
TUOLUMNE CO VIS BUR
MORNING
TWILIGHT
US FOREST SERVICE HEADQUARTERS
SONORA COM HOSP
FS
SIERRA HOSP
WOODS CK DR
FOREST RD
CHURCH
JUNE ST
GOLD ST
BARRETTA
WRIGHTS LN
Sonora Opera Hall
KNOWLES HILL DR
WILLIAM ST
CEMETARY LN
CEM
SONORA
1 LIVINGSTON ST
2 OTIS ST
PINE RD
OAK RD
FAIRVIEW LN
PONDEROSA DR
GERRYMANDER AV
MCGOWAN
TOBY ST
CEM
STEWART ST
GOLDEN ST
DELNERO DR
DELNERO LN
FIR RD
FAIR GROUNDS
LYTTON
MAPLE
HIGH
OLIVE ST
RESTANO WY
221 TOUR
MOUNTAIN VIEW RD
SOUTHGATE DR
HILL ST
FAIR ST
SONORA
BULWER ST
SUNSET ST
PO
BUS STA
MONO WY
BUS 108
LOOP RD
SANGUINETTI RD
SONORA CROSSROADS
TUOLUMNE GEN HOSP
CALAVERAS ST
LIVE OAK DR
TUOLUMNE ST
OREGON ST
NEVADA ST
CO CEM
HOSPITAL RD
SIERRA
MARIPOSA
OLD WARDS FERRY RD
STOCKTON
WOODS CK
S WASHINGTON ST
CROOKED LN
108
SULLIVAN
49 108
HILL VILLA CT
LIME KILN RD
RD
SECO RR
CAMPO SIERRA
GOLD COUNTRY HWY
0
1/4
1/2
MILES
KILOMETERS
0 .1 .2 .5
SEE MAP 41

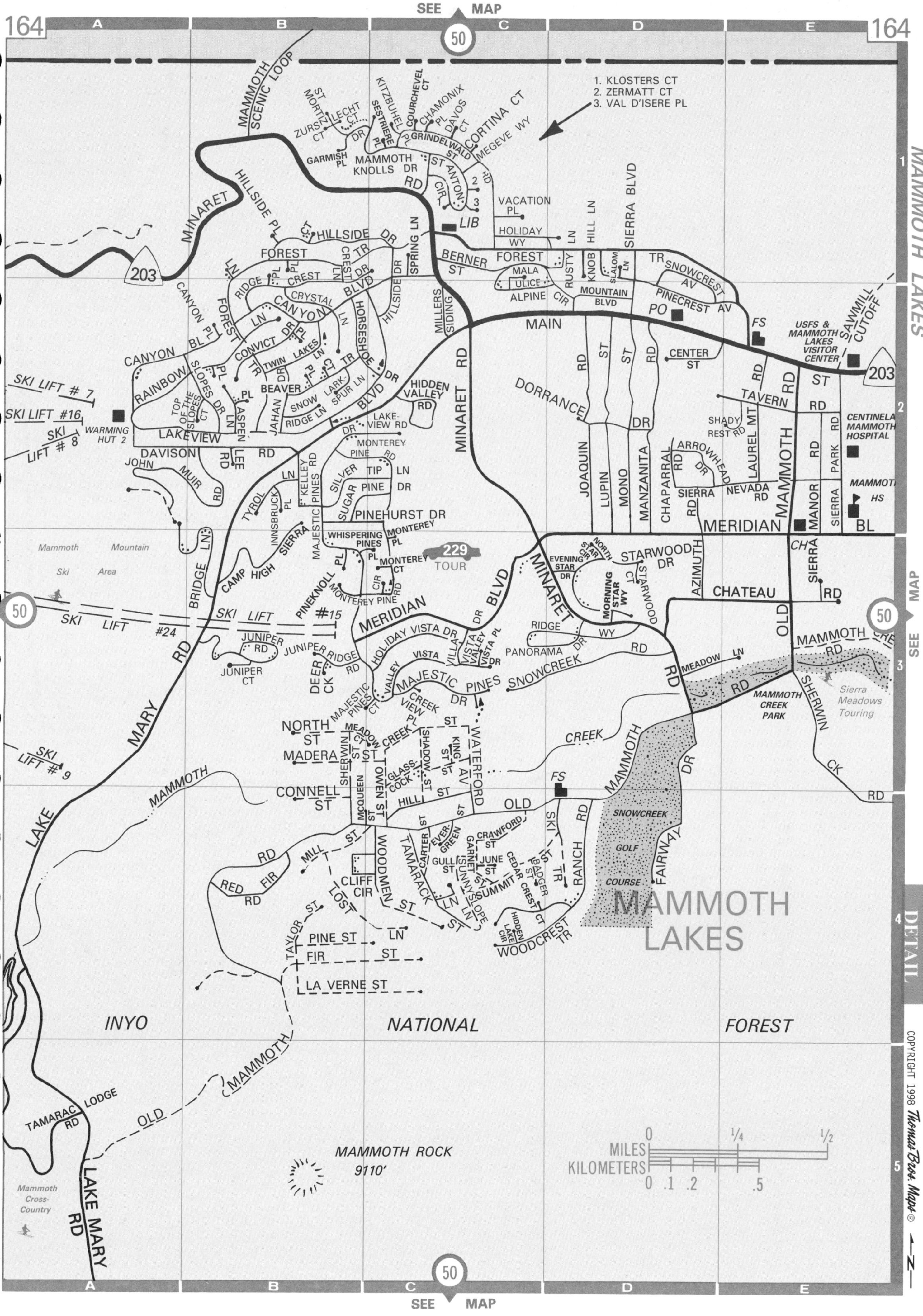
SEE MAP 50
A
B
C
D
E
1. KLOSTERS CT
2. ZERMATT CT
3. VAL D'ISERE PL
MAMMOTH SCENIC LOOP
ST MORITZ
ZURS CT
LECHT CT
DR
GARMISH PL
KITZBUHEL
SESTRIERE PL
COURCHEVEL CT
CHAMONIX PL
DAVOS CT
GRINDELWALD
CORTINA CT
MEGEVE WY
MAMMOTH KNOLLS DR
RD
ST ANTON CIR
VACATION PL
HOLIDAY WY
LIB
MINARET
HILLSIDE PL
HILLSIDE DR
203
FOREST CREST LN
FOREST TR
RIDGE PL
CREST
DR
CRYSTAL
CANYON BLVD
CANYON PL
FOREST LN
CONVICT DR
TWIN LAKES
TR
PL
CT
HORSESHOE DR
HILLSIDE DR
SPRING LN
MILLERS SIDING
BERNER ST
FOREST
MALA ULICE
ALPINE CIR
RUSTY LN
KNOB HILL LN
SLALOM LN
SIERRA BLVD
MOUNTAIN BLVD
TR SNOWCREST AV
PINECREST AV
PO
FS
USFS & MAMMOTH LAKES VISITOR CENTER
SAWMILL CUTOFF
MAIN ST
203
CANYON BL
RAINBOW
SLOPES DR
TOP OF THE SLOPES CT
PL
ASPEN LN
BEAVER DR
JAHAN
SNOW RIDGE LN
LARK-SPUR LN
BLVD
HIDDEN VALLEY RD
LAKE-VIEW RD
MINARET RD
SKI LIFT # 7
SKI LIFT #16
SKI LIFT # 8
WARMING HUT 2
LAKEVIEW
DAVISON RD
JOHN MUIR RD
LEE
RD
MONTEREY PINE RD
SILVER TIP LN
SUGAR PINE DR
KELLEY LN
MAJESTIC PINES RD
TYROL
INNSBRUCK PL
PINEHURST DR
SIERRA HIGH
CAMP HIGH
WHISPERING PINES PL
MONTEREY PL
MONTEREY CT
CIR
RD
229 TOUR
PINEKNOLL PL
MONTEREY PINE
BRIDGE LN
Mammoth Mountain Ski Area
50
SKI LIFT #24
SKI LIFT #15
MERIDIAN BLVD
DORRANCE DR
RD
ST
ST
RD
CENTER ST
JOAQUIN
LUPIN
MONO
MANZANITA
CHAPARRAL RD
ARROWHEAD DR
RD
SIERRA
NEVADA RD
LAUREL MT RD
SHADY REST RD
TAVERN RD
MAMMOTH RD
RD
PARK RD
CENTINELA MAMMOTH HOSPITAL
MAMMOTH HS
MANOR
SIERRA
BL
MERIDIAN
EVENING STAR DR
NORTH STAR CIR
STARWOOD DR
MORNING STAR WY
STARWOOD CT
AZIMUTH
CHA
SIERRA
CHATEAU RD
OLD
MAMMOTH CREEK RD
50 SEE MAP
RIDGE WY
PANORAMA DR
MINARET RD
JUNIPER RD
JUNIPER RIDGE RD
JUNIPER CT
DEER CK
HOLIDAY VISTA DR
VISTA
VILLA
VISTA VALLEY
VISTA PL
DR
VALLEY
MAJESTIC PINES DR
SNOWCREEK RD
MEADOW LN
RD
MAMMOTH CREEK PARK
SHERWIN CK RD
Sierra Meadows Touring
MAJESTIC PINES CT
CREEK VIEW PL
ST
NORTH ST
MADERA ST
SHERWIN ST
MEADOW CT
CREEK
SHADOW ST
KING ST
WATERFORD AV
GLASS-COCK ST
CONNELL ST
MCQUEEN ST
OWEN ST
HILL ST
OLD
CREEK
FS
MAMMOTH DR
SKI TR
RANCH RD
SNOWCREEK GOLF COURSE
FAIRWAY DR
SKI LIFT # 9
MAMMOTH
LAKE MARY RD
ST
MILL ST
RD
RED FIR RD
CLIFF CIR
LOST LN
WOODMEN ST
TAMARACK ST
CARTER ST
EVER-GREEN ST
GULL ST
GARNET ST
SUNNYSLOPE LN
JUNE ST
CRAWFORD ST
CEDAR CREST CT
BADGER ST
SUMMIT
HIDDEN LAKE CIR
WOODCREST TR
MAMMOTH LAKES
TAYLOR ST
PINE ST
FIR ST
LA VERNE ST
INYO NATIONAL FOREST
MAMMOTH
TAMARAC LODGE RD
OLD
MAMMOTH ROCK 9110'
Mammoth Cross-Country
LAKE MARY RD
MILES 0 1/4 1/2
KILOMETERS 0 .1 .2 .5
50
SEE MAP
MAMMOTH LAKES
DETAIL

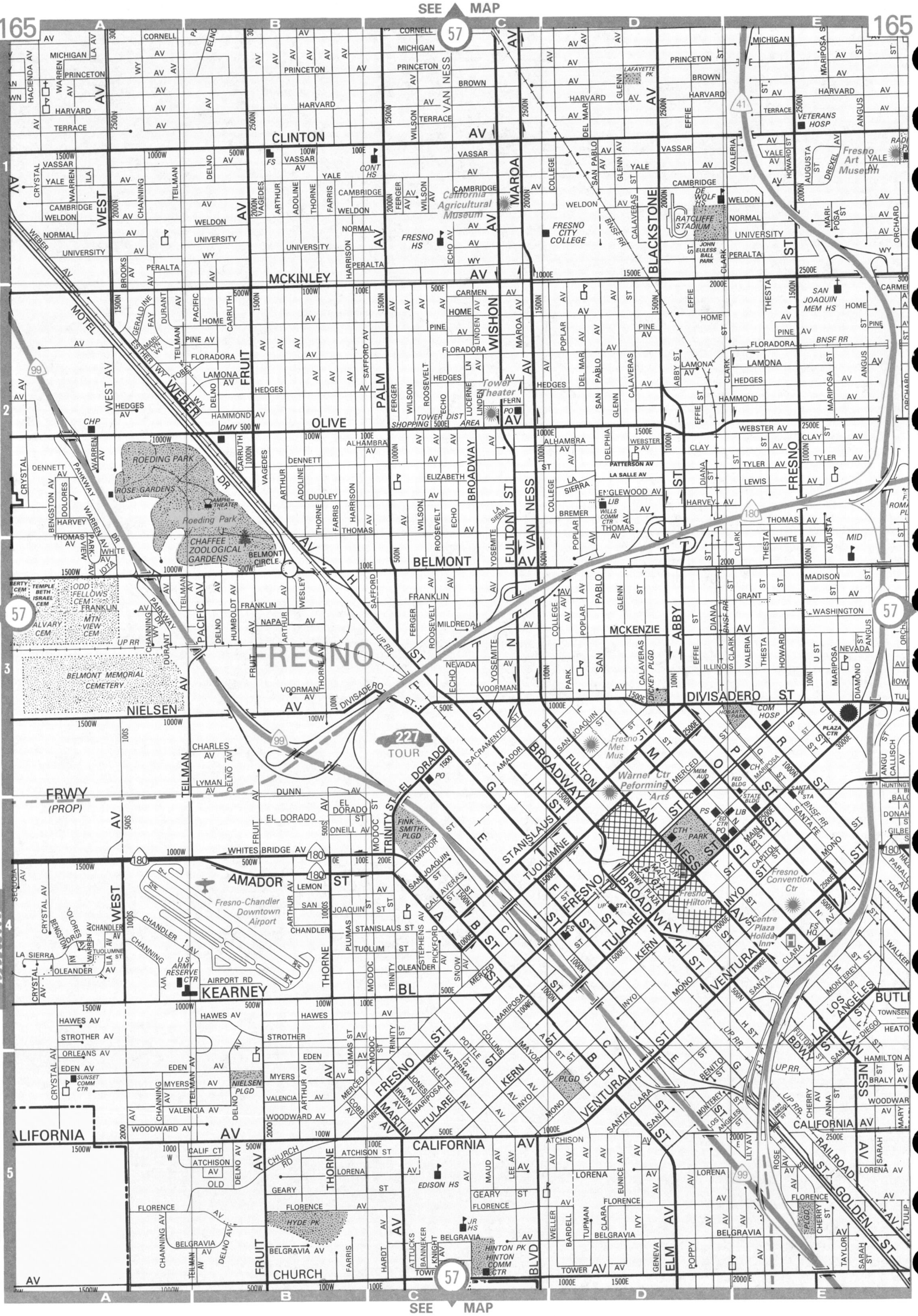
SEE MAP 57
FRESNO
CLINTON AV
MCKINLEY AV
OLIVE AV
BELMONT AV
DIVISADERO ST
NIELSEN AV
WHITES BRIDGE AV
CALIFORNIA AV
CHURCH AV
WEST AV
FRUIT AV
PALM AV
WISHON AV
MAROA AV
VAN NESS
BLACKSTONE AV
FRESNO ST
ABBY ST
BROADWAY
VENTURA AV
TULARE ST
KEARNEY BL
WEBER AV
ELM AV
BLVD
California Agricultural Museum
FRESNO CITY COLLEGE
FRESNO HS
RATCLIFFE STADIUM
Fresno Art Museum
VETERANS HOSP
SAN JOAQUIN MEM HS
Tower Theater
Roeding Park
ROSE GARDENS
CHAFFEE ZOOLOGICAL GARDENS
BELMONT MEMORIAL CEMETERY
MTN VIEW CEM
ODD FELLOWS CEM
TEMPLE BETH ISRAEL CEM
227 TOUR
FRWY (PROP)
Fresno-Chandler Downtown Airport
U.S. ARMY RESERVE CTR
FINK SMITH PLGD
Fresno Met Mus
Warner Ctr Peforming Arts
CTH PARK
Fresno Hilton
Fresno Convention Ctr
Centre Plaza Holiday Inn
COM HOSP
EDISON HS
HYDE PK
HINTON PK
HINTON COMM CTR
NIELSEN PLGD
SUNSET COMM CTR
LAFAYETTE PK
DICKEY PLGD
MID
DETAIL

SEE MAP 78

SEE MAP 78

SEE MAP 54

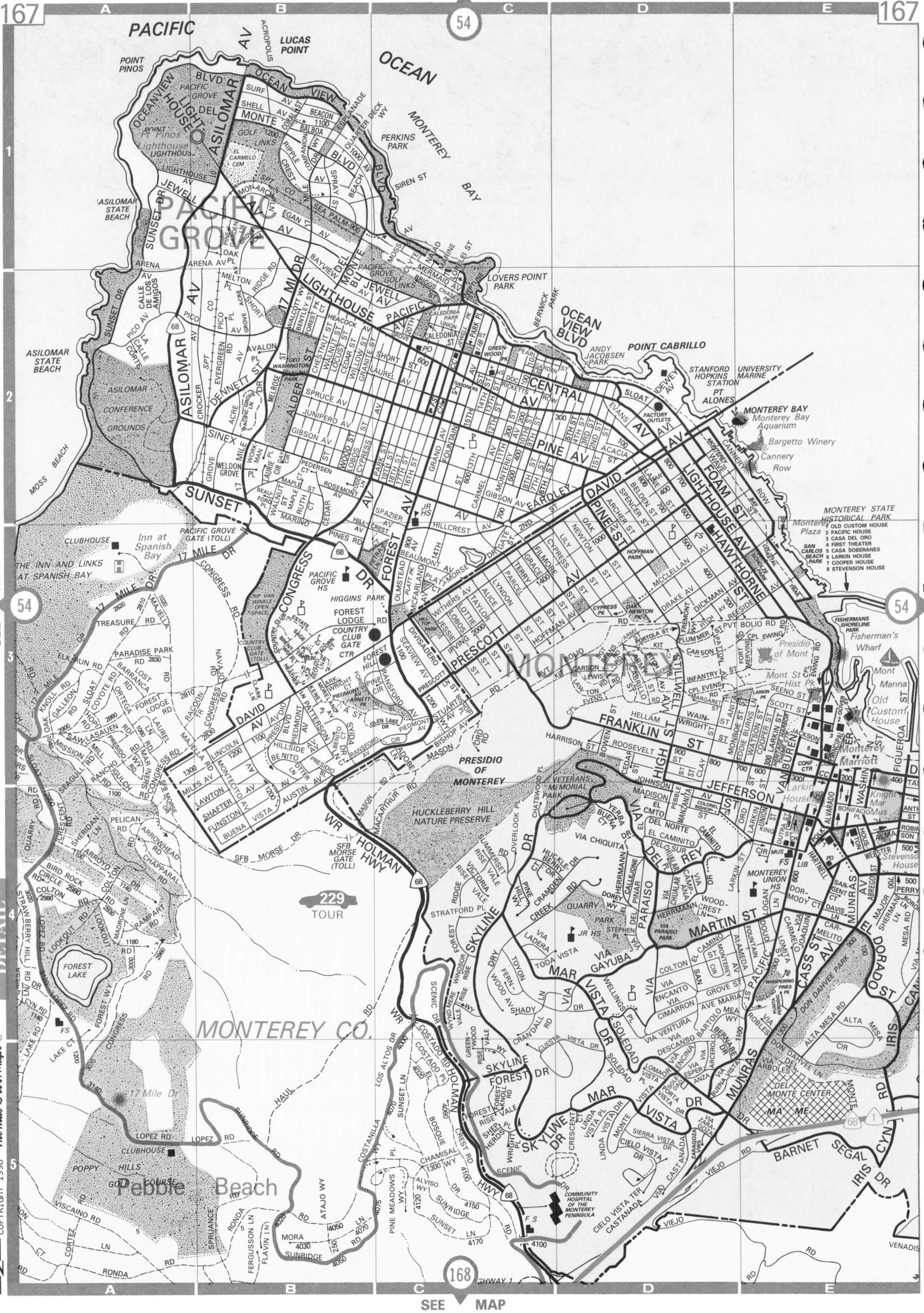

SEE MAP 168

SEE 167 MAP

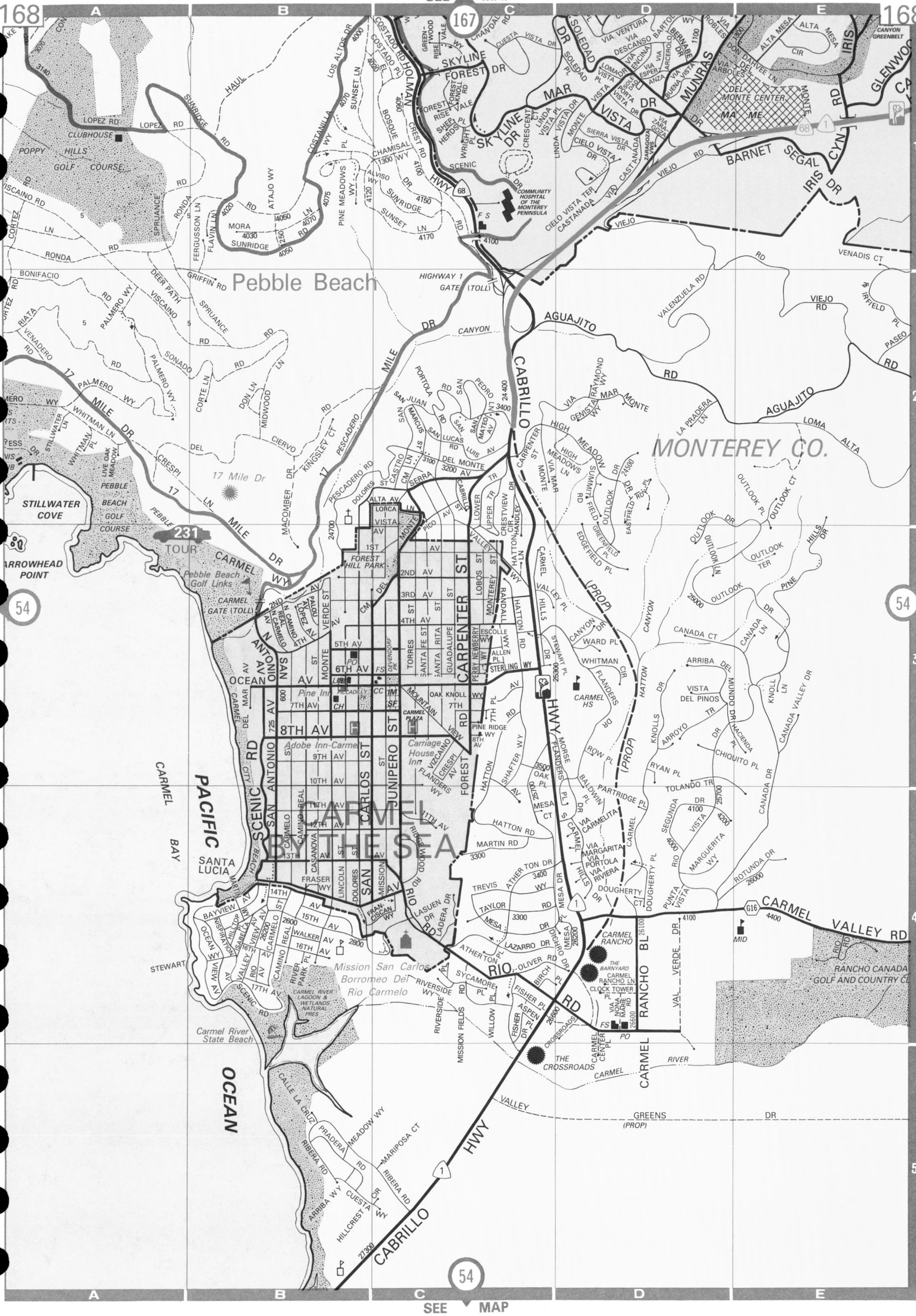

SEE 54 MAP

SEE 54 MAP

SEE 54 MAP

SEE MAP 53

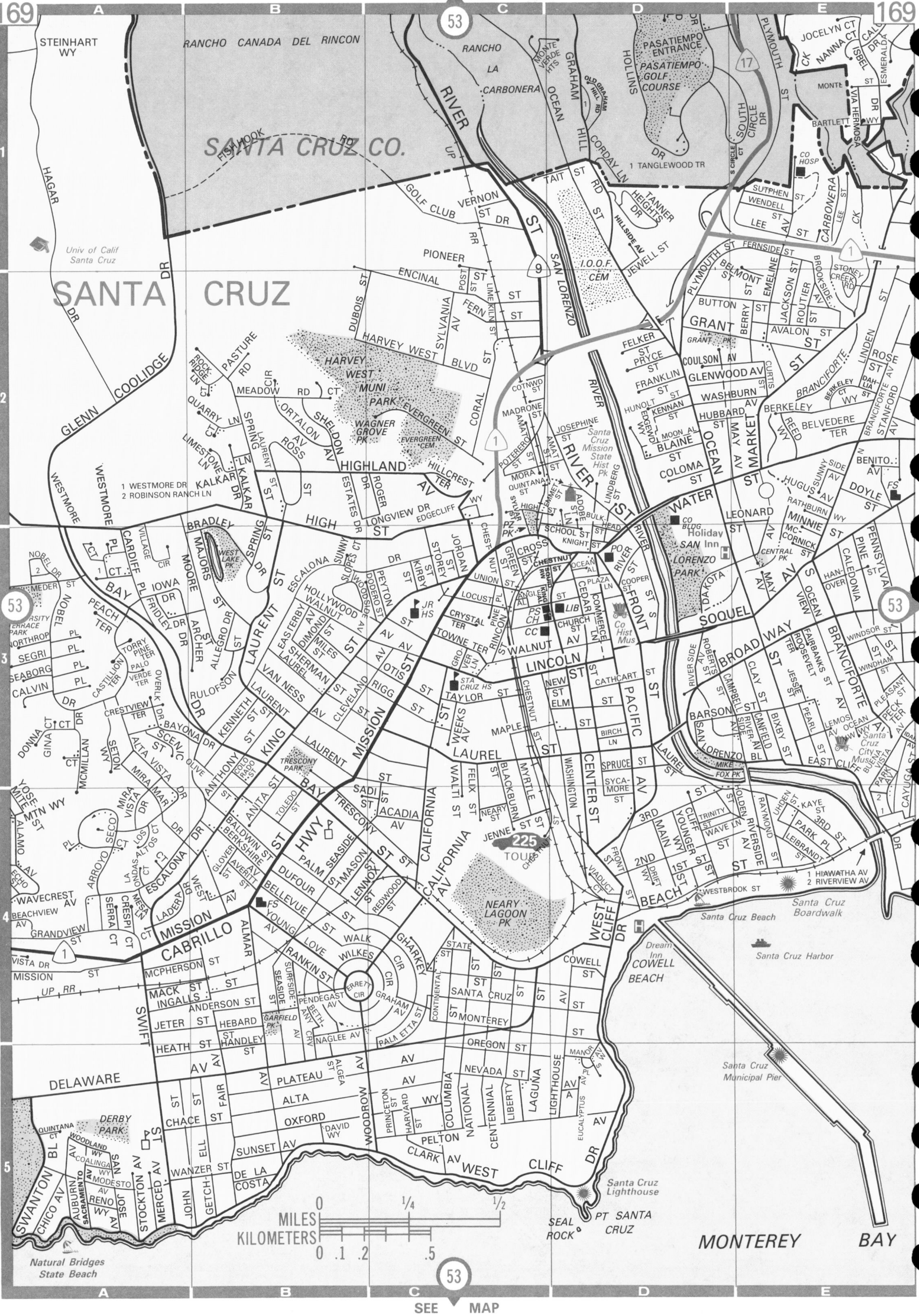

SEE MAP 53

SEE MAP 48

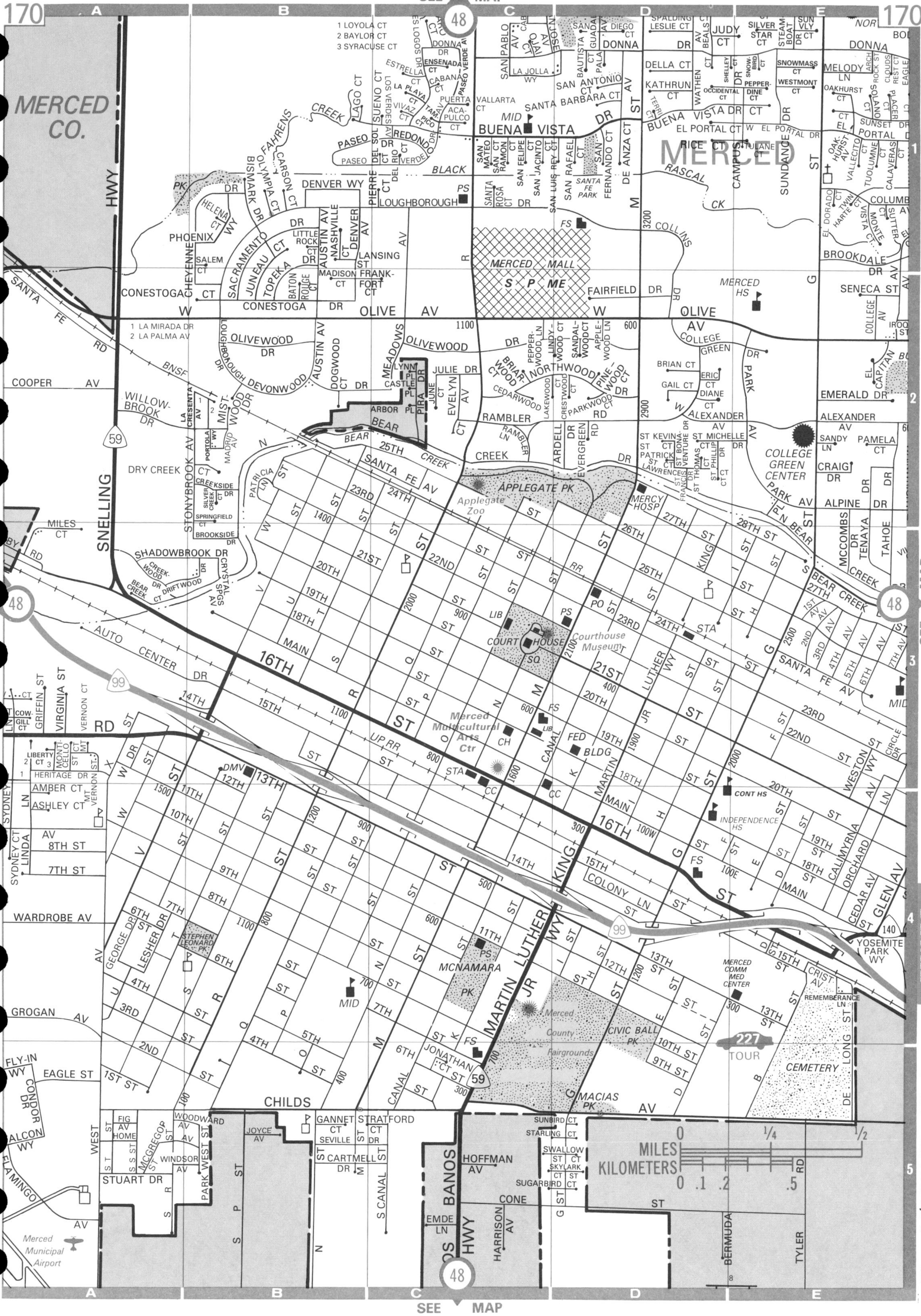

SEE MAP 48

SEE MAP 54

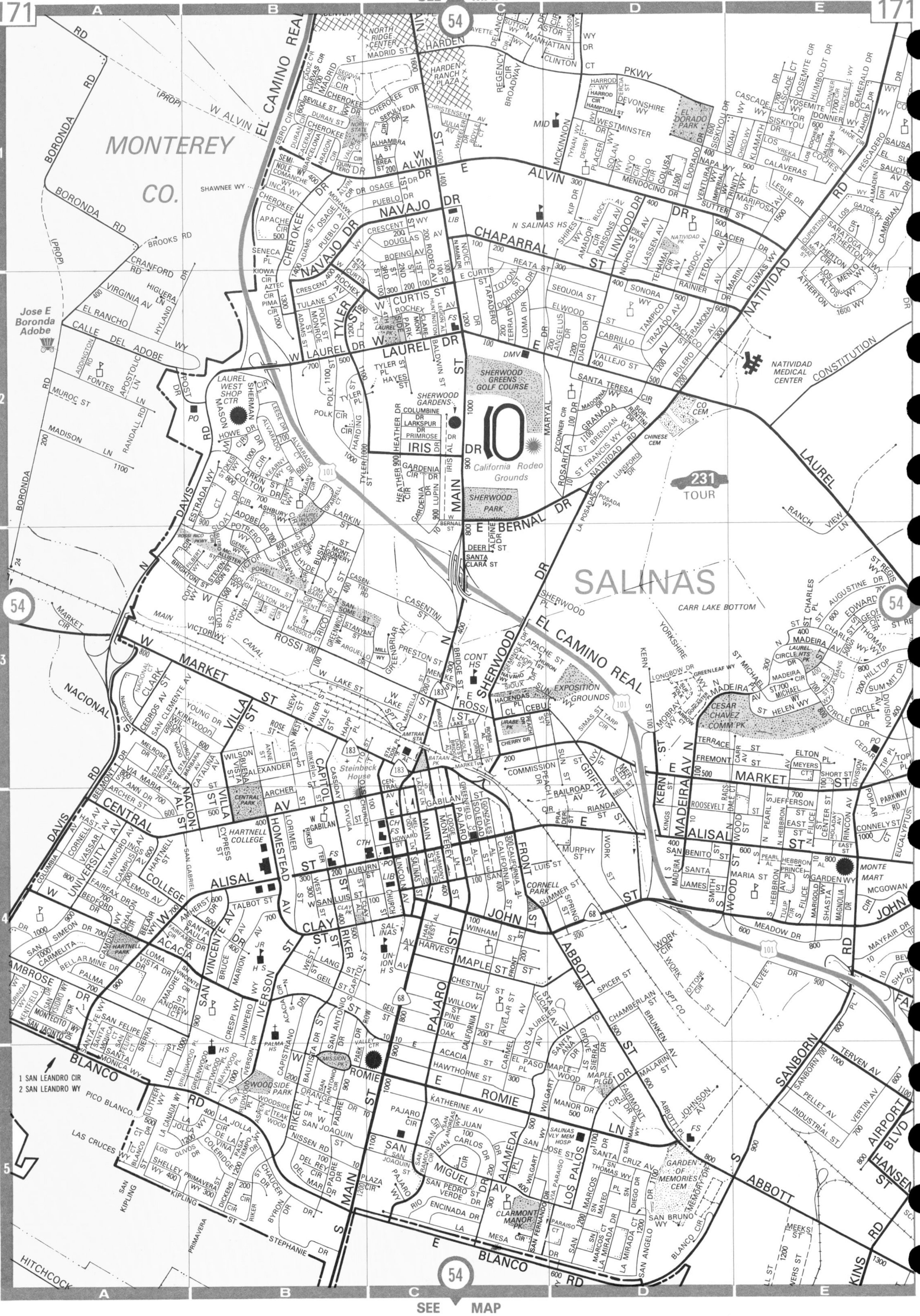

SEE MAP 54

SEE MAP 54

SEE MAP 54

SALINAS

DETAIL

SEE MAP 54

SEE MAP 76

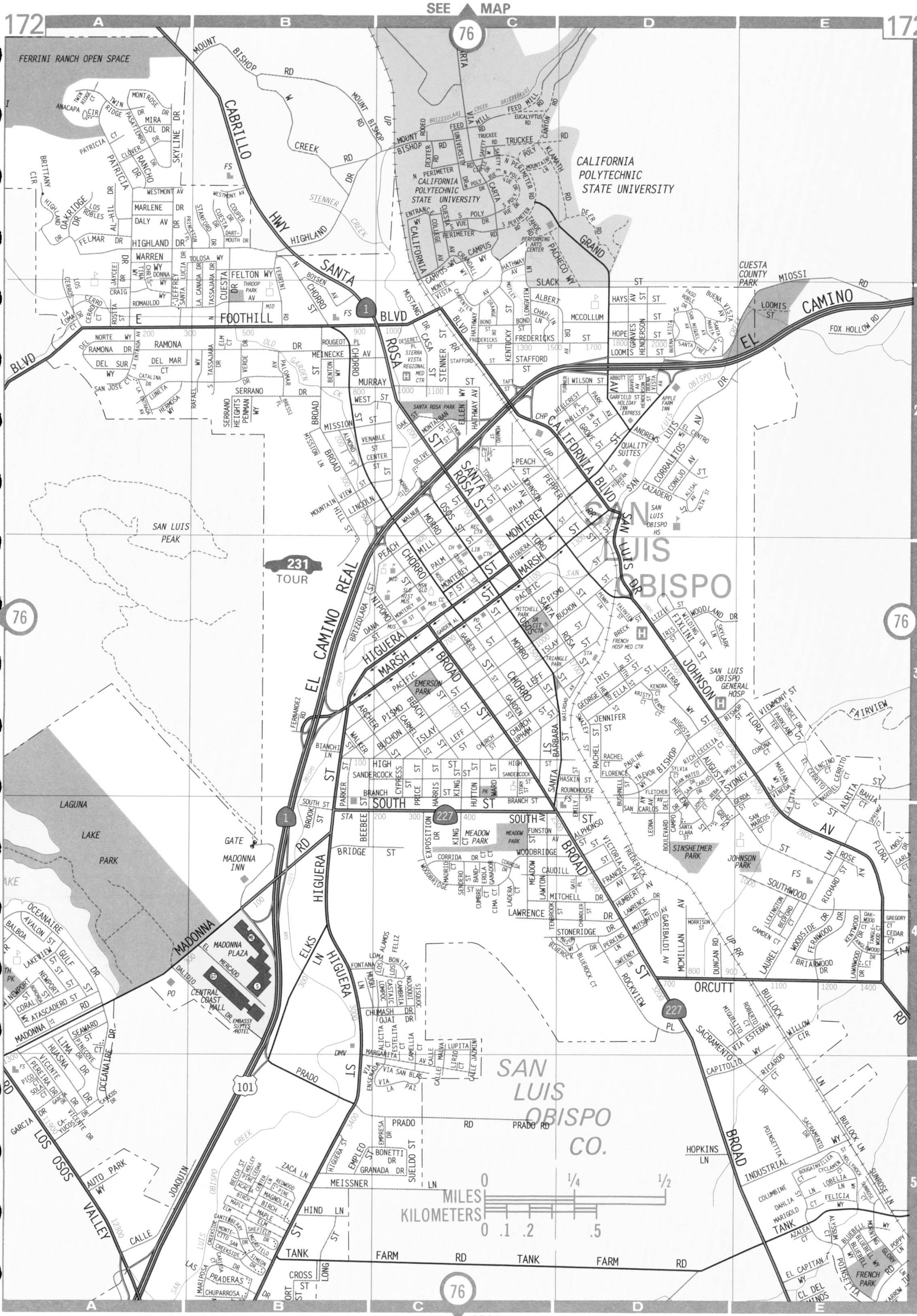
FERRINI RANCH OPEN SPACE
CALIFORNIA POLYTECHNIC STATE UNIVERSITY
SAN LUIS OBISPO
SAN LUIS PEAK
231 TOUR
LAGUNA LAKE PARK
MADONNA INN
MADONNA PLAZA
CENTRAL COAST MALL
EMBASSY SUITES HOTEL
SAN LUIS OBISPO CO.
SAN LUIS OBISPO GENERAL HOSP
FRENCH HOSP MED CTR
SIERRA VISTA REGIONAL MED CTR
SAN LUIS OBISPO HS
CUESTA COUNTY PARK
SANTA ROSA PARK
EMERSON PARK
MEADOW PARK
SINSHEIMER PARK
JOHNSON PARK
FRENCH PARK
MITCHELL PARK
THROOP PARK
PERFORMING ARTS CENTER
QUALITY SUITES
GARFIELD ST HOLIDAY INN EXPRESS
APPLE FARM INN
FOOTHILL BLVD
SANTA ROSA ST
CALIFORNIA BLVD
EL CAMINO REAL
HIGUERA ST
MARSH ST
BROAD ST
JOHNSON AV
SAN LUIS DR
MONTEREY ST
ORCUTT RD
TANK FARM RD
LOS OSOS VALLEY RD
MADONNA RD
PRADO RD
SOUTH ST
HIGHLAND DR
GRAND AV
BISHOP ST
AUGUSTA ST
CABRILLO HWY
SANTA ROSA
MILES 0 1/4 1/2
KILOMETERS 0 .1 .2 .5
1
2
3
4
5
A B C D E
DETAIL
SEE MAP 76

SEE 86 MAP

SEE 86 MAP
SEE 86 MAP
SEE 86 MAP
DETAIL

SEE MAP 87

SEE MAP 87

175
SEE MAP 88

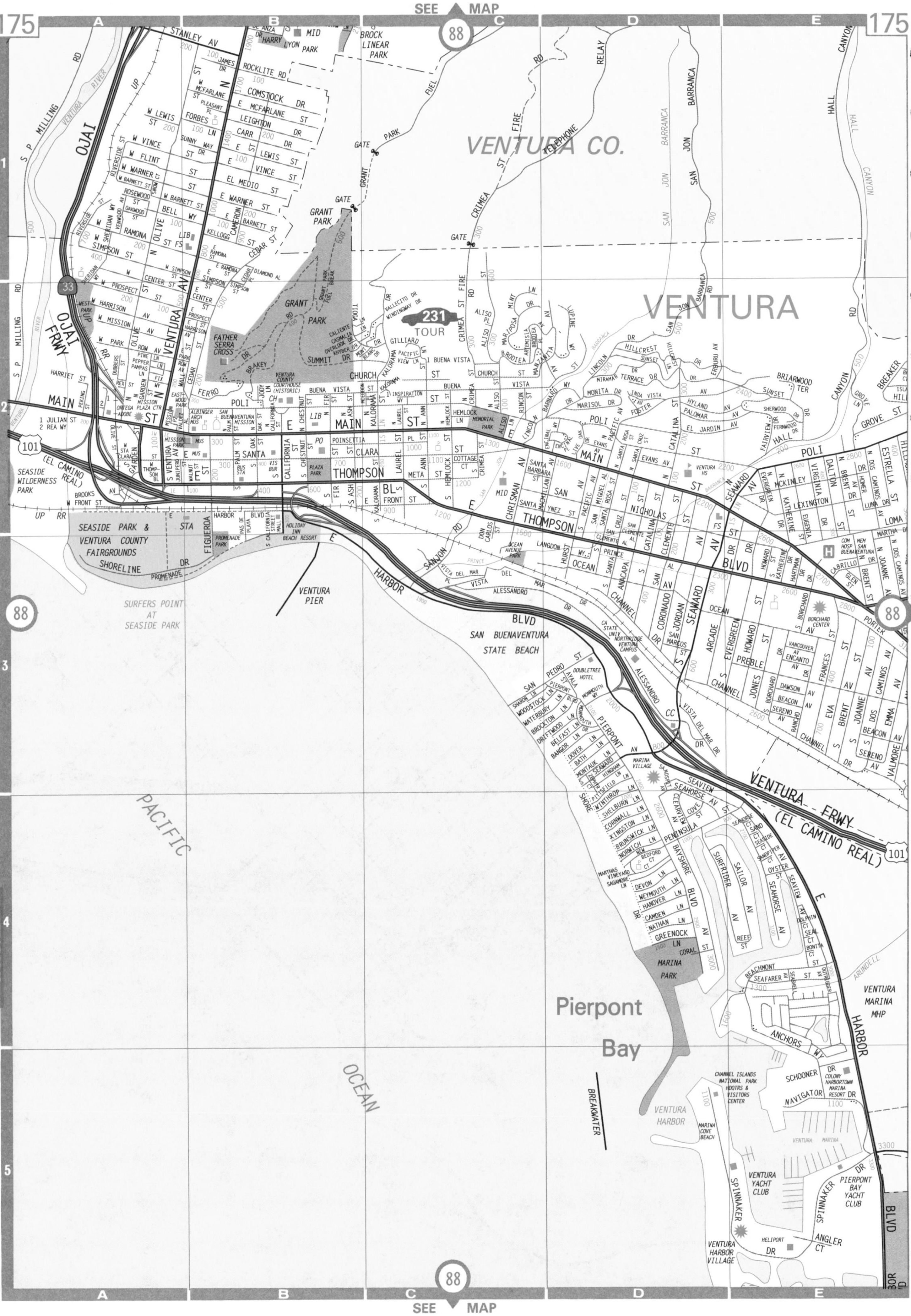

SEE MAP 88
SEE MAP 88
SEE MAP 88
DETAIL

SEE MAP 96

OXNARD DETAIL MAP

SEE MAP Q

SEE MAP Q

SEE MAP 97

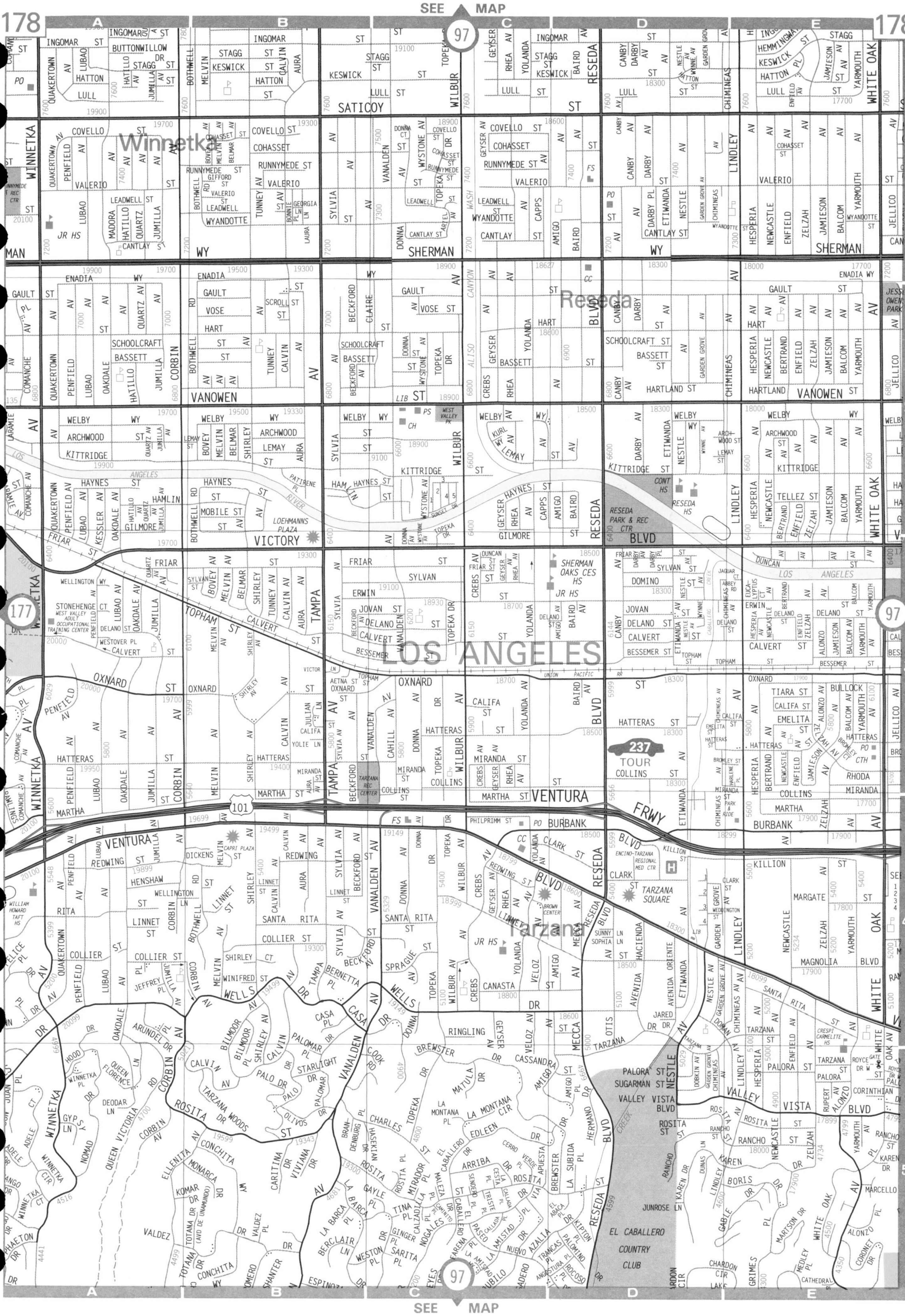

SEE MAP 177

SEE MAP 97

RESEDA-TARZANA

DETAIL

SEE MAP 97

SEE MAP Q
SEE MAP Q

BURBANK
DETAIL

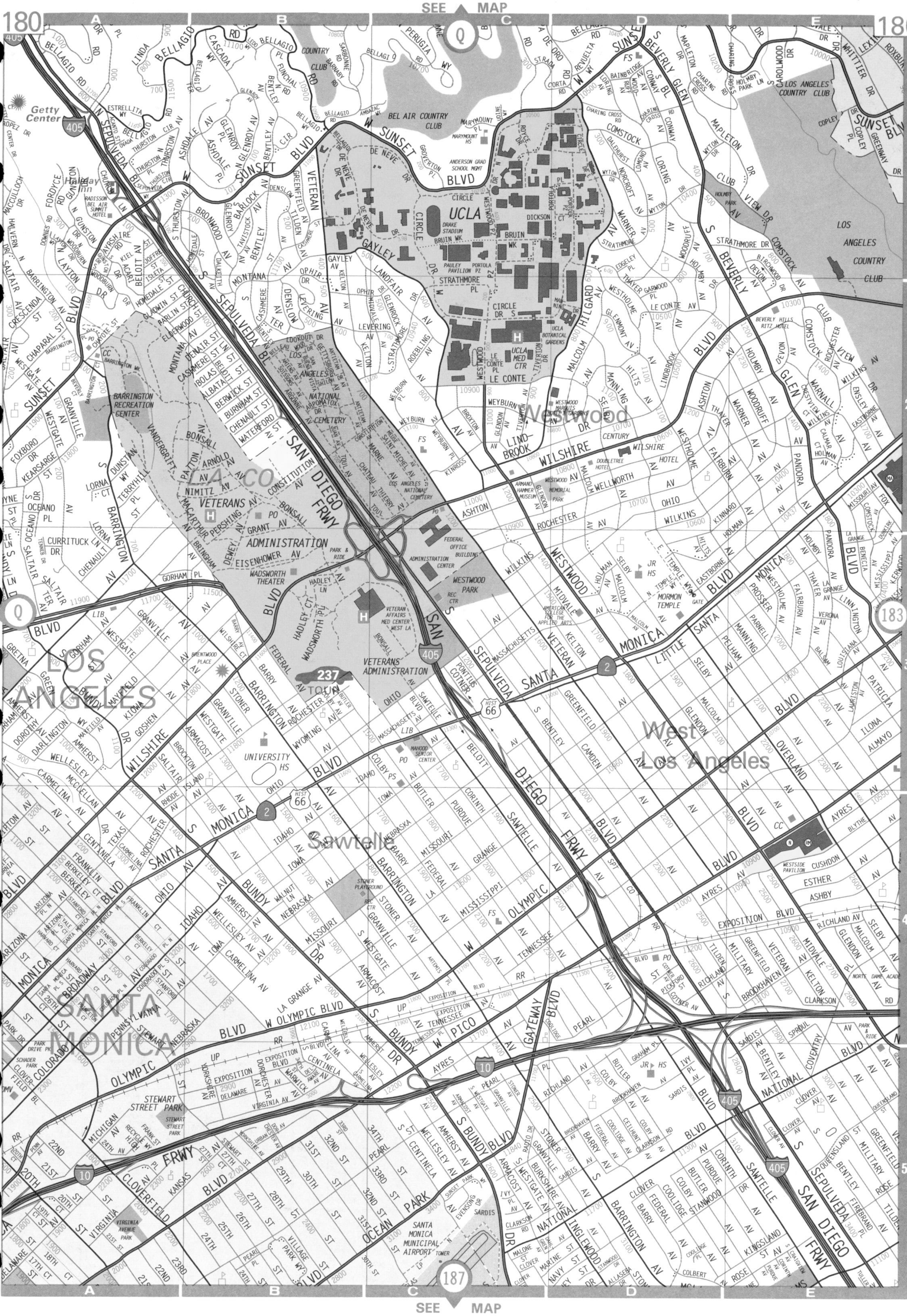

WEST LOS ANGELES-WESTWOOD

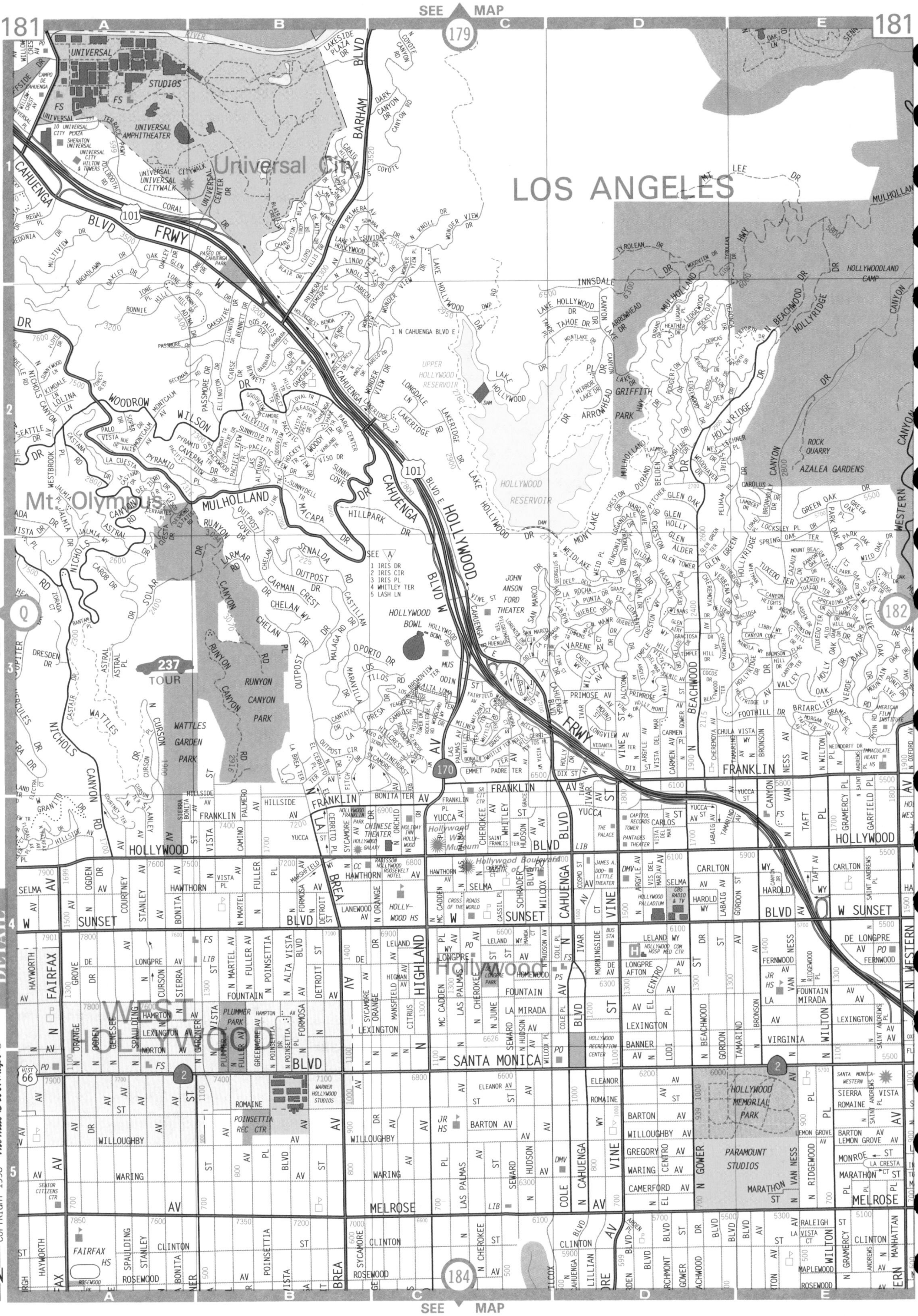
SEE MAP 179
LOS ANGELES
Universal City
UNIVERSAL STUDIOS
UNIVERSAL AMPHITHEATER
UNIVERSAL CITYWALK
Mt. Olympus
UPPER HOLLYWOOD RESERVOIR
HOLLYWOOD RESERVOIR
GRIFFITH PARK
HOLLYWOODLAND CAMP
ROCK QUARRY
AZALEA GARDENS
HOLLYWOOD BOWL
JOHN ANSON FORD THEATER
RUNYON CANYON PARK
WATTLES GARDEN PARK
TOUR
CHINESE THEATER
CAPITOL RECORDS TOWER
PANTAGES THEATER
HOLLYWOOD PALLADIUM
CBS RADIO & TV
WEST HOLLYWOOD
Hollywood
PLUMMER PARK
POINSETTIA REC CTR
WARNER HOLLYWOOD STUDIOS
HOLLYWOOD MEMORIAL PARK
PARAMOUNT STUDIOS
HOLLYWOOD RECREATION CENTER
HOLLYWOOD FWY
CAHUENGA BLVD
MULHOLLAND DR
FRANKLIN AV
HOLLYWOOD BLVD
SUNSET BLVD
SANTA MONICA BLVD
MELROSE AV
LOS ANGELES-HOLLYWOOD
SEE MAP Q
SEE MAP 182
SEE MAP 184
DETAIL
Thomas Bros. Maps®

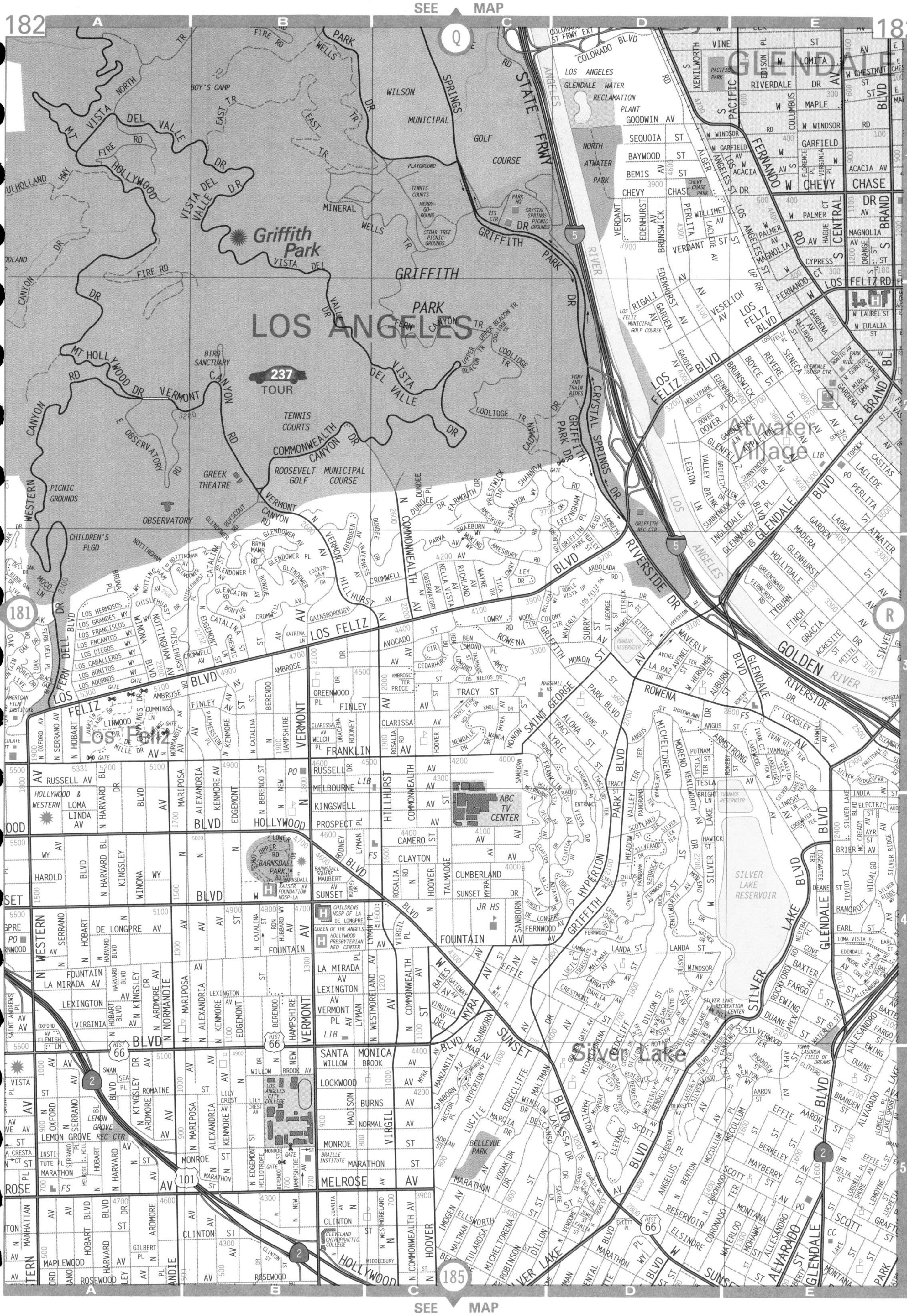

A B C D E
LOS ANGELES
Griffith Park
GRIFFITH PARK
GLENDALE
Atwater Village
Los Feliz
Silver Lake
WILSON MUNICIPAL GOLF COURSE
LOS ANGELES GLENDALE WATER RECLAMATION PLANT
NORTH ATWATER PARK
CRYSTAL SPRINGS PICNIC GROUNDS
ROOSEVELT MUNICIPAL GOLF COURSE
GREEK THEATRE
OBSERVATORY
BIRD SANCTUARY
CHILDREN'S PLGD
LOS FELIZ MUNICIPAL GOLF COURSE
ABC TV CENTER
SILVER LAKE RESERVOIR
IVANHOE RESERVOIR
ROWENA RESERVOIR
BARNSDALL PARK
LOS ANGELES CITY COLLEGE
BELLEVUE PARK
HOLLYWOOD & WESTERN LOMA LINDA AV
LOS ANGELES RIVER
GOLDEN STATE FRWY
LOS FELIZ BLVD
HOLLYWOOD BLVD
SUNSET BLVD
SANTA MONICA BLVD
MELROSE AV
GRIFFITH PARK DR
RIVERSIDE DR
GLENDALE BLVD
VERMONT AV
HYPERION AV
TOUR 237
SEE MAP R
181
185

DETAIL

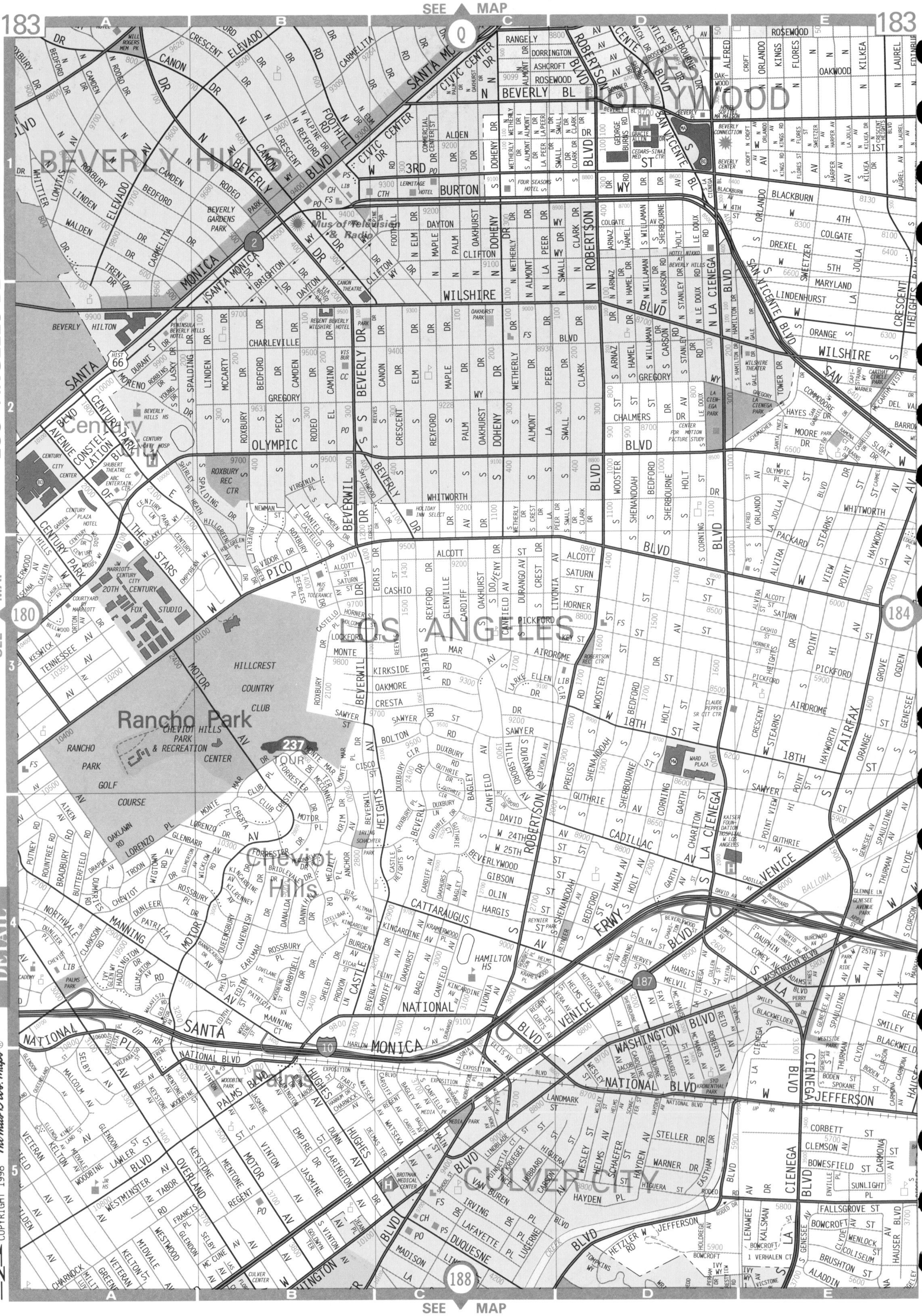
SEE MAP Q
BEVERLY HILLS
LOS ANGELES-BEVERLY HILLS
WEST HOLLYWOOD
Century City
LOS ANGELES
Rancho Park
CHEVIOT HILLS PARK & RECREATION CENTER
RANCHO PARK GOLF COURSE
HILLCREST COUNTRY CLUB
Cheviot Hills
Palms
CULVER CITY
20TH CENTURY FOX STUDIO
Mus of Television & Radio
BEVERLY GARDENS PARK
ROXBURY REC CTR
LA CIENEGA PARK
WARD PLAZA
HAMILTON HS
SANTA MONICA BLVD
WILSHIRE BLVD
OLYMPIC BLVD
PICO BLVD
VENICE BLVD
NATIONAL BLVD
WASHINGTON BLVD
JEFFERSON BLVD
SANTA MONICA FRWY
LA CIENEGA BLVD
ROBERTSON BLVD
BEVERLY DR
MOTOR AV
OVERLAND AV
SEE MAP 180
SEE MAP 184
SEE MAP 188
DETAIL
A B C D E
1 2 3 4 5

SEE MAP 181

SEE MAP 183

SEE MAP 185

SEE MAP Q

LOS ANGELES

DETAIL

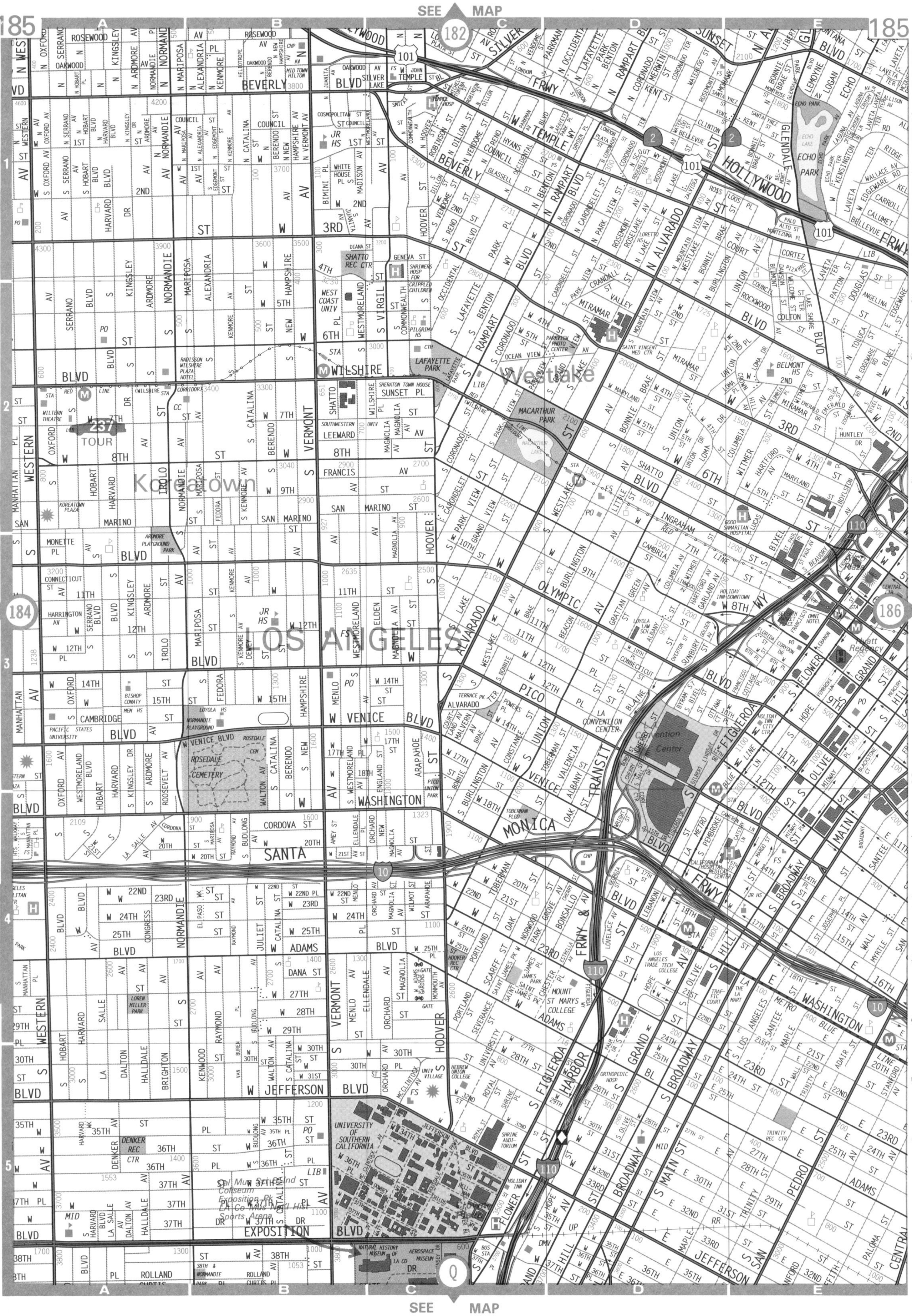
SEE MAP 182
SEE MAP 184
SEE MAP 186
SEE MAP Q
LOS ANGELES
DETAIL
Koreatown
Westlake
LOS ANGELES
MACARTHUR PARK
LAFAYETTE PARK
ECHO PARK
ROSEDALE CEMETERY
UNIVERSITY OF SOUTHERN CALIFORNIA
Convention Center
LA CONVENTION CENTER
HOLLYWOOD
FRWY
WILSHIRE
OLYMPIC
PICO
VENICE BLVD
WASHINGTON
SANTA MONICA
JEFFERSON
EXPOSITION
WESTERN
VERMONT
HOOVER
ALVARADO
FIGUEROA
HARBOR FRWY
BROADWAY
BEVERLY
SUNSET
TEMPLE
MARIPOSA
NORMANDIE
A
B
C
D
E
1
2
3
4
5

SEE MAP

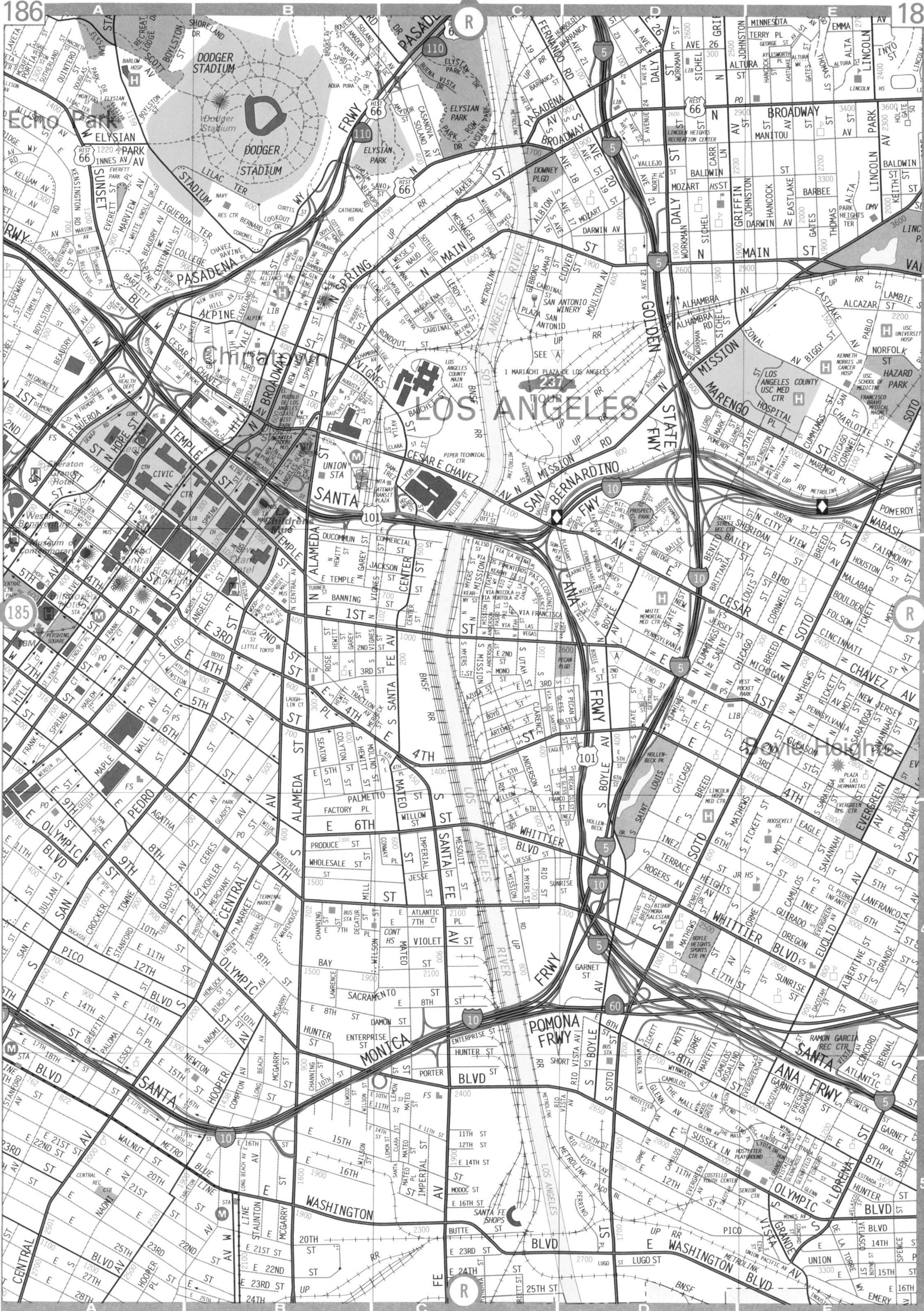

LOS ANGELES

DETAIL

SEE MAP

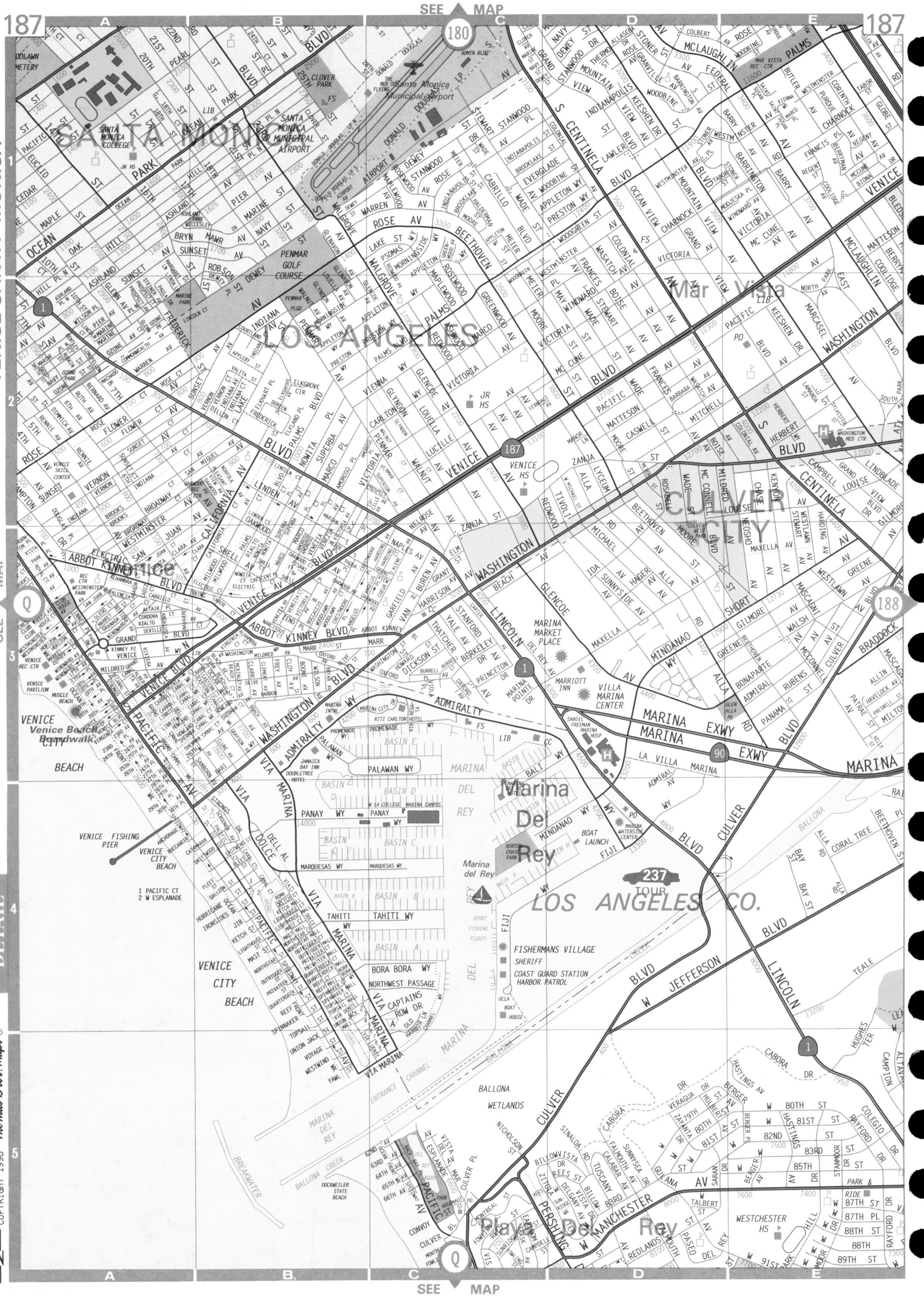
SEE MAP 180
SEE MAP 188
SEE MAP Q
VENICE-SANTA MONICA
DETAIL
SANTA MONICA
LOS ANGELES
Mar Vista
CULVER CITY
Venice
Marina Del Rey
Playa Del Rey
LOS ANGELES CO.
Santa Monica Municipal Airport
SANTA MONICA MUNICIPAL AIRPORT
CLOVER PARK
SANTA MONICA COLLEGE
PENMAR GOLF COURSE
VENICE HS
JR HS
VENICE BEACH
Venice Beach Boardwalk
VENICE CITY BEACH
VENICE FISHING PIER
MARINA MARKET PLACE
VILLA MARINA CENTER
MARRIOTT INN
DANIEL FREEMAN MARINA HOSP
WASHINGTON MED CTR
FISHERMANS VILLAGE
SHERIFF
COAST GUARD STATION HARBOR PATROL
BALLONA WETLANDS
DOCKWEILER STATE BEACH
WESTCHESTER HS
MARINA EXWY
VENICE BLVD
WASHINGTON BLVD
LINCOLN BLVD
CULVER BLVD
W JEFFERSON BLVD
W MANCHESTER AV
PACIFIC AV
ADMIRALTY WY
VIA MARINA
1 PACIFIC CT
2 W ESPLANADE
237 TOUR

SEE MAP 183

SEE MAP 189

SEE MAP 188
LOS ANGELES
INGLEWOOD
EL SEGUNDO-LA AIRPORT
Los Angeles International Airport
LOS ANGELES INTERNATIONAL AIRPORT
PUBLIC PARKING LOT "B"
BUS SERVICE TO TERMINALS
PUBLIC PARKING LOT C
BUS SERVICE TO TERMINALS
LAX CITY BUS CENTER
TWA HANGAR
AMERICAN HANGARS
INTL TERM
IMPERIAL TERMINAL
IMPERIAL CARGO COMPLEX
DELTA MAINTENANCE
UNITED MAINTENANCE
CARL E NIELSEN YOUTH PARK
WESTCHESTER PKWY
CENTURY BLVD
SEPULVEDA BLVD
AVIATION BLVD
GLENN ANDERSON FWY
IMPERIAL HWY
SAN DIEGO FWY
LA CIENEGA
L.A. CO.
SEE MAP Q
EL SEGUNDO
RECREATION PARK
HILLTOP PARK
DEL AIRE PARK
MARIPOSA AV
GRAND AV
E EL SEGUNDO BLVD
XEROX CENTRE DR
HACIENDA HOTEL
INTERNATIONAL CENTER
DOUBLETREE CLUB HOTEL
COURTYARD BY MARRIOTT
THE LAKES AT EL SEGUNDO GOLF COURSE
CHEVRON OIL REFINERY
METRO GREEN LINE
HAWTHORNE
ROSECRANS AV
MANHATTAN BEACH
SAND DUNE PARK
MARINE AVENUE PARK
RADISSON PLAZA HOTEL
MANHATTAN VILLAGE
REDONDO BEACH
TRW INC
1 SANTA CRUZ CT
2 LAFAYETTE CT
3 SAN MIGUEL CT
4 GRENADA CT
5 CATALINA CT
6 MALAGA WY
7 NANTUCKET PL
8 DOVER PL
SEE MAP S
DETAIL

SEE MAP R

SEE MAP R

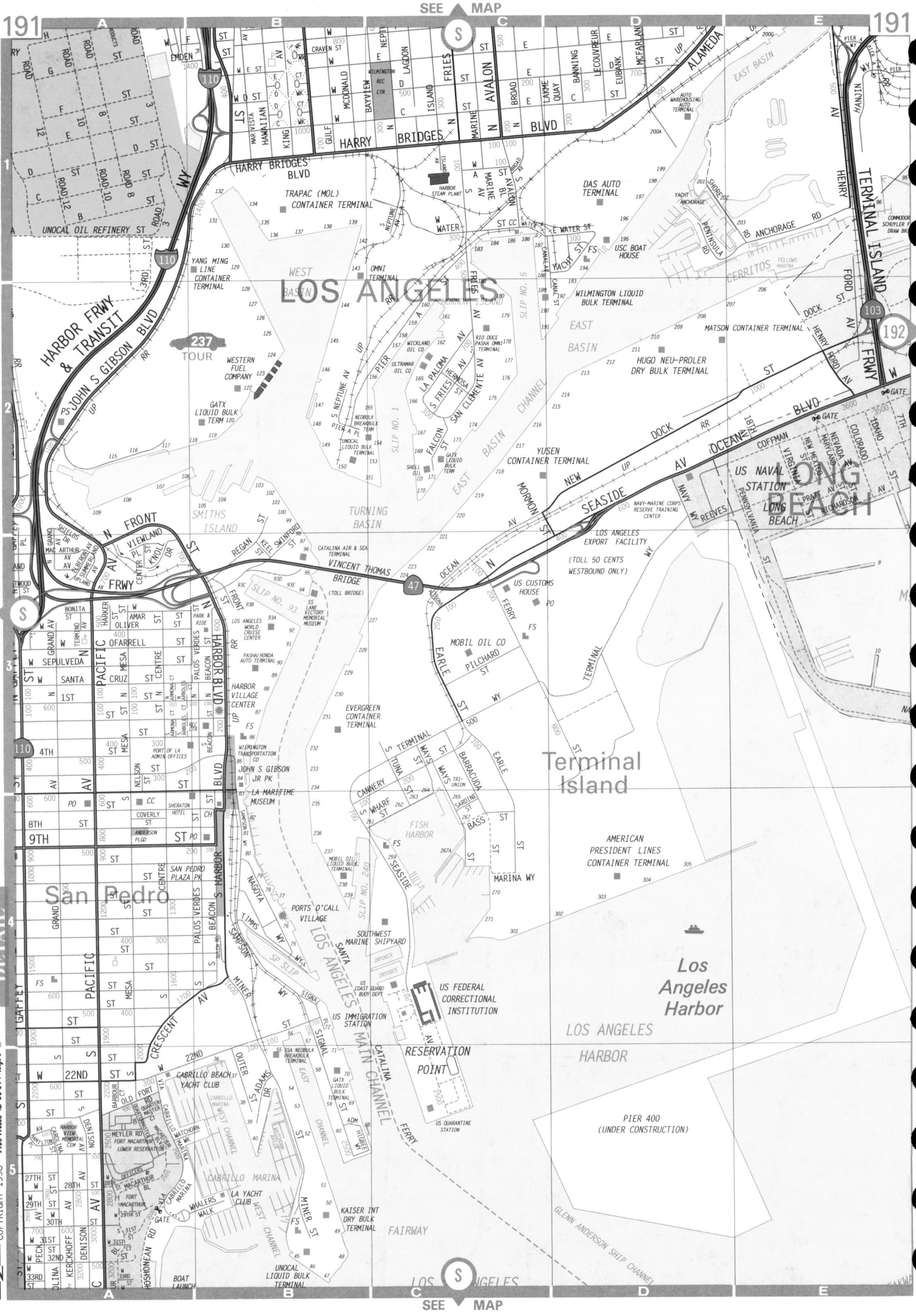
SEE MAP
SAN PEDRO
LOS ANGELES
San Pedro
Terminal Island
LONG BEACH
Los Angeles Harbor
LOS ANGELES HARBOR
LOS ANGELES MAIN CHANNEL
HARBOR FRWY & TRANSIT
JOHN S GIBSON BLVD
HARRY BRIDGES BLVD
UNOCAL OIL REFINERY ST
TRAPAC (MOL) CONTAINER TERMINAL
YANG MING LINE CONTAINER TERMINAL
OMNI TERMINAL
WEST BASIN
EAST BASIN
EAST BASIN CHANNEL
TURNING BASIN
SMITHS ISLAND
WESTERN FUEL COMPANY
GATX LIQUID BULK TERM
DAS AUTO TERMINAL
USC BOAT HOUSE
WILMINGTON LIQUID BULK TERMINAL
MATSON CONTAINER TERMINAL
HUGO NEU-PROLER DRY BULK TERMINAL
YUSEN CONTAINER TERMINAL
US NAVAL STATION LONG BEACH
NAVY-MARINE CORPS RESERVE TRAINING CENTER
LOS ANGELES EXPORT FACILITY
(TOLL 50 CENTS WESTBOUND ONLY)
VINCENT THOMAS BRIDGE (TOLL BRIDGE)
CATALINA AIR & SEA TERMINAL
SS LANE VICTORY MEMORIAL MUSEUM
LOS ANGELES WORLD CRUISE CENTER
PASHA/HONDA AUTO TERMINAL
US CUSTOMS HOUSE
MOBIL OIL CO
HARBOR VILLAGE CENTER
EVERGREEN CONTAINER TERMINAL
WILMINGTON TRANSPORTATION CO
JOHN S GIBSON JR PK
LA MARITIME MUSEUM
PORT OF LA ADMIN OFFICES
SHERATON HOTEL
ANDERSON PLGD
SAN PEDRO PLAZA PK
FISH HARBOR
MOBIL OIL LIQUID BULK TERMINAL
PORTS O'CALL VILLAGE
SOUTHWEST MARINE SHIPYARD
AMERICAN PRESIDENT LINES CONTAINER TERMINAL
US COAST GUARD BUOY DEPT
US FEDERAL CORRECTIONAL INSTITUTION
US IMMIGRATION STATION
RESERVATION POINT
US QUARANTINE STATION
SSA NEOBULK BREAKBULK TERMINAL
GATX LIQUID BULK TERMINAL
CABRILLO BEACH YACHT CLUB
CABRILLO MARINA
WEST CHANNEL
EAST CHANNEL
LA YACHT CLUB
KAISER INT DRY BULK TERMINAL
UNOCAL LIQUID BULK TERMINAL
FORT MACARTHUR
HARBOR VIEW MEMORIAL CEM
PIER 400 (UNDER CONSTRUCTION)
GLENN ANDERSON SHIP CHANNEL
FAIRWAY
TERMINAL ISLAND FRWY
OCEAN BLVD
SEASIDE AV
NEW DOCK ST
HARBOR BLVD
PACIFIC AV
GAFFEY ST
ALAMEDA ST
AVALON BLVD
DETAIL
237 TOUR

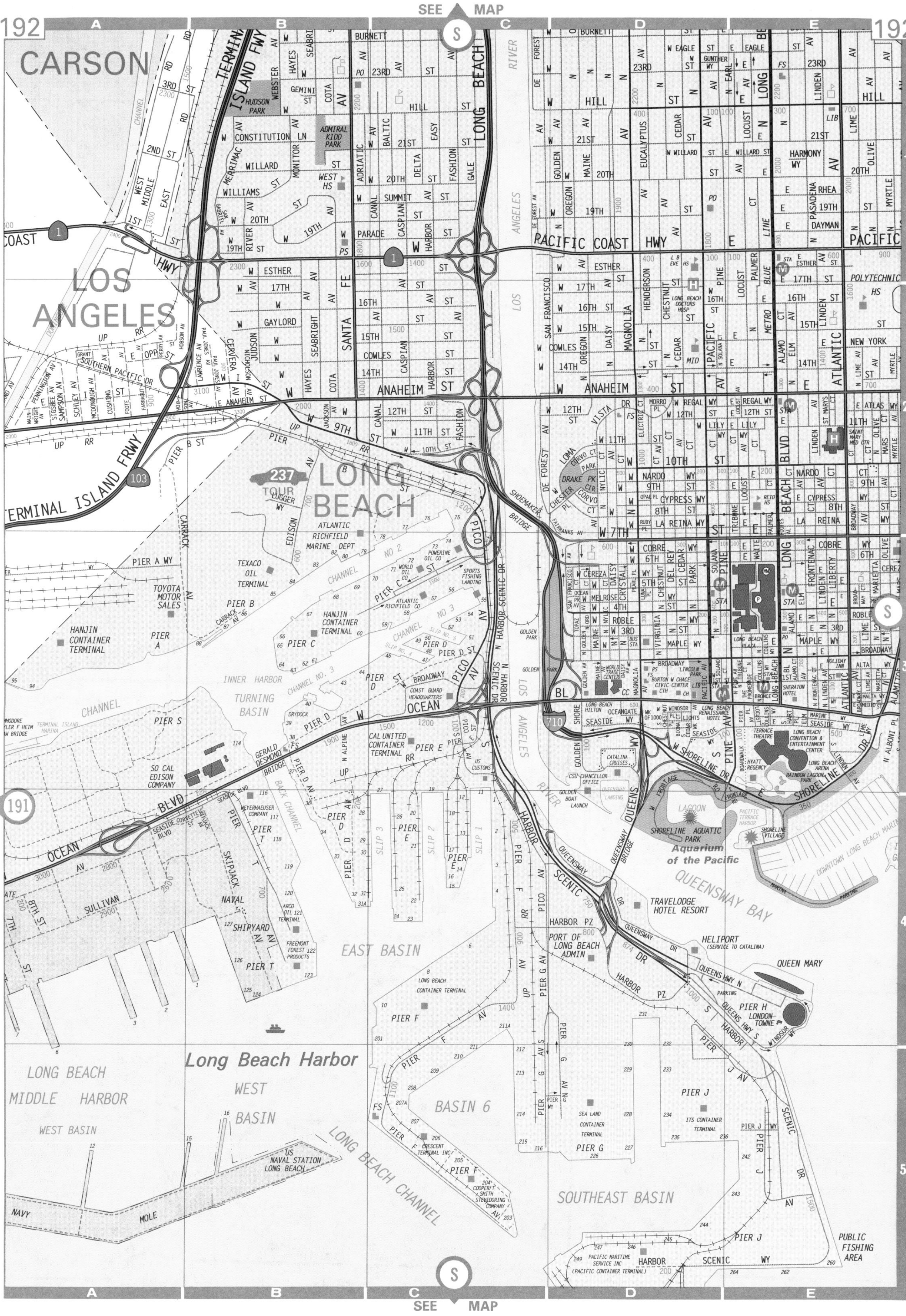
SEE MAP
CARSON
LOS ANGELES
LONG BEACH
PACIFIC COAST HWY
TERMINAL ISLAND FWY
LONG BEACH FWY
ANAHEIM ST
OCEAN BLVD
SHORELINE DR
QUEENSWAY BRIDGE
QUEENSWAY BAY
GERALD DESMOND BRIDGE
HUDSON PARK
ADMIRAL KIDD PARK
DRAKE PK
GOLDEN PARK
RAINBOW LAGOON PARK
SHORELINE AQUATIC PARK
Aquarium of the Pacific
SHORELINE VILLAGE
DOWNTOWN LONG BEACH MARINA
LONG BEACH CONVENTION & ENTERTAINMENT CENTER
LONG BEACH ARENA
TERRACE THEATRE
HYATT REGENCY
SHERATON HOTEL
QUEEN MARY
LONDON TOWNE
HELIPORT (SERVICE TO CATALINA)
TRAVELODGE HOTEL RESORT
PORT OF LONG BEACH ADMIN
CATALINA CRUISES
US CUSTOMS
COAST GUARD HEADQUARTERS
SPORTS FISHING LANDING
ATLANTIC RICHFIELD MARINE DEPT
TEXACO OIL TERMINAL
TOYOTA MOTOR SALES
HANJIN CONTAINER TERMINAL
SO CAL EDISON COMPANY
WEYERHAEUSER COMPANY
CAL UNITED CONTAINER TERMINAL
LONG BEACH CONTAINER TERMINAL
SEA LAND CONTAINER TERMINAL
ITS CONTAINER TERMINAL
CRESCENT TERMINAL INC
COOPER/T SMITH STEVEDORING COMPANY
PACIFIC MARITIME SERVICE INC (PACIFIC CONTAINER TERMINAL)
US NAVAL STATION LONG BEACH
EAST BASIN
WEST BASIN
BASIN 6
SOUTHEAST BASIN
INNER HARBOR
TURNING BASIN
BACK CHANNEL
CHANNEL NO 2
CHANNEL NO 3
Long Beach Harbor
LONG BEACH MIDDLE HARBOR
LONG BEACH CHANNEL
NAVY MOLE
PUBLIC FISHING AREA
PIER A
PIER B
PIER C
PIER D
PIER E
PIER F
PIER G
PIER H
PIER J
PIER S
PIER T
SLIP 1
SLIP 2
SLIP 3
LOS ANGELES RIVER
LONG BEACH DETAIL
A B C D E
1 2 3 4 5

ANAHEIM
GARDEN GROVE
ORANGE
DISNEYLAND
Disneyland
ANAHEIM CONVENTION CENTER
Edison International Field
ANAHEIM CEM
PEARSON PARK
LA PALMA PARK
LINCOLN PARK
JULIANNA PARK
EDISON PARK
BOYSEN PARK
JUAREZ PARK
PONDEROSA PARK
ANGELS LAWN CEMETERY
GRAND PARK
STODDARD PARK
LITTLE PEOPLES PARK
Mother Colony House
ANAHEIM HS
KATELLA HS
JR HS
SHERATON ANAHEIM HOTEL
DISNEYLAND HOTEL
THE PAN PACIFIC HOTEL
CONESTOGA HOTEL
ANAHEIM MARRIOTT HOTEL
ANAHEIM HILTON & TOWERS
HOLIDAY INN
HILTON SUITES
THE RESIDENCE INN
WESTERN MED CTR HOSP ANAHEIM
EAST ANAHEIM CENTER
TOWNE CTR
ANAHEIM VISITORS & CONVENTION BUREAU
GRANADA SQ
LA PALMA AV
E LA PALMA
SYCAMORE
LINCOLN AV
BROADWAY
SOUTH
SANTA ANA
VERMONT
BALL RD
CERRITOS AV
KATELLA AV
ORANGEWOOD AV
CHAPMAN AV
HARBOR BLVD
ANAHEIM BLVD
EAST ST
N STATE COLLEGE BLVD
S STATE COLLEGE BLVD
SUNKIST ST
WEST ST
WALNUT
GILBUCK
HASTER ST
HAMPSTEAD ST
MANCHESTER AV
SANTA ANA FRWY
5
239
TOUR
GENE AUTRY WY
METROLINK
SCRRA
UP RR
RIVER
STATE COLLEGE BLVD
THE CITY DR N
SEE MAP
T
194
195
DETAIL

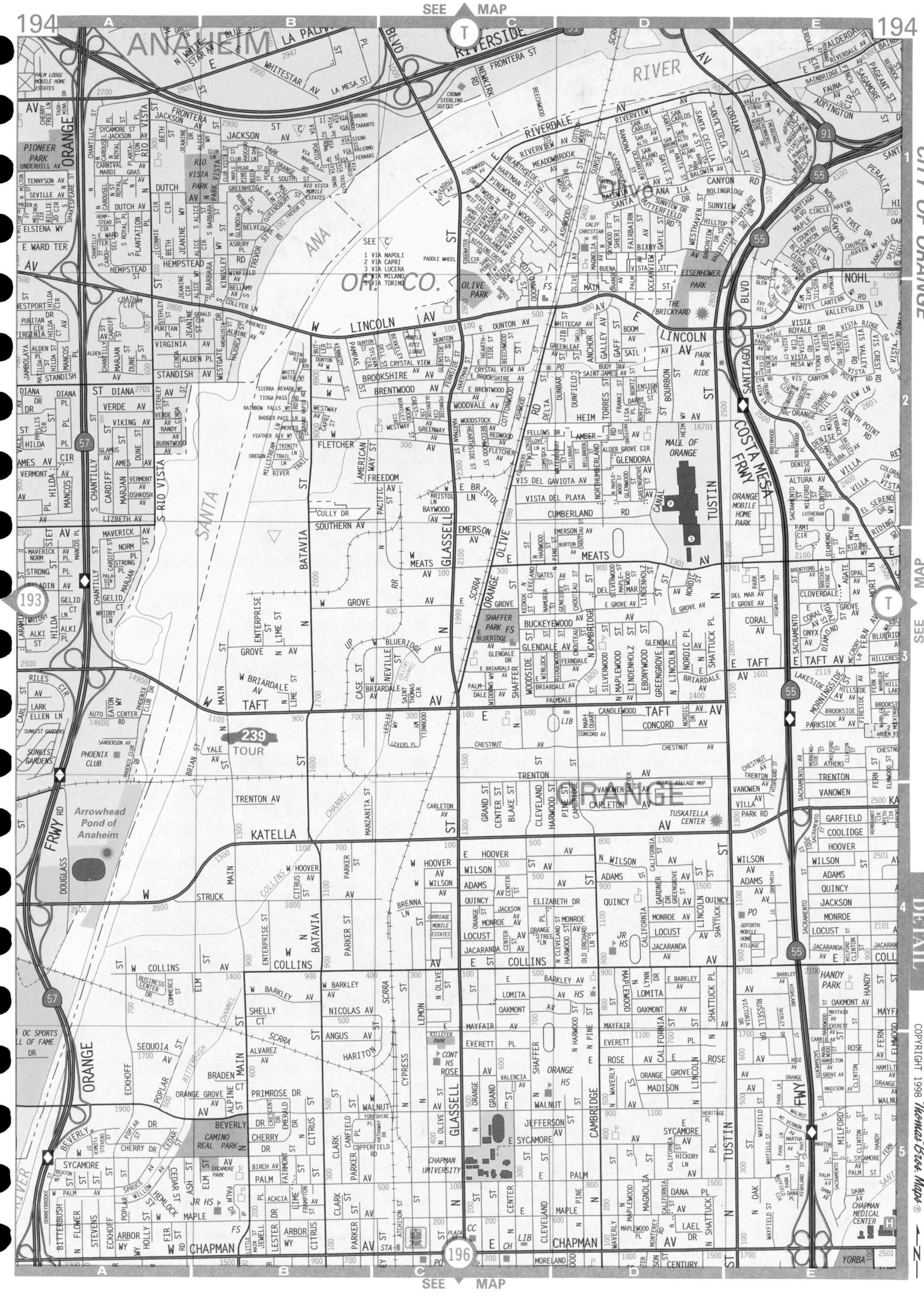
SEE MAP T
SEE MAP 196
SEE MAP 193
SEE MAP T
CITY OF ORANGE
DETAIL
ANAHEIM
ORANGE
OR. CO.
SANTA ANA RIVER
RIVERSIDE
LA PALMA
LINCOLN AV
TAFT AV
KATELLA AV
CHAPMAN AV
COLLINS AV
MEATS AV
GROVE AV
ORANGE FRWY
COSTA MESA FRWY
GLASSELL ST
BATAVIA ST
TUSTIN ST
MAIN ST
SANTIAGO BLVD
PIONEER PARK
RIO VISTA PARK
OLIVE PARK
EISENHOWER PARK
THE BRICKYARD
MALL OF ORANGE
ORANGE MOBILE HOME PARK
SHAFFER PARK
TUSKATELLA CENTER
PHOENIX CLUB
SUNKIST GARDENS
Arrowhead Pond of Anaheim
CAMINO REAL PARK
HANDY PARK
KILLEFER PARK
CHAPMAN UNIVERSITY
CHAPMAN MEDICAL CENTER
ORANGE HS
JR HS
239 TOUR
CROWN STERLING SUITES
PALM LODGE MOBILE HOME ESTATES
OC SPORTS HALL OF FAME
SEE C
1 VIA NAPOLI
2 VIA CAPRI
3 VIA LUCERA
4 VIA MILANO
5 VIA TORINO

SEE MAP 193
SEE MAP 196
SEE MAP 197
SEE MAP T
DETAIL
GARDEN GROVE
ORANGE
SANTA ANA
FOUNTAIN VALLEY
OR. CO.
THE CITY CENTER
UC IRVINE MED CTR
CRYSTAL CATHEDRAL
WESTHAVEN PARK
HARBOR PLAZA
GARDEN GROVE CENTER
BRISTOL VILLAGE PLAZA
BRISTOL MARKET PLACE
RANCHO SANTIAGO COLLEGE SANTA ANA
RIVER VIEW GOLF COURSE
WILLOWICK MUNICIPAL GOLF COURSE
CAMPESINO PARK
SPURGEON PARK
EL SALVADOR PARK
LAKE PARK SANTA ANA
ROSITA PARK
SANTA ANITA PARK
HERITAGE PARK
JEROME PARK
WINDSOR PARK
MORRISON PARK
GARDEN GROVE FRWY
GARDEN GROVE BLVD
W MEMORY LN
WESTMINSTER AV
17TH ST
HAZARD AV
5TH ST
1ST ST
MCFADDEN AV
EDINGER AV
HARBOR BLVD
FAIRVIEW ST
BRISTOL ST
CHAPMAN AV
LAMPSON AV
TRASK AV
CITY PKWY W
METROPOLITAN DR
SANTA ANA RIVER
22
239 TOUR

SEE MAP 194

SEE MAP 198

SEE MAP 198
SEE MAP T
SEE MAP 199

SEE MAP 196
SEE MAP 197
SEE MAP T
SEE MAP 200
SANTA ANA
TUSTIN
IRVINE
COSTA MESA
NEWPORT BEACH
TUSTIN MARINE CORPS AIR STATION
JOHN WAYNE AIRPORT (SEE TABLE OF CONTENTS FOR AIRPORT MAP)
ORANGE COUNTY
COSTA MESA FRWY
SAN DIEGO FRWY
DETAIL
SEE B
1 MOAT PL
2 PARAPET PL
3 DAMSEL WY
4 NORTON PL
5 COMMONS WY
6 PRINCE WY
7 ROYAL PL
8 VAUXHALL PL
9 CROWN WY
10 SHREWSBURY PL
11 MILTON WY
12 HORSHAM PL
13 SOMERSET WY
14 KIPLING PL
15 MATCHLESS WY
16 THRONE WY
17 S SCEPTOR ST
RANCHO SAN JOAQUIN GOLF COURSE
COPYRIGHT 1998 Thomas Bros. Maps ®

SEE 197 MAP

SEE T MAP

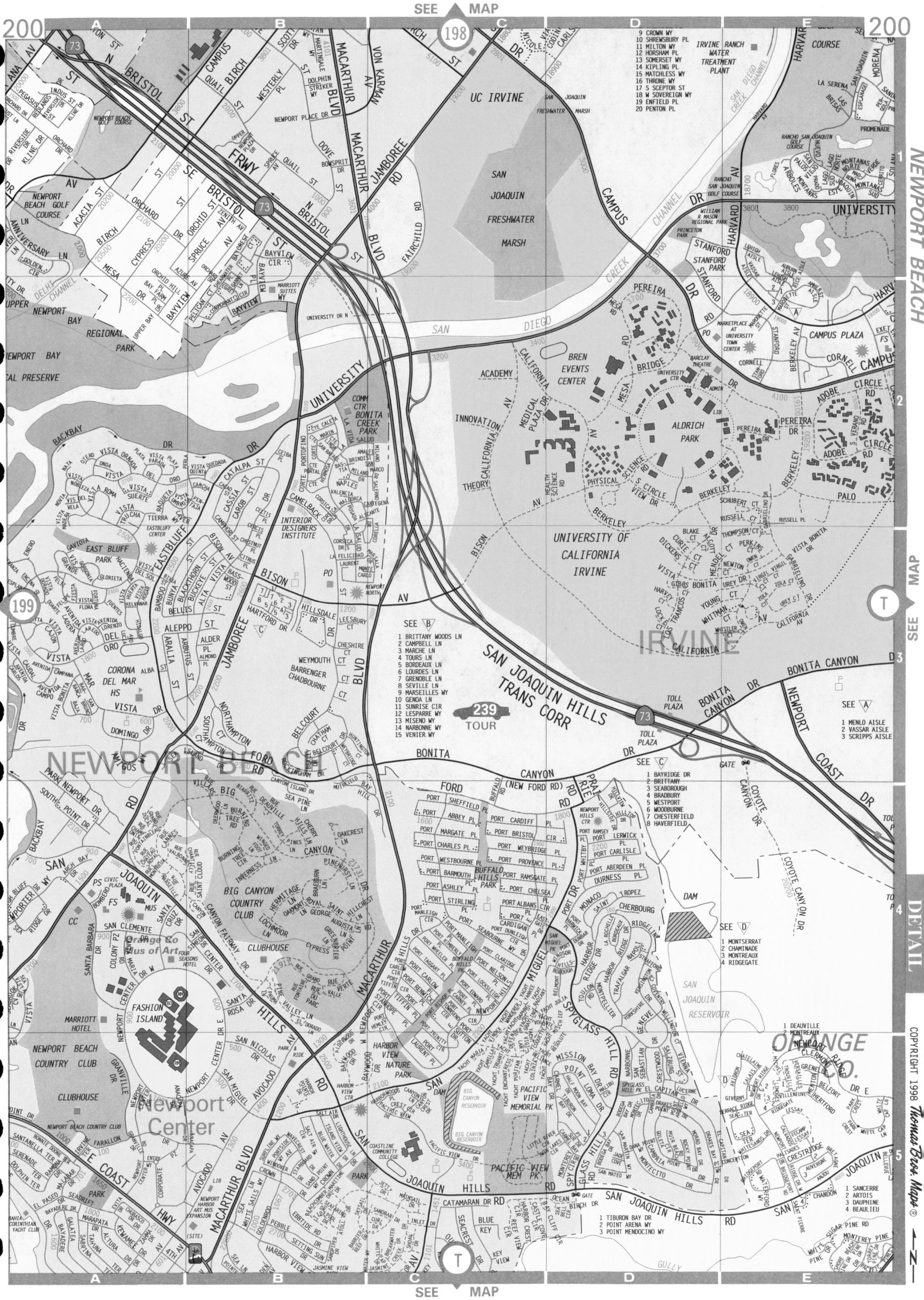
SEE MAP 198
UC IRVINE
SAN JOAQUIN FRESHWATER MARSH
IRVINE RANCH WATER TREATMENT PLANT
9 CROWN WY
10 SHREWSBURY PL
11 MILTON WY
12 HORSHAM PL
13 SOMERSET WY
14 KIPLING PL
15 MATCHLESS WY
16 THRONE WY
17 S SCEPTOR ST
18 W SOVEREIGN WY
19 ENFIELD PL
20 PENTON PL
NEWPORT BEACH GOLF COURSE
UPPER NEWPORT BAY REGIONAL PARK
NEWPORT BAY ECOLOGICAL PRESERVE
SAN DIEGO CREEK CHANNEL
BREN EVENTS CENTER
ALDRICH PARK
UNIVERSITY OF CALIFORNIA IRVINE
IRVINE
CAMPUS PLAZA
EAST BLUFF PARK
INTERIOR DESIGNERS INSTITUTE
BONITA CREEK PARK
CORONA DEL MAR HS
NEWPORT BEACH
SAN JOAQUIN HILLS TRANS CORR
239 TOUR
SEE B
1 BRITTANY WOODS LN
2 CAMPBELL LN
3 MARCHE LN
4 TOURS LN
5 BORDEAUX LN
6 LOURDES LN
7 GRENOBLE LN
8 SEVILLE LN
9 MARSEILLES WY
10 GENOA LN
11 SUNRISE CIR
12 LESPARRE WY
13 MISENO WY
14 NARBONNE WY
15 VENIER WY
SEE A
1 MENLO AISLE
2 VASSAR AISLE
3 SCRIPPS AISLE
SEE C
1 BAYRIDGE DR
2 BRITTANY
3 SEABOROUGH
4 BRADBURY
5 WESTPORT
6 WOODBURNE
7 CHESTERFIELD
8 HAVERFIELD
SEE D
1 MONTSERRAT
2 CHAMINADE
3 MONTREAUX
4 RIDGEGATE
BIG CANYON COUNTRY CLUB
BUFFALO HILLS PARK
FASHION ISLAND
Orange Co Mus of Art
MARRIOTT HOTEL
NEWPORT BEACH COUNTRY CLUB
Newport Center
HARBOR VIEW NATURE PARK
BIG CANYON RESERVOIR
PACIFIC VIEW MEMORIAL PK
COASTLINE COMMUNITY COLLEGE
SAN JOAQUIN RESERVOIR
DAM
ORANGE CO.
1 DEAUVILLE
2 MONTREAUX
1 SANCERRE
2 ARTOIS
3 DAUPHINE
4 BEAULIEU
1 TIBURON BAY DR
2 POINT ARENA WY
3 POINT MENDOCINO WY
SAN JOAQUIN HILLS RD
MACARTHUR BLVD
JAMBOREE RD
BONITA CANYON DR
NEWPORT COAST DR
E COAST HWY
SEE MAP 199
SEE MAP T
NEWPORT BEACH
DETAIL
COPYRIGHT 1998 Thomas Bros. Maps ®

SEE MAP T

SEE MAP T
SEE MAP 98

LAGUNA NIGUEL
SAN JUAN CAPISTRANO
DANA POINT
SAN CLEMENTE
Capistrano Beach
SALT CREEK CORRIDOR REGIONAL PARK
PACIFIC OCEAN
DOHENY STATE BEACH
Dana Point Marina
WEST BASIN
EAST BASIN
MARINE STUDIES INSTITUTE
LANTERN BAY COUNTY PARK
HERITAGE PARK
CAPISTRANO BEACH COUNTY PARK
SAN JUAN HILLS GOLF COURSE
MARCO FORSTER ATHLETIC FIELDS
SAN JUAN CAPISTRANO SPORTS PARK
AGRICULTURAL PRESERVE
SAN DIEGO FRWY
CAMINO CAPISTRANO
PACIFIC COAST HWY
ORTEGA HWY
CM DEL AVION
DEL OBISPO ST
GOLDEN LANTERN
STONEHILL DR
CAMINO LAS RAMBLAS
SAN JUAN CREEK
TRABUCO CREEK
239 TOUR
SEE MAP 105
1 VIA LA MORA
2 VIA LA CARTA
1 SANDY BEACH PL
1 MAINSAIL WY
2 SURFSIDE DR
3 PORT MARINE DR
4 BRIDGEWATER LN
5 BLUEWATER LN
6 OCEANWOOD LN
7 HARBOR POINT DR
SAN JUAN CAPISTRANO
DETAIL

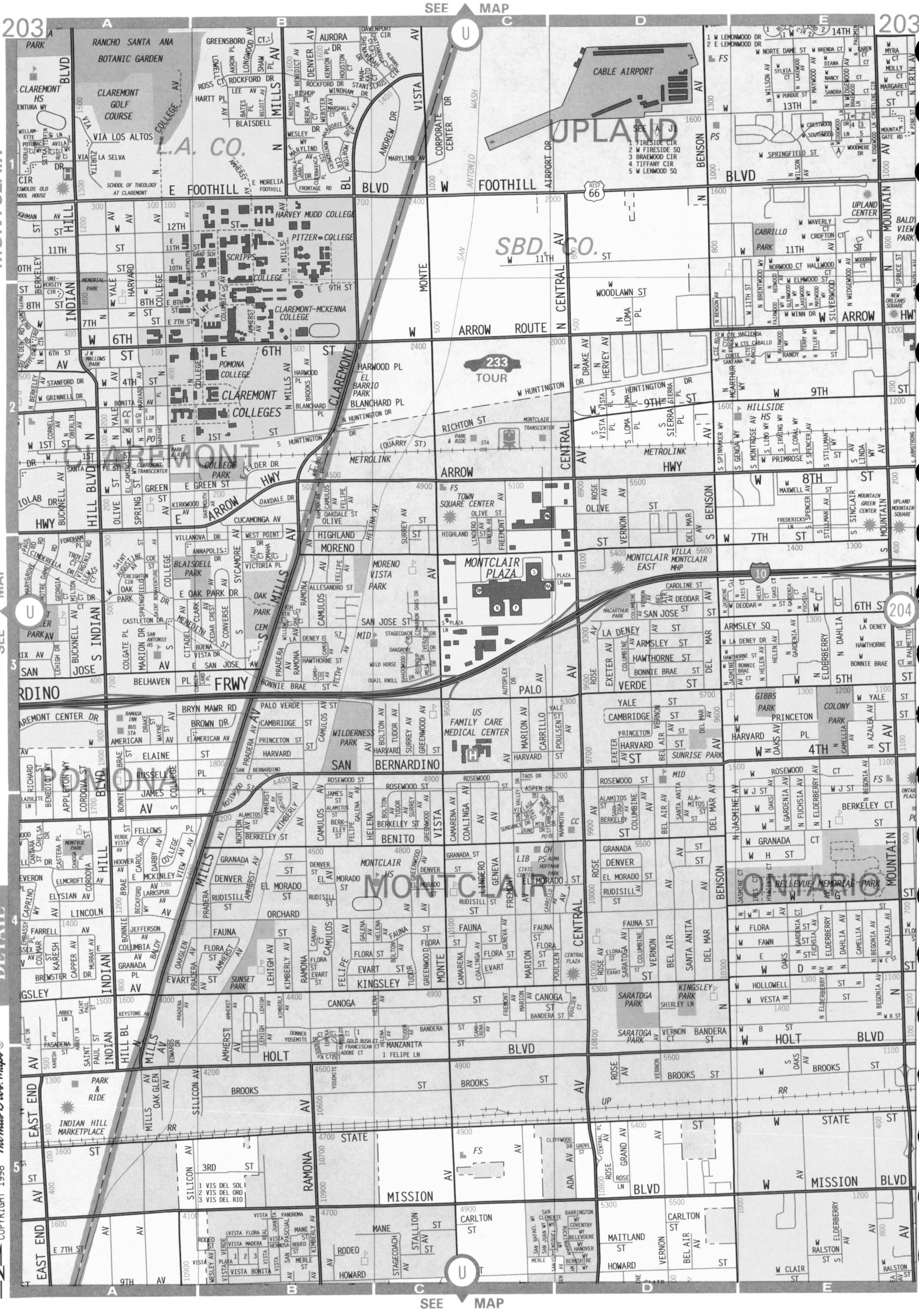
SEE MAP U
RANCHO SANTA ANA BOTANIC GARDEN
CLAREMONT GOLF COURSE
CLAREMONT HS
L.A. CO.
SBD. CO.
CABLE AIRPORT
UPLAND
SEE A J1
1 FIRESIDE CIR
2 W FIRESIDE SQ
3 BRAEWOOD CIR
4 TIFFANY CIR
5 W LENWOOD SQ
SCHOOL OF THEOLOGY AT CLAREMONT
E FOOTHILL BLVD
W FOOTHILL BLVD
HIST 66
MONTCLAIR
HARVEY MUDD COLLEGE
PITZER COLLEGE
SCRIPPS COLLEGE
CLAREMONT-MCKENNA COLLEGE
POMONA COLLEGE
CLAREMONT COLLEGES
CLAREMONT
MEMORIAL PARK
CABRILLO PARK
UPLAND CENTER
BALDY VIEW PARK
W ARROW ROUTE
233 TOUR
EL BARRIO PARK
HILLSIDE HS
METROLINK
ARROW HWY
MONTCLAIR TRANSCENTER
COLLEGE PARK
TOWN SQUARE CENTER
MOUNTAIN GREEN CENTER
UPLAND MOUNTAIN SQUARE
BLAISDELL PARK
MORENO VISTA PARK
MONTCLAIR PLAZA
MONTCLAIR EAST
VILLA MONTCLAIR MHP
10
SEE MAP U
OAK PARK CEM
MACARTHUR PARK
204
SAN ANTONIO HS
FRWY
SAN BERNARDINO
US FAMILY CARE MEDICAL CENTER
WILDERNESS PARK
GIBBS PARK
COLONY PARK
SUNRISE PARK
POMONA
MONTCLAIR HS
MONTCLAIR
CIVIC CENTER
ALMA HOFFMAN PARK
ONTARIO
BELLEVUE MEMORIAL PARK
MONTVUE PARK
SUNSET PARK
CENTRAL PLAZA
KINGSLEY PARK
SARATOGA PARK
HOLT BLVD
BROOKS ST
PARK & RIDE
INDIAN HILL MARKETPLACE
STATE ST
MISSION BLVD
1 VIS DEL SOL
2 VIS DEL ORO
3 VIS DEL RIO
DETAIL
SEE MAP U

SEE MAP U
UPLAND
ONTARIO
RANCHO CUCAMONGA
RED HILL COUNTRY CLUB
CLUBHOUSE
W FOOTHILL BLVD
E FOOTHILL BLVD
UPLAND MEMORIAL PARK
SAN ANTONIO COMMUNITY HOSP
SAN BERNARDINO RD
ARROW HWY
UPLAND HS
BALDY VIEW PARK
METROLINK
8TH ST
FERN RESERVOIR PARK
CITRUS PARK
OLIVEDALE PARK
UPLAND MOUNTAIN SQUARE
SAN BERNARDINO FWY
CHAFFEY HS
JOHN GALVIN PARK
VINEYARD FREEWAY CENTER
ONTARIO PLAZA
GROVE MEMORIAL PARK
FLORA D STREET PARK
JAMES GALANIS PARK
SAN ANTONIO PARK
ONTARIO VILLAGE
HOLT BLVD
Museum Of History & Art
STATE ST
ONTARIO INTERNATIONAL AIRPORT
AIRPORT PARKING
MISSION BLVD
CYPRESS PARK
BON VIEW PARK
SAM ALBA MINI PARK
MOUNTAIN AV
SAN ANTONIO AV
EUCLID AV
CAMPUS AV
GROVE AV
4TH ST
6TH ST
9TH ST
5TH ST
SEE MAP U

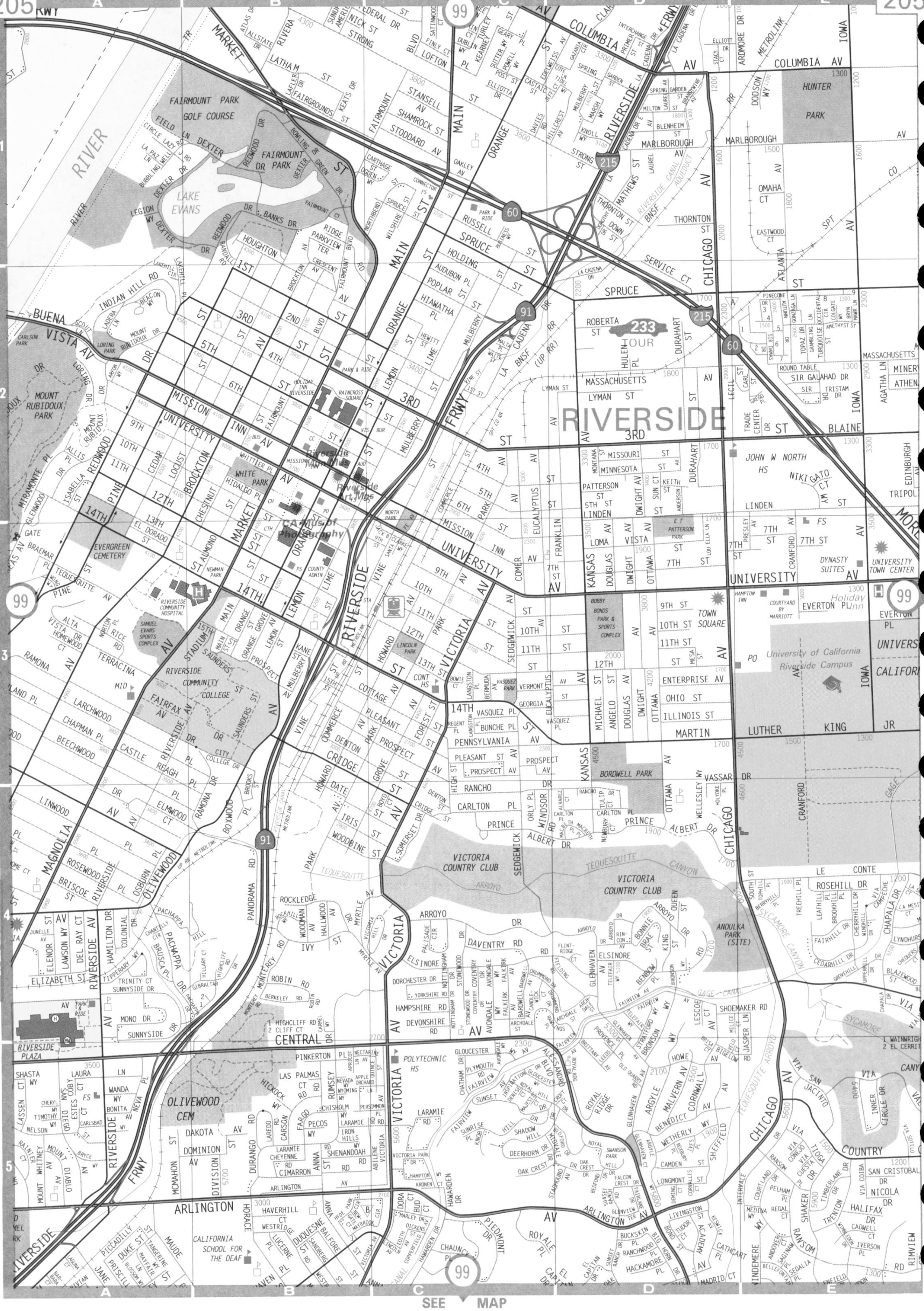
RIVERSIDE
RIVER
FAIRMOUNT PARK GOLF COURSE
FAIRMOUNT PARK
LAKE EVANS
MOUNT RUBIDOUX PARK
EVERGREEN CEMETERY
RIVERSIDE COMMUNITY HOSPITAL
SAMUEL EVANS SPORTS COMPLEX
RIVERSIDE COMMUNITY COLLEGE
WHITE PARK
Riverside Mun Mus
Riverside Art Mus
CA Mus of Photography
RAINCROSS SQUARE
HOLIDAY INN RIVERSIDE
COUNTY ADMIN
LINCOLN PARK
HUNTER PARK
JOHN W NORTH HS
TOWN SQUARE
BOBBY BONDS PARK & SPORTS COMPLEX
UNIVERSITY TOWN CENTER
DYNASTY SUITES
University of California Riverside Campus
BORDWELL PARK
VICTORIA COUNTRY CLUB
ANDULKA PARK (SITE)
POLYTECHNIC HS
OLIVEWOOD CEM
CALIFORNIA SCHOOL FOR THE DEAF
RIVERSIDE PLAZA
TEQUESQUITE CANYON
SYCAMORE CANYON
233 TOUR
60
91
215
99
UNIVERSITY
MISSION INN AV
MAIN ST
MARKET ST
ORANGE ST
LEMON ST
CHICAGO AV
IOWA AV
COLUMBIA AV
SPRUCE ST
BLAINE ST
MARTIN LUTHER KING JR
CENTRAL AV
ARLINGTON AV
VICTORIA AV
MAGNOLIA AV
BUENA VISTA AV
RIVERSIDE FRWY
COUNTRY CLUB DR
CANYON CREST DR
LE CONTE DR
ALESSANDRO BLVD
3RD ST
14TH ST
CHICAGO

SEE MAP
100
PALM SPRINGS
PALM SPRINGS COUNTRY CLUB
WHITEWATER
PALM SPRINGS REGIONAL AIRPORT
AIR 21
ALASKA
AMERICAN
AMERICAN EAGLE
AMERICA WEST EXPRESS
DELTA CONNECTION
RENO AIR
UNITED
UNITED EXPRESS
US AIR EXPRESS
DESERT HOSP
RUTH HARDY PARK
RIVIERA RESORT & RACQUET CLUB
SUNRISE MARKET PLACE
SUNRISE SQUARE
LOEHMANNS PLAZA
VICTORIA PARK
RACQUET CLUB RESORT HOTEL
ODONNELL GOLF CLUB
HYATT REGENCY SUITES
DESERT FASHION PLAZA
Palm Springs Desert Museum
SPA HOTEL & MINERAL SPRINGS
PALM SPRINGS HILTON RESORT
WYNDHAM PALM SPRINGS HOTEL
CONV CTR
PALM SPRINGS MARQUIS HOTEL & VILLAS
LAS BRISAS RESORT HOTEL
PLAZA AT SUNRISE
PALM SPRINGS STADIUM
SUNRISE PARK
PALM SPRINGS HS
PALM SPRINGS MALL
SCH ADM
AIRPORT TERMINAL
MESQUITE COUNTRY CLUB
TAHQUITZ CREEK
TOMMY JACOBS BEL AIR GREENS
RAMADA HOTEL RESORT
SMOKE TREE PLAZA
TAHQUITZ CREEK RESORT
TAHQUITZ FALLS
DMV
TOUR
235
111
CEM
PO
CTH
CO ADM
FS
LIB
BOYS CLUB
DETAIL
SEE A
1 ALESANDRO RD
2 ARAPAHOE ST
3 BIG CHIEF ST
4 BLACK HAWK ST
5 CHEROKEE ST
6 COCOMO ST
7 DIVINA ST
8 DIABLO
9 ESCANABA ST
10 FONDULAC ST
11 GERONIMO ST
12 HIAWATHA ST
13 INDIAN PAW ST
14 POCAHONTAS ST
15 WIGWAM ST
16 TOTEM POLE
17 TOMAHAWK ST
SEE B
1 VIA ACAPULCO N
2 N MAJORCA CIR
3 N VALLARTA CIR
4 N PALOMAR CIR
5 N MADRID CIR
1 EUCALYPTUS DR N
2 CAMELLIA ST
3 REDWOOD DR N
4 EUCALYPTUS DR S
SAN RAFAEL RD
RACQUET CLUB
N PALM CANYON DR
N INDIAN CANYON DR
AVENIDA CABALLEROS
SUNRISE WY
FARRELL DR
GENE AUTRY
VISTA CHINO
TACHEVAH DR
ALEJO RD
AMADO RD
ANDREAS
TAHQUITZ CANYON WY
ARENAS RD
BARISTO RD
SATURNINO RD
RAMON RD
SUNNY DUNES RD
MESQUITE AV
S PALM CANYON DR
E PALM CANYON DR
SONORA RD
RIVERSIDE DR
SAN LORENZO RD
TAMARISK RD
ALAMEDA
CIVIC DR
E VIA ESCUELA
W VIA ESCUELA
MIRADOR
A B C D E
1 2 3 4 5

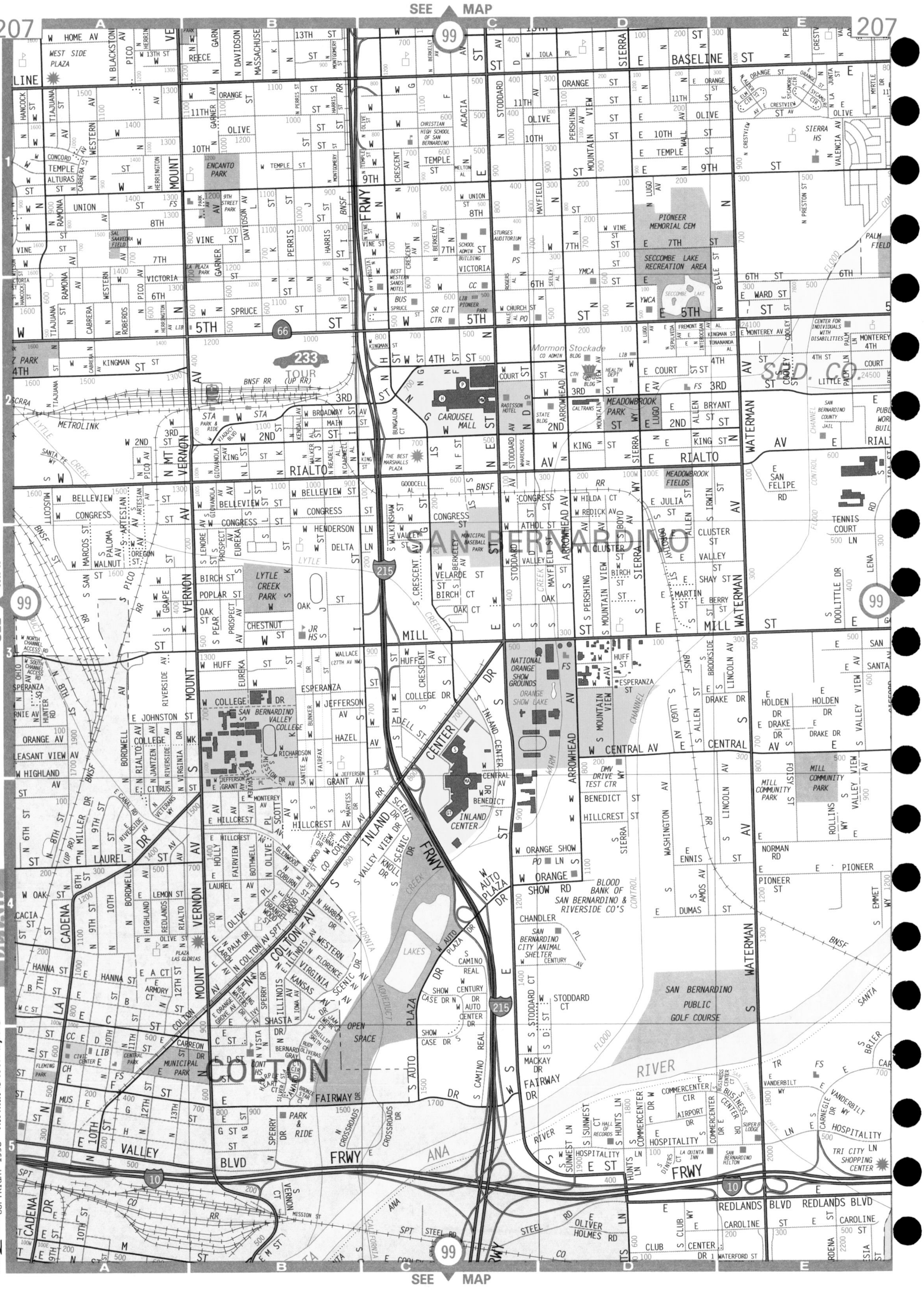
SEE MAP 99
SAN BERNARDINO
DETAIL
SAN BERNARDINO
COLTON
SBD. CO
W BASELINE ST
E BASELINE ST
W HIGHLAND AV
W 5TH ST
5TH ST
E 5TH ST
W MILL ST
E MILL ST
RIALTO AV
E RIALTO AV
W CENTRAL AV
E CENTRAL AV
VALLEY BLVD
REDLANDS BLVD
WATERMAN AV
MOUNT VERNON AV
ARROWHEAD AV
SIERRA WY
MOUNTAIN VIEW
INLAND CENTER DR
FRWY
66
233
215
10
99
MEADOWBROOK PARK
MEADOWBROOK FIELDS
CAROUSEL MALL
INLAND CENTER
LYTLE CREEK PARK
PIONEER MEMORIAL CEM
SECCOMBE LAKE RECREATION AREA
NATIONAL ORANGE SHOW GROUNDS
ORANGE SHOW LAKE
SAN BERNARDINO VALLEY COLLEGE
SAN BERNARDINO PUBLIC GOLF COURSE
SAN BERNARDINO CITY ANIMAL SHELTER
MILL COMMUNITY PARK
ENCANTO PARK
MUNICIPAL PARK
CENTRAL PARK
FLEMING PARK
OPEN SPACE
LAKES
SANTA ANA RIVER
TRI CITY SHOPPING CENTER
BLOOD BANK OF SAN BERNARDINO & RIVERSIDE CO'S
DMV DRIVE TEST CTR
MORMON STOCKADE
METROLINK
BNSF RR
TOUR
CALIFORNIA AQUEDUCT
FLOOD CONTROL CHANNEL
SEE MAP 99

SEE MAP 91

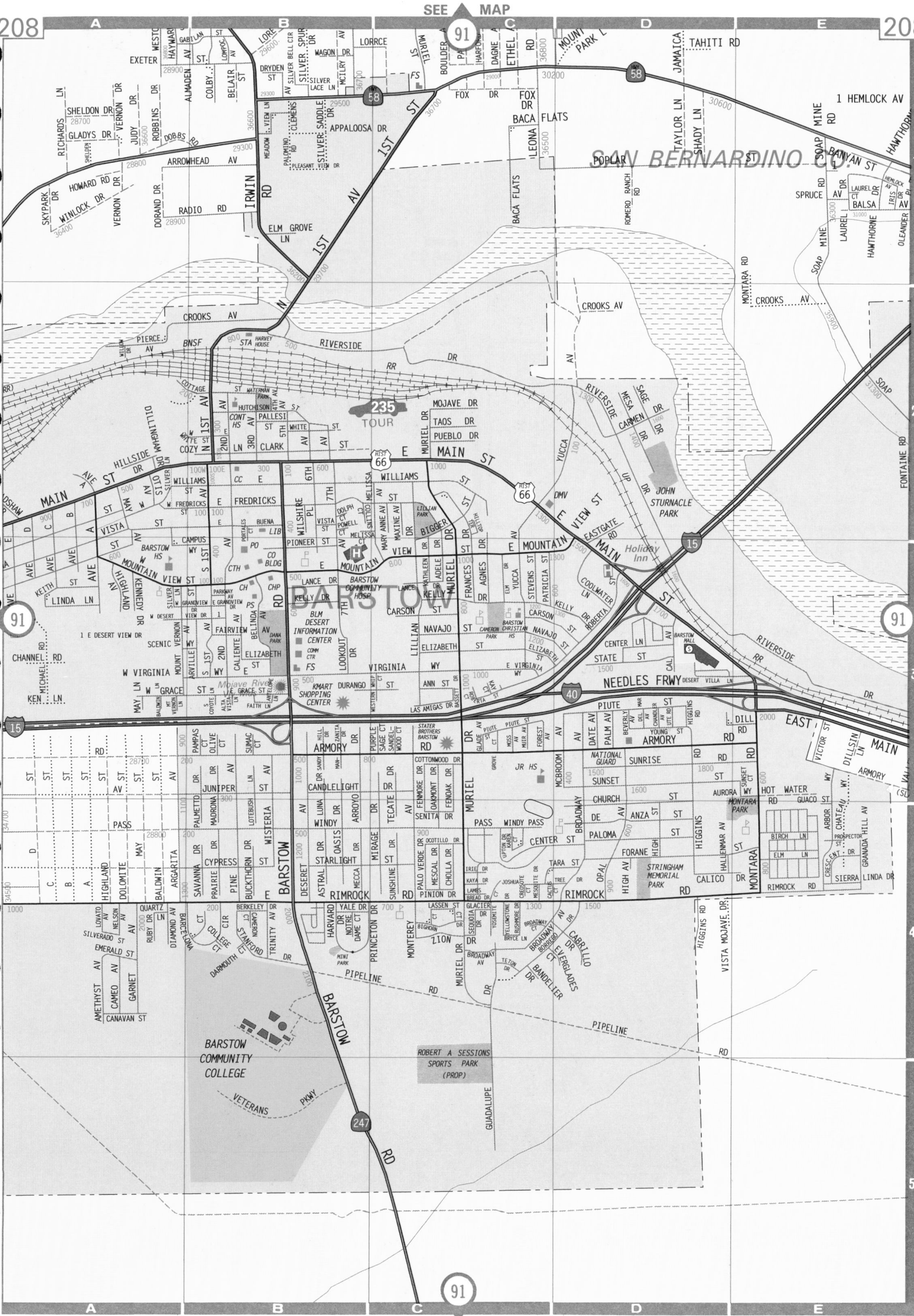

SEE MAP 91

SEE MAP 91

SEE MAP 91

DETAIL

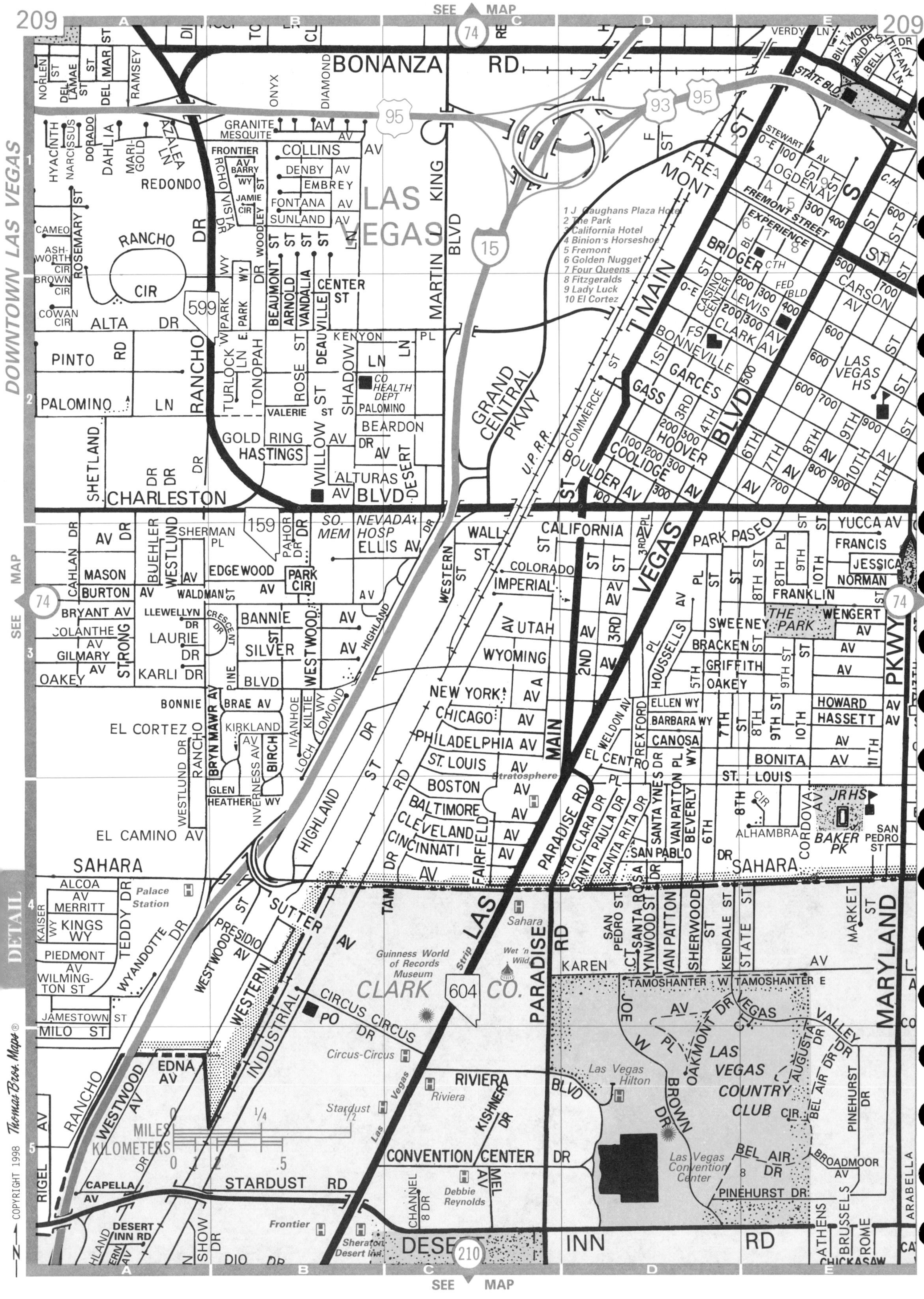
SEE MAP 74
SEE MAP 74
SEE MAP 210
DOWNTOWN LAS VEGAS
DETAIL
LAS VEGAS
CLARK CO.
1 J. Gaughans Plaza Hotel
2 The Park
3 California Hotel
4 Binion's Horseshoe
5 Fremont
6 Golden Nugget
7 Four Queens
8 Fitzgeralds
9 Lady Luck
10 El Cortez
BONANZA RD
CHARLESTON BLVD
SAHARA
DESERT INN RD
RANCHO DR
MARTIN KING BLVD
GRAND CENTRAL PKWY
LAS VEGAS BLVD
MAIN ST
FREMONT ST
FREMONT STREET EXPERIENCE
PARADISE RD
MARYLAND PKWY
CONVENTION CENTER DR
STARDUST RD
RIVIERA BLVD
INDUSTRIAL RD
HIGHLAND DR
WESTERN AV
SUTTER AV
CIRCUS CIRCUS DR
CO HEALTH DEPT
SO. NEVADA MEM HOSP
THE PARK
JRHS
BAKER PK
LAS VEGAS HS
LAS VEGAS COUNTRY CLUB
Las Vegas Hilton
Las Vegas Convention Center
Stratosphere
Sahara
Wet 'n Wild
Guinness World of Records Museum
Circus-Circus
Riviera
Stardust
Debbie Reynolds
Frontier
Sheraton Desert Inn
Palace Station
PO
FS
CTH
FED BLD
STATE BLD
U.P.R.R.
MILES 0 1/4 1/2
KILOMETERS 0 .1 .2 .5
Thomas Bros. Maps ®
COPYRIGHT 1998

SEE MAP 209
LAS VEGAS
CONVENTION/CENTER DR
Las Vegas Convention Center
PINEHURST DR
STARDUST RD
CAPELLA AV
DESERT INN RD
Frontier
Sheraton Desert Inn
DESERT INN RD
Desert Inn Country Club
PINKS PL
POLLUX AV
ALDEBARAN AV
HIGHLAND DR
WESTERN AV
FASHION SHOW DR
DIO DR
FASHION SHOW MALL
SPRING MTN RD
BLACK CANYON AV
Treasure Island
PERSHING AV
HIGHLAND DR
CINDER
INDUSTRIAL
LYON DR
VEGAS PLAZA DR
UP RR
EMERSON
EDISON AV
FRANKLIN BLVD
BURBANK AV
GREEN LAWN DR
COUNTRY CLUB LN
COUNTRY CLUB
PARADISE RD
SIERRA VISTA DR
LISBON
OAKBROOK LN
ROYAL CREST CIR
GILSON LN
WISCONSIN LN
ELM DR
TWAIN AV
Venetian (opens 1999)
Mirage
Las Vegas Strip
SANDS
SUZANNE CIR
CENTRAL PARK DR
HUGHES PKWY
HOWARD HUGHES
CORPORATE DR
CASSELLA
NORTH CIR
VIKING CIR
KOLSON
CALCATERRO CIR
NORTHROP AV
CAMBRIDGE
WESTCHESTER
Harrahs
IDA AV
WINNICK
Imperial Palace
Caesars Palace
ALBERT AV
MANHATTAN
MC KELLAR
FRED-RIKA
SWENSON ST
FLAMINGO RD
Rio
Bellagio
Ballys
592
Paris (opens 1999)
1 Flamingo Hilton
2 Barbary Coast
3 Bourbon St
4 Maxim
AVIS AV
LA CIENEGA
FREDDA
CHARLOTTE DR
Emerald Springs Inn
Continental Hotel
ROCHELLE AV
DEBBIE WY
ALADDIN GOLF COURSE
AUDRIE ST
LANA
SADIE ST
SALTON ST
605
Hard Rock
SWENSON ST
COTTAGE GROVE AV
CHATHAM CIR
CLAYMONT ST
Univ of Nevada, Las Vegas
74
SEE MAP
BUSINESS LN
HARMON AV
JOEL AV
KISNER DR
The Mirage Golf Club
604
NAPLES AV
LA MAR CIR
San Tropez
NAPLES DR
SEE A
1 S BARBARA WY
2 SARA LEE CIR
3 S CAROL CIR
4 JANE WY
TOMPKINS AV
Monte Carlo
Alexis Park Resort Hotel
KOVAL LN
DECKOW LN
NICK KELLY
BERMUDA RD
BATES ST
MGM Grand
POLARIS
New York New York
Hotel San Remo
PARADISE PK
593
TROPICANA AV
Travelodge Hotel
Excalibur
Tropicana
ELLINGTON ST
PLACID ST
SAGE AV
SHIRLEY ST
Luxor
BELL DR
PALO VERDE RD
CLARK CO.
RENO AV
GARY ST
JANIS PL
DURANTE ST
BOYER ST
TONI ST
DUKE ST
ALI BABA
LA CIENEGA ST
DEMET DR
PONCHO CIR
MONIKA WY
HACIENDA AV
RENT CAR RD
KITTY HAWK WY
WESTMINSTER AV
COUNT WUTSKE AV
MESA VISTA AV
DANVILLE LN
PRINCE SCOTTY
RICHARD AV
Paradise (opens 1998)
McCarran Int'l Airport
KING ST
LADY MARLENE AV
GILES ST
BETHEL
INDUSTRIAL RD
15
LAS VEGAS BLVD S
DIABLO DR
DEWEY DR
COUNT CARLSON
BLACK KNIGHT
MILES 0 1/4 1/2
KILOMETERS 0 .1 .2 .5
WAYNE NEWTON BLVD
RUSSELL RD
QUAIL AV
HAVEN
AIR TERMINAL
HOFFMAN DR
CHULA WY
OQUENDO RD
74
SEE MAP
LAS VEGAS STRIP
DETAIL

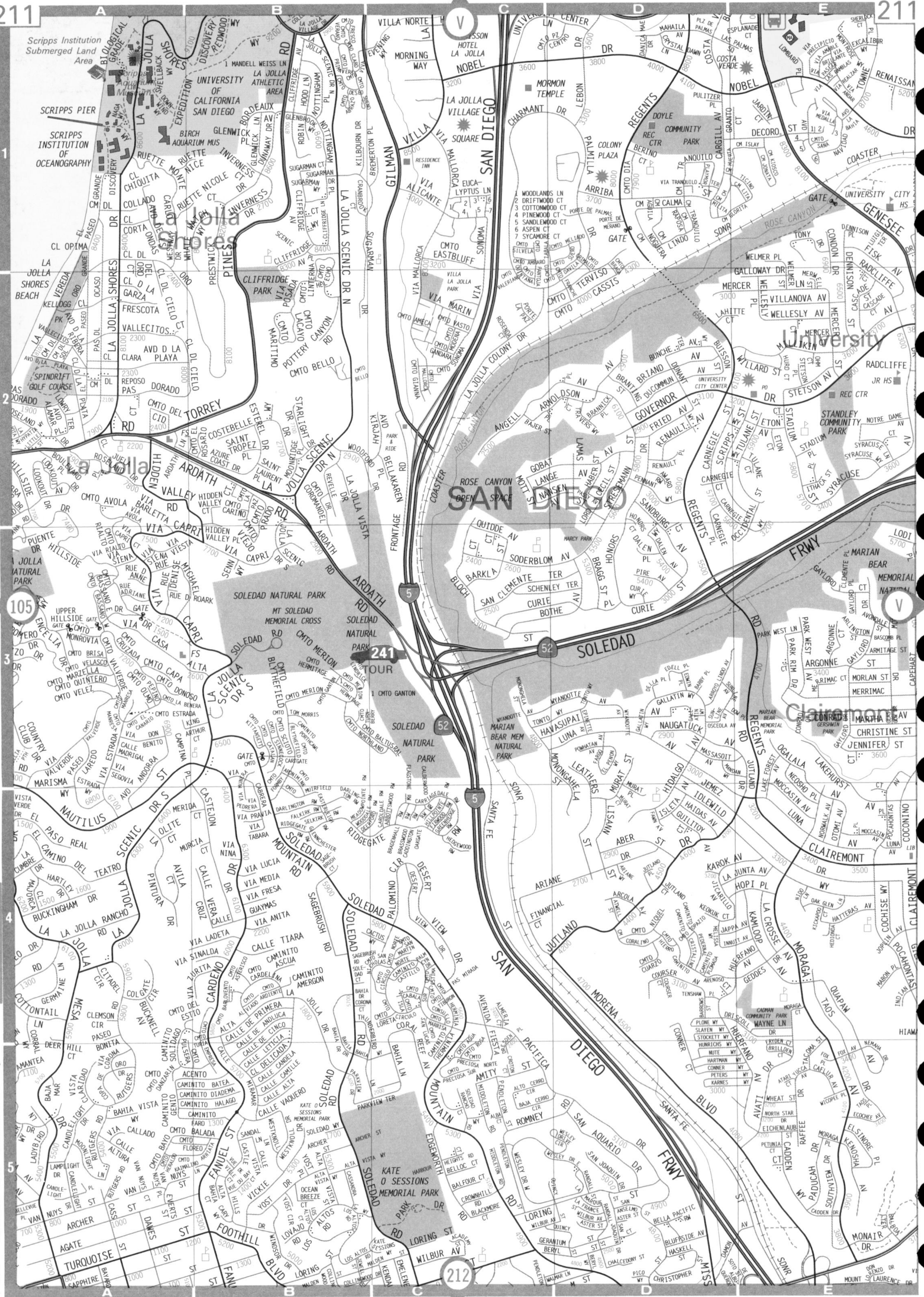
Scripps Institution Submerged Land Area
BIOLOGICAL GRADE
SCRIPPS PIER
SCRIPPS INSTITUTION OF OCEANOGRAPHY
BIRCH AQUARIUM MUS
UNIVERSITY OF CALIFORNIA SAN DIEGO
LA JOLLA ATHLETIC AREA
1 MANDELL WEISS LN
SAN DIEGO
La Jolla Shores
LA JOLLA SHORES BEACH
SPINDRIFT GOLF COURSE
CLIFFRIDGE PARK
La Jolla
LA JOLLA NATURAL PARK
SOLEDAD NATURAL PARK
MT SOLEDAD MEMORIAL CROSS
SOLEDAD NATURAL PARK
TOUR
1 CMTO GANTON
KATE O SESSIONS MEMORIAL PARK
KATE O SESSIONS MEMORIAL PARK
LA JOLLA VILLAGE SQUARE
MORMON TEMPLE
HYATT REGENCY LA JOLLA
DOYLE COMMUNITY PARK
COLONY PLAZA
ROSE CANYON OPEN SPACE
SAN DIEGO
ROSE CANYON
University
UNIVERSITY CITY CENTER
STANDLEY COMMUNITY PARK
UNIVERSITY CITY HS
MARIAN BEAR MEMORIAL NATURAL PARK
MARIAN BEAR MEM NATURAL PARK
Clairemont
CADMAN COMMUNITY PARK
MARCY PARK
1 WOODLANDS LN
2 DRIFTWOOD CT
3 COTTONWOOD CT
4 PINEWOOD CT
5 SANDLEWOOD CT
6 ASPEN CT
7 SYCAMORE CT
ARDATH RD
LA JOLLA SCENIC DR N
LA JOLLA SCENIC DR S
GILMAN DR
VILLA LA JOLLA DR
NOBEL DR
GENESEE AV
REGENTS RD
SOLEDAD MOUNTAIN RD
SOLEDAD RD
NAUTILUS ST
TORREY PINES RD
LA JOLLA VILLAGE DR
LA JOLLA COLONY DR
GOVERNOR DR
CLAIREMONT DR
SAN DIEGO FRWY
SOLEDAD FRWY
MORENA BLVD
SANTA FE
MOUNT SOLEDAD
5
52
241
SEE MAP 105
SEE MAP 212
DETAIL
COPYRIGHT 1998 Thomas Bros. Maps ®

SEE MAP 211

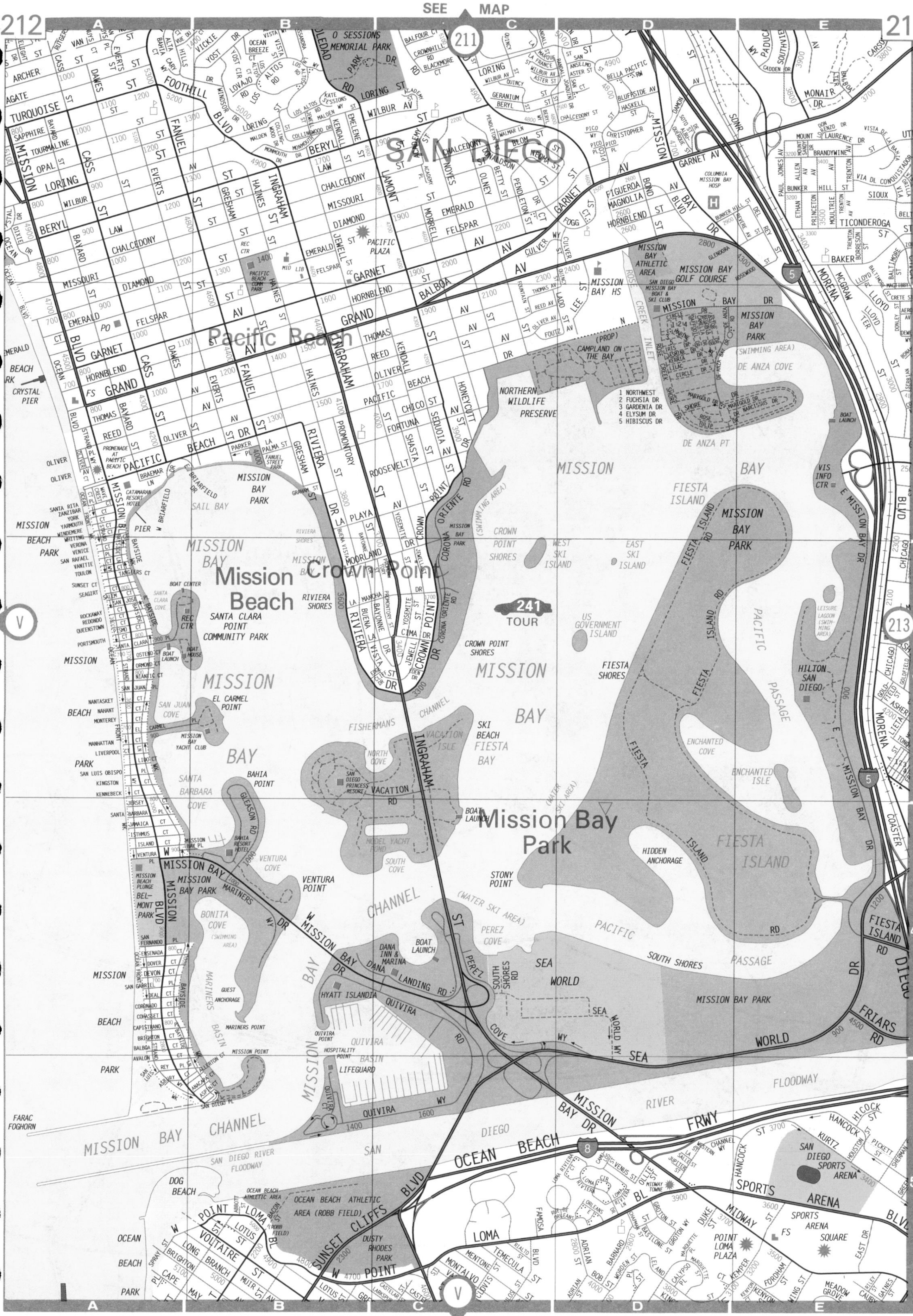

SEE MAP 213

SEE MAP V

SEE MAP V

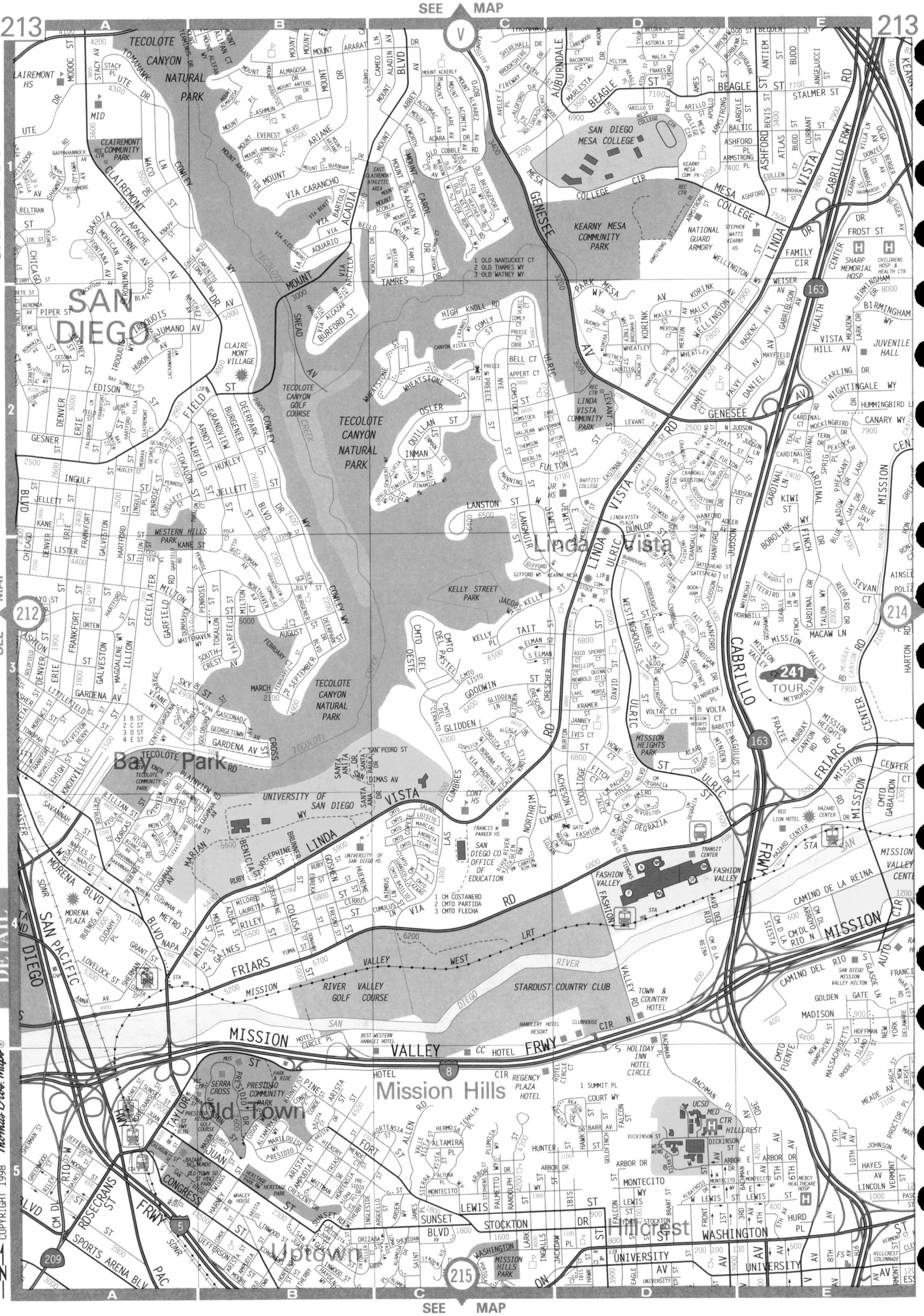

SEE MAP 212
SEE MAP 214
SEE MAP 215

SEE MAP V

SEE MAP 216

SEE MAP 213

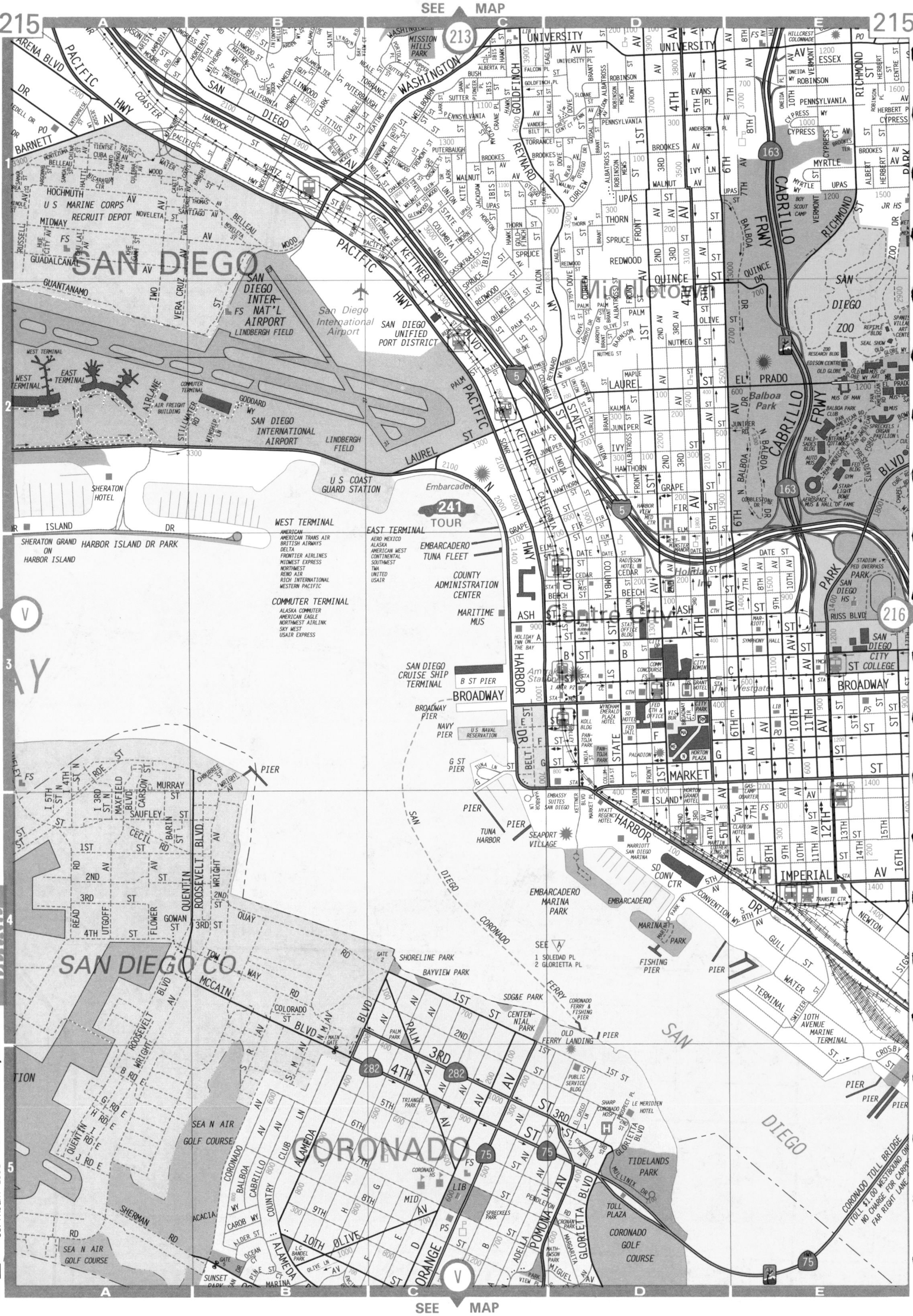
SAN DIEGO-DOWNTOWN
SAN DIEGO
SAN DIEGO INTER-NAT'L AIRPORT
LINDBERGH FIELD
San Diego International Airport
SAN DIEGO UNIFIED PORT DISTRICT
U S MARINE CORPS RECRUIT DEPOT
U S COAST GUARD STATION
SHERATON HOTEL
SHERATON GRAND ON HARBOR ISLAND
HARBOR ISLAND DR PARK
WEST TERMINAL
EAST TERMINAL
COMMUTER TERMINAL
EMBARCADERO TUNA FLEET
COUNTY ADMINISTRATION CENTER
MARITIME MUS
SAN DIEGO CRUISE SHIP TERMINAL
B ST PIER
BROADWAY PIER
NAVY PIER
G ST PIER
TUNA HARBOR
SEAPORT VILLAGE
SD CONV CTR
EMBARCADERO MARINA PARK
MARINA PARK
FISHING PIER
10TH AVENUE MARINE TERMINAL
Middletown
Centre City
HORTON PLAZA
Balboa Park
SAN DIEGO ZOO
CABRILLO FRWY
PACIFIC HWY
HARBOR DR
SAN DIEGO CO.
CORONADO
SEA N AIR GOLF COURSE
TIDELANDS PARK
CORONADO GOLF COURSE
TOLL PLAZA
CORONADO TOLL BRIDGE
SAN DIEGO BAY
216

SEE MAP 214
SEE MAP 215
SEE MAP V
SAN DIEGO
North Park
Balboa Park
BALBOA PARK
BALBOA PARK MUNICIPAL GOLF COURSE
City Heights
South Park
Golden Hill
Mount Hope
Stockton
Grant Hill
Sherman Heights
Logan Heights
Mountain View
Memorial
Barrio Logan
Southcrest
GREENWOOD CEM
HOLY CROSS CEM
U S NAVAL RESERVATION
NASSCO SHIPYARD
BAY
DETAIL

SEE MAP 112

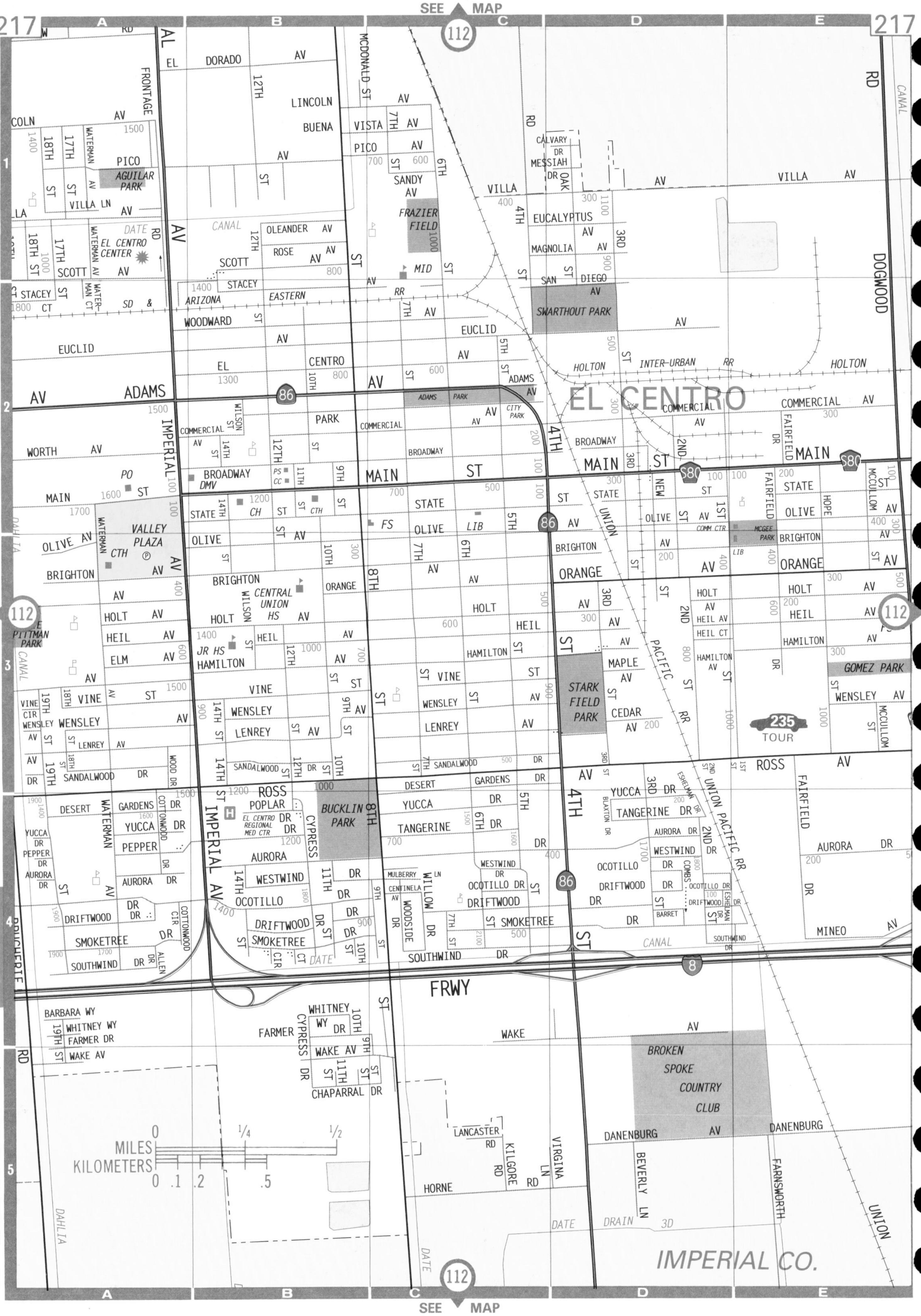

SEE MAP 112

Discover California

This section shows twelve Driving Tours which highlight different regions of California. Each Tour designates a scenic route, and briefly describes some of the points of interest along the way. In addition to the designated Tours, each of the twelve regions is filled with points of interest, some of which are listed on the pages accompanying each Tour section.

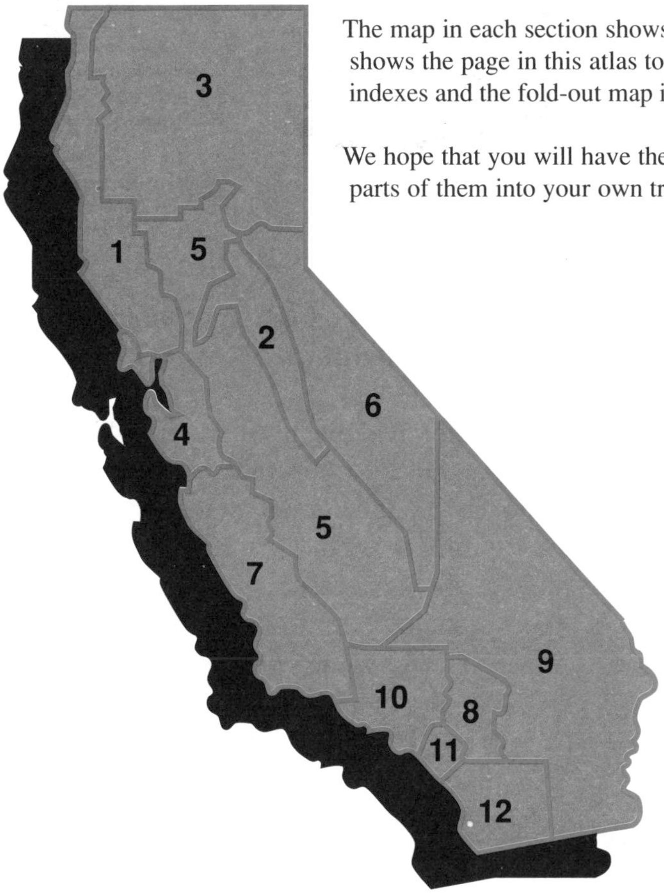

The map in each section shows the tours highlighted in yellow. Each Tour section also shows the page in this atlas to refer to for a more detailed map. Also, the extensive indexes and the fold-out map in the back of the atlas will provide additional information.

We hope that you will have the opportunity to take all of the Tours, or at least integrate parts of them into your own travel plans.

Table of Contents

1. North Coast 219
2. Gold Country 221
3. Shasta-Cascade 223
4. San Francisco Bay Area 225
5. Central Valley 227
6. High Sierra 229
7. Central Coast 231
8. Inland Empire 233
9. Deserts 235
10. Greater Los Angeles Area 237
11. Orange County 239
12. San Diego County 241

General Information Numbers and Web Sites

California Road Conditions Information

Caltrans 24-Hour Service
On a touchtone phone, press Highway Number & Pound (#) Key
Northern California Conditions: (916) 445-7623
Southern California Conditions: (213) 628-7623

General Tourism and Travel Information

California Trade & Commerce Agency, Office of Tourism
(916) 322-2881

We invite your comments and recommendations.
Please write to:

Thomas Bros. Maps®
17731 Cowan, Irvine, CA 92614
c/o CRA Driving Tours

Thomas Bros. Maps® updates this Atlas annually based on field research and available sources, but changes can and do occur. We hope that you will not be inconvenienced by any information that becomes obsolete or inaccurate.

Travel Web Site Information

State of California	www.ca.gov
California Highway Conditions	www.dot.ca.gov/hq/roadinfo
California State Dept of Parks & Recreation	ceres.ca.gov/parks
California Guidebook	www.gocalif.ca.gov
California Highway Patrol	www.chp.ca.gov
California Snow Reports	www.aminews.com
California Travel Parks Association	www.campgrounds.com
Caltrans	www.dot.ca.gov
Department of Motor Vehicles	www.dmv.ca.gov
GORP - Calif Scenic Byways & Recreational Drives	www.gorp.com/gorp/activity/byway/ca.htm
National Park Service	www.nps.gov:80
Off Highway Vehicles	www.calohv.ca.gov
US Forest Service	www.fs.fed.us

The web site addresses are subject to change without notice. Thomas Bros. Maps is not responsible for any changes, omissions, errors or information contained within these web sites.

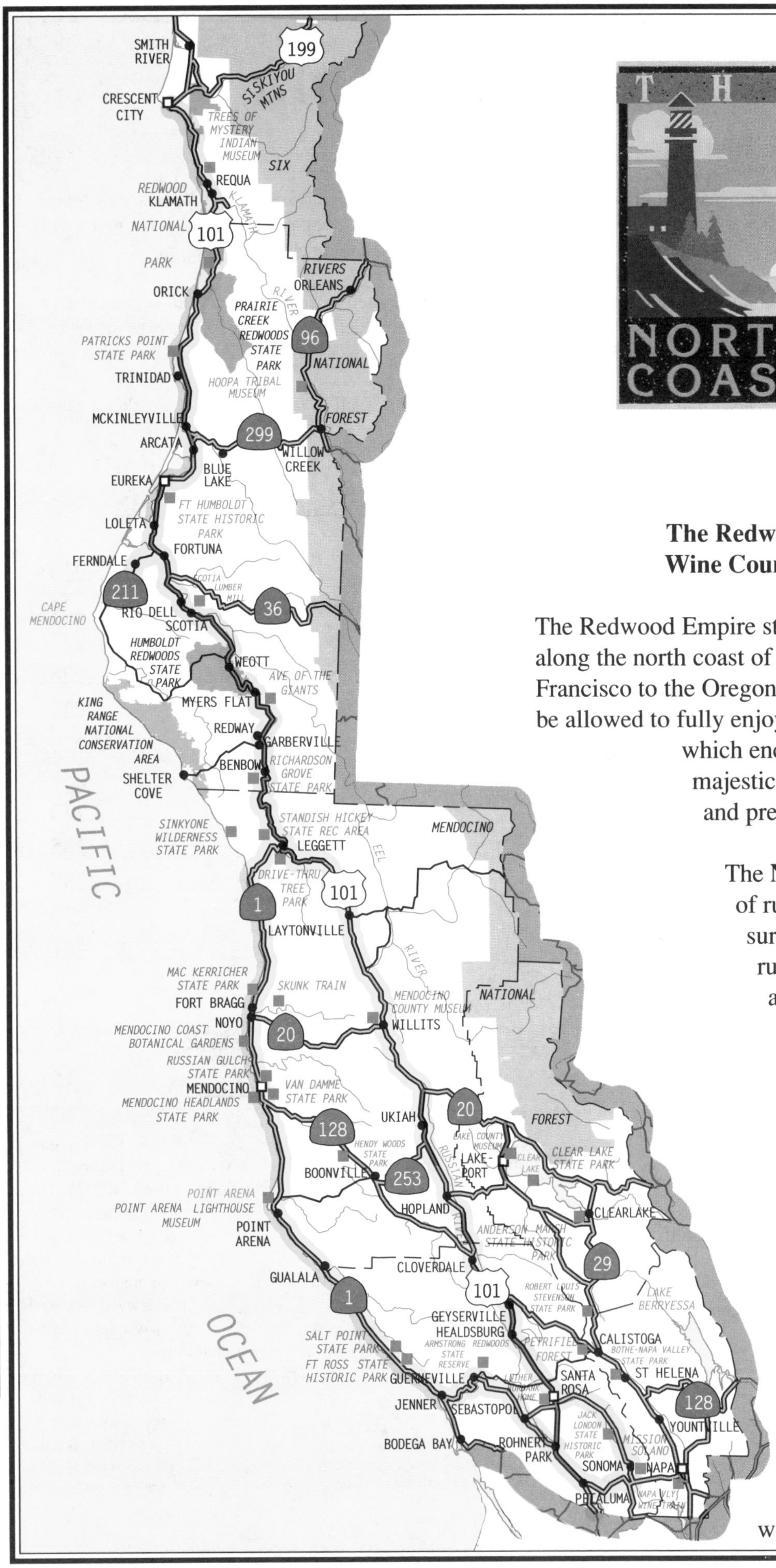

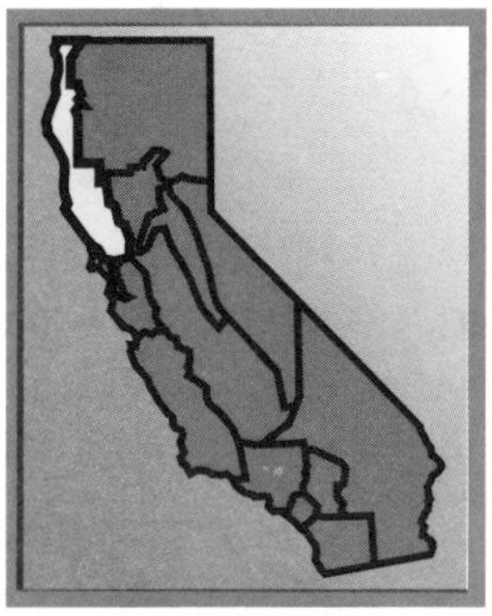

1 Inch to 28 Miles

Scale

0 Miles 28

The Redwood Empire from Wine Country to Redwoods

The Redwood Empire stretches more than 400 miles along the north coast of California, north of San Francisco to the Oregon border. Several days should be allowed to fully enjoy the spectacular scenery, which encompasses rugged coastline, majestic redwood forests, lush valleys and premier wine country.

The **North Coast** is the California of rugged shores and pounding surf, of towering redwoods and rushing streams, of verdant hills and bountiful vineyards.

www.gocalif.ca.gov/guidebook/NC/

Driving Tour Points of Interest:

BODEGA BAY - *(Page 37, C3)* The bay was discovered in 1775 by Spanish explorers. Russian fur hunters settled at nearby Bodega in 1809. Fishing, a landmark Catholic church, hillside and waterfront lodgings and restaurants abound. Golf is available at Bodega Harbor Golf Links, an 18-hole championship course overlooking the ocean. At Spud Point Marina, you'll find boat charters for cruises, whale watching, and deep-sea fishing. **Doran Regional Park** is an on-the-bay sand-spit (swim, camp, fish). **Westside Park** is in the inner-bay (camp, fish, boat launch). The UC Marine Lab offers tours Fridays 2-4 p.m., groups by reservation: (707) 875-2211. At **Bodega Head State Park** at the north end of Bodega Bay, a three-mile trail climbs north and down to Salmon Creek Beach at Sonoma Coast State Beach.

SONOMA COAST STATE BEACH - *(Page 37, C2)* Broad, shining beaches and secluded coves, rocky coastline, and tide pools are protected and maintained by the State. Open to the public at several access points with fire rings on the sand and numerous developed campsites. (707) 875-3483

The drive along the Russian River, named for the fur traders who flourished there in the 19th century, is dotted with small towns, wineries and peaceful orchards. The road winds through forests of redwoods which have been preserved rather than destroyed for the sake of the pavement.

FORT ROSS STATE HISTORIC PARK - *(Page 37, A1)* Eleven miles north of Jenner on Highway 1. In the early 1800s, Ross, a Russian word for "Russia," was established as a base to hunt otter and seal and to grow food for the Russian colonies in Alaska. The Russians competed with the Spanish in Bodega Bay for control of this rich hunting ground and the verdant Russian River valley. Today, you'll see restored and reconstructed redwood structures: the stockade, block-houses, a Russian chapel, officers' barracks, a Russian well and a storehouse. Living history events, Orthodox Easter church service and Ranch Day events are presented annually. Call for information about the picnic area: (707) 847-3286. See Bufano's 72-foot Peace statue on the access trail from Highway 1, north of the fort.

MOUNT KONOCTI - *(Page 31, E3)* This 4,300-foot dormant volcano with four peaks last erupted a few thousand years ago, and is a landmark for the entire Clear Lake area and the subject of Native American legends. Many enjoy rockhounding for Lake County "diamonds," semi-precious stones of volcanic origin found only in the county. This area also offers golf courses, tennis courts at resorts and parks, and a country club at the lakeside base of the mountain.

SINKYONE WILDERNESS STATE PARK - *(Page 22, B2)* The south gateway to the spectacular isolated Lost Coast, 50 miles north of Fort Bragg. Exit Highway 1 above Rockport, following unpaved Usal Road (County Road No. 431) to primitive campsites at Usal Creek. Rugged Lost Coast Trail winds 21 miles north through a 7,000-acre coastal plateau, with ocean vistas, waterfalls, cliffs, access to black sand beaches, tide pools, and trail campsites. The Visitor Center in a ranch house at Needle Rock is open in the summer. (707) 986-7711

HUMBOLDT REDWOOD STATE PARK - *(Page 16, A4)* A 51,222 acre park that protects 2,000 year old trees in a 20 million year old forest - the largest remaining stand of virgin redwoods in the world. Camping is permitted. (707) 946-2409

AVENUE of the GIANTS - *(Page 16, C4)* World famous 31-mile scenic drive parallels Highway 101. The road meanders through solemn groves of redwoods, some 300 feet tall. There are numerous attractions and gift shops along the way. Contact The Avenue of the Giants Association at (707) 923-2555.

SCOTIA - *(Page 16, A3)* A stylized "company town" built almost entirely of redwood. The sprawling mill, **Pacific Lumber**, offers free, self-guided tours of their redwood processing plant and museum. (707) 764-2222

FERNDALE - *(Page 15, D2)* Five miles west of Highway 101, a Victorian town of splendid gingerbread style homes and shops. The entire town is a designated State Historical Landmark. (707) 786-4477

EUREKA - *(Page 15, E1)* In the Old Town historic district there are specialty shops, art galleries and studios, Humboldt Cultural Center and antiques. The Carson Mansion is the 1885 redwood Queen of Victorians.

PATRICK'S POINT STATE PARK - *(Page 9, E3)* A gorgeous, 630-acre park with 12 hiking trails that allow visitors to walk out near the edge of steep bluffs or onto the sandy beach. For camping information, call (707) 677-3570.

PRAIRIE CREEK REDWOODS STATE PARK - *(Page 10, A1)* A large meadowland of tall grasses bordered by dense redwoods and fern canyons. Elk may be seen in the open areas. The Visitors Center has displays and information. (707) 464-6101, ext. 5301

www.gocalif.ca.gov/guidebook/GC/

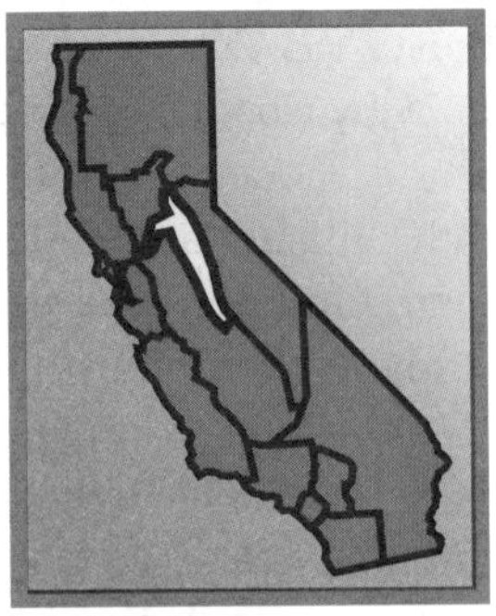

1 Inch to 22 Miles

Scale

0 Miles 22

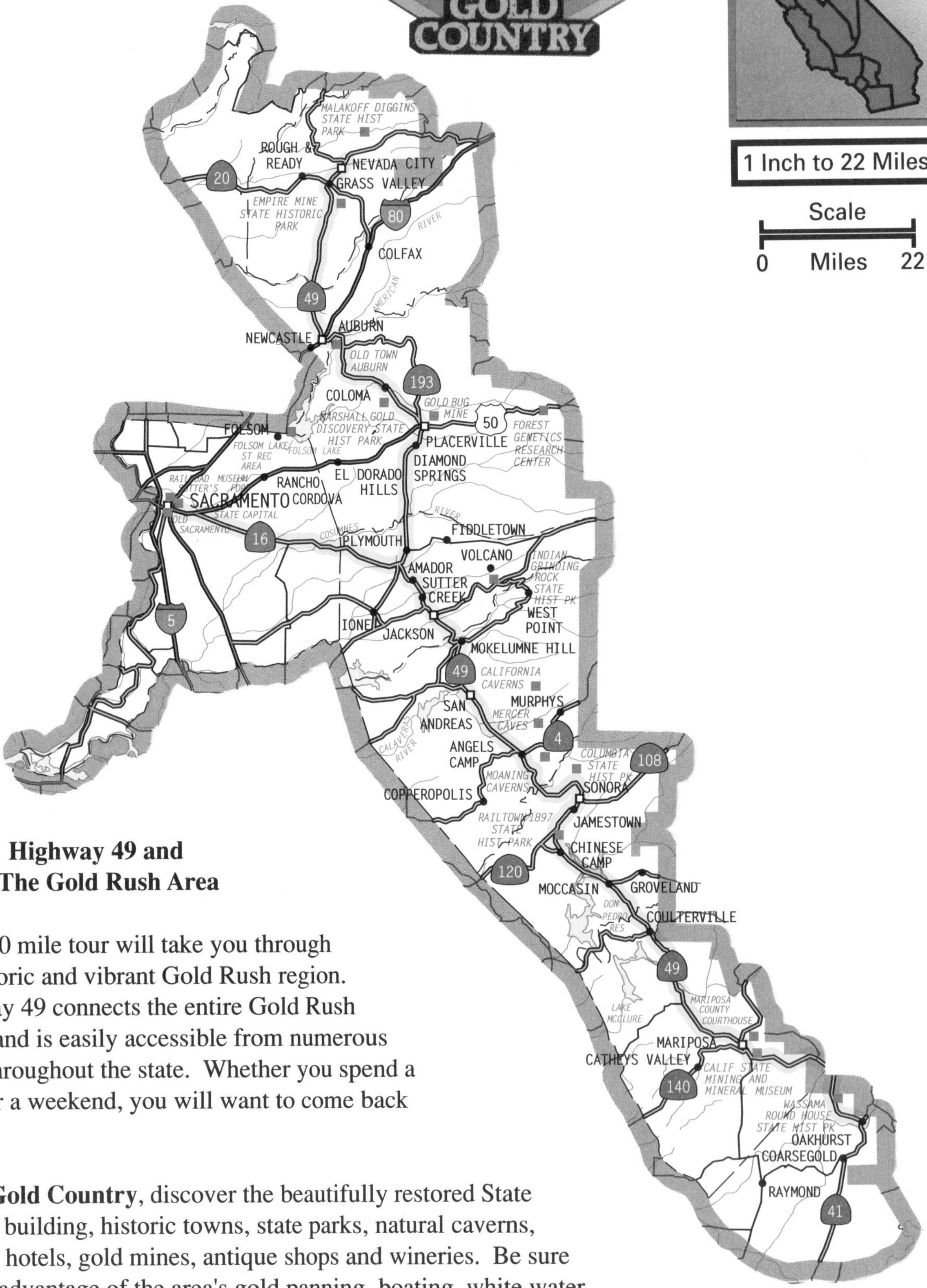

Highway 49 and The Gold Rush Area

This 300 mile tour will take you through the historic and vibrant Gold Rush region. Highway 49 connects the entire Gold Rush region and is easily accessible from numerous roads throughout the state. Whether you spend a week or a weekend, you will want to come back often.

In the **Gold Country**, discover the beautifully restored State Capitol building, historic towns, state parks, natural caverns, historic hotels, gold mines, antique shops and wineries. Be sure to take advantage of the area's gold panning, boating, white water rafting, camping, picnicking and a wide variety of recreational activities.

Driving Tour Points of Interest:

JAMESTOWN - *(Page 41, C5)* Affectionately called "Jimtown" by its residents. This gold camp had an especially bawdy reputation as a rough and tumble town. Visit the **Railtown 1897 State Park**. (209) 984-3953

COLUMBIA - *(Page 41, C4)* "The Gem of the Southern Mines" once attracted 15,000 fortune-seeking miners. Today, Columbia invites visitors to experience that heyday by taking part in Living Histories and special events, or to stroll through town on a walking tour led by authentically-costumed guides. (209) 532-4301 or 532-0150

ANGELS CAMP - *(Page 41, B4)* Made famous twice, first as an important Gold Rush center and again by Mark Twain's short story "The Celebrated Jumping Frog of Calaveras County." Each May, the town hosts its Jumping Frog Jubilee and frog-jumping contest. (209) 754-4009

Mercer Caverns - *(Page 41, B4)* 1.5 miles west of Murphys. Open since 1885, the caves invite explorers into eight rooms of crystalline formations. (209) 728-2101

The Sierra foothills from Jackson to Plymouth (Page 40) *are blanketed with oak trees and vineyards. Amador County is gaining recognition for its premium wineries. Amador County Chamber of Commerce: (209) 223-0350.*

SACRAMENTO - *(Page 39, E1)* The State Capital since 1854. The city has a colorful history, well-preserved amid a modern and dynamic environment of current political activity.

Old Sacramento State Historic Park - *(Page 137, A2)* A ten-block district along the Sacramento River which recreates the flavor of the Gold Rush days. Museums, saloons and shops line the western-style streets. The **California State Railroad Museum** features dozens of historic exhibits and 21 lavishly restored locomotives and cars. **Old Sacramento Visitors Center**, located in the Old Sacramento State Historic Park, provides information and walking tours of the city. (916) 442-7644

Sutter's Fort *(Page 137, D3)* Site of the first settlement founded by Captain John Sutter in 1839. The fort has been restored and houses exhibits and memorabilia of the Gold Rush days. (916) 445-4422

State Capitol - *(Page 137, B3)* Constructed between 1861 and 1874. The main building is a formidable structure with a 210-foot gold dome, marble floors and radiant, crystal chandeliers. It is the dominant landmark among the state buildings in the area, and is surrounded by a 40-acre park of trees and plants from around the world. Tours of the main building, its chambers, and some executive offices are available, as well as historical exhibits, murals and a film. (916) 324-0333

COLOMA - *(Page 34, D4)* "Birthplace of the Gold Rush." John Marshall discovered gold here on January 24, 1848. The **James W. Marshall Gold Discovery Park** is a 300-acre State Park that captures the spirit of the Old West through living history exhibits, museums, and walking tours. (916) 622-3470

AUBURN - *(Page 34, C3)* One of the first mining camps in California. Old Town Auburn boasts California's oldest operating post office and the oldest volunteer fire department "West of Boston," both established in 1852.

GRASS VALLEY - *(Page 34, C1)* An active mining town for 100 years. The large, commercial operations continued into the 1950s.

Empire Mine State Park - *(Page 127, D4)* Documents 107 years of mining history with displays, exhibits, films and tours. Call the Visitors Center at (916) 273-8522.

NEVADA CITY - *(Page 34, C1)* "Queen City of the Northern Mines," once the third largest city in California. Many fine buildings and homes remain, including California's oldest, still-operating hotel and the state's oldest theatre building.

www.gocalif.ca.gov/guidebook/SC/

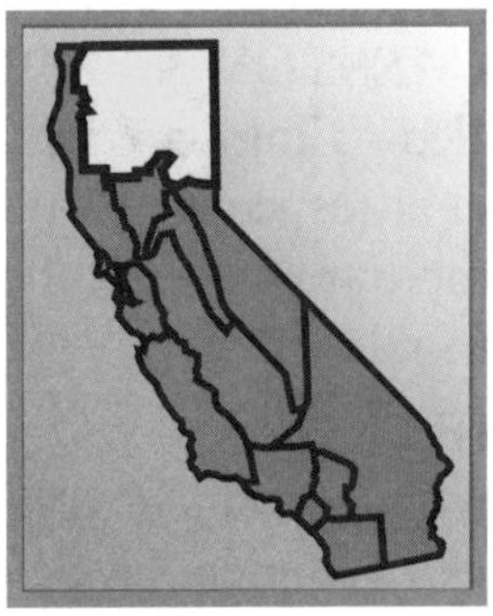

1 Inch to 35 Miles

Scale

0 Miles 35

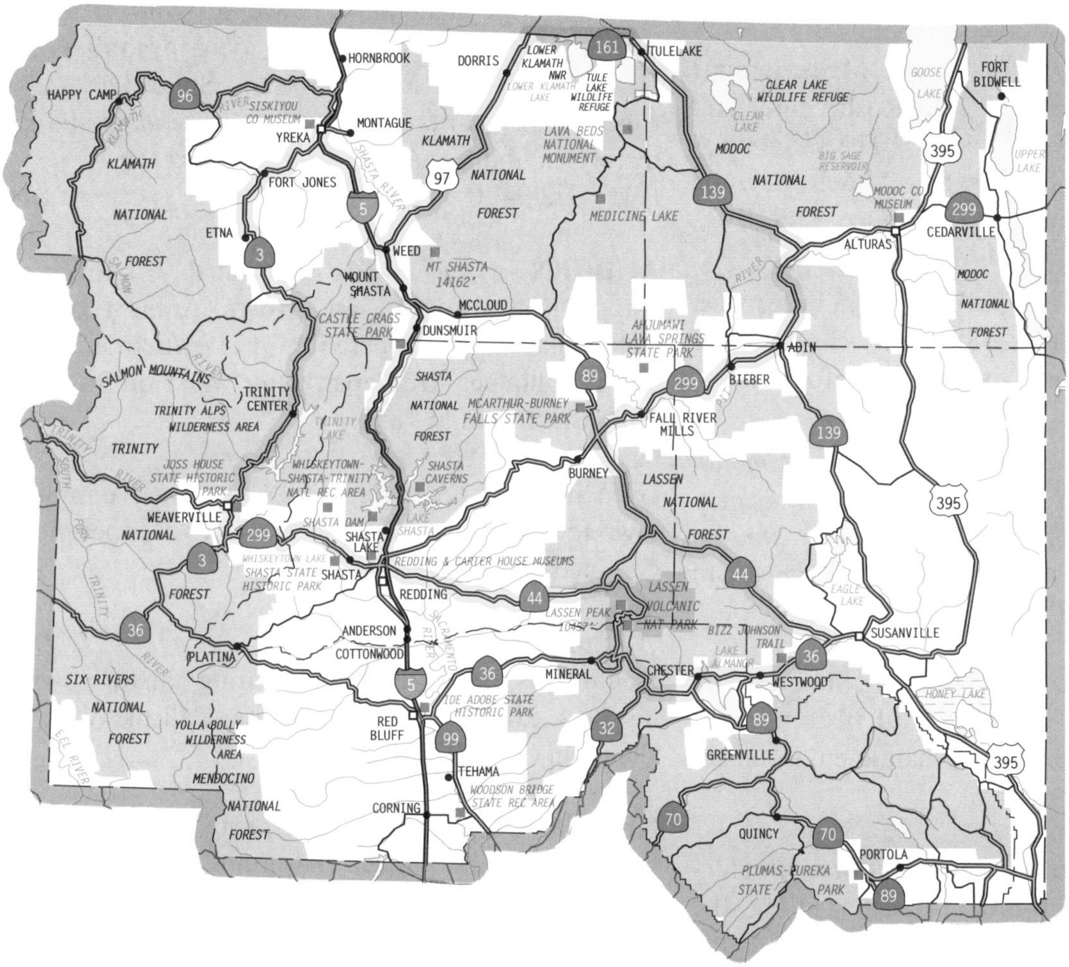

Towering Mountains, Caves and Crags

This approximately 560-mile round trip provides a lovely drive through countryside dotted with historical sites and natural wonders. If you take time to stop and visit some of each, allow at least two extra days.

The **Shasta-Cascade** is big country - over 28,000 square miles with snow capped mountains, volcanoes, glaciers, waterfalls, white water rivers, dense forests, alpine lakes, and rugged canyons. It is home to seven national forests, one national park, one national monument, six state parks, the Trinity Alps, and the California Cascade Range.

Driving Tour Points of Interest

LASSEN VOLCANIC NATIONAL PARK - *(Page 19, E2)* Located 45 minutes east of Redding and Red Bluff. The park encompasses a remarkable wilderness area scarred by massive volcanic eruptions which occurred a mere 75 years ago. The park's scenic 35-mile main road winds through conifer forests, among clear lakes and hydrothermal areas of boiling mud pots and steaming sulphur vents. The park features over 150 miles of hiking trails, camping, fishing and boating facilities, plus special naturalist activities throughout the summer months. (916) 595-4444

REDDING - *(Page 18, C2)* Gateway city to Northern California and vital crossroads for travelers and commerce.

Shasta-Cascade Wonderland Association - 1250 Parkview Ave., *(Page 122, C3)* Provides extensive maps, brochures and detailed information of the area. (800) 474-2782

SHASTA STATE HISTORIC PARK - *(Page 18, B2)* Three miles west of Redding. This town of restored buildings depicts the Gold Rush days when the area was a thriving center for wagon trains. (916) 243-8194

WHISKEYTOWN LAKE - *(Page 18, A2)* A man-made Alpine lake popular with water sports enthusiasts. Camping is available.

WEAVERVILLE - *(Page 17, D1)* A Chamber of Commerce walking-tour map of this Gold Rush town highlights 116 historic points of interest. Especially noteworthy are the **Joss House** and **Jackson Memorial Museum**. (916) 623-6101

LAKE SHASTA CAVERNS - *(Page 18, C1)* A fascinating and educational two-hour excursion for all ages. The tour includes a 15-minute catamaran cruise across Lake Shasta, a shuttle bus ride up the mountain side and a tour through the natural caverns. Guides tell the history, folklore, and geological development of the area. 1-800-795-CAVE

MOUNT SHASTA CITY - *(Page 12, C2)* An Alpine-like town nestled at the foot of the "Friendly Giant," Mount Shasta.

Mount Shasta/Sisson Museum - (916) 926-5508; Located on the grounds of California's oldest fish hatchery (est. 1888). Antiques and photographs document the history of the hatchery and the city of Mt. Shasta. Self-guided tours only of the hatchery grounds (Feeding the fish is encouraged). (916) 926-2215

McARTHUR-BURNEY FALLS MEMORIAL STATE PARK - *(Page 13, C4)* One hour north of Lassen Volcanic National Park. The main attractions are the spectacular **Burney Falls** that cascade over a 129-foot cliff into an emerald pool. A one-mile, self-guided nature trail highlights numerous geological formations, local fauna and lush flora. The 875-acre park is open year round and offers 118 family campsites, six miles of hiking trails, fishing and boat launch facilities onto adjoining Lake Britton. (916) 335-2777

From Highway 89, follow the roadway signs for Medicine Lake. At the junction of Medicine Lake Highway (Page 5, D5), *the road turns north to the Lava Beds National Monument. This stretch of remote highway slices through thick forests and ancient lava flows. The drive from Highway 89 at Bartle to the Visitors Center at Lava Beds takes about 1-1/2 hours. The nearest food and gas are at Canby or Tulelake.*

LAVA BEDS NATIONAL MONUMENT - *(Page 5, D4)* A surreal area of lava flows, mud holes and caves. The Visitors Center at the south entrance is open during the summer months and provides maps and information highlighting the park's fascinating historical and geological points of interest. Just outside the north entrance is the Petroglyph Section (intriguing Rock Art), etched into the cliffs over 2,000 years ago. (916) 667-2282

TULE LAKE AND LOWER KLAMATH WILDLIFE REFUGES - *(Page 5, D3 and C3)* Vast lake areas which sustain massive concentrations of waterfowl. Several turnouts along Highway 161 enable bird watchers to observe this unique nature reserve.

Highway 97 to Weed cuts through wide open spaces and tranquil farmlands. There are few towns, with limited services, along this 56-mile stretch.

Other Points of Interest:

Highway 96 follows 150 miles of the wild and scenic Klamath River. The area is a recreational paradise where salmon and steelhead fishing, rafting, canoeing, kayaking, and wilderness horse packing challenge rugged sportsmen from around the world.

HAPPY CAMP - *(Page 2, E4)* A small, friendly rural mountain community with full services. The Ranger Station provides maps and camping information. (916) 493-2900

San Francisco Bay Area Sampler... "The Scenic City" Natural Wonders and Family Fun

This three-day tour begins with a full day exploring the highlights of San Francisco along the city's Scenic 49 Mile Drive. Circle the Bay on day two, visiting the East and North Bay regions. The route includes the cities of Oakland, Berkeley and Vallejo as well as Marin County's seaside villages and the historic redwood forest, Muir Woods. Conclude the day with an evening drive across the Golden Gate Bridge into San Francisco. Head south on day three along I-280. Visit the Silicon Valley cities of San Jose and Santa Clara filled with high-tech and high adventure. Family attractions abound in the natural wonders of the California coastline including the beachside communities of Santa Cruz and Half Moon Bay.

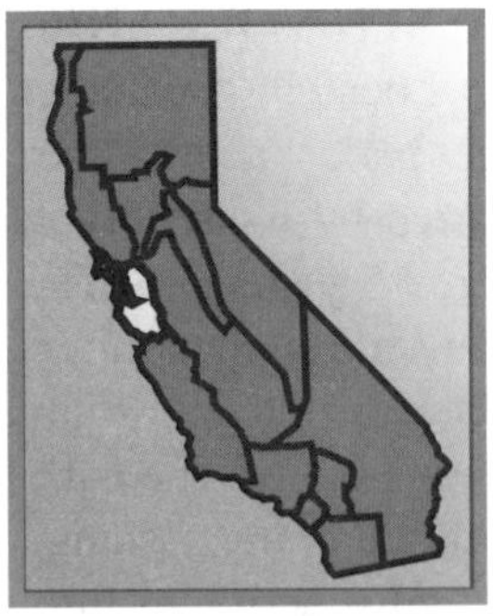

1 Inch to 17 Miles

Scale

0 Miles 17

With a population of more than 6 million, the **San Francisco Bay Area** is the nation's fourth largest metropolitan area. It is a bounty of beaches, historical sites and parks - all in one of the most exquisite natural settings on earth.

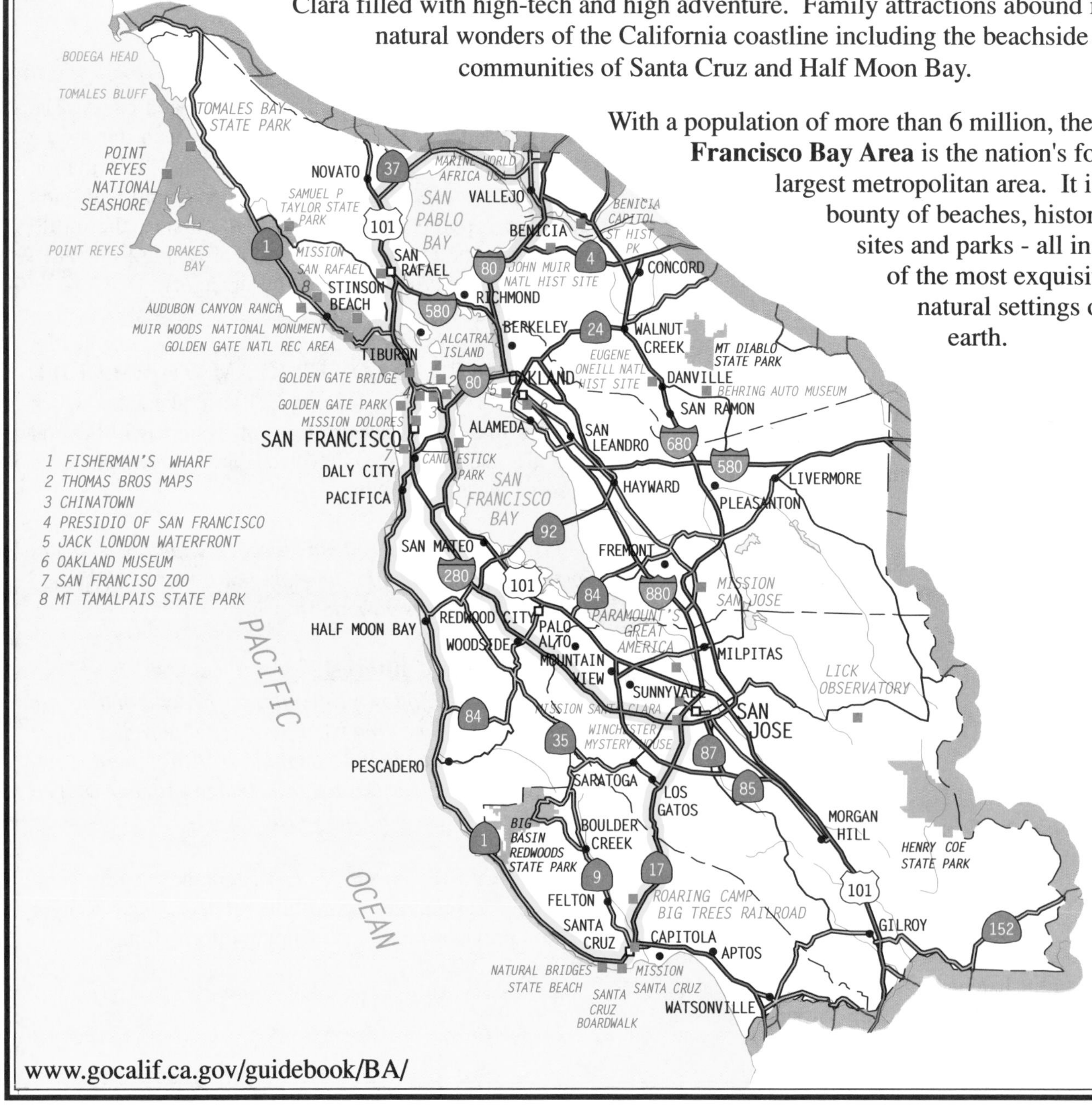

www.gocalif.ca.gov/guidebook/BA/

Driving Tour Points of Interest:

SANTA CRUZ - *(Page 169, E4)* Enjoy a natural setting between ocean and forest with close proximity to the big cities. The **Boardwalk,** (408) 423-5590, is California's only operating seaside amusement park.
Visitors Center: (408) 425-1234

BIG BASIN REDWOODS STATE PARK - *(Page 53, E1)* Towering redwoods, some over 330 feet tall and 18 feet in diameter, create a lush canopy over the road; rich green mosses thrive on the stone bridges, wooden fences, and tree trunks. Unfortunately, the road is not suitable for trailers or large RVs. (408) 338-8860

SAN JOSE - *(Page 46, B4)* Located in a region known equally for fine wines and high-technology industries.

Winchester Mystery House - *(Page 151, B5)* Created by the heiress of the Winchester Rifle fortune. The 160-room mansion and six acres of gardens were designed according to the bizarre superstitious obsessions of their eccentric owner. (408) 247-2101

Rosicrucian Park - *(Page 151, D4)* Contains elaborate fountains, tiled walkways, gardens and statues in the style of ancient Egypt. The **Rosicrucian Museum** features the largest collection of ancient Egyptian relics in the western U.S. (408) 947-3636

MISSION SAN FRANCISCO DE ASIS (Mission Dolores) - *(Page 142, B4)* Established in 1776 as the sixth in the chain of 21 Franciscan missions. It is the oldest building in San Francisco. (415) 621-8203

GOLDEN GATE PARK - *(Page 141)* Formerly 1,000 acres of sand dunes. This park has been transformed into one of the most beautiful metropolitan parks in the world featuring miles of pleasant drives, green lawns, playing fields, bridle paths, and bicycle routes. There are also lakes and gardens, a stadium, and a golf course.

California Academy of Sciences - (415) 750-7145; **Conservatory of Flowers; Japanese Tea Garden; Strybing Arboretum; M.H. De Young Memorial Museum**.

SAN FRANCISCO ZOO - *(Page L, A5)* Ranks among the top city zoos in the U.S. The collection boasts over 1,000 animals and birds. http://www.sfzoo.com/ (415) 753-7080

SAN FRANCISCO CIVIC CENTER - *(Page 143, B4)* Includes an impressive group of federal, state and city buildings: City Hall, Civic Auditorium, Performing Arts Center, War Memorial, Opera House, Main Public Library and San Francisco Museum of Modern Art.

UNION SQUARE - *(Page 143, C3)* The heart of downtown shopping. This attractive outdoor square is used for many civic events, fashion shows, rallies, and concerts. Around the square and spreading southward are many of San Francisco's fine shops and department stores.

JAPANTOWN - *(Page 143, A3)* Traditional shops, restaurants, a theatre, tea houses, sushi bars, Japanese baths, and a five-tiered, 35-foot Peace Pagoda reflect the spirit of the 12,000 San Francisco residents of Japanese descent.

CHINATOWN - *(Page 143, C2)* A 24-block area of pagoda-style architecture, curio shops, street markets, restaurants , and temples. Home to the largest Chinese community outside the Orient.

During your visit, please stop by **Thomas Bros. Maps and Books**, *550 Jackson Street, (415) 981-7520 (Page 143, D2).*

FISHERMAN'S WHARF - *(Page 143, B1)* The famous waterfront area of seafood restaurants, harbor cruises, excellent shopping, galleries, and entertainment. The refurbished brick buildings of Ghirardelli Square, The Cannery, and Pier 39 are especially popular restaurant and shopping meccas.

LOMBARD STREET - *(Page 143, B2)* Called "The Crookedest Street in the World." The steep, one-way, brick avenue, trimmed in flowers, is open to all vehicles except motorhomes and trailers.

TELEGRAPH HILL - *(Page 143, C2)* Includes **Coit Tower**, a 210-foot monument built in 1934 as a memorial to the city's volunteer firemen. An elevator takes visitors to the top for a panoramic view of San Francisco, the East Bay, the waterfront, the bay bridges, and Alcatraz Island.

FORT MASON CENTER - *(Page 143, A1)* A former Army base converted into a cultural center. This artisan's showplace includes 45 studios, three theatres, and five museums. (415) 979-3010

PALACE OF FINE ARTS - *(Page 142, A1)* Built for the 1915 Panama-Pacific International Exposition. It has been beautifully restored and now houses the **Exploratorium**, a science museum, (415) 561-0362, and the 1,000 seat **Palace of Fine Arts Theatre**. (415) 567-6642

PRESIDIO OF SAN FRANCISCO - *(Page 141, C2)* Former U.S. Sixth Army headquarters. The 1,500 acres of park-like hills and beaches are open to the public. **The Presidio Army Museum** chronicles over 100 years of San Francisco military history. (415) 561-4323

SAUSALITO - *(Page L, B4)* Historic artist's colony. Its picturesque marina is filled with over 350 houseboats, while the hillsides are filled with unusual homes perched precariously above the bay. Sausalito is a popular retreat offering numerous restaurants with spectacular day and evening views of the bay.

MUIR WOODS NATIONAL MONUMENT - *(Page L, A4)* Located two miles off the Panoramic Highway. A network of trails threads the 553 acres of redwood forests. No camping, picnicking or fishing permitted. (415) 388-2595

STINSON BEACH *(Page 45, A1)* A small town and popular park now a part of the Golden Gate National Recreation Area. The sandy beaches and good surf attract over one million visitors each year. (415) 868-0942

Audubon Canyon Ranch - *(Page 38, A5)* Wildlife sanctuary and educational center. Open March through July. (415) 868-9244

MT. TAMALPAIS STATE PARK - *(Page L, A4)* Beautiful area of redwoods laced with roads and trails. The view from "Mt. Tam" encompasses the Pacific Ocean and Farallon Islands, San Francisco Bay, and on a clear day, as far as the Great Central Valley. Hiking and camping are available, and a natural amphitheater seats 3,750 people.

SAN RAFAEL - *(Page L, B3)* Visit the **Mission San Rafael Archangel**, a replica built in 1949 on the approximate site of the original 1817 mission.
(415) 456-3016

Marin County Civic Center - Designed by Frank Lloyd Wright. The 140-acre complex is a combination of futuristic structures and landscapes.
(415) 499-7407

BERKELEY - *(Page L, C4)* Notoriously described as "radical," "revolutionary" and "avant garde." It is regarded as one of the nation's leading educational centers with the **University of California** *(Page 156, B2)* and its academic populace having shaped the city through the decades. The top of the 307-foot Campanile affords a view of the campus, the East Bay area and San Francisco. Campus information: (510) 642-5215

OAKLAND - *(Page L, D4)* Named for the extensive groves of live oak trees that once flourished here. The city has grown into a major urban center with one of the largest commercial ports in the world. It is also a residential district for thousands of bay area commuters. Call the Visitors Center at (510) 839-9000.

Lake Merritt - *(Page 158, B3)* A 155-acre body of salt water in the center of the city surrounded by Lakeside Park. It is a favorite recreation spot with a garden center, Children's Fairyland, Gamebird Refuge, Natural Science Center, sailboats for rent, and 122 acres of green lawns. At night, the entire lake is adorned with a string of white lights called the "necklace of lights" which gives an enchanting radiance to the park.

Oakland Museum - *(Page 158, A3)* Covering four square blocks, this three-tiered complex is really three different museums in one: history, natural science and art, with exhibits as intriguing as the building's architecture. (510) 238-3401

Jack London Square - *(Page 157, E4)* A 10-block area of waterfront considered the historical center of Oakland. Fine restaurants and shops line the wharf where the famous adventure writer spent much of his time.

Paramount Theatre - *(Page 158, A2)* A sublime example of Art Deco form. The 3,000-seat theatre, built in 1931, has been restored and is an active facility. Tours are available by calling (510) 465-6400.

MARINE WORLD AFRICA USA - *(Page 134, E1)* A unique combination of wildlife park and oceanarium, 160-acre Marine World Africa USA is home to more than 100 species of animals. Other attractions include the largest display of robotic dinosaurs in the U.S., water-ski and boat shows, a playground, restaurants, snack bars, and picnic areas. (707) 643-6722 or (707) 644-4000
www.freerun.com/napavalley/outdoor/marinewo/marinewo.html

THE CENTRAL VALLEY

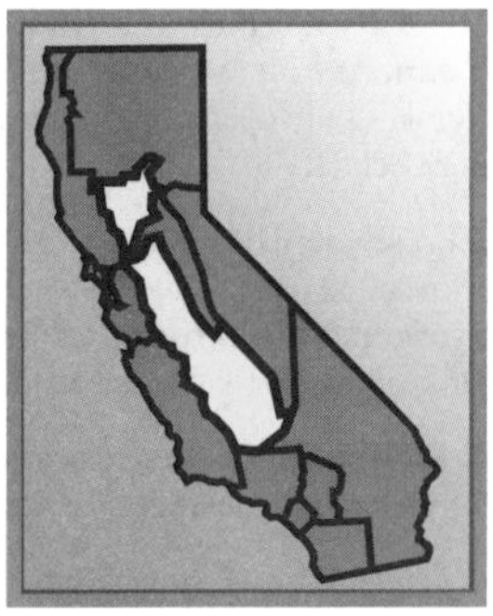

1 Inch to 47 Miles

Scale

0 Miles 47

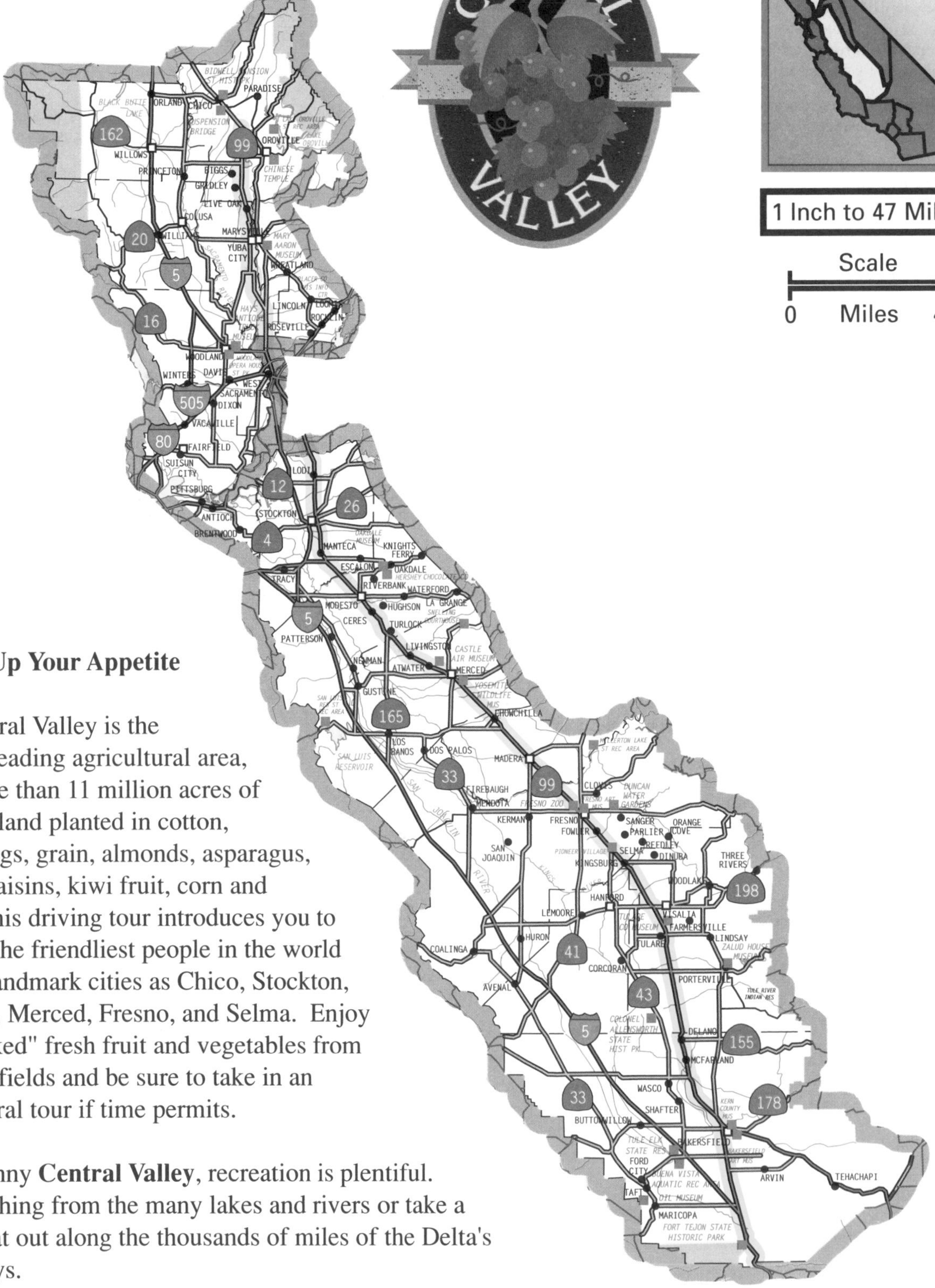

Pack Up Your Appetite

The Central Valley is the nation's leading agricultural area, with more than 11 million acres of irrigated land planted in cotton, grapes, figs, grain, almonds, asparagus, carrots, raisins, kiwi fruit, corn and more. This driving tour introduces you to some of the friendliest people in the world in such landmark cities as Chico, Stockton, Modesto, Merced, Fresno, and Selma. Enjoy "just picked" fresh fruit and vegetables from roadside fields and be sure to take in an agricultural tour if time permits.

In the sunny **Central Valley**, recreation is plentiful. Enjoy fishing from the many lakes and rivers or take a houseboat out along the thousands of miles of the Delta's waterways.

www.gocalif.ca.gov/guidebook/CV/

Driving Tour Points of Interest

BAKERSFIELD

Kern County Museum - *(Page 166, C2)* The museum's 16-acre outdoor complex is the beginning of a walk through history. With over 60 structures, the museum displays a wide variety of historic buildings depicting scenes from the past. Diverse artifacts relating to Kern County life between the 1860s and 1930s are displayed in genuine and recreated residences, businesses, and civic buildings. (805) 861-2132

VISALIA

Tulare County Museum - *(Page 68, B2)* Beautifully landscaped and home to the remainder of a great oak forest that once existed in the area, **Mooney Grove Museum** is the largest and most complete museum in the county with many historical items. The original "End of the Trail" Statue was on display in the park until 1968, when it was moved to the Cowboy Hall of Fame and replaced by a bronze replica. (209) 733-6616

Chinese Cultural Center - *(Page 68, B1)* Guarding the entrance to the center are two 12-ton marble TZU-SHIH lions which are used in China to act as guards for important buildings. Inside, the center features ongoing arts and crafts exhibits as well as unique artifacts of China and its culture. To visit the Chinese Center is to experience over 12,000 years of Chinese culture. Free, but call ahead for reservations. (209) 625-4545

FRESNO

Wild Water Adventures - *(Page 57, D3)* A family water amusement park with more than 52 acres of grass, trees and "Wet and Wild" water fun, Wild Water Adventures has more than 17 rides and attractions including 15,000 gallons of splashin' kiddie areas and the West's largest wave pool. Open daily mid-June through Labor Day. Limited days and hours in May and September. (209) 297-5640

Chaffee Zoological Gardens - *(Page 165, B2)* Located in Roeding Park, the zoological and botanical gardens have more than 600 specimens of mammals, birds, and reptiles. Highlights include the Tropical Rainforest, the Asian Elephant Compound, and the world's first computerized Reptile House. Open every day of the year from 10:00 a.m. (209) 498-2671

Fresno Art Museum - *(Page 165, E1)* The Fresno Art Museum is the area's only modern-art museum. Featuring up to 22 separate exhibitions per year, the museum collects and exhibits American sculpture, Californian art, Mexican art, and works on paper. An extensive collection of Ansel Adams photographs, Robert Cremean sculpture, French post-Impressionist graphics, and pre-Columbian Mexican sculpture makes these exhibits unique in the West. (209) 485-4810

Shaver and Huntington Lakes - *(Page 58, B1)* This beautiful resort area has it all. Camping, fishing, sailing/boating, four-wheeling, and horse pack trips in the summer, downhill and cross-country skiing, and snowmobiling in the winter. Services include lodging and condominium rentals, restaurants, and shopping. The Shaver Lake Chamber of Commerce also sponsors several special events throughout the year. (209) 841-3350

MERCED

Castle Air Museum - *(Page 48, B4)* This museum is a history lesson that the whole family can share. It alone houses one of the country's finest collections of World War II aircraft along with vintage planes restored to their original appearance. Displays of military equipment, uniforms, medals, and other memorabilia can be viewed at an indoor museum. (209) 723-2178

Courthouse Museum - *(Page 170, D3)* This three-story courthouse, which was built in 1875, was designed by Albert A. Bennett, one of the architects of the State Capitol. In the architectural style of Italianate, it is situated in the center of beautiful Courthouse Park. The museum houses 8,500 square feet of exhibits which depict the history of early settlers to the Great Central Valley. (209) 723-2401

Lake Yosemite - *(Page 48, C4)* Lake Yosemite County Park is a favorite with sailors, boaters, and windsurfers alike. The lake is used for fishing, boating, swimming, and water-skiing while shaded picnic and sports areas dot the rest of the park. A paved bike path leads from the park back into Merced, connecting into the twelve miles of class one, grade-separated bike trails. In all, 29 tree-shaded parks enhance the city. (209) 384-3333

MODESTO

Hershey's Chocolate Company & Visitors Center - *(Page 47, E1)* Visitors can watch chocolate being made during a free factory tour of the Hershey plant in Oakdale. Tours are offered Monday - Friday, 8:30 a.m. to 3:00 p.m. (209) 848-8126

McHenry Mansion and Museum - *(Page 162, B3)* Catch a glimpse of turn-of-the-century living at both the McHenry Mansion and McHenry Museum in Modesto. The mansion is a fully-restored and furnished Victorian house built in 1883, offering free tours Tuesdays - Thursdays and Sundays, 1:00 p.m. to 4:00 p.m., (209) 577-5344. The museum is open Tuesdays-Sundays, 12:00 p.m. to 4:00 p.m. (209) 577-5366

STOCKTON - *(Page 40, B5)* Surrounded by 1,000 miles of winding California Delta waterways, Stockton is the state's largest inland seaport, providing large ocean-going vessels with access from the San Francisco Bay to the Port of Stockton. The Delta provides outdoor and water recreation such as houseboating, swimming, and water skiing, fishing, waterfowl hunting, and bird watching. (209) 547-2770

Children's Museum of Stockton - *(Page 160, C4)* A center of learning and discovery for children, providing interactive exhibits in a warm, inviting environment. Exhibits encourage creative play and expression among children and provide insight into people and cultures. (209) 465- 4386

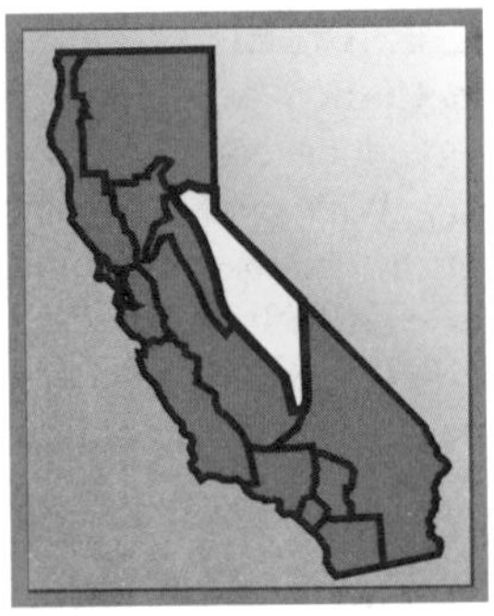

1 Inch to 39 Miles

Scale

0 Miles 39

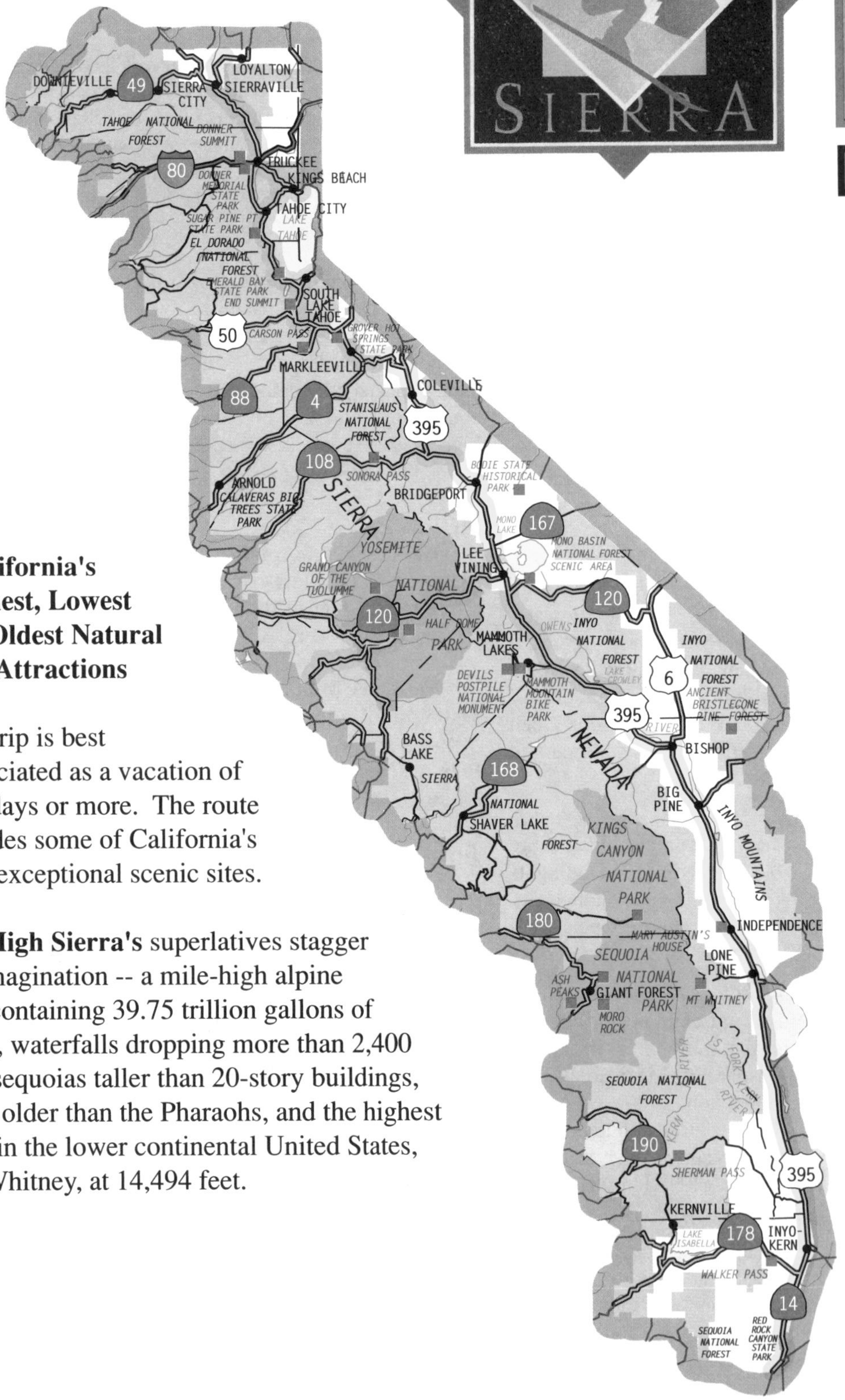

California's Highest, Lowest and Oldest Natural Attractions

This trip is best appreciated as a vacation of four days or more. The route includes some of California's most exceptional scenic sites.

The **High Sierra's** superlatives stagger the imagination -- a mile-high alpine lake containing 39.75 trillion gallons of water, waterfalls dropping more than 2,400 feet, sequoias taller than 20-story buildings, pines older than the Pharaohs, and the highest peak in the lower continental United States, Mt. Whitney, at 14,494 feet.

www.gocalif.ca.gov/guidebook/HS/

Driving Tour Points of Interest:

KINGS CANYON / SEQUOIA NATIONAL PARK - Perhaps one of the most beautiful and peaceful places on earth. The headquarters for both parks, Ash Mountain, is located seven miles north of Three Rivers on Highway 198 *(Page 58, E5)*. The Visitors Center provides information, maps, and brochures of the parks. (209) 565-3341

Along the 46-mile Generals Highway which links the two parks, there are numerous *points of interest*. The main attractions, of course, are the incredible sequoias, the largest living things on earth. They have survived the last ice age and are found only along the western slope of the Sierra Nevada. Unbelievably, these 2,000 year old giants were in danger of being destroyed by greedy loggers. Evidence of this careless harvest is on display at Big Stump Basin and should be a reminder to us of our responsibility to protect these and all natural wonders.

At **Moro Rock** *(Page 59, A4)* climbers can get a 100-mile panorama of surrounding mountains and valleys. At **Giant Forest** *(Page 59, A4);* the 2,500 year old General Sherman Tree stands 272 feet high, the largest living thing on earth. The Congress Trail is a two-mile hike through several stands of sequoias; park rangers lead groups of visitors and explain the history of the trees. **Grant Grove** is the location of four or five of the largest sequoias in the world.

There are several full-service campgrounds within the two parks. Hiking and fishing are popular and horses may be rented for trips into the back country. The parks are open all year, although some roads are closed in the winter.

WESTERN SLOPE - The western portion of the Southern Sierra is dominated by Kings Canyon and Sequoia National Parks, twin treasures joined end to end. The main entrance for both parks, Ash Mountain, can be reached by the main road, Highway 180, east from Fresno *(Page 58, D3)*; but if time allows, we recommend taking the zigzag route that threads through the Sequoia National Forest from Lake Isabella. Forests of tall trees, craggy granite rocks, waterfalls, and numerous campgrounds line the way. The county-maintained road is closed during the winter. Call CALTRANS for road conditions. (916) 445-1534

EASTERN SLOPE - Highway 395 is a straight course due north and south through the Owens Valley, flanked by dramatic granite walls of the Sierra Nevada to the west and Inyo-White mountains and Mojave Desert to the east. Joshua trees and volcanic rock pepper the roadside landscape.

Visitors Center - Located at the Junction of Highway 395 and Highway 136. This excellent center provides extensive information, maps, exhibits, and information concerning the Eastern Sierra & High Desert. Books and gift items are also for sale. (619) 876-6222

LONE PINE - *(Page 60, A4)* Gateway to both Death Valley and Mt. Whitney. This is a great place to stock up on provisions before tackling either of these formidable giants.

Alabama Hills - A rocky area northwest of town that has been used in countless movie westerns.

Whitney Portal - *(Page 59, E4)* 13 miles west of Lone Pine, it is the trail head for hikers attempting to ascend Mt. Whitney.

Mt. Whitney Ranger District: (619) 876-6200.

BISHOP - *(Page 51, D4)* Business and recreational center of Owens Valley. Visitors Information: (619) 873-8405.

Laws Railroad Museum - splendid restoration of the once-active town of Laws. In addition to a locomotive and cars, the 11-acre area has several buildings which display antique collections of everything from bottles to baggage. (619) 873-5950

MAMMOTH LAKES - *(Page 50, D2)* One of California's year-round getaways. While snow skiing is the wintertime focus, the area offers such summertime activities as hiking, camping, pack trips, water sports and excellent trout fishing. Mammoth Lakes Visitors Bureau: (800) 367-6572.

DEVIL'S POSTPILE NATIONAL MONUMENT - *(Page 50, C2)* The monument consists of a sheer wall of symmetrical basaltic columns more than 60 feet high. The unusual formation was created eons ago by the crystallization of volcanic matter. A trail leads to the top where the surface resembles mosaic tiles. (619) 934-2289

YOSEMITE NATIONAL PARK - *(Page 49)* The grandeur cannot be adequately captured in the words of John Muir or the photographs of Ansel Adams. Yosemite must be experienced firsthand. The park covers nearly 1,200 square miles of glacier-carved valleys, massive cliffs and Alpine wilderness. It is one of the nation's most popular attractions with nearly 3 million visitors each year. Summer (June-Sept.) is the busiest time. Check with park service for seasonal road closures and trail information as well as accommodations, campsite reservations and activities. Park headquarters *(Page 63, D1)* in Yosemite Valley provides guides, maps and information.

MONO LAKE - **Tufa State Reserve** *(Page 43, D5)* A surrealistic landscape of limestone formations rise from the lake. The area has scant vegetation and the water is three times as salty as the ocean. The salt water sustains a unique ecosystem of algae, brine shrimp and brine flies which in turn attract 80 species of waterfowl. Some of the tufa has been exposed by the declining water level and walking trails allow a close-up view.

BODIE STATE HISTORIC PARK - *(Page 43, C3)* A "genuine" gold-mining ghost town. What remains of the original town has been left to natural decay and presents an authentic glimpse of the once booming Old West Town. The road to Bodie is partially unpaved, so call for road conditions. (619) 647-7445

SOUTH LAKE TAHOE - *(Page 36, A3)* The more populated end of the lake with luxury hotels, restaurants, and shops. The Nevada side allows gambling casinos.

Vikingsholm - *(Page 35, E3)* A private residence built in 1929, in classic Scandinavian design. A steep, one-mile hike is necessary to tour this lovely, secluded estate.

LAKE TAHOE - *(Page 35 & 36)* "The Lake of the Sky." This is a premier resort area offering a full spectrum of outdoor activities for the entire family. The 72 miles of shoreline provide access to the incredibly clear blue lake; the surrounding mountains are dotted with everything from campsites to casinos. Lake Tahoe's Visitor Authority: (916) 544-5050.

TAHOE CITY - *(Page 35, E2)* The north shore of Lake Tahoe includes many popular ski resorts. Pine forests and mountain lodges dominate, making it a quiet, more rustic experience.

DOWNIEVILLE - *(Page 26, D4)* Once a boom town of 5,000 miners. Today, a self-guided walking tour highlights 23 historic sites and buildings. The museum and courthouse exhibits are especially interesting. Call for hours: (916) 289-3261.

Other Points of Interest:

ANCIENT BRISTLECONE PINE FOREST - *(Page 52, A3)* A 28,000 acre area of the White Mountains that contains the oldest living things on earth. These gnarled pine trees are over 4,000 years old. (619) 873-2500

The view southwest provides a spectacular panorama of the Sierra Nevada and Mount Whitney.

CALAVERAS BIG TREES STATE PARK - *(Page 41, D3)* Two groves of giant redwoods and pines. These sequoias were the first of their kind to receive world-wide attention. Scientists and journalists flocked to the forests in the 1850s to examine and report on these natural phenomena. (209) 795-2334

The Enchanting Middle Kingdom and a Castle on the Hill

CENTRAL COAST

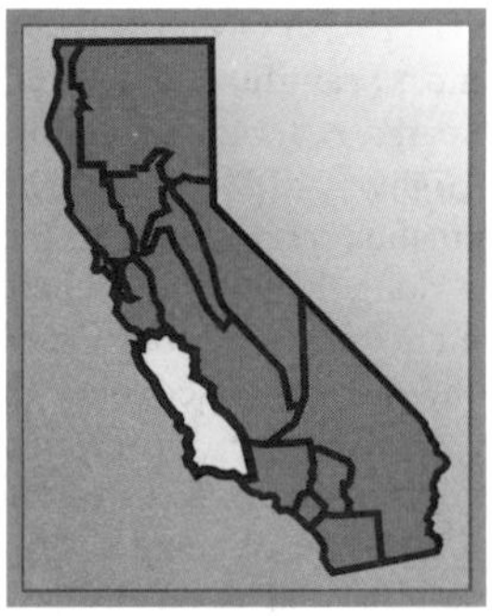

1 Inch to 29 Miles

Scale

0 Miles 29

Plan a minimum of three to five days to fully enjoy all the attractions and points of interest that this 388 mile round trip offers. From Ventura Harbor to the red tile roofs of Santa Barbara, to walnut groves, to a Danish Hamlet and the Lompoc Flower Fields, through the "Barbecue Capital of the World" to the home of the Pismo Clam, from the state's burgeoning new wine regions to Hearst's famous Castle to Monterey's Aquarium by-the-bay and world class golf, you'll be amazed at the stunning sites of this tour.

The **Central Coast**, with its austere cypress trees, fog-shrouded cliffs, and crashing surf immortalized in photographs by Ansel Adams and Edward Weston, continues to draw vacationers year after year.

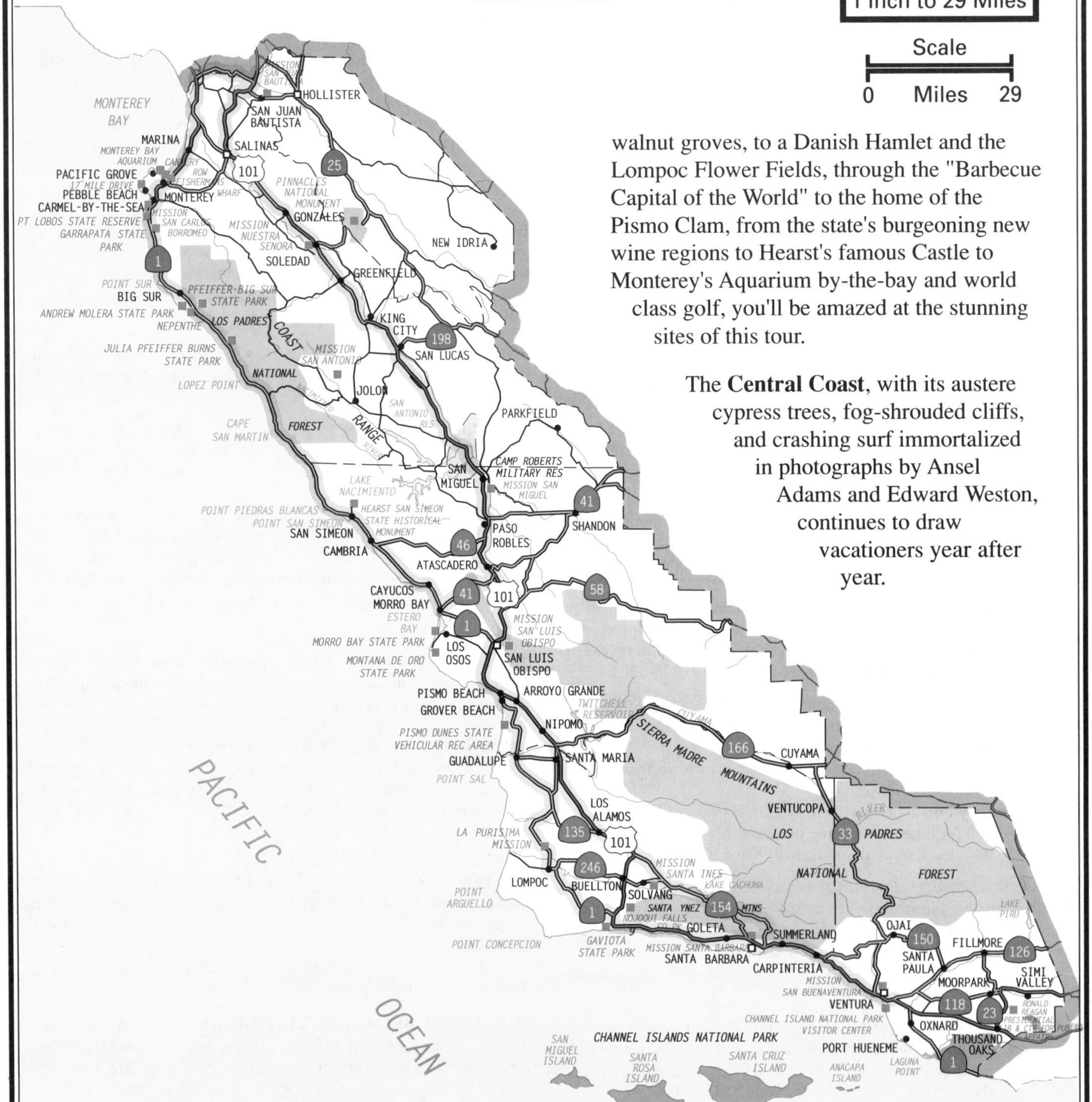

www.gocalif.ca.gov/guidebook/CC/

Driving Tour Points of Interest

SANTA BARBARA - *(Page 87, C4)* A charming city of adobe buildings, red tile roofs and palm trees. Among the fine galleries, restaurants and shops in the downtown area, there are many historical plaques and markers identifying early buildings *(Page 174)* The Visitors Center, 1 Santa Barbara Street, (805) 965-3021, provides copies of a Red Tile Walking Tour which will guide you to over a dozen points of interest in a 12-block area.

CACHUMA LAKE RECREATION AREA - *(Page 87, A3)* A large, full-service campground. In addition to 600 campsites, there are hiking trails, a boating and fishing marina, horseback riding, bicycle rentals, a general store, a Weekend Fireside Theatre, and special 2-hour cruises on the lake to view migrating eagles. (805) 688-4568

SOLVANG - *(Page 86, D3)* A Danish village established in 1911 with old-country architecture, windmills, cobblestone sidewalks, and good-luck storks. This enchanting town celebrates its Hans Christian Andersen heritage with authentic shops, bakeries, and many fine restaurants. Solvang Information Center: (805) 688-6144.

Old Mission Santa Ines - located a short distance from the heart of downtown Solvang. Established in 1804, it is the 19th Franciscan mission and one of the best preserved.

NOJOQUI FALLS COUNTY PARK - *(Page 86, E3)* A 164-foot waterfall, seven miles south of Solvang. This unique local "natural wonder" is a popular picnic and hiking spot.

LOMPOC - *(Page 86, B3)* Lompoc Valley is known as the "Flower Seed Capital of the World." Experts agree that 50-75% of all flower seeds in the world come from this tiny area. A map outlining a 19-mile self-guided tour called the "Valley Flower Drive" is available from the Lompoc Chamber of Commerce. (805) 736-4567

La Purisima Mission - *(Page 86, C2)* Founded in 1787, it was the 11th Franciscan mission and well known as the most fully restored, located in the most original setting. It has nine buildings with 900 acres of park and 12 miles of foot trails. (805) 733-3713

PISMO BEACH - *(Page 76, B4)* Bordered by groves of tall eucalyptus trees which were planted at the turn of the century and today are a haven for migrating Monarch butterflies that travel from as far away as Canada each Fall to seek protection until Spring. The sand dunes are the most extensive coastal dunes remaining in California. **Pismo** is a Chumash Indian word for "blobs of tar," known today as Pismo clams.

Pismo Dunes State Vehicular Recreation Area - Provides access to 12 miles of beach where you may drive your car. Camping, hiking, surf fishing, and clam digging are permitted on the dunes. (805) 473-7220

SAN LUIS OBISPO - *(Page 76, B3)* The County Seat and bustling town of 42,050 residents. For county-wide visitors information, call (805) 541-8000.

Mission San Luis Obispo de Tolosa - *(Page 172, C3)* Established in 1772, it is named for a 13th century French saint. The mission is fifth in the chain of 21 missions and still serves as a parish church. (805) 543-6850 or (805) 781-8220

MORRO BAY - *(Page 75, E3)* The huge dome-shaped rock for which Morro Bay is named, is actually a centuries-old, 476-foot volcanic dome. The Chamber of Commerce, (805) 772-4467, provides a map of the city and other helpful information. Walk along the Embarcadero to watch the fishermen at work, or browse through the interesting shops.

CAMBRIA - *(Page 75, C2)* This quiet village, tucked away among the pines, was a former lumbering, shipping, mining, and whaling station. Today, the restored town is a popular artists colony, filled with unique galleries, antique stores, and gift shops. (805) 927-3624

HEARST SAN SIMEON STATE HISTORICAL MONUMENT - *(Page 75, B1)* Popularly known as the "Hearst Castle." The gargantuan estate of the late William Randolph Hearst with its lavish architecture, furnishings, and landscaping was donated to the state and is open to the public. Tours are conducted and reservations are necessary. (800) 444-4445

PFEIFFER BIG SUR STATE PARK - *(Page 64, B2)* Pine trees, chaparral and redwoods create a peaceful refuge. Though the park is not large, 807 acres, it provides access to the Los Padres National Forest and the Ventana Wilderness. Combined, there are over 300,000 acres for hiking, camping, and fishing along Big Sur River. (408) 667-2315

Nepenthe - means "no sorrow." This fine restaurant was designed by a student of Frank Lloyd Wright. Redwood and adobe were used so that the building became "one with the landscape and the earth it stands on." Located on the ocean side of the highway, three miles south of Big Sur State Park.

POINT LOBOS - *(Page 54, A5)* One of the most strikingly beautiful areas of California coastline. This state reserve takes special care to preserve the unspoiled shoreline and natural flora. The area is strictly for day use and the number of visitors is limited.

CARMEL BY THE SEA - *(Page 54, A5)* The village flavor of Carmel reflects the creativeness and individuality of its many artists and writers. Hilly streets, whimsical architecture, and natural landscaping combine to create a storybook aura.

Mission San Carlos Borromeo - *(Page 168, B4)* Founded in 1770 as the 2nd in the eventual chain of 21 missions. Father Serra, the "Father of the Missions," has his final resting place here. It is a fine example of the typical mission architecture. (408) 624-3600

17-Mile Drive - *(Page 53)* Beginning at the north end of Carmel, it winds through scenic, wooded areas of the Del Monte Forest and fabulous shoreline, past the famous **Pebble Beach Golf Course** and on to Monterey.

MONTEREY - *(Page 54, A4)* A favorite year-round resort. The Chamber of Commerce, (408) 649-1770, can provide detailed information and walking tour maps. **Cannery Row** and **Fisherman's Wharf** are popular areas for restaurants and shopping. The scenic peninsula along Ocean View Boulevard to the Pt. Pinos Lighthouse is lined with Victorian homes, many converted into Bed and Breakfast Inns.

Monterey Bay Aquarium - *(Page 167, E2)* This "hands-on" aquarium is one of the largest in the world with special exhibits and habitats for over 5,000 sea creatures. (408) 648-4888

MISSION SAN JUAN BAUTISTA - *(Page 54, D3)* The 15th Franciscan Mission. It is well preserved and still an active Catholic church. The beautiful plaza where it is located also has several other historic buildings. (408) 389-4485

PINNACLES NATIONAL MONUMENT - *(Page 55, B5)* This area is a geological phenomenon, created from an ancient volcano that erupted along the San Andreas Rift Zone, just east of the park. Hiking, rock climbing, cave exploring, picnicking, and camping are permitted. Since crags and spires create a ridge through the center of the park, there is no road connecting both entrances. (408) 389-4485

SOLEDAD MISSION - *(Page 65, A1)* The Mission Nuestra Senora de la Soledad, "Our Lady of Solitude," was founded in 1791 as the 13th in a chain of 21 California Missions. It has been restored and offers a museum and chapel. (408) 678-2586

www.gocalif.ca.gov/guidebook/IE/

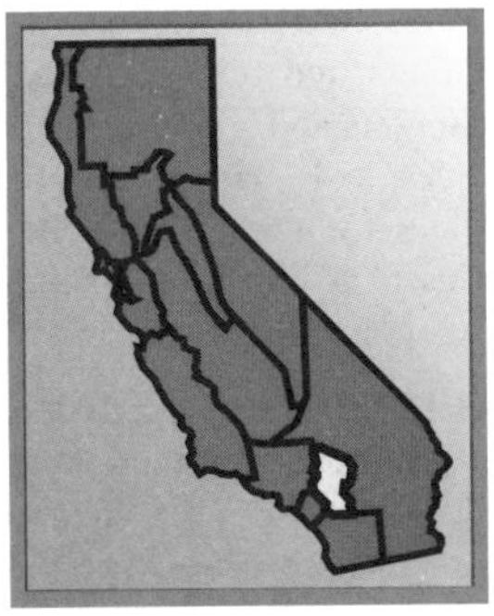

1 Inch to 14 Miles

Scale

0 Miles 14

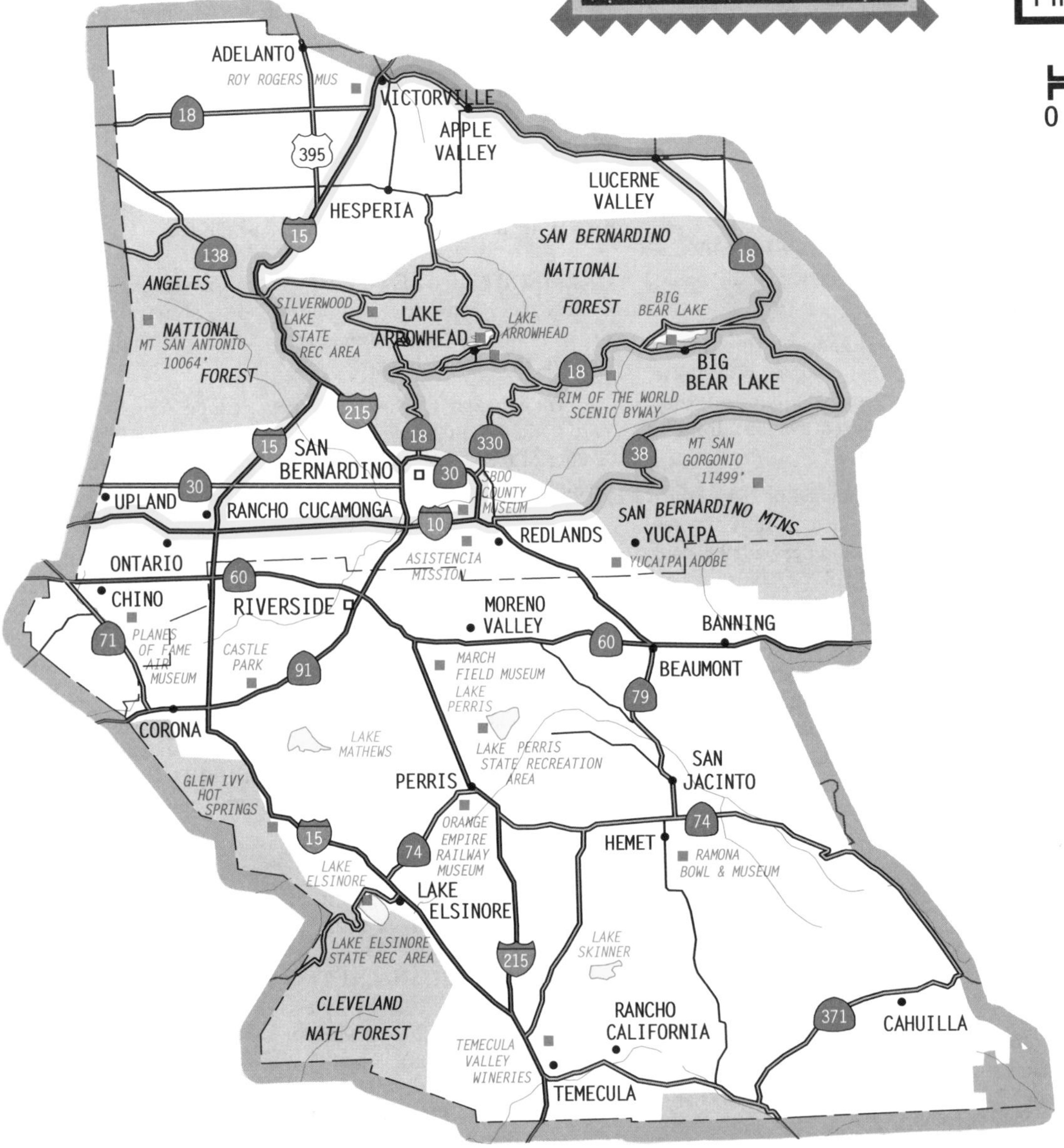

Valleys and Peaks of the Inland Empire

Southern California's Inland Empire is a land of towering mountain peaks, fertile valleys and vibrant communities. The region is rich in history and provides a wealth of recreational opportunities. This tour requires a minimum of two days to fully enjoy the diverse attractions found in the area.

The **Inland Empire** gave rise to the popular conception that in Southern California, one can water-ski and snow-ski in the same day... it's really possible. Lakes for warm weather sports are just a short trip from snow-clad mountains. Wine tasting from local vineyards, picking apples in season or camping in a national forest, or shopping at its best, this region has it all.

Driving Tour Points of Interest:

ROY ROGERS MUSEUM - *(Page 91, B3)* Western film stars Roy Rogers and Dale Evans, family memorabilia including Roy's famous horse, Trigger; walk-through exhibits. Open seven days a week 9 a.m. to 5 p.m., except Thanksgiving and Christmas. (760) 243-4547

SILVERWOOD LAKE STATE RECREATION AREA - *(Page 91, B5)* On Highway 138. The park is a forest of Ponderosa pine, cedar, oak, and fir. The area provides excellent camping and picnicking while the man-made lake offers fishing, swimming, water-skiing and boating. (760) 389-2303

RIM OF THE WORLD HIGHWAY - *(Page 99, C1)* A 40-mile scenic drive along Highway 18 north of San Bernardino. The route threads along the 5,000 to 7,000 foot crest of the San Bernardino Mountains, through several rustic communities and resort areas.

Lake Arrowhead - *(Page 91, C5)* A beautiful man-made lake in an Alpine setting. It is a year-round resort for nature lovers and sports enthusiasts. Restaurants, both quaint and luxurious, lodges, shops, and theatres complete the vacation package.

Big Bear Lake - *(Page 91, E5)* Known for crisp air and spectacular scenery, a wide range of accommodations, restaurants, and activities. In the summer, the seven-mile lake is a playground for water sports; in the winter, the surrounding mountains offer several snow-skiing areas and cozy cabin retreats.

San Bernardino County Museum - *(Page 99, C2)* An especially exciting place for children because of its "hands-on" exhibits of small animals and reptiles. The museum also boasts a collection of 100,000 bird eggs. Located in Redlands. (909) 798-8570

Other Points of Interest:

RIVERSIDE ART MUSEUM - *(Page 205, B2)* Built in 1929 in the Mission Revival tradition, the museum offers art exhibits, a gallery, and a restaurant. Placed on the National Register of Historic places in 1982. Open Mon.-Sat. 10 a.m. to 4 p.m. (909) 684-7111

RIVERSIDE MUNICIPAL MUSEUM - *(Page 205, B2)* Italian Renaissance structure contains a large collection of Native American Indian artifacts and exhibits of the citrus industry's early days and local history. (909) 782-5273

MARCH FIELD MUSEUM - *(Page 99, C3)* Static displays of aircraft, flying memorabilia, and vintage planes. With prior notice, a film titled "The March Field Story" can be viewed. Open Mon.-Fri. 10 a.m. to 4 p.m.; Sat. and Sun. noon to 4 p.m. Closed holidays. (909) 697-6600

LAKE PERRIS STATE RECREATION AREA - *(Page 99, C3)* Boating, camping, fishing, swimming, water slide, wind surfing, jet skiing, and water skiing. Boat rentals available, sailing, bicycling, horseback riding trails, hiking trails, rock climbing, and picnicking. (909) 657-0676

ORANGE EMPIRE RAILWAY MUSEUM - *(Page 99, B4)* Railroad and trolley memorabilia. Walk-through exhibits and picnicking. Trolley rides on weekends. All-day passes. Open Sat., Sun., and on major holidays (except Thanksgiving and Christmas). Grounds open daily. (909) 943-3020

LAKE ELSINORE RECREATION AREA - *(Page 99, B4)* This 2,954-acre area includes 600 developed campsites; fishing, swimming, boating, and food service available. (909) 674-3124

PLANES OF FAME MUSEUM - *(Page U, D3)* The museum houses a unique collection of World War II airplanes and fighter jets, many of them flyable; and exhibits of military aviation memorabilia. Open daily except for Christmas, 9 a.m. to 5 p.m. (909) 597-3722 or 597-3514

SKI AREAS

Bear Mountain - *(Page 92, A5)* P.O. Box 6812, Big Bear Lake 92315, (909) 585-2519. Two quad chairs, five double chairs, three triple chairs, and three pomas. Summit elevation 8,800 ft.

Mountain High - *(Page 90, D5)* P.O. Box 428, Wrightwood 92397, (760) 249-5477. Eleven chairs and one tow. Summit elevation 8,200 ft.

Ski Sunrise - *(Page 90, D4)* P.O. Box 645, Wrightwood 92397, (760) 249-6150. Off Hwy. 2. Summit elevation 7,600 ft.

Snow Summit - *(Page 100, A1)* 880 Summit Blvd., P.O. Box 77, Big Bear Lake 92315, (909) 866-5766. Eleven chairs, 230 skiable acres, three food service lodges, ski school, and rentals. Summit elevation 8,200 ft.

Snow Valley - *(Page 99, D1)* P.O. Box 2337, Running Springs 92382, (909) 867-2751. Located in the San Bernardino Mountains off Highway 18, four miles east of Running Springs. 13 chair lifts and 230 acres of skiing terrain. Just 85 miles from Los Angeles. Group rates available.

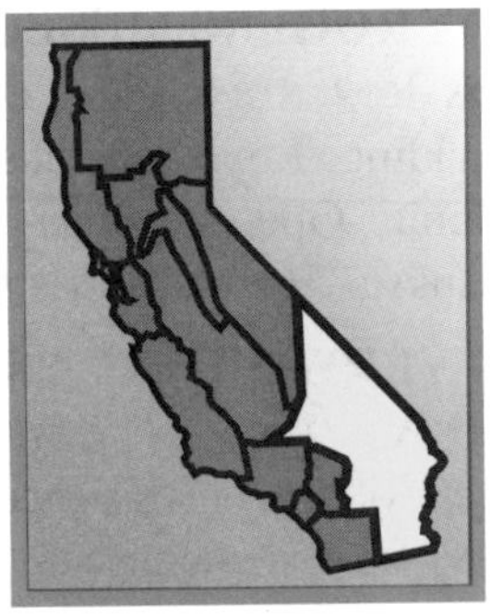

1 Inch to 43 Miles

Scale

0 Miles 43

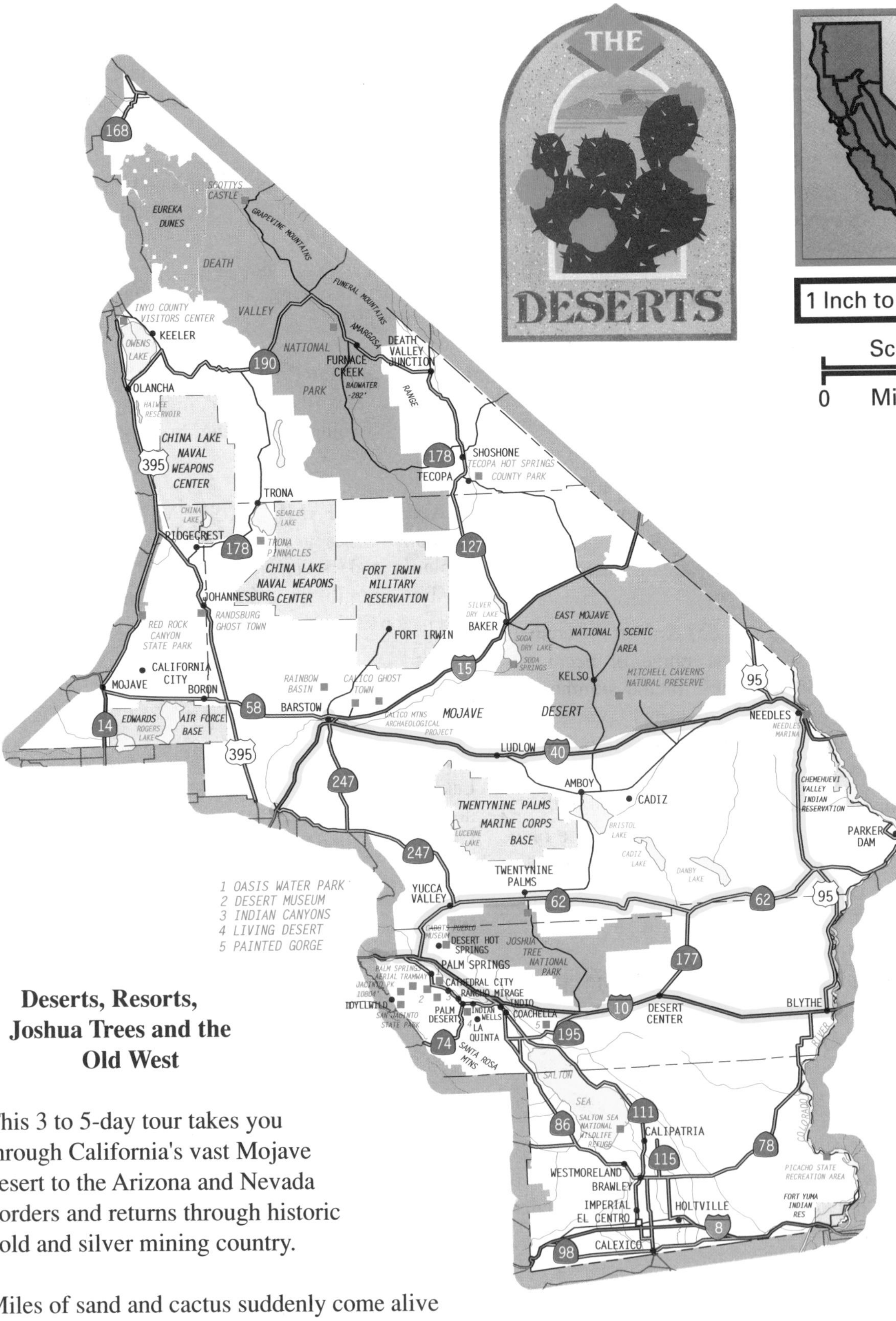

Deserts, Resorts, Joshua Trees and the Old West

This 3 to 5-day tour takes you through California's vast Mojave desert to the Arizona and Nevada borders and returns through historic gold and silver mining country.

Miles of sand and cactus suddenly come alive in an explosion of color in the **Deserts**; the warm desert in bloom is unforgettable. But most of the year the vast expanses of cholla, prickly pear, and Joshua trees create a desolate grandeur.

www.gocalif.ca.gov/guidebook/DE/

Driving Tour Points of Interest:

PALMS-TO-PINES HIGHWAY - The 64-mile scenic drive through the San Bernardino National Forest and San Jacinto Mountains.

Idyllwild - *(Page 100, B4)* Small, mountain community with lots of shops and restaurants. The Idyllwild Visitors Center has a splendid museum and a wealth of information.
(909) 659-3850

INDIO - *(Page 101, A4)* "The Date Capital of the World." 200,000 date palms yield 40 million pounds of many varieties of dates. Stop at Shield's Date Gardens for blackdate ice cream and a 20-minute slide show on the romance of the date.
(619) 347-0996

LIVING DESERT - *(Page 100, E4)* A 1,200-acre park containing the plants and animals of various desert regions. Fascinating exhibits and six miles of trails introduce visitors to desert life beyond the civilized world. Closed in August.
(619) 346-5694

PALM SPRINGS - *(Page 206)* World-class resort with exclusive shops, fine restaurants, and luxury hotels galore. Nicknamed the "Golf Capital of the World," Palm Springs also boasts 8,000 swimming pools and an average of 330 days of sunshine each year. Call the Visitors Bureau for information.
(619) 770-9000

Desert Museum - *(Page 206, A4)* A unique structure which houses an eclectic combination of contemporary art exhibits, regular concerts and dance performances.
(619) 325-7186

Moorten Botanical Garden - *(Page 100, D3)* A 4-acre garden filled with 3,000 varieties of desert plants representing several regions of the world. (619) 327-6555

Aerial Tramway - *(Page 100, C3)* Called the "Eighth Engineering Wonder of the World," it is the longest singlelift passenger tramway in the world. Two 80-passenger trams rise from the desert floor to 8,516 feet in elevation for a breathtaking view of Palm Springs, the Coachella Valley, and the Salton Sea. At the top is a restaurant, gift shop, and picnic area. A six mile hike leads to the top of Mt. San Jacinto (10,840' elev.), where on a clear day the view extends to the mountain ranges of Las Vegas. (619) 325-1391

Mt. San Jacinto State Park - *(Page 100, B3)* Combines granite peaks and sub-Alpine forests of mostly untouched wilderness. Camping and extensive hiking and riding trails are available. (909) 659-2607

Indian Canyons - *(Page 100, C4)* Four canyons, once inhabited by the Agua Caliente Cahuilla Indians. Palm and Andreas Canyons have the most and second-most palm trees in the world, with Murray Canyon listed as fourth. Tahquitz Canyon is noted for its magnificent waterfalls and pools. Each canyon is a lush and tranquil oasis. Excellent for hiking, picnicking, and bird watching.

DESERT HOT SPRINGS - *(Page 100, D2)* Another popular resort, just northeast of Palm Springs, across Highway 10. It is known for natural hot mineral waters which reach temperatures of 200 degrees F. (800) FIND-DHS

JOSHUA TREE NATIONAL PARK - *(Page 101, A2)* Encompasses two desert regions:

The Eastern Half is representative of the "low" Colorado Desert, arid and rocky, with the distinctive Ocotilla Cacti and numerous other plants and wildlife unique to the region.

The Western Half is the "high" Mojave Desert, where Joshua Trees grow to 40 feet tall. A giant member of the lily family, it was supposedly named by the Mormons for its upstretched "praying" arms. The **Keys View** provides a dramatic view of the Coachella Valley and San Jacinto Mountains. There are no services within the park, but the well-maintained roads provide turnouts with information plaques and picnic tables. The unusual rock formations have been used as protection by Indians and hideouts by cattle rustlers in the past, and more recently were the backdrop to a private ranch.

Brochures and trail maps are available at the West Entrance Information Station. There are two visitor centers in the park. **The Oasis Visitor Center** at the Twentynine Palms entrance has a museum and short, self-guided nature walk, (619) 367-7511. **The Cottonwood Visitor Center** is at the south entrance. *(Page 101, D4)*

Other Points of Interest:

DEATH VALLEY NATIONAL MONUMENT - *(Page 61)* Far from desolate, this reserve is home to countless species of flora and fauna. The desert bighorn, golden eagle, mountain lion, and desert tortoise also find sanctuary here. Highway 190 crosses a series of peaks and salt bogs, multicolored vistas, and unspoiled wilderness. There is a distinct drop in elevation as the road descends to **Badwater**, *(Page 72, A2)* the lowest spot in the western hemisphere, 282 feet below sea level. A few communities survive in the harsh desert where summer temperatures may reach 130 degrees F and average less than 2" of rainfall each year. The Visitors Center provides information, brochures, and exhibits concerning the two million acres of monument territory. (760) 786-2331

Scotty's Castle - *(Page 61, B1)* Lavishly decorated Spanish/Moorish estate built in the 1920s is now owned by the National Park Service. Daily tours are conducted.

Stovepipe Wells - *(Page 61, D4)* A small town with a motel and store. Nearby is a great location to play on the huge sand dunes.

SALTON SEA STATE RECREATION AREA - *(Page 108)* Created in 1905 when the Colorado River flooded. This 35-mile long inland sea is 230 feet below sea level and is one of the world's largest bodies of inland salt water. Gradual leaching of minerals from the land has made the water several times saltier than the ocean. Fish originally introduced in the 1950s by the Department of Fish and Game have adapted and survived. Seventy-five species of birds make this their permanent home while as many as 300 other species have migrated here at one time or another. The 17,868-acre Salton Sea area is undeveloped, but is a popular area for boaters and fishermen. Campsites are available. (619) 393-3052

L.A.'s The Place

This driving tour is designed to capture the diversity of the Los Angeles area. From Pacific Coast Highway, to the magic of Hollywood, to historic landmarks and to various ethnic communities of the downtown, you'll enjoy shopping, dining, accommodations and the friendly people that make up this world-class destination.

THE GREATER LOS ANGELES AREA

1 Inch to 15 Miles

Scale
0 Miles 15

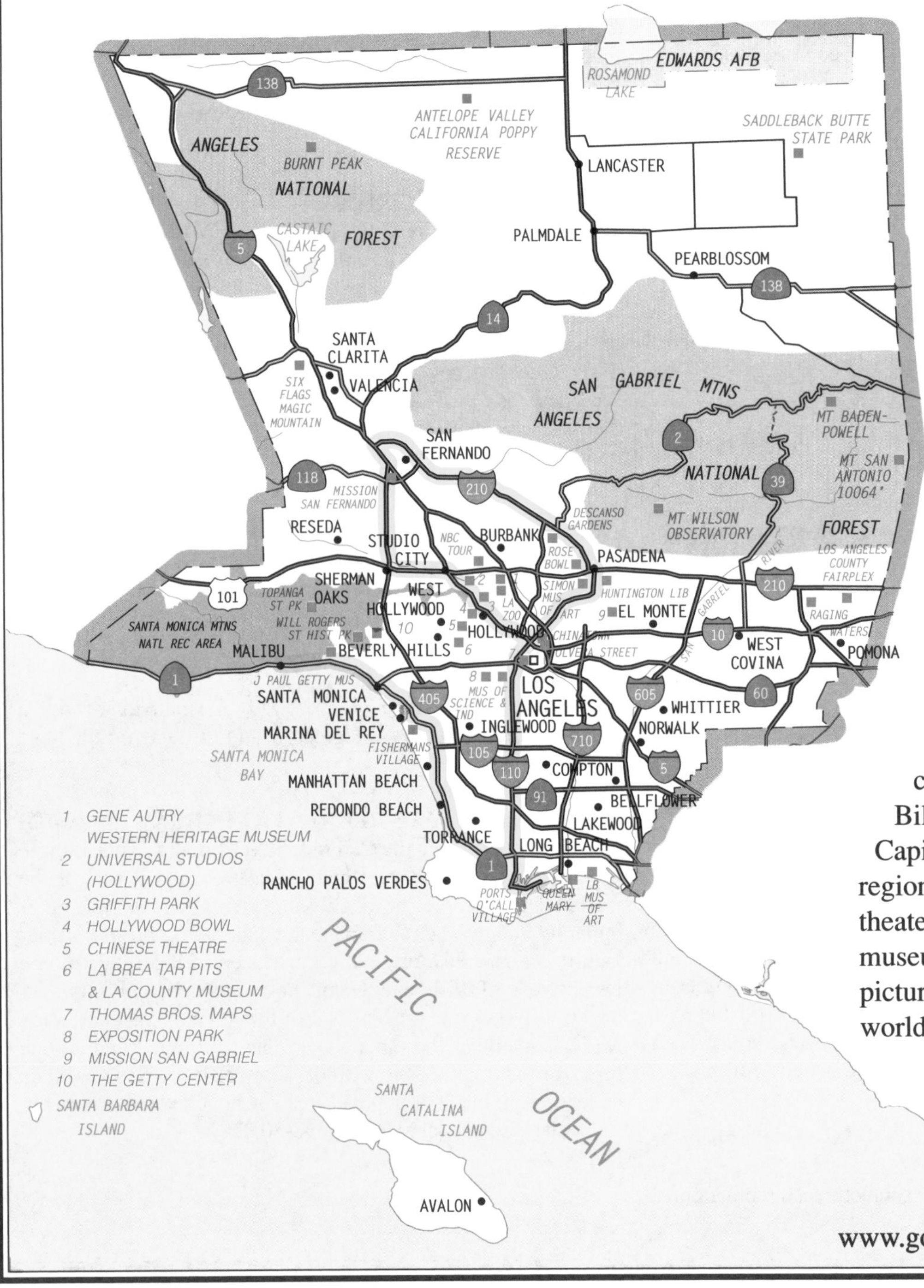

Los Angeles County is 4,083 square miles filled with an infinite variety of recreational and cultural opportunities. Billed as the "Entertainment Capital of the World", the region features the best in theater and music, art and museums, television and motion pictures, sporting events and world-famous attractions.

www.gocalif.ca.gov/guidebook/LA/

TOURS

Driving Tour Points of Interest:

While the people of other cities talk about the local weather, the people of Los Angeles and Orange County talk about the local traffic. The Southland has the most intricate freeway system in the world. Driving the freeways is often compared to an amusement park ride and a visit to Southern California would not be complete, or possible, without it (see pages Q, R, S, and T or the fold-out map for an overview.)

RANCHO PALOS VERDES - *(Page S, B3)* An area of rolling hills and exclusive homes. The **Wayfarer's Chapel** is an inspiring glass church designed by Lloyd Wright in 1946. (310) 377-1650

Highway 1 provides access to many beach cities, each with a unique personality (page 97.) *Redondo Beach has the surfers, Manhattan Beach has the yuppies, Marina Del Rey has the yachts, and Venice has the bizarre.*

SANTA MONICA - *(Page 97, C2)* A broad, sparkling beach community with a very special pier. **Santa Monica Pier** – built in 1908 – is a popular California landmark. Souvenir shops, restaurants, an arcade, and a historic carousel share this unique setting. It is a popular Hollywood film location. (310) 458-8900

J. PAUL GETTY MUSEUM - *(Page Q, A4)* The museum and surrounding gardens are a re-creation of a Roman country villa. The museum houses a permanent collection of Greek and Roman antiquities and pre-twentieth century Western European art. The museum is temporarily closed. (310) 458-2003

THE GETTY CENTER - *(Page 180, A1)* A tram ride to the summit starts the new Getty adventure. The Getty Center is the home for the new J. Paul Getty Museum and the other Getty art and education organizations. The breathtaking buildings, views and exhibits offer the visitor a new perspective on art and its meanings. Parking reservations are required. (310) 440-7300

TOPANGA - *(Page 97, B2)* This rustic mountain town and canyon became a popular mecca for the "counterculture" in the 1960s. The **Topanga State Park** is the nation's second largest urban park and the world's largest wildland situated within the boundaries of a major city. (310) 455-2465

Universal Studios - *(Page 181, A1)* A tram ride through the backlots and stages of a movieland park: (818) 777-3801; **Hollywood Bowl** - *(C3)* Magnificent outdoor amphitheater and park: (213) 850-2000; **Mann's Chinese Theatre** - *(C4)* Hosts gala movie premieres: (213) 464-8111; **Hollywood Wax Museum** - *(C4)* Movie legends immortalized in wax: (213) 462-8860; **Walk of Fame** - *(C4)* The stars of the stars.

QUEEN MARY - *(Page 192, E4)* One of the largest passenger ships ever built. (562) 435-3511.

BEVERLY HILLS - *(Page 183)* One of the most glamorous celebrity residential communities in Southern California and one of the world's most exclusive shopping districts. Visitors Bureau: (310) 271-8174.

HANCOCK PARK AREA - *(Page 184)* Another cluster of intriguing and diverse points of interest is only moments away: **Los Angeles County Museum of Art** - *(A2)* One of the most comprehensive art collections in the world: (213) 857-6000; **George C. Page Museum of La Brea Discoveries** - *(A2)* Showcases the research and outstanding fossils recovered from the adjacent **Rancho La Brea Tar Pits**: (213) 934-PAGE; **Farmer's Market** - *(A1)* Open-air market since 1934: (213) 933-9211; **CBS Studios** - *(A1)* Television programs in production.

EXPOSITION PARK - *(Page 185, C5)* South of the downtown area on Highway 110, take the Exposition Blvd. exit. **Natural History Museum** - More than 14,000,000 specimens, artifacts, and 300 million years of earth history on display in the nation's fourth largest natural history museum. (213) 763-DINO

Also in this area: **California State Museum of Science and Industry**, **Aerospace Building**, **Los Angeles Memorial Coliseum**, **Sports Arena,** and **Exposition Park Rose Gardens**. (213) 748-6131.

Nearby is the **University of Southern California Campus** and the **Shrine Civic Auditorium**.

DOWNTOWN LOS ANGELES - *(Pages 185 & 186)* The "City of Angels." Stop at **Thomas Bros. Maps and Books**, 521 W. 6th St., *(Page 186, A3).* (213) 627-4018

Olvera Street and El Pueblo de Los Angeles Historic Monument - *(Page 186, B2)* Founding site of Los Angeles includes 27 historic buildings. (213) 628-1274

Museum of Contemporary Art - *(Page 186, A3)* Sleek and geometric, devoted to the art and culture of 1940 to the present. (213) 626-6222

Music Center - *(Page 186, A2)* Performing arts complex which includes three major theatres. Tour information: (213) 972-7211.

GRIFFITH PARK - *(Page 182)* One of the world's largest municipal parks. In addition to hiking and horseback riding trails, a golf course and lots of picnic areas, the 4,000-acre park encompasses numerous other attractions: **Los Angeles Zoo**: (213) 666-4090; **Gene Autry Western Heritage Museum**: (213) 667-2000; **Griffith Observatory**: (213) 664-1191.

Sunshine, Beaches, Attractions, Resorts and More!

If you're searching for some of the world's finest restaurants and shopping experiences, look no further. The same goes for charming seaside communities, world-class theme parks, prime surfing and original art work. Again, look no further. Add to that outstanding recreational facilities, numerous parks and museums and it all adds up to this special driving tour of Orange County.

Orange County has long been famous for its family-oriented theme parks, 42 miles of shoreline and the citrus groves that gave the area its name. Today, the region has taken on an international sophistication undreamed of 50 years ago.

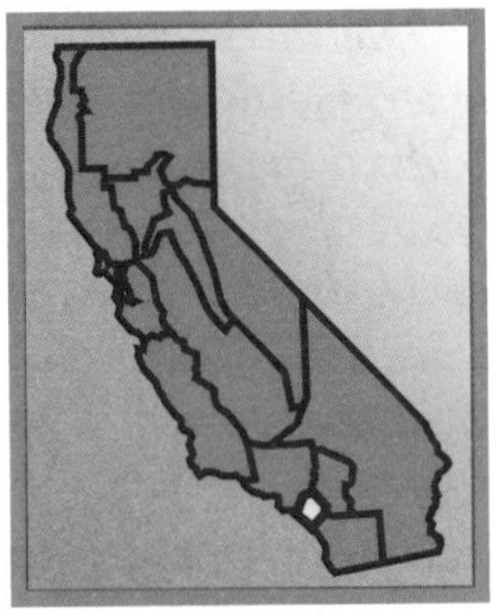

1 Inch to 7 Miles

Scale

0 Miles 7

www.gocalif.ca.gov/guidebook/OC/

TOURS

Driving Tour Points of Interest:

SAN JUAN CAPISTRANO - *(Page 105, D1)* Home of the **Mission San Juan Capistrano** - *(Page 202, E1)* Founded in 1776. The restored structure contains a museum; a self-guided tour explains the Mission's history. The famous Mission, the seventh built, is the place where thousands of swallows return each year on St. Joseph's Day, March 19th. (714) 248-2047

DOHENY STATE BEACH - *(Page 202, B4)* 120 developed campsites and large beach area. (714) 496-6172

LAGUNA BEACH - *(Page 201)* A captivating town with an emphasis on art. The attractive streets are lined with galleries, shops, and cafes. Chamber of Commerce: (714) 494-1018.

Laguna Art Museum - *(Page 201, A2)* Exhibitions highlight historical and contemporary American art, with special emphasis on works produced in California. Open Tues. - Sun. 11 a.m. to 5 p.m. (714) 494-6531

WILD RIVERS WATERPARK - *(Page 98, D4)* Family waterpark with 40 rides and attractions for all ages. Open mid-May through Sept. Call for schedule and hours. (714) 768-WILD

CRYSTAL COVE STATE PARK - *(Page T, E4)* Between Corona del Mar and Laguna Beach. 2,800 acres, with three miles of beach and an underwater preserve for divers to explore. Open 6 a.m. to sunset. (714) 494-3539

BALBOA ISLAND - *(Page 199, D5)* A tiny island jammed with cozy, pricey beach houses. The main street is lined with boutiques and cafes selling everything from bikinis to frozen bananas. Take the car ferry across to the **"Fun Zone"** for a ride on the ferris wheel, a cruise of the harbor, or an ocean cruise to Catalina Island.

Balboa Pavilion - *(Page 199, D5)* Designated a California Historical Landmark, built in 1905, Balboa Pavilion has been restored to authentic "waterfront Victorian." (714) 673-5245

ORANGE COUNTY MUSEUM OF ART - *(Page 200, A4)* Offers modern and contemporary art. Changing exhibitions and a permanent collection of post-WWII California art. Gift shop, restaurant. Call for group discount (10 or more.) Handicapped access. Open Tues. - Sat. 10 a.m. to 5 p.m. Sun. 12 p.m. to 5 p.m. (714) 759-1122

NEWPORT BEACH FASHION ISLAND - *(Page 200, A4)* more than 200 shops located in an open-air Mediterranean-style village atmosphere. Ocean view dining. Handicapped facilities. (714) 721-2000

UPPER NEWPORT BAY ECOLOGICAL RESERVE - *(Page 199, E2)* Meandering coastal lagoon surrounded by prominent bluffs and cliffs. Nature study, photography, hiking, bicycling, and boating. Kayak and canoe tours, campfire programs monthly. (714) 640-6746

HUNTINGTON STATE BEACH - *(Page T, B4)* Fire rings, cold showers, a bicycle trail, and a paved ramp for beach wheelchair access. Popular beach area. (714) 536-1454

BOLSA CHICA STATE BEACH - *(Page T, A3)* Three miles up the coast from Huntington Beach, on Hwy. 1. A popular swimming and surfing beach that has fire rings, dressing rooms, cold showers, bicycle trails, and a paved ramp for beach wheelchair access. (714) 846-3460

ORANGE COUNTY PERFORMING ARTS CENTER - *(Page 198, A3)* Includes a 3,000-seat, three-tiered main theatre for musical theatre, symphony, opera, and dance. (714) 556-ARTS

SOUTH COAST PLAZA - *(Page 197, E3)* Contains the finest collection of shops and restaurants, including: Gucci, Cartier, Saks, Tiffany, Emporio Armani, Chanel, and Escata. (714) 435-2000

SOUTH COAST REPERTORY THEATRE - *(Page 198, A3)* This Tony Award winning professional resident theatre presents an eleven-month season, Sept. through July, of 12 classic and contemporary plays on two stages. (714) 957-4033

THOMAS BROS. MAPS - *(Page 198, C3)* Corporate headquarters and retail showroom. Please stop by and say "Hello." 17731 Cowan, Irvine. (714) 863-1984 or (800) 899-MAPS

BOWERS MUSEUM OF CULTURAL ART - *(Page 196, B3)* Housed in a recently expanded Spanish-style 1930s building, the museum specializes in the cultural arts of the Americas and Pacific Rim and has permanent galleries on the arts of Native America, Africa and Oceania. (714) 567-3600

EDISON INTERNATIONAL FIELD OF ANAHEIM - *(Page 193, E5)* Home of the California Angels baseball club. Guided tours of the stadium daily except Sunday. Parking for tour guests is free. (714) 940-2000

ARROWHEAD POND OF ANAHEIM - *(Page 194, A4)* Known as "The Pond" - home of The Mighty Ducks National Hockey League team. Opened in 1993, this state-of-the-art arena is open year round for many other sporting events and concerts. For general information call (714) 704-2400.

DISNEYLAND - *(Page 193, B4)* The "Magic Kingdom" known throughout the world as the spectacular showcase for Mickey Mouse and all the Disney characters. The $200 million amusement park is divided into several theme "lands." A full day is needed to enjoy all of the attractions. (714) 999-4565; www.disney.com/Disneyland/_index.html

KNOTT'S BERRY FARM - *(Page T, B2)* A popular family amusement park with six theme areas, shows, and over 150 rides. In addition, the Market Place has restaurants and specialty shops featuring the original Mrs. Knott's jams and preserves. Located at 8039 Beach Blvd. in Buena Park. (714) 220-5200; www.knotts.com

MOVIELAND WAX MUSEUM - *(Page T, B2)* Features more than 258 wax likenesses of movie and TV stars. Facilities for the handicapped. Free parking. Open every day and night of the year. (714) 522-1154

RICHARD NIXON LIBRARY - *(Page T, D1)* Museum archives and birthplace offers exhibits on Vietnam, China, the Soviet Union, the White House, and Watergate. Gift shop. Open 10 a.m. to 5 p.m. daily. Handicapped access. (714) 993-3393

One of the Most Ideal Climates in the Nation

San Diego's 59 mile scenic drive is a beautiful way to spend a day. It can be driven in three hours with few stops, or one could spend days visiting the many museums, parks, restaurants, shops and countless attractions.

Highlights of this tour include Coronado, Fort Rosecrans Cemetery, Cabrillo National Monument, Sunset Cliffs, Mission Bay Park, Sea World, La Jolla, Old Town, Balboa Park, the San Diego Zoo and the zoo's sister park - the Wild Animal Park, Escondido, Seaport Village, the San Diego Convention Center and the Gaslamp Quarter.

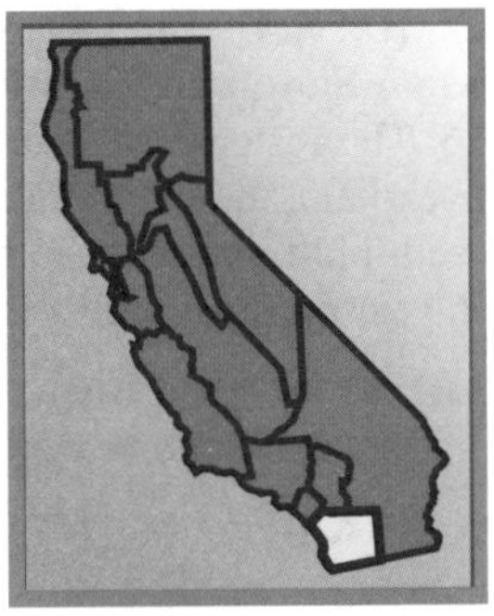

1 Inch to 15 Miles

Scale

0 Miles 15

San Diego, the hub of this region, is famous for its mild, temperate climate and 70 miles of sandy beaches.

For history buffs, San Diego offers preserved historic sections to tour. In the mountains east of San Diego is the gold-mining town of Julian. The eastern portion of San Diego County comprises the Anza-Borrego Desert State Park.

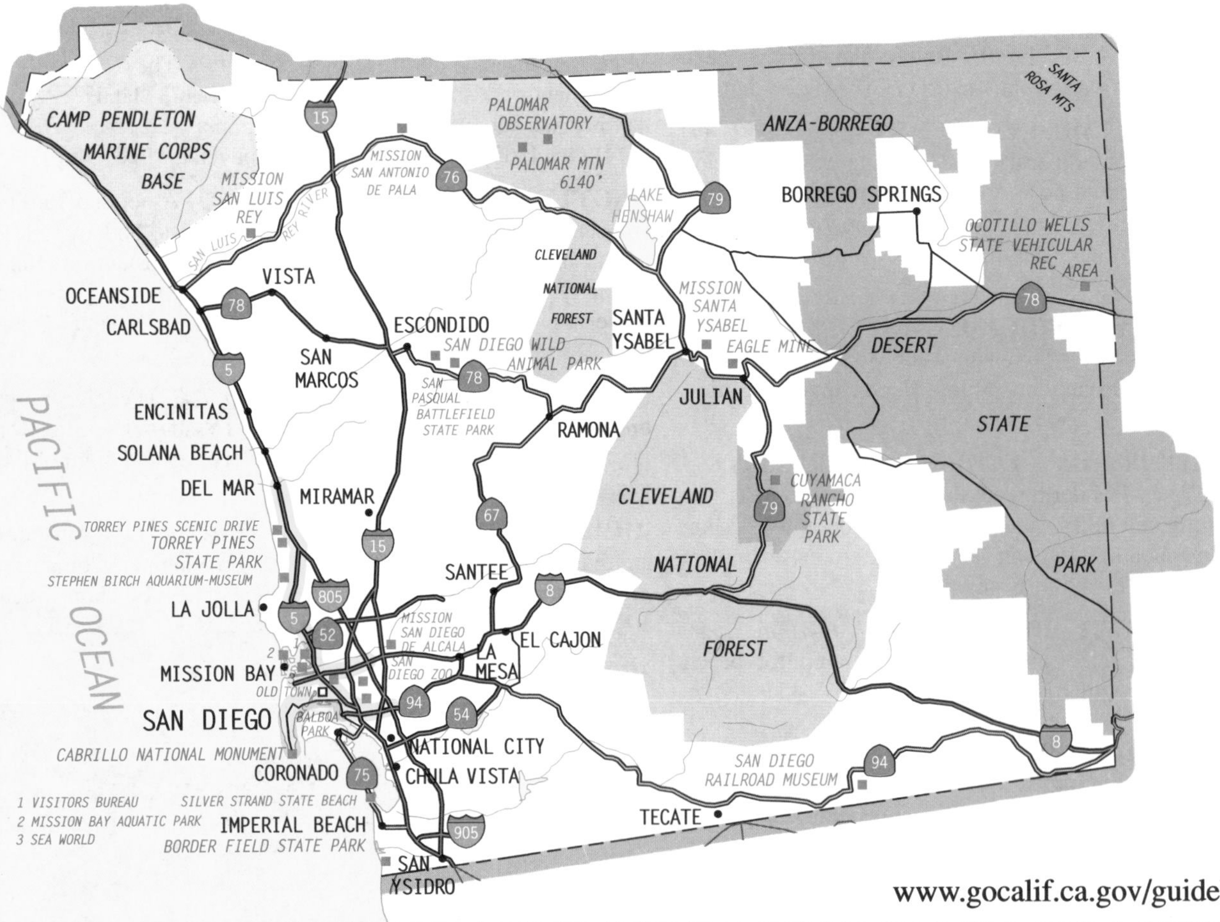

www.gocalif.ca.gov/guidebook/SD/

Driving Tour Points of Interest:

CABRILLO NATIONAL MONUMENT - *(Page V, A4)* Named for the Portuguese explorer Juan Rodriguez Cabrillo, who claimed the area for Spain in 1542. Point Loma provides a view of the city and the bay, as well as a vantage point to watch migratory whales at certain times of the year. A lighthouse, museum, and hiking trails are maintained year-round. (619) 557-5450

DOWNTOWN - *(Page 215, D3)* Easy to navigate by car, on foot, or through the Old Town Trolley Tours. Start at the International Visitors Information Center (619) 236-1212, located at **Horton Plaza Center**, a multi-tiered shopping complex with 160 shops, restaurants and cinemas. The **Embarcadero** is the busy waterfront area where visitors can watch the fleets come in, tour a Navy ship, or take a harbor cruise. The **Maritime Museum** features three restored ships, including the Star of India, the oldest merchant vessel afloat. (619) 234-9153

BALBOA PARK - *(Page 216)* Over 1,000 acres of fascinating museums, theatres, gardens, shops and restaurants. This unique park was the site of two World's Fairs and continues to greet millions of visitors from around the world. The **San Diego Zoo**, located within the park, proudly exhibits a renowned collection of rare birds and animals in their natural habitats.
(619) 234-3153; www.sandiegozoo.org

OLD TOWN SAN DIEGO STATE HISTORIC PARK - *(Page 213, A5)* The location of the first permanent Spanish settlement in what is now California. The small cluster of adobe buildings has been restored and the area revitalized into a charming plaza of museums, galleries, shops, and restaurants. A walking tour map is available at the Visitors Center. (619) 220-5422

MISSION SAN DIEGO DE ALCALA - *(Page 214, E2)* Established in 1769 as the first Franciscan Mission. The restored church and impressive bell tower are surrounded by attractive gardens. Open year round. (619) 281-8449

MISSION BAY PARK - *(Page 212)* An aquatic playground for water sports enthusiasts. Twenty-seven miles of shoreline are open for public swimming, fishing, and picnicking. Several boat launches are located around the bay as motor-boating, water-skiing, and sailing are popular.

Sea World - *(Page 212, C4)* One of California's most popular theme parks, featuring 135 acres of entertaining and educational marine exhibits and performances. This is an all-day excursion in itself. (619)226-3901;
www.bev.net/education/SeaWorld/homepage.html

LA JOLLA - *(Page 105, C3)* The "jewel" of San Diego. Reminiscent of the French Riviera, this gorgeous residential community has a village area along Prospect Street *(Page 105, B2)* with swank restaurants, boutiques, and galleries.

La Jolla Cave - *(Page 105, B2)* Wave-eroded sandstone cliffs have formed several impressive caves, one of which can be reached by an 80-foot staircase through a curio shop. (619) 454-6080

Birch Aquarium at Scripps - *(Page 211, A1)* Several displays emphasize the fish and animals found in Southern California's waters. Changing displays explore the latest oceanography developments. (619) 534-3474

TORREY PINES SCENIC DRIVE - *(Page V, A1)* Curves north of La Jolla to **Torrey Pines State Reserve**. The clifftop park protects over 7,000 gnarled Torrey pines which exist naturally only one other place in the world, on Santa Rosa Island. Several short, interpretive nature trails, a museum, and Visitors Center provide information. (619) 755-2063

DEL MAR - *(Page V, A1)* Where "The Turf Meets the Surf." The oceanside **Del Mar Racetrack** was founded in 1937 by a group of Hollywood celebrities. Each year, July through September, the pink and green art deco grandstand is open to the public for championship thoroughbred racing. Other events are held throughout the year. (619) 755-1141

Other Points of Interest:

ENCINITAS - *(Page 106, B4)* Take the Encinitas Boulevard exit to **Quail Botanical Gardens**, a peaceful setting of foot trails that meander through 30 acres of rare and exotic plants, trees and flowers. Nationally recognized for its diverse and botanically important plant collections. Gift shop and plant sales. (619) 436-3036

SAN DIEGO WILD ANIMAL PARK - *(Page 106, D3)* Located six miles south of Escondido. This wildlife sanctuary exists in conjunction with the San Diego Zoo. Animals are often relocated from one park to the other. Within the compound, many of the 2,400 animals are allowed to roam freely in natural settings. A special monorail takes visitors on a one-hour safari-like adventure. (619) 480-0100

PALOMAR MOUNTAIN STATE PARK - *(Page 107, A2)* Thick fir and cedar forests resemble those of the Sierra Nevada. Fishing and camping are permitted.

PALOMAR OBSERVATORY - *(Page 107, A2)* Showcases a 200-inch Hale telescope, one of the largest in the world. There is a visitors gallery, photographs, a videotape and a small gift shop. (619) 742-2119

JULIAN - *(Page 107, C3)* A turn-of-the-century mining town and self-proclaimed "Apple Capital of San Diego." Old West storefronts harbor quaint shops and home-style restaurants. The Chamber of Commerce provides information, local maps, and a calendar of events. (619) 765-1857

Eagle & High Peak Mines - *(Page 107, C3)* Visitors travel 1,000 feet into an authentic gold mine. There is a museum and displays of tools, machinery, and antique engines.
(619) 765-9921

CUYAMACA RANCHO STATE PARK - *(Page 107, C4)* A peaceful area of oak and pine trees, meadows, and streams. There are hundreds of miles of riding and hiking trails within the park. The 3-1/2 mile Cuyamaca Peak trail leads to the 6,512 foot summit where the view encompasses the Pacific Ocean, the desert, Mexico, and the Salton Sea. Camping is permitted. (619) 765-0755

ANZA-BORREGO DESERT STATE PARK - *(Page 107, D2)* 600,000 acres of peaceful, isolated desert, the largest in California. Even though the area may appear desolate, it is actually a complex and fragile ecosystem; steep canyon walls and feathery palms protect numerous bird and wildlife species. In the spring, the desert is a carpet of colorful wildflowers. Camping is permitted. The Visitors Center, just west of Borrego Springs, provides trail maps and information. (619) 767-5311

LIST OF ABBREVIATIONS

ABBR	NAME
AL	ALLEY
AR	ARROYO
ARR	ARROYO
AV	AVENUE
AVD	AVENIDA
AVD D LS	AVENIDA DE LOS
BCH	BEACH
BL	BOULEVARD
BLVD	BOULEVARD
CEM	CEMETERY
CIR	CIRCLE
CK	CREEK
CL	CALLE
CL DL	CALLE DEL
CL D LS	CALLE DE LAS CALLE DE LOS
CL EL	CALLE EL
CLJ	CALLEJON
CL LA	CALLE LA
CL LS	CALLE LAS CALLE LOS
CM	CAMINO
CM D	CAMINO DE
CM D LA	CAMINO DE LA
CM D LS	CAMINO DE LAS CAMINO DE LOS
CMTO	CAMINITO
CN	CANAL
COM	COMMON
CR	CRESCENT
CRES	CRESCENT
CSWY	CAUSEWAY
CT	COURT
CTE	CORTE
CTO	CUT OFF
CTR	CENTER
CV	COVE
CY	CANYON
CYN	CANYON
D	DE
DL	DEL
DR	DRIVE
DS	DOS
E	EAST
EST	ESTATE
EXWY	EXPRESSWAY
EXT	EXTENSION
FRWY	FREEWAY
FWY	FREEWAY
FY	FREEWAY
GN	GLEN
GRDS	GROUNDS
GRN	GREEN
GRV	GROVE
HTS	HEIGHTS
HWY	HIGHWAY
HY	HIGHWAY
JCT	JUNCTION
KPN	KEY PENINSULA NORTH
KPS	KEY PENINSULA SOUTH
L	LA
LN	LANE
LP	LOOP
LS	LAS, LOS
MDW	MEADOW
MHP	MOBILE HOME PARK
MNR	MANOR
MT	MOUNT
MTN	MOUNTAIN
MTWY	MOTORWAY
MTY	MOTORWAY
N	NORTH
PAS	PASEO
PAS DE	PASEO DE
PAS DL	PASEO DEL
PAS D LS	PASEO DE LAS PASEO DE LOS
PGD	PLAYGROUND
PK	PARK
PK	PEAK
PKWY	PARKWAY
PL	PLACE
PT	POINT
PY	PARKWAY
PZ	PLAZA
RCH	RANCH
RCHO	RANCHO
RD	ROAD
RDG	RIDGE
RES	RESERVOIR
RIV	RIVER
RV	RIVER
RO	RANCHO
S	SOUTH
SN	SAN
SPG	SPRING
SPGS	SPRINGS
SQ	SQUARE
SRA	SIERRA
ST	SAINT
ST	STREET
STA	SANTA
STA	STATION
TER	TERRACE
THTR	THEATER
TKTR	TRUCK TRAIL
TR	TRAIL
VIA D	VIA DE
VIA D LS	VIA DE LAS VIA DE LOS
VIA DL	VIA DEL
VIS	VISTA
VLG	VILLAGE
VLY	VALLEY
VW	VIEW
W	WEST
WK	WALK
WY	WAY

INDEX OF CITIES

CITY NAME	ABBR	PAGE
ALAMEDA	A	157
ANAHEIM	ANA	193
AUBURN	AUB	126
AVALON	AVLN	97
BAKERSFIELD	BKD	166
BARSTOW	BARS	208
BELMONT	BLMT	145
BENICIA	BEN	153
BERKELEY	B	156
BEVERLY HILLS	BH	183
BURBANK	BUR	179
CARMEL BY THE SEA	CAR	168
CHICO	C	124
CLAREMONT	CLA	203
COLTON	CLTN	207
CORONADO	COR	215
CORTE MADERA	CRTM	140
COSTA MESA	CM	197
CULVER CITY	CUL	188
CUPERTINO	CPTO	149
DANA POINT	DPT	202
DAVIS	DVS	136
EL CENTRO	EC	217
EL CERRITO	ELC	155
EL SEGUNDO	ELS	189
EUREKA	EUR	121
FAIRFIELD	FRFD	135
FOSTER CITY	FCTY	145
FOUNTAIN VALLEY	FTNV	197
FRESNO	FRE	165
GARDEN GROVE	GG	195
GRASS VALLEY	GV	127
HAWTHORNE	HAW	189
HAYWARD	H	146
INGLEWOOD	ING	189
IRVINE	IRV	198
LAGUNA BEACH	LAG	201
LAGUNA NIGUEL	LN	202
LAS VEGAS	LV	209
LONG BEACH	LB	192
LOS ALTOS	LSAL	149
LOS ANGELES	LA	177
MANHATTAN BEACH	MB	189
MAMMOTH LAKES	ML	164
MANTECA	MAN	161
MARTINEZ	M	154
MENLO PARK	MP	147
MERCED	MER	170
MILLBRAE	MLBR	144
MILL VALLEY	MV	140
MODESTO	MDO	162
MONTCLAIR	MTCL	203
MONTEREY	MONT	167
MOUNTAIN VIEW	MVW	148
NAPA	NAP	133
NEVADA CITY	NEVC	128
NEWPORT BEACH	NB	199
OAKLAND	O	157
ONTARIO	ONT	204
ORANGE	ORA	194
OXNARD	OXN	176
PACIFIC GROVE	PAC	167
PALM SPRINGS	PMSP	206
PALO ALTO	PA	147
PASADENA	PAS	190
PIEDMONT	P	158
PLACERVILLE	PLCV	138
POMONA	POM	203
RANCHO CUCAMONGA	ROC	204
REDDING	RED	122
REDWOOD CITY	RC	145
RENO	RENO	130
RICHMOND	R	155
RIVERSIDE	RIV	205
ROSS	ROSS	139
SACRAMENTO	SCTO	137
SALINAS	SAL	171
SAN ANSELMO	SANS	139
SAN BERNARDINO	SBDO	207
SAN BRUNO	SBR	144
SAN CLEMENTE	SCL	202
SAN DIEGO	SD	211
SAN FRANCISCO	SF	141
SAN JOSE	SJ	152
SAN JUAN CAPISTRANO	SJC	202
SAN LUIS OBISPO	SNLO	172
SAN MATEO	SM	145
SAN PABLO	SP	155
SAN RAFAEL	SR	139
SANTA ANA	SA	196
SANTA BARBARA	STB	174
SANTA CLARA	SCLR	150
SANTA CRUZ	SC	169
SANTA MARIA	SMA	173
SANTA MONICA	SMON	180
SANTA ROSA	STR	131
SONOMA	SNMA	132
SONORA	SNRA	163
SOUTH LAKE TAHOE	SLT	129
SOUTH SAN FRANCISCO	SSF	144
STOCKTON	S	160
SUISUN CITY	SUIS	135
SUNNYVALE	SVL	149
TUSTIN	TUS	198
UKIAH	U	123
UPLAND	UPL	204
VALLEJO	VAL	134
VENTURA	VENT	175
WEST HOLLYWOOD	WHOL	181
YUBA CITY	YUBA	125

INDEX OF COUNTIES

COUNTY NAME	ABBR	PAGE
CALIFORNIA		
ALAMEDA	ALA	45
ALPINE	ALP	42
AMADOR	AMA	40
BUTTE	BUT	25
CALAVERAS	CAL	41
COLUSA	COL	32
CONTRA COSTA	CC	38
DEL NORTE	DN	2
EL DORADO	ED	35
FRESNO	FRCO	57
GLENN	GLE	24
HUMBOLDT	HUM	16
IMPERIAL	IMP	109
INYO	INY	59
KERN	KER	78
KINGS	KIN	67
LAKE	LAE	31
LASSEN	LAS	20
LOS ANGELES	LACO	97
MADERA	MAD	49
MARIN	MAR	38
MARIPOSA	MPA	49
MENDOCINO	MEN	22
MERCED	MCO	48
MODOC	MOD	6
MONO	MNO	43
MONTEREY	MON	64
NAPA	NAPA	38
NEVADA	NEV	34
ORANGE	ORCO	98
PLACER	PLA	34
PLUMAS	PLU	26
RIVERSIDE	RCO	99
SACRAMENTO	SAC	39
SAN BENITO	SBT	54
SAN BERNARDINO	SBD	91
SAN DIEGO	SDCO	106
SAN FRANCISCO	SFCO	45
SAN JOAQUIN	SJCO	40
SAN LUIS OBISPO	SLO	75
SAN MATEO	SMCO	45
SANTA BARBARA	SB	86
SANTA CLARA	SCL	46
SANTA CRUZ	SCR	53
SHASTA	SHA	18
SIERRA	SIE	27
SISKIYOU	SIS	4
SOLANO	SOL	39
SONOMA	SON	37
STANISLAUS	STA	47
SUTTER	SUT	33
TEHAMA	TEH	18
TRINITY	TRI	17
TULARE	TUL	68
TUOLUMNE	TUO	42
VENTURA	VEN	88
YOLO	YOL	33
YUBA	YUB	33
ARIZONA		
LA PAZ	LPAZ	104
MOHAVE	MOH	85
YUMA	YUMA	112
NEVADA		
CARSON CITY	CRSN	36
CLARK	CLK	74
DOUGLAS	DGL	36
ESMERALDA	ESM	52
LYON	LYON	43
MINERAL	MIN	44
NYE	NYE	62
STOREY	STOR	28
WASHOE	WSH	28
OREGON		
CURRY	CUR	1
JACKSON	JKSN	3
JOSEPHINE	JOS	2
KLAMATH	KLAM	5
LAKE	LAKE	7
MEXICO		
BAJA CALIFORNIA	BAJA	111

STREET	CO.	PAGE	GRID
A			
A ST	ALA	L	E5
A ST	ALA	45	E2
A ST	DVS	136	C3
A ST	DN	1	D4
A ST	H	146	E2
A ST	SBD	92	A1
A ST	SD	215	D3
A ST	TEH	18	E5
A ST W	ALA	L	E5
A ST W	ALA	N	E1
A ST W	H	146	B3
ABBOTT DR	KER	80	B3
ABBOTT RD	LACO	R	A5
ABBOTT ST	MON	54	D4
ABBOTT ST	SAL	171	D4
ABBOT KINNEY BL	LA	187	A3
ABBY ST	FRE	165	D3
ABEL ST	SCL	P	B3
ABELIA ST	SBD	92	B3
ABELOR RD	INY	51	C4
ABERDEEN DR	SBD	100	E1
ABERDEEN STA RD	INY	59	E1
ABERNATHY RD	SOL	L	E1
ABERNATHY RD	SOL	M	A1
ABERNATHY RD	SOL	38	E3
ABERNATHY RD	YUB	26	A4
ABLE RD	COL	32	E2
ABORN RD	SCL	P	C3
ABORN RD	SCL	46	C4
ABRAM DR	RCO	100	A5
ACACIA AV	STA	47	C3
ACACIA AV	SUT	33	C2
ACACIA ST	SAL	171	A4
ACADEMY AV	FRCO	57	E4
ACAMPO RD	SJCO	39	E4
ACARI RD	KER	78	B3
ACKERMAN LN	HUM	16	B3
ACME RD	SUT	33	B3
ACMITE ST	KER	91	E3
ACOMA TR	SBD	100	D1
ADA RD	KER	78	B3
ADAIR RD	IMP	108	E5
ADAIR RD	STA	47	C2
ADAM FOX FRM RD	HUM	9	E4
ADAMS AV	CM	197	C5
ADAMS AV	EC	217	A2
ADAMS AV	FRCO	56	D4
ADAMS AV	FRCO	57	C4
ADAMS AV	FRCO	58	A4
ADAMS AV	ORCO	T	C4
ADAMS AV	SD	214	B4
ADAMS AV	SDCO	V	C3
ADAMS AV	SDCO	111	D1
ADAMS BLVD	LA	184	A4
ADAMS BLVD	LA	185	B4
ADAMS BLVD	LACO	Q	D4
ADAMS DR	KER	79	E1
ADAMS RD	TEH	18	C4
ADAMS ST	IMP	109	A5
ADAMS ST	RCO	99	A2
ADAMS ST	RCO	101	A4
ADDISON RD	BUT	25	C1
ADELAIDA RD	SLO	75	E1
ADELAIDA RD	SLO	76	A1
ADELINE ST	B	156	A4
ADELINE ST	O	157	D2
ADELANTO RD	SBD	91	B3
ADIN CUTOFF RD	LAS	14	B3
ADML CALLAHN LN	VAL	134	E3
ADMIRALTY WY	LACO	187	B3
ADOBE DR	KER	79	E2
ADOBE DR	KER	80	A2
ADOBE PL	MON	65	C4
ADOBE RD	BUT	25	C4
ADOBE RD	COL	25	A5
ADOBE RD	KER	78	D4
ADOBE RD	SBD	101	B1
ADOBE RD	SLO	76	A1
ADOBE RD	SHA	18	D3
ADOBE RD	SON	L	A1
ADOBE RD	SON	38	A3
ADOBE RD	TEH	18	D4
ADOBE CREEK RD	LAK	31	D3
ADOBE MTN RD	SBD	90	D2
ADOBE RANCH RD	MNO	44	A5
ADOHR RD	KER	78	A3
ADOLFO LOPEZ BL	BAJA	112	B4
AERO DR	SD	214	A1
AERO DR	SDCO	V	B2
AERO DR	SDCO	111	D1
AEROPUERTO HWY	BAJA	111	E2
AFTON BLVD	GLE	25	A4
AFTON RD	BUT	25	B5
AFTON CANYON RD	SBD	82	D5
AGATE RD	SBD	91	D1
AGER RD	SIS	4	B3
AGER RD	SIS	5	D2
AGER BESWICK RD	SIS	4	C3
AGGEN RD	VEN	88	C5
AGNES WILSON RD	LPAZ	104	A2
AGNES WILSON RD	RCO	103	E2
AGOURA RD	LACO	96	E1
AGUA CALIENT BL	BAJA	111	E3
AGUA CALIENT RD	SB	87	D4
AQUA CALIENT RD	SON	132	A1
AGUA DULCE CYN	LACO	89	D4
AGUA FRIA RD	MPA	49	A3
AGUAJITO RD	MON	53	E4
AGUAJITO RD	MON	168	D2
AGUA MANSA RD	RCO	99	B2

STREET	CO.	PAGE	GRID
AGUAS FRIAS RD	BUT	25	B4
AGUEREBERRY PT	INY	71	D1
AHERN RD	SJCO	47	A2
AHLF RD	SUT	33	C2
AIKENS MINE RD	SBD	83	D4
AINSWORTH PL	RCO	107	A1
AIR BASE PKWY	FRFD	135	C2
AIR BASE PKWY	SOL	M	A1
AIR BASE PKWY	SOL	38	E3
AIR BASE RD	SBD	91	B3
AIRD CIR	BUT	25	E3
AIROLA	CAL	41	B4
AIROSA DR	SBD	90	E3
AIROX RD	SB	86	B1
AIR PARK DR	IMP	108	C2
AIRPORT BLVD	KER	80	A5
AIRPORT BLVD	LA	189	D1
AIRPORT BLVD	LACO	Q	D5
AIRPORT BLVD	RCO	101	A4
AIRPORT BLVD	SAL	171	E5
AIRPORT BLVD	SMCO	N	C1
AIRPORT BLVD	SSF	144	C1
AIRPORT BLVD	SJ	151	D1
AIRPORT BLVD	SCR	54	B2
AIRPORT BLVD	SON	37	E1
AIRPORT BLVD S	SSF	144	C2
AIRPORT DR	O	159	D5
AIRPORT RD	ALP	36	C4
AIRPORT RD	DGL	36	C3
AIRPORT RD	HUM	9	E4
AIRPORT RD	KER	78	A4
AIRPORT RD	MEN	22	B5
AIRPORT RD	MEN	30	C1
AIRPORT RD	MOD	8	A1
AIRPORT RD	MNO	50	E2
AIRPORT RD	NAPA	L	D1
AIRPORT RD	NAPA	38	C3
AIRPORT RD	SLO	76	B1
AIRPORT RD	SHA	18	C3
AIRPORT RD	SIS	4	B3
AIRPORT RD	SOL	M	D1
AIRPORT RD	SOL	39	C3
AIRPORT RD	TRI	17	D1
AIRPORT WY	SJCO	40	B5
AIRPORT WY	SJCO	47	B2
AIRWAY DR	KLAM	5	C1
AKER AV	STA	47	D1
AKERS RD	TUL	68	B1
AKINS RD	SIS	5	D2
AKRICH ST	SHA	18	C2
ALABAMA ST	SBD	99	C2
ALAMEDA AV	BUR	179	C5
ALAMEDA AV	LACO	Q	D3
ALAMEDA AV	SAL	171	C5
ALAMEDA AV	YOL	39	D2
ALAMEDA BLVD	COR	215	C5
ALAMEDA ST	LA	186	B4
ALAMEDA ST	LACO	97	E2
ALAMEDA ST	LACO	S	D2
ALAMEDA ST	MAN	161	C3
ALAMEDA ST	VAL	134	C4
ALAM D LS PULGS	BLMT	145	B5
ALAM D LS PULGS	SMCO	N	C1
ALAM D LS PULGS	SMCO	N	D2
ALAM D LS PULGS	SM	145	A4
ALAM D LS PULGS	SMCO	45	D4
ALAMEDA PAD SER	STB	174	C2
ALAMEDA, THE	SJ	151	E3
ALAMITOS AV	LACO	S	D3
ALAMO DR	MPA	48	D2
ALAMO RD	IMP	109	B5
ALAMO ST	LACO	88	E5
ALAMO ST	SIS	5	A2
ALAMO ST	VEN	88	E5
ALAMO ST	VEN	89	A5
ALAMO CREEK RD	SLO	76	D5
ALAMO PINTADO	SB	86	E3
ALASKA AV	FRFD	135	B2
ALBA RD	SCR	N	E5
ALBA RD	SCR	53	E1
ALBAUGH RD	LAS	14	C3
ALBERS RD	STA	47	E2
ALBRT ETTER RCH	HUM	16	A5
ALBERTON AV	BUT	25	A3
ALBION LTL RIV	MEN	30	B1
ALBION RIDGE RD	MEN	30	C1
ALBRIGHT RD	IMP	109	B3
ALCALDE RD	FRCO	66	D3
ALCATRAZ AV	ALA	L	D4
ALCATRAZ AV	O	156	A4
ALCOSTA BLVD	CC	M	B5
ALDEN ST	KER	78	E4
ALDER AV	SBD	80	E1
ALDER AV	SBD	99	B1
ALDER ST	PAC	167	B2
ALDER CAMP RD	DN	1	E5
ALDER CAMP RD	DN	9	E1
ALDER CAMP RD	DN	10	A1
ALDER CREEK RD	NEV	27	D5
ALDER CK BCH RD	MEN	30	C3
ALDRCRFT HTS RD	SCL	P	B5
ALDRCRFT HTS RD	SCL	54	A1
ALDERPOINT RD	HUM	16	C3
ALDER PT BLUFF	TRI	16	D5
ALDER SPGS RD	GLE	23	D3
ALDER SPGS RD	GLE	24	A3
ALDERWOOD DR	SIS	4	A4
ALDINE DR	SD	214	A1
ALDINE DR	SDCO	V	C3
ALDINE DR	SDCO	111	D1
ALDRIDGE RD	SHA	19	A2
ALEJO DR	RCO	100	C3
ALESSANDRO BLVD	RCO	99	B3

STREET	CO.	PAGE	GRID
ALEXANDER AV	BUT	33	C1
ALEXANDER AV	SHA	18	C3
ALEXANDER LN	LAS	21	C3
ALEXANDR VLY RD	SON	31	D5
ALFALFA AV	STA	47	C4
ALFRD HARRL HWY	KER	78	D2
ALGA RD	SDCO	106	C3
ALGERINE RD	TUO	41	C5
ALGODON RD	YUB	33	D3
ALGRN WRDS FRRY	TUO	41	C5
ALGOMAN AV	SBD	91	E3
ALHAMBRA	CC	38	E5
ALHAMBRA AV	CC	L	E3
ALHAMBRA AV	M	154	B2
ALHAMBRA BLVD	SCTO	137	D4
ALHAMBRA RD	LACO	R	B3
ALHAMBRA VLY RD	CC	L	D3
ALHAMBRA VLY RD	CC	38	D5
ALHAMBRA VLY RD	CC	154	C5
ALHAMBRA VLY RD	M	154	C4
ALICE AV	HUM	16	C5
ALICIA AV	YUB	33	D2
ALICIA PKWY	ORCO	98	D5
ALIPAZ ST	SJC	202	C2
ALISAL RD	MON	54	D4
ALISAL RD	SB	86	E3
ALISAL ST E	SAL	171	D4
ALISAL ST W	SAL	171	B4
ALISO CANYON RD	LACO	89	E4
ALISO CANYON RD	SB	87	C1
ALISO CANYON RD	VEN	88	B5
ALISO PARK RD	SB	87	C1
ALISOS AV	SB	87	A3
ALISOS CYN RD	SB	86	D2
ALLA RD	LA	187	E3
ALLAN RD	AMA	41	A1
ALLEGHANY RD	YUB	26	C5
ALLEN AV	LACO	R	C2
ALLEN AV	MCO	48	C3
ALLEN RD	IMP	108	D3
ALLEN RD	KER	78	C3
ALLEN RD	SJCO	47	C1
ALLENDALE RD	SOL	39	A2
ALLIANCE RD	HUM	9	E5
ALLIANCE RD	HUM	10	A5
ALLISON RCH RD	NEV	34	C2
ALLUVIAL AV	FRCO	57	C3
ALMA AV	KER	79	D5
ALMA AV	SJ	152	C5
ALMA ST	PA	147	A2
ALMA ST	SCL	N	E2
ALMA ST	SCL	45	D4
ALMADEN AV	SJ	152	C5
ALMADEN BLVD	SJ	152	B4
ALMADEN EXPWY	SCL	P	B4
ALMADEN EXPWY	SCL	46	B5
ALMANOR DR W	PLU	20	B4
ALMER RD	COL	32	D2
ALMOND AV	CLO	32	E3
ALMOND AV	MCO	48	A4
ALMOND AV	STA	47	C3
ALMOND DR	MCO	55	D2
ALMOND DR	MCO	56	A2
ALMOND DR	SLO	76	B2
ALMOND RD	KER	77	B1
ALMND ORCHRD RD	SUT	33	B1
ALMONDWOOD DR	SJCO	47	B2
ALMONTE BLVD	MAR	140	B4
ALOHA ST	TEH	18	D5
ALONA ST	KER	80	A4
ALONDRA BLVD	LACO	97	E3
ALONDRA BLVD	LACO	98	A3
ALOSTA AV	LACO	98	C1
ALOSTA AV	LACO	U	A2
ALPHA RD	NEV	26	E5
ALPINE AV	FRCO	56	D4
ALPINE AV	SJCO	40	A5
ALPINE AV	S	160	A3
ALPINE BLVD	SDCO	107	A5
ALPINE RD	MOD	7	C5
ALPINE RD	MOD	8	C1
ALPINE RD	SJCO	40	B4
ALPINE RD	SMCO	N	D3
ALPINE RD	SMCO	45	D4
ALPINE ST	LA	186	B2
ALPINE MINE RD	ALP	36	A4
ALPS DR	KER	79	C5
ALT CT	RCO	107	C1
ALTA	FRCO	58	A4
ALTA ST	MON	54	E5
ALTA ST	NEV	34	C1
ALTA BONNY NOOK	PLA	34	E1
ALTADENA DR	LACO	98	A1
ALTADENA DR	LACO	R	B2
AL TAHOE BLVD	SLT	129	A4
ALTAIR AV	SDCO	106	D5
ALTA LAGUNA BLVD	LAG	201	D1
ALTA LOMA DR	SBD	100	E1
ALTAMONT PS RD	ALA	M	D5
ALTA SIERRA DR	NEV	34	C2
ALTA MESA DR	SHA	18	C2
ALTA MESA RD	SAC	40	B2
ALTAMONT PSS RD	ALA	46	C2
ALTA VISTA	AVLN	97	A4
ALTA VISTA	BKD	166	E2
ALTA VISTA DR	KER	78	D3
ALTHEA AV	FRCO	56	A2
ALTON AV	SA	197	D2
ALTON PKWY	IRV	198	D3
ALTUS AV	KER	80	B5
ALUM ROCK AV	SCL	P	C3
ALUM ROCK AV	SCL	46	B4
ALVARADO BLVD	ALA	N	E1

STREET	CO.	PAGE	GRID
ALVARADO BLVD	ALA	P	A1
ALVARADO BLVD	ALA	45	E3
ALVARADO RD	MON	65	D4
ALVARADO RD	STA	47	E2
ALVARADO ST	LA	185	C3
ALVARADO ST	LACO	Q	E4
ALVARADO ST	SDCO	106	C2
ALVARADO TR	MCO	55	D2
ALVARADO-NLS RD	ALA	45	E3
ALVARADO-NLS RD	ALA	P	A1
ALVES RD	MCO	48	A3
ALVIN AV	SMA	173	B2
ALVIN DR E	SAL	171	D1
ALVIN DR W	SAL	171	C1
ALVISO-MLPTS RD	SCL	46	A4
ALVORD MTN RD	SBD	82	C5
ALWARD RD	SHA	19	B3
AMADOR AV	FRCO	56	D5
AMADOR ST	FRE	165	B4
AMADOR ST	VAL	134	D4
AMADOR CREEK RD	AMA	40	E2
AMAR RD	LACO	98	B2
AMAR RD	LACO	R	E4
AMARGOSA RD	SBD	91	B3
AMARGOSA ST	SBD	92	C2
AMBOY CUTOFF	SBD	93	E3
AMBOY RD	SBD	93	D4
AMBOY RD	SBD	101	C1
AMBROSE DR	SAL	171	A4
AMEDEE RD	LAS	21	D4
AMELIA AV	LACO	U	B1
AMEN LN	TEH	18	C3
AMERICAN AV	FRCO	57	A4
AMERICAN AV	FRCO	58	B4
AMERICAN AV	MCO	47	D5
AMERICAN AV	STA	47	C2
AMERICAN CYN RD	NAPA	L	D2
AMERICAN CYN RD	NAPA	38	D4
AMERICN FLAT RD	AMA	40	E2
AMRICAN FLT SDE	AMA	40	E1
AMERICN GIRL MN	IMP	110	B5
AMERICN MINE RD	SHA	18	A1
AMERIGO	SJCO	40	C5
AMES ST	ALA	M	D5
AMES ST	ALA	46	C2
AMESTI RD	SCR	54	B2
AMOROSE ST	RCO	99	B4
AMSTERDAM RD	MCO	48	B3
ANACAPA ST	STB	174	A2
ANAHEIM BLVD	ANA	193	C4
ANAHEIM BLVD	ORCO	98	C3
ANAHEIM BLVD	ORCO	T	C2
ANAHEIM ST	LB	192	D2
ANAHEIM ST	LACO	97	D5
ANAHEIM ST	LACO	S	C2
ANAPAMU ST	STB	174	C3
ANCHO ERIE MINE	NEV	26	E5
ANCHO MINE RD	NEV	26	E5
ANCHOR	FRCO	58	B4
ANDERHOLT RD	IMP	112	B4
ANDERSON DR W	SHA	18	C3
ANDERSON LN	HUM	15	D2
ANDERSON RD	DVS	136	B3
ANDERSON RD	SLO	76	A1
ANDERSON RD	SOL	39	C2
ANDERSON RD	STA	47	C4
ANDERSON RD	TUL	68	C2
ANDERSON ST	SBD	99	C2
ANDERSON CK RD	JKSN	3	D1
ANDERSON GRADE	SIS	4	D4
ANDERSON RCH RD	LAS	14	D4
ANDERSON VLY WY	MEN	30	E3
ANDESITE RD	SIS	4	D5
ANDESITE RD	SIS	12	D1
ANDESITE LOG RD	SIS	12	D1
ANDRADE RD	ALA	P	B1
ANDRADE RD	ALA	46	B3
ANDRE RD	IMP	109	A4
ANDRESSEN RD	PLA	34	A3
ANDREW AV	SB	86	C1
ANDREWS RD	LAS	14	C3
ANDREWS RD	SIS	4	E3
ANGELES CRST HY	LACO	R	B1
ANGELES FRST HY	LACO	90	A4
ANGELES FRST HY	LACO	R	B1
ANITA RD	BUT	25	A2
ANNADALE AV	FRCO	57	B4
ANNADALE AV	FRCO	58	A3
ANNAPOLIS RD	SON	30	E5
ANNAPOLIS RD	SON	31	A5
ANNETTE RD	KER	76	E1
ANNIN AV	KER	78	B1
ANTELOPE DR	LAS	8	B4
ANTELOPE HWY	LACO	90	D4
ANTELOPE RD	MNO	42	E1
ANTELOPE RD	MNO	43	A1
ANTELOPE RD	RCO	99	C4
ANTELOPE RD	SAC	34	A5
ANTELOPE RD	SLO	66	E5
ANTELOPE SPGS	MNO	50	E2
ANTELOPE VLY FY	LACO	89	E2
ANTELOPE VLY RD	SIE	27	C3
ANTHONY RD	LACO	89	D4
ANTOLA RD	LAS	21	C3
ANTONIO PKWY	ORCO	98	E5
ANZA RD	IMP	112	A4
ANZA RD	RCO	106	D1
ANZAR RD	SBT	54	D2
ANZA TRAIL RD	IMP	111	C4
APACHE TR	RCO	100	B3
APACHE CYN RD	VEN	88	A2
APPALOOSA RD	CAL	41	A2
APPIAN WY	CC	L	C3

STREET	CO.	PAGE	GRID
APPIAN WY	CC	38	C5
APPLE AV	STA	47	C3
APPLE RD	TEH	24	C2
APPLE CANYON RD	RCO	100	C4
APPLE COLONY RD	TUO	41	D5
APPLEGATE RD	MCO	48	B4
APPLE RANCH RD	TUO	41	E4
APPLE SEED LN	RCO	100	A5
APPLE VALLEY RD	SBD	91	C3
APPLEWHITE	SBD	91	A5
APRICOT AV	STA	47	C3
APRIL LN	VEN	88	C4
AQUEDUCT RD	KER	79	E5
AQUEDUCT RD	KER	80	A5
AQUEDUCT RD	SBD	103	A2
AQUEDUCT RD	SBD	104	A1
ARAMAYO WY	TEH	24	E1
ARATA LN	SON	37	E1
ARBINI RD	STA	47	E1
ARBOGA RD	YUB	33	D2
ARBOLEDA DR	MCO	48	C5
ARBOR RD	SLO	76	A1
ARBOR WY	MCO	56	C1
ARBORETUM RD	PA	147	A3
ARBOR VITAE ST	LA	189	D1
ARBOR VITAE ST	LACO	Q	D5
ARBURUA RD	MCO	55	D2
ARC RD	INY	51	D5
ARCH RD	SJCO	40	B5
ARCH AIRPORT RD	SJCO	40	B5
ARCHER AV	SUT	33	C1
ARCHER RD	SHA	18	A3
ARCHERDALE RD	SJCO	40	C5
ARCHIBALD AV	RCO	98	E3
ARCHIBALD AV	SBD	U	E4
ARCHIE BROWN RD	SHA	13	D4
ARDATH RD	SD	211	B3
ARDATH RD	SDCO	V	A2
ARDATH RD	SDCO	106	C5
ARDEN DR	LACO	R	C3
ARDEN WY	SAC	40	A1
ARDENWOOD BLVD	ALA	N	E1
ARDENWOOD BLVD	ALA	P	A1
ARDMORE AV	MB	189	E5
ARENA WY	MCO	48	A4
ARGO ST	KER	80	D1
ARGONAUT RD	LAK	31	D3
ARGONNE DR	S	160	B4
ARGYLE RD	MON	65	B3
ARLINGTON AV	CC	L	C3
ARLINGTON AV	LA	184	E4
ARLINGTON AV	LACO	Q	D4
ARLINGTON AV	LACO	S	B2
ARLINGTON AV	RIV	205	D5
ARLINGTON AV	RCO	99	A2
ARLINGTON AV S	RENO	130	A5
ARLINGTON BLVD	A	155	D2
ARLINGTON BLVD	DVS	136	A3
ARLINGTON RD	PLU	20	D5
ARLINGTON MN RD	RCO	103	B3
ARMORY RD	BARS	208	B3
ARMOUR RD	SUT	33	C4
ARMOUR RANCH RD	SB	86	E3
ARMOUR RANCH RD	SB	87	A3
ARMSTRONG	SJCO	40	A4
ARMSTRONG AV	FRCO	57	D2
ARMSTRONG AV	FRCO	57	D3
ARMSTRONG RD	CAL	41	C3
ARMSTRONG RD	LAS	14	D3
ARMSTRONG RD	RCO	99	A2
ARMSTRONG RD	STA	47	C4
ARMSTRONG RD	YUB	33	D1
ARMSTRNG WDS RD	SON	37	C1
ARMY RD	RCO	110	B1
ARMY ST	SFCO	L	B5
ARMY ST	SFCO	45	C2
ARNO RD	SAC	40	A3
ARNOLD DR	SON	L	B2
ARNOLD DR	SON	38	B3
ARNOLD DR	SON	132	A3
ARNOLD RD	IMP	112	C5
ARNOLD WY	SDCO	107	B5
AROSA RD	KER	79	C4
ARQUES RD	SCL	P	A3
ARRECHE RD	MOD	7	D5
ARRELLAGA ST	STB	174	C3
ARROW HWY	CLA	203	B2
ARROW HWY	LACO	98	B1
ARROW HWY	LACO	U	A2
ARROW HWY	MTCL	203	C2
ARROW HWY	ROC	204	E1
ARROW HWY	SBD	98	D1
ARROW HWY	SBD	U	D2
ARROW HWY	UPL	204	A2
ARROW ROUTE	SBD	203	C2
ARROWHEAD AV	SBDO	207	D3
ARROWHEAD BLVD	RCO	103	D5
ARROWHEAD BLVD	RCO	110	D1
ARROWHEAD RD	LAK	32	A3
ARROWHEAD ST	CAL	41	A5
ARROWHEAD TR	SBD	82	E4
ARROWHEAD TR	SBD	83	A4
ARROWHEAD LK RD	SBD	91	C5
ARROYA AV	MCO	56	A1
ARROYO AV	KER	79	E5
ARROYO AV	KER	80	A5
ARROYO BLVD	LACO	R	B2
ARROYO BLVD	PAS	190	A3
ARROYO PKWY	PAS	190	C5
ARROYO RD	ALA	P	C1
ARROYO RD	ALA	46	C2
ARROYO RD	SBD	92	A4
ARROYO BURRO RD	SB	87	C4

STREET INDEX

STREET	CO.	PAGE	GRID
ARROYO GR GUADL	SLO	76	B5
ARROYO GR GUADL	SLO	86	A1
AR GRANDE HUASNA	SLO	76	D4
ARROYO SECO RD	MON	64	E2
ARROYO SECO RD	MON	65	A1
ARTESIA AV	SB	86	B3
ARTESIA BLVD	LACO	97	D3
ARTESIA BLVD	LACO	98	A3
ARTESIA BLVD	LACO	S	B1
ARTESIA FRWY	LACO	98	A3
ARTESIA FRWY	LACO	S	D1
ARTESIA FRWY	LACO	T	A1
ARTHUR	SJCO	47	C1
ARTHUR RD	CC	L	E3
ARTHUR RD	CC	M	A3
ARTHUR ST	RCO	101	C5
ARTICHOKE RD	SMCO	N	C4
ARTICHOKE RD	SMCO	45	C5
ARTIC MINE RD	NEV	26	E5
ARTISTS DR	INY	72	A1
ASH AV	SHA	13	C5
ASH AV	STA	47	C3
ASH ST	SD	215	D3
ASH ST	SDCO	107	A4
ASHBY AV	ALA	L	D4
ASHBY AV	B	156	C3
ASHBY RD	SHA	18	C2
ASH CREEK RD	INY	60	B5
ASH CREEK RD	SHA	18	E3
ASH CREEK RD	SIS	4	A3
ASH CK SINK RD	SIS	13	A2
ASHE RD	KER	78	D4
ASHFORD ST	SD	213	E1
ASHLAN AV	FRCO	56	C3
ASHLAN AV	FRCO	57	A5
ASHLEY LN	SJCO	40	B4
ASH VALLEY RD	LAS	8	A3
ASH VALLEY RD	LAS	14	D3
ASHWORTH RD	MPA	49	B3
ASILOMAR AV	PAC	167	A2
ASPEN VALLEY RD	TUO	49	C1
ASPEN VALLEY RD	TUO	63	A4
ASSOCIATED RD	SB	86	B1
ASSOCIATED RD	SIS	4	E3
ASSOCIATED RD	SIS	5	A3
ASTER RD	SBD	91	A3
ASTORIA AV	KER	89	C1
ATEN RD	IMP	109	A5
ATHEL ST	KER	80	C1
ATHERTON AV	MAR	L	A2
ATHERTON BLVD	MAR	38	B4
ATHERTON ST	LACO	S	E2
ATHERTON ST	LACO	T	A2
ATHLONE RD	MCO	48	D5
ATKINS RD	SJCO	40	C4
ATLANTIC AV	A	157	D5
ATLANTIC AV	LB	192	E2
ATLANTIC AV	LACO	97	E3
ATLANTIC AV	LACO	S	D1
ATLANTIC AV	LACO	S	D2
ATLANTIC AV E	FRFD	135	D2
ATLANTIC BLVD	LACO	98	A2
ATLANTIC BLVD	LACO	R	B4
ATLAS	CC	38	C5
ATLAS RD	CC	L	C3
ATLAS PEAK RD	NAPA	38	D2
ATTERBERRY CT	KER	79	E2
ATTILA RD	SBD	84	C4
ATWATER	MCO	47	E4
ATWELL AV	TUL	67	E4
ATWELL AV	TUL	68	A4
ATWOOD	PLA	34	C3
AUBERRY RD	FRCO	57	E1
AUBERRY RD	FRCO	58	A1
AUBERRY RD	MAD	49	E5
AUBREY AV	MCO	56	A2
AUBURN BLVD	SAC	34	A5
AUBURN RD	NEV	34	C2
AUBURN RD	PLA	34	B3
AUBURN-FOLSOM RD	AUB	126	C5
AUBURN RAVNE RD	AUB	126	C3
AUCTION SNIVELY	TEH	18	D4
AUDUBON DR	FRCO	57	C2
AUGUST AV	MCO	47	D4
AUGUST RD	STA	47	D4
AUGUSTINE RD	RCO	109	C1
AUKLET RD	SBD	92	C1
AULD RD	RCO	99	D5
AURORA CYN RD	MNO	43	B3
AUSTIN RD	IMP	109	A5
AUSTIN RD	SJCO	40	B5
AUSTIN RD	SJCO	47	B1
AUSTIN CREEK RD	SON	37	C2
AUSTIN MDWS RD	NEV	27	A4
AUSTRIAN RD	CAL	41	B4
AUTO CIR	SD	213	E4
AUTO PLAZA DR	SBDO	207	C4
AUTOPSTA TIJ-EN	BAJA	111	D3
AUTUMN AV	SJ	152	B4
AVALON AV	SBD	100	E1
AVALON BLVD	LA	191	C1
AVALON BLVD	LACO	97	E3
AVALON BLVD	LACO	S	C1
AVALON CYN RD	AVLN	97	A5
AVENA	SJCO	47	C1
AVENAL CUTOFF	KIN	67	A3
AVD BERMUDAS	RCO	100	E4
AVD CABALLEROS	PMSP	206	B1
AVD DEL CAPITAN	SB	87	A4
AVD D LS ARBLES	VEN	88	D5
AVD D LS ARBLES	VEN	96	D1
AVENIDA DEL SOL	KER	80	C1
AVENIDA ENCINO	RCO	100	D5

STREET	CO.	PAGE	GRID
AVD LA CUMBRE	RCO	100	D5
AVD LOS FELIZ	RCO	100	D5
AVENIDA OBREGON	RCO	100	E4
AVENUE A	KER	89	E1
AVENUE A	YUMA	112	D5
AVENUE B	LACO	89	D2
AVENUE B	LACO	90	C2
AVENUE C	LACO	89	D2
AVENUE C	LACO	90	D2
AVENUE C	YUMA	112	C5
AVENUE D	LACO	90	B2
AVENUE E	LACO	89	E2
AVENUE E	LACO	90	A2
AVENUE E	RCO	99	B3
AVENUE E	YUMA	112	C5
AVENUE E-8	LACO	90	B2
AVENUE F	LACO	89	B2
AVENUE F	LACO	89	D2
AVENUE F	LACO	90	C2
AVENUE F	SBD	99	D2
AVENUE F-4	LACO	89	C2
AVENUE F-4	LACO	90	A2
AVENUE F-8	LACO	89	C2
AVENUE F-8	LACO	90	D2
AVENUE G	LACO	89	E2
AVENUE G-2	LACO	90	C2
AVENUE G-3	LACO	90	C2
AVENUE G-4	LACO	90	C2
AVENUE G-6	LACO	90	C2
AVENUE G-8	LACO	90	B2
AVENUE H	LACO	89	E2
AVENUE I	LACO	89	E2
AVENUE J	LACO	89	E3
AVENUE J	LACO	90	C2
AVENUE J-8	LACO	90	A2
AVENUE K	LACO	89	E3
AVENUE K	LACO	90	C3
AVENUE K-8	LACO	89	D3
AVENUE L	LACO	89	E3
AVENUE L	LACO	90	B3
AVENUE L	RCO	99	D2
AVENUE M	LACO	89	E3
AVENUE M	LACO	90	B3
AVENUE M-8	LACO	89	E3
AVENUE N	LACO	89	E3
AVENUE N	LACO	90	C3
AVENUE O	LACO	90	A3
AVE OF THE STARS	LA	183	A2
AVENUE ONE	MCO	48	B4
AVENUE P	LACO	89	E3
AVENUE P	LACO	90	A3
AVENUE P	LACO	90	D3
AVENUE P-8	LACO	90	A3
AVENUE P-8	LACO	90	C3
AVENUE Q	LACO	90	C3
AVENUE Q	LACO	90	C3
AVENUE S	LACO	89	E3
AVENUE S	LACO	90	A3
AVENUE SAN LUIS	LA	177	A4
AVENUE STANFORD	LACO	89	B4
AVENUE T	LACO	90	B3
AVENUE T	LACO	90	C3
AVENUE TWO	MCO	48	B4
AVENUE U	LACO	90	C3
AVENUE Z	LACO	90	D4
AVENUE 2	TUL	68	D5
AVENUE 4 1/2	MAD	56	E3
AVENUE 5	MAD	56	E3
AVENUE 5 1/2	MAD	56	E3
AVENUE 5 1/2	MAD	57	A3
AVENUE 6	MAD	56	E3
AVENUE 6	MAD	57	A3
AVENUE 6 1/2	MAD	57	A3
AVENUE 7 1/2	MAD	56	D3
AVENUE 7 1/2	MAD	56	E3
AVENUE 7 1/2	MAD	57	C3
AVENUE 8	MAD	56	E3
AVENUE 8	MAD	57	A2
AVENUE 8	MAD	57	C2
AVENUE 8	TUL	68	B5
AVENUE 8 1/2	MAD	57	A2
AVENUE 9	MAD	56	E2
AVENUE 9	MAD	57	C2
AVENUE 9 1/2	MAD	56	E2
AVENUE 10	MAD	56	E2
AVENUE 10	MAD	57	B2
AVENUE 10 1/2	MAD	56	E2
AVENUE 10 1/2	MAD	57	A2
AVENUE 11	MAD	56	E2
AVENUE 11	MAD	57	A2
AVENUE 11 1/2	MAD	56	E2
AVENUE 11 1/2	MAD	57	A2
AVENUE 12	MAD	56	E2
AVENUE 12	MAD	57	B2
AVENUE 12	TUL	68	B5
AVENUE 12	TUL	68	C5
AVENUE 12 1/2	MAD	57	B2
AVENUE 13	MAD	56	E2
AVENUE 13 1/2	MAD	56	E2
AVENUE 13 1/2	MAD	57	A2
AVENUE 14	MAD	56	E2
AVENUE 14	MAD	57	C2
AVENUE 14 1/2	MAD	56	E2
AVENUE 14 1/2	MAD	57	A2
AVENUE 14 1/2	MAD	57	C2
AVENUE 15	MAD	56	E2
AVENUE 15 1/2	MAD	56	E2
AVENUE 15 1/2	MAD	57	B2
AVENUE 16	MAD	56	E2
AVENUE 16	TUL	68	B4
AVENUE 16	TUL	68	C4
AVENUE 16 1/2	MAD	56	E2
AVENUE 17	MAD	56	D2

STREET	CO.	PAGE	GRID
AVENUE 17 1/2	MAD	56	E2
AVENUE 18	MAD	56	D2
AVENUE 18 1/2	MAD	56	D2
AVENUE 19	MAD	56	D1
AVENUE 19 1/2	MAD	56	D1
AVENUE 20	LA	186	D1
AVENUE 20	MAD	56	D1
AVENUE 20 1/2	MAD	56	D1
AVENUE 21	MAD	56	D1
AVENUE 21	MAD	57	A1
AVENUE 21 1/2	MAD	56	D1
AVENUE 22	MAD	56	D1
AVENUE 22 1/2	MAD	56	D1
AVENUE 23 1/2	MAD	56	D1
AVENUE 24	MAD	56	D1
AVENUE 24	TUL	68	B4
AVENUE 24 1/2	MAD	56	E1
AVENUE 25	MAD	56	D1
AVENUE 25 1/2	MAD	56	D1
AVENUE 26	MAD	56	D1
AVENUE 26 1/2	MAD	56	E1
AVENUE 27	MAD	48	D5
AVENUE 27 1/2	MAD	48	E5
AVENUE 28	MAD	48	E5
AVENUE 28	TUL	68	C4
AVENUE 32	TUL	68	B4
AVENUE 40	TUL	68	C4
AVENUE 42	TUL	67	E4
AVENUE 42	TUL	68	C4
AVENUE 42	TUL	68	A4
AVENUE 44	TUL	68	B4
AVENUE 46	TUL	67	E4
AVENUE 46	TUL	68	C4
AVENUE 50	TUL	67	E4
AVENUE 52	TUL	68	B4
AVENUE 52	TUL	68	C4
AVENUE 54	TUL	67	E4
AVENUE 56	TUL	68	B4
AVENUE 58	TUL	68	A4
AVENUE 62	TUL	68	A4
AVENUE 64	TUL	68	D4
AVENUE 66	TUL	68	D4
AVENUE 68	TUL	68	A4
AVENUE 68	TUL	68	D4
AVENUE 70	TUL	68	D4
AVENUE 74	TUL	68	D4
AVENUE 76	TUL	68	D4
AVENUE 78	TUL	68	D4
AVENUE 80	TUL	68	B4
AVENUE 80	TUL	68	C4
AVENUE 84	TUL	68	A4
AVENUE 86	TUL	68	D4
AVENUE 88	TUL	67	E4
AVENUE 88	TUL	68	A4
AVENUE 88	TUL	68	D4
AVENUE 90	TUL	68	D4
AVENUE 92	TUL	68	D4
AVENUE 94	TUL	68	D4
AVENUE 95	TUL	68	C4
AVENUE 96	TUL	68	D4
AVENUE 100	TUL	68	D3
AVENUE 102	TUL	68	D3
AVENUE 104	TUL	67	E3
AVENUE 104	TUL	68	C3
AVENUE 108	TUL	68	A3
AVENUE 108	TUL	68	D3
AVENUE 112	TUL	67	E3
AVENUE 112	TUL	68	D3
AVENUE 116	TUL	68	B3
AVENUE 116	TUL	68	D3
AVENUE 120	TUL	67	E3
AVENUE 120	TUL	68	D3
AVENUE 124	TUL	68	C3
AVENUE 128	TUL	67	E3
AVENUE 128	TUL	68	C3
AVENUE 132	TUL	68	C3
AVENUE 136	TUL	67	E3
AVENUE 136	TUL	68	C3
AVENUE 138	TUL	68	E3
AVENUE 144	TUL	68	A3
AVENUE 152	TUL	68	B3
AVENUE 152	TUL	68	C3
AVENUE 156	TUL	68	D3
AVENUE 160	TUL	68	A3
AVENUE 160	TUL	68	D3
AVENUE 164	TUL	68	B3
AVENUE 168	TUL	68	A3
AVENUE 168	TUL	68	C3
AVENUE 169	TUL	68	D3
AVENUE 172	TUL	68	C3
AVENUE 176	TUL	68	A3
AVENUE 176	TUL	68	C3
AVENUE 178	TUL	68	D3
AVENUE 180	TUL	68	B3
AVENUE 182	TUL	68	D3
AVENUE 184	TUL	68	C2
AVENUE 188	TUL	68	D2
AVENUE 190	TUL	68	A2
AVENUE 192	TUL	68	A2
AVENUE 192	TUL	68	B2
AVENUE 196	TUL	68	B2
AVENUE 196	TUL	68	D2
AVENUE 198	TUL	68	A2
AVENUE 199	TUL	67	E2
AVENUE 200	TUL	68	A2
AVENUE 200	TUL	68	C2
AVENUE 204	TUL	67	E2
AVENUE 204	TUL	68	A2
AVENUE 204	TUL	68	C2
AVENUE 204	TUL	68	C4
AVENUE 206	TUL	68	D2
AVENUE 208	TUL	67	E2
AVENUE 208	TUL	68	A2

STREET	CO.	PAGE	GRID
AVENUE 208	TUL	68	C2
AVENUE 212	TUL	68	D2
AVENUE 212	TUL	68	D2
AVENUE 216	TUL	68	A2
AVENUE 216	TUL	68	D2
AVENUE 222	TUL	68	D2
AVENUE 224	TUL	68	B2
AVENUE 226	TUL	68	D2
AVENUE 228	TUL	68	B2
AVENUE 232	TUL	68	D2
AVENUE 236	TUL	68	A2
AVENUE 236	TUL	68	D2
AVENUE 240	TUL	68	A2
AVENUE 244	TUL	68	A2
AVENUE 248	TUL	68	A2
AVENUE 252	TUL	68	A2
AVENUE 256	TUL	67	E2
AVENUE 260	TUL	68	A2
AVENUE 264	TUL	68	B2
AVENUE 268	TUL	68	A2
AVENUE 271	TUL	68	B1
AVENUE 272	TUL	68	A1
AVENUE 272	TUL	68	D1
AVENUE 276	TUL	68	C1
AVENUE 280	TUL	68	A1
AVENUE 300	TUL	68	C1
AVENUE 304	TUL	68	A1
AVENUE 306	TUL	68	D1
AVENUE 308	TUL	68	A1
AVENUE 312	TUL	68	D1
AVENUE 318	TUL	68	C1
AVENUE 320	TUL	68	A1
AVENUE 320	TUL	68	D1
AVENUE 324	TUL	68	C1
AVENUE 328	TUL	68	A1
AVENUE 328	TUL	68	C1
AVENUE 332	TUL	68	C1
AVENUE 332	TUL	58	C5
AVENUE 334	TUL	58	D5
AVENUE 334	TUL	68	D1
AVENUE 336	TUL	68	B1
AVENUE 336	TUL	58	C5
AVENUE 337	TUL	68	C1
AVENUE 340	TUL	68	B1
AVENUE 340	TUL	58	C5
AVENUE 344	TUL	68	B1
AVENUE 344	TUL	58	C5
AVENUE 346	TUL	68	D1
AVENUE 348	TUL	68	C1
AVENUE 350	TUL	58	D5
AVENUE 352	TUL	57	E5
AVENUE 352	TUL	58	C5
AVENUE 356	TUL	58	B5
AVENUE 356	TUL	58	C5
AVENUE 360	TUL	57	E5
AVENUE 360	TUL	58	C5
AVENUE 364	TUL	58	C5
AVENUE 368	TUL	58	B5
AVENUE 368	TUL	58	C5
AVENUE 376	TUL	57	E5
AVENUE 376	TUL	58	C5
AVENUE 380	TUL	58	C5
AVENUE 384	TUL	58	A5
AVENUE 386	TUL	58	C5
AVENUE 388	TUL	58	C5
AVENUE 390	TUL	57	E5
AVENUE 390	TUL	58	C5
AVENUE 392	TUL	58	A5
AVENUE 394	TUL	58	C5
AVENUE 396	TUL	57	E5
AVENUE 396	TUL	58	A5
AVENUE 398	TUL	58	C5
AVENUE 400	TUL	58	B5
AVENUE 404	TUL	58	B5
AVENUE 404	TUL	58	C5
AVENUE 408	TUL	57	E5
AVENUE 408	TUL	58	B5
AVENUE 410	TUL	57	E5
AVENUE 416	TUL	58	C5
AVENUE 424	TUL	58	A4
AVENUE 428	TUL	58	B4
AVENUE 432	TUL	58	B4
AVENUE 436	TUL	58	B4
AVENUE 438	TUL	58	B4
AVENUE 440	TUL	58	B4
AVENUE 444	TUL	58	B4
AVENUE 448	TUL	58	B4
AVENUE 450	TUL	58	B4
AVENUE 452	TUL	58	B4
AVENUE 456	TUL	58	B4
AVENUE 460	TUL	58	B4
AVENUE 464	TUL	58	B4
AVENUE 468	TUL	58	B4
AVENUE 472	TUL	58	B4
AVERY RD	FRCO	55	E3
AVERY RD	MCO	55	D3
AVERY SHEEP RCH	CAL	41	C3
AVIATION BLVD	ELS	189	E4
AVIATION BLVD	HAW	189	D4
AVIATION BLVD	LA	188	E5
AVIATION BLVD	LA	189	E2
AVIATION BLVD	LACO	97	D3
AVIATION BLVD	LACO	S	B1
AVIATION BLVD	MB	189	D5
AVOCADO BLVD	SDCO	V	E5
AVOCADO BLVD	SDCO	111	E1
AVOCADO RD	BUT	25	E5
AYERS AV	SJCO	47	C1
AYRES HOLMES RD	PLA	34	B3
AZALEA TR	RCO	100	B3
AZEVEDO	MCO	47	D5
AZEVEDO RD	SOL	39	C4
AZEVEDO RD	STA	47	C4

STREET	CO.	PAGE	GRID
AZTEC AV	RCO	102	C4
AZUSA AV	LACO	98	B2
AZUSA AV	LACO	R	E4
AZUSA CANYON RD	LACO	R	E3
B			
B ST	BUT	25	C5
B ST	DVS	136	C3
B ST	FRE	165	C4
B ST	H	146	E2
B ST	IMP	109	A4
B ST	KER	68	B5
B ST	SD	216	B3
B ST	LACO	97	E4
B ST	LACO	S	C2
B ST	SD	215	D3
B ST	SJCO	40	B5
B ST	YUBA	125	D3
B ST	YUB	33	D2
B ST N	SCTO	137	B2
BABCOCK RD	LAS	14	B4
BABCOCK CNDR RD	LAS	14	B4
BABEL SLOUGH RD	YOL	39	D2
BACHELOR VLY RD	LAK	31	C2
BACK BONE RD	NEV	26	D5
BACKBONE RD	SHA	13	A5
BACKBONE RD	SHA	18	E1
BACKES LN	KER	79	C4
BACKUS RD	KER	79	E5
BACON RD	STA	47	B2
BACON ST	SDCO	V	A3
BACON ST	SDCO	111	C1
BACON ISLAND	SJCO	39	E5
BADDAGE RD	RCO	107	B1
BADENOUGH CY RD	SIE	27	D3
BADGER RD	SON	38	A2
BADGER FLAT	MCO	55	D1
BAGDAD HWY	SBD	93	C4
BAGDAD HWY	SBD	101	C1
BAGDAD WY	SBD	93	D4
BAGDAD CHASE RD	SBD	93	B2
BAGGTT MARYSVLL	BUT	25	D5
BAGLEY RD	COL	32	D2
BAILEY AV	KER	70	A5
BAILEY AV	MCO	48	B4
BAILEY AV	SB	86	B3
BAILEY AV	SCL	P	D4
BAILEY RD	COL	32	E3
BAILEY RD	CC	M	B3
BAILEY RD	CC	39	A5
BAILEY RD	DN	1	D3
BAILEY RD	IMP	110	D5
BAILEY RD	RCO	107	B1
BAILEY RD	SBD	84	A2
BAILEY RD	SCL	46	C5
BAILEY RD	SUT	33	C3
BAILEY FLATS RD	MAD	49	B5
BAILEY HILL RD	SIS	4	A2
BAILY RD	KER	79	B4
BAILY RIDGE RD	CAL	41	C2
BAIN ST	RCO	99	A2
BAIR RD	HUM	10	B4
BAIRD RD	SON	38	A2
BAKER AV	ONT	204	E3
BAKER AV	ORCO	T	C3
BAKER AV	ROC	204	E2
BAKER RD	COL	32	C2
BAKER RD	MCO	55	E1
BAKER RD	SJCO	40	B4
BAKER RD	STA	47	C3
BAKER RD	TEH	18	D5
BAKER RD	SUT	33	C4
BAKER RD	YUB	26	B5
BAKER ST	CM	197	C4
BAKER ST	CM	198	A4
BAKER CREEK RD	INY	51	D5
BAKER RILEY WY	CAL	41	B3
BKRSFLD-GLNVLLE	KER	68	E5
BKRSFLD-GLNVLLE	KER	69	A5
BKRSFLD-GLNVLLE	KER	78	D2
BAKRSFLD-MCKITT	KER	78	A3
BALBOA AV	SD	212	C2
BALBOA AV	SDCO	V	A2
BALBOA AV	SDCO	106	C5
BALBOA BLVD	LACO	97	C1
BALBOA BLVD	LACO	Q	B1
BALBOA BLVD	NB	199	B5
BALBOA BLVD	ORCO	T	C4
BALCH PARK RD	TUL	69	A2
BALCOM CYN RD	VEN	88	D5
BALDERSTON	ED	34	E3
BALD HILL RD	PLA	34	C3
BALD HILLS RD	DN	1	E4
BALD HILLS RD	DN	2	A4
BALD HILLS RD	HUM	10	A2
BALD MTN RD	CAL	41	B2
BALD MTN RD	HUM	10	B5
BALD MTN RD	MEN	23	A2
BALD MTN RD	MNO	50	D1
BALD MTN RD	SHA	13	E4
BALD MTN RD	YUB	33	E1
BALD MTN RD N	CAL	41	C2
BALD MTN LKOUT	SIS	3	D4
BALD MT SPGS RD	MNO	50	E1
BALD ROCK RD	BUT	25	E3
BALDWIN AV	LACO	R	C3
BALDWIN RD	STA	47	D2
BALDWIN RD	STA	47	B3
BALDWIN RD	VEN	88	A4
BALDWIN ST	CAL	40	D4
BALDWIN PARK BLVD	LACO	R	D4
BALDY RD	SBD	90	E5

STREET	CO.	PAGE	GRID
BALDY MCCULY RD	SHA	13	E4
BALDY MESA RD	SBD	91	A4
BALE LN	NAPA	29	B2
BALFOUR RD	CC	M	C3
BALFOUR RD	CC	39	C5
BALIS RD	TEH	18	C5
BALIS BELL RD	TEH	18	B5
BALL RD	ANA	193	A3
BALL RD	ORCO	98	B3
BALL RD	ORCO	T	B2
BALL RD	TEH	17	E4
BALLANTREE LN	NEV	34	B2
BALLARAT RD	INY	71	C3
BALLARD RD	TEH	24	E2
BALL FERRY PK RD	SHA	18	D3
BALLICO AV	MCO	48	A4
BALLINGER RD	RCO	99	E5
BALLINGR CYN RD	VEN	87	E1
BALL MT LTL SHA	SIS	4	B4
BALL MT LTL SHA	SIS	5	A4
BALL MTN LKOUT	SIS	4	D3
BALL ROCK RD	TEH	23	E1
BALLS FERRY RD	SHA	18	D3
BALSAM RD	SBD	91	B4
BALSAMO RD	SBD	81	A5
BALTIMORE MN RD	PLA	34	E3
BANCROFT DR	SDCO	V	D3
BANCROFT DR	SDCO	111	E1
BANCROFT RD	CC	M	A3
BANCROFT RD	STA	47	C3
BANCROFT WY	ALA	L	D4
BANCROFT WY	B	156	A3
BANDERILLA DR	MPA	48	D2
BANDINI BLVD	LACO	R	A4
B & R LN	SOL	39	C3
BANDUCCI RD	KER	79	B4
BANGOR AV	KIN	57	E5
BANGOR PARK CTO	BUT	25	E5
BANGOR PARK RD	BUT	25	D5
BANGS AV	STA	47	C2
BANNER RD	CAL	41	B3
BANNER QUAKR HL	NEV	34	D1
BANNER RDG LAVA	NEV	34	C1
BANNING IDYLLWD	RCO	100	A3
BANNISTER AV	SCL	P	E5
BANNISTER RD	IMP	108	E4
BANNON ST	SCTO	137	B1
BANTA RD	SJCO	47	E2
BAR RD	MAD	49	E5
BAR RD	MAD	50	A5
BARBARA WRTH RD	IMP	112	B4
BARBER	SJCO	39	E3
BARBER LN	RCO	107	B1
BARBER RD	ALP	36	B4
BARBER RD	TEH	25	A2
BARBER MTN RD	SDCO	112	B1
BARD RD	IMP	110	D5
BARDSDALE AV	VEN	88	D4
BARHAM AV	TEH	24	D2
BARHAM BLVD	LA	181	B1
BARHAM BLVD	LACO	Q	D3
BAR K RD	TRI	17	C2
BARKER RD	KER	67	B5
BARKER CREEK RD	TRI	17	B2
BARKER MINE RD	MNO	51	C2
BARKHOUSE CK RD	SIS	3	D3
BARKSHANTY RD	SIS	10	D2
BARLOW LN	INY	51	D4
BAR MTN LOOKOUT	SIS	3	C4
BARNES LN	MEN	23	B2
BARNES RD	KER	90	B1
BARNES RD	SBD	92	D4
BARNES RD	SLO	66	A5
BARNES RD	SLO	76	A1
BARNETT AV	SD	215	A1
BARNETT AV	SDCO	V	B3
BARNETT RD	STA	48	B2
BARNEY GULCH RD	TRI	11	B5
BARNHART RD	STA	47	C3
BARNY OLDFLD RD	IMP	110	C5
BARR RD	HUM	10	B5
BARRANCA AV	LACO	U	A3
BARRANCA PKWY	IRV	198	D2
BARRANCA PKWY	ORCO	98	C4
BARRANCA PKWY	ORCO	T	D3
BARRANCA PKWY	TUS	198	D2
BARREL SPGS RD	LACO	90	A3
BARREL SPGS RD	MOD	7	E3
BARRETT	CC	38	C5
BARRETT AV	ELC	155	E3
BARRETT AV	FRCO	57	B5
BARRETT AV	FRCO	57	C5
BARRETT LAKE RD	SDCO	112	B2
BARRINGTON AV	LACO	180	A2
BARRINGTON LN	SIE	27	C4
BARRY RD	SUT	33	D2
BARRYS RD	HUM	16	A1
BARSTOW AV	FRCO	57	A3
BARSTOW AV	FRCO	57	C3
BARSTOW AV	KIN	57	E5
BARSTOW FRWY	SBD	91	A5
BARSTOW FRWY	SBD	99	B1
BARSTOW RD	BARS	208	B4
BARSTOW RD	KER	80	D5
BARSTOW RD	SBD	91	E2
BARSTOW RD	SBD	92	A4
BARTEL ST	SHA	13	C5
BARTELL RD	INY	51	E5
BARTH RD	IMP	108	E3
BARTLE GAP RD	SIS	13	B3
BARTLETT RD	SOL	39	B3
BARTLETTE RD	INY	60	B5
BARTLETT SPG RD	LAK	31	E2

STREET	CO.	PAGE	GRID
BARTOLOMEI	SJCO	40	C5
BARTOLOMEI	SJCO	47	C1
BARTON	PLA	34	B5
BARTON RD	SBD	99	C2
BARTON ST	RCO	99	B3
BARTON HILL RD	YUB	26	B4
BAR W RD	HUM	16	B3
BASCOM AV	SCL	46	B4
BASCOM AV	SJ	151	C4
BASCOM AV	SCL	P	B3
BASE LINE AV	SB	86	E3
BASELINE RD	LACO	98	D1
BASE LINE RD	LACO	U	A2
BASE LINE RD	PLA	33	E5
BASELINE RD	SBD	U	D2
BASELINE RD	SBD	98	E1
BASELINE RD	SBD	101	C1
BASELINE ST	SBDO	207	D1
BASELINE ST	SBD	102	C1
BASIC SCHOOL RD	KER	78	B5
BASILONE RD	SDCO	105	E1
BASIN RD	SBD	82	E5
BASIN ST	KER	79	C2
BASLER RD	TEH	18	B4
BASS	FRCO	56	C3
BASSET RD	LAS	14	C3
BASSETT AV	KER	68	C5
BASS HILL RD	LAS	21	A3
BASS LAKE RD	ED	34	C5
BASS VALLEY RD	MAD	49	D4
BASTANCHURY RD	ORCO	T	C1
BATAVIA RD	SOL	39	B2
BATAVIA ST	ORA	194	B3
BATCHELDER RD	SB	86	C2
BATEMAN RD	SHA	19	B2
BATES	SUT	33	C4
BATH ST	STB	174	B3
BATTERY ST	SF	142	E2
BATTERY ST	SF	143	D2
BATTL CK BTM RD	SHA	19	A3
BATTLES RD	SMA	173	C4
BAUGHMAN RD	IMP	108	E4
BAUMBACH AV	KER	79	B4
BAUTISTA RD	RCO	100	A4
BAXTER AV	NAP	133	B2
BAXTER RD	MCO	48	E5
BAXTER RD	RCO	99	C5
BAXTERS RD	MNO	43	E5
BAXTERS RD	MNO	50	E1
BAY DR	SC	169	A3
BAY HWY	SON	37	C3
BAY RD	SMCO	N	D2
BAY RD	SMCO	45	D3
BAY ST	SF	142	B1
BAY ST	SC	169	B3
BAYLEY RES RD	MOD	8	A2
BAYLIS BLUE GUM	GLE	24	D4
BAYOU RD	SAC	33	D5
BAYSHORE BLVD	SMCO	L	C5
BAYSHORE BLVD	SMCO	45	C2
BAYSHORE FRWY	BLMT	145	D4
BAYSHORE FRWY	MLBR	144	D3
BAYSHORE FRWY	MVW	148	D3
BAYSHORE FRWY	SJ	151	D1
BAYSHORE FRWY	SJ	152	C1
BAYSHORE FRWY	SM	145	A1
BAYSHORE FRWY	SMCO	45	D3
BAYSHORE FRWY	SMCO	144	D2
BAYSHORE FRWY	SSF	144	C2
BAYSHORE FRWY	SVL	148	D3
BAYSHORE RD	BEN	153	D5
BAYSIDE DR	NB	199	D5
BAY VIEW AV	NAPA	38	C3
BAY VIEW RD	MCO	55	C1
BEACH BLVD	ORCO	98	B3
BEACH BLVD	ORCO	T	B1
BEACH RD	HUM	22	A1
BEACH RD	IMP	109	A2
BEACH RD	MPA	49	B4
BEACH RD	SCR	54	B3
BEACH PARK BL	FCTY	145	E1
BEACON RD	SLO	76	B1
BEACON ST	AVLN	97	B4
BEAGLE ST	SD	213	D1
BEAL RD	IMP	109	B2
BEALE RD N	YUB	33	D2
BEALE RD S	YUB	33	E3
BEALEVILLE RD	KER	79	B3
BEAL RANCH RD	CAL	40	E3
BEAMER ST	YOL	33	B5
BEAN CLIPPER RD	YUB	26	B4
BEAN CREEK RD	BUT	25	E4
BEAN CREEK RD	SCR	P	A5
BEAN CREEK RD	SCR	54	A1
BEAN HOLLOW RD	SMCO	N	C4
BEAN HOLLOW RD	SMCO	45	C5
BEAR ST	CM	197	E4
BEAR ST	ORCO	T	D3
BEAR ST	SA	197	E3
BEAR BASIN RD	DN	2	B3
BEAR BUTTE RD	HUM	16	B5
BEAR CANYON RD	FRCO	66	B2
BEAR CREEK DR N	MCO	48	C4
BEAR CREEK DR S	MCO	48	C4
BEAR CREEK LOOP	TRI	12	A3
BEAR CREEK RD	CC	L	D3
BEAR CREEK RD	CC	38	D5
BEAR CREEK RD	LAK	31	D1
BEAR CREEK RD	SCL	P	A4
BEAR CREEK RD	SCR	N	E5
BEAR CREEK RD	SCR	P	A5
BEAR CREEK RD	SCR	45	E5
BEARD RD	NAP	133	C2

STREET	CO.	PAGE	GRID
BEAR GULCH RD	SMCO	N	C3
BEAR MTN BLVD	KER	78	D4
BEAR MTN RD	FRCO	58	B3
BEAR MTN RD	SHA	18	C1
BEAR MTN RD	SIS	13	C2
BEAR MTN LKOUT	SHA	18	D1
BEAR MT WINE RD	KER	78	E3
BEAR MT WINE RD	KER	79	A3
BEAR RANCH HILL	BUT	25	E2
BEAR RIVER	AMA	41	D1
BEAR RIVER S	AMA	41	D1
BEAR RIVER DR	SUT	33	D3
BEAR RIV RDG RD	HUM	15	D3
BEAR SPRINGS RD	LAS	14	A3
BEAR TRAP DR	MPA	49	A3
BEAR TRAP RD	NEV	26	C5
BEAR VALLEY	MPA	48	E3
BEAR VLY CUTOFF	SBD	91	B4
BEAR VLY PKWY	SDCO	106	D4
BEAR VALLEY RD	COL	32	B2
BEAR VALLEY RD	KER	79	B4
BEAR VALLEY RD	SBD	90	E4
BEAR VALLEY RD	SIE	27	D4
BEASON ST	KER	78	A1
BEASORE RD	MAD	49	E4
BEATIE RD	SHA	18	D3
BEAUCHAMP RD	COL	32	D2
BEAUMONT AV	O	158	D3
BEAUMONT AV	RCO	99	E3
BEAUMONT ST	SBD	91	E3
BEAVER CREEK RD	SIS	3	D3
BECHELLI LN	RED	122	E2
BECHELLI LN	SHA	18	C2
BECK AV	SOL	L	E1
BECK AV	SOL	M	A1
BECKER	SUT	33	C4
BECKER RD	SOL	39	C1
BECKET CT	KER	79	C5
BECKWITH RD	SIE	27	D3
BECKWITH RD	STA	47	B2
BECKWRTH CALPNE	PLU	27	C3
BECKWRTH GENESE	PLU	26	E1
BECKWRTH GENESE	PLU	27	B1
BECKWRTH LOYLTN	PLU	27	C3
BCKWRTH TYLRSVL	PLU	26	E1
BCKWRTH TYLRSVL	PLU	27	B2
BEDFORD DR	SBD	92	B1
BEE CANYON RD	RCO	100	A4
BEECH AV	KER	78	B2
BEECH AV	SBD	99	A2
BEECH ST	BKD	166	B2
BEECH ST	SDCO	106	C2
BEECHER RD	SJCO	40	B5
BEE GULCH RD	ALP	42	A1
BEEGUM RD	SHA	17	D4
BEEGUM GORGE RD	SHA	17	D4
BEEKLEY RD	RCO	102	C4
BEEKLEY RD	SBD	90	E4
BEETHOVEN ST	LA	187	C1
BEEROCK RD	SLO	65	D5
BEHYMER	FRCO	56	C2
BEHYMER AV	FRCO	57	D2
BELCHER AV	MCO	48	B4
BELFAST RD	LAS	21	B3
BELFIELD RD	SBD	92	E5
BELL	MCO	48	A4
BELL LN	PLU	26	D1
BELL RD	AMA	40	E1
BELL RD	BUT	25	A3
BELL RD	KER	77	E2
BELL RD	KER	78	A2
BELL RD	PLA	34	B3
BELL RD	SB	87	C1
BELL RD	STA	47	C4
BELL ST	SB	86	D2
BELLAGIO RD	LA	180	A1
BELLAM BLVD	SR	139	E5
BELLA ROSA DR	HUM	16	C4
BELLA VISTA DR	KER	79	D1
BELLE TER	KER	166	D5
BELLE GRAVE AV	RCO	99	A2
BELLEVUE AV	SUT	33	D3
BELLEVUE RD	MCO	48	B4
BELLFLOWER BLVD	LACO	98	A3
BELLFLOWER BLVD	LACO	S	E2
BELLFLOWER BLVD	LACO	T	A2
BELLFLOWER ST	SBD	91	B3
BELL HILL RD	LAK	31	D3
BELL MTN RD	SBD	91	C3
BELL SPRINGS RD	HUM	16	C5
BELL SPRINGS RD	MEN	22	D1
BELLVIEW RD	MAD	57	C1
BELMONT AV	FRE	165	C3
BELMONT AV	FRCO	56	C3
BELMONT AV	FRCO	57	C3
BELOMY ST	SCLR	151	B3
BELSBY AV	RCO	102	C4
BELTLINE RD	SHA	18	C2
BELVIN RD	YUBA	125	A1
BENA RD	KER	79	A3
BENBOW DR	HUM	22	C1
BEND	TEH	18	D4
BENDER	SJCO	40	A3
BENDER AV	KER	78	B2
BENDER RD	SHA	18	A3
BENDLER RD	STA	47	E2
BENEDICT CYN DR	LACO	Q	C3
BENHAM LN	CUR	1	D2
BEN HUR RD	MPA	49	B4
BENICIA AV	KIN	57	E5
BENICIA RD	SOL	38	D4
BENICIA RD	VAL	134	D5
BENITO ST	MTCL	203	C4

STREET	CO.	PAGE	GRID
BENITO ST	UPL	203	C4
BENIT JUAREZ BL	BAJA	112	B4
BENNER AV	KER	68	B5
BENNET RD	LACO	89	A5
BENNET RD	VEN	88	E5
BENNETS WELL RD	INY	72	A2
BENNETT RD	BUT	25	A2
BENNETT RD	MCO	55	E2
BENNETT RD	NEV	34	C1
BENNETT RD	RCO	100	D3
BENNETT VLY RD	SON	38	A2
BENNETT VLY RD	STR	131	D4
BENSON AV	MTCL	203	D4
BENSON AV	SBD	U	D3
BENSON AV	SBD	203	D2
BENSON AV	UPL	203	D1
BENSON DR	SHA	18	B2
BENSON RD	TEH	18	C4
BENT RD	STA	47	D2
BENTLEY RD	STA	47	D2
BENTON DR	SHA	18	C2
BENTON RD	RCO	99	D5
BENTON RD E	RCO	99	E5
BENTON ST	SCLR	150	D3
BENTON CROSSING	MNO	51	B2
BERDOO CYN RD	RCO	101	B3
BERKELEY AV	STA	47	E3
BERKSHIRE RD	KER	79	A3
BERNAL AV	ALA	M	B5
BERNAL AV	ALA	P	B1
BERNAL DR E	SAL	171	C3
BERNARD ST	KER	78	D3
BERNARD WY	SHA	18	C1
BERRELLESA ST	M	154	B2
BERRY RD	SUT	33	D3
BERRY CREEK RD	BUT	25	E3
BERRYESSA RD	SJ	152	C1
BERRYESSA RD	SCL	P	B3
BERRYESSA RD	SCL	46	B4
BERRYSSA KNX RD	NAPA	32	C4
BERT RD	LAS	27	E1
BERTAS RD	HUM	15	E1
BERT CRANE RD	MCO	48	B5
BERTRAM CIR	KER	79	C4
BERYL ST	LACO	97	D3
BERYL ST	LACO	S	B1
BERYL ST	SD	212	B1
BERYLWOOD RD	VEN	88	C5
BESSEMR MINE RD	SBD	92	B4
BEST RD	IMP	109	B4
BEST RD	MPA	49	C3
BEST RD	RCO	99	E5
BEST RD	SUT	33	C3
BEST RANCH RD	YOL	33	C5
BETHANY RD	SJCO	46	D1
BETHEL AV	FRCO	57	E4
BETHEL RD	SLO	76	A2
BETHEL ISLND RD	CC	M	D3
BETHEL ISLND RD	CC	39	C5
BETTERAVIA RD	SB	86	B1
BETTERAVIA RD	SMA	173	C5
BETTS RD	TRI	23	A1
BETTY WY	SIS	4	B4
BETZ RD	SUT	33	D3
BEVERLY BLVD	LA	184	A1
BEVERLY BLVD	LA	185	C1
BEVERLY BLVD	LACO	97	D2
BEVERLY BLVD	LACO	98	A2
BEVERLY BLVD	LACO	183	C1
BEVERLY BLVD	LACO	Q	D4
BEVERLY DR	BH	183	B1
BEVERLY DR	LAS	20	E3
BEVERLY DR	LACO	Q	C3
BEVERLY GLEN BL	LA	180	E2
BEVERLY GLEN BL	LACO	97	C1
BEVERLY GLEN BL	LACO	Q	C3
BEVERWIL DR	BH	183	B2
BEVERWIL DR	LA	183	B3
BEYER BLVD	SDCO	V	D5
BEYER BLVD	SDCO	111	D2
BEYER LN	SJCO	40	B5
BEYER WY	SDCO	V	C5
BEYER WY	SDCO	111	D2
BEYERS LN	NEV	34	B2
BIANCHI RD	S	160	B1
BIDDLE	SLO	76	B4
BIDWELL RD	SHA	13	D5
BIDWELL CK RD	MOD	7	D3
BIEBER LKOUT RD	LAS	14	B3
BIG BAR DUMP RD	TRI	17	A1
BIG BAR MTN RD	BUT	25	E2
BIG BEN	PLA	34	B3
BIG BEND DR	CLK	85	B5
BIG BEND RD	BUT	25	D3
BIG BEND RD	SHA	13	A4
BIG CANYON	LAK	32	A4
BIG CREEK RD	PLU	26	B2
BIG CREEK RD	TRI	17	B2
BIG CK SHAFT RD	TUO	48	E1
BIG COVE RD	PLU	20	B4
BIG DIPPER	PLA	34	E2
BIGELOW RD	SIS	13	A2
BIGELOW RD	SUT	33	B1
BIG FLAT RD	DN	2	B4
BIG FRCH CK RD	TRI	17	A1
BIGGAR LN	MEN	23	A2
BIGGS EAST HWY	BUT	25	C5
BIG HILL RD	TUO	41	D4
BIG HILL LKOUT	HUM	10	C3
BIG HORN DR	RCO	100	D5
BIG INCH PIPELN	KER	79	E5
BIG INCH PIPELN	KER	80	A5
BIG LAKES RD	MOD	14	D2

STREET	CO.	PAGE	GRID
BIG MEADOWS RD	SIS	3	C5
BIG OAK DR	MEN	31	B3
BIG PINES HWY	LACO	90	C4
BIG PN REPTR RD	INY	51	E5
BIG RANCH RD	NAPA	29	E5
BIG RANCH RD	NAPA	38	C2
BIG RANCH RD	NAPA	133	C1
BIG RESRVOIR RD	PLA	34	E2
BIG ROCK CK RD	LACO	90	C4
BIG SAGE RD	MOD	6	E5
BIG SAGE RD	MOD	7	A5
BIG SANDY RD	MON	66	B4
BIG SPRING DR	NEV	34	B2
BIG SPRING RD	SHA	19	A2
BIG SPRINGS RD	MNO	50	D1
BIG SPRINGS RD	SIS	4	C5
BIG SPRINGS RD	SIS	12	E2
BIG SPRINGS CTO	PLU	20	B4
BIG STUMP RD	SIS	5	A2
BIG TRAILS DR	MEN	22	E4
BIG TREES RD	INY	51	C4
BIG TUJUNGA BL	LACO	Q	E1
BIG TUJUNGA CYN	LACO	89	E5
BIG VALLEY RD	LAK	31	D3
BILBY RD	SAC	39	E2
BILLE RD	BUT	25	C3
BILLIE ST	KER	78	D4
BILLINGS AV	KER	78	B1
BILLINGS LN	RCO	99	B4
BILLY WRIGHT RD	MCO	55	C2
BINET RD	BUT	26	B4
BINGHAMTON RD	SOL	39	B2
BIOLA AV	FRCO	57	B3
BIR RD	INY	51	C4
BIRCH AV	MON	65	A1
BIRCH ST	NB	198	C5
BIRCH ST	ORCO	98	C3
BIRCH ST	ORCO	T	D1
BIRCH ST	ORCO	U	A4
BIRCH CREEK RD	INY	59	E1
BIRCHIM LN	INY	51	C3
BIRCHIN FLAT RD	MNO	42	E2
BIRCHIN FLAT RD	MNO	43	A2
BIRCHVILLE RD	NEV	26	B5
BIRD RD	SJCO	47	A2
BIRDS LANDNG RD	SOL	39	B4
BIRD SPG CYN RD	KER	80	A1
BIRKHEAD	FRCO	57	C2
BIRMINGHAM DR	SDCO	106	B4
BISCH CT	KER	79	E2
BISHOP AV	FRCO	57	B4
BISHOP AV	FRCO	67	B1
BISHOP AV	SUT	33	C1
BISHOP CK RD E	INY	51	C4
BISHOP CK RD W	INY	51	C4
BISIGNANI RD	MCO	55	E1
BISON AV	NB	200	B3
BISSET STN RD	MAD	49	D4
BITNEY SPGS RD	NEV	34	B1
BITTERWATER RD	MON	65	C2
BITTRWTR VLY RD	KER	77	A1
BIXBY RD	VEN	88	D5
BIXLER RD	CC	39	D5
BLACK RD	SB	86	B1
BLACK BART RD	BUT	25	E4
BLACK BEAR RD	SIS	11	B2
BLACK BUTTE RD	GLE	24	B3
BLACK BUTTE RD	SHA	19	A3
BLACK BUTTE RD	TEH	24	C2
BLK BTTE BSN RD	LACO	90	D3
BLACK CANYON RD	INY	51	E4
BLACK CANYON RD	MNO	44	B5
BLACK CANYON RD	MNO	51	B1
BLACK CANYON RD	SBD	81	C5
BLACK CANYON RD	SBD	84	B5
BLACK CANYON RD	SBD	94	C1
BLACK CANYON RD	SDCO	107	A3
BLACK DIAMND WY	CC	39	B5
BLACK DIAMND MN	BUT	25	D1
BLK EAGLE MN RD	RCO	101	E3
BLACK FOX MTN	SIS	13	B2
BLACK GULCH RD	KER	79	C1
BLACK GULCH RD	LAS	14	A5
BLACK HAWK RD	CC	M	B4
BLACK HAWK RD	CC	46	A1
BLACKHAWK RD	PLU	26	C1
BLACK HILLS RD	RCO	100	D4
BLACKIE RD	MON	54	C3
BLACK LAKE RD	LAS	14	B5
BLACKMER RD	SUT	33	B2
BLACKMORE	SJCO	47	C1
BLACK MTN RD	IMP	110	B3
BLACK MTN RD	SDCO	106	D4
BLACK MTN RD	SMCO	N	C2
BLACK MTN RD	SMCO	45	C3
BLACK MTN RD	SIS	4	B3
BLACK MTN TR	RCO	100	B3
BLACK MTN LO RD	SLO	76	D3
BLACK RANCH RD	SHA	13	C4
BLACK ROCK RD	RCO	103	C5
BLACK ROCK CYN	SBD	100	E2
BLACK RCK MN RD	MNO	51	C2
BLACK ROCK SPGS	INY	59	E2
BLACKS CYN RD	MOD	14	D1
BLACKS RDG LKOT	LAS	14	B5
BLACKSTONE AV	FRE	165	D1
BLACKSTONE ST	TUL	68	B2
BLACKWELL LN	DN	1	D4
BLAGEN RD	CAL	41	C3
BLAINE ST	RIV	205	E2
BLAINE ST	RCO	99	B2
BLAIR RD	IMP	109	B3
BLAIS RD	IMP	109	A4

STREET INDEX

STREET	CO.	PAGE	GRID
BLAKE RD	SAC	40	B2
BLAKE ST	SBD	99	B1
BLAKER RD	STA	47	D3
BLANCHARD FT RD	TRI	17	D2
BLANCO	MON	54	C4
BLANCO RD	MPA	48	D2
BLANCO RD E	MON	171	C5
BLANCO RD E	SAL	171	C5
BLANCO RD W	MON	171	A5
BLANCO RD W	SAL	171	A5
BLAND RD	SHA	17	E3
BLANEY AV	CPTO	150	A4
BLANKENSHIP AV	KER	78	A1
BLANKO RD	SBD	90	E4
BLATCHLEY RD	TEH	24	D2
BLAZING STAR AV	SBD	91	A3
BLEDSOE RD	MCO	48	B3
BLEVENS RD	LPAZ	104	C5
BLEWETT RD	STA	47	B2
BLICKENSTAFF RD	LAS	21	B4
BLISS DR	RCO	107	C1
BLISS RD	MCO	48	C5
BLISS RD	YUB	33	D2
BLITHEDALE AV	MAR	L	B4
BLITHEDALE AV E	MV	140	A3
B L M DUMP RD	LAS	20	E1
BLOCK RD	BUT	25	C5
BLOCK RD	BUT	33	C1
BLODGETT RD	IMP	109	B5
BLOODY CAMP RD	HUM	10	C3
BLOOMR HLL LKOT	BUT	25	D3
BLOOMFIELD AV	LACO	T	A2
BLOOMFIELD AV	SCL	54	D2
BLOOMFIELD RD	SON	37	D3
BLOOMFLD GRNTVL	NEV	26	D5
BLOOMINGTON RD	SBD	99	B2
BLOSS AV	MCO	47	D4
BLOSSER RD	STB	173	A2
BLOSSER RD	SB	86	B1
BLOSSER RD	SMA	173	A5
BLOSSOM	SJCO	39	E3
BLOSSOM AV	MCO	56	A2
BLOSSOM RD	STA	47	E2
BLOSSOM HILL RD	SCL	P	B4
BLOSSOM HILL RD	SCL	46	A5
BLOWERS DR	RCO	99	A4
BLUE GILL RD	SIS	4	B3
BLUE GULCH RD	SIS	11	B3
BLUE GUM AV	STA	47	C2
BLUE LAKE BLVD	HUM	10	A5
BLUE LAKE RD	MOD	8	C3
BLUE LK MPLE CK	HUM	16	B1
BLUE LAKES RD	ALP	36	B5
BLUE LAKES RD	LAK	31	C2
BLUE MTN RD	CAL	41	C2
BLUE MTN RD	KER	69	A5
BLUE MTN LKT RD	CAL	41	C2
BLUE RIDGE RD	SOL	38	E2
BLUE RIDGE RD	TEH	19	C3
BLUE SLIDE RD	HUM	15	E3
BLUFF ST	RCO	100	A2
BLUFF CREEK RD	TRI	16	E5
BLYTHE AV	FRCO	57	C3
BLYTHE AV	FRCO	67	B1
BLYTHE-VIDAL RD	RCO	103	D2
BOARDER ST	RCO	100	A3
BOARTS RD	IMP	109	A4
BOAT HARBOR RD	LAS	20	E2
BOBCAT TR	RCO	100	A5
BOB HOPE DR	RCO	100	E4
BOBS GAP RD	LACO	90	C4
BOB WHITE WY	INY	73	A4
BOCA RD	NEV	27	E5
BOCA SPRINGS RD	NEV	27	E5
BOCA SPGS RD E	NEV	27	E5
BODEGA AV	SON	38	A3
BODEGA HWY	SON	37	D2
BODEM ST	MDO	162	D2
BODFISH CYN RD	KER	79	D1
BODIE RD	MNO	43	C3
BODIE MASONC RD	MNO	43	C3
BOESSOW RD	SAC	40	B3
BOGARD RD	LAS	14	B5
BOGGS RD	COL	24	E5
BOGGS & CHAMLIN	TEH	24	C2
BOGUE RD	STA	47	E3
BOGUE RD	STA	48	A3
BOGUE RD	SUT	33	C2
BOHAN DILLON RD	SON	37	B1
BOHEMIAN HWY	SON	37	C2
BOHN BLVD	SHA	18	B3
BOLAM RD	SIS	4	D5
BOLAM RD	SIS	12	D1
BOLAM LOGGNG RD	SIS	12	D1
BOLES RD	COL	32	E3
BOLEY RD	IMP	108	E5
BOLLINGER CY RD	CC	M	A4
BOLINGER CYN RD	CC	45	E1
BOLINGER CYN RD	CC	46	A1
BOLO RD	SBD	94	A3
BOLSA AV	ORCO	98	B4
BOLSA CHICA RD	ORCO	98	B4
BOLSA CHICA RD	ORCO	T	B3
BON ST	MCO	48	D5
BONANZA AV	TRI	17	D1
BONANZA RD	CLK	74	D2
BONANZA RD	LV	209	B1
BONANZA RD	SBD	101	A1
BONANZA TR	SBD	91	C2
BONANZA WY	NEV	34	B1
BONANZA KING RD	TRI	12	A4
BOND RD	SJCO	40	A2
BOND RD	STA	47	E2

STREET	CO.	PAGE	GRID
BONDS CORNER RD	IMP	112	C4
BONDS FLAT RD	TUO	48	C2
BONDURANT	MPA	49	A2
BONE STEEL RD	IMP	112	C4
BONETTI RD	SJCO	46	D1
BONITA AV	LACO	98	C1
BONITA AV	LACO	U	B2
BONITA RD	MCO	55	D2
BONITA RD	SDCO	V	D4
BONITA RD	SDCO	111	D2
BONITA CYN DR	IRV	200	C3
BONITA CYN DR	ORCO	98	C4
BONITA CYN DR	ORCO	T	D4
BONITA LATERAL	SB	76	C5
BONITA LATERAL	SB	86	B1
BONITA SCHL RD	SLO	76	C5
BONITA SCHL RD	SB	76	C5
BONITA SCHL RD	SB	86	B1
BONITA VISTA RD	RCO	100	C4
BONNER RD	MCO	48	D4
BONNEYVIEW RD E	SHA	18	C2
BONNEYVIEW RD S	SHA	18	C2
BONNIE CT	KER	79	C3
BONNY LN	RCO	107	B1
BONNY DOON RD	SCR	53	D2
BOOKER RD	TUO	41	D5
BOONE LN	FRCO	66	B3
BOONE ST	SMA	173	C3
BOOTH RD	LPAZ	104	B2
BOOT JACK	MPA	49	C3
BORAX RD	KER	80	D5
BORAX MILL RD	INY	62	A5
BORBA	SJCO	40	A5
BORBA	SJCO	47	A1
BORCHARD	VEN	96	D1
BORDEN RD	SAC	40	B3
BORDEN ST	MAD	57	A2
BORDER AV	RCO	U	E5
BORDER AV	SBD	100	E1
BOREL RD	RCO	99	D5
BORMAN LN	LAK	32	B4
BORNT RD	IMP	112	C4
BORON AV	KER	80	E5
BORREGO SLTN SEA	SDCO	108	A2
BORREGO SPGS RD	SDCO	107	E2
BORREGO VLY RD	SDCO	107	E2
BOSCOVICH RD	IMP	112	D5
BOSTON AV	LACO	Q	E2
BOTTINI	TUO	41	E4
BOTTLE CREEK RD	BUT	25	D1
BOTTLE HILL RD	BUT	25	D1
BOTTLE ROCK RD	LAK	31	E4
BOUCHO RD	COL	32	E3
BOULDER AV	SBD	99	C1
BOULDER HWY	CLK	74	D2
BOULDER RD	SBD	91	C3
BOULDER CK RD	SDCO	107	C5
BOULDER CK RD	SIS	3	C5
BL D L AMERICAS	BAJA	112	B4
BOULEVARD, THE	GLE	24	E4
BOULTON RD	SUT	33	C3
BOUNDARY ST	SD	216	C1
BOUNDARY TR	DN	2	A4
BOUNDARY CONE RD	MOH	85	D5
BOUQUET CYN RD	LACO	89	C4
BOUSE QUARTZITE	LPAZ	104	C4
BOW AV	KER	80	C1
BOWEN RD	COL	32	D1
BOWEN RANCH RD	SBD	91	C4
BOWERS AV	SCL	P	B3
BOWERS AV	SCLR	150	E1
BOWKER RD	IMP	112	B3
BOWKER RD	IMP	112	B4
BOWL PL	SB	86	E3
BOWMAN RD	KER	80	D1
BOWMAN RD	MOD	7	B5
BOWMAN RD	SBDO	81	A1
BOWMAN RD	SJCO	47	A1
BOWMAN RD	TEH	18	B4
BOWMAN LAKE RD	NEV	27	A5
BOWMAN LAKE RD	NEV	35	A1
BOX CANYON RD	RCO	101	C5
BOX CAR RD	MCO	55	E1
BOX ELDER ST	RCO	100	C4
BOX SPRINGS BL	RCO	99	B2
BOX SPRINGS RD	RCO	99	C2
BOYCE RD	SOL	39	A1
BOYD	CC	38	E5
BOYD DR	TUL	58	C4
BOYD RD	IMP	109	B5
BOYD SPRINGS RD	LAS	14	B4
BOYER RD	MPA	49	C3
BOYER RD	YUB	33	D1
BOYES BLVD	SON	132	A2
BOYLE AV S	LA	186	D3
BOYLE RD	IMP	109	A3
BOYLE RD	SHA	18	D2
BOYLES AV	LAK	32	A3
BOY SCOUT CP RD	VEN	88	B2
BRACE RD	PLA	34	B4
BRACK RD	SON	31	D5
BRACK RD	SON	37	D1
BRADBURY RD	MCO	47	E3
BRADBURY RD	MCO	48	A3
BRADBURY RD	STA	47	C3
BRADDOCK DR	LA	188	A2
BRADFORD AV	ORCO	T	D1
BRADFORD RD	BUT	25	B4
BRADFORD RD	RCO	107	B1
BRADLEY AV	SDCO	V	E2
BRADLEY AV	SDCO	106	E5
BRADLEY RD	MON	65	A4
BRADLEY RD	RCO	99	C4

STREET	CO.	PAGE	GRID
BRADLEY RD	VEN	88	C5
BRADLY HENLY RD	SIS	4	B3
BRADLEY LOCK RD	MON	65	C4
BRADSHAW RD	IMP	109	A5
BRADSHAW RD	SAC	40	A2
BRADSHAW RD	YUB	33	E3
BRADSHW TR, THE	RCO	102	A5
BRADSHW TR, THE	RCO	110	B1
BRADY RD	TRI	17	B2
BRAGG RD	RCO	100	A5
BRAMLETT RCH RD	MNO	44	C5
BRAMLOT RD	TRI	17	B3
BRANCH RD	SLO	76	B1
BRANCH RD E	HUM	22	C1
BRANCH RD W	SIS	3	D4
BRANCH CAMP W	BUT	25	D1
BRANCH MILL RD	SLO	76	B4
BRANCIFORTE DR	SCR	54	A2
BRANCO RD	MCO	55	E1
BRAND BLVD	LACO	Q	E2
BRANDON RD	ED	40	D1
BRANDT	IMP	109	A3
BRANDT RD	SJCO	40	C4
BRANDT RD	KER	78	A2
BRANDY CITY RD	SIE	26	C4
BRANDY CREEK RD	SHA	18	A2
BRANFORD ST	LACO	Q	C2
BRANHAM LN	SCL	P	B4
BRANHAM LN	SCL	46	B5
BRANNAN ST	SF	142	D4
BRANNAN ST	SF	143	D5
BRANNAN ISLD RD	SAC	39	C4
BRANNAN ISLD RD	SAC	M	D2
BRANNAN MTN RD	HUM	10	C4
BRANNIGAN MN RD	SBD	83	C4
BRANNIN RD	TEH	24	C2
BRANNON AV	FRCO	56	B2
BRANSCOMB RD	MEN	22	D4
BRANSTETTER LN	SHA	18	C2
BRANT RD	SBD	84	C3
BRANT CIMA RD	SBD	84	B3
BRAWLEY	IMP	108	C2
BRAWLEY AV	FRCO	57	C5
BRAY AV	TEH	18	D5
BRAZO RD	MCO	47	C4
BREA BLVD	ORCO	98	C3
BREA BLVD	ORCO	U	A4
BREA BLVD	ORCO	T	C1
BREA CYN CUTOFF	LACO	U	A3
BREA CYN CUTOFF	LACO	98	C2
BREA CANYON RD	LACO	98	C2
BRECKENRIDGE RD	KER	78	E3
BRECKENRIDGE RD	KER	79	A2
BREEDLOVE RD	ED	34	E3
BRENDA ST	KER	70	A5
BRENT RD	TEH	18	D4
BRENTWOOD AV	CC	M	D3
BRENNAN	SJCO	47	C1
BRENTWOOD AV	CC	39	C5
BRETZ RD	FRCO	58	B1
BREUING RD	MCO	55	D1
BREUNER AV	COL	32	E3
BREWER RD	NEV	34	C2
BREWER RD	PLA	33	E4
BREWER CREEK RD	SIS	12	E1
BRICELAND RD	HUM	16	B5
BRICELAND RD	MEN	22	A1
BRICELND THORNE	HUM	16	B5
BRIDESTEIN RD	IMP	109	C5
BRIDGE RD	VEN	88	C4
BRIDGE ST	COL	33	A2
BRIDGE ST	RCO	99	D3
BRIDGE ST	SUT	33	C2
BRIDGE ST	SUT	125	A3
BRIDGE ST	YUBA	125	D3
BRIDGE ARBOR	LAK	31	D2
BRIDGE CK SPGS	LAS	20	C2
BRIDGE GULCH RD	TRI	17	B3
BRDGPORT SCH RD	ED	41	A1
BRIDGEWAY	MAR	140	D5
BRIDLE PATH DR	SCL	P	E5
BRIGGS AV	LACO	R	A2
BRIGGS RD	RCO	99	D4
BRIGGS RD	VEN	88	C5
BRIGGS GRIDLY W	BUT	25	C5
BRIGGSMORE AV	STA	47	C2
BRIGHTON AV	MDO	162	E1
BRIGHTWOOD	MAD	57	B1
BRIM RD	COL	32	B2
BRIMHALL RD	KER	78	B3
BRINKERHOFF AV	SB	86	E3
BRINKERHOFF AV	SB	87	A3
BRIONES VLY RD	CC	39	B5
BRISTOL PKWY	CUL	188	C3
BRISTOL RD	VEN	88	B5
BRISTOL ST	CM	197	E4
BRISTOL ST	ORCO	98	C4
BRISTOL ST	ORCO	T	D3
BRISTOL ST	SA	195	D3
BRISTOL ST	SA	197	E3
BRISTOL ST N	NB	200	A1
BRITE RD	KER	78	A3
BRITTO RD	MCO	56	A2
BROAD ST	NEVC	128	B2
BROAD ST	SNLO	172	D4
BROAD ST W	NEVC	128	B2
BROADWAY	A	159	A2
BROADWAY	ALA	L	D4
BROADWAY	ALA	45	D1
BROADWAY	AMA	40	E2
BROADWAY	ANA	193	B2
BROADWAY	EUR	121	A4
BROADWAY	FRE	165	C3

STREET	CO.	PAGE	GRID
BROADWAY	LAG	201	B2
BROADWAY	LB	192	D3
BROADWAY	LA	185	D5
BROADWAY	LA	186	B2
BROADWAY	LACO	Q	E3
BROADWAY	LACO	S	C1
BROADWAY	O	156	C4
BROADWAY	O	158	A2
BROADWAY	SCTO	137	B4
BROADWAY	SBD	92	D5
BROADWAY	SD	215	E3
BROADWAY	SD	216	B3
BROADWAY	SDCO	V	B3
BROADWAY	SDCO	106	E5
BROADWAY	SDCO	111	D2
BROADWAY	SF	143	B4
BROADWAY	SFCO	L	B4
BROADWAY	SB	76	E3
BROADWAY	SC	169	E3
BROADWAY	SMA	173	B3
BROADWAY	SMON	180	A4
BROADWAY	SOL	134	C1
BROADWAY	SNMA	132	D5
BROADWAY	SON	L	B1
BROADWAY	SUT	33	C2
BROADWAY	VAL	134	C2
BROADWAY	YUB	33	D3
BROADWAY N	LA	186	C1
BROADWAY N	LACO	R	A3
BROADWAY RD	LACO	R	C5
BROADWAY RD	VEN	88	D5
BROADWAY ST	C	124	B4
BROADWAY ST	FRFD	135	B4
BROADWAY ST	SBD	101	A1
BROADWAY TER	O	156	C5
BROCK RD	IMP	112	A3
BROCKMAN LN	INY	51	D4
BROCKMAN RD	KER	78	C1
BROCKMAN RD	LAS	8	A4
BROCKMAN MLL RD	AMA	41	A1
BROCK MTN LKOUT	SHA	12	E5
BROCKTON AV	RIV	205	B2
BROKAW RD	SCL	P	B3
BROKAW RD	SCL	46	B4
BROKEOFF MDWS	SHA	19	C2
BROOKDALE RD	SHA	18	D2
BROOKHILL RD	MAD	57	C2
BROOKHURST ST	ORCO	98	B4
BROOKHURST ST	ORCO	T	C2
BROOKS RD	MCO	48	B4
BROOKS ST	SB	86	D1
BROOKSIDE	FRCO	58	D4
BROOKSIDE AV	RCO	99	E2
BROOKSIDE AV	SBD	99	C2
BROOKSIDE RD	CAL	41	C2
BROOKSIDE RD	S	160	A2
BROPHY RD	YUB	33	D2
BROWN RD	KER	70	C5
BROWN RD	KER	80	C1
BROWN RD	SB	86	A1
BROWN RD	SHA	13	D4
BROWN RD	SOL	39	B3
BROWN RD	SUT	33	C3
BROWN ST	NAP	133	C3
BROWN ST	RCO	99	B3
BROWNLL LAVA BD	SIS	5	D3
BROWNING	PLA	33	E5
BROWNING RD	COL	33	B3
BROWNING RD	KER	68	C5
BROWNING RD	SUT	33	C3
BROWN MATERL RD	KER	77	C1
BROWNS CREEK RD	TRI	17	D2
BROWNS MTN RD	TRI	17	D1
BROWNS RANCH RD	TRI	17	D1
BROWNS RAVINE	BUT	25	D1
BROWNS VALLEY	SBT	55	B4
BROWN VALLEY RD	SOL	39	A2
BROWN VALLEY RD	SCR	54	B2
BROYLE RD	STA	47	C3
BROYLES RD	BUT	25	A2
BROYLES RD	STA	47	C2
BRUCE RD	BUT	25	B3
BRUCE CRUM	SHA	13	E4
BRUCEVILLE RD	SAC	39	E3
BRUCITE ST	KER	91	E3
BRUELLA RD	SJCO	40	B4
BRUGGA LN	HUM	15	D2
BRUNDAGE LN	BKD	166	C5
BRUNDAGE LN	KER	166	C5
BRUNSWICK RD	NEV	34	C1
BRUS	MOD	8	B3
BRUSH LN	STA	47	C3
BRUSH CREEK RD	SIS	4	B3
BRUSH CREEK RD	SON	38	A2
BRUSHY MTN LKOT	HUM	10	C5
BRYAN AV	FRCO	57	B5
BRYANT	FRCO	56	B2
BRYANT ST	SBD	99	D2
BRYANT ST	SF	142	D4
BRYANT ST	SF	143	D4
BRYANT RAVIN RD	BUT	26	A4
BRYANTS CYN RD	MON	55	A5
BRYANTS CYN RD	MON	65	A1
BUCHANAN RD	CC	M	B3
BUCHANAN RD	CC	39	B5
BUCHANAN RD	MAD	49	B5
BUCHANAN RD	TUO	41	E5
BUCHANAN ST	RCO	101	B5
BUCHANAN HLW RD	MCO	48	D5
BUCK RD	RCO	99	D5
BUCK RD	SJCO	40	B3
BUCKEYE RD	MPA	49	A3
BUCKEYE RD	NEV	34	D1

STREET	CO.	PAGE	GRID
BUCKEYE ARM RD	TRI	11	D5
BUCKEYE CK RD	SON	31	A5
BUCKEYE CK RD	TRI	12	A4
BUCKEYE RDG RD	TRI	11	D5
BUCKHORN	TEH	24	C2
BUCKHORN AV	KER	89	C1
BUCKHORN RD	SIS	4	C5
BUCKHORN RDG RD	AMA	41	B2
BUCKHORN STA LP	TRI	17	E1
BUCKLEY RD	SLO	76	B4
BUCKMAN FUNCK	SJCO	40	D5
BUCK MEADOWS	MPA	49	A1
BUCKNELL RD	KER	80	D3
BUCKS BAR RD	ED	34	E5
BUCKS FLAT RD	TEH	19	B4
BUCKSKIN RD	CAL	41	A4
BUCKS LAKE RD	PLU	26	C1
BUCKTHRN CYN RD	SBD	90	E2
BUCKWHEAT RD	SBD	90	E4
BUDDY CT	KER	79	B3
BUELL RD	SHA	18	A3
BUENA CREEK RD	SDCO	106	C3
BUENA VISTA	AMA	40	D3
BUENA VISTA	LACO	97	D1
BUENA VISTA	SCL	54	D1
BUENA VISTA AV	A	157	E5
BUENA VISTA AV	A	158	B5
BUENA VISTA AV	A	159	A1
BUENA VISTA AV	RIV	205	A2
BUENA VISTA AV	RCO	U	E5
BUENA VISTA AV	SCL	P	E5
BUENA VISTA BL	KER	78	D4
BUENA VISTA BL	KER	79	A4
BUENA VISTA DR	MER	170	C1
BUENA VISTA DR	SBD	100	E1
BUENA VISTA DR	SLO	76	A1
BUENA VISTA DR	SCR	54	B2
BUENA VISTA RD	AMA	40	D3
BUENA VISTA RD	KER	78	C3
BUENA VISTA RD	SBD	91	E4
BUENA VISTA RD	SJCO	40	C3
BUENA VISTA ST	BUR	179	C2
BUENA VISTA ST	LACO	Q	D2
BUENA VISTA ST	LACO	R	D3
BUENA VISTA ST	VEN	88	D5
BUERER LN	SJCO	47	C1
BUERKLE RD	KER	78	A3
BUFFALO RUN RD	RCO	102	C4
BUFFUM LN	LAS	21	B3
BUFFUM RD	SHA	13	A5
BUHACH RD	MCO	48	B5
BUHNE ST	EUR	121	C2
BULKLEY RD	SOL	39	C2
BULLARD AV	FRCO	56	C3
BULLARD AV	FRCO	57	B3
BULL CANYON RD	SLO	76	D5
BULL CREEK RD	MPA	49	B2
BULLION MTN RD	SBD	101	C1
BULLIS RD	LACO	S	D1
BULLRIDGE WHEEL	KIN	67	B4
BULL RUN ST	KER	80	C1
BULL SKIN RIDGE	SHA	19	A1
BULLY CHOOP RD	SHA	17	E3
BULS RD	KER	87	E1
BUMMERVILLE RD	CAL	41	B2
BUNCE RD	SUT	33	D2
BUNCH GRASS LKT	SHA	13	B5
BUNDY DR	LA	180	B4
BUNDY DR	LACO	Q	C4
BUNDY CANYON RD	RCO	99	C5
BUNKER RD	MCO	47	C5
BUNKER RD	MCO	55	C1
BUNKER HILL RD	SIE	26	D3
BUNKER STATN RD	SOL	39	C3
BUNNY LN	RCO	100	C5
BUNSELMEIER RD	LAS	14	B3
BUNTE RD	MON	65	C3
BUNTGVLL CUMMGS	LAS	21	B4
BURBANK BLVD	BUR	179	B2
BURBANK BLVD	LA	177	C4
BURBANK BLVD	LA	178	D4
BURBANK BLVD	LACO	97	C1
BURBANK BLVD	LACO	Q	C2
BURBANK ST	KER	78	A2
BURCH RD	SUT	33	C3
BURCHELL AV	MCO	48	D5
BURCHELL RD	SCL	54	C1
BURCH HAVEN RD	MCO	55	B2
BURGESS RCH RD	TRI	16	E5
BURKE LN	SOL	39	B3
BURLANDO RD	KER	69	D5
BURLINGAME AV	SMCO	N	C1
BURLNGTN RDG RD	NEV	34	E1
BURMA RD	NEV	34	C2
BURNETT	PLA	34	B3
BURNHAM RD	VEN	88	A4
BURNS AV	KER	78	C1
BURNS CUTOFF	SJCO	40	A5
BURNS FRWY	HUM	9	E5
BURNS FRWY	HUM	10	A5
BURNS RD	LPAZ	104	A2
BURNS CANYON RD	SBD	100	B1
BURNSIDE LK RD	ALP	36	B4
BURNS VALLEY RD	LAK	32	A3
BURNT RCH DUMP	TRI	10	E5
BURNT TREE RD	SBD	81	C5
BURRELL RD	HUM	15	E4
BURRIS LN	MEN	31	C1
BURRIS RD	SUT	33	B2
BURROUGH N RD	FRCO	58	A2
BURROUGH VLY RD	FRCO	58	A2
BURSON RD	CAL	40	D4
BURTON WY	BH	183	C1

STREET	CO.	PAGE	GRID
BURTON MESA BL	SB	86	B2
BURWOOD RD	SJCO	47	D2
BUSH ST	AMA	40	D2
BUSH ST	SF	142	A3
BUSHARD ST	ORCO	T	C3
BUSHEY RD	MOD	14	C1
BUSSEL RD	KER	78	B2
BUSTER RD	COL	33	A2
BUTANO CUTOFF	SMCO	N	C4
BUTANO CUTOFF	SMCO	45	C5
BUTCHER RCH RD	SIE	26	E3
BUTLER AV	FRCO	57	C3
BUTLER RD	COL	25	A5
BUTLER RD	STA	47	B2
BUTLER VLY RD	HUM	16	A1
BUTTE AV	FRCO	66	E1
BUTTE AV	SUT	33	C2
BUTTE RD	LAS	14	D3
BUTTE RD E	SUT	33	C2
BUTTE RD N	SUT	33	B1
BUTTE RD S	SUT	33	B2
BUTTE RD W	SUT	33	B1
BUTTE CITY HWY	BUT	25	A5
BUTTE CREEK RD	HUM	16	B2
BUTTE HOUSE RD	SUT	33	C2
BUTTE HOUSE RD	YUBA	125	A2
BUTTEMER RD	SBD	90	E4
BUTTE MTN RD	AMA	40	E2
BUTTE MTN RD	TEH	24	C2
BUTTERBREDT CYN	KER	79	E2
BUTTERBREDT CYN	KER	80	A2
BUTTERCUP CT	KER	79	C4
BUTTERFIELD RD	MAR	L	A3
BUTTRFLD STG RD	MAD	49	D5
BUTTRFLD STG RD	MAD	57	D1
BUTTRFLD STG RD	RCO	99	D5
BUTTERFLY PK RD	RCO	100	C5
BTRFLY VLY TWAN	PLU	26	C1
BUTTERMILK RD	INY	51	B4
BUTTERS RD	IMP	109	C4
BUTTE SLOUGH RD	COL	33	A2
BUTTE VALLEY RD	INY	72	A3
BUTTE VLY RD E	SIS	5	A3
BUTTE VLY RD W	SIS	4	E3
BUTTE VLY AIRPT	SIS	5	A3
BUTTONHOOK RD	SB	86	D3
BUTTONWILLOW AV	FRCO	58	A4
BUTTONWILLOW DR	KER	77	E3
BUTTONWILLOW DR	KER	78	A3
BUTTS RD	MCO	47	C5
BUTTS RD	MCO	55	C1
BUTTS CANYON RD	LAK	32	B5
BUZZARD ROOST	SHA	19	A1
BVD AV	MCO	48	C5
BYERS PASS RD	LAS	21	B3
BYINGTON RD	SUT	33	C4
BYOFF RD	TRI	10	E5
BYRON HWY	CC	M	D3
BYRON HWY	CC	39	C5
BYRON RD	SJCO	46	D1
BYRON RD	CC	M	E4
BYRON RD	CC	46	D1
BYSTRUM RD	STA	47	D3
BYWOOD DR	TEH	18	C4

C

STREET	CO.	PAGE	GRID
C ST	KER	68	B5
C ST	SD	216	A3
C ST	YOL	137	A2
C ST E	CLTN	207	A4
CABALLERO CT	LAK	32	A4
CABIN RD	LAS	14	B4
CABRILLO AV	LACO	S	C2
CABRILLO BLVD	STB	174	D4
CABRILLO DR	AVLN	97	B5
CABRILLO FRWY	SD	213	E3
CABRILLO FRWY	SD	215	E2
CABRILLO FRWY	SDCO	V	B3
CABRILLO HWY	MONT	167	D5
CABRILLO HWY	MONT	168	C2
CABRILLO HWY	MON	53	E5
CABRILLO HWY	MON	54	B4
CABRILLO HWY	MON	168	C2
CABRILLO HWY	SLO	75	B1
CABRILLO HWY	SLO	76	B5
CABRILLO HWY	SLO	172	B1
CABRILLO HWY	SMCO	N	B2
CABRILLO HWY	SMCO	45	B3
CABRILLO HWY	SB	86	B1
CABRILLO HWY	SC	169	A4
CABRILLO HWY	SCR	N	D5
CABRILLO HWY	SCR	53	D1
CABRILLO HWY	SCR	54	A2
CACHAGUA RD	MON	54	C5
CACHAGUA RD	MON	64	C1
CACHUMA RD	SB	87	A2
CACTUS AV	RCO	99	C3
CACTUS AV	SBD	99	B1
CACTUS DR	MCO	55	D2
CACTUS FLATS	INY	70	B2
CACTUS VLY RD	RCO	99	E4
CADET RD	KER	78	A4
CADILLAC AV	LA	183	D4
CADIZ DR	SBD	102	C1
CADIZ RD	SBD	94	B3
CADIZ RD	SBD	103	A1
CADY RD	IMP	109	A4
CAHUENGA BLVD	LA	179	A3
CAHUENGA BLVD	LA	181	D5
CAHUENGA BLVD	LACO	Q	D3
CAHUENGA BLVD W	LA	181	A1
CAHUILLA RD	RCO	100	B5

STREET	CO.	PAGE	GRID
CAHUILLA RD	SBD	91	C3
CAHUILLA HTS RD	RCO	100	A5
CAIRO	KIN	57	D5
CAJALCO RD	RCO	99	A3
CAJON BLVD	SBD	91	A5
CAJON ST	SBD	99	C2
CALAVERAS AV	FRCO	56	D4
CALAVERAS AV	FRCO	66	D2
CALAVERAS RD	ALA	P	C1
CALAVERAS RD	ALA	46	B3
CALAVERAS RD	SCL	46	B4
CALAVERITAS RD	CAL	41	A3
CALDOR RD	ED	41	B1
CALICO BLVD	SBD	92	A1
CALICO RD	SBD	92	A1
CALIENT-BODF RD	KER	79	B3
CALIENT-BODF RD	KER	79	C2
CALIENTE CK RD	KER	79	C3
CALIFORNIA AV	BKD	166	B3
CALIFORNIA AV	COL	32	E3
CALIFORNIA AV	FRE	165	A5
CALIFORNIA AV	FRCO	56	C3
CALIFORNIA AV	FRCO	57	C3
CALIFORNIA AV	KER	78	D3
CALIFORNIA AV	LA	187	B2
CALIFORNIA AV	LACO	R	A5
CALIFORNIA AV	MDO	162	A4
CALIFORNIA AV	RENO	130	A3
CALIFORNIA AV	RCO	98	E3
CALIFORNIA AV	RCO	99	D4
CALIFORNIA AV	SCL	P	D5
CALIFORNIA AV	SCL	54	C1
CALIFORNIA AV	SC	169	C4
CALIFORNIA AV	STA	47	B2
CALIFORNIA BLVD	LACO	R	B3
CALIFORNIA BLVD	NAP	133	B2
CALIFORNIA BLVD	PAS	190	A5
CALIFORNIA BLVD	SNLO	172	D2
CALIFORNIA BLVD	SLO	172	D2
CALIFORNIA DR	IMP	108	C2
CALIFORNIA DR	NAPA	29	D4
CALIFORNIA ST	BUR	179	B3
CALIFORNIA ST	EUR	121	C2
CALIFORNIA ST	LACO	98	A1
CALIFORNIA ST	RED	122	B1
CALIFORNIA ST	SBD	99	B1
CALIFORNIA ST	SDCO	106	B3
CALIFORNIA ST	SF	141	B3
CALIFORNIA ST	SF	142	D2
CALIFORNIA ST	SF	143	C3
CALIFORNIA ST	SFCO	L	B4
CALIFORNIA ST	SFCO	45	B1
CALIFORNIA ST	SJCO	40	A5
CALIFORNIA ST	S	160	D2
CALIFORNIA ST	VENT	175	B2
CALIF CITY BLVD	KER	80	B4
CALIFRNIA FARMS	SJCO	47	C1
CALIF PINES BL	MOD	14	E2
CALISTOGA AV	NAP	133	C4
CALISTOGA RD	SON	38	A1
CALKINS RD	FRCO	57	E1
CALLAHAN RD	TEH	18	C5
CALLAHAN RD E	SIS	11	D1
CALLE DEL SOL	AVLN	97	B4
CALLE ECUESTRE	SB	87	A4
CALLEGUAS RD	VEN	96	C1
CALLE H COLEGIO	BAJA	112	B4
CALLE LIPPIZANA	SB	87	A4
CALLENDR BLK LK	SLO	76	B5
CALLE QUEBRADA	SB	87	A4
CALLE REAL	SB	86	E4
CALLE REAL	SB	87	A4
CALLOWAY DR	KER	78	C3
CALNEVA RD	LAS	21	E5
CALPACK RD	SJCO	46	E1
CALPINE RD	SIE	27	B3
CALPINE LO RD	SIE	27	B3
CALVIN CREST RD	MAD	49	D4
CALVINE RD	SAC	39	E2
CALVINE RD	SAC	40	A2
CALZ	BAJA	112	B4
CALZADA AV	SB	86	E3
CAMANCHE PKWY N	AMA	40	C3
CAMANCHE PKWY S	CAL	40	D3
CAMARES DR	LACO	90	A3
CAMARILLO ST	LA	179	A4
CAMARILLO ST	LACO	Q	D3
CAMBRIA AV	FRCO	56	A2
CAMBRIA RD	SBD	91	E4
CAMBRIDGE DR	BUR	179	D1
CAMBRIDGE RD	SHA	18	C3
CAMBRIDGE ST	ORA	196	D1
CAMBRIDGE ST	SA	196	D1
CAMBRIDGE ST N	ORA	194	D5
CAMDEN AV	SCL	P	B4
CAMDEN AV	SCL	46	A5
CAMERON AV	LACO	98	C2
CAMERON AV	LACO	U	A2
CAMERON RD	MEN	30	C2
CAMERON CYN RD	KER	79	D5
CAMERON PARK DR	ED	34	C5
CAMINO AV	IMP	108	C2
CAMINO ALTO	MAR	L	B4
CAMINO ALTO	MV	140	B3
CM CAPISTRANO	SJC	202	C3
CAMINO CIELO	SB	87	A3
CM DE FLORES	AVLN	97	B4
CM DEL AVION	LN	202	B2
CM DEL AVION	SJC	202	C2
CAMINO DL MONTE	AVLN	97	A4
CAMINO DL MONTE	CAR	53	D5
CAMINO DL MONTE	CAR	168	C3
CAMINO DL MONTE	MON	168	C3

STREET	CO.	PAGE	GRID
CM DL RIO W	SD	213	A5
CAMINO DIABLO	CC	M	D4
CAMINO DIABLO	CC	46	C1
CM DOS RIOS	VEN	96	D1
CM LAS RAMBLAS	SJC	202	D4
CM MIRA COSTA	SCL	202	E5
CAMINO ORO	SHA	19	A2
CAMINO PABLO	CC	L	D4
CAMINO PABLO	CC	L	E4
CAMINO REAL	LACO	S	A2
CAMINO REAL	SHA	19	A3
CAMINO SANTA FE	SDCO	106	C5
CM SANTA FE DR	SDCO	V	B2
CM TASSAJARA RD	CC	M	B4
CM TASSAJARA RD	CC	46	A1
CAMINO VISTA	SHA	19	A2
CAMMATTI-SHN RD	SLO	76	D1
CAMP RD	SAC	39	E3
CAMP RD E	COL	32	D2
CAMPBELL	SJCO	47	D1
CAMPBELL AV	BUT	33	C1
CAMPBELL AV	SCL	P	B3
CAMPBELL AV	SCL	46	A5
CAMPBELL DR	KER	78	E4
CAMPBELL RD	IMP	111	E3
CAMPBELL RD	SBD	101	D1
CAMPBELL RD	SB	86	C3
CAMPBELL RD	SOL	39	B1
CAMPBL HOT SPGS	SIE	27	C4
CAMPBELL RDG RD	TRI	10	D5
CAMPBLLS FLT RD	TUO	41	C5
CAMP CREEK RD	BUT	25	E2
CAMP CREEK RD	SIS	4	B2
CAMP FAR WST RD	PLA	34	A3
CAMPHORA RD	MON	54	E5
CAMPHORA RD	MON	55	A5
CAMP KIMTU RD	HUM	16	C5
CAMP NINE RD	CAL	41	C4
CAMPO RD	SDCO	V	D3
CAMPO RD	SDCO	111	E1
CAMPODONICA RD	MCO	48	A3
CAMPOS LN	SOL	39	A1
CAMP ROCK RD	SBD	92	A1
CAMPO SECO RD	CAL	40	D3
CAMPO SECO RD	TUO	41	C5
CAMP THREE RD	SIS	10	E2
CAMPTON RD	EUR	121	D4
CAMPTON RD	HUM	15	E1
CAMPTONVILLE RD	SIE	26	C5
CAMPUS AV	ONT	204	C3
CAMPUS AV	UPL	204	C2
CAMPUS DR	IRV	198	C5
CAMPUS DR	KER	78	E4
CAMPUS DR	NB	198	C5
CAMP WEOTT RD	HUM	15	D2
CMP 1 TEN MI RD	MEN	22	C4
CMP 2 TEN MI RD	MEN	22	C4
CAMP 8 RD	SLO	76	C2
CAMUESA RD	SB	87	D3
CANA HWY	BUT	25	A2
CANADA AV	PAS	190	A1
CANADA BLVD	LACO	97	E1
CANADA BLVD	LACO	R	A2
CANADA RD	SMCO	N	D2
CANADA RD	SMCO	45	C3
CANADA RD	SCL	54	D2
CANAL AV	FRCO	57	E1
CANAL BLVD	SJCO	46	E1
CANAL BLVD	SJCO	47	A1
CANAL DR	MCO	47	E4
CANAL DR	MCO	48	A4
CANAL RD	GLE	24	E3
CANAL RD	KER	77	E2
CANAL RD	KER	78	A2
CANAL ST	PLCV	138	C2
CANAL BANK RD	STA	47	E2
CANAL BANK RD	STA	48	A2
CANAL GULCH RD	SIS	4	A4
CANAL SCHOOL RD	MCO	47	C4
CANA PINE CREEK	BUT	25	A2
C AND D BLVD	RCO	103	D5
CANFIELD RD	SDCO	107	A2
CANFIELD RD	SON	37	E3
CANNIBAL RD	HUM	15	D2
CANNON RD	SDCO	106	B3
CANNON RD	TEH	18	B5
CANNON ST	SDCO	V	A3
CANOGA AV	LA	177	C3
CANON DR	BH	183	A1
CANON RD	SOL	39	A3
CANON ST	SDCO	111	C1
CANON PERDIDO	STB	174	C3
CANRIGHT RD	SOL	39	C3
CANTELOW RD	SOL	38	E2
CANTELOW RD	SOL	39	A2
CANTON RD	MCO	48	C5
CANYON DR	RCO	100	C3
CANYON DR	SBD	82	A5
CANYON RD	INY	52	B3
CANYON RD	MEN	23	A5
CANYON RD	MNO	52	B3
CANYON RD	SBD	93	B5
CANYON RD	SBD	100	C2
CANYON RD	SMCO	N	C4
CANYON RD	SMCO	45	C5
CANYON RD	SHA	18	C3
CANYON RD	SON	31	D5
CANYON WY	PLA	34	D2
CANYON CREEK RD	MOD	14	E1
CANYON CREEK RD	SIS	3	B5
CANYON CREEK RD	TRI	17	C1
CANYON CREST DR	RCO	99	B2
CANYON VW LOOP	TEH	19	B4

STREET	CO.	PAGE	GRID
CANYON VIEW RD	SBD	91	D4
CAPAY AV	GLE	24	E3
CAPAY RD	TEH	24	D2
CAPE GLOUCESTER	SBD	91	E2
CAPEZZOLI LN	LAS	21	C4
CAPITAL BLVD	GLE	24	E4
CAPITAN TK TR	SDCO	107	B5
CAPITOL AV	SCTO	137	C3
CAPITOL AV	SCL	P	C3
CAPITOL AV	SCL	46	B4
CAPITOL AV	YOL	137	A2
CAPITOL AV	YOL	39	D1
CAPITOL EXPWY	SCL	P	C4
CAPITOL EXPWY	SCL	46	B5
CAPITOL ST	SAL	171	B3
CAPITOLA RD	SCR	54	A2
CAPPELL RD	HUM	10	C2
CAPPS CROSSING	ED	35	B5
CAPRI AV	MCO	55	D1
CARBINE TR	KER	79	D5
CARBON CYN RD	ORCO	98	C3
CARBON CYN RD	ORCO	T	E1
CARBON CYN RD	ORCO	U	B4
CARBON CYN RD	SBD	98	C3
CARBON CYN RD	SBD	U	B4
CARBONDALE RD	AMA	40	C2
CARBONDALE RD	SAC	40	C2
CARDELLA RD	MCO	48	B4
CARDENO DR	SD	211	B4
CARDIFF ST	SDCO	V	D3
CAREY RD	IMP	109	A4
CARGIL LN	RCO	107	C1
CARIBOU RD	SIS	11	C3
CARLETON RD	MPA	49	B3
CARLIN RD	SJCO	46	E1
CARLSBAD BLVD	SDCO	106	B3
CARLSON	CC	38	C5
CARLSON BLVD	CC	L	C3
CARLSON BLVD	R	155	B4
CARLSON RD	BUT	25	B4
CARLSON RD	SUT	33	C3
CARLTON RD	SCR	54	C2
CARLTON RD	SIS	4	B4
CARLUCCI RD	MCO	56	A1
CARLYLE RD	NEV	27	A5
CARMEL RD	KER	77	D1
CARMELLIA AV	FRCO	56	B2
CARMEL MTN RD	SDCO	106	D4
CARMEL RCHO BL	MON	168	D5
CARMEL VLY RD	MON	54	B5
CARMEL VLY RD	MON	64	C1
CARMEL VLY RD	MON	168	E4
CARMEL VLY RD	SDCO	V	A1
CARMEL VLY RD	SDCO	106	C4
CARMEN LN	BUT	25	A3
CARMENCITA AV	SJCO	40	A2
CARMENITA AV	LACO	T	B1
CARNATION RD	MCO	47	D5
CARNELIAN BAY	PLA	35	E1
CARNEROS AV	NAPA	38	C3
CARPENTER RD	HUM	10	D5
CARPENTER RD	SJCO	40	B5
CARPENTER RD	STA	47	E1
CARPENTER ST	CAR	53	D5
CARPENTER ST	CAR	168	C3
CARPENTER ST	MON	168	C3
CARPENTERIA	MON	54	C3
CARPENTER RIDGE	BUT	25	D1
CARQUINEZ SC DR	CC	L	E3
CARR AV	SBT	54	C2
CARRIAGE LN	SHA	18	B3
CARRIER GLCH RD	TRI	17	C3
CARRILLO ST	STB	174	B4
CARRIZO GRGE RD	SDCO	111	A4
CARROLL RD	SAC	39	E3
CARROLL CK RD	INY	60	B5
CARROLTON	SJCO	47	C1
CARROT LN	RCO	107	B1
CARRVILLE LOOP	TRI	11	E4
CARRVILLE LOOP	TRI	12	A4
CARSON RD	ED	34	E5
CARSON ST	LACO	97	D5
CARSON ST	LACO	S	B2
CARSTENS RD	MPA	49	B3
CARTER RD	MPA	49	B3
CARTER ST	SBD	99	D2
CARTMILL AV	TUL	68	A2
CARUTHERS AV	FRCO	57	C5
CARVER LN	RCO	99	B4
CASA DR	LA	178	B4
CASADEL RD	MAD	49	E5
CASADEL RD	MAD	50	A5
CASA DIABLO CTO	MNO	51	B2
CASA DIABLO MN	MNO	51	B2
CASA GRANDE RD	SON	L	A1
CASALE RD	TEH	18	D5
CASA LOMA RD	SCL	P	C5
CASA LOMA RD	SCL	54	B1
CASCADE BLVD	SHA	18	C2
CASCADE RD	SBD	101	E4
CASCADIAN AV	SBD	91	D3
CASE RD	RCO	99	C4
CASEY AV	KER	68	B5
CASEY AV	SB	86	E3
CASEY RD	IMP	109	B5
CASEY RD	SOL	39	B2
CASINO DR	CLK	85	D5
CASITAS VIS RD	VEN	88	A5
CASPR LTL LK RD	MEN	22	C5
CASS ST	MONT	167	E4
CASS ST	MON	53	E5
CASS ST	SD	212	A2
CASS ST	SDCO	V	A2

STREET	CO.	PAGE	GRID
CASS ST	SDCO	106	C5
CASSEL RD	SHA	13	D5
CASSEL FALL RIV	SHA	13	D4
CASSERLY RD	SCR	54	C2
CASSIDY ST	SDCO	106	B3
CASTAIC RD	LACO	89	B4
CASTAIC CYN RD	LACO	89	B3
CASTERLINE RD	HUM	16	D4
CASTILLO ST	STB	174	B3
CASTLE CT	BUT	25	C3
CASTLE ST	S	160	C3
CASTLE CREEK RD	SHA	12	C3
CASTLE HEIGHTS AV	LA	183	B4
CASTLE LAKE RD	SIS	12	C2
CASTRO	CC	38	C5
CASTRO RD	CC	38	D5
CASTRO RD	RCO	99	D4
CASTRO ST	MVW	148	A4
CASTRO RANCH RD	CC	L	D3
CASTROVILLE BL	MON	54	C3
CATALINA AV	AVLN	97	B5
CATALINA BLVD	SDCO	V	A3
CATALINA DR	DVS	136	C1
CAT CANYON RD	SB	86	D2
CATERPILLAR RD	SHA	18	C2
CATFISH BCH RD	PLU	20	B4
CATHEDRAL RD	ED	36	A3
CATHEY RD	HUM	16	B4
CATLETT RD W	SUT	33	D4
CATRINA RD	MCO	56	B1
CATTARAUGUS AV	LA	183	C4
CATTLE DR	TUL	68	E3
CATTLE DRIVE RD	MNO	51	C1
CATTLEMEN RD	MON	65	D3
CATWAY RD	SB	87	A2
CAUGHLIN RD	SBD	91	A3
CAVE CITY RD	CAL	41	B3
CAVEDALE RD	SON	38	B2
CAVIN RD	VEN	88	E4
CAVITT & STLLMN	PLA	34	B4
CAWELTI RD	VEN	96	C1
CAWSTON AV	RCO	99	E4
CAYLEY DR	KER	79	B4
CAYTON VLY RD	SHA	13	C4
CAYUCOS CK RD	SLO	75	D2
CAZADERO HWY	SON	37	C1
CCMO RD	KER	77	D3
CEBADA CYN RD	SB	86	C3
CECIL AV	KER	68	B5
CECIL RD	COL	33	B3
CECILVILLE RD	SIS	11	C3
CEDAR AV	FRCO	57	C5
CEDAR AV	RCO	100	C4
CEDAR AV	SBD	99	B2
CEDAR DR	MOD	14	B2
CEDAR ST	SBD	80	E1
CEDAR ST	SDCO	107	A4
CEDAR CAMP RD	HUM	10	C2
CEDAR CAMP RD	SIS	10	C1
CEDAR CAMP RD	TRI	17	A4
CEDAR CANYON RD	SBD	84	B4
CEDAR CREEK RD	ED	41	A1
CEDAR CREEK RD	HUM	10	C5
CEDAR CK LP RD	BUT	25	C1
CEDAR GROVE RD	SIS	5	A2
CEDAR RAVINE RD	ED	34	E5
CEDAR RAVINE ST	PLCV	138	E3
CEDARVILLE DUMP	MOD	8	E1
CEDAR WELL	SIS	5	A4
CEDARWOOD CT	SHA	19	A3
CEDROS DR	SBD	90	E2
CEMENT HILL RD	FRFD	135	C2
CEMENT HILL RD	NEV	34	C1
CEMETERY DR	MOD	14	C3
CEMETERY RD	COL	32	D1
CEMETERY RD	HUM	16	D4
CEMETERY RD	MCO	47	D4
CEMETERY RD	MNO	43	C4
CEMETERY RD	SBD	82	A5
CEMETERY RD	SHA	19	B2
CEMETERY RD	SIS	5	A2
CENTENNIAL RD	HUM	15	D3
CENTER AV	MCO	154	C4
CENTER RD	LAS	21	A3
CENTER RD	STA	47	B2
CENTER ST	CAL	41	A3
CENTER ST	LA	186	C3
CENTER ST	MAN	161	A4
CENTER ST	RCO	99	B2
CENTER ST	SBD	99	C2
CENTER ST	SC	169	D3
CENTER ST	S	160	D3
CENTER ST EXT	RCO	99	C2
CENTER ST S	TEH	24	E1
CTR SCH HOUSE	LAS	14	C3
CENTER VLY RD	MEN	23	A5
CENTERVILLE LN	DGL	36	B3
CENTERVILLE RD	BUT	25	C3
CENTERVILLE RD	HUM	15	D2
CENTERVILLE RD	MOD	8	A1
CENTERVILLE RD	MOD	14	D1
CENTINELA AV	CUL	187	E2
CENTINELA AV	LA	188	C3
CENTINELA AV	LA	187	D1
CENTINELA AV	LACO	Q	C4
CENTINELLA RD	MCO	55	C1
CENTRAL AV	FRCO	56	D4
CENTRAL AV	FRCO	57	B4
CENTRAL AV	HUM	9	E4
CENTRAL AV	HUM	10	A4
CENTRAL AV	KER	78	A2
CENTRAL AV	LA	186	B5
CENTRAL AV	LACO	97	E2

INDEXES

STREET	CO.	PAGE	GRID
CENTRAL AV	LACO	Q	E2
CENTRAL AV	LACO	S	C1
CENTRAL AV	MCO	47	D4
CENTRAL AV	MON	65	B2
CENTRAL AV	MTCL	203	D2
CENTRAL AV	ORCO	T	C1
CENTRAL AV	ORCO	U	A4
CENTRAL AV	PAC	167	C2
CENTRAL AV	RCO	99	B2
CENTRAL AV	RIV	205	B4
CENTRAL AV	SAL	171	A4
CENTRAL AV	SBD	U	D3
CENTRAL AV	SBD	98	D2
CENTRAL AV	RCO	99	B4
CENTRAL AV	SBD	203	C2
CENTRAL AV	SB	86	B3
CENTRAL AV	STA	47	D3
CENTRAL AV	SUT	33	B3
CENTRAL AV	TEH	24	D1
CENTRAL AV	VEN	88	C5
CENTRAL AV	YOL	39	D2
CENTRAL AV E	SBDO	207	D3
CENTRAL AV W	SBDO	207	D3
CENTRAL RD	SBD	91	C3
CENTRAL EXPWY	MVW	148	B4
CENTRAL EXPWY	SCL	N	E2
CENTRAL EXPWY	SCL	P	B3
CENTRAL EXPWY	SCLR	151	B1
CENTRAL EXPWY	SVL	148	B4
CENTRAL FRWY	SF	143	B5
CENTRAL SKYWAY	SF	142	C4
CENTRAL ST	RCO	99	C5
CENTRAL CAMP RD	MAD	49	E4
CENTRAL HILL RD	CAL	40	E3
CENTRAL HILL RD	CAL	41	A3
CENTRL HOUSE RD	BUT	25	D5
CENTRALIA ST	LACO	S	E2
CENTRALIA ST	LACO	T	A2
CENTRAL VLY HWY	KER	78	B1
CENTURY BLVD	LA	189	C1
CENTURY BLVD	LACO	97	D2
CENTURY BLVD	LACO	Q	D5
CENTURY PARK EAST	LA	183	A2
CENTURY PARK WEST	LA	183	A2
CERINI AV	FRCO	57	B5
CERINI AV	FRCO	57	C5
CERRITOS AV	ANA	193	D4
CERRITOS AV	ORCO	T	B2
CERRO GORDO RD	INY	60	C5
CERRO GORDO RD	INY	60	D4
CERRO NOROESTE	KER	78	A5
CERRO NOROESTE	KER	87	E1
CERVANTES BLVD	SF	142	A1
CESAR CHAVEZ AV	LACO	R	A4
CESAR E CHAVEZ AV	LA	186	C2
CHADBOURNE RD	CC	39	B5
CHADBOURNE RD	SOL	38	E3
CHADWICK RD	SBD	101	E1
CHAHLIP LN	FRCO	58	C1
CHALET DR	KER	79	C4
CHALFANT RD	MNO	51	D3
CHALFANT LP RD	MNO	51	D3
CHALK BLUFF RD	INY	51	C4
CHALK BLUFF RD	NEV	34	D1
CHALK HILL RD	SON	37	E1
CHALLNGE CTO RD	YUB	26	A4
CHALLENGER WY	LACO	90	A3
CHALONE RD	SBT	55	A5
CHAMBERLAIN	PLA	34	A3
CHAMBERLAIN RD	MCO	48	B5
CHAMBERS RD	HUM	15	D4
CHAMBERS WLS RD	SBD	103	E1
CHAMPAGNE AV	KER	89	C1
CHAMPS FLAT RD	LAS	20	C2
CHANAC RD	KER	79	B4
CHANDLER	YUB	33	D1
CHANDLER BLVD	BUR	179	B2
CHANDLER BLVD	LACO	Q	C2
CHANDLER RD	PLU	26	D1
CHANDON AV	BUT	33	C1
CHANNEL ISLD BL	VEN	96	B1
CHAPALA ST	STB	174	A2
CHAPARAJOS ST	CAL	41	A4
CHAPARRAL DR	SHA	18	B2
CHAPMAN AV	ORA	193	D5
CHAPMAN AV	ORA	196	B1
CHAPMAN AV	ORCO	98	C3
CHAPMAN AV	ORCO	T	B2
CHAPMAN AV	ORCO	T	C1
CHAPMAN AV E	ORA	194	D5
CHAPMAN AV W	ORA	194	A5
CHAPMAN RD	RCO	107	C1
CHAPPIUS LN N	LAS	21	B3
CHAPPIUS LN S	LAS	21	B4
CHAPULNIK RD	IMP	109	B4
CHARD AV	TEH	18	D5
CHARLEBOIS RD	MNO	42	E1
CHARLES ST	KER	80	D1
CHARLES ST	SHA	18	C3
CHARLES HILL RD	CC	L	E4
CHARLESTON BLVD	LV	209	A2
CHARLESTON BL E	CLK	74	D2
CHARLESTON RD	MCO	55	D2
CHARLESTON RD	SCL	N	E3
CHARLESTON RD	SCL	P	A3
CHARLESTON RD	SCL	45	E4
CHARLESTON RD W	PA	147	E5
CHRLSTN VOLCANO	AMA	41	A2
CHAROLAIS RD	SLO	76	A1
CHARTER WY	SJCO	40	B5
CHARTER OAK DR	TUL	68	C1
CHASE AV	KER	79	E2
CHASE AV	KER	80	A2

STREET	CO.	PAGE	GRID
CHASE AV	SDCO	V	E3
CHASE AV	SDCO	111	E1
CHASE AV	TEH	24	D2
CHASE DR	RCO	98	E3
CHASE SCHOOL RD	RCO	100	E3
CHATEAU DR	SMCO	45	C3
CHATEAU RD	ML	164	D3
CHATEAU FRESNO	FRCO	57	B4
CHATEAU FRESNO	FRCO	57	B5
CHATSWORTH BLVD	SDCO	V	A3
CHATSWORTH BLVD	SDCO	111	C1
CHECKMATE RD	RCO	100	A5
CHELSEY AV	CC	L	C3
CHEMEHUEVI BLVD	MOH	96	B4
CHEMISE MTN RD	HUM	22	A1
CHEROKEE LN	SAC	40	B3
CHEROKEE LN	SJCO	40	B3
CHEROKEE RD	BUT	25	D4
CHEROKEE RD	MCO	55	D1
CHEROKEE RD	SBD	82	C5
CHEROKEE RD	SJCO	40	B5
CHERRY AV	FRCO	57	C4
CHERRY AV	FRCO	57	C5
CHERRY AV	KER	78	B2
CHERRY AV	LACO	97	E4
CHERRY AV	LACO	S	D2
CHERRY AV	RCO	99	E3
CHERRY AV	SBD	99	A2
CHERRY AV	SBR	144	A2
CHERRY AV	STA	47	C4
CHERRY ST	SUT	33	C2
CHERRY CREEK RD	SON	31	C4
CHERRY GLEN RD	SOL	38	E3
CHERRY VLY BLVD	RCO	99	E2
CHERT RD	RCO	107	B1
CHESEBORO RD	LACO	90	B4
CHESTER AV	BKD	166	C4
CHESTER AV	KER	78	D3
CHESTER LN	BKD	166	B4
CHESTR JNPR LK RD	PLU	20	A3
CHESTER SKI RD	PLU	20	A4
CHESTR WRNR VLY	PLU	19	E3
CHESTR WRNR VLY	PLU	20	A3
CHESTNUT AV	FRCO	57	C2
CHESTNUT AV	FRCO	57	C5
CHESTNUT AV	SMCO	N	B1
CHESTNUT AV	SA	196	D4
CHESTNUT AV	TEH	18	D5
CHESTNUT ST	SHA	18	C3
CHESTNUT WY	CAL	41	B5
CHEVALIER RD	KER	78	D4
CHEVY CHASE DR	LACO	97	E1
CHEVY CHASE DR	LACO	R	A3
CHEZEM RD	HUM	10	B5
CHICAGO AV	RIV	205	D4
CHICAGO AV	STA	47	C2
CHICK RD	IMP	112	B3
CHICK RD	RCO	108	E1
CHICKEN HAWK RD	PLA	34	E2
CHICKEN RCH RD	LAS	8	C5
CHICKEN RCH RD	TUO	41	C5
CHICO AV	KIN	57	E5
CHICO CANYON RD	BUT	25	C2
CHICORB LN	SOL	39	B2
CHICO RIVER RD	BUT	25	A3
CHIDAGO LOOP	MNO	51	C2
CHIDAGO CYN RD	MNO	51	B2
CHIHUAHUA VLY	SDCO	107	B2
CHILD RD	TUO	163	D3
CHILDS AV	MER	170	B5
CHILDS AV	MCO	48	C4
CHILE CAMP RD	CAL	40	D3
CHILENO VLY RD	SON	37	E3
CHILENO VLY RD	SON	38	A3
CHILES RD	YOL	39	C1
CHILES POPE VLY	NAPA	29	D1
CHILES POPE VLY	NAPA	38	C1
CHILI HILL RD	PLA	34	B3
CHIMNEY ROCK RD	SLO	75	D1
CHINA CAMP RD	MCO	55	D1
CHINA CREEK RD	MAD	49	D4
CHINA GRADE	SIS	3	A3
CHINA GRADE LP	KER	78	D2
CHINA GRADE RD	PLU	26	D1
CHINA GULCH DR	SHA	18	B3
CHINA LAKE BLVD	KER	80	D1
CHINA PK LO RD	SIS	3	A3
CHINA POINT RD	BUT	25	D2
CHINA RANCH RD	INY	73	A5
CHINO AV	SBD	U	C3
CHINO AV	SBD	98	D2
CHINQUAPIN RD	MAD	49	E4
CHINQUAPIN RD	MAD	50	A4
CHINQUAPIN DR	MEN	23	A5
CHIRIACO RD	RCO	101	E4
CHITTENDEN RD	TEH	24	C2
CHLORIDE RD	SBD	92	B1
CHLORIDE CLF RD	INY	62	A3
CHOLAME RD	MON	66	C4
CHOLAME VLY RD	SLO	66	D5
CHOLLA RD	SBD	91	C4
CHOLLA RD	SBD	92	C5
CHORRO ST S	SNLO	172	C3
CHOWCHILLA	MAD	56	D3
CHOWCHILLA BLVD	MAD	56	D1
CHOWCHILLA MTN	MPA	49	C3
CHRISMAN RD	SJCO	47	A2
CHRISTENSEN RD	SAC	40	A3
CHRISTIAN RD	TEH	24	D2
CHRISTIE LN	MNO	51	C1
CHRISTN VLY RD	PLA	34	C3
CHROME MINE RD	TRI	17	B3
CHUALAR RD	MON	54	D4

STREET	CO.	PAGE	GRID
CHUALAR CYN RD	MON	54	E4
CHUALAR RIV RD	MON	54	D5
CHUCKWAGON DR	CAL	41	A5
CHUCKWALLA RD	SBD	91	D3
CHUCKWL SPGS RD	RCO	102	D5
CHUCKWLA VLY RD	RCO	102	D4
CHUCKWLA VLY RD	RCO	103	A5
CHURCH AV	FRE	165	B5
CHURCH AV	FRCO	57	A3
CHURCH AV	FRCO	57	D3
CHURCH AV	SCL	54	D1
CHURCH AV	SCL	P	E5
CHURCH LN	HUM	15	E2
CHURCH LN	SCL	P	E5
CHURCH RD	SOL	M	D2
CHURCH RD	SOL	39	C4
CHURCH ST	HUM	16	D4
CHURCH ST	SBD	99	C2
CHURCH ST	STA	47	D2
CHURCH ST	S	160	C5
CHURCH HILL RD	CAL	41	A3
CHURCHILL MN RD	INY	51	D3
CHURCH SPGS RD	STA	48	A1
CHURN CREEK RD	SHA	18	C2
CIBOLA RD	LPAZ	103	E5
CIBOLA RD	LPAZ	110	D1
CIENAGA RD	KER	78	A5
CIENEGA RD	SBT	54	E3
CIENEGA RD	SBT	55	A4
CIMA RD	SBD	83	E2
CIMA RD	SBD	84	A2
CIMA MESA RD	LACO	90	B4
CINCHA ST	CAL	41	A4
CINDER RD	INY	70	C3
CINDER PIT RD	MOD	14	D1
CIPRIANI BLVD	BLMT	145	A5
CIRCLE DR	INY	70	E1
CIRCLE DR	RCO	100	B4
CIRCLEA CT	BUT	25	C3
CIRCLE C LN	SOL	39	B2
CITRACADO PKWY	SDCO	106	D3
CITRUS AV	LACO	98	C2
CITRUS AV	LACO	U	A2
CITRUS AV	SBD	99	A2
CITRUS AV	SBD	99	D2
CITRUS AV	SDCO	106	C3
CITRUS AV	SDCO	106	D3
CITY DR, THE	ORA	195	E1
CITY CAMP	MNO	43	C5
CIVIC CENTER BLVD	FRFD	135	C4
CIVIC CENTER DR	BH	183	C1
CIVIC CENTER DR	SR	139	C1
CIVIC CENTER DR	SA	195	D3
CIVIC CENTER DR	SA	196	B3
CLAIREMONT DR	SD	211	E4
CLAIREMONT DR	SD	213	A1
CLAIREMONT DR	SDCO	V	B2
CLAIREMONT DR	SDCO	106	C5
CLAIRMNT MSA BL	SDCO	V	B2
CLAIREMONT MESA	SDCO	106	C5
CLARATINA AV	STA	47	D2
CLAREMONT AV	ALA	L	D4
CLAREMONT AV	B	156	B4
CLAREMONT AV	O	156	B4
CLAREMONT BLVD	CLA	203	B2
CLARENDON AV	SF	141	D5
CLARIBEL RD	STA	47	D2
CLARISSA AV	AVLN	97	B5
CLARK AV	COL	24	E5
CLARK AV	LACO	S	E2
CLARK AV	SB	86	C1
CLARK AV	TEH	24	E2
CLARK AV	YUBA	125	C4
CLARK RD	BUT	25	C3
CLARK RD	IMP	109	A5
CLARK RD	IMP	112	A4
CLARK RD	MEN	30	D2
CLARK RD	MON	65	A1
CLARK RD	SLO	76	C1
CLARK RD	SOL	39	B2
CLARK RD	STA	47	C2
CLARK RD	SUT	33	C1
CLARKE RD	HUM	15	D4
CLARK MTN RD	SBD	84	A2
CLARK RANCH RD	MNO	51	C1
CLARKSBURG	YOL	39	D2
CLARKS FORK RD	ALP	42	B2
CLARKSON AV	FRCO	56	D5
CLARKSON AV	FRCO	57	C5
CLARKS VLY RD	GLE	24	B4
CLARKS VLY RD	LAS	8	D4
CLAUS RD	STA	47	D2
CLAUSEN RD	MCO	48	E5
CLAWITER RD	ALA	45	E2
CLAWITER RD	ALA	146	B5
CLAWITER RD	ALA	N	E1
CLAWITER RD	H	146	B5
CLAY RD	INY	72	D1
CLAY ST	SAL	171	B4
CLAY ST	U	123	B3
CLAY BANK RD	FRFD	135	E3
CLAY BANK RD	SOL	39	A3
CLAY MINE RD	KER	80	C5
CLAY RIVER RD	SBD	91	E1
CLAY STATION RD	SAC	40	B3
CLAYTON AV	FRCO	56	D4
CLAYTON AV	FRCO	58	A4
CLAYTON RD	CC	39	A5
CLAYTON RD	NEV	34	B2
CLAYTON RD	SON	32	A5
CLAYTON RD	STA	47	D3
CLAYTON CREEK	LAK	32	A4
CLEAR CREEK RD	KER	79	B4

STREET	CO.	PAGE	GRID
CLEAR CREEK RD	SBT	65	E1
CLEAR CREEK RD	SBT	66	A1
CLEAR CREEK RD	SHA	18	B3
CLEAR LAKE RD	MOD	6	C3
CLEGHORN RD	LAS	14	D5
CLEGHORN CYN RD	SBD	91	B5
CLEM	SJCO	40	C5
CLEMENCEAU AV	FRCO	57	D5
CLEMENTE AV	AVLN	97	B5
CLEMENTS RD	SJCO	40	C4
CLEMENTS RD	SUT	33	C2
CLEVELAND AV	MAD	57	A2
CLEVELAND AV	SBD	U	E3
CLEVELAND AV	SD	214	A5
CLEVELAND AV	STA	47	D1
CLEVELAND RD	MCO	56	C1
CLEVELAND ST	RCO	101	C5
CLIFF DR	LAG	201	B2
CLIFF DR	STB	174	C5
CLIFF DR W	SC	169	D4
CLIFF RIDGE RD	MEN	30	C2
CLIFTON CT RD	SJCO	46	D1
CLINE GULCH RD	SHA	18	A1
CLINTON AV	FRE	165	B1
CLINTON AV	FRCO	56	E3
CLINTON AV	FRCO	57	A3
CLINTON AV	KIN	57	E5
CLINTON AV S	SJCO	47	B1
CLINTON RD	AMA	41	A2
CLINTON RD	STA	47	D2
CLINTON RD E	AMA	41	A2
CLINTON RD W	AMA	41	A2
CLINTN KEITH RD	RCO	99	C5
CLIO STATE RD	PLU	27	B3
CLOSE AV	TUL	68	D1
CLOUGH RD	HUM	15	D2
CLOUTIER ST	DN	1	D3
CLOVER LN	SB	86	E2
CLOVER LN	SB	87	A2
CLOVER LN	SHA	18	B3
CLOVER CREEK RD	KLAM	5	A1
CLOVERDALE DR	SHA	18	B3
CLOVERDALE RD	RCO	U	E3
CLOVERDALE RD	RCO	98	E2
CLOVERDALE RD	SMCO	N	C4
CLOVERDALE RD	SMCO	45	C5
CLOVERFIELD BL	SMON	180	A5
CLOVERLEAF DR	MAD	57	B2
CLOVER VLY RD	LAK	31	D2
CLOVIS AV	FRCO	57	D5
CLUB DR	DN	1	E3
CLYDE AV	MCO	48	B5
COACHELLA CANAL	RCO	108	D1
COACHLA CN RD	IMP	109	B2
COACHLLA CYN RD	RCO	101	D5
COAL RD	RCO	99	B4
COAL CANYON RD	BUT	25	C4
COAL CANYON RD	ORCO	U	D5
COAL CANYON RD	ORCO	98	D3
COALINGA RD	SBT	65	D1
COALINGA RD	SBT	66	A1
COALNGA MNL SPG	FRCO	66	B3
COAL MINE RD	AMA	40	D3
COAST HWY	LAG	201	A2
COAST HWY	ORCO	202	D5
COAST HWY	SON	30	D5
COAST HWY E	NB	199	D5
COAST HWY E	NB	200	A5
COAST HWY W	NB	199	C5
COAST RD	MON	64	B1
COAST RIDGE TR	MON	64	E4
COCHRANE RD	SCL	P	D4
COCHRAN RD	SCL	54	C1
COCK RBN ISL RD	HUM	15	D2
COCOPAH RD	IMP	112	D5
COD DR	SIS	4	B3
CODONI AV	STA	47	D2
COFFEE RD	KER	78	C2
COFFEE RD	MDO	162	E2
COFFEE RD	STA	47	D2
COFFEE ST	MCO	48	C5
COFFEE CREEK RD	HUM	15	D2
COFFEE CREEK RD	TRI	11	D3
COGSWELL RD	STA	47	E2
COGSWELL RD	STA	48	A2
COHASSET RD	BUT	25	B2
COHASSET RD	C	124	A2
COHEN RD	SJCO	47	A1
COHN AV	FRCO	66	D3
COLBY RD	IMP	110	D5
COLBY MTN LKOUT	TEH	19	D2
COLDEN AV	LACO	Q	E5
COLD CANYON RD	LACO	97	B2
COLD CREEK RD	TRI	17	B3
COLD SPRINGS RD	ED	34	D4
COLD SPRINGS RD	LAS	8	C4
COLDWATR CYN AV	LACO	97	C1
COLDWATR CYN AV	LACO	Q	C2
COLDWATR CYN DR	LACO	97	D1
COLDWELL AV	MDO	162	A2
COLDWELL LN	FRCO	66	B3
COLE AV	LACO	181	D5
COLE RD	IMP	112	B4
COLE RD	MPA	49	B3
COLE GRADE RD	SDCO	106	B3
COLEMAN AV	MP	147	A1
COLEMAN AV	SMCO	147	A1
COLEMAN AV	SCL	P	B3
COLEMAN AV	SJ	151	D2
COLEMN FSH HTCH	SHA	18	D3
COLEMAN VLY RD	SON	37	C2
COLES RD	SUT	33	B3
COLES LEVEE RD	KER	78	B4

STREET	CO.	PAGE	GRID
COLEY RD	IMP	112	D5
COLFAX	PLA	34	D2
COLFAX AV	GV	127	C4
COLFAX AV	LACO	Q	D3
COLFAX AV	NEV	127	C4
COLGATE RD	KER	80	D3
COLIMA RD	LACO	98	B3
COLIMA RD	LACO	R	D5
COLIN RD	SBD	80	E1
COLISEUM ST	LA	184	C5
COLLEGE AV	ALA	L	D4
COLLEGE AV	B	156	B4
COLLEGE AV	MAR	139	B5
COLLEGE AV	MDO	162	A2
COLLEGE AV	O	156	B4
COLLEGE AV	SDCO	V	C3
COLLEGE AV	SDCO	111	D1
COLLEGE AV	SIS	12	C1
COLLEGE AV	SON	37	E2
COLLEGE AV	STR	131	C3
COLLEGE AV W	STR	131	B3
COLLEGE BLVD	SDCO	106	B3
COLLEGE DR	SAL	171	A4
COLLEGE DR	SMA	173	C4
COLLEGE CITY RD	COL	33	A3
COLLEGE HTS BL	KER	80	E1
COLLIER RD	MCO	47	E4
COLLIER RD	MCO	48	A4
COLLIER RD	SJCO	40	B3
COLLIER CYN RD	ALA	46	B2
COLLINS AV	ORA	194	C4
COLLINS AV	ORCO	T	D2
COLLINS RD	IMP	110	D5
COLLINS RD	INY	51	D4
COLLINSVILLE RD	SOL	M	B2
COLLINSVILLE RD	SOL	39	B4
COLLYER DR	SHA	18	C2
COLOMA RD	ED	34	D4
COLOMA RD	ED	138	B1
COLOMA RD	SAC	40	A1
COLOMBERO DR	SIS	12	D2
COLOMBO MINE RD	SIE	26	E4
COLOMBO MINE RD	SIE	27	A4
COLOMBUS AV	MCO	47	D4
COLONY RD	BUT	25	B4
COLONY RD	MON	64	E1
COLONY RD	MON	65	A1
COLONY RD	SAC	40	B2
COLORADO AV	RCO	99	A3
COLORADO AV	SCL	N	E2
COLORADO AV	SMON	180	A5
COLORADO BLVD	LACO	97	E1
COLORADO BLVD	LACO	98	A1
COLORADO BLVD	LACO	R	D3
COLORADO BLVD	PAS	190	E4
COLORADO RD	FRCO	57	A5
COLORADO RD	MPA	49	B3
COLORADO ST	GLEN	182	E1
COLORADO ST	LACO	Q	E3
COLORADO ST	LACO	S	E2
COLORADO ST	LACO	T	A2
COLORADO RV RD	RCO	103	D4
COLOSEUM	INY	59	E2
COLOSSEUM RD	SBD	84	B2
COLSEN CYN RD	SB	86	D1
COLT LN	CAL	41	A5
COLTON AV	CLTN	207	B4
COLTON AV	SBD	99	B2
COLUMBIA AV	RIV	205	D1
COLUMBIA AV	RCO	99	B2
COLUMBIA RD N	KER	80	D3
COLUMBIA RD S	KER	80	D4
COLUMBINE RD	SIS	12	C2
COLUMBUS AV	SF	142	C1
COLUMBUS AV	SF	143	B1
COLUMBUS AV	SFCO	45	C1
COLUMBUS PKWY	SOL	L	D2
COLUMBUS PKWY	SOL	38	D4
COLUMBUS ST	KER	78	D3
COLUSA AV	CC	L	D4
COLUSA AV	FRCO	56	E4
COLUSA AV	FRCO	66	E1
COLUSA AV	SUT	125	A2
COLUSA AV	YUBA	125	A2
COLUSA HWY	BUT	25	B5
COLUSA RD	SBD	91	B3
COLUSA CO RD	COL	31	E1
COLUSA-PRNTN RD	COL	32	E1
COLYEAR SPGS RD	TEH	17	E5
COMANCHE DR	KER	78	E4
COMANCHE DR	KER	79	A3
COMANCHE PT RD	KER	79	A4
COMBELLACK RD	PLCV	138	B2
COMBIE RD	NEV	34	C3
COMBIE RD	PLA	34	C3
COMETA RD	SJCO	47	D1
COMM BLVD	SBD	91	C1
COMMERCE AV	LACO	Q	E1
COMMERCIAL ST	SD	216	A4
COMMONS RD	STA	47	D3
COMMONWEALTH	ORCO	98	B3
COMMONWEALTH AV N	LA	182	C3
COMMONWEALTH AV	ORCO	T	B1
COMMONWEALTH AV	RCO	99	E4
COMPTCHE UKIAH	MEN	30	B1
COMPTON AV	LACO	Q	E5
COMPTON BLVD	LACO	S	B1
COMSTOCK	WSH	130	B3
COMSTOCK RD	SBT	55	A2
COMSTOCK RD	SJCO	40	B4
CONARD RD	LAS	20	D3
CONCHO ST	CAL	41	A4
CONCORD AV	CC	39	C5

STREET	CO.	PAGE	GRID
CONCORD BLVD	CC	M	A3
CONCORD BLVD	CC	39	A5
CONCOW RD	BUT	25	D1
CONDIT AV	STA	47	B3
CONDOR RD	SBD	92	B1
CONDOR RD	SBD	101	C1
CONDUIT	SUT	33	C3
CONE RD	INY	51	D5
CONE RD 3	LAS	20	B1
CONE GROVE RD	TEH	18	D5
CONEJO AV	FRCO	57	B5
CONEJO AV	FRCO	57	C5
CONEJO DR	SBD	90	E3
CONE PEAK RD	MON	64	E3
CONFER RD	SJCO	40	B5
CONGRESS AV	MONT	53	D3
CONGRESS AV	PAC	167	B3
CONGRESS ST	SD	213	A5
CONGRSS SPGS RD	SCL	45	E5
CONGRSS SPGS RD	SCL	N	E4
CONGRSS SPGS RD	SCL	P	A4
CONKLIN BLVD	KER	80	C4
CONKLIN RD	MOD	8	D1
CONKLIN CK RD	HUM	15	D4
CONKLING RD	IMP	112	A3
CONN CREEK RD	NAPA	29	D4
CONNECTION	LAS	21	E4
CONNELLY RD	IMP	112	C3
CONRAD GROVE LP	TEH	19	D3
CONSTANCE AV	STB	174	A2
CONSTANTIA RD	LAS	27	E1
CONSTELLATN AV	KER	89	C1
CONSTELLATION BLV	LA	183	A2
CONSTITUTION WY	A	157	E5
CONSUMNES MINE	ED	35	B5
CONTADAS	CC	45	D1
CONTOUR AV	RCO	99	D3
CONTRA COSTA AV	FRCO	56	D4
CONTRA COSTA BL	CC	L	E3
CONTRA COSTA BL	CC	M	A3
CONTRA LOMA BL	CC	M	C3
CONVENTN CTR DR	CLK	209	C5
CONVICT CPGD RD	MNO	50	E2
CONVICT CPGD RD	MNO	51	A2
CONVICT CK EXP	MNO	51	A2
CONVICT LAKE RD	MNO	50	E2
CONVICT LAKE RD	MNO	51	A2
CONVOY ST	SDCO	V	B2
CONVOY ST	SDCO	106	D5
CONWAY RANCH RD	MNO	43	B4
COOK LN	SOL	39	B3
COOK RD	AMA	40	C3
COOK ST	RCO	100	E4
COOK ST	SMA	173	A3
COOK CAMPBLL RD	SIS	4	E4
COOK PEAK LKOUT	KER	79	D1
COOKS CAMP RD	CAL	41	C2
COOKS SPRING RD	COL	32	B1
COOLEY RD	IMP	109	B5
COOLEY RD	SIS	4	B3
COOLGARDIE RD	SBD	81	D4
COOLIDGE AV	SCL	P	D5
COOMBS ST S	NAP	133	D4
COOMBSVILLE RD	NAPA	L	D1
COOMBSVILLE RD	NAPA	38	D3
COON HOLLOW CK	BUT	25	D1
COOPER RD	IMP	109	C5
COOPER RD	MON	54	C4
COOPER RD	NEV	34	D1
COOPR CIENG T T	RCO	100	B5
COOPERSTOWN RD	STA	48	B2
COPA DE ORA AV	MCO	55	D1
COPCO RD	SIS	4	B3
COPENHAGEN	HUM	15	D2
COPP AV	KER	89	B1
COPPER	FRCO	57	D2
COPPER AV	FRCO	56	A2
COPPER CYN RD	SHA	18	C1
COPPER CITY RD	SBD	81	D4
COPPER COVE DR	CAL	41	A5
COPPER HEAD RD	MON	65	C4
COPPER MTN RD	SBD	101	B1
COPPEROPOLIS	SJCO	40	C5
COPPEROPOLIS RD	TRI	17	B5
COPPER VISTA WY	SDCO	106	C3
COPP PIT RD	MOD	14	D2
COPUS RD	KER	78	B4
CORAL RD	MCO	47	E5
CORAL RD	MCO	55	E1
CORAM RD	SHA	18	B1
CORBETT CYN RD	SLO	76	B4
CORBIN AV	LA	178	A3
CORBIN RD	COL	32	D1
CORCORAN RD	KER	77	E1
CORD	SJCO	40	C3
CORDA RD	MON	54	E5
CORDELIA RD	SOL	L	E1
CORDELIA RD	SOL	M	A1
CORDELIA RD	SOL	38	E3
CORDELIA RD	SOL	135	A5
CORE RD	SAC	39	E2
CORKILL RD	RCO	100	D3
CORN CAMP RD	KER	77	E3
CORNELIA AV	FRCO	57	B4
CORNELIUS AV	SUT	33	D3
CORNING RD	TEH	24	C2
CORN SPRINGS RD	RCO	102	C5
CORONA AV	KIN	57	E5
CORONA EXPWY	RCO	98	D2
CORONA EXPWY	SBD	98	D2
CORONA FRWY	RCO	98	E3
CORONA RD	SON	L	A1
CORONA RD	SON	38	A3

STREET	CO.	PAGE	GRID
CORONA D MAR FY	ORCO	98	C4
CORONADO AV	SDCO	V	C5
CORONADO AV	SDCO	111	D2
CORRAL RD	SHA	19	D2
CORRAL CYN RD	SDCO	112	C1
CORRL DE TIERRA	MON	54	C5
CORRAL HOLLW RD	SJCO	46	E2
CORRALITOS RD	SCR	54	B2
CORREIA RD	SJCO	39	E4
CORRELL RD	SUT	33	B3
CORTE MADERA AV	CRTM	140	B1
CORTEZ AV	MCO	47	E3
CORTEZ AV	MCO	48	A3
CORTEZ WY	KER	79	E2
CORTINA SCH RD	COL	32	D3
CORTINA VNYD RD	COL	32	D3
CORTO RD	SBD	91	D4
CORWIN RD	SBD	91	C3
CORWIN RANCH RD	RCO	99	B5
CORYDON RD	RCO	99	B5
COSGROVE	CAL	41	B4
COSTA RD	YUB	26	A4
COSTA MESA FRWY	CM	197	E5
COSTA MESA FRWY	SA	198	B3
COSTA MESA FRWY	SA	196	E3
COSTA MESA FRWY	TUS	196	E5
COSTA MESA FRWY	ORA	194	E2
COSTA MESA FRWY	ORCO	98	B4
COSTA MESA FRWY	ORCO	T	C4
COSTNER RD	STA	47	C2
COTA ST	STB	174	C4
COTHARIN RD	VEN	96	D2
COTTA RD	SJCO	39	E4
COTTAGE AV	MAN	161	E1
COTTAGE AV	SJCO	161	E1
COTTLE RD	STA	47	D1
COTTON RD	MCO	55	E2
COTTON CREEK	MPA	48	D2
COTTON GIN RD	MCO	55	E2
COTTNTAIL CK RD	SLO	75	D2
COTTONWOOD AV	RCO	99	C3
COTTONWOOD AV	RCO	99	D4
COTTONWOOD DR	SBD	92	C1
COTTONWOOD RD	BUT	25	C4
COTTONWOOD RD	INY	60	B5
COTTONWOOD RD	KER	78	D3
COTTONWOOD RD	MCO	47	C5
COTTONWOOD RD	RCO	100	A2
COTTONWOOD RD	SBT	55	B4
COTTONWD CYN RD	MNO	43	C4
COTTONWD CYN RD	RCO	99	C4
COTTONWD CYN RD	SB	77	B5
COTTONWD CK RD	SIS	4	A2
COTTONWD SPG RD	RCO	101	D4
COUCH ST	VAL	134	C3
COULTERVILLE RD	MPA	49	C2
COUNCIL HILL RD	SIE	26	C4
COUNCILMAN RD	HUM	10	D5
COUNTRY	SJCO	40	C5
COUNTRY RD	SIS	4	C5
COUNTRY CLUB BL	SJCO	40	A5
COUNTRY CLUB BL	SJCO	160	A3
COUNTRY CLUB DR	RIV	205	E5
COUNTRY CLUB DR	RCO	100	A4
COUNTRY CLUB RD	AVLN	97	A5
COUNTRY CLUB RD	HUM	10	D4
COUNTRY CLUB RD	YUB	33	D3
COUNTRYMAN DR	PLU	26	B2
COUNTY RD	INY	51	D5
COUNTY RD	MOD	8	A1
COUNTY RD	MOD	14	E1
COUNTY RD B	GLE	24	C4
COUNTY RD BB	GLE	24	C4
COUNTY RD C	GLE	24	C3
COUNTY RD D	GLE	24	D4
COUNTY RD F	GLE	24	D3
COUNTY RD H	GLE	24	D3
COUNTY RD I	GLE	24	D3
COUNTY RD J	GLE	24	D3
COUNTY RD M	GLE	24	D4
COUNTY RD MM	GLE	24	D3
COUNTY RD N	GLE	24	D4
COUNTY RD NN	GLE	24	D3
COUNTY RD P	GLE	24	D4
COUNTY RD PP	GLE	24	D4
COUNTY RD QQ	GLE	24	D3
COUNTY RD R	GLE	24	E4
COUNTY RD RR	GLE	24	E3
COUNTY RD S	GLE	24	E4
COUNTY RD SS	GLE	24	E4
COUNTY RD T	GLE	24	E4
COUNTY RD TT	GLE	24	E4
COUNTY RD U	GLE	24	E3
COUNTY RD V	GLE	24	E4
COUNTY RD VV	GLE	24	E3
COUNTY RD W	GLE	24	E4
COUNTY RD WW	GLE	24	E4
COUNTY RD XX	GLE	24	E3
COUNTY RD Y	GLE	25	A5
COUNTY RD YY	GLE	25	A5
COUNTY RD Z	GLE	25	A4
COUNTY RD ZZ	GLE	25	A4
COUNTY RD 5	YOL	33	A4
COUNTY RD 6	YOL	33	A4
COUNTY RD 7	YOL	33	A4
COUNTY RD 8	YOL	32	E4
COUNTY RD 9	GLE	24	D3
COUNTY RD 10	YOL	32	E4
COUNTY RD 11	GLE	24	E3
COUNTY RD 11	YOL	32	E4
COUNTY RD 11	YOL	33	B4
COUNTY RD 11A	YOL	33	B4
COUNTY RD 11B	YOL	33	B4

STREET	CO.	PAGE	GRID
COUNTY RD 12	YOL	33	B4
COUNTY RD 12A	YOL	33	A4
COUNTY RD 13	YOL	32	E4
COUNTY RD 14	YOL	33	A4
COUNTY RD 14A	YOL	33	B4
COUNTY RD 15	GLE	24	E3
COUNTY RD 15	YOL	33	B4
COUNTY RD 15B	YOL	32	E4
COUNTY RD 16	GLE	24	E3
COUNTY RD 16	YOL	33	A5
COUNTY RD 16A	YOL	32	E5
COUNTY RD 17	YOL	33	A5
COUNTY RD 18	GLE	24	E3
COUNTY RD 18	YOL	33	B5
COUNTY RD 18B	YOL	33	C5
COUNTY RD 18C	YOL	33	C5
COUNTY RD 19	GLE	24	E3
COUNTY RD 19	YOL	33	B5
COUNTY RD 19A	YOL	33	A5
COUNTY RD 20	GLE	24	E3
COUNTY RD 20	YOL	33	C5
COUNTY RD 20A	YOL	32	E5
COUNTY RD 21	GLE	24	E3
COUNTY RD 21A	YOL	32	E5
COUNTY RD 23	GLE	25	A3
COUNTY RD 23	YOL	33	A5
COUNTY RD 24	GLE	24	D3
COUNTY RD 24	YOL	33	B5
COUNTY RD 25	GLE	24	D3
COUNTY RD 25	YOL	33	A5
COUNTY RD 25A	YOL	33	A5
COUNTY RD 26	GLE	24	C3
COUNTY RD 26	YOL	33	A5
COUNTY RD 26A	YOL	33	C5
COUNTY RD 27	GLE	24	D3
COUNTY RD 27	YOL	33	B5
COUNTY RD 28	GLE	24	D3
COUNTY RD 28	YOL	39	A1
COUNTY RD 28H	YOL	39	C1
COUNTY RD 29	GLE	24	E3
COUNTY RD 29	GLE	25	A3
COUNTY RD 29	YOL	39	A1
COUNTY RD 29A	YOL	39	A1
COUNTY RD 30	GLE	24	D3
COUNTY RD 30	GLE	25	A3
COUNTY RD 30	YOL	39	B1
CO RD 30 1/2	GLE	25	A3
COUNTY RD 31	GLE	24	D4
COUNTY RD 31	GLE	25	A3
COUNTY RD 31	YOL	39	A1
COUNTY RD 32	GLE	24	E4
COUNTY RD 32	GLE	25	A4
COUNTY RD 32	YOL	39	B1
CO RD 32 1/2	GLE	24	E4
COUNTY RD 33	GLE	24	D4
COUNTY RD 33	GLE	25	A4
COUNTY RD 34	GLE	24	E4
COUNTY RD 34	GLE	25	A4
COUNTY RD 35	GLE	24	D4
COUNTY RD 36	GLE	24	E4
COUNTY RD 36	YOL	39	C2
COUNTY RD 37	GLE	24	E4
COUNTY RD 38	GLE	24	E4
COUNTY RD 38	YOL	39	C2
COUNTY RD 38A	YOL	39	C2
COUNTY RD 39	GLE	24	D4
COUNTY RD 40	GLE	24	E4
COUNTY RD 41	GLE	24	E4
COUNTY RD 43	GLE	24	E4
COUNTY RD 43	YOL	32	D4
COUNTY RD 44	GLE	24	E4
COUNTY RD 44	YOL	32	D4
COUNTY RD 45	GLE	24	D4
COUNTY RD 45	YOL	32	D4
COUNTY RD 46	GLE	24	E4
COUNTY RD 47	YOL	32	D4
COUNTY RD 48	GLE	24	D4
COUNTY RD 49	GLE	24	D4
COUNTY RD 50	GLE	24	E4
COUNTY RD 50	GLE	25	A4
COUNTY RD 53	GLE	24	E4
COUNTY RD 57	GLE	24	E4
COUNTY RD 58	GLE	24	C4
COUNTY RD 59	GLE	24	C5
COUNTY RD 59	YOL	32	D4
COUNTY RD 60	GLE	24	D5
COUNTY RD 61	GLE	24	E5
COUNTY RD 61	YOL	32	D4
COUNTY RD 62	GLE	24	C5
COUNTY RD 63	GLE	25	A5
COUNTY RD 63	YOL	32	D4
COUNTY RD 64	GLE	24	E5
COUNTY RD 65A	GLE	24	E5
COUNTY RD 65B	GLE	24	E5
COUNTY RD 65C	GLE	24	C5
COUNTY RD 66A	GLE	24	D5
COUNTY RD 66B	GLE	24	E5
COUNTY RD 67	GLE	25	A5
COUNTY RD 68	GLE	24	D5
COUNTY RD 69	GLE	24	C5
COUNTY RD 69	GLE	25	A5
COUNTY RD 70	GLE	25	A5
COUNTY RD 70	YOL	32	D4
COUNTY RD 71	GLE	24	D5
COUNTY RD 71	YOL	32	D4
COUNTY RD 75A	YOL	32	D4
COUNTY RD 76	YOL	32	D5
COUNTY RD 78	YOL	32	D5
COUNTY RD 78A	YOL	32	D5
COUNTY RD 79	YOL	32	D5
COUNTY RD 79A	YOL	32	E5
COUNTY RD 79B	YOL	32	E5
COUNTY RD 80	YOL	32	E5

STREET	CO.	PAGE	GRID
COUNTY RD 81	YOL	32	E5
COUNTY RD 82	YOL	32	E5
COUNTY RD 82B	YOL	32	E5
COUNTY RD 84A	YOL	32	E4
COUNTY RD 84B	YOL	32	E4
COUNTY RD 85	YOL	32	E5
COUNTY RD 85B	YOL	32	E5
COUNTY RD 86	YOL	32	E4
COUNTY RD 86A	YOL	33	A5
COUNTY RD 87	YOL	33	A5
COUNTY RD 87B	YOL	33	A5
COUNTY RD 88	YOL	33	A4
COUNTY RD 88A	YOL	33	A5
COUNTY RD 88B	YOL	33	A5
COUNTY RD 89	YOL	33	A4
COUNTY RD 90	YOL	39	A1
COUNTY RD 90A	YOL	33	A5
COUNTY RD 91	YOL	33	A5
COUNTY RD 91A	YOL	39	A1
COUNTY RD 91B	YOL	33	A4
COUNTY RD 92	YOL	33	B4
COUNTY RD 92B	YOL	33	A4
COUNTY RD 92C	YOL	33	B5
COUNTY RD 92F	YOL	39	B1
COUNTY RD 93	YOL	33	B5
COUNTY RD 93A	YOL	33	B4
COUNTY RD 93B	YOL	33	B4
COUNTY RD 94	YOL	33	B4
COUNTY RD 94A	YOL	33	B5
COUNTY RD 94B	YOL	33	B5
COUNTY RD 95	YOL	33	B4
COUNTY RD 95A	YOL	39	B1
COUNTY RD 96	YOL	33	B5
COUNTY RD 96B	YOL	33	B5
COUNTY RD 97	YOL	33	B5
COUNTY RD 97D	YOL	39	B1
COUNTY RD 98	YOL	33	B4
COUNTY RD 99	YOL	33	B5
COUNTY RD 99E	YOL	33	C5
COUNTY RD 100	YOL	33	C5
COUNTY RD 101	YOL	33	C5
COUNTY RD 101A	DVS	136	C1
COUNTY RD 101A	YOL	39	C1
COUNTY RD 102	YOL	33	C5
COUNTY RD 102B	YOL	33	C5
COUNTY RD 103	YOL	33	C5
COUNTY RD 104	YOL	39	C1
COUNTY RD 105	YOL	39	C2
COUNTY RD 106	YOL	39	C2
COUNTY RD 107	YOL	33	C4
COUNTY RD 107A	YOL	33	D4
COUNTY RD 108	YOL	33	B4
COUNTY RD 116	YOL	33	C4
COUNTY RD 119	YOL	33	D5
COUNTY RD 122	YOL	33	D5
COUNTY RD 124	YOL	33	D5
COUNTY RD 126	YOL	39	D1
COUNTY RD 128A	YOL	39	D1
COUNTY RD 152	YOL	39	C2
COUNTY RD 155	YOL	39	C2
COUNTY RD 200	GLE	24	D3
COUNTY RD 303	GLE	24	B4
COUNTY RD 304	GLE	24	B4
COUNTY RD 307	GLE	24	A3
COUNTY RD 310	GLE	23	E4
COUNTY RD 314	GLE	24	B3
COUNTY RD 315	GLE	24	A3
COUNTY RD 400	GLE	24	B5
COUNTY HOSP RD	PLU	26	C1
COUNTY LINE RD	KER	68	B5
CO LINE RD E	TRI	17	E2
CO LINE CK RD	TRI	16	D3
COURCHEVEL RD	PLA	35	D2
COURSE RD	KER	78	B4
COURT ST	RED	122	B2
COURTLAND RD N	YOL	39	D2
COURTLANDT CT	KER	79	C4
COUTOLENC RD	BUT	25	D2
COVE AV	FRCO	58	B4
COVE RD	SBD	91	E4
COVE RD	SHA	13	A5
COVELL BLVD	DVS	136	B2
COVELO RD	MEN	23	A3
COVELO RD	MEN	22	E4
COVELO RFUSE RD	MEN	23	A2
COVERT RD	STA	47	C2
COVINA BLVD	LACO	R	E3
COWBOY CNTRY TR	RCO	107	B1
COWBOY JOE RD	LAS	21	D5
COW CAMP RD	BUT	25	E2
COW CAMP RD	MNO	43	C3
COW CREEK RD S	SHA	18	E2
COW CREEK RD S	SHA	19	A2
COWEL RD	CC	38	E5
COWELL BLVD	DVS	136	E3
COW GULCH RD	SHA	17	D3
COW HAVEN CY RD	KER	80	B1
COW MTN ACCESS	MEN	31	B2
COX AV	SCL	P	A4
COX AV	SCL	45	E5
COX LN	BUT	25	D5
COX RD	IMP	109	A3
COX RD	SJCO	40	C4
COX RD	SHA	18	B3
COX RD	STA	47	B3
COX ST	RCO	99	C4
COXCOMB TR	SBD	102	C1
COXEY	SBD	91	D4
COX FERRY RD	MCO	48	B3
COYOTE RD	MCO	56	B1
COYOTE RD	SBD	101	A2
COYOTE #1 RD	IMP	111	C4
COYOTE #2 RD	IMP	111	C4

STREET	CO.	PAGE	GRID
COYOTE CYN RD	INY	71	D4
COYOTE CYN RD	RCO	107	C1
COYOTE GAP RD	BUT	25	E2
COYOTE LAKE RD	SBD	82	B5
COYOTE RES RD	SCL	P	E5
COYOTE SPGS RD	MNO	43	C4
COYOTE VLY RD	INY	51	C4
COYOTE VLY RD	SBD	93	A5
COYOTE VLY RES	LAS	14	C5
COZZI AV	MCO	56	A1
CRABTREE RD	LAS	8	D4
CRABTREE RD	STA	48	B2
CRAFTON AV	SBD	99	D2
CRAIG	SJCO	47	C1
CRAIG AV	SON	132	B3
CRAIG AV	TEH	18	E5
CRAIG RD	SUT	33	B1
CRAMER	PLA	34	B3
CRAM GULCH RD	SIS	4	B5
CRANE AV	MCO	47	D4
CRANE RD	STA	47	D2
CRANE CANYON RD	SON	38	A2
CRANE FLAT	MPA	63	B5
CRANE FLAT RD	MPA	49	C2
CRANE VALLEY RD	MAD	49	E5
CRANMORE RD	SUT	33	B3
CRANMORE RD	SUT	33	C4
CRANNELL RD	HUM	9	E4
CRANNELL RD	HUM	10	A4
CRATER RD	SBD	93	E3
CRATER HILL RD	PLA	34	B3
CRAWFORD AV	FRCO	58	A4
CRAWFORD RD	CLO	32	E2
CRAWFORD RD	MEN	23	A3
CRAWFORD RD	STA	47	D2
CRAY CROFT RDG	SIE	26	D4
CRAZY HORSE CYN	MON	54	D3
CREED RD	SOL	39	B3
CREEK RD	MCO	55	D2
CREEK RD	RED	122	A4
CREEK RD	VEN	88	B4
CREEKSIDE CT	KER	79	C4
CREEKSIDE LN	STA	47	E2
CREIGHTON DR	SHA	13	D3
CRENSHAW BLVD	LA	184	D3
CRENSHAW BLVD	LACO	97	D3
CRENSHAW BLVD	LACO	Q	D5
CRENSHAW BLVD	LACO	S	B2
CREOLE MINE RD	SBD	92	E4
CRESCENT AV	AVLN	97	B4
CRESCENT AV	LA	191	A4
C RESERVOIR RD	MOD	6	D4
CRESSEY WY	MCO	48	A4
CRESSMAN RD	FRCO	58	B1
CREST DR	RCO	99	B2
CREST RD	LACO	S	B2
CRESTLINE RD	SDCO	107	A2
CRESTON RD	SLO	76	B1
CRESTON EUREKA	SLO	76	B2
CRESTN ODONOVAN	SLO	76	C2
CRESTVIEW DR	MNO	51	D2
CRESTVIEW ST	KER	80	C1
CREWS RD	SCL	54	D2
CRIDGE ST	RIV	205	B3
CRIPE RD	FRCO	58	A1
CRIPPEN AV	SBD	91	A3
CRIPPLE CK RD	SLO	76	B2
CRISPIN RD	MEN	30	C3
CRISS RD	SIS	4	E3
CRISS RD	SIS	5	A3
CRISTIANITOS RD	SDCO	105	E1
CRISWELL AV	MCO	55	E1
CROCKER AV	P	158	D2
CROCKER RD	SJCO	46	E1
CROCKER SPGS RD	KER	77	D4
CRONESE LAKE RD	SBD	82	E4
CRONESE LAKE RD	SBD	83	A4
CROOKED MDW RD	MNO	50	E1
CROSBY RD	HUM	15	D2
CROSBY ST	SD	216	A4
CROSBY HAROLD	PLA	34	B3
CROSS RD	COL	32	E3
CROSS RD	MON	65	C4
CROSS CYNS RD	SLO	66	B5
CROSS CTRVILLE	MEN	31	B1
CROSS CNTRY RD	MON	66	B4
CROUCH AV	BUT	25	A3
CROW RD	STA	47	E2
CROW CANYON RD	ALA	M	A5
CROW CANYON RD	ALA	45	E2
CROWDER	PLA	33	E5
CROWDER FLAT RD	MOD	6	E5
CROWLEY RD	SUT	33	C3
CROWLEY LAKE DR	MNO	51	A3
CROWLEY LAKE PL	MNO	51	A2
CROWLY LK DM RD	MNO	51	B2
CROWN RD	MCO	48	C4
CROWN & PICKLE	SBD	92	D5
CROWN POINT DR	SD	212	C3
CROWN POINT RD	BUT	25	C2
CROWN VLY PKWY	ORCO	98	D5
CROWN VALLEY RD	LACO	89	E4
CROWS LANDNG RD	MDO	162	C5
CROWS LANDNG RD	STA	47	C4
CROWS LANDNG RD	STA	162	C5
CROY RD	SCL	P	C5
CROY RD	SCL	54	C1
CRUCERO RD	SBD	83	A5
CRUCERO RD	SBD	93	B1
CRUICKSHANK RD	IMP	112	B3
CRUMP LN	FRCO	66	B3
CRUZON GRADE RD	NEV	26	C5
CRYSTAL AV	MOH	96	A3

STREET	CO.	PAGE	GRID
CRYSTAL CK RD	SHA	18	A2
CRYSTAL SPGS DR	LA	182	C1
CRYSTAL SPGS DR	LACO	Q	E3
CRYSTAL SPGS RD	KLAM	5	C1
CRYSTAL SPGS RD	SBR	144	A4
CRYSTAL SPGS RD	SMCO	N	C2
CRYSTAL SPGS RD	SMCO	45	C3
CUDA DR	KER	78	E4
CUDDEBACK RD	SBD	80	E3
CUDDEBACK RD	SBD	81	A3
CUDDY VALLEY RD	KER	88	C1
CUDDY VALLEY RD	VEN	88	C2
CUFF RD	IMP	109	B2
CUIN RD	IMP	108	E5
CULL CANYON RD	ALA	M	A5
CULL CANYON RD	ALA	45	E1
CULLEN AV	SCL	P	E5
CULVER BLVD	CUL	188	A2
CULVER BLVD	LACO	97	C2
CULVER BLVD	LA	187	D5
CULVER DR	ORCO	98	C4
CULVER DR	ORCO	T	E4
CUMMINGS RD	HUM	15	E1
CUMMINGS RD	VEN	88	B5
CUMMINGS SKYWAY	CC	38	D4
CUMMINGS VLY RD	KER	79	B4
CUNEO RD	MPA	48	E1
CUNNINGHAM LN	MNO	42	E1
CUNNINGHAM RD	CAL	41	C3
CUNNINGHAM RD	MCO	48	D5
CUNNINGHAM RD	MEN	31	B2
CURRAN RD	AMA	40	D3
CURREY RD	SOL	39	B1
CURRIE RD	SOL	39	B4
CURRIER RD	BUT	25	C4
CURTIS ST W	SAL	171	C2
CURTNER AV	SCL	P	B4
CURTNER AV	SCL	46	B5
CURTOLA PKWY	VAL	134	C5
CUSTER AV	FRCO	56	B2
CUSTER AV	SBD	91	E4
CUTCA TRUCK TR	RCO	106	E1
CUTLER AV	GLE	24	E3
CUT OFF RD	LAS	21	C3
CUTOFF RD	MEN	23	C5
CUTTING	CC	38	C5
CUTTING AV	GLE	24	E3
CUTTING BLVD	CC	L	C3
CUTTING BLVD	R	155	A4
CUTTNGS WHRF RD	NAPA	L	C1
CUTTNGS WHRF RD	NAPA	38	C3
CUYAMA ST	SB	87	D1
CYA RD	MPA	49	A3
CYPRESS AV	LACO	R	E3
CYPRESS AV	RED	122	C2
CYPRESS AV	SHA	18	C2
CYPRESS AV	SUT	33	D3
CYPRESS FRWY	O	157	D2
CYPRESS RD	CC	M	D3
CYPRESS RD	CC	39	C5
CYPRESS RD	MCO	56	A1
CYPRESS RD	SBD	80	E1
CYPRESS ST	C	124	C4
CYPRESS ST	LACO	98	B2
CYPRESS MTN DR	SLO	75	D1
CYPRUS AV	U	123	B2
CYRMIC RD	KER	77	D3
CYRUS CANYON RD	KER	79	D1
D			
D AV	COR	215	C5
D ST	MAR	L	B3
D ST	MDO	162	C4
D ST	ONT	203	D4
D ST	ONT	204	B4
D ST	SR	139	C4
D ST	SON	L	A1
D ST	SON	38	A3
DAGGETT YERMO	SBD	92	A1
DAGNINO RD	ALA	M	C5
DAGNINO RD	ALA	46	C2
DAHLIN RD	SJCO	47	C1
DAHLSTROM RD	COL	32	E3
DAILEY RD	KER	79	C2
DAINTY AV	CC	M	D3
DAINTY AV	CC	39	C5
DAIRY AV	LACO	S	D1
DAIRY LN	MCO	56	A1
DAIRY RD	AUB	126	C1
DAIRY RD	BUT	25	A3
DAIRY RD	KER	78	A3
DAIRY RD	STA	47	B2
DAIRY RD	YUB	33	B2
DAIRY MART RD	SDCO	V	C5
DAIRY MART RD	SDCO	111	D2
DAKIN RD	LAS	21	C4
DAKOTA AV	FRCO	57	C3
DAKOTA AV	FRCO	56	E3
DAKOTA AV	STA	47	C2
DALBY	PLA	33	E3
DALE LN	SHA	18	B3
DALE RD	KER	79	B4
DALE RD	STA	47	C2
DALE RD	TEH	24	E2
DALE TR	SBD	101	E1
DALE VISTA RD	SBD	101	E1
DALLY RD	SOL	39	B3
DALTON AV	ALA	M	D5
DALTON AV	ALA	46	C2
DALY ST	LA	186	D1
DAMIEN AV	LACO	98	C1
DANA DR	SHA	18	C2
DANA FOOTHILL RD	SLO	76	C5
DANA PT HARBOR RD	DPT	202	A4
DANBY RD	SBD	101	D1
DANENBERG RD	IMP	112	B3
DANIELS AV	VAL	134	A3
DANLEY LATERAL	COL	32	C1
DANLEY RD	COL	32	D1
DAN MCNAMARA RD	MCO	48	A5
DANTES VIEW	INY	72	B1
DANVILLE BLVD	CC	M	A4
DANVILLE BLVD	CC	45	E1
DARBY RD	BUT	25	E5
DARBY RD	CAL	41	C3
DARGATE RD	KER	77	E2
DARK CANYON RD	BUT	25	D3
DARLING RD	LACO	89	D4
DARLING RDG RD	ED	34	E4
DARMS LN	NAPA	38	C2
DARRAH RD	MPA	49	B3
DATE ST	SB	86	C1
DATE PALM DR	RCO	100	D4
DATONI RD	YUB	33	D2
DAUBENBERGER RD	STA	47	E3
DAULTON RD	MAD	56	B1
DAULTON RD	MAD	57	B1
DA VALL DR	RCO	100	D3
DAVENPORT RD	LACO	89	D4
DAVID AV	MONT	53	C3
DAVID AV	MONT	167	B3
DAVID AV	PAC	167	B3
DAVID RD	KER	78	E5
DAVIDSON	FRCO	56	B2
DAVIDSON RD	HUM	9	E2
DAVIDSON RD	HUM	10	A2
DAVIS AV	FRCO	57	A5
DAVIS AV	FRCO	57	C5
DAVIS AV	KER	78	B1
DAVIS RD	BUT	25	B5
DAVIS RD	IMP	109	A2
DAVIS RD	KER	76	E1
DAVIS RD	MON	54	C4
DAVIS RD	MON	171	A4
DAVIS RD	RCO	99	D3
DAVIS RD	SJCO	40	A4
DAVIS RD	SIS	4	C4
DAVIS RD	SIS	5	C4
DAVIS RD	STA	47	C4
DAVIS RD	STA	48	B3
DAVIS RD	SUT	33	B2
DAVIS ST	ALA	L	D5
DAVIS ST	ALA	45	D2
DAVIS ST	LAK	32	A3
DAVIS CK CEM RD	MOD	7	C4
DVS CK TRNS STA	MOD	7	C4
DAWN RD	KER	89	E1
DAWN RD	KER	90	A1
DAWSON RD	RCO	99	C3
DAWSON RANCH RD	MNO	51	D2
DAY AV	SHA	19	E1
DAY RD	MOD	13	E3
DAY RD	SCL	54	C1
DAY RD	SHA	13	E3
DAY ST	RCO	99	C3
DAY RD	SCL	P	E5
DAYBREAK CT	TUO	163	D5
DAYLIGHT PASS	INY	61	E4
DAYLIGHT PS CTO	INY	61	E3
DAYTON RD	BUT	25	B3
DAYTON WEST RD	BUT	25	A3
DEAD HRSE CY RD	SIS	13	B3
DEAD INDIAN RD	JKSN	4	A1
DEADMAN CK RD	MNO	50	D2
DEAD MANS GULCH	MON	65	E4
DEADWOOD RD	BUT	25	D3
DEADWOOD RD	PLA	35	A2
DEADWOOD RD	TRI	17	E1
DEADWOOD LO RD	SIS	3	D4
DEALWOOD RD	IMP	109	B5
DEAN CREEK RD	HUM	16	C5
DE ANGELIS RD	MCO	47	D4
DE ANZA BLVD	CPTO	149	E4
DE ANZA DR	RCO	99	E3
DE ANZA TR	SDCO	107	D1
DEARBORN RD	IMP	111	E3
DEARDORFF RD	CAL	41	B2
DEARWOOD DR	MEN	31	B2
DEATH VALLEY RD	INY	52	B5
DEAVER AV	KER	70	A5
DECPTION CYN RD	RCO	100	E3
DECKER AV	SBD	92	E5
DECKER RD	SUT	33	B2
DECORD DR	LACO	89	A4
DECOTO RD	ALA	P	A1
DECOTO RD	ALA	45	E3
DEE KNOCH RD	SHA	13	E4
DEEP CREEK RD	MOD	8	D1
DEEP CREEK RD	SBD	91	C5
DEEP SPRINGS RD	SBD	84	A3
DEEP SPGS RANCH	INY	52	B4
DEEP WELL RD	MCO	55	E1
DEEP WY	RCO	100	B5
DEER CREEK AV	TUL	68	B5
DEER CREEK RD	SBD	91	C4
DEER CREEK RD	VEN	96	D2
DEER FLAT RD	SHA	19	C2
DEERHORN VLY RD	SDCO	112	B1
DEER LICK KNOB	TRI	17	D2
DEER LICK SPGS	TRI	17	D3
DEER MTN RD	SIS	4	D5
DEER PARK RD	BUT	26	A3
DEER PARK RD	NAPA	29	B2
DEER PARK RD	NAPA	38	B1
DEER SPRING RD	MNO	51	B2
DEER VALLEY	ED	34	C5
DEER VALLEY RD	CC	M	C3
DEER VALLEY RD	CC	39	B5
DEETZ RD	SIS	12	C2
DEFENDER GRADE	AMA	41	B2
DEFRAIN BLVD	RCO	103	D5
DE HARVEY ST	KER	78	D4
DEHESA RD	SDCO	107	A5
DE LA CRUZ BL	SCL	P	B3
DE LA CRUZ BL	SCLR	151	C1
DE LA GUERRA ST	STB	174	D3
DEL AMO BLVD	LACO	98	A3
DEL AMO BLVD	LACO	S	D2
DE LA VINA ST	STB	174	A2
DELAWARE AV	SC	169	A5
DELAWARE RD	STA	47	E2
DELAWARE ST	SM	145	A2
DELCERRO BLVD	SDCO	V	C3
DELCERRO BLVD	SDCO	111	D1
DEL DIOS HWY	SDCO	106	D4
DELEVAN RD	COL	32	D1
DELFATTI LN	KLAM	5	B1
DELFERN RD	KER	77	D2
DELFIND RD	KER	77	D2
DELHI RD	SOL	39	C2
DELIMA RD	SJCO	47	A1
DEL MAR AV	LACO	R	C4
DEL MAR AV	CM	199	D1
DEL MAR BLVD	PAS	190	C4
DEL MAR HTS RD	SDCO	106	C4
DEL MAR HTS RD	SDCO	V	A1
DEL MONTE AV	SUT	33	C4
DEL MONTE BLVD	MONT	167	B1
DEL NORTE AV	FRCO	57	A4
DEL NORTE DR	TEH	18	C4
DEL OBISPO ST	ORCO	98	D5
DEL OBISPO ST	DPT	202	B4
DEL OBISPO ST	SJC	202	C2
DEL ORO RD	SBD	91	C4
DEL ORTO RD	CAL	40	E3
DEL ORTO RD	CAL	41	A3
DEL PASO RD	SAC	33	D5
DEL PRADO AV	DPT	202	A4
DELPHOS RD	CLO	32	D2
DEL PUERTO AV	STA	47	C3
DEL PUERTO CYN	STA	46	E4
DEL PUERTO CYN	STA	47	A3
DEL REY AV	FRCO	57	E3
DEL REY AV	FRCO	57	E5
DEL ROSA AV	SBD	99	C1
DELTA AV	SJCO	46	E1
DELTA AV	SJCO	47	A1
DELTA RD	CC	M	D3
DELTA RD	CC	39	C5
DELTA RD	MCO	55	E1
DE LUZ RD	SDCO	106	B1
DEMAREE RD	TUL	68	B1
DEMAREST MNE RD	CAL	41	A4
DEMPSEY RD	SCL	P	B2
DENISE AV	KER	80	A5
DENNETT ST	PAC	167	B2
DENNISON RD	KER	79	D4
DENNY RD	TRI	10	E5
DENNY RD	TRI	11	A4
DENTON RD	MCO	56	A1
DENTON RD	STA	48	A2
DENTN & LEAK RD	MCO	56	B1
DENVER AV	FRCO	56	E4
DENVER AV	KIN	57	E5
DENVERTON RD	SOL	39	B3
DE PORTOLA RD	RCO	99	E5
DEPOT AV	SB	86	C1
DEPOT RD	ALA	146	B5
DEPOT RD	H	146	B5
DEPOT ST	SMA	173	B3
DERRICK BLVD	FRCO	66	C2
DERRICK RD	BUT	25	D4
DERRICK RD	IMP	111	E3
DERRICK RD	LAS	14	B3
DERRICK FT RD N	TRI	11	E3
DERRICK FT RD N	TRI	12	A3
DERRICK FT RD S	TRI	12	A3
DERSCH RD	SHA	18	C3
DESCANSO AV	AVLN	97	B5
DESCHUTES RD	SHA	18	D2
DESERT RD	CLK	85	D5
DESERT RD	IMP	112	D3
DESERT CTR RICE	RCO	102	C4
DESERT INN RD	CLK	209	C5
DESERT INN RD	CLK	210	C1
DSRT SHORES DR	IMP	108	C1
DESERT VIEW AV	SBD	91	D4
DESERT WILLW TR	SBD	100	D2
DESEVADO RD	SIS	4	C3
DE SOTO AV	LA	177	D3
DESSIE DR	LAK	31	C3
DETLOW RD	BUT	25	D3
DETOUR RD	GLE	24	D3
DETWEILER RD	MPA	48	D2
DEVILS CORRL RD	LAS	20	D3
DEVILS DEN RD	KIN	67	B5
DEVOE RD	SUT	33	C4
DEVONSHIRE BLVD	LACO	97	C1
DEVORE RD	SBD	99	B1
DEVOSE DR	LAS	8	A4
DE VRIES	SJCO	40	A4
DEWITT RD	STA	47	D2
DE WOLF AV	FRCO	57	D2
DE WOLF AV	FRCO	57	D5
DE WOLF AV	SB	86	B3
DE 1 FIRST ST	COL	32	D1
DIABLO RD	CC	M	B4
DIABLO RD	CC	46	A1
DIABLO MINE RD	INY	51	C3
DIABLO MINE RD	MNO	51	C3
DIABLO OASIS DR	RCO	100	C3
DIAGONAL 7	MAD	56	C3
DIAGONAL 11	MAD	56	D1
DIAGONAL 232	TUL	68	D4
DIAGONAL 252	TUL	68	D3
DIAGONAL 254	TUL	68	D3
DIAMOND RD	ED	138	C5
DIAMOND BAR BL	LACO	98	C2
DIAMOND BAR BL	LACO	U	D3
DIAMOND MTN RD	PLU	20	E4
DIAMOND VLY RD	ALP	36	C4
DIAZ LN	INY	51	D4
DIAZ ST	KER	80	A4
DICK COOK	PLA	34	B4
DICKERMAN RD	IMP	109	B4
DICKINSON AV	FRCO	57	B4
DICKINSON AV	FRCO	67	B1
DICKNSN FRRY RD	MCO	48	B5
DICKSON HILL RD	FRFD	135	E1
DIDO AV	SBD	92	A3
DIEHL RD	IMP	111	E3
DIEHL RD	STA	47	C4
DIENSTAG RD	STA	48	A2
DIERSSEN RD	SAC	39	E3
DIETRICH	SJCO	40	C5
DIETRICH RD	IMP	109	B4
DIGGER RAVNE RD	PLU	26	C1
DI GIORGIO RD	KER	78	D3
DI GIORGIO RD	KER	79	A3
DIGIORGIO RD	SDCO	107	E2
DILLARD RD	SAC	40	A3
DILLION RD	SIS	10	D1
DILLON RD	HUM	15	D2
DILLON RD	RCO	100	E3
DILLON RD	RCO	100	C3
DILLON BEACH RD	MAR	37	D3
DINKELSPIEL RD	SOL	39	B4
DINKEY CREEK RD	FRCO	58	B1
DINKY AV	KER	89	B1
DINUBA AV	FRCO	56	E4
DINUBA AV	FRCO	57	C4
DINUBA AV	FRCO	58	A4
DIPS RD	TRI	17	B3
DIRKS RD	COL	24	D5
DISCH RD	SJCO	40	C4
DISTELRATH DR	DN	1	D3
DISTRICT CTR DR	BUT	25	D5
DITCH RD	KER	78	A5
DITCH RD	SIE	26	C4
DITCH CREEK RD	SIS	4	A3
DIVISADERO ST	FRE	165	B3
DIVISADERO ST	SF	142	A2
DIVISION ST	LACO	89	E2
DIVISION ST	SDCO	V	C4
DIVISION ST	SDCO	111	D1
DIVISION ST	SLO	76	B5
DIVISION CK RD	INY	59	E2
DIXIE RD	BUT	25	D2
DIXIE RD	SBD	91	D1
DIXIE CYN RND VLY	PLU	20	C5
DIXIE VALLEY RD	LAS	14	D4
DIXON AV E	SOL	39	B2
DIXON AV W	SOL	39	B2
DIXON LN	INY	51	D4
DIXON HILL RD	YUB	26	A5
DIXON MINE RD	ALP	42	C1
DOBBINS ST	KER	70	A5
DOBIE LN	MEN	23	B3
DOBIE MEADOWS	MNO	43	D4
DOBIE MEADOWS	MNO	43	E4
DOBIE MEADOWS	MNO	44	A4
DOBSON RD	SBD	81	E4
DODDS	SJCO	47	C1
DODDS RD	STA	47	C4
DODGE RD	COL	24	E5
DODGE RDG LP RD	TUO	42	A3
DOE MILL RD	BUT	25	C2
DOERKSEN RD	STA	47	E3
DOG BAR RD	NEV	34	C2
DOG CREEK RD	SHA	12	B4
DOGGIE TR	SBD	101	A2
DOGTOWN RD	CAL	41	B2
DOGTOWN RD	MPA	48	E2
DOGTOWN RD	MPA	49	A2
DOG VALLEY RD	SIE	27	E5
DOGWOOD RD	IMP	217	E1
DOGWOOD RD	ALP	36	A5
DOGWOOD RD	IMP	109	A5
DOGWOOD RD	IMP	112	A4
DOHENY DR	BH	183	C2
DOHENY DR	LACO	Q	D4
DOHENY PARK RD	DPT	202	C4
DOLAN RD	MON	54	B3
DOLAN HARDNG RD	YUB	34	A1
DOLLARHIDE RD	NAPA	38	C1
DOLORES ST	SF	142	B5
DOLPHIN AV	KER	80	C1
DOLPHIN DR	IMP	108	C2
DOME AV	TUL	68	D3
DOME ST	SB	86	D1
DOMINION RD	SB	86	C1
DOMINO CT	KER	79	B4
DON RD	SBD	101	D1
DONAHUE RD	SUT	33	C4
DONKIN RD	STA	47	B3
DONLON,JAMES BL	CC	M	C3
DONNER PASS RD	NEV	27	B5
DONNER PASS RD	VAL	134	B1
DONOVAN RD	SMA	173	B2
DON PEDRO RD	STA	47	C3
DONS RD	MOD	8	B2
DOOLITTLE DR	A	159	B2
DOOLITTLE DR	ALA	L	D5
DOOLITTLE DR	ALA	45	D2
DOOLITTLE DR	O	159	E4
DOOLITTLE CK RD	SIS	2	E3
DOON GRADE	BUT	25	D2
DORA RD	SUT	33	B2
DORA ST	U	123	C3
DORAN SCENIC DR	SBD	82	A5
DORFF LN	HUM	15	D2
DORIS AV	VEN	96	B1
DORNES RD	PLA	34	A3
DORRETT DR	BUT	25	C2
DORRIS AV	FRCO	66	E2
DORRIS BROWNELL	SIS	5	B3
DORRIS TEHNER	SIS	5	A3
DORSEY RD	STA	47	D1
DOS CABEZA RD	IMP	111	B3
DOSE RD	TRI	10	E5
DOS PALMAS RD	SBD	90	E4
DOS REIS RD	SJCO	47	A1
DOS RIOS DR	SBD	90	E3
DOS RIOS LN	STA	47	B3
DOS RIOS RD	BUT	25	C5
DOSTER RD	CAL	41	A3
DOTTA LN	PLU	27	D3
DOTTA GUIDCI RD	PLU	27	D2
DOTY RD	SHA	13	D5
DOUBLE SPGS RD	CAL	40	E3
DOUGHERTY RD	CC	M	B4
DOUGHERTY RD	CC	46	B1
DOUGHERTY RD	SUT	33	C3
DOUGLAS	KIN	67	D1
DOUGLAS AV	FRCO	56	C4
DOUGLAS AV	SB	86	B3
DOUGLAS LN	SBD	100	E1
DOUGLAS RD	SAC	40	B1
DOUGLAS ST	ELS	189	D3
DOUGLAS RGR STA	MAD	49	E5
DOVE	SJCO	47	D1
DOVER AV	FRFD	135	D3
DOVER AV	KIN	67	E1
DOVER DR	NB	199	C4
DOVER DR	ORCO	T	C4
DOVER CANYON RD	SLO	75	E1
DOVE SPG CYN RD	KER	80	A2
DOW BUTTE RD	LAS	20	D1
DOW BUTTE LO RD	LAS	20	D1
DOWD RD	PLA	34	A3
DOWD RD	PLA	33	E4
DOWDEN RD	IMP	109	B3
DOWER AV	FRCO	57	B3
DOWER AV	FRCO	57	B5
DOW FLAT RD	LAS	20	D1
DOWNEY AV	LACO	S	E1
DOWNEY RD	INY	73	A4
DOWNEY RD	LACO	R	A4
DOWNEY ST	MDO	162	C3
DOWNIE RD	STA	47	E3
DOWNIE RD	STA	48	A3
DOWS PRAIRIE RD	HUM	9	E4
DOYLE DR	SF	141	D1
DOYLE GRADE	LAS	27	D1
DOYLE RD	MCO	47	C5
DOYLE RANCH RD	KER	69	E5
DOYLE RANCH RD	KER	79	E1
DRAIN 10 RD	SIS	5	E2
DRAIS AV	SJCO	40	C5
DRAKE AV	COL	32	E3
DRAKE RD	HUM	15	E2
DRAPER RD	STA	47	C4
DRAPER RD	TEH	18	C3
DREDGR CP MORGN	TRI	17	C1
DRESSER AV	KER	78	A2
DREW RD	IMP	111	E3
DREXLER	SUT	33	B2
DRIFTWOOD DR	FRFD	135	C4
DRIVE 212	TUL	58	C5
DRIVE 244	TUL	68	D2
DRIVE 254	TUL	58	D4
DRIVER AV	LACO	97	A1
DRIVER RD	KER	68	C5
DRIVER RD	KER	78	C2
DROBISH RD	BUT	25	E5
DROGE	SJCO	47	C1
DRUM CANYON RD	SB	86	D3
DRUMMOND AV	KER	80	C1
DRY CREEK CTO	MNO	50	D2
DRY CREEK RD	LAK	32	A5
DRY CREEK RD	MCO	48	B3
DRY CREEK RD	MNO	50	D2
DRY CREEK RD	NAPA	29	C4
DRY CREEK RD	NAPA	38	B2
DRY CREEK RD	PLA	34	C3
DRY CREEK RD	SJCO	40	B3
DRY CREEK RD	SLO	76	B1
DRY CREEK RD	SHA	18	D1
DRY CREEK RD	SIS	4	B3
DRY CREEK RD	SON	31	C5
DRY CREEK RD	TUL	58	D5
DRY CREEK RD W	SON	31	D5
DRY CREEK RD W	SON	37	D1
DRY CK BASIN RD	MOD	8	C1
DRY CK CMP GRND	LAS	8	B3
DRYDEN AV	SCL	P	E5
DRY GENESEO RD	SLO	76	B1
DRY SLOUGH RD	COL	33	A2
DRYTOWN AMADOR-			
-VIA BUNKERHILL	AMA	40	E2
DU BOIS ST	SR	139	D4
DUBOIS TK TR	SDCO	107	B5
DUCK CREEK RD	AMA	40	C3
DUCK LAKE RD	LAS	21	E4

STREET	CO.	PAGE	GRID
DUDLEY RD	MON	65	D3
DUFAU	VEN	96	C1
DUGGANS RD	NEV	34	C2
DUMETZ RD	LA	177	C5
DUMP RD	HUM	16	B3
DUMP RD	INY	60	A3
DUNAWAY RD	IMP	111	D3
DUNAWEAL LN	NAPA	29	A2
DUNBAR LN	SDCO	107	A5
DUNCAN RD	SBD	90	E4
DUNCAN RD	SJCO	40	C5
DUNCAN ST	KER	78	E4
DUNCAN CYN RD	SBD	99	A1
DUNCAN CREEK RD	SHA	17	E3
DUNDERBURG MDW	MNO	43	B4
DUNE RD	SBD	92	B1
DUNES RD	CLK	210	B2
DUNFORD RD	KER	78	A3
DUNLAP DR	RCO	99	C3
DUNLAP RD	FRCO	58	C3
DUNLAP RD	KER	69	B5
DUNN LN	CAL	41	B5
DUNN RD	MCO	48	C4
DUNN RD	SBD	82	D5
DUNN RD	STA	47	B2
DUNNE AV	SCL	P	D5
DUNNE AV E	SCL	P	D5
DUNSTONE DR	BUT	25	D5
DUNTON RD	STA	40	E5
DUPONT RD	RCO	102	D5
DURANT AV	B	156	A3
DURBROW RD	NEV	128	A4
DURFEE AV	LACO	R	C4
DURHAM HWY	BUT	25	C3
DURHAM RD	ALA	P	B2
DURHAM RD	SIS	5	A3
DURHAM DAYTN HY	BUT	25	B3
DURHAM FERRY RD	SJCO	47	A2
DURKEE RD	LAS	14	A3
DURNEL RD	BUT	25	B4
DUSK LN	TUO	163	D3
DUSTIN RD	SJCO	40	B4
DUSTIN AKERS RD	KER	78	A4
DUSTY LN	STA	47	D2
DUSTY WY	TEH	18	D5
DUSTY MILE RD	SBD	92	D5
DUTCH CREEK RD	SIS	3	E3
DUTCH CREEK RD	TRI	17	C2
DUTCHER CK RD	SON	31	C5
DUTCH MINE RD	TUO	41	C5
DUTTON AV	SON	131	C4
DUTTON AV N	STR	131	B3
DUVALL ST	KER	78	A4
DUZEL CREEK RD	SIS	3	E5
DUZEL CREEK RD	SIS	11	E1
DUZEL RCK LO RD	SIS	3	E5
DUZEL RCK LO RD	SIS	11	E1
DWIGHT WY	B	156	A3
DWIGHT WY	MCO	48	A4
DWINNELL WY	SIS	12	C1
DWINNELL WY	SIS	12	C1
DYE RD	SDCO	107	A4
DYER DR	PLU	20	C4
DYER LN	PLA	33	E5
DYER RD	ORCO	T	D3
DYER RD	SA	198	D2
DYER ST	ALA	N	E1
DYER ST	ALA	P	A1
DYER ST	ALA	45	E3
DYERVILLE LOOP	HUM	16	B4
DYERVILLE LP RD	HUM	16	C4
DYSERT RD	SIS	4	E3
DYSON LN	PLU	27	C3
E			
E ST	DVS	136	D3
E ST	EUR	121	C1
E ST	FRE	165	C4
E ST	OXN	176	C4
E ST	SBD	99	B2
E ST	SDCO	V	C4
E ST	SDCO	111	D2
E ST	YUB	33	D2
EABY RD	SBD	90	E4
EADY RD	IMP	112	A4
EAGER RD	SUT	33	C2
EAGLE AV	FRCO	56	A2
EAGLE BORAX WLL	INY	72	A2
EAGLE CK LP RD	TRI	11	E3
EAGLE CK LP RD	TRI	12	A3
EAGLE FIELD RD	MCO	55	E2
EAGLE LAKE RD	NEV	27	A5
EAGLE MTN RD	RCO	102	B4
EAGLE PK LKOUT	TEH	24	A2
EAGLE ROCK BLVD	LACO	R	A3
EAGLE ROCK RD	TRI	17	A1
EAGLE RCK LKOUT	SIS	4	D3
EAGLES NEST RD	MNO	43	A4
EAGLES NEST RD	SAC	40	B2
EAGLEVL DUMP RD	MOD	8	E2
EAGLEVILLE LOOP	MOD	8	E2
EARDLEY AV	PAC	167	C2
EARLHAM ST	SDCO	107	A4
EARP RD	COL	33	A2
EAST AV	ALA	M	D5
EAST AV	ALA	46	C2
EAST AV	BUT	25	B3
EAST AV	BUT	124	B1
EAST AV	C	124	A1
EAST AV	FRCO	57	C5
EAST AV	MCO	48	A3
EAST AV	TEH	24	D2

STREET	CO.	PAGE	GRID
EAST LN	MEN	23	B3
EAST RD	LACO	R	E5
EAST ST	ANA	193	C1
EAST ST	NAP	133	E3
EAST ST	ORCO	T	D2
EAST ST	RED	122	B1
EASTBLUFF DR	NB	200	A3
EAST END AV	POM	203	A5
EAST END RD	SBD	92	A4
EASTERN AV	LACO	98	A2
EASTERN AV	LACO	R	B5
EAST FORK RD	SHA	18	A1
EAST FORK RD	TRI	11	B5
EAST FORK RD	TRI	12	A4
EAST FORK RD	TRI	17	C3
E FK HAYFORD RD	TRI	17	C3
E FK INDIAN CK	SHA	2	E3
E FK STUART CPG	TRI	11	E5
EAST GRADE RD	SDCO	107	A2
EAST GRADE RD	TRI	16	E2
EASTIN RD	STA	47	C5
EASTMAN RD	STA	40	D5
EASTMAN RD	STA	47	D1
EASTMONT RD	KER	78	E2
EASTSHORE FRWY	ELC	155	D4
EASTSHORE FRWY	R	155	D2
EASTSHORE FRWY	SP	155	C1
EASTSHORE RD	SHA	18	B2
EAST SIDE	PLU	20	D5
EASTSIDE LN	MNO	42	E1
EASTSIDE RD	INY	51	D4
EASTSIDE RD	MEN	23	A5
EAST SIDE RD	MEN	31	B2
EASTSIDE RD	MNO	42	E1
EASTSIDE RD	RED	122	B4
EASTSIDE RD	SHA	18	C2
EASTSIDE RD	SHA	18	C3
EASTSIDE RD	SIS	3	D5
EASTSIDE RD	SIS	11	D1
EAST SIDE RD	TRI	12	A4
E SIDE CALPELLA	MEN	31	B1
E SDE PORTR VLY	MEN	31	B1
E SDE REDWD VLY	MEN	31	B1
EAST WEST RD	SIS	5	D2
EASY ST	KER	79	C4
EASY ST	SHA	18	D2
EATON RD	BUT	25	A3
EATON RD	STA	47	E1
EBERLE RD	KER	78	C4
ECHO VALLEY RD	MON	54	C3
EDDINS RD	IMP	109	A3
EDDY RD	COL	33	A3
EDDY RD	LPAZ	104	A2
EDDY GULCH RD	SIS	11	B2
EDDY GLH LKOUT	SIS	11	B3
EDEN PLAINS RD	CC	M	D3
EDGAR AV	BUT	25	B3
EDGER RD	IMP	108	E5
EDGEWATER BLVD	FCTY	145	D2
EDGEWOOD AV	MAR	L	A4
EDGEWOOD RD	SMCO	N	C2
EDGEWOOD RD	SMCO	45	D3
EDGEWOOD RD	SIS	12	C1
EDINGER AV	ORCO	98	B4
EDINGER AV	ORCO	T	B3
EDINGER AV	SA	196	A5
EDINGER AV	SA	197	C5
EDINGER AV	SA	198	E1
EDINGER ST	SA	195	C5
EDISON AV	SBD	98	D2
EDISON AV	SBD	U	D3
EDISON BLVD	BUR	179	A3
EDISON HWY	KER	78	E3
EDISON HWY	KER	79	A3
EDISON RD	KER	78	E3
EDISON ST	SB	86	E3
EDISON WY	CLK	85	D5
EDITH AV	TEH	24	D2
EDMINSTER RD	MCO	47	D4
EDMUNDSON AV	SCL	P	D5
EDMUNDSON AV	SCL	54	C1
ED POWERS RD	INY	51	C4
ED RAU RD	SAC	39	E2
EDSEL LN	STA	47	C2
EDWARD ST	KER	79	B5
EDWARDS	SJCO	47	D1
EDWARDS ST	ORCO	T	B3
EEL RIVER RD	MEN	23	B5
EEL RIVER RD	MEN	31	C1
EEL ROCK RD	HUM	16	C4
EGAN RD	TUO	41	C5
EGGERT RD	SOL	39	C2
EHRLICH RD	STA	47	C3
EICKHOFF RD	LAK	31	D2
EIGHMY RD	TEH	18	C4
EIGHTH ST	C	124	C5
EIGHT MILE RD	SJCO	39	E4
EISENHOWER DR	RCO	100	E5
ELBERTA ST	KER	89	E1
EL CAJON BLVD	SD	214	A5
EL CAJON BLVD	SDCO	V	D3
EL CAJON BLVD	SDCO	111	D1
EL CAMINO AV	SAC	40	A1
EL CAMINO DR	SHA	18	C3
EL CAMINO RD	SBD	101	D1
EL CAMINO CIELO	SB	87	C4
EL CAMINO REAL	BLMT	145	C4
EL CAMINO REAL	BURL	144	E5
EL CAMINO REAL	STAN	147	B3
EL CAMINO REAL	SVL	149	D1
EL CAMINO REAL	MLBR	144	D4
EL CAMINO REAL	MON	54	D4
EL CAMINO REAL	MON	65	A1

STREET	CO.	PAGE	GRID
EL CAMINO REAL	MON	66	A5
EL CAMINO REAL	MON	171	B1
EL CAMINO REAL	MVW	148	B5
EL CAMINO REAL	PA	147	D4
EL CAMINO REAL	SAL	171	D3
EL CAMINO REAL	SBT	54	D2
EL CAMINO REAL	SBR	144	A2
EL CAMINO REAL	SDCO	106	B3
EL CAMINO REAL	SNLO	172	B3
EL CAMINO REAL	SLO	66	A5
EL CAMINO REAL	SLO	76	B2
EL CAMINO REAL	SMCO	N	D2
EL CAMINO REAL	SMCO	45	C3
EL CAMINO REAL	VEN	175	E3
EL CAMINO REAL	SB	86	C1
EL CAMINO REAL	SCL	P	A3
EL CAMINO REAL	SCLR	150	B2
EL CAMINO REAL	SVL	149	D1
EL CAMINO REAL	SCL	46	A4
EL CAMINO REAL	SCL	54	D2
EL CAMINO REAL	SMA	173	C1
EL CAMINO REAL	SSF	144	A1
EL CAMINO REAL	SVL	150	B2
EL CAMPO RD	MCO	55	E2
EL CAMPO RD	RCO	100	C5
EL CAMPO RD	SLO	76	B5
EL CAPITAN WY	MCO	47	E4
EL CAPITAN WY	MCO	48	A4
EL CAPTN SCH RD	MCO	48	B5
EL CARISO TK TR	RCO	99	B4
EL CENTRO AV	NAPA	38	C3
EL CENTRO AV	NAP	133	A1
EL CENTRO BLVD	SUT	33	D3
EL CENTRO RD	SAC	33	D5
EL CENTRO ST	IMP	111	E3
EL CERRITO RD	RCO	98	E3
EL CERRO BLVD	CC	M	A4
EL CIELO DR	RCO	100	D3
EL CIELO RD	PMSP	206	E5
EL CONQUISTA RD	RCO	107	A1
ELDER AV	KIN	67	B1
ELDER ST	SBDO	106	C2
ELDER CREEK RD	RCO	107	B1
ELDER CREEK RD	SAC	39	E1
ELDER CREEK RD	SAC	40	A1
EL DIABLO RD	SBD	92	E5
EL DORADO AV	FRCO	56	E4
EL DORADO AV	FRCO	66	E2
EL DORADO AV	S	160	C1
EL DORADO DR	RCO	100	C3
EL DORADO DR	SBD	102	C1
EL DORADO ST	AUB	126	E3
EL DORADO ST	FRE	165	C3
EL DORADO ST	MONT	167	E4
EL DORADO ST	SJCO	40	A5
EL DRDO HLLS RD	ED	34	C5
EL DORADO MN RD	RCO	101	C2
ELDRIDGE RD	LAS	14	A5
ELEANOR AV	STA	47	D2
ELEVADO AV	BH	183	A2
ELEVADO RD	SBD	91	B3
ELECTRA RD	AMA	41	A3
ELEVATOR RD	SOL	39	D3
ELFERS RD	STA	47	B3
ELGIN	MCO	56	B1
ELGIN AV	KIN	67	B1
ELHOLM RD	MCO	47	C5
ELINOR RD N	HUM	16	A3
ELINOR RD S	HUM	16	A3
ELIZA GULCH RD	SIS	3	E4
ELIZABETH LK RD	LACO	89	C3
ELIZABETH LK RD	LACO	90	A3
ELZBTH LK P CYN	LACO	89	B2
ELK	MCO	48	A4
ELK AV	BUT	25	B3
ELK CT	KER	79	B4
ELK CREEK RD	HUM	16	B4
ELK CREEK RD	SIS	3	A4
ELK GROVE BLVD	SAC	39	E2
ELK GRV FLRN RD	SAC	39	E2
ELK HILLS RD	KER	77	E3
ELK HILLS RD	KER	78	A3
ELKHORN AV	FRCO	56	D5
ELKHORN AV	FRCO	57	D5
ELKHORN BLVD	SAC	33	D5
ELKHORN RD	MEN	31	A4
ELKHORN RD	MON	54	C3
ELKHORN RD	SLO	77	D4
ELKHORN GRAD RD	KER	78	A5
ELKHORN GRADE	FRCO	57	B5
ELK MOUNTAIN RD	LAK	23	C5
ELK MOUNTAIN RD	LAK	31	C1
ELK RIVER RD	HUM	121	A5
ELK RIVER RD	HUM	15	E1
ELKS LN	SNLO	172	B4
ELK VALLEY RD	DN	1	D4
ELK VALLEY RD	SIS	10	D1
ELK VLY CRSS RD	DN	1	D3
ELLA AV	YUB	33	D2
ELLA RICHTER RD	SHA	18	A3
ELLENA ST	FRCO	57	B5
ELLENWOOD DR	STA	47	E2
ELLENWOOD RD	STA	48	A2
ELLER LN	SIS	3	D5
ELLER LN	SIS	11	D1
ELLIOT	SJCO	40	B3
ELLIOT AV	MCO	48	B4
ELLIOT ST	SBD	93	B2
ELLIOT RCH RD	PLA	34	E2
ELLIOTT RD	BUT	25	C3
ELLIOTT CK RD	SIS	3	B2
ELLIOTT RCH RD	SAC	39	E2
ELLIS AV	RCO	99	C4

STREET	CO.	PAGE	GRID
ELLIS RD	AMA	41	C1
ELLIS RD	YUB	33	D2
ELM AV	FRCO	57	C4
ELM AV	MON	65	B1
ELM AV	AUB	126	C3
ELM AV	SDCO	106	B3
ELM ST	BKD	166	B2
ELM ST	RCO	99	C5
ELM ST	SDCO	107	A4
ELM ST	TUL	68	B3
EL MARGARITA RD	SUT	33	C2
EL MEDIO RD	SBD	90	E3
ELMER AV	SUT	33	C2
ELMER ST	RCO	99	B4
ELMIRA RD	SOL	39	A2
EL MIRAGE RD	SBD	90	E3
EL MIRAGE RD	SBD	91	A3
ELMO HWY	KER	78	A1
EL MONTE AV	LACO	R	D3
EL MONTE AV	TUL	58	A4
EL MONTE RD	SCL	N	E3
EL MONTE RD	SCL	45	E4
ELNA RD	INY	59	E1
EL NIDO RD	MCO	48	C5
EL NORTE PKWY	SDCO	106	D3
ELORDY LN	SUT	33	E4
EL PASTA RD	RCO	107	A1
EL POMAR AV	STA	47	E2
EL POMAR DR	SLO	76	A2
EL POMAR RD	SLO	76	B2
EL POMAR RO RD	SLO	76	B2
EL PORTAL	CC	38	C5
EL PORTAL DR	SP	155	D1
EL POZO GRADE	SLO	76	D3
EL PRADO	SD	215	E2
EL RANCHO DR	KER	79	C4
EL REPOSO RD	RCO	107	A1
EL RIO DR	TUL	68	C1
EL ROBLAR	VEN	88	A4
EL ROBLAR ST	SB	87	E1
EL SEGUNDO BLVD	ELS	189	D4
EL SEGUNDO BLVD	LACO	97	D3
EL SEGUNDO BLVD	LACO	Q	D5
EL SEGUNDO BLVD	LACO	S	C1
EL SERENO RD	MCO	55	C2
EL SOBRANTE RD	RCO	99	B3
EL TEJON HWY	KER	78	E4
EL TEJON HWY	KER	79	A4
EL TORO DR	BKD	166	C5
EL TORO RD	ORCO	98	D5
ELVERTA RD	SAC	33	D5
EL VICINO AV	MDO	162	D2
ELWOOD RD	FRCO	58	B3
ELY RD	SON	L	A1
ELY RD	SUT	33	C4
ELYSIAN PARK AV	LA	186	A1
ELYSIAN VLY RD	LAS	21	A4
EMBARCADERO,THE	SF	142	E1
EMBARCADERO, THE	SF	143	D1
EMBARCADERO RD	PA	147	D2
EMBARCADERO RD	SCL	N	E2
EMERALD AV	RCO	100	E3
EMERALD AV	STA	47	C2
EMERALD DR	SDCO	106	C3
EMERALD RD	SBD	91	E4
EMERSON RD	MOD	8	D2
EMERSON RD	TEH	18	D4
EMERY RD	STA	47	E2
EMERY RD	STA	48	A2
EMIGH RD	SOL	39	C4
EMIGRANT RD	PLU	26	D1
EMIGRANT TR	SHA	19	B3
EMMERT RD	COL	33	A3
EMMIGRANT TR	ALP	36	B4
EMPIRE	CC	39	C5
EMPIRE AV	BUR	179	B2
EMPIRE AV	CC	M	D3
EMPIRE ST	GV	127	B4
EMPIRE ST	NEV	127	C4
EMPIRE CREEK RD	SIS	3	E3
EMPIRE GRADE	SCR	N	E5
EMPIRE GRADE	SCR	53	D1
EMPIRE MINE RD	CC	M	C3
EMPIRE MINE RD	CC	39	B5
ENCHNTD FRST RD	RCO	100	A4
ENCINAL	MON	54	D4
ENCINAL AV	A	159	A1
ENCINAL AV	ALA	L	D5
ENCINAL AV	ALA	45	D1
ENCINAL RD	SUT	33	C1
ENCINITAS BLVD	SDCO	106	C4
ENCINITAS RD	SDCO	106	C4
END RD W	HUM	10	A5
ENDERTS BCH RD	DN	1	E4
ENGLEHART AV	FRCO	58	A4
ENGLISH RD	IMP	109	A3
ENGLISH COLONY	PLA	34	B5
ENGLISH HILLS	SOL	39	A2
ENNIS RD	FRCO	58	C3
ENNIS RD	SUT	33	B2
ENOS LN	KER	78	B3
ENSLEY RD	SUT	33	C4
ENTERPRISE	SJCO	47	D1
ENTERPRISE RD	BUT	25	E4
ENTERPRISE ST	TUL	68	A2
ERBES RD	VEN	96	E1
EREISTIN DR	SBD	92	E5
ERHIT RD	TUO	48	E1
ERHIT RD	TUO	49	A1
ERICKSON RD	BUT	25	B4
ERLE RD	MCO	48	C5
ERNST	MPA	48	E2
ERNST	MPA	49	A2

STREET	CO.	PAGE	GRID
ERRECA RD	MCO	48	A5
ERRINGER RD	VEN	88	E5
ERRINGER RD	VEN	89	A5
ERRINGER RD	VEN	96	E1
ERRINGER RD	VEN	97	A1
ERSKINE RD	IMP	108	E5
ERSKINE CK RD	KER	79	D1
ERTESZEK DR	KER	79	C4
ERWIN ST	LA	177	C3
ESCALON BELLOTA	SJCO	40	C5
ESCALON BELLOTA	SJCO	47	C1
ESCHINGER RD	SAC	39	E2
ESCHINGER RD	SAC	40	A2
ESCOBA DR	PMSP	206	E5
ESCOBAR ST	M	154	B1
ESCOLLE RD	MON	54	D5
ESCONDIDO AV	SDCO	106	C3
ESCONDIDO FRWY	RCO	99	C3
ESCONDIDO FRWY	SD	216	D3
ESCONDIDO FRWY	SDCO	106	D2
ESCONDIDO RD	LACO	89	D4
ESMERALDA RD	CAL	41	B4
ESPERANZA AV	RCO	100	B3
ESPERANZA RD	MON	54	D4
ESPERANZA RD	SIS	13	A2
ESPINOSA RD	MON	54	C3
ESPINOSA RD	MON	65	B1
ESPLANADE	BUT	25	A2
ESPLANADE AV	RCO	99	D4
ESPLANADE, THE	C	124	B3
ESPOLA RD	SDCO	106	D4
ESQUON RD	BUT	25	B4
ESSEX LN	HUM	10	A5
ESSEX RD	SBD	94	D2
ESTHER AV	MCO	56	B2
ESTRELLA RD	SLO	66	A5
ESTRELLA RD	SLO	76	B1
ESTUDILLO AV	ALA	L	E5
ETHANAC RD	RCO	99	C4
ETHEREDGE ST	KER	68	D5
ETIWANDA AV	SBD	98	E2
ETTERBG HONEYDW	HUM	16	A5
ETTING RD	VEN	96	C1
ETZEL RD	SOL	39	C2
EUCALYPTUS AV	MCO	48	A4
EUCALYPTUS AV	RCO	99	C3
EUCALYPTUS AV	SBD	U	E3
EUCALYPTUS AV	STA	47	B3
EUCALYPTUS RD	BUT	25	B5
EUCALYPTUS RD	MCO	56	A2
EUCALYPTUS ST	AVLN	97	B5
EUCALYPTUS ST	SBD	91	B4
EUCLID AV	ALA	L	D4
EUCLID AV	LA	186	E4
EUCLID AV	ONT	204	B4
EUCLID AV	SBD	U	D3
EUCLID AV	SBD	98	D2
EUCLID AV	SDCO	V	C3
EUCLID AV	SDCO	111	D1
EUCLID AV	SF	141	E3
EUCLID AV	STA	47	E3
EUCLID AV	UPL	204	B1
EUCLID ST	FTNV	197	A2
EUCLID ST	ORCO	98	B3
EUCLID ST	ORCO	T	C2
EUREKA RD	PLA	34	B5
EUREKA RD S	INY	52	D5
EUREKA WY	RED	122	B1
EUREKA WY	SHA	18	C2
EUREKA CYN RD	SCR	P	C5
EUREKA CYN RD	SCR	54	B1
EUREKA HILL RD	MEN	30	C3
EUREKA MINE RD	SIE	26	C4
EUREKA VLY RD	INY	52	D4
EUROPE AV	KER	79	D5
EVAN HEWES HWY	IMP	111	D3
EVAN HEWES HWY	IMP	112	D3
EVANS	TUL	68	D1
EVANS AV	FRCO	56	B2
EVANS RD	COL	32	D2
EVANS RD	RCO	107	C1
EVANS RD	SIS	4	E3
EVNS REIMR RD W	BUT	25	B5
EVELYN AV	SCL	P	A3
EVELYN AV	SVL	148	D5
EVELYN AV	SVL	150	A1
EVERETT AV	KIN	67	C1
EVERETT ST	KER	80	D1
EVERETT MEM HWY	SIS	12	C2
EVERGLADE	SUT	33	C3
EVERGREEN AV	LA	186	E4
EVERGREEN RD	CAL	40	D4
EVERGREEN RD	TEH	18	C3
EVERGREEN RD	TUO	42	B5
EVERGREEN RD	TUO	63	A3
EVERITT RD	SUT	33	C2
EXCELSIOR AV	FRCO	66	E1
EXCELSIOR AV	FRCO	67	C1
EXCELSIOR AV	KIN	67	D1
EXCELSIOR RD	SAC	40	A2
EXCELSIOR MN RD	SBD	73	D5
EXCELSIOR MN RD	SBD	83	D1
EXCELSIOR PT RD	NEV	34	E1
EXCHEQUER	MPA	48	D3
EXCHEQUER DR	FRCO	58	C1
EXCHEQUER DAM	MPA	48	D3
EXP MINE RD	TUO	41	C4
EXPOSITION BLVD	LA	184	C5
EXPOSITION BLVD	LA	185	B5
EXPOSITION BLVD	LACO	97	D2
EXPOSITION BLVD	LACO	Q	D4
EXPOSITION BLVD	SAC	39	E1

INDEXES

F

STREET	CO.	PAGE	GRID
F ST	DVS	136	C2
F ST	EUR	121	D3
F ST	FRE	165	D4
F ST	HUM	15	E1
F ST	SD	215	D3
F ST	SBD	99	B1
F ST	SDCO	V	C4
F ST	SDCO	111	D2
F ST E	CLTN	207	A5
FABRY RD	MON	55	B5
FAHEY RD	MCO	55	C1
FAIR DR	CM	199	B1
FAIR ST	BUT	25	B3
FAIR ST	BUT	124	E5
FAIRBANKS RD	MEN	23	A3
FAIRCHILD LN	SJCO	40	B5
FAIRFAX	FRCO	56	B3
FAIRFAX AV	KIN	67	C1
FAIRFAX AV	LA	181	A1
FAIRFAX AV	LA	183	E3
FAIRFAX AV	LA	184	A1
FAIRFAX AV	LACO	Q	D4
FAIRFAX RD	KER	78	E3
FAIRFAX BOLINAS	MAR	38	A5
FAIRFIELD AV	FRFD	135	B3
FAIRFIELD AV	SBD	91	C3
FAIRFIELD ST	EUR	121	B3
FAIRGROUND DR	NAPA	L	D1
FAIRGROUNDS DR	VAL	134	E2
FAIRHAVEN AV	ORCO	T	E2
FAIRHAVEN AV	SA	196	C2
FAIRLANE RD	SBD	92	A4
FAIRMEAD BLVD	MAD	56	E1
FAIRMONT AV	SDCO	V	C3
FAIRMONT AV	SDCO	111	D1
FAIRMONT AV E	MDO	162	D1
FAIRMONT RD	LACO	89	C2
FAIRMOUNT AV	SD	216	E1
FAIROAKS AV	LACO	R	B2
FAIR OAKS AV	LACO	190	B1
FAIR OAKS AV	PAS	190	B3
FAIR OAKS AV	SCL	45	E4
FAIR OAKS AV	SCL	46	A4
FAIR OAKS BLVD	SAC	40	A1
FAIR OAKS BLVD	SAC	34	A5
FAIR PLAY RD	ED	41	A1
FAIRVIEW AV	ALA	P	A1
FAIRVIEW AV	CC	M	D3
FAIRVIEW AV	CC	39	C5
FAIRVIEW AV	RCO	100	A4
FAIRVIEW AV	SB	87	B4
FAIRVIEW RD	COL	32	D1
FAIRVIEW RD	CM	199	C1
FAIRVIEW RD	MON	54	E5
FAIRVIEW RD	ORCO	98	C4
FAIRVIEW RD	ORCO	T	C4
FAIRVIEW RD	SBT	54	E2
FAIRVIEW RD	SBT	55	A2
FAIRVIEW RD	SBD	92	C1
FAIRVIEW RD	VEN	88	B4
FAIRVIEW ST	SA	195	C4
FAIRWAY DR	CLTN	207	B5
FAIRWAY DR	EUR	121	C5
FAIRWAY PL	SB	86	E3
FAITH HOME RD	MCO	47	D4
FAITH HOME RD	STA	47	D3
FALL RD	INY	70	B2
FALLBROOK AV	LA	177	A4
FALL CREEK RD	SIS	4	C2
FALLEN LEAF RD	ED	35	E3
FALLING LEAF RD	SHA	18	C2
FALLON RD	SBT	54	E2
FALLON RD	SBT	55	A2
FALL RIVER RD	SHA	13	E4
FALLS CYN RD	AVLN	97	A5
FAMOSO HWY	KER	78	A1
FAMOSO-PRTVL HY	KER	78	C1
FANDANGO PSS RD	MOD	7	D3
FANNING	SJCO	40	B5
FANOE RD	MON	54	E5
FANUEL ST	SD	212	A1
FARGO AV	KIN	67	C1
FARGO CANYON RD	RCO	101	B4
FARINA ST	RCO	100	A5
FARLEY MINE RD	SBD	91	D3
FARMER RANCH RD	TRI	17	B2
FARMERSVILLE RD	TUL	68	C2
FARM HILL BLVD	SMCO	N	D2
FARM HILL BLVD	SMCO	45	D3
FARMLAN RD	SUT	33	B2
FARMLAND AV	MCO	48	C4
FARNHAM RDG RD	ED	41	A1
FARQUHAR RD	TEH	18	B4
FARRELL DR	PMSP	206	D2
FARRIS DR	CAL	40	D4
FARRIS RD	BUT	25	B5
FARRIS RD	BUT	33	B1
FASIG RD	SUT	33	B3
FAUST RD	STA	47	C2
FAWCETT RD	IMP	112	A3
FAWN LODGE RD	TRI	17	D1
FAXON RD	COL	33	B3
FAY LN	SIS	11	D1
FAY RD	MCO	47	D4
FAY RANCH RD	KER	69	E5
FAY RANCH RD	KER	79	E1
FAY RIDGE RD	KER	78	C1
FEATHER LAKE HY	LAS	20	A2
FEATHER LAKE RD	SHA	19	E1
FEATHER RIV BL	YUB	33	D3

STREET	CO.	PAGE	GRID
FEDERAL BLVD	SD	216	D3
FEDERAL BLVD	SDCO	V	C3
FEDERAL BLVD	SDCO	111	D1
FEE RD	MOD	7	D3
FEENSTRA RD	SLO	76	B2
FEE RESRVOIR RD	MOD	7	D3
FELCIANA MTN RD	MPA	49	B3
FELDMILLER RD	TRI	16	E3
FELDSPAR AV	KER	80	B1
FELICIANO DR	LA	177	B5
FELICITA RD	SDCO	106	D3
FELIZ CREEK RD	MEN	31	B3
FELL ST	SFCO	L	B5
FELL ST	SF	141	E4
FELL ST	SF	142	A4
FELL ST	SFCO	45	B1
FELLOWSHIP RD	STB	174	A5
FELTER RD	SCL	46	B4
FELTON EMPRE RD	SCR	53	E1
FENDERS FERRY	SHA	13	A5
FENSLER RD	SIS	5	D2
FENTEM RD	MCO	47	C5
FERGUSON RD	IMP	110	E4
FERN RD	SHA	19	A2
FERN RD E	SHA	19	A1
FERN ST	SD	216	B3
FERN ST	SDCO	V	C3
FERN ST	SDCO	111	D1
FERN CANYON DR	MEN	31	B2
FERNDALE DMP RD	HUM	15	D2
FERN DELL DR	LA	182	A3
FERRELL RD	IMP	112	A4
FERRETTI RD	TUO	41	D5
FERRETTI RD	TUO	48	D1
FERRY RD	TEH	18	D4
FERRY RD E	HUM	15	E2
FESLER ST	SMA	173	A2
FICKLE HILL RD	HUM	10	A5
FIDDLETOWN RD	AMA	40	E2
FIDLTWN QTZ MTN	AMA	40	E1
FIDDLTWN SLV LK	AMA	41	A1
FIDDYMENT	PLA	33	E4
FIELD RD	SBD	82	C5
FIELDBROOK RD	HUM	10	A4
FIELDS RD	MCO	48	C3
FIELDS RD	RCO	100	A3
FIELDS RIDGE RD	BUT	26	B4
FIESTA ISLND RD	SD	212	E4
FIFIELD RD	IMP	109	B4
FIFIELD RD	SUT	33	D4
FIFTH AV	C	124	B3
FIFTH ST	C	124	B5
FIG AV	FRE	165	C5
FIG AV	FRCO	57	C4
FIG AV	FRCO	57	C5
FIG AV	STA	47	C3
FIGMOND AV	MCO	48	C3
FIG TREE LN	SHA	18	C3
FIGUEROA ST	LA	185	D5
FIGUEROA ST	LACO	R	A3
FIGUEROA ST	LACO	S	C2
FIGUEROA ST	MONT	167	E3
FIGUEROA MTN RD	SB	87	B2
FILBURN AV	KER	78	A1
FILIPPINI RD	SIE	27	C3
FILLMAN RD	LAS	8	A4
FILLMORE ST	RCO	101	B5
FILLMORE ST	SF	142	B2
FILLY LN	CAL	41	B5
FIMPLE RD	BUT	25	B3
FINCK RD	SJCO	46	E1
FINE AV	SJCO	40	C5
FINE AV	STA	47	D2
FINK RD	STA	47	C4
FINKS RD	COL	32	D1
FINLEY LN	LAS	14	C3
FINNEL AV	TEH	24	D1
FINNEY RD	IMP	109	B5
FINNEY RD	STA	47	C2
FINNING HILL RD	PLA	34	E2
FIR ST	C	124	E4
FIR ST	RCO	100	C4
FIRE CAMP RD	BUT	25	E4
FIRESTONE	FRCO	66	C3
FIRESTONE BLVD	LACO	97	E2
FIRESTONE BLVD	LACO	R	A5
FIRETHORN RD	SBD	92	B3
FIRST AV	C	124	B3
FIRST AV	STA	47	C3
FIRST AV E	C	124	D3
FIRST ST	SIS	12	D3
FISCHER RD	IMP	111	E4
FISH & GAME RD	LAS	21	C3
FISHER AV	KER	89	C1
FISHER DR	TUL	68	C1
FISHER RD	HUM	15	E2
FISHER RD	IMP	110	D5
FISHER RD	LPAZ	104	A2
FISHER RD	MCO	48	B4
FISHER RD	TRI	10	E5
FISHERS LANDING	YUMA	110	E4
FISH HATCHRY RD	INY	59	E3
FISH ROCK RD	MEN	31	A4
FISH ROCK RD	MEN	30	D4
FISH SLOUGH RD	MNO	51	D2
FISH SPRINGS RD	INY	59	E1
FISKE	MPA	48	E5
FISKE	MPA	49	A1
FITCH MTN RD	SON	37	D1
FITZGERALD DR	BUT	25	C2
FITZGERALD RD	SCL	P	D5
FITZGERALD RD	SCL	54	D1
FITZHUGH CK RD	MOD	8	B2

STREET	CO.	PAGE	GRID
FIVE BRIDGES RD	INY	51	D4
FIVE MILE DR	AMA	40	D2
FIVE MILE CK RD	TUO	41	D4
FIVE MI STA RD	SBD	95	D2
FLAMINGO RD	CLK	210	C2
FLANAGAN RD	SHA	18	C1
FLANNERY RD	SOL	39	B3
FLATTOP MTN RD	KIN	67	A4
FLEA VALLEY RD	BUT	25	D2
FLEMING AV E	VAL	134	E3
FLEMING RD	PLA	34	A3
FLETCHER DR	LACO	Q	E3
FLETCHER PKWY	SDCO	V	D3
FLETCHER PKWY	SDCO	111	E1
FLINT AV	KIN	67	C1
FLINT AV	MCO	47	E4
FLINT AV	MCO	48	A4
FLINT ST	KER	80	C5
FLOOD RD	IMP	110	D5
FLOOD RD	SJCO	40	C5
FLORADALE AV	SB	86	B3
FLORAL AV	C	124	D1
FLORAL AV	FRCO	56	D4
FLORAL AV	FRCO	57	B4
FLORENCE AV	ING	188	E5
FLORENCE AV	LACO	97	D2
FLORENCE AV	LACO	Q	D5
FLORES AV	TEH	18	D5
FLORES RD	YUB	34	A1
FLORIDA AV	RCO	99	D4
FLORIDA DR	SD	216	A2
FLORIDA ST	VAL	134	B4
FLORIN RD	SAC	40	A1
FLORIN MILL RD	SHA	13	D3
FLORIN PERKINS	SAC	40	A2
FLOURNOY AV	TEH	24	D2
FLOWER ST	LA	185	E3
FLOWER ST	SA	196	A3
FLOWERS LN	SHA	18	B3
FLOWING WELLS	IMP	109	B3
FLOYD AV	FRCO	57	B3
FLOYD AV	STA	47	D2
FLYNN RD	INY	51	D4
FLYNN CREEK RD	MEN	30	D2
FOAM ST	MONT	167	D2
FOAM ST	MON	53	E2
FOBES RANCH RD	RCO	100	C4
FOGARTY RD	STA	47	E1
FOGARTY RD	STA	48	A1
FOGG RD	SAC	39	E2
FOLETTA RD	MON	54	D5
FOLEY AV	KER	79	D3
FOLSOM AV	FRCO	56	B2
FOLSOM BLVD	SAC	34	B5
FOLSOM BLVD	SAC	39	E1
FOLSOM BLVD	SAC	40	A1
FONSECA RD	COL	24	E5
FONTANA AV	SBD	99	A2
FOOLISH PLSR RD	RCO	107	A1
FOOTE RD	SIE	26	C5
FOOTHILL BLVD	ALA	146	D1
FOOTHILL BLVD	BUT	25	D4
FOOTHILL BLVD	CLA	203	B1
FOOTHILL BLVD	CPTO	149	A4
FOOTHILL BLVD	H	146	E2
FOOTHILL BLVD	LACO	89	E5
FOOTHILL BLVD	LACO	98	B1
FOOTHILL BLVD	LACO	Q	B1
FOOTHILL BLVD	LACO	U	A1
FOOTHILL BLVD	NAP	133	B2
FOOTHILL BLVD	O	158	B3
FOOTHILL BLVD	ORCO	T	E3
FOOTHILL BLVD	ROC	204	E1
FOOTHILL BLVD	SBD	99	A1
FOOTHILL BLVD	SD	212	A1
FOOTHILL BLVD	SDCO	V	A2
FOOTHILL BLVD	SDCO	106	C5
FOOTHILL BLVD	SNLO	172	B2
FOOTHILL BLVD	UPL	203	C1
FOOTHILL BLVD	UPL	204	B1
FOOTHILL DR	SBD	102	C1
FOOTHILL DR	SIS	4	A4
FOOTHILL DR	SOL	39	A2
FOOTHILL EXPWY	PA	147	B5
FOOTHILL EXPWY	SCL	N	E3
FOOTHILL EXPWY	SCL	45	E4
FOOTHILL EXPWY	SCCO	149	B3
FOOTHILL FRWY	LACO	97	D1
FOOTHILL FRWY	LACO	98	A1
FOOTHILL FRWY	LACO	R	B2
FOOTHILL FRWY	LACO	R	C3
FOOTHILL FRWY	PAS	190	B2
FOOTHILL RD	ALA	P	B1
FOOTHILL RD	ALA	46	B2
FOOTHILL RD	BH	183	B1
FOOTHILL RD	DGL	36	B3
FOOTHILL RD	INY	59	E3
FOOTHILL RD	MNO	51	C1
FOOTHILL RD	MON	64	E1
FOOTHILL RD	MON	65	A1
FOOTHILL RD	SBD	91	D4
FOOTHILL RD	SBD	92	A4
FOOTHILL RD	SLO	76	A3
FOOTHILL RD	STB	174	C1
FOOTHILL RD	SB	87	D1
FOOTHILL RD	SCL	P	E5
FOOTHILL RD	SCL	54	D1
FOOTHILL RD	TEH	18	E5
FOOTHILL RD	VEN	88	B4
FOOTHILL RD	VEN	88	B5
FOOTHILL TRANS- -CORRRIDOR	ORCO	98	E4
FOPPIANO LN	SJCO	40	B5

STREET	CO.	PAGE	GRID
FORBES N	PLA	34	B3
FORBES S	PLA	34	A3
FORBESTOWN RD	BUT	25	E4
FORBESTOWN RD	BUT	26	A4
FRBSTOWN RES RD	BUT	26	A4
FORD RD	NB	200	B3
FORD ST	RCO	100	E3
FORD ST	SBD	99	C2
FORDYCE LAKE RD	NEV	27	B5
FOREMAN CIR RD	BUT	25	D4
FOREST	MPA	49	D3
FOREST AV	MONT	53	D2
FOREST AV	PAC	167	C3
FOREST BLVD	KER	80	B4
FOREST CIR	BUT	25	C2
FOREST DR	BUT	25	C2
FOREST RD	CAR	168	C4
FOREST TR	ML	164	B1
FOREST HOME BL	SBD	99	E2
FORST HM CRBNDL	AMA	40	D2
FOREST HOUSE	SIS	3	E4
FOREST LAKE	SJCO	40	A3
FOREST LAWN DR	LA	179	D5
FOREST LAWN DR	LACO	Q	D3
FOREST RANCH RD	BUT	25	C2
FOREST RANCH WY	BUT	25	C2
FORGAY RD	PLU	20	D5
FORNI RD	PLCV	138	A4
FORREST ST	BKD	166	C4
FORRESTER RD	IMP	109	A4
FORSMANS PL	NEV	128	A4
FORSYTHE RD	YUB	26	A5
FT BRAGG SHERWD	MEN	22	C5
FT CADY RD	SBD	92	C1
FORT INDEPNDNCE	INY	59	E3
FORTNA RD	SUT	33	C2
FORT ROMIE RD	MON	64	E1
FORT ROMIE RD	MON	65	A1
FORT ROSS RD	SON	37	B1
FORT SAGE RD	LAS	21	E5
FORT SEWARD RD	HUM	16	C5
FORT STOCKTN DR	SD	213	B5
FORT STOCKTN DR	SDCO	V	B3
FORT STOCKTN DR	SDCO	111	C1
FORT TEJON RD	LACO	90	B3
FORTUNA BLVD	HUM	15	E2
FORTY MILE RD	YUB	33	D3
FORTYNINE LN	MOD	7	D5
FORTYNINE PALMS	SBD	101	B1
FORWARD RD	TEH	19	B3
FORWARDS MILL	SHA	19	C3
FOSS RD	JKSN	3	D1
FOSS HILL	SON	32	A5
FOSSIL BED RD	SBD	81	C5
FOSTER	MON	54	C4
FOSTER RD	LACO	R	B5
FOSTER RD	LACO	S	E1
FOSTER RD	LACO	T	A1
FOSTER RD	NAP	133	B5
FOSTER RD	SHA	18	B3
FOSTER RD	SIS	4	C3
FOSTER CITY BL	FCTY	145	D1
FOSTER CITY BL	SMCO	N	D1
FOSTER CITY BL	SMCO	45	D3
FOSTER MTN RD	MEN	23	B5
FOULDS RD	IMP	108	E3
FOULKE LN	SIS	4	B5
FOUNTN HOUSE RD	YUB	26	B5
FOUR CORNERS RD	LAS	14	B3
FOUR MILE RD	COL	24	E5
FOUR MILE RD	COL	32	E1
FOUR MIL RDG RD	BUT	25	E3
FOURTEENTH ST	EUR	121	B2
FOURTH AV	SUT	33	D3
FOURTH ST	C	124	B5
FOUSSAT RD	SDCO	106	B3
FOUTS SPGS RD	COL	24	A5
FOWLER AV	FRCO	57	D2
FOWLER AV	FRCO	57	D5
FOWLER RD	PLA	34	B3
FOWLER PBLC CMP	SIS	13	A2
FOX RD	LAS	21	B4
FOX RD	MCO	48	B4
FOX RD	STA	47	D2
FOX RD	SOL	39	B2
FOXEN CANYON RD	SB	86	D1
FOXWORTHY AV	SCL	P	B4
FOXWORTHY AV	SCL	46	B5
FRAGUERO RD	TUO	41	C5
FRANCESCHI RD	KER	79	D3
FRANCISCO BLVD	SR	139	E4
FRANCISQUITO AV	LACO	R	E4
FRANCISQITO CYN	LACO	89	C3
FRANCIS SPGS RD	SBD	83	C2
FRANCO WSTRN RD	KER	77	D3
FRANK AV	KER	70	A5
FRANK COX RD	STA	47	B3
FRANKENHEIMR RD	STA	47	E1
FRANKLIN AV	LA	181	E3
FRANKLIN AV	LA	182	C4
FRANKLIN AV	LACO	Q	E3
FRANKLIN AV	YUBA	125	C4
FRANKLIN BLVD	SAC	39	E2
FRANKLIN BLVD	SCTO	137	D4
FRANKLIN RD	MCO	48	B4
FRANKLIN RD	SBD	84	C4
FRANKLIN RD	SUT	33	B2
FRANKLIN RD	SUT	125	A4
FRANKLIN ST	MDO	162	A4
FRANKLIN ST	MONT	167	D3
FRANKLIN ST	MON	53	E3
FRANKLIN ST	SF	142	C2
FRANKLIN ST	SF	143	A2

STREET	CO.	PAGE	GRID
FRANKLIN ST	SA	195	D4
FRANKLIN LEVEE	SUT	33	B2
FRANK SNATRA DR	RCO	100	D4
FRANKWOOD AV	FRCO	58	A4
FRASER RD	KER	78	C3
FRATES RD	SON	L	A1
FRATES RD	SON	38	A3
FRAZIER LN	MEN	23	B2
FRAZIER RD	FRCO	57	E1
FRAZIER RD	SJCO	40	C4
FRAZIER MTN RD	VEN	88	C2
FRAZR MTN PK RD	KER	88	C2
FRAZIER PK RD	SCL	54	D2
FRAZINE RD	STA	47	D2
FREDERICK AV	SJCO	47	B2
FREDERICK ST	RCO	99	C3
FREDERICKSBURG	ALP	36	C4
FREDERICKSON LN	CC	M	C3
FREDERICKSON RD	LAS	8	D5
FRED HAIGHT DR	DN	1	E3
FREDRICK ST	SF	141	E4
FREDRICKS RD	IMP	109	A4
FREEBORN RD	KER	78	A3
FREEDOM BLVD	SCR	54	B2
FREEMAN FLAT RD	MON	65	C2
FREEMN SCH HSE	TEH	24	C2
FREEMONT BLVD	ALA	P	B2
FREEPORT BLVD	SCTO	137	C4
FREITAS PKWY	MAR	38	B5
FREITAS RD	STA	47	C4
FREMONT AV	KER	79	E2
FREMONT AV	KIN	67	B1
FREMONT AV	LSAL	149	B2
FREMONT AV	LACO	R	B4
FREMONT AV	SCL	P	A3
FREMONT AV	SCL	45	E4
FREMONT AV	SVL	149	C2
FREMONT BLVD	ALA	46	A3
FREMONT DR	SON	L	B1
FREMONT RD	SBD	92	C1
FREMONT RD	SJCO	40	B5
FREMONT ST	CLK	74	D2
FREMONT ST	LV	209	D1
FREMONT ST	SBD	99	D2
FREMONT ST	SF	143	D3
FREMONT ST	S	160	A4
FREMONT PEAK RD	SBD	81	A4
FRENCH AV	BUT	33	C1
FRENCH RD	HUM	16	B5
FRENCH&SUGAR CK	SIS	11	D2
FRENCH BAR RD	AMA	40	E3
FRENCH CAMP RD	HUM	10	C3
FRENCH CAMP RD	SJCO	40	B5
FRENCH CAMP RD	SJCO	47	B1
FRENCH CREEK RD	BUT	25	E3
FRENCH CREEK RD	ED	40	D1
FRENCH CREEK RD	SIS	11	D2
FRENCH FLAT RD	TUO	41	B5
FRENCH GULCH RD	CAL	41	B4
FRENCH GULCH RD	SHA	18	A1
FRENCH HILL RD	DN	2	A3
FRENCHMAN LK RD	PLU	27	D2
FRENCHTOWN RD	YUB	26	A5
FRENZEN RD	COL	32	E3
FRESHWATER RD	COL	32	C2
FRESHWTR KNEELD	HUM	15	E1
FRESHWATER POOL	HUM	16	A1
FRESNO AV	KER	78	B2
FRESNO AV	KER	78	C2
FRESNO AV	SJCO	40	A5
FRESNO RD	MCO	48	D5
FRESNO ST	FRE	165	E2
FRESNO ST	FRCO	57	C3
FRESNO-COALINGA	FRCO	66	E1
FRESNO FLAT RD	MAD	49	D4
FRESZ RD	RCO	106	E1
FREWERT RD	SJCO	47	A1
FREY AV	KER	77	E2
FREY AV	KER	78	A2
FREY RANCH RD	BUT	26	B3
FRIANT RD	FRCO	57	C2
FRIANT RD	MAD	57	D2
FRIARS RD	SD	212	E4
FRIARS RD	SD	213	B4
FRIARS RD	SD	214	D2
FRIARS RD	SDCO	V	B3
FRIARS RD	SDCO	111	D1
FRICOT CITY RD	CAL	41	B4
FRIDAY RIDGE RD	HUM	10	C5
FRIEDRICH RD	TRI	16	E1
FRIEL RD	CLO	33	A3
FRINK RD	IMP	109	A2
FRISBY RD	SHA	19	A1
FRITZ DR	TUL	68	D1
FRONT ST	BUR	179	E2
FRONT ST	DN	1	D4
FRONT ST	LA	191	A2
FRONT ST	SAL	171	C4
FRONT ST	SF	143	D2
FRONT ST	SC	169	D3
FRONT ST	SOL	39	C4
FRONTAGE RD	CAL	41	A3
FRONTIER RD	SBD	91	C2
FRUCHTENICHT RD	COL	33	B3
FRUDDEN RD	MON	65	D4
FRUIT AV	FRE	165	B2
FRUIT AV	FRCO	57	C4
FRUIT AV	FRCO	57	C5
FRUIT AV	STA	47	B3
FRUITLAND AV	MCO	48	A4
FRUITLAND RD	YUB	33	D1
FRUITRIDGE RD	SAC	39	E1
FRUITRIDGE RD	SAC	40	A1

STREET	CO.	PAGE	GRID
FRUITVALE AV	ALA	L	D4
FRUITVALE AV	ALA	45	D1
FRUITVALE AV	KER	78	D3
FRUITVALE AV	O	158	E4
FRUITVALE AV	O	159	B1
FRUITVALE AV	SCL	P	A4
FRUITVALE RD	BUT	25	B4
FRUITVALE RD	PLA	34	B3
FRY RD	SOL	39	B2
FRYMIRE RD	STA	48	A1
FUENTE ST	ORCO	T	C1
FUERTE DR	SDCO	V	E3
FUERTE DR	SDCO	111	E1
FUGLER RD	SB	86	C1
FULKERTH RD	STA	47	C3
FULLEN RD	CAL	41	C3
FULLER LN	AMA	40	E3
FULLER RD	INY	59	E1
FULLERTON RD	LACO	98	B2
FULLERTON RD	LACO	R	E5
FULMOR RD	HUM	15	D2
FULMOR TOPPEN	HUM	15	D2
FULTON AV	SAC	40	A1
FULTON LN	NAPA	29	C2
FULTON RD	SON	37	E2
FULTON ST	SF	141	B4
FULTON ST	SF	142	A3
FULTON ST	SFCO	L	B5
FULTON ST	SFCO	45	B1
FULTON ST	S	160	B2
FULTON ST N	FRE	165	C3
FULWEILER AV	AUB	126	B3
FURLONG AV	SCL	54	D2
FURNACE CK RD	SBD	91	E4
FURNC CK WSH RD	INY	72	C2
FURNC CK WSH RD	INY	73	A4
FUZZY LN	SHA	18	C3
G			
G ST	DVS	136	D3
G ST	FRE	165	C4
G ST	HUM	9	E5
G ST	HUM	10	A5
G ST	SBDO	207	C3
G ST	SD	215	D3
G ST	MER	170	D4
G ST	MCO	48	C4
G ST	MCO	48	C4
G ST	ONT	203	E4
G ST	ONT	204	C4
G ST	SCTO	137	C2
GABY AV	COL	32	E3
GADDINI	SOL	39	A1
GADING RD	H	146	E4
GAFFERY RD	STA	47	A3
GAFFEY ST	LA	191	A4
GAFFEY ST	LACO	S	C3
GAFFNEY RD	YOL	39	D2
GAGE AV	LACO	Q	E5
GAGE RD	BUT	25	C4
GAINES LN	SHA	18	D3
GALE AV	FRCO	66	C2
GALE RD	SBD	91	E2
GALENA ST	RCO	99	A2
GALENA CYN RD	INY	72	A3
GALEPPI RD	LAS	21	C4
GALLAGHER AV	TEH	24	D2
GALLAGHER RD	SUT	33	E3
GALLATIN RD	LAS	20	D2
GALLATIN RD	TEH	24	C1
GALLAWAY RD	SIE	26	D4
GALLOPADE TR	SBD	80	E1
GALVEZ AV	FRCO	56	B2
GAMBLE RD	MCO	48	B3
GAMMA GULCH RD	SBD	100	D1
GAMMEL RD	SBD	101	C1
GANESHA BLVD	LACO	U	B2
GANGER RD	SIS	5	D2
GANN RD	CAL	40	E4
GAP FOLSOM RD	CAL	41	C2
GARAPATOS RD	MON	64	B1
GARATE RD	LAS	8	C5
GARBAGE DUMP RD	LAS	14	B3
GARBAGE PIT RD	MNO	43	B3
GARBAGE PIT RD	MNO	50	D1
GARBONI RD	RCO	99	D4
GARCES HWY	KER	67	E5
GARCES HWY	KER	68	C5
GARCES HWY	KER	69	A5
GARCIA RIVER RD	MEN	30	C3
GARDEN DR	LAK	31	D2
GARDEN HWY	SAC	39	D1
GARDEN HWY	SUT	33	D2
GARDEN HWY	SUT	125	D5
GARDEN HWY	YUBA	125	E4
GARDEN RD	SDCO	106	E4
GARDEN ST	STB	174	B2
GARDENA BLVD	LACO	S	C1
GARDEN BAR RD	PLA	34	B3
GARDEN BAR RD	NEV	34	B2
GARDENDALE ST	LACO	R	B5
GARDENDALE ST	LACO	S	E1
GARDEN GROVE BL	GGR	195	D2
GARDEN GROVE BL	ORCO	98	B4
GARDEN GROVE BL	ORCO	T	C2
GARDEN GROVE FY	GGR	195	C2
GARDEN GROVE FY	ORA	196	B1
GARDEN GROVE FY	ORCO	98	B4
GARDEN GROVE FY	ORCO	T	C3
GARDEN TRACT RD	CC	L	C3
GARDEN VLY RD	ED	34	D4
GARDEN VLY RD	YUB	26	B5

STREET	CO.	PAGE	GRID
GARDINER FRY RD	TEH	24	E2
GARDNER AV	MCO	48	C4
GARDNER LN	CAL	41	B4
GARDNER ST	LA	184	A1
GARDNER ST	VAL	134	B2
GARDNER FLD RD	KER	78	A4
GAREY AV	LACO	98	D2
GAREY AV	LACO	U	C3
GAREY AV	SB	86	C1
GARFIELD AV	FRCO	57	B3
GARFIELD AV	FRCO	57	B5
GARFIELD AV	LACO	98	A2
GARFIELD AV	LACO	R	B5
GARFIELD AV	LACO	S	D1
GARFIELD AV	ORCO	98	B4
GARFIELD AV	ORCO	T	B3
GARFIELD AV	SAC	34	A5
GARFIELD ST	RCO	101	C5
GARIN RD	MON	54	C2
GARLAND RD	BUT	25	C2
GARLOCK RD	KER	80	D2
GARMIRE RD	SUT	33	B2
GARNER LN	BUT	25	A2
GARNER PL	CAL	40	C4
GARNER RD	STA	47	D2
GARNET AV	SD	212	A2
GARNET AV	SDCO	V	A2
GARNET AV	SDCO	106	C5
GARNET ST	SBD	99	D2
GARNETT LN	SOL	39	D2
GARNIER RD	LAS	21	D5
GARRARD	CC	38	C5
GARRET	PLA	34	D2
GARRETT DR	RCO	100	A5
GARRISON AV	STA	47	C2
GARST RD	IMP	109	A3
GARST RD	STA	47	D2
GARVEY AV	LACO	98	A2
GARVEY AV	LACO	R	C4
GARVEY RD	IMP	108	E4
GARWOOD RD	SUT	33	D4
GARZOLI AV	KER	78	B1
GAS COMPANY RD	KER	78	A4
GASKELL RD	KER	89	B2
GASKELL RD	KER	89	D1
GAS LINE RD	RCO	102	B5
GASPERS RD	SHA	18	D2
GAS POINT RD	SHA	18	B3
GASQUET FLAT RD	DN	2	A3
GASTENBIDE RD	MCO	55	C2
GASTON RD	NEV	26	E5
GATES RD	STA	47	B2
GATES RD	TRI	16	D1
GATES CANYON RD	SOL	38	E2
GATEWAY	CC	39	D5
GATEWAY BLVD	LA	180	C4
GATEWAY BLVD	KER	80	E1
GATEWAY RD	CC	M	D3
GATOS TR	SBD	100	E1
GAVILAN DR	RCO	99	B3
GAVILAN RD	SDCO	106	C1
GAVIOTA	AVLN	97	A4
GAVIOTA BCH RD	SB	86	D4
GAVIOTA STA RD	SB	86	D4
GAWNE CARTER RD	SJCO	40	C5
GAWNE CARTER RD	SJCO	47	C1
GAYLEY AV	LA	180	C1
GAZELLE CALLAHN	SIS	4	B5
GAZELLE CALLAHN	SIS	11	E2
GAZELLE CALLAHN	SIS	12	A1
GAZELLE MTN LKT	SIS	12	A1
GAZOS CREEK RD	SMCO	N	C4
GAZOS CREEK RD	SMCO	45	C5
G-BAR-T RCH RD	MNO	44	C5
G-BAR-T RCH RD	MNO	51	C1
GEARY BLVD	SF	141	A3
GEARY BLVD	SF	142	D3
GEARY BLVD	SFCO	L	B4
GEARY BLVD	SFCO	45	B1
GEARY RD	CC	L	E3
GEARY RD	CC	M	A3
GEARY RD	CC	38	E5
GEARY ST	SF	143	C3
GECKO RD	IMP	109	D4
GEER AV	MCO	47	D4
GEER RD	STA	47	E3
GELDING RD	CAL	41	B4
GENASCI RD	SIE	27	C3
GENE AUTRY TR	PMSP	206	E2
GENERL BEALE RD	KER	79	A3
GENRL PETROLEUM	KER	79	E5
GENRL PETROLEUM	KER	80	A5
GENRL PETROLEUM	KER	89	C1
GENERALS HWY	TUL	58	E3
GENERALS HWY	TUL	59	A5
GENESEE AV	SD	211	E1
GENESEE AV	SD	213	C1
GENESEE AV	SDCO	V	B2
GENESEE AV	SDCO	106	C5
GENESEE RD	PLU	26	D1
GENESEE INDN CK	PLU	26	E1
GENESEO RD	SLO	76	B1
GENEVA AV	KIN	67	C1
GENOA LN	DGL	36	C3
GENTRY RD	IMP	109	A3
GENTRY RD	INY	72	E4
GENTRY RD	INY	73	A4
GEORGE RD	IMP	112	A4
GEORGE SMITH RD	FRCO	58	B3
GEORGETOWN	ED	34	E3
GEORGETOWN RD	ED	34	E4
GEO WSHNTN BL S	SUT	33	C3
GEORGIA LN	STA	47	E2

STREET	CO.	PAGE	GRID
GEORGIA RD	SBD	81	C5
GEORGIA ST	VAL	134	D4
GEORGIA ST	SOL	L	D2
GEORGIA SLID RD	ED	34	E3
GEPHART RD	KER	80	D5
GERARD AV	MCO	48	C4
GERBER RD	SAC	40	A2
GERBER RD	TEH	24	D1
GERKIN RD	INY	51	D4
GERRIE LN	RCO	107	C1
GETTYSBURG AV	FRCO	56	C3
GETTYSBURG AV	FRCO	57	A3
GEYSERS RD	SON	31	C4
GEYSRS RESRT RD	SON	31	D4
GHOST TOWN RD	SBD	92	A1
GIANT RD	CC	L	C3
GIANT ROCK RD	SBD	92	E5
GIANT ROCK RD	SBD	93	A5
GIBRALTAR RD	SB	87	C3
GIBSON RD	COL	32	D2
GIBSON RD	YOL	33	B5
GIBSON CYN RD	SOL	39	A2
GIDDINGS AV	TUL	68	B1
GIELOW LN	MEN	31	B2
GIFFORD RD	SUT	33	C4
GILBERT RD	STA	47	D1
GILLAM RD	CAL	40	E3
GILLESPIE RD	IMP	109	A2
GILLESPIE ST	STB	174	A3
GILLETT RD	IMP	109	B5
GILLETT RD	MON	65	C4
GILLETTE RD	KER	79	D3
GILLETTE RD	MCO	48	D5
GILLILAND RD	LAS	8	C5
GILLIS CYN RD	SLO	76	D1
GILLMAN AV	KER	89	D1
GILL RANCH RD	PLU	26	E2
GILL STA COSO	INY	70	C3
GILMAN DR	SD	211	C1
GILMAN DR	SDCO	V	A2
GILMAN DR	SDCO	106	C5
GILMAN RD	SCL	54	D2
GILMAN RD	SHA	12	D4
GILMAN SPGS RD	RCO	99	D3
GILMORE	SJCO	40	C4
GILMORE RCH RD	TEH	18	D5
GILROY HT SP RD	SCL	54	D1
GIRARD LO RD	SHA	12	C3
GIRARD LOOKOUT	SHA	12	C3
GIRARD RIDGE RD	SHA	12	C4
GIRAUDO RD	KER	79	B4
GIRD RD	SDCO	106	C2
GIRDNER RD	SUT	33	B2
GIRVAN RD	SHA	18	C2
GIVENS LUSTR RD	MCO	48	C5
GLACIER LODG RD	INY	51	D5
GLACIER PT RD	MPA	49	D2
GLACIER PT RD	MPA	63	C5
GLADDING RD	PLA	34	A3
GLADSTONE ST	LACO	U	A2
GLASSCOCK RD	SJCO	39	D4
GLASSELL ST	ORA	194	C5
GLASSELL ST	ORA	196	C1
GLASSELL ST	ORCO	98	C3
GLASSELL ST	ORCO	T	D2
GLASS FLOW RD	MNO	50	D1
GLEASON RD	SBD	92	D5
GLEN AV	MER	170	E4
GLEN RD	SB	87	B4
GLEN ALPINE RD	ED	35	E4
GLEN ANNIE RD	SB	87	B4
GLEN ARBOR RD	SCR	N	E5
GLEN ARBOR RD	SCR	P	A5
GLEN ARBOR RD	SCR	53	E1
GLENBURN RD	SHA	13	D4
GLEN CANYON RD	SCR	54	A1
GLENCO AV	GLE	24	D3
GLENCOE AV	LA	187	D3
GLENDALE AV	LACO	97	E1
GLENDALE AV	LACO	Q	E3
GLENDALE BLVD	LA	182	E3
GLENDALE BLVD	LA	185	E2
GLENDALE BLVD	LACO	Q	E3
GLENDALE DR	HUM	10	A5
GLENDALE FRWY	LACO	R	A3
GLENDORA AV	LACO	98	B2
GLENDORA AV	LACO	U	A2
GLENDORA MTN RD	LACO	98	C1
GLENDORA MTN RD	LACO	U	A1
GLENISON GAP RD	TRI	17	C1
GLENN AV	FRCO	66	E3
GLENN DR	GLE	24	A4
GLENN RD	TEH	24	C2
GLENN RD E	COL	25	A5
GLENN RD W	COL	24	D5
GLENN-ALLEN AV	KER	68	D5
GLENN COOLDG DR	SC	169	A2
GLENN COOLDG DR	SCR	169	A2
GLENNDENNING RD	SIS	3	D5
GLENNEYRE	LAG	201	B2
GLENN M ANDERSN			
-FWY & TRANSIT	LACO	Q	C5
GLENOAKS BLVD	BUR	179	C1
GLENOAKS BLVD	LACO	89	D5
GLENOAKS BLVD	LACO	97	D1
GLENOAKS BLVD	LACO	Q	C1
GLENOAKS RD	RCO	99	D5
GLENSHIRE DR	NEV	27	D5
GLENWOOD DR	SCR	54	A1
GLENWOOD LN	FRCO	58	B1
GLOBE DR	TUL	69	A3
GLOBE MINE RD	SBD	84	A5
GLORIA RD	MON	54	E5

STREET	CO.	PAGE	GRID
GLORIA RD	MON	55	A5
GLORIETTA BLVD	CC	L	E4
GLORIETTA BLVD	CC	45	D1
GLORIETTA BLVD	COR	215	D5
G-O RD	DN	2	B4
GOAT MTN RD	COL	32	A1
GOAT MTN RD	SBD	100	E1
GOBBI ST	U	123	C4
GOBLE LN	HUM	15	D2
GODDELL RD	CAL	40	E3
GODFREY AV	SCL	P	E5
GODFREY RCH RD	SLO	75	E1
GODLEY RD	PLA	34	B3
GODWIN RD	SBD	101	C1
GOETZ RD	RCO	99	C4
GOFFS RD	SBD	94	D2
GOFFS RD	SBD	95	A1
GOGNA	SJCO	40	B5
GOLD CROWN RD	RCO	101	E2
GOLD CROWN RD	SBD	101	E1
GOLDEN AV	SBD	99	C1
GOLDEN RD	SIS	5	D2
GOLDEN ST	SBD	100	E1
GOLDEN CYN RD	INY	72	A1
GOLDEN CTR FRWY	GV	127	D3
GOLDEN CTR FRWY	NEV	128	A4
GOLDEN EAGLE AV	PLU	26	C1
GOLDEN GATE AV	SF	142	A3
GOLDEN GATE DR	HUM	16	B3
GOLDEN GATE RD	MNO	42	D1
GOLDENROD AV	FRCO	57	A4
GOLDEN SPGS DR	LACO	U	B3
GOLDEN STATE AV	BKD	166	C2
GOLDEN STATE BL	FRCO	57	E5
GOLDEN STATE BL	STA	47	D3
GOLDEN STATE DR	MAD	57	A2
GOLDEN STATE FY	BUR	179	B1
GOLDEN STATE FY	LA	182	D1
GOLDEN STATE FY	LACO	89	B4
GOLDEN STATE FY	LACO	97	D1
GOLDEN STATE FY	LACO	Q	B1
GOLDN TROUT CRS	BUT	26	B4
GOLDENWEST AV	ORCO	98	B4
GOLDEN WEST ST	ORCO	T	B3
GOLD HILL RD	ED	34	D4
GOLDHILL RD	PLA	34	B3
GOLD HILL RD	SOL	38	D4
GOLD HILL RD	VEN	88	D2
GOLD LAKE RD	PLU	27	A3
GOLD LAKE RD	SIE	27	A3
GOLD LK FOREST	PLU	26	E3
GOLD PARK	SBD	101	C2
GOLD RCK RCH RD	IMP	110	B5
GOLD RUN RD	LAS	20	E3
GOLDRUSH RD	RCO	107	B1
GOLDSBOROUGH GL	SHA	17	D3
GOLD STONE LN	SHA	18	B2
GOLDSTONE RD	SBD	81	E3
GOLD STRIKE RD	CAL	41	A3
GOLER RD	KER	80	E2
GOLF RD	MCO	48	C4
GOLF CLUB RD	CC	L	E3
GOLF CLUB RD	CC	M	A3
GOLF COURSE RD	HUM	10	A5
GOLF LINK RD	MCO	47	E4
GOLF LINKS RD	AVLN	97	B5
GOLF LINKS RD	ALA	L	E5
GOLF LINKS RD	ALA	45	E1
GOMAN AV	TUL	70	A3
GOMER AV	KER	78	A1
GOMEZ RD	SHA	13	D4
GONDER RD	IMP	109	B4
GONSALVES RD	TEH	18	C5
GONZAGA RD	MCO	55	C1
GONZALES RD	MCO	55	C2
GONZALES RD	OXN	176	B2
GONZALES RD	VEN	88	B5
GONZALES RD	VEN	96	B1
GONZALES RIV RD	MON	54	E5
GOODALE RD	INY	59	E2
GOODE HILL RD	LACO	89	E3
GOODENOUGH RD	VEN	88	D4
GOODFELLOW AV	FRCO	57	E4
GOODWATER AV	SHA	18	C2
GOODWIN DR	SBD	91	A4
GOODWIN RD	STA	47	D2
GOODYEAR RD	SOL	38	E4
GOODYEAR CK RD	SIE	26	D4
GOOLSBY RCH RD	MNO	51	C1
GOOSE CREEK RD	AMA	40	C3
GOOSE HAVEN RD	SOL	39	B3
GOOSE RANCH RD	TRI	17	D1
GOOSE VALLEY RD	SHA	13	C4
GOPHER CYN RD	SDCO	106	C2
GOPHR HLL LNDFL	PLU	26	C1
GORDEN RD	HUM	16	C2
GORDONS FRRY RD	SIS	3	A3
GORDON VLY RD	NAPA	38	C3
GORDON VLY RD	SOL	L	E1
GORDON VLY RD	SOL	38	E3
GORGE RD	INY	51	C3
GORMAN RANCH	PLA	34	E3
GOSFORD RD	KER	78	C3
GOSS RD	SBD	90	E4
GOUDIE TRUCK TR	SDCO	107	C5
GOUGER NECK RD	MOD	14	B3
GOUGH ST	SF	142	B2
GOUGH ST	SF	143	A2
GOULD AV	LACO	S	B1
GOULD RD	COL	32	E1
GOULD RD	LPAZ	104	A2
GOVE RD	MCO	48	B5
GOVER RD	SHA	18	D3

STREET	CO.	PAGE	GRID
GOVERNOR DR	SD	211	D2
GOVERNOR DR	SDCO	V	B2
GOVERNOR DR	SDCO	106	C5
GOVERNOR MN RD	LACO	89	E4
GOWER ST	LA	181	D5
GOWLING RD	IMP	109	B5
G P RD	KER	77	C1
GRACE RESORT RD	SHA	19	B3
GRACIE RD	NEV	34	C1
GRACIOSA RD	SB	86	C2
GRAEAGLE RD	SIE	26	E3
GRAEAGLE RD	SIE	27	A3
GRAEAGL JHNSVLL	PLU	26	E2
GRAESER RD	IMP	112	C3
GRAHAM	SIS	12	C1
GRAHAM AV	RCO	99	B4
GRAHAM RD	FRCO	57	A4
GRAHAM RD	IMP	111	E3
GRAHAM RD	SJCO	40	B3
GRAHAM RD	TEH	19	B3
GRAHAM HILL RD	SC	169	D1
GRAHAM HILL RD	SCR	54	A1
GRAHAM HILL RD	SCR	169	D1
GRAHAM PASS RD	RCO	109	E1
GRAINLAND RD	BUT	25	A4
GRAMERCY DR	SD	214	B1
GRAMERCY DR	SDCO	V	C2
GRAMERCY DR	SDCO	111	D1
GRANADA AV	SAL	171	D2
GRAND AV	ALA	L	D4
GRAND AV	BUT	25	C4
GRAND AV	ELS	189	B3
GRAND AV	LA	185	E1
GRAND AV	LACO	97	E2
GRAND AV	LACO	98	C2
GRAND AV	LACO	Q	C5
GRAND AV	LACO	U	A2
GRAND AV	LACO	S	A1
GRAND AV	O	158	A2
GRAND AV	ORCO	98	C4
GRAND AV	ORCO	T	D3
GRAND AV	P	158	C2
GRAND AV	RCO	99	D4
GRAND AV	RCO	99	B4
GRAND AV	RCO	99	E4
GRAND AV	SA	196	C4
GRAND AV	SA	198	C1
GRAND AV	SD	212	B2
GRAND AV	SDCO	V	A3
GRAND AV	SNLO	172	D1
GRAND AV	SLO	76	B4
GRAND AV	SMCO	L	B5
GRAND AV	SMCO	N	B1
GRAND AV	SMCO	45	C2
GRAND AV	SR	139	D3
GRAND AV	SB	86	E3
GRAND AV	TUL	68	D3
GRAND AV	VEN	88	D4
GRAND AV	YUB	33	D2
GRAND AV E	SSF	144	D1
GRAND AV W	O	157	D2
GRAND BLVD	LA	187	A3
GRAND ST	H	146	D2
GRAND ST	MDO	162	C3
GRAND CIRCLE BL	RCO	U	E5
GRANDE PUMICE	MOD	8	A1
GRANDE VISTA S	LA	186	E5
GRAND ISLAND RD	SAC	M	E1
GRAND ISLAND RD	SAC	39	C4
GRANDON RD	RCO	107	C1
GRAND VIEW AV	LACO	R	C2
GRANDVILLE RD	MCO	56	B2
GRANGE RD	LAK	32	B4
GRANGE RD	SOL	M	A1
GRANGE RD	SON	38	A2
GRANGE RD	TEH	24	D2
GRANGER CK RD	MOD	8	D1
GRANGEVILLE BL	KIN	67	C1
GRANGEVLLE BYPS	KIN	67	B1
GRANITE RD	KER	78	D1
GRANITE RD	KER	79	A1
GRANITE RD	MAD	49	B5
GRANITE RD	SBD	92	A4
GRANITE CK RD	SCR	54	A2
GRNIT MTN VW RD	SDCO	107	D3
GRANITE SPGS RD	MPA	48	D2
GRANITE VIEW RD	INY	60	A4
GRANITEVILLE RD	NEV	27	A4
GRANIT WELLS RD	SBD	81	A3
GRANT AV	COL	32	E3
GRANT RD	LSAL	149	A2
GRANT RD	MCO	56	C1
GRANT RD	MVW	148	A5
GRANT RD	SCL	N	E3
GRANT RD	SCL	P	A3
GRANT RD	SCL	45	E4
GRANT ST	RCO	101	C5
GRANT LAKE RD	MNO	50	C1
GRANTLAND AV	FRCO	57	B2
GRANTLAND AV	FRCO	67	B1
GRANT LINE RD	SAC	40	A2
GRANT LINE RD	SJCO	47	A2
GRAPE WY	BUT	25	A3
GRAPEFRUIT BLVD	RCO	101	B4
GRAPEVNE CYN RD	KER	70	C5
GRAPEVNE CYN RD	SBD	91	D5
GRAPEVINE GULCH	AMA	40	D3
GRAPP LN	RCO	107	C1
GRASS RD	SBD	100	A1
GRASSHOPPR RD S	LAS	13	A5
GRASSHOPPR RD S	LAS	14	E5
GRASSHOPPER FLT	TRI	11	C5
GRASS VALLEY RD	SBT	54	E3

STREET	CO.	PAGE	GRID
GRASS VALLEY RD	SBT	55	A3
GRATON RD	SON	37	D2
GRATTON RD	STA	47	E3
GRAVEL PIT RD	RCO	103	C5
GRAVEN RES RD	MOD	8	A2
GRAVEN RES RD	MOD	14	E2
GRAVES RD	SJCO	47	B1
GRAVEYARD GULCH	SIS	3	C4
GRAY AV	YUBA	125	C2
GRAYSON	CC	38	E5
GRAYSON RD	STA	47	B3
GREAT HWY	SFCO	L	B5
GREAT HWY	SFCO	45	B2
GREAT CIR DR	KER	80	B4
GREAT NORTHERN	MOD	5	E3
GREAT SO OVRLND	SDCO	108	A5
GREELEY RD	KER	78	C3
GREELY HILL RD	MPA	48	E1
GREELY HILL RD	MPA	49	A1
GREEN RD	COL	32	D3
GREEN RD	IMP	109	C4
GREEN RD	SAC	40	B2
GREEN RD	SBD	90	D4
GREEN ST	PAS	190	C4
GREENBACK LN	SAC	34	B5
GREENBAY RD	COL	32	E3
GREENFIELD AV	VAL	134	D3
GREENFIELD DR	SDCO	107	A5
GREEN HILL RD	SON	37	D2
GREENHORN RD	NEV	34	C1
GREENHORN RD	SIS	4	A4
GREEN HOUSE RD	MCO	47	E5
GREEN HOUSE RD	MCO	48	A5
GREEN LAKES RD	MNO	43	B4
GREENLEAF AV	LACO	R	C5
GREENLEY RD	TUO	41	C5
GREENLEY RD	TUO	163	D3
GREEN MTN RD	MAD	49	B5
GREEN MTN LKOUT	MPA	49	B5
GREEN RIVER RD	RCO	U	D5
GREEN RIVER RD	RCO	98	D3
GREENSPOT RD	SBD	99	C1
GREENSPOT RD	SBD	99	D2
GREEN SPRING RD	TUO	48	B1
GREENSTONE	ED	34	D5
GREENS WELL RD	SBD	84	A1
GREENTREE BLVD	SBD	91	B4
GREEN VALLEY RD	CC	M	B4
GREEN VALLEY RD	CC	46	A1
GREEN VALLEY RD	ED	34	D5
GREEN VALLEY RD	ED	34	C5
GREEN VALLEY RD	SAC	34	C5
GREEN VALLEY RD	SCR	54	B2
GREEN VALLEY RD	SOL	L	E1
GREEN VALLEY RD	SOL	38	D3
GREEN VALLEY RD	SON	37	D2
GREENVILLE RD	ALA	46	C2
GREENVILLE ST	ORCO	T	C3
GREENVILLE-			
-ROUND VLY RD	PLU	20	C5
GRNVL WOLF CK RD	PLU	20	C5
GREENWALD AV	RCO	99	B4
GREENWOOD AV	FRCO	57	E4
GREENWOOD AV	LACO	R	B4
GREENWOOD RD	ED	34	D4
GREENWOOD RD	SJCO	47	A2
GREENWD HTS DR	HUM	10	A5
GREEN, W S RD	COL	32	E2
GREGORY AV	YOL	39	D1
GREGORY RD	CAL	40	D4
GREGORY CK RD	SHA	12	C5
GREILICH RD	AMA	40	D2
GREVIE RD	COL	33	A3
GREY OWL CT	NEV	127	B1
GRIDER RD	SIS	3	B3
GRIDER CREEK RD	SIS	3	B4
GRIDLEY RD	COL	25	A5
GRIFFIN AV	LA	186	D1
GRIFFIN RD	IMP	109	B4
GRIFFIN RD	STA	47	C2
GRIFFIN ST	SAL	171	D3
GRIFFITH AV	KER	78	B2
GRIFFITH AV	MCO	47	E4
GRIFFITH AV	YUB	33	D2
GRIFFITH PK DR	LA	182	D2
GRIFFITH PK DR	LACO	Q	E3
GRIMES AV	STA	47	C2
GRIMES RD	SJCO	46	E1
GRIMES-ARBKL RD	CLU	32	E3
GRIMES CYN RD	VEN	88	D5
GRIMSEL DR	KER	79	C5
GRINDSTONE RD	GLE	23	E3
GRINDSTONE RD	GLE	24	A3
GRIZZLY RD	PLU	27	B2
GRIZZLY RD	TUO	48	D1
GRIZZLY BLUF RD	HUM	15	D2
GRIZZLY GLCH RD	SHA	18	A2
GRIZZLY HLL RD N	NEV	26	C5
GRIZZLY ISLD RD	SOL	M	A1
GRIZZLY ISLD RD	SOL	38	E3
GRIZZLY ISLD RD	SOL	39	A3
GRIZZLY PEAK BL	O	156	C2
GRZZLY PK LKOUT	SIS	13	B3
GROOMS	SJCO	47	D1
GROSJEAN	MPA	49	B3
GROTTO CANYON	INY	61	D4
GROUSE CREEK RD	SIS	11	E2
GROUSE RIDGE RD	NEV	27	A5
GROVE AV	GLE	24	D3
GROVE AV	MCO	48	B4
GROVE AV	ONT	204	D3
GROVE AV	ROC	204	D2
GROVE AV	SBD	U	D3
GROVE AV	SBD	98	E2
GROVE AV	U	123	B3
GROVE RD	SUT	33	D3
GROVE ST	ALA	M	A5
GROVE ST	SON	132	A3
GROVE WY	ALA	L	E5
GROVE WY	ALA	P	A1
GROVE WY	ALCO	146	E1
GROVE SHFTR FWY	O	157	E2
GROVE SHFTR FWY	O	158	A1
GRUB GULCH RD	MAD	49	B5
GRUBBS RD	BUT	25	D5
GSCHWEND RD	MEN	30	D2
GUADALUPE FRWY	SJ	152	A3
GUADALUPE PKWY	SJ	151	E1
GUADALUPE ST	SB	86	A1
GUALALA LOOKOUT	MEN	30	D4
GUALALA RDG RD	MEN	30	E1
GUERNEVILLE HWY	SON	37	C1
GUERNEVILLE RD	STR	131	A2
GUERNEVILLE RD	SON	37	E2
GUERRERO ST	SF	142	C5
GUERRERO ST	SFCO	L	B5
GUERRERO ST	SFCO	45	C2
GUIBAL AV	SCL	P	E5
GUIBERSON RD	VEN	88	D4
GUIDIVILLE RES	MEN	31	B2
GUINTOLI LN	HUM	9	E5
GULCH RD	TRI	17	B3
GULLETT RD	IMP	109	A5
GULLEY VIEW DR	RCO	107	C1
GULLING ST N	PLU	27	B2
GULLING ST S	PLU	27	B2
GUM AV	GLE	25	A4
GUN CLUB RD	KER	77	E2
GUN CLUB RD	MCO	47	D5
GUNN AV	LACO	R	C5
GUNST RD	HUM	9	E2
GUNST RD	HUM	10	A2
GURR RD	MCO	48	B5
GUTHERIE RD	IMP	108	E5
GUTIERREZ ST	STB	174	D3
GUTTRY RD	LAS	14	B3
GUY KERR RCH RD	HUM	10	C5
GUYS GULCH RD	SIS	4	A5
GWIN MINE RD	CAL	40	E3
GYLE RD	TEH	24	D1
GYPSUM CYN RD	ORCO	U	C5
GYPSUM CYN RD	ORCO	98	D3
H			
H ST	BKD	166	C4
H ST	BEN	153	C5
H ST	EUR	121	D1
H ST	FRE	165	B3
H ST	IMP	109	A4
H ST	KER	78	D3
H ST	MCO	55	D1
H ST	OXN	176	B3
H ST	SCTO	137	C2
H ST	SAC	39	E1
H ST	SBD	91	D1
H ST	SDCO	V	C4
H ST	SDCO	106	B4
H ST	SDCO	111	D2
H ST	SR	139	C4
H ST	SB	86	B3
H ST N	SBDO	207	C2
HAAS RD	COL	32	D2
HACIENDA AV	RCO	100	D2
HACIENDA BLVD	LACO	98	B2
HACIENDA BLVD	LACO	R	D5
HACIENDA BLVD	KER	80	B4
HACIENDA RD	SHA	18	D3
HACKAMORE PL	MNO	43	A3
HACKETT RD	STA	47	C3
HACKLEMAN RD	IMP	109	A5
HACKMAN RD	SOL	39	C2
HACKNEY DR	MNO	42	E1
HACKSTAFF RD	LAS	21	E5
HAGATA RD	LAS	21	A2
HAGEMAN RD	KER	78	C3
HAGEMAN RD	SUT	33	B2
HAGEN RD	NAPA	38	D3
HAGEN RD	NAPA	133	E2
HAGEN FLAT RD	SHA	13	A4
HAHN RD	COL	32	D3
HAIGHT MTN RD	SIS	5	A5
HAILES RD	VEN	96	C1
HAILLE RD	TEH	25	A2
HALE AV	COL	32	E3
HALE AV	SCL	P	D4
HALE RD	AMA	41	A1
HALEY RD	IMP	109	C3
HALEY RD	MCO	47	C5
HALEY ST	STB	174	C4
HLF MOON BAY RD	SMCO	45	C3
HALFWAY RD	SDCO	107	B2
HALL AV	SJCO	47	D1
HALL RD	LAS	27	E1
HALL RD	MON	54	C3
HALL RD	SON	37	E2
HALL RD	STA	47	E3
HALL RD	STA	48	A2
HALL RD	TEH	24	D2
HALL RD	VEN	88	D4
HALL WY	SHA	19	E2
HALL CITY CK RD	TRI	17	C3
HALLEY RD	SOL	39	A2
HALLOCK	VEN	88	C5
HALLORAN SPG RD	SBD	83	B3
HALLORAN SUMMIT	SBD	83	D2
HALLOWELL RD	STA	47	C4
HALLS FLAT RD	LAS	20	A2
HALLS GRADE RD	RCO	100	B3
HALLWOOD BLVD	YUB	33	D2
HALLWOOD BLVD W	YUB	33	D2
HALSTEAD	SBD	81	C5
HAM LN	SJCO	40	A4
HAMBONE RD	SIS	13	C2
HAMBURG RD	MCO	55	E2
HAMES RD	SCR	54	B2
HAMILTON	ORCO	98	B4
HAMILTON	YOL	39	D2
HAMILTON AV	ORCO	T	B4
HAMILTON AV	SCL	P	B3
HAMILTON AV	SCL	46	E1
HAMILTON AV	TEH	24	D1
HAMILTON RD	DN	1	E4
HAMILTON RD	KER	89	D1
HAMILTON RD	STA	47	B3
HAMILTON RD E	BUT	25	C5
HAMILTON RD W	BUT	25	C5
HAMLTN NORD CNA	BUT	25	A3
HAMLIN RD	BUT	25	C3
HAMLIN GULCH RD	SIS	3	E5
HAMLOW RD	STA	47	E3
HAMMER LN	SJCO	40	A5
HAMMER LOOP RD	TEH	18	A5
HAMMETT RD	STA	47	C2
HAMMIL RD	MNO	51	D2
HAMMONTON RD	YUB	33	E2
HAMMNTN SMRTVLL	YUB	33	E2
HAMNER AV	RCO	U	E4
HAMNER AV	RCO	98	E3
HAMPTON RD	CC	L	D3
HANAUPAH CYN RD	INY	72	A2
HANAWALT AV	KER	78	A1
HANCOCK RD	SBD	84	C4
HANEY VIEW DR	SHA	13	E4
HANFORD ARMONA	KIN	67	C1
HANKINS RD	COL	32	D2
HANKS RD	MOD	7	D4
HANSEN	FRCO	58	B4
HANSEN AV	RCO	99	D3
HANSEN RD	LAS	21	B1
HANSEN RD	SJCO	46	D2
HANSEN ST	SAL	171	E5
HAPGOOD RD	SB	86	C3
HAPPY TR	SBD	92	D5
HAPPY CAMP LKOT	MOD	14	B1
HAPPY CAMP RD	VEN	88	D5
HAPPY CAMP DUMP	SIS	3	A3
HAPPY CANYON RD	SB	87	A3
HAPPY GAP RD	TUL	58	D3
HAPPY VALLEY RD	ALA	P	B1
HAPPY VALLEY RD	CC	L	E4
HAPPY VALLEY RD	ED	35	A5
HAPPY VALLEY RD	SHA	18	C3
HARBERS LN	HUM	15	E2
HARBISON RD	COL	32	E1
HARBISON CYN RD	SDCO	107	A5
HARBOR	YOL	39	D1
HARBOR BLVD	ANA	193	B1
HARBOR BLVD	CM	197	B3
HARBOR BLVD	CM	199	B2
HARBOR BLVD	FTNV	197	B1
HARBOR BLVD	GGR	195	B2
HARBOR BLVD	LA	191	B3
HARBOR BLVD	LACO	S	C3
HARBOR BLVD	ORCO	98	B3
HARBOR BLVD	ORCO	T	C2
HARBOR BLVD	SMCO	N	D2
HARBOR BLVD	SA	195	B5
HARBOR BLVD	SA	197	B2
HARBOR BLVD	SMCO	145	D5
HARBOR BLVD	VENT	175	C3
HARBOR BLVD	VEN	96	B1
HARBOR BLVD	VEN	175	E4
HARBOR DR	IMP	108	C2
HARBOR DR	SD	215	D4
HARBOR DR	SD	216	A5
HARBOR DR	SDCO	V	B4
HARBOR DR N	SD	215	C3
HARBOR FRWY	LA	185	D5
HARBOR FRWY	LA	191	A2
HARBOR FRWY	LACO	97	D4
HARBOR FRWY	LACO	S	C2
HARBOR WY	R	155	A3
HARBOR BAY PKWY	A	159	A4
HARBOR SCNIC DR	LB	192	C3
HARDEN FLAT	TUO	49	B1
HARDER RD	ALA	N	E1
HARDER RD	ALA	P	A1
HARDER RD	ALA	45	E2
HARDER RD W	H	146	E4
HARDIN RD	NAPA	38	C1
HARDING AV	STA	47	D3
HARDING RD	MCO	47	E3
HARDING RD	MCO	48	A3
HARDING WY	SJCO	40	A5
HARDING WY	S	160	A4
HARDMAN AV	NAPA	38	D2
HARDRK DAVIS RD	SBD	91	B3
HARDY RD	IMP	111	E3
HARE CANYON RD	MON	65	E4
HARE CANYON RD	MON	66	A4
HARKINS	MON	54	C4
HARKINS RD	SAL	171	E5
HARKINS SLGH RD	SCR	54	B2
HARKNESS DR	PLU	20	A3
HARKNESS ST	NAP	133	A1
HARLAN AV	FRCO	66	D1
HARLAN AV	FRCO	57	C5
HARLAN RD	COL	32	C2
HARLAN MTN RD	SBT	54	E4
HARLAN MTN RD	SBT	55	A4
HARLEY LEIGHTON	SHA	18	C2
HARMON RD	MCO	56	B1
HARMON RD	TUL	67	E2
HARMONY GRVE RD	SDCO	106	C3
HARMONY VLY RD	SLO	75	C2
HARNEY	SJCO	40	A4
HARP RD	TEH	18	C3
HARPER LN	MCO	55	C2
HARPER LN	SOL	39	B2
HARPER RD	IMP	112	D5
HARPER LAKE RD	SBD	81	B5
HARPOLD RD	KLAM	5	D1
HARRIGAN RD	IMP	111	E3
HARRINGTON AV	COL	32	E3
HARRIS	MPA	49	C3
HARRIS RD	BUT	25	B4
HARRIS RD	HUM	16	D5
HARRIS RD	IMP	109	B5
HARRIS RD	MON	54	C4
HARRIS RD	SUT	33	C3
HARRIS ST	EUR	121	B3
HARRIS ST	HUM	9	E5
HARRIS ST	HUM	15	E1
HARRISON AV	HUM	9	E5
HARRISON AV	HUM	15	E1
HARRISON RD	TRI	17	B2
HARRISON ST	O	158	B1
HARRISON ST	RCO	101	B5
HARRISON ST	SF	142	D3
HARRISON ST	SF	143	D4
HARRISN GLCH RD	SHA	17	C3
HARRIS RANCH RD	MNO	51	D2
HARROD RD	SBD	92	A4
HARROLD RD	SJCO	47	D1
HARRY CASH RD	SIS	4	C4
HART AV	KER	68	C5
HART RD	IMP	109	C4
HART RD	SIS	4	C4
HART RD	STA	47	C2
HART FLAT RD	KER	79	B3
HARTLEY DR	BUT	25	C2
HARTMANN RD	LAK	32	B4
HART MINE RD	SBD	84	D3
HARTNELL	RED	122	E4
HARTNELL AV	SHA	18	C2
HART OAKS DR	KER	79	B3
HARTSHORN RD	IMP	109	C5
HARTS MEADOW	SIS	12	E1
HARTS MTN RD	SIS	4	E5
HARTVICKSON LN	CAL	40	E4
HARVARD AV	IRV	198	E5
HARVARD AV	ORCO	T	E3
HARVARD RD	SBD	92	C1
HARVARD MINE RD	TUO	41	C5
HARVEY RD	BUT	25	C2
HARVEY RD	SAC	40	A3
HARVEY RD	STA	47	C4
HARVEY RD 1	LAS	20	C1
HARVEY RD 2	LAS	20	C1
HARVEY RD 4	LAS	20	C1
HARVY MTN LO RD	LAS	20	C1
HARVY PETTIT RD	MCO	48	D5
HARVEY VLY RD	LAS	20	C1
HARWOOD RD	SCL	P	B4
HARWOOD RD	SCL	46	B5
HASKELL AV	LACO	Q	B2
HASKINS RD	SIS	5	D2
HASKINS VALLEY	BUT	26	A3
HASLEY CYN RD	LACO	89	A4
HASSLER RD	ED	34	E4
HASTAIN RD	IMP	109	B4
HASTE ST	B	156	A3
HASTER ST	ANA	193	C5
HASTER ST	GGR	195	C1
HASTER ST	ORCO	T	C2
HASTINGS DR	BEN	153	A2
HATCHET CK RD	TRI	11	E4
HAT CREEK PK RD	SHA	13	D4
HAT CK PWRHOUSE	SHA	13	D4
HAT CK PWRHS #2	SHA	13	D4
HATCH RD	BUT	25	B5
HATCH RD	MCO	48	C4
HATCH RD	STA	47	C2
HATCHET CK RD	NEV	34	B2
HATCHET CK RD	TRI	12	A4
HATHAWAY ST	RCO	100	A3
HAUSER BLVD	LA	184	A3
HAUSER BR RD	SON	37	A1
HAVASU LAKE RD	SBD	95	D4
HAVEN AV	SBD	U	E2
HAVEN AV	SBD	98	E2
HAVEN RD	SBD	80	E5
HAVENS RD	IMP	108	E5
HAVERFORD RD	SDCO	107	A4
HAVLINA ST	SIS	5	D2
HAWEE CANYON RD	INY	70	B2
HAWKEYE AV	STA	47	E3
HAWKINS RD	SOL	39	B2
HAWKINS RD	STA	48	A3
HAWKINS BAR RD	TRI	10	D5
HAWKNSVLLE HMBG	SIS	3	E3
HAWKNSVLLE HMBG	SIS	4	A4
HAWKS HILL RD	HUM	15	D2
HAWLEY GRADE	ED	36	A4
HAWTHORNE AV	C	124	D3
HAWTHORNE AV	SHA	18	B3
HAWTHORNE BLVD	LACO	97	D3
HAWTHORNE BLVD	LACO	S	B2
HAWTHORNE ST	MONT	167	D3
HAWTHORNE ST	RCO	99	C5
HAWVER RD	CAL	41	A3
HAYDEN RD	MCO	48	D4
HAYDEN HILL RD	LAS	14	C4
HAYDN HLL CTO	LAS	14	D4
HAYDN HLL LKOUT	LAS	14	D4
HAYES AV	FRCO	57	B3
HAYES AV	FRCO	57	B5
HAYES ST	RCO	101	C5
HAYNES RD	SBD	91	E3
HAYNES RD	SHA	13	C5
HAYS CANYON RD	MOD	8	E2
HAYWARD BLVD	ALA	M	A5
HAYWARD BLVD	ALA	P	A1
HAYWARD RD	MCO	48	C2
HAZEL AV	SAC	34	B5
HAZELDEAN RD	STA	48	A2
HAZEL DELL RD	SCR	54	C2
HAZEL VALLEY RD	ED	35	B4
HAZELTINE AV	LACO	Q	C2
HAZELTON AV	S	160	E5
HAZEN RD	TEH	19	B3
HEACOCK ST	RCO	99	C2
HEAD DAM RD	BUT	25	D1
HEALDSBURG AV	SON	37	D2
HEALY RD	MCO	48	C5
HEARST RD	MCO	47	D5
HEARST RD	MCO	55	D1
HEARST POST OFC	MEN	23	B4
HEARST WLLTS RD	MEN	23	A5
HEATH RD	KER	78	C3
HEATHER AV	KER	70	C5
HEATHER AV	MAD	57	B1
HEBER RD	IMP	112	B3
HECKER PASS HWY	SCL	54	C2
HECTOR RD	SBD	92	D2
HEDDING ST	SJ	151	B4
HEDDING ST	SJ	152	B2
HEDDING ST	SCL	P	B3
HEDGER RD	SUT	33	C1
HEFFERNAN AV	IMP	112	A4
HEGAN LN	BUT	25	B3
HEGENBRGR EXPWY	ALA	45	D2
HEGENBERGER RD	ALA	L	D5
HEGENBERGER RD	ALA	45	D2
HEGENBURGER RD	O	159	E3
HEIDI RD	TUL	68	E1
HEINSEN RD	MON	65	D4
HEINZELMAN DR	SIS	4	C5
HEISKELL DR	MAD	57	B1
HEITT AV	KER	68	B5
HELEN DR	MLBR	144	B5
HELENA AV	STA	47	E2
HELENDALE RD	SBD	91	B2
HELLMAN AV	RCO	U	E4
HELLMAN AV	RCO	98	E3
HELLS HALF ACRE	SIE	26	D4
HELLS HALF ACRE	TUO	41	D3
HELLS HALF ACRE	TUO	42	A3
HELLS HOLLOW RD	TUO	48	E1
HELMS CT	KER	79	C3
HEMET LAKE RD	RCO	100	B4
HEMPHILL RD	LAS	21	B4
HENDERSON AV	TUL	68	D3
HENDERSON RD	FRCO	57	C4
HENDERSON RD	RED	122	D3
HENDERSON ST	EUR	121	C3
HENDERSN CYN RD	SDCO	107	E2
HENDRICKS DR	SBD	101	E1
HENDRICKS RD	LAK	31	C2
HENLEY RD	KLAM	5	C1
HENNESSEY RD	HUM	10	D5
HENNESSEY RD	TRI	10	E5
HENNESS PASS RD	SIE	26	D4
HENNESS PASS RD	SIE	27	A4
HENRY RD	SBD	101	D1
HENRY RD	SJCO	40	D5
HENRY RD	SJCO	47	D1
HENRY ST	B	156	A1
HENRY DOTA RD	SIE	27	C4
HENRY FORD AV	LA	191	E1
HENRY FORD AV	LB	191	E1
HENRY MILLER AV	MCO	56	A1
HENRY MILLER RD	MCO	55	C1
HENSLEY RD	MAD	57	B1
HEREFORD RD	MCO	47	E5
HEREFORD RD	MCO	48	A5
HEREFORD RD	MCO	55	E1
HEREFORD RD	SBD	92	B1
HERIOT LN	PLU	27	C3
HERIOT LN	SIE	27	C3
HERITAGE CT	SHA	18	B2
HERITAGE RD	SDCO	V	D5
HERITAGE RD	SDCO	111	E2
HERLONG ACCESS	LAS	21	D5
HERMOSA AV	LACO	S	A1
HERMOSA RD	KER	78	E3
HERMOSA RD	VEN	88	B4
HERNANDEZ DR	LACO	90	A3
HERNANDEZ DR	MPA	48	C2
HERNDON AV	FRCO	56	B3
HERNDON AV	FRCO	57	C3
HERNLEY RD	RCO	107	B1
HERON AV	SBD	101	A1
HERRICK RD	HUM	121	B5
HERRING RD	KER	78	C4
HERZOG RD	SAC	M	E1
HERZOG RD	SAC	39	D3
HESPELER RD	SOL	38	E2
HESPERIA RD	MON	65	C5
HESPERIA RD	SBD	91	B4
HESPERIAN BLVD	ALA	N	E1
HESPERIAN BLVD	ALA	P	A1
HESPERIAN BLVD	ALA	45	E2
HESPERIAN BLVD	ALCO	146	B2

STREET	CO.	PAGE	GRID
HESPERIAN BLVD	H	146	B2
HESSE RD	TEH	18	B5
HETCH HETCHY RD	TUO	42	B5
HETTENSHAW RD	TRI	16	E4
HETZEL RD	IMP	108	E5
HEWES AV	ORCO	98	C4
HEWES AV	ORCO	T	E3
HEWITT RD	SJCO	40	C5
HEWLTT STURTVNT	MEN	31	B3
HEYSER RD	IMP	110	D5
HIALEAH WY	RCO	100	C5
HIATT RD	SUT	33	B4
HIAWATHA AV	AVLN	97	B4
HIBBARD RD	MEN	31	A4
HIBBARD RD	SJCO	40	B4
HICKEY BLVD	SMCO	N	B1
HICKEY BLVD	SMCO	45	B2
HICKMAN LN	TEH	18	C4
HICKMAN RD	STA	47	E3
HICKMAN RD	STA	48	A3
HICKS	LAS	21	B4
HICKS LN	BUT	25	B2
HICKS RD	SUT	33	E3
HIDALGO ST	MPA	48	C2
HIDDEN HILLS RD	SBD	94	A2
HIDDEN OAKS DR	KER	79	B4
HIDDEN VLY RD	SB	87	B4
HIDDEN VALLEY RD	SD	211	A2
HIDEAWAY HAVEN	SHA	13	D3
HIEROGLYPH RD	MNO	51	C2
HIETT AV	KER	78	B1
HIGDON RD	CAL	41	B2
HIGGINS AV	BUT	33	C1
HIGGNS PRSMA RD	SMCO	N	B2
HIGGNS PRSMA RD	SMCO	45	C3
HIGH RD	SBD	91	D4
HIGH RD	SIS	3	E4
HIGH ST	ALA	L	D4
HIGH ST	A	159	A2
HIGH ST	AUB	126	C4
HIGH ST	MONT	167	D3
HIGH ST	MON	53	E3
HIGH ST	O	159	B1
HIGH ST	SC	169	B3
HIGH ST	SCR	53	E2
HIGHGRADE RD	MOD	7	D2
HIGHLAND AV	FRCO	57	D2
HIGHLAND AV	LA	181	C4
HIGHLAND AV	LA	184	C1
HIGHLAND AV	LACO	97	D3
HIGHLAND AV	LACO	Q	D4
HIGHLAND AV	LACO	S	A1
HIGHLAND AV	P	158	D2
HIGHLAND AV	SBD	98	E1
HIGHLAND AV	SBD	99	C2
HIGHLAND AV	SDCO	V	C4
HIGHLAND AV	SDCO	111	D1
HIGHLAND AV	U	123	B3
HIGHLAND BLVD	RCO	99	D2
HIGHLAND DR	CLK	209	A5
HIGHLAND DR	LACO	R	A2
HIGHLAND RD	CC	M	C5
HIGHLAND RD	CC	46	B1
HIGHLAND WY	P	158	D1
HIGHLAND WY	SCR	P	B5
HIGHLAND WY	SCR	54	B1
HIGHLND HOME RD	RCO	99	E3
HIGHLAND LK RD	ALP	42	B1
HIGHLND SPG RD	LAK	31	D3
HIGHLND SPGS RD	RCO	99	E3
HIGHLAND VLY RD	SDCO	106	E4
HIGHLANDS LK RD	SHA	12	B4
HIGHLANDS VW DR	TUO	163	D3
HIGHLINE RD	IMP	109	C5
HIGHLINE RD	KER	79	B4
HIGHLINE RD	KER	79	C4
HIGH PRAIRIE RD	HUM	10	C5
HIGHRIDGE RD	LACO	S	B3
HIGH ROCK RD	LAS	21	E4
HIGH SCHOOL RD	SON	37	D2
HIGH VALLEY RD	KER	88	D1
HIGH VALLEY RD	LAK	31	E2
HIGH VALLEY RD	LAK	32	A3
HY TO THE STARS	SDCO	107	A2
HIGUERA ST	SLO	76	A4
HIGUERA ST	SNLO	172	C3
HILBORN RD	NAPA	135	B1
HILDRETH LN	SJCO	40	B4
HILDRETH RD	MAD	57	D1
HILGARD AV	LA	180	D2
HILL	FRCO	58	B4
HILL AV	PAS	190	E3
HILL RD	COL	32	D2
HILL RD	CC	38	E5
HILL RD	KER	78	C4
HILL RD	KLAM	5	C2
HILL RD	MEN	23	B3
HILL RD	SMCO	N	C4
HILL RD	SCL	P	D5
HILL RD	SCL	54	D1
HILL RD	SIS	5	D3
HILL RD E	MEN	23	A5
HILL ST	AVLN	97	B4
HILL ST	LA	185	D4
HILL ST	LA	186	B3
HILL ST	LACO	S	D2
HILL ST	ML	164	C4
HILL ST	SDCO	V	A3
HILL ST	SDCO	106	B3
HILL ST	SDCO	111	C1
HILLCREST AV	BEN	153	C3
HILLCREST AV	CC	39	B5
HILLCREST BLVD	LACO	R	D3
HILLCREST BLVD	MLBR	144	C5
HILLCREST BLVD	SMCO	N	C1
HILLCREST BLVD	SMCO	45	B3
HILLCREST RD	CC	M	C3
HILLCREST ST	KER	80	E1
HILLDALE AV	MCO	55	C1
HILLDALE AV	MCO	86	E1
HILLER RD	HUM	9	E4
HILLGATE RD	COL	32	E3
HILLHURST AV	LA	182	C3
HILLSDALE AV	SCL	P	B4
HILLSDALE AV	SMCO	N	C2
HILLSDALE BL E	FCTY	145	C2
HILLSDALE BL E	SM	145	B3
HILLSDALE BL W	SM	145	A4
HILLS FERRY RD	MCO	47	C4
HILLSIDE AV	RCO	98	E3
HILLSIDE BLVD	SMCO	L	B5
HILLSIDE BLVD	SMCO	N	B1
HILLSIDE BLVD	SMCO	45	C2
HILLSIDE DR	MPA	49	C3
HILLSIDE DR	SMCO	N	C1
HILLSIDE DR	SMCO	45	C3
HILLSIDE DR	SHA	18	D2
HILL SIDE STA	LAS	14	B3
HILLSIDE VIS RD	RCO	107	C1
HILLS VALLEY RD	FRCO	58	B4
HILLTOP	SHA	18	C2
HILLTOP DR	CC	L	C3
HILLTOP RD	SIS	5	A2
HILL VIEW TK TR	SBD	91	C2
HILMAR RD	STA	47	D4
HILT RD	SIS	4	A2
HILT HUNGRY RD	SIS	4	A2
HILTON PACK STA	MNO	51	A3
HILTONS RD	HUM	9	E2
HILTONS RD	HUM	10	A2
HIME RD	IMP	112	A3
HI MOUNTAIN RD	SLO	76	C3
HINDS RD	STA	47	D1
HINKLEY RD	SBD	81	C5
HINTON AV	MCO	47	E4
HIRSCH RD	MPA	49	B4
HIRSCHDALE RD	NEV	27	E5
HITCHCOCK RD	MON	54	C4
HI YOU GULCH RD	SIS	3	D4
HOADLEY PKS RD	SHA	17	E1
HOAG RD	TEH	24	D2
HOAGLAND RD	HUM	16	D5
HOAGLIN RD	TRI	16	E5
HOAGLIN SCH RD	TRI	16	E5
HOBART AV	FRCO	56	B2
HOBART MILLS RD	NEV	27	D5
HOBBS RD	IMP	109	A2
HOBBS RD	SUT	33	C3
HOBO GULCH RD	TRI	11	B5
HOBSON AV	MON	65	B2
HOBSON WY	OXN	176	B4
HOBSON WY	RCO	103	C5
HOFFMAN LN	CC	46	C1
HOFFMAN RD	SBD	80	E3
HOFFMAN RD	SBD	81	A3
HOFFMAN RD	YUB	33	D3
HOFFMAN ST	AMA	40	E2
HFMN PLUMAS RD	YUB	33	D3
HOGAN	FRCO	58	A4
HOGAN LN	SJCO	40	B4
HOGAN DAM RD	CAL	40	E4
HOGBACK RD	INY	60	A4
HOG CANYON RD	KER	79	D3
HOG CANYON RD	SLO	76	B1
HOG CANYON EXT	SLO	66	B5
HOGIN RD	STA	47	C4
HOG LAKE TK TR	RCO	100	B5
HOGSBACK RD	TEH	18	D5
HOGSBACK RD	TEH	19	B4
HOKE RD	SUT	33	C2
HOLBROOK RD	MCO	48	D5
HOLBROOK WY	NEV	127	C1
HOLCOMB CK RD	SBD	91	E5
HOLCOMB VLY RD	SBD	91	E5
HOLCOMBS RD	SIE	27	D4
HOLDEN	SJCO	40	C5
HOLDNER RD	SOL	39	B2
HOLDRIDGE DR	TUL	68	E3
HOLDRIDGE RD	IMP	112	C3
HOLE AV	RCO	99	A3
HOLENBECK	SJCO	40	C5
HOLIDAY AV	KER	89	C1
HOLIDAY RD	DN	2	B3
HOLLAND	YOL	39	D2
HOLLAND AV	BUT	25	B3
HOLLAND RD	RCO	99	C4
HOLLAND RD	SOL	39	C3
HOLLND TRACT RD	CC	39	D5
HOLLENBECK AV	LACO	U	A3
HOLLENBECK AV	SVL	149	D3
HOLLISTER AV	SB	87	B4
HOLLISTER ST	SDCO	V	C5
HOLLISTER ST	SDCO	111	D2
HOLLOW LN	SHA	18	C2
HOLLOW RD	CC	39	A5
HOLLOWAY RD	COL	32	E1
HOLLOWAY RD	KER	77	C1
HOLLOW LOG RD	PLA	34	E2
HOLLY AV	LACO	R	C3
HOLLY RD	SBD	91	A3
HOLLY RD	TRI	17	A4
HOLLY ST	SMCO	N	D2
HOLLYWOOD BLVD	LA	181	A4
HOLLYWOOD BLVD	LA	182	B4
HOLLYWOOD BLVD	LACO	97	D2
HOLLYWOOD BLVD	LACO	Q	D3
HOLLYWOOD FRWY	LA	181	C2
HOLLYWOOD FRWY	LA	185	E1
HOLLYWOOD FRWY	LACO	97	D1
HOLLYWOOD FRWY	LACO	Q	D3
HOLLYWOOD LN	SBD	101	D1
HOLLYWOOD WY	BUR	179	B2
HOLLYWOOD WY	LACO	97	D1
HOLLYWOOD WY	LACO	Q	D2
HOLMAN HWY	MONT	167	C5
HOLMAN HWY	MON	53	D4
HOLMAN HWY	MON	168	C1
HOLMES AV	KER	78	B5
HOLMES LN	SOL	39	A2
HOLMES RD	SBD	84	C4
HOLMES RD	TEH	24	E1
HOLMES ST	ALA	P	C1
HOLMES ST	ALA	46	B2
HOLMS FLAT RD	HUM	16	B3
HOLOHAN RD	SCR	54	C2
HOLSTEAD RD	SBD	81	C5
HOLT AV	LACO	U	C2
HOLT BLVD	MTCL	203	B5
HOLT BLVD	ONT	203	E5
HOLT BLVD	ONT	204	A5
HOLT BLVD	SBD	U	C2
HOLT BLVD	SBD	98	D2
HOLT RD	IMP	109	C5
HOLT RD	KER	79	E5
HOLT RD	KER	80	A5
HOLTON RD	IMP	109	B5
HOLTVLE DUMP RD	IMP	109	C5
HOLTZWL	MPA	48	E2
HOLTZWL	MPA	49	A2
HOLWORTHY DR	TUL	68	D2
HOLZHAUSER LN	SIS	11	D1
HOME AV	SD	216	D3
HOME AV	SDCO	V	C3
HOME AV	SDCO	111	D1
HOMEDALE RD	KLAM	5	C1
HOMES RD	SBD	91	E4
HOMESTEAD AV	SAL	171	B4
HOMESTEAD RD	SLO	76	B2
HOMESTEAD RD	SCL	P	A3
HOMESTEAD RD	SCL	45	E4
HOMESTEAD RD	SCLR	150	D3
HOMESTEAD RD	SCLR	151	B3
HOMESTEAD RD	SVL	149	C3
HOMESTEAD RD	SVL	150	D3
HOMEWOOD CYN RD	INY	71	B4
HONDA RD	SB	86	B3
HONEY BEE RD	SHA	18	B3
HONEY RUN RD	BUT	25	C3
HONEY SPGS RD	SDCO	112	B1
HONEY WAGON RD	IMP	108	E2
HONOLULU AV	IMP	108	C2
HONOLULU AV	LACO	Q	E2
HONOLULU RD	KER	78	A4
HOOD FRANKLN RD	SAC	39	E2
HOOKER CREEK RD	HUM	16	C5
HOOKER CREEK RD	TEH	18	C4
HOOKTON RD	HUM	15	D1
HOOPER AV	LA	186	B5
HOOPER RD	SUT	33	C2
HOOPER RD	YUB	33	D2
HOOVER RD	MCO	56	C1
HOOVER ST	LA	185	C3
HOOVER ST	LACO	Q	E4
HOOVER FLAT RD	LAS	14	C4
HOPE ST	KLAM	5	C1
HOPKINS ST	ALA	L	C4
HOPLAND ST	SBD	91	B3
HOPPER RD	STA	47	E2
HOPYARD RD	ALA	M	B5
HOPYARD RD	ALA	46	B2
HORIZON CIR	NEV	127	B1
HORIZON RD	SBD	91	B3
HORIZON ST	SBD	91	C4
HORN LN	SIS	11	D5
HORN RD	LAS	8	D5
HORNBROOK RD	SIS	4	B3
HORNITOS RD	MPA	48	D3
HORR RD	SHA	13	D3
HORSE CANYON RD	KER	80	B1
HORSE CREEK RD	SIS	3	C3
HORSE LAKE RD	LAS	21	B1
HORSE LINTO RD	HUM	10	D4
HORSE RDG LKOUT	TRI	17	A4
HORSESHOE RD	STA	47	E1
HORSESHOE RD	STA	48	A1
HORSESHOE BR RD	PLA	34	B4
HORSESHOE HL RD	MAR	37	E5
HORSESHOE MDWS	INY	60	A4
HORTON CREEK RD	INY	51	C4
HOSFIELD DR	TUL	68	B2
HOSKING RD	KER	78	D3
HOSLER AV	BUT	25	A3
HOSTETTER RD	SCL	P	B3
HOTCHKISS RD	TRI	22	E1
HOT CK RANCH RD	MNO	50	E2
HOT CK RANCH RD	MNO	51	A2
HOTLUM	SIS	12	C1
HOT SPRINGS RD	ALP	36	B5
HOT SPRINGS RD	RCO	108	D1
HOT SPRINGS RD	TUL	68	E4
HOT SPRINGS RD	TUL	69	A4
HOUGHTON AV	TEH	24	D2
HOUGHTON RD	KER	78	C4
HOUSE RD	IMP	108	E5
HOUSE RD	LAS	14	C3
HOUSTON AV	KIN	67	D1
HOUSTON AV	TUL	68	B1
HOUT RD	AMA	40	D2
HOVLEY RD	IMP	109	A4
HOWARD	SJCO	47	A1
HOWARD AV	FRCO	57	A5
HOWARD AV	FRCO	57	A3
HOWARD AV	MCO	47	E4
HOWARD AV	MCO	48	A4
HOWARD RD	MCO	47	E4
HOWARD RD	RCO	107	B1
HOWARD RD	STA	47	B3
HOWARD RD	SJCO	47	A1
HOWARD RD	TUL	68	B4
HOWARD ST	MEN	23	A3
HOWARD CREEK RD	SIE	27	A3
HOWRDS GLCH FTG	MOD	14	C1
HOWE RD	CC	L	E3
HOWE RD	M	154	C3
HOWE CREEK RD	HUM	15	E3
HOWELL AV	KER	80	C1
HOWELL AV	SIS	11	D1
HOWELL RD	IMP	109	A2
HOWELL MTN RD	NAPA	29	C2
HOWELL MTN RD	NAPA	38	B1
HOWELLS RD	PLU	26	B1
HOWLAND HILL RD	DN	1	D4
HOWSLEY RD	SUT	33	D4
HOY RD	SIS	12	C1
HOY RD	TEH	18	D5
HOYER RD	STA	47	C4
HUASNA RD	SLO	76	C4
HUASNA TOWNSITE	SLO	76	D4
HUB CT	CAL	41	A5
HUBBARD	PLA	34	B3
HUBBARD RD	LACO	89	E4
HUBBARD ST	LACO	89	C5
HUBBARD ST	LACO	Q	C1
HUDSON AV	FRCO	56	B2
HUDSON RD	MON	65	A1
HUDSON RD	SIS	4	A3
HUDSON RD	SUT	33	E3
HUDSON ST	SMCO	N	D2
HUDSON ST	SHA	13	C5
HUERHUERO L PNZ	SLO	76	C2
HUEY RD	SLO	76	A1
HUFF RD	IMP	108	E5
HUFF RD	SBD	91	E3
HUFF ST	RCO	107	C1
HUFFAKER RD	SUT	33	E3
HUFFMASTER RD	COL	32	C2
HUFFORD RD	HUM	9	E2
HUFFORD RD	HUM	10	A2
HUGHES AV	FRCO	57	C4
HUGHES AV	FRCO	67	C1
HUGHES AV	LA	183	B5
HUGHES LN	KER	78	D3
HUGHES RD	GV	127	C2
HUGHES RD	NEV	127	C2
HUGHES RD	SUT	33	C2
HULEN RD	MCO	47	C5
HULEN RD	MCO	55	C1
HULL AV	MCO	48	B4
HULL RD	GLE	24	A3
HULL CREEK RD	TRI	23	A1
HULL MTN RD	LAK	23	D5
HULL VALLEY RD	MEN	23	A2
HULTBERG RD	MCO	47	D4
HULTBERG RD	STA	47	D3
HUMBOLDT AV	FRCO	56	E3
HUMBOLDT AV	FRCO	57	A3
HUMBOLDT RD	BUT	19	D5
HUMBOLDT RD	BUT	25	B3
HUMBOLDT RD	C	124	E4
HUMBOLDT RD	DN	1	D4
HUMBOLDT RD	PLU	19	E5
HUMBOLDT RD	PLU	20	A5
HUMBOLDT ST	VAL	134	E4
HUMBLDT HILL RD	HUM	15	E1
HUMBUG RD	PLU	19	E5
HUMBUG RD	PLU	20	A5
HUMBUG CREEK RD	SIS	4	A4
HUMBUG HUMBOLDT	PLU	20	B4
HUME AV	KIN	67	E1
HUME RD	FRCO	58	E3
HUMPHREY CIR	PLU	20	D5
HUMPHREY RD	SUT	33	C2
HUN RD	SBD	84	C4
HUNEWILL RCH RD	MNO	43	B3
HUNGRY CK LO RD	SIS	4	A2
HUNGRY CK MTWY	PLU	20	E5
HUNGRY VLY RD	VEN	88	D2
HUNT RD	CAL	40	E4
HUNT RD	CAL	41	A4
HUNT RD	IMP	112	B3
HUNT RD	LAS	14	C3
HUNT RD	MCO	47	C5
HUNTER	MON	54	C4
HUNTER BLVD	RCO	103	D4
HUNTER CREEK RD	DN	1	E5
HUNTER CREEK RD	DN	2	A5
HUNTER MTN RD	INY	61	A4
HUNTERS VLY RD	MPA	48	E2
HUNTINGTON AV	SSF	144	B1
HUNTINGTON DR	LACO	97	E2
HUNTINGTON DR	LACO	R	B3
HUNTINGTON RD	MAD	57	C2
HUNTINGTON RD	STA	47	B2
HUNTLEY MINE RD	MNO	50	E2
HUNTSMAN AV	FRCO	56	E4
HUNTSMAN AV	FRCO	57	C4
HUNTSMAN AV	FRCO	58	A4
HUPP COUTOLENC	BUT	25	D2
HURDS GULCH RD	SIS	3	D5
HURLES CIR	BUT	25	E4
HURLETON RD	BUT	25	E4
HURLTN SWDS FLT	BUT	25	E4
HURLEY FLATS RD	RCO	100	B3
HURRICANE RD	SLO	77	D4
HUSMAN RD	MCO	47	C5
HUSMAN RD	MCO	55	C1
HUSTED RD	COL	32	E2
HUSTON RD	IMP	109	B5
HUTCHINS	MCO	56	B1
HUTCHINS ST	SJCO	40	A4
HUTCHINSON RD	SJCO	47	B2
HUTCHINSON RD	SUT	33	C3
HUTSELL RD	MEN	30	E3
HYAMPOM RD	TRI	17	A2
HYDE RD	IMP	111	E3
HYDE ST	FRCO	57	B5
HYDRIL RD	KIN	67	A3
HYPERION AV	LA	182	D4
I			
I AV	SBD	91	C4
I ST	SBDO	207	B3
I ST	EUR	121	D1
I ST	MDO	162	B3
IBEX SPRING RD	SBD	72	D5
ICE HOUSE RD	ED	35	C3
ICE HOUSE RD	ED	35	C4
ICELAND RD	NEV	27	E5
IDAHO AV	KIN	67	D2
IDAHO AV	LA	180	C4
IDAHO RD	STA	47	D3
IDAHO ST	SDCO	V	C3
IDAHO ST	SDCO	111	D1
IDAHO-MARYLD RD	GV	127	D3
IDAHO-MARYLD RD	NEV	34	C1
IDAHO-MARYLD RD	NEV	127	D3
IDALEONA DR	RCO	99	B3
IDLEWOOD LN	HUM	9	E3
IDLEWOOD LN	HUM	10	A3
IGNACIO BLVD	MAR	L	A2
IKE CROW RD	STA	47	C4
ILLINOIS AV	STA	47	C2
ILLINOIS AV	TEH	24	E2
ILLINOIS VLY RD	DN	2	D2
IMLER RD	IMP	108	E4
IMOLA AV	NAPA	L	D1
IMOLA AV	NAP	133	C5
IMOLA AV W	NAP	133	B5
IMPERIAL AV	EC	217	B4
IMPERIAL AV	IMP	109	A5
IMPERIAL AV	SD	216	A4
IMPERIAL AV	SDCO	V	C3
IMPERIAL AV	SDCO	111	D1
IMPERIAL HWY			
IMPERIAL HWY	IMP	111	B3
IMPERIAL HWY	LA	189	B2
IMPERIAL HWY	ELS	189	B2
IMPERIAL HWY	LACO	97	D3
IMPERIAL HWY	LACO	98	B3
IMPERIAL HWY	LACO	Q	C5
IMPERIAL HWY	LACO	R	E5
IMPERIAL HWY	LACO	S	A1
IMPERIAL HWY	ORCO	R	E5
IMPERIAL HWY	ORCO	T	C1
IMPERIAL ST	KER	77	E2
IMPERIAL ST	KER	78	B2
IMPERIAL DAM RD	IMP	110	E5
IMPERL GABLS RD	IMP	110	B3
INCLINE RD	MPA	49	B2
INCLINE RD	MPA	63	A5
INDEPENDENCE RD	CAL	41	B2
INDPNDCE CEM RD	CAL	41	B2
INDEPNDNC LK RD	SIE	27	C5
INDEPNDNCIA MAT	BAJA	112	B4
INDIAN AV	RCO	100	C3
INDIAN RD	LAS	21	A4
INDIAN TR	SBD	91	C2
INDIAN TR	SBD	101	B1
INDIANA AV	MCO	56	B1
INDIANA AV	STA	47	E2
INDIANA ST	LACO	R	B4
INDIANA RCH RD	YUB	26	A5
INDIANA SCH RD	YUB	26	A5
INDIAN CYN DR	PMSP	206	B4
INDIAN CYN RD	KER	70	C5
INDIAN CYN RD	KER	80	C1
INDIAN CEM RD	ALP	36	B4
INDIAN COVE CIR	SBD	101	B2
INDIAN CV E RD	SBD	101	B2
INDIAN CV W RD	SBD	101	B2
INDIAN CV MT RD	SBD	101	B2
INDIAN CREEK RD	ALP	36	C5
INDIAN CREEK RD	KER	79	D3
INDIAN CREEK RD	MNO	51	D2
INDIAN CREEK RD	PLU	21	A5
INDIAN CREEK RD	RCO	100	A4
INDIAN CREEK RD	SIS	2	D2
INDIAN CREEK RD	SIS	3	D4
INDIAN CREEK RD	TRI	17	D2
INDIAN DIGGINS	ED	41	B1
INDIAN FLAT RD	NEV	34	C1
INDIAN GUIDE	FRCO	58	B3
INDIAN GULCH RD	MPA	48	E3
INDIAN GULCH RD	MPA	49	A4
INDIAN GLCH EXT	MPA	48	D4
INDIAN HILL BL	CLA	203	A3
INDIAN HILL BL	LACO	98	D1
INDIAN HILL BL	POM	203	A4
INDIAN HILL RD	RCO	100	C5
INDIAN HILL RD	SIE	26	C4
INDIAN HILL RD	STA	48	C2
INDIANOLA AV	FRCO	57	E4
INDIANOLA CTO	HUM	9	E5
INDIANOLA CTO	HUM	10	A5

STREET INDEX

STREET	CO.	PAGE	GRID
INDIANOLA RESRV	HUM	15	D2
INDIAN OLE RD	LAS	20	C4
INDIAN PAINT DR	RCO	100	C5
INDIAN PASS RD	IMP	110	B4
INDIAN PEAK RD	MPA	49	B3
INDIAN POINT RD	KER	79	B4
INDIAN RANCH RD	INY	71	C2
INDIAN RES RD	AMA	40	D3
INDIAN ROCK RD	IMP	112	D5
INDIANS RD	MON	64	D2
INDIAN SCHL RD	LPAZ	104	A2
INDIAN SERVICE RD	TUL	69	A3
INDIAN SPRINGS RD	ALP	36	D5
INDIAN SPRINGS RD	NEV	34	B2
INDIAN SPRINGS RD	SBD	81	D4
INDIAN TOM LAKE	SIS	5	B2
INDIAN VALLEY RD	MAR	38	A4
INDIAN VLY RD	MON	66	A5
INDIAN VLY RD	SIE	26	C4
INDIAN VLY RD	SLO	66	A5
INDIAN VLY RD	TRI	17	A2
INDIAN WELLS ST	KER	80	D1
INDIO AV	SBDO	100	E1
INDUSTRIAL BLVD	H	146	B5
INDUSTRIAL BLVD	MOH	96	B4
INDUSTRIAL PKWY	ALA	N	E1
INDUSTRIAL PKWY	ALA	P	A1
INDUSTRIAL PKWY	ALA	45	E2
INDUSTRIAL WY	SMCO	145	E5
INDSTRL FARM RD	KER	78	C2
INGHRAM RD	TEH	24	D2
INGLEWOOD AV	LACO	S	B1
INGLEWOOD BLVD	LA	188	A3
INGOMAR GRADE	MCO	55	D1
INGOMAR RD	MCO	47	D5
INGOMAR RD	MCO	55	D1
INGRAHAM ST	SD	212	B1
INGRAHAM ST	SDCO	V	A3
INGRAM LN	SUT	33	B1
INGRAM CREEK RD	STA	47	A3
INK GRADE	NAPA	32	B5
INK GRADE	NAPA	38	B1
INLAND DR	SJCO	39	E5
INLAND CTR DR	SBDO	207	C4
INSKIP RD	TEH	19	A4
INTAKE BLVD	RCO	103	D5
INTERLAKE RD	SLO	65	D5
INTERNATIONL AV	FRCO	57	D2
INTERNATIONL AV	IMP	109	B3
INTERNATIONAL BLVD	O	158	B3
INTERNATIONAL BLVD	O	159	D1
INVESTOR AV	RCO	102	C4
INWOOD RD	SHA	19	A3
INYO N	INY	51	D3
INYO ST	DN	1	D4
INYOKERN RD	KER	80	D1
IONA AV	KIN	67	D2
IONE RD	SAC	40	C2
IONE MICHIGAN BR	AMA	40	C2
IOWA AV	RCO	99	B2
IOWA AV	RIV	205	E2
IOWA AV	STA	47	C3
IOWA CITY RD	YUB	33	D1
IOWA HILL RD	PLA	34	E2
IRIS AV	RCO	99	B3
IRIS CT	KER	79	C1
IRIS DR	SAL	171	C2
IRIS LN	SDCO	106	D3
IRIS WY	CAL	41	B2
IRIS CANYON RD	MONT	167	E5
IRIS CANYON RD	MONT	168	E1
IRISH HILL RD	AMA	40	D2
IRISH TOWN PNE-			
-GRV WIELAND RD	AMA	41	A2
IRMULCO RD	MEN	22	D5
IROLO ST	LA	185	A2
IRONAGE RD	SBD	101	E1
IRONE AV	KER	89	C1
IRON MTN RD	SBD	91	C1
IRON MTN RD	SHA	18	B1
IRON MTN PUMPNG	SBD	102	E1
IRONWOOD AV	RCO	99	C2
IRONWOOD CT	KER	79	B4
IRVINE AV	CM	199	D3
IRVINE AV	NB	199	C4
IRVINE BLVD	ORCO	98	C4
IRVINE BLVD	ORCO	T	E3
IRVINE RD	IMP	109	C4
IRVINE CTR DR	ORCO	98	C4
IRVINE CTR DR	ORCO	T	E3
IRVINE LODGE RD	MEN	22	E4
IRWIN RD	SBD	81	E5
IRWIN RD	SBD	82	A5
IRWIN RD	SBD	208	B1
IRWIN RD	TEH	24	C2
IRWINDALE AV	LACO	R	E3
ISABELLA BLVD	KER	80	B4
ISABELA-WLKR PS	KER	79	D1
ISABELA-WLKR PS	KER	80	B1
ISHI PISHI RD	HUM	10	D2
ISLAND DR	A	159	A3
ISLAND RD	SHA	13	D3
ISLAND RD	SIS	3	D5
ISLAND RD	SIS	11	D1
ISLAND BAR HILL	BUT	25	E4
ISLAND MTN RD	HUM	22	D1
ISLAND MTN RD	TRI	22	D1
ISLAND PARK RD	FRCO	58	B2
ISLETON RD	SAC	M	E1
ISPEN AV	MCO	48	E5
ITALIAN BAR RD	FRCO	50	A5
ITALIAN BAR RD	TUO	41	C4
IVANHOE RD	SBD	91	E4

STREET	CO.	PAGE	GRID
IVANPAH RD	SBD	84	C2
IVANPAH CIMA RD	SBD	84	B3
IVERSON LN	LAS	14	B3
IVERSON RD	MEN	30	D4
IVERSON RD	MON	54	E5
IVERSON ST	SAL	171	B4
IVESGROVE DR	LACO	89	D3
IVORY MILL RD	GLE	24	A4
IVY AV	MCO	56	C1
IVY ST	C	124	B5

J

STREET	CO.	PAGE	GRID
J ST	DVS	136	D2
J ST	MDO	162	B3
J ST	MER	170	C5
J ST	OXN	176	B5
J ST	SCTO	137	D3
J ST	SDCO	V	C4
J ST	SDCO	111	D2
JACALITOS CK RD	FRCO	66	D3
JACARANDA DR	KER	79	B4
JACK AV	KER	78	B2
JACKASS FLTS RD	NEV	26	C5
JACKASS GRADE	SBT	55	E4
JACKASS GRADE	SBT	56	A4
JACKASS HILL RD	TUO	41	C5
JACK CREEK RD	SLO	75	E2
JACK CREEK RD	SLO	76	A2
JACKLIN RD	SCL	P	B2
JACKLIN RD	SCL	46	B3
JACK PINE AV	KER	79	E5
JACK RABBIT TR	RCO	99	D3
JACK RANCH RD	KER	69	B5
JACK RANCH RD	KER	80	D1
JACKS RD	MON	54	E5
JACK SHAW RD	HUM	16	B2
JACK SLOUGH RD	YUB	33	D2
JACKSNIPE RD	SOL	38	E3
JACKSON	PLA	33	E4
JACKSON AV	KER	77	E1
JACKSON AV	KER	78	B1
JACKSON AV	KIN	67	D2
JACKSON AV	SJCO	47	D1
JACKSON DR	SDCO	V	D2
JACKSON DR	SDCO	106	D5
JACKSON RD	IMP	109	B4
JACKSON RD	SAC	40	A1
JACKSON RD	SBD	91	D3
JACKSON RD	STA	47	C2
JACKSON ST	ALA	L	E5
JACKSON ST	ALA	M	A5
JACKSON ST	ALA	N	E1
JACKSON ST	ALA	P	A1
JACKSON ST	ALA	45	E2
JACKSON ST	RCO	99	A3
JACKSON ST	RCO	101	A4
JACKSON ST	TEH	18	D5
JACKSON ST W	ALA	N	E1
JACKSON ST W	H	146	E3
JACKSON GATE RD	AMA	40	E2
JACKSON MDWS RD	SIE	27	C4
JACKSON RCH RD	HUM	9	E5
JACKSON SLGH RD	SAC	M	D2
JACKSON VLY RD	AMA	40	D3
JACKSONVILLE RD	TUO	41	C5
JACKS VALLEY RD	DGL	36	B2
JACK TONE RD	SJCO	40	B4
JACOB DEKEMA FY	SD	214	B3
JACOB DEKEMA FY	SD	216	C1
JACOB DEKEMA FY	SDCO	V	D4
JACOB DEKEMA FY	SDCO	106	C5
JACOB DEKEMA FY	SDCO	111	D2
JACOBS	FRCO	58	B4
JACOBS RD	SJCO	40	A5
JACOBS WY	RCO	99	B4
JACOBY CREEK RD	HUM	10	A5
JACQUELINE	SIS	4	C2
JADE AV	SIS	4	C4
JAHANT	SJCO	40	A3
JAHANT RD	SJCO	40	B3
JAIL RD	AVLN	97	B5
JAKE RD	RCO	100	A5
JALAMA RD	SB	86	B4
JAMACHA BLVD	SDCO	V	D3
JAMACHA RD	SDCO	V	E3
JAMACHA RD	SDCO	111	A3
JAMAICA BLVD	MOH	96	B4
JAMBOREE RD	IRV	198	E4
JAMBOREE RD	NB	200	B1
JAMBOREE RD	ORCO	98	C5
JAMBOREE RD	ORCO	T	E3
JAMES RD	FRCO	56	E4
JAMES RD	IMP	109	B5
JAMES RD	KER	78	D2
JAMES DONLON BL	CC	M	C3
JAMES LICK FRWY	SF	142	D5
JAMES LICK FRWY	SFCO	45	C2
JAMESON AV	FRCO	57	B5
JAMESON AV	FRCO	57	B4
JAMESON RD	COL	32	E1
JAMESON RD	KER	79	D4
JAMISON CK RD	SCR	N	D5
JAMISON CK RD	SCR	53	D1
JANE RD	SBD	92	D4
JANES RD	HUM	10	A5
JANESVILLE GRADE	LAS	21	B4
JANICE AV	KER	79	E1
JANICE AV	KER	80	A1
JANICE RD	SIS	4	C2
JANICE ST	KER	80	A4
JANOPAUL AV	STA	162	C5
JANSS RD	VEN	96	D1

STREET	CO.	PAGE	GRID
JAPATUL LN	SDCO	107	B5
JAPATUL LN	SDCO	112	B1
JAPATUL RD	SBD	91	C4
JAPATUL RD	SBD	91	D3
JAPATUL RD	SDCO	107	B5
JAPATUL RD	SDCO	112	B1
JAPATUL VLY RD	SDCO	107	C5
JAPATUL VLY RD	SDCO	112	C1
JAQUIMA DR	CAL	41	A4
JARDINE RD	SLO	76	B1
JARED LN	SB	86	E2
J ARTHR YNGR FY	FCTY	145	D1
J ARTHR YNGR FY	SM	145	A2
J ARTHR YNGR FY	SMCO	45	D3
JARVIS AV	ALA	N	E2
JARVIS AV	ALA	P	A2
JARVIS AV	ALA	45	E3
JARVIS RD	ALP	36	C4
JASMINE RD	SBD	92	B3
JASPER LN	YUB	33	E2
JASPER RD	IMP	112	B4
JASPER RD	TUO	48	B1
JASPER SEARS BR	MCO	55	C1
JASPER SEARS RD	MCO	55	C1
JAVA AV	KIN	67	C2
JAVIS AV	KER	80	E1
JAWBONE CYN RD	KER	79	E2
JAWBONE CYN RD	KER	80	B3
JAY DEE LN	RCO	100	C5
JAYMAR RD	HUM	16	B3
JAYNE AV	FRCO	66	D3
JAYNE AV	FRCO	67	A2
JEAN BLANC RD	INY	51	D3
JEANESE	TUO	41	C5
JEAN NICHOLS RD	RCO	99	D5
JEFF ST	KER	80	C1
JEFFERSON AV	FRCO	56	E4
JEFFERSON AV	FRCO	57	C4
JEFFERSON AV	FRCO	58	A4
JEFFERSON AV	RCO	99	C5
JEFFERSON AV	SM	N	D2
JEFFERSON BLVD	CUL	188	B3
JEFFERSON BLVD	LA	185	B5
JEFFERSON BLVD	LACO	97	D2
JEFFERSON BLVD	LACO	Q	D4
JEFFERSON BLVD	LA	187	D4
JEFFERSON BLVD	LACO	188	A4
JEFFERSON BLVD	YOL	39	D2
JEFFERSON BLVD W	LA	184	D5
JEFFERSON ST	MONT	167	D4
JEFFERSON ST	NAP	133	C4
JEFFERSON ST	ORCO	T	D1
JEFFERSON ST	RCO	101	A4
JEFFERSON ST	SDCO	106	B3
JEFFERY RD	IMP	111	E3
JEFFREY RD	ORCO	98	C4
JEFFREY RD	ORCO	T	E4
JEFFREY RCH RD	MNO	51	D2
JELLYS FERRY RD	TEH	18	D4
JENKINS RD	KER	78	C3
JENKS LAKE RD	SBD	100	A1
JENNINGS RD	STA	47	C3
JENNY LIND RD	CAL	40	D4
JENSEN AV	COL	32	E3
JENSEN AV	FRCO	56	C4
JENSEN AV	FRCO	57	A3
JENSEN RD	SLO	75	E1
JERROLD AV	FRCO	56	B2
JERRY COLLINS AV	MCO	48	B5
JERSEY	MCO	55	E2
JERSEY AV	KIN	67	C2
JERSEYDALE RD	MPA	49	C3
JERSEY ISLAND	CC	39	C4
JERSEY ISLND RD	CC	M	D3
JERUSALEM GRADE	LAK	32	B4
JESS VALLEY RD	MOD	8	B3
JESSICA DR	SUT	125	A4
JESUS MARIA RD	CAL	41	A3
JETTY RD S	HUM	15	D1
JEWELL AV	PAC	167	A1
JEWELL RD	TEH	18	C4
JEWELL VLY RD	SDCO	111	A4
JEWETT RD	HUM	16	D5
JEWETT RD	SUT	33	C3
JEWETTA AV	KER	78	C3
J HART CLINTON DR	SM	145	B1
J HELT RD	HUM	15	D2
JIM DAY RD	SHA	13	E4
JIM HARVEY RD	SHA	18	C2
JIMMY DURNTE BL	SDCO	106	C4
JIM NEGRA RD	MCO	55	C2
JOAQUIN RD	ML	164	D2
JOAQUIN RDG LKT	FRCO	66	C2
JOEGER	PLA	34	C3
JOE SMITH RD	INY	51	D4
JOHANSEN RD	STA	47	D2
JOHN ST	RCO	100	E3
JOHN ST	SAL	171	C4
JOHN DALY BLVD	SMCO	L	B5
JOHN DALY BLVD	SMCO	45	B2
JOHN F FORAN FRWY	SF	142	E4
J F KENNEDY DR	RCO	99	C3
J F KENNEDY DR	SF	141	B4
JOHN FOX RD	STA	47	E2
JOHN GIBSON BL	LA	191	A2
JOHN LADD CHROM	SIS	3	B3
JOHN MUIR PKWY	CC	L	D3
JOHN MUIR PKWY	CC	38	D5
JOHN MUIR PKWY	M	154	D3
JOHNNY MDW RD	MNO	43	E5
JOHNNY MDW RD	MNO	50	E1
JOHNNY MDW RD	MNO	51	A1
JOHNS DR	TUL	68	D3

STREET	CO.	PAGE	GRID
JOHNS RD	KER	79	C3
JOHN SCHOOL RD	COL	33	A3
JOHN SCHOOL RD	YOL	33	A3
JOHN SMITH RD	SBT	55	A3
JOHNSON AV	MCO	47	D4
JOHNSON AV	SDCO	V	E2
JOHNSON AV	SDCO	106	E5
JOHNSON AV	SNLO	172	D3
JOHNSON AV	SLO	76	B3
JOHNSON CT	KER	79	C4
JOHNSON DR	TUL	58	B4
JOHNSON LN	DGL	36	C3
JOHNSON RD	HUM	10	B3
JOHNSON RD	HUM	15	E2
JOHNSON RD	KER	78	C3
JOHNSON RD	LAS	21	B3
JOHNSON RD	LACO	89	D3
JOHNSON RD	LACO	89	D4
JOHNSON RD	MCO	55	E1
JOHNSON RD	SBD	90	E3
JOHNSON RD	SBD	90	E4
JOHNSON RD	SBD	91	C3
JOHNSON RD	SJCO	40	C4
JOHNSON RD	TEH	18	B5
JOHNSON RD	TEH	18	D4
JOHNSON RD N	MCO	55	D1
JOHNSON ST	RCO	101	B5
JOHNSON ST	RCO	108	B1
JOHNSON ST	SBD	91	E3
JOHNSON ST	SB	87	D1
JOHNSON CYN RD	INY	72	A3
JOHNSON CYN RD	MON	54	E5
JOHNSON CYN RD	MON	55	A5
JOHNSON RCH RD	PLU	20	D5
JOHNSON SCH RD	LAS	21	B3
JOHNSTON AV	KER	80	D1
JOHNSTON AV	RCO	99	E4
JOHNSVILLE RD	SIE	26	D3
JOHNSVLL MCCREA	PLU	26	E3
JOHN T. KNOX FRWY	RIV	155	B4
JOHN WEST RD	MAD	49	D4
JOINES RD	YUB	33	E1
JOINT HWY 14	LAS	21	A3
JOINT HWY 14	LAS	21	A3
JOINT RD	TEH	18	B5
JOJOBA RD	RCO	107	A1
JOJOBA RD E	RCO	107	A1
JOJOBA ST	RCO	102	C4
JOLON RD	MON	65	B3
JOLON PLEYTO	MON	65	B4
JONATA PARK RD	SB	86	D3
JONATHAN ST	SBD	91	B3
JONES AV	COL	32	E3
JONES LN	MOD	8	B1
JONES RD	LAS	8	B5
JONES RD	MCO	48	B4
JONES RD	SJCO	47	D1
JONES ST	FRCO	57	B5
JONES ST	SMA	173	D3
JONES BAR RD	NEV	34	C1
JONES BRADWAY	SBD	92	A3
JONES VALLEY RD	SIE	27	E4
JORDAN RD	HUM	16	A3
JORDAN RD	MCO	47	E4
JORDAN RD	MCO	48	A4
JORDAN CREEK RD	MPA	48	E1
JORDAN CREEK RD	MPA	49	A1
JORDON HILL RD	BUT	25	D2
JORGENSEN RD	MCO	47	C5
JORGENSEN RD	STA	47	C4
JOSE BASIN RD	FRCO	50	A5
JOSE BASIN RD	MAD	58	A1
JOSEPH PL	SIS	4	C2
JOSEPH CREEK RD	MOD	7	C5
JOSHUA BLVD	KER	80	C5
JOSHUA DR	SBD	100	D2
JOSHUA LN	SBD	100	E2
JOSHUA RD	SBD	91	C3
JOSHUA RD	SBD	91	D4
JOSHUA WY	KER	79	D5
JOSHUA TREE RD	SBD	92	C5
JOY RD	SON	37	C2
JOY ST	KER	70	A5
J T CROW RD	STA	47	C4
JUAN ST	SD	213	B5
JUAN ST	SDCO	V	B3
JUAN DIEGO-			
-FLATS RD	RCO	100	A5
JUBILEE PASS RD	INY	72	C4
JUDAH ST	SF	141	B5
JUDSON ST	SBD	99	C2
JULIAN AV	KER	89	D1
JULIAN AV	SDCO	107	A5
JULIAN RD	SDCO	107	A4
JULIAN ST	SCL	P	C3
JULIAN ST	SCL	46	B4
JULIAN ST	SJ	152	C3
JULIE ST	KER	79	C3
JUMAR CT	RCO	107	B1
JUMPER AV	KER	78	A2
JUNCAL RD	SB	87	D4
JUNE ST	SBD	99	B1
JUNE LK BCH RD	MNO	50	C1
JUNIPER AV	MCO	48	B4
JUNIPER LN	SIS	4	C5
JUNIPER RD	LAS	14	C3
JUNIPER RD	RCO	99	B3
JUNIPER ST	SD	216	B2
JUNIPER ST	SDCO	106	C2
JUNIPER FLTS RD	RCO	99	D4
JUNIPER FLTS RD	RCO	101	A2
JUNIPER HILL RD	LACO	90	B4
JUNIPR KNOLL RD	SIS	5	A3

STREET	CO.	PAGE	GRID
JUNIPER LAKE RD	LAS	20	A3
JUNIPERO ST	CAR	168	C4
JUNIPERO SRA BL	SCL	N	D3
JUNIPERO SRA BL	SCL	45	D4
JUNIPERO SRA FY	CPTO	150	A4
JUNIPERO SRA FY	SJ	150	D5
JUNIPERO SRA FY	SMCO	45	C3
JUNIPER RDG RD	LAS	8	C5
JUNIPER STA RD	MOD	7	B5
JUNKANS RD	SHA	18	A3
JURS RD	CAL	41	B2
JURUPA AV	RCO	99	A2
JURUPA AV	SBD	99	A2
JURUPA RD	RCO	99	A2
JUSTICE CT	KER	79	D2
JUSTICE RD	TRI	16	E5
JUTLAND DR	SD	211	D4

K

STREET	CO.	PAGE	GRID
K ST	BEN	153	B3
K ST	MDO	162	B3
KADOTA AV	MCO	48	D5
KAGEL CANYON RD	LACO	Q	D1
KAISER	SJCO	40	B5
KAISER RD	IMP	109	C3
KAISER RD	RCO	102	C4
KAISER RD	STA	47	D3
KALIN RD	IMP	109	A4
KAMM AV	FRCO	56	E5
KAMM AV	FRCO	57	C5
KAMM AV	TUL	57	D5
KAMM RD	IMP	109	C5
KANDRA RD	SIS	5	D2
KANE RD	HUM	9	E3
KANE RD	SBD	91	E2
KANSAS AV	KIN	67	D2
KANSAS AV	MDO	162	A3
KANSAS AV	RIV	205	D3
KANSAS AV	STA	47	C2
KANSAS AV	TEH	18	E5
KAPAPA RD	SBD	80	E1
KAPRANOS RD	LAK	23	C5
KARCHNER RD	PLA	34	A3
KAREN AV	RCO	100	C3
KARLO RD	LAS	21	C2
KARNAK RD	SUT	33	C4
KASSON RD	SJCO	47	A2
KATELLA AV	ANA	193	A4
KATELLA AV	ANA	194	B4
KATELLA AV	ORA	194	B4
KATELLA AV	ORCO	98	B3
KATELLA AV	ORCO	T	D2
KATHERINE RD	VEN	97	A1
KAUFENBERG RD	LAS	14	A4
KAUFFMAN AV	TEH	18	E5
KAUFMAN RD	STA	47	E2
KAUT RD	TRI	10	E5
KAVANAUGH RD	IMP	112	C3
KEARNEY AV	FRCO	57	A3
KEARNEY BLVD	FRE	165	B4
KEARNY ST	SF	142	D2
KEARNY ST	SF	143	D2
KEARNY VILLA RD	SD	214	A1
KEARNY VILLA RD	SDCO	V	C2
KEARNY VILLA RD	SDCO	106	D5
KEATON RD	MCO	47	D4
KECKS RD	KER	77	A1
KEEFER RD	BUT	25	A2
KEEGAN RD	COL	32	C2
KEELE RD	RCO	110	C1
KEHOE AV	SM	145	B1
KEIM BLVD	RCO	110	C1
KELBAKER RD	SBD	83	C3
KELBAKER RD	SBD	84	A5
KELBAKER RD	SBD	93	E2
KELBAKER RD	SBD	94	A1
KELLEMS LN	SIS	3	D5
KELLEMS LN	SIS	11	D1
KELLER RD	RCO	99	C5
KELLEY RD	SBD	101	D1
KELLOG RD	SUT	33	B2
KELLOGG DR	ORCO	98	C3
KELLOGG DR	ORCO	T	E1
KELLOGG RD	DN	1	D3
KELLOGG SRRA BL	RCO	100	C3
KELLY	SJCO	47	D1
KELLY RD	HUM	16	C2
KELLY RD	NAPA	L	D1
KELLY RD	NAPA	38	D1
KELLY RD	TEH	24	A2
KELLY RD	YUB	26	B5
KELLY GULCH RD	SIS	11	B2
KELSEY CREEK RD	SIS	3	B4
KELSEY CREEK RD	LAK	31	D3
KELSO AV	KER	79	E1
KELSO RD	ALA	M	E4
KELSO RD	ALA	46	D1
KELSO RD	KER	79	E1
KELSO RD	SBD	83	C4
KELSO CIMA RD	SBD	83	E5
KELSO CIMA RD	SBD	84	A4
KELSO CK VLY RD	KER	79	E1
KELSO VALLEY RD	KER	79	E2
KELSO VALLEY RD	KER	80	A2
KEMP CT	HUM	16	B3
KEMPER RD	KER	80	A5
KEMPER RD	STA	47	D2
KEMPTON RD	SUT	33	D3
KENDALL AV	KER	80	D1
KENDALL DR	SBD	99	B1
KENDALL RD	SBD	91	E4
KENDLE RD	IMP	109	C4

STREET	CO.	PAGE	GRID
KENMAR LN	KER	79	A4
KENMAR RD	HUM	15	E2
KENNEBRAW LN	HUM	16	C4
KENNEDY AV	BUT	25	A3
KENNEDY RD	STA	48	A1
KENNEDY RD	TRI	17	B1
KENNEDY MEADOW	TUL	70	A3
KENNEDY MEM DR	SHA	18	B2
KENNEFICK RD	SJCO	40	B4
KENNETH AV	SAC	34	B5
KENNETH RD	LACO	Q	D2
KENNETT RD	SHA	18	C1
KENNEY AV	TEH	18	C4
KENNY AV	MCO	48	B4
KENNY CAMP RD	TRI	11	D5
KENO WORDEN RD	KLAM	5	A1
KENSINGTON WY	S	160	B2
KENT AV	KIN	67	B2
KENT AV	KIN	67	C2
KENT AV	MAR	139	A5
KENT AV	SUT	33	C1
KENTUCKY AV	YOL	33	B5
KENWOOD	SDCO	111	E1
KENWOOD DR	SDCO	V	D3
KEOUGH HOT SPGS	INY	51	D5
KERN RD	SBD	101	D1
KERN ST	SAL	171	D4
KERN CANYON RD	KER	79	A2
KERN RIV CYN RD	KER	79	B2
KERTO RD	KER	78	A5
KERSHAW RD	IMP	109	B4
KESTER AV	LACO	Q	C3
KETTLEMAN LN	SJCO	40	A4
KETTNER BLVD	SD	215	C2
KETTNER BLVD	SDCO	V	B3
KEYES RD	MCO	48	B3
KEYES RD	STA	47	D3
KEYES RD	STA	48	A3
KEYES ST	SJ	152	C5
KEYS RD	SUT	33	D4
KEYSTONE RD	IMP	109	A5
KEYSVILLE RD	KER	79	C1
KEZAR DR	SF	141	D4
KIBBE RD	YUB	33	D1
KICKAPOO TR	SBD	100	D2
KIDDER CREEK RD	SIS	3	C5
KIDDER CK RD S	SIS	3	D5
KIDDER CK RD S	SIS	11	D1
KID LAKES	PLA	35	C1
KIDWELL RD	SOL	39	B1
KIEFER BLVD	SAC	39	E1
KIEFER BLVD	SAC	40	B1
KIEFER RD	IMP	112	C4
KIELY BLVD	SJ	150	E5
KIELY BLVD	SCLR	150	E3
KIERNAN AV	STA	47	B2
KIETZKE LN	RENO	130	E3
KILAGA SPGS RD	PLA	34	B3
KILAGA SPG RD N	PLA	34	B3
KILBURN RD	NAP	133	A4
KILBURN RD	STA	47	C4
KILE RD	SJCO	39	E3
KILER CANYON RD	SLO	75	E1
KILER CANYON RD	SLO	76	A1
KILGORE RD	SUT	33	A2
KILKARE RD	ALA	46	B2
KILLGORE HLS RD	SIS	4	A4
KILROY	STA	47	D3
KILROY RD	MCO	47	D4
KIMBALL LN	YUB	33	D2
KIMBALL RD	TEH	18	D5
KIMBERLINA RD	KER	78	B1
KIMBERLY CT	KER	79	C5
KIMBERLY DR	KER	79	C5
KIMBERLY RD	SHA	18	D3
KIMTU CT	HUM	16	B5
KINCAID RD	SCL	P	D3
KINCAID RD	SCL	46	C4
KINE AV	RCO	99	C3
KINEVAN RD	SB	87	B4
KING AV	KIN	67	C2
KING RD	COL	32	C2
KING RD	IMP	112	C3
KING RD	KER	67	C5
KING RD	PLA	34	B4
KING RD	SJ	152	D1
KING RD	SCL	P	C3
KING RD	SCL	46	B4
KING RD	SOL	39	C2
KING RD	TEH	18	C5
KING RD	TRI	12	A4
KING ST	BKD	166	E4
KING ST	SF	143	E4
KING CITY RD	SBT	65	C1
KINGDON	SJCO	40	A4
KING RANCH RD	BUT	25	E5
KING RIDGE RD	SON	37	A1
KINGS AV	FRCO	66	D2
KINGS RD	SBD	90	E4
KINGS RD	TUO	48	E1
KINGS RD	TUO	49	A1
KINGSBURY RD	TRI	17	B2
KINGS CANYON RD	FRCO	58	A3
KINGS HILL RD	PLA	34	D2
KINGSLEY ST	MTCL	203	C4
KINGS MTN RD	SMCO	N	D2
KINGS MTN RD	SMCO	45	C4
KINGS PEAK RD	HUM	16	A5
KINGSTON RD	SBD	83	E2
KINGS VALLEY RD	DN	1	E3
KINNEY RD	MEN	30	C3
KIOWA BLVD	MOH	96	B4
KIOWA RD	RCO	102	C3

STREET	CO.	PAGE	GRID
KIOWA RD	SBD	91	C4
KIP ST	KER	80	C1
KIRBY RD	MCO	48	C4
KIRBY ST	CAL	40	D4
KIRK RD	SCL	P	B4
KIRKER PASS RD	CC	M	B3
KIRKVILLE RD	SUT	33	C3
KIRSCHENMANN RD	SB	87	D1
KIT CARSON RD	AMA	35	E5
KIT CARSON CPGD	ALP	36	B4
KITCHEN CK RD	SDCO	112	D1
KLAMATH BCH RD	DN	1	E5
KLAMATH BCH RD	DN	9	E1
KLAMATH BCH RD	DN	10	A1
KLAMATH MILL RD	DN	2	A5
KLAMATHON RD	SIS	4	B3
KLAMATH RIV RD	SIS	3	D3
KLASSETTE ST	KER	80	A4
KLAU MINE RD	SLO	75	D1
KLIPSTEIN ST	KER	78	A5
KLIPSTEIN CY RD	KER	78	A5
KLOKE RD	IMP	112	B4
KLONDIKE RD	SBD	93	C3
KLONDIKE MINE RD	TRI	17	A3
KNEELAND RD	HUM	16	B1
KNIEBES RD	MCO	47	D5
KNIGHTON RD	SHA	18	C3
KNIGHTS RD	SUT	33	C3
KNIGHTSEN AV	CC	M	D3
KNIGHTSEN AV	CC	39	C5
KNOB HILL RD	MEN	31	B2
KNOB PK LKOT RD	SHA	17	D3
KNOTT AV	ORCO	98	B3
KNOTT AV	ORCO	T	B2
KNOWLES RD	MAD	49	B5
KNOWLES RD	MCO	56	C1
KNOX RD	STA	47	E1
KNOXVL DVLHD RD	NAPA	32	C4
KOALA RD	SBD	91	A3
KOCH RD	KER	78	B2
KOENIGSTEIN RD	VEN	88	C4
KOESTER RD	KER	79	D3
KONOCTI RD	LAK	31	D3
KOPTA RD	TEH	24	E2
KOSTER RD	SJCO	47	A2
KOSTER ST	EUR	121	B1
KOWOLOWSKI RD	MOD	6	A2
KRAEMER BLVD	ORCO	T	D1
KRAFFT RD	MCO	48	D4
KRAFT RD	KER	78	E5
KRAMAR RD	IMP	111	E3
KRAMER BLVD	ORCO	98	C3
KRAMER RD	LAS	14	B3
KRAMER RD	SBD	91	A1
KRATZMEYER RD	KER	78	C2
KREHE RD	SUT	33	C1
KROSENS RD	YUB	25	E5
KRUSE RD	COL	32	D1
KT RD	SBT	54	E3
KT RD	SBT	55	A3
KUBLER RD	IMP	111	E4
KUCK RD	SIS	4	B4
KUENZLI ST	RENO	130	D2
KUMBERG RD	IMP	112	C4
KUNA AV	SBD	92	E5
KURT RD	KER	77	E1
KUTZ RD	IMP	108	E5
KYLE AV	KER	70	A5
KYTE AV	KER	78	C2
L			
L ST	BEN	153	C4
L ST	CC	M	C3
L ST	DVS	136	D2
L ST	DN	1	D4
L ST	MDO	162	B3
L ST	SCTO	137	D3
L ST	SDCO	V	C4
L ST	SDCO	111	D2
LA BARR MDWS RD	NEV	34	C2
LABP & L RD	SBD	91	A4
LA BREA AV	LA	181	B4
LA BREA AV	LA	184	B3
LA BREA AV	LACO	97	D2
LA BREA AV	LACO	Q	D5
LA BREA CK RD	SB	77	A5
LA BRISA DR	SBD	100	E1
LA BRISTA DR	SBD	100	D1
LA BRUCHERIE RD	IMP	112	A3
LA CADENA DR	CLTN	207	A4
LA CADENA DR	SBD	90	E3
LA CADENA DR	SBD	99	B2
LACEY BLVD	KIN	67	C1
LA CIENEGA BLVD	BH	183	D2
LA CIENEGA BLVD	CUL	183	E4
LA CIENEGA BLVD	LA	188	E4
LA CIENEGA BLVD	ING	189	E1
LA CIENEGA BLVD	LA	183	D4
LA CIENEGA BLVD	LACO	97	D2
LA CIENEGA BLVD	LACO	Q	D4
LA CIENEGA BLVD	LACO	188	E2
LA CIENEGA BLVD	LACO	189	E2
LAC JAC	FRCO	58	A4
LACK RD	IMP	109	A4
LA COLINA	TUL	68	E3
LA COLINA LN	RCO	107	C1
LA CONTENTA RD	SBD	100	E2
LA COSTA AV	SDCO	106	C3
LA CRESCENTA AV	LACO	R	A2
LA CRESTA DR	SDCO	107	A5
LA CUARTA ST	LACO	R	D5
LADD RD	STA	47	C2

STREET	CO.	PAGE	GRID
LADDER RIDGE RD	LAK	31	D2
LADINO AV	MCO	48	B4
LA ENTRADA AV	LACO	R	D5
LAFAYETTE RD	SIE	26	D5
LAFAYETTE ST	SCLR	151	B1
LAFAYETTE ST	S	160	D5
LA GLORIA RD	SBT	55	B5
LAGOMARSINO AV	MON	65	B2
LAGOON DR	KER	78	A2
LA GRANADA	SDCO	106	C4
LA GRANDE RD	COL	32	C2
LA GRANGE RD	MCO	48	C2
LA GRANGE RD	STA	48	C2
LA GRANGE RD	TUO	48	C1
LA GRANGE DM RD	STA	48	C2
LAGUE RD	YUB	26	A5
LAGUNA AV	FRCO	67	B1
LAGUNA FRWY	ORCO	98	D4
LAGUNA FRWY	ORCO	T	E4
LAGUNA RD	SON	37	D2
LAGUNA RD	VEN	96	C1
LAGUNA ST	STB	174	A2
LAGUNA CYN RD	LAG	201	B2
LAGUNA CYN RD	ORCO	98	C5
LAGUNA CYN RD	ORCO	T	E5
LAGUNA CREEK TR	SOL	38	E3
LAGUNA MTN RD	SDCO	107	D5
LAGUNA SECA DR	SBD	91	D4
LAGUNA SECA RD	MCO	55	D3
LA HABRA BLVD	ORCO	R	E5
LA HABRA BLVD	ORCO	T	C1
LA HONDA RD	SMCO	N	C3
LA HONDA RD	SMCO	45	C4
LAIRD RD	PLA	34	B4
LAIRD RD	STA	47	C3
LAIRO RED ROCK	SIS	5	C3
LA JOLLA AV	SDCO	106	C5
LA JOLLA BLVD	SDCO	V	A2
LA JOLLA BLVD	SDCO	106	C5
LA JOLLA AMAGO	SDCO	107	A2
LA JOLLA S DR N	SD	211	B2
LA JOLLA S DR S	SD	211	A4
LA JOLLA MESA DR	SD	211	A4
LA JOLLA SHR DR	SD	211	A2
LA JOLLA VLG RD	SDCO	V	A2
LAKE AV	FRCO	56	E3
LAKE AV	FRCO	57	A3
LAKE AV	KER	79	C2
LAKE AV	LACO	98	A1
LAKE AV	LACO	R	B3
LAKE AV	PAS	190	D4
LAKE AV	SCR	54	C2
LAKE BLVD	SHA	18	C2
LAKE DR	SBD	91	C5
LAKE RD	FRCO	50	B5
LAKE RD	KER	80	C3
LAKE RD	MCO	48	C4
LAKE RD	STA	47	E2
LAKE RD	STA	48	A2
LAKE RD N	INY	51	B5
LAKE RD S	INY	51	C5
LAKE RD S	KER	78	B4
LAKE RD S	KER	78	C4
LAKE ST	MAD	57	A2
LAKE ST	RCO	99	B4
LK ALMANOR W DR	PLU	20	B4
LK ALMANR RD E	PLU	20	C4
LK ALPINE RD E	ALP	42	A1
LK ALPINE RD W	ALP	42	A2
LAKE ANNIE RD	MOD	7	D3
LK BRITTON LOOP	SHA	13	C4
LK BRITTON RAMP	SHA	13	C4
LAKE CALIF DR	TEH	18	D3
LAKE CANYON RD	LACO	89	B3
LAKE CANYON RD	LACO	89	C3
LAKE CITY RD	NEV	26	C5
LK CITY DUMP RD	MOD	7	D5
LAKE CREST RD	LAS	21	B4
LAKE DAVIS RD	PLU	27	B2
LAKE EARL DR	DN	1	D4
LAKE FOREST DR	ORCO	98	D4
LAKE FRANCES RD	YUB	26	B5
LAKE HERMAN RD	SOL	L	E2
LAKE HERMAN RD	SOL	38	D4
LK JENNINGS PK	SDCO	107	A5
LAKELAND RD	LACO	R	C5
LAKELAND RD	LACO	T	A1
LAKE LEAVITT RD	LAS	21	B3
LAKE MARY RD	ML	164	A4
LAKE MARY RD	MNO	50	D2
LAKE MATHEWS DR	RCO	99	B3
LAKE MCCUMBER	SHA	19	B2
LAKE MEAD DR	CLK	74	E3
LAKE MORENA DR	SDCO	112	D1
LAKE MURRAY BL	SDCO	V	D3
LAKE MURRAY BL	SDCO	106	D5
LAKEPORT BLVD	LAK	31	D3
LAKE POWAY RD	SDCO	106	D4
LAKERIDGE RD	SHA	19	A3
LAKE SHORE AV	O	158	B3
LAKESHORE BLVD	LAK	31	D3
LAKESHORE RD	KLAM	5	B1
LAKESHORE DR	LAK	32	A3
LAKESHORE DR	SHA	12	C5
LAKE SHORE DR	SIS	12	C1
LAKESHORE RD	MOD	7	B4
LAKESIDE DR	O	158	A3
LAKE SIDE LN	SIS	4	C2
LAKE STATION RD	KER	78	B4
LAKE TAHOE BLVD	SLT	129	A4
LAKEVIEW	KIN	67	C2
LAKEVIEW	PLA	34	A3
LAKEVIEW AV	ORCO	T	E2

STREET	CO.	PAGE	GRID
LAKEVIEW AV	RCO	99	D3
LAKEVIEW DR	AMA	40	D3
LAKEVIEW DR	LAK	31	D2
LAKE VIEW DR	LAS	21	B4
LAKE VIEW DR	SLO	75	D1
LAKEVIEW RD	MPA	49	B3
LAKEVIEW RD	SCR	54	C2
LAKEVIEW RD	SDCO	107	A5
LAKE VIEW RD	SIS	4	C3
LAKEVIEW RD	SON	38	B3
LAKEVIEW CEM RD	SIS	5	A3
LAKEVILLE HWY	SON	L	A1
LAKEVILLE RD	SON	L	B2
LK WILDWOOD DR	NEV	34	B1
LAKEWOOD BLVD	LACO	98	A3
LAKEWOOD BLVD	LACO	S	E2
LAKEWOOD DR	MEN	23	A5
LAKIN DAM RD	SIS	13	A2
LA LOMA AV	B	156	B2
LA LOMA AV	MDO	162	C3
LA LOMA AV	VEN	88	C5
LA LOMA RD	LACO	R	B3
LAMB BLVD	CLK	74	E2
LAMB CANYON RD	RCO	99	E3
LAMBERT LN	LAS	21	C4
LAMBERT RD	LACO	R	C5
LAMBERT RD	ORCO	U	A4
LAMBERT RD	ORCO	T	C1
LAMBERT RD	SAC	39	D3
LAMBIE RD	SOL	39	B3
LAMBUTH RD	STA	47	D1
LAMERT LN	GLE	24	D5
LA MESA RD	SBD	90	E4
LA MIRADA AV	LACO	R	D5
LA MIRADA AV	LACO	T	B1
LA MIRADA BLVD	LACO	98	B3
LAMMERS RD	SJCO	46	E2
LAMONT ST	SD	212	C1
LAMPLEY RD	STA	48	A2
LAMPSON AV	GGR	195	C1
LAMPSON AV	ORCO	T	B2
LANCASTER BLVD	KER	90	B1
LANCASTER BLVD	LACO	90	A4
LANCASTER RD	LACO	88	E2
LANCASTER RD	LACO	89	A2
LANCASTER RD	STA	47	E1
LANCASTER RD	STA	48	A1
LANCHA PLANA-			
-BUENA VISTA RD	AMA	40	D3
LANDACRE RD	TRI	17	B2
LANDAU BLVD	RCO	100	D3
LANDECENA DR	TRI	17	D1
LANDER AV	MCO	47	D5
LANDER AV	STA	47	E3
LANDERGEN RD	HUM	15	E4
LANDES RD	TEH	18	C4
LANDESS RD	SCL	46	B4
LANDIS GULCH	TRI	17	C3
LAND PARK DR	SCTO	137	B4
LANDRAM AV	MCO	48	B4
LANDVALE RD	O	156	D4
LANES RD	FRCO	57	C2
LANES VALLEY RD	TEH	19	A3
LANFAIR RD	SBD	84	D3
LANFAIR RD	SBD	94	E1
LANGDON RD	MCO	55	D2
LANGLL VLY RD E	KLAM	5	E1
LANGLL VLY RD E	KLAM	6	A1
LANGLL VLY RD W	KLAM	5	E1
LANGLL VLY RD W	KLAM	6	A1
LANGWORTH RD	STA	47	D2
LANINI RD	MON	54	E5
LANINI RD	MON	55	A5
LANKERSHIM BLVD	LACO	97	D1
LANKERSHIM BLVD	LACO	Q	D2
LANNAGAN RD	TRI	11	B5
LANNAGAN RD	TRI	17	B1
LA NOVIA AV	SJC	202	E2
LANPHERE RD	HUM	9	E5
LANSING AV	KIN	67	C2
LA PALMA AV	ANA	193	D1
LA PALMA AV	ANA	194	B1
LA PALMA AV	KER	80	A5
LA PALMA AV	ORCO	98	A3
LA PALMA AV	ORCO	T	B2
LA PALOMA	AVLN	97	A4
LA PALOMA DR	TUL	68	E3
LA PALOMA RD	MCO	48	C4
LA PANZA AV	SB	87	E2
LA PAZ RD	ORCO	98	D5
LA PORTE RD	BUT	25	D5
LA PORTE RD	BUT	26	B4
LA PORTE RD	YUB	26	A5
LA POSTA RD	SDCO	112	D1
LA PUENTE RD	LACO	U	A3
LARGO GRANDE	RCO	107	B1
LARGO VISTA RD	LACO	90	D4
LARKELLEN AV	LACO	R	E4
LARKIN RD	BUT	25	C4
LARKIN RD	SUT	33	C1
LARKIN ST	SF	143	B3
LARKIN VALLEY	SCR	54	B3
LARKMEAD LN	NAPA	29	B2
LARKSPUR DR	MLBR	144	B5
LARREA AV	SBD	101	B3
LARRY FLAT	MOD	7	D3
LARSEN RD	IMP	109	A5
LARSON LN	MNO	42	E1
LARSON RD	RCO	107	C1
LA SALLE CANYON	SB	86	B3
LAS AMIGAS RD	NAPA	38	C3
LAS ANIMAS RD	SCL	46	C5
LAS FLORES AV	KER	80	C1

STREET	CO.	PAGE	GRID
LAS GALLINAS AV	SR	139	B1
LA SIERRA AV	RCO	99	A3
LAS LOMAS AV	AVLN	97	A5
LAS PALMAS AV	STA	47	C3
LASPINA DR	TUL	68	B2
LAS PLUMAS AV	BUT	25	D4
LAS POSAS	VEN	96	C1
LS PULGAS CY RD	SDCO	106	A2
LAS ROCAS	RCO	100	D4
LASSELLE ST	RCO	99	C3
LASSEN AV	BUT	25	B3
LASSEN AV	FRCO	67	A1
LASSEN AV	FRCO	57	A3
LASSEN LN	SIS	12	C2
LASSEN RD	TEH	25	A2
LASSEN ST	LAS	8	B4
LASSEN TRAIL	TEH	19	D4
LASSEN CREEK RD	MOD	7	C4
LASSEN PARK HWY	SHA	19	D2
LASSICS LKOT RD	TRI	16	E4
LAST CHANCE CYN	KER	80	C2
LAST CHANCE MNE	NEV	26	E5
LAST CHANCE MNE	NEV	35	A1
LAS TUNAS DR	LACO	R	C3
LAS VARAS RD	SB	87	A4
LAS VEGAS BLVD	CLK	74	D3
LAS VEGAS BL S	CLK	209	C4
LAS VEGAS BL S	CLK	210	B5
LAS VEGAS BL S	LV	209	C4
LAS VIRGENES RD	LACO	97	A1
LATHAM RD	SUT	33	B3
LATHROP RD	MAN	161	A1
LATHROP RD	SJCO	47	A1
LATHROP RD	SJCO	161	D1
LATIGO CYN RD	LACO	97	A2
LA TIJERA BLVD	LA	188	D5
LA TIJERA BLVD	LACO	Q	D5
LATKA LN	TEH	19	B4
LATROBE RD	AMA	40	D1
LATROBE RD	ED	40	C1
LATROBE RD	SAC	40	B1
LA TUNA CYN RD	LACO	97	D1
LA TUNA CYN RD	LACO	Q	D2
LAUFFER RD	HUM	22	D1
LAUGHLIN RD	STA	47	E2
LAUGHLIN CVC DR	CLK	85	D4
LAURA DR	LAS	27	E1
LAUREL AV	KIN	67	B2
LAUREL AV	SUT	33	D3
LAUREL DR E	MON	171	E2
LAUREL DR E	SAL	171	E2
LAUREL DR W	SAL	171	A2
LAUREL DR W	MON	171	A2
LAUREL LN	YUB	33	D1
LAUREL ST	NAP	133	A4
LAUREL ST	SD	215	C2
LAUREL ST	SDCO	V	B3
LAUREL ST	SC	169	C3
LAUREL ST	VAL	134	E5
LAUREL ST E	CLTN	207	A4
LAUREL WY	TEH	18	C4
LAUREL CYN BLVD	LACO	97	D1
LAUREL CYN BLVD	LACO	Q	C1
LAUREL DELL RD	LAK	31	C2
LAURELES GRADE	MON	54	C5
LAUREL GLEN RD	SCR	P	B5
LAUREL GLEN RD	SCR	54	A1
LAUREL GROVE AV	MAR	L	A3
LAUREL GROVE AV	ROSS	139	A4
LAURELLEN RD	YUB	33	D2
LAURENT ST	SC	169	B3
LAURJOE RD	SBD	91	E3
LAUSTEN RD	COL	32	D1
LAUX RD	COL	33	A1
LAVA BED RD	BUT	25	B3
LAVA BDS NAT MN	MOD	6	A4
LAVA BDS MED LK	SIS	5	C5
LAVAL RD	KER	78	E5
LAVER CROSSING	LAS	21	D5
LA VETA AV	ORA	196	B1
LAVEZZOLA RD	SIE	26	D4
LAVIC RD	SBD	92	E2
LA VISTA AV	VEN	88	C5
LAWRENCE EXPWY	SCL	P	A3
LAWRENCE EXPWY	SCLR	150	C4
LAWRENCE EXPWY	SJ	150	C4
LAWRENCE EXPWY	SVL	150	C4
LAWSON LN	HUM	15	E2
LAXAQUE RD	MOD	8	D1
LAYTNVL DOS RIO	MEN	22	E3
LAZARO CARDENAS	BAJA	112	B4
LAZARUS LN	RCO	100	A5
L B CROW RD	STA	47	C4
LEACH RD	YUB	33	D3
LEAR AV	SBD	101	B1
LEARY RD	SAC	M	E1
LEARY RD	SAC	39	D3
LEASTALK AV	SBD	84	C3
LEATHER RD	IMP	110	D5
LEAVENWORTH ST	SF	143	B2
LEAVESLEY RD	SCL	P	E5
LEAVESLEY RD	SCL	54	D1
LEAVITT RD	LAS	21	B3
LEE RD	MCO	48	A3
LEE RD	PLU	26	D1
LEE RD	SHA	13	E4
LEE RD	SUT	33	D4
LEEDS	MCO	48	C4
LEEGE AV	SB	86	B3
LEEK RD	STA	47	D2
LEE SCHOOL RD	SAC	40	B2
LEESVILLE RD	COL	32	C2
LEESVL-LODGA RD	COL	32	B1

STREET INDEX

STREET	CO.	PAGE	GRID
LEFF RD	RCO	107	B1
LEFFINGWELL RD	LACO	R	C5
LEFFINGWELL RD	LACO	T	B1
LEGION AV	MCO	47	E4
LEGION AV	MCO	48	A4
LEGION PARK DR	MDO	162	E5
LE GRAND RD	MCO	48	D5
LEGRAY RD	KER	78	E5
LEIGHTON, H RD	SHA	18	C2
LEILA LN	SBD	101	E1
LEIMERT BLVD	LACO	Q	D4
LEININGER RD	TEH	25	A1
LEISER RD	SUT	33	C4
LEISURE TOWN RD	SOL	39	A2
LELITER RD	KER	70	C5
LEMON AV	SDCO	V	D3
LEMON AV	SDCO	111	E1
LEMON AV	SJCO	47	D1
LEMON AV	STA	47	B3
LEMON RD	SBD	91	C4
LEMON ST	ORCO	T	C1
LEMON ST	RIV	205	B3
LEMON ST	VAL	134	D5
LEMON CANYON RD	SIE	27	C4
LEMOS RD	SIS	4	A2
LENAHAN RD	COL	32	D1
LENARD RD	LAS	14	C3
LENINGER RD	BUT	25	A2
LENTELL RD	HUM	15	E1
LENWOOD RD	SBD	91	D1
LEO RD	RCO	107	A1
LEON AV	MCO	56	B2
LEON RD	RCO	99	D4
LEONA AV	LACO	89	D3
LEONARD AV	FRCO	57	D4
LEONARD AV	KER	78	A2
LEONARD RD	MPA	49	C3
LEONI RD	ED	35	B5
LEOTA ST	MCO	55	D1
LEPRECHAUN LN	RCO	107	B1
LERDO HWY	KER	77	D2
LERDO HWY	KER	78	A2
LEROY AV	SJCO	47	B1
LESSING ST	SBD	91	A3
LETTS VALLEY RD	COL	31	E1
LEVEE RD	FRCO	56	E4
LEVEE RD	IMP	112	D5
LEVEE RD	YOL	39	C2
LEVERONI RD	SON	L	B1
LEVERONI RD	SON	38	B3
LEVERONI RD	SON	132	B5
LEVIATHAN LKOUT	ALP	36	D5
LEVIATHAN RD	ALP	36	D5
LEWELLING BLVD	ALA	146	B1
LEWELLING BL E	ALA	L	E5
LEWIS RD	MON	54	C2
LEWIS RD	SHA	13	E4
LEWIS RD	SOL	39	B3
LEWIS RD	STA	47	C4
LEWIS RD	VEN	96	C1
LEWIS RD	YUB	33	E3
LEWIS CREEK RD	MON	65	D2
LEWIS RIDGE RD	BUT	26	B4
LEWISTON AV	FRCO	67	C1
LEWISTON RD	SHA	18	A1
LEWISTON RD	TRI	17	D1
LEWISTON TURNPK	TRI	17	E1
LEXINGTON AV	MCO	56	A2
LEXINGTON AV	SDCO	106	E5
LEXINGTN HLL RD	PLU	26	C3
LIBERAL AV	TEH	24	D2
LIBERTY AV	MCO	48	A4
LIBERTY RD	SJCO	40	B3
LIBERTY RD W	BUT	25	B5
LIBERTY ISLD RD	SOL	M	D1
LIBERTY ISLD RD	SOL	39	C3
LIBRAMIENTO SUR	BAJA	111	D3
LIBRAMNT ORIENT	BAJA	111	D2
LICHEN WY	RCO	107	B1
LICHENS RD	SIS	4	B4
LIEBERT RD	IMP	111	E3
LIGGET AV	COL	32	E3
LIGHTHILL RD	SIS	3	D5
LIGHTHOUSE AV	MONT	167	D2
LIGHTHOUSE AV	MON	53	E2
LIGHTHOUSE AV	PAC	167	B2
LIGHTHOUSE RD	HUM	15	D4
LIGHTHOUSE RD	MEN	30	C3
LILI VALLEY WY	CAL	41	C2
LILLEY MTN DR	MAD	49	C5
LILY GAP RD	CAL	41	C2
LIM RD	LAS	14	C3
LIME CREEK RD	CAL	40	E3
LIMEDYKE LKOUT	TRI	16	E2
LIMEKILN RD	MON	54	D5
LIME KILN RD	NEV	34	C2
LIMEKILN RD	SBT	54	E4
LIMEKILN RD	SBT	55	A4
LIME KILN RD	TUO	41	C5
LIME SADDLE RD	BUT	25	C3
LIMONITE AV	RCO	99	A2
LINCOLN	LACO	97	C2
LINCOLN	MCO	48	B5
LINCOLN AV	A	159	A1
LINCOLN AV	ANA	193	B2
LINCOLN AV	ANA	194	B2
LINCOLN AV	FRCO	56	D4
LINCOLN AV	FRCO	57	A4
LINCOLN AV	FRCO	58	A4
LINCOLN AV	KIN	67	C2
LINCOLN AV	LACO	R	B2
LINCOLN AV	ORA	194	D2
LINCOLN AV	ORCO	98	B3

STREET	CO.	PAGE	GRID
LINCOLN AV	ORCO	T	B2
LINCOLN AV	PAS	190	B2
LINCOLN AV	RCO	U	E5
LINCOLN AV	RCO	98	E3
LINCOLN AV	SAL	171	C4
LINCOLN AV	SD	214	A5
LINCOLN AV	SDCO	106	D3
LINCOLN AV	SR	139	D3
LINCOLN AV	SA	196	C3
LINCOLN AV	SCL	P	B3
LINCOLN AV	SCL	46	B4
LINCOLN AV	SJ	152	A5
LINCOLN AV	YUB	33	E1
LINCOLN AV W	NAP	133	B2
LINCOLN BLVD	BUT	25	D5
LINCOLN BLVD	LA	187	C3
LINCOLN BLVD	LACO	Q	B4
LINCOLN BLVD	LACO	187	D4
LINCOLN BLVD	MCO	47	E4
LINCOLN BLVD	MCO	48	A4
LINCOLN BLVD	SF	141	B3
LINCOLN BLVD	SMON	187	A2
LINCOLN RD	SBD	91	E4
LINCOLN RD	SUT	33	C2
LINCOLN RD	SUT	125	A5
LINCOLN RD	YUBA	125	A5
LINCOLN ST	NAPA	29	A1
LINCOLN ST	RCO	101	B5
LINCOLN ST	SC	169	D3
LINCOLN ST	S	160	D5
LINCOLN ST N	KER	77	E4
LINCOLN ST N	KER	78	A4
LINCOLN WY	AUB	126	D2
LINCOLN WY	SFCO	L	B5
LINCOLN WY	SF	141	C4
LINCOLN WY	SFCO	45	B1
LINDA DR	SIS	4	B2
LINDA VISTA AV	LACO	98	A1
LINDA VISTA AV	LACO	R	B2
LINDA VISTA AV	NAP	133	A2
LINDA VISTA AV	PAS	190	A3
LINDA VISTA AV	TUL	68	D3
LINDA VISTA DR	SB	87	A3
LINDA VISTA RD	SBD	91	D1
LINDA VISTA RD	SD	213	B4
LINDA VISTA RD	SDCO	V	B3
LINDA VISTA RD	SDCO	111	C1
LINDBERGH BLVD	KER	80	B4
LINDBLOOM RD	MCO	55	D3
LINDBROOK BLVD	LA	180	D2
LINDEN AV	MCO	56	A1
LINDEN AV	SBD	99	B2
LINDEN AV	SSF	144	B1
LINDENBERGER RD	RCO	99	D4
LINDERO CYN RD	LACO	96	E1
LINDLEY AV	LA	178	E4
LINDLEY AV	LACO	97	C1
LINDLEY RD	HUM	15	E4
LINDSAY RD	IMP	109	A3
LINDSAY RD	KER	78	C4
LINDSEY AV	GLE	24	E3
LINE RD	YOL	39	D2
LINEA DEL CIELO	SDCO	106	C4
LINGARD RD	MCO	48	C5
LINN RD	SJCO	40	C4
LINNE RD	SJCO	46	E2
LINNE RD	SLO	76	B1
LINSON AV	SBD	91	A3
LINWOOD AV	STA	47	C3
LINWOOD RD	MCO	47	E3
LINWOOD RD	MCO	48	A3
LISBON ST	MCO	48	A5
LISBON ST	SDCO	V	D3
LISCOMB HILL RD	HUM	10	A5
LIST AV	TUL	68	C1
LITT RD	STA	47	D2
LITTLE AV	BUT	25	C5
LITTLE RD	LPAZ	104	A2
LITTLE BEAR RD	RCO	102	C4
LTL BLACK ROCK	TRI	17	C4
LTL BRWNS CK RD	TRI	17	D1
LTL BRWNS CK RD	TRI	17	D1
LTL GIANT MILL	TEH	19	B4
LITTL GRASS VLY	PLU	26	C3
LITTL HONKR BAY	SOL	39	B3
LITTLE JOHN	SJCO	40	C5
LITTLE JOHN RD	CAL	41	A5
LITTLE LAKE RD	INY	70	C4
LITTLE LAKE RD	MEN	30	C1
LITL MORONGO DR	SBD	100	D1
LITL PANOCHE RD	FRCO	55	D4
LITL PANOCHE RD	SBT	55	D4
LITTLE RIVER	MEN	30	B1
LTL SLATE CK RD	SHA	12	B4
LTL SYCAMOR CYN	LACO	96	D2
LTL TUJUNGA RD	LACO	89	D5
LITTLE VLY RD	LAS	14	A4
LITTLE VLY RD	MEN	22	C4
LITTLE VLY DUMP	LAS	14	B5
LITL VIRGNIA LK	MNO	43	B4
LITTLE WALKR RD	MNO	42	E3
LITTLE WALKR RD	MNO	43	A3
LITTON DR	NEV	127	C2
LIVELY RD	BUT	25	B5
LIVE OAK	FRCO	58	B3
LIVE OAK AV	LACO	98	B1
LIVE OAK AV	SBD	99	A2
LIVE OAK AV	SCL	P	D5
LIVE OAK AV	SCL	54	C1
LIVEOAK DR	BUT	25	B3
LIVE OAK DR	SBD	99	D1
LIVE OAK RD	SBT	55	B4
LIVE OAK RD	SJCO	40	B4

STREET	CO.	PAGE	GRID
LIVEOAK RD	SLO	76	A1
LIVE OAK RD	TEH	18	C5
LIVE OAK CYN RD	ORCO	98	E4
LIVE OAK CYN RD	SBD	99	D2
LIVERMORE RD	NAPA	32	A5
LIVNGSTN CRESSY	MCO	47	E4
LIVNGSTN CRESSY	MCO	48	A4
LIVORNA RD	CC	M	A4
LLAGAS RD	SCL	P	D5
LLAGAS RD	SCL	54	C1
LLANO RD	SON	37	E2
LLOYD LN	SHA	18	C3
LOBATA RD	YUB	33	E1
LOCAN AV	FRCO	57	D3
LOCH LOMOND RD	LAK	31	E4
LOCKHART RD	SBD	81	B4
LOCKWOOD RD	STA	47	D3
LOCKWOOD CEM RD	MON	65	C5
LOCKWD JOLON RD	MON	65	C4
LOCKWD SAN ARDO	MON	65	C4
LOCKWD SN LUCAS	MON	65	C3
LOCKWOOD VLY RD	VEN	88	C2
LOCO BILL RD	KER	79	D3
LOCUST AV	RCO	99	C2
LOCUST AV	SBD	81	A5
LOCUST AV	SBD	91	E4
LOCUST AV	STA	47	C3
LOCUST RD	SHA	18	D3
LOCUST TREE RD	SJCO	40	B5
LODGE RD	FRCO	58	A1
LODI LN	NAPA	29	B2
LODI RD	COL	33	A3
LOFGREN RD	BUT	25	B4
LOGAN AV	SD	216	E5
LOGAN LN	MEN	23	B2
LOG CABIN MINE	MNO	43	C5
LOGGING CAMP RD	MNO	50	E1
LOG HOUSE RD	SIS	4	E2
LOKERN RD	KER	77	D3
LOKOYA RD	NAPA	38	B2
LOLETA AV	TEH	24	D2
LOLETA RD	HUM	15	D2
LOMA AV	MCO	56	B1
LOMA ALTA DR	LACO	98	A1
LOMA ALTA DR	LACO	R	B2
LOMA ALTA DR	STB	174	B4
LOMA PRIETA AV	SCR	P	B5
LOMA PRIETA RD	SCR	54	A1
LOMA RICA DR	NEV	34	C1
LOMA RICA RD	YUB	33	D1
LOMAS CANTADAS	CC	156	E2
LOMAS SANTA FE	SDCO	106	C4
LOMA VERDE RD	RCO	102	C4
LOMA VISTA DR	NAPA	38	C2
LOMBARD ST	SFCO	L	B4
LOMBARD ST	SF	142	A2
LOMBARD ST	SF	141	E2
LOMBARD ST	SFCO	45	B1
LOMBARDY AV	MCO	47	E3
LOMBARDY AV	MCO	48	A3
LOMITA	VEN	88	A4
LOMITA BLVD	LACO	97	D3
LOMITA BLVD	LACO	S	B2
LOMITAS DR	TUL	58	D5
LOMITAS DR	TUL	68	D1
LOMPOC-CASML RD	SB	86	B2
LONDALE RD	STA	47	B1
LONE BUTTE RD	KER	80	A5
LONE COMPANY RD	MNO	42	E1
LONE HILL AV	LACO	U	B2
LONE MTN RD	JOS	2	C2
LONE OAK AV	STA	47	E2
LONE PINE LN	SON	38	A1
LONE PINE CYN	SBD	90	E5
LONE PN NRRW GG	INY	60	B4
LONE STAR MN RD	MNO	51	C2
LONE STAR RD	COL	32	E2
LONE STAR RD	MNO	51	C2
LONE STAR RD	PLA	34	B3
LONE STAR RD	SBD	91	C2
LONE TREE	SJCO	47	C1
LONE TREE RD	BUT	25	D5
LONE TREE RD	MCO	48	B5
LONE TREE RD	SBT	55	A2
LONE TREE RD	SHA	18	D3
LONE TREE WY	CC	M	C3
LONE TREE WY	CC	39	B5
LONG BARN	TUO	41	E4
LONG BEACH BLVD	LB	192	E3
LONG BEACH BLVD	LACO	97	E3
LONG BEACH BLVD	LACO	S	D1
LONG BEACH BL N	LACO	S	D1
LONG BEACH FRWY	LB	192	C1
LONG BEACH FRWY	LACO	97	E3
LONG CANYON RD	SB	86	D1
LONG CANYON RD	RCO	100	D3
LONGCOR RD	TEH	18	C3
LONGDEN AV	LACO	R	C3
LONG FELLOW AV	BUT	25	B3
LONG GULCH RD	SIS	4	A4
LONG HAY FLAT	SHA	19	B3
LONG HOLLOW DR	MAD	49	C5
LONG HOLLOW DR	TEH	24	C2
LONGHORN DR	LAS	8	B4
LONGHORN LN	KER	79	B4
LONG PRAIRIE RD	SIS	5	A5
LONG RAVINE RD	NEV	34	B2
LONG RIDGE RD	TRI	16	E5
LONG VALLEY RD	ALP	36	C4
LONG VALLEY RD	LAK	32	A3
LONG VALLEY RD	SIE	27	E3
LONG VALLEY RD	PLU	20	C5
LONGVIEW AV	MCO	47	E4

STREET	CO.	PAGE	GRID
LONGVIEW AV	MCO	48	A4
LONGVIEW RD	LACO	90	C3
LONOAK RD	MON	65	C2
LOOKOUT RD	CAL	41	C2
LKOUT-HACKMR RD	MOD	6	B5
LKOUT-HACKMR RD	MOD	14	B1
LKOUT INDIAN RD	MOD	14	B3
LOOKOUT MTN RD	SLO	76	C3
LOONEY RD	MCO	48	B3
LOOP BLVD N	KER	80	B4
LOOP BLVD S	KER	80	B4
LOOP RD	HUM	16	A2
LOOP RD	RCO	101	B2
LOOP RD	SHA	19	C2
LOPES RD	SOL	38	E4
LOPEZ DR	SLO	76	B4
LOPEZ CANYON RD	LACO	Q	C1
LOPEZ CANYON RD	SLO	76	C4
LOQUAT AV	STA	47	B3
LORAINE AV	LACO	U	A1
LORENA ST	LA	186	E5
LORENSON	PLA	34	B3
LORENTZ RD	AMA	40	D1
LORENZEN RD	SJCO	47	A2
LORETZ RD	CLO	32	D1
LORRAINE RD	SBD	92	E5
LORT DR	TUL	68	C1
LOS ALAMITOS BL	ORCO	T	A2
LOS ALAMOS RD	RCO	99	C5
LOS ALTOS DR	LACO	R	D4
LOS ANGELES AV	VEN	88	C5
LOS ANGELES AV	VEN	89	A5
LOS ANGELES ST	KER	78	A2
LS ANGLS AQDUCT	KER	80	B2
LS BERROS ARRYO	SLO	76	B4
LOS BURROS RD	MON	64	E4
LOS BURROS RD	MON	65	A4
LOS CERRITOS RD	MCO	48	B3
LOS CERRITOS RD	STA	48	B2
LOS COCHES RD	MON	65	A1
LOS COCHES RD	SDCO	V	E2
LOS COCHES RD	SDCO	107	A5
LS COYOTES DIAG	LACO	S	E2
LS COYOTES DIAG	LACO	T	A2
LOS FELIZ BLVD	GLEN	182	E2
LOS FELIZ BLVD	LA	182	C3
LOS FELIZ BLVD	LACO	97	D1
LOS FELIZ BLVD	LACO	Q	E3
LOS FLORES RD	SBD	91	B5
LOS GATOS BLVD	SCL	P	B4
LOS GATOS BLVD	SCL	46	A5
LOS GATOS RD	FRCO	66	C2
LOS LOBOS RD	MON	65	D4
LOS NIETOS RD	LACO	98	A2
LOS NIETOS RD	LACO	R	C5
LOS OLIVOS ST	STB	174	B2
LOS OSOS VLY RD	SLO	75	E3
LOS OSOS VLY RD	SLO	76	A3
LOS PADRES RD	SBD	91	C3
LOS PALOS DR	SAL	171	D5
LOS PINOS DR	RCO	100	D5
LOS PINOS RD	SDCO	112	D1
LS RANCHITOS RD	SR	139	B2
LOS ROBLES AV	LACO	R	B3
LOS ROBLES AV	PAS	190	C2
LOS ROBLES AV N	PAS	190	C2
LOS ROBLES RD	LACO	98	A1
LOST RD	RCO	99	C4
LOST CREEK RD	TEH	19	E4
LOST CK DAM RD	YUB	26	B4
LOST HILLS AV	FRCO	66	D3
LOST HILLS RD	KER	77	D2
LOST LAKE RD	ALP	36	A5
LOST LAKE RD	FRCO	57	D2
LOST SECTION S	INY	72	C3
LOST SECTION RD	INY	72	C3
LOS VERJELES RD	BUT	25	E5
LOS VERJELES RD	YUB	25	E5
LOTT RD	BUT	25	B3
LOTUS RD	ED	34	D5
LOUIE RD	SIS	4	C5
LOUIS AV	BUT	25	B5
LOUISE AV	MAN	161	A2
LOUISE AV	SJCO	47	C1
LOUMAS LN	KER	79	C4
LOUPE AV	SCL	P	C3
LOUPE AV	SCL	46	B4
LOVE CREEK RD	CAL	41	C3
LOVEKIN BLVD	RCO	103	D5
LOVELAND RD	IMP	109	A4
LOVELOCK RD	BUT	25	D2
LOVENESS RD	MOD	14	B1
LOW RD	IMP	111	E3
LOWDEN RD	RED	122	E3
LOWDEN RD	SHA	122	E3
LOW DIVIDE RD	DN	1	E3
LOW DIVIDE RD	DN	2	A3
LOWE RD	IMP	110	B3
LOWELL ST	SDCO	V	A3
LOWELL HILL RD	NEV	34	E1
LOWER RD	AVLN	97	B5
LOWER AZUSA RD	LACO	98	A2
LOWER AZUSA RD	LACO	R	D3
LOWR CHILES VLY	NAPA	29	E2
LOWR CHILES VLY	NAPA	38	C1
LOWER COLFAX RD	NEV	34	C2
LOWER DORRAY RD	CAL	41	E3
LOWER E TER	AVLN	97	B5
LOWR ENTRPRS RD	BUT	25	E4
LOWER FIRE RD	SIS	4	D5
LOWER FORBESTWN	BUT	26	A4
LOWER GAS PT RD	SHA	18	B3
LOWR GLACIER RD	INY	51	E5

STREET	CO.	PAGE	GRID
LOWER HONCUT RD	BUT	25	D5
LOWER JONES	SJCO	39	D5
LOWER KLAMTH HY	KLAM	5	B1
LOWER KUCK RD	SIS	4	C3
LOWER LAKE RD	DN	1	D3
LOWER LAKE RD	LAK	31	E3
LOWER LAKE RD	LAK	32	A3
LWR LITL SHASTA	SIS	4	B4
LOWER MAD RIVER	TRI	16	E3
LOWER RATLSNAKE	TRI	17	A3
LOWER SACRAMNTO	SJCO	40	A4
LOWER SPGS RD	SHA	18	B2
LWR WESTSIDE RD	TRI	16	E4
LOWR WYANDTT RD	BUT	25	D5
LOWERY RD	HUM	15	D3
LOWERY RD	TEH	18	B5
LOWERY CEM RD	TEH	24	A1
LOWES CANYON RD	SLO	66	B5
LOW GAP RD	MEN	30	D1
LOW GAP RD	MEN	31	A2
LOW GAP RD	MEN	123	A2
LOW GAP RD	U	123	A2
LOYALTON RD	SIE	27	D3
LOYALTON RD	SIE	27	C3
LOZANO RD	MPA	48	D2
LOZANOS RD	PLA	34	B4
LUBKEN RD	INY	60	B4
LUCAS VALLEY RD	MAR	L	A3
LUCAS VALLEY RD	MAR	38	A4
LUCE GRISWLD RD	TEH	18	B4
LUCERNE VLY CTO	SBD	91	D2
LUCILLE	FRCO	66	D3
LUCILLE LN	RCO	107	C1
LUCINDA RD	SBD	81	C5
LUCKEHE RD	SUT	33	C1
LUCKY HILL RD	SIE	26	C3
LUCY BROWN RD	SLO	76	D1
LUDEMAN LN	MLBR	144	C4
LUDLOW RD	SBD	93	A2
LUDY BLVD	RCO	110	C1
LUIS AV	MCO	55	C1
LUISENO RD	RCO	107	B1
LUKENS LN	RCO	99	C3
LULU MINE RD	TUO	41	C5
LULU MINE RD	TUO	48	C1
LUMGREY RD	SIS	3	E3
LUMPKIN RD	BUT	25	E4
LUMPKIN RD	BUT	26	B4
LUMPKIN-			
-LA PORTE RD	BUT	26	A4
LUMPKIN RDG RD	BUT	26	B3
LUNA RD	IMP	109	B3
LUNA VISTA LN	SBD	100	D1
LUNDY AV	SCL	P	B3
LUNDY AV	SJ	152	D1
LUNDY LAKE RD	MNO	43	B4
LUNING AV	TEH	24	D1
LUNT RD	BUT	25	D3
LUPIN AV	MCO	48	B4
LUPINE	FRCO	58	B3
LUPINE LN	RCO	100	C5
LURLINE AV	COL	32	D2
LUTHER RD	PLA	34	C3
LUTHER RD	PLA	126	C1
LUTHER RD	TEH	18	D5
LUTHER E GIBSON	SOL	38	E4
LUTIE AV	KER	80	A4
LUX AV	MCO	56	B1
LYERLY RD	IMP	109	B3
LYNCH RD	NAPA	38	D3
LYNCH CANYON DR	SLO	65	D5
LYNCH MDWS RD	BUT	25	D2
LYNN RD	VEN	96	D1
LYNN RD W	VEN	96	D1
LYON AV	FRCO	56	C2
LYON AV	RCO	99	E3
LYON RD	STA	47	E2
LYON RD	STA	48	A2
LYONS AV	LACO	89	B4
LYONS AV	SLT	129	A3
LYONS RD	IMP	111	E4
LYONS RD	IMP	112	A4
LYONS ST	SNRA	163	C3
LYTLE AV	KER	68	B5
LYTLE CREEK RD	SBD	90	E5
LYTLE CREEK RD	SBD	99	A1
LYTTON ST	SDCO	V	A3

M

STREET	CO.	PAGE	GRID
M ST	EUR	121	D1
M ST	FRE	165	D3
M ST	MCO	48	C4
M ST	MER	170	C5
M ST E	CLTN	207	A5
M 1	TUL	69	A5
M 3	TUL	69	B5
M 8	LACO	90	C3
M 9	TUL	69	B5
M 10	TUL	69	B5
M 15	TUL	69	A4
M 33	TUL	68	E4
M 52	TUL	69	A4
M 56	TUL	69	B4
M 99	TUL	69	C4
M 107	TUL	69	C3
M 109	CAL	68	E4
M 109	TUL	69	A4
M 112	TUL	69	A4
M 117	TUL	68	D3
M 120	TUL	68	E3
M 176	TUL	68	E3
M 220	TUL	69	A2

STREET	CO.	PAGE	GRID
M 231	TUL	69	A2
M 240	TUL	68	E2
M 276	TUL	69	A1
M 296	TUL	68	D1
M 348	TUL	68	E1
M 357	TUL	58	E5
M 357	TUL	59	A4
M 375	TUL	59	B5
M 453	TUL	58	D4
M 461	TUL	58	D4
M 465	TUL	58	D4
M 468	TUL	58	D4
M 469	TUL	58	D4
MABURY RD	SJ	152	D1
MAC RD	RCO	107	C1
MACARTHUR BLVD	ALA	L	D5
MACARTHUR BLVD	ALA	45	D1
MACARTHUR BLVD	CM	197	B3
MACARTHUR BLVD	IRV	198	C3
MACARTHUR BLVD	IRV	200	B5
MACARTHUR BLVD	NB	200	B5
MACARTHUR BLVD	O	157	E1
MACARTHUR BLVD	O	158	B2
MACARTHUR BLVD	ORCO	98	C4
MACARTHUR BLVD	ORCO	T	C3
MACARTHUR BLVD	SA	197	D3
MACARTHUR BLVD	SA	198	B3
MACARTHUR FRWY	ALA	45	D1
MACARTHUR FRWY	O	158	A1
MCCARTNEY RD	A	159	A3
MACDOEL DIST RD	SIS	4	E4
MACDOEL DIST RD	SIS	5	A3
MACDONALD AV	CC	L	C3
MACDONALD AV	R	155	C3
MACDONALD LN	SIS	4	C5
MACE BLVD	YOL	39	C1
MACEDONA CYN RD	SBD	84	A4
MACHADO LN	SIS	4	C5
MACHADO ST	RCO	99	B4
MACKERT RD	SUT	33	C4
MACKS GULCH RD	SIS	4	A5
MACKS GULCH RD	SIS	12	A1
MACKVILLE RD	SJCO	40	C3
MACLAY AV	LACO	89	D5
MACLAY AV	LACO	Q	C1
MACY ST	LACO	97	E2
MACY ST	LACO	R	A4
MADDALENA RD	PLU	27	C2
MADDEN AV	SUT	33	C2
MADDOCK RD	SUT	33	C4
MADEIRA AV N	MON	171	D3
MADEIRA AV N	SAL	171	D3
MADELINE RD	LAS	8	B4
MADERA AV	FRCO	57	A4
MADERA AV	KER	78	B2
MADERA AV	KER	78	C2
MADERA AV	MAD	57	A2
MADERA RD	MCO	55	D1
MADERA RD	SBD	90	E3
MADERA ST	SDCO	V	D3
MADERA ST	SDCO	111	D1
MADISON AV	KIN	67	C2
MADISON AV	SAC	34	A5
MADISON AV	SAC	34	B5
MADISON AV	SD	214	A4
MADISON ST	KER	166	E5
MADISON ST	RCO	99	B2
MADISON ST	RCO	101	A4
MADISON ST	S	160	D3
MADONNA RD	SLO	76	A4
MADONNA RD	SNLO	172	B4
MAD RIVER RD	HUM	9	E5
MAD RIVER ROCK	TRI	16	E3
MADRONA ST	NAPA	29	B3
MADRONE RD	SON	38	B3
MADSEN	FRCO	57	E2
MADSEN AV	FRCO	57	E5
MAGEE CANYON RD	MNO	44	A5
MAGEE CANYON RD	MNO	51	B1
MAGEE HILLS RD	RCO	99	E5
MAGIC MTN PKWY	LACO	89	B4
MAGNOLIA	MAR	38	B5
MAGNOLIA	SJCO	47	D1
MAGNOLIA AV	FRCO	57	C5
MAGNOLIA AV	GLE	24	D3
MAGNOLIA AV	KER	78	A2
MAGNOLIA AV	LB	192	D2
MAGNOLIA AV	MAR	L	A3
MAGNOLIA AV	MCO	47	E4
MAGNOLIA AV	MCO	48	A4
MAGNOLIA AV	ORCO	98	B4
MAGNOLIA AV	ORCO	T	C2
MAGNOLIA AV	RCO	99	A3
MAGNOLIA AV	RIV	205	A4
MAGNOLIA AV	SDCO	V	E2
MAGNOLIA AV	SDCO	106	E5
MAGNOLIA AV	SDCO	107	A4
MAGNOLIA AV	MLBR	144	C5
MAGNOLIA AV	STA	47	B3
MAGNOLIA BLVD	BUR	179	C3
MAGNOLIA BLVD	LACO	Q	C3
MAGNOLIA RD	YUB	33	D1
MAGNUS ORCHD RD	SIE	26	D5
MAGONIGAL RD	NEV	27	B5
MAHER RD	MON	54	C3
MAHOGANY WY	LAS	20	E2
MAHOGANY FLAT	INY	71	C2
MAHOGANY PK RD	SIS	5	B3
MAHON AV	SJCO	47	D1
MAHONEY RD	SLO	75	E1
MAHONEY RD	SB	86	B1
MAIDEN LN	AVLN	97	B4
MAIL RD	SB	86	D3

STREET	CO.	PAGE	GRID
MAIL RT	LAS	8	C5
MAIN AV E	SCL	P	D5
MAIN AV E	SCL	54	C1
MAIN RD N	KLAM	5	E2
MAIN RD S	MOD	7	A3
MAIN ST	A	157	C5
MAIN ST	AMA	40	D2
MAIN ST	BARS	208	A2
MAIN ST	CC	L	E4
MAIN ST	CC	M	A3
MAIN ST	CC	M	A4
MAIN ST	EC	217	C2
MAIN ST	ELS	189	A3
MAIN ST	GV	127	C3
MAIN ST	HUM	15	E3
MAIN ST	IMP	109	A5
MAIN ST	IMP	109	B2
MAIN ST	INY	51	D4
MAIN ST	IRV	198	C4
MAIN ST	KER	78	E3
MAIN ST	LAK	31	D3
MAIN ST	LAS	8	B4
MAIN ST	LAS	21	B4
MAIN ST	LV	209	C3
MAIN ST	LA	185	E4
MAIN ST	LA	186	C1
MAIN ST	LACO	88	E4
MAIN ST	LACO	Q	C5
MAIN ST	LACO	Q	E5
MAIN ST	LACO	R	B3
MAIN ST	LACO	S	A1
MAIN ST	LACO	S	C2
MAIN ST	MAN	161	C4
MAIN ST	MEN	30	C4
MAIN ST	MOD	14	B3
MAIN ST	NAPA	38	A1
MAIN ST	ORA	194	B5
MAIN ST	ORA	196	B1
MAIN ST	ORCO	98	B4
MAIN ST	ORCO	T	D3
MAIN ST	PLCV	138	D3
MAIN ST	RCO	U	E5
MAIN ST	RCO	98	E3
MAIN ST	RCO	99	B4
MAIN ST	RCO	99	E4
MAIN ST	RIV	205	C1
MAIN ST	SAL	171	C4
MAIN ST	SBD	91	B4
MAIN ST	SBD	91	D1
MAIN ST	SBD	93	B2
MAIN ST	SD	216	B5
MAIN ST	SDCO	V	C5
MAIN ST	SDCO	V	E3
MAIN ST	SDCO	106	C2
MAIN ST	SDCO	107	A4
MAIN ST	SDCO	111	D2
MAIN ST	SJCO	40	B5
MAIN ST	SLO	75	C2
MAIN ST	SLO	76	A2
MAIN ST	SA	196	B3
MAIN ST	SA	198	C2
MAIN ST	SB	76	C5
MAIN ST	SB	86	B1
MAIN ST	SMA	173	B3
MAIN ST	SHA	18	C1
MAIN ST	SIE	26	D4
MAIN ST	SIS	3	D5
MAIN ST	SON	37	C2
MAIN ST	STA	47	E3
MAIN ST	S	160	E4
MAIN ST	SUIS	135	C4
MAIN ST	TEH	18	D3
MAIN ST	TUL	68	B1
MAIN ST	TUL	68	D3
MAIN ST	VENT	175	A2
MAIN ST	YUBA	125	D5
MAIN ST E	STA	47	E3
MAIN ST N	AMA	40	E2
MAIN ST N	LA	186	D1
MAIN ST N	LACO	R	A4
MAIN ST N	MON	54	C4
MAIN ST N	SAL	171	C2
MAIN ST S	SAL	171	B5
MAIN ST W	GV	127	A3
MAIN ST W	SB	76	B5
MAIN ST W	SB	86	A1
MAIN ST W	STA	47	D3
MAIN DRAIN RD	KER	77	D2
MAINE AV	LACO	R	E3
MAINE ST	SOL	38	D4
MAINE ST	VAL	134	B4
MAIN EAST WEST	MOD	5	E3
MAIN PRAIRIE RD	SOL	39	B3
MAITLAND DR	A	159	B3
MAJESTC OAK CIR	SHA	18	E3
MAJESTIC VW DR	SHA	18	C3
MALAGA AV	FRCO	56	E4
MALAGA AV	FRCO	57	C4
MALAGA RD	KER	78	E3
MALIBU CYN RD	LACO	97	A2
MALIN HWY	MOD	5	E2
MALLARD RD	MCO	55	E2
MALLARD RD	YOL	39	D2
MALLOTT RD	SUT	33	C2
MALTON AV	TEH	24	D2
MALUM RIDGE RD	MAD	49	E4
MALVERN AV	ORCO	T	C1
MAMELUKE HLL RD	ED	34	E3
MAMMTH POOL RD	MAD	49	E5
MAMMTH POOL RD	MAD	50	A5
MAMMTH SCNC LP	MNO	50	D2
MAMMOTH TVRN RD	ML	164	D2
MANCHESTER AV	ANA	193	A2

STREET	CO.	PAGE	GRID
MANCHESTER AV	LA	187	D5
MANCHESTER AV	LA	188	A5
MANCHESTER AV	LACO	97	D2
MANCHESTER AV	LACO	Q	D5
MANCHESTER AV	SDCO	106	C4
MANDEVLL CYN RD	LACO	97	C2
MANDRAPA RD	IMP	111	E4
MANGALAR RD	RCO	100	C5
MANGO ST	SBD	80	E5
MANGROVE AV	BUT	124	B2
MANGROVE AV	C	124	C3
MANHATTAN AV	LACO	97	D3
MANHATTAN AV	LACO	S	A1
MANHATTAN BLVD	LACO	97	D3
MANHATTAN BLVD	LACO	S	B1
MANIER DR	TUL	69	A3
MANKAS CORNR RD	SOL	L	E1
MANKAS CORNR RD	SOL	M	A1
MANKAS CORNR RD	SOL	38	E3
MANLY RD	KER	89	D1
MANNEL AV	KER	78	B2
MANNING AV	FRCO	56	B4
MANNING AV	FRCO	57	E4
MANNING AV	LA	183	A4
MANNING RD	ALA	M	C5
MANNING RD	ALA	46	C1
MANOR RD	COL	32	C2
MANOR ST	KER	78	D2
MANTECA AV	KIN	67	C2
MANTECA RD	SJCO	47	B2
MANTON RD	TEH	18	E4
MANTON RD	TEH	19	A3
MANTON SCH RD	TEH	19	B3
MANUAL DOMINGOS	SB	86	C3
MANZANA DR	RCO	100	D3
MANZANITA AV	BUT	25	B3
MANZANITA AV	BUT	124	C2
MANZANITA AV	RCO	99	C2
MANZANITA RD	ML	164	C2
MANZANITA RD	RCO	100	B5
MANZANITA RD	TRI	16	D1
MANZANITA LK RD	MAD	49	E5
MANZANITA LKOUT	MOD	14	D2
MANZNR REWRD RD	INY	60	A3
MAPES RD	LAS	21	C3
MAPES RD	RCO	99	C4
MAPLE AV	FRCO	57	C2
MAPLE AV	FRCO	67	C1
MAPLE AV	SBD	91	B4
MAPLE AV	STR	131	D4
MAPLE LN	NAPA	29	B2
MAPLE LN	SBD	100	A1
MAPLE ST	RCO	98	E3
MAPLE ST	SAL	171	C4
MAPLE ST	SDCO	107	A4
MAPLE CREEK RD	HUM	10	B5
MAPLE HILLS RD	HUM	16	B5
MARBLE HOT-			
-SPRINGS RD	PLU	27	C2
MARCH LN	S	160	A1
MARCIEL DR	MAD	57	B2
MARCONI AV	SAC	40	A1
MARCO POLO AV	RCO	100	A5
MARCUM RD	SUT	33	D4
MARCUSE RD	SUT	33	D3
MAR DE CORTEZ	AVLN	97	A4
MARE ISLAND BL	VAL	134	B4
MARE ISLAND WY	VAL	134	B4
MARE ISL CAUSWY	VAL	134	A4
MARENGO AV	LACO	R	B3
MARENGO RD	COL	32	D2
MARENGO ST	LA	186	D2
MARENGO ST N	LACO	190	C1
MARGUERITE AV	TEH	24	D2
MARGUERITE PKWY	ORCO	98	D5
MARGUERITE RD	MCO	48	E5
MARGUERTE MN RD	AUB	126	C2
MARICOPA HWY	KER	78	B5
MARIE AV	KER	89	E1
MARIE DR	PLU	20	D5
MARILLA AV	AVLN	97	B4
MARIN AV	FRCO	56	D4
MARIN ST	VAL	134	B4
MARINA AV	ALA	P	C1
MARINA AV	ALA	46	C2
MARINA BLVD	ALA	L	D5
MARINA BLVD	ALA	45	D2
MARINA BLVD	SF	142	A1
MARINA BLVD	SUIS	135	C5
MARINA DR	IMP	108	C2
MARINA DR	MEN	31	B1
MARINA EXPWY	LA	187	D3
MARINA FRWY	LACO	97	C2
MARINA VISTA	M	154	C1
MARINE AV	COL	32	E3
MARINE AV	MB	189	C5
MARINE AV	RB	189	E5
MARINE PKWY	RC	145	E4
MARINERS ISL BL	SM	145	C1
MARINETTE	TUL	68	B1
MARINE WORLD PY	SMCO	N	D2
MARINE WORLD PY	SMCO	45	D3
MARINO LN	KER	79	E2
MARIPOSA AV	BUT	25	B3
MARIPOSA AV	C	124	D2
MARIPOSA AV	ELS	189	B3
MARIPOSA AV	RCO	99	B3
MARIPOSA AV	TUL	68	B1
MARIPOSA RD	SJCO	40	B5
MARIPOSA RD	SJCO	47	C1
MARIPOSA RD	STA	47	D2
MARIPOSA ST	FRE	165	C4
MARIPOSA ST	VAL	134	E3

STREET	CO.	PAGE	GRID
MARIPOSA WY	MCO	48	C5
MARIPOSA DUMP	MPA	49	B3
MARITIME ST	O	157	B2
MARKET AV	CC	L	C3
MARKET ST	COL	33	A2
MARKET ST	O	157	E2
MARKET ST	RED	122	B3
MARKET ST	RIV	205	B3
MARKET ST	RCO	99	B2
MARKET ST	SD	215	D3
MARKET ST	SD	216	A3
MARKET ST	SFCO	L	B5
MARKET ST	SF	142	B4
MARKET ST	SF	143	B4
MARKET ST	SFCO	45	C1
MARKET ST	SJ	152	B2
MARKET ST	SCLR	151	B3
MARKET ST	S	160	E5
MARKET ST	YUBA	125	D1
MARKET ST W	MON	171	B3
MARKET ST W	SAL	171	B3
MARKHAM ST	RCO	99	D5
MARK HOPKINS AV	SUT	33	D3
MARKLEEVLLE LKT	ALP	36	C5
MARKS	FRCO	57	C5
MARKS AV	FRCO	57	C4
MARKS RD	SBD	101	D1
MARK SPGS W RD	SON	37	E1
MARKWEST STA RD	SON	37	D1
MARLAY AV	SBD	99	A2
MAR MONTE AV	SCR	54	B2
MARNI CT	KER	79	C4
MAROA AV	FRE	165	C1
MAROA AV	FRCO	57	C5
MARQUARDT AV	LACO	T	B1
MARR RD	LAS	8	D5
MARSH RD	SCL	46	B3
MARSH RD	SMCO	N	D2
MARSH ST	SNLO	172	C3
MARSH ST	SLO	76	A3
MARSHALL RD	ED	34	D4
MARSHALL RD	MCO	55	C1
MARSHALL RD	STA	47	C4
MARSHALL ST	RCO	99	C4
MARSHAL-PETALMA	MAR	37	D4
MARSHALL RCH RD	TRI	17	C2
MARSH CREEK RD	CC	M	B3
MARSH CREEK RD	CC	M	D4
MARSH CREEK RD	CC	39	A5
MARSH CREEK RD	CC	39	A5
MARSHES FLAT RD	TUO	48	D1
MARSHVIEW RD	SOL	38	E4
MART AV	STA	47	E2
MATHILDA AV	SVL	149	E2
MARTIN AV	FRE	165	C5
MARTIN AV	KER	78	B2
MARTIN LN	AMA	40	D3
MARTIN RD	FRCO	56	D4
MARTIN RD	IMP	109	A4
MARTIN RD	MON	64	D1
MARTIN RD	YUB	25	E5
MARTIN ST	LAK	31	D3
MARTIN ST	MONT	167	D4
MARTIN ST	MON	53	E3
MARTIN ST	RCO	99	B3
MARTINEZ RD	MON	65	C4
MARTINEZ CYN RD	CAL	89	A4
MARTINGALE LN	CAL	41	A4
MRTN LTHR KG BL	LA	184	B5
MRTN LTHR KG BL	LACO	Q	D4
ML KING JR BL	RIV	205	D3
M L KING JR WY	ALA	L	D4
M L KING JR WY	O	156	A4
M L KING JR WY	O	157	E2
MARTIS PEAK RD	PLA	35	E1
MARTY RD	SUT	33	E1
MARVIN RANCH RD	SIE	26	C4
MAR VISTA	SDCO	106	C3
MAR VISTA DR	MONT	168	D1
MAR VISTA DR	MONT	167	D4
MAR VISTA DR	MON	53	E5
MARX RD NO 1	SHA	18	A3
MARX RD NO 2	SHA	18	A3
MARY AV	SVL	149	C1
MARY AV N	SVL	148	D4
MARY AV S	SVL	148	D5
MARYSVILLE BLVD	SAC	33	E5
MARYSVILLE RD	YUB	26	A5
MARYSVILLE RD	YUB	33	E1
MASON AV	LA	177	E1
MASON ST	STB	174	E3
MASON DIXON RD	SBD	100	E1
MASONIC AV	SFCO	L	B5
MASONIC AV	SF	141	E3
MASONIC AV	SF	142	A3
MASONIC RD	MNO	43	C2
MASSACHUSTTS AV	SDCO	V	D3
MASSACHUSTTS AV	SDCO	111	D1
MASSACK RD	PLU	26	D2
MASSEY RD	MPA	49	C3
MAST AV	KER	78	B1
MASTEN AV	SCL	P	E5
MASTEN RD	TEH	18	B5
MASTERS AV	FRCO	56	D4
MASTERSONS RD	SIS	11	E2
MATEO ST	LA	186	C3
MATHER FIELD RD	SAC	40	A1
MATHESON RD	SHA	18	B2
MATHEWS RD	LAS	14	B4
MATHEWS RD	SJCO	40	E5
MATHEWS RD	SJCO	47	A1
MATHEWS RD	SIS	5	A2
MATHILDA AV	SCL	P	A3

STREET	CO.	PAGE	GRID
MATHILDA AV	SCL	45	E4
MATHILDA AV	SVL	148	E4
MATHILDA AV	SVL	149	E2
MATILIJA RD	VEN	88	A4
MATLOCK LP	TEH	18	C4
MATTERHORN DR	KER	79	C5
MATTHEWS LN	YUB	33	D1
MATTOLE RD	HUM	15	C3
MATTOLE RD	HUM	15	E4
MAUDE AV W	SVL	148	D4
MAUI RD	SBD	92	C1
MAURICO AV	RCO	99	C4
MAWSON RD	SUT	33	A2
MAXSON RD	FRCO	58	B2
MAXWELL LN	SOL	39	C2
MAXWELL RD	AMA	40	C2
MAXWELL CYN RD	NAPA	38	C1
MAXWLL SITES RD	COL	32	C1
MAY	CC	38	C5
MAYARADA	SBD	101	E1
MAYARO LODGE RD	BUT	25	E2
MAYBECK	SJCO	40	A5
MAYBERT RD	NEV	26	E5
MAYER AV	KER	78	B2
MAYER RD	YUB	33	D2
MAYFIELD RD	RCO	102	A4
MAYHEW AV	TEH	24	D2
MAYNARD RD	SHA	18	D2
MAY SCHOOL RD	ALA	M	C5
MAY SCHOOL RD	ALA	46	C2
MAYS CANYON RD	SON	37	C2
MAYTEN RD	SIS	4	C5
MAZE BLVD	MDO	162	A3
MAZE BLVD	STA	47	C2
MAZOURKA CANYON	INY	60	A3
MCADAMS CK RD	SIS	3	D5
MCADAMS INDN CK	SIS	3	D4
MCARTHUR RD	SHA	13	C3
MCARTHUR RD	SUT	33	B2
MCAULIFFE RD	SHA	18	A3
MCAUSLAND RD	COL	24	E5
MCBEAN PKWY	LACO	89	B4
MCCABE RD	IMP	112	A3
MCCABE RD	MCO	47	B5
MCCABE RD	MCO	55	B1
MCCAHILL LN	HUM	15	E2
MCCAIN BLVD	COR	215	B4
MCCAIN VLY RD	SDCO	111	A3
MCCALL AV	FRCO	57	D3
MCCALL BLVD	RCO	99	C4
MCCANN RD	HUM	16	B4
MCCART RD	KER	68	A5
MCCARTHY RES RD	CAL	41	B2
MCCARTY RD	RCO	U	D4
MCCARTY RD	TEH	24	B2
MCCATER RD	MCO	48	E5
MCCAY	MPA	48	E3
MCCLAIN LN	RCO	107	B1
MCCLATCHY RD	SUT	33	B2
MCCLELLAN RD	CPTO	149	C5
MCCLELLAN RD	LAS	14	C3
MCCLELLAND LN	LAS	21	C3
MCCLELLN MTN RD	HUM	16	C3
MCCLINTOCK RD	STA	47	C4
MCCLOSKEY RD	SBT	54	E3
MCCLOSKEY RD	SBT	55	A3
MCCLOSKEY RD	SOL	39	C3
MCCLOUD DUMP RD	SIS	12	E2
MCCLURE AV	TEH	24	D1
MCCLURE RD	STA	47	D2
MCCLURE SUB RD	MEN	31	B2
MCCOMBS RD	KER	77	E1
MCCOMBS RD	KER	78	B1
MCCONAHUE GL RD	SIS	11	E1
MCCONNELL RD	IMP	109	B5
MCCORMACK RD	SOL	39	B3
MCCOURTNEY RD	NEV	34	B2
MCCOURTNEY RD	NEV	127	A5
MCCOURTNEY RD	PLA	34	A3
MCCOY AV	KER	77	E1
MCCOY RD	LAS	20	C3
MCCOY RD	MON	54	E5
MCCOY RD	MON	55	A5
MCCOY RD	TEH	18	C4
MCCRACKEN RD	STA	47	B3
MCCREERY RCH RD	SBT	55	C3
MCCRORY RD	SOL	39	A3
MCCULLACH RD	MCO	47	D4
MCCULLOCK BLVD	MOH	96	B4
MCCULLY RD	MOD	7	D5
MCCUNE RD	SOL	39	A2
MCDANIEL RD	IMP	112	D5
MCDERMOTT RD	COL	32	D1
MCDERMOTT RD	RCO	99	E4
MCDOEL DORRS RD	SIS	5	A3
MCDONALD	SJCO	39	E5
MCDONALD AV	STA	47	C2
MCDONALD RD	IMP	109	A3
MCDOWELL BLVD	SON	L	A1
MCEWEN RD	CC	L	D3
MCEWEN RD	CC	38	D5
MCEWEN RD	STA	47	E2
MCFADDEN	MON	54	C4
MCFADDEN AV	SA	195	A5
MCFADDEN AV	SA	196	C5
MCFADDEN ST	TUS	196	E5
MCFARLND-WDY RD	KER	78	C1
MCGARY RD	SOL	38	D4
MCGEE AV	STA	47	D2
MCGEE CREEK RD	MNO	51	A3
MCGOWAN	YUB	33	D2
MCGRATH RD	SUT	33	B2
MCHENRY AV	MDO	162	C3

STREET	CO.	PAGE	GRID
MCHENRY AV	SJCO	47	C2
MCHENRY RD	MCO	48	C5
MCINTIRE RD	SJCO	40	C3
MCINTOSH RD	HUM	10	D4
MCKEAN RD	SCL	P	C4
MCKEAN RD	SCL	46	C5
MCKEE RD	MCO	48	C4
MCKEE RD	SJ	152	E2
MCKEE RD	SCL	P	C3
MCKEE RD	SCL	46	B4
MCKEE ST	MCO	48	D5
MCKEEN RD	SIS	11	D2
MCKELL RD	LAK	32	A5
MCKENZIE AV	FRE	165	D3
MCKENZIE RD	SAC	40	A3
MCKERNIE ST	RCO	99	E4
MCKIBBEN RD	KER	78	A1
MCKIM RD	IMP	109	B5
MCKINLEY AV	FRE	165	B5
MCKINLEY AV	FRCO	57	A3
MCKINLEY AV	SJCO	47	A1
MCKINLEY ST	RCO	99	A3
MCKINLEYVLLE AV	HUM	9	E4
MCKINNEY CK RD	SIS	3	D4
MCKNNEY RUBICN	PLA	35	D2
MCLAIN RD	YUB	26	B4
MCLAUGHLIN AV	LA	187	D1
MCLAUGHLIN AV	SCL	P	C3
MCLAUGHLIN AV	SJ	152	E3
MCMASTER RD	MCO	48	C5
MCMILLAN CYN RD	SLO	76	C1
MCMULLIN	SJCO	47	A2
MCMULLIN GRADE	FRCO	57	A4
MCMURRY MDWS RD	INY	59	D1
MCNAMARA RD	MCO	48	C5
MCNEILL LN	SOL	39	B1
MCNELLA LN	PLU	27	C3
MCNERNEY RD	IMP	109	A3
MCRAE RD	BUT	25	B4
MCRAE RD	TUO	41	C5
MCSWAIN RD	MER	170	A3
MCSWAIN RD	MCO	170	A3
MEACHAM RD	KER	78	B3
MEAD RD	IMP	109	B4
MEADE AV	SD	214	A5
MEADOW DR	AMA	41	B2
MEADOW DR	MCO	48	A4
MEADOW RD	TRI	17	D1
MEADOW GLEN RD	CAL	41	C2
MEADOW LAKE RD	NEV	26	E5
MEADOW LAKE RD	NEV	27	B4
MEADOW LAKE RD	SIE	27	B5
MEADOW RIDGE RD	MAD	49	D5
MEADOWS DR	VAL	134	C1
MEADOWS RD	IMP	112	B4
MEADOW VLY RD	YUB	26	A5
MEADOW VIEW DR	SHA	18	C3
MEADOWVIEW RD	SAC	39	D2
MEADOW VISTA RD	PLA	34	C3
MEALEY RD	IMP	108	E5
MEAMBER CK RD	SIS	3	C4
MEARS RIDGE RD	SHA	12	C3
MEATS AV E	ORA	194	D3
MECARTNEY RD	A	159	A3
MECCA AV	LA	178	D4
MECCA DALE RD	RCO	101	E3
MECHAM RD	SON	37	E3
MEDFORD AV	KIN	67	C2
MEDFORD RD	FRCO	57	E1
MEDICINE LK HWY	MOD	5	E5
MEDICINE LK HWY	SIS	5	D5
MEDICINE LK RD	SIS	5	C5
MEDICINE LK RD	SIS	13	B2
MEDLIN RD	STA	47	C4
MEEKLAND AV	ALA	L	E5
MEEKLAND AV	ALA	M	A5
MEEKLAND AV	ALA	N	E1
MEEKLAND AV	ALA	P	A1
MEEKS RD	SBD	92	D5
MEHRING RD	IMP	110	D5
MEHRTEN DR	TUL	68	D1
MEIER RD	STA	47	E2
MEIER RD	STA	48	A2
MEIGS RD	STB	174	A5
MEIKLE RD	STA	47	E2
MEIKLE RD	STA	48	A2
MEISS RD	SAC	40	B2
MEISS LAKE- -SAMS NECK RD	SIS	4	E3
MEISS LAKE- -SAMS NECK RD	SIS	5	A3
MELCHER RD	KER	78	B1
MELLA DR	AMA	41	A2
MELLO AV	SJCO	47	C1
MELLOR RD	STA	48	A2
MELODY CT	HUM	10	A5
MELOLANO RD	IMP	109	B5
MELON ST	RCO	102	C4
MELONES CT	TUO	41	B5
MELROSE AV	LA	181	C5
MELROSE AV	LA	182	C5
MELROSE AV	LACO	Q	D3
MELROSE AV	SDCO	106	C3
MELROSE DR	SDCO	106	C3
MEMORY LN	SA	195	E2
MEMORY LN	SA	196	A2
MENDENHALL RD	TEH	18	C5
MENDIBOURE RD	LAS	8	B4
MENDIBURN	KER	79	D5
MENDIBURN RD	KER	80	B4
MENDOCINO AV	FRCO	57	E2
MENDOCINO AV	STR	131	C1
MENDOCINO PASS	MEN	23	B2

STREET	CO.	PAGE	GRID
MENDOCINO ST	LACO	190	D1
MENIFEE RD	RCO	99	C4
MENLO AV	RCO	99	E4
MERCED AV	FRCO	66	D3
MERCED AV	KER	78	A2
MERCED AV	LACO	R	E4
MERCED AV	MCO	47	E4
MERCEDES AV	MCO	48	B4
MERCED FALLS RD	MPA	48	D3
MERCED FALLS RD	TUO	48	D2
MERIDIAN AV	SJ	151	E5
MERIDIAN BLVD	ML	164	C3
MERIDIAN RD	BUT	25	A3
MERIDIAN RD	SBD	91	E2
MERIDIAN RD	SCL	P	B3
MERIDIAN RD	SCL	46	B4
MERIDIAN RD	SOL	39	B3
MERIDIAN RD	SUT	33	A2
MERLE AV	STA	47	D2
MERRIAM RD	STA	47	E3
MERRIAM RD	YUB	26	B5
MERRILL AV	FRCO	56	B2
MERRILL RD	TEH	24	E2
MERRILL RD S	KLAM	5	C2
MERRILL ST	SBD	99	A2
MERRILL FLAT RD	LAS	20	D2
MERRILLVILLE RD	LAS	20	E2
MERRIMAC CTO RD	BUT	25	E3
MERRITT	LAK	31	D3
MERRITT DR	TUL	57	E5
MERRITT DR	TUL	58	A5
MERRITT LN	PLA	34	A3
MERVEL AV	MCO	55	E2
MESA DR	RCO	103	C5
MESA DR	RCO	110	C1
MESA DR	SBD	100	E1
MESA DR	SDCO	106	B3
MESA RD	MAR	37	E5
MESA RD	SBD	92	E5
MESA TK TR W	SDCO	107	C5
MESA COLLEGE DR	SD	213	E1
MESA COLLEGE DR	SDCO	V	B2
MESA GRANDE RD	SDCO	107	B3
MESA VERDE DR	CM	197	A4
MESQUITE AV	PMSP	206	C5
MESQUITE RD	INY	61	B2
MESQUITE CYN RD	KER	80	C2
MESQUITE PSS RD	SBD	84	A1
MESQUITE SPG RD	SBD	101	B1
MESQUITE VLY RD	INY	73	C3
MESSICK	SJCO	40	C4
MESSICK RD	SUT	33	D3
MESSILLA VLY RD	BUT	25	D3
MESSING RD	CAL	40	D4
MESTMAKER ST	KER	68	D5
METCALF RD	NEV	34	B2
METCALFE RD	SCL	P	D4
METCALFE RD	SCL	46	C5
METROPOLE AV	AVLN	97	B5
METROPOLITAN DR	ORA	195	D1
METROPOLITAN RD	HUM	15	E2
METTER RD	SUT	33	C1
METTLER AV	KER	68	B5
METTLER AV	KER	78	B2
METTLER RD	SJCO	40	A4
METTLER RD	STA	47	D1
METZ RD	MON	65	B1
METZGER RD	SHA	13	D3
MEXICAN LAKE RD	SBT	66	B1
MEYER RD	LACO	R	D5
MEYER RD	LACO	T	B1
MEYERS LN	SUT	33	B1
MEYERS GRADE RD	SON	37	B1
MICA RD	RCO	107	C1
MICHAEL RD	MCO	48	B5
MICHEL RD	CAL	41	B3
MICHELLE DR	SUT	125	A4
MICHELSON DR	IRV	198	C4
MICHELTORENA ST	STB	174	A4
MICHIGAN BAR RD	SAC	40	C2
MICHILLINDA BL	LACO	R	C2
MICHOACAN AVD	BAJA	112	B4
MICKE GROVE RD	SJCO	40	B4
MIDDLE AV	SCL	P	E5
MIDDLE AV	SCL	54	D1
MIDDLE RD	MAR	37	D3
MIDDLE RD	SJCO	46	E1
MIDDLE BAR RD	AMA	40	E3
MIDDLE CREEK RD	SHA	18	C3
MIDDLE CREEK RD	SIS	3	C3
MIDDLE CK RCH	SIS	3	C3
MIDDLE E TER	AVLN	97	B5
MIDDLEFIELD RD	PA	147	C2
MIDDLEFIELD RD	SCL	N	E2
MIDDLEFLD RD E	MVW	148	C3
MIDDLE FORK RD	MON	66	B4
MIDDL FK GASQUET	DN	2	A3
MID FK HUMBG RD	SIS	3	E4
MIDDLE HARBR RD	O	157	B2
MIDDL HONCUT RD	BUT	25	D5
MIDDLE RIDGE RD	MEN	30	B2
MIDDLETON DR	DN	1	D3
MIDDLETON RD	SUT	33	B2
MIDDLETON RD	TRI	11	E3
MIDDLETOWN RD	PLCV	138	B2
MIDDLETWN PK DR	SHA	18	B2
MDL TWO ROCK RD	SON	37	E3
MIDLAND AV	SDCO	106	D4
MIDLAND RD	RCO	103	B2
MIDLAND TR	KER	80	C2
MIDOIL RD	KER	77	E4
MIDWAY	BUT	25	B5
MIDWAY DR	SDCO	V	A3

STREET	CO.	PAGE	GRID
MIDWAY RD	ALA	M	E5
MIDWAY RD	KER	77	E4
MIDWAY RD	SBD	101	D1
MIDWAY RD	SOL	39	A2
MIDWAY WELLS	INY	61	D3
MIKISHA BLVD	SBD	92	D5
MILAN RD	KER	77	E2
MILE END	MON	64	E1
MILE END	MON	65	A1
MILES RD	MCO	48	C5
MILFORD RD	SBDO	81	A1
MILFORD CEM RD	LAS	21	C5
MILFORD GRADE	LAS	21	C5
MILGEO RD	SJCO	47	C2
MIL-GOR RD	SBD	101	E1
MILHAM AV	KIN	67	B3
MILITAR	BAJA	112	B4
MILITARY E	BEN	153	C4
MILITARY W	BEN	153	A3
MILITARY W	SOL	38	D4
MILITARY RD	SIS	13	A2
MILITARY PASS	SIS	12	D1
MILITARY PASS	SIS	13	A2
MILL AV	KER	78	B1
MILL RD	BUT	26	B4
MILL RD	MNO	52	C3
MILL RD	SLO	76	B1
MILL RD	TEH	19	C4
MILL RD	YUB	26	B4
MILL ST	GV	127	B4
MILL ST	NEV	34	C1
MILL ST	RENO	130	C3
MILL ST	SBD	99	C2
MILL ST	SBDO	207	C3
MILL ST	U	123	C3
MILLARD CYN RD	RCO	100	B2
MILLBRAE AV	MLBR	144	E5
MILLBRAE AV	SMCO	N	C1
MILLBRAE AV	SMCO	45	C3
MILLBROOK AV	FRCO	57	C2
MILL CANYON RD	MNO	42	E2
MILL CREEK RD	HUM	10	C3
MILL CREEK RD	MEN	31	B2
MILL CREEK RD	SBD	99	E1
MILL CREEK RD	SIS	3	C5
MILL CREEK RD	SON	37	C5
MILL CK PWR HS	MNO	43	B4
MILLER	MAR	45	B1
MILLER AV	FRCO	56	B2
MILLER AV	MAR	L	B4
MILLER AV	MV	140	A3
MILLER AV	VAL	134	E4
MILLER RD	COL	32	A3
MILLER RD	IMP	112	C3
MILLER RD	MCO	48	D4
MILLER RD	TRI	22	E1
MILLER RD	YOL	39	C2
MILLER ST	SMA	173	C4
MILLER WAY	SCTO	137	E4
MILLER RANCH RD	SIE	26	D4
MILLERTON RD	FRCO	57	D2
MILLERTON RD	MAD	57	D1
MILLIKEN AV	SBD	U	E3
MILLIKEN AV	SBD	98	E2
MILLS AV	CLA	203	B1
MILLS AV	LACO	R	D5
MILLS AV	MTCL	203	B4
MILLS RD	MCO	47	C5
MILLS RD	SOL	39	C2
MILLS RD	SUT	33	B2
MILLS ORCHRD RD	COL	32	D1
MILLS PARK RD	SIE	27	A3
MILLUX AV	FRCO	56	B2
MILLUX RD	KER	78	C4
MILLVL PLAIN RD	SHA	18	D3
MILLWOOD DR	TUL	58	C5
MILLWOOD RD	FRCO	58	C3
MILNES RD	STA	47	D2
MILPAS DR	SBD	91	D4
MILPAS ST	STB	174	D3
MILPITAS BLVD	SCL	P	B2
MILPITAS BLVD	SCL	46	B4
MILPITAS RD	MON	64	E3
MILPITAS RD	MON	65	B3
MILPITAS WSH RD	IMP	110	B2
MIL POTRERO HWY	KER	88	B1
MILSAP BAR RD	BUT	25	E3
MILSAP BAR RD	BUT	26	A3
MILSTEAD RD	MEN	22	D1
MILTON RD	CAL	40	E5
MILTON RD	NAPA	L	C1
MILTON RD	NAPA	38	C3
MILTON RD	SJCO	40	C5
MILTON RD	STA	40	E5
MINA RD	MEN	23	A1
MINDANAO WY	LA	187	D3
MINE RD	VEN	89	A5
MINER RD	CC	L	D4
MINER ST	S	160	E4
MINERAL RD	IMP	108	E1
MINERAL RD	SHA	19	C3
MINERAL KING AV	TUL	68	A1
MINERAL KING RD	TUL	59	B5
MINERAL SCHOOL	SHA	19	A1
MINERET RD	ML	164	C2
MINERS CREEK RD	SIS	11	D2
MINES RD	ALA	P	D1
MINES RD	ALA	46	C2
MINES RD	SCL	46	D3
MING AV	KER	78	C3
MINI DR	VAL	134	C1
MINNEOLA RD	SBD	92	B1
MINNESOTA ST	SDCO	106	C2

STREET	CO.	PAGE	GRID
MINNEWAWA AV	FRCO	57	D2
MINNEWAWA AV	FRCO	57	D5
MINNIEAR RD	STA	47	B3
MINNIETTA RD	INY	71	B2
MINT RD	MCO	56	B1
MINTURN RD	MCO	48	D5
MIRABEL RD	SON	37	D2
MIRAMAR RD	SDCO	V	B1
MIRAMAR RD	SDCO	106	D5
MIRAMAR WY	SDCO	V	B2
MIRAMAR WY	SDCO	106	D5
MIRA MESA BLVD	SDCO	V	B1
MIRA MESA BLVD	SDCO	106	C5
MIRANDA AV	CC	M	A4
MIRASOL AV	KER	77	E3
MIRASOL AV	KER	78	A3
MISSION AV	MCO	48	C5
MISSION AV	SD	214	A4
MISSION AV	SDCO	106	B3
MISSION AV	SR	139	C4
MISSION BLVD	ALA	45	E2
MISSION BLVD	ALA	146	C1
MISSION BLVD	H	146	D2
MISSION BLVD	MTCL	203	C5
MISSION BLVD	ONT	203	E5
MISSION BLVD	ONT	204	A5
MISSION BLVD	POM	203	A5
MISSION BLVD	RCO	99	A2
MISSION BLVD	SBD	U	D2
MISSION BLVD	SBD	98	D2
MISSION BLVD	SBD	203	A5
MISSION BLVD	SD	212	A1
MISSION BLVD	SDCO	V	A2
MISSION BLVD	SDCO	106	C5
MISSION DR	LACO	R	C3
MISSION FRWY	SDCO	V	A3
MISSION RD	LA	186	C2
MISSION RD	LACO	98	A2
MISSION RD	LACO	R	B3
MISSION RD	MON	65	B3
MISSION RD	SDCO	106	C2
MISSION RD	SMCO	L	B5
MISSION RD	SMCO	N	B1
MISSION RD	SMCO	45	B2
MISSION ST	SFCO	L	B5
MISSION ST	SF	142	C5
MISSION ST	SF	143	B4
MISSION ST	STB	174	A3
MISSION ST	SC	169	A4
MISSION TR	RCO	99	B5
MISSION BAY DR	SD	212	D1
MISSN BAY DR W	SD	212	B4
MISSION CTR RD	SD	213	E4
MISSION CK RD	RCO	100	C2
MISSION GORGE RD	SD	214	B3
MISSION GRGE RD	SDCO	V	C2
MISSION GRGE RD	SDCO	106	E5
MISSION INN AV	RIV	205	B2
MISSION LKS BL	RCO	100	C2
MISSN OLIVE RD	BUT	25	E5
MISSION RDGE RD	STB	174	D2
MISSION VLY FWY	SD	213	B4
MISSION VLY FWY	SD	214	A4
MISSION VLGE DR	SD	214	C1
MISSION VLGE DR	SDCO	V	C2
MISSION VLGE DR	SDCO	106	D5
MISSOURI AV	STA	47	E2
MISSOURI FLAT RD	ED	138	A5
MISTLETOE DR	VEN	88	C4
MITCHELL RD	HUM	10	C3
MITCHELL RD	HUM	15	E1
MITCHELL RD	LAS	8	E5
MITCHELL RD	LAS	14	E5
MITCHELL RD	STA	47	D4
MITCHLLS CMP RD	IMP	110	C3
MIX CANYON RD	SOL	38	E2
MOANING CAVE RD	CAL	41	B4
MOBLEY	SJCO	40	C5
MOBLEY	SJCO	47	C1
MOCAL RD	KER	77	E4
MOCAL RD	KER	78	D4
MOCKINGBIRD CYN	RCO	99	B3
MODJESKA CYN RD	ORCO	98	E3
MODOC AV	FRCO	57	A3
MODOC COUNTY RD	MOD	5	D3
MOFFAT BLVD	MAN	161	C4
MOFFAT BLVD	SJCO	161	C4
MOFFAT RANCH RD	INY	60	A4
MOFFATT RD	MCO	47	D5
MOFFETT BLVD	MVW	148	A3
MOFFETT BLVD	SCL	N	E3
MOFFETT BLVD	SCL	P	A3
MOFFETT DR	TUL	68	D1
MOFFETT RD	STA	47	D3
MOFFETT CK RD E	SIS	3	E5
MOFFETT CK RD W	SIS	3	E5
MOHAVE RD	LPAZ	103	E3
MOHAVE ROSE DR	LACO	89	D3
MOHAVE VLY HWY	MOH	85	D5
MOHLER RD	SJCO	47	B2
MOJAVE AV	KER	89	C1
MOJAVE DR	SBD	91	B3
MOJAVE RD	SBD	91	B4
MOJAVE RD	SBD	101	C4
MOJAVE-RANDSBRG	KER	80	C1
MOJVE TRPICO RD	KER	79	E5
MOJVE TRPICO RD	KER	80	A5
MOJVE TRPICO RD	KER	89	E1
MOKELUMNE HILL- -CMP SECO TP RD	CAL	41	C3
MOLERA RD	MON	54	B3
MOLINO AV	MV	140	A3
MOLLER AV	TEH	24	E2

STREET	CO.	PAGE	GRID
MONARCH MINE RD	SIE	26	E4
MONARCH MINE RD	SIE	27	A4
MONO DR E	MONO	43	C4
MONO WY	TUO	163	D4
MONROE	MCO	55	D1
MONROE AV	FRCO	57	B3
MONROE AV	FRCO	57	B5
MONROE AV	TEH	18	D5
MONROE ST	RCO	101	A4
MONROE ST	SCLR	150	C1
MONSON	FRCO	58	B4
MONTGUE AGER RD	SIS	4	B4
MONTAGUE EXPWY	SCL	P	B3
MONTAGUE GRNADA	SIS	4	B4
MONTANA AV	LACO	97	C2
MONTANA AV	SHA	18	C2
MONTANA ST	PAS	190	A1
MONTARA RD	SBD	91	E1
MONTARA RD	SD	208	E4
MONTE RD	IMP	109	A4
MONTEBELLO BLVD	LACO	R	C4
MONTE BELLO RD	SCL	N	E3
MONTE BELLO RD	SCL	45	E4
MONTE BLOYD RD	MEN	30	D2
MONTECITO RD	SDCO	107	A4
MONTECITO RD	SLO	75	E2
MONTECITO ST	STB	174	D3
MONTE DIABLO AV	S	160	A4
MONTEREY AV	FRCO	56	D4
MONTEREY AV	FRCO	66	D2
MONTEREY AV	MDO	162	D4
MONTEREY AV	RCO	100	E4
MONTEREY BLVD	SFCO	L	B5
MONTEREY BLVD	SFCO	45	B2
MONTEREY HWY	SCL	P	D4
MONTEREY HWY	SCL	54	D1
MONTEREY RD	LACO	R	B3
MONTEREY RD	SLO	76	A1
MONTEREY RD	SLO	76	A2
MONTEREY HWY	SCL	46	B4
MONTEREY ST	SAL	171	C4
MONTEREY ST	SNLO	172	C2
MONTEREY PSS RD	LACO	R	B4
MONTE VERDE AV	CAR	168	B3
MONTE VISTA AV	CLA	203	C1
MONTE VISTA AV	MCO	48	A3
MONTE VISTA AV	MTCL	203	C4
MONTE VISTA AV	SBD	U	C2
MONTE VISTA AV	SBD	80	E1
MONTE VISTA AV	SBD	203	C2
MONTE VISTA AV	STA	47	C3
MONTE VISTA AV	STA	48	A3
MONTE VISTA DR	SDCO	106	C3
MONTE VISTA RD	SHA	18	B3
MONTEZUMA RD	SDCO	V	C3
MONTEZUMA RD	SDCO	111	D1
MONTEZUMA HL RD	SOL	39	B4
MONTGOMERY AV	BUT	25	A3
MONTGOMERY DR	STR	131	D3
MONTGOMERY RD	IMP	109	B3
MONTGOMERY RD	TRI	11	B5
MONTGOMERY ST	SF	142	D2
MONTGOMERY ST	SF	143	D2
MONTGOMERY ST	MCO	48	C3
MONTGOMRY CK RD	TRI	11	D5
MONTGMRY RCH RD	SHA	18	B2
MONTICELLO RD	NAPA	133	E1
MONTPELIER RD	STA	47	E3
MONTPELIER RD	STA	48	A3
MONUMENT BLVD	CC	M	A3
MONUMENT RD	HUM	15	E3
MOODY RD	MEN	22	B2
MOODY ST	ORCO	T	B2
MOONEY BLVD	TUL	68	B2
MOONEY RD	LAS	20	C3
MOONEY FLAT RD	NEV	34	A1
MOONRIDGE RD	SBD	100	A1
MOONSHINE RD	YUB	26	B5
MOONWIND ST	KER	80	D1
MOORE RD	LAS	21	E4
MOORE RD	PLA	33	E4
MOORE RD	PLA	34	A4
MOORE RD	SUT	33	B2
MOOREHEAD RD	STA	47	C5
MOORES FLAT RD	NEV	26	D5
MOORPARK AV	SJ	150	E5
MOORPARK RD	VEN	96	D1
MOORPARK ST	LACO	Q	C3
MOORPARK WY	LA	179	A5
MOORVILL RDG RD	BUT	26	B4
MOOSE CAMP RD	SHA	13	B5
MORADA LN	SJCO	40	A4
MORAGA AV	ALA	L	D4
MORAGA AV	ALA	45	D1
MORAGA AV	MCO	55	D1
MORAGA AV	P	158	C1
MORAGA AV	SD	211	E4
MORAGA RD	CC	L	E4
MORAGA RD	CC	45	E1
MORAGA WY	CC	L	E4
MORAN AV	MCO	48	A4
MORAN RD	CAL	41	C3
MORAN RD	STA	47	C4
MORAN RD	TEH	24	D1
MORCOURT AV	KER	80	C1
MOREHEAD RD	DN	1	D3
MOREHEAD RD	SUT	33	B2
MORELLO AV	CC	L	E3
MORELLO AV	CC	154	E3
MORELLO AV	M	154	D4
MORENA BLVD	SD	211	D4
MORENA BLVD	SD	212	E1
MORENA BLVD	SD	213	A4

STREET	CO.	PAGE	GRID
MORENA BLVD	SDCO	V	A2
MORENA BLVD	SDCO	111	C1
MORENA BLVD W	SD	213	A4
MORENA RES DR	SDCO	112	D1
MORENO AV	SDCO	V	E1
MORENO AV	SDCO	106	E5
MORENO ST	MTCL	203	B3
MORENO BEACH DR	RCO	99	C2
MORGAN RD	CAL	41	B5
MORGAN RD	HUM	15	D2
MORGAN RD	LAS	21	C1
MORGAN RD	SBD	101	D1
MORGAN RD	STA	47	D3
MORGAN WY	LPAZ	104	A5
MORGAN CYN RD	FRCO	57	E2
MORGAN TERRITRY	CC	46	B1
MORGAN VLY RD	LAK	32	B4
MORLEY AV	MCO	48	D5
MORLEY FIELD DR	SD	216	A1
MORMON ST	LA	191	C2
MORMN EMGRNT TR	ED	35	C5
MORNING DR	KER	78	E3
MORNING STAR CT	TUO	163	C3
MORNING STAR CTO	SBD	84	B3
MORNING STAR DR	TUO	163	C4
MORNING STAR MN	SBD	84	B3
MORNING STAR RD	ALP	36	C5
MORONGO RD	RCO	100	A3
MORONGO RD	SBD	101	B1
MORONI RD	SUT	33	B2
MORRETTI CYN RD	SLO	76	B4
MORRILL RD	STA	47	D2
MORRIS AV W	MDO	162	A2
MORRIS RD	COL	33	A2
MORRIS RD	KER	78	A3
MORRIS RD	STA	47	C4
MORRIS MINE RD	MNO	51	C2
MORRISON RD	STA	48	A1
MORRISN BRYN RD	TEH	24	B2
MORRISON CYN RD	ALA	P	B1
MORRISON CYN RD	ALA	46	A3
MORRIS RANCH RD	RCO	100	C5
MORRO RD	KER	91	C3
MORSE RD	SJCO	40	B4
MORSE RD	YOL	39	D3
MORTON AV	TUL	68	D3
MORTON BL S	MDO	162	C4
MOSAIC CANYON	INY	61	D4
MOSELEY RD	DN	1	D3
MOSHER	MPA	49	A3
MOSQUITO RD	ED	34	E4
MOSQUITO RDG RD	PLA	34	E3
MOSS OLD MLL RD	TRI	10	E5
MOTHER LODE DR	ED	34	D5
MOTHER LODE TR	MAD	49	C4
MOTOR AV	LA	183	B3
MOTOR AV	LACO	Q	C4
MOTT AIRPORT RD	SIS	12	D2
MOULTAN LOOP	TEH	19	A3
MOULTON PKWY	ORCO	98	D5
MOUND SPGS RD	SBD	100	C1
MT ACADIA BLVD	SD	213	B1
MOUNTAIN AV	LACO	R	D2
MOUNTAIN AV	ONT	203	E4
MOUNTAIN AV	ONT	204	A4
MOUNTAIN AV	RCO	100	A5
MOUNTAIN AV	SBD	U	D2
MOUNTAIN AV	SBD	98	D1
MOUNTAIN AV	STB	174	A3
MOUNTAIN AV	UPL	203	E1
MOUNTAIN BLVD	O	156	E5
MOUNTAIN DR	STB	174	B2
MOUNTAIN RD	SBD	90	D4
MOUNTAIN RD S	VEN	88	C5
MOUNTAIN ST	LACO	Q	E2
MTN CLIMBER WY	KER	79	C5
MTN HOME CK RD	SBD	99	E1
MTN HOME RCH RD	SON	38	A1
MTN HOUSE RD	ALA	M	E4
MTN HOUSE RD	ALA	46	D1
MTN HOUSE RD	MEN	31	B4
MTN HOUSE RD	SIE	26	D4
MTN LEMON RD S	VEN	88	C5
MTN MEADOW RD	SHA	19	C2
MTN QUAIL LN	MOD	7	B5
MOUNTAIN RCH RD	CAL	41	B3
MTN SCHOOL RD	SHA	13	B5
MTN SPRINGS RD	SBD	91	B2
MTN SPRINGS RD	SBD	94	E1
MTN SPRINGS RD	SLO	76	A1
MOUNTAIN VW AV	FRCO	56	C5
MOUNTAIN VW AV	FRCO	57	D5
MOUNTAIN VW AV	SBD	99	C2
MOUNTAIN VW AV	RCO	99	E2
MOUNTAIN VW RD	HUM	16	B1
MOUNTAIN VW RD	KER	78	E3
MOUNTAIN VW RD	KER	79	A3
MOUNTAIN VW RD	MEN	30	E3
MOUNTAIN VW RD	RCO	100	D3
MOUNTAIN VW RD	SBD	90	E3
MOUNTAIN VW RD	SBD	91	C1
MOUNTAIN VW RD	SBD	92	B1
MOUNTAIN VW RD	STB	174	A4
MOUNTAIN VW RD	SCR	P	B5
MOUNTAIN VW RD	SCR	54	A1
MOUNTAIN VW RD	SHA	13	C5
MOUNTAIN VW RD	STA	47	D3
MOUNTAIN VW ST	BARS	208	A3
MTN VW-ALVSO RD	MVW	148	B4
MTN VW-ALVSO RD	SCL	P	B3
MTN VIEW RCH RD	SON	31	C5
MT AUKUM RD	ED	40	E1
MT AUKUM RD	ED	41	A1
MT BALDY LKOUT	SIS	2	E3
MT BULLION CTO	MPA	49	A3
MT DIABLO SC BL	CC	M	B4
MT EATON RD	TUO	41	D5
MT EDEN RD	SCL	N	E4
MT EDEN RD	SCL	P	A4
MT EDEN RD	SCL	45	E5
MT EMMA RD	LACO	90	A4
MT GAINES	MPA	48	E3
MT GLEASON AV	LACO	Q	E2
MT HAMILTON RD	SCL	P	C3
MT HAMILTON RD	SCL	46	C4
MT HERMON RD	SCR	P	A5
MT HERMON RD	SCR	53	E1
MT HOUGH CRYSTL	PLU	26	D1
MT HOLLYWOOD DR	LA	182	A2
MT HOUSE RD	YUB	26	C5
MT MADONNA RD	SCL	54	C2
MT OLIVE RD	NEV	34	C2
MT OPHIR RD	MPA	49	A3
MT PIERCE LKOUT	HUM	15	E3
MT PINOS RD	KER	88	D2
MT PINOS RD	VEN	88	A1
MT PINOS RD	VEN	88	C2
MT REBA RD	ALP	42	A1
MT SHASTA DR	SIS	12	E2
MT VEEDER RD	NAPA	29	C4
MT VEEDER RD	NAPA	38	C2
MT VERNON AV	CLTN	207	B4
MT VERNON AV	KER	78	D3
MT VERNON AV	RCO	99	B2
MT VERNON AV	SBD	91	D1
MT VERNON AV	SBD	99	B2
MT VERNON AV	SBDO	207	A2
MT VERNON RD	PLA	34	B3
MT VERNON RD	PLA	126	A2
MT WHITNEY	FRCO	57	C5
MT WHITNEY AV	FRCO	66	D1
MT WHITNEY ST	KER	70	C5
MT WILSON	LACO	98	A1
MT WILSON RD	LACO	R	C2
MT ZION RD	AMA	41	A2
MOVIE RD	INY	60	A4
MOWRY AV	ALA	P	A2
MOWRY AV	ALA	46	A3
M T FREITAS PKY	SR	139	A1
MUCK VALLEY RD	LAS	14	B4
MUDD RD	IMP	109	A5
MUD LAKE RD	ALP	36	C4
MUD LAKE RD	MOD	6	A5
MUD LAKE RD	MOD	14	A1
MUELLER	SJCO	40	A5
MUELLER	SJCO	47	A1
MUIR AV	BUT	25	A3
MUIR MILL RD	MEN	22	E5
MUIR WOODS RD	MAR	L	A4
MUIR WOODS RD	MAR	45	A1
MULBERRY AV	MCO	48	B4
MULBERRY AV	RCO	99	A2
MULBERRY DR	LACO	R	C5
MULBERRY ST	C	124	D5
MULE BRIDGE RD	SIS	11	C2
MULE CANYON RD	SBD	92	A1
MULE CREEK RD	TRI	11	D5
MULE DEER LN	MOD	7	B5
MULE TOWN RD	SHA	18	B2
MULHOLLAND DR	LA	181	B2
MULHOLLAND DR	LACO	97	C1
MULHOLLAND DR	LACO	Q	C3
MULHOLLAND HWY	LACO	97	A1
MULLER LN	DGL	36	B3
MULLER RD	KER	78	E3
MULLER RD	KER	79	A3
MULLOY RD	SIS	4	C3
MUMMA RD	COL	33	A3
MUMY RD	INY	51	C4
MUNCY RD	STA	47	C3
MUNJAR RD	BUT	25	A2
MUNRAS AV	MONT	167	D5
MUNRAS AV	MON	53	E4
MUNSEY RD	KER	80	C3
MUNRAS AV	MONT	168	D1
MUNZER RD	KER	78	B3
MURIEL DR	BARS	208	C3
MURPHY AV	SCL	P	B3
MURPHY LN	SCL	P	E5
MURPHY LN	SCL	54	D1
MURPHY LN	SHA	19	A1
MURPHY RD	IMP	112	A3
MURPHY RD	MON	54	C2
MURPHY RD	NEV	26	C5
MURPHY RD	SBT	55	B3
MURPHY RD	SCR	54	C2
MURPHY RD	SJCO	47	C1
MURPHY RD	STA	47	C2
MURPHY RD	TUO	41	C5
MURPHYS GRD RD	CAL	41	B4
MURRAY RD	HUM	9	E4
MURRAY RD	HUM	10	A4
MURRAY RD	SJCO	40	C5
MURRAY RD	SUT	33	C3
MURRAY CK RD E	CAL	41	B3
MURRAY CK RD W	CAL	41	B3
MURRAY RIDGE RD	SD	214	A2
MURRIETA HT SPG	RCO	99	C5
MURRIETTA RD	RCO	99	C3
MUSCAT AV	FRCO	57	B4
MUSCAT AV	FRCO	57	D4
MUSTANG RD	RCO	100	A5
MUSTANG SPGS RD	SLO	76	A1
MUTAU FLAT RD	VEN	88	C5
MYER AV	TUL	68	C2
MYERS LN	COL	32	E2
MYERS RD	COL	32	D2
MYERS RD	SIS	4	E3
MYERS RD	SIS	5	A3
MYERS ST	BUT	25	D4
MYKLE OAKS RD	MPA	49	A3
MYRA AV	LA	182	C5
MYRTLE AV	DN	1	E5
MYRTLE AV	EUR	121	E1
MYRTLE AV	HUM	9	E5
MYRTLE AV	HUM	15	E1
MYRTLE AV	LACO	R	D2
MYRTLEWOOD DR	MAD	57	C2
N			
N ST	SCTO	137	D3
NABORLY RD	SBD	101	D1
NACIMNTO-FER RD	MON	64	E3
NACIMNTO-FER RD	MON	65	A3
NACIMIENTO LAKE	MON	65	E4
NACMIENTO LK DR	SLO	75	E1
NACMIENTO LK DR	SLO	76	A1
NACIONAL ST	SAL	171	A3
NADEAU RD	INY	71	B1
NADER RD	PLA	34	A3
NAGEL CANYON RD	KER	79	D3
NAGLEE AV	SJ	151	D4
NANTES AV	MCO	55	E1
NAPA AV	FRCO	56	E5
NAPA RD	SBD	92	E5
NAPA RD	SON	38	B3
NAPA RD	SON	L	B1
NAPA RD	SON	132	D5
NAPA ST	SON	L	B1
NAPA ST E	SNMA	132	E4
NAPA ST E	SON	38	B3
NAPA ST W	SNMA	132	C4
NARANJO BLVD	TUL	58	D5
NARANJO BLVD	TUL	68	D1
NARBONNE AV	LACO	S	B2
NARRAGANSETT AV	SDCO	V	A3
NARRAGANSETT AV	SDCO	111	C1
NASHUA RD	MON	54	C3
NASON RD	MON	64	C1
NASON ST	RCO	99	C3
NATIONAL AV	SD	216	A4
NATIONAL AV	SDCO	V	C4
NATIONAL AV	SDCO	111	D1
NATIONAL BLVD	CUL	183	C5
NATIONAL BLVD	LA	180	E5
NATIONAL BLVD	LA	183	C4
NATIONAL BLVD	LACO	Q	C4
NATL TRAILS HWY	SBD	91	B2
NATL TRAILS HWY	SBD	92	A1
NATL TRAILS HWY	SBD	93	A2
NATL TRAILS HWY	SBD	94	A4
NATIVIDAD RD	MON	54	D4
NATOMAS RD	SUT	33	D4
NATURAL BRDG RD	INY	72	B1
NAUMAN RD	VEN	96	B1
NAUTILUS ST	SD	211	A4
NAVAJO DR	SAL	171	C1
NAVAJO RD	RCO	99	C4
NAVAJO RD	SBD	91	C3
NAVAJO RD	SDCO	V	D2
NAVAJO RD	SDCO	111	D1
NAVARO ST	SDCO	V	A3
NAVARRO RDG RD	MEN	30	C2
NAVELENCIA AV	FRCO	58	A4
NAVY DR	SJCO	40	A5
NEAL SPRING RD	SLO	76	B1
NEBO ST	SBD	92	A1
NEBRASKA AV	FRCO	57	B4
NEBRASKA AV	FRCO	57	C4
NEBRASKA AV	TUL	58	A4
NEBRASKA ST	VAL	134	C3
NECKLE RD	IMP	112	A3
NECTAR RD	RCO	107	B1
NEEDHAM RD	STA	47	B3
NEEDHAM ST	MDO	162	A3
NEEDLE PEAK RD	SLT	129	D4
NEELEY	SJCO	40	A4
NEENACH RD	LACO	89	E2
NEES AV	FRCO	56	C3
NEES AV	FRCO	57	C3
NEGRO CREEK DR	TUL	58	C4
NEGRO HOLE RD	SIS	5	C4
NEIGHBORS BLVD	RCO	103	D5
NEIGHBORS BLVD	RCO	110	D1
NEILSON RD	CAL	40	E3
NELANDER	MCO	47	E4
NELSON	SJCO	40	C5
NELSON	SJCO	47	C1
NELSON AV	BUT	25	C4
NELSON DR	TUL	69	B2
NELSON RD	BUT	25	B4
NELSON RD	TRI	17	C2
NELSON BAR RD	BUT	25	D3
NELSON CREEK RD	SHA	13	B4
NELSON PIT RD	IMP	112	C3
NELSON RES RD	LAS	8	B3
NELSONS CROSSNG	BUT	26	A3
NELSN SHPPEE RD	BUT	25	B4
NEROLY RD	CC	39	C5
NEROLY RD	CC	M	C3
NESTLE AV	LA	178	D5
NETHERLANDS RD	YOL	39	D2
NETHERTON RD	MCO	47	C5
NEUGERBAUER	SJCO	39	E5
NEUMARKEL RD	KER	79	A3
NEURALIA RD	KER	80	B4
NEVA AV	TEH	24	D2
NEVADA AV	KIN	67	B2
NEVADA AV	KIN	67	C2
NEVADA ST	AUB	126	B3
NEVADA ST	NEVC	128	C2
NEVADA ST	NEV	128	D2
NEVADA CITY HWY	GV	127	D2
NEVADA CITY HWY	NEV	127	D2
NEVADA CITY HWY	NEV	128	A5
NEVIS AV	KER	78	C1
NEW AV	LACO	R	C4
NEW AV	SCL	P	E5
NEW AV	SCL	54	D1
NEWARK BLVD	ALA	P	A2
NEWARK BLVD	ALA	45	E3
NEWBERRY RD	SBD	92	C1
NEW BIG OAK FLT	MPA	49	C1
NEW BIG OAK FLT	MPA	63	B4
NEWCASTLE	PLA	34	C3
NEWCASTLE RD	SJCO	40	B5
NEW CEMETERY RD	LAS	14	B3
NEW CHESTR DUMP	PLU	20	B4
NW CHG QRTZ MTN	AMA	40	E2
NEWCOMB AV	FRCO	56	C4
NEWCOMB ST	TUL	68	D3
NEW DIXIE MN RD	SBD	92	C5
NEW DOCK ST	LA	191	D2
NEW DOCK ST	LACO	S	C3
NEWHALL AV	LACO	89	B4
NEWHALL RD	MCO	48	B5
NEWHALL RD	SUT	33	B2
NEW HOPE RD	SAC	39	E3
NEW HOPE RD	SAC	40	A3
NEWHOPE ST	FTNV	197	A1
NEWHOPE ST	GGR	195	A3
NEWHOPE ST	ORCO	T	C3
NEWHOPE ST	SA	195	A4
NEW IDRIA RD	SBT	55	E5
NEW IDRIA RD	SBT	56	A4
NEWLAND ST	ORCO	T	B3
NEWMARK AV	FRCO	57	E4
NEW PLEYTO RD	MON	65	D4
NEW PEORIA FLAT	TUO	41	B5
NEWPORT AV	GLE	24	D3
NEWPORT AV	ORCO	98	C4
NEWPORT AV	ORCO	T	E2
NEWPORT BLVD	CM	199	C2
NEWPORT BLVD	NB	199	B4
NEWPORT RD	MCO	48	A3
NEWPORT RD	RCO	99	C4
NEWPORT RD	RCO	99	D4
NEWPORT CST DR	ORCO	T	D5
NEWPORT CST DR	IRV	200	E3
NEWPORT CST DR	ORCO	98	C5
NEWPORT CST DR	ORCO	T	D5
NEWRIVER RD	TRI	11	A4
NEW ROME RD	NEV	34	C1
NEWSOM RD	MCO	47	C5
NEWSOM RD	MCO	55	C1
NEWTON AV	KIN	67	C3
NEWTOWN RD	ED	34	E5
NEWVILLE RD	GLE	24	B3
NEWVILLE RD	TEH	24	A2
NEW YORK DR	LACO	R	B2
NEW YRK FLAT RD	YUB	26	A4
NEW YRK HOUS RD	YUB	26	A5
NEW YORK MTN RD	SBD	84	C4
NEW YORK RCH RD	AMA	40	E2
NIAGARA AV	COL	33	A2
NICASIO VLY RD	MAR	37	E4
NICE LUCERNE	LAK	31	D2
NICHOLAS RD	MAD	57	E2
NICHOLLS RD	NEV	34	B2
NICHOLS RD	IMP	112	A3
NICHOLS RD	RCO	99	B4
NICHOLS CYN RD	LA	181	A3
NICHOLS MILL RD	SIE	27	B4
NICKEL RD	MCO	48	A5
NICOLAS RD	RCO	99	D5
NICOLAUS	PLA	33	E4
NICOLAUS AV	SUT	33	D3
NIDER RD	IMP	109	B3
NIDERER RD	SLO	75	E1
NIDERER RD	SLO	76	A1
NIELSEN AV	FRCO	57	A3
NIELSON AV	FRE	165	A3
NIELSON RD	CAL	41	A3
NIESTRATH RD	SON	37	B1
NIHELL ST	NEV	128	C2
NILAND AV	IMP	109	B3
NILAND MRINA RD	IMP	109	A2
NILE AV	SJCO	47	B1
NILE RD	SJCO	47	B1
NILES AV	KIN	67	D3
NILES ST	BKD	166	E2
NILES ST	KER	78	E3
NILES CANYON RD	ALA	P	B1
NILES CANYON RD	ALA	46	A3
NILL AV	KER	78	C1
NIMITZ BLVD	SD	212	C5
NIMITZ BLVD	SDCO	V	A3
NIMITZ BLVD	SDCO	111	C1
NIMITZ FRWY	ALA	45	D2
NIMITZ FRWY	ALA	146	D4
NIMITZ FRWY	H	146	D4
NIMITZ FRWY	O	158	C4
NIMITZ FRWY	O	159	D1
NIMITZ FRWY	SJ	151	E3
NIMITZ FRWY	SJ	152	A1
NINE RD	CAL	41	C4
NINE MILE CYN	INY	70	B4
NINTH ST	C	124	C5
NIPTON RD	SBD	84	C2
NIPTON DESRT RD	SBD	84	C2
NIPTON MOORE RD	SBD	84	C2
NISQUALLY RD	SBD	91	B4
NISSEN RD	HUM	15	D2
NM 1	TUL	68	E5
NM 14	TUL	68	E4
NM 18	TUL	69	C4
NM 23	TUL	69	B4
NM 24	TUL	69	B4
NM 45	TUL	69	C4
NM 50	TUL	69	B4
NM 88	TUL	69	C4
NM 93	TUL	69	C4
NM 112	TUL	69	C3
NM 117	TUL	70	A3
NM 121	TUL	69	B3
NM 127	TUL	69	B3
NM 133	TUL	70	A3
NM 163	TUL	69	B3
NM 175	TUL	69	B3
NM 231	TUL	69	B2
NM 232	TUL	69	A2
NM 276	TUL	69	A1
NOBEL DR	SD	211	C1
NOBLE RD	YUB	33	D2
NOFFSINGER RD	IMP	109	B3
NOLAN RD	IMP	109	B4
NOLINA CIR	RCO	100	D4
NO NINE	MPA	48	E3
NONPAREIL AV	COL	32	E3
NOPEL AV	BUT	25	C2
NORD AV	BUT	124	A4
NORD AV	KER	78	C3
NORD HWY	BUT	25	A3
NORDAHL RD	IMP	110	D5
NORD GIANELLA	BUT	25	A3
NORDOFF ST	LACO	97	C1
NORFOLK ST	SM	145	A1
NORHAM PL	SBD	101	A1
NORIEGA RD	KER	78	C3
NORMA ST S	KER	80	E1
NORMAL ST	SD	214	A5
NORMAL ST	SDCO	V	B3
NORMAL ST	SDCO	111	D1
NORMAN	SUT	33	B2
NORMAN AV	KER	80	B5
NORMAN RD	COL	24	E5
NORMANDIE AV	LA	182	B5
NORMANDIE AV	LA	185	A4
NORMANDIE AV	LACO	Q	E5
NORMANDIE AV	LACO	S	C2
NORMANDY CT	NEV	127	C2
NORMAN HILLS RD	RCO	107	C1
NORRBOM RD W	SON	38	B3
NORRBOM RD	SON	132	D3
NORRIS RD	KER	78	C2
NORRIS CYN RD	CC	M	A5
NORRIS CYN RD	CC	46	A1
NORRISH RD	IMP	109	C5
NORTH AV	FRCO	56	C4
NORTH AV	FRCO	57	B4
NORTH AV	KIN	57	D5
NORTH AV	MCO	47	E3
NORTH AV	MCO	48	A3
NORTH AV	ORCO	T	C2
NORTH AV	SDCO	106	D3
NORTH AV	STA	47	C2
NORTH HWY	INY	61	D3
NORTH RD	STA	47	B2
NORTH ST	MAN	161	C3
NORTH ARM	PLU	20	D5
N BNK CHETKO RD	CUR	1	D2
NORTH BUSCH RD	MEN	23	B5
NORTH BUSCH RD	MEN	31	B1
NORTHCREST DR	DN	1	D4
NORTHRLY BR GRN	SLO	75	D2
NORTH FORK RD	HUM	15	D4
NORTH FORK RD	MAD	49	D5
NORTH FORK RD	SBT	66	A2
NORTH FORK RD	TUO	41	E4
N FK MAD RIV RD	TRI	17	B5
NORTHGATE BLVD	SAC	39	E1
NORTHGATE BLVD	SCTO	137	D1
NORTH GATE RD	CC	M	A4
NORTH GATE RD	CC	39	A5
NORTH GATE RD	SOL	39	A3
NORTH POINT ST	SF	142	C1
NORTH POINT ST	SF	143	B1
N LIVERMORE AV	ALA	46	C2
NORTH RIDGE RD	SBD	100	C2
NORTHRUP RD	MCO	47	D4
NORTHRUP RD	MOD	8	A1
NORTHRUP RD	MOD	14	E1
NORTH SHORE	PLA	35	E1
NORTH SHORE DR	SBD	92	A5
NORTH SHORE RD	SIS	12	C2
NORTHSIDE DR	MPA	63	B2
NORTH SIDE RD	SBD	91	E3
NORTH STAR TR	SBD	100	C2
NORTH VALLEY RD	PLU	20	D5
NORTHWOODS BLVD	NEV	27	D5
NORTON RD	KER	80	B3
NORTON RD	SBT	55	E4
NORTON RD	SOL	39	C3
NORTONVILLE	CC	39	B5
NORVEL RD	LAS	20	C3
NORWALK BLVD	LACO	98	A3
NORWALK BLVD	LACO	R	C5
NORWALK BLVD	LACO	T	A2
NORWGIAN RCH RD	TRI	11	E4
NOVATO BLVD	MAR	L	A2
NOVATO BLVD	MAR	38	A4
NOYES VALLEY RD	SIS	11	E2
NTU RD	SB	86	B1
NUESTRO RD	SUT	33	C2

STREET	CO.	PAGE	GRID
NUEVO RD	RCO	99	C3
NUNES LN	SHA	19	C2
NUNNIEMAKER RD	HUM	16	C4
NURSE SLOUGH LN	SOL	39	A3
NURSERY ST	NEV	128	C2
NYON RD	SBD	100	B1
O			
O ST	FRE	165	D3
OAHU RD	SBD	92	C1
OAK AV	LAKE	7	B1
OAK AV	MCO	48	B4
OAK AV	SUT	33	D3
OAK AV	TRI	17	B2
OAK DR	SDCO	112	D1
OAK RD	MPA	49	B3
OAK ST	BKD	166	A4
OAK ST	MCO	47	E4
OAK ST	MCO	48	A4
OAK ST	SF	141	E4
OAK ST	SF	142	B4
OAK ST	SF	143	A4
OAK ST	SHA	18	B3
OAK ST	S	160	B4
OAK ST	U	123	C2
OAK WY	BUT	25	A3
OAK CREEK RD	KER	79	D5
OAK CREEK RD N	INY	59	E3
OAK CREEK RD S	INY	59	E3
OAKDALE RD	MCO	48	A3
OAKDALE RD	MCO	48	B3
OAKDALE RD	STA	47	D2
OAKDL WTRFRD HY	STA	47	E2
OAK FLAT RD	SLO	75	E1
OAK FLAT RD	SLO	76	A1
OAK FLAT RD	STA	47	B4
OAK GLEN AV	SCL	P	D5
OAK GLEN AV	SCL	54	C1
OAK GLEN RD	RCO	100	A5
OAK GLEN RD	SBD	99	E2
OAK GROVE	CC	38	E5
OAK GROVE	MPA	49	B4
OAK GROVE RD	CC	M	A3
OAK GRV SCHOOL	MPA	49	B4
OAK HILL RD	ED	34	E5
OAK HILL RD	SBD	91	A4
OAK KNOLL AV	LACO	R	B3
OAK KNOLL AV	NAPA	29	E5
OAK KNOLL AV	NAPA	38	C2
OAK KNL RNG STA	SIS	3	D3
OAKLAND AV	FRCO	67	A1
OAKLAND AV	O	158	B2
OAKLAND AV	P	158	B1
OAKLAND CP RD	PLU	26	D1
OAKLEA RD	STA	47	B3
OAKLEY LN	YUB	33	E3
OAK MEADOW RD	NEV	34	B2
OAKMONT TR	SHA	18	C1
OAKMORE ST	TUL	68	B2
OAK PARK BLVD	CC	L	E3
OAK PARK BLVD	CC	M	A3
OAK RANCH RD	SIE	26	D4
OAK RIDGE RD	SCL	P	D2
OAK RIDGE RD	TRI	17	A2
OAK RUN RD	SHA	18	D2
OAK RUN RD	SHA	18	E1
OAK RUN TO FERN	SHA	19	A1
OAK SPG RCH RD	SBD	90	E4
OAK SPRINGS RD	SBD	91	D4
OAKS RANCHO RD	KER	79	B4
OAK TREE RD	NEV	26	B5
OAK VALLEY DR	SIS	4	A4
OAK VALLEY RD	YUB	26	C4
OAK VIEW CT	KER	79	B4
OAKVLLE CRSS RD	NAPA	29	D3
OAKVLLE CRSS RD	NAPA	38	C2
OAKVILLE GRADE	NAPA	29	C4
OAKVILLE GRADE	NAPA	38	C2
OAKWAY	BUT	25	D2
OAKWOOD	SJCO	40	C5
OAKWOOD	SJCO	47	C1
OASIS RD	MON	65	C3
OASIS RD	INY	52	C3
OASIS RD	RCO	102	C4
OASIS RD	SBD	90	D4
OASIS RD	SHA	18	C2
OAT GAP RD	MEN	23	C5
OAT HILL RD	LAK	32	B5
OAT HILL RD N	NAPA	32	B5
OATMN TOPOCK HY	MOH	95	E1
OBANION RD	SUT	33	C3
OBERLIN RD	SIS	4	A4
OBRIEN RD	JOS	2	C2
OBSIDAN DOME RD	MNO	50	D1
O'BYRNES FERRY	TUO	41	B5
OCCIDENTAL RD	SON	37	D2
OCEAN AV	CAR	53	D5
OCEAN AV	CAR	168	B3
OCEAN AV	SFCO	L	B5
OCEAN AV	SFCO	45	B2
OCEAN AV	SB	86	B3
OCEAN BLVD	LB	191	E2
OCEAN BLVD	LB	192	C3
OCEAN BLVD	LACO	98	A4
OCEAN BLVD	LACO	S	D2
OCEAN DR	DN	1	D3
OCEAN DR	HUM	9	E4
OCEAN DR	MEN	22	C4
OCEAN BEACH FWY	SD	212	C5
OCEAN PARK BLVD	LA	180	C5
OCEAN PARK BLVD	LACO	Q	C4
OCEAN PARK BLVD	SMON	180	C5
OCEAN PARK BLVD	SMON	187	A1
OCEAN PARK RD	SB	86	A2
OCEANSIDE BLVD	SDCO	106	B3
OCEAN VIEW AV	INY	51	B3
OCEAN VIEW BLVD	LACO	R	A2
OCEAN VIEW BLVD	PAC	167	A1
OCEAN VIEW BLVD	SD	216	B4
OCEAN VIEW BLVD	SDCO	V	C4
OCEAN VIEW BLVD	SDCO	111	D1
OCEANVIEW DR	CUR	1	D2
OCEAN VIEW DR	DN	1	D3
OCONNOR WY	SLO	76	A3
OCOTILLO WY	SBD	91	C4
ODD FELLW PK RD	HUM	16	A3
ODOM LN	MEN	22	C5
O'FARRELL ST	SF	142	C3
O'FARRELL ST	SF	143	B3
OFFAL RD	MNO	42	E1
OFFIELD LOOKOUT	SIS	10	E1
OFFUTT RD	KER	78	B1
OGBURN CEM RD	SHA	19	A2
OGIER RD	IMP	112	C3
OGILBY RD	IMP	110	B4
OGULIN CANYON	LAK	32	A3
O'HARA AV	CC	M	D3
O'HARA AV	CC	39	C5
OHIO AV	FRCO	56	C3
OHIO AV	LA	180	A4
OHM RD	COL	32	E2
OHM RD	TEH	18	D5
OIL CANYON RD	FRCO	66	D2
OIL CITY RD	FRCO	66	D2
OILER CT	KER	79	C3
OILFIELDS RD	KER	78	D2
OIL PLANT RD	MNO	43	C5
OIL WELL RD	HUM	15	E2
OJAI DR	SHA	18	C3
OJAI FRWY	VEN	88	A5
OJAI ST	VEN	88	B4
OKEEFFE RD	SIS	5	D2
OKLAHOMA AV	TEH	18	D5
OKLAHOMA SCH RD	SIS	5	B3
OLANCHA DRWN RD	INY	70	E1
OLD HWY	COL	32	D1
OLD HWY	LAS	21	D5
OLD HWY	MPA	49	A4
OLD HWY	PLU	26	D1
OLD AIRLINE HWY	SBT	55	B4
OLD ALLRED RD	MPA	49	B3
OLD ALTURAS HWY	MOD	5	E2
OLD ALTURAS HWY	MOD	6	A2
OLD ALTURAS RD	SHA	18	C2
OLD ARCATA RD	HUM	9	E5
OLD ARCATA RD	HUM	10	A5
OLD AUBURN RD	SAC	34	B5
OLD BANNING- -IDYLLWILD RD	RCO	100	A3
OLD BAYSHRE HWY	SJ	152	A1
OLD BREA CYN RD	LACO	U	A3
OLD CAMP TWO RD	SIS	13	C2
OLD CASTLE RD	SDCO	106	B2
OLD CEMETERY RD	LAS	14	B3
OLD CHAMPS FLAT	LAS	20	D1
OLD CHISHOLM DR	SBD	101	B1
OLD COAST HWY	SB	86	D3
OLD COPPER CITY	SBD	81	D3
OLD CORNING RD	TEH	24	D2
OLD COULTRVLLE- -YOSEMITE RD	MPA	49	C1
OLD COULTRVLLE- -YOSEMITE RD	MPA	63	A4
OLD CUTOFF RD	LAS	21	B4
OLD DAVIS RD	SOL	39	C1
OLD DON PDRO RD	TUO	48	C1
OLD DRYTOWN- -PLYMOUTH RDYMT	AMA	40	D2
OLD EEL RIV RD	LAK	23	C5
OLD EEL ROCK	HUM	16	C4
OLD EL MIRAGE	SBD	90	D3
OLD ELSINORE RD	RCO	99	C3
OLDENBERG RD	SBD	91	D3
OLD FT TEJON RD	LACO	90	B3
OLD FRIANT RD	FRCO	57	C2
OLD GASQUET TLL	DN	2	B3
OLD GULCH RD	CAL	41	B4
OLD HRLD PLM RD	LACO	90	A3
OLD HAUN RD	PLU	20	C4
OLD HERNANDZ RD	SBT	55	C5
OLD HIGHWAY 99	SIS	12	B1
OLD HWY 138	LACO	89	D2
OLD HWY RD	LAS	14	A4
OLD HWY RD	PLU	26	C1
OLD HWY RT 29	LAS	21	C5
OLD HWY S FORK	DN	2	A3
OLD HONEY RUN	BUT	25	C3
OLD KANE SPG RD	SDCO	108	A3
OLD KNOX RD	YUB	26	B4
OLD LAMBERT RD	AMA	40	C2
OLD LANDMARK DR	SBD	91	D1
OLD LEESVL GRAD	COL	32	C2
OLD LOMA RD	BUT	25	C1
OLD LONG VLY RD	LAK	32	A3
OLD MAIL RT	LAS	8	C5
OLD MAMMOTH RD	ML	164	A5
OLD MAMMOTH RD	MNO	50	D2
OLD MATTOLE RD	HUM	15	C4
OLD MIDLAND RD	KLAM	5	B1
OLD MILL RD	DN	1	D4
OLD MINE RD	SBD	101	A1
OLD MINE TR	RCO	100	B5
OLD MIRAMAR RD	SDCO	V	B2
OLD MIRAMAR RD	SDCO	106	C5
OLD MORGN HL RD	TRI	17	B2
OLD MORRO RD	SLO	76	A2
OLD NATL TR HWY	SBD	94	B2
OLD OAK FLAT RD	MPA	49	C1
OLD OAKLAND RD	SJ	152	B1
OLD OAKLAND RD	SCL	P	B3
OLD OAKLAND RD	SCL	46	B4
OLD PARKER RD	SBD	103	E2
OLD PIEDMONT RD	SCL	46	B4
OLD PLYMTH SAC- -VIA FIN RCH RD	AMA	40	D2
OLD PONY EXPRSS	ALP	36	B4
OLD RAILROAD GR	SHA	12	B4
OLD RANCH RD	KER	79	C5
OLD REDWOOD HWY	SON	37	E1
OLD RENO RD	NEV	27	D5
OLD RDG ROUTE RD	LACO	89	A2
OLD RIVER RD	KER	78	C3
OLD RIVER RD	KER	78	E4
OLD RIV SCHL RD	LACO	R	B5
OLD SN FRANCSCO	SVL	149	E1
OLD SCHOOL RD	SHA	13	D3
OLD SCH HOUS RD	TRI	22	E1
OLD SEIAD HWY	SIS	3	B3
OLD SEIAD CK RD	SIS	3	B3
OLD SHASTA RIV	SIS	4	A4
OLD SHERWIN GRD	INY	51	B3
OLD SHERWOOD RD	MEN	22	E4
OLD SKYLINE	KIN	67	A3
OLD SONOMA RD	NAP	133	B5
OLD SONOMA RD	NAPA	L	C1
OLD SONOMA RD	NAPA	38	C3
OLD SPANISH TR	INY	72	E4
OLD SPANISH TR	INY	73	B4
OLD STAGE RD	MEN	30	D4
OLD STAGE RD	MON	54	D3
OLD STAGE RD	SIS	12	C2
OLD STAGE RD N	SIS	12	C1
OLD STAGEROAD	MEN	30	D4
OLD STATE HWY	HUM	9	E2
OLD STATE HWY	HUM	10	A2
OLD STATE HWY	INY	72	E3
OLD STATE HWY	INY	73	A3
OLD STATE HWY	KIN	67	B4
OLD STATE HWY	LAK	31	C2
OLD STATE HWY	MNO	43	C5
OLD STATE HWY	MNO	50	D2
OLD STATE HWY	SIS	4	E3
OLD STATE HWY	SIS	5	A4
OLD STEWRTS PT- -SKAGGS SPGS RD	SON	31	B5
OLD STOCKTON RD	AMA	40	D3
OLD STOCKTON- -IONE HWY	AMA	40	D2
OLD STRWBRRY RD	TUO	41	E3
OLD STRWBRRY RD	TUO	42	A3
OLD SUTTER CK- -AMADOR CITY HY	AMA	40	E2
OLD STTR HLL RD	AMA	40	E2
OLD TELEGRPH RD	VEN	88	E4
OLD TELEGRPH RD	VEN	89	A4
OLD THREE CK RD	HUM	10	C5
OLD TIM BELL RD	STA	47	E2
OLD TOLL	MPA	49	A3
OLD TOLL RD	INY	71	A1
OLD TOLL RD	LAS	14	A3
OLD TOLL RD	MEN	31	C3
OLD TOLL RD	YUB	26	B5
OLD TOPANGA CYN	LACO	97	B2
OLD TRUCKEE RD	SIE	27	C4
OLD WESTSIDE RD	SIS	4	B5
OLD WILBUR RD	COL	32	C2
OLD WITR SPG RD	LAK	31	C2
OLD WMN SPGS RD	SBD	92	A4
OLD WMN SPGS RD	SBD	100	D1
OLD YERMO CTO	SBD	91	E1
OLD YOSEMITE RD	MPA	49	A1
OLD 44 DR	SHA	18	C2
OLEANDER	SJCO	47	B2
OLEANDER AV	BKD	166	C4
OLEANDER AV	RCO	99	B3
OLEMA ST	SBD	80	E1
OLINDA RD	SHA	18	C3
OLIVAS LN	SOL	39	A2
OLIVE AV	BUR	179	C4
OLIVE AV	COR	215	B5
OLIVE AV	FRE	165	B2
OLIVE AV	FRCO	57	A3
OLIVE AV	FRCO	57	C3
OLIVE AV	GLE	24	D3
OLIVE AV	MAR	L	A2
OLIVE AV	MCO	48	A4
OLIVE AV	MCO	48	C4
OLIVE AV	RCO	99	B5
OLIVE AV	RCO	99	D4
OLIVE AV	SDCO	106	C3
OLIVE AV	SJCO	47	B2
OLIVE AV	STA	47	B3
OLIVE AV	STA	47	E1
OLIVE AV	STA	48	A1
OLIVE AV	TEH	24	D1
OLIVE AV	TUL	68	D3
OLIVE AV W	MER	170	B2
OLIVE DR	KER	78	D2
OLIVE DR E	DVS	136	D3
OLIVE HWY	BUT	25	D4
OLIVE LN	GLE	25	A4
OLIVE RD	TEH	24	D2
OLIVE RD	VEN	88	B5
OLIVE ST	AVLN	97	B4
OLIVE ST	LA	185	E3
OLIVE ST	LACO	R	C3
OLIVE ST	MAR	38	B4
OLIVE ST	RCO	99	B4
OLIVE ST	SDCO	107	A4
OLIVE ST	SHA	18	B3
OLIVEHURST	YUB	33	D2
OLIVE LAKE BLVD	RCO	103	D5
OLIVENHAIN RD	SDCO	106	C4
OLIVE ORCHRD RD	CAL	40	D4
OLIVER RD	SBT	55	D4
OLIVERA DR	TUL	58	C5
OLIVE SCHOOL LN	SOL	39	A2
OLIVET RD	SON	37	D2
OLIVEWOOD AV	TEH	24	D2
OLNEY PARK DR	SHA	18	B2
OLSEN RD	MCO	48	B3
OLSEN RD	VEN	88	D5
OLSEN CREEK RD	TRI	16	E2
OLSON RD	LAS	8	B4
OLYMPIC	LAK	32	A3
OLYMPIC BLVD	BH	183	B2
OLYMPIC BLVD	LA	184	B2
OLYMPIC BLVD	LA	185	D4
OLYMPIC BLVD	LA	186	B4
OLYMPIC BLVD	LA	180	C4
OLYMPIC BLVD	LACO	97	D2
OLYMPIC BLVD	LACO	Q	D4
OLYMPIC BLVD	SMON	180	A5
OLYMPIC RD	MAD	57	B1
OLYMPIC RD	SBD	100	E1
OMAHA AV	KIN	67	B3
OMAHA AV	KIN	67	E3
OMEGA RD	NEV	26	E5
OMO RANCH RD	ED	41	B1
ONEAL RD	BUT	25	C4
ONEAL RD	MAD	57	D1
ONE HOLE SPG RD	SBD	92	C5
ONION VALLEY RD	ED	35	B3
ONION VALLEY RD	INY	59	E3
ONSTOTT RD	SUT	33	C2
ONTARIO AV	RCO	U	E5
ONTARIO AV	RCO	98	E3
ONTARIO FRWY	SBD	99	A1
ONYX AV	SIS	4	C5
OPAL RD	MCO	48	D4
OPAL WY	SHA	18	C1
OPAL FERRY RD	KER	88	D1
OPAL MTN RD	SBD	81	C4
OPENSHAW RD	BUT	25	C4
OPEN SHAW RD	PLU	20	D5
OPHIR RD	BUT	25	D5
OPHIR RD	INY	71	A2
ORANGE AV	BUT	25	E5
ORANGE AV	EC	217	D3
ORANGE AV	FRCO	57	C4
ORANGE AV	FRCO	57	D4
ORANGE AV	KIN	67	A3
ORANGE AV	KIN	67	D3
ORANGE AV	LACO	Q	E2
ORANGE AV	LACO	R	D4
ORANGE AV	LACO	S	D2
ORANGE AV	ORCO	T	B2
ORANGE AV	RCO	99	C3
ORANGE AV	SDCO	V	B4
ORANGE AV	SDCO	V	D5
ORANGE AV	SDCO	111	C1
ORANGE AV	SDCO	111	D2
ORANGE AV	SJCO	47	D1
ORANGE AV	SON	132	A4
ORANGE AV	STA	47	C3
ORANGE AV W	SSF	144	A1
ORANGE FRWY	ANA	194	A5
ORANGE FRWY	ORCO	98	C3
ORANGE FRWY	ORCO	194	A5
ORANGE FRWY	ORCO	T	D1
ORANGE RD	SDCO	107	A3
ORANGE ST	KER	78	B2
ORANGE ST	RCO	99	B2
ORANGE ST	SBD	99	C2
ORANGE BLSSM RD	STA	48	A1
ORANGEBURG AV E	MDO	162	D2
ORANGEBURG AV W	MDO	162	B1
ORANGE GROVE AV	LACO	R	C3
ORANGE GROVE AV	LACO	U	B2
ORANGE GROVE BL	LACO	R	B3
ORANGE GROVE BL	PAS	190	C3
ORANGE-OLIVE RD	ORA	194	C3
ORANGE-OLIVE RD	ORCO	98	C3
ORANGE-OLIVE RD	ORCO	T	D2
ORANGE PARK BL	ORCO	T	E2
ORANGE SHOW RD	SBDO	207	D4
ORANGETHORPE AV	ORCO	98	B3
ORANGETHORPE AV	ORCO	98	C3
ORANGETHORPE AV	ORCO	T	B1
ORANGEWOOD AV	ORCO	T	B2
ORANGEWOOD RD	TEH	24	D1
ORCHARD AV	SLO	76	C5
ORCHARD AV	TEH	24	D2
ORCHARD DR	FRCO	58	D4
ORCHARD DR	MCO	48	C5
ORCHARD DR	IMP	112	C3
ORCHARD RD	MCO	47	C5
ORCHARD RD	SJCO	40	B4
ORCHARD RD	STA	47	B2
ORCHARD ST	RCO	99	E2
ORCHARD WY	MCO	56	C1
ORCHARD PARK AV	MCO	48	B4
ORCHARD SPGS RD	NEV	34	D2
ORCUTT RD	SLO	76	B4
ORCUTT RD	VEN	88	C4
ORCUTT-GAREY RD	SB	86	C1
ORD ST	SB	86	B2
ORD FERRY RD	BUT	25	A4
ORD MOUNTAIN RD	SBD	91	E2
ORD RANCH RD	BUT	25	C5
ORDWAY RD	SIS	12	C1
OREGON DR	MDO	162	D4
OREGON EXPWY	PA	147	D3
OREGON EXPWY	SCL	45	E4
OREGON EXPWY	SCL	N	E2
OREGON CREEK RD	SIE	26	D4
OREGON GULCH RD	BUT	25	D4
OREGON HILL RD	YUB	26	B5
OREGON MTN RD	DN	2	C3
ORESTIMBA RD	STA	47	C4
ORLEANS AV	FRCO	55	E3
ORMONDE RD	SLO	76	B4
ORMSBY AV	FRCO	56	C2
ORMSBY ST	SDCO	106	C2
ORNBAUN RD	MEN	30	E3
ORO FINO RD	SIS	3	D5
OROVILLE BANGOR	BUT	25	D4
OROVLL CHICO HY	BUT	25	B3
OROVLLE DM BL E	BUT	25	D4
OROVLLE DM BL W	BUT	25	C4
OROVLLE GRIDLEY	BUT	25	C5
OROVLE QUNCY HY	BUT	25	D4
OROVLE QUNCY HY	BUT	25	E3
OROVLE QUNCY HY	BUT	26	A3
ORR RD	SAC	40	A3
ORR & DAY RD	LACO	R	C5
ORR & DAY RD	LACO	T	A1
ORR CREEK LN	PLA	34	B3
ORRIS RD	RCO	102	A4
ORRLAND AV	TUL	68	B3
ORR MTN LOOKOUT	SIS	5	A4
ORR SPRINGS RD	MEN	30	E1
ORR SPRINGS RD	MEN	31	A1
ORSI RD	STA	47	E1
ORTEGA HWY	ORCO	98	E5
ORTEGA HWY	SCL	202	E1
ORTIGALITA RD	MCO	55	D2
OSAGE RD	SOL	39	B2
OSBORN RD	SIS	5	D2
OSBORN RD	TEH	24	B2
OSBORNE AV	RCO	102	C4
OSBORNE RD	SBD	91	D2
OSBORNE ST	LACO	97	C1
OSBORNE ST	LACO	Q	C2
OSBORNE PARK RD	IMP	109	D4
OSDICK RD	SBD	80	E3
OSGOOD RD	ALA	P	B2
OSO PKWY	ORCO	98	D5
OSO FLACO LK RD	SLO	76	B5
OSOS ST	SNLO	172	C2
OSPITAL RD	CAL	40	D4
OSTROM RD	YUB	33	E2
OSWALD RD	SUT	33	B2
OSWELL ST	KER	78	D3
OTAY LAKES RD	SDCO	V	D4
OTAY LAKES RD	SDCO	111	E2
OTAY MESA RD	SDCO	V	D5
OTAY MESA RD	SDCO	111	E2
OTAY VALLEY RD	SDCO	V	D5
OTAY VALLEY RD	SDCO	111	E2
OTIS DR	A	159	A2
OTIS ST	LACO	R	A5
OTOE RD	SBD	91	C3
OUR HSE DAM RD	SIE	26	C5
OUTINGDALE	ED	40	E1
OUTLAW MINE RD	RCO	102	A2
OVERLAND AV	CUL	188	B1
OVERLAND AV	LA	183	A5
OVERLAND AV	LACO	Q	C4
OVERLAND AV	MCO	55	D1
OVERLAND DR	SHA	18	C3
OWENS	SJCO	47	D1
OWENS AV	CLK	74	E2
OWENS RD	INY	51	D4
OWENS RD	SIS	5	A2
OWENS GORGE RD	MNO	51	B2
OWENS RIVER RD	MNO	50	E1
OWENS RV RCH RD	MNO	50	E1
OWENYO LONE PNE	INY	60	B4
OWL HOLE SPG RD	SBD	82	B1
OXALIS AV	FRCO	56	B2
OXBOW PL	SB	86	E3
OXFORD AV	FRCO	56	A2
OXFORD RD	SOL	39	D3
OXFORD ST	B	156	A2
OXNARD BLVD	OXN	176	C1
P			
P ST	BKD	166	D5
P ST	FRE	165	E3
P ST	KER	166	D5
P ST	SCTO	137	C3
P ST	SBD	91	D1
PACHECO BLVD	CC	L	E3
PACHECO BLVD	CC	38	E5
PACHECO BLVD	CC	154	C2
PACHECO BLVD	M	154	C2
PACHECO RD	KER	78	D3
PACHECO PASS HY	SCL	54	E2
PACHECO PASS RD	SCL	54	D2
PACIFIC AV	DN	1	D4
PACIFIC AV	LB	192	C2
PACIFIC AV	LA	187	A3
PACIFIC AV	LA	191	A4
PACIFIC AV	LACO	97	D4
PACIFIC AV	LACO	S	C3
PACIFIC AV	LACO	S	D2
PACIFIC AV	PAC	167	C2
PACIFIC AV	SC	169	D3
PACIFIC AV	S	160	B1
PACIFIC AV	SUT	33	D3
PACIFIC AV	SUT	33	D4
PACIFIC AV	TUL	68	B2

STREET	CO.	PAGE	GRID
PACIFIC BLVD	LACO	97	E2
PACIFIC BLVD	LACO	R	A4
PACIFIC BLVD	SM	145	B3
PACIFIC HWY	SD	213	A4
PACIFIC HWY	SD	215	C2
PACIFIC ST	MONT	167	E4
PACIFIC ST	SBD	99	C1
PACIFIC BCH DR	SD	212	A2
PACIFIC BCH DR	SDCO	V	A3
PACIFIC CST HWY	LB	192	D1
PACIFIC CST HWY	LA	192	D1
PACIFIC CST HWY	LACO	97	B2
PACIFIC CST HWY	LACO	S	B1
PACIFIC CST HWY	LACO	T	A3
PACIFIC CST HWY	ORCO	98	C5
PACIFIC CST HWY	ORCO	T	A3
PACIFIC CST HWY	VEN	96	C2
PACIFC GRV-CRML	MONT	167	B4
PACIFC GRV-CRML	MON	53	D3
PACIFC GRV-CRML	MON	167	B4
PACIFC GRV-CRML	PAC	167	B4
PACIFIC HTS RD	BUT	25	C5
PACIFIC LUMBER	HUM	16	A1
PACIFIC MINE RD	SIE	26	C3
PACIFIC VIEW DR	MEN	30	C3
PACIFIC VIEW RD	VEN	96	C2
PACKER RD	COL	32	E1
PACKER LAKE RD	SIE	26	E3
PACKER LAKE RD	SIE	27	A3
PAC MINE RD	SIE	26	D3
PAGE AV	FRCO	67	B1
PAGE RD	STA	47	B2
PAGE MILL RD	PA	147	C4
PAGE MILL RD	SCL	N	E3
PAGE MILL RD	SCL	45	D4
PA HA LN	INY	51	D4
PAIGE AV	TUL	68	B2
PAIGE BAR RD	SHA	18	B2
PAINE RD	AMA	40	D2
PAINT RD	CAL	41	B4
PAINTED CAVE	SB	87	C4
PAINTED GRGE RD	IMP	111	C3
PAINTER AV	LACO	98	B2
PAINTER AV	LACO	R	D4
PAJARO ST	SAL	171	C4
PALA RD	DN	1	D3
PALA RD	RCO	106	D1
PALA TEMECLA RD	SDCO	106	D1
PALAZZO RD	MCO	47	E5
PALAZZO RD	MCO	48	A5
PALAZZO RD	MCO	55	E1
PALERMO RD	BUT	25	D5
PALRMO HONCT HY	BUT	25	D5
PALISADE AV	SBD	91	E3
PALISADES AV	RED	122	E1
PALISADES DR	LACO	97	C2
PALLETT CK RD	LACO	90	C4
PALM AV	AUB	126	C3
PALM AV	COR	215	C4
PALM AV	FRE	165	C2
PALM AV	FRCO	57	C3
PALM AV	KER	78	B1
PALM AV	KER	78	C3
PALM AV	LACO	R	C5
PALM AV	MCO	48	A4
PALM AV	RCO	99	B2
PALM AV	RCO	99	E4
PALM AV	SBD	99	B1
PALM AV	SDCO	V	C5
PALM AV	SDCO	V	D3
PALM AV	SDCO	111	D2
PALM AV	SDCO	111	E1
PALM AV	SCL	P	D4
PALM AV	SCL	54	C1
PALM AV	SHA	18	B3
PALM DR	RCO	100	D3
PALM DR	SDCO	106	C4
PALM DR	SCL	N	E2
PALM ST	BKD	166	B4
PALM CANYON DR	PMSP	206	B5
PALM CANYON DR	RCO	100	D4
PALM CANYON DR	SDCO	107	E2
PALM CYN DR E	PMSP	206	B5
PALM CYN DR N	PMSP	206	A1
PALMDALE BLVD	LACO	90	B3
PALMDALE RD	SBD	90	E4
PALMDALE RD	SBD	91	A3
PALMER AV	FRCO	66	C2
PALMER RD	SB	86	C2
PALMER CREEK RD	HUM	15	E2
PALMETTO AV	BUT	124	C3
PALMETTO AV	C	124	C3
PALMETTO ST	SBD	80	E5
PALMETTO ST	SBD	81	A5
PALMETTO WY	LAS	20	D2
PALMS TO PINES	RCO	100	E4
PALO COLORDO RD	MON	64	B1
PALOMA RD	CAL	40	E3
PALOMAR AV	SDCO	V	C5
PALOMAR AV	SDCO	111	D2
PALOMAR ST	RCO	99	C5
PALOMAR APRT RD	SDCO	106	B3
PALOMAR DIV TK	RCO	106	D1
PALOMARES RD	ALA	M	A5
PALOMARES RD	ALA	P	A1
PALOMARES RD	ALA	46	A2
PALOMAS AV	KER	77	E3
PALOMAS AV	KER	78	A3
PALOMINO RD	SDCO	106	C2
PALOMINO WY	HUM	22	C1
PALO PRIETA CHO	SLO	76	D1
PALOS VERDES BL	LACO	S	B2
PALOS VRDS DR E	LACO	97	D4

STREET	CO.	PAGE	GRID
PALOS VRDS DR E	LACO	S	B3
PALOS VRDS DR N	LACO	97	D3
PALOS VRDS DR N	LACO	S	B2
PALOS VRDS DR S	LACO	S	A3
PALOS VRDS DR S	LACO	97	D4
PALOS VRDS DR W	LACO	97	D4
PALOS VRDS DR W	LACO	S	A2
PALO VERDE AV	LACO	S	E2
PALO VERDE BLVD	MOH	96	B4
PALO VERDE RD	IMP	110	C1
PALO VERDE RD	SBD	100	C2
PALO VERDE ST	MTCL	203	C3
PAMELA ST	KER	79	C2
PAMO RD	SDCO	107	A3
PAMPA RD	KER	79	A3
PANAMA LN	KER	78	B3
PANAMA LN	KER	79	A3
PANAMA RD	KER	78	D3
PANAMA RD	KER	79	A3
PANAMINT VLY RD	INY	71	B1
PANCHO RD	RCO	107	A1
PANCHORICO RD	MON	65	E3
PANGBORN LN	INY	60	B4
PANOCHE RD	FRCO	56	D3
PANOCHE RD	SBT	55	B4
PANOCHE RD	SBT	56	A4
PANORAMA DR	KER	78	E2
PANORAMA PT RD	SHA	18	D3
PANORAMIC HWY	MAR	38	A5
PANORAMIC HWY	MAR	L	A4
PANORAMIC HWY	MAR	45	A1
PANTHER CK RD	TEH	19	C3
PANTHER GAP RD	HUM	16	A4
PAPPAS RD	KER	80	C3
PARADISE AV	MDO	162	A4
PARADISE AV	STA	47	C3
PARADISE DR	CRTM	140	D1
PARADISE DR	MAR	L	B3
PARADISE DR	RCO	100	C5
PARADISE RD	CLK	74	D2
PARADISE RD	CLK	209	C4
PARADISE RD	CLK	210	E3
PARADISE RD	COL	24	E5
PARADISE RD	LV	209	C4
PARADISE RD	SJCO	46	E1
PARADISE RD	SJCO	47	A1
PARADISE RD	SB	87	B3
PARADISE RD	STA	47	C2
PARADISE SPG RD	SBD	81	E4
PARADISE SPG RD	SBD	82	B5
PARADISE VLY RD	SDCO	V	D4
PARADISE VLY RD	SDCO	111	D1
PARAISO SPGS RD	MON	64	E1
PARAISO SPGS RD	MON	65	A1
PARAMOUNT BLVD	LACO	98	A3
PARAMOUNT BLVD	LACO	R	C4
PARAMOUNT BLVD	LACO	S	E1
PARDEE DAM RD	CAL	40	D3
PARDOES	AMA	41	D1
PARIS AV	KIN	67	D3
PARIS VALLEY RD	MON	65	D3
PARK AV	BUT	25	B3
PARK AV	C	124	C5
PARK AV	LAG	201	B2
PARK AV	SJ	151	D4
PARK AV	SJ	152	A4
PARK AV	SCLR	151	C3
PARK AV	TRI	17	D2
PARK BLVD	ALA	L	D4
PARK BLVD	ALA	45	D1
PARK BLVD	O	158	D3
PARK BLVD	SD	214	A5
PARK BLVD	SD	215	E3
PARK BLVD	SD	216	A1
PARK BLVD	SDCO	V	B3
PARK RD	BEN	153	D4
PARK RD	IMP	109	B4
PARK RD	SBT	55	A3
PARK RD E	COL	24	B5
PARK ST	ALA	L	D5
PARK ST	HUM	9	E5
PARK ST	S	160	B4
PARK ST	TUL	68	B3
PARK WY	LAK	31	D2
PARK CREEK RD	ED	35	B4
PARKER AV	CC	L	D3
PARKER RD	SBD	101	E1
PARKER RD	STA	47	D2
PARKER CREEK RD	MOD	8	C1
PARKER CREEK RD	MOD	8	B1
PARKER CK RD W	MOD	8	C1
PARKER DAM RD	SBD	104	B1
PARKER LAKE RD	MNO	43	C5
PARKER LAKE RD	MNO	50	C1
PARKER-POSTN RD	LPAZ	103	E4
PARKFIELD GRADE	FRCO	66	C3
PARKFLD CEM RD	MON	66	C4
PARKFLD-COALNGA	FRCO	66	C4
PARK HILL RD	SLO	76	B3
PARKMAN RD	IMP	110	D5
PARK MARINA DR	RED	122	D1
PARK MOABI	SBD	95	E2
PARKMONT DR	LACO	89	D3
PARKS RD	SUT	33	C3
PARKSIDE DR	RCO	101	D5
PARKSIDE DR N	CC	M	B3
PARKVIEW AV	RED	122	C3
PARKVIEW LN	KER	79	C5
PARKVILLE RD	SHA	18	D3
PARKWAY DR	DN	1	D4
PARKWAY DR	TEH	18	D4
PARLIER AV	FRCO	56	E4
PARLIER AV	FRCO	57	D4

STREET	CO.	PAGE	GRID
PARLIER AV	FRCO	58	B4
PARR	CC	38	C5
PARR BLVD	CC	L	C3
PARROTTS FERRY	TUO	41	C4
PARSONS RD	FRCO	66	C2
PASADENA AV	LA	186	C1
PASADENA FRWY	LA	186	B2
PASADENA FRWY	LACO	97	E2
PASADENA FRWY	LACO	R	A3
PASCOE RD	KER	69	B5
PASEO AV	SUT	33	C1
PASEO DEL MAR	LACO	97	D4
PASEO DEL MAR	LACO	S	B3
PASKENTA RD	TEH	18	C5
PASKENTA RD	TEH	24	C1
PASKENTA CEM RD	TEH	24	B2
PASO ST	KER	78	A5
PASO NOGAL	CC	38	E5
PASO ROBLES BL	SLO	76	A1
PASO ROBLES HWY	KER	77	E1
PASQUALE RD	NEV	34	D1
PASS RD	SUT	33	A2
PASSONS BLVD	LACO	R	C5
PAST TIME LN	RCO	100	A5
PATHFINDER RD	LACO	U	B3
PATRICIA AV	SIS	4	C2
PATRICIA LN	CAL	41	C3
PATRICIA LN	MNO	42	E1
PATRICIA LN	MNO	43	A1
PATRICK RD	LPAZ	104	A2
PATRICK WY	SBD	100	E1
PATRICKS CK RD	DN	2	B3
PATRICKS PT	HUM	9	E3
PATTERSON AV	SB	87	B4
PATTERSON LN	MOD	8	E1
PATTERSON RD	HUM	10	D4
PATTERSON RD	KER	89	B1
PATTERSON RD	STA	47	D2
PATTERSON RD	VEN	96	B1
PATTERSON CK RD	SIS	3	D5
PATTERSON CK RD	SIS	11	D1
PATTRSN MILL RD	MOD	8	E3
PATTERSON PS RD	ALA	M	D5
PATTERSON PS RD	ALA	46	C2
PATTERSON PS RD	SJCO	46	D2
PATTERSN RCH RD	TRI	17	A1
PATTERSN SAWMLL	LAS	8	D3
PATTISON RD	CAL	40	D3
PATTON	MCO	55	E1
PATTON MILLS RD	TEH	24	A2
PATTYMOCUS-			
-LOOKOUT RD	TEH	17	D4
PATWIN RD	SBD	90	E3
PAUBA RD	RCO	106	D1
PAUI RD	RCO	107	B1
PAULARINO AV	CM	197	E4
PAULINE AV	STA	47	C2
PAUL NEGRA RD	MCO	55	E3
PAXTON RD	SBDO	100	E1
PAXTON ST	LACO	Q	C1
PAYEN RD	SAC	40	C1
PAYMASTER MN RD	SBD	83	C4
PAYNE AV	CC	39	C5
PAYNE RD	IMP	108	E5
PAYNE RD	SUT	33	B2
PAYNE WY	KER	79	D3
PAYNES CK LOOP	TEH	19	A4
PAYNES CREEK RD	TEH	19	A4
PAYNES CREEK RD	TEH	18	D4
PEABODY CT	NEV	127	B3
PEABODY RD	SOL	M	B1
PEABODY RD	SOL	39	A3
PEACEFUL GLEN	SOL	39	A2
PEACH AV	FRCO	57	D2
PEACH AV	FRCO	57	D5
PEACH AV	GLE	24	E4
PEACH AV	MCO	47	E4
PEACH AV	MCO	48	A4
PEACH AV	SBD	91	C4
PEACH TREE RD	MON	65	E2
PEACH TREE RD	MON	66	A2
PEACHY CYN RD	SLO	75	E1
PEACHY CYN RD	SLO	76	A1
PEAK RD	TRI	16	D5
PEAR AV	GLE	25	A4
PEAR AV	STA	47	C4
PEARBLOSSOM HWY	LACO	90	A4
PEARL RD	SJCO	40	B3
PEARL ST	SDCO	V	A2
PEARL ST	SDCO	106	C5
PEAR MAIN ST	SBD	91	B3
PEARSON RD	BUT	25	C3
PEARSON RD	INY	70	C5
PEASE RD	SUT	33	C2
PEAVINE RDG RD	ED	35	B4
PEBBLE BEACH DR	DN	1	D4
PEBBLY BEACH RD	AVLN	97	B5
PECHO VALLEY RD	SLO	75	E3
PECK RD	LACO	98	B1
PECK RD	LACO	R	D4
PEDERSON	FRCO	58	A3
PEDLEY RD	RCO	99	A2
PEDRICK RD	SOL	39	B2
PEDRICK RD	SOL	39	B1
PEDRO RANCH RD	MNO	51	C1
PEDROS RD	STA	47	D3
PEGASUS DR	KER	78	D2
PEGASUS ST	KER	79	B4
PEG LEG RD	SDCO	107	E2
PELGER RD	SUT	33	B3
PELICAN RD	STA	47	B2
PELLERIN RD	STA	47	E2
PELLET RD	IMP	108	E4

STREET	CO.	PAGE	GRID
PELLISER RD	KER	79	B4
PELTIER RD	SJCO	39	E3
PELTIER RD	SJCO	40	A3
PENCIL RD	MOD	7	B5
PENDLETON RD	SBD	92	A1
PENDOLA RD	YUB	26	B4
PENDOLA EXT	YUB	26	C4
PENDOLA GARDEN	MPA	49	A3
PENINSULA AV	SMCO	N	C1
PENINSULA DR	HUM	15	E5
PENINSULA DR	PLU	20	B4
PENMAN SPGS RD	SLO	76	B1
PENNINGTON RD	BUT	33	B1
PENNINGTON RD	SUT	33	C1
PENNSYLVANIA AV	LACO	Q	E2
PENNSYLVANIA AV	RCO	99	E3
PENNSYLVANIA AV	SOL	L	E1
PENNSYLVANIA AV	SOL	M	A1
PENNSYLVANIA AV	SOL	135	B4
PENNSYLV GCH RD	CAL	41	C4
PENON LOOKOUT	MPA	48	D1
PENOYAR GRSS LK	SIS	4	E5
PENROSE ST	LACO	Q	D2
PENTLAND RD	KER	78	B5
PENTZ RD	BUT	25	C3
PEORIA RD	YUB	34	A1
PEPPER AV	SBD	99	B2
PEPPER DR	KER	78	E3
PEPPER RD	SON	37	E3
PEPPER ST	MCO	47	E4
PEPPER ST	MCO	48	A4
PEPPER ST	SBD	80	E5
PEPPER ST	SBD	81	A5
PERALTA BLVD	ALA	P	A1
PERALTA BLVD	ALA	46	A3
PERALTA ST	ALA	L	C4
PERALTA ST	O	157	C2
PERCH ST	KER	79	C4
PERCY AV	YUBA	125	D3
PERCY RD	KER	79	D1
PEREZ RD	IMP	112	D5
PERI RD	MON	65	D4
PERIMETER RD	NEV	34	B2
PERINI RD	LAK	32	A4
PERKINS AV	KER	78	B1
PERKINS RD	CLO	33	A3
PERKINS RD	SB	87	C1
PERKINS ST	U	123	B3
PERRAL RD	KER	77	D2
PERRIN AV	FRCO	57	D2
PERRIN RD	SJCO	47	B2
PERRIS BLVD	RCO	99	C3
PERRY RD	COL	32	D1
PERRY RD	RCO	99	B4
PERRY CREEK RD	ED	41	A1
PERSHING AV	S	160	A1
PERSHING AV	SJCO	40	A5
PERSHING DR	LA	187	D5
PERSHING DR	LACO	Q	C5
PERSHING DR	SD	216	A3
PERSHING DR	SDCO	V	C3
PESCADERO RD	SMCO	N	C4
PESCADERO CK RD	SMCO	45	C5
PETALUMA AV	SON	132	B4
PETALUMA HLL RD	STR	131	D4
PETALUMA HLL RD	SON	38	A2
PETALUMA HLL RD	SON	131	D4
PETE MILLER RD	STA	47	C5
PETERSBOURGH S	CAL	40	E3
PETERSBURG RD	SIS	11	B3
PETERSON DR	NAPA	29	B2
PETERSON LN	LAK	31	D3
PETERSON RD	COL	32	C1
PETERSON RD	FRCO	58	B1
PETERSON RD	IMP	109	B3
PETERSON RD	KER	68	C5
PETERSON RD	KER	77	E1
PETERSON RD	KER	78	B1
PETERSON RD	LPAZ	104	A3
PETERSON RD	LACO	89	D4
PETERSON RDG RD	YUB	26	B5
PETRIFIED FORST	NAPA	38	A1
PETRIFIED FORST	SON	38	A1
PETRO RD	INY	72	C2
PETROGLYPH RD	MNO	51	D3
PETRLEUM CLB RD	KER	78	A4
PETTINGER RD	CAL	40	D4
PETTYJOHN RD	TEH	17	E5
PEW RD	SBD	85	C5
PEZZI RD	SJCO	40	B4
PFE RD	PLA	33	E5
PFITZER RD	MCO	47	D5
PHEASANT CT	KER	79	B4
PHEASANT DR	MOD	7	B5
PHEASANT LN	SIS	4	B4
PHELAN RD	HUM	15	D1
PHELAN RD	SBD	91	A4
PHELPS AV	FRCO	66	D2
PHILADELPHIA ST	LACO	98	D2
PHILADELPHIA ST	SBD	U	C3
PHILADELPHIA ST	SBD	98	D2
PHILBRIC RD	SB	86	C1
PHILBROOK RD	BUT	25	D1
PHILDOW RD	LAS	20	E3
PHILIP	PLA	33	E4
PHILIPS RD	MCO	55	E1
PHILLIPE LN	SIS	4	A5
PHILLIPS	LAK	32	A3
PHILLIPS BLVD	SBD	U	C3
PHILLIPS DR	SBD	82	A5
PHILLIPS RD	KER	78	C1
PHILLIPS RD	KER	78	D4
PHILLIPS RD	KER	80	B4

STREET	CO.	PAGE	GRID
PHILLIPS RD	SHA	19	A1
PHILLIPS RD	SOL	39	B1
PHILLIPSVLLE RD	HUM	16	C4
PHILO GRNWD RD	MEN	30	C2
PHOENIX LAKE RD	TUO	41	D5
PHYLLIS RD	TEH	18	C4
PICACHO RD	IMP	110	D5
PICADOR BLVD	SDCO	V	D5
PICADOR BLVD	SDCO	111	D2
PICARD RD	SIS	4	E2
PICARD RD	SIS	5	A2
PICRD SAMS NECK	SIS	4	E2
PICARDY DR	S	160	B4
PICAYUNE RD	MAD	49	D5
PICKENS RD	LAS	21	D5
PICKERING AV	LACO	R	C5
PICKETT RD	IMP	109	B4
PICO BLVD	LA	180	C4
PICO BLVD	LA	183	B3
PICO BLVD	LA	184	A3
PICO BLVD	LA	185	C3
PICO BLVD	LACO	Q	C4
PICO BLVD	SMON	187	A1
PICO CANYON RD	LACO	89	B4
PIEDMONT AV	O	158	B1
PIEDMONT RD	SCL	P	C3
PIEDRA RD	FRCO	58	A3
PIEDRA AZUL	MCO	55	D3
PIEDRAS DR	RCO	99	B3
PIER AV	LACO	S	B1
PIERCE LN	SOL	38	E4
PIERCE RD	SCL	P	A4
PIERCE RD	SCL	45	E5
PIERCE RD	SUT	33	C3
PIERCE ST	BKD	166	A2
PIERCE ST	RCO	99	A3
PIERCE ST	RCO	101	B4
PIERCE CK MTWY	PLU	21	A4
PIERCE POINT RD	MAR	37	D4
PIERI RD	KER	78	B4
PIERLE RD	IMP	108	E5
PIERSON BLVD	RCO	100	C2
PIGEON PASS RD	RCO	99	C2
PIGEON POINT RD	HUM	15	E1
PIGEON SPG RD	KER	79	C5
PIKE RD	STA	47	D3
PIKE CITY RD	SIE	26	C5
PIKE CITY RD	YUB	26	C5
PILAR RD	SIS	4	D5
PILE ST	SDCO	107	A4
PILGRIM CK RD	SIS	12	E2
PILITAS HUERHRO	SLO	76	C2
PILOT SPRING RD	MNO	43	D5
PILOT SPRING RD	MNO	50	E1
PIMLICO DR	RCO	100	C5
PINAL ST	SB	86	D1
PINE AV	BUT	25	B3
PINE AV	LB	192	D3
PINE AV	MEN	31	C1
PINE AV	PAC	167	C2
PINE AV	SBD	U	D4
PINE AV	SBD	98	D2
PINE AV	TRI	17	B2
PINE DR	HUM	16	B4
PINE DR	LAS	20	E2
PINE DR	MPA	48	E1
PINE ST	C	124	C4
PINE ST	CC	L	E3
PINE ST	MONT	167	D2
PINE ST	MON	53	E2
PINE ST	RED	122	B1
PINE ST	RCO	100	C4
PINE ST	SDCO	107	A4
PINE ST	SF	142	A3
PINE ST	SHA	18	C3
PINE ST	U	123	C2
PINE CANYON RD	MON	65	B3
PINE CANYON RD	SB	76	E5
PINE COVE TR	KER	79	D2
PINE CREEK BLVD	MOD	8	B1
PINE CREEK RD	INY	51	B4
PINE CREEK RD	HUM	10	C3
PINE CREEK RD	SIS	2	E3
PINE FLAT	SON	31	E5
PINE FLAT RD	SBD	91	E5
PINE FLAT RD	SCR	N	E5
PINE FLAT RD	SCR	53	D1
PINE GROVE	VEN	88	C4
PINE GROVE RD	KLAM	5	C1
PINE GRV TABEAU	AMA	41	A2
PINE GULCH RD	AMA	40	E2
PINE HILLS RD	SDCO	107	C4
PINE HOLLOW RD	CC	M	B3
PINEHURST RD	CC	45	D1
PINE MTN DR	TUO	48	E1
PINE MTN RD	KER	78	E1
PINE MTN RD	KER	79	A1
PINE MTN RD	MEN	31	D4
PINE NUT RD	MNO	42	E1
PINE RIDGE	FRCO	58	C3
PINE RIDGE RD	HUM	10	C3
PINE RIDGE RD	MEN	31	A2
PINES TO PALMS HWY	RCO	100	B4
PINE TREE CY RD	KER	80	A4
PINE VALLEY RD	MON	65	D3
PINEVISTA CIR	RCO	100	A3
PINEWOOD LN	FRCO	58	B1
PINEY CK LOOP	MON	64	D^
PINKSTON CYN RD	BUT	25	D3
PINNACLE RD	SBD	81	A1
PINOLE VLY RD	CC	L	D3
PINOLI RIDGE RD	NEV	26	E4
PINOLI RIDGE RD	NEV	27	A4

STREET	CO.	PAGE	GRID
PINON CANYON RD	KER	79	C4
PINON VILLGE RD	TUL	70	A3
PINTO DR	CAL	41	B4
PINTO RD	RCO	101	E4
PINTO BASIN RD	RCO	101	D4
PINTO MTN RD	SBD	101	C1
PIONEER AV	STA	47	D1
PIONEER BLVD	LACO	98	A3
PIONEER BLVD	LACO	T	A2
PIONEER DR	KER	78	E3
PIONEER RD	DN	2	B3
PIONEER RD	MCO	55	D1
PIONEER RD	STA	47	D3
PIONEER TR	SLT	129	C4
PIONEER CK RD	AMA	41	B2
PIONEERTOWN RD	SBD	100	D1
PIONEER TR RD	ED	36	A3
PIPE CREEK RD	RCO	100	C5
PIPE LINE AV	SBD	U	C3
PIPE LINE AV	SBD	98	D2
PIPER RD	CC	M	D3
PIPES RD	SBD	100	C1
PIPES CANYON RD	SBD	100	D1
PIPI RD	ED	41	C1
PIRCEN RD	LAS	14	B3
PIRU CANYON RD	LACO	89	A4
PIRU CANYON RD	VEN	88	E4
PISGAH CRATR RD	SBD	92	E2
PISTACHIO RD	KER	77	B1
PIT RD	MNO	51	A2
PIT #1 PWRHS RD	SHA	13	D4
PITTMAN HILL RD	FRCO	58	A2
PITT RIV CYN RD	LAS	14	A4
PITT SCHOOL RD	SOL	39	B2
PITTVILLE RD	LAS	20	A1
PITTVILLE RD	SHA	13	E4
PITTVILLE BENCH	LAS	14	A4
PITTZER RD	IMP	112	B3
PIUMA RD	LACO	97	A2
PIUTE MTN RD	KER	79	D2
PIUTE PINES RD	KER	79	D3
PLACENTIA AV	ORCO	T	C4
PLACER AV	FRCO	56	E4
PLACER CT	KER	79	D2
PLACER RD	SHA	18	B2
PLACER RD	SUT	33	E3
PLACER ST	RED	122	A2
PLACER ST	SHA	18	B2
PLACER ST	TRI	17	D1
PLACER HILLS RD	PLA	34	C3
PLACERITA CYN	LACO	89	C5
PLACERVILLE DR	PLCV	138	A3
PLACERVILLE RD	SAC	34	B5
PLAINS RD	CC	39	C5
PLAINSBURG RD	MCO	48	D5
PLANO ST	TUL	68	D3
PLANTATION ST	RCO	102	C4
PLANT FIVE RD	INY	51	C4
PLANZ RD	KER	78	D3
PLASKETT RDG RD	MON	64	E4
PLATEAU CIR	SHA	18	B2
PLATEAU PINE RD	SHA	19	B3
PLATFORM RD	MAR	37	E4
PLATINA RD	SHA	18	A3
PLATINA RD	SHA	17	D3
PLATINA SCH RD	SHA	17	D4
PLAYA AZUL	AVLN	97	B4
PLAZA ST	SDCO	106	C4
PLEASANT	CC	38	E5
PLEASANT AV	SON	37	E1
PLEASANT RD	SLO	66	B5
PLEASANT GROVE	PLA	33	D4
PLEASANT GROVE	SUT	33	E4
PLEASANT GRV LN	BUT	25	E5
PLEASANT HILL	SON	37	D2
PLEASANT HLL RD	CC	L	E4
PLEASANT HLL RD	CC	M	A3
PLEASANT OAK DR	TUL	68	E3
PLEASNTN SNL RD	ALA	P	B1
PLEASNTN SNL RD	ALA	46	B2
PLEASANT PT RD	HUM	15	E2
PLEASNTS VLY RD	SOL	38	E2
PLEASANT VLY AV	O	156	B5
PLEASANT VLY RD	ALP	36	C5
PLEASANT VLY RD	ED	34	E5
PLEASANT VLY RD	NEV	34	B1
PLEASANT VLY RD	STA	47	D1
PLEASANT VLY RD	VEN	96	B1
PLEASNT VLY DAM	INY	51	C3
PLESANTE RD	MON	54	C3
PLEYTO CEM RD	MON	65	C4
PLINCO MINE RD	PLU	21	C5
PLUMAS AV	FRCO	57	A3
PLUMAS ST	RENO	130	B4
PLUMAS ARBGA RD	YUB	33	D3
PLUMB LN E	RENO	130	D5
PLUMB LN W	RENO	130	C5
PLUMBAGO RD	SIE	26	D5
PLUM CREEK RD	TEH	19	A4
PLUMMER LKOT RD	TRI	17	B3
PLUM VALLEY RD	MOD	7	C4
PLUNKETT RD	HUM	10	A5
PLYMIRE RD	TEH	18	C4
PLYMOUTH AV	KIN	67	A3
PLYMOUTH RD	SBD	80	E5
PLYMTH SHNDOAH	AMA	40	E1
POCK LN	SJCO	40	B5
POCKET RD	SAC	39	D2
POE RD	IMP	108	E3
POE POWERHOUSE	BUT	25	E3
POINSETTIA LN	SDCO	106	B3
PT CABRILLO DR	MEN	30	B1
PT LAKEVIEW RD	LAK	32	A3
POINT LOMA AV	SDCO	V	A3
POINT LOMA AV	SDCO	111	C1
POINT LOMA BL W	SDCO	V	A3
POINT LOMA BL W	SD	212	B5
PT OF TIMBER RD	CC	39	C5
PT PLEASANT RD	SAC	39	E3
POINT RANCH RD	MNO	43	B3
PT REYES PETLMA	MAR	37	E4
POINT SAL RD	SB	86	A1
PT SAN PEDRO RD	MAR	L	B3
POKER BAR RD	TRI	17	D1
POKER FLAT RD	SIE	26	D3
POLE LINE RD	MCO	55	E2
POLELINE RD	SBD	93	A5
POLE LINE RD	SHA	13	E5
POLETA RD	INY	51	D4
POLETA LAWS RD	INY	51	D4
POLHEMUS RD	SMCO	N	C2
POLI ST	VENT	175	E2
POLK AV	FRCO	57	B3
POLK AV	FRCO	67	B1
POLK AV	FRCO	57	B5
POLK ST	LACO	Q	C1
POLK ST	RCO	101	B5
POLLACK FLAT	SIS	5	A5
POLSON RD	NAPA	38	D3
POMEGRANATE AV	STA	47	C3
POMELO AV	STA	47	C3
POMERADO RD	SDCO	V	C1
POMERADO RD	SDCO	106	D5
POMEROY LS BERS	SLO	76	C5
POMONA AV	COR	215	C5
POMONA AV	TEH	24	D1
POMONA BLVD	LACO	R	B4
POMONA FRWY	LACO	98	A2
POMONA FRWY	LACO	R	E4
POMONA ST	CC	38	D5
POMPONIO CK RD	SMCO	N	C3
POND RD	KER	68	A5
PONDER WY	SHA	18	B3
PONDEROSA BLVD	LAS	21	B4
PONDEROSA RD	CAL	41	C4
PONDEROSA WY	AMA	41	B3
PONDEROSA WY	BUT	25	C2
PONDEROSA WY	BUT	25	D3
PONDEROSA WY	BUT	26	A4
PONDEROSA WY	CAL	41	B3
PONDEROSA WY	MPA	49	B3
PONDEROSA WY	PLA	34	D3
PONDEROSA WY	SHA	19	B2
PONDEROSA WY	TEH	19	B3
PONDOSA WY	SIS	13	C3
PONY RD	SBD	92	C4
PONY WY	CAL	41	A4
PONY EXPRESS TR	ED	35	A4
POOLE AV	KER	80	C1
POOLE LN	SIE	27	D3
POOLE RD	HUM	15	D2
POOLE RD	MCO	48	D5
POOL STATION RD	CAL	41	A3
POONKINNEY RD	MEN	23	A3
POOP OUT HL RD	SBD	100	A1
POOR BOY CK RD	ALP	36	C5
POORE RD	IMP	109	C3
POPE ST	NAPA	29	C2
POPE CANYON RD	NAPA	38	C1
POPE VALLEY RD	NAPA	29	B5
POPE VALLEY RD	NAPA	32	B5
POPE VALLEY RD	NAPA	38	B1
POPLAR AV	KER	78	B2
POPLAR AV	SMCO	N	C1
POPPET FLAT RD	RCO	100	B3
POPPY BLVD	KER	80	B4
PORTAL RD W	MNO	43	C5
PORT CHICAGO HY	CC	M	A3
PORTER	FRCO	58	A4
PORTER AV	RCO	99	C3
PORTER RD	SOL	39	B2
PORTER CREEK RD	SON	37	E1
PORTERVILLE HWY	KER	68	D5
PORTERVILLE HWY	KER	78	D1
PORTERVILLE WY	KER	78	C1
PORT KENYON RD	HUM	15	D2
PORTOLA AV	ALA	M	C5
PORTOLA AV	RCO	100	E4
PORTOLA BLVD	ALA	46	C2
PORTOLA DR	SFCO	L	B5
PORTOLA DR	SFCO	45	B2
PORTOLA RD	SLO	76	A2
PORTOLA RD	SMCO	N	D3
PORTOLA RD	SMCO	45	D4
PORTLA ST PK RD	SMCO	45	D5
PORTLA ST PK RD	SMCO	N	D4
PORTOLA MCLEARS	PLU	27	B3
PORTUGUESE BEND	SUT	33	C4
PORTUGUESE CYN	MON	66	B4
PORT WINE RIDGE	PLU	26	C3
PORT WINE RIDGE	SIE	26	C4
PORTY ST	KER	78	D4
POSO AV	KER	77	E1
POSO AV	KER	78	A1
POSO FLAT RD	KER	79	A1
POST AV	TEH	24	E2
POST RD	RCO	99	B4
POST MTN RD	TRI	17	B3
POTRERO RD E	VEN	96	D1
POTRERO RD W	VEN	96	D1
POTRERO ST	SFCO	L	C5
POTRERO GRDE BL	LACO	R	C4
POTTER RD	MON	54	D4
POTTEROFF RD	CAL	41	B3
POUND RD	IMP	109	A3
POUNDSTONE RD	COL	33	B3
POURROY RD	RCO	99	D5
POVERTY RD	SAC	M	E1
POVERTY RD	SAC	39	D3
POVERTY HILL RD	SIE	26	C4
POWAY RD	SDCO	V	C1
POWAY RD	SDCO	106	D4
POWDER HILL RD	SIS	5	C5
POWDER HILL RD	SIS	13	C1
POWELL AV	SON	37	D1
POWELL RD	SBD	92	D5
POWELL RD	SUT	33	B1
POWELL RD	VEN	88	E4
POWELLTOWN RD	BUT	25	D2
POWER RD	TRI	17	C1
POWER HOUSE RD	FRCO	57	E1
POWERHOUSE RD	TRI	11	E5
POWERHOUSE RD S	TEH	19	B3
POWER HSE HL RD	BUT	25	E5
POWER INN RD	SAC	39	E1
POWER LINE RD	LAS	20	A1
POWER LINE RD	MNO	52	C3
POWER LINE RD	RCO	106	E1
POWER LINE RD	SAC	33	D5
POWER LINE RD	SBD	83	A3
POWER LINE RD	SBD	91	C3
POWER LINE RD	SHA	18	B2
POWER LINE RD	SUT	33	D4
POWERS AV	MAN	161	D3
POZOS RD	RCO	99	C3
PRADO RD	SNLO	172	B5
PRAHSER RD	SJCO	40	C5
PRAIRE WY	MEN	30	C1
PRAIRE WY	MEN	30	B1
PRAIRIE AV	LACO	S	B1
PRAIRIE AV	SBD	91	C1
PRAIRIE DR	LAS	8	A5
PRAIRIE CK RD	TRI	17	A1
PRAIRIE FLWR RD	STA	47	D3
PRAIRIE FLWR RD	STA	47	D4
PRATT RD	TUL	68	B1
PRATT RANCH RD	MEN	31	C3
PRATVLL BTT RES	PLU	20	B5
PREFUMO CYN RD	SLO	75	E4
PREFUMO CYN RD	SLO	76	A4
PRELL RD	SB	86	C1
PRESCOTT AV	MONT	167	C5
PRESCOTT AV	MON	53	D3
PRESCOTT AV	PAC	167	C3
PRESCOTT RD	SJCO	47	B1
PRESIDIO AV	SF	141	E2
PRESIDIO BLVD	SF	141	C3
PRESIDIO BLVD	SFCO	L	B5
PRESIDIO BLVD	SFCO	45	B1
PRESSLEY RD	SON	38	A2
PRESTON	MPA	49	A5
PRESTON RD	BUT	25	C4
PRESTON RD	IMP	111	E4
PRESTON RD	MCO	47	C4
PREVITALI RD	AMA	41	A2
PRICE CREEK RD	HUM	15	D3
PRICE CK CAMPBL	TRI	17	B1
PRICE CK SCH RD	HUM	15	E2
PRICE CANYON RD	SLO	76	B4
PRIEST COLTRVLL	MPA	48	D1
PRIEST COLTRVLL	TUO	48	E1
PRIEST VLY RD	MON	66	A2
PRIM RD	IMP	109	B5
PRIMROSE MN RD	SIE	26	E4
PRINCE AV	FRCO	56	A2
PRINCE RD	MCO	47	C4
PRINCESS PAT MN	SBD	90	E2
PRINCETON	FRCO	58	A3
PRINCETON RD	MCO	48	B3
PROGRESS RD	SUT	33	B2
PROSPECT AV	KER	78	A1
PROSPECT AV	ORCO	T	E2
PROSPECT AV	SDCO	V	E2
PROSPECT RD	SCL	45	E4
PROSPECT RD	SCL	P	A3
PROSPECT ST	SDCO	V	A2
PROSPECT ST	SDCO	106	C5
PROSPERITY AV	TUL	68	A2
PROSSER DAM RD	NEV	27	D5
PROUTY RD	SJCO	40	B3
PROVIDENCE RCH	SBD	84	B4
PRUNE AV	STA	47	C3
PRUNERIDGE AV	CPTO	150	B4
PRUNERIDGE AV	SCLR	150	B4
PRUNERIDGE AV	SCL	151	A4
PRUSSIAN HILL RD	CAL	41	B3
PUDDING CK RD	MEN	22	B5
PUEBLO AV	KIN	67	C3
PUENTE AV	LACO	98	B2
PUENTE AV	LACO	R	D4
PULGA RD	BUT	25	D2
PULLMAN RD	IMP	111	E4
PUMICE MINE RD	MNO	50	D1
PUMICE MINE RD	MNO	51	C1
PUMICE MILL RD	MNO	51	D3
PUMP RD	MCO	55	E2
PUMP RD	STA	47	C4
PUMPHOUSE RD	COL	32	D2
PUMPHOUSE RD	SIS	4	B5
PUMPHOUSE RD	YOL	39	D2
PUNKIN CTR RD	LAS	14	B4
PURDON RD	NEV	26	C5
PURDY AV	KER	80	A5
PURISIMA RD	SB	86	B3
PURISIMA CK RD	SMCO	45	C4
PURITAN MINE RD	LACO	89	E4
PUTAH LN	LAK	32	A4
PUTAH CREEK RD	SOL	39	A1
PUTNAM RD	COL	25	A5
PUTNAM WY	COL	32	E3
PYLE RD	CAL	41	B5
PYLE RD	LAK	31	D2
PYRAMID HILLS	KIN	67	A5
PYRITE RD	RCO	99	A2
Q			
QUAIL AV	KIN	67	B3
QUAIL DR	RCO	100	B5
QUAIL HILL RD	HUM	16	A2
QUAIL ST	KER	80	C1
QUAIL WY	RCO	100	A5
QUAIL HILL RD	CAL	41	A5
QUAIL HOLLOW RD	SCR	N	E5
QUAIL SPGS RD	SBD	101	A1
QUAIL SPGS SPUR	SBD	101	E3
QUAKER ST	HUM	9	E5
QUAKR HL CRS RD	NEV	34	D1
QUALITY RD	KER	68	C5
QUARRY RD	HUM	9	E4
QUARRY RD	MAD	49	B5
QUARRY RD	SDCO	V	D4
QUARRY RD	SDCO	111	E1
QUARRY RD S	HUM	10	A5
QUARTZ AV	SIS	4	C5
QUARTZ ST	BUT	25	D2
QUARTZ ST	SBD	84	C3
QUARTZ ST	TUO	41	C5
QUARTZ HILL RD	SHA	18	C2
QUARTZ MT LKOUT	SIS	3	D5
QUARTZ MTN RD	MAD	49	D5
QUARTZ VLY DR	SIS	3	C5
QUARTZ VLY RD	SIS	3	C5
QUARTZ VLY RD E	SIS	3	C5
QUATAL CYN RD	KER	87	E2
QUATAL CYN RD	SB	87	E2
QUATAL CYN RD	VEN	88	A1
QUEBEC AV	KIN	67	E3
QUEBEC AV	KIN	67	A3
QUEEN OF SHEBA	INY	72	A3
QUEENS AV	YUBA	125	A1
QUEENS WY	LB	192	D4
QUESTHAVEN RD	SDCO	106	C3
QUICK RD	IMP	112	C5
QUIEN SABE RD	SBT	55	B3
QUIEN SABE RCH	SBT	55	B3
QUIMBY RD	SCL	P	C3
QUIMBY RD	SCL	46	B4
QUINCY RD	SIE	26	D3
QUINCY RD	STA	47	E3
QUINCY JCT RD	PLU	26	D1
QUINCY LA PORTE	PLU	26	D2
QUINCY LA PORTE	PLU	26	C4
QUINLEY AV	MCO	48	B5
QUINN RD	HUM	15	D1
QUINN RD	KER	68	D5
QUISENBERRY RD	STA	47	C3
QUITO RD	SCL	P	A4
QUITO RD	SCL	46	A5
R			
R ST	FRE	165	E3
R ST	MER	170	B4
RABBIT BRUSH LN	SIS	4	B3
RABBIT RANCH RD	MNO	51	C2
RABBIT SPGS RD	SBD	91	E4
RABBIT SPGS RD	SBD	92	A4
RABER ST	KER	80	A5
RACE ST	SJ	151	E4
RACE ST	SCL	P	B3
RACE TRACK RD	SAC	M	E1
RACE TRACK RD	SAC	39	D3
RACE TRACK RD	TUO	163	A3
RACETRACK VLY	INY	61	A2
RACINE AV	KIN	67	E3
RADIO LN	RED	122	C5
RADIO STATN RD	SOL	39	B2
RAGAN MEADWS RD	TRI	17	A3
RAG DUMP RD	BUT	25	D2
RAGLIN RIDGE RD	TEH	23	E1
RAGLIN RIDGE RD	TEH	24	A1
RAGSDALE RD	RCO	102	B4
RAHILLY RD	MCO	48	B5
RAIL CANYON RD	COL	24	B5
RAIL CANYON RD	GLE	24	B5
RAIL CREEK RD	SIS	12	B3
RAILROAD AV	CC	M	B3
RAILROAD AV	DN	1	D4
RAILROAD AV	HUM	16	D4
RAILROAD AV	RED	122	B3
RAILROAD AV	SMA	173	B2
RAILROAD AV	SOL	135	E3
RAILROAD AV	SUT	33	D2
RAILROAD AV	VAL	134	A5
RAILROAD ST	SBD	84	C3
RAILROAD CYN RD	RCO	99	C4
RAILRD FLAT RD	CAL	41	B3
RAINBOW	FRCO	57	E3
RAINBOW BASN RD	SBD	81	D5
RAINBOW CYN RD	SBD	93	B4
RAINBOW GLEN RD	SDCO	106	C1
RAINBOW LAKE RD	SHA	18	B3
RAINES RD	STA	47	B3
RAIN TREE LN	BUT	25	A2
RAJNUS RD	KLAM	5	E2
RALPH RD	IMP	109	A5
RALSTON AV	BLMT	145	A5
RALSTON AV	SMCO	N	C1
RALSTON AV	SMCO	45	C3
RAMAL RD	SON	38	C3
RAMBLA PACIFICO	LACO	97	B2
RAMELI GREIG RD	PLU	27	D2
RAMIREZ RD	YUB	33	D1
RAMON RD	PMSP	206	C4
RAMON RD	RCO	100	D3
RAMONA AV	LACO	U	B1
RAMONA AV	MTCL	203	B5
RAMONA AV	SBD	U	C3
RAMONA AV	SBD	91	C3
RAMONA AV	SBD	98	D2
RAMONA BLVD	LACO	R	D3
RAMONA BLVD	RCO	99	E3
RAMONA EXPWY	RCO	99	C3
RAMONA FRWY	SDCO	V	D3
RAMONA FRWY	SDCO	106	E5
RAMOS RD	MCO	55	D1
RAMP RD	MNO	43	B3
RAMSEY RD	RCO	107	B1
RAMSEY RD	SOL	38	E3
RAMSEY MINE RD	LPAZ	104	D4
RAMS HILL DR	SDCO	107	E3
RAMSHORN RD	TRI	12	A3
RAMS HORN GRADE	AMA	41	A2
RAMSHN MUMBO CK	TRI	12	B3
RANCH RD	HUM	15	D2
RANCH RD	MCO	48	C5
RANCH RD	MNO	52	C3
RANCHERIA RD	KER	69	C5
RANCHERIA RD	KER	78	E2
RANCHERIA RD	KER	79	A2
RANCHERIA RD	MEN	30	C3
RANCHERIA CK RD	SIS	4	A3
RANCHERIAS RD	SBD	91	C3
RANCHERIA-SAWML	KER	79	B1
RANCHERO	SBD	91	B4
RANCHITA CYN RD	MON	66	C5
RANCHITA CYN RD	SLO	66	B5
RANCHITO RD	MPA	48	D2
RANCHITOS RD	MAR	L	A3
RANCHLAND DR	SHA	18	B2
RANCH LAND RD	SDCO	106	E4
RANCHO AV	SBD	99	B2
RANCHO DR	KER	78	E4
RANCHO DR	KER	79	A4
RANCHO DR	SBD	91	A3
RANCHO RD	KER	78	E5
RANCHO RD	KER	79	A5
RANCHO RD	LV	209	A2
RANCHO RD	SB	76	C5
RANCHO RD	SB	86	B1
RANCHO RD	SHA	18	C2
RNCHO ALISAL RD	SB	86	E3
RCHO BAUTSTA RD	RCO	100	B5
RO BERNARDO RD	SDCO	106	D4
RANCHO CALIF RD	RCO	99	D5
RANCHO CALIF RD	RCO	106	C1
RANCHO CANADA	SDCO	107	A5
RNCHO CONEJO BL	VEN	96	D1
RO SANTA FE RD	SDCO	106	C3
RANCHO VIEJO RD	SJC	202	E1
RANDALL AV	SBD	99	A2
RANDALL RD	KER	77	E4
RANDOLPH RD	MCO	47	E4
RANDOLPH RD	SAC	40	A2
RANDSBURG RD	SBD	81	C2
RANDSBRG CTO	KER	80	A4
RANDSBRG CTO	SBD	80	E3
RANDSBG INYOKRN	KER	80	D1
RANDSBG WASH RD	SBD	80	E1
RANDSBG WASH RD	SBD	81	A1
RANGE RD	MCO	48	B5
RANGER STA RD	INY	51	B3
RANGER STA RD	INY	60	A4
RANGER STA RD	TRI	17	B1
RANGO WY	SDCO	107	E3
RANNELS BLVD	RCO	103	C5
RANNELS BLVD	RCO	110	C1
RASOR RD	SBD	83	A4
RATTLESNAKE RD	NEV	34	C2
RATTLESNAKE RD	TRI	17	B3
RATTLSNK BTT RD	MOD	14	E1
RATTLSNK CYN RD	SBD	92	C5
RATTLSNAK CK RD	SIS	3	D5
RAWHIDE RD	TUO	41	C5
RAWSON RD	TEH	18	D5
RAY	SJCO	40	A3
RAY RD	SB	86	B1
RAYHOUSE RD	YOL	32	C4
RAYMOND AV	ORCO	T	C1
RAYMOND RD	ALA	M	D5
RAYMOND RD	ALA	46	C2
RAYMOND RD	MAD	49	C5
RAYMOND RD	MAD	57	B1
RAYNOR RANCH	MCO	48	E5
READING RD	TEH	18	D5
REAL RD	BKD	166	A4
REAL RD	KER	166	A5
REALTY RD	SJCO	40	B4
REATA RD	INY	51	D4
RECALDE RD	SBT	55	E4
RECHE RD	SBD	92	D5
RECHE RD	SDCO	106	C2
RECHE CANYON RD	RCO	99	C2
RECLAMATION RD	LAK	31	D2
RECLAMATION RD	SUT	33	C3
RECTOR RD	NEV	34	C1
RED BANK RD	TEH	18	B5
RED BANK RD	TEH	24	C1
RED BOX RD	LACO	R	C2
RED CAP RD	HUM	10	D2
RED CLOUD MN RD	RCO	102	B4
REDDING AV	KIN	67	D3
REDDING CYN RD	INY	51	E4
REDDING CK RD	TRI	17	D2

STREET INDEX

STREET	CO.	PAGE	GRID
REDDINGTON AV	COL	32	E3
RED DOG RD	NEV	34	C1
RED GRADE RD	TRI	17	D1
RED HEAD CYN RD	MON	65	D3
RED HILL AV	CM	198	A5
RED HILL AV	IRV	198	B3
RED HILL AV	ORCO	98	C4
RED HILL AV	ORCO	T	D3
REDHILL RD	CAL	41	B4
RED HILL RD	IMP	109	A3
RED HILL RD	INY	51	C4
RED HILL RD	TRI	17	C1
REDHILL RD	TUO	48	C1
REDINGER LK RD	MAD	49	E5
REDINGER LK RD	MAD	50	A5
REDLANDS BLVD	RCO	99	C2
REDLANDS BLVD	SBDO	207	E5
REDLANDS BLVD	SBD	99	C2
REDLANDS FRWY	RCO	99	D2
REDLANDS FRWY	SBD	99	D2
REDLANDS ST	SBD	99	D2
REDMEYER RD	MEN	31	B2
REDMOND RD	HUM	9	E5
RED MOUNTAIN RD	KER	80	E3
RED MOUNTAIN RD	MCO	55	B1
RED MOUNTAIN RD	RCO	100	A5
RED MOUNTAIN RD	SBD	80	E3
RED MOUNTAIN RD	SHA	13	C3
RED MOUNTAIN RD	TRI	17	B4
RED MTN LKOUT	GLE	24	A3
RED MTN MTWY	TRI	17	B4
RED MTN TK TR	RCO	106	C1
RED OAK CYN RD	SIE	26	E3
REDONDO AV	LACO	98	A4
REDONDO AV	LACO	S	E2
REDONDO BLVD	LA	184	B3
REDONDO BCH BL	LACO	S	B1
REDPARK RD	HUM	9	E1
RED ROCK RD	LAS	27	E2
RED ROCK RD	SIS	5	A3
REDROCK-INYOKRN	KER	80	C1
REDROCK-INYOKRN	KER	80	C2
REDROCK-RANDSBG	KER	80	B3
RED ROVER MN RD	LACO	89	E4
RED SHANK LN	RCO	100	A5
REDSTONE AV	KER	79	C3
RED TOP RD	SOL	38	D3
RED TOP MTN RD	MAD	57	C1
RED VISTA RD	ALP	36	A5
REDWING RD	SBD	91	D3
REDWOOD BLVD	KER	80	B4
REDWOOD DR	HUM	16	C5
REDWOOD DR	TUL	69	B2
REDWOOD HWY	CRTM	140	C3
REDWOOD HWY	DN	1	E3
REDWOOD HWY	DN	2	A5
REDWOOD HWY	DN	9	E3
REDWOOD HWY	HUM	15	E3
REDWOOD HWY	HUM	16	B4
REDWOOD HWY	MAR	L	A2
REDWOOD HWY	MAR	38	A4
REDWOOD HWY	MAR	140	C3
REDWOOD HWY	MEN	22	C2
REDWOOD HWY	STR	131	C2
REDWOOD HWY	SON	31	B3
REDWOOD HWY	SON	37	E2
REDWOOD HWY	SON	38	A3
REDWOOD RD	ALA	L	E4
REDWOOD RD	ALA	45	E1
REDWOOD RD	ALA	47	E1
REDWOOD RD	NAPA	29	D5
REDWOOD RD	NAPA	38	C2
REDWOOD RD	STA	47	D3
REDWOOD ST	SOL	L	D2
REDWOOD ST	VAL	134	B3
REDWD HOUSE RD	HUM	16	B3
REDWD RETREAT RD	SCL	P	D5
REDWD RETREAT RD	SCL	54	C1
REED	FRCO	58	A4
REED AV	KER	80	A5
REED AV	SVL	150	A1
REED LN	SCL	P	A3
REED RD	KER	68	C5
REED RD	SUT	33	C2
REEDER RD	KLAM	5	C1
REED MTN RD	HUM	22	C1
REED ORCHARD RD	TEH	25	A1
REEDS CREEK RD	TEH	18	B5
REEDS TURNPIKE	CAL	41	A5
REED VALLEY RD	RCO	100	A5
REESE AV	COL	33	A1
REESE RD	BUT	25	A2
REEVES RD	VEN	88	B4
REEVES CYN RD	MEN	31	A1
REFUGIO RD	SB	86	E3
REGENTS RD	SD	211	D2
REGENTS RD	SDCO	V	A2
REGENTS RD	SDCO	106	C5
REGLI LN	HUM	15	E2
REICHART RCH RD	MNO	51	C1
REID AV	TUL	68	D3
REID RD	KER	79	E2
REID RD	KER	80	A2
REILLY RD	MCO	48	C5
REINA RD	KER	78	C2
REINO RD	VEN	96	D1
REIS AV	VAL	134	E5
RELIEF HILL RD	NEV	26	D5
RELIEZ RD	CC	38	E5
RELIEZ VLY RD	CC	L	E3
RELIZ CANYON RD	MON	65	A2
REMANN AV	SHA	19	E1
REMBACH WY	KER	79	C1
RENFRO RD	KER	78	C3
RENGSTORFF RD	SCL	N	E2
RENGSTORFF RD	SCL	P	A2
RENO AV	TEH	24	D1
RENWICK AV	SB	86	B3
REQUA RD	DN	1	E5
REQUA RD	DN	2	A5
RESEDA BLVD	LA	178	D2
RESEDA BLVD	LACO	97	C1
RESERVATION RD	COL	32	E1
RESERVATION RD	MON	54	B4
RESERVATION RD	TUL	68	E3
RESERVE RD	KER	77	D3
RESERVOIR RD	BUT	25	D5
RESERVOIR RD	ED	34	D3
RESERVOIR RD	SOL	38	E4
RESERVOIR RD	STA	48	A2
RETRAC WY	NEV	34	C2
RETSON RD	BUT	25	D2
REVIS RD	MAD	49	C5
REWARD RD	KER	77	D3
REYES ADOBE RD	LACO	96	E1
REYNARD WY	SD	215	C1
REYNOLDS AV	MCO	56	B2
REYNOLDS HWY	MEN	23	A5
REYNOLDS RD	SHA	13	E4
REYNLDS FRRY RD	TUO	41	B5
RHEEM BLVD	CC	L	E4
RHELM	CC	38	C5
RHONDA RD	SHA	18	C3
RIALTO AV	SBD	99	B1
RIALTO AV	SBDO	207	B2
RIATA RD	LAK	32	A4
RIATA WY	CAL	41	A4
RICE AV	SBD	101	A1
RICE AV	VEN	96	B1
RICE RD	FRCO	57	C2
RICE RD	MCO	48	B5
RICE RD	STA	47	E2
RICE RD	VEN	88	A4
RICE CANYON RD	LAS	21	B3
RICE CREEK RD	LAK	23	D5
RICE CREEK RD	LAK	31	D1
RICES CRSSG RD	NEV	34	B1
RICES CRSSG RD	YUB	26	A5
RICES TEX HL RD	YUB	26	A5
RICETON HWY	BUT	25	C5
RICH LN	RCO	106	E1
RICH RD	KER	68	C5
RICHARD RD	SIS	4	D5
RICHARD ST	KER	70	A5
RICHARDS AV	BUT	33	C1
RICHARDS BLVD	DVS	136	D3
RICHARDSON RD	SBD	91	A3
RICHARDSON RD	SIS	4	E3
RICHARDSON RD	SIS	5	A2
RICHARDSON SPGS	BUT	25	B2
RICH BAR RD	PLU	26	B1
RICHEY RD	CLO	33	A3
RICHFIELD RD	TEH	24	D1
RICH GULCH RD	PLU	26	B1
RICHLAND RD	SUT	125	B5
RICHMOND RD	LAS	21	A3
RICHMOND ST	SD	215	E1
RICHVALE HWY	BUT	25	B4
RIDER ST	RCO	99	B3
RIDGE DR	SHA	18	B2
RIDGE RD	AMA	40	E2
RIDGE RD	CAL	41	B2
RIDGE RD	NEV	34	C1
RIDGE RD	NEV	127	A2
RIDGE RD	NEV	128	A4
RIDGE RD	SIE	26	C5
RIDGE RD	SIS	3	E4
RIDGE RD	TEH	18	C5
RIDGECREST BLVD	KER	80	D1
RIDGE ROUTE RD	ED	34	E4
RIDGEWAY DR	ED	35	B4
RIDGEWAY HWY	MEN	23	B5
RIDGEWOOD	MEN	23	A5
RIDGEWOOD DR	HUM	15	E1
RIDGEWOOD RD	SHA	18	C2
RIEBLI RD	SON	37	E1
RIEBLI RD	SON	38	A1
RIEFF RD	LAK	32	B4
RIEGO RD	SUT	33	D5
RIGGIN AV	TUL	68	A1
RIGGINS RD	SUT	33	C4
RIGGS RD	SBD	83	B2
RIKER ST	SAL	171	B5
RILEY RD	BUT	25	B5
RILEY RD	SB	86	E3
RILEY RD	SAC	40	A2
RIM O T WRLD HY	SBD	91	C5
RIM O T WRLD HY	SBD	99	D1
RIMROCK RD	BARS	208	D4
RIM ROCK RD	RCO	107	C1
RIMROCK RD	SBD	91	D1
RIMROCK RD	SBD	100	C1
RIM ROCK CANYON	RCO	107	C1
RINCON AV	SDCO	106	D3
RINCON AV	SON	38	A2
RINCON RD	SBD	91	C4
RINCNADA LS PIL	SLO	76	C3
RINGWOOD AV	SMCO	N	D2
RIO RD	CAR	168	C4
RIO RD	MON	168	C4
RIO BLANCO	SJCO	39	E4
RIO BONITO RD E	BUT	25	C5
RIO BONITO RD W	BUT	25	C5
RIO DEL SOL RD	RCO	100	E3
RIOLINDA AV	FRCO	57	B4
RIO LINDA BLVD	SAC	33	E5
RIO OSO RD	SUT	33	D3
RIORDON RD	COL	32	D1
RIOSA RD	PLA	33	E3
RIOSA RD	PLA	34	A3
RIO VISTA AV	FRCO	58	A4
RIO VISTA AV W	TEH	18	D4
RIO VISTA RD	SUIS	135	D4
RIO VISTA ST	ORCO	T	D2
RIPONE RD	STA	47	C2
RIPPON RD N	SJCO	47	C1
RIPPON RD W	SJCO	47	B2
RISING HILL RD	SIS	4	C5
RITTER RD	SHA	13	D3
RITTS MILL RD	SHA	19	B2
RIVER AV	BUT	33	C1
RIVER BLVD	KER	78	D3
RIVER RD	BUT	25	A3
RIVER RD	COL	33	A1
RIVER RD	HUM	15	D3
RIVER RD	HUM	16	D5
RIVER RD	MAD	49	C5
RIVER RD	MAD	57	B1
RIVER RD	MCO	47	D4
RIVER RD	MON	54	D4
RIVER RD	RCO	U	E4
RIVER RD	RCO	98	E3
RIVER RD	RCO	99	C4
RIVER RD	SAC	M	E1
RIVER RD	SBD	85	C5
RIVER RD	SBD	95	D1
RIVER RD	SJCO	47	C1
RIVER RD	SLO	66	A5
RIVER RD	SLO	76	A1
RIVER RD	SLO	76	C3
RIVER RD	SON	37	D1
RIVER RD	STA	47	B3
RIVER RD	STA	47	D1
RIVER RD	TEH	24	D1
RIVER RD S	YOL	39	D2
RIVER ST	SC	169	C1
RIVER ST	SCR	169	C1
RIVER ST	SON	31	C4
RIVER BENCH RD	LAS	20	E3
RIVERBEND AV	FRCO	57	E3
RIVERCREST DR	HUM	16	B5
RIVEREDGE RD	SDCO	106	C1
RIVERFORD RD	SDCO	V	E2
RIVERFORD RD	SDCO	106	E5
RIVER GRADE RD	LACO	R	D3
RIV JCT FRMS RD	SJCO	47	B2
RIVER RANCH RD	SHA	18	C3
RIVER ROCK RD	TRI	17	D1
RIVERSIDE	WSH	130	B3
RIVERSIDE AV	MCO	47	D4
RIVERSIDE AV	RCO	103	C5
RIVERSIDE AV	SBD	99	B1
RIVERSIDE AV	SHA	18	C3
RIVERSIDE AV	TEH	18	D5
RIVERSIDE BLVD	SCTO	137	B4
RIVERSIDE BLVD	SAC	39	D1
RIVERSIDE DR	LA	179	A5
RIVERSIDE DR	LA	182	D3
RIVERSIDE DR	LACO	Q	E3
RIVERSIDE DR	RED	122	A1
RIVERSIDE DR	RCO	99	B4
RIVERSIDE DR	SBD	U	C3
RIVERSIDE DR	SBD	98	D2
RIVERSIDE DR	SDCO	V	E2
RIVERSIDE DR	SDCO	106	E5
RIVERSIDE DR	SHA	18	C2
RIVERSIDE DR	SON	132	B3
RIVERSIDE DR	STA	47	D2
RIVERSIDE FRWY	ANA	194	C1
RIVERSIDE FRWY	ORCO	98	C3
RIVERSIDE FRWY	ORCO	T	E1
RIVERSIDE FRWY	RCO	99	A3
RIVERSIDE RD	HUM	10	A5
RIVERSIDE RD	INY	51	D4
RIVERSIDE RD	SBD	92	C1
RIVERSIDE ST	KER	78	A2
RIVERSIDE PK RD	HUM	16	A3
RIVER SPRINGS	MNO	44	B5
RIVERVIEW DR	SHA	12	C5
RIVER VIEW RD	SBD	91	C1
RIVERVIEW RD	TRI	17	B2
RIVER WAY DR	TUL	68	B1
RIVIERA	RED	122	A5
RIVIERA DR	SD	212	B2
RIVIERA DR	SDCO	V	A3
RIVIERA DR	SHA	18	C2
RIVIERA RD	SUT	33	C1
ROAD 1	LAS	20	B1
ROAD 1	MAD	56	B1
ROAD 4	LAS	20	B1
ROAD 4	MAD	56	C1
ROAD 5	MAD	56	C1
ROAD 5 1/2	MAD	56	C2
ROAD 6	MAD	56	C1
ROAD 7	MAD	56	C1
ROAD 8	MAD	56	C1
ROAD 8 1/2	MAD	56	C3
ROAD 9	LAS	20	B1
ROAD 9	MAD	56	C1
ROAD 10	MAD	56	D1
ROAD 10 1/2	MAD	56	D2
ROAD 11	MAD	56	D1
ROAD 12	MAD	56	D1
ROAD 12	TUL	57	E5
ROAD 13	MAD	56	D1
ROAD 14	MAD	56	D1
ROAD 14 1/2	MAD	56	D1
ROAD 15	MAD	56	D1
ROAD 15 1/2	MAD	56	D1
ROAD 16	MAD	56	D2
ROAD 16	TUL	57	E5
ROAD 16 1/2	MAD	56	D2
ROAD 17	MAD	56	D2
ROAD 18	MAD	56	E1
ROAD 18 1/2	MAD	56	E1
ROAD 19	MAD	56	E1
ROAD 19 1/2	MAD	56	E2
ROAD 20	MAD	56	E2
ROAD 20 1/2	MAD	56	E2
ROAD 21	MAD	56	E2
ROAD 21 1/2	MAD	56	E2
ROAD 22	MAD	48	E5
ROAD 22 1/2	MAD	48	E5
ROAD 23	MAD	48	E5
ROAD 23 1/2	MAD	56	E1
ROAD 24	MAD	56	E1
ROAD 24	TUL	57	E5
ROAD 24	TUL	67	E2
ROAD 24 1/2	MAD	56	E2
ROAD 24 1/2	MAD	57	A2
ROAD 25	LAS	20	B1
ROAD 25	MAD	57	A2
ROAD 26	MAD	57	A2
ROAD 26 1/2	MAD	57	A2
ROAD 27	MAD	57	A1
ROAD 28	MAD	57	A2
ROAD 28	TUL	57	E5
ROAD 28	TUL	67	E2
ROAD 28 1/2	MAD	57	A2
ROAD 29	MAD	49	B5
ROAD 29 1/2	MAD	57	B2
ROAD 30	MAD	57	B2
ROAD 30 1/2	MAD	57	B2
ROAD 31	MAD	57	B3
ROAD 31 1/2	MAD	57	B2
ROAD 32	MAD	57	B2
ROAD 32	TUL	57	E5
ROAD 33	MAD	57	B2
ROAD 33 1/2	MAD	57	B2
ROAD 34	MAD	57	B3
ROAD 34	TUL	67	E4
ROAD 34	TUL	68	A4
ROAD 34 1/2	MAD	57	B2
ROAD 35	MAD	57	B2
ROAD 36	MAD	57	B2
ROAD 36	TUL	57	E5
ROAD 37	MAD	57	B2
ROAD 37 1/2	MAD	57	C2
ROAD 38	MAD	57	C2
ROAD 38	TUL	67	E4
ROAD 39	MAD	57	C2
ROAD 39 1/2	MAD	57	C2
ROAD 40	MAD	57	C2
ROAD 40	TUL	57	E5
ROAD 40 1/2	MAD	57	C2
ROAD 42	TUL	57	E4
ROAD 44	TUL	57	E5
ROAD 46	TUL	68	A4
ROAD 48	TUL	57	E4
ROAD 48	TUL	68	A1
ROAD 50	TUL	68	A4
ROAD 52	TUL	58	A4
ROAD 52	TUL	68	A1
ROAD 56	TUL	58	A5
ROAD 56	TUL	68	A1
ROAD 60	TUL	58	A5
ROAD 60	TUL	68	A1
ROAD 64	TUL	58	A4
ROAD 64	TUL	68	A1
ROAD 68	TUL	58	A5
ROAD 68	TUL	68	A1
ROAD 72	TUL	58	A4
ROAD 74	TUL	58	A5
ROAD 76	TUL	58	A5
ROAD 76	TUL	68	A1
ROAD 78	TUL	58	A4
ROAD 80	TUL	58	A5
ROAD 80	TUL	68	A2
ROAD 84	TUL	58	A5
ROAD 84	TUL	68	A1
ROAD 88	TUL	58	A5
ROAD 88	TUL	68	A3
ROAD 92	TUL	68	A2
ROAD 96	TUL	58	A4
ROAD 100	TUL	58	B5
ROAD 100	TUL	68	B1
ROAD 104	TUL	58	B5
ROAD 108	TUL	68	B1
ROAD 109	TUL	58	B4
ROAD 110	MEN	31	B3
ROAD 112	TUL	58	B5
ROAD 114	TUL	58	B4
ROAD 116	TUL	58	B5
ROAD 120	TUL	58	B5
ROAD 124	TUL	58	B4
ROAD 124	TUL	68	B2
ROAD 128	TUL	58	B4
ROAD 128	TUL	68	B3
ROAD 132	TUL	58	B4
ROAD 132	TUL	68	B1
ROAD 136	TUL	58	B4
ROAD 136	TUL	68	B3
ROAD 138	TUL	68	B1
ROAD 140	TUL	58	B4
ROAD 140	TUL	68	B1
ROAD 143	TUL	58	B4
ROAD 144	TUL	58	B5
ROAD 148	TUL	58	B5
ROAD 148	TUL	68	B1
ROAD 152	TUL	58	B4
ROAD 152	TUL	68	B1
ROAD 156	TUL	58	B5
ROAD 156	TUL	68	B1
ROAD 158	TUL	68	B1
ROAD 164	TUL	68	C1
ROAD 166	TUL	68	C1
ROAD 168	TUL	68	C1
ROAD 172	TUL	68	C2
ROAD 176	TUL	68	C3
ROAD 180	TUL	58	C5
ROAD 180	TUL	68	C1
ROAD 182	TUL	58	C5
ROAD 182	TUL	68	C1
ROAD 184	TUL	58	C5
ROAD 188	TUL	68	C3
ROAD 190	TUL	68	C1
ROAD 192	TUL	68	C1
ROAD 194	TUL	58	C5
ROAD 196	TUL	58	C5
ROAD 196	TUL	68	C1
ROAD 197	TUL	58	C5
ROAD 200	TUL	58	C5
ROAD 200	TUL	68	C1
ROAD 202	TUL	68	C3
ROAD 204	MAD	57	C2
ROAD 204	TUL	58	C5
ROAD 205	MAD	57	C2
ROAD 206	TUL	58	C5
ROAD 208	TUL	58	C5
ROAD 208	TUL	68	C1
ROAD 209	MAD	57	C1
ROAD 210	TUL	68	C1
ROAD 212	TUL	58	C5
ROAD 212	TUL	68	C1
ROAD 216	MAD	57	D1
ROAD 216	TUL	68	C2
ROAD 220	TUL	58	D5
ROAD 220	TUL	68	D1
ROAD 222	TUL	68	D1
ROAD 224	TUL	68	D4
ROAD 228	TUL	68	D1
ROAD 232	TUL	68	D2
ROAD 235	MAD	50	A5
ROAD 236	TUL	68	D1
ROAD 240	TUL	68	D4
ROAD 244	TUL	68	D1
ROAD 248	TUL	68	D1
ROAD 252	TUL	68	D2
ROAD 256	TUL	68	D3
ROAD 260	TUL	68	D2
ROAD 264	TUL	68	D3
ROAD 266	TUL	68	D4
ROAD 268	TUL	68	D3
ROAD 272	TUL	68	D4
ROAD 276	TUL	68	D2
ROAD 296	TUL	68	E3
ROAD 320	TUL	68	E3
ROAD 406	MAD	57	C1
ROAD 434	MAD	49	D4
ROAD 601	MAD	49	D4
ROAD 602	MAD	57	B1
ROAD 612	MAD	49	C5
ROAD 810	MAD	49	C4
ROAD 812	MAD	49	C4
ROAD RUNNER RUT	SBD	100	D1
ROAN RD	CAL	41	B4
ROBB RD	RCO	99	B4
ROBBEN RD	SOL	39	B3
ROBBEN RD	SOL	39	B2
ROBBINS RD	SUT	33	B3
ROBBINS RCH RD	NEV	26	D5
ROBBY RD	KER	79	B4
ROBERTA AV	LAKE	7	C1
ROBRTNO RIGHETI	SLO	76	B4
ROBERTS LN	KER	78	D2
ROBERTS RD	SJCO	40	A5
ROBERTS RD	SJCO	47	A1
ROBERTS RD	SON	38	A3
ROBERTS FRRY RD	STA	48	B2
ROBERTSON BLVD	BH	183	D1
ROBERTSON BLVD	LA	183	C4
ROBERTSON BLVD	LACO	Q	D4
ROBERTSON BLVD	LACO	183	D1
ROBERTSON BLVD	MAD	56	D1
ROBERTS RES RD	MOD	14	B3
ROBIN AV	MCO	47	E4
ROBIN AV	MCO	48	A4
ROBINSON	SJCO	47	C1
ROBINSON RD	IMP	109	A5
ROBINSON RD	MCO	48	C3
ROBINSON RD	SOL	39	B3
ROBINSON CYN RD	MON	54	B5
ROBINSON CK RD	MEN	31	A2
ROBINSN MILL RD	BUT	25	E5
ROBNSN RCHRIA W	LAK	31	D2
ROBLAR AV	SB	86	E3
ROBLAR RD	SON	37	D3
ROBLEY POINT RD	BUT	25	D2
ROBS RD	MOD	8	B3
ROCA LN	SBD	90	E2
ROCK CANYON RD	LAS	14	A3
ROCK CANYON RD	RCO	107	C1
ROCK CREEK DR	BUT	25	B2
ROCK CREEK RD	CAL	40	E4
ROCK CREEK RD	CAL	41	A4
ROCK CREEK RD	ED	34	E3
ROCK CREEK RD	INY	51	A3
ROCK CREEK RD	MNO	51	A3
ROCK CREEK RD	NEV	34	C1
ROCK CREEK RD	SHA	18	B2
ROCK CREEK RD	SHA	19	B3
ROCK CK GRBG PT	MNO	51	B3
ROCKERFELLER RD	BUT	25	E3
ROCKHAVEN	SBD	101	A2
ROCKING CHR RD	SBD	101	A2

STREET	CO.	PAGE	GRID
ROE RD	BUT	25	C3
ROCKLIN	PLA	34	B4
ROCK PILE RD	KER	79	A4
ROCKPILE RD	SON	31	B4
ROCKRIDGE RD	RCO	100	A5
ROCK RIVER RD	STA	48	B1
ROCK RIVER RD	TUO	48	B1
ROCK SPRINGS RD	SBD	91	C4
ROCKVILLE RD	SOL	L	E1
ROCKVILLE RD	SOL	38	D3
ROCKWOOD RD	IMP	112	A4
ROCKY CT	KER	79	D5
ROCKY LN	KER	79	D3
ROCKY RD	RCO	99	B5
ROCKY BAR RD	ED	41	A1
ROCKY BLUFF RD	RCO	99	B4
ROCKY CANYON RD	SLO	76	B2
ROCKYDALE RD	JOS	2	D1
ROCKY PT CMPGRD	PLU	20	B4
RODDEN RD	STA	47	E1
RODEO AV	TEH	24	D1
RODEO BLVD	LACO	Q	D4
RODEO RD	LA	184	A5
RODEO RD	SBD	91	C2
RODEO GULCH RD	SCR	54	A2
RODUNER RD	MCO	48	B5
ROEDING RD	STA	47	D3
ROEN RD	STA	48	A2
ROGERS RD	KER	80	B3
ROGERS RD	STA	47	B3
ROGERS CREEK RD	SIS	10	E1
ROHNERVILLE RD	HUM	15	E2
ROLAND DR	SIS	4	C5
ROLINDA AV	FRCO	57	B5
ROLLING HLLS RD	LACO	S	B2
ROLLINS RD	MLBR	144	E5
ROLLINS LAKE RD	PLA	34	D2
ROMEL ST	CAL	41	A4
ROMERO	MCO	55	C1
ROMERO RD	MCO	47	C5
ROMERO CYN RD	SB	87	D4
ROMERS DAIRY RD	MEN	31	B3
ROMIE LN E	SAL	171	C5
RONALD REAGAN FY	LA	89	B5
RONALD REAGAN FY	VEN	88	E5
RONNIE AV	KER	79	B5
ROOP RD	SCL	P	E5
ROOP RD	SCL	54	D1
ROOSEVELT RD	MCO	48	C5
ROOST AV	KER	79	B4
ROOT AV	KER	78	B1
ROOT RD	RCO	99	E5
ROOT RD	STA	47	D2
ROSA RD	MCO	47	D4
ROSAMOND BLVD	KER	80	C5
ROSAMOND BLVD	KER	89	D1
ROSAMOND BLVD	KER	90	B1
ROSAMND HLLS RD	RCO	107	C1
ROSARITA DR	SAL	171	D2
ROSCOE BLVD	LACO	97	C1
ROSCOE RD	HUM	15	E4
ROSCOE RD	STA	47	E2
ROSE AV	FRCO	56	E4
ROSE AV	FRCO	57	C4
ROSE AV	LA	187	C1
ROSE AV	MCO	47	E4
ROSE AV	MCO	48	B4
ROSE AV	VEN	88	B5
ROSE AV	VEN	96	B1
ROSE DR	ORCO	T	D1
ROSE RD	KER	79	E2
ROSE RD	KER	80	A2
ROSE RD	SIS	5	D2
ROSE RD	TRI	17	B1
ROSE RD	YOL	39	D2
ROSE ST	SDCO	106	D3
ROSEBURG AV	MDO	162	A1
ROSECRANS	LACO	97	D3
ROSECRANS AV	ELS	189	C5
ROSECRANS AV	MB	189	A5
ROSECRANS AV	ORCO	98	B3
ROSECRANS AV	ORCO	T	C1
ROSECRANS BLVD	SDCO	111	C1
ROSECRANS ST	SDCO	V	A3
ROSE GARDEN RD	MCO	47	C5
ROSEDALE HWY	KER	78	C3
ROSE HILLS RD	LACO	R	D4
ROSE LAWN AV	MCO	47	E3
ROSELAWN AV	MDO	162	A5
ROSE LAWN AV	STA	47	E3
ROSELLE AV	STA	47	D2
ROSE MARIE LN	S	160	A1
ROSEMARY RD	SB	86	C1
ROSEMEAD BLVD	LACO	98	A2
ROSEMEAD BLVD	LACO	R	C5
ROSE MINE RD	SBD	92	B5
ROSEMORE AV	STA	47	C2
ROSER RD	TEH	24	C2
ROSES RD	LACO	R	C3
ROSE VALLEY RD	VEN	88	B3
ROSEWOOD AV	VEN	96	C1
ROSEWOOD BLVD	KER	80	B5
ROSITA ST	LA	178	B5
ROSS AV	EC	217	E3
ROSS RD	IMP	111	E3
ROSS RD	IMP	112	D5
ROSSI ST	SAL	171	C3
ROSSMORE AV	LA	184	D2
ROSSMORE AV	LACO	Q	C4
ROSY RIDGE RD	RCO	107	B1
ROUGH&READY RD	NEV	34	B1
ROULTS RD	MNO	51	B3
ROUND HOUSE RD	MAD	49	D4

STREET	CO.	PAGE	GRID
ROUND MTN LKOUT	SIS	13	D1
ROUND MTN RD	KER	78	D2
ROUND MTN RD	MNO	51	B2
ROUND ROBIN DR	RCO	100	B4
ROUNDUP WY	SBD	91	C4
ROUND VALLEY RD	SBD	100	B1
ROUND VALLEY RD	TEH	23	D2
ROUND VLY RD N	INY	51	B4
ROUND VLY RD S	INY	51	C4
RND VLY TUNGSTN	INY	51	C4
ROUNDY RD	TRI	17	D1
ROUSE AV	STA	162	A5
ROUSE RD	RCO	99	C4
RT OLYMPC TORCH	LAS	20	D2
ROUTE 4 FRWY	CC	154	D3
ROUTE 4 FRWY	M	154	D3
ROUTE 47 FRWY	LB	191	E1
ROUTE 47 FRWY	LA	191	E1
ROUTE 47 FRWY	LACO	97	E4
ROUTE 47 FRWY	LACO	S	D2
ROUTE 101 FRWY	SB	86	D4
ROUTE 101 FRWY	SB	87	D4
ROWDY CREEK RD	DN	1	E3
ROWENA AV	LA	182	D3
ROWLEE RD	KER	77	E2
ROWLEE RD	KER	78	A2
ROWLES RD	TEH	24	E2
ROXBURY DR	SIS	3	C4
ROXBURY RD	MCO	56	B1
ROXFORD ST	LACO	89	C5
ROXFORD ST	LACO	Q	B1
ROYAL AV	VEN	88	E5
ROYAL AV	VEN	89	A5
ROYAL OAKS DR	LACO	R	D5
ROY JONES RD	SIS	4	B3
ROYO RNCHERO DR	SUT	33	C2
RUBIDOUX BLVD	RCO	99	B2
RUBLE RD	STA	47	C3
RUCKER AV	SCL	P	E5
RUCKER AV	SCL	54	D1
RUDD RD	KER	78	C3
RUDDICK	MEN	31	B2
RUDGEAR RD	CC	M	A4
RUDNICK RD	KER	80	C4
RUDOLPH DR	KER	79	C4
RUDOLPH RD	INY	51	D3
RUEGGER RD	IMP	109	A3
RUFF LN	GLE	24	E5
RUFFIN RD	SDCO	V	C2
RUFFIN RD	SDCO	106	D5
RUGGED TRAIL RD	RCO	107	C1
RUMBLE RD	STA	47	C2
RUNGE RD	SOL	39	C2
RUSH ST	RCO	107	C1
RUSH CREEK DR	TRI	11	D5
RUSH CREEK RD	MNO	43	C5
RUSH CREEK RD	TRI	17	D1
RUSH CK SHORTCT	TRI	17	D1
RUSH CK CAMP RD	TRI	11	D5
RUSHING HILL LKT	TUO	48	B1
RUSS LN	HUM	15	D2
RUSSEL AV	KER	79	A4
RUSSELL AV	FRCO	56	A3
RUSSELL BLVD	DVS	136	B3
RUSSELL BLVD	YOL	39	A1
RUSSELL RD	CAL	41	A3
RUSSELL RD	SAC	39	D3
RUSSELL RD	STA	47	B2
RUSSELL RD	TEH	18	C3
RUTH DUMP RD	TRI	17	A4
RUTHERFORD	NAPA	29	D3
RUTHERFORD RD	IMP	109	A4
RUTH HILL RD	FRCO	58	C3
RUTH HILL RD	FRCO	58	B3
RUTH ZENIA RD	TRI	16	E4
RYAN AV	KER	80	A4
RYAN RD	LAS	21	B3
RYAN RD	SLO	76	C2
RYAN CREEK RD	MEN	23	A5
RYE CANYON RD	LACO	89	B4
RYE GRASS SWALE	MOD	8	A1
RYE GRASS SWALE	MOD	14	E1
RYER RD E	SOL	39	D3
RYER ISLAND RD	SOL	M	D1
S			
S ST	EUR	121	E2
SABINANA RD	YUB	33	E1
SABODAN ST	KER	78	D5
SACHREITER RD	COL	33	A2
SACRAMENTO AV	BUT	25	A3
SACRAMENTO AV	C	124	A4
SACRAMENTO AV	FRCO	56	D4
SACRAMENTO AV	SUT	33	D3
SACRAMENTO DR	SHA	18	C2
SACRAMENTO ST	PLA	34	D1
SACRAMENTO ST	PLCV	138	C3
SACRAMENTO ST	VAL	134	B2
SACRMNTO VLY BL	SUT	33	C4
SACRMNTO VLY RD	SUT	33	C3
SADDLE CT	KER	79	C5
SADDLEBACK RD	SIE	26	D4
SADDLEHORN RD	SBD	84	C3
SADDLE PEAK RD	LACO	97	B2
SADDLE TRAIL RD	SHA	18	B3
SADDLE VIEW CT	SHA	13	E4
SAGE AV	SBD	100	D1
SAGE RD	HUM	15	D2
SAGE RD	RCO	99	E4
SAGEBRUSH LN	SIS	4	E3
SAGE CANYON RD	KER	80	B1
SAGE FLATS DR	INY	70	B2

STREET	CO.	PAGE	GRID
SAGE HEN RD	MNO	51	A2
SAGE HEN RD	NEV	27	D5
SAGE HN MDWS RD	MNO	43	E5
SAGE HN MDWS RD	MNO	50	E1
SAGE HN MDWS RD	MNO	51	A1
SAGEHORN RD	MOD	7	D3
SAGELAND CT	KER	79	B4
SAGE VALLEY RD	LAS	21	D5
SAGINAW AV	FRCO	57	E4
SAHARA AV	LV	209	A4
SAHARA AV E	CLK	74	D2
SAHARA AV W	CLK	74	C2
ST CATHERINE WY	AVLN	97	B4
ST FRANCIS AV	STA	47	C2
ST GEORGE ST	LA	182	D3
ST HELENA HWY	NAPA	29	D4
ST HELENA RD	SON	38	A1
ST JAMES ST	SJ	152	C3
ST JOHN RD	TRI	16	E2
ST JOHN LOOP RD	TRI	16	E2
ST LOUIS AV	KER	80	A4
ST LOUIS RD	HUM	9	E5
ST LOUIS RD	HUM	10	A5
ST LOUIS RD	PLU	26	C3
ST MARYS AV	TEH	18	D5
ST MARYS RD	CC	L	E4
ST MARYS RD	CC	M	A4
ST MARYS RD	CC	45	E1
SALE LN	TEH	18	D5
SALEM AV	KIN	67	E3
SALEM RD	SOL	39	B3
SALINAS RD	MON	54	C2
SALINE VLY ALT	INY	70	E1
SALINE VLY RD	INY	60	C3
SALINE VLY RD	INY	60	D5
SALMON CREEK RD	HUM	16	B4
SALMON FALLS RD	ED	34	C5
SALMON LAKE RD	SIE	26	E3
SALMON LAKE RD	SIE	27	A3
SALMON RIVER RD	SIS	10	E2
SALMON RIVER RD	SIS	11	A2
SALT RD N	SHA	12	C4
SALT CREEK RD	MCO	55	D2
SALT CREEK RD	SHA	12	D5
SALTDALE RD	KER	80	C3
SALTON DR	IMP	108	C2
SALTON RD	SBD	80	E5
SALTON RD	SBD	81	A5
SALTON BAY DR	IMP	108	C2
SALTON VIEW RD	RCO	101	B3
SALT POOL RD	INY	72	A1
SALT SPG VLY RD	CAL	41	A5
SALT SPG VLY RD	CAL	41	A4
SALTUS RD	SBD	93	E3
SALTUS RD	SBD	94	A3
SALVADORI RD	SIS	4	B5
SAM ALLEY RIDGE	LAK	31	D2
SAMEL DR	SBD	100	D2
SAMPLE RD	FRCO	57	E2
SAMPSON ST	SD	216	A5
SAMSON AV	TEH	18	D5
SAMSON AV	TEH	24	D2
SAN ANDREAS RD	SCR	54	B2
SAN ANDREAS RD	SBD	100	E2
SAN ANDREAS ST	STB	174	A3
SN ANTONE CP RD	CAL	41	B4
SAN ANTONIO AV	CAR	53	D5
SAN ANTONIO AV	ONT	204	A5
SAN ANTONIO AV	UPL	204	A1
SN ANTONIO AV N	CAR	168	B4
SAN ANTONIO DR	LACO	S	D2
SAN ANTONIO DR	LACO	T	A1
SAN ANTONIO RD	MON	65	D5
SAN ANTONIO RD	SB	86	B2
SAN ANTONIO RD	SCL	N	E3
SAN ANTONIO RD	SCL	P	A3
SAN ANTONIO RD	SCL	P	E3
SAN ANTONIO RD	SCL	45	E4
SAN ANTONIO ST	SJ	152	D3
SAN ANTONIO VLY	SCL	46	D4
SAN BENACIO RD	MON	54	C4
SAN BENITO AV	FRCO	56	D4
SAN BENITO AV	TEH	18	D5
SN BERNARDNO AV	FRCO	56	C3
SN BERNARDNO AV	SBD	98	D2
SN BERNARDNO FY	CLA	203	A3
SN BERNARDNO FY	LA	186	D2
SN BERNARDNO FY	LACO	98	B2
SN BERNARDNO FY	LACO	R	D4
SN BERNARDNO FY	MTCL	203	B3
SN BERNARDNO FY	ONT	204	B3
SN BERNARDNO FY	SBD	98	D2
SN BERNARDNO FY	UPL	204	B3
SN BERNARDNO RD	LACO	U	A2
SN BERNARDNO RD	SBD	80	E1
SN BERNARDNO RD	UPL	204	D1
SN BERNARDNO ST	MTCL	203	B3
SN BERNARDNO ST	SBD	U	D2
SN BERNARDNO CK	SLO	75	E3
SN BERNARDNO CK	SLO	76	A3
SANBORN RD	SUT	33	C2
SANBORN RD S	SAL	171	E5
SAN BRUNO AV	SBR	144	B3
SAN BRUNO AV	SMCO	45	B2
SAN CARLOS AV	SMCO	N	D2
SAN CARLOS AV	SMCO	45	D3
SAN CARLOS RD	MCO	55	D2
SAN CARLOS ST	CAR	168	B4
SAN CARLOS ST	SJ	151	C4
SAN CARLOS ST	SJ	152	C4
SANCHES RD	MCO	47	C4
SANCHEZ RD	MON	54	E5
SAND CANYON AV	ORCO	98	C4

STREET	CO.	PAGE	GRID
SAND CANYON AV	ORCO	T	E4
SAND CANYON RD	INY	51	C4
SAND CANYON RD	KER	70	E5
SAND CANYON RD	KER	79	D4
SAND CANYON RD	LACO	89	C4
SAND CANYON RD	SBD	99	D2
SAND CREEK RD	COL	32	D3
SAND CREEK RD	FRCO	58	B4
SAND CREEK RD	TUL	58	B4
SAND CREST DR	IMP	108	C2
SANDERS RD	STA	47	C3
SANDERS RD	SUT	33	C2
SANDERSON AV	RCO	99	E4
SAND FLAT RD	SIS	12	D3
SAND FLAT CTO	MNO	50	E1
SAND HILL RD	SMCO	N	D3
SAND HILL RD	SMCO	45	D4
SANDIA CREEK DR	SDCO	106	C1
SAN DIEGO AV	FRCO	56	D4
SAN DIEGO FRWY	IRV	198	D4
SAN DIEGO FRWY	LA	180	C2
SAN DIEGO FRWY	LA	188	D4
SAN DIEGO FRWY	LACO	97	C2
SAN DIEGO FRWY	LACO	180	C3
SAN DIEGO FRWY	LACO	189	E2
SAN DIEGO FRWY	LACO	S	B1
SAN DIEGO FRWY	ORCO	98	D4
SAN DIEGO FRWY	ORCO	197	A3
SAN DIEGO FRWY	ORCO	202	C4
SAN DIEGO FRWY	ORCO	T	B3
SAN DIEGO FRWY	SD	211	C4
SAN DIEGO FRWY	SDCO	V	A2
SAN DIEGO FRWY	SDCO	106	B3
SAN DIEGO FRWY	SDCO	111	D2
SAN DIEGO FRWY	SJC	202	C4
SAN DIEGO ST	KER	78	D2
SN DIEGO MSN RD	SD	214	D2
SAN DIMAS AV	LACO	U	B1
SN DIMAS CYN RD	LACO	U	B1
SANDMOUND BLVD	CC	39	D5
SAN DOMINGO RD	CAL	41	B4
SAND RIDGE RD	ED	34	E5
SAND RIDGE RD	ED	40	E1
SANDRINI RD	KER	78	D4
SANDROCK RD	SD	214	A1
SANDROCK RD	SDCO	V	B3
SANDROCK RD	SDCO	106	D5
SAND SLOUGH RD	MCO	47	E5
SAND SLOUGH RD	MCO	48	A5
SANDY AV	KER	80	C1
SANDY DR	RCO	107	C1
SANDY RD	MON	66	B4
SANDY ST	KER	80	C1
SANDY HILLS RD	RCO	107	C1
SANDY MUSH RD	MCO	48	B5
SANDY PRAIRIE	HUM	15	E2
SAN FELIPE RD	SBT	54	E2
SAN FELIPE RD	SBT	55	A2
SAN FELIPE RD	SDCO	107	C2
SAN FELIPE RD	SCL	P	C3
SAN FELIPE RD	SCL	46	C4
SAN FERNANDO BL	BUR	179	B1
SAN FERNANDO RD	BUR	179	D1
SAN FERNANDO RD	LACO	89	B5
SAN FERNANDO RD	LACO	89	C5
SAN FERNANDO RD	LACO	97	E1
SAN FERNANDO RD	LACO	Q	C1
SANFORD RD	SON	37	D2
SANFORD RCH RD	MEN	31	B2
SN FRANCSQT CYN	LACO	89	B4
SAN GABRIEL BL	LACO	98	A2
SAN GABRIEL BL	LACO	R	C3
SAN GABRIEL FWY	LACO	98	A3
SAN GABRIEL FWY	LACO	S	E1
SAN GABRIEL RD	LACO	R	E3
SAN GABRIEL CYN	LACO	98	C1
SN GABRL CYN RD	LACO	R	E3
SN GABRL RIV FY	LACO	T	A1
SN GABRL RIV PY	LACO	R	C4
SAN GORGONIO AV	RCO	100	A3
SN GUILLERMO RD	VEN	88	B2
SANHEDRIN RD	GLE	24	A4
SAN IGNACIO RD	RCO	99	E5
SANITARIUM RD	NAPA	29	C2
SAN JACINTO RD	RCO	99	C4
SAN JACINTO ST	SBD	100	C2
SAN JACINTO RDG	RCO	100	A4
SAN JOAQUIN AV	FRCO	66	D3
SAN JOAQUIN AV	LAK	32	A3
SAN JOAQUIN RD	ORCO	T	E3
SAN JOAQUIN ST	S	160	D3
SN JQUIN HLS RD	NB	200	A4
SN JQN HLS TRNS COR	ORCO	T	E5
SN JQN HLS TRNS COR	ORCO	98	C5
SN JQN HLS TRNS COR	ORCO	200	C3
SAN JOSE RD	CLO	32	E2
SAN JOSE RD	SCR	P	B5
SN JOSE AVNALES	SLO	76	D3
SN JOSE L PANZA	SLO	76	E3
SN JOSE-STA MAR	SLO	76	B3
SN JS ST MAR LK	SLO	76	C3
SN JS ST MAR MT	SLO	76	D3
SAN JUAN AV	SAC	34	A5
SAN JUAN HWY	SBT	54	D2
SAN JUAN RD	MCO	56	B1
SAN JUAN RD	MON	54	C2
SAN JUAN CYN RD	SBT	54	D3
SAN JUSTO RD	SBT	54	D3
SANKEY RD	SUT	33	D4
SAN LUCAS RD	MON	65	C3
SAN LUIS BAY DR	SLO	76	A4
SAN LUISITO CK	SLO	75	E3
SAN LUISITO CK	SLO	76	A3

STREET	CO.	PAGE	GRID
SAN MARCOS RD	SLO	76	A1
SAN MARCOS RD	SB	87	B4
SN MARCOS PS RD	SB	87	B3
SAN MARIN DR	MAR	L	A2
SAN MARTIN AV	SCL	P	E5
SAN MARTIN AV	SCL	54	D1
SN MARTNZ CHQT	LACO	89	A4
SN MARTNZ GD CN	LACO	89	A4
SAN MATEO AV	FRCO	56	D5
SAN MATEO AV	SBR	144	B3
SAN MATEO AV	SSF	144	B1
SAN MATEO RD	SDCO	105	E1
SAN MATEO ST	SBD	99	C2
SAN MIGUEL AV	SAL	171	C5
SAN MIGUEL DR	CC	M	A4
SAN MIGUEL DR	NB	200	C5
SN MGUEL CYN RD	MON	54	C3
SN MIGUELITO RD	SB	86	B3
SAN PABLO AV	ALA	L	D4
SAN PABLO AV	ALA	45	D1
SAN PABLO AV	CC	L	C3
SAN PABLO AV	CC	38	C5
SAN PABLO AV	ELC	155	E4
SAN PABLO AV	O	157	E1
SAN PABLO AV	R	155	C2
SAN PABLO AV	SP	155	C1
SN PABLO DAM RD	CC	L	D3
SN PABLO DAM RD	CC	38	C5
SN PABLO DAM RD	SP	155	D1
SAN PASQUAL RD	SDCO	106	D3
SAN PASQUAL RD	SB	86	B3
SAN PASQUAL VLY	SDCO	106	E3
SAN PEDRO AV	SBD	84	C3
SAN PEDRO RD N	MAR	L	B3
SAN PEDRO RD N	MAR	38	B5
SAN PEDRO RD N	MAR	139	D2
SAN PEDRO ST	LA	186	A4
SAN PEDRO ST	LACO	S	C1
SAN RAFAEL AV	PAS	190	A4
SAN RAFAEL DR	RCO	100	C3
SN RAMON VLY BL	CC	M	B5
SN RAMON VLY BL	CC	46	A2
SANS BAKER RD	FRCO	58	C3
SN SIMEON CK RD	SLO	75	C1
SANTA ANA AV	CM	199	C3
SANTA ANA AV	NB	199	B4
SANTA ANA AV	ORCO	T	C4
SANTA ANA AV	SBD	99	A2
SANTA ANA BLVD	SA	196	B3
SANTA ANA FRWY	ANA	193	C4
SANTA ANA FRWY	LA	186	B2
SANTA ANA FRWY	LACO	98	A2
SANTA ANA FRWY	LACO	T	B1
SANTA ANA FRWY	ORCO	98	A2
SANTA ANA FRWY	ORCO	T	B1
SANTA ANA FRWY	SA	196	B2
SANTA ANA RD	VEN	88	A5
STA ANA CYN RD	ORCO	98	C3
STA ANA CYN RD	ORCO	T	E2
STA ANA VLY RD	SBT	55	A3
SANTA ANITA AV	LACO	98	B2
SANTA ANITA AV	LACO	R	C4
SANTA ANITA AV	LACO	R	D2
SANTA ANITA RD	SBT	55	B3
STA BARBARA ST	SDCO	111	C1
STA BARBARA ST	STB	174	B2
STA BARBARA ST	SDCO	V	A3
STA BARB CYN RD	SB	87	D1
SANTA CLARA AV	SA	196	D2
SANTA CLARA AV	VEN	88	B5
SANTA CLARA ST	SJ	152	C3
SANTA CLARA ST	SCL	P	C3
SANTA CLARA ST	SCL	46	B4
SANTA CLARA ST	VAL	134	B4
SANTA CRUZ AV	SCL	P	A4
STA CRZ GUN CLB	MCO	55	E2
STA CRZ GUN CLB	MCO	56	A2
SANTA FE	MCO	48	C4
SANTA FE AV	KIN	67	E3
SANTA FE AV	LB	192	B2
SANTA FE AV	LA	186	C4
SANTA FE AV	LACO	R	A4
SANTA FE AV	LACO	S	D2
SANTA FE AV	MCO	48	D5
SANTA FE AV	SBD	81	B5
SANTA FE AV	SDCO	106	C2
SANTA FE AV	SJCO	47	D1
SANTA FE AV	STA	47	D2
SANTA FE BLVD	MAD	57	B2
SANTA FE DR	MCO	48	A3
SANTA FE DR	SDCO	106	C4
SANTA FE GRADE	FRCO	56	C3
SANTA FE GRADE	MCO	47	D4
SANTA FE RD	SBD	92	B4
SANTA FE ST	SBD	92	A1
SANTA FE WY	KER	78	B2
STA FE FIRE RD	SBD	91	A5
STA FE SPGS RD	LACO	R	C5
SANTA ISABEL	CM	199	D1
SANTA LUCIA AV	CAR	168	B4
SANTA LUCIA AV	MCO	55	D1
SANTA LUCIA RD	SLO	76	A2
SANTA MARIA WY	SB	86	C1
STA MAR MESA RD	SB	86	C1
SANTA MONICA BL	LA	180	A4
SANTA MONICA BL	LA	182	A5
SANTA MONICA BL	LA	183	A2
SANTA MONICA BL	LACO	97	D2
SANTA MONICA FY	LA	184	A4
SANTA MONICA FY	LA	185	B4
SANTA MONICA FY	LA	186	A5
SANTA MONICA FY	LACO	97	C2
SANTA MONICA FY	LACO	Q	C4

STREET	CO.	PAGE	GRID
SANTA PAULA FWY	VEN	88	B5
SANTA PAULA ST	VEN	88	C5
STA RITA GRADE	MCO	56	B1
SANTA RITA RD	ALA	M	B5
SANTA RITA RD	ALA	46	B2
STA RITA OLD CK	SLO	75	E2
SANTA ROSA AV	SON	37	E2
SANTA ROSA AV	STR	131	D4
SANTA ROSA RD	INY	60	D5
SANTA ROSA RD	RCO	99	B4
SANTA ROSA RD	SBD	91	D4
SANTA ROSA RD	SB	86	C3
SANTA ROSA RD	VEN	88	D5
SANTA ROSA ST	SNLO	172	C2
STA ROSA CK RD	SLO	75	C2
STA ROSA MTN TK	RCO	100	D5
SANTA TERESA BL	SCL	P	C4
SANTA TERESA BL	SCL	46	B5
SANTA TERESA BL	SCL	54	D2
SANTA YSABEL RD	SLO	75	E3
SANTIAGO BLVD	ORA	194	E2
SANTIAGO BLVD	ORCO	98	C3
SANTIAGO BLVD	ORCO	T	E2
SANTIAGO CYN RD	ORCO	98	D3
SANTIAGO CYN RD	ORCO	T	E2
SN TIMTEO CY RD	RCO	99	D2
SN TIMTEO CY RD	SBD	99	D2
SAN TOMAS EXPWY	SJ	150	E5
SAN TOMAS EXPWY	SCL	P	B3
SAN TOMAS EXPWY	SCLR	150	E2
SANTOS AV	SJCO	47	C1
SANTOS RD	SB	86	D3
SANTOS ST	SB	86	B1
SAN VICENTE BL	LA	183	E1
SAN VICENTE BL	LACO	97	C2
SAN VICENTE BL	LACO	Q	D4
SAN VICENTE RD	MON	55	A5
SAN VICENTE RD	MON	65	A1
SAN VICENTE RD	SDCO	107	A4
SAN VINCENTE AV	SAL	171	B4
SAPAQUE RD	MON	65	C5
SARATOGA AV	KER	80	E1
SARATOGA AV	SJ	150	E5
SARATOGA AV	SCL	P	A4
SARATOGA AV	SCLR	150	E5
SARATOGA AV	SCLR	151	A4
SARATOGA AV	SCL	46	A5
SARATGA-LS G RD	SCL	P	A4
SARTGA-LS GATOS	SCL	46	A5
SARATOGA SPGS	LAK	31	C2
SARATOGA SPG RD	SBD	72	D5
SARATOGA SPG RD	SBD	82	D1
SARATOGA-SVL RD	SCL	P	A4
SARATOGA-SVL RD	SCL	45	E4
SARATOGA-SVL RD	SVL	149	E3
SARBO RD	MCO	55	D1
SARDINE LAKE RD	SIE	27	A4
SARGENT RD	SJCO	40	A4
SARGENTS RD	MON	65	E4
SARGENTS RD	MON	66	A4
SARIDA AV	KER	79	C4
SARINA RD	DN	1	D3
SARON FRUIT COL	TEH	18	D4
SASIA RD	KER	79	B4
SATICOY AV	VEN	88	B5
SATICOY ST	LA	177	C1
SATICOY ST	LA	178	B1
SAUGUS VNTRA RD	LACO	89	A4
SAVANA	MCO	48	D5
SAVIERS RD	OXN	176	C5
SAWMILL	INY	51	C4
SAW MILL RD	ALP	36	B5
SAWMILL RD	BUT	25	C3
SAWMILL RD	KER	69	C5
SAWMILL RD	KER	79	C1
SAWMILL RD	MNO	50	E2
SAW MILL CREEK	SBT	66	B1
SAWMILL CRSSOVR	MNO	51	B1
SAWMILL CTO	MNO	50	D2
SAWMILL FLAT RD	TUO	41	C4
SAWMILL MDWS RD	MNO	51	B1
SAWTELLE AV	SUT	33	C3
SAWTELLE BLVD	CUL	188	A1
SAWTELLE BLVD	LA	180	C4
SAWTELLE BLVD	LA	188	B2
SAWTOOTH PEAK	KER	80	C1
SAWYER AV	STA	47	D1
SAWYERS BAR RD	SIS	11	C1
SAYLOR RD	STA	47	E3
SAYRE ST	LACO	Q	C1
SCALA LN	SIS	4	B4
SCALES RD	YUB	26	C4
SCANDIA RD	SOL	M	B1
SCANDIA RD	SOL	39	A3
SCARFACE RD	SIS	3	E5
SCARFACE RD	SIS	4	A5
SCARLT BUGLE RD	RCO	100	C5
SCARONI AV	KER	78	B2
SCENIC DR	STA	47	D2
SCENIC DR	MDO	162	D2
SCENIC DR	STA	162	D2
SCENIC RD	CAR	168	B4
SCHAAD RD	COL	32	D2
SCHADD RD	CAL	41	C2
SCHAEFFER RD	SB	87	D1
SCHAFER AV	TEH	18	E5
SCHAGLE RD	SUT	33	C3
SCHALLOCK RD	KER	78	C5
SCHARTZ RD	IMP	109	B4
SCHATZ RD	KER	79	C4
SCHEAFER	MPA	49	B3
SCHEIBER RD	SUT	33	D3
SCHELL RD	IMP	112	C3

STREET	CO.	PAGE	GRID
SCHILLING	MPA	48	E2
SCHILLING AV	FRCO	67	B1
SCHLAG RD	SUT	33	C2
SCHMIDT DR	RCO	107	A1
SCHMIDT RD	MCO	47	C5
SCHOBER LN	INY	51	D4
SCHOOL RD	IMP	112	D5
SCHOOL RD	MNO	50	E2
SCHOOL RD	MNO	51	A2
SCHOOL ST	HUM	15	E2
SCHOOL ST	MEN	30	C3
SCHOOL ST	U	123	C2
SCHOOLER RD	SBD	101	D1
SCHOOL HOUSE RD	LAS	21	C1
SCHOOL HOUSE RD	MPA	49	A4
SCHLHOUSE HL RD	SIS	4	D3
SCHOTT RD	BUT	25	C2
SCHOTT RD	LAS	14	B3
SCHROEDER AV	SUT	33	C1
SCHROEDER MINE	SIS	3	E4
SCHUETTE RD	LAK	31	C2
SCHULMEYER RD	SIS	4	A5
SCHULTE RD	SJCO	46	E2
SCHULTZ RD	KER	80	D5
SCHUSTER RD	KER	68	B5
SCIARONE RD	ED	35	B5
SCOFIELD AV	KER	78	A1
SCOTIA PINES CIR	NEV	127	A3
SCOTT AV	LACO	R	D5
SCOTT BLVD	SCL	P	B3
SCOTT BLVD	SCLR	151	A2
SCOTT RD	CAL	41	C3
SCOTT RD	LAS	27	E2
SCOTT RD	MPA	49	C3
SCOTT RD	RCO	99	C4
SCOTT RD	SAC	40	C1
SCOTT RD	SIS	5	D2
SCOTT BAR RD	SIS	3	D4
SCOTT CREEK RD	ALA	P	B2
SCOTT CREEK RD	ALA	46	B3
SCOTT DAM RD	LAK	23	C5
SCOTT FORBES RD	YUB	34	A1
SCOTT LUMBER RD	SHA	19	C1
SCOTT MTN RD	SIS	11	E2
SCOTT MTN RD	TRI	11	E2
SCOTT RIVER RD	SIS	3	B4
SCOTTS CREEK RD	LAK	31	C3
SCOTTS FLAT RD	NEV	34	D1
SCOTTS VLY RD	LAK	31	C2
SCOTTS VLY RD	SCR	54	A1
SCOTT VALLEY DR	SCR	P	A5
SCOTT VALLEY RD	SIS	3	D5
SCOTT VALLEY RD	SIS	11	D1
SCOTT VLY AIRPT	SIS	3	D5
SCOUT RD	BUT	19	D5
SCOUT ST	SHA	18	B3
SCOVELL AV	RCO	99	E4
SCRANTON AV	TUL	68	D3
SEAL BEACH BLVD	ORCO	98	A4
SEAL BEACH BLVD	ORCO	T	A3
SEARLES STA RD	KER	80	E2
SEARLES STA RD	SBD	80	E2
SEARLES STA CTO	SBD	80	E2
SEARS RD	LAS	21	B4
SEARS POINT RD	SOL	38	C4
SEARS POINT RD	SOL	134	A3
SEARS POINT RD	SON	L	B2
SEARS POINT RD	VAL	134	A3
SEASIDE AV	LA	191	D2
SEASIDE BLVD	LACO	S	C3
SEATTLE AV	KIN	67	D3
SEA VIEW DR	IMP	108	C2
SEAVIEW RD	SON	37	A4
SEAVW QUARRY RD	SON	37	B1
SEAWARD AV	VENT	175	D3
SEBASTIAN RD	KER	78	E5
SEBASTIAN RD	KER	79	A5
SEBASTOPOL AV	STR	131	C5
SEBASTOPOL FRWY	STR	131	B4
SEBASTOPOL FRWY	SON	131	B4
SEBASTOPOL RD	SON	131	B4
SECO ST	PAS	190	A3
SECOND ST	C	124	B5
SECRETARIAT RD	KER	79	A4
SECRET SPGS RD	SIS	4	E3
SECTION OLD-			
-RED BLUFF RD	PLU	19	E3
SEE CANYON RD	SLO	75	E4
SEE CANYON RD	SLO	76	A4
SEE VEE LN	INY	51	D4
SEIAD CREEK	SIS	3	B3
SEIAD OAKS RD	SIS	3	B3
SEIDNER	SJCO	47	D1
SEIGLER CYN RD	LAK	32	A4
SEIGLER SPGS RD	LAK	31	E4
SEIGLER SPGS			
-NORTH RD	LAK	32	A4
SELLERS AV	CC	M	D4
SELLERS AV	CC	39	C5
SELMADOLPH ST	SBD	91	E3
SELVA RD	DPT	202	A4
SEMINARY AV	ALA	L	D5
SEMINARY AV	ALA	45	D1
SEMINARY AV	O	159	E1
SEMINARY DR	MAR	140	C4
SEMINARY DR	MV	140	C4
SENATOR WASH RD	IMP	110	E5
SENECA RD	PLU	20	B5
SENECA RD	SBD	91	B4
SENECA RD	SBD	91	E3
SENILIS AV	SBD	100	C2
SENTER RD	SCL	P	C3
SENTER RD	SCL	46	B4

STREET	CO.	PAGE	GRID
SEPULVEDA BLVD	CUL	188	B2
SEPULVEDA BLVD	ELS	189	C4
SEPULVEDA BLVD	LA	180	C3
SEPULVEDA BLVD	LA	188	C4
SEPULVEDA BLVD	LA	189	C1
SEPULVEDA BLVD	LACO	97	C1
SEPULVEDA BLVD	LACO	Q	C2
SEPULVEDA BLVD	LACO	S	B2
SEPULVEDA BLVD	LACO	180	B2
SEQUOIA BLVD	KER	80	B4
SEQUOIA RD	FRCO	58	D3
SEQUOIA RD	HUM	16	C4
SERENADE DR	SBD	80	E1
SERENE DR	SHA	18	B2
SERENO DR	VAL	134	C2
SERFAS CLUB DR	RCO	U	E5
SERFAS CLUB DR	RCO	98	E3
SERPA LN	SIS	3	D5
SERPA LN	SOL	39	B2
SERRAMONTE BLVD	SMCO	L	B5
SERRAMONTE BLVD	SMCO	N	B1
SERRANO RD	VEN	96	C2
SERVICE RD	SIE	26	C4
SERVICE RD	STA	47	C3
SESPE ST	VEN	88	D5
SESPE RIVER RD	VEN	88	B3
SEVEN HILLS RD	ALA	L	E5
SEVEN HILLS RD	ALA	M	A5
SEVEN MILE LN	BUT	25	A4
SEVEN MILE RD	SLO	77	B3
SEVEN MI SLOUGH	HUM	15	D2
SEVEN OAK RD	SBD	100	A1
SEVERE RD	IMP	109	A3
SEWARD DR	HUM	16	C4
SEXTON	SJCO	47	C1
SEYMOUR RD	SUT	33	B4
SEYMOUR CK RD	VEN	88	C2
SHABELL LN	INY	59	E3
SHACKELFORD RD	STA	47	B2
SHADOW CYN RD	SLO	75	E2
SHADOW MTN RD	SBD	83	D2
SHADOW MTN RD	SBD	90	E2
SHADOW MTN RD	SBD	91	A2
SHADOW MTN RD	SBD	101	D1
SHADY DELL RD	SIS	5	A3
SHAFFER RD	MCO	48	B3
SHAFTER AV	KER	78	C3
SHAFTER RD	KER	78	C4
SHAIN AV	FRCO	56	B2
SHAKELEY LN	AMA	40	D2
SHAKE RIDGE RD	AMA	40	E2
SHAKE RIDGE RD	AMA	41	A2
SHALE RD	KER	77	E4
SHAMROCK RD	SIS	4	A4
SHANDON CEM RD	SLO	76	D1
SHANDON-SN JUAN	SLO	76	D1
SHANK RD	IMP	109	B4
SHANNON DR	SBD	101	D1
SHANNONDALE RD	LACO	89	E4
SHANNON VLY RD	LACO	89	E4
SHARON RD	MCO	55	E2
SHARP PARK RD	SMCO	N	B1
SHARP PARK RD	SMCO	45	B2
SHASTA AV	FRCO	56	E3
SHASTA AV	FRCO	57	A3
SHASTA BLVD	TEH	18	E5
SHASTA BLVD	TEH	24	E1
SHASTA WY	C	124	B4
SHASTA WY	KLAM	5	C1
SHASTA CO RD	MOD	13	E3
SHA DAM ACCS RD	SHA	18	B1
SHA SPG MCCLOUD	SIS	12	D2
SHASTA VIEW DR	MOD	14	E1
SHASTA VIEW DR	SHA	18	C2
SHASTA VISTA DR	SIS	4	C5
SHATTUCK AV	B	156	A2
SHATTUCK AV	O	156	A4
SHAVES AV	SBD	91	C1
SHAW AV	FRCO	57	C3
SHAWMUT RD	TUO	41	C5
SHAWMUT RD	TUO	48	C1
SHAW PIT RD	MOD	14	B2
SHAWS FLAT RD	SNRA	163	A2
SHAWS FLAT RD	TUO	163	A2
SHAWS FLAT RD	TUO	41	C5
SHAWS FT JMSTWN	TUO	41	C5
SHAY CREEK RD	ALP	36	B5
SHEEP CAMP RD	MNO	51	B2
SHEEP CREEK RD	SBD	90	E4
SHEEP CK SPG RD	SBD	82	E1
SHEEP CK TK TR	SBD	90	E5
SHEEP MTN RD	SIS	5	A3
SHEEP RANCH RD	CAL	41	B3
SHEEPY CREEK RD	SIS	5	B2
SHEEPY ISLND RD	SIS	5	B2
SHEFFIELD RD	SUT	33	C3
SHEKELL	VEN	88	D5
SHELBY ST	KER	78	B5
SHELDON RD	SAC	39	E2
SHELDON ST	LACO	Q	C2
SHELL AV	CC	L	E3
SHELL AV	MCO	56	A1
SHELL BLVD	CC	38	E5
SHELL RD	FRCO	66	D2
SHELL RD	TUO	41	C5
SHELL CANYON RD	IMP	111	C3
SHELLCO RD	KER	67	C5
SHELL GULCH RD	SIS	11	D1
SHELL NO 2	YUB	33	D1
SHELLEY	SJCO	40	D4
SHELLEY RD	SIS	4	B4
SHELTER COVE RD	HUM	22	A1
SHELTER ISLD DR	SDCO	V	A3

STREET	CO.	PAGE	GRID
SHELTON RD	SBD	101	D1
SHELTON RD	SJCO	40	C4
SHELTN BUTTE RD	HUM	10	D3
SHENANDOAH SCHL	AMA	40	E1
SHEPHERD AV	FRCO	57	C2
SHEPHERD RD	MOD	14	B3
SHEPPARD RD	VEN	88	C5
SHERIDAN	FRCO	58	A4
SHERIDAN RD	ALA	P	B2
SHERIDAN RD	ALA	46	B3
SHERIDAN RD	SLO	76	B5
SHERMAN RD	HUM	16	C4
SHERMAN RD	SBD	100	C2
SHERMAN WY	LA	177	A1
SHERMAN WY	LA	178	C1
SHERMAN WY	LACO	97	C1
SHERMAN ISLAND-			
-E LEVEE RD	SAC	M	D2
SHERWIN CK RD	MNO	50	E2
SHERWOOD AV	KER	77	E1
SHERWOOD AV	KER	78	B1
SHERWOOD BLVD	TEH	24	E1
SHERWOOD DR	SAL	171	C3
SHERWOOD RD	MEN	22	E4
SHERWD RNCHERIA	MEN	22	D4
SHETLAND CT	CAL	41	B5
SHIELDS AV	FRCO	56	A3
SHIELDS AV	FRCO	57	A3
SHIELDS RD	SHA	17	C3
SHIELLS RD	STA	47	C4
SHILOH RD	SOL	39	B4
SHILOH RD	SON	37	E1
SHIMMINS RDG RD	MEN	22	E4
SHINGLE RD S	ED	40	C1
SHINGLETWN DUMP	SHA	19	B3
SHINGLETOWN RDG	SHA	19	A3
SHINN RANCH RD	LAS	21	D2
SHIPPEE RD	BUT	25	C4
SHIPPEE RD	MCO	48	B5
SHIRK RD	TUL	68	A1
SHIRLAND	PLA	34	C4
SHIRLEY RD	CAL	41	A5
SHIRLEY MDWS RD	KER	79	C1
SHIRT TAIL CYN	PLA	34	D2
SHIVELY RD	HUM	16	A3
SHOEMAKE AV	STA	47	B2
SHOEMAKER AV	LACO	T	B1
SHOEMAKER RD	HUM	10	C4
SHOEMAKER RD	SIS	4	E4
SHOP RD	MNO	42	E1
SHOP ST	INY	70	B2
SHORE RD	SBT	54	E2
SHORELINE DR	LB	192	D3
SHORELINE DR	STB	174	C5
SHORELINE HWY	MAR	L	A4
SHORELINE HWY	MAR	37	D4
SHORELINE HWY	MEN	22	C3
SHORELINE HWY	MEN	30	C4
SHORELINE HWY	MAR	140	A4
SHORT AV	KER	91	C3
SHORT LN	TUO	163	C3
SHORT RD	KER	78	A5
SHORT CREEK RD	MEN	23	B2
SHORTYS WELL RD	INY	72	A2
SHOSHONE VLY RD	SBD	93	B5
SHOSHONI LOOP	SHA	13	E4
SHOUP AV	LA	177	B4
SHOUP RD	SHA	18	A3
SHOWER PASS RD	HUM	16	B2
SHRODE LN	LAS	21	C3
SHULTZ RD	MCO	56	C1
SHUMWAY RCH RD	RCO	100	D5
SHUTE MTN RD	BUT	25	E3
SHUTT ST	DN	1	D3
SHY ST	MCO	47	C5
SHY ST	MCO	55	C1
SICARD FLAT RD	YUB	34	A1
SIDDING RD	KER	78	B3
SIDEWINDER RD	IMP	110	C5
SIDEWINDER RD	RCO	102	C3
SIDEWINDER RD	SBD	91	D2
SIDNEY GULCH RD	TRI	17	D1
SIERRA AV	FRCO	57	C3
SIERRA AV	SBD	99	A2
SIERRA DR	MPA	48	E1
SIERRA DR	MDO	162	B4
SIERRA HWY	KER	80	A5
SIERRA HWY	KER	90	A1
SIERRA HWY	LACO	89	C4
SIERRA PKWY	CAL	41	D3
SIERRA RD	LAS	20	E3
SIERRA RD	SCL	P	C3
SIERRA RD	SCL	46	B4
SIERRA RD	STA	47	E1
SIERRA ST	RENO	130	B2
SIERRA WY	KER	69	D5
SIERRA WY	KER	79	D1
SIERRA WY	SBDO	207	D3
SIERRA WY	SBD	99	C1
SIERRA WY	TUL	58	A5
SIERRA CTR DR	SHA	13	E4
SRA COLLEGE BL	PLA	34	B4
SRA COLLEGE DR	NEV	127	C1
SIERRA DEL SOL	RCO	100	E3
SIERRA MADRE AV	LACO	98	C1
SIERRA MADRE AV	LACO	U	A1
SIERRA MADRE BL	LACO	98	A1
SIERRA MADRE BL	LACO	R	C3
SIERRA MADRE BL	LACO	R	C2
SIERRA VISTA AV	TEH	24	D1
SIERRA VISTA ST	KER	80	C1
SIERRA VLY RD	PLU	27	C3
SIEVERS RD	SOL	39	B1
SIGNAL RD	IMP	111	E4

STREET	CO.	PAGE	GRID
SIGNAL BUTTE RD	LAS	20	E1
SIGNAL RIDGE RD	MEN	30	D3
SIKES RD	SOL	39	C2
SILAXO AV	FRCO	56	C2
SILLS RD	COL	32	D3
SILSBEE RD	IMP	112	A3
SILURIAN LK RD	SBD	83	B2
SILVA RD	MPA	49	B3
SILVA RD	SIS	4	C3
SILVERA CT	BUT	25	C3
SILVERADO TR	NAP	133	E4
SILVERADO TR	NAPA	29	A1
SILVERADO TR	NAPA	38	C2
SILVER BAR RD	MPA	49	B4
SILVER BRDG RD	SHA	18	D2
SILVER CYN RD	INY	51	E4
SILVRADO CYN RD	ORCO	98	E4
SILVER CREEK RD	MOH	85	D4
SILVER CREEK RD	SCL	P	C3
SILVER CREEK RD	SCL	46	B4
SILVER CK CMPGD	ALP	42	C1
SILVER HILL RD	ALP	36	C5
SILVER KING RD	SHA	18	B2
SILVER LAKE BL	LA	182	E5
SILVER LAKE BL	LACO	Q	E4
SILVER LAKE RD	LAS	20	B3
SILVER BAR RD	MPA	49	B4
SILVER PUFF DR	KER	89	E3
SILVER QUEEN RD	KER	79	E5
SILVER QUEEN RD	KER	80	A5
SILVER RAPIDS RD	CAL	40	D4
SILVR STRAND BL	SDCO	V	B4
SILVR STRAND BL	SDCO	111	D2
SILVERTHORN RD	SHA	18	D1
SLVR TIP CPGRD	ALP	42	A2
SILVER VLY RD	SBD	92	B1
SILVEYVILLE RD	SOL	39	B2
SIMAS ST	SB	86	B1
SIMMERHORN RD	SAC	40	A3
SIMMLER RD	SLO	77	A2
SIMMLR BITTRWTR	SLO	76	E1
SIMMLR BITTRWTR	SLO	77	A1
SIMMLR SN DIEGO	SLO	77	C4
SIMMONS RD	LAK	23	C5
SIMMONS RD	SHA	18	B2
SIMMONS RD	STA	47	C3
SIMPSON LN	MEN	22	C5
SIMPSON LN	YUB	33	D2
SIMPSON RD	IMP	109	B3
SIMPSON RD	RCO	99	D4
SIMPSON RD	TEH	24	C1
SIMPSN DATNI RD	YUB	33	D2
SIMS RD	TUO	41	C5
SIMS RD	TUO	48	C1
SIMS CREEK RD	TRI	17	C3
SIMS LOOKOUT RD	SHA	12	C4
SINCLAIR FRWY	ALA	46	A3
SINCLAIR FRWY	SCL	46	A3
SINCLAIR RD	IMP	109	A3
SINEX AV	PAC	167	B2
SINGLE SPRINGS	SIS	4	E5
SINGLETON RD	RCO	99	D2
SINGLE TREE	SBD	100	E2
SINGLETREE DR	CAL	41	A5
SINGLEY RD	HUM	15	E2
SINNARD AV	SUT	33	C1
SINTON RD	SB	86	B1
SIR F DRAKE BL	MAR	37	E4
SIR F DRAKE BL	MAR	38	A3
SIR F DRAKE BL	MAR	L	A3
SIR F DRAKE BL	ROSS	139	A4
SISK RD	STA	47	C2
SISKIYOU AV	FRCO	57	A3
SISKIYOU AV	FRCO	67	A2
SITES-LODOGA RD	COL	24	B5
SITES-LODOGA RD	COL	32	B1
SIX MILE RD	CAL	41	B4
SKAGGS ISLND RD	SOL	38	C3
SKAGGS SPGS RD	SON	31	C5
SKIDOO RD	INY	71	D1
SKI HILL RD	MOD	7	C5
SKI RUN BLVD	SLT	129	C3
SKITTONE RD	STA	47	D2
SKULL FLAT RD	CAL	41	B2
SKUNK RANCH RD	CAL	41	C4
SKYLINE BLVD	ALA	L	D4
SKYLINE BLVD	ALA	45	D1
SKYLINE BLVD	KIN	67	A3
SKYLINE BLVD	SMCO	N	B1
SKYLINE BLVD	SMCO	N	C2
SKYLINE BLVD	SMCO	45	C3
SKYLINE BLVD	SCL	N	E4
SKYLINE DR	KER	79	B4
SKYLINE DR	MONT	167	C4
SKYLINE DR	MON	53	D3
SKYLINE DR	SBD	100	E1
SKYLINE DR	SDCO	V	D4
SKYLINE DR	SDCO	111	D1
SKYLINE MTWY	PLU	20	D4
SKYLINE RD	KER	77	E3
SKYLINE RD	KIN	67	A3
SKYLINE RD	SON	31	A5
SKY LINE DR	VAL	134	E3
SKYLINE FRST DR	MONT	167	C5
SKYLINE FRST DR	MONT	168	C1
SKYLINE FRST DR	MON	53	D4
SKYLINE RCH RD	SBD	100	D1
SKY RANCH RD	MON	54	C5
SKY VALLEY RD	RCO	100	E3
SKY VALLEY RD	SOL	38	D4
SKY VIEW DR	IMP	108	C2
SKYVIEW RD	MAD	57	C2
SKYWAY	BUT	25	C2

STREET	CO.	PAGE	GRID
SKYWAY DR	SB	86	B1
SKYWAY RD	BUT	19	D5
SKYWAY RD	BUT	25	D1
SLACKS CYN RD	MON	66	B3
SLASH X RCH RD	SBD	91	C2
SLATE RD	YUB	26	A4
SLATE CREEK RD	SHA	12	B4
SLATE CREEK RD	TRI	11	D5
SLATE GULCH	MPA	48	E3
SLATE MTN RD	TRI	12	A4
SLATE MTN LO RD	SHA	12	B4
SLATER AV	ORCO	T	B3
SLATER RD	HUM	16	B2
SLATE RANGE	INY	71	B2
SLATER BUTTE LO	SIS	3	A3
SLAUGHTERHOUSE	MPA	49	B3
SLAUSON AV	CUL	188	C3
SLAUSON AV	LACO	97	D2
SLAUSON AV	LACO	Q	E4
SLAUSON AV	LACO	R	C5
SLAUSON AV	LACO	188	E3
SLAYTON RD	IMP	109	C5
SLIGER MINE RD	ED	34	D3
SLOAT BLVD	SFCO	L	B5
SLOAT BLVD	SFCO	45	B2
SLOAT RD	PLU	26	E2
SLOUGH RD	SIS	4	B5
SLOUGH RD	SIS	12	B1
SLOUGHHOUSE RD	SAC	40	B2
SLOVER AV	SBD	99	A2
SLUG GULCH RD	ED	41	A1
SLUSSER RD	SON	37	D2
SLY PARK RD	ED	35	A5
SMALLEY RD	FRCO	57	E1
SMARTS RANCH RD	SBD	92	B5
SMARTVILLE RD	YUB	34	A1
SMITH	YUB	33	E1
SMITH AV	FRCO	57	E4
SMITH AV	KER	78	B1
SMITH AV	KER	70	A5
SMITH GRADE	SCR	53	D1
SMITH RD	MON	65	C5
SMITH RD	SBD	80	E1
SMITH MTN RD	MON	66	B3
SMITH PK LKOUT	TUO	48	E1
SMITH PK LKOUT	TUO	49	A1
SMITHNECK RD	SIE	27	D4
SMITHSON RD	SBD	91	B2
SMITH STA RD	MPA	48	E1
SMITH STA RD	MPA	49	A1
SMITH STA RD	TUO	48	E1
SMITH STA RD	TUO	49	A1
SMITH TALC RD	SBD	73	B5
SMOKE CK RCH RD	LAS	21	D3
SMOKE TREE RD	SBD	90	E4
SNAVELY RD	DN	1	E3
SNEATH LN	SMCO	N	B1
SNEATH LN	SMCO	45	B2
SNEATH LN	SBR	144	A2
SNELL ST	SNRA	163	B3
SNELLING HWY	MER	170	A3
SNELLING RD	MCO	48	C3
SNELL VALLEY RD	NAPA	32	B5
SNOW RD	KER	77	E2
SNOW RD	KER	78	C2
SNOW ST	KER	79	E1
SNOW ST	KER	80	A1
SNOW CAMP RD	HUM	10	B5
SNOWDN HOVEY GL	SIS	4	C4
SNOWS RD	ED	35	A5
SNOWSHOE SPGS	ALP	36	B4
SNOW TENT RD	NEV	26	D5
SNYDER RD	IMP	109	C5
SNYDER RD	MCO	47	C5
SOAP CREEK RD	SIS	3	E5
SOBOBA RD	RCO	99	E3
SOBOBA ST	RCO	100	A4
SOBRANTE AV	CC	L	D3
SOBRANTE AV	CC	38	C5
SODA BAY RD	LAK	31	D3
SODA CANYON RD	NAPA	38	C2
SODA CREEK RD	SHA	12	C3
SODA LAKE RD	KER	78	A5
SODA LAKE RD	KER	87	E1
SODA LAKE RD	SLO	77	B3
SODA LAKE CK RD	SLO	77	B3
SODA LK SN DIEG	SLO	77	B3
SODA LK SN DIEG	SLO	77	D4
SODA ROCK LN W	SON	31	D5
SODA SPRINGS RD	BUT	19	D5
SODA SPRINGS RD	SON	30	E5
SOETH RD	GLE	24	B5
SOLANO AV	ALA	L	D4
SOLANO AV	NAP	133	A2
SOLANO AV	VAL	134	D4
SOLANO WY	CC	M	A3
SOLDIER MTN DR	SHA	13	D3
SOLDIER MTN RD	SHA	13	D3
SOLEDAD DR	MONT	167	D4
SOLEDAD DR	MONT	168	D1
SOLEDAD DR	MON	53	E4
SOLEDAD FRWY	SDCO	V	B2
SOLEDAD FRWY	SDCO	106	C5
SOLEDAD CYN RD	LACO	89	E4
SOLEDAD MTN RD	SD	211	B4
SOLOMAN RD	SB	86	B1
SOMAVIA RD	MON	54	D4
SOMEO ST	SB	86	B1
SOMERSVILLE RD	CC	M	B3
SOMERSVILLE RD	CC	39	B5
SONOMA AV	FRCO	56	D4
SONOMA AV	FRCO	66	D1
SONOMA AV	STR	131	E3

STREET	CO.	PAGE	GRID
SONOMA BLVD	NAPA	L	D2
SONOMA BLVD	VAL	134	C5
SONOMA HWY	SNMA	132	C3
SONOMA MTN RD	SON	38	A2
SONORA	SJCO	40	D5
SONORA	STA	48	A1
SONORA RD	STA	40	D5
SONORA RD	STA	47	D1
SONORA RD	STA	48	A1
SOPHIE ST	RCO	99	C4
SOQUEL AV	SC	169	D3
SOQUEL DR	SCR	54	A2
SOQUEL-SAN JOSE	SCR	54	A2
SORENSON RD	HUM	16	B3
SORENSON RD	RCO	107	B1
SORREL WY	CAL	41	A4
SORRENTO VLY RD	SDCO	106	C4
SORRENTO VLY RD	SDCO	V	A1
SOSCOL AV	NAP	133	D3
SOSCOL RD	NAPA	38	D3
SOTO ST	LA	186	C3
SOTO ST	LACO	R	A4
SOULE LN	SIS	4	C4
SOULSBYVILLE RD	TUO	41	D5
SOUTH AV	FRCO	56	E4
SOUTH AV	FRCO	57	B4
SOUTH AV	MCO	47	E4
SOUTH AV	MCO	48	A4
SOUTH AV	TEH	24	E2
SOUTH RD	MNO	51	C1
SOUTH ST	ANA	193	B3
SOUTH ST	GLE	24	D3
SOUTH ST	LACO	98	A3
SOUTH ST	LACO	S	D1
SOUTH ST	LACO	T	B1
SOUTH ST	ORCO	T	C2
SOUTH ST	RED	122	B2
SOUTH ST	SBD	90	E4
SOUTH ST	SNLO	172	C4
SOUTH ST	SHA	18	C3
SOUTHAM RD	COL	24	E5
SOUTHAMPTON RD	BEN	153	A3
SOUTH BANK RD	DN	1	E3
S BNK CHETKO RD	CUR	1	D2
SOUTH BAY FRWY	SDCO	V	D4
SOUTH BAY FRWY	SDCO	111	D1
SOUTHBAY FRWY	SVL	148	D3
SOUTHERN AV	SIS	12	D2
S EMBARCADRO FY	SFCO	45	C2
SOUTH FORK DR	TUL	58	E5
SOUTH FORK DR	TUL	68	E1
SOUTH FORK DR	TUL	69	A1
SOUTH FORK RD	DN	1	E4
SOUTH FORK RD	DN	2	A4
SOUTH FORK RD	SHA	18	B3
SOUTH FORK RD	SIS	2	E3
SOUTH FORK RD	TRI	10	D5
SOUTH FORK RD	TRI	16	E2
SOUTH FORK RD	TUO	41	D4
S FK LOOKOUT RD	SHA	18	B2
S FK MAD RIV RD	TRI	17	B5
S FORK MTN RD	LAS	8	B3
S FORK MTN RD	TRI	16	E3
S FK SALMON RIV	SIS	11	A2
SOUTH GRADE RD	SDCO	107	A2
SOUTH GRADE RD	SDCO	107	B5
SOUTH LNDG RD	MNO	51	A3
SOUTHSIDE DR	MPA	63	B2
SOUTHSIDE RD	SBT	54	E3
SOUTHSIDE RD	SBT	55	A3
SOUTH VLY FRWY	SCL	54	C1
SW EXPWY	SCL	P	B3
SOUTHWORTH RD	CAL	40	D4
SOUZA RD	TRI	17	A4
SOWLES RD	SJCO	40	B3
SPA RD	IMP	108	E1
SPACER DR	TUL	68	B2
SPANGLE GOLD RD	MAD	49	C5
SPANGLER RD	KER	68	C5
SPANISH DAGGER	RCO	100	C5
SPANISH DRY DGN	ED	34	D3
SPANISH RCH RD	PLU	26	B1
SPANSH RCH BUTE	PLU	25	E2
SPANSH RCH BUTE	PLU	26	A2
SPANISH VALLEY	NAPA	32	C5
SPARKS RD	MCO	47	C5
SPARKS RANCH RD	SOL	39	B1
SPAULDING RD	LAS	20	D1
SPEAR AV	HUM	10	A5
SPECIMAN SPG RD	MAD	49	B4
SPENCE RD	MON	54	D4
SPENCER LN	SON	32	A5
SPENCER LN	SON	38	A1
SPENCER RD	COL	24	E5
SPENCER RD	STA	47	A2
SPENCEVILLE RD	NEV	34	B2
SPENCEVILLE RD	YUB	33	E5
SPERRY AV	STA	47	B3
SPERRY RD	STA	47	E3
SPAGNOLI MINE RD	AMA	41	A2
SPICER RD	COL	33	A3
SPILLWAY RD	MNO	51	B2
SPINELLI RD	MAD	49	C5
SPINK RD	CAL	41	B2
SPOONER RD	LAS	8	A4
SPOONER RD	LAS	14	E4
SPORTS ARENA BL	SD	212	E5
SPORTS ARENA BL	SD	213	A5
SPRECKELS BLVD	MON	54	C4
SPRING ST	LACO	S	E2
SPRING ST	NAPA	29	C3
SPRING ST	U	123	B3
SPRING ST N	LA	186	B2

STREET	CO.	PAGE	GRID
SPRING TR	LAK	31	D2
SPRING BRNCH RD	TEH	18	D3
SPRING BRNCH RD	TEH	19	A3
SPRINGBROOK RD	CC	L	E4
SPRINGBROOK RD	CC	M	A4
SPRING CREEK RD	SHA	13	D3
SPRINGDALE ST	ORCO	T	A3
SPRINGER RD	SCL	N	E3
SPRINGFIELD AV	FRCO	56	E4
SPRINGFIELD AV	FRCO	57	B4
SPRING GAP RD	TUO	41	E3
SPRING GAP RD	TUO	42	A3
SPRING GARDEN	PLA	34	D3
SPRING GULCH RD	LAS	14	B4
SPRING GULCH RD	SHA	18	C3
SPRING HILL RD	LAS	14	E4
SPRING HILL RD	SON	37	E3
SPRING HILL RD	SON	38	A3
SPRING LAKE RD	KLAM	5	B1
SPRING MDWS RD	SIS	12	A3
SPRING MTN RD	NAPA	29	A2
SPRING MTN RD	NAPA	38	B1
SPRINGS RD	SOL	L	D2
SPRINGS RD	SOL	38	D4
SPRING VLY LTRL	COL	32	D2
SPRING VLY RD	COL	32	C2
SPRING VLY RD	MEN	31	B1
SPRING VLY RD	YUB	33	E1
SPRINGVILLE AV	TUL	68	D3
SPRINGVLLE MILO	TUL	69	A2
SPROUL CREEK RD	HUM	22	B1
SPRUCE AV	SSF	144	B1
SPRUCE RD	TUL	68	C2
SPRUCE RD EXT	LAK	32	A4
SPRUCE ST	B	156	A1
SPRUCE CAMP RD	MCO	55	E2
SPRUCE GROVE RD	LAK	32	B4
SPUNKY CYN RD	LACO	89	C3
SPUR ST	CAL	41	A4
SPYROCK RD	MEN	22	D2
SQUAW BUSH RD	SBD	92	B4
SQUAW FLAT RD	VEN	88	D3
SQUAW GULCH RD	SIS	11	D2
SQUAW VALLEY RD	SIS	12	D3
SQUAW VLY LP RD	SIS	12	D3
SQUIRREL CK RD	PLU	26	D2
STABLER LN	YUBA	125	A1
STADIUM WY	LACO	Q	E3
STADIUM WY	SD	214	A3
STADIUM WY	SDCO	V	B3
STADIUM WY	SDCO	111	D1
STAFFORD RD	HUM	16	A3
STAGE RD	AVLN	97	A4
STAGE RD	BUT	25	C2
STAGE RD	LAS	8	D5
STAGE RD	LACO	T	B1
STAGE RD	SMCO	N	C4
STAGE RD	SMCO	45	C5
STAGE COACH LN	SDCO	106	C2
STAGECOACH RD	HUM	9	E4
STAGECOACH RD	SB	87	B3
STAGECOACH CYN	NAPA	32	C5
STAGE GULCH RD	SON	L	A1
STAGHORN RD	RCO	107	C1
STAHL RD	IMP	109	B4
STALLARD RD	IMP	110	C2
STALLION WY	CAL	41	B4
STAMPEDE DAM RD	SIE	27	C5
STAMPFLI LN RD	PLU	20	D5
STANDARD RD	TUO	41	D5
STANDARD MNE RD	PLU	20	C5
STANDIFORD AV	STA	47	C2
STANDISH PIT RD	LAS	21	B3
STANDLEY ST	U	123	B3
STANISLAUS AV	FRCO	66	D1
STANISLAUS RD W	STA	47	B3
STANLEY	SJCO	40	C5
STANLEY AV	VEN	88	A5
STANLEY BLVD	ALA	M	C5
STANLEY BLVD	ALA	P	C1
STANLEY BLVD	ALA	46	B2
STANLEY RD	CAL	41	B2
STANLEY RD	IMP	109	B3
STANLEY RD	RCO	100	A5
STANWOOD DR	STB	174	E1
STANYAN ST	SF	141	E3
STAPP RD	HUM	16	C2
STAR AV	STA	47	E2
STARBRIGHT MINE	SBD	82	A4
STARDUST RD	CLK	210	B1
STAR HILL RD	SMCO	N	C3
STARK	SJCO	47	A1
STARK RD	STA	47	B3
STARKEY RD	SLO	76	C1
STARLING ST	LACO	90	C2
STARLITE DR	INY	51	C4
STARR RD	IMP	109	C5
STATE LN	SBD	100	B1
STATE ST	LACO	R	A5
STATE ST	MTCL	203	B5
STATE ST	ONT	203	E5
STATE ST	ONT	204	C5
STATE ST	RCO	99	E4
STATE ST	SB	87	C4
STATE ST	SD	215	D3
STATE ST	SDCO	V	B4
STATE ST	STB	174	A2
STATE ST N	MEN	31	B2
STATE ST N	U	123	C2
STATE ST S	MEN	123	D3
STATE ST S	U	123	D3
STATE COLLGE BL	ORCO	98	C3
STATE COLLGE BL	ORCO	T	D2

STREET	CO.	PAGE	GRID
STATE COL BL	ANA	193	E5
STATE COL PKWY	SBD	99	B1
STATE FRSTRY RD	SON	31	A5
STATE LINE RD	MOD	5	D2
STATE LINE RD	MNO	52	C3
STATE LINE RD	INY	72	D1
STATE LINE RD	SIS	5	B2
STATEN ISLND RD	SJCO	39	D4
STATE RANCH RD	SUT	33	C3
STATION RD	KER	78	A3
STAVERVILLE RD	SIE	27	D3
STEARNS RD	STA	47	E2
STEARNS ST	LACO	S	E2
STEARNS ST	VEN	89	A5
STEEG RD	SBD	101	D1
STEEL BRIDGE RD	TRI	17	D1
STEELE LN	MEN	22	E3
STEELE LN W	STR	131	B2
STEELE CYN RD	NAPA	38	D2
STEELHEAD CIR	TRI	17	D1
STEELHEAD RD	HUM	16	D5
STEEL SWAMP RD	MOD	6	C3
STEFFAN ST	VAL	134	E5
STEIDLMAYER RD	CLU	33	A2
STEINEGUL	SJCO	47	D1
STEINER RD	SUT	33	B3
STEINER FLAT RD	TRI	17	C1
STELLAR RD	SBD	92	A4
STELLING RD N	CPTO	149	D4
STENT CUTOFF	TUO	41	C5
STEPHANIE LN	DGL	36	C2
STEPHENSON BLVD	RCO	110	C1
STEPHENS RIDGE	BUT	25	E3
STERCHI LN	SIS	4	C5
STERLING AV	SBD	99	C2
STERLING RD	INY	70	C4
STERLING LAKE	NEV	27	B5
STETSON AV	RCO	99	E4
STEVEN ST	KER	78	B5
STEVENS RD	IMP	111	E3
STEVENS CK BLVD	CPTO	150	E5
STEVENS CK BLVD	SCL	P	B3
STEVENS CK BLVD	SCLR	150	E5
STEVENS CK BLVD	SCL	46	A4
STEVENS CK FRWY	MVW	148	B5
STEVENS CK RD	SCL	N	E3
STEVENS CK RD	SCL	P	A3
STEVENS CK RD	SCL	45	E4
STEVENSON BLVD	ALA	P	A2
STEVENSN BDG RD	SOL	39	B1
STEVENS MINE RD	SBD	80	E2
STEVENS MINE RD	SBD	81	A2
STEVENS PASS RD	SIS	5	A5
STEVENS PASS RD	SIS	13	B1
STEWART	MOD	14	D1
STEWART AV	BUT	124	A5
STEWART LN	INY	51	E5
STEWART LN	SOL	39	B4
STEWART RD	HUM	16	C4
STEWART RD	INY	51	D4
STEWART RD	SJCO	47	A1
STEWART RD	SUT	33	D2
STEWART RD	TEH	18	C5
STEWART ST	SB	86	C1
STEWARTS POINT-			
-SKAGGS SPGS RD	SON	30	E5
STEWARTS POINT-			
-SKAGGS SPGS RD	SON	31	A5
STEWART RCH RD	HUM	16	D4
STEWART SPGS RD	SIS	12	B1
STICE RD	TEH	18	D4
STIERLIN RD	SCL	N	E2
STIERLIN RD	SCL	P	A2
STILLWELL AV	MONT	167	D3
STILLWELL AV	MON	53	E3
STILSON CYN RD	BUT	25	B3
STIMPSON RD	BUT	25	D5
STIMPSON RD	BUT	33	D1
STINE RD	BKD	166	A5
STINE RD	KER	78	D3
STINGY LN	SHA	18	C3
STOCKDALE HWY	KER	78	A3
STOCKDALE RD	SLO	76	A1
STOCKER ST	LACO	Q	D4
STOCKTON AV	MCO	48	B4
STOCKTON BLVD	SCTO	137	E4
STOCKTON BLVD	SAC	39	E1
STOCKTON RD	VEN	88	D5
STOCKTON ST	SNRA	163	A5
STOCKWLL MNE RD	INY	71	B4
STODDARD RD	STA	47	C2
STODDARD RD	STA	47	E2
STODDARD MTN RD	SBD	91	C2
STODDARD WELLS	SBD	91	D2
STOEKEL RD	SHA	18	B3
STONE AV	STA	47	C2
STONE RD	LAS	20	E1
STONE RD	MCO	55	D1
STONEBORO RD	MEN	30	C3
STONE CANYON RD	MON	66	B3
STONE COAL RD	MOD	14	B2
STONEHEDGE DR	YUB	25	E5
STONEHILL DR	DPT	202	A3
STONE HOUSE RD	SAC	40	C1
STONEHURST AV	LACO	Q	D2
STONERIDGE DR	ALA	46	A2
STONE VALLEY RD	CC	M	A4
STONE VALLEY RD	CC	46	A1
STONEWLL CYN RD	MON	65	A1
STONEY CREEK RD	LAS	21	D2
STONY CREEK RD	AMA	40	D3
STONYFD-LDGA RD	COL	24	B5
STONY POINT RD	STR	131	A3

STREET	CO.	PAGE	GRID
STONY POINT RD	SON	37	E2
STONY POINT RD	SON	37	E3
STONY POINT RD	SON	131	A4
STOREY	FRCO	56	C2
STORRIE RD	PLU	25	E2
STORY RD	SCL	P	C3
STORY RD	SCL	46	B4
STORY RD	STA	47	E3
STOVALL RD	COL	32	D2
STOVEPIPE WELLS	INY	61	D4
STOVER RD	HUM	10	B4
STOW	SJCO	40	C5
STOW	SJCO	47	C1
STOWELL RD	SB	86	B1
STOWELL RD	SMA	173	A4
STRADLEY AV	KER	68	B5
STRAND, THE	LAS	20	E1
STRATTON LN	SOL	39	B4
STRAWBERRY DR	MAR	140	D3
STRAWBERRY LN	SHA	18	C3
STRAWBERRY RD	MON	54	C3
STREETER AV	RCO	99	B2
ST OF GL LNTERN	DPT	202	A4
STREET 200	MAD	57	D1
STREET 225	MAD	50	A5
STREET 600	MAD	49	B1
STREET 600	MAD	49	C4
STREET 603	MAD	57	B1
STREIBY RD	IMP	109	B4
STRINGTOWN RD	BUT	25	E4
STRIPLIN RD	SUT	33	D4
STROUD AV	FRCO	57	C5
STRUCKMAN RD	CAL	41	B3
STUBBLEFIELD RD	KER	78	A5
STUBBLEFIELD RD	KER	87	E1
STUBBY SPGS TR	RCO	101	A2
STUDEBAKER RD	LACO	98	A3
STUDEBAKER RD	LACO	S	E1
STUDEBAKER RD	LACO	S	E2
STUDEBAKER RD	LACO	T	A1
STUHR RD	STA	47	C4
STUKEY ST	DN	1	D3
STUMPFIELD MTN	MPA	49	C3
STUMPTOWN RD	HUM	9	E4
STUNT RD	LACO	97	B2
STURGIS RD	VEN	96	B1
STURM RD	HUM	16	C3
SUBACO RD	SUT	33	B3
SUBSTATION RD	MNO	50	E2
SUCCESS DR	TUL	68	D3
SUCCESS VLY DR	TUL	68	E3
SUCKER RUN RD	BUT	26	A4
SUCKOW RD	KER	80	D5
SUDDEN RD	SB	86	B3
SUE AV	KER	89	C1
SUE ST	KER	80	B5
SUEY RD	SMA	173	E3
SUEY CREEK RD	SLO	76	D5
SUGAR CREEK RD	SIS	11	D2
SUGARLOAF RD	FRCO	58	A1
SUGAR LOAF RD	INY	51	D5
SUGARLF LKSHR RD	SHA	12	B5
SUGRLOAF LKT RD	SHA	12	B5
SUGARLOAF TK TR	SBD	99	E1
SUGAR PINE	PLA	34	E2
SUGAR PINE PL	BUT	25	C2
SUGAR PINE RD	TUO	41	E4
SUGAR PINE SPG	LAS	14	A3
SUISUN VLY RD	SOL	L	E1
SUISUN VLY RD	SOL	38	E3
SULFUR RD	INY	52	D5
SULKEY CT	CAL	41	A5
SULLENGER RD	SUT	33	B2
SULLIVAN RD	KER	78	A2
SULLIVAN RD	MPA	49	B3
SULLIVAN RD	STA	47	C5
SULPHUR BANK DR	LAK	32	A3
SULPHUR MTN RD	VEN	88	B4
SULPHR MTN RD E	VEN	88	B4
SULPHUR SPGS RD	MON	65	B3
SULTANA DR	MCO	48	A4
SULTZE AV	KER	78	B5
SUMMERHILL DR	TUO	42	A3
SUMMER HOMES RD	ML	164	C2
SUMMERS LN	KLAM	5	B1
SUMMERS RD	LAS	21	E5
SUMMERSET RD	SBD	91	C1
SUMMIT AV	GLE	24	D3
SUMMIT AV	SBD	99	A1
SUMMIT RD	BUT	25	D5
SUMMIT RD	KER	79	C4
SUMMIT RD	SCL	P	C5
SUMMIT RD	SCR	P	A5
SUMMIT RD	SCR	54	B1
SUMMIT CREEK RD	TRI	17	C2
SUMMIT LAKE DR	NAPA	38	B1
SUMMIT LEVEL RD	CAL	41	C3
SUMMITROSE ST	LACO	Q	E1
SUMMIT TRUCK TR	SBD	91	B5
SUMMY	SUT	33	B2
SUMNER AV	AVLN	97	B5
SUMNER AV	FRCO	56	E4
SUMNER AV	FRCO	58	B4
SUMNER ST	BKD	166	E3
SUNBURST AV	SBD	100	E1
SUNDOWN LN	TUO	163	C3
SUNEVER RD	SBD	101	A1
SUNFAIR RD	SBD	101	A1
SUNFLOWER AV	CM	197	D3
SUNFLOWER AV	CM	198	A3
SUNFLOWER AV	LACO	U	A2
SUNFLOWR SPG RD	SBD	94	D2
SUNFLR SPGS SPR	SBD	94	E3

STREET	CO.	PAGE	GRID
SUNKIST ST	ANA	193	E3
SUNKIST ST	ORCO	T	D2
SUNKIST TR	LPAZ	104	C4
SUNLAND BLVD	LACO	97	D1
SUNLAND BLVD	LACO	Q	D2
SUNLAND DR	INY	51	D4
SUNNY LN	AVLN	97	B5
SUNNY ACRES AV	MCO	47	E3
SUNNY ACRES AV	MCO	48	A3
SUNNY BRAE LN	HUM	10	A5
SUNNY HILL RD	SHA	18	A3
SUNNYSIDE AV	FRCO	57	D3
SUNNYSIDE AV	FRCO	57	D4
SUNNYSIDE AV	MAD	57	A1
SUNNYSIDE RD	LAS	21	B4
SUNNYSLOPE	FRCO	58	B2
SUNNYSLOPE RD	SBD	90	E4
SUNNYVALE AV	CPTO	149	E1
SUNNYVALE AV	SVL	148	E5
SUNNY VISTA RD	SBD	100	E1
SUNOL BLVD	ALA	P	B1
SUNRISE	SBD	101	B1
SUNRISE BLVD	SAC	34	A5
SUNRISE BLVD	SJCO	40	B1
SUNRISE HWY	SDCO	107	D4
SUNRISE HWY	SDCO	107	D5
SUNRISE WY	PMSP	206	C5
SUNRISE WY	RCO	100	D3
SUNRISE SPGS RD	SBD	93	A5
SUNSET	SAC	34	B5
SUNSET AV	KER	79	E5
SUNSET AV	LACO	R	D4
SUNSET AV	MAD	57	A2
SUNSET AV	MCO	55	D1
SUNSET AV	RCO	99	E3
SUNSET BLVD	KER	79	A4
SUNSET BLVD	LA	181	A4
SUNSET BLVD	LA	182	A4
SUNSET BLVD	LA	186	A1
SUNSET BLVD	LACO	97	C2
SUNSET BLVD	LACO	Q	D2
SUNSET BLVD	SD	213	C5
SUNSET BLVD	SDCO	V	B3
SUNSET BLVD	SFCO	L	B5
SUNSET BLVD	SF	141	A5
SUNSET BLVD	SFCO	45	B1
SUNSET BLVD	LA	180	C1
SUNSET BLVD W	PLA	33	E4
SUNSET BLVD W	PLA	34	A4
SUNSET DR	IMP	108	C2
SUNSET DR	INY	60	B4
SUNSET DR	MCO	47	E4
SUNSET DR	MCO	48	A4
SUNSET DR	MONT	53	C2
SUNSET DR	PAC	167	B2
SUNSET DR	SDCO	106	C3
SUNSET PKWY	MAR	38	B4
SUNSET RD	CC	M	D3
SUNSET RD	CC	39	C5
SUNSET RD	CLK	74	D3
SUNSET RD	GLE	24	D3
SUNSET RD	SBD	100	E1
SUNSET ST	FRCO	66	D2
SUNSET CYN DR	LACO	Q	D2
SUNSET CLFFS BL	SD	212	B5
SUNSET CLFFS BL	SDCO	V	A3
SUNSET CLFFS BL	SDCO	111	C1
SUNSET CRSSG RD	LACO	U	B3
SUNSET LAKE RD	ALP	42	B1
SUNSHINE MNE RD	KER	80	E3
SUPERIOR AV	CM	199	B3
SUPERIOR AV	NB	199	A3
SUPERIOR RD	KER	78	B3
SURPRISE CYN RD	INY	71	C3
SURPRISE SPG RD	SBD	100	E1
SURPRISE VLY RD	LAS	8	E3
SURPRISE VLY RD	MOD	7	E3
SURPRISE VLY RD	MOD	8	E3
SUSAN HILLS DR	LAS	20	E3
SUSANVILLE RD	LAS	14	B3
SUSQUEHANNA RD	SIS	4	D3
SUTLIFF RD	SJCO	47	D1
SUTTENFIELD RD	SJCO	40	B3
SUTTER AV	FRCO	56	E4
SUTTER AV	FRCO	66	E3
SUTTER AV	MDO	162	A5
SUTTER LN	AMA	40	D2
SUTTER RD	HUM	9	E4
SUTTER RD	HUM	10	A4
SUTTER RD	YOL	39	D3
SUTTER ST	AMA	40	E2
SUTTER CK IONE-			
-BACK CUTOFF RD	AMA	40	D2
SUTTR CK VOLCNO	AMA	40	E2
SUTTER ISLND RD	SAC	M	E1
SUTTER ISLND RD	SAC	39	D3
SUTTERVILLE RD	SAC	39	D1
SWAN RD	MCO	48	B4
SWAN RD	SOL	39	C2
SWAN MTN RD	PLU	20	B3
SWANSEA RD	LPAZ	104	D3
SWANSON AV	FRCO	57	B5
SWANSON AV	FRCO	57	C5
SWANSON RD	STA	47	E3
SWANTON RD	SCR	N	D5
SWANTON RD	SCR	53	D1
SWARTHOT CYN RD	SBD	91	A5
SWASEY DR	SHA	18	B2
SWEDE CREEK RD	SHA	18	D2
SWEDE CREEK RD	TRI	11	A5
SWEDES FLAT RD	BUT	25	E5
SWEENEY RD	ED	35	A5
SWEENEY RD	SB	86	C3

STREET	CO.	PAGE	GRID
SWEENEY RD	SOL	39	A2
SWEENEY PASS RD	SDCO	108	A5
SWEENY RD	MCO	55	C2
SWEET RD	IMP	109	A5
SWEETEN LN	SBD	91	D1
SWEETLAND RD	NEV	26	B5
SWEETSER RD	KER	89	E1
SWEETWATER RD	SDCO	V	C4
SWEETWATER RD	SDCO	111	E1
SWEETWATER RD	SDCO	111	D2
SWEETWR SPGS BL	SDCO	V	E3
SWEETWTR SPG RD	SON	37	D1
SWEITZER LN	SBD	92	D5
SWENSEN RD	MCO	47	D4
SWETZER RD	SUT	33	E3
SWIFT AV	MCO	56	A2
SWIFT RD	SBD	80	E5
SWIFT ST	SC	169	A4
SWIFT CREEK	TRI	11	E4
SWIGART RD	SIS	4	B4
SWISS RANCH RD	CAL	41	B3
SX RD	MOD	14	E1
SYCAMORE AV	FRCO	57	A4
SYCAMORE AV	SDCO	106	C3
SYCAMORE DR	LACO	88	E5
SYCAMORE LN	DVS	136	B3
SYCAMORE RD	ALA	P	B1
SYCAMORE RD	KER	78	E4
SYCAMORE RD	KER	79	A4
SYCAMORE RD	SDCO	V	C5
SYCAMORE RD	SDCO	111	D2
SYCAMORE RD	VEN	88	D4
SYCAMORE ST	MCO	47	E3
SYCAMORE ST	MCO	48	A3
SYCAMORE CYN RD	SB	87	C4
SYCAMORE CYN RD	STB	174	E3
SYCAMORE CUTOFF	CLU	33	A2
SYCAMRE FLAT RD	MON	65	A2
SYCAMORE SL RD	COL	33	A2
SYCAMORE VLY RD	CC	M	B4
SYCAMORE VLY RD	CC	46	A1
SYDNOR AV	KER	80	D1
SYKES RD	INY	70	B3
SYLVAN AV	STA	47	D2
SYLVESTER RD	MCO	55	D1
SYMMES CREEK RD	INY	59	E3
T			
T ST	BKD	166	D4
T ST	STA	47	C4
TABL MTN OVRCRS	BUT	25	C4
TABLE BLUFF RD	HUM	15	D1
TABLE MTN BL	BUT	25	C4
TABLE MTN RD	FRCO	57	D2
TABLE MTN RD	RCO	100	C5
TABLE MTN TK TR	RCO	107	C1
TABLEROCK RD	SIS	4	C4
TABOOSE CK RD	INY	59	E1
TABOR AV	SOL	39	A3
TABOR AV E	FRFD	135	C3
TAECKER RD	IMP	109	B4
TAFT AV	ORA	194	B3
TAFT AV	ORCO	98	C3
TAFT AV	ORCO	T	D2
TAFT HWY	KER	78	C3
TAFT ST	TEH	24	E1
TAGE RD	SBD	101	D1
TAGLIO RD	MCO	47	D5
TAHOE ST	MCO	48	B4
TALBERT AV	ORCO	98	B4
TALBERT AV	ORCO	T	B3
TALBERT LN	SOL	39	B4
TALBOT ST	SDCO	V	A3
TALC CITY RD	INY	70	D1
TALMAGE RD	U	123	D4
TAMALPAIS AV	MAR	38	B5
TAMARACK AV	SDCO	106	B3
TAMARACK RD	SHA	19	C1
TAMARACK RD	TEH	19	C4
TAMARACK LK RD	TRI	12	B3
TAMARACK PK RD	SHA	13	C5
TAMPA AV	LA	178	B3
TAMPA AV	LACO	97	B1
TANABE RD	YUB	33	D1
TANATEA ST	RCO	107	C1
TANK FARM RD	KER	78	A4
TANK FARM RD	SLO	76	B4
TANNERY GLCH RD	TRI	11	D5
TAPADERO ST	CAL	41	A4
TAPIA LN	SBD	90	E2
TAPLIN RD	NAPA	29	C3
TAPO RD	VEN	89	A5
TAPO CANYON RD	VEN	89	A5
TARA AV	KER	69	B5
TAR CANYON RD	KIN	66	E4
TARKE RD	SUT	33	B2
TARPON DR	SIS	4	B3
TASSAJARA RD	ALA	46	B2
TASSAJARA RD	ALA	M	B5
TASSAJARA RD	MON	64	D2
TATE CREEK RD	SIS	13	A2
TAVERN RD	SDCO	107	B5
TAVERNETTI RD	MON	54	E5
TAVERNETTI RD	MON	55	A5
TAVERNOR RD	SAC	40	B2
TAYLOR AV	KER	78	B1
TAYLOR BLVD	CC	L	E3
TAYLOR BLVD	CC	M	A3
TAYLOR BLVD	CC	38	E5
TAYLOR LN	SIS	5	B4
TAYLOR RD	CC	39	C4
TAYLOR RD	STA	47	C3

STREET	CO.	PAGE	GRID
TAYLOR ST	SJ	151	E3
TAYLORSVL TRANS	PLU	20	D5
TEAFORD SDLE RD	MAD	49	E4
TEAGUE AV	FRCO	57	D2
TEAGUE AV	MON	65	B2
TEAL DR	MOD	7	A5
TEALE RD	KER	78	D4
TEALE RD	KER	79	A4
TEAPOT	TUL	68	C3
TECHNR RBSN RD	SIS	5	A4
TECOLOTE RD	SDCO	V	B3
TECOLOTE RD	SDCO	111	C1
TECOPA HOT SPGS	INY	73	A4
TED ELDER RD	SHA	13	D3
TED KIPF RD	IMP	109	C3
TED KIPF RD	IMP	110	A4
TEDOC RD	TEH	17	D4
TEFFT ST	SLO	76	C5
TEGAN RD	SAC	39	E2
TEGNER RD	MCO	47	D4
TEHACHAPI BLVD	KER	79	D4
TEHACHP-WLW SPG	KER	79	D5
TEHAMA AV	KIN	67	A4
TEHAMA AV	TEH	24	D1
TEHAMA ST	GLE	24	D4
TEHAMA & VNA RD	TEH	24	E1
TEJON RD	LACO	90	C4
TELEGRAPH AV	O	156	A4
TELEGRAPH AV	O	158	B2
TELEGRAPH AV	S	160	A2
TELEGRAPH RD	CAL	40	E5
TELEGRAPH RD	CAL	41	A5
TELEGRAPH RD	LACO	89	A4
TELEGRAPH RD	LACO	98	A2
TELEGRAPH RD	LACO	R	B4
TELEGRAPH RD	MPA	49	B3
TELEGRAPH RD	VEN	88	E4
TELEGRPH CYN RD	SDCO	V	D4
TELEGRPH CYN RD	SDCO	111	D2
TELEGRAPH CK RD	HUM	22	A1
TELEGRAPH MN RD	SBD	83	D3
TELEPHONE RD	SB	86	C1
TELEPHONE RD	VEN	88	B5
TELESCOPE PK RD	RD	10	C4
TELL BLVD	DN	1	D3
TEMESCAL CYN RD	RCO	99	A3
TEMPERANCE AV	FRCO	57	D2
TEMPERANCE AV	FRCO	57	D5
TEMPLE AV	LACO	R	D4
TEMPLE AV	LACO	S	E2
TEMPLE ST	LA	185	C1
TEMPLE ST	LA	186	A2
TEMPLE CITY BL	LACO	R	C3
TEMPLE CREEK	SJCO	47	C1
TEMPLE HILLS DR	LAG	201	C3
TEMPLETON RD	SLO	76	A2
TENAJA RD	RCO	99	B5
TENAJA TRUCK TR	RCO	99	B5
TENMILE RD	MEN	30	D4
TENMILE CTO	MEN	30	D4
TENNANT AV	SCL	P	E5
TENNANT AV	SCL	54	D1
TENNANT RD	SIS	4	E5
TENNANT RD	SIS	5	A5
TENNANT LAVA BD	MOD	5	D4
TENNANT LAVA BD	SIS	5	B5
TENNESSEE ST	SBD	99	C2
TENNESSEE ST	VAL	134	C4
TENNYSON RD	ALA	N	E1
TENNYSON RD	ALA	P	A1
TENNYSON RD	ALA	45	E2
TEPUSQUET RD	SB	86	B3
TEQUEPIS CYN RD	SB	87	A3
TERCEIRA RD	MCO	55	E2
TERMINAL IS FWY	LB	191	E1
TERMINAL IS FWY	LA	191	E1
TERMINAL IS FWY	LACO	S	D2
TERMINOUS RD	SAC	39	D4
TERMO GRASSHPPR	LAS	8	A5
TERMO GRASSHPPR	LAS	14	E5
TERRA BELLA ST	LACO	Q	C2
TERRACE	FRCO	58	A3
TERRACE RD	RCO	100	D4
TERRY MILL RD	SHA	13	A5
TERWER RIFFL RD	DN	10	A1
TERWILLIGER RD	RCO	107	C1
TESLA RD	ALA	M	D5
TESLA RD	ALA	P	D1
TESLA RD	ALA	46	C2
TESORO RD	SBD	90	E3
TEST STATION	MNO	43	C5
TEXAS AV	KER	79	E5
TEXAS AV	KER	80	A5
TEXAS RD	STA	47	C2
TEXAS ST	FRFD	135	C3
TEXAS ST	SD	214	B5
TEXAS ST	SD	216	A1
TEXAS ST	SDCO	V	B3
TEXAS ST	SDCO	111	D1
TEXAS ST N	SOL	M	A1
TEXAS ST N	SOL	38	E3
TEXAS HILL	MPA	48	E2
TEXAS HILL RD	YUB	26	A5
TEXAS SPGS RD	SHA	18	B2
THATCHER RD	SHA	19	C2
THATCHER MLL RD	SHA	19	C2
THATCHER RDG RD	BUT	25	D1
THE BRADSHAW TR	RCO	102	A5
THEDA ST	RCO	99	C4
THE INDIAN RD	MOD	8	B3
THEODORE ST	RCO	99	D3
THEODORIC RD	SBD	84	C4
THING RD	SDCO	112	C2

STREET	CO.	PAGE	GRID
THIRD ST	C	124	B5
THISSELL RD	SOL	39	B2
THOMAS	SON	31	E5
THOMAS	SON	37	E1
THOMAS RD	HUM	16	B5
THOMAS RD	KER	90	C1
THOMAS RD	MCO	55	C2
THOMAS RD	SBT	55	A3
THOMAS RD	SHA	18	B3
THOMAS RD	SHA	19	A1
THOMAS ST	KER	80	A4
THOME RD	YUB	33	D1
THOMES AV	TEH	24	D1
THOMPSON AV	FRCO	57	D3
THOMPSON AV	FRCO	57	D5
THOMPSON BLVD	VENT	175	B2
THOMPSON RD	IMP	109	A5
THOMPSON RD	LAS	14	B4
THOMPSON RD	MNO	43	B4
THOMPSON RD	SBD	81	C5
THOMPSON RD	SLO	76	C5
THOMPSON RD	SUT	33	C3
THOMPSON CYN AV	KER	79	C2
THOMPSON CYN RD	MON	65	B2
THOMSEN RD	SOL	39	C2
THORNBERRY RD	MAD	49	D4
THORNE AV	FRE	165	B4
THORNTON AV	ALA	P	A1
THORNTON AV	ALA	45	E3
THORNTON AV	ALA	46	A3
THORNTON RD	MCO	48	B4
THORNTON RD	SJCO	40	A4
THOUSND OAKS BL	LACO	96	E1
THOUSND OAKS BL	VEN	96	D1
THOUSND PLMS RD	RCO	100	E3
THOUSAND SPGS	SHA	13	D3
THREE CHOP RD	MEN	22	D5
THREE FLAGS HWY	KER	80	D1
THREE PINES CYN	KER	80	B1
THREE POINTS RD	LACO	89	B2
THREE SLASHS RD	IMP	110	C2
THRIFT RD	MCO	48	C5
THRUSH DR	SIS	4	C3
THUNDER	SDCO	106	B3
THUNDERBIRD BL	KER	80	C4
THUNDERBIRD RD	SBD	91	C3
THUNDER CYN RD	SLO	75	D2
TIBURON BLVD	MAR	L	B4
TIBURON BLVD	MAR	140	E3
TICE VALLEY BL	CC	L	E4
TICE VALLEY BL	CC	M	A4
TICINO ST	SB	86	B1
TIEDEMAN RD	STA	47	B2
TIERNEY RD	HUM	16	B3
TIERRA BUENA RD	SUT	33	C2
TIERRA DEL SOL	SDCO	112	E2
TIERRA RJADA RD	VEN	88	E5
TIERRA SANTA BL	SDCO	V	C2
TIERRA SANTA BL	SDCO	106	D5
TIFFANY RCH RD	SLO	76	B4
TIGER CREEK RD	SIS	11	D2
TILTON AV	SCL	P	D4
TILTON DR	LACO	89	E3
TIM BELL RD	STA	48	A2
TIMBER COVE RD	SON	37	A1
TIMBER CRATER	SHA	13	D3
TIMBUCTOO RD	YUB	34	A1
TIMM RD	SOL	39	A2
TIMMONS AV	KER	68	B5
TIMMONS RD	SIS	4	B5
TIM MULLEN RD	HUM	16	B1
TIMS RD	SB	86	E2
TIN BARN RD	SON	31	A5
TIN BARN RD	SON	37	A1
TINDALL RCH RD	MEN	31	B2
TINEMAHA RD	INY	59	E1
TIOGA PASS RD	MPA	42	E5
TIOGA PASS RD	MPA	43	A5
TIOGA PASS RD	MPA	50	A1
TIOGA PASS RD	MPA	63	D3
TIOGA PASS RD	MNO	43	A5
TIOGA PASS RD	TUO	42	E5
TIOGA PASS RD	TUO	50	A1
TIOGA PASS RD	TUO	63	A4
TIONESTA RD	MOD	5	E5
TIONESTA RD	MOD	6	A4
TIONESTA RD	SIS	5	D5
TIPPECANOE ST	SBD	99	C2
TIPTOP RD	MPA	49	C3
TISDALE	SUT	33	B3
TITLOW HILL RD	HUM	10	C5
TITSWORTH RD	IMP	109	C4
TIZON RD	RCO	107	B1
TOBACCO	SJCO	40	C5
TOBIN DR	VAL	134	B1
TODCO RD	KER	69	B5
TODD RD	SON	37	E2
TODD EYMANN RD	FRCO	58	D3
TODD VALLEY	PLA	34	D3
TOEWS AV	MCO	48	D4
TOFT DR	RCO	99	A4
TOKAVANA WY	PLA	34	D2
TOKAY COLONY RD	SJCO	40	B4
TOLAND LN	SOL	39	C4
TOLAND RD	VEN	88	C4
TOLAND PARK RD	VEN	88	C4
TOLL GATE WY	BUT	25	C2
TOLL HOUSE RD	FRCO	57	D2
TOLL HOUSE RD	FRCO	58	A2
TOMALES RD	SON	37	E3
TOMALES PETALMA	MAR	37	D3
TOM GREEN MN RD	SHA	18	A1
TOMKI RD	MEN	23	B5

STREET	CO.	PAGE	GRID
TOMPKNS HILL RD	HUM	15	E2
TOM SHAW RD	HUM	16	B2
TOM WELLS RD	LPAZ	104	A5
TONNER CYN RD	ORCO	U	A4
TONZI RD	AMA	40	D2
TOOME CAMP	TEH	24	A2
TOOMES RD	STA	47	C2
TOPA LN	VEN	88	C4
TOPANGA CYN BL	LA	177	B4
TOPANGA CYN BL	LACO	97	B1
TOPAZ LN	MNO	42	E1
TOPAZ RD	SBD	91	B3
TOPO RD	MON	65	B1
TOPO VALLEY RD	SBT	65	C1
TOPOCK DAVIS DM	MOH	95	E1
TOPPEN DORFF LN	HUM	15	D2
TORO CANYON RD	SB	87	D4
TORO CREEK RD	SLO	75	E2
TORO CREEK RD	SLO	76	A2
TORRANCE BLVD	LACO	97	D3
TORRANCE BLVD	LACO	S	B2
TORREY PINES RD	SD	211	B2
TORREY PINES RD	SDCO	V	A2
TORREY PINES RD	SDCO	106	C5
TORREY RD N	VEN	88	E4
TORREY RD S	VEN	88	E4
TOTH RD	HUM	22	A1
TOTTEN RD	SHA	13	E4
TOVEY AV	LACO	90	A3
TOWER RD	MCO	48	C4
TOWER RD	SLO	76	B1
TOWER LINE RD	KER	79	A4
TOWNE AV	LACO	U	C2
TOWNSEND RD	IMP	109	C5
TOWNSEND RD	SIS	4	C4
TOWNSEND ST	SBD	91	D1
TOWNSHIP AV	VEN	88	E5
TOWNSHIP AV	VEN	89	A5
TOWNSHIP RD	KLAM	5	B2
TOWNSHIP RD	YUB	34	A1
TOWNSHIP RD N	SUT	33	C2
TOWNSHIP RD S	SUT	33	C3
TOZER ST	MAD	57	A2
TRABUCO RD	ORCO	98	D4
TRABUCO RD	ORCO	T	E3
TRACTOR AV	FRCO	66	D2
TRACY AV	KER	78	A2
TRACY BLVD	SBD	100	D1
TRACY BLVD	SJCO	46	E1
TRAGEDY SPGS RD	AMA	35	D5
TRAIL CANYON RD	INY	72	A1
TRAILS END LN	RCO	107	C1
TRAILS END RD	SIS	4	C5
TRAILS END CAMP	SBD	96	B5
TRAMPA CYN RD	MON	64	C1
TRAMWAY RD	TEH	19	C4
TRANCAS ST	NAP	133	B2
TRANSMSN LNE RD	SBD	92	A4
TRASK AV	GGR	195	A2
TRASK AV	ORCO	T	B3
TRAUTWEIN RD	RCO	99	B3
TRAVIS BLVD	FRFD	135	B3
TRAVIS BLVD	SOL	L	E1
TRAVIS BLVD	SOL	M	A1
TRAYNHAM RD	COL	33	A3
TREAT BLVD	CC	M	A3
TREAT BLVD	CC	38	E5
TREDWAY	SJCO	40	A4
TREFOIL LN	SHA	18	D3
TREMONT RD	SOL	39	C1
TREMONT ST	AVLN	97	B5
TRENTHAM RD	IMP	109	B5
TRES CERITOS AV	RCO	99	D4
TRESTLE GLEN	MAR	45	B1
TRETHEWAY RD	SJCO	40	B4
TRIANGLE RD	MPA	49	B3
TRIANGLE RCH RD	MOD	6	D4
TRIANGLE RCH RD	STA	47	D2
TRIMBLE RD	SCL	P	B3
TRIMMER SPGS RD	FRCO	58	A3
TRIMMER SPGS RD	INY	58	C2
TRINDADE RD	MCO	48	B4
TRINIDAD SCNC DR	HUM	9	E4
TRINITY	TEH	18	D5
TRINITY AV	FRCO	56	E3
TRINITY AV	FRCO	57	A4
TRINITY RD	SON	38	B2
TRINITY ST	FRE	165	C4
TRINITY ST	RED	122	B1
TRINITY ALPS RD	TRI	11	D5
TRINITY DAM BL	TRI	11	D5
TRINITY DAM BL	TRI	17	D1
TRINITY MTN RD	SHA	18	A1
TRINITY PINE DR	TRI	17	B3
TRIPP FLATS RD	RIV	100	B5
TRIUNFO CYN RD	LACO	96	E1
TRONA RD	SBD	80	E2
TRONA RD	SBD	81	A1
TRONA AIRPRT RD	INY	71	B4
TRONA WLDRSE RD	INY	71	B4
TROPICANA AV	CLK	74	D3
TROPICANA AV	CLK	210	C4
TROWER	MPA	49	A3
TROWER AV	NAP	133	A1
TROY RD	SBD	92	C2
TRUCKEE AV	TEH	24	D1
TRUCKE ARPRT RD	NEV	27	D5
TRUCKE-TAHO ARP	NEV	35	E1
TRUESDALE RD	SLO	76	D1
TRUEX RD	BUT	25	D3
TRUMAN RD	KER	89	D1
TRUMAN MDWS RD	MNO	44	C5
TRUMBULL RD	LAS	21	D2

STREET	CO.	PAGE	GRID
TRUXTUN AV	BKD	166	B3
TRUXTUN AV	KER	78	D3
TSCHIRKY RD	SIS	5	D2
TUBBS RD	SOL	39	A2
TUCACOTA HLS RD	RCO	99	E5
TUCKER RD	KER	79	C4
TUCKER RD	LAS	21	D5
TUCKER CYN RD	SLO	76	D1
TUCSON AV	KIN	67	D4
TUDOR RD	SUT	33	C3
TUGG WY	CAL	41	A5
TUJUNGA AV	LACO	Q	D3
TUJUNGA CYN BL	LACO	Q	E1
TULARE AV	KER	77	E2
TULARE AV	FRCO	57	C3
TULARE AV	TUL	68	B1
TULARE ST	FRE	165	D4
TULAROSA RD	SB	86	C3
TULE LN	CC	39	C5
TULE LN	GLE	24	E4
TULE RD	COL	33	A3
TULE RD	YOL	39	D2
TULE CYN TK TR	RCO	107	C1
TULE CREEK RD	TRI	17	B2
TULEDAD RD	LAS	8	D5
TULE PEAK RD	RCO	107	B1
TULE SPRING RD	INY	72	A2
TULE SPGS TK TR	SDCO	107	B4
TULIP AV	STA	47	C4
TULLOCH RD	MCO	48	B1
TULLOCH RD	TUO	41	B5
TULLY RD	MDO	162	A2
TULLY RD	SJCO	40	C4
TULLY RD	SCL	P	C3
TULLY RD	SCL	46	B4
TULLY RD	STA	47	C2
TULLY CREEK RD	HUM	10	C3
TUMBLEWEED RD	LACO	90	C4
TUNA CANYON RD	LACO	97	B2
TUNGSTEN RD	MNO	51	D3
TUNGSTEN CTY RD	INY	51	C4
TUNITAS CK RD	SMCO	N	C3
TUNITAS CK RD	SMCO	45	C4
TUNNEL RD	B	156	C4
TUOLUMNE AV	FRCO	56	D4
TUOLUMNE BLVD	MDO	162	A4
TUOLUMNE RD	STA	47	C3
TUOLUMNE ST	SOL	L	D2
TUOLUMNE ST	VAL	134	D2
TUPMAN RD	KER	78	B3
TURK ST	SF	142	B3
TURK ST	SF	143	A4
TURKEY AV	BUT	25	D5
TURKEY FLAT RD	MON	66	D4
TURKEY HILL RD	KLAM	5	E2
TURLOCK AV	SCL	P	E5
TURLOCK AV	SCL	54	D1
TURLOCK RD	MCO	48	B3
TURNBULL CYN RD	LACO	98	B2
TURNBULL CYN RD	LACO	R	D4
TURNELL RD	TEH	18	C4
TURNER AV	BUT	33	C1
TURNER AV	MCO	47	D4
TURNER AV	SBD	U	E2
TURNER DR	TUL	68	B2
TURNER RD	AMA	40	E2
TURNER RD	MCO	47	D4
TURNER RD	SJCO	39	E4
TURNER RD	STA	47	D3
TURNER ISLND RD	MCO	56	A1
TURQUOISE ST	SD	212	A1
TURQUOISE ST	SDCO	V	A2
TURQUOISE ST	SDCO	106	C5
TURRI RD	SLO	75	E3
TURRI RD	SLO	76	A3
TURTLE MTN RD	SBD	95	C4
TURTLE VLY RD	SBD	91	C2
TUSCAN SPGS RD	TEH	18	D4
TUSSING RCH RD	SBD	91	C4
TUSTIN AV	CM	199	C3
TUSTIN AV	ORA	194	D2
TUSTIN AV	ORA	196	E1
TUSTIN AV	ORCO	98	C4
TUSTIN AV	SA	196	E2
TUSTIN AV	ORCO	T	D2
TU SU LN	INY	51	D4
TUTTLECREEK RD	INY	60	A4
TUTTLETOWN RD	TUO	41	C5
TUXEDO AV N	S	160	C3
TUXFORD ST	LACO	Q	D2
TWEEDY BLVD	LACO	R	A5
TWENTIETH ST	C	124	E5
TWENTY-EIGHT MI	STA	47	E1
TWNTY MULE TEAM	INY	72	A1
TWNTY MULE TEAM	KER	80	C4
TWNTYNINE PALMS	SBD	100	E1
TWNTYNINE PALMS	SBD	101	D1
TWENTY-SIX MILE	STA	47	D1
TWILIGHT CT	TUO	163	D4
TWILIGHT LN	TUO	163	D3
TWIN RD S	MNO	43	A3
TWIN CITIES RD	SAC	39	E3
TWIN CITIES RD	SAC	40	A3
TWIN LAKES RD	MNO	43	B3
TWIN LAKES RD	TRI	12	B3
TWIN LKS CMPST	ALP	35	E5
TWIN OAKES RD	KER	79	D3
TWIN OAKS VLY	SDCO	106	C3
TWIN PEAKS RD	SDCO	106	D4
TWIN PINES RD	RCO	100	A3
TWIN VALLEY RD	LAK	31	E2
TWIN VIEW BLVD	SHA	18	C2
TWISSELMAN RD	KER	67	B5

STREET	CO.	PAGE	GRID
TWIST RD	TUO	41	C5
TWIST RD	TUO	48	C1
TWITCHLL ISL RD	SAC	M	D2
TWITCHLL ISL RD	SAC	39	C4
TWO MILE RD	COL	32	D1
TWO MILE RD	SBD	101	B1
TYLER AV	LACO	R	C4
TYLER RD	TEH	18	D5
TYLER ST	MONT	167	E3
TYLER ST	RCO	99	A3
TYLER ST	RCO	101	B4
TYLER ST	SAL	171	B2
TYLER ST	SDCO	V	D3
TYLER ST	SDCO	111	D1
TYLER FOOT CRSG	NEV	26	B5
TYLER GULCH RD	SIS	3	D4
TYLER ISLAND RD	SAC	M	E2
TYLER ISLAND RD	SAC	39	D4

U

STREET	CO.	PAGE	GRID
U ST	FRE	165	E3
UBEHEBE RD	INY	60	E4
UGO ST	MCO	48	A4
UKIAH RD	MEN	31	B2
UKIAH BOONVILLE	MEN	30	E3
UKIAH BOONVILLE	MEN	31	A3
UKONOM LKOUT RD	SIS	2	E5
ULLREY AV	SJCO	47	C1
ULRIC ST	SD	213	D3
ULRIC ST	SDCO	V	B3
ULRIC ST	SDCO	111	C1
UNDERPASS RD	MEN	22	E4
UNDERSTOCK DR	BUT	25	C2
UNDERWOOD LN	INY	51	D4
UNDERWOOD RD	MON	54	C5
UNDERWD MTN RD	TRI	16	E1
UNDINE RD	SJCO	46	E1
UNION AV	BKD	166	E3
UNION AV	KER	166	E5
UNION AV	FRFD	135	C4
UNION AV	SB	86	C1
UNION AV	SCL	P	B4
UNION AV	SCL	46	A4
UNION AV	SOL	38	E3
UNION RD	KER	78	B4
UNION RD	MAN	161	A3
UNION RD	SBT	54	E3
UNION RD	SJCO	47	B1
UNION RD	SLO	76	B1
UNION ST	EUR	121	C2
UNION ST	HUM	15	E1
UNION CITY BLVD	ALA	N	E1
UNION CITY BLVD	ALA	P	A1
UNION CITY BLVD	ALA	45	E3
UNION HILL RD	TRI	17	D1
UNION RIDGE RD	ED	34	E5
UNION SCHOOL RD	SHA	18	C1
UNION SUGAR AV	SB	86	B3
UNITED ST	KER	80	A5
UNIVERSITY AV	ALA	L	D4
UNIVERSITY AV	KER	78	E2
UNIVERSITY AV	PA	147	B2
UNIVERSITY AV	RIV	205	C3
UNIVERSITY AV	RCO	99	B2
UNIVERSITY AV	SAL	171	A4
UNIVERSITY AV	SD	214	D5
UNIVERSITY AV	SD	215	D1
UNIVERSITY AV	SDCO	V	B3
UNIVERSITY AV	SDCO	111	D1
UNIVERSITY AV	SMCO	N	E2
UNIVERSITY DR	IRV	200	B2
UNIVERSITY DR	ORCO	98	C4
UNIVERSITY DR	ORCO	T	D4
UPAS ST	SD	216	A1
UPHAM RD	BUT	25	E5
UPHILL RD	SBD	101	A1
UPJOHN RD W	KER	80	D1
UPLAND RD	VEN	88	C5
UPPER E TER	AVLN	97	B5
UPPER BEAR RIV	HUM	15	D3
UPPR COUGR FIRE	SIS	4	D5
UPPR COUGR FIRE	SIS	12	D1
UPPER DIVISN CK	INY	59	E2
UPPER DORRAY RD	CAL	41	A2
UPPER FALL RD	SIS	13	A2
UPPER LK CTY RD	MOD	7	D5
UPR MAD RIV RD	TRI	17	A4
UPPER PALMRO RD	BUT	25	D5
UPPER SHOTGN RD	SHA	12	C4
UPPER S FORK RD	TRI	16	E2
UPPR SUMMRS MDW	MNO	43	B3
UPPER TOBY RCH	HUM	16	C5
UPPER WILLOW CK	SIS	4	C3
USAL RD	MEN	22	B2
USFS CAMP RD	TRI	17	A1
USONA RD	MPA	49	C4
USTICK RD	STA	47	C3
UTAH DR	INY	70	E1
UTAH TR	SBD	101	C1
UTAH MINE RD	BUT	25	D2
UTICA AV	KIN	67	D4
UTICA PWRHSE RD	CAL	41	C4
UVAS RD	SCL	54	C1
UXMAL	BAJA	112	B4

V

STREET	CO.	PAGE	GRID
V ST	MER	170	A4
VADNEY AV	TEH	24	E2
VAIL	SJCO	39	E3
VAIL RD	IMP	109	A3
VAIRA RANCH RD	AMA	40	D2

STREET	CO.	PAGE	GRID
VALDOR RD	TRI	17	C1
VALENCIA AV	LACO	89	B4
VALENCIA AV	ORCO	98	C3
VALENCIA AV	ORCO	T	D1
VALENCIA BLVD	TUL	58	C5
VALENCIA BLVD	TUL	68	C1
VALENCIA RD	SCR	54	B2
VALENSIN RD	SAC	40	A3
VALENTINE AV	FRCO	57	C4
VALENTINE AV	FRCO	67	C1
VALERIA AV	FRCO	56	B2
VALK RD	STA	47	E2
VALLECITO ST	SHA	18	C1
VALLECITOS RD	ALA	P	C1
VALLECITOS RD	ALA	46	B2
VALLE VISTA AV	VAL	134	C3
VALLE VISTA RD	SBD	101	B1
VALLEY AV	ALA	M	B5
VALLEY AV	ALA	P	B1
VALLEY AV	ALA	46	B2
VALLEY BLVD	LACO	97	E2
VALLEY BLVD	LACO	98	B2
VALLEY BLVD	LACO	R	C3
VALLEY BLVD	SBD	99	A2
VALLEY PKWY	SDCO	106	D3
VALLEY RD	KER	80	C3
VALLEY RD	MEN	23	A5
VALLEY RD	PLA	34	A3
VALLEY RD E	SB	87	D4
VALLEY RD W	MOD	8	B3
VALLEY CTR RD	SBD	92	B1
VALLEY CTR RD	SDCO	106	E3
VALLEY CIR BL	LACO	97	B1
VALLEY CTO RD	LAS	14	B3
VALLEY FORD RD	SON	37	D3
VLY FRD/FRNKLN-			
-MARSH RD	MAR	37	D3
VLY FRD/FRNKLN-			
-SCHOOL RD	MAR	37	D3
VALLEY HOME RD	STA	47	D1
VALLEY SAGE RD	LACO	89	D4
VALLEY VIEW DR	CAL	41	C3
VALLEY VIEW DR	SBD	102	C1
VALLEY VIEW RD	JKSN	3	E1
VALLEY VIEW RD	SBD	91	C1
VALLEY VIEW ST	ORCO	98	B3
VALLEY VIEW ST	ORCO	T	B2
VALLEY VW LKOUT	TEH	24	A2
VALLEY VISTA BL	LA	178	E5
VALLEY WELLS RD	INY	71	B4
VALLEY WELLS RD	SBD	81	C5
VALLEY WEST RD	KER	78	A4
VALLOMBROSA AV	BUT	25	B3
VALLOMBROSA AV	BUT	124	D4
VALLOMBROSA AV	C	124	D4
VALOS RD	KER	78	E5
VALPARAISO AV	SMCO	N	D2
VALPARAISO AV	SCL	45	D4
VALPREDO AV	KER	78	D5
VAL VERDE	PLA	34	B4
VALYERMO	LACO	90	C4
VAN ALDEN AV	LA	178	C4
VAN ALLEN	SJCO	40	C5
VAN ALLEN	SJCO	47	C1
VAN ARSDALE RD	MEN	23	B5
VAN BRMMR LKOUT	SIS	5	B4
VAN BUREN BLVD	RCO	99	A2
VAN BUREN ST	MONT	167	E4
VAN BUREN ST	RCO	101	A4
VANCE AV	HUM	15	E1
VAN CLIFF	MCO	47	E5
VANDEGRIFT BLVD	SDCO	106	B2
VANDEGRIFT RD	SDCO	106	B2
VANDEN RD	SOL	39	A3
VANDENBERG RD	SB	86	B2
VANDER LINDN RD	IMP	112	C3
VANDER POEL RD	IMP	112	A3
VANDER VEER RD	RCO	101	C5
VAN DOLLEN RD	SLO	66	B5
VAN DUSEN CYN	SBD	92	A5
VAN DUZEN RD	TRI	16	E4
VAN DUZEN RD E	TRI	16	E3
VAN GORDN CK RD	SLO	75	C1
VAN LOON CUTOFF	MNO	51	D2
VAN NESS AV	FRE	165	D3
VAN NESS AV	FRCO	57	C3
VAN NESS AV	LACO	Q	D5
VAN NESS AV	SF	142	C2
VAN NESS AV	SF	143	B2
VAN NESS AV	SFCO	L	B4
VAN NESS AV	SFCO	45	C1
VAN NESS AV S	SF	142	C5
VAN NESS RD	TRI	12	A5
VAN NUYS BLVD	LACO	89	C5
VAN NUYS BLVD	LACO	97	C1
VAN NUYS BLVD	LACO	Q	C1
VANOWEN ST	LA	177	A2
VANOWEN ST	LA	178	B2
VAN SICKLE RD	SOL	39	A4
VANS RANCH RD	SBD	92	E5
VARGAS RD	ALA	P	B1
VARGAS RD	ALA	46	B3
VARNER RD	RCO	100	D3
VARNI RD	SCR	54	B2
VASCO RD	ALA	M	D5
VASCO RD	ALA	46	C2
VASCO RD	CC	M	D4
VASCO RD	CC	46	C1
VASQUEZ CYN RD	LACO	89	C4
VASQUEZ CK RD	SBT	55	D4
VASSAR AV	MCO	48	C5
VASSAR ST	RENO	130	C4
VAUGHN AV	MCO	48	B4

STREET	CO.	PAGE	GRID
VAUGHN RD	RCO	108	E1
VAUGHN RD	SOL	39	B2
VAWTER RD	COL	32	E3
VAWTER RANCH RD	RCO	99	E5
VEDDER RD	SHA	13	C5
VEE BEE ST	RCO	100	E3
VENCILL RD	IMP	112	C3
VENDEL RD	IMP	108	E4
VENICE BLVD	LA	183	D3
VENICE BLVD	LA	184	D3
VENICE BLVD	LA	185	C3
VENICE BLVD	LA	187	C2
VENICE BLVD	LACO	97	C2
VENICE BLVD	LACO	Q	C4
VENTURA AV	FRCO	57	D3
VENTURA AV	MAD	56	D1
VENTURA AV	VEN	88	A5
VENTURA AV	VEN	175	A2
VENTURA BLVD	LA	177	C4
VENTURA BLVD	LA	178	A4
VENTURA BLVD	LACO	97	C1
VENTURA FRWY	BUR	179	A5
VENTURA FRWY	LA	177	C4
VENTURA FRWY	LA	178	D4
VENTURA FRWY	LA	179	C5
VENTURA FRWY	LACO	97	A1
VENTURA FRWY	VEN	175	E3
VENTURA FRWY	VEN	88	A5
VENTURA FRWY	VEN	96	C1
VENTURA RD	MCO	48	B5
VENTURA RD	OXN	176	A4
VENTURA RD	VEN	96	B1
VENTURA ST	FRE	165	D5
VENTURA ST	VEN	88	D4
VENTURE VLY RD	SDCO	107	D3
VENZKE RD	SHA	18	D3
VERA AV	KER	80	D1
VERANO AV	SON	132	C3
VERBENA AV	C	124	E2
VERBENA AV	SBD	91	B3
VERBENA DR	RCO	100	D2
VERDE AV	MCO	47	D4
VERDEMNT RCH RD	SBD	99	B1
VERDE SCHOOL RD	IMP	112	C3
VERDI PEAK RD	SIE	27	E4
VERDUGO AV	BUR	179	C4
VERDUGO AV	LACO	Q	D3
VERDUGO BLVD	LACO	R	A2
VERDUGO LN	KER	78	C2
VERDUGO RD	LACO	R	A3
VERMICULITE MN	SBD	100	E2
VERMONT AV	LA	182	C5
VERMONT AV	LA	185	B4
VERMONT AV	LACO	97	D3
VERMONT AV	LACO	S	C2
VERMONT CYN RD	LA	182	B2
VERNON AV	LACO	97	D2
VERNON AV	LACO	Q	E4
VERNON AV	LACO	U	A1
VERNON RD	SUT	33	D4
VESTA ST	SDCO	111	D1
VESTA ST	SDCO	V	C4
VESTAL RD	TEH	18	A4
VETERAN AV	LACO	Q	C5
VETERANS HALL	TRI	10	E5
VIA CAPRI	SD	211	A3
VIA DE LA VALLE	SDCO	106	C4
VIA DEL REY	MONT	167	D4
VIA DEL REY	MON	53	E3
VIADUCT BLVD	SBDO	207	B2
VIA GAYUBA	MONT	167	D4
VIA PARAISO	MONT	167	D4
VIA RANCHO PKWY	SDCO	106	D4
VIA SECO ST	SBD	92	A3
VIA VERDE	LACO	U	A2
VICHY SPGS RD	MEN	31	B2
VICKREY LN	SOL	38	E2
VICKY LN	DGL	36	C3
VICTOR AV	SHA	18	C2
VICTOR RD	SJCO	40	B4
VICTOR ST	KER	80	D1
VICTORIA AV	RCO	99	A3
VICTORIA AV	RIV	205	C4
VICTORIA CT	KER	79	C4
VICTORIA DR	SDCO	107	B5
VICTORIA DR	SHA	18	B2
VICTORIA ST	LACO	97	E3
VICTORIA ST	LACO	S	C1
VICTORIA ST	ORCO	T	C4
VICTORIA ST	CM	199	B2
VICTORIA ST	STB	174	B4
VICTORY AV	STA	47	D1
VICTORY BLVD	BUR	179	B2
VICTORY BLVD	LA	177	C2
VICTORY BLVD	LA	178	B3
VICTORY BLVD	LACO	97	D1
VICTORY BLVD	LACO	Q	C2
VICTORY HWY	CC	M	C3
VICTORY HWY	CC	39	C5
VICTORY HWY	SAC	M	E1
VICTORY PL	BUR	179	D2
VICTORY PL	LACO	Q	D2
VICTORY RD	SJCO	47	D1
VIEJAS GRADE	SDCO	107	B5
VIERRA RD	YUB	26	A5
VIEUDELOU AV	AVLN	104	B4
VIEW DR	TUL	58	B4
VIEW LAND RD	LAS	21	D3
VILAS RD	BUT	25	C2
VILLA AV	SR	139	D3
VILLA RD	IMP	109	B5
VILLA ST	SAL	171	B3
VILLA CREEK RD	SLO	75	D2

STREET	CO.	PAGE	GRID
VILLAGE DR	AMA	40	D3
VILLAGE RD	SDCO	106	C5
VLLA MANUCHA RD	STA	47	C4
VILLA PARK RD	ORCO	T	E2
VINA RD	TEH	24	E2
VINCENT AV	LACO	R	E3
VINCENT RD	MCO	47	E3
VINCENT RD	MCO	48	A3
VINCENT RD	STA	47	E3
VINCENT RD	STA	48	A3
VINE AV	MCO	48	B4
VINE AV	SJCO	47	D1
VINE ST	LA	181	D5
VINE ST	LACO	Q	D3
VINE ST	SDCO	V	E2
VINE ST	SDCO	107	A5
VINE ST	SJ	152	B4
VINE WY	KER	79	C1
VINE HILL RD	SCR	P	B5
VINE HILL RD	SCR	54	A1
VINELAND AV	FRCO	57	A4
VINELAND AV	LACO	97	D1
VINELAND AV	LACO	Q	D2
VINELAND RD	KER	78	E4
VINEWOOD AV	MCO	47	E4
VINEWOOD AV	MCO	48	A4
VINEYARD AV	ALA	M	C5
VINEYARD AV	ALA	P	C1
VINEYARD AV	ALA	46	B2
VINEYARD AV	OXN	176	B1
VINEYARD AV	SBD	98	E2
VINEYARD AV	SBD	U	E3
VINEYARD AV	VEN	176	C1
VINEYARD DR	SLO	75	E1
VINEYARD DR	SLO	76	A1
VINEYARD RD	PLA	34	A5
VINEYARD RD	SJCO	40	A2
VINEYARD RD	STA	47	B3
VINEYARD RD	YUB	34	A2
VINEYARD WY	MCO	56	B1
VINEYARD CYN RD	MON	66	B4
VINNUM RD	HUM	16	B4
VINTON GULCH RD	BUT	25	D3
VINTON LOYALTON	PLU	27	D3
VIOLA AV	TEH	24	D2
VIOLA MINERAL	TEH	19	C3
VIRGIL AV	LACO	Q	E4
VIRGINIA	SBD	92	D5
VIRGINIA AV	KIN	67	E4
VIRGINIA AV	MDO	162	B2
VIRGINIA RD	LACO	R	B3
VIRGINIA RD	STA	47	E2
VIRGINIA RD	STA	48	A2
VIRGINIA RD	YUB	33	E1
VIRGINIA ST	RCO	99	D3
VIRGINIA ST N	RENO	130	B2
VIRGINIA ST S	RENO	130	B3
VIRGINIA LK RD	MNO	43	B4
VIRGINIATOWN RD	PLA	34	B3
VISALIA RD	FRCO	58	D4
VISALIA RD	TUL	68	C1
VISTA AV	MCO	48	D5
VISTA LN	LAS	21	B4
VISTA RD	SBD	91	B2
VISTA WY	SDCO	106	B3
VISTA CHINO	PMSP	206	D2
VISTA CHINO	RCO	100	D3
VISTA DEL MAR	LACO	97	C2
VISTA DL MAR BL	LACO	Q	C5
VISTA DEL VALLE	LA	182	A1
VISTA DE ORO	RCO	100	E3
VISTA ENCINA AV	MDO	162	D3
VISTA GRANDE DR	KER	79	D1
VISTA MINE RD	IMP	110	A4
VIVIAN RD	STA	47	C3
VLASNIK RD	KER	77	E2
VOGEL RD	IMP	111	E3
VOGEL RD	KER	79	D5
VOLCANO CIR	BUT	25	B3
VOLCANO PIONEER	AMA	41	A2
VOLCANOVILLE RD	ED	34	E3
VOLLEY RD	PLA	34	C3
VOLTA RD	MCO	55	D1
VOLTAIRE ST	SDCO	V	A3
VOLTAIRE ST	SDCO	111	C1
VON GLAHN	SJCO	47	C1
VOORHESS RD	MCO	48	D5
VORDEN RD	SAC	M	E1
VORDEN RD	SAC	39	D3
VOTAW RD	AMA	40	E1
VULCAN MINE RD	SBD	84	A5
VULCAN MINE RD	SBD	94	A1

W

STREET	CO.	PAGE	GRID
WAALEW RD	SBD	91	C3
W A BARR RD	SIS	12	C2
WABASH AV	EUR	121	B2
WABASH AV	SBD	99	D2
WABASH BLVD	SD	216	C5
WABASH BLVD	SDCO	111	D1
WABASH BLVD	SDCO	V	C4
WACHTEL WY	SAC	34	B5
WACKERMAN RD	TEH	24	C2
WADDELL ST	TUL	68	C2
WADDINGTON RD	HUM	15	D2
WADE AV	MCO	48	E5
WADLEIGH RD	COL	32	D1
WAGNER	SJCO	47	C1
WAGNER AV	COL	32	E3
WAGON RD	BUT	25	C2
WAGON WHEEL	SBD	101	A1
WAGSTAFF RD	BUT	25	C3

STREET	CO.	PAGE	GRID
WAHL RD	IMP	112	A3
WAINWRIGHT RD	MCO	47	D4
WAKEFIELD	FRCO	58	A4
WALCH AV	TEH	24	E2
WALDO RD	YUB	34	A2
WALERGA	PLA	33	E5
WALGROVE AV	LA	187	C1
WALKER DR	SHA	13	D4
WALKER PL	MNO	51	C1
WALKER RD	DN	1	E3
WALKER RD	IMP	108	E3
WALKER RD	LAS	14	C3
WALKER RD	MEN	23	A5
WALKER RD	MEN	31	A1
WALKER RD	NAPA	32	B5
WALKER RD	PLU	20	B4
WALKER RD	SBD	92	C5
WALKER RD	SIS	3	D3
WALKER RD	SON	37	E3
WALKER ST	GLE	24	D3
WALKER ST	ORCO	T	B2
WALKER WY	IMP	110	B5
WALKER BASIN RD	KER	79	C3
WALKER CREEK RD	INY	70	B2
WALKER CREEK RD	SIS	3	B3
WALKR LANDNG RD	SAC	M	E1
WALKR LANDNG RD	SAC	39	D3
WALKER MINE RD	PLU	26	E1
WALKER MINE RD	SHA	18	B1
WALKER PLAINS	BUT	25	E2
WALKUP RD	COL	32	B1
WALL RD	SJCO	40	C4
WALLACE RD	KER	78	C1
WALLACE RD	SON	38	A2
WALLACE CK RD	SON	37	D1
WALLEN RD	TEH	18	D4
WALLER ST	SF	141	E4
WALLIS RD	STA	48	A3
WALLY HILL RD	CAL	41	B4
WALMORT RD	SAC	40	A2
WALNUT AV	CC	M	A3
WALNUT AV	CC	38	E5
WALNUT AV	FRE	165	C5
WALNUT AV	FRCO	57	C4
WALNUT AV	LACO	Q	E2
WALNUT AV	MCO	48	A4
WALNUT AV	ORCO	T	E3
WALNUT AV	STA	47	C3
WALNUT AV	STA	47	D1
WALNUT AV	TUL	68	B1
WALNUT AV	U	123	B3
WALNUT AV	YUB	33	D2
WALNUT BLVD	CC	M	A4
WALNUT BLVD	CC	M	D4
WALNUT BLVD	CC	39	C5
WALNUT BLVD	CC	46	C1
WALNUT DR	COL	32	D2
WALNUT DR	HUM	15	E1
WALNUT DR	NAPA	29	D4
WALNUT DR	SJCO	40	C4
WALNUT LN	GLE	25	A4
WALNUT RD	TEH	24	D2
WALNUT ST	ANA	193	A4
WALNUT ST	C	124	A5
WALNUT ST	ORCO	T	C1
WALNUT ST	PAS	190	B3
WALNUT ST	TEH	18	C5
WALNUT GROVE AV	LACO	R	C4
WALNUT GROVE RD	SJCO	39	E3
WALSER RD	KER	79	C2
WALTERS RD	LAS	14	C3
WALTERS RD	SOL	39	A3
WALTERS CAMP RD	IMP	110	C2
WALTERS MINE RD	BUT	26	B3
WALTHERS RD	SOL	M	A1
WALTON AV	SUT	33	C2
WALTON AV	SUT	125	A5
WALTZ RD	PLA	33	E3
WAMBLE RD	STA	47	E1
WAMBLE RD	STA	48	A1
WANGENHEIM RD	STA	47	C4
WARD AV	STA	47	B4
WARD RD	HUM	10	B5
WARD RD	LACO	89	E4
WARD RD	MCO	55	E1
WARD CREEK RD	PLU	26	E1
WARD LAKE RD	LAS	21	B3
WARDLOW RD	LACO	98	A3
WARDLOW RD	LACO	S	E2
WARDLOW RD	LACO	T	A2
WARDROBE AV	MCO	48	B4
WARDS FERRY RD	TUO	41	D5
WARDS FERRY RD	TUO	48	D1
WARE RD	COL	32	E2
WARE RD	IMP	112	B4
WARING RD	SDCO	V	C3
WARING RD	SDCO	111	D1
WARING RD	STA	47	E3
WARM SPGS BLVD	ALA	P	B2
WARM SPGS BLVD	ALA	46	B3
WARM SPRINGS RD	INY	51	D4
WARM SPRINGS RD	SON	38	B2
WARNER AV	FTNV	197	B2
WARNER AV	ORCO	98	B4
WARNER AV	ORCO	T	C3
WARNER AV	ORCO	T	E3
WARNER AV	SA	197	C1
WARNER AV	SA	198	B2
WARNER AV	TUS	198	D1
WARNER RD S	LAS	8	C3
WARNER RD W	MOD	8	C1
WARNER ST	C	124	A3
WARNERVILLE RD	STA	47	E2
WARNERVILLE RD	STA	48	A2
WARREGARD RD	CAL	41	B3
WARREN AV	RCO	99	C4
WARREN AV	TEH	18	C4
WARREN FRWY	ALA	45	D1
WARREN FRWY	O	156	E5
WARREN RD	CAL	40	D4
WARREN RD	RCO	99	D5
WARREN RD	RCO	99	D4
WARREN VISTA AV	SBD	100	E1
WASCO WY	KER	78	A3
WASCO POND RD	KER	68	B5
WASHBURN WY	KLAM	5	B1
WASHINGTON AV	RCO	99	C5
WASHINGTON AV	SBD	99	B2
WASHINGTON AV	SDCO	V	E3
WASHINGTON AV	SDCO	106	E5
WASHINGTON AV	SA	195	D3
WASHINGTON AV	SA	196	B3
WASHINGTON BLVD	ALA	P	B2
WASHINGTON BLVD	CUL	183	D5
WASHINGTON BLVD	CUL	187	C3
WASHINGTON BLVD	CUL	188	A2
WASHINGTON BLVD	DN	1	D4
WASHINGTON BLVD	LA	184	D4
WASHINGTON BLVD	LA	185	C4
WASHINGTON BLVD	LA	186	B5
WASHINGTON BLVD	LA	187	B3
WASHINGTON BLVD	LACO	97	E2
WASHINGTON BLVD	LACO	98	A2
WASHINGTON BLVD	LACO	R	B2
WASHINGTON BLVD	LACO	R	A4
WASHINGTON BLVD	MCO	47	E4
WASHINGTON BLVD	MCO	48	A4
WASHINGTON BLVD	PAS	190	A2
WASHINGTON RD	MCO	56	B1
WASHINGTON RD	NEV	26	D5
WASHINGTON RD	SBD	92	A3
WASHINGTON RD	STA	47	D3
WASHINGTON ST	SB	87	C1
WASHINGTON ST	FRCO	66	D3
WASHINGTON ST	MONT	167	E4
WASHINGTON ST	RCO	99	B3
WASHINGTON ST	RCO	100	E4
WASHINGTON ST	RIV	99	D5
WASHINGTON ST	SD	213	D5
WASHINGTON ST	SD	215	C1
WASHINGTON ST	SDCO	V	B3
WASHINGTON ST	SDCO	111	C1
WASHINGTON ST	SCLR	151	C3
WASHINGTON ST	SNRA	163	B2
WASHINGTON ST	S	160	C5
WASHINGTON ST	TUO	163	B2
WASHINGTON ST E	SON	L	A1
WASHINGTON ST E	SON	38	A3
WASHOE	FRCO	56	C4
WASHOE AV	FRCO	56	C3
WASIOJA RD	SB	77	C5
WASIOJA RD	SB	87	B1
WATER LN	SMCO	N	C4
WATER ST	AMA	40	E2
WATER ST	SC	169	D2
WATER ST	SCR	54	A2
WATER CANYON RD	KER	80	B3
WATER CANYON RD	KER	79	C5
WATERFRONT RD	CC	L	E3
WATERFRONT RD	CC	M	A3
WATERFRONT RD	CC	154	E1
WATERLOO LN	DGL	36	C3
WATERLOO RD	SJCO	40	B5
WATERMAN AV	SBD	99	C2
WATERMAN AV	SBDO	207	E3
WATERMAN RD	AMA	40	D2
WATERMAN RD	SAC	40	B2
WATERS RD	VEN	88	D5
WATERS END RD	SLO	76	C4
WATERTOWN RD	CAL	40	E3
WATER TROUGH RD	SON	37	D2
WATKINS DR	RCO	99	B2
WATKINS RD	TEH	24	D2
WATKINS TR	KER	79	C5
WATKINSON RD	SJCO	40	B3
WATMAUGH RD	SON	L	B1
WATSON RD	MEN	31	B2
WATSONVILLE RD	SCL	P	D5
WATSONVILLE RD	SCL	54	C1
WATT AV	SAC	34	A5
WATT AV	SAC	40	A1
WATT LN	BUT	25	C5
WATTENBURG RD	MEN	23	A3
WATTRSN TROUGHS	MNO	51	B2
WATTS AV	SUT	33	D3
WATTS DR	KER	79	C3
WATTS VALLEY RD	FRCO	57	E3
WATTS VALLEY RD	FRCO	58	A3
WAUCOBA SALINE	INY	60	C2
WAUKEENA RD	YOL	39	D2
WAVERLY	SBD	91	D1
WAVERLY	SJCO	40	D5
WAWONA RD	MPA	49	D2
WAY RD	MCO	55	E1
WAYBUR RD	SUT	33	C3
WEAVER CREEK E	TRI	17	D1
WEAVER CT	KER	79	D3
WEAVER RD	IMP	109	A4
WEAVER HILLS DR	RCO	107	A1
WEAVERVLL SCOTT	TRI	12	C1
WEAVERVLL SCOTT	TRI	11	D5
WEAVERVLL SCOTT	TRI	11	E3
WEBB RD	IMP	109	C5
WEBB RD	SHA	18	D3
WEBB RD	SUT	33	C4
WEBER AV	FRE	165	A2
WEBER AV	S	160	C5
WEBER RD	SOL	39	B2
WEBSTER AV	RCO	99	C3
WEBSTER RD	SBD	91	E1
WEBSTER ST	A	157	E5
WEBSTER ST	ALA	45	D1
WEBSTER ST	FRFD	135	B4
WEDEL AV	KER	77	E1
WEED RD	IMP	112	A4
WEEDPATCH HWY	KER	78	E3
WEEDS POINT RD	YUB	26	C4
WEEKS RD	SCL	P	C5
WEEMASOUL RD	TEH	18	A5
WEGIS RD	KER	78	C3
WEIMAR CROSS RD	PLA	34	C3
WEINERT RD	IMP	109	A5
WEIR AV	MCO	47	E4
WEIR CANYON RD	ORCO	U	C5
WEIR CANYON RD	ORCO	98	D3
WEISS RD	SUT	33	B2
WEISER RD	KER	77	C1
WEITCHER RD	MOD	14	E1
WELCH CT	CAL	41	B5
WELCOME AV	KER	80	D1
WELDON	FRCO	58	A3
WELLBARN AV	FRCO	57	E1
WELLOCK RD	TRI	17	D1
WELLS AV	RENO	130	C3
WELLS AV N	RENO	130	C2
WELLS DR	LA	177	D5
WELLS RD	COL	32	D1
WELLS RD	MAD	49	C5
WELLS RD	RCO	103	D4
WELLS RD	VEN	88	B5
WELLSFORD RD	STA	47	D2
WELLSONA RD	SLO	76	A1
WELTY RD	STA	47	A3
WENDEL RD	LAS	21	C3
WENGLER HILL RD	SHA	19	A2
WENTE ST	ALA	P	C1
WENTE ST	ALA	46	C2
WENTWORTH ST	LACO	89	D5
WENTWORTH ST	LACO	Q	D1
WENTWTH SPGS RD	ED	34	E3
WENTWTH SPGS RD	ED	35	B3
WERICK RD	RCO	99	A3
WESCOTT RD	COL	33	A2
WEST AV	FRE	165	A1
WEST AV	FRCO	57	C4
WEST AV	FRCO	67	C1
WEST AV	RCO	110	C1
WEST DR	RCO	100	D2
WEST LN	MCO	48	B4
WEST LN	S	160	E1
WEST LN	SJCO	40	A4
WEST LN	SJCO	160	E1
WEST LN	TUO	163	C3
WEST RD	COL	33	A3
WEST RD	LACO	R	D5
WEST RD	MEN	31	B1
WEST RD	STA	47	C4
WEST ST	ANA	193	A4
WEST ST	EUR	121	E1
WEST ST	ORCO	T	C2
WEST ST	TUL	68	A2
WESTBOROUGH	SMCO	N	B1
WESTBROOK LN	DN	1	D3
WESTCLIFF DR	NB	199	C4
WEST COAST RD	HUM	16	C5
WEST CREEK WY	NEV	127	B1
W END OREGN MTN	TRI	17	C1
WESTERN AV	KER	78	A2
WESTERN AV	LA	182	A4
WESTERN AV	LA	185	A4
WESTERN AV	LACO	97	D3
WESTERN AV	LACO	Q	E5
WESTERN AV	LACO	Q	E2
WESTERN AV	LACO	S	C3
WESTERN AV	ORCO	T	B2
WESTERN CYN RD	LA	182	A3
WESTERN HILL RD	RCO	100	B5
WESTERN MINE	LAK	32	A5
WESTRN MINERALS	KER	78	A5
WESTERN TALC RD	INY	73	A5
WESTERN TALC RD	SBD	73	A5
WESTFALL	MPA	49	C3
WESTFALL W	MPA	49	A4
WESTGATE AV	HUM	9	E3
WESTGATE DR	HUM	15	E1
WESTGATE DR	NAPA	38	D2
WESTHAVEN DR	HUM	9	E4
WESTLAKE BLVD	VEN	96	E1
WEST LAWN AV	FRCO	57	B4
WEST LAWN AV	FRCO	57	B5
WESTMINSTER AV	GGR	195	A3
WESTMINSTER AV	ORCO	98	A4
WESTMINSTER AV	ORCO	T	A3
WESTMINSTER AV	SA	195	C3
WESTMORELAND RD	IMP	108	E5
WESTON RD	TEH	24	B2
WESTOVER DR	TEH	18	D5
WESTOVER RD	TEH	24	D1
WEST PORTAL RD	MNO	50	D1
WESTRIDGE RD	TRI	17	B3
WESTSIDE BLVD	MCO	47	E4
WESTSIDE BLVD	MCO	48	A4
WESTSIDE FRWY	FRCO	56	B4
WESTSIDE FRWY	FRCO	66	E2
WEST SIDE FRWY	KER	77	D1
WEST SIDE FRWY	KER	78	D4
WESTSIDE FRWY	KIN	67	B4
WESTSIDE FRWY	MCO	55	D1
WESTSIDE FRWY	STA	47	B3
WEST SIDE HWY	INY	72	A1
WEST SIDE HWY	KER	67	B5
WEST SIDE HWY	KER	78	A4
WESTSIDE RD	IMP	111	E3
WEST SIDE RD	JOS	2	C1
WEST SIDE RD	LAS	8	A5
WESTSIDE RD	MOD	7	B3
WESTSIDE RD	MOD	8	A2
WESTSIDE RD	SHA	18	B1
WESTSIDE RD	SIE	27	B3
WESTSIDE RD	SON	37	D1
WSIDE POTTR VLY	MEN	31	B1
WESTWOOD BLVD	LACO	Q	C4
WESTWOOD ST	TUL	68	D3
WET MEADOW RD	MNO	50	E1
WETMORE RD	ALA	P	C1
WETMORE RD	ALA	46	C2
WEYER RD	STA	47	E2
WEYMOUTH BLUFF	HUM	15	E2
WHEALAN RD	MCO	48	D5
WHEATLAND RD	SUT	33	E3
WHEDBEE DR	SOL	38	E3
WHEELER RD	IMP	108	D5
WHEELER RD	SBD	91	C2
WHEELER CYN RD	VEN	88	B5
WHEELER NURSERY	SHA	12	E5
WHEELER RDG RD	KER	78	E5
WHEEL GULCH RD	TRI	17	B1
WHEELOCK RD	BUT	25	C3
WHIPPLE AV	SMCO	N	D2
WHIPPLE RD	ALA	P	A1
WHISKEY CK RD	COL	32	E3
WHISKEY CK RD	SHA	18	B2
WHISKEY SLIDE RD	CAL	41	B3
WHISLER RD	KER	78	B1
WHITAKER BLF RD	MAR	37	D3
WHITE AV	LACO	U	C2
WHITE DR	BUT	25	B4
WHITE LN	KER	78	D3
WHITE LN	NAPA	29	C3
WHITE LN	SJCO	40	B5
WHITE RD	COL	33	D3
WHITE RD	MCO	47	D3
WHITE RD	MON	66	C4
WHITE RD	SBD	91	A4
WHITE RD	SCL	P	C3
WHITE RD	SCL	46	B4
WHITE COTTGE RD	NAPA	29	C2
WHITE COTTGE RD	NAPA	38	B1
WHITE CRANE RD	MCO	47	E4
WHITE CRANE RD	MCO	48	A4
WHITEHORSE RD	MOD	13	E2
WHITEHORSE RD	MOD	14	A2
WHITEHURST RD	SCL	54	C2
WHITE MTN RD	INY	51	E4
WHITE MTN RD	INY	60	D4
WHITE OAK DR	SHA	18	C3
WHITE PINE LN	SB	86	E2
WHITE PINE LN	SB	87	A2
WHITEPINE ST	SIS	4	B3
WHITE RIVER RD	KER	69	A5
WHITE ROCK RD	ED	40	C1
WHITE ROCK RD	MPA	49	A4
WHITE ROCK RD	MPA	48	E5
WHITE ROCK RD	MCO	48	E5
WHITE ROCK RD	SAC	40	A1
WHITE ROCK RD	SHA	17	D3
WHTE ROCK LK RD	NEV	27	B5
WHITES BRDGE AV	FRCO	56	D3
WHITES BRDGE AV	FRCO	57	C3
WHITES GULCH RD	SIS	11	C2
WHITES MILL RD	KER	69	B5
WHITES MILL RD	KER	79	B1
WHITEWTR CYN RD	RCO	100	C2
WHITE WOLF RD	TUO	42	D5
WHITE WOLF RD	TUO	63	C3
WHITLEY AV	KIN	67	D3
WHITLOCK RD	IMP	109	C5
WHITLOCK RD	MPA	49	A3
WHITLOCK RD E	MPA	49	B3
WHITLOW RD	HUM	16	C4
WHITMORE AV	STA	47	D2
WHITMORE RD	SHA	18	C2
WHITMORE RD	SHA	19	A2
WHITMRE TUBS RD	MNO	50	E2
WHITMRE TUBS RD	MNO	51	A2
WHITNEY AV	VAL	134	D1
WHITNEY PORTL RD	INY	60	A4
WHITSETT AV	LACO	Q	C3
WHITTIER AV	RCO	99	E4
WHITTIER BLVD	LA	186	D4
WHITTIER BLVD	LACO	98	B2
WHITTIER BLVD	LACO	R	B4
WHITTIER BLVD	LACO	R	D5
WHITTIER BLVD	ORCO	R	D5
WHITTLE RD	CAL	41	B4
WHITTLEY AV E	AVLN	97	B5
WHITWELL WY	RCO	107	C1
WHITWORTH RD	MCO	47	C5
WHITWORTH RD	MCO	55	C1
WIASMUL RD	RCO	107	B1
WIBLE RD	KER	166	B5
WIBLE RD	KER	78	D4
WICKENDEN WY	MOD	8	A1
WICKMAN RD	BUT	25	B5
WICKS ST	SB	86	C1
WIDGEON RD	YOL	39	D3
WIDOW SPGS DR	SIS	12	E2
WIDOW VALLEY RD	MOD	13	E3
WIDOW VALLEY RD	MOD	14	A3
WIGHT WY	LAK	31	D3
WILBUR	CC	39	B5
WILBUR AV	LA	178	C3
WILBUR RD	BUT	25	C4
WILBUR SPGS RD	COL	32	B3
WILCOX RD	SHA	19	D1
WILCOX RD	TEH	18	D4
WILCOX RANCH RD	TUO	41	C5
WILD RD	SBD	91	B2
WILDASS RD	SBT	66	B1
WILDCAT RD	MCO	55	C2
WILDCAT RD	SHA	18	E3
WILDCAT RD	SHA	19	A3
WILDCAT RD	TEH	19	A3
WILD CAT TR	RCO	100	A5
WILDCAT CK RD	SIS	11	D2
WILDCAT CYN RD	CC	L	D4
WILDCAT CYN RD	CC	45	D1
WILDCAT CYN RD	SDCO	107	A5
WILD DUCK RD	MCO	55	E2
WILDER RD	HUM	16	A2
WILDER RD	TEH	18	D5
WLDRNSS LDGE RD	MEN	22	C3
WILDER RIDGE RD	HUM	16	A4
WILDHORSE RD	SBD	92	B1
WILDHRSE CYN RD	MON	65	C2
WILDHRSE CYN RD	SBD	84	B4
WILDMAN RD	KER	78	E4
WILD PLUM RD	SIE	27	A4
WILDROSE RD	INY	61	C5
WILD WASH RD	SBD	91	C2
WILDWOOD AV	SLT	129	D3
WILDWOOD RD	COL	32	E3
WILDWOOD RD	KER	78	A2
WILDWOOD RD	SJCO	47	C1
WILDWOOD RD	TRI	17	C2
WILDWOOD CYN RD	SBD	99	E2
WILEY WELLS RD	RCO	103	B5
WILFRED CYN RD	MNO	51	B2
WILHOLT RD	SJCO	40	A5
WILKIE AV	SUT	33	D3
WILKINS AV	STA	47	D1
WILKINS RD	IMP	109	B2
WILKINS RD	IMP	112	D5
WILKINSON RD	IMP	109	A3
WILLARD RD	TEH	18	C5
WILLARD CK RD	LAS	20	E3
WILLIAM RD	BUT	25	C3
WILLIAM ST	SJ	152	C4
WILLIAMS	SJCO	47	C1
WILLIAMS AV	MCO	47	D4
WILLIAMS RD	IMP	109	B4
WILLIAMS RD	KER	79	C2
WILLIAMS RD	KER	80	D4
WILLIAMS RD	LAS	8	B4
WILLIAMS RD	MON	54	D4
WILLIAMS RD	SHA	13	E4
WILLIAMS CK RD	HUM	15	D2
WILLIAMSON RD	KER	79	D4
WILLIAMSON RD	RCO	107	A1
WILLIAMSON RD	TUO	41	B5
WILLIAM TELL TR	KER	79	C5
WILLIAMS VLY RD	PLU	20	C5
WILLIAMS WLL RD	SBD	81	E5
WILLIS RD	MCO	56	B1
WILLISTON RD	SUT	33	C1
WILLMOTT RD	MCO	55	D1
WILLMS RD	STA	48	A1
WILLOUGHBY RD	IMP	112	A4
WILLOW AV	FRCO	57	D2
WILLOW AV	GLE	24	E5
WILLOW AV	KER	89	C1
WILLOW DR	KER	78	A2
WILLOW DR	MAD	57	B1
WILLOW RD	MP	147	B1
WILLOW RD	SBD	91	C4
WILLOW RD	SDCO	107	A5
WILLOW RD	SLO	76	B5
WILLOW RD	SMCO	N	E2
WILLOW RD	SMCO	45	D3
WILLOW ST	LACO	97	E3
WILLOW ST	LACO	S	D2
WILLOW ST	SJ	152	C5
WILLOW WY	LAS	20	E2
WILLOW CREEK RD	AMA	40	D2
WILLOW CREEK RD	INY	52	D4
WILLOW CREEK RD	SBT	55	C5
WILLOW CREEK RD	SLO	75	E1
WILLOW CREEK RD	SLO	76	A1
WILLOW CREEK RD	SIS	4	C3
WILLOW CREEK RD	YUB	26	B5
WILLW CK RED RCK	SIS	5	B3
WILLOW GLEN DR	SDCO	111	E1
WILLOW GLEN RD	YUB	26	A5
WILLOW PASS RD	CC	M	A3
WILLOW PASS RD	CC	M	B3
WILLOW PASS RD	CC	39	A5
WILLOW POINT RD	YOL	39	D2
WILLOW RCH RD S	MOD	7	C3
WILLOWS RD	SDCO	107	B5
WILLOW SPGS EXT	SIS	12	E2
WILLOW SPGS RD	KER	79	D5
WILLOW SPGS RD	KER	89	D1
WILLOW SPGS RD	KER	90	A1
WILLOW SPGS RD	LAS	14	A5
WILLOW SPGS RD	LACO	89	C3
WILLOW SPGS RD	SCL	P	D5
WILLOW SPGS RD	SCL	54	C1
WILLOW VLY RD	NEV	34	C1
WILL S GREEN RD	COL	32	E2
WILMINGTON AV	LACO	97	E3
WILMINGTON AV	LACO	S	D2
WILMINGTON BLVD	LACO	S	C2
WILSHIRE AV	SBD	101	C1
WILSHIRE BLVD	BH	183	C2
WILSHIRE BLVD	LA	180	D2

STREET INDEX

STREET	CO.	PAGE	GRID
WILSHIRE BLVD	LA	185	B2
WILSHIRE BLVD	LACO	97	D2
WILSHIRE BLVD	LACO	Q	D4
WILSHIRE BLVD	LACO	180	D2
WILSHIRE RD	SBD	92	A4
WILSON AV	COL	32	E3
WILSON AV	MAR	38	A4
WILSON AV	VAL	134	A3
WILSON DR	TUL	68	E3
WILSON RD	IMP	112	D5
WILSON RD	KER	78	D3
WILSON RD	MCO	55	D1
WILSON RD	SBD	101	D1
WILSON RD	SUT	33	D3
WILSON ST	KER	79	C3
WILSON ST	RIV	100	A3
WILSON ST	TEH	24	E1
WILSON WY	PLA	34	B3
WILSON WY	SJCO	40	B5
WILSON BEND RD	COL	33	B3
WILSON CREEK RD	DN	1	E5
WILSON HILL RD	MAR	37	E4
WILSON HILL RD	SHA	19	B3
WILSON LAKE RD	TEH	19	D4
WILSON LANDING	BUT	25	A2
WILSON RANCH RD	SBD	90	E4
WILSON SPGS RD	LAS	14	A5
WILSON VLY RD	RCO	107	A1
WILTON PL	LA	181	E4
WILTON PL	LA	184	E2
WILTON RD	SAC	40	A2
WIMER RD	SJCO	40	D4
WINCHESTER BLVD	SCL	P	B3
WINCHESTER BLVD	SCL	46	A5
WINCHESTER RD	RCO	99	D4
WINCHUCK RD	CUR	1	D2
WINDING WY	SIS	12	E2
WINDLASS DR	RCO	101	C5
WINDSONG WY	RCO	107	B1
WINDSOR AV	LACO	R	B2
WINDSOR RIV RD	SON	37	D1
WINE CREEK RD	SON	31	D5
WINE CREEK RD	SON	37	D1
WINEMAN RD	SLO	76	C5
WINEVILLE AV	SBD	99	A2
WINGATE RD	INY	71	C3
WINGFIELD RD	LAS	21	A3
WING LEVEE RD	SJCO	46	E1
WINNETKA AV	LA	178	A3
WINNETKA AV	LACO	97	B1
WINSHIP RD	SOL	39	C2
WINSHIP RD	YUBA	125	D4
WINSLOW RD	IMP	109	A2
WINSOME WY	SHA	18	B2
WINTER GRDNS BL	SDCO	V	E2
WINTER GRDNS BL	SDCO	106	E5
WINTERGREEN RD	SBD	90	E4
WINTERS RD	SBD	100	E1
WINTERS RD	SOL	39	A1
WINTRS GULCH RD	SIS	4	A5
WINTON AV W	ALA	45	E2
WINTON AV W	H	146	D3
WINTON AV W	ALA	L	E5
WINTON AV W	ALA	N	E1
WINTON RD	CAL	41	B2
WINTON WY	MCO	48	B4
WINTOON WY	SIS	12	E2
WIRT RD	IMP	109	B3
WISCONSIN AV	COL	32	E3
WISCONSIN AV	TEH	24	E2
WISE RD	PLA	33	E3
WISE RD	PLA	34	A3
WISHON AV	FRE	165	C2
WISHON DR	TUL	69	B2
WISTOS LN	LAS	21	B3
WITHERS AV	CC	L	E3
WITHERS AV	CC	38	E5
WITHROW RD	SHA	19	A2
WITTER SPG E RD	LAK	31	C2
WIXOM RD	IMP	111	E3
WOHLFORD RD	SDCO	106	E3
WOLF RD	NEV	34	C2
WOLF CREEK RD	ALP	36	C5
WOLF CREEK RD	NEV	34	C2
WOLFE RD	CPTO	150	A4
WOLFE RD	SCL	P	A3
WOLFE RD	SCL	45	E4
WOLFE RD	SCL	46	A4
WOLFE RD	SVL	150	A3
WOLFE RD	VEN	96	C1
WOLFE GRADE	MAR	L	B3
WOLFE GRADE	MAR	139	C5
WOLFSEN	MCO	47	E5
WOLFSEN	MCO	55	E1
WOLFSKILL	SOL	39	A1
WONDER AV	KER	80	A4
WONDERLAND BLVD	SHA	18	C1
WONDERLAND DR	RCO	100	A3
WONDER STUMP RD	DN	1	D3
WONDERVIEW RD	RCO	100	A3
WOO RD	MCO	55	E2
WOOD RD	RCO	99	B3
WOOD RD	SUT	33	B2
WOOD RD	VEN	96	C1
WOOD ST	GLE	24	D4
WOODBINE RD	RCO	100	C5
WOODBRIDGE RD	SJCO	39	E4
WOODBRIDGE RD	SJCO	40	B4
WOODBURY RD	LACO	R	B2
WOODBURY RD	PAS	190	B1
WOOD CANYON RD	INY	71	D1
WOODCUTTERS WY	SHA	19	B3
WOODEN VLY RD	NAPA	38	D2

STREET	CO.	PAGE	GRID
WOODFORD-TEH RD	KER	79	C4
WOODHILL DR	SHA	13	A5
WOODHOUSE MINE	CAL	41	B2
WOODLAND AV	MCO	48	C4
WOODLAND AV	SR	139	E5
WOODLAND AV	STA	47	C2
WOODLAND AV	TEH	24	D1
WOODLAND DR	MPA	49	C3
WOODLAND WY	SHA	19	B3
WOODLF TUNNL RD	BUT	26	B4
WOODLEY RD	SDCO	106	C4
WOOLEY RD E	VEN	96	B1
WOODMAN AV	LACO	97	C1
WOODMAN AV	LACO	Q	C2
WOOD RANCH RD	LAS	21	B2
WOODRIDGE RD	SHA	19	B3
WOODROW AV	SC	169	C5
WOODRW WILSON DR	LA	181	A2
WOODRUFF AV	LACO	S	E2
WOODRUFF AV	LACO	T	A2
WOODRUFF LN	YUB	33	D1
WOODSBRO RD	SJCO	40	A5
WOODSIDE AV	SDCO	V	E2
WOODSIDE AV	SDCO	106	E5
WOODSIDE RD	SMCO	45	D3
WOODSIDE RD	SMCO	N	D2
WOODS LAKE RD	ALP	36	A5
WOODSON AV	TEH	24	D2
WOODSON RD	SJCO	40	A3
WOOD VALLEY RD	SDCO	106	E3
WOODVIEW LN	MPA	49	B4
WOODWARD AV	SJCO	47	A1
WOODY RD	KER	78	D1
WOODY ST	KER	78	E1
WOODY-GRANIT RD	KER	68	E5
WOODY-GRANIT RD	KER	69	A5
WOODY-GRANIT RD	KER	78	E1
WOODY-GRANIT RD	KER	79	A1
WOOKEY RD	BUT	25	A2
WOOLEY RD	OXN	176	B4
WOOLLOMES AV	KER	68	A5
WOOLNER AV	FRFD	135	A4
WORDEN AV	MCO	48	C5
WORDEN RD	CAL	41	B3
WORK RD	KER	90	B1
WORKMAN ST	LACO	Q	C1
WORKMAN MILL RD	LACO	98	A2
WORKMAN MILL RD	LACO	R	C4
WORMWOOD RD	IMP	111	E4
WORSLEY RD	RCO	100	C2
WORTH AV	TUL	68	D3
WORTH RD	SUT	33	D4
WORTHINGTON RD	IMP	108	E5
WORTHINGTON RD	MCO	47	C5
WORTHINGTON ST	KER	79	E1
WRAGG CANYON RD	NAPA	38	D2
WRAN RD	LAS	21	C4
WREN RD	STA	47	E2
WRIGHT AV	TUL	68	B3
WRIGHT RD	IMP	109	C5
WRIGHT RD	SIS	5	D3
WRIGHTS LAKE RD	ED	35	D4
WRIGLEY RD	HUM	15	E1
WRIGLEY TER RD	AVLN	97	B5
WUNPOST RD	MCO	65	E4
WYANDOTTE AV	BUT	25	D4
WYNDTT MNRS RCH	BUT	25	D4
WYE RD	INY	51	D4
WYER RD	COL	32	E3
WYLIE DR	MDO	162	E1
WYLIE ST	SB	87	D1
WYMAN CREEK RD	INY	52	A3
WYNCOOP RD	SUT	33	B2
WYNDHAM LN	RED	122	C4
WYNDHAVEN DR	TEH	18	D4
WYO AV	GLE	24	E3
WYSE RD	LACO	89	D4
X			
XIMENO AV	LACO	S	E3
Y			
YAJOME ST	NAP	133	C2
YANKEE HILL RD	TUO	41	C4
YAQUI GULCH RD	MPA	49	B3
YAQUI PASS RD	SDCO	107	E3
YARD RD	TEH	18	D4
YELLOW BUTTE RD	SIS	4	D5
YELLW JACKET RD	MNO	51	C1
YELLW JACKET RD	TEH	19	C4
YERBA BLVD	KER	80	B4
YERBA BUENA RD	VEN	96	D2
YERMO RD	SBD	82	C5
YERMO RD	SBD	92	A1
YERMO CUTOFF	SBD	81	E5
YERMO CUTOFF	SBD	82	A5
YGNACIO VLY RD	CC	M	A3
YMCA RD	FRCO	58	D3
YOAKIM BRDG RD	SON	31	C5
YOCUM RD	IMP	109	B3
YOKE ST	SHA	18	C3
YOLANDA AV	KER	89	C2
YOLANO RD	SOL	39	C2
YOLO AV	FRCO	56	E4
YOLO ST	STA	47	C4
YOLO CO LINE RD	COL	32	E3
YOLO CO LINE RD	COL	33	A3
YORBA LN	SBD	90	E3
YORBA LINDA BL	ORCO	98	C3
YORBA LINDA BL	ORCO	T	D1
YORK AV	KIN	67	A5

STREET	CO.	PAGE	GRID
YORK BLVD	LACO	97	E1
YORK BLVD	LACO	R	A3
YORK RD	IMP	110	D5
YORK RD	SIS	4	C3
YOSEMITE AV	MAN	161	A4
YOSEMITE AV	MCO	48	C4
YOSEMITE AV	SJCO	47	B1
YOSEMITE BLVD	MDO	162	E3
YOSEMITE BLVD	STA	47	D2
YOSEMITE BLVD	STA	48	B2
YOSEMITE RD	TUO	41	D5
YOSEMTE OAKS RD	MPA	49	B3
YSMTE SPGS PKWY	MAD	49	C5
YOU BET RD	NEV	34	D2
YOUD RD	MCO	48	B3
YOUNG AV	COL	32	E3
YOUNG RD	COL	24	E5
YOUNG RD	IMP	109	B3
YOUNG RD	STA	47	C3
YOUNG ST	RCO	99	E4
YOUNG LOVE AV	SC	169	B4
YOUNGS HILL RD	YUB	26	C4
YOUNGSTOWN RD	MCO	47	E4
YOUNT ST	NAPA	29	D4
YOUNTVLL CRS RD	NAPA	29	D4
YOUNTVLL CRS RD	NAPA	38	C2
YOWELL RD	MOD	14	B3
YREKA AGER RD	SIS	4	B4
YREKA WALKER RD	SIS	3	D3
YREKA WALKER RD	SIS	4	A4
YTURRIARTE RD	SBT	55	D4
YUBA AV	FRCO	56	E3
YUBA NEVADA RD	YUB	26	B5
YUBA PASS RD	SIE	27	B4
YUCAIPA BLVD	SBD	99	D2
YUCCA RD	RCO	107	C1
YUCCA RD	SBD	90	E3
YUCCA TR	SBD	100	E1
YUCCA LOMA RD	SBD	91	C4
Z			
ZABALA RD	MON	54	D4
ZABRISKIE PT RD	INY	72	A1
ZACA STATION RD	SB	86	E2
ZACHARIAS RD	STA	47	B3
ZACHARY AV	KER	78	C1
ZANES RD	HUM	15	E1
ZAYANTE RD	SCR	54	A1
ZAYANTE RD E	SCR	P	A5
ZEDIKER AV	FRCO	57	E3
ZEDIKER AV	FRCO	57	E4
ZEERING RD	STA	47	C3
ZEIGLER PT RD	HUM	10	D5
ZELDA LN	SBD	101	E1
ZENIA RD	MEN	23	A2
ZENIA BLUFF RD	HUM	16	D5
ZENIA LK MTN RD	TRI	17	A5
ZENIA LK MTN RD	TRI	22	E1
ZENO RD	LAK	31	D2
ZERKER RD	KER	78	C2
ZERMATT DR	KER	79	C5
ZINC HILL RD	INY	70	E1
ZINC MINE RD	SBD	84	A3
ZINFANDEL DR	SAC	40	A1
ZINFANDEL LN	NAPA	29	C3
ZINK RD	BUT	25	E3
ZITZMAN RD	SIS	3	C5
ZLABEK RD	SIS	5	D2
ZOGG MINE RD	SHA	18	B2
ZOO DR	LACO	Q	E3
ZULU QUEN MN RD	RCO	102	A2
ZUMWALT	SJCO	47	C1
ZUMWALT AV	TUL	68	A2
ZUMWALT RD	COL	32	D2
ZZYZX RD	SBD	83	B4
NUMERICAL STREETS			
1ST AV	BARS	208	B1
1ST AV	BUT	25	B3
1ST AV	GLE	24	E3
1ST AV	IMP	112	D5
1ST AV	LPAZ	104	B2
1ST AV	LACO	R	D5
1ST AV	LACO	T	B1
1ST AV	MCO	47	E4
1ST AV	PLU	20	A4
1ST AV	SBD	208	C1
1ST AV	SD	215	D3
1ST AV	SDCO	V	B3
1ST AV	SDCO	V	C4
1ST AV	SDCO	111	D2
1ST ST	ALA	M	C5
1ST ST	ALA	46	C2
1ST ST	BEN	153	C4
1ST ST	DN	1	D3
1ST ST	DVS	136	C3
1ST ST	FRCO	57	C3
1ST ST	LA	186	A2
1ST ST	LACO	Q	E4
1ST ST	NAPA	L	C1
1ST ST	NAP	133	C4
1ST ST	ORCO	98	C4
1ST ST	ORCO	T	D3
1ST ST	RCO	U	E4
1ST ST	RCO	98	E3
1ST ST	SF	143	D3
1ST ST	SCL	P	B3
1ST ST	SJ	151	E1
1ST ST	SJ	152	A2
1ST ST	SA	195	A4
1ST ST	SA	196	A4

STREET	CO.	PAGE	GRID
1ST ST	SCL	46	A4
1ST ST	SCL	54	D2
1ST ST	SHA	18	C3
1 1/2 AV	KIN	68	A1
2ND AV	COL	33	B3
2ND AV	GLE	24	E3
2ND AV	KIN	68	A1
2ND AV	LPAZ	104	B1
2ND AV	MCO	47	D4
2ND AV	RCO	103	D4
2ND AV S	MCO	48	A4
2ND ST	FRFD	135	A4
2ND ST	KER	68	B5
2ND ST	LA	186	A3
2ND ST	LACO	S	E3
2ND ST	MER	170	A5
2ND ST	SDCO	106	E5
2ND ST	SDCO	106	E5
2ND ST	SR	139	C4
2ND ST E	BEN	153	C4
2ND ST E	RENO	130	B3
2ND ST E	SOL	38	D4
2ND ST W	RENO	130	A3
2 1/2 AV	KIN	67	E2
3RD AV	FCTY	145	C1
3RD AV	GLE	24	E3
3RD AV	LPAZ	104	B1
3RD AV	MCO	47	D4
3RD AV	NAPA	38	D3
3RD AV	RCO	103	D4
3RD AV	SBD	99	B1
3RD AV	SDCO	V	C4
3RD AV	SDCO	111	D2
3RD AV	SMCO	N	C1
3RD AV	SMCO	45	C3
3RD AV	TEH	18	E5
3RD AV	TEH	24	E1
3RD ST	BH	183	C1
3RD ST	CC	38	C5
3RD ST	COR	215	C5
3RD ST	DVS	136	C3
3RD ST	EUR	121	C1
3RD ST	LA	184	A1
3RD ST	LA	185	B1
3RD ST	LA	186	B3
3RD ST	LACO	Q	B4
3RD ST	NAP	133	C4
3RD ST	RIV	205	C2
3RD ST	SBDO	207	D2
3RD ST	SBD	99	C1
3RD ST	SFCO	L	C5
3RD ST	SF	142	E3
3RD ST	SR	139	C4
3RD ST	SHA	18	C3
3RD ST	TEH	24	D2
3RD ST	YOL	137	A3
4TH AV	CAR	168	C3
4TH AV	GLE	24	E3
4TH AV	KIN	67	E1
4TH AV	MCO	47	D4
4TH AV	MON	168	C3
4TH AV	RCO	103	D4
4TH AV	SD	215	D3
4TH AV	SDCO	V	C4
4TH AV	SDCO	111	D2
4TH AV	ALA	L	D4
4TH ST	BKD	166	C4
4TH ST	COR	215	C5
4TH ST	EC	217	D4
4TH ST	EUR	121	C1
4TH ST	KER	166	C4
4TH ST	LA	186	A3
4TH ST	MAR	L	A3
4TH ST	MAR	38	B5
4TH ST	MOD	8	B3
4TH ST	ONT	203	E3
4TH ST	ONT	204	A3
4TH ST	RCO	99	C4
4TH ST	SBD	99	D2
4TH ST	SDCO	V	C4
4TH ST	SDCO	111	C1
4TH ST	SJ	152	B3
4TH ST	SR	139	B3
4TH ST	SA	196	A3
4TH ST	SCL	54	E3
4TH ST	SHA	18	C3
4TH ST	STR	131	D3
4TH ST E	RENO	130	B2
4TH ST W	RENO	130	A2
5TH AV	CAR	168	B3
5TH AV	GLE	24	E3
5TH AV	GLE	24	E3
5TH AV	KIN	67	E1
5TH AV	LPAZ	104	A2
5TH AV	LACO	R	D3
5TH AV	SBD	92	D5
5TH AV	SBD	99	D2
5TH AV	SDCO	106	D3
5TH AV	SR	139	C4
5TH AV E	SIS	4	B4
5TH ST	DVS	136	C3
5TH ST	EUR	121	C1
5TH ST	HUM	9	E5
5TH ST	LA	186	A3
5TH ST	RCO	99	A3
5TH ST	SCTO	137	A3
5TH ST	SBD	99	C1
5TH ST	SBDO	207	C2
5TH ST	SA	195	C4
5TH ST	SOL	L	D2
5TH ST	TEH	24	E1
5TH ST	VAL	134	D5
5TH ST	VEN	96	B1

STREET	CO.	PAGE	GRID
5TH ST E	BEN	153	C4
5TH ST E	OXN	176	D4
5TH ST E	VEN	176	D4
5TH ST W	LACO	90	A2
5 1/2 AV	KIN	67	E2
6TH AV	CAR	168	B3
6TH AV	GLE	24	E3
6TH AV	KIN	67	E1
6TH AV	MCO	47	E4
6TH AV	RCO	103	D4
6TH AV	SD	215	E3
6TH AV	SDCO	V	B3
6TH ST	GLE	24	D3
6TH ST	LA	184	A2
6TH ST	LA	185	B2
6TH ST	LA	186	A3
6TH ST	ONT	203	E3
6TH ST	ONT	204	B3
6TH ST	RCO	99	A3
6TH ST	YUB	33	E2
6 1/2 AV	KIN	67	E2
7TH	CC	38	C5
7TH AV	CAR	168	B3
7TH AV	KIN	67	E1
7TH AV	LPAZ	104	A2
7TH AV	LACO	R	D4
7TH AV	SF	141	D5
7TH AV	SFCO	L	B5
7TH AV	SFCO	45	B1
7TH AV	SCR	54	A2
7TH AV	YUB	33	D2
7TH ST	EUR	121	C1
7TH ST	IMP	109	A4
7TH ST	KER	78	B1
7TH ST	LB	192	D2
7TH ST	LA	186	A3
7TH ST	LACO	97	C2
7TH ST	LACO	98	A4
7TH ST	LACO	S	E2
7TH ST	O	157	C3
7TH ST	O	158	A3
7TH ST	RCO	99	B2
7TH ST	RCO	99	E4
7TH ST	SBD	91	B4
7TH ST	SBD	99	B2
7TH ST	SBD	99	D2
7TH ST	SJ	152	B3
7TH ST	SLO	75	E3
7TH ST	STA	47	E3
7TH ST	UPL	204	C2
7TH ST N	MDO	162	B3
7TH ST S	MDO	162	C4
7TH ST S	STA	162	C4
7TH ST W	BEN	153	B3
7TH STANDARD RD	KER	77	C2
7 1/2 AV	KIN	57	E5
8TH AV	CAR	53	D5
8TH AV	CAR	168	B3
8TH AV	KIN	67	D1
8TH AV	RCO	103	D4
8TH AV	SD	215	E4
8TH ST	ALA	L	C4
8TH ST	BKD	166	C4
8TH ST	BUT	25	C5
8TH ST	EC	217	C3
8TH ST	IMP	112	A3
8TH ST	LA	185	A2
8TH ST	LA	186	A4
8TH ST	RCO	99	E3
8TH ST	SBD	U	E2
8TH ST	SDCO	V	C4
8TH ST	SDCO	106	B3
8TH ST	SDCO	111	D1
8TH ST	SJCO	40	B5
8TH ST	SON	L	B1
8TH ST	UPL	204	C2
8 1/2 AV	KIN	57	D5
9TH AV	KER	68	C5
9TH AV	KIN	67	D1
9TH AV	LPAZ	104	A2
9TH AV	SD	215	E3
9TH AV	SDCO	106	D3
9TH ST	GGR	193	A5
9TH ST	LA	185	E3
9TH ST	LA	186	A4
9TH ST	LA	191	A4
9TH ST	LACO	S	C3
9TH ST	MDO	162	B3
9TH ST	SBD	203	D2
9TH ST	SBDO	207	C1
9TH ST	SF	143	C4
9TH ST	UPL	203	E2
9TH ST	UPL	204	B2
9TH ST S	MDO	162	C4
9TH ST S	STA	162	C4
9 1/2 AV	KIN	67	D1
10 MI HOUSE TR	BUT	25	C2
10TH	CC	38	C5
10TH AV	KIN	67	D1
10TH AV	RCO	103	D5
10TH ST	LB	192	D2
10TH ST	RCO	99	D3
10TH ST	SF	142	D4
10TH ST	SJ	152	B2
10TH ST	YUB	33	D2
10TH ST E	LACO	90	A3
10TH ST W	BEN	153	A3
10TH ST W	CC	M	C3
10TH ST W	LACO	89	E3
10 1/2 AV	KIN	67	D2
11TH AV	KIN	67	D1
11TH AV	LPAZ	104	A2
11TH AV	RCO	103	D5

STREET INDEX

STREET	CO.	PAGE	GRID
11TH AV	SBD	91	E1
11TH AV	SD	215	E3
11TH AV	SDCO	V	B3
11TH ST	LAK	31	D3
11TH ST	MDO	162	B3
11TH ST	SBD	91	B4
11TH ST	SJCO	47	A2
12TH AV	KIN	67	D1
12TH AV	LPAZ	104	A2
12TH AV	SD	215	E4
12TH AV	SDCO	V	B3
12TH ST	BUT	25	C4
12TH ST	HUM	15	E2
12TH ST	MOD	8	A1
12TH ST	YUB	33	D2
12TH ST E	O	158	C4
12TH ST N	SCTO	137	D1
12 3/4 AV	KIN	67	D1
13TH AV	ALA	L	D4
13TH AV	ALA	45	D1
13TH AV	CAR	168	B4
13TH AV	KIN	67	D1
13TH AV	LPAZ	104	A2
13TH ST	CC	38	C5
13TH ST	SJ	152	C2
13 1/4 AV	KIN	67	D1
14 MILE HOUSE	BUT	25	C2
14TH AV	KIN	67	D1
14TH AV	LPAZ	104	A2
14TH AV	O	158	C4
14TH AV	RCO	100	D3
14TH AV	RCO	103	D5
14TH ST E	ALA	L	E5
14TH ST E	CC	M	C3
14TH ST	CC	39	B5
14TH ST	EUR	121	B2
14TH ST	MDO	162	B3
14TH ST	O	157	D2
14TH ST	RIV	99	E2
14TH ST	RIV	205	B3
14TH ST	RCO	99	B2
14TH ST	SBD	99	D2
14TH ST E	ALA	45	E2
14 1/2 AV	KIN	67	D2
15TH AV	KIN	67	D1
15TH AV	RCO	103	C5
15TH AV	SDCO	106	D3
15TH ST	KER	80	A5
15TH ST	MDO	162	B3
15TH ST	SCTO	137	B3
15 1/2 AV	KIN	67	C1
16TH AV	KIN	67	C1
16TH AV	RCO	100	D3
16TH AV	RCO	103	D5
16TH ST	MER	170	B3
16TH ST	SCTO	137	C3
16TH ST	SBD	98	D1
16TH ST	SBD	99	D2
16TH ST	SD	215	E4
16TH ST	SD	216	A4
16TH ST	SDCO	V	B3
16TH ST	YUMA	112	C5
17 MILE DR	MON	53	B3
17 MILE DR	MON	167	A3
17 MILE DR	PAC	167	B2
17TH AV	KIN	67	C1
17TH AV	SCR	54	A2
17TH ST	CM	199	C3
17TH ST	MDO	162	C3
17TH ST	ORCO	98	C4
17TH ST	ORCO	T	B4
17TH ST	ORCO	T	C4
17TH ST	ORCO	T	D3
17TH ST	SF	141	E5
17TH ST	SA	195	D3
17TH ST	SA	196	C3
18TH AV	KIN	67	C1
18TH AV	RCO	100	D3
18TH AV	RCO	103	D5
18TH ST	BKD	166	B3
18TH ST	LAK	32	A3
18TH ST	SDCO	V	C4
18TH ST	SDCO	111	D2
18 3/4 AV	KIN	67	C1
19TH AV	KIN	67	C3
19TH AV	SFCO	L	B5
19TH AV	SFCO	45	B2
19TH ST	BKD	166	B3
19TH ST	CM	199	A2
19TH ST	KER	80	A5
19TH ST	ORCO	T	C4
19TH ST	SBD	98	D1
20TH AV	KIN	67	C1
20TH AV	RCO	100	D3
20TH AV	RCO	103	C5
20TH ST	KER	80	B5
20TH ST	KIN	80	A5
20TH ST E	LACO	90	A3
20TH ST W	KER	89	E1
20 1/2 AV	KIN	67	C2
21ST AV	KIN	67	C3
21ST ST	BKD	166	B3
21ST ST	MER	170	D3
21ST ST	SCTO	137	C4
21 1/2 AV	KIN	67	C1
22ND AV	KIN	67	C1
22ND AV	RCO	100	E3
22ND AV	RCO	103	C5
22ND ST	RCO	100	A3
22ND ST	YUB	33	D2
22 1/2 AV	KIN	67	C1
23RD AV	KIN	67	C1
23RD AV	O	158	B4
23RD ST	BKD	166	C3
23RD ST	CC	L	C3
23RD ST	CC	38	C5
23RD ST	R	155	B3
23RD ST	SP	155	B1
23RD ST	SMON	187	B1
23 1/2 AV	KIN	67	B1
24TH AV	KIN	67	B1
24TH AV	RCO	100	E3
24TH AV	RCO	103	C5
24TH ST	BKD	166	C2
24TH ST	KER	78	D3
24TH ST	SAC	39	E1
24TH ST	SDCO	V	C4
24TH ST	SDCO	111	D2
24TH ST	SJ	152	D3
24TH ST	YUMA	112	C5
24 1/2 AV	KIN	67	B1
25TH AV	KIN	67	B1
25TH AV	KIN	67	B4
25TH AV	RCO	103	C5
25TH AV	SF	141	B4
25TH AV	SM	145	A3
25TH ST	LACO	S	C3
25TH ST	SD	216	A4
25TH ST	SDCO	V	B3
25TH ST E	LACO	90	A3
25TH ST W	KER	89	E1
26TH AV	RCO	101	A3
26TH AV	RCO	103	C5
26TH ST	SD	216	B5
26 1/4 AV	KIN	67	B1
27TH AV	KIN	67	B1
27TH ST	SDCO	V	C5
27TH ST	SDCO	111	D2
28TH AV	KIN	67	B2
28TH AV	RCO	101	A3
28TH AV	RCO	110	D1
28TH AV	SM	145	A3
28TH ST	SD	216	B4
28TH ST	SDCO	V	C3
28TH ST	SDCO	111	D1
29TH AV	ALA	L	D4
29TH ST	SCTO	137	D4
30TH AV	KIN	67	B3
30TH AV	RCO	100	D3
30TH AV	RCO	110	C1
30TH ST	BKD	166	D2
30TH ST	KER	80	B5
30TH ST	SD	214	C5
30TH ST	SD	216	B4
30TH ST	SDCO	V	C4
30TH ST	SDCO	111	D1
30TH ST	SDCO	111	D2
30TH ST E	LACO	90	A3
30TH ST W	KER	89	E1
30TH ST W	LACO	89	E2
31ST AV	SM	145	A3
32ND AV	RCO	101	A3
32ND AV	RCO	110	C1
32ND ST	KER	80	B5
32ND ST	LAK	32	A3
32ND ST	SD	216	C4
32ND ST	SDCO	111	D1
32ND ST	YUMA	112	C5
34TH AV	RCO	100	D3
34TH AV	RCO	110	C1
34TH ST	BKD	166	C2
35TH AV	ALA	L	D4
35TH AV	O	158	D5
35TH AV	RCO	110	C1
36TH AV	KIN	67	A4
36TH AV	RCO	100	D4
36TH AV	RCO	110	D1
36TH ST	LAK	32	A3
37TH ST	KER	80	B5
38TH AV	RCO	101	A4
38TH AV	RCO	110	D1
38TH ST	SD	216	D5
40TH AV	RCO	101	A4
40TH ST	SBD	99	B1
40TH ST	SD	214	D5
40TH ST	SDCO	V	C4
40TH ST E	LACO	90	A3
40TH ST W	KER	89	E1
40TH ST W	LACO	89	E2
41ST AV	SCR	54	A2
41ST ST	LACO	Q	E4
42ND AV	RCO	101	A4
42ND AV	SM	145	B4
43RD ST	SD	216	E1
44TH AV	RCO	100	E4
47TH AV	RCO	101	A4
47TH AV	SAC	39	E1
47TH ST E	LACO	90	A3
48TH AV	RCO	101	A4
50TH AV	RCO	101	A4
50TH ST E	LACO	90	A3
50TH ST W	KER	89	E1
50TH ST W	LACO	89	E2
51ST ST	LACO	Q	E4
52ND AV	RCO	101	A4
54TH AV	RCO	101	A4
54TH ST	RCO	99	A2
54TH ST	SDCO	V	C3
54TH ST	SDCO	111	D1
55TH ST E	LACO	90	B3
57TH ST E	LACO	90	B3
58TH AV	RCO	101	A5
60TH AV	RCO	101	A5
60TH ST	SDCO	V	C4
60TH ST E	LACO	90	B2
60TH ST W	KER	89	E2
60TH ST W	LACO	89	E2
62ND AV	RCO	101	B5
64TH AV	RCO	101	B5
65TH EXPWY	SAC	39	E1
65TH ST E	LACO	90	B2
65TH ST W	LACO	89	E2
66TH AV	RCO	101	B5
67TH ST	RCO	101	A5
68TH AV	RCO	101	B5
68TH AV	TEH	18	E5
70TH AV	RCO	101	B5
70TH ST	SDCO	V	D3
70TH ST	SDCO	111	D1
70TH ST E	LACO	90	B3
70TH ST W	LACO	89	E2
72ND AV	RCO	101	B5
73RD AV	ALA	L	D5
74TH AV	RCO	101	B5
76TH AV	RCO	101	B5
76TH ST E	LACO	90	B3
78TH AV	RCO	108	B1
80TH AV	RCO	107	C1
80TH AV	RCO	108	B1
80TH ST E	LACO	90	B3
80TH ST W	KER	89	D2
80TH ST W	LACO	89	D3
81ST AV	RCO	108	B1
82ND AV	RCO	108	B1
82ND ST	LACO	90	B3
84TH AV	RCO	108	B1
85TH ST W	LACO	89	D3
87TH ST E	LACO	90	B4
87TH ST W	LACO	89	D3
90TH ST E	LACO	90	B3
90TH ST W	KER	89	D2
90TH ST W	LACO	89	D3
92ND ST	LACO	Q	E5
92ND ST W	LACO	89	D3
95TH ST W	LACO	89	D3
96TH ST E	LACO	90	B4
97TH ST W	LACO	89	D3
98TH AV	ALA	L	E5
98TH AV	ALA	45	D2
98TH AV	O	159	E4
98TH ST W	LACO	89	D3
99-97 CUTOFF	SIS	4	B5
100TH ST E	LACO	90	B2
100TH ST W	KER	89	D2
103RD ST	LACO	Q	E5
105TH ST E	LACO	90	B3
106TH ST E	LACO	90	B4
110TH ST E	LACO	90	B3
110TH ST W	KER	79	D5
110TH ST W	LACO	89	D2
115TH ST W	KER	79	D5
120TH ST E	LACO	90	B2
120TH ST W	LACO	89	D2
121ST ST E	LACO	90	B4
130TH ST E	LACO	90	C2
130TH ST W	LACO	89	D2
131ST ST E	LACO	90	C4
135TH ST	LACO	S	C1
137TH ST E	LACO	90	C2
140TH ST E	LACO	90	C2
140TH ST W	KER	89	D1
145TH ST	KER	89	D1
145TH ST E	LACO	90	C3
146TH ST	KER	89	D1
147TH ST	KER	89	C1
149TH ST	KER	89	C1
150TH ST E	LACO	90	C3
152ND ST W	KER	89	C1
155TH ST	KER	89	C1
157TH ST W	KER	89	C1
160TH ST W	LACO	89	C2
164TH ST	LACO	S	B1
165TH ST E	LACO	90	C3
170TH ST E	LACO	90	C3
170TH ST W	KER	89	C2
170TH ST W	LACO	89	C2
175TH ST E	LACO	90	C3
176TH ST	KER	89	C1
177TH ST	KER	89	C1
180TH ST E	LACO	90	C3
180TH ST W	LACO	89	C2
182ND ST	LACO	S	C1
185TH ST E	LACO	90	C3
185TH ST W	KER	89	C2
190TH ST	LACO	97	D3
190TH ST	LACO	S	B1
190TH ST E	LACO	90	C2
190TH ST W	LACO	89	C2
195TH ST	LACO	S	E2
195TH ST	LACO	T	A2
195TH ST E	LACO	90	C2
195TH ST W	KER	89	C2
200TH ST E	LACO	90	D2
200TH ST E	LACO	90	C3
204TH ST E	LACO	90	D4
210TH ST	KER	89	C1
210TH ST E	LACO	90	D3
215TH ST W	KER	89	C2
220TH ST	LACO	S	C2
220TH ST E	LACO	90	D3
223RD ST	LACO	S	C2
223RD ST E	LACO	90	D4
225TH ST E	LACO	90	D2
228TH ST	LACO	S	C2
230TH ST E	LACO	90	D3
230TH ST W	KER	89	B2
233RD ST E	LACO	90	D4
235TH ST E	LACO	90	D3
235TH ST W	KER	89	B2
235TH ST W	LACO	89	B2
240TH ST E	LACO	90	D3
295TH ST W	KER	89	B2
300TH ST W	KER	89	B2
8001	MAD	50	A5
8003	MAD	50	A4
8004	MAD	50	A4
8005	MAD	50	A4
8006	MAD	50	A4
8007	MAD	50	A4
8008	MAD	50	A5
8009	MAD	50	A4
8009	MAD	50	A5
8013	MAD	50	B4
8014	MAD	50	B4
8015	MAD	50	B4
8016	MAD	50	A4
8020	MAD	50	A4
8021	MAD	49	E4
8023	MAD	50	B3
8024	MAD	50	A3
8026	MAD	50	B3
8027	MAD	50	B3
8029	MAD	50	A4
8041	MAD	49	E4
8042	MAD	49	D3
8046	MAD	49	D3
8063	MAD	57	C1
8066	MAD	57	D1
8067	MAD	57	E1
8080	MAD	57	D1
8081	MAD	49	D5
8082	MAD	49	D5
8083	MAD	49	D5
8086	MAD	49	C5
8087	MAD	57	C1

FEDERAL

ROUTE NO.	CO. ABBR.	PAGE	GRID
6	ESM	44	E4
6	MIN	44	D5
6	MNO	51	C1
50	CRSN	36	B2
50	DGL	36	B2
50	ED	35	B4
50	ED	36	A3
50	LYON	36	D1
50	SAC	40	A1
60	LPAZ	104	D4
93	CLK	74	E2
93	MOH	85	E1
95	CLK	74	D2
95	LPAZ	103	E5
95	MIN	44	A1
95	NYE	62	B2
95	RCO	103	E2
95	SBD	85	B4
95	SBD	95	B1
95	SBD	103	D1
95	YUMA	112	E5
97	KLAM	5	B1
97	SIS	4	D5
97	SIS	5	A3
97	SIS	12	C1
101	CUR	1	C1
101	DN	10	A1
101	HUM	9	E3
101	HUM	10	A2
101	HUM	15	D2
101	HUM	16	B4
101	HUM	22	C1
101	LACO	97	B1
101	LACO	Q	B3
101	MAR	38	B5
101	MAR	45	B1
101	MAR	L	A2
101	MEN	22	C2
101	MEN	31	A1
101	MON	54	C3
101	MON	55	A5
101	MON	65	B2
101	SB	86	C1
101	SB	87	A4
101	SBT	54	D3
101	SCL	46	A4
101	SFCO	45	B1
101	SFCO	L	B3
101	SLO	76	A1
101	SMCO	45	C2
101	SMCO	L	C5
101	SMCO	N	D2
101	SCL	54	D1
101	SCL	P	C3
101	SON	32	D5
101	SON	37	E1
101	SON	33	A3
101	VEN	88	A5
101	VEN	96	D1
197	DN	1	E3
199	DN	1	E3
199	DN	2	C3
395	CRSN	36	C2
395	DGL	36	C3
395	INY	51	C3
395	INY	59	E1
395	INY	60	A3
395	INY	70	B1
395	KER	70	C5
395	KER	80	D1
395	LAKE	7	C1
395	LAS	8	B3
395	LAS	21	B3
395	LAS	27	E1
395	MOD	7	C3
395	MOD	8	B2
395	MNO	42	E2
395	MNO	43	A2
395	MNO	50	D1
395	SBD	80	E3
395	SBD	91	A2
395	WSH	28	A3

INTERSTATE

ROUTE NO.	CO. ABBR.	PAGE	GRID
5	COL	32	D1
5	COL	33	A3
5	FRCO	55	E3
5	FRCO	56	B4
5	FRCO	66	D1
5	GLE	24	D3
5	JKSN	4	A1
5	KER	77	E2
5	KER	78	B3
5	KER	88	D1
5	KIN	67	C4
5	LACO	88	E2
5	LACO	89	A3
5	LACO	97	E1
5	LACO	98	B3
5	LACO	Q	C2
5	LACO	R	B5
5	MCO	47	C5
5	MCO	55	E2
5	ORCO	98	B3
5	ORCO	105	E1
5	ORCO	T	E3
5	SAC	39	E2
5	SDCO	106	A2
5	SDCO	111	D2
5	SDCO	V	A2
5	SJCO	39	E4
5	SJCO	40	A4
5	SJCO	47	A2
5	SHA	12	C3
5	SHA	18	C2
5	SIS	4	B3
5	SIS	12	D2
5	STA	47	A3
5	TEH	18	D4
5	TEH	24	D1
5	YOL	33	A4
8	IMP	111	B4
8	SDCO	107	A5
8	SDCO	111	C1
8	SDCO	112	D1
8	SDCO	V	C3
8	YUMA	112	D5
10	LPAZ	103	E5
10	LACO	97	D2
10	LACO	98	A2
10	LACO	Q	C4
10	LACO	U	A2
10	RCO	99	E3
10	RCO	100	A3
10	RCO	101	A4
10	RCO	102	D4
10	RCO	103	B5
10	SBD	99	A1
10	SBD	U	D2
15	CLK	74	E1
15	RCO	99	B4
15	SBD	82	C5
15	SBD	83	D3
15	SBD	84	A2
15	SBD	91	D2
15	SBD	92	B1
15	SBD	99	A1
15	SBD	98	E2
15	SDCO	106	D3
15	SDCO	V	C1
40	SBD	92	A1
40	SBD	93	D2
40	SBD	94	D2
40	SBD	95	C1
80	ALA	L	C4
80	CC	38	C5
80	CC	L	C4
80	NEV	27	C6
80	NEV	35	D1
80	PLA	34	D2
80	PLA	35	A1
80	SAC	33	E5
80	SAC	34	A5
80	SAC	39	E1
80	SFCO	45	C1
80	SFCO	L	C4
80	SOL	38	E3
80	SOL	39	A2
80	WSH	28	A4
80	YOL	39	D1
105	LACO	Q	E5
105	LACO	S	C1
110	LACO	97	D3
110	LACO	Q	E4
110	LACO	S	C2
205	SJCO	46	D2
210	LACO	89	E5
210	LACO	97	E1
210	LACO	98	B1
210	LACO	Q	C1
210	LACO	R	A2
210	LACO	U	A2
215	SBD	99	B1
238	ALA	45	E2
238	ALA	L	E5
280	SCL	45	E4
280	SCL	N	E3
280	SFCO	45	B2
280	SFCO	L	B5
280	SMCO	45	B2
280	SMCO	N	E3
380	SMCO	45	C2
380	SMCO	N	B1
405	LACO	97	C1
405	LACO	Q	B3
405	LACO	S	D2
405	ORCO	98	B4
405	ORCO	T	B3
505	SOL	39	A2
505	YOL	33	A4
505	YOL	39	A1
580	ALA	45	A1
580	ALA	46	A2
580	ALA	L	E5
580	ALA	M	A5
580	CC	L	E5
580	MAR	38	B5
580	SJCO	46	D2
605	LACO	98	B2
605	LACO	R	D3
605	LACO	T	A2
680	ALA	46	B2
680	ALA	P	B1
680	CC	38	E5
680	CC	46	A1
680	CC	L	E3
680	CC	M	A3
680	SCL	46	B4
680	SCL	P	B2
680	SOL	38	E4
710	LACO	97	E2
710	LACO	R	B5
710	LACO	S	D2
780	SOL	38	D4
780	SOL	L	D2
805	SDCO	106	C5
805	SDCO	111	D2
805	SDCO	V	B1
880	ALA	45	E2
880	ALA	157	C3
880	ALA	P	B2
880	SCL	46	B4
980	ALA	45	D1
980	ALA	L	D4

STATE

ROUTE NO.	CO. ABBR.	PAGE	GRID
1	HUM	15	D3
1	LACO	96	D2
1	LACO	97	B2
1	LACO	Q	C4
1	LACO	S	B2
1	MAR	37	E4
1	MAR	45	A1
1	MAR	L	A4
1	MEN	22	C2
1	MEN	30	C3
1	MON	54	B3
1	MON	64	B2
1	MON	65	A4
1	ORCO	98	C5
1	ORCO	105	D1
1	ORCO	T	B4
1	SFCO	45	B1
1	SFCO	L	B4
1	SLO	65	A5
1	SLO	75	B1
1	SLO	76	A4
1	SMCO	45	B2
1	SMCO	L	A4
1	SMCO	N	B1
1	SB	86	B2
1	SCR	53	C1
1	SCR	54	B2
1	SCR	N	C5
1	SON	30	D5
1	SON	37	B1
1	VEN	96	C1
2	LACO	90	C4
2	LACO	97	E1
2	LACO	Q	D3
2	LACO	R	A2
2	SBD	90	E5
3	SIS	3	D5
3	SIS	4	A4
3	SIS	11	D1
3	SIS	12	A2
3	TRI	11	E4
3	TRI	12	A3
3	TRI	17	B2
4	ALP	36	C5
4	ALP	42	B1
4	CAL	41	D2
4	CC	38	D5
4	CC	39	C5
4	CC	L	E3
4	CC	M	B3
4	SJCO	39	E5
4	SJCO	40	B5
4	STA	40	E5
9	SCL	45	E5
9	SCL	N	E4
9	SCL	P	A4
9	SCR	53	D1
9	SCR	N	E4
9	SCR	P	A5
12	CAL	40	D4
12	CAL	41	A3
12	NAPA	38	C3
12	NAPA	L	D1
12	SAC	39	C4
12	SAC	M	E2
12	SJCO	39	E4
12	SJCO	40	A1
12	SOL	38	E3
12	SOL	39	A3
12	SOL	M	C1
12	SON	37	E2
12	SON	38	A2
13	ALA	45	D1
13	ALA	L	D4
14	KER	80	C1
14	KER	89	E1
14	LACO	89	E2
15	SBD	98	E2
15	SDCO	V	C3
16	COL	32	C3
16	SAC	39	E1
16	SAC	40	A1
16	YOL	32	D4
17	SCR	54	A1
17	SCR	P	A4
18	LACO	90	D4
18	SBD	91	A4
18	SBD	92	A4
18	SBD	99	C1
19	LACO	98	A3
19	LACO	R	C3
19	LACO	S	E2
20	COL	32	E2
20	COL	33	A2
20	LAK	31	E3
20	LAK	32	A3
20	MEN	22	D5
20	MEN	31	C2
20	NEV	34	C1
20	SUT	33	C2
20	YUB	33	E1
22	ORCO	98	B4
22	ORCO	T	C2
23	LACO	96	E2
23	VEN	88	D5
23	VEN	96	E1
24	ALA	L	D4
24	CC	38	E5
24	CC	45	E1
24	CC	L	D4
25	MON	65	D2
25	SBT	55	A3
25	SBT	65	D1
26	CAL	41	B2
26	SJCO	40	D4
27	LACO	97	B1
27	LACO	Q	A3
28	CRSN	36	B2
28	PLA	35	E1
28	WSH	36	A1
29	LAK	31	D2
29	LAK	32	A4
29	NAPA	38	B1
29	NAPA	L	D1
29	SOL	38	D4
30	LACO	98	D1
30	LACO	U	C2
30	SBD	98	E1
30	SBD	99	B1
31	RCO	98	E2
31	RCO	U	E4
32	BUT	25	A3
32	GLE	24	D3
32	TEH	19	E4
33	FRCO	56	B2
33	FRCO	66	D2
33	KER	67	B5
33	KER	77	B1
33	KER	78	A5
33	KIN	67	A4
33	MCO	47	C5
33	MCO	55	C1
33	SJCO	47	A2
33	SLO	87	E1
33	SB	87	E1
33	STA	47	B3
33	VEN	88	A2
34	VEN	88	C5
34	VEN	96	C1
35	SFCO	45	B2
35	SFCO	L	B5
35	SMCO	45	C3
35	SMCO	L	B5
35	SMCO	N	C2
35	SCL	46	A5
36	HUM	15	E2
36	HUM	16	C3
36	LAS	20	E3
36	LAS	21	A3
36	PLU	20	A4
36	SHA	17	E4
36	TEH	17	E4
36	TEH	18	C4
36	TEH	19	C4
36	TRI	16	E3
36	TRI	17	A3
37	MAR	L	B2
37	SOL	38	D4
37	SOL	L	C2
37	SON	38	C4
38	SBD	91	E5
38	SBD	92	A5
38	SBD	99	E1
38	SBD	100	B1
39	KLAM	5	C1
39	LACO	98	C1
39	LACO	R	E2
39	LACO	U	A1
39	ORCO	98	B4
39	ORCO	T	B2
41	FRCO	57	C3
41	KIN	67	C2
41	MAD	49	D4
41	MAD	57	C2
41	MPA	63	C5
41	SLO	66	D5
41	SLO	76	A2
42	LACO	97	E2
42	LACO	Q	E5
43	FRCO	57	D5
43	KER	68	B5
43	KER	78	B2
43	KIN	67	E2
43	TUL	68	A3
44	LAS	20	A2
44	SHA	18	C2
44	SHA	19	C2
45	COL	32	E1
45	COL	33	A2
45	GLE	24	E3
45	YOL	33	C4
46	JOS	2	D1
46	KER	77	A1
46	KER	78	B1
46	SLO	66	D5
46	SLO	75	E2
46	SLO	76	B1
47	LACO	191	C3
48	LACO	89	A3
49	AMA	40	D1
49	CAL	41	A3
49	ED	34	D4
49	MAD	49	D4
49	MPA	48	E2
49	MPA	49	A3
49	NEV	34	C1
49	PLA	34	C3
49	PLU	27	D3
49	SIE	26	C4
49	SIE	27	C4
49	TUO	41	C5
49	TUO	48	D1
49	YUBA	26	C4
50	ED	34	C5
50	SAC	39	E1
50	SAC	40	A1
52	SDCO	106	C5
52	SDCO	V	B2
53	LAK	32	A3
54	SDCO	111	E1
54	SDCO	V	C4
55	ORCO	98	C4
55	ORCO	T	D3
56	SDCO	106	D4
57	LACO	98	C2
57	LACO	U	B3
57	ORCO	98	C3
57	ORCO	T	D1
58	KER	77	E3
58	KER	78	B3
58	KER	80	A4
58	SBD	91	C1
58	SLO	76	B3
58	SLO	77	A3
59	MCO	48	C4
60	LACO	98	B2
60	LACO	R	D4
60	RCO	99	B4
60	SBD	98	D2
60	SBD	U	C3
61	ALA	45	D2
61	ALA	L	D5
62	RCO	100	C2
62	RCO	102	E2
62	SBD	101	A1
62	SBD	102	A2
62	SBD	103	B2
63	FRCO	58	B4
63	TUL	58	B5
63	TUL	68	B2
65	KER	68	D6
65	KER	78	D2
65	PLA	34	A3
65	TUL	68	C2
65	YUB	33	D3
66	JKSN	4	A1
66	KLAM	4	D1
66	SBD	98	E1
66	SBD	99	B1
66	SBD	U	D2
67	SDCO	106	E4
67	SDCO	107	A4
67	SDCO	V	E1
68	MOH	85	D4
68	MON	54	B4
70	BUT	25	D3
70	KLAM	5	D1
70	LAS	27	E2
70	PLU	26	A1
70	SUT	33	D4
70	YUB	33	D1
71	LACO	98	D2
71	LACO	U	B2
71	RCO	98	D2
71	SBD	98	D2
71	SBD	U	D4
72	LPAZ	104	B2
72	LACO	97	E2
72	LACO	98	A2
72	LACO	R	B4
73	ORCO	98	C4
73	ORCO	T	D4
74	ORCO	98	E5
74	ORCO	99	A5
74	RCO	99	C4
74	RCO	100	A4
75	SDCO	111	C1
75	SDCO	V	C4
76	SDCO	106	D2
76	SDCO	107	B2
77	ALA	L	D5
77	ALA	45	D1
77	ALA	159	C1
78	IMP	108	C3
78	IMP	109	A4
78	IMP	110	C2
78	RCO	103	D5
78	RCO	110	C1
78	SDCO	106	C3
78	SDCO	107	C3
78	SDCO	108	A3
79	RCO	99	E3
79	RCO	106	D1
79	SDCO	107	B1
80	SFCO	L	C4
82	SCL	46	A4
82	SCL	P	A3
82	SMCO	45	C2
82	SMCO	N	C1
83	SBD	98	D2
83	SBD	U	D3
84	ALA	45	E3
84	ALA	46	B3
84	ALA	P	C1
84	SMCO	45	D4
84	SMCO	N	D3
84	YOL	39	D1
85	SCL	45	E4
85	SCL	P	A3
86	IMP	108	C2
86	IMP	109	A4
86	RCO	101	B4
86	RCO	108	B1
87	SCL	46	B4
87	SCL	P	B4
88	ALP	36	C4
88	AMA	35	D5
88	AMA	41	A2
88	DGL	36	C3
88	SJCO	40	C3
89	ALP	36	B4
89	ED	35	E3
89	ED	36	A4
89	MNO	36	D5
89	NEV	27	D5
89	PLA	35	D1
89	PLU	20	A4
89	PLU	26	C1
89	SHA	13	C3
89	SHA	19	E1
89	SIE	27	C4
89	SIS	12	E2
89	SIS	13	B3
89	TEH	19	D3
90	LACO	Q	C5
90	ORCO	98	C3
90	ORCO	T	D1
90	ORCO	U	B4
91	LACO	97	E3
91	LACO	S	C1
91	ORCO	98	C3
91	ORCO	T	C2
91	RCO	99	A3
91	RCO	U	C5
92	ALA	45	D3
92	ALA	N	E1
92	SMCO	45	D3
92	SMCO	N	C2
94	SDCO	111	E1
94	SDCO	112	D2
94	SDCO	V	D3

HIGHWAY INDEX

ROUTE NO.	CO. ABBR.	PAGE	GRID
95	LPAZ	104	B2
95	MOH	85	D5
95	MOH	95	D1
95	MOH	96	B3
96	HUM	10	C3
96	SIS	2	E4
96	SIS	3	C3
96	SIS	10	E1
98	IMP	111	C3
98	IMP	112	C4
99	BUT	25	B3
99	FRCO	57	B3
99	JKSN	3	E1
99	KER	68	B5
99	KER	78	C2
99	MAD	56	D1
99	MAD	57	B2
99	MCO	48	B4
99	MCO	56	D1
99	SAC	39	E2
99	SAC	40	A2
99	SJCO	40	B4
99	SJCO	47	B1
99	STA	47	D3
99	SUT	33	C3
99	TEH	18	D5
99	TUL	57	E5
103	LACO	97	E4
103	LACO	S	D2
104	SAC	40	C2
107	LACO	97	D3
107	LACO	S	B2
108	MNO	42	E2
108	STA	47	D2
108	TUO	41	D4
108	TUO	42	B2
110	LACO	97	E2
110	LACO	R	B3
111	IMP	108	D1
111	IMP	109	B3
111	IMP	112	B3
111	RCO	100	C3
111	RCO	101	A4
111	RCO	108	D1
112	ALA	45	D2
113	SOL	39	B2
113	SOL	M	C1
113	SUT	33	C3
113	YOL	33	C5
114	SMCO	N	D2
115	IMP	109	B3
115	IMP	112	C3
116	SON	37	D2
116	SON	38	A3
116	SON	L	B1
117	SDCO	111	E2
117	SDCO	V	D5
118	LACO	89	B5
118	LACO	Q	A1
118	VEN	88	C5
118	VEN	89	A5
119	KER	78	B3
120	MNO	43	C5
120	MNO	51	B1
120	SJCO	47	B1
120	STA	48	A1
120	TUO	41	C5
120	TUO	48	C1
120	TUO	49	B1
121	NAPA	38	D2
121	NAPA	L	B1
121	SON	38	B3
121	SON	L	B1
123	ALA	L	C4
124	AMA	40	D2
125	SDCO	106	E4
125	SDCO	V	D3
126	LACO	89	A4
126	VEN	88	D4
126	VEN	89	A4
127	INY	72	D2
127	SBD	72	E5
127	SBD	83	B2
128	MEN	30	C2
128	MEN	31	B4
128	NAPA	38	B2
128	SON	31	D5

ROUTE NO.	CO. ABBR.	PAGE	GRID
128	SON	38	A1
128	YOL	39	A1
129	SCR	54	D2
130	SCL	46	C4
130	SCL	P	C3
131	MAR	38	B5
131	MAR	45	B1
132	MPA	48	D2
132	SJCO	47	A2
132	STA	47	B2
132	STA	48	B2
133	ORCO	98	D5
133	ORCO	T	E4
134	LACO	97	D1
134	LACO	Q	D3
134	LACO	R	A3
135	SB	86	C1
136	INY	60	B4
137	TUL	68	B2
138	LACO	88	E2
138	LACO	89	A2
138	LACO	90	A3
138	SBD	91	A5
139	LAS	14	C3
139	LAS	20	E1
139	LAS	21	A3
139	MOD	5	E3
139	MOD	6	A4
139	MOD	14	D1
139	SIS	5	E3
140	KLAM	5	C1
140	LAKE	7	A1
140	MCO	47	D4
140	MCO	48	A4
140	MPA	48	E4
140	MPA	49	C2
142	ORCO	T	E1
142	ORCO	U	B4
142	SBD	98	D2
144	SB	87	C4
145	FRCO	57	A4
145	FRCO	66	E1
145	MAD	57	B2
146	CLK	74	E3
146	MON	55	B5
146	SBT	55	C5
147	PLU	20	C4
149	BUT	25	C4
150	SB	87	E4
150	VEN	88	B4
151	SHA	18	C1
152	MAD	56	C1
152	MCO	55	E1
152	MCO	56	B1
152	SCL	54	D2
152	SCR	54	C2
154	SB	87	A3
155	KER	68	B5
155	KER	69	B5
155	KER	79	C1
156	CLK	72	E1
156	CLK	74	A1
156	MON	54	C3
156	SBT	54	E2
156	SBT	55	A2
157	CLK	73	E2
157	CLK	74	A2
158	CLK	73	E1
158	CLK	74	A1
158	MNO	50	C1
160	CLK	73	E3
160	CLK	74	B3
160	NYE	73	C2
160	SAC	39	E1
160	SAC	M	D2
161	CLK	74	C5
161	SIS	5	B2
162	BUT	25	B5
162	GLE	24	B4
162	GLE	25	B5
162	MEN	22	E4
162	MEN	23	A3
163	CLK	85	C4
163	SDCO	106	D5
163	SDCO	V	C2
164	CLK	84	E2
164	LACO	98	A1

ROUTE NO.	CO. ABBR.	PAGE	GRID
165	MCO	47	E5
165	MCO	55	E2
166	KER	77	A4
166	KER	78	B5
166	SB	86	B1
166	SLO	76	D5
167	MNO	43	E4
168	FRCO	50	B5
168	FRCO	57	E2
168	FRCO	58	A1
168	INY	51	E5
168	INY	52	C3
168	MNO	52	C3
169	DN	1	E5
169	DN	2	A5
169	DN	10	A1
169	HUM	10	C3
170	LACO	97	D1
170	LACO	Q	C2
172	TEH	19	D4
173	SBD	91	C5
174	NEV	34	D2
175	LAK	31	E3
175	LAK	32	A5
175	MEN	31	C3
176	SB	86	C1
177	RCO	102	D2
178	INY	72	D3
178	INY	73	A3
178	KERN	69	E5
178	KER	70	A5
178	KER	78	E2
178	KER	79	A2
178	KER	80	B1
178	SBD	81	A1
180	FRCO	56	E3
180	FRCO	57	C3
180	FRCO	58	B3
180	FRCO	59	A3
182	MNO	43	C2
183	MON	54	C3
184	KER	78	E3
185	ALA	45	D1
188	SDCO	112	C2
189	SBD	91	C5
190	INY	61	D4
190	INY	70	C1
190	INY	72	C1
190	TUL	68	B3
190	TUL	69	A3
191	BUT	25	C3
192	SB	87	C4
193	ED	34	E4
193	PLA	34	B3
195	RCO	101	B5
198	FRCO	66	E2
198	KIN	67	C2
198	MON	65	D2
198	MON	66	A2
198	TUL	58	E5
198	TUL	59	A5
198	TUL	68	B1
200	HUM	9	E5
200	HUM	10	A5
201	TUL	58	B5
202	KER	79	C4
203	MNO	50	D2
204	KER	78	D3
206	DGL	36	B3
206	SBD	99	B1
207	DGL	36	B3
208	DGL	36	E4
208	MEN	22	B2
209	SDCO	111	C1
209	SDCO	V	A4
213	LACO	S	C3
213	LACO	97	D3
215	RCO	99	C3
216	TUL	68	C1
217	SB	87	B4
218	MON	54	B4
219	STA	47	C2
220	SOL	39	D3
221	NAPA	38	D3
223	KER	78	D4
223	KER	79	A4
224	SB	87	E4

ROUTE NO.	CO. ABBR.	PAGE	GRID
225	SB	87	C4
227	SLO	76	B4
229	SLO	76	B2
232	VEN	88	B5
233	MAD	56	D1
236	SCR	53	D1
236	SCR	N	D4
237	SCL	46	B4
237	SCL	P	B3
238	ALA	46	A2
238	ALA	P	A1
241	ORCO	98	D4
242	CC	M	A3
243	RCO	100	A3
245	FRCO	58	D4
245	TUL	58	C4
245	TUL	68	C1
246	SB	86	C3
247	SBD	91	E2
247	SBD	92	B4
247	SBD	100	D1
250	ORCO	98	C3
253	MEN	31	A3
254	HUM	16	B4
255	HUM	9	E5
255	HUM	10	A5
259	SBD	99	B1
262	ALA	46	A3
262	ALA	P	B2
263	SIS	4	A4
264	ESM	52	A1
265	ESM	52	E1
266	MNO	52	C3
267	ESM	61	C1
267	PLA	35	E1
267	PLA	36	A1
269	FRCO	67	A1
270	MNO	43	B3
271	MEN	22	C1
273	SHA	18	C2
274	SDCO	106	C5
274	SDCO	V	B2
281	LAK	31	E3
282	SDCO	111	C1
282	SDCO	V	B4
284	PLU	27	D2
299	HUM	10	B4
299	LAS	14	A3
299	MOD	7	C5
299	MOD	8	B1
299	MOD	14	D1
299	SHA	13	B5
299	SHA	18	B2
299	TRI	10	D5
299	TRI	16	E1
299	TRI	17	D1
330	SBD	99	C1
338	LYON	43	B1
341	LYON	36	D1
341	WSH	28	C5
359	MIN	44	B2
360	MIN	44	E3
371	RCO	100	B5
372	NYE	73	B2
373	NYE	62	D5
374	NYE	62	A3
380	SMCO	N	B1
428	WSH	36	C1
429	WSH	36	B1
430	WSH	28	B4
431	WSH	28	B5
431	WSH	36	B1
445	WSH	28	D1
446	WSH	28	E2
447	WSH	28	E2
512	CRSN	36	C2
513	CRSN	36	C2
604	CLK	74	E2
759	DGL	36	C3
905	SDCO	V	D5
COUNTY			
1	LPAZ	103	E3
1	LPAZ	104	A1
3	LPAZ	104	B2
10	LPAZ	104	A2
14	LPAZ	103	E2

ROUTE NO.	CO. ABBR.	PAGE	GRID
14	LPAZ	104	A2
17	LPAZ	103	E2
17	LPAZ	104	A2
21	LPAZ	103	E3
21	LPAZ	104	A3
25	LPAZ	103	E3
29	LPAZ	103	E2
30	LPAZ	103	E3
30	LPAZ	104	A3
34	LPAZ	103	E3
38	LPAZ	103	E3
44	LPAZ	103	E3
44	LPAZ	104	A3
50	LPAZ	103	E4
56	LPAZ	103	E4
A 1	LAS	20	D2
A 2	LAS	14	C3
A 3	LAS	21	B4
A 5	TEH	18	C3
A 6	TEH	18	E4
A 6	TEH	19	B3
A 7	TEH	18	D5
A 8	TEH	18	D5
A 9	TEH	24	D2
A10	SIS	12	C2
A11	TEH	24	D1
A12	SIS	4	B5
A13	PLU	20	B4
A14	PLU	27	A3
A15	PLU	27	B2
A16	SHA	17	E3
A16	SHA	18	A3
A16	SHA	122	A2
A17	SHA	18	D3
A17	SHA	19	A3
A18	SHA	18	C2
A19	SHA	13	D3
A21	LAS	20	C3
A22	PLU	20	D5
A23	PLU	27	C2
A23	SIE	27	C3
A24	PLU	27	D3
A25	LAS	21	D5
A26	LAS	21	D5
A27	LAS	21	B3
B 2	BUT	25	D4
D 1	DN	1	E3
D 2	DN	1	D4
D 3	DN	1	D3
D 5	DN	1	D2
E 1	ALP	36	C5
E 4	YOL	32	E4
E 4	YOL	33	A4
E 6	YOL	39	B1
E 6	YOL	136	B2
E 7	SOL	39	B1
E 7	YOL	33	B5
E 8	YOL	33	C4
E 8	YOL	39	C1
E 9	YOL	39	D2
E10	YOL	33	B4
E11	YOL	33	B4
E13	SAC	39	D3
E16	AMA	40	E1
E16	ED	35	B4
G 1	SBT	54	E3
G 2	SCL	46	A4
G 2	SCL	P	A3
G 2	SCLR	150	C1
G 3	PA	147	D3
G 3	SCL	45	D4
G 3	SCL	147	C6
G 3	SCL	N	D3
G 4	SCL	46	A4
G 4	SCL	P	B3
G 4	SCLR	150	E1
G 4	SCLR	151	A1
G 5	PA	147	C6
G 5	SCL	45	E4
G 5	SCL	147	A4
G 5	SCL	149	A3
G 5	SCL	P	A3
G 5	SCL	N	E3
G 6	SCL	45	E4
G 6	SCL	46	A4
G 6	SCL	148	C5
G 6	SCLR	151	B1

ROUTE NO.	CO. ABBR.	PAGE	GRID
G 7	SCL	54	D2
G 8	SCL	46	B5
G 8	SCL	54	C1
G 8	SCL	P	B4
G 9	SCL	54	D2
G10	SCL	46	B5
G10	SCL	P	B4
G11	MON	54	C3
G12	MON	54	C3
G13	MON	65	C2
G13	SBT	65	C1
G14	MON	65	B3
G15	MON	65	B1
G16	MON	54	B5
G16	MON	64	C1
G16	MON	65	B1
G16	MON	168	E4
G17	MON	54	C4
G17	MON	65	A1
G18	MON	65	D4
G19	MON	65	E5
G20	MON	54	C5
J 1	FRCO	55	E3
J 1	FRCO	56	A3
J 1	SBT	55	B4
J 2	ALA	46	C2
J 2	ALA	P	D1
J 2	SJCO	46	E1
J 3	SJCO	47	B2
J 4	CC	46	D1
J 4	SJCO	46	E2
J 4	SJCO	47	A2
J 5	SJCO	40	B4
J 5	SJCO	47	C1
J 6	SJCO	40	C5
J 6	SJCO	47	D1
J 7	MCO	47	E3
J 7	MCO	48	A3
J 7	SJCO	40	B5
J 7	SJCO	47	C1
J 7	STA	47	D2
J 8	SCTO	137	D5
J 9	SJCO	47	C1
J 9	STA	47	D1
J 9	STA	48	A3
J11	SAC	39	D3
J11	SJCO	39	D3
J12	SJCO	40	C3
J13	SJCO	46	E1
J14	STA	40	E5
J14	STA	47	E1
J15	TUL	68	B2
J16	MPA	48	E3
J16	MCO	48	B3
J16	STA	47	D3
J17	MCO	48	A3
J17	STA	47	C3
J18	STA	47	C4
J19	FRCO	58	B4
J19	TUL	58	A5
J20	MPA	48	E2
J20	TUO	48	E1
J21	TUL	58	D5
J22	TUL	68	B4
J23	TUL	58	C5
J23	TUL	68	C2
J24	TUL	68	B4
J25	TUL	68	A1
J27	TUL	68	C2
J28	TUL	68	C2
J29	TUL	68	D2
J30	TUL	68	B1
J32	TUL	68	A1
J34	TUL	68	A1
J38	TUL	57	E5
J38	TUL	58	B5
J40	TUL	58	A5
J41	TUL	70	B4
J42	TUL	68	E3
J42	TUL	69	A3
J44	TUL	68	C5
J59	MCO	48	C2
J59	TUO	48	C1
N 1	LACO	97	B2
N 2	LACO	89	A2
N 3	LACO	89	E5
N 3	LACO	90	A4

ROUTE NO.	CO. ABBR.	PAGE	GRID
N 5	LACO	90	A2
N 6	LACO	90	C4
N 7	LACO	S	B3
N 8	LACO	98	C2
N 8	LACO	R	D5
N 9	LACO	96	E2
N 9	LACO	97	A2
R 2	RCO	102	B4
R 3	RCO	99	E5
R 3	RCO	100	A5
R 3	RCO	106	E1
R 3	RCO	107	A1
S 1	SDCO	107	D4
S 1	SDCO	112	D1
S 2	IMP	111	B3
S 2	SDCO	107	C3
S 2	SDCO	108	A4
S 2	SDCO	111	B3
S 3	SDCO	107	E3
S 4	SDCO	106	D4
S 4	SDCO	V	C1
S 5	SDCO	106	D4
S 6	SDCO	106	E2
S 6	SDCO	107	A2
S 7	SDCO	107	A2
S 8	SDCO	106	C4
S 9	SDCO	106	C4
S10	SDCO	106	C3
S11	SDCO	106	C3
S12	SDCO	106	D3
S13	SDCO	106	C1
S14	SDCO	106	C3
S15	SDCO	106	C2
S16	RCO	106	D1
S16	SDCO	106	D1
S17	SDCO	V	E3
S17	SDCO	111	E1
S17	SDCO	112	A1
S18	ORCO	T	E4
S18	ORCO	98	D4
S19	ORCO	98	E4
S20	SB	86	B2
S21	SDCO	V	A1
S21	SDCO	106	C5
S22	IMP	108	C2
S22	SDCO	107	E2
S22	SDCO	108	B2
S24	IMP	112	D5
S24	IMP	110	D5
S26	IMP	109	A4
S27	IMP	109	A5
S28	IMP	109	A5
S28	IMP	112	C3
S29	IMP	108	E5
S29	IMP	111	E3
S30	IMP	109	A3
S30	IMP	112	A3
S31	IMP	109	B4
S31	IMP	112	B3
S32	IMP	109	C4
S32	IMP	112	C3
S33	IMP	109	C4
S33	IMP	112	C4
S34	IMP	110	B4
S80	IMP	108	C5
S80	IMP	109	A5
S80	IMP	111	D3
S80	IMP	112	A3

HIGHWAY INDEX

HIGHWAY NAME	HWY NO.	CO. ABBR.	PAGE	GRID
ANDERSON, GLENN FWY	105	LACO	Q	C5
ANDERSON, GLENN FWY	105	LACO	189	C2
ANGELES CREST HWY	2	LACO	90	B5
ANGELES CREST HWY	2	SBD	90	E5
ANTELOPE VALLEY FWY	14	KER	89	E2
ANTELOPE VALLEY FWY	14	KER	90	A2
ANTELOPE VALLEY FWY	14	LACO	89	D4
ANTELOPE VALLEY FWY	14	LACO	90	A2
ARROYO PKWY	110	LACO	190	C5
ARTESIA FWY	91	LACO	97	E3
ARTESIA FWY	91	LACO	S	C1
ARTESIA FWY	91	ORCO	98	A3
BAKERSFIELD-MCKITTRICK HWY	58	KER	78	A3
BARSTOW FWY	15	SBD	82	C5
BARSTOW FWY	15	SBD	83	D3
BARSTOW FWY	15	SBD	84	A2
BARSTOW FWY	15	SBD	91	B5
BARSTOW FWY	15	SBD	92	B1
BARSTOW FWY	215	SBD	99	B1
BAY HWY	1	SON	37	C3
BAYSHORE FWY	101	BLMT	145	D4
BAYSHORE FWY	101	SCL	N	E3
BAYSHORE FWY	101	SCL	P	A3
BAYSHORE FWY	101	SCL	46	A4
BAYSHORE FWY	101	SCL	148	A3
BAYSHORE FWY	101	SCL	151	D1
BAYSHORE FWY	101	SCL	152	B1
BAYSHORE FWY	101	SMCO	L	C5
BAYSHORE FWY	101	SMCO	N	D2
BAYSHORE FWY	101	SMCO	45	D3
BAYSHORE FWY	101	SMCO	144	C2
BOULDER HWY	93	CLK	74	E2
BOULDER HWY	95	CLK	74	E2
BURNS FWY	101	HUM	9	E5
BURNS FWY	101	HUM	10	A5
BURNS FWY	101	HUM	15	E1
CABRILLO FWY	163	SDCO	V	B3
CABRILLO FWY	163	SDCO	111	C1
CABRILLO FWY	163	SDCO	213	E1
CABRILLO FWY	163	SDCO	215	E2
CABRILLO HWY	1	MAR	53	D4
CABRILLO HWY	1	MON	54	B4
CABRILLO HWY	1	MON	64	B2
CABRILLO HWY	1	MON	65	A4
CABRILLO HWY	1	MON	168	C2
CABRILLO HWY	1	SB	86	B1
CABRILLO HWY	1	SCR	N	D5
CABRILLO HWY	1	SCR	53	C1
CABRILLO HWY	1	SCR	54	B2
CABRILLO HWY	1	SCR	169	A4
CABRILLO HWY	1	SLO	65	A5
CABRILLO HWY	1	SLO	75	B1
CABRILLO HWY	1	SLO	76	B5
CABRILLO HWY	1	SLO	172	B1
CABRILLO HWY	1	SMCO	L	B5
CABRILLO HWY	1	SMCO	N	B2
CABRILLO HWY	1	SMCO	45	B3
CALF CANYON HWY	58	SLO	76	C2
CENTRAL EXPWY	82	SCL	N	E3
CENTRAL FWY	101	SFCO	142	C5
CENTRAL SKYWAY	101	SFCO	142	C4
CENTRAL VALLEY HWY	43	KER	78	B1
CENTURY FWY	105	LACO	Q	D5
CHARLES BROWN HWY	178	INY	73	A3
COAST HWY	1	ORCO	105	D1
COAST HWY	1	ORCO	199	C4
COAST HWY	1	ORCO	201	A2
COAST HWY	1	ORCO	202	D5
COAST HWY	1	SON	30	D5
COAST HWY	1	SON	37	B2
COAST HWY E	1	ORCO	200	A5
CORONA DEL MAR FWY	73	ORCO	T	D4
CORONA DEL MAR FWY	73	ORCO	98	C4
CORONA DEL MAR FWY	73	ORCO	197	D4
CORONA DEL MAR FWY	73	ORCO	198	A5
CORONA EXPWY	71	LACO	U	C3
CORONA EXPWY	71	LACO	98	D2
CORONA EXPWY	71	RCO	98	D2
CORONA EXPWY	71	SBD	U	C3
CORONA EXPWY	71	SBD	98	D2

HIGHWAY NAME	HWY NO.	CO. ABBR.	PAGE	GRID
CORONA FWY	15	RCO	99	B4
COSTA MESA FWY	55	ORCO	T	C4
COSTA MESA FWY	55	ORCO	98	C4
COSTA MESA FWY	55	ORCO	194	E3
COSTA MESA FWY	55	ORCO	196	E3
COSTA MESA FWY	55	ORCO	197	E5
COSTA MESA FWY	55	ORCO	198	B3
DEKEMA, JACOB FWY	805	SDCO	V	D4
DEKEMA, JACOB FWY	805	SDCO	106	C5
DEKEMA, JACOB FWY	805	SDCO	111	D2
DEKEMA, JACOB FWY	805	SDCO	214	A3
DEKEMA, JACOB FWY	805	SDCO	216	C1
EASTSHORE FWY	80	ALA	L	D3
EASTSHORE FWY	80	CC	L	D3
EASTSHORE FWY	80	CC	38	C5
EASTSHORE FWY	80	CC	155	D3
EL CAMINO REAL	101	MON	54	D4
EL CAMINO REAL	101	MON	55	A5
EL CAMINO REAL	101	MON	65	B2
EL CAMINO REAL	101	MON	66	A5
EL CAMINO REAL	101	MON	171	D3
EL CAMINO REAL	101	SB	86	C1
EL CAMINO REAL	101	SB	87	A4
EL CAMINO REAL	101	SBT	54	D2
EL CAMINO REAL	101	SCL	54	D2
EL CAMINO REAL	82	SCL	147	B3
EL CAMINO REAL	82	SCL	149	E2
EL CAMINO REAL	82	SCL	150	B2
EL CAMINO REAL	82	SCL	151	A2
EL CAMINO REAL	101	SLO	66	A5
EL CAMINO REAL	101	SLO	76	A4
EL CAMINO REAL	101	SLO	172	B3
EL CAMINO REAL	82	SMCO	145	A3
EL DORADO FWY	50	SAC	40	A1
ELVAS FWY	80	SAC	137	E2
ESCONDIDO FWY	215	RCO	99	C4
ESCONDIDO FWY	15	SDCO	214	D4
ESCONDIDO FWY	15	SDCO	V	C1
ESCONDIDO FWY	15	SDCO	106	D2
ESCONDIDO FWY	15	SDCO	216	D3
EVAN HEWES HWY	8	IMP	111	B4
EVAN HEWES HWY	8	IMP	112	A5
EVAN HEWES HWY	8	IMP	112	D3
FAMOSO HWY	46	KER	78	A1
FOOTHILL FWY	210	LACO	Q	B1
FOOTHILL FWY	210	LACO	R	B2
FOOTHILL FWY	210	LACO	U	A2
FOOTHILL FWY	210	LACO	89	D5
FOOTHILL FWY	210	LACO	97	D1
FOOTHILL FWY	210	LACO	98	A1
FOOTHILL FWY	210	LACO	190	B2
FOOTHILL TRANS. CORRIDOR	241	ORCO	98	E4
GARDEN GROVE FWY	22	ORCO	T	C3
GARDEN GROVE FWY	22	ORCO	98	B4
GARDEN GROVE FWY	22	ORCO	195	B2
GARDEN GROVE FWY	22	ORCO	196	B1
GIBSON, LUTHER E FWY	680	SOL	L	E2
GIBSON, LUTHER E FWY	680	SOL	38	E4
GIBSON, LUTHER E FWY	680	SOL	153	E4
GLENDALE FWY	2	LACO	R	A3
GLENDALE FWY	2	LACO	97	E1
GLENN ANDERSON FWY	105	LACO	Q	C5
GLENN ANDERSON FWY	105	LACO	189	C2
GOLD COUNTRY HWY	49	AMA	40	D1
GOLD COUNTRY HWY	49	CAL	41	A3
GOLD COUNTRY HWY	49	ED	34	C4
GOLD COUNTRY HWY	49	ED	40	A1
GOLD COUNTRY HWY	49	ED	138	B1
GOLD COUNTRY HWY	49	MPA	48	D1
GOLD COUNTRY HWY	49	MPA	49	A3
GOLD COUNTRY HWY	49	NEV	34	C1
GOLD COUNTRY HWY	49	PLA	34	C3
GOLD COUNTRY HWY	49	PLA	126	B1
GOLD COUNTRY HWY	49	PLU	27	D3
GOLD COUNTRY HWY	49	SIE	26	C4
GOLD COUNTRY HWY	49	SIE	27	C3
GOLD COUNTRY HWY	49	TUO	41	A3
GOLD COUNTRY HWY	49	TUO	48	D1
GOLD COUNTRY HWY	49	TUO	163	B1
GOLDEN CENTER FWY	20	NEV	127	D3

HIGHWAY INDEX

HIGHWAY NAME	HWY NO.	CO. ABBR.	PAGE	GRID
GOLDEN CENTER FWY	20	NEV	128	A4
GOLDEN GATE FWY	101	MAR	L	B4
GOLDEN GATE FWY	101	SFCO	L	B4
GOLDEN GATE FWY	101	SFCO	45	B1
GOLDEN STATE FWY	5	LACO	Q	B1
GOLDEN STATE FWY	5	LACO	R	C5
GOLDEN STATE FWY	5	LACO	88	E2
GOLDEN STATE FWY	5	LACO	89	B4
GOLDEN STATE FWY	5	LACO	97	D1
GOLDEN STATE FWY	5	LACO	179	C1
GOLDEN STATE FWY	5	LACO	182	D2
GOLDEN STATE FWY	5	LACO	186	D3
GROVE SHAFTER FWY	980	ALA	L	D4
GROVE SHAFTER FWY	980	ALA	45	D1
GROVE SHAFTER FWY	24	ALA	156	A5
GROVE SHAFTER FWY	980	ALA	158	A2
GUADALUPE PKWY	87	SCL	151	D1
GUADALUPE FWY	87	SCL	152	A3
HARBOR FWY	110	LACO	Q	E5
HARBOR FWY	110	LACO	S	C2
HARBOR FWY	110	LACO	97	D4
HARBOR FWY	110	LACO	185	D4
HARBOR FWY	110	LACO	191	A2
HOLLYWOOD FWY	170	LACO	Q	C2
HOLLYWOOD FWY	101	LACO	Q	D3
HOLLYWOOD FWY	101	LACO	97	D1
HOLLYWOOD FWY	170	LACO	97	D1
HOLLYWOOD FWY	101	LACO	181	C2
HOLLYWOOD FWY	101	LACO	185	D1
HOLLYWOOD FWY	101	LACO	186	A2
HOLMAN HWY	68	MON	168	C1
IDYLLWILD NATL FOREST HWY	74	RCO	100	A4
JACOB DEKEMA FWY	805	SDCO	V	D4
JACOB DEKEMA FWY	805	SDCO	106	C5
JACOB DEKEMA FWY	805	SDCO	111	D2
JACOB DEKEMA FWY	805	SDCO	214	A1
JACOB DEKEMA FWY	805	SDCO	216	C1
JAMES LICK FWY	80	SFCO	L	C4
JAMES LICK FWY	80	SFCO	45	C1
JAMES LICK FWY	101	SFCO	142	D5
JAMES LICK SKYWY	80	SFCO	142	D4
JAMES LICK SKYWY	101	SFCO	143	C5
JOHN T KNOX FWY	580	CC	L	C3
JOHN T KNOX FWY	580	CC	155	B4
JUNIPERO SERRA FWY	280	SCL	N	D2
JUNIPERO SERRA FWY	280	SCL	P	A3
JUNIPERO SERRA FWY	280	SCL	45	D3
JUNIPERO SERRA FWY	101	SCL	149	B3
JUNIPERO SERRA FWY	101	SCL	150	A4
JUNIPERO SERRA FWY	280	SMCO	N	B1
JUNIPERO SERRA FWY	280	SMCO	45	B2
KNOX, JOHN T FWY	580	CC	L	C3
KNOX, JOHN T FWY	580	CC	155	B4
LAGUNA FWY	133	ORCO	T	E4
LAGUNA FWY	133	ORCO	98	D5
LAKEVILLE HWY	116	SON	L	A1
LICK, JAMES FWY	80	SFCO	L	C4
LICK, JAMES FWY	80	SFCO	45	C1
LICK, JAMES FWY	101	SFCO	142	D5
LICK, JAMES SKYWY	80	SFCO	142	D4
LICK, JAMES SKYWY	101	SFCO	143	C5
LONG BEACH FWY	710	LACO	R	B4
LONG BEACH FWY	710	LACO	S	D2
LONG BEACH FWY	710	LACO	97	E3
LONG BEACH FWY	710	LACO	192	C2
LOS BANOS HWY	59	MCO	170	C5
LUTHER E GIBSON FWY	680	SOL	L	E2
LUTHER E GIBSON FWY	680	SOL	38	E4
LUTHER E GIBSON FWY	680	SOL	153	E4
MACARTHUR FWY	580	ALA	L	D4
MACARTHUR FWY	580	ALA	45	D1
MACARTHUR FWY	580	ALA	158	B2
MARICOPA HWY	166	KER	78	B5
MARINA EXPWY	90	LACO	187	D3
MARINA FWY	90	LACO	Q	C4
MARINA FWY	90	LACO	97	C2
MARINA FWY	90	LACO	188	A3
MARINE WORLD PKWY	37	SOL	134	B2
MIDLAND TRAIL	14	KER	80	C2
MISSION VALLEY FWY	8	SDCO	V	B3

HIGHWAY NAME	HWY NO.	CO. ABBR.	PAGE	GRID
MISSION VALLEY FWY	8	SDCO	111	C1
MISSION VALLEY FWY	8	SDCO	213	B4
NEEDLES FWY	40	SBD	92	A1
NEEDLES FWY	40	SBD	93	D2
NEEDLES FWY	40	SBD	94	D2
NEEDLES FWY	40	SBD	208	D3
NEEDLES FWY	40	SBD	95	C1
NIMITZ FWY	880	ALA	L	E5
NIMITZ FWY	880	ALA	P	B2
NIMITZ FWY	880	ALA	45	D2
NIMITZ FWY	880	ALA	46	A3
NIMITZ FWY	880	ALA	146	C4
NIMITZ FWY	880	ALA	157	D3
NIMITZ FWY	880	ALA	158	B4
NIMITZ FWY	880	ALA	159	C1
NORTH HWY	190	INY	72	B1
OCEAN BEACH FWY	8	SDCO	212	C5
OJAI FWY	33	VEN	88	A5
OJAI FWY	33	VEN	175	A2
ONTARIO FRWY	15	SBD	98	E2
ONTARIO FRWY	15	SBD	99	A1
ORANGE FWY	57	LACO	U	B3
ORANGE FWY	57	LACO	98	C3
ORANGE FWY	57	ORCO	T	D1
ORANGE FWY	57	ORCO	U	A4
ORANGE FWY	57	ORCO	98	C3
ORANGE FWY	57	ORCO	194	A4
ORTEGA HWY	74	ORCO	98	E5
ORTEGA HWY	74	ORCO	99	A5
ORTEGA HWY	74	ORCO	202	E1
PACIFIC COAST HWY	1	LACO	Q	C4
PACIFIC COAST HWY	1	LACO	S	B1
PACIFIC COAST HWY	1	LACO	96	E2
PACIFIC COAST HWY	1	LACO	97	B2
PACIFIC COAST HWY	1	ORCO	T	A3
PACIFIC COAST HWY	1	ORCO	98	C5
PACIFIC COAST HWY	1	VEN	96	C2
PASADENA FWY	110	LACO	R	A3
PASADENA FWY	110	LACO	97	E2
PASADENA FWY	110	LACO	186	B2
PASO ROBLES HWY	46	KER	77	A1
PINES TO PALMS HWY	74	RCO	100	B4
POMONA FWY	60	LACO	R	E4
POMONA FWY	60	LACO	98	B2
POMONA FWY	60	SBD	U	D3
POMONA FWY	60	SBD	98	D2
PORTERVILLE HWY	65	KER	68	D5
PORTERVILLE HWY	65	KER	78	D1
PORTERVILLE HWY	65	TUL	68	C2
RAMONA FWY	125	SDCO	V	D2
REDLANDS FWY	10	RCO	99	D2
REDLANDS FWY	10	RCO	100	A3
REDLANDS FWY	10	SBD	99	D2
REDONDO BEACH FWY	91	KER	97	E3
REDONDO BEACH FWY	91	LACO	S	C1
REDWOOD HWY	101	DN	1	E3
REDWOOD HWY	199	DN	2	B3
REDWOOD HWY	101	DN	10	A1
REDWOOD HWY	101	HUM	9	E3
REDWOOD HWY	101	HUM	10	A2
REDWOOD HWY	101	HUM	15	E3
REDWOOD HWY	101	HUM	16	B4
REDWOOD HWY	101	HUM	22	C1
REDWOOD HWY	101	MAR	L	A2
REDWOOD HWY	101	MAR	38	A4
REDWOOD HWY	101	MAR	45	B1
REDWOOD HWY	101	MAR	139	D2
REDWOOD HWY	101	MAR	140	C2
REDWOOD HWY	101	MEN	22	C2
REDWOOD HWY	101	MEN	31	A1
REDWOOD HWY	101	SON	L	A2
REDWOOD HWY	101	SON	31	C4
REDWOOD HWY	101	SON	37	D1
REDWOOD HWY	101	SON	38	A3
REDWOOD HWY	101	SON	131	C2
RIVERSIDE FWY	91	ORCO	T	D2
RIVERSIDE FWY	91	ORCO	U	C5
RIVERSIDE FWY	91	ORCO	98	C3
RIVERSIDE FWY	91	ORCO	194	D1
RIVERSIDE FWY	91	RCO	U	C5

HIGHWAY INDEX

HIGHWAY NAME	HWY NO.	CO. ABBR.	PAGE	GRID
RIVERSIDE FWY	91	RCO	99	A3
RIVERSIDE FWY	91	RCO	205	C2
RIVERSIDE FWY	91	RIV	205	B3
RIVERSIDE FWY	215	RCO	205	D1
RIVERSIDE FWY	215	SBD	99	B2
RONALD REAGAN FRWY	118	LACO	Q	C1
RONALD REAGAN FRWY	118	LACO	89	B5
RONALD REAGAN FRWY	118	VEN	88	E5
RONALD REAGAN FRWY	118	VEN	89	B5
ROSEDALE HWY	58	KER	78	C3
ROUTE 4 FWY	4	CC	M	B3
ROUTE 4 FWY	4	CC	154	C3
ROUTE 8 FWY	8	SDCO	106	D5
ROUTE 8 FWY	8	SDCO	107	A5
ROUTE 8 FWY	8	SDCO	111	A4
ROUTE 8 FWY	8	SDCO	112	D1
ROUTE 17 FWY	17	SCL	46	A5
ROUTE 17 FWY	17	SCR	P	B4
ROUTE 17 FWY	17	SCR	54	A1
ROUTE 52 FWY	52	SDCO	211	E3
ROUTE 67 FWY	67	SDCO	106	E5
ROUTE 78 FWY	78	SDCO	106	C3
ROUTE 94 FWY	94	SDCO	V	D3
ROUTE 94 FWY	94	SDCO	216	D3
ROUTE 101 FWY	101	SB	86	D2
ROUTE 101 FWY	101	SB	173	C1
SAN BERNARDINO FWY	10	LACO	U	B2
SAN BERNARDINO FWY	10	LACO	98	B2
SAN BERNARDINO FWY	10	LACO	186	D3
SAN BERNARDINO FWY	10	SBD	U	D2
SAN BERNARDINO FWY	10	SBD	98	D2
SAN BERNARDINO FWY	10	SBD	99	A1
SAN BERNARDINO FWY	10	SBD	203	B3
SAN BERNARDINO FWY	10	SBD	204	D3
SAN DIEGO FWY	405	LACO	Q	B3
SAN DIEGO FWY	405	LACO	S	B2
SAN DIEGO FWY	405	LACO	97	C2
SAN DIEGO FWY	405	LACO	180	C2
SAN DIEGO FWY	405	LACO	188	D4
SAN DIEGO FWY	405	LACO	189	E2
SAN DIEGO FWY	405	ORCO	T	B3
SAN DIEGO FWY	405	ORCO	98	B4
SAN DIEGO FWY	5	ORCO	98	D4
SAN DIEGO FWY	5	ORCO	105	D1
SAN DIEGO FWY	405	ORCO	197	A3
SAN DIEGO FWY	405	ORCO	198	D4
SAN DIEGO FWY	5	ORCO	202	D3
SAN DIEGO FWY	5	SDCO	V	A2
SAN DIEGO FWY	5	SDCO	106	A2
SAN DIEGO FWY	5	SDCO	111	D2
SAN DIEGO FWY	5	SDCO	211	C4
SAN DIEGO FWY	5	SDCO	212	E3
SAN DIEGO FWY	5	SDCO	213	A4
SAN DIEGO FWY	5	SDCO	216	B5
SAN GABRIEL RIVER FWY	605	LACO	R	D4
SAN GABRIEL RIVER FWY	605	LACO	S	E2
SAN GABRIEL RIVER FWY	605	LACO	T	A2
SAN GABRIEL RIVER FWY	605	LACO	98	A2
SAN JOAQUIN HILLS TRANS CORR	73	ORCO	T	E5
SAN JOAQUIN HILLS TRANS CORR	73	ORCO	98	C5
SAN JOAQUIN HILLS TRANS CORR	73	ORCO	200	C3
SANTA ANA FWY	5	LACO	98	A2
SANTA ANA FWY	5	LACO	186	D3
SANTA ANA FWY	5	ORCO	T	B1
SANTA ANA FWY	5	ORCO	U	A5
SANTA ANA FWY	5	ORCO	98	A2
SANTA ANA FWY	5	ORCO	193	C4
SANTA ANA FWY	5	ORCO	196	B3
SANTA MONICA FWY	10	LACO	Q	C4
SANTA MONICA FWY	10	LACO	97	D2
SANTA MONICA FWY	10	LACO	180	B5
SANTA MONICA FWY	10	LACO	183	B4
SANTA MONICA FWY	10	LACO	184	D4
SANTA MONICA FWY	10	LACO	185	D4
SANTA MONICA FWY	10	LACO	186	A5
SANTA PAULA FWY	126	VEN	88	B5
SAN VICENTE FWY	67	SDCO	106	E5
SEBASTOPOL FWY	12	SON	131	B4
SHORELINE HWY	1	MAR	L	B4
SHORELINE HWY	1	MAR	37	D4

HIGHWAY NAME	HWY NO.	CO. ABBR.	PAGE	GRID
SHORELINE HWY	1	MAR	45	A1
SHORELINE HWY	1	MAR	140	B4
SHORELINE HWY	1	MEN	22	C3
SHORELINE HWY	1	MEN	30	C4
SILVERADO TRAIL	121	NAPA	133	E4
SINCLAIR FWY	680	ALA	P	B2
SINCLAIR FWY	680	ALA	46	B2
SINCLAIR FWY	680	CC	46	A1
SINCLAIR FWY	680	SCL	P	B2
SINCLAIR FWY	680	SCL	46	B4
SINCLAIR FWY	280	SCL	151	D5
SINCLAIR FWY	280	SCL	152	D4
SNELLING HWY	59	MCO	170	C5
SOLEDAD FWY	52	SDCO	V	B2
SOLEDAD FWY	52	SDCO	106	C5
SOLEDAD FWY	52	SDCO	211	D3
SONOMA HWY	12	SON	132	C3
SOUTH BAY EXPWY	54	SDCO	V	D4
SOUTH BAY EXPWY	54	SDCO	111	D1
SOUTHBAY FWY	237	SCL	P	A3
SOUTHBAY FWY	237	SCL	46	A4
SOUTHBAY FWY	237	SCL	148	C4
SOUTHRN EMBARCADERO FY	280	SFCO	L	C5
SOUTHRN EMBARCADERO FY	280	SFCO	45	C2
SOUTHRN EMBARCADERO FY	280	SFCO	143	E5
SOUTH VALLEY FWY	101	SCL	54	C1
STEVENS CREEK FWY	85	SCL	N	E3
STEVENS CREEK FWY	85	SCL	P	A3
STEVENS CREEK FWY	85	SCL	45	E4
STEVENS CREEK FWY	85	SCL	148	A4
TAFT HWY	119	KER	78	C3
TERMINAL ISLAND FWY	103	LACO	S	D2
TERMINAL ISLAND FWY	103	LACO	191	E1
TERMINAL ISLAND FWY	103	LACO	192	A2
THREE FLAGS HWY	395	KER	80	D1
TWENTYNINE PALMS HWY	62	RCO	100	C2
TWENTYNINE PALMS HWY	62	RCO	102	C2
TWENTYNINE PALMS HWY	62	SBD	100	C2
TWENTYNINE PALMS HWY	62	SBD	101	C1
TWENTYNINE PALMS HWY	62	SBD	102	A2
VENTURA FWY	134	LACO	Q	E3
VENTURA FWY	134	LACO	R	A3
VENTURA FWY	101	LACO	97	B1
VENTURA FWY	134	LACO	97	B1
VENTURA FWY	101	LACO	177	C4
VENTURA FWY	101	LACO	178	D4
VENTURA FWY	101	LACO	179	A5
VENTURA FWY	101	VEN	87	E5
VENTURA FWY	101	VEN	88	A5
VENTURA FWY	101	VEN	96	D1
VENTURA FWY	101	VEN	175	C3
WARREN FWY	13	ALA	L	D4
WARREN FWY	13	ALA	45	D1
WARREN FWY	13	CC	156	E5
WESTSIDE FWY	5	FRCO	55	E3
WESTSIDE FWY	5	FRCO	56	B4
WESTSIDE FWY	5	FRCO	66	E2
WEST SIDE FWY	5	KER	77	D1
WEST SIDE FWY	5	KER	78	B3
WEST SIDE FWY	5	KER	88	D1
WESTSIDE FWY	5	KIN	67	C4
WESTSIDE FWY	5	MCO	47	C5
WESTSIDE FWY	5	MCO	55	D1
WESTSIDE FWY	5	SAC	39	E2
WESTSIDE FWY	5	SJCO	39	E4
WESTSIDE FWY	5	SJCO	40	A4
WESTSIDE FWY	5	SJCO	47	A2
WESTSIDE FWY	5	STA	47	B3
WESTSIDE FWY	5	YOL	33	A4
WEST SIDE HWY	33	KER	67	B5
WEST SIDE HWY	33	KER	77	C1
WEST SIDE HWY	33	KER	78	A4
YOUNGER FWY	92	ALA	N	D1
YOUNGER FWY	92	ALA	45	D2
YOUNGER FWY	92	SMCO	N	D1
YOUNGER FWY	92	SMCO	45	D2
YOUNGER FWY	92	SMCO	145	D1

POINTS OF INTEREST INDEX

NAME & ADDRESS	PAGE	GRID
AIRPORTS	280	
AMUSEMENT PARKS	280	
BEACHES	280	
CAMPGROUNDS	282	
COLLEGES & UNIVERSITIES	283	
GOLF COURSES	284	
HARBORS	284	
HISTORICAL SITES	284	
HOTELS	287	
MISSIONS	292	
PARKS & NATIONAL FORESTS	293	
POINTS OF INTEREST	295	
RECREATION LAKES, RIVERS & MARINAS	301	
SKI AREAS	304	
THEATER	304	
WINERIES	304	

AIRPORTS

NAME & ADDRESS	PAGE	GRID
ALTURAS MUNICIPAL AIRPORT, 1 mi W of Alturas	8	A1
AMADOR COUNTY AIRPORT, near Amador	40	D2
ANTIOCH AIRPORT, Lone Tree Wy, Antioch	M	C3
ARCATA AIRPORT, off Hwy 101 at Airport Rd	10	A4
AUBURN AIRPORT, 4 mi N of Auburn	34	C3
BAKERSFIELD AIRPARK, Watts Dr & Union Av	78	D3
BARSTOW-DAGGETT, Nat'l Trails Hwy, Barstow	92	B1
BENTON AIRPARK, Gold St, Redding	122	A3
BIG BEAR CITY AIRPORT, Big Bear City	92	A5
BISHOP AIRPORT, 2 mi E of Bishop	51	D4
BRACKETT FIELD, McKinley Av, La Verne	U	C2
BUCHANAN FIELD AIRPORT, John Glenn Dr, Concord	M	A3
BURBANK-GLENDALE-PASADENA, 2627 N Hollywood Wy	179	A1
CALAVERAS COUNTY AIRPORT, Hwy 49 S of San Andreas	41	A4
CARSON AIRPORT, Carson City, Nevada	36	C1
CATALINA AIR & SEA TERMINAL, Harbor Blvd	191	B3
CHICO MUNICIPAL AIRPORT, 5 mi NW of Chico	25	B2
CHINO AIRPORT, Hwy 83, Chino	U	D3
COLUMBIA AIRPORT off Hwy 49, Columbia	41	C4
COLUSA COUNTY AIRPORT, 3 mi S of Colusa	33	A2
DELANO MUNICIPAL AIRPORT, Hwy 99, Delano	68	B5
DOUGLAS COUNTY AIRPORT, Minden, Nevada	36	C3
FANTASY HAVEN AIRPORT, 2 mi SE of Tehachapi	79	D4
FRESNO AIR TERMINAL, 5175 E Clinton Av	57	D3
FRESNO-CHANDLER DOWNTOWN AIRPORT, Amador & Thorne	165	B4
FROGTOWN AIRPORT, Off Hwy 49, Angels Camp	41	B4
IMPERIAL COUNTY AIRPORT, Hwy 86 at Main, Imperial	109	A5
INYOKERN COUNTY AIRPORT, Hwy 395, Inyokern	80	D1
JOHN MCNAMARA FIELD, nr Crescent City	1	C4
JOHN WAYNE AIRPORT, MacArthur Blvd, Orange Co	198	B5
KERN VALLEY AIRPORT, Sierra Wy N of Lake Isabella	69	D5
LAKEVIEW MUNICIPAL AIRPORT, near jct of 140 & 395	7	B1
LAMPSON AIRPORT, SW of Clear Lake off Hwy 175	31	D3
LIVERMORE AIRPORT, Stanley Blvd, Livermore	M	C5
LONE PINE AIRPORT, 1 mile south of Lone Pine	60	B4
LONG BEACH MUNICIPAL, 4100 Donald Douglas Dr	S	E2
LOS ANGELES INTERNATIONAL, 1 World Wy	189	C2
MADERA AIRPORT, Hwy 99 & Av 17	57	A2
MARIPOSA YOSEMITE AIRPORT, near Mariposa	49	A3
McCARRAN INTERNATIONAL, 5 miles S of Las Vegas	210	C5
MEADOWS FIELD, Skyway & Airport Drs	78	D2
MENDOCINO COUNTY AIRPORT, Hwy 1 S of Little River	30	B1
MERCED MUNICIPAL AIRPORT, 2 mi SW of Merced	170	A5
MODESTO CITY-COUNTY AIRPORT, E of Hwy 99, Modesto	162	E4
MONTEREY PENINSULA AIRPORT, off Hwy 68	54	B1
NAPA COUNTY AIRPORT, 2030 Airport Rd, Napa	L	D1
NEEDLES MUNICIPAL, Airport Rd & Hwy 95, Needles	95	D2
NORTH LAS VEGAS AIR TERMINAL, 3.5 miles NW of Las Vegas	74	D2
OAKDALE AIRPORT, 8191 Laughlin Rd, Oakdale	47	E1
OAKLAND INTERNATIONAL, Doolittle & Airport Wy	159	B4
OCOTILLO WELLS AIRPORT, Hwy 78, Ocotillo	108	B3
ONTARIO INTERNATIONAL AIRPORT, 2 mi E of Ontario	204	E5
OROVILLE AIRPORT, 3 mi SW of Oroville	25	C4
OXNARD AIRPORT, Ventura Rd & 5th St, Oxnard	176	A4
PALMDALE AIRPORT, Sierra Hwy	90	A3
PALM SPRINGS REGIONAL, 2 mi E of Palm Springs	206	E3
PEARCE AIRPORT, Hwy 53 S of Clearlake	32	A3
PLACERVILLE AIRPORT, S of Hwy 50 near Smithflat	34	E5
REDDING MUNICIPAL AIRPORT, 7 miles SE of Redding	18	C2
RENO-CANNON INTERNL AIRPORT, 2 miles from Reno	28	C4
SACRAMENTO CO METRO AIRPORT, 12 mi NW of Sacramento	33	D5
SACRAMENTO EXECUTIVE AIRPORT, 6151 Freeport Blvd	39	D1
SALINAS MUNICIPAL AIRPORT, off Hwy 101	54	D4
SAN DIEGO INTERNATIONAL AIRPORT, Lindbergh Field	215	B2
SAN FRANCISCO INTL' AIRPORT, Airport Wy off Bayshore Fwy	144	D3
SAN JOSE INTERNATIONAL AIRPORT, 1661 Airport Bl	151	D1
SAN LUIS OBISPO AIRPORT, 901 Airport Dr	76	B4
SANTA BARBARA AIRPORT, James Fowler Rd	87	B4
SANTA MARIA PUBLIC AIRPORT, Skyway Dr, Santa Maria	86	B1
SANTA MONICA MUNICIPAL AIRPORT	187	C1
SHAFTER-KERN COUNTY AIRFIELD, Lerdo Hwy	78	B2
SISKIYOU COUNTY AIRPORT, Montague	4	C4
STOCKTON METRO AIRPORT, 5000 S Airport Wy	40	B5
SUSANVILLE AIRPORT, 5 mi SE of Susanville	21	B3
SUTTER COUNTY AIRPORT, off Samuel Dr	125	E4
TAFT-KERN AIRPORT, West Side Hwy, Taft	78	A4
TAHOE AIRPORT, Pioneer Trail Rd	36	A3
TEHACHAPI-KERN CO AIRPORT, Green & J Sts	79	D4
TRUCKEE AIRPORT, 4 miles E of Truckee	35	E1
TULELAKE MUNICIPAL AIRPORT, N of Hwy 139 near Newell	5	E3
TURLOCK MUNICIPAL AIRPORT, 13099 Newport Rd, Ballico	48	A3
UKIAH AIRPORT, State St	123	D5
VENTURA COUNTY AIRPORT, Oxnard	176	A4
WILLITS MUNI AIRPORT, 3 mi N of Willits on US 101	23	A5
YUBA COUNTY AIRPORT, Olivehurst	33	D2
YUCCA VALLEY AIRPORT, Hwys 62 & 247, Yucca Valley	100	D1

AMUSEMENT PARKS

NAME & ADDRESS	PAGE	GRID
DISNEYLAND, Harbor Blvd, Anaheim Amusement park-8 theme sections, rides & shops.	193	B4
GREAT AMERICA, 1 Great America Pkwy, Santa Clara Family amusement park, American history theme.	P	B3
KNOTTS BERRY FARM, 8039 Beach Bl, Buena Park Amusement Pk-6 theme areas, rides, shops & restaurants.	T	B2
MARINE WORLD AFRICA USA, 1000 Fairgrounds, Vallejo Land & sea animal shows; natural setting	134	D1
OASIS WATER PARK, 1500 Gene Autry Tr, Palm Springs Wave pool, speed slide, hydro tubes & lagoon.	100	D3
RAGING WATERS, 111 Via Verde, San Dimas Pools, slides & picnic area.	U	B2
RAGING WATERS, off Capitol Expressway, San Jose Pools, slide &, picnic area.	P	C3
SAN DIEGO WILD ANIMAL PARK, 5 mi W of Escondido Tour through preserve for endangered species.	106	D3
SEA WORLD, 1720 S Shores Rd, Mission Bay Park Marine life amusement park, shows & attractions.	212	C4
SIX FLAGS HURRICANE HARBOR, I-5 at Valencia Av Theme waterpark, pools & slides.	89	B4
SIX FLAGS MAGIC MOUNTAIN, I-5 at Valencia Av Family amusement park; thrill rides & shops.	89	B4
UNIVERSAL STUDIOS & AMPHITHEATER, Universal City Plaza Features tours of movie and TV sets; shows.	181	A1
WATERWORLD USA, 1600 Exposition Blvd, Sacramento Water amusement park, pools & slides.	39	E1
WET 'N WILD, 2600 Las Vegas Blvd, Las Vegas Wave pool, flumes & water roller coaster.	209	C4
WILD RIVERS, Irvine Center Dr, Irvine Water slides & activities.	T	E4
WILD WATER ADVENTURES, 11413 E Shaw, Clovis Water amusement park with 17 water rides.	57	D3
WINDSOR WATERWORKS, 8225 Conde, Windsor Pool, flumes & picnic area.	37	E1

BEACHES

NAME & ADDRESS	PAGE	GRID
ARROYO BURRO BEACH COUNTY PARK, 2981 Cliff Dr Picnic, swimming & surf fishing.	87	C4
ASILOMAR STATE BEACH, Sunset Dr, Pacific Grove Conference facilities in a beautiful setting.	167	A1
ATASCADERO STATE BEACH, Junction of Hwy 1 and Hwy 41 Swim, fishing & camping.	75	D3
AVILA STATE BEACH, Front St, Avila Beach Fire rings, fishing & swimming.	76	A4
BAKER BEACH, NW shore Presidio, San Francisco Fishing & hiking nearby, no swimming.	141	B2
BEAN HOLLOW STATE BEACH, S of Half Moon Bay Fishing & camping on the beach.	N	B4

POINTS OF INTEREST INDEX

NAME & ADDRESS	PAGE	GRID
BOLSA CHICA STATE BEACH, N of Huntington Beach Sandy beach, body surfing & picnicking.	T	A3
BOOMER BEACH, Coast Blvd, La Jolla Scenic beach, swimming & fishing.	105	B2
CABRILLO BEACH, E of Pacific Av, San Pedro Public boat ramp, surf fishing & barbeque pits.	S	C3
CAPISTRANO BEACH, San Juan Capistrano Sandy beach, body surfing & picnicking.	202	D5
CAPITOLA CITY BEACH, 30th Av, Capitola Swimming & fishing.	54	A2
CARDIFF STATE BEACH, Cardiff by the Sea Fine beach for fishing & swimming.	106	B4
CARLSBAD STATE BEACH, Carlsbad Bl, Carlsbad Store, concessions, fish, swim, surfing & camping.	106	A3
CARMEL RIVER STATE BEACH, Scenic Rd, Carmel by the Sea Skin diving, fishing & bird watching sites.	168	B4
CARPINTERIA STATE BEACH, Linden Av, Carpinteria Camp, picnic, fishing pier & boat ramp.	87	D4
CASA BEACH, Coast Blvd, La Jolla Swimming & fishing.	105	A3
CASPER HEADLANDS STATE RESERVE, Hwy 1 near Casper Scenic environment with good fishing.	22	A5
CASPER STATE BEACH, off Hwy 1 near Casper Scenic area for picnicking & fishing.	22	B5
CAYUCOS STATE BEACH, on Ocean Front Rd, Cayucos Fishing pier, barbeque & picnic facilities.	75	D2
CORAL BEACH, Hwy 1 W of Malibu Beach Picnic, fishing & swimming.	97	A2
CORONA DEL MAR STATE BEACH, Corona Del Mar Sandy beach, picnic, tidepools & body surfing.	T	D5
DAN BLOCKER BEACH, PCH & Corral Canyon, Malibu Swim, surfing & sunbathing.	97	A2
DOCKWEILER STATE BEACH, Venice Picnic, swimming & fishing.	187	A4
DOHENY STATE BEACH, Puerto & Del Obispo Sts, Dana Point Fire rings, picnic areas, surfing & camping.	202	B4
EL CAPITAN STATE BEACH, Avenida del Capitan Surf, boat rentals, hiking & camping.	87	A4
EL DORADO BEACH, off Hwy 50, South Lake Tahoe On the south shore of lovely Lake Tahoe.	129	A3
EMMA WOOD STATE BEACH, Hwy 101 & Hwy 33 Camp, fishing & swimming.	88	A5
GAZO CREEK ANGLING ACCESS, Gazo Creek Rd Beach access for fishing.	N	C4
GOLETA BEACH COUNTY PARK, 5990 Sandspit Rd Fishing pier, swimming & boat hoist.	87	B4
GRAY WHALE COVE STATE BEACH, N of Half Moon Bay Good beach for fishing.	N	A1
GREENWOOD CREEK STATE BEACH, Hwy 1 near Elk. Exhibits, picnic & fishing.	30	C2
HALF MOON BAY STATE BEACH, near Half Moon Bay Camp on bluffs above beaches, picnic & hiking.	N	B2
HERMOSA BEACH, between Redondo & Manhattan Beaches Public fishing pier, swimming & surfing.	S	A1
HUNTINGTON BEACH STATE PARK, Huntington Beach Sandy beach, picnic & good surfing.	T	B4
ISLA VISTA COUNTY BEACH PARK, Camino Del Sur Sandy beach & tidepools.	87	B4
J D PHELAN BEACH, El Camino del Mar, San Francisco Swimming cove protected from the wind.	141	A2
LAS TUNAS BEACH, near Junction of Hwy 1 & Hwy 27 Swimming in the surf, fishing & picnicking.	Q	A4
LEADBETTER BEACH, Shoreline Dr, Santa Barbara Very wide, sandy beach & picnic facilities.	174	C5
LEO CARRILLO STATE BEACH, S of Hwy 101 Good surfing, diving & swimming.	96	D2
LEUCADIA STATE BEACH, Leucadia Scenic beach for fishing & swimming.	106	B4
LITTLE RIVER STATE BEACH, South of Trinidad Beautiful beaches, delta & nature trails.	9	E4
MALIBU LAGOON STATE BEACH, near Malibu Site of famous surfrider beach, swimming.	97	B2
MANCHESTER STATE BEACH, near Point Arena Beaches, sand dunes, Point Arena Lighthouse.	30	B3
MANHATTAN BEACH, Manhattan Beach Public fishing pier, swimming & surfing.	S	A1
MANRESA STATE BEACH, off San Andreas Rd Sandy beach & tide pools.	54	B2
MARINA STATE BEACH, 10 mi N of Monterey Good fishing area.	54	B4

NAME & ADDRESS	PAGE	GRID
MARINE STREET BEACH, La Jolla Fish, swimming & sunbathing.	105	A3
MCGRATH STATE BEACH, S of Santa Clara River Hike, camping & fishing.	96	A1
MONTARA STATE BEACH, N of Half Moon Bay Fishing beach.	N	A2
MONTEREY STATE BEACH, Park Av, Monterey Sandy beach, fishing & swimming in summer.	54	B4
MOONLIGHT STATE BEACH, Encinitas Sandy beach for swimming & fishing.	106	B4
MORRO STRAND STATE BEACH, end of Yerba Buena Rd Sand dunes, streams; camping permitted.	75	D2
MOSS LANDING STATE BEACH, off Hwy 1, Moss Landing Fishing & equestrian trails.	54	B3
NATURAL BRIDGES STATE BEACH, W Cliff Dr, Santa Cruz Natural sandstone formation; picnics & fishing.	169	A5
NEW BRIGHTON STATE BEACH, off Hwy 1, Capitola Sandy beach, tide pools.	54	A2
NEWPORT DUNES AQUATIC PARK, off PCH, Newport Beach Swimming and other aquatic recreation.	199	D4
OCEANSIDE CITY BEACH, The Strand & Pacific, Oceanside Popular resort; 4 mi beach, swimming & skin diving.	106	A3
PACIFICA STATE BEACH, Hwy 1, Pacifica Tidepools, fishing & hiking.	N	B1
PELICAN STATE BEACH, 21 miles N of Crescent City Fishing; no swimming.	1	D2
PESCADERO STATE BEACH, Hwy 1 S of Half Moon Bay Good beach for fishing.	N	B4
PISMO STATE BEACH, off Hwy 101, Pismo Beach Camping & hiking among sandy beaches & dunes.	76	B5
POINT DUME BEACH, Hwy 1, N of Malibu Good beach for picnic, hiking & fishing.	96	E2
POINT REYES NATIONAL SEASHORE, near Olema Sandy beach, tidepools, picnic, camping & hiking.	37	D5
POINT SAL STATE BEACH, Sal Point Rd Many varieties of marine life.	86	A1
POMPONIO STATE BEACH, Hwy 1 S of Half Moon Bay Lovely beach for picnic & fishing.	N	B3
PORT HUENEME BEACH, off Hueneme Rd Fishing pier, playground & bike paths.	96	B1
REDONDO BEACH, Redondo Beach Adjacent to King Harbor Marina; swimming & fishing.	S	A2
REFUGIO STATE BEACH, Refugio Rd Tidepools, camping & fishing.	86	E4
RIO DEL MAR STATE BEACH, Rio Del Mar Blvd, Aptos Clean sandy beach, jetty; nearby shopping.	54	B2
ROBERT H MEYER MEM STATE BEACH, Hwy 1 W of Malibu Picnic facilities, swimming & fishing.	96	E2
ROBERT W. CROWN MEMORIAL STATE BEACH, Alameda Day use only; youth programs offered.	L	D5
ROYAL PALMS BEACH, Paseo dl Mar, Los Angeles Good beach for picnic, swimming & fishing.	S	C3
SALINAS RIVER STATE BEACH, Potrero Rd, Castroville Wide sandy beach & dunes; clamming & fishing.	54	B3
SAN BUENAVENTURA STATE BEACH, Harbor Bl, Ventura Good swimming, beach equipment rentals.	175	C3
SAN CLEMENTE STATE BEACH, San Clemente Picnic & BBQ facilities, surfing & camping.	105	D1
SAN ELIJO STATE BEACH, Cardiff by the Sea Good beach for camp, fishing & swimming.	106	B4
SAN GREGORIO STATE BEACH, Hwy 1 S of Half Moon Bay Good fishing beach; picnicking.	N	B3
SAN ONOFRE STATE BEACH, San Onofre Surf fishing, clamming, surfing & camping.	105	E2
SANTA CRUZ BEACH, Beach St, Santa Cruz Swim, surfing & surf fishing.	169	D4
SANTA MONICA STATE BEACH, Palisades Beach Rd, Santa Monica Most popular beach in the Los Angeles area.	Q	B4
SCHOONER GULCH STATE BEACH, Hwy 1 S of Point Arena Picnic, fishing and a scenic overlook.	30	C4
SEACLIFF STATE BEACH, 5 mi S of Hwy 1, Santa Cruz Co Swimming; marine museum - open in summer.	54	B2
SILVER STRAND STATE BEACH, 5000 Hwy 75, Coronado Beautiful beach for picnic, swimming & fishing.	V	B4
SONOMA COAST STATE BEACH, N of Bodega Bay Scenic beaches, picnic, camping & hiking.	37	B2
SOUTH CARLSBAD STATE BEACH, S of Carlsbad Camp, fishing & swimming.	106	B3
STILLWATER COVE, Hwy 1 S of Walsh Landing Good swimming & fishing.	37	A1

POINTS OF INTEREST INDEX

NAME & ADDRESS	PAGE	GRID
SUNSET STATE BEACH, W of Watsonville Scenic bluffs; picnic, camp, fishing & clamming.	54	B2
THORNTON STATE BEACH, off Hwy 35 E of Daly City Good fishing & hiking trails.	L	B5
TOPANGA STATE BEACH, Topanga Canyon Blvd Swimming in the surf & picnicking.	Q	A4
TORREY PINES STATE BEACH, S of Del Mar Scenic beach for hike, swimming & exploring.	V	A1
TRINIDAD STATE BEACH, off Hwy 101, Trinidad Beaches, bluffs, nature trails & picnicking.	9	E4
TWIN LAKES STATE BEACH, Santa Cruz Swimming, fire pits; day use only-no camping.	54	A2
WEST BEACH, Cabrillo Bl, Santa Barbara Sandy beach; restaurants & specialty shops.	174	D4
WESTPORT-UNION LANDING STATE BEACH, N of Westport Fishing & camping.	22	B3
Wm. RANDOLPH HEARST STATE BEACH, Hwy 1, San Simeon Picnic facilities; boat, fishing & swimming.	75	B1
WILL ROGERS STATE BEACH, N of Santa Monica Wide sandy beach; picnic & surfing.	Q	B4
WINDANSEA BEACH, foot of Palomar St Surfboarding & spectator beach; no swimming.	V	A2
WIPEOUT BEACH, Coast Blvd, La Jolla Sandy beach, swimming & fishing.	105	A3
ZMUDOWSKI STATE BEACH, 1 mi N of Moss Landing Fishing & horseback riding.	54	B3

CAMPGROUNDS

NAME & ADDRESS	PAGE	GRID
ANDREW MOLERA STATE PARK, W of Hwy 1, Big Sur Sandy beaches, meadows, camping & hiking.	64	B2
ANTELOPE LAKE, 45 miles NE of Quincy 200+ dev sites; hike, boat, waterskiing & fishing.	21	A4
ANZA BORREGO DESERT STATE PARK, San Diego County Beautiful wildflowers in spring; camping & hiking.	108	A4
ATASCADERO STATE BEACH, Jct of Hwy 1 & Hwy 41 Camping and picnic facilities.	75	D3
AUSTIN CREEK STATE RECREATION AREA, E of Ft Ross Primitive camping & picnic area.	37	C1
BASS LAKE, E of Oakhurst 220+ dev sites; hike, boat, waterskiing & fishing.	49	E4
BENBOW LAKE STATE REC AREA, 2 mi S of Garberville Camp, picnic, horse trails, swimming & fishing.	22	B1
BIG BASIN REDWOODS STATE PARK, on Hwy 236 Camping alongside the historic redwoods.	N	D4
BIG PINE CANYON, 10 miles W of Big Pine Campgrounds, picnic areas & hiking.	51	C5
BOLSA CHICA STATE BEACH, N of Huntington Beach Camp, picnic, body surfing, & swimming.	T	A3
BOTHE-NAPA VALLEY STATE PARK, on Hwy 29 Camp, picnic, swimming & hiking.	38	A1
BRANNAN ISLAND STATE RECREATION AREA, S of Rio Vista Visitors center, camp, fish, swimming & boating.	M	D2
BUTANO STATE PARK, E of Hwy 1 at Gazos Creek Rd Camping and recreational facilities.	N	C4
CALAVERAS BIG TREES STATE PARK, E of Arnold Camping among the redwood groves.	41	D3
CAMANCHE RESERVOIR, W of San Andreas 1150+ dev sites; boat, fish, hiking & swimming.	40	C3
CARPINTERIA STATE BEACH, Linden Av Camp, picnic, fishing pier & boat ramp.	87	D4
CASTLE CRAG STATE PARK, S of Dunsmuir Camp, fish, hiking & swimming.	12	D3
CASTLE ROCK STATE PARK, near Junction of Hwy 9 & Hwy 35 Scenic park for picnic, camping & hiking.	N	E4
CASWELL MEMORIAL STATE PARK, Hwy 99 S of Manteca Camp, fish, swimming & hiking.	47	B2
CHINA CAMP STATE PARK, N of San Rafael Camping & recreation facilities.	L	B3
CLEAR LAKE STATE PARK, near Lakeport Camp, picnic, hiking & boating.	31	D3
COL. ALLENSWORTH STATE HISTORIC PARK, 20 mi N of Wasco Camping & historical exhibits.	68	B4
COLUSA-SACRAMENTO RIVER STATE REC AREA, Colusa Camp, fish, boating & waterskiing.	33	A1
CUYAMACA RANCHO STATE PARK, on Hwy 79, Julian In old Indian territory; camp, hiking & equestrian.	107	C4
DEL NORTE COAST REDWOODS STATE PARK, S of Crescent City Exhibits, camp, picnic, hiking & fishing.	1	E4
D. L. BLISS STATE PARK, N of Emerald Bay Camp, beach, trails & dense forest.	35	E3
DOHENY STATE BEACH, 25300 Harbor Dr, Dana Point 115+ sites, fire rings, beach, swimming & fishing.	202	B4
DONNER MEMORIAL STATE PARK, 2 mi W of Truckee Open mid-May to mid-Sept., Memorial Museum.	35	D1
EAGLE LAKE, 20 mi N of Susanville 300+ dev sites; boat, waterski, fishing & hiking.	20	E2
EL CAPITAN STATE BEACH, Avenida del Capitan Surf, hike, camping & boat rentals.	87	A4
EMERALD BAY STATE PARK, Hwy 89 near Emerald Bay Scenic; camp, picnic & swimming.	35	E3
EMMA WOOD STATE BEACH, Junction of Hwy 101 & Hwy 33 Camp, swimming & fishing.	88	A5
FALLEN LEAF LAKE, Southwest of Lake Tahoe 200+ dev sites; boat, fish, swimming & horses.	35	E3
FOLSOM LAKE STATE REC AREA, 1 mile N of Folsom Camp, boat, fish, waterskiing & horses.	34	B5
FOREST OF NISENE MARKS, 4 miles N of Aptos Camp, picnic & hiking trails.	P	B5
FREMONT PEAK STATE PARK, S of San Juan Bautista Picnic, camping & hiking trails.	54	D3
FURNACE CREEK CAMPGROUND, Furnace Creek Ranch Camping facilities in the heart of Death Valley.	62	A5
GAVIOTA STATE PARK, Gaviota Beach Rd Camp, picnic areas, fishing & boat launch.	86	D4
GEORGE HATFIELD STATE REC AREA, 28 mi W of Merced Camp, picnic, hiking & fishing.	47	D4
GOLD HILL CAMPGROUND, SW of Gorman Primitive camping near Hungry Valley SVRA	88	D2
GRIZZLY CREEK REDWOODS STATE PARK, E of Fortuna Scenic; nature trails, creeks, camping & fishing.	16	B3
GROVER HOT SPRINGS STATE PARK, W of Markleeville Camp, fishing & swimming in hot creeks.	36	B5
HALF MOON STATE BEACH Near Half Moon Bay 51 dev sites; no swimming, fish, picnic.	N	B2
HARRIS BEACH STATE PARK, N of Crescent City Camp, lodging & dining.	1	C2
HENDY WOODS STATE PARK, near Philo on Hwy 128 Camp, picnic, fish, hiking & swimming.	30	D3
HENRY COE STATE PARK, 14 mi NE of Morgan Hill Picturesque camping and picnic grounds.	P	E4
HENRY COWELL REDWOODS STATE PARK, N of Santa Cruz Equestrian trails, camp, hiking & fishing.	N	E5
HIDDEN VIEW, 17 miles N of Madera Scenic area to camp, swim & fish.	49	B5
HOLLISTER HILLS VEHICULAR REC AREA, Cienega Rd Camping, motorcycling & 4-wheel drive trails.	54	E3
HUMBOLDT REDWOODS STATE PARK, Redwood Highway Tallest redwoods; camp, picnic, fishing & hiking.	16	A4
HUNGRY VALLEY STATE VEHICULAR REC AREA, Gorman Primitive camping; off-road vehicle use.	88	E2
HUNTINGTON LAKE, North of Camp Sierra 300+ dev sites; boat, waterski, fishing & horses.	50	B5
INDIAN GRINDING ROCK STATE HISTORIC PARK, S of Volcano Restored Miwok Indian Village; camping facilities.	41	A2
JENKINSON LAKE, 18 miles E of Placerville 290+ dev sites; boat, fish, swimming & hiking.	35	B5
J SMITH REDWOODS STATE PARK, NE of Crescent City Exhibits, camp, picnic, hiking & fishing.	1	E4
JUNE LAKE LOOP, 18 miles N of Mammoth Lakes 280+ dev sites; boat, fish, backpacking & horses.	50	A1
LAKE ELSINORE STATE RECREATION AREA, near I-15 & Hwy 74 Camp, swim, fishing & boating.	99	B4
LAKE HENSHAW, off Hwy 76, Santa Ysabel 400+ dev sites; fish, boating & hiking.	107	B3
LAKE MCCLURE, S of Coulterville 550+ dev sites; picnic, swim, houseboating & fishing.	48	D2
LAKE MENDOCINO, N of Ukiah 300+ dev sites; boat, waterski, fishing & hiking.	31	B2
LAKE NACIEMENTO, 40 mi NW of Paso Robles 350+ dev sites; swim, hike, boating & waterskiing.	65	D5
LAKE OROVILLE STATE REC AREA, NE of Oroville Camp, fish, boat, waterskiing & horseback riding.	25	D4
LAKE PERRIS STATE REC AREA, off Ramona Expressway Camp, bicycle trails & boat rentals.	99	C3
LAKE SAN ANTONIO RECREATION AREA, W of Bradley 650+ dev sites; boat, fish, swim, hiking & horses.	65	D4
LEO CARRILLO STATE BEACH, S of Hwy 101 Good surfing, diving & swimming.	96	D2

POINTS OF INTEREST INDEX

NAME & ADDRESS	PAGE	GRID
LITTLE GRASS VALLEY LAKE, W of Gibsonville Camping and recreational facilities.	26	C3
LOPEZ LAKE, 23 miles N of Santa Maria 300+ sites, picnic area, boat, fishing & waterskiing.	76	C4
MacKERRICHER STATE PARK, N of Fort Bragg Rocky beaches, sand dunes, nature trails.	22	B5
MALAKOFF DIGGINS STATE HIST PARK, NE of Nevada City Camping along colorful slopes.	26	D5
MANCHESTER STATE BEACH, near Point Arena Camping on sandy beaches among sand dunes.	30	B3
McARTHUR-BURNEY FALLS MEM STATE PARK, NE of Burney Well developed park with camping & fishing.	13	C4
McCONNELL STATE RECREATION AREA, 5 mi SE of Delhi Camp, picnic, fishing & swimming.	48	A3
MCGRATH STATE BEACH, Off Hwy 101, Oxnard 174 sites, visitor center, hiking & fishing.	96	A1
MILLERTON LAKE REC AREA, 22 miles E of Madera Camp, boat, fishing & horseback riding.	57	D1
MONTANA DE ORO STATE PARK, Pecho Valley Rd Barbeque facilities; camp, riding & hiking.	75	E3
MORRO BAY STATE PARK, on Morro Bay Camp, fish, clamming & boating.	75	D3
MT DIABLO STATE PARK, Diablo Rd Camp on the Peak, hiking trails.	M	B4
MT SAN JACINTO STATE PARK, Hwy 111 near Palm Springs Picnic, hiking & limited camping.	100	B3
MOUNT TAMALPAIS STATE PARK, 6 mi N of Hwy 1 Camp, hiking & equestrian trails.	L	A3
NEW BRIGHTON STATE BEACH, off Hwy 1 Scenic camp, fishing & swimming.	54	A2
OAKWOOD LAKE RESORT, off I-5 S of Manteca Camp, watersports & shopping.	47	A1
OCOTILLO WELLS STATE VEHICULAR REC AREA, Hwy 78 Off-road 4-wheel drive vehicle trails.	108	B3
PALOMAR MOUNTAIN STATE PARK, Birch Hill Rd Beautiful area to camp or enjoy a picnic.	107	A2
PATRICKS POINT STATE PARK, N of Trinidad Camp, picnic, hiking & biking.	9	D3
PAUL M. DIMMICK WAYSIDE CAMPGROUND, W of Navarro Primitive campgrounds; picnic, swimming & fishing.	30	C2
PFEIFFER BIG SUR STATE PARK, E of Hwy 1, Big Sur Hike, camp, swimming & fishing.	64	B2
PICACHO STATE RECREATION AREA, W of Picacho Camp, fish, hiking & sailing.	110	C4
PISMO DUNES STATE VEHICULAR REC AREA, Pismo Beach Off-road, 4-wheel drive trails; camp & picnic.	76	B5
PISMO STATE BEACH, off Hwy 101, Pismo Beach Camping & hiking along sandy beaches & dunes.	76	B5
PLUMAS EUREKA STATE PARK, Hwy A14 at Johnsville Camping, scenic creeks, trails, lakes & mountains.	26	E2
POINT MUGU STATE PARK, Hwy 1, S of Oxnard Camp near the ocean; hike, swimming & fishing.	96	C2
PORTOLA STATE PARK, W of Hwy 35, S of Portola Valley Camping, recreational facilities.	N	D4
PRAIRIE CREEK REDWOODS STATE PARK, N of Orick Camp, picnic areas, fishing & hiking.	10	A1
PROVIDENCE MOUNTAINS STATE REC AREA, Essex Rd Camping facilities in scenic surroundings.	94	B1
RED ROCK CANYON STATE PARK, Hwy 14 at Ricardo Exhibits, picnic, camping & hiking.	80	B3
REFUGIO STATE BEACH, Refugio Rd Tidepools; camping & fishing.	86	E4
RICHARDSON GROVE STATE PARK, S of Garberville Scenic camping area; fish, swimming & hiking.	22	B1
ROCK CREEK LAKE, SW of Toms Place 220+ dev sites, fish, hike, backpacking & boating.	51	A3
ROLLINS RESERVOIR, N of Colfax 240+ dev sites, hike, fish, boating & waterskiing.	34	D2
RUSSIAN GULCH STATE PARK, S of Fort Bragg Camp, hike to waterfall, rocky headlands.	30	A1
SADDLEBACK BUTTE STATE PARK, E of Lancaster Camp, picnicking & hiking trails.	90	C3
SALTON SEA STATE RECREATION AREA, off Hwy 111 Good area to camp, boat, waterski, or hike.	108	E2
SALT POINT STATE PARK, N of Fort Ross off Hwy 1 Camping, beaches, underwater preserve, trails.	37	A1
SAMUEL P. TAYLOR STATE PARK, off Hwy 1 near Olema Camp, winter sports, fishing & riding.	37	E4
SAN CLEMENTE STATE BEACH, San Clemente Camp, picnic facilities, BBQ, surfing & camping.	105	D1
SAN ELIJO STATE BEACH, Cardiff by the Sea Camp & picnic on the beach; swimming.	106	B4
SAN LUIS RES STATE REC AREA, 16 mi W of Los Banos Lovely area to camp, waterski, fish & hike.	55	C1
SAN ONOFRE STATE BEACH, San Onofre Surf fishing, surf, clamming & camping.	105	E2
SAN SIMEON STATE BEACH, Hwy 1, Morro Bay Camping & hiking; sand dunes to explore.	75	B1
SEACLIFF STATE BEACH, 5 mi S of Hwy, Aptos Camping & swimming.	54	B2
SHASTA LAKE, off I-5 N of Redding 400+ sites, fish, boating & waterskiing.	18	B1
SILVER STRAND STATE BEACH, 5000 Hwy 75, Coronado RV camp, picnic, fish, boating & swimming.	V	B4
SILVERWOOD LAKE STATE RECREATION AREA, Hwy 138 Camp, swim, boating & fishing.	91	B5
SINKYONE WILDERNESS STATE PARK, Humboldt & Mendocino Co Tent camping, picnic, hiking & fishing.	22	A1
SMITH RIVER NATIONAL RECREATION AREA, Hwy 199 Camp, raft, fish, hiking & hunting.	2	B3
SONOMA COAST STATE BEACH, N of Bodega Bay Scenic beaches; picnic, camping & hiking.	37	B2
SOUTH CARLSBAD STATE BEACH, S of Carlsbad Scenic beach for camp, fishing & swimming.	106	B3
STAMPEDE RESERVOIR, Sierra Co 250+ dev sites, boat, waterski, fishing & hiking.	27	D4
STANDISH HICKEY STATE REC AREA, 1 mi N of Leggett Camp, hiking trails, fishing & swimming.	22	C2
STOVEPIPE WELLS CAMPGROUND, Death Valley National Park 200 campsites (RV & tents) in the valley.	61	C4
SUGARLOAF RIDGE STATE PARK, Adobe Canyon Rd Camp, fishing & riding.	38	A2
SUGAR PINE POINT STATE PARK, N of Meeks Bay Camp, swim, fishing & hiking.	35	E2
SUNSET CAMPGROUND, Furnace Creek Ranch, Death Valley Campsites near the heart of Death Valley.	62	A5
SUNSET STATE BEACH, W of Watsonville Scenic beach for camp, fishing & clamming.	54	B2
TAHOE STATE RECREATION AREA, N of Tahoe City Camp, picnic, swim, fishing & boating.	35	E2
TEXAS SPRINGS CAMPGROUND, Furnace Creek Ranch RV and tent campsites in scenic Death Valley.	62	A5
TOPAZ LAKE, east of Markleeville 200+ dev sites, boat, waterski, fishing & swimming.	36	E5
TRINITY LAKE, 44 miles NW of Redding 400+ sites, sail, waterski, fishing & horseback riding.	12	A4
TUOLUMNE MEADOWS, Tioga Pass Rd Camp, fish, backpack, mountain climbing & horses.	43	A5
TURLOCK LAKE STATE REC AREA, SW of La Grande Waterski, fish, boat, hiking & camping.	48	B2
UNION VALLEY RESERVOIR, 17 mi N of Riverton 270+ dev sites; boat, fish, swimming & hiking.	35	C4
VAN DAMME STATE PARK, S of Fort Bragg 73 sites, hike, nearby swimming.	30	C1
WESTPORT UNION LANDING STATE BEACH, N of Westport Camping & fishing.	22	B3
WOODSON BRIDGE STATE REC AREA, SE of Corning Nature trail, camp, fishing & swimming.	24	D2

COLLEGES & UNIVERSITIES

NAME & ADDRESS	PAGE	GRID
CALIF STATE UNIV, BAKERSFIELD, 9001 Stockdale Hwy Small campus; good student-professor ratio.	78	C3
CALIF STATE POLYTECH UNIV, POMONA, 3801 W Temple Outstanding programs in architecture.	U	B2
CALIF STATE POLYTECH UNIV, SAN LUIS OBISPO Noted for studies in agriculture & business.	172	B1
CALIF STATE UNIVERSITY, CHICO, W 1st St Offers a variety of quality academic programs.	124	B4
CALIF STATE UNIV, DOMINGUEZ HILLS, 1000 E Victoria Noted as a leader in innovative programs.	S	D1
CALIF STATE UNIV, FRESNO, Shaw & Cedar Av Noted for agriculture, business, engineering.	57	C3
CALIF STATE UNIV, FULLERTON, 800 N State College Bl Good academic opportunities in many subjects.	T	D1
CALIF STATE UNIV, HAYWARD, 25800 Carlos Bee Bl Strong programs in sciences & liberal arts.	M	A5
CALIF STATE UNIV, LONG BEACH, 1250 Bellflower Bl One of largest universities in CSU system.	T	A2

POINTS OF INTEREST INDEX

NAME & ADDRESS	PAGE	GRID
CALIF STATE UNIV, LOS ANGELES, 5151 State College Dr Wide spectrum of programs with an urban focus.	R	B4
CALIF STATE UNIV, MONTEREY BAY, 100 Campus Center Added to the CSU system in 1995.	54	B4
CALIF STATE UNIV, NORTHRIDGE, 18111 Nordhoff St A broad range of educational opportunities.	Q	B2
CALIF STATE UNIV, SACRAMENTO, 6000 J St Situated halfway between S F & the Sierras.	39	E1
CALIF STATE UNIV, SAN BERNARDINO, 5000 University On a 3-3 system: 3 quarters, 3 classes.	99	B1
CALIF STATE UNIV, SAN MARCOS, 333 Twin Oaks Valley Rd Newest addition to the CSU system.	106	C3
CALIF STATE UNIV, STANISLAUS, 801 W Monte Vista Av Small, intimate campus in San Joaquin Valley.	47	D3
CALIF TECH-CALIF INSTITUTE OF TECH, 1201 E Calif Bl, Pasadena Largest private technical college in California.	190	D4
CLAREMONT COLLEGES, College Av & Foothill Bl, Claremont Distinguished group of six schools & colleges.	203	A1
CLAREMONT GRADUATE SCHOOL, Claremont Colleges, Claremont Studies in education, business, history & English.	203	A1
CLAREMONT McKENNA COLLEGE, Claremont Colleges, Claremont Studies in political science & economics.	203	B2
HARVEY MUDD COLLEGE, Claremont Colleges, Claremont Studies in sciences, engineering & mathematics.	203	A1
HUMBOLDT STATE UNIVERSITY, Arcata Beautiful campus in a redwood forest.	10	A5
LOYOLA-MARYMOUNT UNIV, LOS ANGELES, Loyola Bl & W 80th St Fine academic Catholic university.	188	A4
PEPPERDINE UNIVERSITY, 24255 W Pacific Coast Hwy, Malibu Private univ; noted for studies in business.	97	A2
PITZER COLLEGE, Scott Hall, Claremont Colleges, Claremont Studies in liberal arts and humanities.	203	B1
POMONA COLLEGE, Sumner Hall, Claremont Colleges, Claremont Studies in history, social & natural sciences.	203	B2
ST MARYS COLLEGE, St Marys Rd, Moraga Studies in liberal arts & economics.	L	E4
SAN DIEGO STATE UNIVERSITY, 5300 Campanile Dr, San Diego Largest in the CSUC system.	V	C3
SAN FRANCISCO STATE UNIVERSITY, 1600 Holloway Av, SF Many interdisciplinary programs.	L	A5
SAN JOSE STATE UNIVERSITY, 125 S 7th St, San Jose Campus of 27,000 students in Santa Clara Valley.	152	C4
SCRIPPS COLLEGE, Balch Hall, Claremont Colleges, Claremont Studies in social science, literature, fine arts.	203	B1
SCRIPPS INSTITUTE OF OCEANOGRAPHY, San Diego Branch of UCSD, oceanographic research.	211	A1
SCRIPPS INSTITUTE SUBMERGED LAND AREA, San Diego Part of Scripps Institute of Oceanography.	211	A1
SONOMA STATE UNIV, 1801 E Cotati Av, Rohnert Park Offers programs in sciences and liberal arts.	38	A3
STANFORD UNIVERSITY, Junipero Serra Blvd Distinguished univ; beautiful church on campus.	147	A3
UNIV OF CALIF, BERKELEY, 2200 University Av Oldest & largest of the Univ Of Cal campuses.	156	B2
UNIV OF CALIF, DAVIS, Russell Bl & La Rue Studies in law, medicine, agriculture & sciences.	136	B3
UNIV OF CALIF, IRVINE, Campus Dr Good programs in sciences & medicine.	200	D2
UNIV OF CALIF, LOS ANGELES, 405 Hilgard Av Outstanding liberal arts & medical schools.	180	C1
UNIV OF CALIF, RIVERSIDE, 900 University Av Desert campus lies at base of foothills.	205	E3
UNIV OF CALIF, SAN DIEGO, La Jolla Village Dr Specializes in physical, natural science & medicine.	V	A2
UNIV OF CALIF, SAN FRANCISCO, 3rd & Parnassus Avs Small campus, tours available.	141	E5
UNIV OF CALIF, SANTA BARBARA, Ward Memorial Bl Beautiful campus beside the ocean.	87	A4
UNIV OF CALIF, SANTA CRUZ, Hill St Overlooks bay, excellent marine research dept.	169	A1
UNIVERSITY OF NEVADA, LAS VEGAS, Flamingo Rd Noted for music & theater; concert hall.	210	E3
UNIVERSITY OF NEVADA, RENO, N Virginia & 9th Sts Beautiful site overlooking Truckee Meadows.	130	B1
UNIVERSITY OF THE PACIFIC, Stadium Dr, Stockton Noted for Liberal Arts & Sciences.	160	B2
UNIVERSITY OF SAN DIEGO, Alcala Park Fine academic programs, small campus.	213	B4
UNIVERSITY OF SAN FRANCISCO, 2130 Fulton St Fine academic programs on a small campus.	141	E3
UNIVERSITY OF SANTA CLARA, The Alameda, Santa Clara. Mission Santa Clara is on this campus.	151	C3
UNIV OF SOUTHERN CALIF, 3551 University Av, Los Angeles Largest private university in California.	185	C5

GOLF COURSES

NAME & ADDRESS	PAGE	GRID
ALMADEN GOLF & COUNTRY CLUB, San Jose	P	B4
BERMUDA DUNES COUNTRY CLUB, 42360 Adams St, Indio	101	A4
CYPRESS POINT COUNTRY CLUB, 17 Mile Dr, Monterey Co	53	A4
DESERT INN & COUNTRY CLUB, Las Vegas	210	C1
ELDORADO COUNTRY CLUB, Indian Wells	100	E4
FAIRBANKS RANCH COUNTRY CLUB, San Diego	106	C4
GRAEAGLE MEADOWS, Graeagle	27	A3
INDIAN WELLS COUNTRY CLUB, 4600 Club Dr, Riverside	100	E4
LA COSTA COUNTRY CLUB, Carlsbad	106	C3
LA QUINTA COUNTRY CLUB, Eisenhower Dr & 50th Av	101	A4
LOS ANGELES COUNTRY CLUB, 10101 Wilshire Bl, Westwood	180	E1
MISSION HILLS COUNTRY CLUB, Rancho Mirage	100	D4
OAKMONT COUNTRY CLUB, Glendale	Q	E2
PEBBLE BEACH GOLF LINKS, off 2nd Av	168	B3
PLUMAS PINES COUNTRY CLUB, Blairsden	27	A2
RIVIERA COUNTRY CLUB, Pacific Palisades	Q	B4
SPYGLASS HILL GOLF COURSE, Spyglass Hill Rd & Stevenson Dr	53	B4
TAMARISK COUNTRY CLUB, 70240 F Sinatra Dr, Rancho Mirage	100	D4
THE MIRAGE GOLF CLUB, 3650 S Las Vegas Bl, Las Vegas	210	A3
TORREY PINES GOLF COURSE, La Jolla	V	A1

HARBORS

NAME & ADDRESS	PAGE	GRID
ALAMEDA HARBOR, Embarcadero & 9th Av Major shipping center of northern California.	158	B4
BODEGA HARBOR, Hwy 1 at Bodega Bay Small but busy harbor; parks near harbor & bay.	37	C3
INNER HARBOR, between Oakland & Alameda Busy commercial section of San Francisco Bay.	157	D4
LONG BEACH HARBOR, Ocean Blvd, Long Beach Shares largest man-made harbor with Los Angeles.	192	A5
LOS ANGELES HARBOR, Seaside Av, Los Angeles Busy commercial port of state's largest city.	191	C5
PORT HUENEME HARBOR, end of Hueneme Rd, Port Hueneme Dominated by US Naval installation.	96	B1
PORT OF SACRAMENTO, off Lake Washington, Sacramento Furthest inland port of Sacramento deep-water channel.	39	D1
PORT OF STOCKTON, off Hwy 5, Stockton Busy inland agricultural seaport.	160	A5
RICHMOND INNER HARBOR, Richmond Commercial port in San Francisco Bay.	155	B5
SAN DIEGO BAY, W of I-5, San Diego Busy deepwater port, home of US Navy 11th Fleet.	V	C4
SAN FRANCISCO HARBOR, Fisherman's Wharf, San Francisco Major commercial port; 1st in W Coast shippng.	L	B4
SANTA CRUZ HARBOR Small commercial harbor in Monterey Bay.	169	E4

HISTORICAL SITES

NAME & ADDRESS	PAGE	GRID
ALPINE COUNTY HISTORIC COMPLEX, Hwy 89, Markleeville Historic museum and restored buildings.	36	C5
ANDERSON MARSH STATE HISTORIC PARK, near Clear Lake Buildings from Anderson Ranch & Indian site.	32	A3
ANGELS HOTEL, Angels Camp Hotel in Twains, 'The Jumping Frog of Calaveras County'.	41	B4
ARROYO DE CANTUA, off Hwy 5, Fresno Co Headquarters of the notorious bandit Joaquin Murieta.	66	D1
ASTRONOMICAL OBSERVATORY, off Shake Ridge Rd, Amador Co First observatory in California - discovered Great Comet 1861.	41	A2
AVERY HOTEL, Moran Rd, Avery Wooden hotel built in 1853.	41	C3
BALE GRIST MILL STATE HISTORIC PARK, on Hwy 29 Restored mill was built in 1846.	38	B1
BANNING PARK, 401 E M St, Wilmington House built in 1850s by General Phineas Banning.	S	C2
BARNSDALL PARK, 4800 Hollywood Bl, Los Angeles Site of Frank Lloyd Wright's Hollyhock House.	182	B4

INDEXES

NAME & ADDRESS	PAGE	GRID
BENICIA CAPITOL STATE HISTORIC PARK, H & 1st Sts Capitol of California in 1853.	153	B4
BIDWELL MANSION STATE HIST PARK, 525 Esplanade, Chico Restored Victorian home of Chico founder.	124	B4
BODIE STATE HISTORICAL PARK, Bodie, off Hwy 395 Gold boom town, now a restored ghost town.	43	C3
BOK KAI TEMPLE (CHINESE JOSS HOUSE), Marysville Only temple in USA for worship of River God.	33	D2
BORAX MUSEUM, Furnace Creek Ranch, Death Valley Memorabilia from the old borax mine.	62	A5
BOWERS MANSION, Washoe Valley Granite home built 1864 wth rewards of mining.	36	B1
BRAND PARK, San Fernando Mission Blvd, Los Angeles Picturesque atmosphere of early Calif missions.	Q	C1
BRIDGEPORT COVERED BRIDGE, Bridgeport Longest single-span wood-covered bridge in US.	34	B1
BURBANK MEMORIAL GARDENS, Santa Rosa Av A living memorial dedicated to the naturalist.	131	D4
CALICO GHOST TOWN, 10.5 miles NE of Barstow Restored mining town - tour of mine & museum.	92	A1
CALIFORNIA CITRUS STATE HISTORIC PARK, Van Buren Blvd Visitor center, grove with 80 varieties.	99	B3
CALIFORNIA STANDARD OIL WELL, McKittrick Field Discovery well started new oil field in 1899.	77	E3
CALIF STATE MINING & MINERAL MUSEUM, Mariposa Displays of Calif gold, diamonds and fossils.	49	B3
CAMP CURTIS, 1 mi N of Arcata. Estab for the protection of white settlers.	9	E5
CAMP SALVATION, Calexico Refugee ctr for emigrants in search of gold.	112	B4
CAMRON STANFORD HOUSE, 14418 Lakeside Dr Built in 1876 it serves as the Oakland Museum.	158	A3
THE CASTLE, 70 S B St, Virginia City Built 1868 - restored; antique furnishings.	36	D1
CATALINA ISLAND MUSEUM, Casino Building Features displays on the island's history.	97	B4
CHARCOAL KILNS, near Wildrose, Death Valley National Park Large old kilns used during the mining days.	71	D2
CHILDREN'S PARK, S Morton Bl, Modesto Childrens playground wth old train & airplane.	162	D4
CHINESE TEMPLE, E of Oroville A temple of worship for over 10,000 Chinese.	25	D4
CHUMASH PAINTED CAVE STATE HIST PARK, Painted Cave Rd Chumash cave painted with native artwork	87	C4
COL THOMAS BAKER MEMORIAL, City Hall, Bakersfield Civic Center commemorates friend of travelers.	166	C3
COLUMBIA CITY HOTEL, Main St, Columbia Hotel built in 1856 which is still in use.	41	C4
COLUMBIA STATE HISTORIC PARK, N of Columbia Gold boom town in 1850s, now preserved.	41	C4
CONCANNON VINEYARD, S of Livermore Estab Livermore Valley as a select wine district.	P	D1
CONGREGATIONAL CHURCH, Jesus Maria Rd Built 1853 - oldest Congregational Church in Ca.	41	A3
COTTONWOOD CHARCOAL KILNS, N of Cartago Built 1870s to char wood for mines at Owens Lake.	70	B1
DEATH VALLEY GATEWAY, mouth of Furnace Creek Natural entrance to Death Valley used by settlers.	72	B1
DE LA GUERRA PLAZA, 15 E De La Guerra St Shopping arcade in historic adobes.	174	C3
DEL NORTE COUNTY HISTORICAL MUSEUM, Crescent City Largest museum in Northern California.	1	D4
DIEGO SEPULVEDA ADOBE, 1900 Adams Av, Costa Mesa Old ranch adobe now houses a museum.	197	A5
DRYTOWN, N of Amador 1st town in Amador, in which gold was discovered.	40	E2
D STEWART COUNTY STORE, in Ione The 1st brick bldg, built in Ione Valley, 1856.	40	C2
DUNSMUIR HOME & GARDENS, 2960 Peralta Oaks Ct Built 1899, Greek revival mansion, 48 acre garden.	L	E5
EL PRESIDIO DE SANTA BARBARA, 210 E Canon Perdido One of four presidios built in Calif, 1782.	174	C3
EL PUEBLO DE LOS ANGELES, Main & Arcadia Sts State historic park with many historic landmarks.	186	B3
EMPIRE MINE STATE HISTORIC PARK, Colfax Rd Oldest quartz mine in operation for over 100 yrs.	127	D4
ESTUDILLO HOME, S of San Leandro Home of the family which founded San Leandro.	L	E5
EUGENE O'NEILL NATIONAL HISTORIC SITE, NW of Danville Ranger-guided tour of ONeills 1937 Tao House.	M	A4

NAME & ADDRESS	PAGE	GRID
FELTON COVERED BRIDGE, off Graham Hill Rd, Felton 1 of 3 remaining covered bridges in Santa Cruz Co.	P	A5
FERNANDO PACHECO ADOBE, Concord Restored adobe house originally built in 1843.	M	B3
FORT HUMBOLDT STATE HISTORIC PARK, Eureka Exhibits of logging & military life.	121	A3
FORT JANESVILLE, near Janesville Fort built for protection from Indian attacks.	21	B4
FORT MASON, Golden Gate National Recreation Area Former army headquarters houses museum; cultural center.	143	A1
FORT POINT NATIONAL HISTORIC PARK, Golden Gate Park Built in 1861 to control access to San Francisco Bay.	141	C1
FORT ROSS STATE HISTORIC PARK, at Fort Ross Restored Russian outpost; museum and beach.	37	A1
FORT TEJON STATE HISTORIC PARK, Ft Tejon Rd, Lebec Former military center; summer programs.	88	D1
FRESNO FLATS HISTORIC PARK, Rd 427, Oakhurst Historic buildings and artifacts of Madera Co.	49	D4
GASLAMP QUARTER, Downtown San Diego Victorian bldgs, shops, nightclubs & theaters.	215	E4
GIANT DESERT FIGURES, 18 miles north of Blythe 3 giant figures - 2 animals, 1 coiled serpent.	103	C3
GOLD BUG MINE, off Bedford Rd, Placerville Exposed gold veins in old mine shaft; tours.	138	E1
GOLD COUNTRY, HIGHWAY 49, from Mariposa to Vinton 300 mi drive through the historic Mother Lode.	41	A3
GRANVILLE P SWIFT ADOBE, N of Orland Rodeos were held annually at this site.	24	D3
GRASS VALLEY MUSEUM, Chapel St, Grass Valley Built in 1855; artifacts from early Grass Valley.	127	B4
HARMONY BORAX WORKS, Furnace Creek, Death Valley Preserved processing plant near borax discovery.	62	A5
HAROLD LLOYD ESTATE, 1740 Greenacres, Beverly Hills Once home to the silent screen actor.	Q	C3
HEARST SAN SIMEON STATE HISTORIC MONUMENT, off Hwy 1 Tours of fabulous estate of William R Hearst.	75	B1
HERITAGE HILL, Lake Forest Dr & Serrano, Lake Forest Restored historic buildings of central Orange Co.	98	D4
HOTEL LEGER, Main St, Mokelumne Hill Victorian style hotel, garden pool & theatre.	41	A3
INDIAN GRINDING ROCK STATE HISTORIC PARK, S of Volcano Restored Miwok Indian village, museum.	41	A2
IOOF HALL, Mokelumne Hill 1st 3-story building in the interior of the state.	41	A3
JACK LONDON STATE HISTORIC PARK, Glen Ellen Museum is in House of Happy Walls.	38	B2
JACOBY BUILDING, 8th & H, Arcata Princpal supply store for Klamath-Trinity miners.	10	A5
J. J. JACKSON MUSEUM, Highway 299, Weaverville Trinity Co. history; Indian & mining displays.	17	D1
JOHN MUIR NATIONAL HISTORIC SITE, 4204 Alhambra House built 1882; visitor's center & tours.	154	B3
JOSE E BORONDA ADOBE, 333 Boronda Rd, Salinas Restored adobe, artifacts & historic photos.	171	A2
KEANE WONDER MINE & MILL, off Daylight Pass Cutoff Well-preserved historic remains of silver mine.	61	E4
KENTUCKY MINE HISTORIC PARK, NE of Sierra City Restored stamp mill & old gold mine buildngs.	27	A4
KERN CO MUSEUM & PIONEER VILLAGE, 3801 Chester Exhibits of pioneer and Indian history.	166	C2
KEYESVILLE, 4 miles W of Isabella Center of placer & quartz gold mining,1853-70.	79	C1
KIT CARSON MARKER, Kit Carson Replica of original inscription cut from Kit's tree.	35	D5
LAKE COUNTY MUSEUM, 255 N Forbes St, Lakeport In old courthouse, Indian & pioneer displays.	31	D3
LAKEPORT HISTORICAL MUSEUM, 175 3rd St, Lakeport Displays of indian baskets & other artifacts.	31	C3
LA PURISIMA MISSION STATE HISTORIC PARK, 3 mi NE of Lompoc Restored mission, exhibits. Open 9-4:30 daily.	86	C2
LARKIN HOUSE, Jefferson St & Calle Principal Served as American Consulate 1843 to 1846.	167	E4
LAWS RAILROAD MUSEUM & HISTORIC SITE, NE of Bishop Restored 1880's RR depot, locomotive & equipment.	51	D3
LELAND STANFORD WINERY, off Hwy 680 Founder of Stanford University, operated here in 1869.	P	B2
LIVERMORE MEMORIAL MONUMENT, Livermore Remembrance of the 1st settler of Livermore.	P	C1
LA CO MUSEUM OF NATURAL HISTORY, 900 Exposition Bl Exhibits include Indian artifacts, gems & mummy.	185	C5

POINTS OF INTEREST INDEX

NAME & ADDRESS	PAGE	GRID
LOS ENCINOS STATE HISTORIC PARK, 16756 Moorpark St This historic park features 1849 Osa Adobe.	Q	B3
LOS ROBLES ADOBE, 3 mi N of Lemoore Restored adobe house, built in 1849.	67	C1
LOTT HOME, 1735 Montgomery St, Oroville Restored; furnished 1856 home of Judge C Lott.	25	C4
LOWER LAKE STONE JAIL, Lower Lake Claimed to be smallest jail in US, built 1876.	32	A3
LUMMIS HOME STATE HISTORIC MONUMENT, 200 E Av 43, LA Built 1895 by Charles F Lummis.	R	B3
MALAKOFF DIGGINS STATE HISTORIC PARK, NE of Nevada City Colorful slopes exposed by hydraulic mining.	26	D5
MARE ISLAND HISTORICAL PARK, I-80 to Tennessee St. West Former naval shipyards established in 1854.	134	A4
MARIPOSA COUNTY COURTHOUSE, Mariposa Built 1854 after Mariposa became the County seat.	49	B3
MARIPOSA CO HISTORIC CENTER & MUSEUM, 12th St & Jessie St Early Gold Rush equipment, stamp mill & buildings.	49	B3
MARSHALL'S BLACKSMITH SHOP, Gold Trail Park Marshall was a smithy & qualified carpenter.	34	E4
MARSHALL GOLD DISCOVERY STATE HISTORIC PARK, Hwy 49 Marshall's discovery in 1848 started Gold Rush.	34	D4
MARY AARON MUSEUM, 704 D St, Marysville Restored home - gold rush tools & pictures.	33	D2
MARY AUSTIN'S HOUSE, Independence Wrote books depicting beauty of Owens Valley.	59	E3
McKITTRICK BREA PIT, 1/2 mi W of McKittrick Animals were trapped in ancient asphalt pit.	77	E3
MENDOCINO PRESBYTERIAN CHURCH, Main St, Mendocino Built 1868 of redwood, 1 of oldest still in use.	30	C1
METHODIST CHURCH, S of Ione Dedicatd Lone City Centenary Church in 1866.	40	C3
MINERS FOUNDRY, 325 Spring St, Nevada City Manufactured machinery for gold miners.	128	C3
MONO COUNTY HISTORICAL MUSEUM, Bridgeport City Park Restored elementary school, houses many historic artifacts.	43	B3
MONTEREY STATE HISTORIC PARK, 210 Olivier St Includes many buildings of historic interest.	167	E3
MORMON STATION STATE HIST MONUMENT, N of Gardnerville Museum has pioneer items & displays; old fort.	36	B3
MORMON STOCKADE, Court St, San Bernardino Site of 1851 stockade built for protection.	207	D2
MORRO ROCK, off the coast of Morro Bay Important navigational landmark for 300+ yrs.	75	D3
MOTHER COLONY HOUSE, 400 N West St, Anaheim First house built in Anaheim.	193	B2
MURPHYS, 9 mi NE of Angels Camp Victorian houses, old jail, hotels, church.	41	C4
MURPHY'S HOTEL, off Hwy 4 in Murphys Early guests included Mark Twain & Gen Grant.	41	C4
MUSEUM OF NATURAL HISTORY, State Park Rd, Santa Barbara Displays, films & lectures.	174	B2
NAPA COUNTY HISTORICAL MUSEUM, in Calistoga County history of the late 1800s.	38	A1
NAPA VALLEY RAILROAD DEPOT, Calistoga Built 1868, is now the Southern Pacific depot.	38	B1
NATIONAL HISTORIC SHIPS, Hyde St Pier, Aquatic Pk Museum of 5 ships; includes the Balclutha.	143	B1
NATIONAL HOTEL, 2 Water St, Jackson Built in 1849, survived the 1862 fire.	40	E2
NATIONAL HOTEL, 77 Main St, Jamestown Built in 1859, Antiques & saloon.	41	C5
NEVADA STATE HISTORIC MUSEUM, 1650 N Virginia St, Reno Indian, pioneer, mineral & gambling exhibits.	28	B4
OCTAGON HOUSE, 2645 Gough St, San Francisco Eary San Francisco home built in 1861.	143	A2
ODD FELLOWS MEMORIAL, Kirkwood Here rests the Unknown Pioneer, 1849.	36	A5
OLD CUSTOM HOUSE, Fisherman's Wharf Oldest government building in California.	167	E3
OLDEST HOUSE NORTH OF SAN FRANCISCO BAY, N of Novato Built 1776 by an Indian chief.	L	A2
OLD FIREHOUSE No 1, 214 Main St, Nevada City Indian baskets, pioneer and Donner Party items.	128	C2
OLD FOLSOM POWERHOUSE, Folsom Long distance generating plant built in 1890s.	34	B5
OLD HOMESTEAD, Crockett Built in 1867 - 1st American home in Crockett.	L	D3
OLD POINT LOMA LIGHTHOUSE, 1800 Cabrillo Memorial Dr Built in 1854, one of the first pacific lighthouses.	V	A4
OLD SACRAMENTO STATE HISTORIC PARK, 2nd & I Sts Business district during Gold Rush; restored.	137	A2
OLD STOVEPIPE WELL, off Hwy 190, Death Valley Site of underground well marked by stovepipe.	61	D4
OLD TOWN SAN DIEGO STATE HISTORIC PARK Restored Spanish-style bldgs; museums & shops.	213	A5
OLVERA STREET, 130 Paseo de la Plaza Shopping & dining in birthplace of Los Angeles.	186	B2
PEPPARD CABIN, off Hwy 70 in Quincy Cabin built in 1888; made of hand hewn logs.	26	C2
PERALTA HOME, W of Castro Valley The first brick home built in Alameda County.	L	E5
PETALUMA ADOBE STATE HISTORIC PARK, 3325 Adobe Rd Relics displayed in 1836 adobe house.	L	A1
PETER LASSEN GRAVE, 5 mi E of Susanville In memory of a pioneer killed by Indians.	21	A4
PIGEON POINT LIGHTHOUSE, Pigeon Point Rd, San Mateo Co. Constructed in 1872 and still in use.	N	C4
PIONEER YOSEMITE HISTORY CENTER, Wawona Historical buildings, covered bridge & cabins.	49	C3
PIONEER SCHOOLHOUSE, 2 mi E of Quincy 1st schoolhouse in Plumas Co, built in 1857.	26	C1
PLUMAS COUNTY MUSEUM, 500 Jackson Street, Quincy Artifacts of early Plumas County	26	C2
PLYMOUTH TRADING POST, Plymouth Office & commissary of the many small mines.	40	E2
POINT FERMIN HISTORIC LIGHTHOUSE, Paseo Del Mar Located in Angels Gate Park.	S	C3
POINT SUR STATE HISTORIC PARK, Monterey County Ranger-guided tours of lighthouse & Moro Rock.	64	A1
PONY EXPRESS REMOUNT STATION, off Hwy 88 An important remount station in the 1860s.	36	B4
PRESIDIO OF MONTEREY, Pacific St Now House Defense Language Institute.	167	E3
PRESIDIO OF SAN FRANCISCO, NW end Lombard Former Army Post ; 1450 Acres, part of Golden Gate NRC	141	C2
RAILTOWN 1897 STATE HISTORIC PARK, Jamestown 26 acre park with trains on exhibit.	41	B5
RANCHO OLOMPALI STATE HISTORIC PARK, US 101 N of Novato Historic Miwok village and exhibits.	38	A4
RANDSBURG GHOST TOWN, Hwy 395 S of Ridgecrest Residents live in restored 19th Century buildings.	80	D3
RED BRICK GRAMMAR SCHOOL, Altaville Built 1848 - it is one of the oldest in Calif.	41	A4
RENEGADE CANYON NATURAL HIST LANDMARK, near China Lake Remarkable prehistoric rockpile collection.	70	D5
RHYOLITE, off Hwy 374, Nevada Once a booming silver town, now in ruins.	62	A2
RICHARDSON ADOBE, 2.5 mi S of Soledad Built 1843, later used as stage station & PO.	65	B1
ROCKVILLE STONE CHAPEL, Rockville Volunteer pioneers built chapel in 1856.	L	D1
ROOP'S FORT, Weatherlow St, Susanville Built in 1854 - Emigrant trains stopped here.	20	E3
ST JAMES EPISCOPAL CHURCH, Sonora Oldest Episcopal Church in California.	163	B3
SAINT TERESA'S CHURCH, Bodega Built of redwood in 1859; still in use.	37	C3
SAINT VINCENT'S SCHOOL, north of San Rafael Founded in 1855.	L	B3
SALVIO PACHECO ADOBE, Concord Two-story home was the 1st built in the valley.	M	B3
SAN DIEGO PLAZA, Old Town, San Diego Center of Mexican Pueblo, built 1830s; restored.	213	A5
SAN FRANCISCO MARITIME NATIONAL HIST PARK, end Hyde Av Historic ships, guided & self-guided tours.	143	B1
SAN JUAN BAUTISTA STATE HISTORIC PARK, 2nd St, SJB Includes mission, Plaza Hotel, & house built 1841.	54	D3
SAN PASQUAL BATTLEFIELD STATE HISTORIC PARK, Hwy 78 Battle site between Dragoons & Californios.	106	E3
SAN RAFAEL ADOBE, 1330 Dorothy Dr, Glendale Adobe and hacienda built in 1865.	Q	E2
SANTA BARBARA HISTORICAL MUSEUM, 136 E De La Guerra Exhibits of state & local history.	174	C3
SANTA CRUZ CITY MUSEUM, 1305 E Cliff Dr Natural history of Santa Cruz County.	169	E3
SANTA CRUZ COUNTY HISTORIC MUSEUM, Cooper & Front Sts Artifacts & history of early Santa Cruz Co.	169	D3
SANTA MARIA VALLEY HISTORIC MUSEUM, 616 S Broadway Pioneer Indian & Spanish historical exhibits.	173	C3

NAME & ADDRESS	PAGE	GRID
SCOTT MUSEUM, off Hwy 3 in Trinity Center Features Indian artifacts and antiques.	11	E4
SISSON MUSEUM, off Hwy 5 north of Dunsmuir Features the geology & history of gold mining.	12	C2
SKIDOO, off Skidoo Rd in Death Valley Ruins of mining town that once flourished.	61	D5
SNELLING COURTHOUSE, Snelling 1st courthouse in Merced County, built 1857.	48	C3
SONOMA HISTORIC PARK, W Spain St & 3rd St W Home of General Vallejo built in 1850.	132	D3
SONORA OPERA HALL, 250 S Washington St, Sonora Historic opera house built in 1886.	163	C4
STEVENSON HOUSE, 530 Houston St, Monterey Living quarters of Robert Louis Stevenson.	167	E4
STONE HOUSE, 6 mi N of Middleton Oldest building in Lake County, 1st built 1854.	32	A4
SUSPENSION BRIDGE, S of Chico Bidwell Bar Bridge was the 1st in Calif, 1856.	25	B3
SUTTER'S FORT STATE HISTORIC PARK, 28th & L Sts, Sact Features relics of Gold Rush Era.	137	D3
TEMPLE OF KUAN TI, Albion St, Mendocino Chinese house of worship.	30	B1
TUMCO MINES, 4 mi NE of Ogilby Largest stamp mill in US was located here.	110	C5
VALLECITO BELL MONUMENT, Vallecito Used to call the town together until 1939.	41	B4
VIRGINIA CITY, NE of Carson City, Nevada Old mining town - churches, hotels, homes.	36	D1
VOLCANO, 12 mi NE of Jackson Gold rush bldgs - hotel, jail, brewery, PO.	41	A2
WATTS TOWER STATE HISTORIC PARK, 1765 E 107th St Unusual tower studded with glass & shell.	R	A5
WEAVERVILLE JOSS HOUSE STATE HIST PARK, Weaverville Chinese worship house built in 1874.	17	C1
WILL ROGERS STATE HISTORIC PARK, Sunset Blvd Will Rogers' home located in 186 acre park.	Q	B4
WOODLAND OPERA HOUSE STATE HIST PARK, Woodland Built in 1895 to serve Sacramento Valley.	33	C5
YORBA-SLAUGHTER ADOBE, 5.5 miles south of Chino Early American architecture, built in 1850s.	U	D3
YREKA NATIONAL HISTORICAL DISTRICT, 910 S Main St, Yreka Victorian style houses & shops built in 1890's.	4	A4
YUCAIPA ADOBE, Yucaipa Oldest house in San Bernardino Co, built in 1842.	99	D2

HOTELS

* Indicates information obtained from AAA.

NAME & ADDRESS	PAGE	GRID
*ADOBE INN-CARMEL, Dolores St & 8th Av 19 units; fireplaces, pool & sauna; restaurant.	168	B3
*AHWAHNEE HOTEL, E end of Yosemite Valley 123 rooms; an elegant hotel built in the 1920's.	63	D1
*AIRPORT HILTON, 18800 MacArthur Blvd, Irvine 289 rooms; pool, restaurant & tennis court.	198	C5
AIRPORT MARINA HOTEL, 8601 Lincoln Blvd, LA 770 rooms; pool & dining room; LAX transportation	188	A5
*ALEXIS PARK RESORT, 375 E Harmon Av, Las Vegas 500 rooms; pools, putting green & tennis.	210	D3
*AMERICANA CANTON HOTEL, S Palm Canyon 460 rooms; golf, tennis, health spa & 3 pools.	100	C4
*ANAHEIM INN AT THE PARK, 1855 S Harbor Blvd, Anaheim 500 rooms; pool, restaurant & coffee shop.	193	C4
*ANAHEIM HILTON & TOWERS, 777 W Convention Wy 1576 rooms; restaurants & entertainment.	193	C5
*ANAHEIM MARRIOTT HOTEL, 700 W Convention Wy 1033 units; pools, whirlpool, 4 restaurants 7 shops	193	C5
ANAHEIM PZ RESORT HOTEL, 1700 S Harbor Bl,Anaheim 301 rooms; pool & dining room.	193	C4
*ANA HOTEL SF, 50 3rd St, San Francisco 667 rooms; restaurant & lounge, downtown.	143	D3
*ATRIUM HOTEL, 18700 MacArthur Blvd, Irvine 212 rooms; pool, sauna & dining, across from John Wayne Airport.	198	C5
*BALLY'S CASINO RESORT, 3645 Las Vegas Bl, Las Vegas 2818 rooms; casino, restaurants & entertainment.	210	B2
*BALLYS HOTEL - RENO, 2500 E 2nd St, Reno Casino, restaurants, theatres, shows & shops.	28	C4
*BARBARY COAST HOTEL, 3595 Las Vegas Blvd S 200 rooms; casino, restaurant & entertainment.	210	B2
*BARSTOW HOLIDAY INN, 1511 E Main St, Barstow 148 rooms; pool, whirlpool & restaurant.	208	D3
*BERKELEY MARINA MARRIOTT, 200 Marina Bl, Berkeley 373 rooms; indoor pool, sauna & restaurant.	L	C4
*BEST WESTERN BONANZA INN, 1001 Clark Av, Yuba Cty 125 rooms; convention center & restaurant.	125	C2
*BEST WESTERN CAMERON PARK INN, 3361 Coach Ln 61 rooms; pool. Restaurant adjacent.	34	C5
*BEST WESTERN HANALEI HOTEL, 2270 Hotel Cir, San Diego 412 rooms; pool, whirlpool & entertainment.	213	B4
BEST WESTERN JAMAICA BAY INN, 4175 Admiralty Wy, Los Angeles 42 units; heated pool, whirlpool & bike rentals.	187	B3
*BEST WESTERN OCEANSIDE INN, 1680 Oceanside Blvd, Oceanside 80 rooms; pool, sauna, movies & dining room.	106	B3
*BEST WESTERN PONDEROSA MOTOR INN, 1100 H St, Sacramento 98 units; pool & sauna, 3 blocks from capitol.	137	C2
*BEST WESTERN ROYAL LAS VEGAS, 99 Convention Center Dr 237 units; pool, restaurant & casino.	209	D5
*BEST WESTERN STATION HOUSE INN, 901 Park Av, S Lake Tahoe 100 rooms; near beach, casinos & skiing.	36	A3
BEVERLY HERITAGE HOTEL, 3350 Av of the Arts, Costa Mesa 238 rooms; near the Performing Arts Center	198	A3
*BEVERLY HILLS HOTEL, 9641 Sunset Blvd, Beverly Hills 194 rooms; pool & 2 restaurants.	183	A1
*BEVERLY HILTON HOTEL, 9876 Wilshire Blvd, Beverly Hills Large hotel offers exceptional facilities.	183	A2
BILL'S, Hwy 50 in South Lake Tahoe Casino, shows & restaurant.	129	E1
*BILTMORE HOTEL, 506 S Grand Av, Los Angeles Lovely long established hotel of the 1920's.	186	A3
BINION'S HORSESHOE HOTEL, 128 Fremont, Las Vegas 367 rooms; casino, pool & cafe.	209	C2
BOURBON STREET HOTEL, 120 E Flamingo St, Las Vegas Casino, restaurant & shows.	210	B3
*BREAKERS MOTEL, Morro Bay Bl & Market, Morro Bay 25 rooms; ocean view, pool & restaurant.	75	E3
*BUFFALO BILLS RESORT & CASINO, I - 15 & State Line, Primm 1246 rooms; home of the world's tallest roller coaster	84	C1
*BURBANK AIRPORT HILTON & CONV CENTER, 2500 Hollywood Wy 495 rooms; pool, sauna & whirlpool.	179	B1
*CAESAR'S PALACE, 3570 Las Vegas Bl, Las Vegas 1509 rooms; casino, restaurants, entertainment & shops.	210	B2
*CAESAR'S TAHOE, 1 blk N of US 50, Stateline, Nevada Cafe, convention facilities, golf & health club.	129	E1
*CALIFORNIA HOTEL, 1st & Ogden, Las Vegas 635 rooms; dining room, coffee shop & casino.	209	C2
*CARRIAGE HOUSE INN, Junipero Av near 8th Av, Carmel by the Sea 13 units; fireplaces, bay windows; early Amer.	168	C3
*CARMEL VALLEY RANCH RES, 1 Old Ranch Rd, Carmel Valley 100 rooms; tennis courts, 2 pools, golf.	54	B5
*CATAMARAN RESORT HOTEL, 3999 Mission Bl, San Diego 312 rooms; on Mission Bay, restaurant & recreation.	212	A2
*CENTURY PLAZA HOTEL, 2025 Avenue of the Stars, Century City Near Shubert Theater & ABC Entertainment Center.	183	A2
*CIRCUS-CIRCUS, 2880 Las Vegas Blvd, Las Vegas 2793 rooms; casino, game room & circus acts.	209	B5
*CIRCUS-CIRCUS, 500 N Sierra St, Reno Hotel, casino, restaurant & entertainment.	130	B2
*CLAREMONT RESORT, Ashby & Domingo Avs, Oakland Lovely hotel & tennis club with view of San Francisco Bay.	156	C3
CLARION HOTEL, 20200 Sherman Wy, Los Angeles 100 room suites, pool.	177	E1
*CLARION HOTEL, 401 E Millbrae Av, Millbrae 435 rooms; dining room & coffee shop & pool.	144	E5
*CLARION HOTEL, 700 16th St, Sacramento 239 rooms; near State Capitol; airport transportation.	137	C2
CLARION HOTEL BAY VIEW, 660 K st, San Diego 312 rooms; sauna, exercise room & restaurant.	215	E4
*COLONIAL INN, 910 Prospect St, La Jolla 75 rooms; swimming pool & dining room.	105	B2
*COLONY HARBORTOWN MARINA RESRT,1050 Schoonr Dr, Ventura 154 rooms; pool & restaurant.	175	E5
COLORADO BELLE HOTEL & CASINO, 2100 S Casino Dr, Laughlin 1280 rooms; casino, restaurants, pool, spa, fishing & waterskiing.	85	D5
*CONCORD HILTON, 1970 Diamond Blvd, Concord 328 rooms; pool, whirlpool, exercise room & restaurant.	M	A3
*CONESTOGA INN, 1240 S Walnut St, Anaheim 254 units; pool, whirlpool & restaurant.	193	B4
*CONTINENTAL PLAZA HOTEL, 9620 Airport Blvd, Los Angeles 572 rooms; restaurant, pool & exercise room.	189	D1
*COTO DE CAZA, 14 mi E of I-5 via El Toro Rd, Coto de Caza	98	E5

POINTS OF INTEREST INDEX

NAME & ADDRESS	PAGE	GRID
100 rooms; pools & saunas, fishing & tennis.		
COURTYARD BY MARRIOTT, 2000 E Mariposa Av, El Segundo	189	C3
146 rooms; exercise room, pool & dining room.		
*CROWNE PLAZA, 3540 E Figueroa St, LA	185	C5
241 units; next to USC campus; pool.		
*CROWN STERLING SUITES, 3100 E Frontera, Anaheim	194	C1
224 suites; pool, whirlpool, sauna, steam room & dining.		
*CROWN STERLING SUITES - LAX, 1440 E Imperial Av, El Segundo	189	C2
350 rooms; near Los Angeles International Airport.		
*CROWN STERLING SUITES, 901 Calaveras Bl, Milpitas	P	B2
266 suites; pool, whirlpool, sauna & restaurant.		
CROWN STERLING SUITES, 250 Gateway Bl, S San Francisco	144	C1
Bay views; indoor pool & restaurant.		
*DANA POINT HILTON, 34402 Pacific Coast Hwy, Dana Point	202	B4
200 suites; ocean views, pool, sauna & restaurant.		
*DANISH COUNTRY INN, 1455 Mission Dr, Solvang	86	E3
81 rooms; pool, whirlpool & meeting rooms.		
DEBBIE REYNOLDS HOTEL, 305 Convention Center Dr, Las Vegas	209	C5
200 rooms; restaurants, shows & movie museum.		
*DEL MAR HILTON, 15575 Jimmy Durante Bl, Del Mar	106	B4
245 room; pool, spas & tennis; near beach.		
*DEL WEBB'S HIGH SIERRA, 255 N Sierra St	129	E1
Casino, restaurant, entertainment & shops.		
*DISNEYLAND HOTEL, 1150 W Cerritos Av, Anaheim	193	B4
1131 rooms; served by Disneyland Monorail.		
DOUBLETREE HOTEL, 3100 Camino del Rio Ct, Bakersfield	166	A2
262 units; pool & whirlpool.		
*DOUBLETREE CLUB HOTEL, 1985 E Grand Av, El Segundo	189	C3
215 rooms; pool & exercise room; LAX transportation.		
*DOUBLETREE HOTEL, 191 N Los Robles Av, Pasadena	190	C3
350 rooms; pool, sauna, whirlpool, steamroom & health club.		
*DOUBLETREE CLUB HOTEL, 7 Hutton Centre Dr, Santa Ana	198	B3
168 rooms; pool & exercise room, near John Wayne airport.		
*DOUBLETREE HOTEL, 3555 Round Barn Bl, Santa Rosa	37	E2
247 rooms; pool, golf & tennis.		
*DOUBLETREE HOTEL, 2055 Harbor Bl, Ventura	175	D3
284 rooms; pool, health club & spa.		
*DOUBLETREE HOTEL AT THE CITY, 100 The City Dr, Orange	195	E1
451 rooms; pool, whirlpool, tennis & dining.		
DOUBLETREE HOTEL - LAX, 5400 Century Blvd, Los Angeles	189	E1
731 rooms; pool, sauna, dining & entertainment.		
*DOUBLETREE MARINA DEL REY, 4100 Admirality Wy, Los Angeles	187	B3
300 rooms; pool, dining room & entertainment.		
*DREAM INN, 175 W Cliff Dr, Santa Cruz	169	D4
164 rooms; entertainment, pool & whirlpool; resort on beach		
DUNFEY HOTEL, 1770 S Amphlett Blvd, San Mateo	145	B2
266 rms; pool & 2 restaurants; pets allowed.		
EDGEWATER HOTEL & CASINO, 2020 Casino Dr, Laughlin	85	D5
1450 rooms; casino, restaurant, bowl, waterskiing & fishing.		
EL CORTEZ HOTEL, 600 E Fremont St, Las Vegas	209	E1
316 room with a convenient downtown location.		
*ELDORADO HOTEL, 345 N Virginia St, Reno	130	B2
Casino, restaurant & entertainment.		
*EMBASSY SUITES, 211 E Huntington Dr, Arcadia	R	D3
194 suites, pool & sauna.		
*EMBASSY SUITES, 900 E Birch St, Brea	T	D1
229 suites, restaurant, laundry, pool & sauna.		
*EMBASSY SUITES, 7762 Beach Blvd, Buena Park	T	B2
203 rooms; whirlpool, pool & dining.		
*EMBASSY SUITES, 1211 Garvey, Covina	98	C2
264 rooms; restaurant, attractive grounds.		
*EMBASSY SUITES, 8425 Firestone Blvd, Downey	R	B5
220 rooms; sauna, whirlpool & swimming pool.		
*EMBASSY SUITES, 2120 Main St, Irvine	198	D4
293 suites; pool, whirlpool & restaurant.		
*EMBASSY SUITES, 4130 Lake Tahoe Blvd, Lake Tahoe	129	E4
400 units; pool & fitness room.		
*EMBASSY SUITES, 1117 N H St, Lompoc	86	B3
156 suites; pool, whirlpool & fitness center.		
*EMBASSY SUITES, 9801 Airport Bl, Los Angeles	189	D1
215 suites; near LAX, pool, sauna & exercise room.		
*EMBASSY SUITES, 74-700 Hwy 111, Palm Desert	100	D4
196 rooms; restaurant, pool, sundeck & sauna.		
EMBASSY SUITES HOTEL, 333 Madonna Rd, San Luis Obispo	172	B4
195 rooms; pool, at Central Coast Plaza Mall.		
*EMBASSY SUITES, 101 McInnis Pkwy, San Rafael	139	C1
236 suites; indoor pool, exercise room & laundry.		
EMBASSY SUITES, 1325 E Dyer Rd, Santa Ana	198	D2
303 suites; indoor pool, sauna & dining room.		
*EMBASSY SUITES, 2885 Lakeside Dr, Santa Clara	P	B3
257 rooms; cafe, gift shop, pool & sauna.		
*EMBASSY SUITES, 29345 Rancho California Rd, Temecula	106	D1
136 suites; restaurant & exercise room.		
*EMBASSY SUITES HOTEL, 1345 Treat Blvd, Walnut Creek	M	A3
249 units; indoor pool, exercise room & restaurant.		
*EMBASSY SUITES SAN DIEGO BAY, 601 Pacific Hwy, San Diego	215	D4
337 suites; pool, whirlpool, sauna & restaurant.		
*EMBASSY SUITES, LA JOLLA, 4550 La Jolla Village Dr, La Jolla	V	B2
Near beaches, freeways & unique shopping.		
*EMERALD SPRINGS HOLIDAY INN, 325 E Flamingo Rd, Las Vegas	210	D2
150 rooms; pool, restaurant & entertainment.		
*ENCINA LODGE, 2220 Bath St, Santa Barbara	174	A3
122 units; lovely grounds, pool & sauna.		
ESSEX HOUSE HTL & RACQUET CLUB, 44916 N 10th St, Lancaster	90	A2
151 rooms, pool, tennis, restaurant & lounge.		
*EUREKA INN, 518 7th St, Eureka	113	D1
Historic hotel, pool & restaurant.		
*EXCALIBUR HOTEL & CASINO, 3850 Las Vegas Blvd S, Las Vegas	210	B4
4032 rooms; casino, 7 theme restaurants & entertainment.		
*FAIRMONT HOTEL, 170 S Market St, San Jose	152	B4
541 rooms; sauna, steamroom, health club, pool & restaurant.		
*FAIRMONT HOTEL & TOWER, 950 Mason St, San Francisco	143	C3
Atop Nob Hill, offers excellent view; roof garden.		
*FESS PARKERS RED LION RESORT, Santa Barbara	174	E4
360 units; pool, sauna, tennis & exercise room.		
FITZGERALDS HOTEL, 301 E Fremont St, Las Vegas	209	C2
650 units, casino, restaurant & buffet.		
*FITZGERALDS HOTEL, 255 Virginia St, Reno	130	B2
345 units; casino & restaurant.		
*FLAMINGO HILTON, 3555 Las Vegas Bl, Las Vegas	210	B2
3600 rooms; casino, restaurant, entertainment & shops.		
FLAMINGO HILTON, 1900 Casino Dr, Laughlin	85	D5
2000 rooms, restaurants, tennis & pool.		
*FLAMINGO HILTON RENO, 255 N Sierra St, Reno	130	B3
Lovely hotel with pool, casino & restaurants.		
*FOREST INN SUITES, 1101 Park Av, South Lake Tahoe	129	E2
125 units; lovely grounds, 2 pools & saunas.		
*FOUR POINTS HOTEL, 1100 N Mathilda Av, Sunnyvale	148	E3
174 rooms; pool, restaurant & cocktail lounge.		
*FOUR QUEENS, 202 E Fremont St, Las Vegas	209	C1
709 rooms; casino, restaurant & entertainment.		
*FOUR SEASONS BILTMORE HTL, 1260 Channel Dr, Santa Barbara	87	D4
236 rooms; overlooks ocean; pool & restaurant.		
*FOUR SEASONS CLIFT HOUSE, 495 Geary St, San Francisco	143	C3
329 units; newly renovated rooms & restaurant.		
*FOUR SEASONS HOTEL, 300 S. Doheny Dr, Los Angeles	183	D1
285 rooms; pool, whirlpool, exercise room & dining room.		
*FOUR SEASONS HOTEL, 690 Newport Center Dr, Newport Beach	200	A4
285 rooms; tennis, pool & 3 dining rooms.		
FREMONT HOTEL, 200 Fremont St, Las Vegas	209	E1
Casino, restaurant & game room.		
*FRESNO HILTON INN, 1055 Van Ness Av, Fresno	165	D4
192 units; pool & dining room.		
FRONTIER, 3120 Las Vegas Bl S, Las Vegas	210	C1
1000 rooms; casino, 3 restaurants & pool.		
*FURNACE CREEK INN, off Hwy 190 in Death Valley	62	A5
Tennis, golf & lawn games; airport transportation.		
*GOLDEN NUGGET HOTEL, 129 E Fremont St, Las Vegas	209	E1
1907 rooms; casino, restaurant & video arcade.		
GOLD STRIKE HOTEL / CASINO, 1 Main St , Jean	74	C5
800 rooms; 5 restaurants, pool & 5 cent arcade		
GOLD RIVER, Casino Dr, Laughlin	85	C4
1000 rooms; casino, restaurants, pool & convention center.		
GRAND HOTEL, 1 Hotel Wy, Anaheim	193	C4
243 rooms; entertainment & dinner theater.		
*GRAND HYATT SAN FRANCISCO, 345 Stockton St, San Francisco	143	C3
693 units; 3 restaurants & entertainment.		
GRISWOLDS CLAREMONT CTR, 555 W Foothill Bl, Claremont	203	A1
276 rooms; steambath, pool & whirlpool.		
GROVELAND HOTEL, 18767 Main St, Groveland	48	D1
Historic 17 room hotel established in 1850.		
*HACIENDA HOTEL - LAX, 525 N Sepulveda Bl, El Segundo	189	C3
636 rooms; pool, whirlpool & exercise room; airport transportation		
HARD ROCK HOTEL, 4455 Paradise Rd, Las Vegas	210	D3
340 rooms; casino, 2 restaurants & store.		
*HARRAH'S, on US 50, Stateline, Nevada	129	E1
Casino, cafe, theater, restaurants & sauna.		
HARRAH'S DEL RIO, 2900 S Casino Dr, Laughlin	85	D5
1658 rooms; casino, restaurants, shows, pool, spa & beach.		
*HARRAHS - LAS VEGAS, 3475 Las Vegas Bl S, Las Vegas	210	B2

POINTS OF INTEREST INDEX

NAME & ADDRESS	PAGE	GRID
1711 rooms; 5 restaurants, casino & pool.		
*HARRAH'S RENO, 3131 S Virginia St	130	B2
Name entertainment & recreational facilities.		
*HARVEY'S, on US 50, Stateline, Nevada	129	E1
Casino, pool, cafes & restaurants.		
*HERITAGE INN, 204 Harding Bl, Roseville	34	A4
101 large rooms; spacious grounds & restaurant.		
*HILL HOUSE INN, 10701 Pallette Dr, Mendocino	30	B1
44 rooms; Victorian decor, near ocean.		
*HILTON GARDEN, 27710 The Old Rd, Santa Clarita	89	B4
152 rooms; pool, health club & business center.		
*HILTON HOTEL, 39900 Balentine, Newark	P	A2
318 rooms; pool, sauna, whirlpool & dining.		
*HILTON SUITES - ORANGE, 400 N State College Bl	193	E5
230 suites; pools, sauna, fitness center, cafe & lounge		
HILTON-WATERFRONT, 21100 PCH, Huntington Beach	T	B4
296 rooms; pool, tennis, spa, health club & restaurant.		
*HOLIDAY HOTEL, Mill & Center St, Reno	130	B2
195 units; casino, restaurant & entertainment.		
*HOLIDAY INN, 1511 E Main St, Barstow	208	D3
148 rooms; pool, whirlpool & Garden Court Cafe.		
*HOLIDAY INN, 7000 Beach Bl, Buena Park	T	B2
245 units; whirlpool & swimming pool.		
*HOLIDAY INN, 1755 N Highland Av, Hollywood	181	C4
470 units, pool, laundry & rooftop dining.		
*HOLIDAY INN, 3475 Las Vegas Bl, Las Vegas	210	B2
Casino, entertainment & shops.		
*HOLIDAY INN, 1000 E 6th St, Reno	130	C2
286 units; casino, pool & dining room.		
HOLIDAY INN, 1200 University Av, Riverside	205	E3
207 units; sauna, whirlpool & dining room.		
*HOLIDAY INN, 300 J St, Sacramento	137	B2
Pool, dining room & movies.		
*HOLIDAY INN, 1010 Northgate Dr, San Rafael	139	B1
224 rooms; restaurant, suites & entertainment.		
*HOLIDAY INN ANAHEIM AT THE PARK, 1221 S Harbor Bl, Anaheim	193	B3
254 rooms; pool, whirlpool & restaurant.		
*HOLIDAY INN BAY BRIDGE, 1800 Powell St, Emeryville	L	C4
279 rooms; luxury rooms, dining & entertainment.		
HOLIDAY INN BAYVIEW, 530 W Pico Bl, Santa Monica	Q	B4
309 rooms, cafe, lounge, salon & laundry.		
*HOLIDAY INN BEACH RESORT, 450 E Harbor Bl, Ventura	175	B3
260 rooms; near San Buenaventura State Beach.		
HOLIDAY INN BRENTWOOD, 170 N Church Ln, Los Angeles	180	A1
211 rooms, rooftop restaurant, suites & pool.		
*HOLIDAY INN BURBANK, 150 E Angeleno Av, Burbank	Q	E2
490 rooms; suites & sauna.		
*HOLIDAY INN CENTRE PLAZA, 2233 Ventura St, Fresno	165	E4
320 rooms; near the convention center.		
*HOLIDAY INN CHICO, 685 Manzanita Ct, Chico	124	B2
174 rooms; lounge, restaurant & convention center.		
*HOLIDAY INN CITY CENTER, 1020 S Figueroa St, Los Angeles	185	E3
195 rooms; pool, restaurant & gift shop.		
*HOLIDAY INN CONV CENTER, 500 E 1st St, Long Beach	192	E3
216 rooms; pool, exercise room, restaurant & lounge.		
*HOLIDAY INN COSTA MESA, 3131 Bristol St, Costa Mesa	197	E4
230 rooms; restaurant, pool, sauna & exercise room.		
*HOLIDAY INN CROWNE PLAZA, 600 Airport Bl, Burlingame	N	C1
405 rooms; lounge, gift shop & jogging trail.		
*HOLIDAY INN CROWNE PZ, 5985 W Century Bl, Los Angeles	189	D1
615 rooms; pool, sauna, whirlpool & exercise oorm.		
*HOLIDAY INN CROWN PLAZA, 300 N Harbor Dr, Redondo Beach	S	B2
339 rms; lounge, entertainment, tennis & pool.		
*HOLIDAY INN DOWNTOWN LA, 750 Garland Av, Los Angeles	185	E3
205 rooms, cafe, lounge & pool.		
*HOLIDAY INN FAIRFIELD, 1350 Holiday Ln, Fairfield	135	A3
142 rooms; lounge & restaurant.		
*HOLIDAY INN FINANCIAL DISTRICT, 750 Kearny St, San Francisco	143	D2
566 rooms, rooftop pool & panoramic views.		
*HOLIDAY INN FISHERMANS WHARF, 1300 Columbus Av, SF	143	B1
580 rooms, restaurant, lounge, cafe & suites.		
*HOLIDAY INN FRESNO AIRPORT, 5090 E Clinton Av, Fresno	57	D3
210 rooms, near the airport.		
*HOLIDAY INN GOLDEN GATEWAY, 1500 Van Ness Av, SF	143	B3
500 rooms; cafe, club & rooftop pool.		
HOLIDAY INN HARBOR VIEW, 1617 1st Av, San Diego	215	D3
203 rooms, rooftop restaurant & pool.		
HOLIDAY INN HOTEL CIRCLE, 595 Hotel Circle S, San Diego	213	D4
318 rooms; pool, whirlpool, exercise room & restaurant.		
HOLIDAY INN HUNTINGTON BEACH, 7667 Center Av	T	B3
224 rooms, lounge, gift shop & indoor pool.		
HOLIDAY INN IRVINE, 17941 Von Karman Av, Irvine	198	D4
340 rooms; pool, sauna, whirlpool & dining room.		
HOLIDAY INN LA MIRADA, 14299 Firestone Blvd, La Mirada	T	B1
300 rooms, restaurant, lounge, pool & giftshop.		
HOLIDAY INN - LAX, 9901 S La Cienega Bl, Los Angeles	189	E1
403 rooms; pool, exercise room & dining room; LAX transportation.		
HOLIDAY INN MAINGATE, 1850 Harbor Blvd, Anaheim	193	C4
312 rooms; pool, wading pool & dining room.		
HOLIDAY INN MISSION DE ORO, 13070 S Hwy 33, Santa Nella	55	C1
159 rooms;pool, restaurant & conference center.		
HOLIDAY INN MISSION VALLEY/STADIUM, 3805 Murphy Cyn Rd, SD	214	D1
Pool, whirlpool, exercise room, dining & entertainment.		
HOLIDAY INN NORTH EAST, 5321 Date Av, Sacramento	34	A5
230 rooms; pool, whirlpool, exercise room & dining		
HOLIDAY INN OAKLAND, 500 Hegenberger Rd, Oakland	159	E3
290 rooms; cafe, lounge & fitness room.		
HOLIDAY INN ON THE BAY,1355 N Harbor Dr, San Diego	215	C3
600 rooms; pool, dining room & lounges.		
HOLIDAY INN PALO ALTO, 625 El Camino Real, Palo Alto	147	B2
334 rooms; cafe, club, fitness room & whirlpool.		
HOLIDAY INN - PARK CENTER PZ, 282 Almaden Bl, San Jose	152	B4
230 rooms; downtown, close to airport.		
HOLIDAY INN PASADENA, 303 E Cordova St, Pasadena	190	C4
318 rooms; pool, tennis courts, dining room & laundry		
HOLIDAY INN PLEASANTON, 11950 Dublin Canyon Rd, Pleasanton	M	B5
248 rooms; lounge, pool & exercise room.		
HOLIDAY INN RESORT, 1000 Aguajito Rd, Monterey	54	B4
203 units; pool, sauna, tennis & putting green.		
HOLIDAY INN RIVERSIDE, 3400 Market St, Riverside	205	B2
286 rooms; pool, dining room & entertainment.		
*HOLIDAY INN SAN DIEGO BAYSIDE, 4875 N Harbor Dr, San Diego	V	A3
237 rooms; pool, whirlpool, exercise room & dining.		
HOLIDAY INN SAN FRANCISCO CIVIC CENTER, 50 8th St, SF	143	C4
389 rooms; restaurant, lounge & gift shop.		
HOLIDAY INN SAN FRANCISCO AIRPORT, 275 S Airport Bl, S SF	144	C1
275 rooms; cafe, sports lounge & gift shop.		
HOLIDAY INN SAN JOSE N, 777 Belew Dr, Milpitas	P	B2
305 rooms; Italian restaurant & live entertainment.		
HOLIDAY INN SANTA CRUZ, 611 Ocean St, Santa Cruz	169	D3
167 rooms; restaurant, lounge, pool & spa.		
*HOLIDAY INN SELECT, 1221 Chess Dr, Foster City	145	D1
238 rooms; restaurants, lounge & swimming.		
HOLIDAY INN THOUSAND OAKS, 495 N Ventu Park Rd	96	D1
154 rooms, restaurant, pool & exercise room.		
HOLIDAY INN TORRANCE, 21333 Hawthorne Bl, Torrance	S	B2
386 rooms, restaurant, lounges & giftshop.		
HOLIDAY INN TORRANCE, 19800 S Vermont Av, Torrance	S	C2
336 rooms, restaurant, pool & sundeck.		
*HOLIDAY INN-UNION SQUARE, 480 Sutter St, San Francisco	143	C3
401 units; restaurant & coffee shop.		
HOLIDAY INN VALLEJO, 1000 Fairgrounds Dr, Vallejo	134	E1
165 rooms, restaurant, lounge, pool & spa.		
HOLIDAY INN VICTORVILLE, 15494 Palmdale Rd, Victorville	91	B3
161 rooms, restaurant, lounge w/live entertain & pool.		
HOLIDAY INN VISALIA, 9000 W Airport Dr, Visalia	68	A1
258 rooms; entertainment lounge & indoor pool.		
HORIZON, on US 50, Stateline, Nevada	129	D1
539 deluxe rooms; restaurants, pool & convention center.		
*HOTEL DEL CORONADO, on Coronado Peninsula, San Diego	V	B4
Elegant beachfront hotel built in the 1880's.		
HOTEL SAN REMO, 115 E Tropicana Av, Las Vegas	210	B4
711 rooms; casino, restaurant & entertainment.		
HOWARD JOHNSON, 1380 S Harbor Blvd, Anaheim	193	C5
320 rooms; 2 heated pools, whirlpool & restaurant.		
HYATT FISHERMANS WHARF, 555 N Point St, San Francisco	143	B1
313 units; pool, exercise room.		
HYATT GRAND CHAMPIONS RESORT, 44-600 Indian Wells Ln	100	E4
336 rooms; restaurants, tennis, golf & pools.		
HYATT ISLANDIA, 1441 Quivira Rd, San Diego	212	B4
422 rooms; pool & whirlpool, dining room & lounge.		
*HYATT LAKE TAHOE RESORT HOTEL, Country Club Dr, Lake Tahoe	36	B1
460 rooms; pool, beach, sauna & tennis.		
*HYATT AT LOS ANGELES AIRPORT, 6225 W Century, Los Angeles	189	C1
594 rooms; pool, sauna, dining & entertainment.		
HYATT NEWPORTER, 1107 Jamboree Rd, Newport Beach	199	E4
410 rooms; tennis, pools, golf & restaurant.		
HYATT REGENCY, 3777 La Jolla Village Dr, La Jolla	V	A2
400 rooms; tennis, pool, health club & restaurant.		
*HYATT REGENCY, 1 Old Golf Course Rd, Monterey	54	B4

INDEXES

NAME & ADDRESS	PAGE	GRID
579 rooms; pools whirlpool, golf & tennis.		
HYATT REGENCY, 1001 Broadway, Oakland	157	E3
488 rooms; pool, restaurant & lounge.		
*HYATT REGENCY, 5 Embarcadero Center, San Francisco	143	E3
Striking arch, glass elevator & revolving rooftop bar.		
HYATT REGENCY ALICANTE, 100 Pz Alicante, Garden Grove	193	C5
396 rooms; pool, whirlpool, tennis & dining room.		
HYATT REGENCY IRVINE, 17900 Jamboree Rd, Irvine	198	E4
536 rooms; close to John Wayne Airport.		
HYATT REGENCY LONG BEACH, 200 S Pine Av, Long Beach	192	D3
521 rooms; pool, whirlpool & exercise room.		
HYATT REGENCY LOS ANGELES, 711 S Hope St, Los Angeles	185	E3
487 units; at Broadway Plaza; LAX transport.		
HYATT REGENCY SACRAMENTO, 1209 L St, Sacramento	137	C3
502+ rooms; restaurants, pool & jacuzzi.		
HYATT REGENCY SAN DIEGO, 1 Market Pl, San Diego	215	D4
875 waterview rooms; rooftop lounge & fitness room.		
HYATT REGENCY SF AIRPORT, 1333 Bayshore Hwy, SF	45	C3
791 rooms; swimming pool & beautiful grounds.		
HYATT REGENCY SUITES PALM SPRINGS, 285 N Palm Canyon	206	A3
192 rooms; pool, sauna, whirlpool, restaurants & health club.		
HYATT RICKEYS, 4219 El Camino Real, Palo Alto	147	E5
350 units; health club, pool & putting green.		
*HYATT SAN JOSE, 1740 N 1st St, San Jose	151	E1
475 rooms; putting green & dining room.		
HYATT-WESTLAKE, 880 S Westlake Bl, Westlake Village	96	E1
258 rooms; pool, whirlpool & dining room.		
IMPERIAL PALACE, 3535 Las Vegas Blvd, Las Vegas	210	B2
1500 rooms; pools, entertainment & casino.		
*INN AT NAPA VLY-A CROWN STERLING STE, 1075 California Bl	133	B4
205 suites; located in the heart of wine country.		
INN AT SPANISH BAY, 2700 17 Mile Dr, Pebble Beach	167	A3
270 units; golf, putting green, tennis, pool & sauna		
JACKIE GAUGHANS PLAZA HOTEL, 1 Main St, Las Vegas	209	C1
1037 rooms; casino, restaurant & entertainment.		
JW MARRIOTT HOTEL, 2151 Av of Stars, Century City	183	B3
367 rooms; 2 pools, sauna, whirlpool, health club & dining.		
LA CASA DEL ZORRO, CR S-3, Borrego Springs	107	E2
Studios, suites and casitas.		
*LA COSTA RESORT & SPA, Costa Del Mar Rd, Carlsbad	106	C3
547 rooms & houses; golf, tennis & health spa.		
LA JOLLA MARRIOTT. 4240 La Jolla Village Dr, La Jolla	V	B2
360 rooms; pool, whirlpool & dining room.		
LAKE ARROWHEAD RESORT, Lake Arrowhead Village	91	C5
257 rooms; pool, whirlpool & boat dock.		
*LA QUINTA, 2180 Hilltop Dr, Redding	18	C2
148 rooms; pool, whirlpool & restaurant.		
*LA QUINTA HOTEL GOLF & TENNIS RESORT, Eisenhower Dr	100	E4
269 rooms; lovely grounds, pool, tennis & golf.		
LA SIESTA VILLAS, Hwy 111, Palm Springs	100	C3
18 luxurious villas & swimming pool.		
*LAS VEGAS HILTON, 3000 Paradise Rd, Las Vegas	209	D5
3174 rooms; casino, restaurants & star entertainment.		
LE MERIDIEN SAN DIEGO, 2000 2nd St, Coronado	215	D5
300 rooms; 3 pools, sauna, whirlpool, dock, waterskiing & biking.		
*L'ERMITAGE, 9291 Burton Wy, Beverly Hills	183	C1
Elegant suites in the European tradition.		
LOEWS CORONADO BAY RES, 4000 Crndo Bay Rd, Coronado	V	C4
450 rooms; tennis & exercise room.		
LOEWS SANTA MONICA BEACH HOTEL, 1700 Ocean Av	Q	B4
352 rooms; ocean views & pool.		
LONG BEACH AIRPORT MARRIOTT, 4700 Airport Plaza Dr	S	E2
311 rooms; 2 pools, restaurant & exercise room.		
LONG BEACH HILTON, 2 World Trade Center, Long Beach	192	D3
393 rooms; pool, exercise room, dining & entertainment.		
LA AIRPORT HILTON & TOWERS, 5711 W Century Bl, LA	189	D1
1236 rooms; pool, dining room & entertainment.		
*LOS ANGELES AIRPORT MARRIOTT, 5855 W Century Bl, LA	189	D1
1010 rooms; pool, sauna, dining & entertainment.		
*LOS ANGELES HILTON HOTEL, 930 Wilshire Blvd, Los Angeles	185	E3
900 units; pool, shopping & public facilities.		
*LUXOR LAS VEGAS, 3900 Las Vegas Blvd S, Las Vegas	210	B4
2526 rooms; casino, restaurants & oval arena.		
*MADONNA INN, 100 Madonna Rd, San Luis Obispo	172	B4
109 unusually decorated rooms; restaurant & cafe.		
MANDARIN ORIENTAL, 222 Sansome St, San Francisco	143	D3
View of bay & restaurant.		
MARINA DEL REY HOTEL, 13534 Bali Wy, Marina Del Rey	187	C3
159 rooms; pool, dining room & lounge.		
MARINA DEL REY MARRIOTT, 13480 Maxella Av, Marina Del Rey	187	D3
281 rooms; pool, whirlpool & dining room.		
*MARINA INTERNATIONAL HOTEL, 4200 Admiralty Wy, LA	187	C3
135 units; pool & whirlpool; LAX transportation.		
*MARINERS INN, 6180 Moonstone Beach Dr, Cambria	75	C2
26 rooms; whirlpool. Across from the beach.		
*MARK HOPKINS HOTEL, 1 Nob Hill, San Francisco	143	C3
Elegant landmark hotel, panoramic view Top of Mark.		
MARRIOTTS DESERT SPRINGS RESORT, Palm Desert	100	E3
891 rooms; pool, tennis, golf & restaurant.		
MARRIOTT HOTEL, 2355 N Main St, Walnut Creek	M	A3
337 rooms; pool, exercise room & restaurant.		
MARRIOTT HOTEL IRVINE, 18000 Von Karman Av, Irvine	198	D4
489 rooms; pool, sauna, tennis & exercise room.		
MARRIOTT FISHERMAN'S WHARF, 1250 Columbus Av, SF	143	B1
257 rooms, restaurant & lounge.		
MARRIOTT- LAGUNA CLFS RESORT DANA PT, 25135 Pk Lantern	202	B4
350 rooms; 2 pools, whirlpool, sauna, tennis & restaurant.		
*MARRIOTT'S RANCHO LAS PALMAS RESORT, Bob Hope Dr	100	E4
456 rooms; pools, golf, tennis & bicycles.		
MARRIOTT SAN DIEGO MARINA, 333 W Harbor Dr	215	D4
1355 rooms; pools, sauna, tennis & dining.		
MARRIOTT SAN RAMON, 2600 Bishop Dr, San Ramon	M	B5
372 rooms; pool, whirlpool, sauna & restaurants.		
MARRIOTT SUITES COSTA MESA, 500 Anton Bl	198	A3
253 suites; near Performing Arts Center & shopping.		
MARRIOTT'S TENAYA LODGE, 1122 Hwy 41, Fish Camp	49	D3
242 rooms; restaurants, swimming & horseback riding.		
MARRIOTT TORRANCE, 3635 Fashion Wy, Torrance	S	B2
487 rooms; 2 pools, sauna & whirlpool.		
*MAXIM, 160 E Flamingo, Las Vegas	210	B3
Casino, restaurant, entertainment & shops.		
MENDOCINO HOTEL, 45080 Main St, Mendocino	30	B1
Restored 1878 Victorian hotel.		
MGM GRAND, 3799 Las Vegas Bl S, Las Vegas	210	B3
5005 rooms, restaurants, 4 casinos & theme park.		
MIRAGE, 3400 Las Vegas Bl, Las Vegas	210	B2
3044 rooms, unique hotel, waterfalls, volcano & tigers.		
MIRAMAR SHERATON, 101 Wilshire Bl, Santa Monica	Q	B4
300 rooms, near Santa Monica Beach.		
MONTE CARLO RESORT & CASINO, 3770 S Lake Vegas Bl, LV	210	B3
3,014 rooms and suites,shopping, dinning & 90,000 sq ft casino.		
MONTECITO INN, 1295 Coast Village Rd, Montecito	87	D4
60 rooms & suites; restored historic inn.		
MONTEREY PLAZA, 400 Cannery Row, Monterey	167	E3
291 rooms; pool, restaurant & lounge.		
MONTFIELD PARK HOTEL, 8110 Aero Dr, San Diego	214	A1
225 rooms; pool, sauna, whirlpool, exercise room & restaurant.		
*MOONSTONE INN, 5860 Moonstone Beach Dr, Cambria	75	B2
9 rooms with an ocean view from each.		
MURPHY'S HOTEL, 457 Main St, Murphys	41	C4
Historical monument still in full operation.		
*NAPA VALLEY LODGE BEST WSTRN, 2230 Madison St,Yountville	38	C2
55 rooms; lovely view, pool & whirlpool.		
*NAPA VALLEY MARRIOTT, 3425 Solano Av, Napa	133	A2
191 rooms, tennis courts & pool.		
NEVADA LANDING, I - 15 exit 12, Jean	74	C5
303 rooms; 90,000 sq. foot casino		
NEW OTANI HOTEL, 120 S Los Angeles St, Los Angeles	186	B3
435 rooms; beautiful garden, pool & sauna.		
NEWPORT BEACH MARRIOTT HOTEL, 900 Newport Center Dr	200	A4
570 rooms; 2 pools, tennis, dining & entertainment.		
NEWPORT BEACH MARRIOTT SUITES, 500 Bayview Cir, NB	200	B1
250 rooms; pool, sauna, whirlpool & dining.		
NEW YORK NEW YORK, 3790 Las Vegas Bl S, Las Vegas	210	B4
2035 rooms; casino, restaurant & roller coaster.		
OAKLAND AIRPORT HILTON, 1 Hegenberger Rd, Oakland	159	D4
367 rooms; pool, restaurant & entertainment.		
OJAI VALLEY INN, Off Hwy 150, Ojai	88	B4
218 rms; pools, golf, tennis & dining room.		
ONTARIO AIRPORT HILTON, 700 N Haven Av, Ontario	U	E2
309 rooms; dining, whirlpool & swimming pool.		
OXNARD HILTON, 600 Esplanade, Oxnard	176	C1
160rms;pool,whirlpool,tennis, jogging track & VCRs.		
PALACE STATION, 2411 W Sahara Av, Las Vegas	209	A4
1028 rooms; casino, 5 restaurants & bingo parlor.		
PALA MESA RESORT, 2001 Old Hwy 395, Fallbrook	106	C2
135 rooms; pool, whirlpool, golf & tennis.		
PALM SPRINGS HILTON RESORT, 400 E Tahquitz Wy	206	B4
260 rooms; pool, sauna, whirlpool, tennis, health club & dining.		
PALM SPRINGS RIVIERA RESORT, 1600 N Indian Canyon Dr	206	B2

NAME & ADDRESS	PAGE	GRID
480 rooms; 2 pools, wading pool, tennis & golf.		
PAN PACIFIC HOTEL, 1717 S West St, Anaheim 502 rooms; pool & whirlpool, across from Disneyland	193	B4
PAN PACIFIC HOTEL, 500 Post St, San Francisco 331 units; a preferred hotel & restaurant.	143	C3
PARC FIFTY FIVE, 55 Cyril Magnin St, San Francisco 1015 rooms, downtown, restaurant & lounge.	143	C3
PARK HYATT HOTEL, 333 Battery St, San Francisco 360 rooms, bay views & restaurant.	143	D2
PASADENA HILTON, 150 S Los Robles Av, Pasadena 291 rooms; entertainment, dining room & pool.	190	C4
PENINSULA BEVERLY HILLS, 9882 Santa Monica BH 200 rooms, pool, sauna, steamroom & exercise room.	183	B2
*PEPPER TREE INN, 3850 State St, Santa Barbara 150 rooms; patios, 2 pools, sauna & restaurant.	87	C4
*PICADILLY INN AIRPORT, 5115 E McKinley, Fresno 185 rooms; pool, whirlpool & restaurant.	57	D3
*PICADILLY INN-SHAW, 2305 W Shaw Av, Fresno 203 rooms; pool & restaurant; airport trans.	57	C3
PINE INN, Ocean Av, Carmel 49 rooms; Victorian decor & beautiful view.	168	B3
PLAZA INN, 111 E March Ln, Stockton 195 rooms; restaurant, lounge, dancing & live entertainment.	160	B1
PLEASANTON HILTON, 7050 Johnson Dr, Pleasanton 298 rooms; racquetball, tennis & swimming pool.	M	B5
PRIMADONNA RESORT, I-15 & State Line, Primm 660 rooms, casino, restaurants & pool.	84	C1
*QUAIL LODGE, 8205 Valley Greens Dr, Carmel Valley 100 rooms; scenic grounds, golf & tennis.	54	B5
QUALITY HOTEL-MAINGATE, 616 Convention Wy, Anaheim 284 rooms; pool, dining room & coffee shop.	193	C5
QUEEN MARY, 1126 Queens Hwy, Long Beach Historic British luxury liner, restored rooms.	192	E4
RADISSON BEL-AIR SUMMIT,11461 Sunset Bl, Ls Angeles 162 rms; pool, tennis & VCR in rooms.	180	A1
RADISSON HOLLYWOOD ROOSEVELT HOTEL, 7000 Hollywood Bl 380 rooms; swimming, restaurants & lounge.	181	C4
RADISSON HOTEL, 500 Leisure Ln, Sacramento 309 rooms; private lake, paddleboats, pool & par course.	137	E1
RADISSON HOTEL, 300 S Court St, Visalia 201 rooms; pool, exercise room & restaurant.	68	B1
RADISSON HOTEL HARBOR VIEW, 1646 Front St, San Diego 333 rooms; pool, restaurant & sauna.	215	D2
RADISSON HOTEL SAN DIEGO,1433 Cm del Rio S,San Diego 260 rooms; pool, sauna, dining & entertainment.	214	A4
RADISSON HOTEL SF AIRPORT, 1177 Airport Bl, Burlingame 305 rooms; pools, dining room & coffee shop.	N	D1
*RADISSON HOTEL SANTA BARBARA, 1111 E Cabrillo 174 rooms; ocean view, pool, dining room.	87	D4
RADISSON INN, 700 National City Bl, National City 180 units, harbor views, pool & exercise room.	V	C4
RADISSON PLAZA HOTEL, 1400 Parkview Av, Manhattan Bch 380 rooms; golf, pool, whirlpool, sauna & dining room.	189	D5
RADISSON PLAZA HOTEL, 1471 N 4th St, San Jose 184 rooms; pools, whirlpool & restaurant.	152	A1
RAMADA EXPRESS, 2121 Casino Dr, Laughlin 1501 rooms, restaurants, pool & mini train ride.	85	D5
*RAMADA HOTEL, 6th & Lake St, Reno 250 units; casino & restaurant.	130	B2
RAMADA HOTEL, 2726 Grand Av, Santa Ana 183 rooms; exercise room, pool & whirlpool.	198	D2
*RAMADA INN, 114 E Highway 246, Buellton 98 rooms; pool, convention & conference facilities.	86	D3
RAMADA INN, 5865 Katella Av, Cypress 180 units, dining room & pool.	T	B2
RAMADA INN AIRPORT N 6333 Bristol Pky, Culver City 268 rooms; pool, whirlpool & exercise room.	188	C3
RAMADA SUITES, 2050 N Preisker Ln, Santa Maria 210 suites, pool & restaurant.	173	C1
*RANCHO BERNARDO INN, 17550 Bernardo Oaks Dr 236 rooms; 2 pools, golf, bicycling & tennis.	106	D4
RED LION HOTEL, 3050 Bristol St, Costa Mesa 484 rooms; pool, sauna & near Performing Arts Center.	198	A4
*RED LION HOTEL, 1929 4th St, Eureka 180 rooms; pool & dining room.	121	E1
RED LION HOTEL, 100 W Glenoaks Bl, Glendale 350 rooms, pool, spa, sauna & exercise room.	R	A2
*RED LION HOTEL, 1150 9th, Modesto 265 rooms; restaurants, pools & exercise room.	162	A3
RED LION HOTEL, 222 N Vineyard, Ontario 340 rooms; pool, spa, exercise room & lounge.	U	E2
RED LION HOTEL, 1830 Hilltop Dr, Redding 194 rooms; pool, putting green & dining room.	18	C2
RED LION HOTEL, 1 Red Lion Dr, Rohnert Park 245 rooms, pool, spa, tennis & exercise room.	38	A3
RED LION HOTEL, 2001 Point West Wy, Sacramento 448 rooms; pools, airport trans & dining room.	39	E1
RED LION HOTEL, 7450 Hazard Center Dr, San Diego 300 rooms; fountain cafe, pools & tennis courts.	213	E4
RED LION HOTEL, 2050 Gateway Pl, San Jose 507 rooms; exercise room, jogging track, pool & dining.	151	D1
RED LION HOTEL - LAX, 6161 Centinela Av, Culver City 368 rooms; pool, whirlpool & restaurant.	188	C3
REGENT BEVERLY WILSHIRE, 9500 Wilshire Blvd Long established with excellent accommodations.	183	C2
*RENAISSANCE HOTEL, 9620 Airport Blvd, Los Angeles 505 rooms; 2 restaurants, pool & sauna.	189	D1
RENO HILTON, 2500 E 2nd St, Reno, Nevada 2001 rooms, casino, fitness center, pool & tennis.	28	B4
RESIDENCE INN, 1700 S Clementine St, Anaheim 200 rooms; near Disneyland & convention center.	193	C4
RESIDENCE INN, 201 N State College Bl, Orange 105 rooms & suites; pool, whirlpool & sports court.	193	E5
*RIO BRAVO RESORT, 11200 Lake Ming Rd, Rio Bravo 112 rooms; tennis, golf, pools & airstrip.	78	E2
RIO SUITE HOTEL, 3700 W Flamingo Rd, Las Vegas 1410 rooms; casino, sand-bottom pools, restaurants & buffets	210	A2
RITZ CARLTON, 33533 Ritz Carlton Dr, Dana Point 393 rooms; golf, tennis, pools & ocean view.	105	D1
RITZ CARLTON, 600 Stockton St, San Francisco 336 rooms, indoor pool, health club & entertainment.	143	C3
RITZ CARLTON MARINA DEL REY, 4375 Admiralty Wy 306 rooms & suites, pool, sauna, tennis & dining.	187	C3
RIVERSIDE RESORT, 1650 Casino Dr, Laughlin 1403 rooms, casino, restaurants & 750 RV spaces.	85	D5
*RIVIERA, 2901 Las Vegas Bl, Las Vegas Casino, restaurants, entertainment & shops.	209	C5
SACRAMENTO HILTON, 2200 Harvard St, Sacramento 336 rooms, pool, restaurant & lounge.	39	A3
*SACRAMENTO INN, 1401 Arden Wy, Sacramento 387 rooms; pools, putting green & dining room.	39	E1
*SAHARA (DEL WEBB'S), 2535 Las Vegas Bl, Las Vegas Casino, restaurants, entertainment & shops.	209	C4
SAN BERNARDINO HILTON, 285 E Hospitality Ln 247 rooms; dining room, pool & whirlpool.	207	D5
*SAN DIEGO HILTON, 1775 E Mission Bay Dr 357 rooms; pools, beach, rental boats & bikes.	212	E3
SAN DIEGO MISSION VALLEY HILTON, 901 Camino Del Rio S 350 rooms; pool, sauna & exercise room.	213	E4
SAN DIEGO MARRIOTT-MISSION VALLEY, 8757 Rio San Diego 350 rooms; pool, sauna, health club, tennis & restaurant.	214	B3
SAN DIEGO PRINCESS RESORT, 1404 W Vacation Rd 462 rooms; 5 pools, tennis, golf & dining.	212	B3
*SANDS, 3355 Las Vegas Bl, Las Vegas Casino, restaurants & star entertainment.	210	B2
*SANDS REGENCY, Arlington & 3rd Sts, Reno Casino, cafe & shops.	130	A2
SAN FRANCISCO AIRPORT HILTON, SF INTERNATIONAL AIRPORT Restaurant, entertainment & swimming pool.	144	D4
SAN FRANCISCO AIRPORT MARRIOTT, Bayshore Hwy, Burlingame 689 rooms; dining, health club & pool.	N	C1
SAN FRANCISCO HILTON & TOWERS, 333 O'Farrell, San Francisco Shops, sundeck & pool; air, RR & bus transportation.	143	C3
SAN FRANCISCO MARRIOTT, 55 4th St, San Francisco Indoor pool, health club & restaurant.	143	D3
SAN JOSE HILTON & TOWERS, 300 Almaden Bl, San Jose 355 rooms, business center, health club & pool.	152	B4
SAN TROPEZ SUITE HOTEL, 455 E Hamon Av, Las Vegas 150 rooms; pool, whirlpool & exercise room.	210	D3
*SANTA CLARA MARRIOTT, 2700 Great America Parkway 764 rooms; near Great America Theme Park.	P	B3
SANTA MARIA AIRPRT HILTON, 3455 Skyway Dr 190 rooms, business services & pool.	86	B1
SANTA MARIA INN, 801 S Broadway, Santa Maria 166 rms; pool, sauna, whirlpool & exercise room.	173	B4
SHERATON, 12111 Point East Dr, Rancho Cordova 265 rooms; dining room & swimming pool.	40	B1
SHERATON-ANAHEIM, 1015 W Ball Rd, Anaheim 491 rooms; entertainment, dining & pool.	193	B3
*SHERATON AT FISHERMAN'S WHARF, 2500 Mason St, SF	143	B1

NAME & ADDRESS	PAGE	GRID
525 units; pool, restaurant & coffee shop.		
SHERATON CERRITOS, 12725 Center Court Dr, Cerritos	T	A1
203 rooms, dining room & pool.		
*SHERATON DESERT INN, 3145 Las Vegas Bl, Las Vegas	209	B5
821 rooms; casino, restaurants & entertainment.		
SHERATON GRANDE, 333 S Figueroa St, Los Angeles	186	A3
470 rooms, near Music Center & downtown.		
SHERATON GRANDE TORREY PINES, 10950 N Torrey Pines	V	A1
400 rooms; golf, tennis & health club.		
SHERATON HARBOR ISLAND, 1590 Harbor Island Dr	215	A2
350 rooms, near San Diego International Airport.		
SHERATON HARBOR ISLAND HOTEL, 1380 Harbor Island Dr	215	B2
1050 rooms, tennis courts, swimming pool & dining.		
SHERATON HOTEL & CONF CENTER, 45 John Glenn Dr, Concord	M	A3
331 rooms; conference center & entertainment.		
SHERATON INN, 5101 California Av, Bakersfield	78	C3
200 rooms; pool & restaurant.		
SHERATON LONG BEACH, 333 E Ocean Bl, Long Beach	192	E3
460 rooms, dining room, entertainment & pool.		
SHERATON L A AIRPORT, 6101 W Century Blvd	189	C1
807 rooms; pool, whirlpool, dining & entertainment.		
SHERATON L A HARBOR, 601 S Palos Verdes St, San Pedro	191	B4
244 rooms; fitness center, pool, sauna & dining.		
SHERATON MONTEREY, 350 Calle Principal, Monterey	167	E3
338 rooms, 2 restaurants, pool & jacuzzi.		
*SHERATON NEWPORT BEACH, 4545 MacArthur Blvd, NB	198	B5
338 rooms; pool, whirlpool, tennis & basketball.		
SHERATON NORWALK HOTEL, 13111 Sycamore Dr, Norwalk	T	B1
175 rooms; pool, health club, restaurant & lounge.		
SHERATON-PALACE HOTEL, 2 New Montgomery St, SF	143	D3
551 rooms, lounge, restaurant & historical.		
SHERATON PLEASANTON, 5115 Hopyard Rd, Pleasanton	M	B5
214 rooms, restaurant, lounge, pool & weight room.		
SHERATON RESORT INDUSTRY HILLS, 1 Industry Hills Pky	R	E4
298 rooms; 2 swimming pools, tennis & golf.		
SHERATON RIVERSIDE, 3400 Market, Riverside	205	B2
296 units; dining room & entertainment.		
SHERATON ROSEMEAD HOTEL, 888 Montebello Rd, Rosemead	R	C4
150 rooms; restaurant, pool, health club & lounge.		
SHERATON SAN FRANCISCO AIRPORT, 1177 Airport Bl, Burlingame	N	D1
305 rooms; dining room, coffee shop & pools.		
SHERATON SMUGGLERS INN, 3737 N Blackstone, Fresno	57	C3
210 rooms; beautiful landscape, pool & restaurant.		
SHERATON SUITES FAIRPLEX, 600 W McKinley Av, Pomona	U	B2
247 suites, restaurant, lounge, pool & spa.		
SHERATON TOWNHOUSE, 2961 Wilshire Bl, Los Angeles	185	C2
300 rooms, pool, sauna, tennis & dining room.		
SHERATON UNIVERSAL, 333 Universal Ter Pkwy, Los Angeles	181	A1
475 rooms; entertainment, pool & sauna.		
*SHORE CLIFF LODGE, 2555 Price St, Pismo Beach	76	B4
99 rooms; ocean view, heated pool & restaurant.		
*SILVERADO COUNTRY CLUB RESORT, 1600 Atlas Peak	38	D2
260 rooms; 8 pools, golf, tennis & bicycles.		
SILVER LEGACY, 407 N Virginia St, Reno	130	B2
1720 rooms; casino, 5 restaurants & sauna.		
SOFITEL MA MAISON, 8555 Beverly Bl, Los Angeles	183	E1
311 rooms; pool, sauna, exercise, dining room & restaurant.		
SPA HOTEL & MINERAL SPGS, 100 N Indian Cyn Dr, Palm Springs	206	B3
230 rooms; pool, hot mineral pool & health spa.		
*STANFORD COURT, 905 California St, Nob Hill	143	C3
Gracious 1900s decor in Old Stanford House.		
*STOCKTON HILTON, 2323 Grand Canal Blvd, Stockton	40	A5
202 rooms; 3 pools, dining room & coffee shop.		
STRATOSPHERE, 2000 South Las Vegas Bl, Las Vegas	209	C4
1,500 rooms & suites, Tallest free standing observation tower in the USA		
SUNDANCE HOTEL, 301 E Fremont St, Las Vegas	209	C2
650 units; restaurant, buffet & casino.		
*SUNNYVALE HILTON , 1250 Lakeside Dr, Sunnyvale	P	A3
372 rooms; pool & restaurant; airport trans.		
SURF AND SAND HOTEL, 1555 S Coast Hwy, Laguna Beach	201	C3
157 rooms; oceanfront rooms with view, pool & beach.		
SUTTON PLACE HOTEL, 4500 MacArthur Blvd, Newport Beach	198	C5
435 rooms; pool, whirlpool, sauna & tennis.		
*TAHOE SEASONS RESORT, Saddle & Keller, Lake Tahoe	129	E3
160 units; tennis courts & restaurant.		
*THE AUTRY HOTEL, 4200 E Palm Canyon Dr, Palm Springs	100	D3
180 rooms; 3 pools, tennis & entertainment.		
THE CHATEAU, 4195 Solano Av, Napa	38	C2
115 rooms; Country-French atmosphere & pool.		
THE EMPRESS HOTEL OF LA JOLLA, 7766 Fay Av, La Jolla	105	B3
72 rooms; pools, exercise room & dining room.		
*THE INN AT RANCHO SANTA FE, Linea del Cielo	106	C4
80 rooms and cottages on tree-shaded grounds.		
THE LODGE AT PEBBLE BEACH, on the 17 Mile Drive	53	B5
159 units; pool, sauna & golf course.		
THE PARK HOTEL, 300 N Main St, Las Vegas	209	E1
435 rooms, entertainment & casino.		
*THE TREE HOUSE BEST WESTERN, off I-5, Mt Shasta	12	C2
94 rooms; indoor pool, bicycles & dining room.		
*THE WESTGATE, 1055 2nd Av, San Diego	215	D3
223 units; elegant decor & restaurant.		
*TICKLE PINK MOTOR INN, 155 Highland Dr, Carmel	54	A5
35 rooms; beautiful view and lovely location.		
TOWN & COUNTRY HOTEL, 500 Hotel Circle N, San Diego	213	D4
955 rooms; 4 pools, whirlpool, dining & entertainment.		
TRAVELODGE RESORT HOTEL & MARINA, 700 Queensway Dr, LB	192	D4
Located on the waterfront next to Queen Mary.		
TREASURE ISLAND - MIRAGE, 3300 Las Vegas Bl, Las Vegas	210	B1
2900 rooms, casino, restaurants, shops & shows.		
*TROPICANA, 3801 Las Vegas Bl S, Las Vegas	210	B4
1910 rooms; casino, entertainment, theater & pools.		
UNIVERSAL CITY HILTON, 555 Universal Terrace Pkwy, LA	181	A1
456 rooms, 2 dining rooms & pool.		
U S GRANT HOTEL, 326 Broadway, San Diego	215	D3
280 rooms, 1900's decor, restaurant & lounge.		
VILLA HOTEL, 4000 S El Camino Real, San Mateo	145	B4
286 rooms; pool, restaurant & coffeeshop.		
WARNER CTR HILTON & TOWERS, 6360 Canoga Av, Woodland Hills	177	C3
329 rooms; restaurant, health club, 2 pools & tennis.		
WARNER CENTER MARRIOTT, 21850 Oxnard St, Woodland Hills	177	C3
473 rooms; 2 dining rooms, pools, exercise room & sauna.		
WAWONA HOTEL, S entrance to Yosemite Valley	49	D3
A grand mountain resort built in the 1800's.		
*WELK RESORT CENTER, 8860 Lawrence Welk Dr, Escondido	106	D3
132 rooms; pool, golf, tennis & entertainment.		
*WEST BEACH INN, 306 W Cabrillo Blvd	174	C4
45 units; across from yacht harbor & beach.		
WESTIN HOTEL, 1 Old Bayshore Hwy, Millbrae	144	E5
388 rooms; pool, health club, sauna, restaurant & grill		
WESTIN HOTEL, 5101 Great America Pkwy, Santa Clara	P	A3
500 rooms, health fitness center, restaurants & pool.		
*WESTIN BONAVENTURE, 404 S Figueroa, Los Angeles	186	A3
Rooftop restaurant & revolving cocktail lounge.		
WESTIN RESORT, 71-333 Dinah Shore Dr, Rancho Mirage	100	D3
512 rooms, 3 pools, 2 golf courses & tennis.		
*WESTIN ST FRANCIS, Union Square, San Francisco	143	C3
Fashionable shops, skyline view from elevator.		
*WESTIN SOUTH COAST PLAZA, 666 Anton Bl, Costa Msa	197	E3
390 rooms; pool, exercise room & near Performing Arts Center		
*WESTWOOD MARQUIS HTL & GRDNS, 930 Hilgard Av, Westwood	180	D2
250 elegant suites; pool, sauna & whirlpool.		
WHISKEY PETES, I-15 & Stateline, Primm	84	B1
777 rooms; restaurants, casino & pool.		
WILSHIRE PLAZA HOTEL, 3515 Wilshire Blvd, LA	185	B2
400 rooms; entertainment, dining room & pool.		
WYNDHAM GARDEN HOTEL, 1010 Northgate Dr, San Rafael	139	B1
224 rooms: pets, pool & meeting rooms.		
WYNDHAM PALM SPRINGS, 888 E Tahquitz Wy, Palm Springs	206	C4
410 rooms; health club, pool, sauna & 2 dining rooms.		
MISSIONS		
MISSION BASILICA SAN DIEGO DE ALCALA, 10818 SD Msn Rd	214	E3
1769, 1st mission established along El Camino Real.		
MISSION LA PURISIMA CONCEPCION, 4 mi NE of Lompoc	86	B2
1787, 11th mission, rebuilt by original methods.		
MISSION NUESTRA SENORA DE LA SOLEDAD, off US 101	65	A1
1791, 13th mission, stood in ruins for 100 yrs.		
MISSION SAN ANTONIO DE PADUA, off U S 101	65	B3
1771, 3rd mission, one of the largest restored missions.		
MISSION SAN ANTONIO DE PALA, off Hwy 76	106	E2
Built in 1816 to help the San Luis Rey Mission.		
MISSION SAN BUENAVENTURA, Main & Figueroa Sts	175	B2
1782, 9th mission, the last to be founded by Father Serra.		
MISSION SAN CARLOS BORROMEO, 3080 Rio Dr, Carmel	168	B4
1770, 2nd mission, burial place of Father Serra.		
MISSION SAN FERNANDO REY DE ESPANA, 15151 SF Mission Bl	Q	C1
1797, 17th mission, destroyed by 1971earthquake; restored.		
MISSION SAN FRANCISCO DE ASIS, Dolores & 16th Sts	142	B4

POINTS OF INTEREST INDEX

NAME & ADDRESS	PAGE	GRID
1776, 6th mission, chapel unchanged for 175 yrs.		
MISSION SAN FRANCISCO SOLANO, Spain & 1st Sts	132	D3
1823, 21st mission, northernmost & last of the missions.		
MISSION SAN GABRIEL ARCANGEL, 537 W Mission Dr	R	C3
1771, 4th mission, at crossroads in early California.		
MISSION SAN JOSE, 43300 Mission Blvd	P	B2
1777, 14th mission, noted for outstanding music.		
MISSION SAN JUAN BAUTISTA, off US 101	54	D3
1797, 15th mission, near other buildngs of mission era.		
MISSION SAN JUAN CAPISTRANO, off I-5 at Ortega	202	E1
1776, 7th mission, swallows return annually.		
MISSION SAN LUIS OBISPO, Chorro & Monterey Sts	172	C3
1772, 5th mission, 1st mission to use tile tools.		
MISSION SAN LUIS REY DE FRANCIA, on Hwy 76	106	B3
1798, 18th mission, most successful of all missions.		
MISSION SAN MIGUEL ARCANGEL, 801 Mission St	66	A5
1797, 16th mission, last mission secularized - 1834.		
MISSION SAN RAFAEL ARCANGEL, A St & 5th Av	139	D4
1817, 20th mission, founded to aid sick Indians.		
MISSION SANTA BARBARA, Laguna & Los Olivos Sts	174	B2
1786, 10th mission, famed as most beautiful mission.		
MISSION SANTA CLARA DE ASIS, 820 Alviso St	151	C2
1777, 8th mission, bell dated 1798 still clangs.		
MISSION SANTA CRUZ, School & Emmet Sts	169	D2
1791, 12th mission, destroyed, replica built 1931.		
MISSION SANTA INES, 1760 Mission Dr	86	E3
1804, 19th mission, favorite mission of many.		
MISSION SANTA YSABEL, Hwy 79 near Julian	107	C3
Blt 1818, contains museum & Indian burial grounds.		

PARKS (STATE & FEDERAL) & NATIONAL FORESTS

NAME & ADDRESS	PAGE	GRID
ADM WILLIAM STANDLEY STATE REC AREA, Laytonville	22	C3
Beautiful scenery; no camping facilities.		
AHJUMAWI LAVA SPRINGS STATE PARK, Island Rd	13	E3
Accessible by boat only.		
ALAMEDA PARK, Micheltorea & Anacapa Sts	174	C3
Displays 280 species of plants & shrubs.		
AMERICAN RIVER PARKWAY, from Nimbus Dam	137	B1
23 mi long greenbelt along banks of Sacramento River.		
ANCIENT BRISTLECONE PINE FOREST, White Mountain Rd	52	A3
4600 year old pine forest & nature trails.		
ANDREW MOLERA STATE PARK, W of Hwy 1, Big Sur	64	B2
50 campsites, sandy beach, hiking & meadows.		
ANGELES NATIONAL FOREST, N of Los Angeles	Q	D1
Located in the rugged mountains of LA; hiking & winter sports.		
ANGEL ISLAND STATE PARK, E San Francisco Bay	L	B4
Island Park has hiking, bike rentals & picnic; day use.		
ANNADEL STATE PARK, Channel Dr	38	A2
Riding & hiking.		
ANTELOPE VALLEY CALIF POPPY RESERVE, W of Lancaster	89	D2
Scenic area for picnicking.		
ANZA BORREGO DESERT STATE PARK, San Diego County	108	A4
Beautiful wildflowers in spring; camping & hiking.		
ARMSTRONG REDWOODS STATE RESERVE, E of Fort Ross	37	C1
Giant redwoods, picnicking & hiking trails.		
AUBURN STATE REC AREA, 1 mile South of Auburn	34	D3
Camp; riding & hiking trails on American River.		
AUSTIN CREEK STATE RECREATION AREA, E of Ft Ross	37	C1
Camp, horseback ride, meadows, valleys & forests.		
AZALEA STATE RESERVE, off Hwy 101, Arcata	10	A4
Beautiful azaleas bloom late May - early June.		
BENBOW LAKE STATE REC AREA, 2 mi S of Garberville	22	B1
Horse trails, fishing, hiking, swimming & picnicking.		
BENICIA STATE RECREATION AREA, W of Benicia	L	D2
Good fishing & picnic facilities.		
BIDWELL-SACRAMENTO RIVER STATE PARK, W of Chico	25	A3
River access. picnicking & fishing.		
BIG BASIN REDWOODS STATE PARK, on Hwy 236	N	D4
First state park to preserve redwoods.		
BOGGS MOUNTAIN STATE FOREST, N of Hwy 175	32	A4
Picnicking & hiking trails.		
BONELLI REGIONAL COUNTY PARK, Park Rd, San Dimas	U	B2
Picnicking facilities & hiking trails.		
BORDER FIELD STATE PARK, Monument Rd 15 mi S of SD	V	B5
Good area for picnic, fish, swimming & hiking.		
BOTHE-NAPA VALLEY STATE PARK, on Hwy 29	38	A1
Hike, picnic, swimming pool & camping areas.		
BRANNAN ISLAND, South of Rio Vista	M	D2
Boat, fish, camp, hiking & visitors center.		
BROOKSIDE PARK, Rosemont Av, Pasadena	190	A3
Site of Rosebowl; swim, hiking & golfing.		
BUCKSKIN MOUNTAIN STATE PARK, Hwy 95, Arizona	104	C1
Scenic area to hike & picnic.		
BURTON CREEK STATE PARK, E of Tahoe State Park	35	E1
Camping & picnicking.		
BUTANO STATE PARK, E of Hwy 1 at Gazos Creek Rd	N	C4
Camping & recreational facilities.		
CABRILLO NATIONAL MONUMENT, Point Loma, San Diego	V	A4
Visitors center with historic programs & displays.		
CALAVERAS BIG TREES STATE PARK, E of Arnold	41	D3
2 giant Redwood groves - self-guided tours.		
CANDLESTICK POINT RECREATION AREA, US 101	L	C5
Scenic hiking trails; picnicking & fishing.		
CASTLE CRAGS STATE PARK, S of Dunsmuir	12	D3
Pinnacles, crags, cliffs, green pines & rec.		
CASTLE ROCK STATE PARK, near Jct Hwy 9 and Hwy 35	N	E4
Nature & hiking trails, picnicking & camping.		
CASWELL MEMORIAL STATE PARK, Hwy 99 S of Manteca	47	B2
Camp, fish, picnic,swimming & hiking.		
CHABOT REGIONAL PARK, Lake Chabot	L	E5
5000 acre park; fish, picnic, moto-cross & boating.		
CHANNEL ISLANDS NATIONAL PARK, off Santa Barbara	87	C5
Consists of 5 islands, 20 to 60 miles offshore.		
CHINA CAMP STATE PARK, N of San Rafael	L	B3
Recreational facilities and camping.		
CHINO HILLS STATE PK, off Hwy 71, San Bernardino Co	U	C4
Hiking trails & picnic areas.		
CLEAR LAKE STATE PARK, near Lakeport	31	D3
Camp, boat, waterski, hike, picnic, fishing & swimming.		
CLEVELAND NATIONAL FOREST, San Diego & Orange Co's	107	B4
Hike, boat, ride, fishing & camping.		
COL. ALLENWORTH STATE HISTORICAL PARK, 20 mi N of Wasco	68	B4
Historical exhibits & picnic facilities.		
CRYSTAL COVE STATE PARK, N of Laguna Beach	T	D5
3 miles of beaches for swimming & picnicking.		
CUYAMACA RANCHO STATE PARK, on Hwy 79, Julian	107	C4
In old Indian territory; camp, hiking & horses.		
DAYTON STATE PARK, Hwy 50 near Dayton	36	D1
Hiking & picnic facilities.		
DEATH VALLEY NATIONAL PARK, Hwy 190	61	B3
Vast & colorful desert; record summer temperatures.		
DEL NORTE COAST REDWOODS STATE PARK, S of Crescent Cty	1	E4
Dense forests, giant redwoods & good camping.		
DESOLATION WILDERNESS AREA, SW shore of Lake Tahoe	35	D4
Camp, boat, swim, fishing & hiking.		
DEVIL'S POSTPILE NATIONAL MONUMENT, Mammoth Lakes Area	50	C2
Spectacular mass of hexagonal basalt columns.		
D. L. BLISS STATE PARK, North of Emerald Bay	35	E3
Dense forest, trails, camping & beach area.		
DONNER MEMORIAL STATE PARK, 2 mi W of Truckee	35	D1
Rec at Donner Lake, Donner Party memorial & museum.		
EL DORADO NATIONAL FOREST, north of Hwy 88	36	A4
Rugged mountains, dense foliage & scattered lakes.		
EMERALD BAY STATE PARK, Emerald Bay	35	E3
Scenic; picnic,camping & swimming.		
FLOYD LAMB STATE PARK, 9209 Tule Spgs Rd, Las Vegas	74	D1
Fishing & picnicking.		
FOREST OF NISENE MARKS, 4 mi N of Aptos	P	B5
Picnic, hiking trails & camping.		
FREMONT FORD STATE REC AREA, 5 mi E of Gustine	47	D4
Good area for fishing.		
FREMONT NATIONAL FOREST, SE Oregon	7	D2
Good fishing, camping & rock climbing.		
FREMONT PEAK STATE PARK, S of San Juan Bautista	54	D3
Picnic, hiking trails & camping.		
GARRAPATA STATE PARK, Hwy 1, Carmel	54	A5
Good fishing & hiking trails.		
GAVIOTA STATE PARK, Gaviota Beach Rd	86	D4
Camp, fishing, boat launch & picnic areas.		
GEORGE HATFIELD STATE RECREATION AREA, 28 mi W of Merced	47	D4
Picnic, fish, hiking and camping.		
GOLDEN GATE NATIONAL REC AREA, San Francisco & Marin	141	A2
Gardens, historic sites & recreation facilities.		
GOLDEN GATE PARK, between Lincoln Wy & Fulton St	141	D4
Vast city park, walk, equestrian trails & skating.		
GRIZZLY CREEK REDWOODS STATE PARK, E of Fortuna	16	B3
Scenic; camp, fish, nature trails & creeks.		
GROVER HOT SPRINGS STATE PARK, W of Markleeville	36	B5

POINTS OF INTEREST INDEX

NAME & ADDRESS	PAGE	GRID
Camp, swimming at hot springs & fishing in creeks.		
HARRIS BEACH STATE PARK, N of Crescent City	1	C2
Camp, lodging & dining.		
HARRY A MERLO STATE RECREATION AREA, N of Eureka	9	E3
Boating & fishing.		
HENDY WOODS STATE PARK, near Philo on Hwy 128	30	D3
Picnic, camp, fish, hiking & swimming.		
HENRY COE STATE PARK, 14 mi NE of Morgan Hill	P	E4
Picturesque; camp & picnic grounds, day use fee.		
HENRY COWELL REDWOODS STATE PARK, 5 mi N on Hwy 9	N	E5
Equestrian trails, hike, fishing & picnic grounds.		
HOLLISTER HILLS VEHICULAR RECREATION AREA, S of Hollister	54	E3
Motorcycle trails; picnic, camping &, hiking.		
HUMBOLDT LAGOON STATE PARK, Hwy 101 N of Eureka	9	E3
Visitors Center; camping & hiking.		
HUMBOLDT REDWOODS STATE PARK, Redwood Hwy	16	A4
Tallest Redwoods, picnic, camp, fishing & hiking.		
HUNGRY VALLEY STATE VEHICULAR REC AREA, Gorman	88	E2
Camping & off-road trails.		
INYO NATIONAL FOREST, near California-Nevada border	51	D3
Winter sports, boat facilities & camping.		
JACKSON STATE FOREST, Hwy 20 near Dunlap	30	C1
Scenic area for hiking & picnicking.		
JOAQUIN MILLER PARK, Skyline Bl	L	D4
Named for Poet of the Sierras.		
JOSHUA TREE NATIONAL PARK, S of Hwy 62	101	A2
Camp, hiking & rockclimbing in desert environment.		
J SMITH REDWOODS STATE PARK, NE of Crescent City	1	E4
Giant redwoods, camping & Smith River fishing.		
JUG HANDLE STATE RESERVE, near Noyo	22	C5
Self-guided nature trails & picnicking.		
JULIA PFEIFFER BURNS STATE PARK, E & W of Hwy 1	64	C2
Picnic areas & hiking trail to view McWay Waterfall.		
KERN NAIONAL WILDLIFE REFUGE, 19 mi West of Delano	67	D5
Refuge for migrating & winter waterfowl.		
KING RANGE NATIONAL CONSERVATION AREA, Cape Mendocino	15	E5
Camp, picnic, hike, backpacking & scenic shores.		
KINGS BEACH STATE RECREATION AREA, NE of Tahoe City	36	A1
Picnic, swim, fishing & boating.		
KINGS CANYON NATIONAL PARK, Hwy 180	59	B2
Trails, backpack, horses, camping & fishing.		
KLAMATH NATIONAL FOREST, Siskiyou County	3	D3
Camp, boat, fishing & riding.		
KRUSE RHODODENDRON STATE RESERVE, N of Ft Ross	37	A1
Colorful rhododendrons bloom April thru June.		
LAKE EARL STATE PARK, 8 miles N of Crescent City	1	D3
Fishing & primitive camping sites.		
LAKE HAVASU STATE PARK, S of Interstate 40	96	B4
Resorts, camp, boat rentals & hunting.		
LAKE TAHOE NEVADA STATE PARK, E Lake Tahoe	36	B1
Boat, swim, picnic, fishing & hiking.		
LAKES BASIN RECREATION AREA, Blairsden	27	A2
Old glacial area, cross-country ski, lodging & boats		
LASSEN NATIONAL FOREST, S of Hwy 299	13	D5
Dense foliage throughout this lake recreation area.		
LASSEN PEAK, Lassen Volcanic National Park.	19	D3
Only active volcano in California, last erupted 1921.		
LASSEN VOLCANIC NATIONAL PARK, S of Hwy 44	19	E2
Volcanoes, lava flows, hot springs & lakes.		
LAVA BEDS NATIONAL MONUMENT, 30 mi S of Tulelake	5	D4
Cooled lava forming cones, canyons & caves.		
LOS OSOS OAKS STATE RESERVE, Los Osos Valley Rd	75	E3
Hiking trails through beautiful scenery.		
LOS PADRES NATIONAL FOREST, near Santa Barbara	76	D4
Camp, ride, fish, hiking & hunting.		
MacKERRICHER STATE PARK, Hwy 1 N of Fort Bragg	22	B5
Camp, hiking & fishing.		
MAILLIARD REDWOODS STATE RESERVE, NW of Cloverdale	31	A4
Scenic area for picnicking.		
MALIBU CREEK STATE PARK, Malibu Canyon Rd	97	A2
Picnic, fishing & hiking trails.		
MANCHESTER STATE PARK, W of Manchester	30	C3
Beach, dunes, point arena & lighthouse.		
McARTHUR-BURNEY FALLS MEMORIAL STATE PARK, NE of Burney	13	C4
Well developed scenic park.		
McCONNELL STATE RECREATION AREA, 5 mi SE of Delhi	48	A3
Picnic, fish, swimming & camping.		
MENDOCINO HEADLANDS STATE PARK, S of Fort Bragg	30	A1
Rocky bluffs, hiking & wave carved tunnels.		
MENDOCINO NATIONAL FOREST, E of Hwy 101	24	A4
Scenic wilderness, horseback riding & hiking.		
MITCHELL CAVERNS NATURAL PRESERVE, Essex Rd N of I-40	94	B1
Caverns with interesting limestone formations.		
MODOC NATIONAL FOREST, south of California-Oregon border	13	E1
Good fishing, hunting & volcanic features.		
MOJAVE NATIONAL PRESERVE, 222 E Main, Barstow	84	A4
Desert region, dunes, mines & rock formations.		
MONO BASIN NATIONAL FOREST SCENIC AREA, Hwy 120 S	43	D5
Dedicated by Congress to protect Mono Lake.		
MONTANA DE ORO STATE PARK, Pecho Valley Rd	75	E3
Barbeque, camp, riding & hiking.		
MONTGOMERY WOODS STATE RESERVE, Orr Springs	31	A2
Nature trails & picnicking.		
MORRO BAY STATE PARK, on Morro Bay	75	D3
Camp, fish, clamming & boating.		
MOUNTAIN HOME TRACT STATE FOREST, N of Hwy 90	69	B2
Beautiful streams, mountains & forests.		
MT DIABLO STATE PARK, Diablo Rd	M	B4
Hiking trails & campsites on peak.		
MT SAN JACINTO STATE PARK, Hwy 111 near Palm Spgs	100	B4
Picnic, hiking & some camping.		
MT TAMALPAIS STATE PARK, 6 mi N Hwy 1, Marin Co	L	A3
Hiking, equestrian trails & camping.		
MUIR WOODS NATIONAL MONUMENT, Mt Tamalpais State Park	L	A4
Named for naturalist John Muir; day hikes.		
NEVADA STATE PARK, N of Carson City, Nevada	36	C1
Rec at Washoe Lake-camping, boating & nature trails.		
NOJOQUI FALLS COUNTY PARK, S of Solvang	86	E3
Picnic facilities with a view of the falls.		
NORTH ALGODONES DUNES WILDERNESS, N of Hwy 78	109	D4
Vast dune area, closed to off Hwy vehicles.		
OCEANO DUNES SVRA, 576 Camino Mercado, Arroyo Grande	76	B5
Sand dunes, off-road trails, swimming & camping.		
OCOTILLO WELLS STATE VEHICULAR RECREATION AREA, Hwy 78	108	B3
Trails for off-road vehicle use & camping.		
OLD PERPETUAL GEYSER, Hwy 395, Lakeview	7	C1
Geyser erupts every 90 seconds 60 feet high.		
OREGON CAVES NATIONAL MONUMENT, off Hwy 46	2	E2
Spectacular formations of mineral deposits.		
PALOMAR MOUNTAIN STATE PARK, Birch Hill Rd	107	A2
Sierra-like country, many camp & picnic sites.		
PARK MOABI, off I-40	95	D2
Boat rentals & ramp, camping & fishing.		
PATRICKS POINT STATE PARK, N of Trinidad	9	D3
Camp, picnic,hiking & biking.		
PAUL M. DIMMICK WAYSIDE CAMPGROUND, W of Navarro	30	C2
Primitive campground with swimming & fishing.		
PETRIFIED FOREST, on Petrified Forest Hwy	38	A1
Ancient redwoods preserved in volcanic ash.		
PFEIFFER BIG SUR STATE PARK, E of Hwy 1, Big Sur	64	B2
215+ dev sites - store, hike, swimming & fishing.		
PINNACLES NATIONAL MONUMENT, on Hwy 146	55	B5
Remnant of volcanic mountain; hiking & cave exploration.		
PIO PICO STATE HIST PARK, Whittier Blvd, Whittier	R	D4
Second adobe home of last Mexican governor.		
PLACERITA CANYON STATE PARK, Hwy 14 N of San Fernando	89	C5
Scenic area for picnicking and hiking.		
PLUMAS EUREKA STATE PARK, Hwy A14 at Johnsville	26	E2
Scenic creeks, mountains, lakes & trails.		
PLUMAS NATIONAL FOREST, south of Hwy 36	20	B5
Waterfall, lakes, grassy valleys & woodlands.		
POINT LOBOS STATE RESERVE, W of Hwy 1	54	A5
Spectacular view of coast; swimming in China Cove.		
POINT MUGU STATE PARK, Hwy 1	96	C2
Scenic campsite; fish, picnic, swimming & hiking.		
PORTOLA STATE PARK, W of Hwy 35	N	D4
Camping & recreational facilities.		
PRAIRIE CREEK REDWOODS STATE PARK, N of Orick	10	A1
Good camping & scenic trails through lush forest.		
PROVIDENCE MOUNTAINS STATE RECREATION AREA, Essex Rd	94	B1
Scenic area for camping; exhibits.		
RANCHO SIERRA VISTA, Ventura County	96	C1
Native American Cultural Center.		
RED ROCK CANYON STATE PARK, Hwy 14 at Ricardo	80	B3
Picnicking, hiking trails & camping facilities.		
REDWOOD NATIONAL PARK, Crescent City, Orick	2	A4
Giant redwoods, picturesque coast & rivers.		
RICHARDSON GROVE STATE PARK, south of Garberville	22	B1
Scenic; camp, fish, swimming & hiking trails.		
ROBERT LOUIS STEVENSON STATE PARK, off Hwy 29	32	A5

POINTS OF INTEREST INDEX

NAME & ADDRESS	PAGE	GRID
Scenic area for picnicking & hiking.		
ROEDING PARK, north of Belmont Av, Fresno	165	B2
Picnic areas, boat rides & children's zoo.		
ROGUE RIVER NATIONAL FOREST, South Central Oregon	3	C2
Fishing & white-water rafting on Rogue River.		
RUSSIAN GULCH STATE PARK, S of Fort Bragg	30	A1
Rocky headlands, camping & hiking to waterfall.		
SADDLEBACK BUTTE STATE PARK, E of Lancaster	90	C3
Scenic area for picnic, hiking & camping.		
SALTON SEA STATE RECREATION AREA, off Hwy 111	108	E2
Camp, hike, picnic, boating & waterskiing.		
SALT POINT STATE PARK, N of Fort Ross off Hwy 1	37	A1
Underwater preserve, beachs, tidepools & trails.		
SAMUEL P TAYLOR STATE PARK, off Hwy 1	37	E4
Camp, fish, riding & winter sports.		
SAN BERNARDINO NATIONAL FOREST, Hwy 18	U	D1
Camp, picnicking & year-round sports.		
SAN BRUNO MOUNTAIN STATE PARK, S of Daly City	L	B5
Enjoy a picnic amid the beautiful scenery.		
SAN FRANCISCO BAY WILDLIFE REFUGE, south S F Bay	N	E2
Preservation of nature at its best.		
SAN FRANCISCO FISH & GAME REFUGE, off Hwy 280	N	B1
Lovely area for hiking & picnicking.		
SAN GABRIEL WILDERNESS AREA, off Hwy 2	R	E1
Preserve of natural, rugged mountain country.		
SAN ONOFRE STATE PARK, off I-5, San Onofre	105	E1
Scenic area for hiking & picnicking.		
SAN SIMEON STATE PARK, N of Cambria	75	C1
Picnic, hiking, & dunes.		
SANTA MONICA MOUNTAINS NATIONAL REC AREA, LA Co	96	E2
Ranger program & nature trails for hiking.		
SEQUOIA NATIONAL FOREST, Hwy 198	69	D2
Fish, camp, boating & winter sports.		
SEQUOIA NATIONAL PARK, Hwy 198	59	B5
With Kings Canyon, museum, logging & recreation area.		
SHADOW CLIFFS REGIONAL RECREATION AREA, Pleasanton	P	C1
Bike, picnic,swim, fish, boating, & waterslide.		
SHASTA NATIONAL FOREST, off I-5	13	D2
Large lakes, steep mountains & recreation facilities.		
SHASTA STATE HISTORIC PARK, 6 miles W of Redding	18	B2
Restored buildings were built during the Gold Rush.		
SIERRA NATIONAL FOREST, S of Yosemite National Park	49	C3
Grand sequoias; hunting & watersports at the lakes.		
SINKYONE WILDERNESS STATE PARK, Humboldt & Mendocino Co	22	A2
Tent camping, picnic, hiking & fishing.		
SISKIYOU NATIONAL FOREST, SW Oregon	1	E2
Rugged mountains, winding creeks & old mining towns.		
SIX RIVERS NATIONAL FOREST, NW corner of California	10	D3
Many rivers, good fishing, forest-covered mountains.		
SMITHE REDWOODS STATE RESERVE, E of Hwy 101	22	C2
Trails to waterfall, Eel River & picnicking.		
SMITH RIVER NATIONAL RECREATION AREA, Hwy 199	2	B3
Raft, fish, hike, hunting & camping.		
SPRING MOUNTAIN RANCH, Blue Diamond Rd, Blue Diamond	74	B3
Picnic, tours & hiking.		
STANDISH HICKEY STATE RECREATION AREA, 1 mi N of Leggett	22	C2
Picnic, hike, biking & camping.		
STANISLAUS NATIONAL FOREST, SE of Hwy 4	41	D4
Deep, stream-cut canyons, meadows & evergreens.		
SUGARLOAF RIDGE STATE PARK, Adobe Canyon Rd	38	B2
Fish, riding & camping.		
SUGAR PINE POINT STATE PARK, north of Meeks Bay	35	E2
Grove of sugar pines; camping & cross-country ski.		
TAHOE NATIONAL FOREST, W of Lake Tahoe	26	E3
Good fishing, camp, snow skiing & scenic.		
TAHOE STATE RECREATION AREA, N of Tahoe City	35	E2
Good camping, boat, beach & nature trails.		
TECOLOTE CANYON NATURAL PARK, Linda Vista Rd, San Diego	213	B2
Large natural park in the city of San Diego.		
TOIYABE NATIONAL FOREST, E Sierra Nev into Nevada	73	D1
Camp, fish, hunt; forest, grass & sagebrush.		
TOMALES BAY STATE PARK, Tomales Bay	37	D4
Hike to scenic beaches; rocky, wave-cut coves.		
TOPANGA STATE PARK, Hwy 27, in Santa Monica Mtns	Q	A4
Picnic, hiking & horseback riding.		
TORREY PINES STATE RESERVE, S of Del Mar	V	A1
Beautiful hiking area; nature trail & exhibits.		
TRINITY ALPS WILDERNESS AREA, E of Hwy 3	11	D3
Extremely rugged mountains with meadows & lakes.		
TRINITY NATIONAL FOREST, along Hwy 299	17	B3

NAME & ADDRESS	PAGE	GRID
Good hunting & fishing; rivers & lakes.		
TULE ELK RESERVE STATE PARK, Tupman Rd	78	B3
Several acres grazed by native valley elk.		
TURLOCK STATE RECREATION AREA, Hwy 132 East of Modesto	48	B2
Camp, hike, swimming & fishing.		
VAN DAMME STATE PARK, south of Fort Bragg	30	C1
Camp near beach, hiking trails & Pygmy Forest.		
W. IDE ADOBE STATE HISTORICAL PARK, 2 mi NE of Red Bluff	18	D4
Home of the California Pioneer. Picnicking & swimming.		
WILDER RANCH STATE PARK, Hwy 1 N of Santa Cruz	53	E2
Nature trails, beach & historical exhibits.		
WILL ROGERS STATE HISTORIC PARK, Sunset Bl	Q	B4
Will Roger's home locatd within 186 acre park.		
WOODSON BRIDGE STATE RECREATION AREA, SE of Corning	24	D2
Camp, fish, swimming & nature trail.		
YOSEMITE NATIONAL PARK, off Hwy 120	49	D1
Beautiful waterfalls, lakes, canyons, streams & mountains.		
POINTS OF INTEREST		
ABC ENTERTAINMENT CENTER, 2040 Av of Stars, Century City	183	A2
Galleries, restaurants, boutiques & theaters.		
ABC TV CENTER, 4151 Prospect Av, L. A.	182	C4
Tour sets & watch filming of TV programs.		
ACADEMY OF SCIENCES, Golden Gate Park	141	D4
Renowned science museum including Morrison Planetarium.		
AEROSPACE MUSEUM, Balboa Park, San Diego	215	E2
Aeronautical displays of the past and present.		
ALABAMA HILLS, Off Hwy 136, near Lone Pine	60	A4
Backdrop for motion picture & TV westerns.		
ALCATRAZ ISLAND, San Francisco Bay	L	B4
Former maximum security prison; 1/2 day tours.		
AMADOR COUNTY MUSEUM, 225 Church St, Jackson	40	E2
Working models of old gold mines.		
AMARGOSA OPERA HOUSE; Death Valley Junction.	72	D1
Ballet and pantomine performances.		
AMBOY CRATER, S of Hwy 66, Amboy	93	D3
Large volcanic cinder cone & lava fields.		
AMERICAN CAROUSEL MUSEUM, 633 Beach St, San Francisco	143	B1
Carousel art from New York and Philadelphia.		
AMERICAN FOREST PRODUCTION MILL, North Fork	49	E5
Tours of the lumber mill are conducted daily.		
AMERICAN VICTORIAN MUSEUM, 325 Spring St	128	B2
Collection of Victorian artifacts.		
AMTRAK STATION, Kettner & D St, San Diego	215	C3
Train station with access to zoo & other sites.		
ANAHEIM CONVENTION CENTER, Katella & Harbor	193	B4
Concerts, sports events, shows.		
ANGEL'S CAMP MUSEUM, Main St, Angels Camp	41	B4
History museum; also known for Frog Jumping.		
ANO NUEVO STATE RESERVE, off Hwy 1, San Mateo Co.	N	C5
Reserve for seals, sea lions & elephant seals.		
ANSEL ADAMS CENTER, 250 Fourth St, San Francisco.	143	D4
Five exhibit galleries, library & bookstore.		
ANTELOPE VALLEY INDIAN MUSEUM, 15701 E Avenue M	90	C3
Exhibits of Indian artifacts.		
ANZA-BORREGO VISITOR CENTER, State Park Headquarters	107	E3
Information & Ranger Station.		
APPLEGATE ZOO, 25th St, Merced	170	C2
Wild animals, birds, picnic, rose garden & rides.		
AQUARIUM OF THE PACIFIC, Shoreline Dr, Long Beach	192	D4
Exhibits of Pacific sea life, educational facilities & auditorium.		
ARCO PLAZA, 505 S Flower St, Los Angeles	185	E3
Subterranean shopping center.		
ARMAND HAMMER MUSEUM, 10899 Wilshire Bl, Los Angeles	180	C2
250 million dollar art collection.		
ARROWHEAD POND OF ANAHEIM, Katella Av & Douglas Rd	194	A4
Center for entertainment & sporting events.		
ARTIST'S DRIVE, Death Valley National Park	72	A1
Rainbow-colored canyon of geological interest.		
ASIAN ART MUSEUM, near Japanese Tea Garden, Golden Gate Park	141	C4
Outstanding Oriental collection; jade display.		
ATMOSPHERIUM & PLANETARIUM, University of Nevada	130	A1
Space & star programs shown on dome ceilings.		
AUDUBON CANYON RANCH, N on Hwy 1, Stinson Beach	38	A5
Former dairy ranch now a wildlife sanctuary.		
AVENUE OF THE GIANTS, N of Garberville	16	C4
Scenic route through groves of majestic redwoods.		
BADWATER, in Death Valley, south of Hwy 190	72	A1

POINTS OF INTEREST INDEX

NAME & ADDRESS	PAGE	GRID
Lowest point in N America, 282' below sea level.		
BALBOA PARK, off Hwy 163 in San Diego	216	A2
Large central park; gardens, zoo & museums.		
BALBOA PAVILION, Balboa Bl, Newport Beach	T	C4
Beautiful landmark of Newport Bay; cruises.		
BATTERY POINT LIGHTHOUSE, Crescent City	1	D4
Tours & museum include history of lighthouse.		
BAY MEADOWS RACETRACK, S Delaware, San Mateo	145	B3
Thoroughbred, harness & quarter horse racing.		
BERKELEY AQUATIC PARK, Polk St, San Francisco	L	C4
Curved fishing pier creates cold swimming lagoon.		
BERKELEY ROSE GARDENS, Euclid Av & Bayview	156	A1
1000's of different varieties of roses.		
BIDWELL PARK, E 4th St, Chico	124	D4
Swimming pool, picnic, golf & nature trails.		
BIG PINE CANYON, 10 miles W of Big Pine	51	C5
Campgrounds, picnic areas & hiking.		
BIRD ROCK, Bird Rock Av, La Jolla	105	B5
Birdwatching in a natural coastal setting.		
BISHOP CREEK CANYON, SW of Bishop on Hwy 168	51	B4
Steep canyon walls with waterfalls & trails.		
BOLSA CHICA ECOLOGICAL RESERVE, 3842 Warner Av, Htn Bch	T	B3
Preserved wetlands & migratory birds.		
BOWERS MUSEUM, 2002 N Main St, Santa Ana	196	B3
Historical pioneer, Indian & Spanish displays.		
BRADBURY BUILDING, 304 Broadway, Los Angeles	186	B3
Distinguished 19th Century structure.		
BREN EVENTS CENTER, UC Irvine Campus, Irvine	200	D2
Concerts; campus & community events.		
BRIDALVEIL FALL, Yosemite National Park	63	A2
Beautiful waterfall drops 600' to Yosemite Valley.		
BROOKS HALL, under San Francisco Civic Center	143	B4
Subterranean hall built in 1958 for shows.		
BUFFALO ENCLOSURE, Golden Gate Park	141	A4
10 acres downtown SF used for bison preserve.		
CABLE CAR MUSEUM, Washington & Mason, San Francisco	143	C2
World's first cable car & cable winding machine.		
CABOTS PUEBLO MUSEUM, 67624 Desert View	100	C3
Indian, Eskimo & early settler artifacts.		
CABRILLO MARINE MUSEUM, 3720 Stephen M White Dr	S	B3
Beautiful exhibits of fish, birds & whales.		
CALAVERAS COUNTY FAIRGROUNDS, Gun Club Rd, Angels Camp	41	B4
Home of jumping frog jubilee.		
CALAVERAS COUNTY MUSEUM, 30 N Main, San Andreas	41	A3
In old courthouse; Indian arts, guns & gems.		
CALICO MOUNTAINS ARCHAEOLOGICAL PROJECT, Hwy 15	82	B5
Tours available Wednesday through Sunday.		
CALIFORNIA AGRICULTURAL MUSEUM, 1800 N Maroa Av, Fresno	165	C1
Exhibits farming & dairy equipment of the area		
CALIFORNIA ALMOND GROWERS EXCHANGE, 216 O Street	137	D2
Offers tours & films daily.		
CALIFORNIA CAVERNS, Cave City Rd, San Andreas	41	B3
Tours of the caves available.		
CALIFORNIA DESERT INFO CENTER, 831 Barstow Rd, Barstow	208	B3
Visitor facility with exhibits of desert environment and history.		
CALIFORNIA LIVING MUSEUM, Hwy 178, Rio Bravo	78	E2
Informative contemporary museum.		
CALIF MUSEUM OF PHOTOGRAPHY, 3824 Main St, Riverside	205	B2
Exhibits of early to contemporary photographs, historic cameras.		
CALIF MUSEUM OF SCIENCE & INDUSTRY, 700 State Dr	185	C5
Fascinating do-it-yourself museum in Exposition Park.		
CALIFORNIA RAILROAD MUSEUM, E of I-5 on Front St	137	A2
Exhibits housed in restored railway station.		
CALIFORNIA RODEO GROUNDS, 1034 N Main St	171	C2
Parades & square dancing at rodeo.		
CALIFORNIA STATE ARCHIVES, 1020 O St	137	B3
Features historical documents of California.		
CALIFORNIA STATE CAPITOL MUSEUM, Sacramento	137	B3
Exhibits and tours offered daily from 9 to 5.		
CALIFORNIA WESTERN RAILROAD, Laurel St, Ft Bragg	22	C5
Train trips through picturesque redwoods.		
CAMPANILE, center of The University of Berkeley campus	156	B2
Landmark chimes hourly from 12 bronze bells.		
CANNERY ROW, south of Point Alones, Monterey	167	E2
Famous location of John Steinbeck's novels.		
CARIZZO GORGE RAILROAD TRESTLE, N of Jacumba	111	A4
Highest wooden trestle still in use.		
CARNEGIE ART MUSEUM, 424 South C St, Oxnard	176	C4
Houses permanent & traveling art exhibits.		
CARNEGIE STATE VEHICULAR RECREATION AREA, W of Tracy	P	E1

NAME & ADDRESS	PAGE	GRID
Motorcycle trails & camping facilities.		
CARSON MANSION, 143 M St, Eureka	121	D1
Fabulous Victorian home & carved redwood walls.		
CASINO, St Catherine Wy, Catalina Island	97	B4
Features grand ballroom where big bands play.		
CASTLE AIR MUSEUM, Heritage Wy, Atwater	48	B4
Air Force museum; open daily.		
CATALINA ISLAND, 21 mi SW of Los Angeles.	97	D5
Boats depart from Long Beach & LA Harbors.		
CEC SEABEE MUSEUM, Naval Battalion Center	96	A1
History of the Naval Construction Battalion.		
CEDAR GROVE, Kings Canyon National Park	59	B3
Base for trail trips by horseback or backpack.		
CENTER OF THE WORLD, Felicity, California	112	C5
Pyramid built at point determined world center.		
CHABOT OBSERVATORY & SCIENCE CTR, 4917 Mtn Bl, Oakland	L	E4
Planetarium, telescope viewing & gift shop.		
CHILDRENS MUSEUM OF STOCKTON, 420 W Weber Av	160	C4
Interactive environment, art, dance, music & science		
CHINA LAKE EXHIBIT CENTER	80	E1
Close up look at the defense industry.		
CHINATOWN, 900 N Broadway, Los Angeles	186	C2
Authentic Chinese shops & restaurants.		
CHINATOWN, between Stockton & Kearny Sts, San Francisco	143	C2
Largest Chinese settlement in America.		
CHINESE CULTURAL CENTER, 500 S Akers, Visalia	68	B1
Arts, crafts, exhibits & artifacts.		
CHULA VISTA NAT INTERPRETIVE CENTER, 1000 Gunpowder Pt Dr	V	C4
History of California wetlands.		
CHURCH BUILT FROM ONE TREE, Santa Rosa	131	D4
Built from a single redwood tree.		
CHURCH FINE ARTS BUILDING, University of Nevada	130	B1
Art exhibits & theater productions.		
CIVIC MEMORIAL AUDITORIUM, Center St, Stockton	160	D4
Various shows, conventions, exhibits & displays.		
CLARK BIRD REFUGE, E of Santa Barbara	87	D4
Wild birds in their natural habitat.		
CLARKE MEMORIAL MUSEUM, 240 E St, Eureka	121	C1
Victorian furniture, clothing & antique guns.		
CLEAR LAKE WILDLIFE REFUGE, off Hwy 139	6	B3
Hunting of waterfowl & good photography.		
CLIFF HOUSE, 1090 Point Lobos Av	L	A4
Famous restaurant with magnificent view.		
COIT TOWER, top of Telegraph Hill	143	C2
Volunteer firefighter memorial & good view of the city.		
COLEMAN FISH STATION, 12 mi SE of Anderson	18	D3
Large salmon hatchery; spawning fall & winter.		
COLUSA NATIONAL WILDLIFE REFUGE, on Hwy 20	32	E2
1000's of birds to view on self-guided tour.		
COMMUNITY MEMORIAL MUSEUM, Butte House Rd, Yuba City	125	B2
Memorabilia of early Indians & Pioneers.		
CONSERVATORY OF FLOWERS, Golden Gate Park, San Francisco	141	C4
Suberb seasonal flower displays.		
CORRAL CANYON OFF-ROAD VEH AREA, Los Pinos Rd, SDCO	112	C1
Off road trails & camping.		
COURTHOUSE MUSEUM, Courthouse Park, Merced	170	D3
Restored Victorian courthouse is now a museum.		
COW PALACE, Geneva Av & Santos St, Daly City	L	B5
Arena, exhibition center; sports events.		
CROCKER ART MUSEUM, 210 O Street, Sacramento	137	A3
Paintings, furniture & sculpture.		
CRYSTAL CATHEDRAL, Chapman Av, Garden Grove	195	D1
Features religious & secular concerts.		
DAFFODIL HILL, 3 mi N of Volcano	41	B2
Blossoms from late March through mid-April.		
DANTES VIEW, above Badwater, Death Valley National Park	72	B2
Beautiful view of Badwater & Death Valley from mountain.		
DELEVAN NATIONAL WILDLIFE REFUGE, SE of Delevan	32	E1
Nesting area for migrating waterfowl.		
DESCANSO GARDENS, 1418 Descanso Dr	R	A2
1000s of beautiful flowers from around the world.		
DESERT MINING MUSEUM, Butte St, Randsburg	80	D3
Large gem, mineral exhibits & mine guides.		
DEVIL'S GOLF COURSE, S of Hwy 190, Death Valley	72	A1
Unusual salt formations from ancient lakebed.		
DEVIL'S HOLE, DEATH VALLEY NATIONAL MONUMENT	72	E1
A deep water-filled cave, preserves pupfish.		
DE YOUNG MEMORIAL MUSEUM, Golden Gate Park, San Francisco	141	D4
Oldest municiple US art museum; houses World of Art.		
DISNEY STUDIOS, Alameda Av at Buena Vista, Burbank	179	D4

POINTS OF INTEREST INDEX

NAME & ADDRESS	PAGE	GRID
Creative team for Disney Productions.		
DODGER STADIUM, 1000 Elysian Park Home of the Los Angeles Dodgers	186	B1
DUMONT DUNES OFF HIGHWAY VEHICULAR AREA, Hwy 127 Sand dunes & off road trails.	83	A1
DUNCAN WATER GARDENS, 691 Temperance Av, Fresno Landscaped gardens feature ponds with koi.	57	D3
DUNSMUIR MUSEUM, 4101 Pine, Dunsmuir Railroad history & artifacts for the area.	12	D3
EAGLE AND HIGH PEAK MINES, Hwy 78, Julian Historic gold mines, tours & picnic area.	107	C3
EASTERN CALIFORNIA MUSEUM, Hwy 395, Independence Exhibits of local and natural history.	60	A3
EDISON INTERNATIONAL FIELD, 2000 State College Bl, Anaheim Home of the Anaheim Angels.	193	E5
EDWARD F. BEALE MUSEUM, Beale Air Force Base Museum displays objects from base history & WWII	33	E2
EL DORADO COUNTY HISTORICAL MUSEUM, 100 Placerville Dr Gold Rush era items are displayed.	138	B3
EMBARCADERO, Embarcadero Center on waterfront, San Francisco Centers on 4 towers; shops, hotels & restaurants.	143	D2
EMBARCADERO, Harbor Drive, San Diego Restored old ships, maritime museum & restaurants.	215	C2
EQUESTRIAN CENTER, 34th Av & Kennedy Dr Horses for rent for use in Golden Gate Park.	141	B4
EUREKA VALLEY SAND DUNES, S Eureka Rd, Inyo County Home to a variety of rare plants & animals.	60	D1
EXPLORATORIUM & PALACE OF FINE ARTS, Golden Gate Park, SF A fascinating hands on science museum.	142	A1
EXPOSITION PARK, Exposition Bl, Los Angeles Includes memorial coliseum & sports arena.	Q	E4
FARMER'S MARKET, 3rd St & Fairfax Av Acres of markets, restaurants & gift shops.	184	A1
FEATHER RIVER HATCHERY, Lake Oroville View millions of salmon & steelhead.	25	E4
FEATHER RIVER RAILROAD MUSEUM, Portola Over 50 trains; summer train rides.	27	B2
FEATHER RIVER SCENIC BYWAY, 159 Lawrence, Quincy Historic bridges, tunnels, railroad & waterfalls.	26	B1
FERRY BUILDING EMBARCADERO, foot of Market St, San Francisco Bay traffic history, world trade center & mineral museum.	143	E2
FISHERMANS VILLAGE, 13755 Fiji Wy, Marina Del Rey New England themed shopping & dining complex.	187	C4
FISHERMAN'S WHARF, off Foam St, Monterey Art gallery, shopping & theater.	167	E3
FISHERMAN'S WHARF, foot of Taylor at Jefferson, San Francisco Open air markets, restaurants & view of fishing fleet.	143	B1
FLEET SPACE THEATER & SCIENCE CENTER, Balboa Park Exquisite celestial displays & films.	216	A2
FLYING LADY MUSEUM, 15060 Foothill Rd, Morgan Hill Features vintage airplanes & automobiles.	P	E5
FOLSOM PRISON MUSEUM, House # 8, Folsom Prison, Folsom Artifacts and exhibits & souvenirs.	34	B5
FOREST LAWN MEMORIAL PARK, 1712 S Glendale Av Large collection of stained glass & statuary.	179	D5
THE FORUM, Manchester & Prairie Sts, Inglewood Popular center for sports & entertainment.	Q	D5
FOSSIL FALLS, Cinder Rd Ancient Indian site and petroglyphs.	70	C3
FRESNO ART MUSEUM, 2223 N 1st St, Fresno 8 galleries, American sculpture, Californian & Mexican art.	165	E1
FRESNO CONVENTION CENTER, Tulare & M Sts Various shows, conventions, exhibits & displays.	165	E4
FRESNO COUNTY FAIRGROUNDS, Kings Canyon Rd & Maple Av	57	C3
FRESNO METROPOLITAN MUSEUM, Van Ness Av, Fresno Natural & historical exhibits.	165	D3
FROST AMPHITHEATER, Stanford University, Palo Alto Outdoor theater which seats 9,500.	147	A3
FULLERTON ARBORETUM, CSU Fullerton, Fullerton Botanical gardens & Heritage house.	T	D1
FURNACE CREEK VISITOR CENTER, Death Valley Ranger talks, museum, information & gift shop.	62	A5
GAMBLE HOUSE, 4 Westmoreland Pl, Pasadena Great architectural work &, original furnishings.	190	B3
GENE AUTRY WESTERN HERITAGE MUSEUM, Griffith Park, LA Old West exhibits, firearms & paintings.	Q	E3
GENERAL GRANT GROVE, Redwood Mountain Kings Cyn Nat'l Park Seasonal festivities, horse & foot trails.	58	E4
GENERAL PATTON MEMORIAL MUSEUM, Chiriaco Summit WWII desert training center, exhibits & natural science	101	E4

NAME & ADDRESS	PAGE	GRID
GEORGE G HOBERG VISTA POINT, 875 Lakeport Bl, Clear Lake Picnic, old Indian prayer hill & wildflowers.	31	D3
GETTY CENTER, 1200 Getty Center Dr, Los Angeles Large art collection, rotating exhibits, library & gardens.	180	A1
GHIRARDELLI SQUARE, N Point, Beach & Larkin Sts, San Francisco Shops, outdoor cafes by old chocolate factory.	143	A1
GIANT FOREST, Sequoia National Forest, Tulare County One of largest & finest Sequoia groves.	59	A4
GILROY HISTORICAL MUSEUM, 195 Fifth St, Gilroy Gilroy pioneer families' historical items.	54	D2
GLACIER POINT, S of Curry Village, Yosemite 3200' above the valley, valley view & snow-covered peaks.	63	D2
GOLDEN CANYON, S of Hwy 190, Death Valley Hike through dramatically colored, scenic canyon.	62	A5
GOLDEN GATE BRIDGE, on Hwy 101, San Francisco Famous bridge offers spectacular view.	141	C1
GOLD COUNTRY, HIGHWAY 49, Mariposa to Vinton Historic 300 mi drive through the Mother Lode.	27	D3
GOLD COUNTRY MUSEUM, 1273 High St, Auburn Displays of early mining equipment.	126	C4
GOLDEN GATE PROMENADE, along San Francisco Bay shoreline Walkway along marina green.	141	E1
GRACE HUDSON MUSEUM, 431 S Main St, Ukiah Art, Indian baskets & historic photos.	123	D3
GRAND CANYON OF THE TUOLUMNE, N of White Wolf, Tuolumne Co Trails to deep-cut canyons, waterfalls & meadows.	42	C5
GRAND CENTRAL MARKET, Hill & 4th Sts Food bazaar specializing in foods of Mexico.	186	A3
GREAT PETALUMA MILL, 6 Petaluma Bl N, Petaluma Shops & restaurants in restored grain mill.	L	A1
GREAT VALLEY MUSEUM NATURAL HIST, 1100 Stoddard, Modesto Plants & animals indigenous to the Central Valley.	162	A3
GREYSTONE MANSION, 501 N Doheny Rd, Beverly Hills Historic mansion & surrounding park.	Q	C3
GRIFFITH OBSERVATORY, 2800 Observatory Rd, Griffith Park Features displays, planetarium & laserium shows.	182	A2
GRIFFITH PARK, Los Feliz Bl & Riverside Dr, Los Angeles One of nation's largest municipal parks.	182	B1
GUINNESS WORLD OF RECORDS MUSEUM, 2780 Las Vegas Blvd Displays, films & exhibits; open daily.	209	C4
HAGGIN MUSEUM, Rose St & Pershing Av, Stockton Historical displays, paintings & art objects.	160	B4
HAKONE GARDENS, 21000 Big Basin Wy, Saratoga Picturesque Japanese gardens.	P	A4
HANCOCK PARK, 5801 Wilshire Bl, Los Angeles La Brea Tar Pits & Los Angeles County Museum of Art.	184	A2
HAPPY ISLES NATURE CENTER, Yosemite Valley Museum, ranger explains valley features & Indian caves.	63	D2
HASTINGS BUILDING, 2nd & J Sts, Sacramento Museum featuring the history of Sacramento.	137	A2
HAVASU NATIONAL WILDLIFE REFUGE, Lake Havasu Good fishing & many beaches along river.	96	A3
HAYS ANTIQUE TRUCK MUSEUM, 2000 E Main, Woodland Large collection of trucks dating from 1903.	33	C5
HAYWARD AREA HISTORICAL SOCIETY MUS, 22701 Main, Hayward California & local historical exhibits.	146	E2
HERSHEY CHOCOLATE COMPANY, 120 S Sierra Av, Oakdale Visitors center & tours of chocolate factory.	47	E1
HI-DESERT NATURE MUSEUM, 57117 29 Palms Hwy, Yucca Valley Open Wed-Sun 1 to 5 PM, live desert reptiles.	100	D1
HISTORIC GOVERNOR'S MANSION, 16th & I Sts, Sacramento Victorian gothic mansion built in 1877; tours,	137	C3
HOLLYWOOD BOULEVARD, Los Angeles Possibly the best known street in L A.	181	C4
HOLLYWOOD PARK RACE TRACK, 1050 Prairie St, Inglewood Features thoroughbred & harness racing.	Q	D5
HOLLYWOOD WAX MUSEUM, 6767 Hollywood Bl Life-sized figures of many famous moviestars.	181	C4
HOMESTAKE GOLD MINE, Jct of Napa, Lake & Yolo Co's Tours May-October, gold discovered in 1978.	32	B4
HONEY LAKE, SE of Susanville Sierra Ordnance Depot - military facility.	21	C4
HOOPA TRIBAL MUSEUM, on Hwy 96, Hoopa Baskets, weapons, art & tours of local villages	10	C4
HOT CREEK, 3 miles off US 395 on Owens River Rd Boiling hot springs & paved hiking trails.	50	E2
HUMBOLDT BAY MARITIME MUSEUM, 1410 Second St, Eureka Exhibits & marine artifacts of local sailing history.	15	E1
HUNTINGTON LIBRARY, 1151 Oxford Rd, San Marino Includes an art gallery & botanical gardens.	R	C3

POINTS OF INTEREST INDEX

NAME & ADDRESS	PAGE	GRID
HURD CANDLE FACTORY, 3020 St Helena Hwy North, St Helena Distinctive hand-made candles.	38	B1
IMPERIAL SAND DUNES, S of Hwy 78, Imperial Co. largest area of dunes in California; off-highway vehicle area.	110	A5
INDIAN CULTURAL CENTER, Yosemite Village Indian history in the area, displays & relics.	63	D1
INDIAN VALLEY MUSEUM, Taylorsville Located near an original Maidu settlement.	20	D5
INDIO HILLS PALMS, Thousand Palms Canyon Rd, Riverside Co Palm groves and oasis within Coachella Valley Preserve.	100	F3
INYO VISITOR CENTER Off Hwy 395 1-1/2 mi S Lone Pine Information, exhibits, maps of S Inyo County.	60	B4
IRVINE BOWL PARK, off Laguna Canyon Rd, Laguna Beach Natural amphitheater-Pageant of the Masters.	201	B2
JACK LONDON SQUARE, foot of Broadway, Oakland Site of the 1st & Last Chance Saloon.	157	E4
JACKSON SQUARE, Jackson & Montgomery Sts, San Francisco Former Barbary Coast; now shopping plaza.	143	D2
JAPAN CENTER, Post & Geary Sts, Japantown Hub of growing Japantown; traditional culture.	143	A3
JAPANESE TEA GARDEN, Golden Gate Park, San Francisco Creatd 1894; oriental landscape, cherry trees.	141	C4
JIMTOWN 1849 GOLD MINING CAMP, 18170 Main St, Jamestown Tour and pan for gold at real mining camp.	41	C5
JOHNSON VALLEY OHV AREA, Bessemer Mine Rd, SBCO 154,700 acre off-highway vehicle area	92	C3
J PAUL GETTY MUSEUM, 17985 Pacific Coast Hwy, Malibu Roman and Greek antiquities; art collection. (temporarily closed)	Q	A4
JUNIPERO SERRA MUSEUM, 2727 Presidio Dr, San Diego Artifacts, documents about early California.	213	B5
KELLY GRIGGS MUSEUM, 311 Washington, Red Bluff Restored Victorian home; furnished with antiques.	18	D5
KINGS RIVER, Kings Canyon National Park Middle fork runs through national park; excellent fishing.	59	B2
KLAMATH COUNTY MUSEUM, 1451 Main St, Klamath Falls History of the area.	5	B1
KLAMATH NATL FOREST INTERPRETIVE MUS, 1312 Fairlane Rd Displays & exhibits from wildlife to botany.	4	B4
KNIGHT MARITIME MUSEUM, 550 Cl Principal, Monterey Exhibits feature history of whaling industry.	167	E4
LA BREA TAR PITS, 5801 Wilshire Bl, Los Angeles Displys of prehstoric animals found in pits.	184	A2
LADY BIRD JOHNSON REDWOOD GROVE, US 101, Orick One mile trail through redwoods.	10	A2
LAGUNA SECA RECREATION AREA, Hwy 88, Monterey Laguna Seca Raceway; camping and picnicking.	54	C4
LA JOLLA CAVES, 1325 Coast Bl, La Jolla Formed by wave action; curio shop.	105	C2
LA JOLLA MUSEUM CONTEMPORARY ART, 700 Prospect St Collection of architecture, photos & films.	105	A3
LAKE COUNTY FAIRGROUNDS, Martin St, Lakeport County fair, trade fair, shows, racing.	31	D3
LAKE SHASTA CAVERNS, Shasta Caverns Rd E of I-5 Colorful rock formatns; boat tours available.	18	C1
LA MESA/PACIFIC RR MUSEUM, 4695 Nebo Dr, La Mesa Memorabilia of the Pacific SW Railroad.	V	D3
LAS VEGAS CONVENTION CENTER Conventions & exhibits, banquets.	209	D5
LAWRENCE LIVERMORE NAT'L LABORATORY, East Av, Livermore Energy research project conducted in this lab.	M	D5
LEGION OF HONOR MUSEUM, Lincoln Park Modeled after French Legion; fine art & graphics.	141	A3
LEONIS ADOBE & PLUMMER HOUSE, Calabasas Restored pioneer homes.	97	B1
LICK OBSERVATORY, Mt Hamilton 120" reflecting telescope.	P	D3
LITTLE TOKYO, Central Av & 2nd St, Los Angeles Teahouses, sushi bars, shops & hotels.	186	B3
LIVING DESERT, 47900 Portola Av, Palm Desert Botanical garden and wild animal park.	100	E4
LODGE POLE, Sequoia National Forest, Tulare Co Visitors center has geologic displays in park.	59	B4
LOG CABIN MUSEUM, 980 Star Lake Av at Hwy 50 Displays the history of the Lake Tahoe area.	129	A3
LOMBARD STREET, between Hyde & Leavenworth Sts, San Francisco Worlds Crookedest Street; picturesque.	143	B2
LONG BEACH CATALINA CRUISES, Golden Shore Boats depart daily for 22 mile trip to island.	192	D4
LONG BEACH CONVENTION CENTER, Shoreline Dr, Long Beach Hosts many shows & concerts.	192	E3
LONDON BRIDGE, at Lake Havasu Moved from the Thames River to Lake Havasu.	96	B4
LOS ANGELES CHILDRENS MUSEUM, 310 N Main St, Los Angeles Interactive science exhibits for children.	186	B3
LOS ANGELES MARITIME MUSEUM, Sixth St, San Pedro Largest maritime museum on the West Coast.	191	B4
LOS ANGELES STATE & COUNTY ARBORETUM, Arcadia Beautiful gardens featuring numerous plants.	R	C3
LOS ANGELES COLISEUM, Exposition Park, Los Angeles Major sports events; UCLA vs USC football.	Q	E4
LOS ANGELES CONVENTION CENTER, 1201 S Figueroa A variety of large exhibits & shows.	185	D3
LOS ANGELES COUNTY FAIRGROUNDS, Fairplex Dr, Pomona Various events throughout the year.	U	B2
LOS ANGELES COUNTY MUSEUM OF ART, 5905 Wilshire Blvd, LA Large collection of impressionist paintings.	184	A2
LOS ANGELES COUNTY MUSEUMS, Exposition Park, Los Angeles Natural history, science & many more exhibits.	Q	E4
LOS ANGELES ZOO, 5333 Zoo Dr, Griffith Park 15 acre park features more than 2000 animals.	Q	E2
LOWER KLAMATH NATIONAL WILDLIFE REFUGE, Tulelake Great stopping point for migrating waterfowl.	5	C3
MAD RIVER FISH HATCHERY, Hatchery Rd S of Blue Lake Tours and picnicking.	10	A5
MANZANAR, 10 mi N on Hwy 395, Lone Pine Site of WWII Japanese internment camp.	60	A4
MARCH FIELD MUSEUM, March Air Force Base Exhibits of aircraft & memorabilia.	99	C3
MARIPOSA GROVE, Southern Yosemite National Park Giant Sequoias; Grizzly Giant is oldest here.	49	D3
MARITIME MUSEUM STAR OF INDIA, 1306 N Harbor Dr, San Diego Restored windjammer - oldest iron ship afloat.	215	C3
MATURANGO MUSEUM, Highway 178, Ridgecrest Exhibits of the Upper Mohave Desert.	80	D1
McHENRY MUSEUM, 1402 I St, Modesto Historical displays, photos & models.	162	B3
MENDOCINO COAST BOTANICAL GARDENS, S of Ft Bragg Gardens open daily; admission charged.	22	B5
MENDOCINO COUNTY MUSEUM, 400 E Commercial, Willits Indian, pioneer, art & logging exhibits.	23	A5
MERCED COUNTY FAIRGROUNDS, near Junction of Hwy 99 & 59 Hosts Merced County Fair in mid-July.	170	D4
MERCED MULTICULTURAL ARTS CTR, 645 W Main St, Merced Four galleries, theater, studios.	170	C3
MERCER CAVERNS, 1 mi N of Murphys Colorful limestone formations found in 1885.	41	B4
MICKE GROVE PARK & ZOO, 11793 N Micke Grove Rd, Lodi Pool, softball field, zoo & tropical forest exhibit.	40	B4
MINERAL COUNTY MUSEUM, Tenth & D St, Hawthorne Open daily.	44	B1
MINING MUSEUM, Univ of Nevada, Reno History of mining, equipment & minerals.	130	B1
MOANING CAVERN, 5150 Moaning Cave Rd Limestone formations, Indian relics & bones.	41	B4
MODOC COUNTY MUSEUM, 600 S Main St, Alturas Displays of Indian objects & old firearms.	7	B5
MODOC NATIONAL WILDLIFE REFUGE, south of Alturas Popular nesting area for a variety of birds.	8	B1
MOJAVE RIVER VALLEY MUSEUM, 270 Virginia Wy, Barstow Mining, railroad & Indian artifacts displayed.	208	B3
MONO HOT SPRINGS, northeast of Lakeshore Hot and cold currents, beach, near campsites.	50	D4
MONTEREY BAY AQUARIUM, Cannery Row, Monterey Unique aquarium with hands on exhibits.	167	E2
MORETON BAY FIG TREE, Chapala & Montecito Largest fig tree of its kind in the nation.	174	D4
MORMON TEMPLE, 10777 Santa Monica Bl, West Los Angeles One of the largest Mormon temples in the US.	180	D3
MORO ROCK, 2 miles from Giant Forest 6725 ft above sea level; 100 mile view.	59	A4
MORRISON PLANETARIUM, in Golden Gate Park Interesting celestial films and displays.	141	D4
MORRO BAY AQUARIUM, 595 Embarcadero More than 300 fish & marine animal displays.	75	D3
MORRO BAY NATURAL HISTORY MUSEUM, Morro Bay State Park Chumash Indians, wildlife & marine displays.	75	D3
MT SHASTA, off Hwy 5 N of Dunsmuir Mighty 14,162 ft mountain covered by 5 glaciers.	12	D1
MT SHASTA FISH HATCHERY, 1 mi W of Mt Shasta Trout produced to stock Northern Cal streams.	12	C2

POINTS OF INTEREST INDEX

NAME & ADDRESS	PAGE	GRID
MT WHITNEY, Whitney Portal Rd At 14,495' it is highest mountain in the contiguous United States.	59	E4
MT WHITNEY FISH HATCHERY, Fish Hatchery Rd, Independence Built in 1916, unique stone building, lake.	59	E3
MOUNT WILSON OBSERVATORY, Mt Wilson Rd Famous for huge Hooker telescope & camera.	R	C2
MOVIELAND WAX MUSEUM, 7711 Beach Bl, Buena Park Wax displays of celebrities & movie scenes.	T	B2
MUD BATHS, in Calistoga Attracts visitors year around.	38	A1
MUSIC CONCOURSE, Golden Gate Park, San Francisco Free open air concerts given along tree lined walk.	141	D4
MUSEUM OF CONTEMPORARY ART, 250 S Grand, Los Angeles Permanent collection of international flavor.	186	A3
MUSEUM OF FLYING, 2772 Donald Douglas Lp, Santa Monica 20 vintage planes, exhibits & library.	187	C1
MUSEUM OF HISTORY & ART, 225 S Euclid Av, Ontario Permanent & changing art & history exhibits.	204	B5
MUSEUM OF MINING, Johnsville Historical museum of mining in California.	26	E3
MUSEUM OF TELEVISION & RADIO, 465 N Beverly Dr, Beverly Hills Exhibits, radio listening room & TV show viewing.	183	B1
NAPA VALLEY WINE TRAIN, 1275 McKinstry St, Napa Gourmet dining aboard restored pullman cars.	133	D3
NASA AMES RESEARCH CENTER, Moffett Field, Mountain View Exhibits, visitors center & tours.	148	C2
NASA DRYDEN FLIGHT RESEARCH CENTER, Edwards AFB Space & aircraft displays, tours & gift shop.	90	C1
NATIONAL AUTOMOBILE MUSEUM, 10 Lake St, Reno 200 classic & vintage automobiles.	130	C3
NATIONAL MARITIME MUSEUM, foot of Polk Street, San Francisco Displays nautical models, figureheads & photos.	143	A1
NATURAL BRIDGE, Death Valley National Park Colorful hike to natural arch in Black Mountains.	72	B1
NBC STUDIOS, 3000 W Alameda Av, Burbank A look at behind-the-scenes TV production.	179	C4
NEPENTHE, 26 miles S of Carmel Restaurant, gift shop & vista point overlooks sea.	64	B2
NEVADA STATE CAPITOL, N Carson St, Carson City Built 1871, silver dome caps large stone bldg.	36	B2
NEVADA STATE MUSEUM, N Carson at Robinson, Carson City Mining, pioneer, RR objects & exhibits.	36	B2
NEVADA STATE RAILROAD MUSEUM, 2180 S Carson St Historic trains & memorabilia.	36	C2
NOB HILL, at Calif, Sacramento, Jones & Tyler Sts Symbolic of elegant living & cable car access.	143	C3
NORTH COW MOUNTAIN RECREATION AREA, 8 mi E of Ukiah Camping, hunting, fishing, hiking & horseback riding.	31	C2
NORTH STAR MINING MUSEUM, Allison Ranch Rd, Grass Valley Pelton waterwheel & old mining tools.	127	B4
NORTON SIMON MUSEUM, 411 W Colorado Blvd, Pasadena Outstanding collection of art & sculpture.	190	B4
OAKDALE MUSEUM, 1st & F Sts, Oakdale Features local & natural history artifacts.	47	E2
OAKLAND-ALAMEDA COUNTY COLISEUM, Nimitz Fwy, Av 66 2 building sports complex; indoor arena & outdoor stadium.	159	D2
OAKLAND MUSEUM, 1000 Oak St at 10th St Unusual environmental museum follows California history.	158	A3
OAKLAND ZOO, Knowland Dr & 98th Av Picinic area, amusement park, aerial tram & baby zoo.	L	E5
OAKWOOD LAKE RESORT, off I-5 S of Manteca Water theme park with camping facilities.	47	A1
OIL MUSEUM, Hwy 33, Taft History of oil industry & processing methods.	78	A5
OLD EAGLE THEATER, J & Front Sts, Sacramento First theater in California, opened in 1849.	137	B2
OLD FAITHFUL GEYSER OF CALIFORNIA, on Tubbs Rd, Calistoga Eruptions occur every 50 minutes.	38	A1
OLD TIMERS MUSEUM, Highway 4, Murphys Built 1865; Indian display & historic items.	41	C3
OLD TOWN ART GUILD, G & 2nd Sts, Eureka Galleries, gift shops & art supplies.	121	C1
ONE LOG HOUSE, Phillipsville 2000 year old log home hewn from 40 ton tree.	16	C4
ORANGE CO MUS OF ART/ LAGUNA, 307 Cliff Dr, Laguna Beach Features continually changing collections.	201	A2
ORANGE CO MUS OF ART/ NEWPORT, 850 San Clemente Dr, NB Modern & contemporary art.	200	A4
ORANGE EMPIRE RAILWAY MUSEUM, Perris An extensive collection of early trains.	99	B4
PACIFIC HERITAGE MUSEUM, 608 Commercial St, San Francisco Exhibits of pacific region cultures & history.	143	D3
PAGE MUSEUM, 5801 Wilshire Blvd Exhibits of prehistoric animals from tar pits.	184	A2
PAINTED GORGE, off Hwy 195, N of Salton Sea Bluffs of colorfully layered rock.	101	C5
PALM SPRINGS AERIAL TRAMWAY, Tramway Dr Spectacular view of desert floor below.	100	C3
PALM SPRINGS DESERT MUS, 101 Museum Dr, Palm Spgs Fine art displays, desert exhibits.	206	A4
PALOMAR OBSERVATORY, Hwy 56, Mt Palomar Operated by Cal Tech; tours; 200" telescope.	107	A2
PARDEE HOME MUSEUM, 672 11th St, Oakland Oakland landmark, living history of 3 generations	157	E3
PASADENA HISTORICAL MUSEUM, 470 W Walnut St, Pasadena 1905 mansion, historical library & tours.	190	B3
PAULEY PAVILION, U C L A Campus Features many sports events.	180	C1
PEACH TREE RANCH, 26500 Stockdale Hwy, Kern Co Open daily, peaches, apples & plums.	78	B3
PETERSEN AUTOMOTIVE MUSEUM, 6060 Wilshire Blvd, Los Angeles Showcases over 200 rare & classic cars & gift shop.	184	A2
PIER 39, northern waterfront, San Francisco Recreates old SF street scene; shops & resturants.	143	C1
PLACER COUNTY VISITORS INFORMATION CTR, Newcastle Historical & informational displays 24 hours.	34	B4
PLANES OF FAME MUSEUM, Chino Airport World War II memorabilia & plane collection.	U	D3
PT ARENA LIGHTHOUSE & MUSEUM, off Hwy 101, Pt Arena Daily tours; maritime artifacts.	30	B3
POINT HUENEME, end of Hueneme Rd Marks entrance to Port Hueneme Harbor.	96	B1
POINT LOMA, 10 miles W on Catalina Bl Site Cabrillo National Monument, lighthouse & scenic view.	V	A4
POINT MONTARA LIGHTHOUSE, Cabrillo Hwy, San Mateo Co Historic light station, buildings now a hosel.	N	B2
POINT PINOS LIGHTHOUSE, Monterey Harbor, Pacific Grove Oldest lighthouse still in use on West Coast.	167	A1
PONDEROSA RANCH, Tahoe Blvd, Incline Village Western town amusement park & Bonanza TV show site.	36	B1
PORTS O'CALL VILLAGE, on Harbor Blvd, San Pedro Nautical shopping village with harbor tours.	191	B4
QUALCOMM STM @ JACK MURPHY FLD, Inlnd Fwy (805) @ Friars Home of the San Diego Padres and the Chargers.	214	C3
QUEEN MARY, Pier J, Long Beach Tours, restaurants & hotel on famous liner.	192	E4
RACETRACK, Death Valley National Park Clay playa, rocks tilt during high winds.	60	E3
RAINBOW BASIN NAT'L NATURAL LANDMARK, 10 mi N Barstow Natural landmark of color sediment layers.	81	D5
RAINBOW FALLS, within Devils Postpile Monument San Joaquin River plunges 101 feet.	50	C3
RAMONA BOWL & MUSEUM, 2 mi SE of Hemet Home of the annual Ramona Pageant.	99	E4
RANCHO SANTA ANA BOTANIC GARDEN, Foothill Blvd, Claremont Exclusively native plants of California.	203	A1
RASOR OFF HIGHWAY VEHICLE AREA, Hwy 15 & Rasor Rd Off road trails.	83	A5
REDDING CONV & VISITORS BUREAU, 777 Auditorium Dr Local information & event schedule.	122	D1
REDDING MUSEUM & ART CENTER, 1911 Rio, Redding Interesting Indian relics & art collection displayed.	18	B2
RED ROCK CANYON LANDS, Hwy 160, Clark Co, Nevada Scenic loop, visitors center & hiking.	74	B2
RICE VALLEY DUNES OFF HWY VEHICULAR AREA, Hwy 62 Sand dunes & off road trails.	103	C2
RICHMOND ART CENTER, Barrett Av, Richmond Displays of painting & other art objects.	155	B3
RIM OF THE WORLD HIGHWAY Scenic route leads to mountain resort areas.	99	E1
RIPLEYS BELIEVE IT OR NOT MUSEUM, 7758 Beach Bl, Buena Pk Unusual and bizzare people, places and things.	T	B2
RIPLEYS BELIEVE IT OR NOT MUSEUM, 175 Jefferson St, SF Unusual and bizzare people, places & things.	143	C1
RIVERSIDE ART MUSEUM, 3425 Seventh St, Riverside On register of historic places; art exhibits.	205	C2
RIVERSIDE BOTANICAL GARDENS, UC Riverside, Riverside Over 30 acres of dry-climate plants.	99	B2
RIVERSIDE MUNICIPAL MUSEUM, 3720 Orange, Riverside Indian artifacts & citrus industry exhibits.	205	B2

POINTS OF INTEREST INDEX

NAME & ADDRESS	PAGE	GRID
R M NIXON PRESIDENTIAL LIBRARY & BIRTHPLACE, Yorba Linda Memorabilia; exhibits, photographs & farmhouse	T	E1
ROARING CAMP/BIG TREES NARROW GAUGE RAILROAD, Felton Restored 1880's steam locomotives featured.	P	A5
ROBERT RIPLEY MEMORIAL MUSEUM, Juilliard Park, Santa Rosa Museum is in the Church of One Tree.	131	D4
ROSE BOWL, in Brookside Park, Pasadena Famous stadium of New Year's Football game.	190	A3
ROSICRUCIAN EGYPTIAN MUSEUM & PLANETARIUM, San Jose Largest Egyptian collection on the West Coast.	151	D4
ROY ROGERS MUSEUM, I-15, Victorville Memorabilia of Roy Rogers and Dale Evans.	91	B3
R REAGAN PRESIDENTIAL LIBRARY, 40 Presidential Dr, Simi Valley Life of the 40th U.S. President.	88	E5
SACRAMENTO HISTORICAL MUSEUM, 101 I St, Old Sacramento 17th century maps & gold nugget collections.	137	A2
SACRAMENTO NATIONAL WILDLIFE REFUGE, S of Willows Nesting area for migratory waterfowl.	24	D5
SACRAMENTO SCIENCE CENTER & JR MUSEUM, 3615 Auburn Nature trails and animals to touch.	33	D5
SACRAMENTO ZOO, 3930 W Land Park Dr, Sacramento Over 400 animals in simulated environment.	137	A5
SALTON SEA NATIONAL WILDLIFE REFUGE, E of Hwy 111 Scenic view of nesting birds at Salton Sea.	109	A3
SAN BERNARDINO COUNTY MUSEUM, Redlands Artifacts and history of the early settlers.	99	C2
SAND DUNES, E of Stovepipe Wells, Death Valley Shifting sand creates scenic area for a walk.	61	D4
SAN DIEGO AUTOMOTIVE MUS, 2080 Pan American Pz, San Diego Showcases restored cars with changing displays.	215	E2
SAN DIEGO-LA JOLLA UNDERWATER PARK, Torrey Pines Rd Protected marine life area open to public view.	V	A1
SAN DIEGO MUSEUM OF ART, Balboa Park, San Diego Contains American & European art.	215	E2
SAN DIEGO MUS OF MAN, 1350 El Prado, Balboa Park, San Diego Exhibits and displays of ancient cultures.	215	E2
SAN DIEGO RAILROAD MUSEUM, Highway 94, Campo Exhibits of the Pacific SW Railway.	112	D2
SAN DIEGO WILD ANIMAL PARK, 5 mi W of Escondido, Hwy 78 Tour through preserve for endangered species.	106	D3
SAN DIEGO ZOO, Balboa Park, San Diego One of the largest and loveliest in the world.	215	E1
SAN FRANCISCO ART INSTITUTE, 800 Chestnut, San Francisco Three galleries; tours available.	143	B2
SAN FRANCISCO MUSEUM MODERN ART, Van Ness & McAllister 20th century art, changing exhibits.	143	B4
SAN FRANCISCO-OAKLAND BAY BRIDGE, I-80 Main link to East Bay.	L	C4
SAN FRANCISCO ZOO, Sloat Bl & 45th Av, San Francisco Rated among the top six zoos in the world.	L	B5
SAN JOSE MUSEUM OF ART, 110 S Market St, San Jose Collection of 20th century artwork & art classes.	152	B4
SAN LUIS OBISPO CO HISTORICAL MUSEUM, 696 Monterey, SLO Displays of early Californian & Indian relics.	172	C3
SAN ONOFRE VISITORS CENTER, off I-5 Nuclear power generating plant with displays.	105	E1
SANTA ANA ZOO, 1801 E Chestnut, Santa Ana Primates, birds, large mammals & petting zoo.	196	D4
SANTA ANITA PARK, 285 W Huntington Dr, Acadia One of the nation's famous horseracing tracks.	R	D3
SANTA BARBARA BOTANICAL GARDEN, 1212 Mission Canyon Rd 65 acres of native Calif trees, plants & cacti.	174	B1
SANTA BARBARA CO COURTHOUSE, downtown Santa Barbara One of the most beautiful buildings in West.	174	C3
SANTA BARBARA MUSEUM OF ART, State & Anapamu Sts Oriental & American art glasswares, sculptures.	174	C3
SANTA BARBARA ZOO, 500 Ninos Dr, Santa Barbara Exotic animals in natural habitat; picnic area	87	C4
SANTA CRUZ BIG TREES & PACIFIC RR, 6 mi from S Cruz Historic RR from Roaring Camp to Santa Cruz.	P	A5
SANTA CRUZ BOARDWALK, near Municipal Pier, Santa Cruz Shopping, restaurants, outdoor shows, rides.	169	E4
SANTA CRUZ LIGHTHOUSE, West Cliff Dr, Santa Cruz Historic lighthouse.	169	D5
SANTA CRUZ MUNICIPAL PIER, off West Cliff Dr, Santa Cruz Shops and arcades over the ocean.	169	E5
SANTA MONICA PIER, 200 Santa Monica Pier, Santa Monica Amusement park, fishing & carousel.	Q	B4
SAUSALITO FERRY TERMINAL, Anchor St, Sausalito Commuter service to San Francisco.	L	B4
SAWDUST FESTIVAL, Laguna Canyon Rd, Laguna Beach Annually July-Aug; Arts & crafts festival & tour.	201	B2
SCOTIA LUMBER MILL, Main St, Scotia Tour mill, debarking, sawing & shipping logs.	16	A3
SCOTTY'S CASTLE, Death Valley National Park Tour unique mansion built by Death Valley Scotty.	61	B1
SCRIPPS AQUARIUM MUSEUM, 8602 La Jolla Shores Dr Sea exhibits & tidepools.	211	A1
SEAL ROCKS, Golden Gate National Recreation Area View of seal & bird habitats.	L	A5
SEAPORT VILLAGE, 849 W Harbor Dr, San Diego Unique shops along waterfront setting.	215	C4
SESPE WILDLIFE AREA, E of I-5 off Hwy 126. Established to preserve near-extinct California condors.	88	C4
SEVENTEEN MILE DRIVE, Monterey Peninsula Magnificent drive between Carmel & Monterey	53	B3
SHASTA CAVERNS, off O'Brien, 20 mi N of Redding. Variety of crystal formations, tours & gift shop.	18	C1
SHASTA DAM & POWER PLANT, 15 miles NW of Redding 2nd largest dam in the US; excellent view of Mt Shasta	18	B1
SHRINE DRIVE-THRU TREE, Myers Flat Drive through living tree & logging display.	16	B4
SIERRA BUTTES, N of Sierra City Giant rugged granite outcrops; scenic.	27	A4
SIERRA MONO INDIAN MUSEUM, St 274 & St 225, North Fork Artifacts of Native Indian tribes.	49	E5
SIERRA NEVADA MUSEUM OF ART, 549 Court St, Reno Collections of art from all over the world.	130	A3
SIERRA VALLEY MUSEUM, Loyalton 19th Century & Depression era exhibits.	27	D3
SILVERADO MUSEUM, 1490 Library Ln, Napa Memorabilia of Robert Louis Stevenson.	38	B1
SISKIYOU COUNTY MUSEUM, 910 S Main St, Yreka Indian objects, displays of old & new industry.	4	A4
SOLVANG, Hwy 246 Authentic Danish village.	86	E3
SONY STUDIOS, Culver City Major motion picture studio.	188	B1
SOUTH COAST BOTANICAL GARDENS, 26300 Crenshaw Bl California native plants, trees & man-made lake.	S	B2
SOUTH COW MOUNTAIN OHV REC AREA, 5 mi W of Lakeport Off Hwy trails, camping & picnicking.	31	C2
SOUTHWEST MUSEUM, 234 Museum Dr, Los Angeles American Indian artifacts, library & store.	R	A3
SPORTS ARENA, Exposition Park, Los Angeles Hosts sporting events for college & professional athletes.	185	C5
STANFORD MUSEUM OF ART, Stanford University Rodin Sculpture Garden, paintings & various exhibits.	147	A3
STATE CAPITOL, Capitol Mall, Sacramento Daily guided tours through capitol building.	137	B3
STATE INDIAN MUSEUM, 2618 K St, Sacramento Features various California Indian cultures.	137	D3
STATE LIBRARY, 914 Capitol Mall, Sacramento Founded in 1850, Public Library.	137	B3
STEARNS WHARF, lower State St. Santa Barbara The main pier extends beyond State Street.	174	D4
STEINBECK HOUSE, 132 Central Av, Salinas Birthplace of author, restaurant & gift shop.	171	B3
STEINHART AQUARIUM, Golden Gate Park, San Francisco In Academy of Science; features circular fish tank.	141	D4
STEWART INDIAN MUSEUM, 5366 Snyder Av, Carson City Indian artifacts, open daily.	36	C2
STODDARD VALLEY OHV AREA, I-15 & Sidewinder Rd 33,500 acre off-highway vehicle area.	91	D2
STRYBING ARBORETUM, South Dr, Golden Gate Park, SF More than 5000 plant species displayed.	141	C4
SUPERSTITION MOUNTAIN OHV AREA, Wheeler Rd, Imperial Co Off highway vehicle trails.	108	D4
SUTTER BUTTES, Near West Butte Listed as world's smallest mountain range.	33	B1
TECOPA HOT SPRINGS, west of Hwy 127 Old Indian healing pool, baths open to public.	73	A4
TELEGRAPH HILL, at Lombard & Kearny Sts, San Francisco Park, Coit Tower at top with view; tours.	143	C2
TELEVISION CITY - CBS, 7800 Beverly Blvd, Los Angeles Actual site of many telecasts.	184	A1
THOMAS BROS. MAPS RETAIL STORE, 17731 Cowan, Irvine Corporate office & showroom.	198	C3
THOMAS BROS. MAPS AND BOOKS, 521 W 6th St, Los Angeles Retail store	186	A3

POINTS OF INTEREST INDEX

NAME & ADDRESS	PAGE	GRID
THOMAS BROS. MAPS AND BOOKS, 550 Jackson St, San Francisco Retail store	142	E2
TITUS CANYON, E of Hwy 374, Death Valley Nationall Park Colorful, exciting drive thru a narrow canyon.	62	D3
TOWE FORD MUSEUM, 2200 Front St, Sacramento Most complete collection of antique Fords.	137	A3
TRAINTOWN, 20264 Broadway, Sonoma Rides on minature trains through scaled scenery.	132	D5
TRAVIS AIR FORCE MUSEUM, 3rd & E St, Fairfield Displays of various aircraft.	39	B3
TREES OF MYSTERY, 16 miles S of Crescent City Unusual & handcarved redwood trees & Indian Museum.	1	E5
TRINIDAD MEMORIAL LIGHTHOUSE, Trinity @ Edwards, Trinidad Replica of original 1871 lighthouse.	9	E4
TRINITY HERITAGE NATIONAL SCENIC BYWAY, Hwy 3 Historical sites, mountain regions, lakes & gold mines.	11	E4
TRITON MUSEUM, 1505 Warburton Av, Santa Clara Home of national & international art exhibits.	151	B2
TRONA PINNACLES, S of Trona near Pinnacle Tall pinnacles formed by algae of a sea.	81	B1
TUCKER WILDLIFE SANCTUARY, 28322 Modjeska Canyon Features a variety of hummingbirds.	98	E4
TULARE COUNTY MUSEUM, 27000 S Mooney, Mooney Grove Restored buildings; Indian & Pioneer artifcts.	68	B2
TULE LAKE NATIONAL WILDLIFE REFUGE, S of Tulelake Great stopping point for migrating waterfowl.	5	D3
TUOLUMNE COUNTY MUSEUM, 158 W Bradford, Sonora Located in the old jail; gold rush objects.	163	B3
TUOLUMNE COUNTY VISITORS BUREAU, 55 Stockton Rd Local information and event schedule.	163	C3
20TH CENTURY FOX STUDIO, Pico Blvd, Century City One of the oldest studios in Hollywood.	183	B3
UBEHEBE CRATER, Death Valley National Park Crater created by volcanic steam explosion.	61	A2
UNDERSEA WORLD, Hwy 101 S of Crescent City View sea plants & animals; scuba diving show.	1	D4
UNION SQUARE, Geary, Powell, Post & Stockton Sts Fashionable shopping center; park & fountain.	143	C3
UNION STATION, 800 N Alameda St, Los Angeles One of the landmarks of Los Angeles.	186	C2
U C BOTANICAL GARDENS, Centennial Dr, Berkeley Thousands of plant species displayed by region.	156	C2
UNOCAL OIL MUSEUM, 1003 Main St, Santa Paula History of discovery & drilling of oil in California.	88	B5
VENICE BEACH BOARDWALK, Ocean Front Walk, Venice Bicycling, skating & street performers.	187	A3
VICTORIAN TOUR HOUSE, 401 Pine St, Nevada City Privately owned restored home-tours by appointment.	128	C2
VIKINGSHOLM, at Emerald Bay Large Scandinavian castle with furnishings.	35	E3
VISITOR CENTER YOSEMITE VILLAGE, Yosemite Lodge Displays, films & photos of Yosemite.	63	C1
WARM SPRINGS DAM & FISH HATCHERY, 11 mi NW Healdsburg Visitor center & camping; dam created Lake Sonoma.	31	C5
WARNER BROS STUDIOS, 4000 Warner Blvd, Burbank Offers tours of day's activity on the lot.	179	C5
WARREN FIRE MUSEUM, Curry St, Carson City Old firefighting trucks, equipment & pictures.	36	B2
WASSAMA ROUND HOUSE STATE HIST PARK, 55 mi N of Fresno Picturesque picnic area.	49	C4
WAYFARER'S CHAPEL, 5755 Palos Verdes Dr, R Palos Verdes Striking glass church sits atop hill by sea.	S	B3
WESTERN RAILWAY MUSEUM, Highway 12 E of Fairfield Restored rail cars, rides, exhibits & museum.	M	B1
WHISKEYTOWN-SHASTA-TRINITY REC, NW of Redding Camp, backpack, picnic, boat & water sports.	18	A1
WHITNEY PORTAL, W from Lone Pine Starting point for Mt Whitney trail.	59	E4
WILLIAM S HART PARK, Newhall Av at San Fernando Rd Tour the silent screen actor's beautiful home.	89	B5
WINCHESTER MYSTERY HOUSE, Winchester Bl, San Jose Fascinating house & museum.	151	B5
WINNERS CIRCLE RANCH, 59911 Lakeview Hwy, Petaluma Miniature horses bred & trained; sales.	L	B1
WOODMINSTER AMPHITHEATER, S of Orinda Centerpiece of park, summer concerts & light opera.	L	E4
WORLD WILDLIFE MUSEUM, 1245 W Weber Av, Stockton Largest collection of mounted zoo specimens.	160	B4
WRIGLEY MEMORIAL & BOTANICAL GARDN, Avalon Canyon Rd Beautiful cactus, flowers & trees at monument on Catalina Island.	97	A5
YOSEMITE FALLS, Yosemite National Park Two beautiful waterfalls fall over 2,400 feet.	63	D1
YOSEMITE MOUNTAIN SUGAR PINE RR, Hwy 41 N of Sugar Pine 4 miles trip on a steam-powered railroad.	49	D3
YOSEMITE VALLEY, Mariposa County Picturesque, camping, domes, waterfalls & meadows.	63	A1
YOSEMITE WILDLIFE MUSEUM, 2040 Yosemite Pkwy, Merced M-Sat, 10-5; North American wildlife displays.	48	C4
YREKA WESTERN RR, off I-5 & Central Eureka Exit Blue Goose shortline RR through Shasta Valley.	4	B4
YUMA TERRITORIAL PRISON STATE HIST PARK, off I-8, Yuma Blt 1876, operated until 1909; museum & tour.	112	D5
ZABRISKIE POINT, off Hwy 190 in Death Valley Overlooks Death Valley from badland of Black Mountain.	62	B5
ZALUD HOUSE MUSEUM, 393 N Hocket, Porterville 1891 home with period furniture.	68	D3
3 COM PARK, Gilman Av east of Bayshore Fwy Home of San Francisco 49ers & Giants.	L	C5

RECREATION LAKES, RIVERS & MARINAS

NAME & ADDRESS	PAGE	GRID
ALPINE LAKE, 51 mi NE of Angels Camp 100+ dev sites - boat, backpack, fishing & swimming.	42	A1
ANDERSON RESERVOIR, Hwy 101, S of San Jose Fishing & boating facilities.	P	D5
ANTELOPE LAKE, 45 miles NE of Quincy 200+ dev sites - boat, waterski, fishing & hiking.	21	A4
AQUATIC PARK, foot of Polk St, San Francisco Curved fishing pier creates cold swimming lagoon.	143	A1
BALBOA MARINA, 2751 W Pacific Coast Hwy, Newport Beach One of the largest marinas on the west coast.	199	B4
BARNHILL MARINA, Inner Harbor, Alameda Pleasure boat marina in the Inner Harbor.	157	E4
BASS LAKE, E of Oakhurst 220+ dev sites - boat, waterski, fishing & hiking.	49	E4
BEAR RIVER RESERVOIR, Outside Hams Station Launching for boats, fishing & camping.	41	D1
BENICIA MARINA, end of E 3rd St, Benicia Pleasure boat marina south of Benicia Point.	153	B5
BERKELEY AQUATIC PARK, foot of Bancroft Av, Berkeley Saltwater lake, water sports & model boat racing.	L	C4
BERKELEY MARINA, foot of University Av, Berkeley Fishing pier & base for popular sport fishing fleet.	L	C4
BETHANY RESERVOIR ST REC AREA, Christensen Rd, Alameda Day use only; boat, picnic cycling, & fishing.	M	E4
BIG BEAR LAKE, off Hwy 18 Resort area has many winter & summer sports.	91	E5
BIG BEND RESORT, Parker Dam Rd, S of Lake Havasu Waterski, boating & fishing.	96	C5
BIG SAGE RESERVOIR, NW of Alturas Boat, fishing & no camping facilities.	7	A5
BLACK BUTTE LAKE, 9 miles west of Orland 90+ dev sites - boat, waterski, fishing & hiking.	24	B3
BLUE LAKE, 28 mi SE of Alturas 40+ dev sites - boat, waterski, fishing & hiking.	8	C3
BLUE LAKES, Hwy 20 & Blue Lakes Rd RV & tent camp; boat, fish, swimming & hiking.	31	C2
BOCA RESERVOIR, NE of Truckee 90 primitive sites-boat, waterski, fishing & hiking	27	E5
BOWMAN LAKE, 40 mi NE of Nevada City Primitive sites-fish, backpack, swimming & picnicking.	27	A5
BRANNAN ISLAND STATE REC AREA, S of Rio Vista Visitors center,waterski, fish, swimming & picnicking.	M	D2
BRIDGEPORT RESERVOIR, just north of Bridgeport 60+ dev sites - boat, fish, swimming & backpacking.	43	B3
BUCKS LAKE, southwest of Quincy 70+ dev sites - boat, waterski, fishing & hiking.	26	B2
BUENA VISTA AQUATIC REC AREA, 25 mi SW of Bakersfield Fish, swim, camp, waterskiing & boating.	78	B4
BULLARDS BAR RESERVOIR, W of Camptonville 90+ dev sites - boat, picnic, fishing & waterskiing.	26	B5
BUTTE LAKE, Lassen Volcanic National Park 90+ dev sites - sail, fish, swimming & backpacking.	20	A2
BUTTE VALLEY RESERVOIR, off Prattville Butte Reservoir Rd Sailing & recreational facilities.	20	B5
CAMANCHE RESERVOIR, W of San Andreas 1150+ dev sites - boat, fish, hiking & swimming.	40	C3
CAMP FAR WEST RESERVOIR, 29 mi NW of Auburn 130 dev sites - boat, waterski, fishing & swimming.	34	A2

POINTS OF INTEREST INDEX

NAME & ADDRESS	PAGE	GRID
CAPLES LAKE, near Kirkwood on Hwy 88, Kirkwood 30+ dev sites - boat, fish, hiking & horses.	36	A5
CASTAIC LAKE STATE RECREATION AREA, N of Castaic Picnic, boating & swimming.	89	B4
CATALINA YACHT HARBOR, Avalon Bay, Catalina Island Yacht moorings & glass bottom boat tours.	97	B4
CHANNEL ISLANDS HARBOR, Oxnard Small marina & Channel Islands Museum.	96	A1
CHERRY LAKE, 31 mi E of Tuolumne 40+ dev sites - boat, waterski, fishing & horses.	42	B4
CLEAR LAKE, near Lakeport 140+ dev sites - boat, waterski, fishing & hiking.	31	D2
COLLINS LAKE, Oregon House 115 dev sites; boat, fish, swimming & picnicking.	34	A1
COLORADO RIVER, on the California-Arizona border Camp, hike along the river; boating & swimming.	110	C3
COLUSA-SACRAMENTO RIVER STATE REC AREA, Colusa Undeveloped camps, boat, fish, picnicking & waterskiing.	33	A1
CONVICT LAKE, 37 miles north of Bishop 90+ dev sites - boat, fish, backpacking & horses.	50	E2
COYOTE RESERVOIR, N of Gilroy 70+ dev sites - boat, waterski, fishing & hiking.	P	E5
CUYAMACA RESERVOIR, off Hwy 79 south of Julian Camp, fishing & duck hunting; no swimming.	107	C4
DANA POINT MARINA, S of Del Obispo St Shopping, restaurants & boating facilities.	202	B5
DESERT SHORES MARINA, Hwy 86, near Desert Shores Boating & fishing facilities.	108	B1
DONNER LAKE, 2 mi W of Truckee Boat, picnicking & fishing.	35	D1
DON PEDRO RESERVOIR, W of Coulterville 500+ dev sites - houseboat, waterski, fishing & hiking.	48	C2
DORRIS RESERVOIR, east of Alturas Good fishing & swimming; day use only.	8	B1
DOWNTOWN LONG BEACH MARINA, off Shoreline Dr, LB Shopping, restaurants & boating facilities.	192	E4
EAGLE LAKE, 20 mi N of Susanville 300+ dev sites - boat, waterski, fishing & hiking.	20	E2
EASTMAN LAKE PARK & RECREATION AREA, N of Madera Scenic area for picnicking & water sports.	49	A5
EL CAPITAN RESERVOIR, El Monte Rd E CA 67 N I-8 Fish, boating & camping at nearby Lake Jennings Co Park.	107	A5
ELLERY LAKE, 10 miles west of Lee Vining 10+ dev sites - boat, fish, rock climbing & hiking.	43	B5
ENGELBRIGHT RESERVOIR, NE of Marysville 100+ dev boat-in sites, picnic, swimming & fishing.	34	B1
FALLEN LEAF LAKE, southwest of South Lake Tahoe 200+ dev sites - boat, fish, swimming & horses.	35	E3
FOLSOM LAKE STATE REC AREA, 1 mile N of Folsom Developed camps - boat, fish, waterskiing & horses.	34	B5
FRANKS TRACT STATE RECREATION AREA,S of Rio Vista Accessible by boat; swim, fishing & waterskiing.	M	E3
FRENCHMAN RES STATE REC AREA, 10 mi N of Chilcoot 140+ dev sites - boat, waterski, fishing & hiking.	27	D1
FRENCH MEADOWS RESERVOIR, NE of Michigan Bluff 100+ dev sites - boat, fish, swimming & hiking.	35	C2
GOLDEN GATE NATIONAL REC AREA, San Francisco & Marin Beaches & gardens; hiking & picnicking.	141	D1
GOLDEN GATE YACHT CLUB, off Marina Bl, San Francisco Private yacht club at SF yacht harbor.	142	A1
GOLDEN SHORES MARINA, Hwy 95, Topock Boat, waterskiing & fishing.	95	E2
GOOSE LAKE, off Hwy 395 @ California-Oregon border 48 dev sites; boat, hiking trails & hunting.	7	B3
HELL HOLE RESERVOIR, NE of Michigan Bluff 50+ dev sites - boat, waterski, fishing & hiking.	35	C2
HENSLEY LAKE PARK & REC AREA, 17 mi N of Madera Camp, picnic, waterskiing & swimming.	49	B5
HOGAN RESERVOIR, 3 mi W of San Andreas Dev & undev sites - boat, fish, hiking & swimming.	40	E4
HOLIDAY SHORES MARINA, Hwy 95, Bullhead City Waterski, fishing & boating	85	D4
HUNTINGTON HARBOUR, Huntington Beach Waterfront homes & marina facilities.	T	A3
HUNTINGTON LAKE, north of Camp Sierra 300+ dev sites - boat, waterski, fishing & horses.	50	B5
ICE HOUSE RESERVOIR, 12 mi N of Riverton 80+ dev sites - boat, fish, swimming & hiking.	35	C4
INDIAN CREEK RESERVOIR, north of Markleeville 20+ dev sites - picnic, fish, backpacking & boating.	36	C4
INDIAN VALLEY RESERVOIR, east of Markleeville 70 dev sites, RV & tent; boat, fishing & swimming.	32	B2
IRON GATE RESERVOIR & LAKE COPCO, NE of Henley Camp, picnic, fish, swim, raft, hiking & hunting.	4	C2
JACK LONDON MARINA, Embarcadero, Oakland Pleasure boat marina in the Inner Harbor.	157	D4
JACKSON MEADOW RESERVOIR, SE of Sierra City 120+ dev sites - boat, waterski, fishing & hiking.	27	B4
JENKINSON LAKE, 18 mi E of Placerville 180 dev sites - boat, swimming & hiking.	35	B4
JUNE LAKE LOOP, 18 miles north of Mammoth Lakes 280+ dev sites - boat, fish, backpacking & horses.	50	C1
JUNIPER LAKE, Lassen Volcanic National Park Sail, swim, backpack, picnic, hiking & horses.	20	A3
LAKE ALMANOR, southwest of Susanville 170+ dev sites - boat, waterski, fishing & hiking.	20	B4
LAKE AMADOR, 7 mi S of Ione Dev camps - boat, fish, watersliding & hiking.	40	D3
LAKE ARROWHEAD, Hwy 173 Charming resort area; fishing & winter sports.	91	C5
LAKE BERRYESSA, on Hwy 128, Napa County Camp, fish, waterskiing & resorts.	32	D5
LAKE BRITTON, 13 mi N of Burney 120+ dev sites - boat, waterskiing & fishing	13	C4
LAKE CACHUMA RECREATION AREA, 11 mi S of Solvang Fish, boating & camping; no swimming.	87	A3
LAKE CASITAS RECREATION AREA, 11311 Santa Ana Rd Fish, boating & camping.	88	A4
LAKE CROWLEY, 35 miles north of Bishop Dev campsites - boat, picnic, fishing & waterskiing.	51	A2
LAKE DAVIS, north of Portola 110+ dev sites - boat, picnic, hiking & fishing.	27	B2
LAKE DEL VALLE STATE REC AREA, off Hwy 84 Boating and recreation facilities.	P	D1
LAKE ELSINORE STATE RECREATION AREA, Lake Elsinore Area to swim, fish, camp, waterskiing & boating.	99	B4
LAKE HAVASU MARINA, Hwy 95, Lake Havasu City Boat, fishing & waterskiing.	96	A4
LAKE HEMET, Hwy 74 near Idyllwild Lovely mountain scenery; hike, fishing & boating.	100	B4
LAKE HENSHAW, off CA 76, Santa Ysabel 300 dev sites - fish, boating & hiking.	107	B2
LAKE HODGES, off S6 on Lake Dr, Escondido Owned by SD City for day use only; fishing & boating.	106	D4
LAKE ISABELLA, 48 mi NE of Bakersfield One of the most complete rec lakes in California.	79	D1
LAKE JENNINGS, Jennings Pk Rd N off I-8 RV & tent camping; boat, limited fishing.	107	A5
LAKE KAWEAH, 17 mi E of Visalia via Hwy 198 Campsites, boat, fishing & swimming.	68	D1
LAKE McCLOUD, 12 mi S of McCloud Undeveloped campsites - boat, picnic, fishing & hiking.	12	E3
LAKE McCLURE, S of Coulterville 550+ dev sites - houseboat, picnic, fishing & swimming.	48	D2
LAKE McSWAIN, S of Coulterville Boating, fishing, camping, swimming.	48	D3
LAKE MEAD NATL RECREATION AREA, Hwy 93 & Lakeshore One of largest artificial lakes in the world.	85	C1
LAKE MENDOCINO, N of Ukiah 300+ dev sites - boat, waterski, fishing &, hiking.	31	B2
LAKE MERRITT, downtown Oakland Large natural salt water lake.	158	B3
LAKE MOHAVE, E of Searchlight, Nevada Boat, fish, swim, camp, beaches & marinas.	85	C2
LAKE NACIMIENTO, 40 mi NW of Paso Robles 350+ dev sites - waterski, boat, swimming & hiking.	65	D5
LAKE OROVILLE STATE REC AREA, NE of Oroville 200+ dev sites - boat, waterski, fishing & horses.	25	D4
LAKE PERRIS STATE REC AREA, off Ramona Expressway Fish, water ski, camp; boating & bicycle rentals.	99	C3
LAKE PILLSBURY, near Scott Dam 100+ dev sites - boat, waterski, fishing & hiking.	23	D5
LAKE PIRU, off Piru Canyon Rd, Piru Camp, boat, fishing & picnic area.	88	E4
LAKE SABRINA, 18 mi SW of Bishop Dev sites - boat, picnic, fishing & backpacking.	51	B5
LAKE SAN ANTONIO RECREATION AREA, W of Bradley 650+ dev sites-boat, fish, swim, hiking & horses.	65	D4
LAKE SHASTINA, 7 mi N of Weed 70+ dev sites - boat, waterski, fish, hike.	4	C5

POINTS OF INTEREST INDEX

NAME & ADDRESS	PAGE	GRID
LAKE SISKIYOU, 3 mi W of Mt Shasta 280+ dev sites - boat, fish & windsurfing.	12	C2
LAKE SPAULDING, N of Emigrant Gap 20+ dev sites - boat, waterski, hiking & fishing.	35	B1
LAKE SONOMA REC AREA,Hwy 101 & Dry Ck Rd,Warm Springs Camp, fish, hiking & swimming.	31	C5
LAKE SUCCESS, 20 mi E of Tipton via Hwy 190 100+ dev sites - boat, fish, swimming & hiking.	68	D3
LAKE TAHOE, California-Nevada border Dev camps, boat, waterski, fish, swimming & horses.	35	E2
LAKE TURLOCK STATE REC AREA, SW of La Grange 60+ dev sites - boat, waterski, fishing & hiking.	48	B2
LAKE VALLEY RESERVOIR, E of Emigrant Gap Camp, picnic, boat, fish, swimming & hiking.	35	B1
LEWISTON LAKE, 35 mi NW of Redding 90+ dev sites - sail, canoe, fishing & hunting.	17	E1
LEXINGTON RESERVOIR, Hwy 880, S of San Jose Boating and fishing facilities.	P	B4
LITTLE GRASS VALLEY RES, W of Gibsonville 280 dev sites - boat, waterski, fishing & hiking.	26	C3
LONG BEACH MARINA & MARINE STADIUM, Long Beach One of the largest marinas on the west coast.	S	D3
LOON LAKE, NW of Emerald Bay 50+ dev sites - boat, picnic, fishing & hiking.	35	D3
LOPEZ LAKE, 23 mi N of Santa Maria 300+ sites - boat, picnic, waterskiing & fishing.	76	C4
LOWER NEWPORT BAY, Newport Beach Leads to vast estuary in Upper Newport Bay.	199	C5
LUNDY LAKE, 12 miles north of Lee Vining 30+ dev sites - boat, picnic, fishing & backpacking.	43	B4
MAMMOTH POOL RESERVOIR, east of Bass Lake 60+ dev sites - boat, waterski, fishing & hiking.	50	B4
MANZANITA LAKE, Lassen Volcanic National Park 170+ dev sites - sail, fish, hiking & horses.	19	D2
MARINA DEL REY, Via Marina Berths more than 10,000 yachts.	187	C4
MARTINEZ LAKE, Fishers Landing Rd, Yuma Co. Marina on the Colorado River; boating & fishing.	110	E4
MARTINEZ YACHT HARBOR, Martinez Small pleasure craft marina.	154	B1
MARTIS CREEK RESERVOIR, SE of Truckee 20+ dev sites - sail, fish, swimming & hiking.	35	E1
MEDICINE LAKE, 48 miles NE of McCloud 70+ dev sites - boat, waterski, fishing & horses.	5	D5
MILLERTON LAKE REC AREA, 22 miles East of Madera 130+ dev sites - boat, waterski, fishing & horses.	57	D1
MISSION BAY, Mission Bay Park, W of I-5 Separate courses for diverse water sports.	212	D2
MONO LAKE TUFA STATE RESERVE, Hy 395 @ Lee Vining Interesting salt formations surround saltwater lake.	43	D4
MONTEREY MARINA, Ocean View Blvd Small craft harbor near Fisherman's Wharf.	167	E3
MORENA LAKE, Oak Dr & Buckman Spgs Rd, W of I-8 Campsites, fish, boat, hiking & horses.	112	D1
NEEDLES MARINA, Hwy 40, Needles Waterski, boating & fishing.	95	D2
NEW MELONES LAKE, end of Reynolds Ferry Rd Boat, picnic, fishing & camping; RV parking area.	41	B5
NORTH SHORE MARINA, Hwy 111, near Desert Beach Boating & fishing facilities.	108	C1
NOYO HARBOR, south of Fort Bragg Small, scenic eastern-like fishing village.	22	B5
OCEANSIDE HARBOR, 1540 Harbor Dr N Deep sea & sport fishing; pier fishing & sailing.	106	A3
OTAY RESERVOIR, Wueste Rd, E Chula Vista S D City lake, Co. camp, fishing & boating, no swimming.	V	E4
PARDEE RESERVOIR, 3.5 mi E of Buena Vista 180+ dev sites, pool; boat, fishing & bicycle.	40	D3
PICACHO STATE RECREATION AREA, W of Picacho Fish, boat, picnic, camping & hiking.	110	C4
PINECREST LAKE off Hwy 108 near Pinecrest 300 dev site; boat, picnic, trails, fishing & swimming.	42	A3
PINE FLAT RESERVOIR REC AREA, 20 mi N of Fresno Dev camps - houseboat, waterski, fishing & hiking.	58	B2
PROSSER CREEK RESERVOIR, N of Truckee Dev & undev sites - boat, picnic, fishing & swimming.	27	D5
PYRAMID LAKE RECREATION AREA, off I-5 110 dev sites-boat, waterski, fishing & swimming.	88	E3
RICHMOND MARINA BAY, 1340 Marina Wy S, Richmond Large boat marina on San Francisco Bay.	155	B5

NAME & ADDRESS	PAGE	GRID
ROCK CREEK LAKE, SW of Toms Place 220+ dev sites - boat, picnic, backpacking & fishing.	51	B3
ROLLINS RESERVOIR, N of Colfax 240+ dev sites - boat, waterski, fishing & hiking.	34	D2
RUTH LAKE, N of Ruth 100 dev sites - boat, waterski, fishing & horses.	16	E4
SADDLEBAG LAKE, 12.5 miles north of Lee Vining 20+ dev sites - boat, fish, mountain climbing & hiking.	43	B5
ST FRANCIS YACHT CLUB, off Marina Bl, San Francisco Long established yacht club in the Bay Area.	142	A1
SALTON BAY MARINA, off Hwy 86 near Salton City Fishing & boating facilities.	108	D2
SALTON SEA STATE RECREATION AREA, off Hwy 111 Boat, waterski, picnic, camp, fishing & hiking.	108	E2
SALT SPRINGS RESERVOIR, 20.5 mi SE of Hams Sta 20+ dev sites - boat, fish, swimming & hiking.	41	D1
SAN FRANCISCO BAY Boat tours of the bay, harbor and Alcatraz.	L	C5
SAN LUIS RES STATE REC AREA, 16 mi W of Los Banos 70+ dev sites - boat, waterski, fishing & hiking.	55	C1
SANTA BARBARA YACHT HARBOR, W Cabrillo Bl Boat rentals, hoist, ramp & sport fishing.	174	D4
SANTA MARGARITA LAKE, 19 mi from San Luis Obispo 80+ dev sites - boat, fish, picnic, swimming & hiking.	76	C3
SAN VICENTE RESERVOIR, Moreno Av, off CA 67 S D City lake, day use; boating & fishing, no swimming.	V	E1
SCOTTS FLAT RESERVOIR, E of Nevada City 180+ dev sites - boat, waterski, goldpanning & fishing.	34	D1
SHASTA LAKE, off I-5 north of Redding 400+ sites - houseboat, fishing & waterskiing.	18	C1
SHAVER LAKE, south of Camp Sierra 60+ dev sites - boat, waterski, fishing & hiking.	58	B1
SILVER LAKE, 50 mi NE of Jackson 90+ dev sites - boat, fishing & horseback riding.	35	E5
SILVERWOOD LAKE STATE RECREATION AREA, Hwy 138 Swim, fish, camp, boating & waterskiing.	91	B5
SOUTH LAKE, 22 mi SW of Bishop Dev sites - boat, picnic, fishing & backpacking.	51	C5
SOUTH LAKE TAHOE-EL DORADO STATE REC AREA, Hwy 50 Boat, picnic, swimming & fishing.	129	A3
STAMPEDE RESERVOIR, 15 mi N of Truckee 250+ dev sites - boat, waterski, fishing & hiking.	27	D4
STATE UNDERSEA PARK, Hwy 1 & Temple Hills Good diving area, fishing, shells, rock formations.	201	B3
STONY GORGE RESERVOIR, 20 miles west of Willows 140+ dev sites - boat, waterski, fishing & swimming.	24	B4
STOW LAKE, Stow Lake Dr in Golden Gate Park Largest manmade lake in park; boating.	141	C4
SUGAR PINE RESERVOIR, near Foresthill 60 dev sites; boat, fish, trails, swimming & hiking.	34	E2
SUTHERLAND RESERVOIR, Sutherland Dam Dr, Hwy 78 Fish, boat, camp nearby Black Canyon, El Loro Ranch	107	B3
TIOGA LAKE, 12 miles west of Lee Vining 10+ dev sites - picnic, hike, boating & fishing.	43	B5
TOPAZ LAKE, east of Markleeville 200+ dev sites - boat, waterski, fishing & swimming.	36	E5
TRINITY LAKE, 44 mi NW of Redding 400+ sites - sail, waterski, fishing & horseback riding.	12	A4
TULLOCH RESERVOIR, SE of Copperopolis 60+ dev sites - picnic, boat, fishing & swimming.	41	B5
TWIN LAKES, 13 miles southwest of Bridgeport 400 dev sites - boat, fish, backpacking & horses.	43	A3
UNION VALLEY RESERVOIR, 17 mi N of Riverton 270+ dev sites - boat, fish, swimming & hiking.	35	C4
VALLEJO MARINA, off Mare Island Causeway Recreational marina near Mare Island Naval Reserve.	134	A4
VENTURA HARBOR, 1603 Anchors Way Dr Includes 2 marinas, boat rentals & launch ramp.	175	D5
VIRGINIA LAKES, 18.5 miles north of Lee Vining 40+ dev sites - boat, fish, backpacking & horses.	43	B4
WEST VALLEY RESERVOIR, 22 miles SE of Alturas Camp, boat, waterski, fish, swim, hiking & hunting.	8	B3
WHISKEYTOWN LAKE, S of Hwy 299, W of Redding 150+ sites - sail, fish, waterski, hiking & swimming.	18	A2
WILD & SCENIC RIVER, Middle Fork Feather River Designated by Congress as a wild & scenic river.	26	C2
YOSEMITE LAKE & PARK, N of Merced off Lake Rd Boat, sail, picnic, waterski, fishing & hiking.	48	C4

POINTS OF INTEREST INDEX

SKI AREAS

NAME & ADDRESS	PAGE	GRID
ALPINE MEADOWS, Hwy 89 South of Tahoe City	35	D2
BADGER PASS NORDIC, Yosemite National Park	49	D2
BADGER PASS SKI AREA, Hwy 41 in Yosemite National Park	49	D2
BEAR MOUNTAIN, Big Bear	92	A5
BEAR VALLEY CROSS COUNTRY, across from Bear Valley Village	42	A2
BIG AIR GREEN VALLEY, Hwy 18, W of Big Bear Lake	91	D5
BOREAL SKI AREA, Hwy 80 near Boreal Ridge	35	C1
CASTLE LAKE SKI AREA, end Castle Lake Rd, Lake Shastina	12	C3
CEDAR PASS SKI AREA, on Hwy 299, East of Alturas	7	C5
COPPERVALE SKI HILL, Hwy 36 E of Westwood	20	D4
COTTAGE SPRINGS SKI AREA, Hwy 4, Cottage Springs	41	D2
DIAMOND PEAK RESORT, Hwy 27 near Incline Village	36	B1
DODGE RIDGE, near Pinecrest	42	B3
DONNER SKI RANCH, S of I-80 near Truckee	35	D1
DONNER SUMMIT, Hwy 80 near Donner Pass	35	C1
EAGLE MOUNTAIN NORDIC, off Hwy 80 near Lake Valley Res	35	A1
ECHO SUMMIT, Hwy 50 W of Vade	35	E4
GRANLIBAKKEN, Hwy 89 SW of junction with Hwy 28	35	D1
HEAVENLY VALLEY, Hwy 50 South of Stateline	36	B3
HOMEWOOD SKI AREA, Hwy 89 North of Tahoe Pines	35	D2
HOPE VALLEY CROSS COUNTRY, Hwy 88 E of Kirkwood	36	B4
IRON MOUNTAIN RESORT,on Hwy 88, 98mi E of Stockton	35	D5
JUNE MOUNTAIN, Hwy 158 off 395 at June Lake	50	C1
KIRKWOOD CROSS COUNTRY, Kirkwood Ski Resort	36	A5
KIRKWOOD SKI RESORT, Hwy 88 near Carson Pass	36	A5
KRATKA RIDGE, Junction of Hwy 2 and Hwy 39	90	C4
MAMMOTH CROSS COUNTRY, Mammoth Lakes	164	A5
MAMMOTH MOUNTAIN, Hwy 203 W of Hwy 395 at Mammoth Lake	164	A3
MONTECITO-SEQUOIA CROSS COUNTRY, Sequoia Nat'l Forest	58	D4
MOUNTAIN HIGH, Hwy 2 N of Wrightwood	90	D5
MT BALDY, N of Hwy 83 on Mt Baldy Rd	90	E5
MT REBA SKI AREA, N of Bear Valley	42	A1
MT ROSE, SW of Reno	28	B5
MT SHASTA SKI PARK, off Hwy 89, Mt Shasta	12	D2
MT WATERMAN, Route 2 S of Kratka Ridge	90	B5
NORTHSTAR-AT-TAHOE, Hwy 267 N of Junction with Hwy 28	35	E1
PLUMAS-EUREKA SKI BOWL, Hwy 70 N of Hwy 89	26	D3
RENO SKI BOWL, Hwy 27 East of Incline Village	28	A5
ROCK CREEK, near Pine Grove, Mono County	51	B3
ROYAL GORGE CROSS COUNTRY, S of Serene Lakes	35	C1
SHIRLEY MEADOWS SKI AREA, Hwy 155 W of Alta Sierra	79	C1
SIERRA AT TAHOE SKI RESORT, Hwy 50 east of Kyburz, Phillips	35	E4
SIERRA MEADOWS TOURING, Sherwin Creek Rd, Mammoth Lakes	164	E3
SIERRA SKI RANCH, Hwy 50 east of Kyburz	35	E4
SIERRA SUMMIT, north of Hwy 168 at Huntington Lake	50	C5
SKI SUNRISE, Hwy 2 N of Wrightwood	90	D4
SLIDE MOUNTAIN SKI AREA, Hwy 431 near Slide Mountain	36	B1
SNOW FOREST, Hwy 18 near Big Bear Lake	99	E1
SNOW SUMMIT SKI AREA, Big Bear Lake	100	A1
SNOW VALLEY, Hwy 18 W of Big Bear Lake	99	D1
SODA SPRINGS, Hwy 80 near Soda Springs	35	C1
SPOONER LAKE, Cross Country Hwy 50 E of Glenbrook	36	B2
Cross country skiing.		
SQUAW VALLEY, Off Hwy 89 at Squaw Valley	35	D1
SQUAW VALLEY NORDIC, off Hwy 89 at Olympic Valley	35	D1
STOVER MOUNTAIN SKI AREA, NW of Junction Hwys 36 & 89	20	A4
STRAWBERRY CROSS COUNTRY, Hwy 50 in Kyburz	35	D4
SUGAR BOWL, Hwy 80 South of Norden	35	C1
TAHOE-DONNER, Hwy 80 near junction with Hwy 89	27	C5
TAHOE DONNER CROSS COUNTRY, Hwy 80 W of Truckee	35	D1
TAHOE NORDIC, Tahoe City NW of Lake Tahoe	35	E1
TAHOE SKI BOWL, Hwy 89 South of Tahoe Pines	35	D2
YOSEMITE CROSS COUNTRY, Hwy 41 in the Nat'l Park	49	D2

THEATERS

NAME & ADDRESS	PAGE	GRID
AHMANSON THEATER, 135 N Grand Av, Los Angeles	186	A2
Part of the Music Center; dramatic productions.		
ARLINGTON THEATRE, 1317 State St, Santa Barbara	174	C3
Home of the Santa Barbara Symphony.		
CANON THEATER, Canon Dr, Beverly Hills	183	C2
Features off-Broadway plays.		
CONCORD PAVILION, 2000 Kirker Pass Rd, Concord	M	B3
Outdoor facility; concerts, shows.		
DOROTHY CHANDLER PAVILION, 135 N Grand Av, Los Angeles	186	A2
Part of the Music Center; musical performnces.		
GEARY THEATER, 415 Geary St at Mason St	143	C3
The American Conservatory Theater performs nightly.		
GREEK THEATER, 2700 N Vermont Av, Los Angeles	182	B2
Natural amphitheater in Griffith Park.		
HOLLYWOOD BOWL, 2301 N Highland Av, Los Angeles	181	C3
Natural amphitheater, seats 20,000.		
IRVINE MEADOWS AMPHITHEATER, 8800 Irvine Center Dr, Irvine	T	E4
Concerts under the stars.		
JAMES A DOOLITTLE THEATRE, 1615 N Vine St, Los Angeles	181	D4
More serious drama of well known stars.		
JOHN ANSON FORD THEATER, 2580 Cahuenga Blvd, LA	181	C3
Features occasional outdoor jazz concerts.		
MANN'S CHINESE THEATRE, 6925 Hollywood Bl, Hollywood	181	C4
Famed forecourt with footprints of stars.		
MARK TAPER FORUM, 135 N Grand Av, Los Angeles	186	A2
Part of the Music Center; experimental drama.		
OPEN AIR THEATER, SDSU Campus Aztec Center, San Diego	V	C3
Rock concerts are regularly scheduled here.		
ORANGE CO PERFORMING ARTS CTR, 600 Town Ctr Dr,CM	198	A3
Features musical and theatrical performances.		
PACIFIC AMPHITHEATER, Fairview Rd, Costa Mesa	197	D5
Outdoor concerts & entertainment.		
PANTAGES THEATER, 6233 Hollywood Blvd, Los Angeles	181	D4
Features many Broadway productions.		
PARAMOUNT THEATER, 2050 Broadway, Oakland	158	A2
1930's movie house is now performing arts center.		
PASADENA PLAYHOUSE, 39 S El Molino Av, Pasadena	190	D4
Historic 700 seat theatre founded in 1917.		
S.F. WAR MEMORIAL & PERFORMING ARTS CENTER	143	B4
Opera, ballet and symphony.		
SHRINE AUDITORIUM, Jefferson & Figueroa, Los Angeles	185	D5
A variety of musical programs & exhibits.		
SHUBERT THEATRE, 2020 Avenue of the Stars, Century City	183	A2
The stage for many broadway plays.		
SOUTH COAST REPERTORY, 655 Town Center Dr, Costa Mesa	198	A3
Professional resident theatre.		
TERRACE THEATER, Ocean Blvd, Long Beach	192	E3
Features drama, opera, dance & symphony.		
THE MUSIC CENTER, 135 N Grand Av, Los Angeles	186	A2
3 theatre complex for drama, music & opera.		
TOWER THEATER, 1201 N Wishon Av, Fresno	165	C2
30's movie house is now performing arts center		
WARNORS CENTER OF PERFORMING ARTS, 1400 Fulton, Fresno	165	D3
Landmark building home for community events & theater		
WILSHIRE THEATER, 8440 Wilshire Blvd, Los Angeles	183	E2
Classic theater - features plays & musicals.		

WINERIES

Many of the wineries located in the Napa Valley are shown on Page 29 in this Driver's Guide.

NAME & ADDRESS	PAGE	GRID
ADELAIDA CELLARS, 5805 Adelaida Rd, Paso Robles	75	E1
Winery and tasting room are open daily.		
ALDERBROOK WINERY, 2306 Magnolia Dr, Healdsburg	37	D1
Tasting room open daily; tours by appointment.		
ALEXANDER VALLEY VINEYARDS, 8644 Hwy 128, Healdsburg	31	E5
Wine tasting; tours by appointment.		
ALTAMURA WINERY, 4240 Silverado Tr, Napa	29	E4
Tasting room open daily; appointment suggested.		
AMADOR CITY WINERY, Hwy 49 & Water St, Amador	40	D2
Winery and tasting room are open daily.		
A. NONINI WINERY, 2640 N Dickenson, Fresno	57	B3
Winery tours, tasting and retail sales.		
ARCIERO WINERY, Hwy 46 & Jardine Rd, Paso Robles	76	B1
Winery and tasting room are open daily.		
ARROWHEAD WINERY, 14347 Sonoma Hwy, Glen Ellen	29	B5
Tasting room open daily.		
AUSTIN CELLARS, 2923 Grand Av, Los Olivos	86	E3
Tasting room and retail sales; picnic area.		
BABCOCK VINEYARDS, 5175 Hwy 246, Lompoc	86	C3
Open Saturdays & Sundays, 10 am - 4:30 pm.		
BALLARD CANYON WINERY, 1825 Ballard Canyon Rd, Solvang	86	E3
Tours by appointment only; tasting room.		
BANDIERA WINERY, 555 S. Cloverdale Bl, Cloverdale	31	C4
Tasting & sales open Tuesday through Sunday.		
BARGETTO WINERY, 700 Cannery Row, Monterey	167	E2
Tasting room and gift shop.		
BARGETTOS SANTA CRUZ WINERY, 3535 N Main St, Soquel	54	A2

POINTS OF INTEREST INDEX

NAME & ADDRESS	PAGE	GRID
Tasting room and tours.		
BARON VINEYARDS, 1981 Penman Springs Rd, Paso Robles	76	B1
Tasting room open daily.		
BEAULIEU VINEYARD, 1960 St Helena Hwy, Rutherford	29	C3
Open daily for tasting and guided tours.		
BEAUCANON, 1695 St Helena Hwy, St Helena	29	C3
Open daily for tasting and guided tours.		
BELLA ROSA WINERY, Hwy 99 & Pond Rd, McFarland	68	B5
Winery and tasting room are open daily.		
BELLEROSE VINEYARD, 435 W Dry Ck Rd, Healdsburg	37	A1
Hours Tues-Fri 1-5, Sat-Sun 11-4:30.		
BELVEDERE WINERY, 4035 Westside Rd, Healdsburg	37	D1
Tasting room open daily; group tours by appointment.		
BERGFELD 1885 WINE CELLARS, 401 St Helena Hwy	29	C3
Open daily for tasting and tours.		
BERINGER VINEYARDS, 2000 Main St, St Helena	29	B3
Tours of Rhine House, Beringer caves; tasting.		
BERNARDO WINERY, 13330 Pas Dl Verano N, Escondido	106	D4
Wine tasting, sales & gift shop; picnic area.		
BIANCHI VINEYARDS, 5806 N Modoc Av, Kerman	57	A3
Winery and tasting room are open daily.		
BOEGER WINERY, 1709 Carson, Placerville	35	A4
Wine tasting; self guided tours.		
BONNY DOON VINEYARD, 10 Pine Flat Rd, Santa Cruz	N	E5
Open for tours and tasting.		
BRANDER VINEYARD, Hwy 154 & Refugio, Los Olivos	86	E3
Open Monday-Saturday for wine tasting & tours.		
BRITTON CELLARS, 40620 Calle Contento, Temecula	99	D5
Daily tasting & sales; picnic area.		
BUENA VISTA WINERY, 1800 Old Winery Rd, Sonoma	L	C1
Historic landmark of Cal's first wine cellars.		
BYINGTON WINERY, 21850 Bear Creek Rd, Los Gatos	P	A4
Tasting room open daily; picnic area.		
BYRON WINERY, 5230 Tepusquet Rd, Santa Maria	86	D1
Daily tours, wine tasting and retail sales.		
CACHE CELLARS, Pedrick Rd, Davis	39	B2
Tasting room open daily; groups by appointment.		
CACHE CREEK WINERY, Route 21, Woodland	33	B5
Tours and tasting offered daily.		
CADENASSO WINERY, 1955 W Texas St, Fairfield	135	A4
Winery and tasting room are open daily.		
CAKEBREAD CELLARS, 8300 St Helena Hwy, Rutherford	29	D3
Tasting tours by appointment.		
CALIFORNIA CELLAR MASTERS, 212 W Pine St, Lodi	40	A4
Winery and tasting room are open daily.		
CALLAWAY WINERY, 32720 Rancho California Rd, Temecula	99	D5
Tours and tasting room; picnic facilities.		
CAPARONE WINERY, San Marcos Rd, Paso Robles	66	A5
Tasting and sales available daily.		
CAREY CELLARS, 1711 Alamo Pintado Rd, Solvang	86	E3
Daily tours&tasting; picnic area available.		
CARMENET VINEYARD, 1700 Moon Mountain Dr, Sonoma	38	B3
Open by appointment only.		
CARNEROS CREEK WINERY, 1285 Dealy Ln, Napa	L	C1
Tasting and tours; open Wednesday - Sunday.		
CASA DE FRUTA, 6680 Pacheco Pass Hwy, Hollister	54	E2
Open daily; gourmet deli.		
CASWELL VINEYARDS, 8860 Hwy 12, Kenwood	38	A2
Open for tours and tasting Wednesday - Monday.		
CAYMUS VINEYARDS, 8700 Conn Creek Rd, Rutherford	29	D3
Guided tours and tasting by appointment.		
CHALK HILL, 10300 Chalk Hill Rd, Healdsburg	37	E1
Tours and tasting by appointment.		
CHAMISAL VINEYARD, 7525 Orcutt Rd, San Luis Obispo	76	B4
Wine tasting & retail sales; picnic area.		
CHARLES KRUG WINERY, 2800 Main St, St Helena	29	C2
Guided tours and wine tasting daily.		
CHATEAU DE LEU, 1635 W Mason Rd, Suisun	L	E1
Wine tasting & sales; picnic facilities.		
CHATEAU JULIEN WINERY, 8940 Carmel Vly Rd, Carmel	54	B5
Tasting room open daily; groups by appointment.		
CHATEAU MONTELENA, 1429 Tubbs Ln, Calistoga	29	A1
Tours by appointment; store open daily.		
CHATEAU POTELLE WINERY, 3875 Mt Veeder Rd, Napa	29	C4
Tasting room is open daily.		
CHATEAU ST JEAN, 8555 Sonoma Hwy, Kenwood	38	A2
Tasting, self-guided tours.		
CHATEAU SOUVERAIN, 400 Souverain Rd, Geyserville	31	D5
Open daily for tours and tasting.		
CHATOM VINEYARDS, 1969 highway 4, Murphys	41	C4

NAME & ADDRESS	PAGE	GRID
Winery & tasting room open daily.		
CHIMNEY ROCK WINERY, 5350 Silverado Trail, Napa	29	E4
Hours 10-5 daily.		
CHRISTIAN BROTHERS, 2555 Main St, St Helena	29	B2
Open daily for tasting and tours.		
CILURZO VINEYARD, 41220 Calle Contento, Temecula	99	D5
Informal tours and wine tasting; picnic area.		
CLINE CELLARS, Cypress Rd & Sellars Av, Oakley	M	D3
Daily tasting & sales; picnic area.		
CLOS DU BOIS, 5 Fitch St, Healdsburg	37	E1
Tasting room and sales; tours by appointment.		
CLOS DU VAL VINEYARDS, 5330 Silverado Trail, Napa	29	E4
Tasting & tours by appointment; retail sales.		
CLOS PEGASE, 1060 Dunaweal Ln, Calistoga	29	A1
Open daily for tasting and tours.		
CONCANNON VINEYARD, 4590 Telsa Rd, Livermore	P	D1
Wine tasting room; tours by appointment.		
CONN CREEK WINERY, 8711 Silverado Tr, Napa	29	D3
Open daily for tasting and tours.		
CONROTTO WINERY, 1690 Hecker Pass Hwy, Gilroy	54	D2
Tasting room and retail sales open daily.		
CORBETT CANYON, 353 Shell Beach Rd, San Luis Obispo	76	B4
Wine tasting & sales; picnic facilities.		
COSENTINO, St Helena Hwy, Yountville	29	D4
Hours 10-5 daily.		
CRESTON MANOR VINEYARDS & WINERY, Hwy 58, Creston	76	D2
Tours, wine tasting & sales; picnic area.		
CULBERTSON WINERY, 32575 Ro Calif Rd, Temecula	99	D5
Open daily for tours and tasting.		
CUVAISON WINERY, 4550 Silverado Tr, Calistoga	29	A1
Tasting room; picnic area, tours by appointment.		
DAVID BRUCE WINERY, 21439 Bear Creek Rd, Los Gatos	P	A4
Tasting room open daily; tours by appointment.		
DAVIS BYNUM WINERY, 8075 Westside Rd, Healdsburg	37	D1
Tasting room open daily 10AM-5PM; tours by appointment.		
DEER PARK, 29103 Champagne Blvd, Escondido	106	D3
Tasting & self-guided tours 10-5 daily.		
DEER PARK WINERY, 1000 Deer Park Rd, Deer Park	29	C2
Retail sales; tours by appointment.		
DEHLINGER WINERY, 6300 Guerneville Rd, Sebastopol	37	D2
Wine tasting room & retail sales; picnic area.		
DELICATO VINEYARDS, 12001 S Hwy 99, Manteca	47	B1
Tasting & retail sales; tours by appointment.		
DE LOACH VINEYARDS, 1791 Olivet Rd, Santa Rosa	37	E2
Tasting room open daily; tours by appointment.		
DE MOOR WINERY, 7481 St Helena Hwy, Oakville	29	D4
Winery & tasting room open daily; picnic area.		
DEVLIN WINE CELLARS, 3801 Park Av, Soquel	54	A2
Wine tasting & sales; open weekends Noon-5PM.		
DOMAINE CHANDON, California Dr, Yountville	29	D4
Tours, salon museum and restaurant.		
DOMAINE NAPA WINERY, 1155 Mee Ln, St Helena	29	C3
Tasting room is open daily.		
DRY CREEK, 3770 Lambert Bridge Rd, Healdsburg	31	D5
Tasting room open daily; picnic area.		
DUCKHORN VINEYARD, 3027 Silverado Tr, St Helena	29	B2
Hours 9-5 daily.		
EAGLE RIDGE WINERY, 111 Goodwin Av, Penngrove	38	A3
Tasting and tours by appointment.		
EBERLE WINERY, Highway 46, Paso Robles	76	B1
Tours, tasting & sales; monthly gourmet dinner.		
EDNA VALLEY VINEYARD,2585 Biddle Rch, San Luis Obispo	76	B4
Open daily for tasting and sales.		
EL DORADO VINEYARDS, 3551 Carson Rd, Camino	35	A5
Wine tasting.		
EMILIO GUGLIELMO, 1480 E Main Av, Morgan Hill	P	D5
Winery tours by appointment; tasting & sales.		
FERRARA WINERY, 1120 W 15th Av, Escondido	106	D3
Informal tours; wine tasting and sales.		
FERRARI-CARANO WINERY, 8761 Dry Ck Rd, Healdsburg	31	C5
Tasting room; open daily; tours by appointment.		
FETZER VINEYARDS, 13500 S Hwy 101, Hopland	31	B3
Tasting room; vineyards on Bel Arbes Rd, Redwood Valley.		
FIELD STONE WINERY, 10075 Hwy 128, Healdsburg	31	E5
Retail sales and tasting room; tours by appointment.		
FILIPPI WINERY, 11211 Etiwanda Av, Fontana	99	A2
Tasting room open daily 9-6.		
FIRESTONE VINEYARD, 5017 Zaca Sta Rd, Los Olivos	86	E2
Wine tasting, tours & sales.		
FITZPATRICK WINERY, 7740 Fairplay Rd, Somerset	41	A1

POINTS OF INTEREST INDEX

NAME & ADDRESS	PAGE	GRID
Tasting room open weekends.		
FOLIE A DEUX WINERY, 3070 St Helena Hwy, St Helena	29	B2
Tasting, retail sales, picnic area.		
FOPPIANO, 12707 Old Redwood Hwy, Healdsburg	37	D1
Tasting room; no tours.		
FORTINO WINERY, 4525 Hecker Pass Hwy, Gilroy	54	C2
Wine tasting, retail sales & tours available.		
FRANCISCAN VINEYARDS, 1178 Galleron Rd, Rutherford	29	C3
Tasting room; no tours.		
FRANZIA BROS. WINERY, Hwy 120, Ripon	47	B1
Tasting room & retail sales; picnic area.		
FRASINETTI WINERY, 7395 Frasinetti Rd, Sacramento	40	A2
Winery tasting room; retail sales; open Tu-Sun.		
FREEMARK ABBEY WINERY, Hwy 29, St Helena	29	B2
Guided tours and retail sales daily.		
FREY VINEYARDS, 14000 Tomki Rd, Redwood Valley	31	B1
Retail sales & picnic; tours & tasting by appointment.		
FRITZ CELLARS, 24691 Dutcher Ck Rd, Cloverdale	31	C4
Tours & tasting by appointment; open daily.		
GAINEY VINEYARD, E Highway 246, Santa Ynez	86	E3
Winery tours; tasting & picnic area available.		
GALLEANO WINERY INC, 4231 Wineville Rd, Mira Loma	U	E3
Tours by appointment; tasting & sales; picnic area.		
GEYSER PEAK WINERY, 22281 Chianti Rd, Geyserville	31	D5
Wine tasting daily; tours by appointment.		
G FERRER CHAMPAGNE CAVES, 23555 Hwy 121, Sonoma	38	B3
Open daily, tours & tasting; underground caves		
GIRARD WINERY, 7717 Silverado Tr, Oakville	29	D3
Tours & tasting by appointment; retail sales.		
GIUMARRA VINEYARDS, Edison Hwy, Edison	78	E3
Tasting room open Tu-Sat; tours by appointment.		
GLEN ELLEN WINERY, 1883 London Ranch Rd, Glen Ellen	38	B2
Tours; tasting; retail sales and picnic area.		
GLORIA FERRER CHAMPAGNE CAVES 23555 Hwy121 Sonoma	L	B1
Tasting available for a small fee.		
GOLD MINE WINERY 22265 Parrotts Ferry Rd Columbia	41	C4
Open daily for tasting & sales; picnic area.		
GRAND CRU VINEYARDS, 1 Vintage Ln, Glen Ellen	29	A4
Picnic area for small groups or individuals.		
GREENSTONE WINERY, Hwy 88 & Jackson Valley Rd, Ione	40	C3
Open Fri-Sun 10am-4pm;Wed-Sun summers; no tours		
GREENWOOD RIDGE VINEYARDS ,24555 Greenwood Rd, Philo	30	E2
5501 Hwy128 tasting room; open daily, tour by appointment.		
GRGICH HILLS CELLAR 1828 St Helena Hwy, Rutherford	29	C3
Tours by appointment only.		
GUENOC WINERY, 21000 Butts Canyon Rd, Middletown	32	B6
Wine tasting, tours & retail sales; picnics.		
GUNDLACH-BUNDSCHU, 2000 Denmark St, Sonoma	38	C3
Open daily for tasting and sales; picnic area.		
HALLCREST VINEYARDS, 379 Felton Empire Rd, Felton	N	E5
Open daily for tasting; tours by appointment.		
HANDLEY CELLARS, 3151 Highway 128, Philo	30	D2
Tours by appointment, tasting daily; picnic area.		
HANNS KORNELL CHAMPAGNE CELLARS, 1091 Larkmead Ln	29	B2
Informal tours.		
HARMONY CELLARS, on Hy 1 between Morro Bay & Cambria	75	D2
Tasting room open daily, small family-owned.		
HAYWOOD WINERY, 18701 Gehricke Rd, Sonoma	132	E2
Open daily for tours, tasting, sales, picnic.		
HECKER PASS WINERY, 4605 Hecker Pass Hwy, Gilroy	54	C2
Wine tasting & retail sales; tours by appointment.		
HEITZ WINE CELLARS, 436 St Helena Hwy, St Helena	29	C3
Open daily for tasting; no tours.		
HERITAGE CELLARS, 2310 S Railroad Av, Fresno	57	C3
Winery and tasting room are open daily.		
HIDDEN CELLARS WINERY, 1500 Cunningham Rd, Ukiah	31	B2
Open daily Jun-Oct;weekends Nov-May; taste tours.		
HOPE FARMS WINERY, 2175 Arbor Rd, Paso Robles	76	A1
Open dialy 11 to 5, picnics, tasting.		
HOP KILN WINERY, 6050 Westside Rd, Healdsburg	37	D2
Tours by appointment.		
HUSCH VINEYARDS, 4400 Hwy 128, Philo	30	D2
Tours by appointment only.		
INGLENOOK VINEYARDS, 1991 St Helena Hwy S,Ruthfrd	29	C3
Wine tasting, museum & gift shop; tours.		
JEKEL VINEYARD, 40155 Walnut Av, Greenfield	65	A1
Tours by appointment only.		
JEPSON VINEYARDS, 10400 S Hwy 101, Ukiah	31	B3
Tasting & sales; picnic area; tours by appointment.		
JODAR VINEYARDS, 4103 Carson Rd,Camino	35	A4

NAME & ADDRESS	PAGE	GRID
Tasting room open Thur - Sun.		
J FILIPPI VINTAGE CO, 13052 Jurupa Av, Fontana	U	E3
Winery and tasting room are open daily.		
J LOHR, 1000 Lenzen, San Jose	151	E4
Weekdays 10am-5pm tour by appointment; weekends 11am-2pm.		
JOHNSON'S ALEXANDER VALLEY, 8333 Hwy 128, Healdsburg	31	D5
Informal tours; taste and sales; picnic area.		
JOSEPH MATHEWS WINERY, 1711 Main St, Napa	133	C3
Winery and tasting room are open daily.		
JOSEPH PHELPS VINEYARDS, 200 Taplin Rd, St Helena	29	D3
Guided tours by appointment; sales Mon-Sat.		
J ROCHIOLI VINEYARDS/WINERY 6192 Westside Rd, Healdsburg	37	C1
Tours by appointment; open daily for tasting; picnic.		
J W MORRIS WINERY, 101 Grant Av, Healdsburg	37	E1
Tasting room open Thur-Mon; tours by appointment.		
KAUTZ VINEYARDS, Six Mile Rd, Murphys	4	B4
Winery & caverns open daily.		
KENDALL-JACKSON, 600 Matthews Rd, Lakeport	31	D3
Open daily for tasting; tours by appointment.		
KENWOOD VINEYARDS, 9592 Sonoma Hwy, Kenwood	29	B4
Open daily for tasting; tours by appointment.		
KIRIGIN CELLARS, 11550 Watsonville Rd, Gilroy	P	D5
Tasting room open daily; tours by appointment.		
KONOCTI WINERY, Hwy 29 at Thomas Dr, Kelseyville	31	D3
Tasting room open daily; tours by appointment.		
KORBELL CHAMPAGNE CELLARS 13250 River Rd, Guerneville	37	C1
Tasting room open daily; tours.		
LAKE SONOMA WINERY, 9990 Dry Ck Rd, Geyserville	31	C5
Open daily for tours and tasting.		
LAKESPRING WINERY, 2055 Hoffman Ln, Napa	29	D4
Hours M-F 10-3:30.		
LAMBERT BRIDGE, 4085 W Dry Creek, Healdsburg	31	C5
Daily tasting & sales; picnic area.		
LANDMARK VINEYARDS, 101 Adobe Canyon Rd, Kenwood	29	A4
Tasting room open daily 9-6.		
LAS MONTANAS WINERY, 8860 Highway 12, Kenwood	38	B2
Open for tasting and tours; closed Tuesdays.		
LEEWARD WINERY, 2784 Johnson Dr, Ventura	88	B5
Winery and tasting room are open daily.		
LIVE OAKS WINERY, 3875 Hecker Pass Hwy, Gilroy	54	D1
Tasting room open daily.		
LIVERMORE VLY CELLARS, 1508 Wetmore Rd, Livermore	P	C1
Winery tours daily; wine tasting and sales.		
LOST HILLS WINERY, 3125 E Orange Av, Acampo	40	A4
Open daily 9-5 for tasting & sales.		
LOUIS M MARTINI, 254 St Helena Hwy, St Helena	29	C3
Guided tours and wine tasting room open daily.		
LYETH VINEYARD & WINERY, 24625 Chianti Rd, Geyserville	31	C4
Tasting room; appointment required.		
LYTTON SPRINGS WINERY, 650 Lytton Springs Rd, Healdsburg	31	D5
Tasting room open daily; tours by appointment.		
MAISON DUETZ WINERY, 453 Deutz Dr, Arroyo Grande	76	C4
Winery, tasting room open daily; appointment suggested.		
MARIANA VINEYARDS, 23600 Congress Springs Rd, Saratoga	N	E4
Open daily for tasting tours, by appointment.		
MARKHAM WINERY, 2812 St Helena Hwy, St Helena	29	B2
Tasting room open daily; tours by appointment.		
MARK WEST VINEYARD, 7000 Trenton-Healdsburg Rd, Forestville	37	D2
Tasting room open daily.		
MARTIN BROS. WINERY, Hwy 46, Paso Robles	76	B1
Tasting room and sales; picnic area.		
MARTINELLI VINEYARDS, 3362 River Rd, Windsor	37	D1
Hours 10-5 daily.		
MARTINI & PRATI WINERY, 2191 Laguna Rd, Santa Rosa	37	D2
Open daily for tasting and tours.		
MASTANTUONO, Hwy 46 & Vineyard Dr, Templeton	76	A1
Tasting room open daily.		
MATANZAS CREEK WINERY, 6097 Bennett Valley Rd, Santa Rosa	38	A2
Hours M-Sat 10-4, Sun 12-4.		
MAURICE CARRIE WINERY, 34255 Ranco California Rd, Temecula	99	D5
Winery and tasting room are open daily.		
MAYACAMAS VINEYARDS, 1155 Lokoya Rd, Napa	29	C4
No tasting; tours by appointment.		
MAZZOCCO VINEYARDS, 1400 Lytton Springs Rd, Healdsburg	31	D5
Tasting room open daily 10AM to 4PM.		
McDOWELL VALLEY VINEYARDS, 3811 SR 175, Hopland	31	C3
Tasting room, retail sales; tours by appointment.		
MENDOCINO VINEYARDS, 2399 N State St, Ukiah	31	B2
Tasting room open daily; tours by appointment.		
MENGHINI WINERY, 1150 Julian Orchards Dr, Julian	107	C3

POINTS OF INTEREST INDEX

NAME & ADDRESS	PAGE	GRID
Hours 10-4 Fri-Mon.		
MERLION WINERY, 1224 Adams St, St Helena	29	B3
Open daily; appointment required for tasting.		
MERRYVALE VINEYARDS, 1000 Main St, St Helena	29	C3
Hours 10-5:30 daily.		
MILANO WINERY, 14594 S Hwy 101, Hopland	31	B3
Tasting room, retail sales; tours by appointment.		
MILAT VINEYARDS, 1091 St Helena Hwy, St Helena	29	C3
Hours 10-6 daily.		
MILL CREEK VINEYARDS, 1401 Westside Rd, Healdsbrg	37	D1
Open daily; tasting room and picnic area.		
MILLIAIRE WINERY, 276 Main St, Murphys	41	C4
Winery & tasting room open daily.		
MIRASSOU VINEYARDS, 3000 Aborn Rd, San Jose	P	C4
Tasting room and tours available.		
MISSION VIEW VINEYARDS, 3360 N River Rd, San Miguel	66	A5
Winery & tasting open daily; groups by appointment.		
MONTALI WINERY, 600 Addison St, Berkeley	45	C1
Tasting room and sales; picnic area.		
MONTEREY PENINSULA WINERY, 786 Wave St, Monterey	167	D2
Tasting room, open daily 10AM-5PM; no tours.		
MONTEREY VINEYARDS, 800 S Alta St, Gonzales	54	E5
Tours and tasting available.		
MONTEVINA WINERY 20680 Shenandoah School Rd, Plymouth	40	E1
Tasting room open daily.		
MONTICELLO CELLARS, 4242 Big Ranch Rd, Napa	29	E5
Tasting available for fee; tours.		
MONT ST JOHN CELLARS, 5400 Old Sonoma Rd, Napa	L	C1
Wine tasting & sales; picnic facilities.		
MOSBY WINERY, 9496 Santa Rosa Rd, Buellton	86	D3
Tours and tasting available daily by appointment.		
MT PALOMAR, 33820 Rancho California Rd, Temecula	99	D5
Guided tours, tasting, sales & deli; picnic.		
MUMM NAPA VALLEY, 8445 Silverado Trail, Rutherford	29	D3
Open daily for tours, tasting & retail sales.		
MURPHY GOODE, 4001 Highway 128, Geyserville	31	D5
Open for tasting; tours require appointment.		
NAPA BEAUCANNON, 1695 St Helena Hwy	29	C3
Open daily for tours and tasting.		
NAPA CREEK WINERY, 1001 Silverado Trail, St Helena	29	C3
Tasting room open daily.		
NAVARRO WINERY, 5801 Hwy 128, Philo	30	E2
Tasting room open daily; tours by appointment.		
NERVO WINERY, 19550 Geyserville Av, Geyserville	31	D5
Open daily for tasting; no tours.		
NEVADA CITY WINERY, 321 Spring St, Nevada City	128	B2
Tours and tasting daily; picnic area.		
NICHELINI VINEYARD, 2950 Sage Cyn Rd, St Helena	29	E3
Tasting room; no tours.		
OAK RIDGE VINEYARDS, 6100 E Hwy 12, Lodi	40	B4
Tasting room open daily; Fall tours.		
OBESTER WINERY, 12341 San Mateo, Half Moon Bay	N	C2
Tasting room and retail sales; picnic area.		
OLSON VINEYARDS, 3620 Road B, Redwood Valley	31	B1
Tasting room open daily; tours by appointment.		
OPICI WINERY, 10150 Highland Av, Alta Loma	U	E1
Open daily; by apppointment for groups, tasting.		
PARADISE VINTNERS, 1656 Nunneley Rd, Paradise	25	D3
Winery and tasting room are open daily.		
PARDUCCI WINE CELLARS, 501 Parducci Rd, Ukiah	31	A2
Tasting room, tours hourly.		
PASTORI, 23189 Geyserville Av, Cloverdale	31	D5
Open daily for tasting; no tours.		
PAT PAULSEN VINEYARDS, Asti Rd, Asti	31	D5
Tasting room.		
PAUL MASSON VINEYARD, 13150 Saratoga Av, Saratoga	46	A5
By appointment tours.		
PEDRIZZETTI WINERY, 1645 San Pedro Av, Morgan Hll	P	D4
Tasting room open daily; tours by appointment.		
PEDRONCELLI, 1220 Canyon Rd, Geyserville	31	C5
Open all week for tasting; tours by appointment.		
PEJU PROVINCE WINERY, 8466 St Helena Hy, Rutherford	29	C3
Tasting room and retail sales.		
PESENTI WINERY, 2900 Vineyard Dr, Templeton	76	A2
Informal winery tours; wine tasting & sales.		
PHILLIPS FARMS WINERY & VINEYARDS, 4580 W Hwy 12, Lodi	40	A4
Open daily 8-6, for tasting & retail sales.		
PINA CELLARS, 8060 Silverado Tr, Rutherford	29	D3
Open Mon-Fri for wine tasting, weekends by appointment		
PINE RIDGE WINERY, 5901 Silverado Trail, Napa	29	E4

NAME & ADDRESS	PAGE	GRID
Wine tasting & picnic area; tours by appointment.		
PIPER SONOMA CELLARS, 11457 Old Redwood Hwy	37	D1
Guided tours and tasting room.		
PRESTIGE VINEYARDS, 6115 Paseo del Norte, Carlsbad	106	C3
Winery and tasting room are open daily.		
PRESTON VINEYARDS, 9282 W Dry Ck Rd, Healdsburg	31	C5
Tasting & tours; open Mon - Fri, 11AM to 3 PM.		
QUADY WINERY, 13181 Road 24, Madera	57	A2
Tours and tasting offered Monday - Friday.		
RANCHO SISQUOC WINERY, Foxen Cyn Rd SE of Sisquoc	86	D1
Tours and sales; tasting room.		
R & J COOK WINERY, Netherlands Rd, Clarksburg	39	D2
Tasting & sales daily; picnic area.		
RAPAZZINI WINERY, 4350 Monterey Hwy, Gilroy	54	D2
Tours and wine tasting daily.		
RAYMOND VINEYARD & CELLAR, 849 Zinfandel Ln, St Helena	29	C3
Tours by appointment only.		
RETZLAFF VINEYARDS, 1356 S Livermore Av	M	C5
Open for tasting and tours.		
R H PHILLIPS VINEYARDS, Routes 12A & 87, Esparto	33	A5
Open daily for tasting and tours.		
RIDGE VINEYARDS, 17100 Montebello Rd, Cupertino	N	E3
Open for tasting&retail sales; tours by appointment.		
RIVER OAKS VINEYARDS, Lytton Station Rd, Healdsburg	31	D5
Tasting room open daily; tours by appointment.		
ROBERT KEENAN WINERY, 3660 Spring Mountain Rd, St Helena	29	A2
Open Mon-Sat; appointment suggested.		
ROBERT MONDAVI WINERY, 7801 St Helena Hwy, Oakville	29	A2
Tasting & tours; musical events & art exhibit.		
ROBERT PEPI WINERY, 7585 St Helena Hwy, Oakville	29	D4
Winery tours and tasting by appointment.		
ROBERT SINSKEY VINEYARDS, 6320 Silverado Trail, Napa	29	E4
Tasting room open daily; tours by appointment.		
ROBERT STEMMLER, 3805 Lambert Bridge Rd, Healdsburg	31	D5
Wine tasting and retail sales; picnicking.		
RODNEY STRONG, 11455 Old Redwood Hwy, Healdsburg	37	D1
Tasting & sales; concerts & cultural events.		
ROSS-KELLER, 985 Orchard Av, Nipomo	76	C5
Open daily Apr-Nov; Wed-Sun, Dec-Mar.		
ROSS-KELLER WINERY, 900 McMurray Rd, Buellton	86	D3
Tours and tasting daily.		
ROUDON-SMITH TASTING RM, 2364 Bean Ck Rd, Scotts Valley	P	A5
Tasting room and sales Wed-Sun; no tours.		
ROUND HILL CELLARS, 1097 Lodi Ln, St Helena	29	B2
Tours by appointment; retail sales.		
RUTHERFORD HILL WINERY, 200 Rutherford Hill Rd, Rutherford	29	D3
Tours and tasting daily.		
RUTHERFORD VINTNERS, 1673 St Helena Hwy S, Rutherford	29	C3
Tasting room; group tours by appointment.		
S ANDERSON WINERY, 1473 Yountville Cross Rd, Yountville	29	D4
Tasting room open; tours by appointment.		
ST FRANCIS WINERY, 8450 Sonoma Hwy, Kenwood	38	B2
Tasting & sales daily; tours by appointment.		
ST SUPERY VINEYARDS, 8440 St Helena Hwy, Rutherford	38	B2
Hours 9:30-4:30 daily.		
SAN ANTONIO WINERY, 737 Lamar St, Los Angeles	186	D2
Tours, wine tasting, restaurant; picnic area.		
SANFORD WINERY, 7250 Santa Rosa Rd, Buellton	86	D3
Tasting & sales, Mon-Sat; picnic; tours by appointment.		
SAN MARTIN WINERY, 12900 Monterey Rd, San Martin	P	D5
Tasting room open year around.		
SANTA BARBARA, 202 Anacapa St, Santa Barbara	174	D4
Tasting room open.		
SANTA CRUZ MOUNTAIN VINEYARD, 2300 Jarvis Rd, Santa Cruz	54	A1
Open by appointment for tasting and tours.		
SANTA YNEZ VALLEY, 343 N Refugio Rd, Santa Ynez	86	E3
Tasting daily; tours by appointment.		
SANTINO WINERY, 12225 Steiner Rd, Plymouth	40	E1
Informal tours and tasting room.		
SATIETY, Highways 113 & 25A, Yolo	33	C5
Tasting room and winery are open daily.		
SAUSAL WINERY, 7370 Highway 128, Healdsburg	31	E5
Winery and tasting room are open daily.		
SCHARFFENBERGER CELLARS, 7000 Highway 128, Philo	30	D3
Winery and tasting room open daily.		
SCHRAMSBERG VINEYARDS, 1400 Schramsberg Rd, Calistoga	29	A2
Retail sales & winery tours by appointment.		
SCHUG CARNEROS ESTATE, 602 Bonneau Rd, Sonoma	L	B1
Hours 10-5 daily.		
SEA RIDGE, 13404 Dupont Rd, Occidental	37	D2

POINTS OF INTEREST INDEX

NAME & ADDRESS	PAGE	GRID
Tours by appointment.		
SEBASTIANI VINEYARDS, 389 4th St E, Sonoma Tours and tasting daily by appointment.	132	E4
SEQUOIA GROVE VINEYARDS, 8338 St Helena Hwy, Rutherford Winery tours by appointment; tasting & sales.	29	D3
SHENANDOAH VINEYARDS, 12300 Steiner Rd, Plymouth Winery and tasting room are open daily.	40	E1
SIERRA WINERY, 1925 N Mooney Blvd, Tulare Tasting and sales daily; picnic area.	68	B2
SILVERADO VINEYARDS, 6121 Silverado Trail, Napa Open daily; tours by appointment.	29	E4
SILVER OAK WINE CELLARS, 915 Oakville Cross Rd, Oakville Hours M-Sat 10-4:30.	29	D4
SIMI WINERY, 16275 Healdsburg Av, Healdsburg Wine tasting, guided tours.	31	D5
SMITH & HOOK, 37700 Foothill Rd, Soledad Open for tours and tasting daily.	65	A1
SMOTHERS BROS WINES, 9575 Highway 12, Kenwood Open daily for tours and tasting.	29	A4
SOBON ESTATE, 14430 Shenandoah Rd, Plymouth Tours & tasting; State Historic Landmark.	40	E1
SODA ROCK, 8015 Hwy 128, Healdsburg Wine tasting; historic stone winery building.	31	D5
SONOMA CREEK WINERY, 23355 Millerick Rd, Sonoma Hours 9-4 daily.	L	B1
SOTOYOME WINERY, 641 Limerick Ln, Healdsburg Tasting room & tours; open Fri-Sun, 11AM-4:30.	37	E1
SOUVERAIN, Independence Ln & Hwy 101, Geyserville Open daily for tasting and tours; restaurant.	31	D5
SPRING MOUNTAIN VINEYARDS, 2805 Spring Mtn Rd, St Helena Open daily; tours by appointment.	29	B3
STAG'S LEAP WINE CELLARS, 5766 Silverado Trail, Napa Tasting room open daily; appointment required for tours.	29	E4
STEPHEN ZELLERBACH, 14350 Chalk Hill Rd, Healdsburg Picnic, tasting, retail sales; tours by appointment.	32	B5
STEPHEN ZELLERBACH VINEYARD, 4611 Thomas, Healdsburg Tasting room open daily; appointment required for groups.	37	E1
STERLING VINEYARDS, 1111 Dunaweal Ln, Calistoga Tasting & tours; aerial tramway to hilltop winery.	29	A2
STEVENOT WINERY, 2690 Sn Domingo Rd, Murphys Tasting room and retail sales; tours Mon-Fri.	41	B4
STONEGATE WINERY, 1183 Dunaweal Ln, Calistoga Tours by appointment; retail sales most days.	29	A2
STRINGERS ORCHARD, Hwy 395, New Pine Creek Tasting room, tours, preserves, syrup.	7	C2
SUMMER HILL VINEYARDS, 3920 Hecker Pass Hwy, Gilroy Wine tasting & retail sales; picnic area.	54	D2
SUNRISE CELLARS, 13100 Montebello Rd, Cupertino Tasting room and retail sales.	45	E4
SUTTER HOME WINERY, 227 St Helena Hwy S, St Helena Tasting room and gift shop.	29	C3
SYCAMORE CREEK VINEYARDS, 12775 Uvas Rd, Morgan Hill Tours and tasting offered daily.	P	D5
TALLEY VINEYARDS, 3031 Lopez Dr, Arroyo Grande Tasting room & picnic on grounds of Rincon Adobe.	76	C4
THE WINERY AT ASTI, 26150 Asti Rd, Asti Open daily for tasting and tours.	31	C4
THOS. JAEGER WINERY, 13455 San Pasqual Rd, Escondido Open daily 10 am- 5 pm.	106	D4
THOMAS KRUSE WINERY, 4390 Hecker Pass Hwy, Gilroy Retail sales & wine tasting; picnic area.	54	C2
THOMAS VINEYARD, 8916 Foothill Bl, Rancho Cucamonga Wine tasting & sales; picnic; historic landmark.	U	E2
TOPOLOS AT RUSSIAN RIVER, 5700 Gravenstein Hwy, Forestville Tasting room open daily; tours by appointment.	37	D2
TREFETHEN VINEYARDS, 1160 Oak Knoll Av, Napa Tasting room; tours by appointment.	29	E5
TRENTADUE WINERY, 19170 Redwood Hwy, Geyserville Open daily for tasting; tours by appointment.	31	D5
TWIN HILLS, 2025 Nacimiento Rd, Paso Robles Tasting room; picnic; open daily 11AM to 6PM.	76	A2
VALLEY OF THE MOON, 777 Madrone Rd, Glen Ellen Tasting room, retail sales; no tours.	38	B2
VENTANA VINEYARDS, 2999 Monterey-Salinas Hwy68, Monterey Tasting daily; no tours.	54	B4
VIANO VINEYARDS, 150 Morello Av, Martinez Tasting room open daily; appointment required for groups.	154	E3
VIANSA WINERY, 25200 Arnold Dr, Sonoma Hours 10-5 daily.	L	B1
VICHON WINERY, 1595 Oakville Grade, Oakville Tours by appointment; wine tasting & retail sales.	29	C4
VILLA MT EDEN, Oakville Cross Rd, Oakville Tasting daily; tours weekdays by appointment.	29	D3
V. SATTUI WINERY, 1111 White Ln, St Helena Tasting room, tours, gift shop; founded 1885.	29	C3
WEIBEL CHAMPAGNE, 1250 Stanford Av, Mission San Jose Champagne tasting room.	P	B2
WEIBEL VINEYARDS, 7051 N State St, Redwood Valley Tasting room and gift shop; no tours.	31	B1
WENTE BROS, 5565 Tesla Rd, Livermore 4th generation winery; excellent tour/tasting.	P	D1
WENTE BROS SPARKLNG WINE CELLARS, 5050 Arr Rd, Livermore Hourly tours available; restaurant.	P	D1
WERMUTH WINERY, 3942 Silverado Trail, Calistoga Open daily for tasting and tours.	29	B2
WEST WIND WINERY, 4491 Suisun Valley Rd, Suisun Hours 9-5 daily.	L	E1
WHALER VINEYARD, 6200 Eastside Rd, Ukiah Tasting room open daily; appointment suggested.	31	B2
WHITEHALL LN WINERY, 1563 St Helena Hy S, St Helena Retail sales; tours by appointment.	29	C3
WHITE OAK VINEYARDS, 208 Haydon St, Healdsburg Open daily for wine tasting.	37	E1
WILD HORSE WINERY, Templeton Handcrafted and specialty wines available.	76	B2
WILDHURST VINEYARDS, 11171 Hwy 29, Lower Lake Tasting, tours, picnic area.	32	A4
WILLIAM WHEELER WINERY, 130 Plaza St, Healdsburg Open Thurs-Mon for tasting; tours by appointment.	37	E1
WINDSOR VINEYARDS, 11455 Old Redwood Hwy, Healdsburg Tasting room is open daily.	37	D1
WINTERS WINERY, 15 Main St, Winters Wine tasting and retail sales daily.	39	A1
WOODEN VALLEY WINERY, 4756 Suisun Valley Rd, Suisun Tasting room and sales area are open Tues-Sun.	L	E1
YANKEE HILL WINERY, Yankee Hill Rd, Columbia Wine tasting; tours by appointment.	41	C4
YORK MOUNTAIN WINERY, Hwy 46 at York Mtn Rd, Templeton Tasting room; tours by appointment only.	75	E2
ZACA MESA WINERY, 6905 Foxen Cyn Rd, Los Olivos Tour provides a good overview of winemaking.	86	E2
ZD WINERY, 8383 Silverado Trail, Napa Hours 10-4:30 daily.	29	D3

What is the Thomas Bros. Maps® *Educational Foundation?*

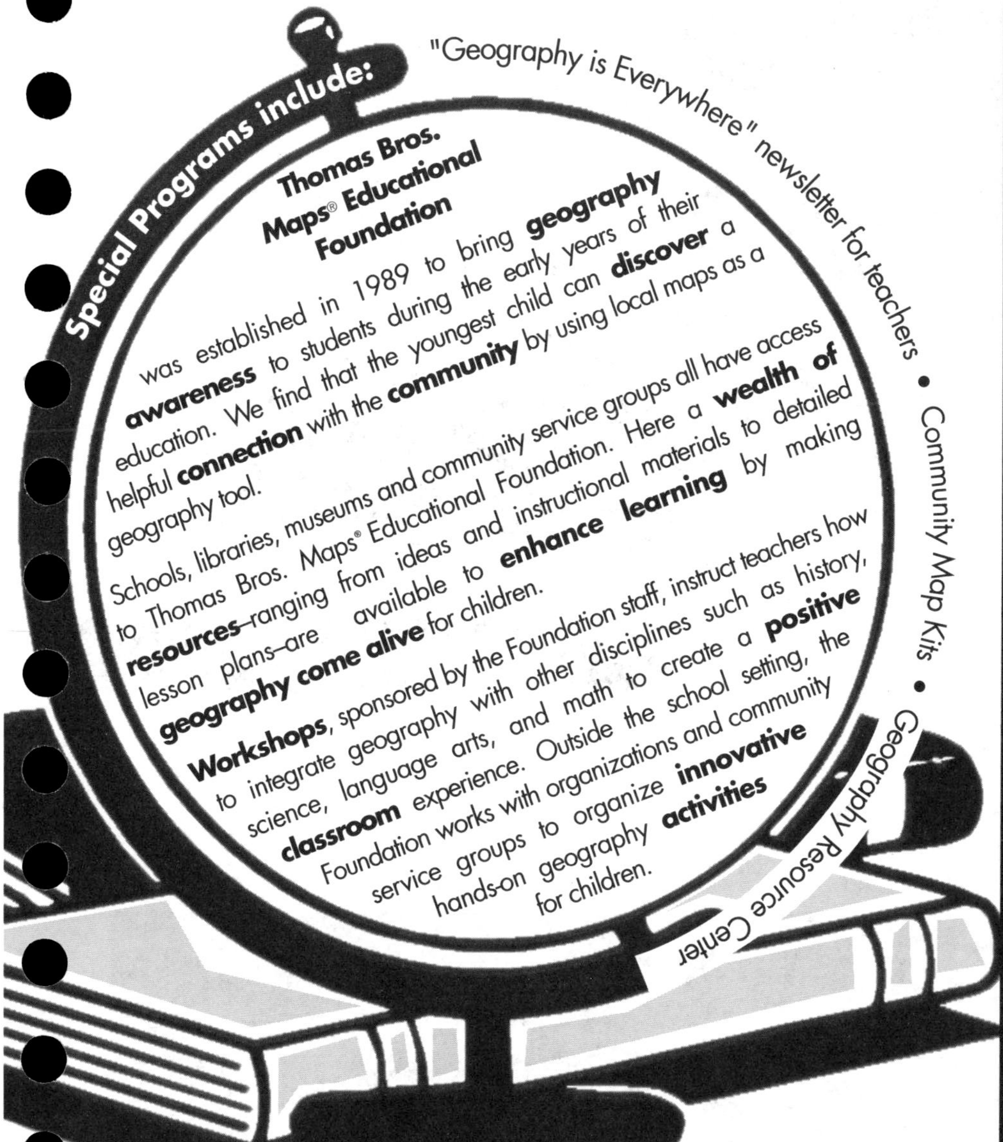

The Foundation's Mission

The Thomas Bros. Maps® Educational Foundation is a public non-profit organization dedicated to expanding students' horizons through the study of geography, ethnic, cultural, social and human values.

The Foundation provides geography programs, assistance and education through:

Researching, designing and producing resource materials for teaching geography.

Showing the value of integrating geographic concepts into various aspects of teaching curricula.

Facilitating the exchange of ideas and resources among teachers and education administrators by providing networking opportunities and sponsoring seminars and workshops.

Establishing and administering scholarships to study cartography and other geography-related disciplines.

With the generous assistance of strategic business partners like The DOT Printer, Leone & Leone, Kodak, Xerox, Zellerbach, Qualex Lab, Spiral Binding, and Consolidated Reprographics, the Educational Foundation continues to grow and expand its impact on our children.

Thomas Bros. Maps Educational Foundation

17731 Cowan, Irvine CA 92614 Tel: 714-863-1984 • 1-800-899-6277 FAX: 714-757-1564

www.thomas.com

EXPRESS MAPS™

Thomas Bros. Maps® Maps for all Reasons

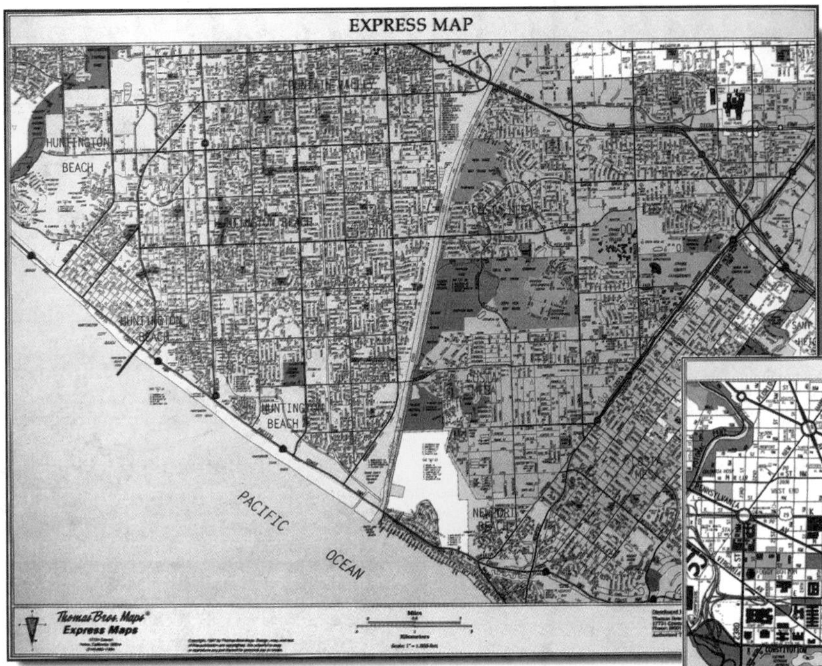

The fastest, most affordable and highest quality custom maps ever published!

Need a larger map to display a sales territory or service area? Need to put a location in the middle of the map? Express Maps™ by Thomas Bros. Maps® give you the ability to put Thomas Guide® quality maps to work solving your business challenges.

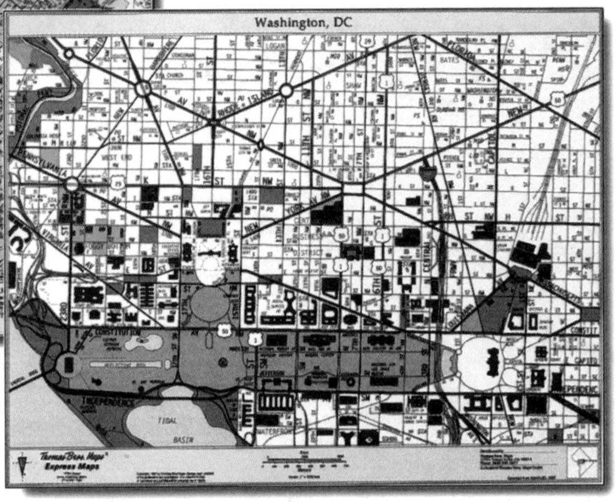

Based on the same "Intelligent Maps" database used for the Thomas Guide®, Express Maps give you the power to choose...

- **The Area - a city, a county, a neighborhood**
- **The Size - from 8 1/2" x 11" to 34" x 44"**
- **The Color - full color or black & white**
- **The Options - laminated, mounted, with or without Thomas Guide® Page and Grid, overlays for ZIP Codes or Census Tracts**

EXPRESS MAPS™

To order, contact your local Express Maps Dealer, or call us at:

1-800-899-6277

Quick 3-5 day Delivery

All at a reasonable price!

Custom Maps

For other special mapping needs, we offer full-service Custom Mapping. Thomas Bros. Custom Maps are built to your specifications, and are used for a wide variety of business and institutional applications, like...

Flat Maps

Folded Maps

Digital or Film Output

Custom Thomas Guides®

BE SURE TO VISIT OUR STORES...

Thomas Bros. Maps®

17731 Cowan
Irvine, CA 92614
1-800-899-6277(Corporate)
1-888-826-6277(Retail)
Page & Grid 859, G-3

Corporate Office & Retail Showroom, Irvine

Thomas Bros. Maps® & Books

550 Jackson Street
San Francisco,
CA 94133
1-800-969-3072
Page & Grid 7, A-4

San Francisco Store

521 W. 6th Street
Los Angeles,
CA 90014
1-888-277-6277
Page & Grid 634, E-4

Los Angeles Store

http://www.thomas.com